MIDLOTHIAN
PUBLIC LIBRARY

Baseball's Best Careers

Also by Michael S. Jones

Baseball Players' Best Seasons: Team by Team Rankings
(McFarland, 2001)

Baseball's Best Careers

Team by Team Rankings

MICHAEL S. JONES

McFarland & Company, Inc., Publishers
Jefferson, North Carolina, and London

Table of Contents

Library of Congress Cataloguing-in-Publication Data

Jones, Michael S., 1956–
Baseball's best careers : team by team rankings / Michael S. Jones.
p.   cm.   /   Includes index.
ISBN 0-7864-1087-6 (softcover : 50# alkaline paper) ∞
1. Baseball — United States — Statistics.   2. Baseball players — Ratings of — United States.   I. Title.
GV877.J66 2001   796.357 — dc21   2001030866

British Library cataloguing data are available

McFarland & Company, Inc., Publishers / Box 611, Jefferson, North Carolina 28640 / www.mcfarlandpub.com

PREFACE

Baseball's tribute to its greatest players lies in a red brick building in a quiet, picturesque town in upstate New York. The films, the plaques on the wall, and the memorabilia provide us with a flavor of the players and their talents. But we don't have to travel to Cooperstown to appreciate these stars. We need only travel through the pages of a baseball statistics book to see for ourselves the Hall of Fame performances of these great legends. And we don't have to limit ourselves to a single Hall of Fame. Using baseball statistics, we can create another Hall of Fame dedicated entirely to players from our favorite team.

More than any other sport, major league baseball is about statistics. As fans, we relate to these statistics in a powerful way. As fans, we also passionately identify with a particular team as our own. We are Mets fans, Tigers fans, or Red Sox fans. We absorb baseball statistics in the same biased fashion. Cardinals fans argue that Ozzie Smith is the greatest shortstop ever, based on his fielding statistics. Orioles fans take exception to Smith as the best, nominating Cal Ripken at short, while Pirates fans look far back in time to see Honus Wagner dominating the position. Yankees fans claim Babe Ruth as the greatest player of all time, while Red Sox fans hold dear the memory of Ted Williams, and Giants fans point to Willie Mays. But we wish we could find one statistic or one set of statistics that could more clearly support our favorite players and teams.

Baseball's Best Careers brings our team spirit as fans to the world of baseball statistics, while giving us the statistical tools to compare the performance of players between teams and through time. Suppose, for a moment, that we are long-suffering Boston Red Sox fans. Even though our team has not won a World Series in more than eighty years, our baseball interest centers on Pedro Martinez and Nomar Garciaparra today, and on Ted Williams,

Carl Yastrzemski, and Smokey Joe Wood in years past. We may even have spent hours sifting through statistical data in a baseball encyclopedia to get some sense of how our Red Sox players of the past and present compare to each other and to their opponents. Now, this work does that analysis, sorting and comparing player performances by position for each team. The resulting statistics give us the tools to create for ourselves a "Hall of Fame" roster for each team, and an overall Hall of Fame roster for all teams.

This book rates the best career performances by position for each team on two levels. On the first level, players are rated according to their *rate of success* compared to their peers. A rate of success metric measures a player's performance for an individual event such as an at bat, or over a short period, such as an inning pitched, a game played, or a short series. On the second level, players are rated according to their *volume of success* over a single season or over their entire careers compared to their peers.

Why use both a rate of success metric and a volume of success metric to evaluate career performance? To illustrate, consider Greg Maddux. His career-based rate of success is excellent, but he doesn't have the innings to compete as effectively in the volume of success metric that considers both a per-batter rate of success and total innings pitched over a career. A hundred years ago, pitchers started and completed every third game, giving them far more innings per season than the best of today's pitchers. Is Maddux having a better or worse career than these early stars? The answer depends on whether we want his great per-game performance, or the other player's greater volume of good performances. We would pick Maddux to represent us in a short series or on a team loaded with much better than average pitchers who can cover his lack of innings. We would pick the volume pitcher to represent us for a full season or over an entire career on a team loaded with average pitchers.

Baseball's Best Careers rates and ranks the greatest players by position based on their entire career performance, and assigns this performance to the player's primary team. Rogers Hornsby had an impressive year at second base for the Cubs in 1929, when he hit .380 with 39 home runs. But Hornsby played less than two full years with the Cubs. He spent most of his career, including his very finest seasons, in a Cardinals uniform. As a result, Hornsby's entire career performance is assigned to the Cardinals, to be rated and ranked against his peers at second. By assigning a player's career entirely to one team, a frequently traded player like Hornsby won't have his career performance cut up into little pieces that dilute his overall historic value. Ryne Sandberg, Johnny Evers, Glenn Beckert, and Billy Herman are left to compete for the honor of the best career Cubs second baseman.

The career-based results are summarized, by both rate of success metrics, and by volume of success metrics, into 25 player All-Star rosters for each team. We can now do a statistical comparison of the greatest Cubs team, excluding Hornsby, to the greatest Cardinals team, which includes Hornsby's entire career contribution. Note that Mark McGwire's career contribution resides with the Oakland Athletics, opening up a roster spot at first base for Cardinals stars Johnny Mize, Jim Bottomley, Bill White, and Keith Hernandez.

This book culminates in the selection of the greatest career-based lineups of all time for the American and National leagues since 1900. These two All-Star teams and the best player careers from the 1800s are merged to create an all-time team featuring the 25 greatest player careers of all time. This process is done both by rate of success performance and by volume of success performance, to give us either the best team ever for a game or short series, or the best team ever based on a player's total career contribution.

We now have the statistical tools to decide who should be in baseball's Hall of Fame. Presented in the All Time Great Players section (pages 220–247) is a rating and ranking of the all-time greatest 25 players for each infield position, the 75 greatest outfielders, the 100 greatest starting pitchers, and the 50 greatest relief pitchers. These 350 players include currently active players, recently retired players, and players who have been retired for at least five years. The highest rated qualified retired players deserve to fill the approximately 180 Hall of Fame spots currently occupied by former major league players.

As an added bonus, the Appendix of this book presents the all time best 125 player careers by season, including 10 players for each infield position, 30 outfielders, 40 starting pitchers, and 5 relief pitchers. Each player's career is presented in two parts. First, we see his raw historical statistics for each season. Next, the adjusted statistics for each season appear, giving us an unbiased look at how this player performed against the historical standard.

Like this work, most historical baseball books analyze player performances at the career level. For a unique alternative, my companion book *Baseball Players' Best Seasons* looks at a player's performance from the perspective of the individual season. The best seasons for players like Ruth, Gehrig, Mays, Spahn, and Clemens are determined and compared to the best seasons from other players. *Baseball Players' Best Seasons* determines the best seasons for each position for each team. The result is a roster of the 25 best player seasons for each team, giving a super-charged lineup for a favorite team to take on the best player performances from other teams. For example, the Yankees lineup includes the best seasons from Ruth, Mantle, DiMaggio, and Gehrig. In the National League, the Cardinals have their own formidable lineup featuring the best years from McGwire, Hornsby, Musial, and Gibson. This companion book is also available from McFarland & Company, Inc., Publishers.

INTRODUCTION

This book is more than a summary of raw, historical statistics about the men who played the game of major league baseball. Much like John Thorn and Pete Palmer's *Total Baseball*, and Bill James' *Stats All-Time Major League Handbook*, this book creates new "sabermetric" statistics from the raw statistics to rate player performances within and between years. These new sabermetrics, or metrics for short, form the basis of all rankings found in this book.

When *The Baseball Encyclopedia* was first published in 1969, raw historic baseball statistics went from being a scarce commodity to a readily available source of enjoyment for baseball fans. However, raw statistics have two limitations that make a historical comparison of players difficult at best. First, no one hitter's statistic, such as hits, home runs, or batting average, is sufficient to make a determination of a player's overall performance. Second, the raw statistics contain natural biases that mask a player's actual performance when compared to other players. Examples of biases are the cyclical periods of pitcher dominance and hitter dominance, the designated hitter rule employed in the American League since 1973, and the shrinking number of innings thrown by starting pitchers over time. Nonbiased metrics for evaluating and ranking players need to be developed to overcome these concerns.

Total Baseball arrived in 1989 with the first widely available metrics comparing all player performances between years. *Total Baseball* introduced two metrics to evaluate hitters. Production, a rate of success metric, is a straightforward sum of slugging average and on-base percentage. Total Player Runs, a volume of success metric, uses several formulas to produce a composite of a player's ability to generate Batting Runs, Stolen Base Runs, and Fielding Runs. All positive and negative run factors are then converted into positive or negative wins for the team. Pitchers have a rate of success metric that compares their

ERA (Earned Run Average) to the league's average ERA for that season. Pitchers also have a second metric, the Total Pitcher's Index, a volume of success metric. This metric analyzes a pitcher's ability to affect runs through his pitching, his batting, and his fielding, with all run factors again converted into positive or negative wins for the team.

The Bill James Historical Baseball Abstract was published in 1985. It introduced the world to the concept of Runs Created as a metric to compare player performances. The basic Runs Created formula was adjusted by 14 technical variations to deal with inconsistencies in rules and data between years. The result is an elaborate list of formulas, each being applicable to certain years. Runs Created received its own voice in the world of baseball encyclopedias in 1999 with the first edition of *Stats All-Time Major League Handbook*.

This work uses the following objectives to select the appropriate metrics for rating player performance:

- Metrics are required for both rate of success and volume of success.
- The metrics used must produce accurate ratings for all players in history.
- These metrics should be simple for the average baseball fan to understand.
- These metrics should be simple for baseball fans to duplicate.

A breakthrough idea led to the development of a new set of metrics to fulfill these objectives. An all-purpose yardstick for measurement exists that allows one to accurately compare player performances across generations. This yardstick is the *historical average* performance of all hitters and of all pitchers.

The sum total of all baseball statistics from 1876 through 2000 is readily available. For instance, batters have made 13,262,794 plate appearances, producing 3,101,789 hits and 209,161 home runs. We can use this data to determine the historic average performance stated in terms of a player who plays a full 162-game schedule. This average hitter has the following statistics:

AB BB HBP TAB HITS 2B 3B HR BA OB SA PRO
615 57   4   676 161 26 6 11 .262 .328 .377 .7059

The average pitcher, regardless of the innings we assign to him, has a 3.76 ERA, and a 4.557 RA/9. (ERA is the number of earned runs allowed per 9 innings pitched. RA/9 is the number of total runs allowed per 9 innings pitched.) We can use this historical average data for hitters and pitchers to develop the four metrics we are interested in — a rate of success metric and a volume of success metric for both hitters and pitchers.

Metrics and Definitions for the Single Season

First, we will calculate a player's rate of success and his volume of success for a single season, and then we will explain how to summarize these results by season to come up with the rate of success and volume of success results for a player's entire career.

Total Factor (TF)— A Rate of Success Metric for Hitters

The rate of success metric for hitters is called *Total Factor (TF)*. Total Factor is the sum of four other factors: a Weighted Production factor (Wtd. PRO), a stolen base factor (SBF), a fielding factor (FF), and a speed factor (SPF): TF = Wtd. PRO + SBF + FF + SPF. These four factors measure each player's impact on creating or saving runs for his team. For ease of presentation for this book, all four factors are stated in whole numbers. This requires us to multiply Production by 1,000 to convert to a whole number. Mark McGwire's 1998 Production of 1.225 becomes 1,225. This approach will henceforth be used when discussing Production numbers.

Weighted Production (Wtd. PRO) is the primary element of the Total Factor metric. Production is the sum of on-base percentage and slugging average. Weighted Production corrects for the differences in Production levels between years by using the historic average Production of 705.9, as follows: Wtd. PRO = PRO × 705.9 / League Average PRO for that Season.

The use of a Production number is both a simple and an accurate means of measuring a player's value. The key to measuring a player's offensive performance is measuring that player's ability to get on base and to drive in runs. Production, a combination of on base percentage and slugging average, provides that measurement far better than the more popular surrogates: batting average and home runs. As support for the use of Production, the authors of *Total Baseball,* who used the complex Batting Runs metric to measure performance, stated on page 633 of the 1999 edition, "the correlation between Batting Runs and Production over the course of an average team season is 99.7 percent."

Weighted Production has one additional advantage. Other published Production metrics correct for cycles in hitting by dividing a player's performance by the league average performance. The result is a ratio, rather than a Production number to which we can relate. Weighted Production, on the other hand, preserves its identity as a Production number, as illustrated by the following example.

In 1981, Mike Schmidt had a .439 on-base percentage and a .644 slugging average, which equals a 1,083 Production. The average Production for the National League that year was 686. Schmidt's Weighted Production = 1,083 × 705.9 / 686 = 1,114. Schmidt's 1,114 Weighted Production exceeds his 1,083 Production by 2.9 percent; this 2.9 percent difference is the adjustment for Schmidt hitting in a pitcher's year.

An adjustment to historic Production data is required to remove the bias related to the designated hitter rule. The DH, hitting in place of a pitcher, increases American League average Production numbers by 3.3 percent in 1973–1996, and by 3.0 percent in 1997–2000, while National League Production numbers increased by 0.3 percent in 1997–2000. This makes it harder for players in these seasons to compete against other players in other seasons when comparing their relative Weighted Production numbers. To correct this bias, we multiply the American League average Production by .967 for 1973–1996 seasons, and by .97 for 1997–2000 seasons. National League average Productions are multiplied by .997 for 1997–2000 seasons.

The *Stolen Base Factor (SBF)* is based on sabermetric studies that show the value of two stolen bases is negated by one time caught stealing. The formula that converts the value of stealing to a rate of success metric is: SBF = (SB - [2 × CS]) × 945 / TAB.

If a player steals 3 bases and is caught once in 676 total at bats, his Stolen Base Factor is (3 - [2 × 1]) × 945 / 676 = 1.4. (Modeling has determined that for the historic average 676 total at bats, one net stolen base above the impact of being caught stealing is equivalent to a Production value of 1.4.) In 1981, Mike Schmidt stole 12 bases and was caught stealing 4 times in 431 total at bats. Schmidt's Stolen Base Factor = $(12 - [2 \times 4]) \times 945 / 431 = +9$.

Records for caught stealing were not kept for many seasons, including in the National League as recently as 1950. A Stolen Base Factor is not computed for those years.

Since a player must be successful two out of every three tries just to break even in Stolen Base Factor, this factor is a slightly negative number overall for the years where it applies. And Stolen Base Factor is a significantly negative number for the few years in the Dead Ball period of 1901–1919 where caught stealing data is available. Even though the number of bases stolen in that period was very high compared to modern times, the rate of successfully stealing a base was much lower. Combine the high attempts and a success rate far below 66.7 percent, and we have a very negative Stolen Base Factor. While a few players such as Ty Cobb managed a positive Stolen Base Factor in some years, in general, a player of that period is fortunate to play in a year where caught stealing information is not available.

Fielding Factor (FF) is the one calculation where, instead of relying on hard statistical data, a judgmental interpretation of this statistical data is used to measure a player's performance. Why a judgmental interpretation of statistical data? Because none of the many statistical approaches ever developed adequately measures fielding performance for all players.

For most of baseball history, fielding percentage was the main measure of fielding performance. Fielding percentage, however, tells us nothing about a player's fielding range. In response, a fielding range statistic has been developed, where range is defined as the sum of a player's putouts and assists per nine innings. Problems with the fielding range statistic include the following:

- The range statistic does not reflect errors made.
- The range statistic is not adjusted to reflect a team having more strikeouts by its pitching staff and, thus, less possible chances available for its fielders.
- Ignoring the strikeout issue, there are only 27 outs in a game to divide up among a team's fielders. A team with nine excellent fielders will have each fielder fare no better statistically than their counterparts on a team with nine average fielders, and no better than their counterparts on a team with nine poor fielders.
- A poor fielder like Albert Belle may have a high range statistic, not because he has great range, but because hitters hit more balls his way in order to avoid hitting them at better fielders.
- The range statistic does not begin to cover all the

skills required of a catcher, while a first baseman's putouts are a function of the abilities of the other players in the infield.

Total Baseball's "Fielding Runs" is the best statistical approach to date. Fielding Runs rates players based on their putouts, assists, double plays, and errors compared to the league average player at that position. Unfortunately, this reliance purely on fielding statistics still produces inconsistent results. A great fielding second baseman, Bill Mazeroski, has the highest career Fielding Runs at +362, while Johnny Bench, perhaps the greatest fielding catcher of all time, has career Fielding Runs of -80. Other players with negative fielding ratings include Mickey Mantle, Roger Maris, Dave Concepcion, Larry Bowa, and Hal Chase. Albert Belle, Jim Rice, Jose Canseco, and Bill Melton are some of the poor fielders who have positive Fielding Runs. Fielding Runs does not produce consistently reliable results because this approach suffers from some of the same problems as the range statistic. Still, more often than not, Fielding Runs approximates the reputation of the player evaluated.

Fielding Factor (FF) combines four sources of information to rate each player's fielding performance: Gold Glove recognition for players since 1957; the player's general fielding reputation, with input for players since 1900 from an independent rating source; the player's *Total Baseball* Fielding Runs rating; and the player's fielding percentage. Fielding Factor, being by nature an estimate, is stated in increments of 10. The historic sum of all Fielding Factors for each position nets to zero.

In 1981, Mike Schmidt produced a +90 Fielding Factor, one of the highest fielding ratings ever. Schmidt's 1981 Fielding Factor reflects his winning his sixth of nine straight Gold Glove awards, his reputation as the greatest fielding third baseman of all time, his solid .956 fielding percentage that year, and a very high +23 Fielding Runs rating for a 107 game schedule.

The *Speed Factor (SPF)* assigned to a player is either +10, 0, or -10. Most elements of speed are already reflected in one of the other three factors. Weighted Production incorporates a player's ability to run out a bunt or extend a single into a double. Stolen Base Factor captures a player's contribution from stealing bases. And Fielding Factor reflects a player's ability to cover ground defensively. What is not covered is a player's ability to run the bases once he is on base. Joe DiMaggio could fly on the base paths; Frank Howard and Harmon Killebrew held up traffic behind them. The sum of all Speed Factors for all players is a small positive number.

In summary, *Total Factor (TF)* enjoys an important advantage over other rate of success metrics, as it goes beyond hitting performance to also incorporate base running and fielding performance. Mike Schmidt was a player who could hit, run, steal, and play great defense. In 1981, his Weighted Production was 1,114, his Stolen Base Factor was +9, his Fielding Factor was +90, and his Speed Factor was +10. Schmidt's Total Factor is 1,223, the highest rate of success performance for any third baseman in major league history. Unfortunately for Schmidt, 1981 was a strike year, and his team played only 107 games. As a result, Schmidt's volume-based statistics such as hits and home runs do not begin to reflect his incredible year. Schmidt's 1981 season is an example of why Total Factor, an all-encompassing rate of success metric, is needed to measure a player's performance.

Hits Contribution (HC) — A Volume of Success Metric for Hitters

Unlike other published metrics, we can convert the Total Factor rate of success metric directly into a volume of success metric, called *Hits Contribution (HC)*. The formula for calculating Hits Contribution is as follows: HC = (TF − Historic Average TF for Position) × TAB / (1000 × [Historic TAB /Historic TAB + Historic TAB/Historic AB]). The historic total at bats (TAB) for the average player is approximately 676, while the historic at bats (AB) is approximately 615. When the first number is divided by the second, the number generated is 1.099. Inserting this new information, the suddenly simple formula for calculating Hits Contribution is now: HC = (TF − A) × TAB / 2,099; Where A = Historic Average TF for Player's Position.

The difference between a player's Total Factor and the historic average Total Factor tells us how much better or worse that player's rate of success is compared to the historic average player at that position. When we multiply this difference by the second half of the equation, we convert the difference into the number of additional (or less) base hits produced by this player as compared to the historic average player at that position, given the same total at bats.

Recall that the historic sum of Fielding Factors equals zero, while a slightly negative sum of Stolen Base Factors is basically offset by a slightly positive sum of Speed Factors. As these three factors net to zero, the historic average Total Factor for *all positions* is roughly equivalent to the historic average Production factor, or 705.9. Based on an analysis of the Production figures for 80 percent of the over 13 million total at bats in history, the historic average Total Factor *for each position* is: C = 677.4, 1B = 770.0, 2B = 685.3, SS = 662.0, 3B = 716.2, OF = 757.4, P = 536.8 (1876-99), P= 442.2 (1900-72), P=370.5 (1973-present).

Each player's performance is compared against the Total Factor for the position he fielded the most games at

during the season. Designated hitters use the historic average Total Factor for the primary position they played in the field or, if they did not appear in the field in that season, the primary position they most recently played.

Total games played by teams vary by year, creating one of the biases making a comparison between years difficult. We already saw how Mike Schmidt's 1981 volume-based statistics are adversely impacted by that strike-shortened season. There were, in fact, many variations in games played over time. Schedules were very irregular in the early days of baseball, with a 154 game schedule not being adopted until 1904. World War I caused a reduction in games played in the 1918 and 1919 seasons. Baseball expanded to a 162 game schedule in the early sixties. And strikes shortened the 1972, 1981, 1994, and 1995 seasons. To correct the impact of this schedule bias on our volume of success metric, we make one addition to the formula: HC = (TF − A) × TAB / 2,099 × 162 / Games in Season where A = 677.4 for catchers, 770.0 for first basemen, 685.3 for second basemen, 662.0 for shortstops, 716.2 for third basemen, 757.4 for outfielders, 536.8 for pitchers (1876–99), 442.2 for pitchers (1900–72), 370.5 for pitchers (1973–present).

The "Games in Season" adjustment does not correct for games lost due to rainouts or extra games played in a season. One hundred fifty-four games are used for "Games in Season" for every year between 1904 and the introduction of expansion teams, except the 1918 and 1919 war years. Likewise, 162 games are used for every year from the introduction of expansion teams to the present, except for the strike-shortened years. For irregular schedule years such as 1896 and 1918, a league average "Games in Season" is used, regardless of the actual games played by each team. This league average "Games in Season" approach is designed to cover nineteenth century situations where teams sometimes failed in midyear.

Mike Schmidt's 1981 Hits Contribution ([1,223 − 716.2] × 431 / 2,099 × 162 / 107) accounts for 157.5 additional base hits compared to the historic average third baseman over a 162-game schedule. Schmidt, through his hitting, his base running, and his fielding, gave the 1981 Philadelphia Phillies almost one additional base hit per game advantage over the competition!

Weighted Runs Allowed Per 9 Innings (Wtd. RA/9) — A Rate of Success Metric for Pitchers

The choice of the basic measure for a pitcher's rate of success is between RA/9 (Runs Allowed per 9 Innings) and the more traditional ERA (Earned Runs Allowed per 9 Innings). Supporters of Earned Run Average argue that a pitcher's performance should not suffer from errors committed by others. However, many unearned runs come after the play where the error is committed, and the pitcher certainly has a major responsibility for those runs scoring. Ultimately, the pitcher is held responsible for giving up runs, whether from legitimate hits, hits that occur because a fielder has limited range, hits from unlucky bounces, errors, walks, hit batsmen, or any other source. Bill James offered the opinion on page 483 of the *Baseball Abstract* that "the distinction between earned runs and unearned runs is silly and artificial...."

A historic analysis supports the use of RA/9 over ERA. Errors were far more prevalent in the early days of the game. In the National Association in 1874, the fielding average was .825, which means one error was committed for every six chances. In that year, RA/9 averaged 8.99, while the league's earned run average was 3.25. If we used ERA to evaluate pitchers, we would be ignoring 64 percent of all runs scored against these pitchers! Pitchers had minuscule ERAs of less than 2.00 that did not reflect their true performance. In 1903, the National League's fielding average was .946, or one error every 19 chances. The league's RA/9 was 4.88, while its ERA was 3.26. Fully one third of all runs scored were unearned. In 1998, the National League's fielding average was .981, or one error for every 53 chances. The league's RA/9 was 4.62, while its ERA was 4.23. Only 8 percent of all runs scored were unearned. As we are comparing players of all time periods, we should avoid the wide variation in results caused by not considering all runs scored.

A case-by-case analysis also typically supports the use of RA/9 over ERA. Jack Pfiester went 14–9 with an incredibly low 1.15 ERA for the 1907 Cubs. While Pfiester's ERA was 47 percent of the National League average ERA, his 2.82 RA/9 was a much higher 81 percent of the National League average RA/9. Pfiester's ERA was remarkably low only because nearly 60 percent of the runs he allowed were unearned! Carl Lundgren went 18–7 and had a superb 1.17 ERA that same year for the Cubs, but he also had a 1.83 RA/9. Lundgren's ERA was 48 percent of the National League average, and his RA/9 was a comparable 52 percent of the National League average. Carl Lundgren was clearly the superior pitcher that year. Yet Lundgren is rated lower than Pfiester based on ERA, even though Lundgren has a far superior RA/9 rating and a higher winning percentage.

Greg Maddux's two best years highlight the advantages of using RA/9. In 1994, Maddux was 16–6 with a 1.56 ERA, while in 1995 he went 19–2 with a 1.63 ERA. Nineteen ninety-four would be considered his better year based on an ERA metric. Now look again at Greg Maddux's two best seasons. In 1994, Maddux was 16–6 with a 1.96 RA/9, while in 1995 he was 19–2 with a 1.67 RA/9. The results are now clearly in favor of 1995.

We will use RA/9 as the basis for the pitcher's rate of success metric. The historic average RA/9 of 4.557 is used to eliminate the historic bias between years. The formula for the rate of success metric, *Weighted Runs Allowed per 9 Innings (Wtd. RA/9)*, is: Wtd. RA/9 = RA/9 × 4.557 / League Average RA/9 for that Season.

Applying the Wtd. RA/9 formula to the previous examples, we determine: Wtd. RA/9 for Maddux in 1994 = 1.96 × 4.557 / 4.65 = 1.92; Wtd. RA/9 for Maddux in 1995 = 1.67 × 4.557 / 4.65 = 1.64; Wtd. RA/9 for Pfiester in 1907 = 2.82 × 4.557 / 3.49 = 3.68; Wtd. RA/9 for Lundgren in 1907 = 1.83 × 4.557 / 3.49 = 2.39.

The 1.64 Wtd. RA/9 performance by Greg Maddux in 1995 is the second best rate of success achieved by a qualifying starting pitcher in major league history, outshining the best seasons for Walter Johnson, Old Hoss Radbourn, Cy Young, Lefty Grove, and Christy Mathewson! We could never have been able to determine how awesome Maddux was that year based on his 1.63 ERA, which appears mundane against Bob Gibson's 1.12 ERA in 1968 or Walter Johnson's 1.14 ERA in 1913. Nor could we have determined his greatness by looking at an ERA-adjusted number, where even Maddux's own 1994 season would have finished ahead of the 1995 season. Given how few runs Maddux allowed in 1995 compared to his competition, is it any wonder he went 19–2?

And who was the starting pitcher with the very best rate of success season? The answer is Pedro Martinez, who blazed to a 1.74 ERA and a far more remarkable 1.55 Wtd. RA/9 for the Boston Red Sox in 2000, while clearly demonstrating that great pitchers can overcome the challenges of pitching in hitter-friendly stadiums like Fenway Park.

Runs per 162 Games (Runs/162)— A Volume of Success Metric for Pitchers

The volume of success metric for pitchers is based on our rate of success metric, Wtd. RA/9. We merely add an innings volume factor, and adjust away the historic bias of uneven schedules. The formula for the volume of success metric, *Runs per 162 Games* is: Runs/162 = (4.557 - Wtd. RA/9) × IP / 9 × 162 / Games in Season. Runs/162 tells us how many runs that pitcher saved (gave up) compared to the historic average pitcher for the same number of innings worked, adjusted to a 162 game schedule. Runs/162 for Maddux in 1994 = (4.557 - 1.92) × 202 / 9 × 162/114.5 = 83.7. Runs/162 for Maddux in 1995 = (4.557 - 1.64) × 210 / 9 × 162/144 = 76.5. Maddux's 1995 season was the second best rate of success season ever. Now his 1994 season comes out ahead? That's right. Not only does Maddux's 1994 season beat out the exemplary 1995 season, so do 32 other pitcher seasons in the twentieth century, and nearly a hundred pitcher seasons from the nineteenth century. We need two metrics for pitchers, and especially for pitchers, because of the enormous volume bias in favor of pitchers who pitched a hundred years ago. Pedro Martinez in 2000 and Greg Maddux in 1995 are the best pitchers ever for the innings they pitched. But they rate far behind the old workhorses like Old Hoss Radbourn and Al Spalding in terms of saving runs for their team over a full season. It all depends on the question we are asking.

Metrics and Definitions for Career Results

Our four career metrics are a simple extension of the four metrics we used to evaluate a single season's performance.

Total Factor (TF)—
A Rate of Success Metric for Hitters

Total Factors (TF) are calculated for each season of a player's career. The Total Factor for a season is multiplied by that season's total at bats per 162 games. These weighted amounts by season are summed, and the sum is divided by the career sum of total at bats per 162 games to calculate the career Total Factor. The career Total Factor is fully adjusted for hitter and pitcher dominance cycle biases, scheduled game biases, etc.

Hits Contribution (HC)—
A Volume of Success Metric for Hitters

We calculate the Hits Contribution (HC) for each season, being careful to use the correct historic average Total Factor by position for each season, as a player's primary position may change from year to year. We must also be careful to use the right number of "Games in Season" for each year. We simply sum the Hits Contribution for each season to produce the career Hits Contribution. This career Hits Contribution has already been corrected for all biases.

Wtd. RA/9—
A Rate of Success Metric for Pitchers

A pitcher's Weighted Runs Allowed per 9 innings (Wtd. RA/9) is calculated for each season. The Wtd. RA/9 for a season is multiplied by that season's innings pitched per 162 games. These weighted amounts by season are summed, and the sum is divided by the career sum of innings pitched per 162 games, to arrive at a career Wtd.

RA/9. The career Wtd. RA/9 has been adjusted for all applicable biases.

Runs/162—
A Volume of Success Metric for Pitchers

We calculate the Runs/162 metric for each season, being careful to use the right number of "Games in Season" for each year. We simply sum the Runs/162 amounts for each season to produce the career Runs/162. This career Runs/162 amount has already been corrected for all biases.

Defining Teams, Players, Rosters, and Other Matters

The Teams

Twenty "teams" have been assembled in this book. Sixteen of these "teams" are the original 16 teams of the twentieth century. These teams keep their identity even after they move to another city, as was the case with the Washington Senators moving to Minnesota in 1961.

Two "teams" consist of the expansion teams for the American and the National League. The expansion teams for each league are grouped together for two reasons. First, these teams have existed for such a short time that their best players do not deserve historic recognition alongside the All-Stars from the original 16 teams. Second, by combining these teams, we generate two teams whose roster can compete effectively against the other 16 teams. These two expansion teams have the disadvantage of missing out on the volume pitching years found earlier in the century. Their main advantage is that they have many quality relievers to choose from, as the relief artist came of age during expansion years.

The remaining two "teams" are comprised of players from 1876 to 1887 and from 1888 to 1899. The nineteenth century squads don't have home run hitters or pitchers with outstanding rate of success results. They do have star hitters and some incredible volume pitchers.

The Players

Results for all major league seasons from 1876 to the present are included in players' career totals. Excluded from consideration are player seasons from the National Association in 1871–1875. The schedules of many of the National Association teams were so short as to make their players' performances of dubious quality for comparison to players from other periods.

The entire career results for a player are assigned to his primary team, i.e., the team for which he has the most total at bats or innings pitched.

A player's primary career position designation is usually the position he plays the most games at during his career. However, if a player plays at least 80 percent as many games in his secondary career position as his primary position, and if he produces at least twice the Hits Contribution at this secondary position, his career position designation is this secondary position. Only 21 out of the several thousand players rated are covered by this exception. One of these exceptions is Ernie Banks, who played slightly more games at first than at short, but who produced nearly all of his career Hits Contribution at short. Banks is considered a career shortstop.

Players who played more games as a designated hitter than any position on the field are assigned to the field position they played the most games at. This is fair, as the career performance of these players reflects poor fielding results in their designated hitter years, representing their true performance value as if they were forced to play a field position. There are no free rides in fielding for DHs.

The Rosters

Each team roster consists of sixteen position players and nine pitchers. Eight reserves back up the starting infielders and outfielders, one for each position. No distinction is made in the outfield between right, center, and left fielders. Five starting pitchers and four relievers round out the roster, reflecting the days when teams did not require a big bullpen. In the case of the nineteenth century squads, when relief pitchers were basically nonexistent, nine starting pitchers have been selected.

Average statistics are presented for the eight starters, the eight reserves, starting pitchers, and relief pitchers. A "weighted average" grand total for hitters gives twice the weighting to the eight starters as compared to the eight reserves.

Minimum Volume Requirement

This work ranks the very best players for each team. For rate of success metrics, where volume doesn't matter, we must set a minimum volume to protect the best players from being crowded out by pretenders to the throne.

For both rate and volume of success, hitters must have at least 2,000 career total at bats, after adjusting to 162 game schedules. (A total of 1,500 minimum at bats are required for currently active players.) Starting pitchers must work at least 800 innings (600 for currently active pitchers), after adjusting to 162-game schedules. Relief pitchers must work at least 200 games in relief (150 for currently active pitchers), after adjusting to 162-game schedules. Or relievers must work at least 400 innings (300 innings for currently active players), after adjusting to 162-game schedules, with a career average of no more than 3 innings per game pitched.

Saves and Other Pitching Statistics

Strikeout pitchers, control pitchers, and pitchers with many wins and a high winning percentage don't gain any advantage because of these attributes. A pitcher's rate of success results are determined by how many runs he gives up per 9 innings pitched, and his volume of success results are also determined by how many innings he works. Everything else is just an element of how many runs a pitcher gives up or, like wins and winning percentage, is heavily dependent on the team for which the pitcher performs.

Including the save as a reduction in RA/9 (Runs Allowed per 9 Innings) would bias pitching ratings toward the modern closer. Because the role of the closer was different in the fifties and sixties, those closers would not receive as much credit as the modern closer, even though they may have more successfully prevented runs. Long relievers and set-up men, who rarely make the All-Star rosters anyway, would be practically shut out from consideration. The final rankings show a predominance of save artists, but only because they are very good at preventing runs, and not because they are save artists.

RBIs, Batting Average, and Other Batting Statistics

Runs batted in and runs scored are extremely unreliable indicators of a player's value, as they are enormously influenced by that hitter's place in the batting order, the other hitters in the lineup, and the cycles of hitter and pitcher dominance. Hack Wilson's 190 RBI record in 1930, aided by huge advantages from all of the above items, is one of the most overrated records in all sports. Another highly overrated statistic is the batting average, which measures how good a player is at hitting singles and extra base hits, but not how good he is at getting on base, hitting for power, and generating runs for his team. Finally, home runs and other batting statistics only serve to the extent they influence the Production statistic.

The Definition of On-Base Percentage

Baseball's Best Careers does not include sacrifice flies in the denominator for computing on-base percentage. A sacrifice fly reflects a hitter doing his job, and it shouldn't penalize his on-base performance to do so. Also, sacrifice flies were not tracked before the 1950s. Instead, they were buried in with sacrifice hits, which do not affect the on-base percentage denominator. Finally, having a sacrifice fly penalize on-base percentage and not penalize batting average is logically inconsistent.

No Ballpark Adjustment

If we insist on adjusting raw statistics for biases, why don't we adjust for one of the greatest potential biases, the ballpark? The problems with a ballpark adjustment are:

- Existing ballpark adjustments demonstrate how complicated this is to accomplish. Two or three pages of extremely complex formulas and elaborate explanations violate the objective that metrics should be simple to understand.
- A ballpark adjustment violates the objective that metrics should be easy to duplicate.
- The ballpark adjustment creates as many problems as it fixes. For example, Larry Walker's home games in 1997 were at incredibly hitter friendly Coors Field. Yet Walker hit 29 of his 49 home runs on the road that year. Adjusting Walker's performance would unfairly penalize him for the incorrect assumption that he hit most of his home runs at Coors. Others would be incorrectly penalized or aided when hitting in ballparks where one field has a "short porch," while the opposite field has deep dimensions. Finally, players like Wade Boggs adapt to a park regardless of its dimensions, while other players fail miserably in ballparks like Fenway because they overswing for the fences.
- Perhaps most important, when we make ballpark adjustments, we are tampering with results that occur within a year. In effect, we are changing the outcome of a season, including who wins the batting title, home run title, ERA title, etc. This book does not in any way alter how one player compares to another player within a year.

Hitting in Fenway may help Fred Lynn, and pitching in Wrigley Field may hurt Ferguson Jenkins. These factors are just the breaks of the game, along with: injuries, lost seasons due to military service, rule changes affecting spitballs and other matters, no competition from black players until the 1940s, and various other factors that produce a player's results within a season.

The statistics in this book are not adjusted for ballpark factors for the above reasons. That adjustment is beyond the scope of this book and, frankly, is a suspect adjustment in metrics used in other books.

Hitter's Inflation

This term simply means the player's batting statistics are inflated by his hitting in a hitter's year, i.e., a year where the league's average Production exceeds the historic average Production of 705.9. The amount of inflation is stated in percentage terms. For example, the National League average Production for 1953 was 747, which represents a hitter's inflation of 5.8 percent when compared to the 705.9 historic average (747 / 705.9 = 1.058).

Hitter's Deflation

A player's batting statistics are deflated by his hitting in a pitcher's year. Nineteen sixty-eight was a well-known pitcher's year, as the average Production in the American League that year was only 639, representing a hitter's deflation of 10.5 percent for all American League hitters (705.9 / 639 = 1.105).

Appendix: The 125 Greatest Players of All Time

The careers for the ten best players of all time for each field position, the forty best starting pitchers, and the five best relief pitchers, are presented by season in the Appendix. These players are the elite of the elite, as their numbers represent only half the number of players actually selected for the Hall of Fame.

Selection Process

Players are selected based on a careful consideration of both career volume of success and career rate of success performances. What is the relative importance of these two metrics? The key factor for hitters is the volume of success, the amount that a player contributes above an average performance over his entire career. But a high rate of success is also an influencing factor. When two players achieve about the same volume of success, the better player is the player with the higher rate of success, even though he will usually have less at bats, hits, and home runs than the other player. Thus, a Joe DiMaggio, Ted Williams, or Roy Campanella will get an extra boost from their higher rate of success despite the impact that lost seasons had on their volume of success. Meanwhile, Eddie Murray and Reggie Jackson will lose in comparison to players with similar volume results, even though their very long careers gave them over 500 home runs and other impressive raw statistics.

In ranking starting pitchers, the advantages that the one, two, or three man rotations had a hundred years ago in accumulating volume results is filtered out. This is accomplished by adjusting every pitcher's volume of success results by the normal frequency of starts for the average team during each pitcher's career. As a result, instead of nearly every great starting pitcher coming from the nineteenth century, only four of the forty chosen come from that era. The volume of success metric is still the most important factor in rating great players, but the volume must now come from many years of above average performance, rather than a few years of above average performance while starting nearly every game.

Currently active players are evaluated on only their career statistics to date, no matter how much potential they have to improve on these statistics. This book does not attempt to predict the future. As a player's career progresses, he will have every opportunity to move up in the ratings in the future.

The Statistics Presented

The top half of the page for each hitter shows his actual raw statistics, as well as the Total Factor (TF) and Hits Contribution (HC) metrics that relate to these unadjusted actual numbers. The bottom half shows his adjusted statistics. The total seasons number appearing on the bottom of the first column is computed by dividing the player's career adjusted total at bats by 676, the historic average total at bats. Once we have this total seasons number, we divide the career actual totals and the career adjusted totals by this amount to display the season average results for each column. (For pitchers, the career totals are divided by innings and multiplied by nine to arrive at the results per 9 innings pitched.)

The adjusted statistics for hitters shows the full power of the concepts in this work, as every raw statistic from hits and home runs to batting average and slugging percentage is adjusted to remove biases. The end result is a world of baseball statistics without bias, truly reflecting how well a player actually performed compared to all players in history. Now we can see for ourselves how Carl Yastrzemski hit for a .332 average in 1968, instead of his unadjusted .301 average during a year that had a 10.5 percent hitter's deflation. We can see how great Mike Schmidt's 1981 season really was when adjusted to a full 162 game schedule. We can see how each season fits into an unbiased career total. And we can judge for ourselves the greatness of each of these 80 talented hitters.

One Example of the Power of the New Metrics

Ty Cobb hit for a consistently high average during his entire career, finishing with a .366 actual batting average — and a .382 adjusted average, after factoring in a 4 percent career hitter's deflation. On the surface, Cobb lost nothing with age as his career progressed, other than some speed on the base paths. But once we adjust for the hitter's deflation of the Dead Ball Era, and the hitter's inflation of the Roaring Twenties, a completely different view of Cobb's career emerges, as shown on his page in the Appendix. Adjusted for hitter's deflation, Cobb hit .405 in 1907, .382 in 1908, and he then hit over .400 for an incredible ten straight years from 1909 to 1918. Cobb's real batting average performance drops off dramatically in 1920, at the same time the league's hitter's inflation takes off. The same pattern can be seen in his Total Factor and Hits Contribution results. Cobb goes from being a historically underrated phenomenon during the Dead Ball Era to an overrated veteran in the twenties.

Cobb has 4,612 adjusted hits over his career — 423 more hits than he actually achieved. The extra hits come from adjusting his results to a 162 game schedule, and from adjusting for the impact of the 4 percent career hitter's deflation. On an adjusted basis, Cobb had 201 more hits than Pete Rose, who finishes with 4,411 adjusted hits (versus Rose's 4,256 actual hits.) The all time hits leader, as it turns out, is neither Cobb nor Rose, but the nineteenth century first baseman Cap Anson. Anson's 2,995 actual hits become 4,818 adjusted hits during his National League career. If we add in adjusted hits from his 1871–1875 performance in the National Association, Anson ends up with more than 6,000 career hits.

Ty Cobb's statistical stories are just the beginning of what lies ahead in this book. Welcome to a whole new world of baseball statistics.

Boston/Milwaukee/ Atlanta Braves (1900–2000)

For nearly 50 years, a lack of talent left the Braves in the humble position of joining the Phillies as the league's doormats. Warren Spahn, Eddie Mathews, and home run king Hank Aaron arrived in the 1940s and 1950s to change the team's fortunes. These three superstars, with help from Johnny Sain, Joe Torre, Del Crandall, Johnny Logan, Rico Carty, and Phil Niekro, produced 21 winning seasons from 1946 to 1974. Atlanta then stumbled for 16 seasons after Aaron's departure, despite a stellar contribution from Dale Murphy in the 1980s. In the 1990s and 2000, Greg Maddux, Tom Glavine, and John Smoltz formed one of the best trios of starting pitchers ever, while leading Atlanta to nine division titles. A supporting cast of hitters included Chipper Jones, Andruw Jones, Fred McGriff, Andres Galarraga, David Justice, and Javy Lopez.

Profiled Braves Players

Hank Aaron

Aaron owns the major league home run record, at least until Ken Griffey, Jr., or another slugger in today's era of easy home runs passes him. Aaron earned his home run crown the hard way, never hitting more than 47 home runs in any one season, and hitting fewer home runs before age 30 than several other great home run hitters. Aaron is the home run king because he had staying power—hitting 20 or more home runs for 20 straight years. Maybe Babe Ruth could have hit over 20 home runs for 20 straight years too, instead of his actual 16 straight

years, if he hadn't been a pitcher for his first five seasons. But Ruth was once a pitcher, and Aaron deserves accolades for owning this significant record.

Aaron demonstrated a full arsenal of abilities. He won three Gold Gloves for fielding, won two batting titles, and even stole 240 bases in 313 attempts in his career. He would have stolen 300 or 400 bases if he had the green light when he first came to the big leagues—he had only 29 attempts in his first six seasons. Aaron's only real weakness was his relatively low .377 lifetime on-base percentage, as he never drew 100 walks in a season.

Aaron hit .305 with 3,771 hits and 755 home runs in 13,798 total at bats. Adjusted for negligible hitter's deflation, Aaron hit .306 with 773 home runs, for a 935 Wtd. Production. His 971 Total Factor ranks third in league rate of success for outfielders, while his 1,429 Hits Contribution ranks second to Willie Mays in league volume of success.

Eddie Mathews

Mathews was already an established home run threat when Hank Aaron arrived in the big leagues in 1954. And, for a while, it looked like Mathews would end up with more career home runs than Aaron. Mathews had an exceptional first ten years, hitting 370 home runs before he turned 30, as compared to Aaron's 342. In fact, in the season Aaron reached that 342 total, he trailed Mathews by 80 home runs. But Mathews hit only 35 home runs after he turned 34, finishing with 512 career home runs. Aaron, on the other hand, hit 274 home runs after he turned 34.

Below are Mathews' first ten seasons, when he was in his twenties, and the remainder of his career:

Years	TAB	HR	BA	Adj. Wtd. BA	PRO	TF	HC
1952–61	6,412	370	.283	.274	907	913	636
1962–68	3,595	142	.250	.256	820	837	193

Mathews hit .271 with 512 home runs in his career. Adjusted for a 1 percent career hitter's inflation, Mathews hit .268 with 524 home runs. His 887 Total Factor ranks fourth in league rate of success for third basemen, while his 829 Hits Contribution ranks second in league volume of success, trailing only Mike Schmidt.

Chipper Jones

Jones has played just six full seasons in the majors, but is already making his mark as one of the greatest third basemen of all time. Jones shows a steady improvement over his career, with a breakout year in 1999 at the age of 27 to win the league's MVP Award. In his career to date, Jones is hitting .303 with 189 home runs, for a 935 Production. Adjusted for a 7 percent career hitter's inflation, Jones hit .284 with 182 home runs, for an 875 Wtd. Production. His 891 Total Factor ranks second in league rate of success among league third basemen — behind only Mike Schmidt. Jones' 343 Hits Contribution currently ranks 10th in league volume of success.

Joe Torre

Torre was a very good player, long before he became manager of the New York Yankees. Torre has been asked to handle many roles in his baseball career. He broke in with the Braves as a catcher, his primary career position. In 1966, his best season with the Braves, Joe Torre the catcher hit .315 with 36 home runs. Torre later played catcher, first, and third for the Cardinals. In 1971, he hit a career high .363 for the Cardinals while playing third base. Traded to the Mets after the 1974 season, Torre finished his career playing both third and first.

In his career, Torre hit .297 with 252 home runs. Adjusted for a 2 percent career hitter's deflation, he hit .304 with 257 home runs, for an 836 Wtd. Production. His 822 Total Factor ranks Torre seventh in league rate of success for catchers, while his 475 Hits Contribution ranks him sixth in league volume of success among catchers.

Dale Murphy

Murphy managed to be an obscure two-time MVP in Atlanta. He broke into the big leagues as an average catcher and first baseman, and he finished his career as an unwanted 37-year-old outfielder who completely lost his hitter's touch. These two challenging periods covered over half his career. But, in the middle of his career, Murphy won five straight Gold Gloves while generating impressive power, speed, and on-base numbers:

Years	TAB	HR	BA	Adj. Wtd. BA	PRO	TF	HC
1982–87	4,149	218	.289	.290	919	968	416
All others	4,825	180	.246	.250	748	763	14

Murphy hit .265 with 398 home runs in his career, along with 161 stolen bases and 21 Fielding Factor points. Adjusted for 1 percent hitter's deflation, Murphy hit .268 with 408 home runs. His 854 Total Factor ranks 47th in league rate of success for outfielders, while his 430 Hits Contribution ranks 24th in league volume of success.

Warren Spahn

Spahn never won more than 23 games in a season, and he lost three seasons to war duty. Yet Spahn managed to win 363 games over his career, the fourth highest wins total in history and the most wins by any pitcher who began his career after the Dead Ball Era. Warren was as steady as they came, winning 20 games 13 times in his career, and throwing as effectively at age 42, when he earned a 23–7 record, as he did when he was a 25-year-old rookie right out of military service.

Spahn was 363–245 with a 3.09 ERA in his career. His 3.59 Wtd. RA/9 ranks 15th in league rate of success. But because he worked 5,244 innings, Spahn was able to save 590 runs from scoring compared to the league average performer, ranking him third in league volume of success.

Greg Maddux

If Greg Maddux could give back the first six years of his career, would he? Maddux struggled to a miserable 8–18 record in his first two seasons, while giving up 39 more runs than the historic average pitcher. He produced respectable seasons for the Cubs in 1988, 1989, and 1991, but none of these seasons came close to Maddux's level of performance in future years.

Years	IP	W–L	SO	ERA	Wtd. RA/9	Runs/162
1986–91	1,174	75–64	738	3.61	4.61	(8)
1992–00	2,144	165–71	1,612	2.40	2.62	484

If Maddux's career started in 1992, he would have the best rate of success for a starting pitcher in history, as his 2.62

Wtd. RA/9 is 8 percent better than the 2.84 number earned by the current number one, Pedro Martinez.

Maddux will be 35 in 2001; he has several years to add to his volume of success. At this point in his career, Maddux is 240–135 with a 2.83 ERA. Maddux's 3.31 Wtd. RA/9 ranks second to Martinez in league rate of success, while his 476 Runs/162 currently ranks sixth in league volume of success.

Tom Glavine

Glavine's career parallels Maddux's. He had a rocky four-year introduction into the majors, before becoming an effective star and the best number two pitcher on any staff. Glavine's best season was in 1998, when he went 20–6 with a 2.47 ERA and 2.59 Wtd. RA/9. Two years later he led the league with 21 wins at age 34.

Years	IP	W–L	SO	ERA	Wtd. RA/9	Runs/162
1987–90	646	33–41	323	4.29	5.38	(59)
1991–00	2,255	175–84	1,488	3.12	3.45	288

Like Maddux, Glavine will be 35 in 2001, giving him several years to add to his current numbers. Glavine is 208–125 lifetime, with a 3.38 ERA, a 3.87 Wtd. RA/9, ranking him 45th in league rate of success, and he saved 229 runs from scoring, ranking him 33rd in league volume of success.

Boston/Milwaukee/Atlanta Braves   **Hitters Volume of Success**

Pos	Years	Name	AB	BB	HBP	TAB	H	2B	3B	HR	BA	OB	SA	PRO	Wtd PRO	SB	CS	SBF	SPF	FF	R TF	V HC
C	1960-77	J.Torre	7,874	779	85	8,738	2,342	344	59	252	.297	.367	.452	819	836	23	29	(4)	(9)	(0)	822	475
1B	1986-	F.McGriff	7,352	1,136	31	8,519	2,103	372	20	417	.286	.384	.512	896	874	70	34	0	(3)	(9)	862	387
2B	1907-14	B.Sweeney	3,692	423	12	4,127	1,004	153	40	11	.272	.349	.344	693	736	172	0	0	9	13	758	139
SS	1912-35	R.Maranville	10,078	839	39	10,956	2,605	380	177	28	.258	.318	.340	658	659	291	93	(3)	8	42	706	220
3B	1952-68	E.Mathews	8,537	1,444	26	10,007	2,315	354	72	512	.271	.378	.509	888	877	68	39	(1)	7	4	887	829
OF	1954-76	H.Aaron	12,364	1,402	32	13,798	3,771	624	98	755	.305	.377	.555	932	935	240	73	6	8	22	971	1,429
OF	1976-93	D.Murphy	7,960	986	28	8,974	2,111	350	39	398	.265	.348	.469	817	824	161	68	3	6	21	854	430
OF	1930-40	W.Berger	5,163	435	38	5,636	1,550	299	59	242	.300	.359	.522	881	857	36	0	0	4	(8)	854	272
Starters	Averages		7,878	931	36	8,844	2,225	360	71	327	.282	.361	.470	831	833	133	42	0	4	10	847	523
C	1992-	J.Lopez	2,761	184	29	2,974	800	130	10	143	.290	.341	.499	840	786	7	16	(8)	(7)	4	775	146
1B	1894-11	F.Tenney	7,595	874	63	8,532	2,231	270	77	22	.294	.371	.358	730	772	285	0	0	10	14	795	122
2B	1978-89	G.Hubbard	4,441	539	33	5,013	1,084	214	22	70	.244	.330	.349	680	684	35	35	(6)	2	45	725	98
SS	1951-63	J.Logan	5,244	451	43	5,738	1,407	216	41	93	.268	.331	.378	710	690	19	13	(1)	0	27	715	150
3B	1993-	C.Jones	3,469	554	5	4,028	1,051	204	18	189	.303	.400	.536	935	875	97	26	10	10	(5)	891	343
OF	1972-87	G.Matthews	7,147	940	21	8,108	2,011	319	51	234	.281	.367	.439	805	815	183	74	5	9	(8)	820	249
OF	1989-	D.Justice	4,846	779	17	5,642	1,373	246	20	276	.283	.384	.513	898	864	48	43	(7)	1	(11)	847	247
OF	1942-52	T.Holmes	4,992	480	24	5,496	1,507	292	47	88	.302	.366	.432	798	807	40	0	0	(3)	27	832	207
Reserves	Averages		5,062	600	29	5,691	1,433	236	36	139	.283	.362	.427	789	785	89	26	(1)	3	12	799	195
Totals	Weighted Ave.		6,939	820	34	7,793	1,961	318	59	264	.283	.361	.460	821	817	118	37	(0)	3	11	831	413

Pitchers Volume of Success

Pos	Years	Name	G	GS	IP	W	L	SV	SO	BB	ERA	RA/9	Wtd RA/9	R V Runs /162
SP	1942-65	W.Spahn	750	665	5,244	363	245	29	2,583	1,434	3.09	3.46	3.59	590
SP	1986-	G.Maddux	471	467	3,318	240	135	0	2,350	733	2.83	3.24	3.31	476
SP	1898-10	V.Willis	513	471	3,996	249	205	11	1,651	1,212	2.63	3.67	3.90	316
SP	1987-	T.Glavine	434	434	2,901	208	125	0	1,811	965	3.38	3.76	3.87	229
SP	1988-	J.Smoltz	356	356	2,414	157	113	0	2,098	774	3.35	3.68	3.84	200
Starters	Averages		505	479	3,575	243	165	8	2,099	1,024	3.02	3.54	3.68	362
RP	1957-74	D.McMahon	874	2	1,311	90	68	153	1,003	579	2.96	3.31	3.70	127
RP	1981-95	S.Bedrosian	732	46	1,191	76	79	184	921	518	3.38	3.75	4.11	61
RP	1993-	G.McMichael	453	0	523	31	29	53	459	193	3.25	3.70	3.62	58
RP	1969-88	G.Garber	931	9	1,510	96	113	218	940	445	3.34	3.90	4.26	51
Relievers	Averages		748	14	1,134	73	72	152	831	434	3.23	3.67	3.98	74
Totals	Averages		1,252	493	4,708	317	237	160	2,929	1,457	3.07	3.57	3.76	436

Boston/Milwaukee/Atlanta Braves   **Hitters Rate of Success**

Pos	Years	Name	AB	BB	HBP	TAB	H	2B	3B	HR	BA	OB	SA	PRO	Wtd PRO	SB	CS	SBF	SPF	FF	R TF	V HC
C	1960-77	J.Torre	7,874	779	85	8,738	2,342	344	59	252	.297	.367	.452	819	836	23	29	(4)	(9)	(0)	822	475
1B	1986-	F.McGriff	7,352	1,136	31	8,519	2,103	372	20	417	.286	.384	.512	896	874	70	34	0	(3)	(9)	862	387
2B	1907-14	B.Sweeney	3,692	423	12	4,127	1,004	153	40	11	.272	.349	.344	693	736	172	0	0	9	13	758	139
SS	1962-74	D.Menke	5,071	698	46	5,815	1,270	225	40	101	.250	.346	.370	717	737	34	54	(12)	4	(11)	718	94
3B	1993-	C.Jones	3,469	554	5	4,028	1,051	204	18	189	.303	.400	.536	935	875	97	26	10	10	(5)	891	343
OF	1954-76	H.Aaron	12,364	1,402	32	13,798	3,771	624	98	755	.305	.377	.555	932	935	240	73	6	8	22	971	1,429
OF	1996-	A.Jones	2,335	238	26	2,599	635	129	21	116	.272	.346	.494	840	781	95	33	11	10	69	870	139
OF	1976-93	D.Murphy	7,960	986	28	8,974	2,111	350	39	398	.265	.348	.469	817	824	161	68	3	6	21	854	430
Starters	Averages		6,265	777	33	7,075	1,786	300	42	280	.285	.367	.480	847	847	112	40	2	4	12	865	430
C	1992-	J.Lopez	2,761	184	29	2,974	800	130	10	143	.290	.341	.499	840	786	7	16	(8)	(7)	4	775	146
1B	1894-11	F.Tenney	7,595	874	63	8,532	2,231	270	77	22	.294	.371	.358	730	772	285	0	0	10	14	795	122
2B	1978-89	G.Hubbard	4,441	539	33	5,013	1,084	214	22	70	.244	.330	.349	680	684	35	35	(6)	2	45	725	98
SS	1951-63	J.Logan	5,244	451	43	5,738	1,407	216	41	93	.268	.331	.378	710	690	19	13	(1)	0	27	715	150
3B	1952-68	E.Mathews	8,537	1,444	26	10,007	2,315	354	72	512	.271	.378	.509	888	877	68	39	(1)	7	4	887	829
OF	1930-40	W.Berger	5,163	435	38	5,636	1,550	299	59	242	.300	.359	.522	881	857	36	0	0	4	(8)	854	272
OF	1989-	D.Justice	4,846	779	17	5,642	1,373	246	20	276	.283	.384	.513	898	864	48	43	(7)	1	(11)	847	247
OF	1942-52	T.Holmes	4,992	480	24	5,496	1,507	292	47	88	.302	.366	.432	798	807	40	0	0	(3)	27	832	207
Reserves	Averages		5,447	648	34	6,130	1,533	253	44	181	.281	.361	.443	805	800	67	18	(3)	2	13	812	259
Totals	Weighted Ave.		5,992	734	33	6,760	1,702	284	42	247	.284	.365	.469	834	831	97	33	0	3	13	847	373

Pitchers Rate of Success

Pos	Years	Name	G	GS	IP	W	L	SV	SO	BB	ERA	RA/9	R Wtd RA/9	V Runs /162
SP	1986-	G.Maddux	471	467	3,318	240	135	0	2,350	733	2.83	3.24	3.31	476
SP	1942-65	W.Spahn	750	665	5,244	363	245	29	2,583	1,434	3.09	3.46	3.59	590
SP	1988-	J.Smoltz	356	356	2,414	157	113	0	2,098	774	3.35	3.68	3.84	200
SP	1997-	K.Millwood	112	105	666	50	31	0	578	198	3.78	4.15	3.86	51
SP	1987-	T.Glavine	434	434	2,901	208	125	0	1,811	965	3.38	3.76	3.87	229
Starters	Averages		425	405	2,909	204	130	6	1,884	821	3.16	3.54	3.63	309
RP	1998-	J.Rocker	180	0	163	6	10	64	223	107	2.54	3.25	2.98	29
RP	1993-	G.McMichael	453	0	523	31	29	53	459	193	3.25	3.70	3.62	58
RP	1957-74	D.McMahon	874	2	1,311	90	68	153	1,003	579	2.96	3.31	3.70	127
RP	1981-95	S.Bedrosian	732	46	1,191	76	79	184	921	518	3.38	3.75	4.11	61
Relievers	Averages		560	12	797	51	47	114	652	349	3.14	3.53	3.80	69
Totals	Averages		984	417	3,706	254	176	119	2,536	1,170	3.16	3.54	3.67	378

Boston/Milwaukee/Atlanta Braves
Catchers

V	R	Years	Name	AB	BB	HBP	TAB	H	2B	3B	HR	BA	OB	SA	PRO	Wtd PRO	SB	CS	SBF	SPF	FF	R TF	V HC
1	1	1960-77	J.Torre	7,874	779	85	8,738	2,342	344	59	252	.297	.367	.452	819	836	23	29	(4)	(9)	(0)	822	475
2	2	1992-	J.Lopez	2,761	184	29	2,974	800	130	10	143	.290	.341	.499	840	786	7	16	(8)	(7)	4	775	146
3	5	1949-66	D.Crandall	5,026	424	21	5,471	1,276	179	18	179	.254	.315	.404	718	701	26	28	(5)	(3)	38	731	146
4	3	1908-21	A.Wilson	2,056	292	15	2,363	536	96	22	24	.261	.357	.364	721	765	50	0	0	(3)	12	774	121
5	4	1910-30	H.Gowdy	2,735	311	30	3,076	738	124	27	21	.270	.351	.358	709	731	59	7	3	(10)	13	737	88
6	8	1939-52	P.Masi	3,468	410	10	3,888	917	164	31	47	.264	.344	.370	714	711	45	1	0	(2)	(3)	706	56
7	7	1970-77	E.Williams	3,058	298	32	3,388	756	115	6	138	.247	.321	.424	745	765	2	5	(2)	(10)	(33)	720	32
8	9	1909-20	B.Rariden	2,877	340	13	3,230	682	105	24	7	.237	.320	.298	618	657	47	0	1	0	19	676	(0)
9	10	1942-52	C.Kluttz	1,903	132	7	2,042	510	90	8	19	.268	.318	.354	671	679	5	0	0	(10)	(4)	665	(13)
10	6	1959-69	G.Oliver	2,216	215	15	2,446	546	111	5	93	.246	.317	.427	744	759	24	21	(7)	(7)	(24)	720	(31)
11	12	1901-14	P.Moran	2,634	142	37	2,813	618	102	24	18	.235	.283	.312	595	655	55	0	0	(7)	(1)	647	(43)
12	11	1884-97	C.Ganzel	2,984	161	18	3,163	774	91	45	10	.259	.301	.330	631	641	60	0	0	(6)	17	653	(47)
13	13	1978-89	B.Benedict	2,878	328	13	3,219	696	98	6	18	.242	.322	.299	621	636	12	20	(8)	(8)	14	634	(70)
14	14	1928-35	A.Spohrer	2,218	124	7	2,349	575	103	25	6	.259	.301	.336	637	603	13	0	0	(1)	(10)	591	(101)
15	15	1919-27	M.O'Neil	1,995	139	12	2,146	475	41	23	4	.238	.292	.288	579	562	18	13	(5)	(10)	20	568	(118)

Boston/Milwaukee/Atlanta Braves
First basemen

V	R	Years	Name	AB	BB	HBP	TAB	H	2B	3B	HR	BA	OB	SA	PRO	Wtd PRO	SB	CS	SBF	SPF	FF	R TF	V HC
1	1	1986-	F.McGriff	7,352	1,136	31	8,519	2,103	372	20	417	.286	.384	.512	896	874	70	34	0	(3)	(9)	862	387
2	2	1894-11	F.Tenney	7,595	874	63	8,532	2,231	270	77	22	.294	.371	.358	730	772	285	0	0	10	14	795	122
3	4	1950-66	J.Adcock	6,606	594	17	7,217	1,832	295	35	336	.277	.339	.485	824	806	20	25	(4)	(10)	(7)	785	64
4	3	1947-61	E.Torgeson	4,969	980	8	5,957	1,318	215	46	149	.265	.387	.417	804	783	133	39	1	10	(3)	791	62
5	9	1991-	B.Hunter	1,555	141	11	1,707	364	90	7	67	.234	.302	.430	733	705	4	9	(7)	0	(13)	684	(75)
6	6	1927-38	B.Jordan	2,980	182	5	3,167	890	153	35	17	.299	.340	.391	731	724	20	0	0	0	(11)	713	(81)
7	8	1909-15	F.Beck	2,130	122	27	2,279	536	78	27	33	.252	.301	.360	661	698	31	0	0	2	(14)	685	(89)
8	5	1983-95	G.Perry	3,144	328	11	3,483	832	150	11	59	.265	.336	.376	712	720	142	75	(2)	9	(9)	716	(89)
9	10	1919-28	D.Burrus	1,760	138	11	1,909	513	87	12	11	.291	.347	.373	720	689	18	12	(8)	0	(7)	673	(93)
10	7	1914-25	W.Holke	4,456	191	16	4,663	1,278	153	58	24	.287	.318	.363	682	691	81	50	(14)	7	11	696	(178)

Boston/Milwaukee/Atlanta Braves
Second basemen

V	R	Years	Name	AB	BB	HBP	TAB	H	2B	3B	HR	BA	OB	SA	PRO	Wtd PRO	SB	CS	SBF	SPF	FF	R TF	V HC
1	1	1907-14	B.Sweeney	3,692	423	12	4,127	1,004	153	40	11	.272	.349	.344	693	736	172	0	0	9	13	758	139
2	2	1978-89	G.Hubbard	4,441	539	33	5,013	1,084	214	22	70	.244	.330	.349	680	684	35	35	(6)	2	45	725	98
3	3	1930-45	T.Cuccinello	6,184	579	18	6,781	1,729	334	43	94	.280	.343	.393	736	726	42	3	0	0	(6)	720	92
4	4	1987-95	J.Treadway	2,119	140	12	2,271	596	103	14	28	.281	.329	.383	712	719	14	13	(5)	0	(1)	713	27
5	5	1942-54	C.Ryan	3,982	518	14	4,514	988	181	42	56	.248	.337	.357	694	690	69	12	1	10	(2)	699	26
6	9	1897-10	E.Abbaticchio	3,044	289	33	3,366	772	99	43	11	.254	.325	.325	650	720	142	0	0	2	(35)	686	18
7	7	1966-77	F.Millan	5,791	318	63	6,172	1,617	229	38	22	.279	.324	.343	667	681	67	43	(3)	7	3	689	10
8	8	1994-	K.Lockhart	1,699	139	10	1,848	465	93	13	33	.274	.332	.402	734	685	29	11	4	0	(1)	688	1
9	6	1939-48	B.Rowell	1,901	113	2	2,016	523	95	26	19	.275	.316	.382	699	703	37	0	0	8	(21)	690	(27)
10	10	1950-62	D.O'Connell	4,035	431	22	4,488	1,049	181	35	39	.260	.335	.351	686	660	48	22	(1)	4	17	679	(34)
11	11	1988-98	M.Lemke	3,230	348	0	3,578	795	125	15	32	.246	.319	.324	643	629	11	19	(7)	0	41	663	(45)
12	12	1906-19	D.Shean	2,167	155	13	2,335	495	59	23	6	.228	.284	.285	569	623	66	0	0	0	23	647	(46)
13	15	1922-31	F.Maguire	2,120	82	13	2,215	545	90	22	1	.257	.289	.322	611	566	23	0	1	3	34	603	(92)
14	13	1914-26	J.Rawlings	3,719	257	27	4,003	928	122	28	14	.250	.303	.309	611	622	92	22	(3)	9	(11)	618	(125)
15	14	1939-54	S.Sisti	2,999	283	16	3,298	732	121	19	27	.244	.313	.324	637	639	30	5	(1)	5	(33)	611	(143)

Boston/Milwaukee/Atlanta Braves
Shortstops

V	R	Years	Name	AB	BB	HBP	TAB	H	2B	3B	HR	BA	OB	SA	PRO	Wtd PRO	SB	CS	SBF	SPF	FF	R TF	V HC
1	4	1912-35	R.Maranville	10,078	839	39	10,956	2,605	380	177	28	.258	.318	.340	658	659	291	93	(3)	8	42	706	220
2	2	1951-63	J.Logan	5,244	451	43	5,738	1,407	216	41	93	.268	.331	.378	710	690	19	13	(1)	0	27	715	150
3	3	1987-99	J.Blauser	4,522	569	91	5,182	1,187	217	33	122	.262	.356	.406	762	741	65	41	(3)	5	(30)	712	113
4	1	1962-74	D.Menke	5,071	698	46	5,815	1,270	225	40	101	.250	.346	.370	717	737	34	54	(12)	4	(11)	718	94
5	7	1985-90	A.Thomas	2,103	59	3	2,165	493	76	4	42	.234	.256	.334	591	601	22	18	(6)	10	18	623	(40)
6	5	1931-37	B.Urbanski	3,046	198	21	3,265	791	123	27	19	.260	.309	.337	646	637	24	0	0	0	(6)	631	(59)
7	9	1969-79	D.Chaney	2,113	238	4	2,355	458	75	17	14	.217	.297	.288	585	595	19	18	(7)	7	13	609	(64)
8	11	1982-98	R.Belliard	2,301	136	23	2,460	508	55	14	2	.221	.271	.259	531	530	43	17	3	10	59	603	(72)
9	10	1963-71	W.Woodward	2,187	169	13	2,369	517	79	14	1	.236	.295	.287	582	596	14	15	(6)	0	16	606	(75)
10	13	1939-47	W.Wietelmann	1,762	156	8	1,926	409	55	6	7	.232	.298	.282	580	593	14	0	0	0	(4)	590	(76)
11	6	1980-92	R.Ramirez	5,494	264	21	5,779	1,432	224	31	53	.261	.297	.342	639	649	112	75	(6)	7	(18)	631	(87)
12	14	1925-35	D.Farrell	1,799	109	10	1,918	467	63	8	10	.260	.306	.320	626	595	14	1	(1)	0	(16)	578	(87)
13	8	1969-78	M.Perez	3,131	245	10	3,386	771	108	22	22	.246	.303	.316	619	629	11	17	(6)	5	(7)	620	(89)
14	12	1963-74	S.Jackson	3,055	250	11	3,316	767	81	28	7	.251	.310	.303	613	629	126	51	7	10	(45)	601	(133)
15	15	1930-40	R.Warstler	4,088	405	11	4,504	935	133	36	11	.229	.300	.287	587	567	42	22	(3)	9	(0)	573	(226)

Boston/Milwaukee/Atlanta Braves
Third basemen

V	R	Years	Name	AB	BB	HBP	TAB	H	2B	3B	HR	BA	OB	SA	PRO	Wtd PRO	SB	CS	SBF	SPF	FF	R TF	V HC
1	2	1952-68	E.Mathews	8,537	1,444	26	10,007	2,315	354	72	512	.271	.378	.509	888	877	68	39	(1)	7	4	887	829
2	1	1993-	C.Jones	3,469	554	5	4,028	1,051	204	18	189	.303	.400	.536	935	875	97	26	10	10	(5)	891	343
3	3	1978-88	B.Horner	3,777	369	16	4,162	1,047	169	8	218	.277	.344	.499	843	853	14	18	(5)	(8)	(25)	814	166
4	4	1911-19	R.Smith	3,907	420	34	4,361	1,087	208	49	27	.278	.353	.377	731	788	117	5	0	0	2	790	159
5	5	1917-23	T.Boeckel	2,880	237	11	3,128	813	130	36	27	.282	.339	.381	720	721	90	46	(9)	10	(15)	707	(14)
6	7	1914-22	W.Barbare	1,777	88	6	1,871	462	52	21	1	.260	.297	.315	612	619	37	16	(3)	0	(21)	595	(89)
7	6	1973-88	J.Royster	4,208	411	11	4,630	1,049	165	33	40	.249	.318	.333	650	653	189	95	(1)	10	(1)	662	(100)

Boston/Milwaukee/Atlanta Braves
Outfielders

V	R	Years	Name	AB	BB	HBP	TAB	H	2B	3B	HR	BA	OB	SA	PRO	Wtd PRO	SB	CS	SBF	SPF	FF	R TF	V HC
1	1	1954-76	H.Aaron	12,364	1,402	32	13,798	3,771	624	98	755	.305	.377	.555	932	935	240	73	6	8	22	971	1,429
2	3	1976-93	D.Murphy	7,960	986	28	8,974	2,111	350	39	398	.265	.348	.469	817	824	161	68	3	6	21	854	430
3	4	1930-40	W.Berger	5,163	435	38	5,636	1,550	299	59	242	.300	.359	.522	881	857	36	0	0	4	(8)	854	272
4	7	1972-87	G.Matthews	7,147	940	21	8,108	2,011	319	51	234	.281	.367	.439	805	815	183	74	5	9	(8)	820	249
5	5	1989-	D.Justice	4,846	779	17	5,642	1,373	246	20	276	.283	.384	.513	898	864	48	43	(7)	1	(11)	847	247
6	6	1942-52	T.Holmes	4,992	480	24	5,496	1,507	292	47	88	.302	.366	.432	798	807	40	0	0	(3)	27	832	207
7	8	1963-79	R.Carty	5,606	642	13	6,261	1,677	278	17	204	.299	.372	.464	836	852	21	26	(5)	(9)	(27)	812	146
8	2	1996-	A.Jones	2,335	238	26	2,599	635	129	21	116	.272	.346	.494	840	781	95	33	11	10	69	870	139
9	12	1987-	R.Gant	5,847	697	30	6,574	1,499	275	46	292	.256	.339	.469	808	790	234	95	6	8	(14)	790	134
10	9	1906-14	J.Bates	3,913	503	49	4,465	1,087	167	73	25	.278	.367	.377	744	805	187	0	0	10	(5)	810	118
11	13	1958-74	F.Alou	7,339	423	57	7,819	2,101	359	49	206	.286	.330	.433	763	780	107	67	(3)	9	(1)	785	93
12	10	1992-	R.Klesko	2,925	392	16	3,333	824	173	20	165	.282	.370	.524	893	841	33	20	(2)	(1)	(30)	808	78
13	11	1961-71	M.Jones	3,091	383	77	3,551	778	132	31	133	.252	.349	.444	792	809	65	40	(4)	6	(14)	798	67
14	14	1956-66	W.Covington	2,978	247	24	3,249	832	128	17	131	.279	.339	.466	805	800	7	4	(0)	(4)	(19)	777	30
15	17	1913-28	L.Mann	4,716	324	28	5,068	1,332	203	106	44	.282	.332	.398	731	766	129	21	(2)	8	(6)	765	22
16	15	1908-15	V.Campbell	2,069	132	18	2,219	642	85	36	15	.310	.357	.408	765	791	92	0	0	0	(15)	776	21
17	16	1950-54	S.Jethroe	1,763	177	25	1,965	460	80	25	49	.261	.337	.418	755	742	98	14	17	10	7	775	17
18	18	1913-29	B.Southworth	4,359	402	14	4,775	1,296	173	91	52	.297	.359	.415	773	770	138	85	(19)	8	5	765	17
19	20	1974-90	C.Washington	6,787	468	36	7,291	1,884	334	69	164	.278	.328	.420	747	759	312	134	6	10	(15)	759	7
20	21	1968-80	R.Garr	5,108	246	19	5,373	1,562	212	64	75	.306	.340	.416	756	770	172	83	1	10	(23)	759	3
21	19	1938-48	M.West	2,676	353	13	3,042	681	136	20	77	.254	.344	.407	751	762	19	0	0	7	(10)	760	(1)
22	23	1995-	M.Tucker	1,995	232	27	2,254	523	101	23	69	.262	.347	.440	787	733	56	27	1	10	10	753	(4)
23	22	1931-45	G.Moore	3,543	317	14	3,874	958	179	53	58	.270	.333	.400	733	740	31	10	(5)	9	11	755	(5)
24	24	1989-97	D.Sanders	2,048	155	19	2,222	545	70	43	38	.266	.324	.398	722	700	183	59	26	10	13	750	(10)
25	25	1914-24	W.Cruise	2,321	238	12	2,571	644	83	39	30	.277	.348	.386	733	761	49	15	(4)	8	(24)	742	(20)
26	28	1983-96	D.James	2,708	318	11	3,037	781	142	21	32	.288	.365	.392	757	754	43	38	(10)	7	(15)	737	(30)
27	26	1959-71	L.Maye	4,048	282	19	4,349	1,109	190	39	94	.274	.324	.410	734	750	59	34	(2)	8	(18)	739	(38)
28	29	1925-30	J.Welsh	2,684	156	47	2,887	778	127	47	35	.290	.340	.411	751	704	37	4	(0)	10	12	726	(46)
29	32	1905-09	D.Howard	1,833	111	36	1,980	482	54	22	6	.263	.318	.326	644	729	67	0	0	7	(21)	715	(47)
30	40	1938-46	C.Workman	1,749	161	15	1,925	423	57	7	50	.242	.311	.368	679	700	24	0	0	10	(19)	691	(52)
31	30	1895-06	C.Dolan	3,174	227	21	3,422	855	99	37	10	.269	.322	.333	656	714	114	0	0	7	0	721	(52)
32	27	1953-64	B.Bruton	6,056	482	29	6,567	1,651	241	102	94	.273	.329	.393	722	703	207	89	4	10	21	738	(63)
33	31	1913-24	R.Powell	3,324	321	19	3,664	890	117	67	35	.268	.336	.375	711	715	51	56	(23)	10	14	716	(70)
34	36	1927-37	R.Moore	2,253	158	3	2,414	627	110	17	27	.278	.326	.378	705	692	11	1	(1)	9	(3)	698	(71)
35	33	1921-32	L.Richbourg	2,619	174	6	2,799	806	101	51	13	.308	.352	.400	752	702	65	1	(0)	10	(7)	705	(73)
36	35	1932-45	D.Garms	3,111	288	16	3,415	910	141	39	17	.293	.355	.379	735	729	18	8	(3)	0	(26)	701	(80)
37	37	1992-	G.Williams	2,573	149	26	2,748	683	154	16	76	.265	.312	.426	739	689	84	51	(7)	10	1	693	(86)
38	38	1920-28	E.Brown	2,902	127	12	3,041	878	170	33	16	.303	.334	.400	735	705	29	9	(3)	0	(9)	693	(99)
39	41	1930-36	H.Lee	2,750	203	9	2,962	755	144	40	33	.275	.326	.392	718	707	15	0	0	(7)	(14)	686	(107)
40	44	1923-27	G.Felix	2,046	189	17	2,252	561	91	25	12	.274	.341	.361	701	672	28	21	(12)	0	(2)	658	(113)
41	42	1972-83	R.Office	2,413	189	16	2,618	626	101	11	32	.259	.317	.350	668	671	27	30	(12)	10	(4)	665	(116)
42	43	1921-44	J.Cooney	3,372	208	6	3,586	965	130	26	2	.286	.329	.342	671	666	30	5	(2)	(1)	(3)	660	(117)
43	39	1967-81	M.Lum	3,554	366	28	3,948	877	128	20	90	.247	.322	.370	692	704	13	29	(11)	6	(7)	692	(136)
44	45	1960-71	T.Cline	1,834	153	21	2,008	437	53	25	6	.238	.304	.304	609	623	22	19	(8)	6	(13)	609	(143)
45	34	1983-	O.Nixon	5,115	585	5	5,705	1,379	142	27	11	.270	.345	.314	660	639	620	186	41	10	14	705	(151)

Boston/Milwaukee/Atlanta Braves
Starting Pitchers

V	R	Years	Name	G	GS	IP	W	L	SV	SO	BB	ERA	RA/9	R Wtd RA/9	V Runs /162
1	2	1942-65	W.Spahn	750	665	5,244	363	245	29	2,583	1,434	3.09	3.46	3.59	589.5
2	1	1986-	G.Maddux	471	467	3,318	240	135	0	2,350	733	2.83	3.24	3.31	476.4
3	6	1898-10	V.Willis	513	471	3,996	249	205	11	1,651	1,212	2.63	3.67	3.90	315.9
4	5	1987-	T.Glavine	434	434	2,901	208	125	0	1,811	965	3.38	3.76	3.87	228.9
5	3	1988-	J.Smoltz	356	356	2,414	157	113	0	2,098	774	3.35	3.68	3.84	199.6
6	14	1964-87	P.Niekro	864	716	5,404	318	274	29	3,342	1,809	3.35	3.89	4.26	183.9
7	10	1928-38	E.Brandt	378	277	2,268	121	146	17	877	778	3.86	4.31	4.14	110.6
8	9	1942-55	J.Sain	412	245	2,126	139	116	51	910	619	3.49	4.01	4.12	107.7
9	11	1910-27	D.Rudolph	279	240	2,049	121	108	8	786	402	2.66	3.42	4.17	96.4
10	13	1915-27	J.Barnes	422	312	2,570	152	150	13	653	515	3.22	4.02	4.25	93.1
11	16	1950-67	L.Burdette	626	373	3,067	203	144	31	1,074	628	3.66	4.11	4.30	91.5
12	15	1953-67	B.Buhl	457	369	2,587	166	132	6	1,268	1,105	3.55	4.04	4.27	85.1
13	7	1937-45	J.Turner	231	119	1,132	69	60	20	329	283	3.22	3.83	4.00	73.4
14	17	1925-37	B.Smith	435	229	2,246	106	139	40	618	670	3.94	4.56	4.31	64.1
15	20	1910-21	L.Tyler	323	267	2,230	127	116	7	1,003	829	2.95	3.83	4.35	56.1
16	4	1997-	K.Millwood	112	105	666	50	31	0	578	198	3.78	4.15	3.86	51.3
17	8	1906-18	T.Hughes	160	85	863	56	39	17	476	235	2.56	3.22	4.10	46.8
18	12	1948-54	V.Bickford	182	149	1,076	66	57	2	450	467	3.71	4.18	4.19	46.5
19	23	1923-35	L.Benton	455	258	2,297	127	128	22	670	691	4.03	4.66	4.40	42.9
20	22	1937-45	J.Tobin	287	227	1,900	105	112	5	498	557	3.44	4.08	4.37	41.5
21	19	1927-37	B.Cantwell	316	163	1,534	76	108	21	348	382	3.91	4.57	4.34	38.2
22	21	1937-49	R.Barrett	253	149	1,263	69	69	7	333	312	3.53	4.13	4.35	30.9
23	26	1966-84	R.Reed	751	236	2,478	146	140	103	1,481	633	3.46	3.94	4.45	29.7
24	18	1921-30	J.Cooney	159	76	795	34	44	6	224	223	3.72	4.62	4.31	22.6
25	29	1927-39	F.Frankhouse	402	215	1,888	106	97	12	622	701	3.92	4.62	4.46	20.7
26	24	1936-47	J.Lanning	278	104	1,071	58	60	13	295	358	3.58	4.22	4.41	18.9
27	30	1952-63	G.Conley	276	214	1,589	91	96	9	888	511	3.82	4.34	4.46	17.0
28	31	1962-72	D.Lemaster	357	249	1,788	90	105	8	1,305	600	3.58	3.92	4.47	16.5
29	27	1980-91	P.Perez	207	193	1,244	67	68	0	822	344	3.44	3.91	4.46	14.4
30	25	1937-46	N.Andrews	127	97	773	41	54	2	216	236	3.46	4.08	4.42	12.7
31	28	1958-65	C.Willey	199	117	876	38	58	1	493	326	3.76	4.19	4.46	9.7
32	32	1966-73	P.Jarvis	249	169	1,284	85	73	3	755	380	3.58	3.92	4.51	7.1
33	33	1958-70	K.Johnson	334	231	1,737	91	106	9	1,042	413	3.46	4.03	4.53	4.7
34	34	1900-07	T.Pittinger	262	227	2,041	115	113	3	832	734	3.10	4.34	4.55	2.6
35	36	1990-99	S.Avery	278	261	1,539	94	83	0	974	562	4.17	4.62	4.64	(14.8)
36	35	1984-96	Z.Smith	360	291	1,919	100	115	3	1,011	583	3.74	4.37	4.63	(15.8)
37	37	1920-35	H.Betts	307	125	1,366	61	68	16	323	321	3.93	4.72	4.68	(19.5)
38	39	1922-30	J.Genewich	272	166	1,402	73	92	12	316	402	4.29	5.00	4.71	(24.5)
39	38	1969-76	C.Morton	255	242	1,649	87	92	1	650	565	3.73	4.24	4.70	(26.0)
40	40	1915-25	D.Fillingim	200	114	1,076	47	73	5	270	313	3.56	4.46	4.76	(26.1)
41	46	1961-67	B.Hendley	216	126	879	48	52	12	522	329	3.97	4.49	4.97	(40.4)
42	42	1940-46	A.Javery	205	147	1,143	53	74	5	470	452	3.80	4.48	4.93	(50.2)
43	41	1949-57	M.Surkont	236	149	1,194	61	76	8	571	481	4.38	4.90	4.92	(50.8)
44	48	1918-24	M.Watson	178	124	942	50	53	4	208	256	4.03	4.98	5.05	(51.6)
45	44	1899-11	P.Flaherty	173	150	1,303	67	84	2	271	331	3.10	4.25	4.95	(60.5)
46	43	1905-11	I.Young	209	161	1,385	63	95	4	560	316	3.11	4.06	4.94	(61.8)
47	49	1916-33	S.Seibold	191	135	1,064	48	85	5	296	405	4.43	5.22	5.08	(65.0)
48	52	1967-75	G.Stone	203	145	1,021	60	57	5	590	270	3.89	4.62	5.16	(69.3)
49	47	1905-13	B.Brown	234	165	1,452	51	103	4	501	631	3.21	4.43	4.99	(73.8)
50	53	1987-98	P.Smith	231	163	1,026	47	71	1	640	404	4.55	4.89	5.19	(75.7)

Boston/Milwaukee/Atlanta Braves
Starting Pitchers

V	R	Years	Name	G	GS	IP	W	L	SV	SO	BB	ERA	RA/9	R Wtd RA/9	V Runs /162
51	56	1908-12	A.Mattern	138	94	844	36	58	4	254	299	3.37	4.77	5.43	(86.2)
52	54	1911-15	H.Perdue	161	122	918	51	64	7	317	199	3.85	4.94	5.36	(86.4)
53	45	1979-91	R.Mahler	392	271	1,951	96	111	6	952	606	3.99	4.48	4.95	(87.4)
54	55	1906-09	V.Lindaman	131	100	904	36	60	2	286	296	2.92	4.16	5.41	(90.3)
55	51	1961-72	T.Cloninger	352	247	1,768	113	97	6	1,120	798	4.07	4.57	5.14	(114.3)
56	50	1914-25	J.Oeschger	365	199	1,818	82	116	8	535	651	3.81	4.69	5.09	(116.9)
57	57	1963-72	W.Blasingame	222	128	864	46	51	5	512	372	4.52	5.06	5.82	(121.3)
58	58	1902-09	G.Dorner	131	106	910	36	69	1	275	330	3.37	4.75	6.04	(159.3)

Boston/Milwaukee/Atlanta Braves
Relief Pitchers

V	R	Years	Name	G	GS	IP	W	L	SV	SO	BB	ERA	RA/9	R Wtd RA/9	V Runs /162
1	3	1957-74	D.McMahon	874	2	1,311	90	68	153	1,003	579	2.96	3.31	3.70	127.2
2	4	1981-95	S.Bedrosian	732	46	1,191	76	79	184	921	518	3.38	3.75	4.11	60.9
3	2	1993-	G.McMichael	453	0	523	31	29	53	459	193	3.25	3.70	3.62	58.3
4	8	1969-88	G.Garber	931	9	1,510	96	113	218	940	445	3.34	3.90	4.26	51.3
5	6	1989-	M.Stanton	680	1	665	37	32	65	566	251	4.00	4.32	4.13	32.9
6	1	1998-	J.Rocker	180	0	163	6	10	64	223	107	2.54	3.25	2.98	28.6
7	5	1966-75	C.Upshaw	348	0	563	34	36	86	323	177	3.13	3.52	4.11	28.0
8	10	1976-85	R.Camp	414	65	942	56	49	57	407	336	3.37	4.01	4.38	19.8
9	7	1991-	M.Wohlers	408	0	414	32	24	112	457	221	3.78	4.17	4.19	18.0
10	9	1933-45	I.Hutchinson	209	32	611	34	33	13	179	249	3.76	4.25	4.37	13.3
11	11	1992-	P.Borbon	218	0	163	10	7	5	129	95	4.41	4.91	4.43	2.3
12	12	1950-59	E.Johnson	273	19	575	40	23	19	319	231	3.77	4.44	4.53	1.9
13	14	1995-	B.Clontz	272	0	278	22	8	8	210	120	4.34	4.76	4.56	(0.2)
14	15	1964-71	D.Kelley	188	61	520	18	30	5	369	215	3.39	3.89	4.57	(0.5)
15	13	1989-	K.Mercker	366	150	1,069	63	61	19	713	488	4.31	4.75	4.56	(0.6)
16	17	1989-	R.Seanez	204	0	210	16	11	10	197	111	4.59	4.98	4.80	(5.9)
17	16	1971-78	T.House	289	21	536	29	23	33	261	182	3.79	4.33	4.67	(7.0)
18	18	1989-96	D.Lilliquist	262	52	484	25	34	17	261	134	4.13	4.56	4.86	(17.0)
19	19	1973-80	A.Devine	217	12	387	26	22	31	194	135	4.21	4.65	5.01	(19.6)
20	20	1983-88	J.Dedmon	250	3	394	20	16	12	210	186	3.84	4.71	5.08	(22.8)
21	21	1962-71	B.Priddy	249	29	536	24	38	18	294	198	4.00	4.42	5.15	(35.6)
22	22	1975-82	P.Hanna	156	47	437	17	25	1	253	279	4.61	5.14	5.74	(59.6)

BOSTON RED SOX
(1901–2000)

An amazing number of talented players contributed impressive seasons for the Red Sox over the years. Babe Ruth, Tris Speaker, Carlton Fisk, Wade Boggs, Harry Hooper, Carl Mays, Reggie Smith, Fred Lynn, Ellis Burks, Roger Clemens, Mo Vaughn, and George Scott started their careers in Boston, and went on to star for other teams as well. Cy Young, Jimmie Foxx, Lefty Grove, Joe Cronin, Jimmy Collins, Pedro Martinez, Vern Stephens, Dennis Eckersley, and Luis Tiant produced big seasons in Boston, and also starred for other teams. Meanwhile, Ted Williams, Carl Yastrzemski, Jim Rice, Bobby Doerr, Dom DiMaggio, Rico Petrocelli, and Nomar Garciaparra played their entire careers with Boston. Dwight Evans also belongs in this last group, despite playing his last season with Baltimore. Is it any wonder Boston has 60 winning seasons and three .500 seasons in 100 years? Excluding 15 losing seasons from 1919 to 1933, when Red Sox ownership stripped the team of all of its stars, the Red Sox were .500 or better in 74 percent of their seasons.

Profiled Red Sox Players

Babe Ruth and Ted Williams

Two players stand far above everyone else in career Wtd. Production numbers: Babe Ruth and Ted Williams. These two sluggers performed at such a high level for so long, that their tenth best season is still better than the very best season for other well-known stars. Ruth's tenth best Wtd. Production was in 1928, when he hit .323 with 54 home runs, for a 1,115 Wtd. Production. Williams' tenth best Wtd. Production was in 1948, when he hit .369

with 25 home runs, for a 1,074 Wtd. Production. Compare these numbers to the very best seasons for other stars:

Willie Mays	1,073 in 1965
Joe DiMaggio	1,047 in 1941
Hank Greenberg	1,039 in 1940
Eddie Mathews	977 in 1954
Tris Speaker	1,069 in 1912
Mel Ott	1,025 in 1938
Ken Griffey Jr.	1,006 in 1994
Al Kaline	1,029 in 1967
Ed Delahanty	1,051 in 1902
Duke Snider	1,018 in 1954

Ted Williams was blessed with the two critical offensive ingredients to generate runs for his team. Williams had the ability to get on base, as reflected by his career .344 batting average and 2,019 walks in 9,764 total at bats, for a major league record .483 on-base percentage. And he could drive in runs, as reflected by his 521 career home runs and .634 slugging average. Adjusting Williams' career 1,116 Production for 2 percent career hitter's inflation yields a Wtd. Production of 1,093, which is also higher than the best season of the above hitters.

Williams was not a fast runner, and he was at best an average fielder, but his hitting was so awesome that he stands among the very best players of all time. His 1,082 Total Factor gives him the second best career rate of success in history behind Ruth. And even though he missed most of five seasons in the prime of his career to two war efforts, Williams' 1,599 Hits Contribution gives him the fourth best volume of success in history. If Williams had just one of those lost seasons back, he would rank second to Ruth in this category as well. If he had all five years back — but, then again, what if Ruth had started out as an outfielder?

Carl Yastrzemski

As a rookie, Yastrzemski faced the burden of replacing the just retired Ted Williams in left field. Yaz performed admirably over his 23-year career, carving out a niche as the second best hitter in Red Sox history. Note that Yastrzemski, like many fellow American League veterans since 1973, used the DH to prolong his career. This gave him a chance to gross up his statistics, as he accumulated 13,873 total at bats, but it cost him in both rate and volume of success. Compare Yastrzemski's actual career results to his career statistics if he had retired after the 1978 season:

Years	TAB	Hits	HR	BA	Adj. BA	Wtd. PRO	TF	HC
1961–83	13,873	3,419	452	.285	.292	864	892	881
1961–78	11,540	2,869	383	.289	.297	884	924	904

Those extra five years gave Yastrzemski a chance to go well over 3,000 in career hits, and hit more than 400 home runs. But they also cost him 23 Hits Contribution, and lowered his career rate of success by 4 percent. His actual career span gives Yastrzemski the 16th best rate of success and eighth best volume of success for American League outfielders. If he had retired five years earlier, Yaz would rank tenth in rate of success and sixth in volume of success.

Yastrzemski's best season was in 1967, when he hit .326 with 44 home runs. Adjusted for 8 percent hitter's deflation, Yaz hit .351 with 46 home runs, for a 1,122 Wtd. Production. His 1,174 Total Factor ranks 15th among league outfielders in rate of success, with only Ruth, Williams, Mantle, and Cobb ahead of him. His 133.8 Hits Contribution ranks 13th in volume of success, with just these same four superstars ahead of him.

Wade Boggs

Boggs hit like a well-oiled machine for Boston in the 1980s, spraying base hits to every field. His claim to fame includes five batting titles, and seven straight years of 200 or more hits, with 100 or more walks in four of these years. Boggs even sported a .356 lifetime batting average seven years into his career. The man who ate only chicken before games ended up producing 3,010 hits and 1,412 walks in 18 seasons. His .328 career batting average and .419 on-base percentage are especially impressive for a modern day third baseman.

Boggs played on such a high level those first seven full seasons that fans were disappointed when he could no longer maintain that 200 hit rate, and he soon struggled even to reach a .300 batting average. Boggs' performance dropped slightly in 1990–1991. He then became a more ordinary hitter the remainder of his career, with the exception of one upbeat season in 1994 with New York. Breaking Boggs' career into two sections, we find:

Years	TAB	HR	BA	Adj. BA	Wtd. PRO	TF	HC
1982–91	6,647	78	.345	.345	909	918	632
1992–99	3,968	40	.300	.287	750	764	97

Boggs hit .328 with 118 home runs in his career. Adjusted for a career 2 percent hitter's inflation, he hit .322 with 121 home runs, a .412 on-base percentage, and an 847 Wtd. Production. Boggs' 858 Total Factor ranks him fifth in rate of success among league third basemen, while his 729 Hits Contribution ranks him second in volume of success behind George Brett. If Boggs had called it a career after his 1991 season, he'd still have the league's second best volume of success, while owning the league's best rate of success at third with that 918 Total Factor.

Joe Cronin

Cronin broke into the big leagues with a few at bats for Pittsburgh in 1926 and 1927. Cronin played his first full season for Washington in 1929. In 1930, Cronin became a star shortstop, hitting .346 for the Senators. In 1933, Cronin became the team's manager, and he hit .309 to lead the Senators to their first pennant in nearly a decade, while finishing second in the AL MVP voting behind Jimmie Foxx. After the 1934 season, Cronin was sold to the Red Sox for $225,000. He assumed a player-manager role for the Sox, and led them to several second place finishes. After his playing days ended, Cronin managed the 1946 Sox to their first pennant in 28 years. Cronin later became the team's general manager, and he was eventually elected president of the American League.

Cronin was a remarkably consistent player over his career, and he contributed equally to the Senators and the Red Sox. If we break his career down by team, we find that Cronin had better fielding statistics with the Senators, and more power with the Red Sox, but about the same overall results.

Team	TAB	HR	BA	Adj. BA	Wtd. PRO	TF	HC
Pirates	113	0	.257	.251	618	675	(1)
Senators	4,064	51	.304	.287	793	847	378
Red Sox	4,495	119	.300	.282	826	829	360

In his career, Cronin hit .301 with 170 home runs. Adjusted for a career 6 percent hitter's inflation, he hit .284 with 171 home runs. His 835 Total Factor ranks third in league rate of success for shortstops, while his 737 Hits Contribution ranks first in the American League in volume of success at short.

Bobby Doerr

Bobby Doerr packed a huge career into his last 12 seasons. Doerr earned 637 Hits Contribution in those 12 years, making him one of the greatest players ever at his position. His success came from his glove, with 48 Fielding Factor points, and from his bat, as he hit .288 with 223 home runs in 7,913 total at bats. Adjusted for a career 2 percent hitter's inflation, Doerr hit .282 with 231 home runs, for an 806 Wtd. Production. His 845 Total Factor ranks fifth in league rate of success for second basemen, while his 637 Hits Contribution ranks fifth in league volume of success at second.

Dwight Evans

Evans performed in the shadow of his outfield teammates during most of his career. Only near the end of his career did Evans emerge as the team's star. Evans broke in with the Red Sox in 1972, when Yastrzemski, Reggie Smith, Tommy Harper, Ben Oglivie, and Rick Miller were vying for playing time in the crowded outfield. Evans earned a starting role in 1974, only to find the outfield even more crowded the next year, with the arrival of Fred Lynn and Jim Rice. Evans hung on to his starter role, but only because he was one of the best defensive right fielders of all time, with a rifle for an arm. Evans was considered an inconsistent hitter, and the fans focused more on Yastrzemski, Rice, and Lynn. It wasn't until Lynn left in 1981 for the Angels that Evans was given a chance to play every day, and it was in that season that his hitting improved dramatically. Evans hit so well in the 1980s that he eventually hit more home runs than Rice, who had a 72 home run lead over the older Evans as late as 1983.

Evans hit .272 with 385 home runs in his career. Adjusted for a 1 percent hitter's deflation, Dewey hit .275 with 399 home runs, and he had 33 Fielding Factor points. Evans' 887 Total Factor ranks 18th among outfielders in league rate of success, while his 657 Hits Contribution ranks 13th in volume of success.

Dwight Gooden and Roger Clemens

Two pitchers with incredible potential arrived in the major leagues in 1984. Gooden was an instant success, going 17–9 with a 2.60 ERA as a 19-year-old rookie, and he then dazzled the league with a 24–4 record and 1.53 ERA in 1985, before slipping to 17–6 in 1986. The other pitcher, Clemens, was 9–4 with a 4.32 ERA as a 21-year-old rookie, and was only 7–5 in his sophomore year, before pitching his own 24–4 season with a 2.48 ERA in 1986, the year the Mets beat the Red Sox in the World Series.

Since Gooden was 2½ years younger and had a 58–19 career record versus Clemens' 40–13 record by 1986, it looked like Gooden would be the bigger star. As it turns out, Gooden's career had already peaked, and he became a .500 pitcher by 1992. Clemens, meanwhile, realized his potential, becoming perhaps the best starting pitcher in the last half century.

Clemens is 260–142 in his career-to-date, with a 3.07 ERA, for a 3.23 Wtd. RA/9, the fourth best rate of success in league history. Clemens saved 555 runs from scoring over 3,667 innings, for 1.3 runs prevented for every 9 innings pitched, the third best volume of success in league history.

Dennis Eckersley

Eckersley's career proved to be truly unique, as he won 20 games one season, while saving 51 in another (to win the 1992 MVP Award). Eck won 197 games and saved 390 games in 1,071 career appearances, proving to be both an effective starting pitcher and a dominating reliever. Eckersley began his career as a starter for 12 seasons with the Indians, Red Sox, and Cubs. He was 151–128 with a 3.67 ERA in 2,496 innings as a starter, with a 4.22 Wtd. RA/9 and 96 runs saved from scoring. As a reliever over 12 seasons with the Athletics, Cardinals, and Red Sox, Eckersley was 46–43 with 387 saves and a 2.96 ERA in 790 innings, earning a 3.12 Wtd. RA/9 and 131 runs saved from scoring. Overall, Eck was 197–171 with a 3.50 ERA, a 3.96 Wtd. RA/9, and he saved 226 runs from scoring, while pitching slightly more than 3 innings per game.

Boston Red Sox   **Hitters Volume of Success**

Pos	Years	Name	AB	BB	HBP	TAB	H	2B	3B	HR	BA	OB	SA	PRO	Wtd PRO	SB	CS	SBF	SPF	FF	R TF	V HC
C	1986-	M.Stanley	4,222	652	48	4,922	1,138	220	7	187	.270	.373	.458	831	795	13	4	1	(8)	(22)	766	134
1B	1991-	M.Vaughn	4,966	652	96	5,714	1,479	250	10	299	.298	.390	.533	923	872	30	17	(1)	(6)	(19)	846	218
2B	1937-51	B.Doerr	7,093	809	11	7,913	2,042	381	89	223	.288	.362	.461	823	806	54	64	(9)	0	48	845	637
SS	1926-45	J.Cronin	7,579	1,059	34	8,672	2,285	515	118	170	.301	.390	.468	857	808	87	71	(6)	7	26	835	737
3B	1982-99	W.Boggs	9,180	1,412	23	10,615	3,010	578	61	118	.328	.419	.443	861	847	24	35	(4)	(4)	19	858	729
OF	1939-60	T.Williams	7,706	2,019	39	9,764	2,654	525	71	521	.344	.483	.634	1,116	1,093	24	17	(1)	(2)	(8)	1,082	1,599
OF	1961-83	C.Yastrzemski	11,988	1,845	40	13,873	3,419	646	59	452	.285	.382	.462	844	864	168	116	(4)	3	30	892	881
OF	1972-91	D.Evans	8,996	1,391	53	10,440	2,446	483	73	385	.272	.373	.470	843	854	78	59	(4)	4	33	887	657
Starters		Averages	7,716	1,230	43	8,989	2,309	450	61	294	.299	.398	.488	886	874	60	48	(3)	(1)	13	883	699
C	1980-92	R.Gedman	3,159	236	16	3,411	795	176	12	88	.252	.307	.399	705	710	3	4	(1)	(10)	5	704	44
1B	1966-79	G.Scott	7,433	699	53	8,185	1,992	306	60	271	.268	.335	.435	770	798	69	57	(5)	5	17	815	207
2B	1987-97	J.Reed	4,554	542	30	5,126	1,231	263	10	27	.270	.352	.350	702	693	40	44	(9)	1	28	714	85
SS	1996-	N.Garciaparra	2,436	184	24	2,644	812	176	29	117	.333	.386	.573	959	893	58	20	6	10	6	915	319
3B	1895-08	J.Collins	6,795	426	84	7,305	1,999	352	116	65	.294	.343	.409	752	786	194	0	0	8	43	837	457
OF	1966-82	R.Smith	7,033	890	33	7,956	2,020	363	57	314	.287	.370	.489	859	882	137	86	(4)	4	21	903	556
OF	1974-90	F.Lynn	6,925	857	30	7,812	1,960	388	43	306	.283	.364	.484	848	851	72	54	(4)	(2)	25	869	423
OF	1974-89	J.Rice	8,225	670	64	8,959	2,452	373	79	382	.298	.356	.502	858	862	58	34	(1)	(2)	(12)	846	389
Reserves		Averages	5,820	563	42	6,425	1,658	300	51	196	.285	.352	.455	807	817	79	37	(2)	2	17	833	310
Totals		Weighted Ave.	7,084	1,008	43	8,134	2,092	400	58	262	.295	.386	.479	865	855	66	44	(3)	0	14	866	569

Pitchers Volume of Success

Pos	Years	Name	G	GS	IP	W	L	SV	SO	BB	ERA	RA/9	Wtd RA/9	R V Runs /162
SP	1984-	R.Clemens	512	511	3,667	260	142	0	3,504	1,186	3.07	3.40	3.23	555
SP	1915-29	C.Mays	490	324	3,021	208	126	31	862	734	2.92	3.61	3.71	309
SP	1975-98	D.Eckersley	1,071	361	3,286	197	171	390	2,401	738	3.50	3.79	3.96	226
SP	1964-82	L.Tiant	573	484	3,486	229	172	15	2,416	1,104	3.30	3.61	4.01	214
SP	1913-25	D.Leonard	331	272	2,192	139	112	13	1,160	664	2.76	3.50	3.79	201
Starters		Averages	595	390	3,130	207	145	90	2,069	885	3.14	3.58	3.73	301
RP	1968-84	T.Burgmeier	745	3	1,259	79	55	102	584	384	3.23	3.73	4.09	67
RP	1977-89	B.Stanley	637	85	1,707	115	97	132	693	471	3.64	4.20	4.24	63
RP	1962-69	D.Radatz	381	0	694	52	43	122	745	296	3.13	3.37	3.80	58
RP	1952-69	B.Henry	527	44	913	46	50	90	621	296	3.26	3.80	4.10	48
Relievers		Averages	573	33	1,143	73	61	112	661	362	3.37	3.87	4.10	59
Totals		Averages	1,168	423	4,273	280	206	201	2,729	1,247	3.20	3.66	3.83	360

Boston Red Sox   **Hitters Rate of Success**

Pos	Years	Name	AB	BB	HBP	TAB	H	2B	3B	HR	BA	OB	SA	PRO	Wtd PRO	SB	CS	SBF	SPF	FF	R TF	V HC
C	1986-	M.Stanley	4222	652	48	4,922	1,138	220	7	187	.270	.373	.458	831	795	13	4	1	(8)	(22)	766	134
1B	1991-	M.Vaughn	4966	652	96	5,714	1,479	250	10	299	.298	.390	.533	923	872	30	17	(1)	(6)	(19)	846	218
2B	1937-51	B.Doerr	7093	809	11	7,913	2,042	381	89	223	.288	.362	.461	823	806	54	64	(9)	0	48	845	637
SS	1996-	N.Garciaparra	2436	184	24	2,644	812	176	29	117	.333	.386	.573	959	893	58	20	6	10	6	915	319
3B	1982-99	W.Boggs	9180	1,412	23	10,615	3,010	578	61	118	.328	.419	.443	861	847	24	35	(4)	(4)	19	858	729
OF	1939-60	T.Williams	7706	2,019	39	9,764	2,654	525	71	521	.344	.483	.634	1,116	1,093	24	17	(1)	(2)	(8)	1,082	1,599
OF	1966-82	R.Smith	7033	890	33	7,956	2,020	363	57	314	.287	.370	.489	859	882	137	86	(4)	4	21	903	556
OF	1961-83	C.Yastrzemski	11988	1,845	40	13,873	3,419	646	59	452	.285	.382	.462	844	864	168	116	(4)	3	30	892	881
Starters	Averages		6,828	1,058	39	7,925	2,072	392	48	279	.303	.400	.497	897	888	64	45	(2)	(0)	9	895	634
C	1906-16	B.Carrigan	1970	206	22	2,198	506	67	14	6	.257	.334	.314	648	710	37	2	(1)	(10)	7	706	31
1B	1914-28	J.Harris	3035	413	31	3,479	963	201	64	47	.317	.404	.472	877	851	36	16	(2)	(2)	(15)	831	120
2B	1966-73	M.Andrews	3116	458	16	3,590	803	140	4	66	.258	.356	.369	724	760	18	25	(8)	0	(22)	730	77
SS	1926-45	J.Cronin	7579	1,059	34	8,672	2,285	515	118	170	.301	.390	.468	857	808	87	71	(6)	7	26	835	737
3B	1895-08	J.Collins	6795	426	84	7,305	1,999	352	116	65	.294	.343	.409	752	786	194	0	0	8	43	837	457
OF	1972-91	D.Evans	8996	1,391	53	10,440	2,446	483	73	385	.272	.373	.470	843	854	78	59	(4)	4	33	887	657
OF	1974-90	F.Lynn	6925	857	30	7,812	1,960	388	43	306	.283	.364	.484	848	851	72	54	(4)	(2)	25	869	423
OF	1987-	E.Burks	6044	657	45	6,746	1,770	334	61	285	.293	.366	.510	876	851	171	79	2	5	7	866	354
Reserves	Averages		5,558	683	39	6,280	1,592	310	62	166	.286	.368	.454	823	822	87	38	(3)	1	13	833	357
Totals	Weighted Ave.		6,405	933	39	7,377	1,912	365	52	241	.298	.391	.485	876	866	71	43	(2)	0	11	874	542

Pitchers Rate of Success

Pos	Years	Name	G	GS	IP	W	L	SV	SO	BB	ERA	RA/9	Wtd RA/9	R V Runs /162
SP	1984-	R.Clemens	512	511	3,667	260	142	0	3,504	1,186	3.07	3.40	3.23	555
SP	1908-20	J.Wood	225	158	1,434	117	57	10	989	421	2.03	3.11	3.50	178
SP	1914-33	B.Ruth	163	148	1,221	94	46	4	488	441	2.28	2.94	3.50	158
SP	1941-49	T.Hughson	225	156	1,376	96	54	17	693	372	2.94	3.30	3.57	158
SP	1915-29	C.Mays	490	324	3,021	208	126	31	862	734	2.92	3.61	3.71	309
Starters	Averages		323	259	2,144	155	85	12	1,307	631	2.78	3.35	3.47	272
RP	1990-	R.Garces	199	0	253	17	8	6	229	127	3.38	3.91	3.50	30
RP	1997-	D.Lowe	231	19	393	15	22	61	288	112	3.94	4.03	3.59	42
RP	1962-69	D.Radatz	381	0	694	52	43	122	745	296	3.13	3.37	3.80	58
RP	1992-99	K.Ryan	240	1	286	14	16	30	225	164	3.91	4.41	4.07	17
Relievers	Averages		263	5	406	25	22	55	372	175	3.50	3.80	3.75	37
Totals	Averages		586	264	2,550	180	107	67	1,679	806	2.90	3.43	3.52	308

Boston Red Sox
Catchers

V	R	Years	Name	AB	BB	HBP	TAB	H	2B	3B	HR	BA	OB	SA	PRO	Wtd PRO	SB	CS	SBF	SPF	FF	R TF	V HC
1	1	1986-	M.Stanley	4,222	652	48	4,922	1,138	220	7	187	.270	.373	.458	831	795	13	4	1	(8)	(22)	766	134
2	3	1980-92	R.Gedman	3,159	236	16	3,411	795	176	12	88	.252	.307	.399	705	710	3	4	(1)	(10)	5	704	44
3	2	1906-16	B.Carrigan	1,970	206	22	2,198	506	67	14	6	.257	.334	.314	648	710	37	2	(1)	(10)	7	706	31
4	4	1951-62	S.White	3,502	218	12	3,732	916	167	20	66	.262	.307	.377	684	677	14	15	(4)	(10)	3	666	(22)
5	5	1962-70	B.Tillman	2,329	228	5	2,562	540	68	10	79	.232	.302	.371	673	688	1	0	0	(10)	(20)	659	(23)
6	7	1925-38	C.Berry	2,018	160	5	2,183	539	88	29	23	.267	.322	.374	696	656	13	5	1	(4)	(7)	647	(34)
7	8	1957-68	R.Nixon	2,504	154	11	2,669	670	115	19	27	.268	.313	.361	674	678	0	7	(5)	(10)	(16)	647	(41)
8	9	1937-45	J.Peacock	1,734	183	1	1,918	455	74	16	1	.262	.333	.325	658	644	14	6	(1)	(6)	(4)	633	(43)
9	6	1896-12	L.Criger	3,202	309	23	3,534	709	86	50	11	.221	.295	.290	584	625	58	0	0	(8)	36	653	(45)
10	10	1930-46	G.Desautels	2,012	232	9	2,253	469	73	11	3	.233	.315	.285	600	571	12	6	0	(3)	24	592	(96)

Boston Red Sox
First basemen

V	R	Years	Name	AB	BB	HBP	TAB	H	2B	3B	HR	BA	OB	SA	PRO	Wtd PRO	SB	CS	SBF	SPF	FF	R TF	V HC
1	1	1991-	M.Vaughn	4,966	652	96	5,714	1,479	250	10	299	.298	.390	.533	923	872	30	17	(1)	(6)	(19)	846	218
2	3	1966-79	G.Scott	7,433	699	53	8,185	1,992	306	60	271	.268	.335	.435	770	798	69	57	(5)	5	17	815	207
3	2	1914-28	J.Harris	3,035	413	31	3,479	963	201	64	47	.317	.404	.472	877	851	36	16	(2)	(2)	(15)	831	120
4	4	1903-13	J.Stahl	3,425	221	94	3,740	894	149	87	31	.261	.323	.382	706	802	178	0	0	6	5	814	90
5	8	1980-86	D.Stapleton	2,028	114	7	2,149	550	118	8	41	.271	.312	.398	710	720	6	11	(8)	0	(6)	707	(20)
6	5	1952-62	D.Gernert	2,493	363	17	2,873	632	104	8	103	.254	.352	.426	778	770	10	11	(4)	(5)	(8)	753	(23)
7	6	1991-	R.Jefferson	2,123	146	20	2,289	637	131	11	72	.300	.351	.474	825	782	2	5	(3)	(7)	(24)	747	(24)
8	7	1940-48	T.Lupien	2,358	241	3	2,602	632	92	30	18	.268	.337	.355	692	705	57	28	(7)	10	0	709	(80)
9	9	1924-31	P.Todt	3,415	207	23	3,645	880	183	58	57	.258	.305	.395	700	655	29	21	(3)	0	20	672	(179)

Boston Red Sox
Second basemen

V	R	Years	Name	AB	BB	HBP	TAB	H	2B	3B	HR	BA	OB	SA	PRO	Wtd PRO	SB	CS	SBF	SPF	FF	R TF	V HC
1	1	1937-51	B.Doerr	7,093	809	11	7,913	2,042	381	89	223	.288	.362	.461	823	806	54	64	(9)	0	48	845	637
2	6	1987-97	J.Reed	4,554	542	30	5,126	1,231	263	10	27	.270	.352	.350	702	693	40	44	(9)	1	28	714	85
3	2	1966-73	M.Andrews	3,116	458	16	3,590	803	140	4	66	.258	.356	.369	724	760	18	25	(8)	0	(22)	730	77
4	5	1982-91	M.Barrett	3,378	304	16	3,698	938	163	9	18	.278	.340	.347	687	684	57	21	4	2	26	715	53
5	3	1952-61	T.Lepcio	2,092	209	18	2,319	512	91	11	69	.245	.319	.398	716	709	11	15	(8)	0	24	726	43
6	8	1901-09	H.Ferris	4,800	161	13	4,974	1,146	192	89	40	.239	.265	.341	606	675	89	0	0	0	29	703	29
7	9	1909-16	S.Yerkes	2,521	207	16	2,744	676	124	32	6	.268	.328	.350	677	717	54	6	0	10	(34)	693	17
8	4	1947-62	B.Goodman	5,644	669	29	6,342	1,691	299	44	19	.300	.377	.378	755	739	37	30	(3)	0	(13)	723	12
9	7	1956-66	F.Mantilla	2,707	256	26	2,989	707	97	10	89	.261	.331	.403	734	731	27	10	2	0	(23)	711	6
10	10	1992-	J.Frye	1,980	200	19	2,199	532	129	10	14	.269	.342	.365	707	669	54	24	3	7	4	683	(3)
11	11	1975-84	J.Remy	4,455	356	4	4,815	1,226	140	38	7	.275	.329	.328	658	670	208	99	2	10	(8)	675	(26)
12	12	1926-31	B.Regan	2,364	122	10	2,496	632	158	36	18	.267	.306	.387	694	651	38	26	(6)	10	0	656	(37)
13	14	1961-65	C.Schilling	1,969	176	11	2,156	470	76	5	23	.239	.305	.317	622	619	11	10	(4)	0	15	630	(57)
14	15	1970-77	D.Griffin	2,136	158	12	2,306	524	70	12	7	.245	.301	.299	600	628	33	23	(5)	7	(2)	628	(63)
15	13	1964-72	D.Jones	2,329	191	11	2,531	548	91	19	41	.235	.296	.343	640	666	20	13	(2)	2	(25)	641	(100)

**Boston Red Sox
Shortstops**

V	R	Years	Name	AB	BB	HBP	TAB	H	2B	3B	HR	BA	OB	SA	PRO	Wtd PRO	SB	CS	SBF	SPF	FF	R TF	V HC
1	2	1926-45	J.Cronin	7,579	1,059	34	8,672	2,285	515	118	170	.301	.390	.468	857	808	87	71	(6)	7	26	835	737
2	1	1996-	N.Garciaparra	2,436	184	24	2,644	812	176	29	117	.333	.386	.573	959	893	58	20	6	10	6	915	319
3	4	1942-54	J.Pesky	4,745	662	25	5,432	1,455	226	50	17	.307	.394	.386	780	771	53	49	(8)	8	14	786	275
4	5	1963-76	R.Petrocelli	5,390	661	26	6,077	1,352	237	22	210	.251	.336	.420	755	788	10	22	(5)	(10)	(3)	770	243
5	3	1992-	J.Valentin	3,649	432	42	4,123	1,031	264	17	120	.283	.365	.463	828	785	47	31	(3)	(1)	12	792	232
6	6	1899-11	F.Parent	4,984	333	51	5,368	1,306	180	74	20	.262	.315	.340	655	727	184	0	0	9	(4)	731	153
7	8	1974-87	R.Burleson	5,139	420	28	5,587	1,401	256	23	50	.273	.331	.361	692	704	72	68	(11)	(0)	18	711	133
8	7	1902-18	H.Wagner	3,333	310	28	3,671	834	128	47	10	.250	.319	.326	645	713	144	4	0	8	(3)	718	97
9	9	1956-67	E.Bressoud	3,672	359	12	4,043	925	184	40	94	.252	.321	.401	721	718	9	13	(4)	0	(8)	706	85
10	10	1956-62	D.Buddin	2,289	410	18	2,717	551	123	12	41	.241	.360	.359	719	707	15	8	(0)	0	(8)	698	49
11	12	1986-98	L.Rivera	2,215	171	14	2,400	516	114	12	28	.233	.292	.333	625	634	20	22	(10)	0	12	637	(31)
12	11	1952-63	B.Klaus	2,513	331	4	2,848	626	106	15	40	.249	.337	.351	688	675	14	7	0	0	(18)	657	(39)
13	14	1980-89	G.Hoffman	2,163	136	20	2,319	524	106	9	23	.242	.293	.331	625	623	5	16	(11)	0	6	618	(60)
14	16	1926-33	H.Rhyne	2,031	184	17	2,232	508	98	22	2	.250	.318	.323	641	609	13	11	(4)	0	(2)	602	(74)
15	13	1914-26	E.Scott	5,837	243	18	6,098	1,455	208	58	20	.249	.281	.315	596	599	69	60	(14)	0	48	633	(91)
16	15	1935-47	S.Newsome	3,716	246	5	3,967	910	164	15	9	.245	.293	.304	597	591	67	35	(3)	10	12	611	(110)
17	17	1911-22	H.Janvrin	2,221	171	19	2,411	515	68	18	6	.232	.292	.287	579	616	79	41	(14)	0	(67)	535	(175)

**Boston Red Sox
Third basemen**

V	R	Years	Name	AB	BB	HBP	TAB	H	2B	3B	HR	BA	OB	SA	PRO	Wtd PRO	SB	CS	SBF	SPF	FF	R TF	V HC
1	1	1982-99	W.Boggs	9,180	1,412	23	10,615	3,010	578	61	118	.328	.419	.443	861	847	24	35	(4)	(4)	19	858	729
2	2	1895-08	J.Collins	6,795	426	84	7,305	1,999	352	116	65	.294	.343	.409	752	786	194	0	0	8	43	837	457
3	3	1908-24	L.Gardner	6,688	654	32	7,374	1,931	301	129	27	.289	.355	.384	739	767	165	68	(12)	7	5	766	196
4	5	1930-42	B.Werber	5,024	701	32	5,757	1,363	271	50	78	.271	.364	.392	756	724	215	68	4	10	13	739	113
5	6	1955-66	F.Malzone	5,428	337	17	5,782	1,486	239	21	133	.274	.318	.399	717	715	14	14	(2)	(3)	29	739	63
6	4	1966-71	J.Foy	2,484	390	18	2,892	615	102	16	58	.248	.354	.372	725	759	99	48	1	10	(15)	755	52
7	7	1990-97	T.Naehring	1,872	236	16	2,124	527	104	4	49	.282	.367	.420	787	745	5	7	(5)	(10)	(1)	729	33
8	8	1938-47	J.Tabor	3,788	286	6	4,080	1,021	191	29	104	.270	.322	.418	739	735	69	54	(10)	10	(19)	715	(2)
9	9	1990-97	S.Cooper	1,801	193	11	2,005	478	94	12	33	.265	.340	.386	726	704	7	10	(7)	(10)	(7)	680	(49)
10	11	1962-74	J.Kennedy	2,110	142	25	2,277	475	77	17	32	.225	.282	.323	605	622	14	10	(3)	6	9	635	(68)
11	10	1975-82	B.Hobson	2,556	183	5	2,744	634	107	23	98	.248	.300	.423	722	727	11	9	(2)	(2)	(59)	663	(74)

Boston Red Sox
Outfielders

V	R	Years	Name	AB	BB	HBP	TAB	H	2B	3B	HR	BA	OB	SA	PRO	Wtd PRO	SB	CS	SBF	SPF	FF	R TF	V HC
1	1	1939-60	T.Williams	7,706	2,019	39	9,764	2,654	525	71	521	.344	.483	.634	1,116	1,093	24	17	(1)	(2)	(8)	1,082	1,599
2	3	1961-83	C.Yastrzemski	11,988	1,845	40	13,873	3,419	646	59	452	.285	.382	.462	844	864	168	116	(4)	3	30	892	881
3	4	1972-91	D.Evans	8,996	1,391	53	10,440	2,446	483	73	385	.272	.373	.470	843	854	78	59	(4)	4	33	887	657
4	2	1966-82	R.Smith	7,033	890	33	7,956	2,020	363	57	314	.287	.370	.489	859	882	137	86	(4)	4	21	903	556
5	5	1974-90	F.Lynn	6,925	857	30	7,812	1,960	388	43	306	.283	.364	.484	848	851	72	54	(4)	(2)	25	869	423
6	8	1974-89	J.Rice	8,225	670	64	8,959	2,452	373	79	382	.298	.356	.502	858	862	58	34	(1)	(2)	(12)	846	389
7	6	1987-	E.Burks	6,044	657	45	6,746	1,770	334	61	285	.293	.366	.510	876	851	171	79	2	5	7	866	354
8	7	1950-61	J.Jensen	5,236	750	23	6,009	1,463	259	45	199	.279	.372	.460	832	822	143	55	5	10	22	859	306
9	14	1909-25	H.Hooper	8,785	1,136	76	9,997	2,466	389	160	75	.281	.368	.387	755	776	375	121	(8)	8	36	812	278
10	9	1940-53	D.DiMaggio	5,640	750	31	6,421	1,680	308	57	87	.298	.383	.419	802	787	100	62	(4)	10	44	838	258
11	13	1894-06	K.Selbach	6,158	783	41	6,982	1,803	299	149	44	.293	.376	.411	787	799	334	0	0	7	14	820	238
12	12	1897-06	C.Stahl	5,069	470	44	5,583	1,546	219	118	36	.305	.369	.416	785	822	189	0	0	10	2	834	226
13	11	1891-07	B.Freeman	4,208	272	66	4,546	1,235	199	131	82	.293	.346	.462	808	855	92	0	0	0	(20)	835	179
14	10	1964-75	T.Conigliaro	3,221	287	33	3,541	849	139	23	166	.264	.330	.476	806	841	20	23	(7)	3	1	838	136
15	17	1985-96	M.Greenwell	4,623	460	39	5,122	1,400	275	38	130	.303	.371	.463	834	820	80	43	(1)	0	(12)	807	127
16	15	1969-80	B.Carbo	2,733	538	19	3,290	722	140	9	96	.264	.389	.427	816	831	26	18	(3)	(2)	(18)	808	82
17	16	1925-33	E.Webb	2,161	260	2	2,423	661	155	25	56	.306	.381	.478	859	813	8	4	(1)	0	(4)	808	61
18	18	1910-21	D.Lewis	5,351	352	40	5,743	1,518	289	68	38	.284	.333	.384	717	762	113	47	(9)	0	23	777	57
19	19	1950-67	J.Piersall	5,890	524	25	6,439	1,604	256	52	104	.272	.334	.386	721	713	115	57	0	10	45	768	43
20	20	1929-38	R.Johnson	4,359	489	12	4,860	1,292	275	83	58	.296	.369	.437	806	761	135	80	(6)	10	(15)	749	(20)
21	23	1960-67	L.Clinton	2,153	188	7	2,348	532	112	31	65	.247	.310	.418	728	732	12	7	(1)	0	4	735	(26)
22	22	1958-70	G.Geiger	2,569	341	17	2,927	633	91	29	77	.246	.339	.394	733	728	62	29	1	8	3	741	(26)
23	25	1930-38	D.Cooke	1,745	290	5	2,040	489	109	28	24	.280	.384	.416	800	755	32	25	(8)	2	(21)	727	(31)
24	21	1917-30	I.Flagstead	4,139	467	53	4,659	1,202	262	50	40	.290	.370	.407	776	734	71	58	(10)	2	16	742	(32)
25	28	1914-23	M.Menosky	2,465	295	40	2,800	685	98	38	18	.278	.364	.370	735	724	90	36	(8)	10	(2)	723	(48)
26	29	1994-	D.Bragg	1,925	253	20	2,198	496	115	10	39	.258	.350	.389	738	685	45	19	3	10	12	710	(50)
27	26	1909-16	C.Engle	2,822	271	25	3,118	748	101	39	12	.265	.335	.341	676	734	128	9	0	0	(8)	726	(50)
28	27	1993-	T.O'Leary	3,222	261	19	3,502	902	197	32	106	.280	.338	.460	797	742	12	17	(6)	2	(13)	725	(56)
29	24	1971-85	R.Miller	3,887	454	16	4,357	1,046	161	35	28	.269	.348	.350	698	712	78	65	(12)	10	19	729	(61)
30	34	1930-33	T.Oliver	1,931	105	6	2,042	534	101	11	0	.277	.316	.340	656	616	12	19	(12)	10	33	647	(113)
31	32	1933-39	M.Almada	2,483	214	5	2,702	706	107	27	15	.284	.342	.367	710	654	56	27	0	10	1	666	(123)
32	35	1952-64	G.Stephens	1,913	233	14	2,160	460	78	15	37	.240	.327	.355	682	675	27	20	(6)	8	(37)	641	(125)
33	31	1943-54	C.Metkovich	3,585	307	22	3,914	934	167	36	47	.261	.323	.367	689	699	61	28	1	9	(16)	693	(134)
34	33	1925-37	J.Rothrock	3,350	299	6	3,655	924	162	35	28	.276	.336	.370	706	667	75	33	(2)	8	(12)	660	(153)
35	30	1929-48	D.Cramer	9,140	572	41	9,753	2,705	396	109	37	.296	.340	.375	715	691	62	73	(8)	6	17	706	(252)

Boston Red Sox
Starting Pitchers

V	R	Years	Name	G	GS	IP	W	L	SV	SO	BB	ERA	RA/9	R Wtd RA/9	V Runs /162
1	1	1984-	R.Clemens	512	511	3,667	260	142	0	3,504	1,186	3.07	3.40	3.23	555.2
2	5	1915-29	C.Mays	490	324	3,021	208	126	31	862	734	2.92	3.61	3.71	308.9
3	10	1975-98	D.Eckersley	1,071	361	3,286	197	171	390	2,401	738	3.50	3.79	3.96	226.1
4	12	1964-82	L.Tiant	573	484	3,486	229	172	15	2,416	1,104	3.30	3.61	4.01	214.4
5	6	1913-25	D.Leonard	331	272	2,192	139	112	13	1,160	664	2.76	3.50	3.79	201.0
6	11	1894-11	J.Tannehill	358	320	2,750	197	117	7	940	477	2.79	3.91	3.97	197.2
7	2	1908-20	J.Wood	225	158	1,434	117	57	10	989	421	2.03	3.11	3.50	178.0
8	4	1941-49	T.Hughson	225	156	1,376	96	54	17	693	372	2.94	3.30	3.57	158.1
9	3	1914-33	B.Ruth	163	148	1,221	94	46	4	488	441	2.28	2.94	3.50	157.6
10	8	1946-57	E.Kinder	484	122	1,480	102	71	102	749	539	3.43	3.81	3.81	129.6
11	15	1939-54	J.Dobson	414	273	2,170	137	103	18	992	851	3.62	4.06	4.06	126.3
12	7	1909-15	R.Collins	199	151	1,336	84	62	4	511	269	2.51	3.33	3.80	118.3
13	16	1898-09	B.Dinneen	391	352	3,075	170	177	7	1,127	829	3.01	4.13	4.25	114.5
14	14	1947-56	M.Parnell	289	232	1,753	123	75	10	732	758	3.50	4.09	4.05	103.0
15	19	1926-43	D.MacFayden	465	332	2,706	132	159	9	797	872	3.96	4.64	4.33	73.2
16	9	1913-17	R.Foster	138	103	842	58	34	3	294	305	2.36	3.25	3.92	63.1
17	13	1912-20	E.Shore	160	121	979	65	43	5	309	270	2.47	3.42	4.03	61.3
18	18	1934-48	F.Ostermueller	390	246	2,067	114	115	15	774	835	3.99	4.62	4.32	57.5
19	17	1953-63	F.Sullivan	351	219	1,732	97	100	18	959	559	3.60	4.14	4.28	56.4
20	22	1980-94	B.Hurst	379	359	2,417	145	113	0	1,689	740	3.92	4.26	4.43	33.4
21	20	1993-	A.Sele	208	208	1,251	92	63	0	968	497	4.46	4.96	4.34	32.3
22	21	1945-50	D.Ferriss	144	103	880	65	30	8	296	314	3.64	4.01	4.36	20.6
23	23	1969-82	B.Lee	416	225	1,944	119	90	19	713	531	3.62	4.10	4.48	16.9
24	24	1982-91	O.Boyd	214	207	1,390	78	77	0	799	368	4.04	4.40	4.52	6.4
25	25	1948-61	M.McDermott	291	156	1,317	69	69	14	757	838	3.91	4.48	4.52	5.2
26	29	1935-46	M.Ryba	240	36	784	52	34	16	307	247	3.66	4.37	4.62	(6.0)
27	27	1992-	T.Wakefield	267	188	1,344	85	77	15	872	571	4.47	5.14	4.60	(6.7)
28	26	1958-68	B.Monbouquette	343	263	1,962	114	112	3	1,122	462	3.68	4.18	4.60	(9.5)
29	28	1901-08	G.Winter	220	182	1,656	83	102	4	568	377	2.87	4.13	4.62	(13.0)
30	32	1961-70	L.Stange	359	125	1,216	62	61	21	718	344	3.56	4.09	4.70	(18.8)
31	30	1926-40	J.Russell	557	182	2,051	85	141	38	418	571	4.46	5.21	4.65	(21.2)
32	36	1940-52	M.Harris	271	109	1,050	59	71	21	534	455	4.18	4.80	4.73	(21.5)
33	37	1912-15	H.Bedient	179	102	937	59	53	19	420	236	3.08	4.08	4.77	(23.5)
34	33	1952-63	I.Delock	329	147	1,238	84	75	31	672	530	4.03	4.58	4.73	(24.2)
35	31	1959-70	E.Wilson	338	310	2,052	121	109	0	1,452	796	3.69	4.10	4.68	(27.3)
36	39	1934-42	J.Wilson	281	121	1,132	68	72	20	590	601	4.59	5.46	4.78	(29.8)
37	35	1954-61	T.Brewer	241	217	1,509	91	82	3	733	669	4.00	4.54	4.73	(30.9)
38	40	1927-45	H.Lisenbee	207	107	969	37	58	1	253	314	4.81	5.53	4.89	(37.3)
39	42	1920-27	B.Karr	177	58	780	35	48	5	180	260	4.60	5.43	4.99	(39.4)
40	41	1906-18	C.Hall	188	80	910	54	47	12	427	391	3.09	4.32	4.98	(44.8)
41	38	1963-73	R.Culp	322	268	1,898	122	101	1	1,411	752	3.58	4.09	4.78	(46.2)
42	45	1929-36	G.Rhodes	200	135	1,049	43	74	5	356	477	4.85	5.81	5.02	(56.2)
43	34	1967-84	M.Torrez	494	458	3,044	185	160	0	1,404	1,371	3.96	4.44	4.73	(59.8)
44	44	1950-58	W.Nixon	225	177	1,234	69	72	3	616	530	4.39	4.92	5.01	(65.9)
45	47	1963-70	D.Morehead	177	134	819	40	64	1	627	463	4.15	4.71	5.37	(73.7)
46	43	1969-81	R.Cleveland	428	203	1,809	105	106	25	930	543	4.01	4.57	5.01	(93.5)
47	46	1918-29	A.Ferguson	257	167	1,242	61	85	10	397	482	4.93	5.61	5.24	(99.1)

Boston Red Sox
Relief Pitchers

V	R	Years	Name	G	GS	IP	W	L	SV	SO	BB	ERA	RA/9	R Wtd RA/9	V Runs /162
1	5	1968-84	T.Burgmeier	745	3	1,259	79	55	102	584	384	3.23	3.73	4.09	66.8
2	7	1977-89	B.Stanley	637	85	1,707	115	97	132	693	471	3.64	4.20	4.24	62.6
3	3	1962-69	D.Radatz	381	0	694	52	43	122	745	296	3.13	3.37	3.80	58.0
4	6	1952-69	B.Henry	527	44	913	46	50	90	621	296	3.26	3.80	4.10	47.9
5	2	1997-	D.Lowe	231	19	393	15	22	61	288	112	3.94	4.03	3.59	42.1
6	1	1990-	R.Garces	199	0	253	17	8	6	229	127	3.38	3.91	3.50	30.1
7	11	1981-95	G.Harris	703	98	1,467	74	90	54	1,141	652	3.69	4.23	4.41	25.7
8	9	1968-82	V.Romo	335	32	646	32	33	52	416	280	3.36	3.75	4.26	21.1
9	8	1951-60	L.Kiely	209	39	523	26	27	29	212	189	3.37	4.11	4.26	18.3
10	4	1992-99	K.Ryan	240	1	286	14	16	30	225	164	3.91	4.41	4.07	16.9
11	10	1937-43	A.McKain	165	34	486	26	21	16	188	208	4.26	4.99	4.37	10.8
12	13	1979-90	M.Clear	481	1	804	71	49	83	804	554	3.85	4.44	4.47	8.3
13	12	1988-99	T.Fossas	567	0	416	17	24	7	324	180	3.90	4.57	4.45	5.3
14	14	1952-63	M.Fornieles	432	76	1,157	63	64	55	576	421	3.96	4.41	4.56	(0.8)
15	15	1984-94	J.Hesketh	339	114	962	60	47	21	726	378	3.78	4.39	4.58	(2.8)
16	16	1995-	J.Wasdin	214	42	524	28	27	3	352	160	5.07	5.43	4.74	(10.7)
17	17	1967-72	G.Waslewski	152	42	410	11	26	5	229	197	3.44	4.03	4.80	(11.3)
18	18	1980-91	S.Crawford	277	16	563	30	23	19	320	186	4.17	4.77	4.91	(23.5)
19	20	1930-34	B.Kline	148	37	442	30	28	7	87	195	5.05	5.76	5.07	(26.6)
20	19	1956-62	D.Sisler	247	59	656	38	44	29	355	368	4.33	4.84	5.02	(35.1)
21	22	1984-91	W.Gardner	189	44	466	18	30	14	358	218	4.90	5.35	5.52	(49.8)
22	24	1990-95	M.Gardiner	136	46	394	17	27	5	239	161	5.21	5.99	5.92	(63.5)
23	23	1966-73	B.Brandon	228	43	590	28	37	13	354	275	4.04	4.74	5.60	(68.7)
24	21	1962-68	J.Lamabe	285	49	712	33	41	15	434	238	4.24	4.75	5.43	(69.1)
25	25	1960-67	A.Earley	223	10	381	12	20	14	310	184	4.48	5.67	6.20	(69.6)

Brooklyn/Los Angeles Dodgers (1900–2000)

The Dodgers produced a few stars in their not-so-successful early years. Zach Wheat, Jeff Pfeffer and Jake Daubert led the Dead Ball teams, and Dazzy Vance starred in the 1920s. The Dodgers then flourished in their golden era during the 1940s and 1950s, led by talented hitters who took advantage of hitter-friendly Ebbets Field. Duke Snider, Jackie Robinson, Roy Campanella, Gil Hodges, Dolph Camilli, Joe Medwick, Pee Wee Reese, Pete Reiser, and Carl Furillo drove up earned run averages throughout the league.

After they moved to Los Angeles, the Dodgers were able to successfully transform themselves into a team dominated by pitching, speed, and defense. Sandy Koufax, Don Drysdale, Don Sutton, Orel Hershisher, Ron Perranoski, and Jim Brewer starred on the mound, while Maury Wills, Willie Davis, Steve Garvey, Davey Lopes, and Brett Butler provided speed and or defense. Mike Piazza and Pedro Guerrero were sluggers who managed to prosper in a pitcher's park.

Profiled Dodgers Players

Roy Campanella

Campanella was 26 when he reached the big leagues. Although his late start cost him many at bats, beginning his career in his prime also meant Campy could immediately achieve a high rate of success. And achieve he did, with six outstanding seasons and two MVP Awards from 1948 to 1953. Campanella then struggled for the first time, dipping to a .207 average in 1954, before roaring back to win his third MVP title in 1955. Two more off years were followed by a car accident, and Campy's career was over in just ten seasons.

How good was Campanella, really? He had a shorter career than catchers like Bench and Fisk for reasons that had nothing to do with talent or desire, so his eleventh place all time volume of success ranking may not be the best way to measure his stature. If we look at his rate of success, where Campanella enjoyed the advantage of playing only during his prime, we find he ranks fifth all time behind Cochrane, Bench, Piazza, and Buck Ewing. Given this information, Campy deserves to be ranked as between the fifth and eleventh best catcher of all time.

In his career, Campanella hit .276 with 242 home runs in 4,768 total at bats. Adjusted for a 3 percent career hitter's inflation, he hit .268 with 248 home runs, for an 835 Wtd. Production. Add 48 Fielding Factor points, and Campy's 877 Total Factor ranks third in league rate of success for catchers, while his 476 Hits Contribution ranks fifth in league volume of success.

Mike Piazza

Piazza is the best hitting catcher ever — period! His career 918 Wtd. Production is 9 percent higher than the 842 number produced by the second highest hitting catcher, Mickey Cochrane. Piazza's problem is that he's not even an average fielder, and he doesn't have any speed. But given his huge hitting advantage over the best catchers in major league history, Piazza is still producing impressive overall rate and volume of success numbers.

In his career-to-date, Piazza is batting .328 with 278 home runs in 4,590 total at bats, for a 974 Production. Adjusted for a career 6 percent hitter's inflation, Piazza has hit .310 with 278 home runs, for a 918 Wtd. Production. After subtracting 31 points for poor fielding and speed, Piazza's 887 Total Factor ranks second in league rate of success for catchers, while his 483 Hits Contribution currently ranks fourth in league volume of success.

Jackie Robinson

Robinson is an American icon, and his personal courage in smashing through baseball's color barrier has at least one historical survey ranking him as the greatest player of all time. While Robinson's on field results don't support this conclusion, these statistics do speak of one of the finest second basemen of all time. And that's before factoring in the lost at bats from not playing in the big leagues until he was 28, let alone the reduced performance from the stress he suffered from the verbal abuse and threats from racists in every city in which he played.

Robinson played only ten seasons, yet, when he retired at the age of 37, had left his mark as a complete ballplayer. As a rookie in 1947, Robinson led the league in steals and won the Rookie of the Year Award. In his third season in 1949, Robinson was the league's MVP, leading the circuit in batting average (.342) and steals (37), while hitting 16 home runs. In 1952, Robinson hit over .300 and drew 106 walks to lead the league in on-base percentage, while hitting 19 home runs. He played multiple positions, and he led the league in fielding percentage three times at second base.

In his career, Robinson hit .311 with 137 home runs and 197 stolen bases. Adjusted for a career 3 percent hitter's inflation, he hit .302 with 141 home runs. His 899 Total Factor ranks second to Rogers Hornsby in league rate of success at second, while his 531 Hits Contribution ranks sixth in league volume of success at second.

Bill Dahlen

Dahlen is one of a handful of players who excelled for extended periods in both the nineteenth and twentieth centuries. Dahlen's most productive seasons occurred while playing for Chicago during the roaring hitter's inflation of 1894 and 1896, but he continued to play at an All-Star level as late as 1908. Dahlen's hitting statistics appear to decline over time more than they actually did, as he was aided by hitter's inflation for much of the 1890s, and plagued by the Dead Ball Era in the 1900s:

Years	TAB	HR	BA	Adj. BA	Wtd. PRO	TF	HC
1891–99	4,954	61	.297	.292	814	887	597
1900–11	5,281	23	.249	.274	721	765	283

Dahlen, a shortstop, played 21 years and set the major league record for errors committed — although he was a good fielder for his day. He appeared in postseason play for the 1900 Brooklyn "Superbas" team, the last postseason series played before the advent of the World Series in 1903. Dahlen also started at shortstop for the Giants in the 1905 World Series.

Dahlen hit .272 with 84 home runs in his career, while stealing 547 bases. Adjusted for a 4 percent hitter's deflation, he hit .283 with 97 home runs. His 826 Total Factor ranks fifth in league rate of success at short, while his 880 Hits Contribution ranks second in major league history in volume of success at short, trailing only the legendary Honus Wagner.

Duke Snider

Snider played in the shadows of two other New York outfield legends— Willie Mays of the Giants and Mickey Mantle of the Yankees. This, despite his having a four year head-start in the majors, and hitting 40 or more home runs five straight seasons from 1953 to 1957, while playing for one of the great hitting dynasties of all time. What reduced Snider to the ranks of a lesser legend was his offensive slide after the Dodgers moved to Los Angeles in 1958, when he was only 31:

Years	TAB	HR	BA	Adj. BA	Wtd. PRO	TF	HC
1947–57	6,024	316	.303	.293	914	935	542
1958–64	2,129	91	.275	.272	846	809	53

Snider hit .295 with 407 home runs in his career, while playing a graceful center field. Adjusted for 2.5 percent hitter's inflation, he hit .288 with 417 home runs, for an 897 Wtd. Production. His 903 Total Factor ranks 12th in league rate of success for an outfielder, while his 596 Hits Contribution ranks 11th in league volume of success in the outfield.

Zach Wheat

Wheat benefited from several factors to achieve a spot in baseball's Hall of Fame. First, he played in a period when all the big name outfielders— Cobb, Speaker, Jackson, and Ruth — played in the other league. As a result, Wheat, who was durable enough to play 19 years, was usually one of the better National League outfielders, in a group that included Roush, Carey, Cravath, and Youngs. Second, those 19 years gave Wheat a high volume of raw statistical results, including 2,884 hits in 9,106 at bats. Third, Wheat was fortunate enough to improve his hitting later in his career — just as the hitting inflation of the

1920s surged, giving him impressive power and batting average numbers that were missing earlier in his career. Finally, he spent 18 seasons with Brooklyn, and it never hurts to be the star player on a team in the media center of the country.

Was Zach Wheat a Hall of Fame caliber player? In his career, he hit .317 with 132 home runs, and an unimpressive 205 steals. Adjusted for a 2 percent career hitter's deflation, Wheat hit .324 with 139 home runs, for an 835 Wtd. Production. His 850 Total Factor ranks 51st in league rate of success among outfielders — hardly a Hall of Fame ranking. His 464 Hits Contribution ranks 21st among league outfielders — and 54th in major league history — in volume of success, putting Wheat on the cusp of deserving Hall recognition for his durability.

Don Sutton

Sutton was never very visible. He pitched well for Dodgers and Astros teams that stockpiled big-name pitchers like Sandy Koufax, Don Drysdale, Andy Messersmith, Tommy John, and Nolan Ryan. Sutton won 20 games just once, in 1976. Yet Sutton managed to pitch effectively for so long that he won 324 games and struck out 3,574 batters in 5,282 innings, with a 3.26 ERA. His 3.89 Wtd. RA/9 ranks 50th in league rate of success, while his 396 Runs/162 ranks an impressive eighth in league volume of success.

Dazzy Vance

Vance appeared briefly in the majors in 1915 and 1918, but he didn't really get started until 1922, when the 31-year-old joined Brooklyn's starting rotation. Dazzy succeeded immediately with 18 wins in each of his first two full seasons with Brooklyn. Vance pitched a truly special season in 1924, leading the league with 28 wins, 262 strikeouts, and a 2.16 ERA. In 1925, Dazzy again led the league in wins with 22. Then, in 1926, the 35-year-old slumped badly with 9 wins and a 3.89 ERA, which could have been a message this late bloomer was already over the hill.

Vance came back to have a solid season in 1927. He then blazed another special season in 1928 at the age of 37, going 22–10 with 200 strikeouts and a 2.09 ERA. Dazzy was the league's strikeout king for the seventh straight season that year — not bad for an old arm. Two years later, the 39-year-old was 17–15 with a league-leading 2.61 ERA in the National League's year of the hitter.

Vance finally retired in 1935 at the age of 44, after 16 seasons. While Dazzy wasn't one of the ten greatest pitchers of all time, he was one of the greatest over–30 pitchers ever. In his career, Vance was 197–140, with a 3.24 ERA. His 3.57 Wtd. RA/9 ranks 13th in league rate of success, while his 342 Runs/162 ranks 12th in league volume of success.

Sandy Koufax

If we could combine Koufax's career, which ended with an aching arm at the age of 30, with Vance's career, which began at age 31, we would have one of the greatest pitchers of all time. This pitcher would have a 362–227 record, 4,369 strikeouts, 3.03 ERA, 3.47 Wtd. RA/9, and 659 Runs/162. Standing on his own record, Koufax was still impressive. Koufax did not start that way, however, as he was prone to wildness the first half of his career. When Koufax found his control in 1962, he put together one of the best five-year stretches of all time:

Years	IP	W–L	SO	BB	ERA	Wtd. RA/9	Runs/162
1955–61	947	54–53	952	501	3.94	4.54	1
1962–66	1,377	111–34	1,444	316	1.95	2.50	315

In his career, Koufax went 165–87 with a 2.76 ERA, while striking out 2,396 batters in 2,324 innings. His 3.36 Wtd. RA/9 ranks third in league rate of success — despite that terrible start. Koufax's 317 Runs/162 ranks 16th in league volume of success.

Don Drysdale

Drysdale was Koufax's partner in crime. Unlike Koufax, Drysdale was effective early in his career, becoming the ace of the Dodgers staff in the late 1950s, at a time when Koufax struggled just to stay on the team. In the 1960s, Koufax took over as the staff ace, even though Drysdale was still going strong. These two pitchers personally lowered many batting averages on opposing teams.

Drysdale was 209–166 in his career, with a 2.95 ERA, while striking out 2,486 batters in 3,432 innings. His 3.72 Wtd. RA/9 ranks 26th in league rate of success, while his 326 Runs/162 ranks just above Koufax in 14th place in league volume of success.

Brooklyn/Los Angeles Dodgers   **Hitters Volume of Success**

Pos	Years	Name	AB	BB	HBP	TAB	H	2B	3B	HR	BA	OB	SA	PRO	Wtd PRO	SB	CS	SBF	SPF	FF	R TF	V HC
C	1992-	M.Piazza	4,135	439	16	4,590	1,356	199	4	278	.328	.395	.580	974	918	17	15	(3)	(10)	(18)	887	483
1B	1933-45	D.Camilli	5,353	947	28	6,328	1,482	261	86	239	.277	.388	.492	880	883	60	0	0	0	5	888	379
2B	1947-56	J.Robinson	4,877	740	72	5,689	1,518	273	54	137	.311	.410	.474	883	858	197	30	6	10	24	899	531
SS	1891-11	B.Dahlen	9,031	1,064	140	10,235	2,457	413	163	84	.272	.358	.382	739	767	547	0	0	9	50	826	880
3B	1971-87	R.Cey	7,162	1,012	62	8,236	1,868	328	21	316	.261	.357	.445	802	811	24	29	(4)	(6)	18	819	408
OF	1947-64	D.Snider	7,161	971	21	8,153	2,116	358	85	407	.295	.381	.540	921	897	99	50	(4)	1	10	903	596
OF	1909-27	Z.Wheat	9,106	650	72	9,828	2,884	476	172	132	.317	.367	.450	817	835	205	49	(4)	5	14	850	464
OF	1926-45	B.Herman	5,603	520	11	6,134	1,818	399	110	181	.324	.383	.532	915	875	94	0	0	8	(26)	857	299
Starters	Averages		6,554	793	53	7,399	1,937	338	87	222	.296	.376	.475	851	847	155	22	(1)	2	9	857	505
C	1948-57	R.Campanella	4,205	533	30	4,768	1,161	178	18	242	.276	.362	.500	861	835	25	15	(2)	(4)	48	877	476
1B	1943-63	G.Hodges	7,030	943	25	7,998	1,921	295	48	370	.273	.361	.487	848	823	63	31	(3)	0	27	847	314
2B	1972-87	D.Lopes	6,354	833	31	7,218	1,671	232	50	155	.263	.351	.388	740	741	557	114	43	10	(29)	765	248
SS	1940-58	P.Reese	8,058	1,210	26	9,294	2,170	330	80	126	.269	.366	.377	743	733	232	45	2	9	19	762	458
3B	1911-26	J.Johnston	5,070	391	20	5,481	1,493	185	75	22	.294	.347	.374	721	728	169	83	(8)	10	(6)	724	23
OF	1978-92	P.Guerrero	5,392	609	32	6,033	1,618	267	29	215	.300	.374	.480	854	865	97	47	(1)	(0)	(18)	847	279
OF	1931-49	D.Walker	6,740	817	16	7,573	2,064	376	96	105	.306	.383	.437	820	815	59	10	(1)	(0)	7	821	241
OF	1919-34	L.O'Doul	3,264	333	23	3,620	1,140	175	41	113	.349	.413	.532	945	893	36	0	0	0	(20)	872	222
Reserves	Averages		5,764	709	25	6,498	1,655	255	55	169	.287	.368	.438	806	795	155	43	4	3	3	805	283
Totals	Weighted Ave.		6,290	765	44	7,099	1,843	311	76	204	.293	.374	.464	837	829	155	29	1	2	7	840	431

Pitchers Volume of Success

Pos	Years	Name	G	GS	IP	W	L	SV	SO	BB	ERA	RA/9	R Wtd RA/9	V Runs /162
SP	1966-88	D.Sutton	774	756	5,282	324	256	5	3,574	1,343	3.26	3.58	3.89	396
SP	1915-35	D.Vance	442	348	2,967	197	140	11	2,045	840	3.24	3.78	3.57	342
SP	1956-69	D.Drysdale	518	465	3,432	209	166	6	2,486	855	2.95	3.39	3.72	326
SP	1955-66	S.Koufax	397	314	2,324	165	87	9	2,396	817	2.76	3.12	3.36	317
SP	1907-16	N.Rucker	336	273	2,375	134	134	14	1,217	701	2.42	3.10	3.62	261
Starters	Averages		493	431	3,276	206	157	9	2,344	911	3.00	3.44	3.68	328
RP	1961-73	R.Perranoski	737	1	1,175	79	74	179	687	468	2.79	3.38	3.87	91
RP	1960-76	J.Brewer	584	35	1,041	69	65	132	810	360	3.07	3.47	3.84	84
RP	1980-94	J.Howell	568	21	845	58	53	155	666	291	3.34	3.57	3.72	82
RP	1981-96	A.Pena	503	72	1,058	56	52	74	839	331	3.11	3.63	3.95	74
Relievers	Averages		598	32	1,029	66	61	135	751	363	3.05	3.51	3.85	82
Totals	Averages		1,091	463	4,306	271	218	144	3,094	1,274	3.01	3.46	3.72	411

Brooklyn/Los Angeles Dodgers   **Hitters Rate of Success**

Pos	Years	Name	AB	BB	HBP	TAB	H	2B	3B	HR	BA	OB	SA	PRO	Wtd PRO	SB	CS	SBF	SPF	FF	R TF	V HC
C	1992-	M.Piazza	4,135	439	16	4,590	1,356	199	4	278	.328	.395	.580	974	918	17	15	(3)	(10)	(18)	887	483
1B	1933-45	D.Camilli	5,353	947	28	6,328	1,482	261	86	239	.277	.388	.492	880	883	60	0	0	0	5	888	379
2B	1947-56	J.Robinson	4,877	740	72	5,689	1,518	273	54	137	.311	.410	.474	883	858	197	30	6	10	24	899	531
SS	1891-11	B.Dahlen	9,031	1,064	140	10,235	2,457	413	163	84	.272	.358	.382	739	767	547	0	0	9	50	826	880
3B	1971-87	R.Cey	7,162	1,012	62	8,236	1,868	328	21	316	.261	.357	.445	802	811	24	29	(4)	(6)	18	819	408
OF	1947-64	D.Snider	7,161	971	21	8,153	2,116	358	85	407	.295	.381	.540	921	897	99	50	(4)	1	10	903	596
OF	1919-34	L.O'Doul	3,264	333	23	3,620	1,140	175	41	113	.349	.413	.532	945	893	36	0	0	0	(20)	872	222
OF	1940-52	P.Reiser	2,662	343	20	3,025	786	155	41	58	.295	.380	.450	829	841	87	3	(0)	10	10	861	160
Starters		Averages	5,456	731	48	6,235	1,590	270	62	204	.292	.380	.476	856	848	133	16	(1)	2	10	859	457
C	1948-57	R.Campanella	4,205	533	30	4,768	1,161	178	18	242	.276	.362	.500	861	835	25	15	(2)	(4)	48	877	476
1B	1912-27	J.Fournier	5,208	587	89	5,884	1,631	252	113	136	.313	.392	.483	875	872	145	94	(13)	5	(4)	860	268
2B	1972-87	D.Lopes	6,354	833	31	7,218	1,671	232	50	155	.263	.351	.388	740	741	557	114	43	10	(29)	765	248
SS	1940-58	P.Reese	8,058	1,210	26	9,294	2,170	330	80	126	.269	.366	.377	743	733	232	45	2	9	19	762	458
3B	1911-26	J.Johnston	5,070	391	20	5,481	1,493	185	75	22	.294	.347	.374	721	728	169	83	(8)	10	(6)	724	23
OF	1926-45	B.Herman	5,603	520	11	6,134	1,818	399	110	181	.324	.383	.532	915	875	94	0	0	8	(26)	857	299
OF	1909-27	Z.Wheat	9,106	650	72	9,828	2,884	476	172	132	.317	.367	.450	817	835	205	49	(4)	5	14	850	464
OF	1978-92	P.Guerrero	5,392	609	32	6,033	1,618	267	29	215	.300	.374	.480	854	865	97	47	(1)	(0)	(18)	847	279
Reserves		Averages	6,125	667	39	6,830	1,806	290	81	151	.295	.368	.443	810	806	191	56	2	5	(0)	814	314
Totals		Weighted Ave.	5,679	710	45	6,433	1,662	277	68	186	.293	.376	.464	840	834	152	29	0	3	6	844	410

Pitchers Rate of Success

Pos	Years	Name	G	GS	IP	W	L	SV	SO	BB	ERA	RA/9	Wtd RA/9	R V Runs /162
SP	1955-66	S.Koufax	397	314	2,324	165	87	9	2,396	817	2.76	3.12	3.36	317
SP	1915-35	D.Vance	442	348	2,967	197	140	11	2,045	840	3.24	3.78	3.57	342
SP	1907-16	N.Rucker	336	273	2,375	134	134	14	1,217	701	2.42	3.10	3.62	261
SP	1956-69	D.Drysdale	518	465	3,432	209	166	6	2,486	855	2.95	3.39	3.72	326
SP	1994-	I.Valdes	197	170	1,132	63	61	1	830	326	3.59	3.94	3.74	106
Starters		Averages	378	314	2,446	154	118	8	1,795	708	2.94	3.43	3.60	270
RP	1995-	A.Osuna	265	0	327	24	21	10	346	141	3.27	3.61	3.47	40
RP	1980-96	S.Howe	497	0	606	47	41	91	328	139	3.03	3.55	3.61	69
RP	1981-90	T.Niedenfuer	484	0	653	36	46	97	474	226	3.29	3.46	3.71	63
RP	1980-94	J.Howell	568	21	845	58	53	155	666	291	3.34	3.57	3.72	82
Relievers		Averages	454	5	608	41	40	88	454	199	3.24	3.54	3.65	64
Totals		Averages	832	319	3,054	195	158	96	2,248	907	3.00	3.45	3.61	334

Brooklyn/Los Angeles Dodgers
Catchers

V	R	Years	Name	AB	BB	HBP	TAB	H	2B	3B	HR	BA	OB	SA	PRO	Wtd PRO	SB	CS	SBF	SPF	FF	R TF	V HC
1	1	1992-	M.Piazza	4,135	439	16	4,590	1,356	199	4	278	.328	.395	.580	974	918	17	15	(3)	(10)	(18)	887	483
2	2	1948-57	R.Campanella	4,205	533	30	4,768	1,161	178	18	242	.276	.362	.500	861	835	25	15	(2)	(4)	48	877	476
3	4	1970-83	J.Ferguson	3,001	562	9	3,572	719	121	11	122	.240	.361	.409	770	775	22	12	(1)	(8)	(1)	765	151
4	3	1931-42	B.Phelps	2,117	160	13	2,290	657	143	19	54	.310	.362	.472	835	833	9	0	0	(10)	(24)	799	140
5	5	1957-70	J.Roseboro	4,847	547	36	5,430	1,206	190	44	104	.249	.329	.371	700	707	67	56	(8)	5	16	720	112
6	6	1980-92	M.Scioscia	4,373	567	22	4,962	1,131	198	12	68	.259	.347	.356	703	712	29	24	(4)	(9)	13	713	89
7	7	1916-30	H.DeBerry	1,850	148	6	2,004	494	81	16	11	.267	.323	.346	669	636	13	5	(1)	(7)	56	684	7
8	8	1928-47	A.Lopez	5,916	556	14	6,486	1,547	206	43	51	.261	.326	.337	663	658	46	1	(0)	(3)	20	675	(9)
9	9	1972-86	S.Yeager	3,584	342	27	3,953	816	118	16	102	.228	.300	.355	655	660	14	18	(5)	(7)	22	669	(16)
10	10	1937-54	M.Owen	3,649	326	13	3,988	929	163	21	14	.255	.318	.322	640	648	36	1	(0)	(2)	13	659	(36)
11	11	1910-22	O.Miller	2,836	104	13	2,953	695	97	33	5	.245	.275	.308	583	608	40	6	(3)	(7)	34	631	(70)
12	12	1920-35	Z.Taylor	2,865	161	16	3,042	748	113	28	9	.261	.304	.329	634	602	9	7	(3)	(10)	6	595	(126)
13	13	1901-11	B.Bergen	3,028	88	0	3,116	516	45	21	2	.170	.194	.201	395	436	23	0	0	(10)	53	479	(319)

Brooklyn/Los Angeles Dodgers
First basemen

V	R	Years	Name	AB	BB	HBP	TAB	H	2B	3B	HR	BA	OB	SA	PRO	Wtd PRO	SB	CS	SBF	SPF	FF	R TF	V HC
1	1	1933-45	D.Camilli	5,353	947	28	6,328	1,482	261	86	239	.277	.388	.492	880	883	60	0	0	0	5	888	379
2	3	1943-63	G.Hodges	7,030	943	25	7,998	1,921	295	48	370	.273	.361	.487	848	823	63	31	(3)	0	27	847	314
3	2	1912-27	J.Fournier	5,208	587	89	5,884	1,631	252	113	136	.313	.392	.483	875	872	145	94	(13)	5	(4)	860	268
4	6	1969-87	S.Garvey	8,835	479	29	9,343	2,599	440	43	272	.294	.333	.446	779	786	83	62	(4)	(0)	19	801	158
5	5	1910-24	J.Daubert	7,673	623	53	8,349	2,326	250	165	56	.303	.360	.401	760	788	251	78	(8)	9	18	807	156
6	4	1901-10	T.Jordan	1,813	254	9	2,076	474	74	24	32	.261	.355	.382	737	843	48	0	0	0	(31)	813	44
7	8	1964-72	W.Parker	4,157	532	24	4,713	1,110	194	32	64	.267	.353	.375	729	748	60	34	(2)	10	32	788	41
8	7	1928-32	D.Bissonette	2,291	233	6	2,530	699	117	50	66	.305	.371	.486	857	798	17	0	0	10	(14)	794	32
9	9	1929-38	S.Leslie	2,460	216	23	2,699	749	123	28	36	.304	.366	.421	787	779	14	0	0	0	0	779	13
10	10	1923-34	H.Hendrick	2,910	239	16	3,165	896	157	46	48	.308	.364	.443	807	772	75	0	1	5	(21)	758	2
11	11	1958-78	R.Fairly	7,184	1,052	40	8,276	1,913	307	33	215	.266	.360	.408	771	784	35	33	(4)	(10)	(15)	755	(36)
12	12	1991-	E.Karros	5,040	439	22	5,501	1,363	254	9	242	.270	.332	.468	800	760	54	28	(0)	(9)	(2)	749	(58)
13	13	1958-63	N.Larker	1,953	211	16	2,180	538	97	15	32	.275	.351	.390	741	727	3	5	(3)	(10)	0	714	(60)
14	15	1984-95	F.Stubbs	2,591	260	10	2,861	602	109	12	104	.232	.305	.404	709	710	74	28	6	0	(12)	704	(87)
15	14	1936-42	B.Hassett	3,517	209	11	3,737	1,026	130	40	12	.292	.333	.362	695	694	53	5	(1)	0	12	705	(120)

Brooklyn/Los Angeles Dodgers
Second basemen

V	R	Years	Name	AB	BB	HBP	TAB	H	2B	3B	HR	BA	OB	SA	PRO	Wtd PRO	SB	CS	SBF	SPF	FF	R TF	V HC
1	1	1947-56	J.Robinson	4,877	740	72	5,689	1,518	273	54	137	.311	.410	.474	883	858	197	30	6	10	24	899	531
2	2	1972-87	D.Lopes	6,354	833	31	7,218	1,671	232	50	155	.263	.351	.388	740	741	557	114	43	10	(29)	765	248
3	3	1943-53	E.Stanky	4,301	996	35	5,332	1,154	185	35	29	.268	.410	.348	758	755	48	5	(0)	0	7	761	205
4	4	1956-63	C.Neal	3,316	337	20	3,673	858	113	38	87	.259	.331	.394	725	711	48	36	(6)	8	11	723	69
5	7	1912-23	G.Cutshaw	5,621	300	26	5,947	1,487	195	89	25	.265	.305	.344	649	687	271	68	(6)	8	15	705	60
6	9	1981-94	S.Sax	6,940	556	24	7,520	1,949	278	47	54	.281	.336	.358	694	696	444	178	10	10	(23)	694	27
7	6	1965-72	J.Lefebvre	3,014	322	13	3,349	756	126	18	74	.251	.326	.378	704	724	8	15	(6)	(10)	(2)	706	20
8	8	1953-66	J.Gilliam	7,119	1,036	33	8,188	1,889	304	71	65	.265	.361	.355	717	702	203	111	(2)	9	(4)	704	10
9	5	1905-18	J.Hummel	3,906	346	11	4,263	991	128	84	29	.254	.316	.352	668	726	117	1	(0)	9	(16)	718	(1)

Brooklyn/Los Angeles Dodgers
Shortstops

V	R	Years	Name	AB	BB	HBP	TAB	H	2B	3B	HR	BA	OB	SA	PRO	Wtd PRO	SB	CS	SBF	SPF	FF	R TF	V HC
1	1	1891-11	B.Dahlen	9,031	1,064	140	10,235	2,457	413	163	84	.272	.358	.382	739	767	547	0	0	9	50	826	880
2	2	1940-58	P.Reese	8,058	1,210	26	9,294	2,170	330	80	126	.269	.366	.377	743	733	232	45	2	9	19	762	458
3	3	1959-72	M.Wills	7,588	552	16	8,156	2,134	177	71	20	.281	.331	.331	662	673	586	208	20	10	18	721	198
4	5	1983-92	D.Anderson	2,026	206	5	2,237	490	73	12	19	.242	.313	.318	631	640	49	30	(5)	8	32	676	(1)
5	4	1990-	J.Offerman	4,596	634	15	5,245	1,277	200	65	39	.278	.367	.375	742	701	157	91	(5)	10	(29)	678	(19)
6	6	1969-86	B.Russell	7,318	483	36	7,837	1,926	293	57	46	.263	.312	.338	650	655	167	69	3	10	(5)	663	(33)
7	7	1911-24	I.Olson	6,111	285	36	6,432	1,575	191	69	13	.258	.295	.318	613	639	156	36	(4)	0	(8)	627	(140)

Brooklyn/Los Angeles Dodgers
Third basemen

V	R	Years	Name	AB	BB	HBP	TAB	H	2B	3B	HR	BA	OB	SA	PRO	Wtd PRO	SB	CS	SBF	SPF	FF	R TF	V HC
1	1	1971-87	R.Cey	7,162	1,012	62	8,236	1,868	328	21	316	.261	.357	.445	802	811	24	29	(4)	(6)	18	819	408
2	2	1911-26	J.Johnston	5,070	391	20	5,481	1,493	185	75	22	.294	.347	.374	721	728	169	83	(8)	10	(6)	724	23
3	4	1934-47	C.Lavagetto	3,509	485	12	4,006	945	183	37	40	.269	.360	.377	737	733	63	0	0	9	18	714	18
4	5	1941-55	B.Cox	3,712	298	7	4,017	974	174	32	66	.262	.318	.380	698	684	42	21	(6)	9	15	702	(0)
5	3	1928-38	J.Stripp	4,211	280	16	4,507	1,238	219	43	24	.294	.340	.384	724	702	50	0	0	10	8	720	(9)
6	6	1954-65	D.Zimmer	3,283	246	13	3,542	773	130	22	91	.235	.291	.372	663	652	45	25	(1)	7	16	673	(31)
7	7	1922-34	A.High	4,400	425	19	4,844	1,250	195	65	44	.284	.350	.388	738	699	33	25	(7)	0	(20)	672	(98)
8	8	1988-	L.Harris	3,282	231	14	3,527	895	136	18	31	.273	.323	.353	677	662	123	50	7	9	(21)	657	(103)
9	9	1928-32	W.Gilbert	2,317	162	17	2,496	624	112	17	7	.269	.322	.341	663	613	21	0	0	0	6	619	(121)

Brooklyn/Los Angeles Dodgers
Outfielders

V	R	Years	Name	AB	BB	HBP	TAB	H	2B	3B	HR	BA	OB	SA	PRO	Wtd PRO	SB	CS	SBF	SPF	FF	R TF	V HC
1	1	1947-64	D.Snider	7,161	971	21	8,153	2,116	358	85	407	.295	.381	.540	921	897	99	50	(4)	1	10	903	596
2	5	1909-27	Z.Wheat	9,106	650	72	9,828	2,884	476	172	132	.317	.367	.450	817	835	205	49	(4)	5	14	850	464
3	4	1926-45	B.Herman	5,603	520	11	6,134	1,818	399	110	181	.324	.383	.532	915	875	94	0	0	8	(26)	857	299
4	6	1978-92	P.Guerrero	5,392	609	32	6,033	1,618	267	29	215	.300	.374	.480	854	865	97	47	(1)	(0)	(18)	847	279
5	9	1931-49	D.Walker	6,740	817	16	7,573	2,064	376	96	105	.306	.383	.437	820	815	59	10	(1)	(0)	7	821	241
6	2	1919-34	L.O'Doul	3,264	333	23	3,620	1,140	175	41	113	.349	.413	.532	945	893	36	0	0	0	(20)	872	222
7	13	1981-97	B.Butler	8,180	1,129	38	9,347	2,375	277	131	54	.290	.379	.376	755	752	558	257	5	10	31	799	192
8	15	1960-79	W.Davis	9,174	418	51	9,643	2,561	395	138	182	.279	.314	.412	726	741	398	131	13	10	31	795	175
9	7	1993-	R.Mondesi	3,875	262	26	4,163	1,109	212	39	187	.286	.336	.506	841	792	162	60	9	10	27	838	169
10	12	1968-86	D.Baker	7,117	762	30	7,909	1,981	320	23	242	.278	.351	.432	782	792	137	73	(1)	2	8	800	166
11	3	1940-52	P.Reiser	2,662	343	20	3,025	786	155	41	58	.295	.380	.450	829	841	87	3	(0)	10	10	861	160
12	14	1946-60	C.Furillo	6,378	514	47	6,939	1,910	324	56	192	.299	.356	.458	814	791	48	26	(5)	(6)	18	797	138
13	8	1904-10	H.Lumley	2,653	204	9	2,866	728	109	66	38	.274	.328	.408	737	832	110	0	0	0	(6)	826	99
14	10	1929-34	J.Frederick	3,102	210	26	3,338	954	200	35	85	.308	.357	.477	833	790	23	0	0	10	13	813	92
15	16	1912-25	C.Stengel	4,288	437	39	4,764	1,219	182	89	60	.284	.356	.410	766	805	131	43	(10)	0	(3)	792	82
16	11	1926-36	D.Taylor	2,190	267	5	2,462	650	121	37	44	.297	.374	.446	821	801	56	2	(1)	10	(3)	806	60
17	17	1937-46	G.Rosen	1,916	218	4	2,138	557	71	34	22	.291	.364	.398	762	771	12	0	0	0	11	782	26
18	19	1964-77	W.Crawford	3,435	431	9	3,875	921	152	35	86	.268	.351	.408	759	774	47	36	(6)	8	(11)	765	13
19	18	1938-42	E.Koy	1,846	137	9	1,992	515	108	29	36	.279	.332	.427	759	765	40	0	0	7	(4)	768	11
20	20	1943-53	G.Hermanski	1,960	289	22	2,271	533	85	18	46	.272	.372	.404	776	763	43	2	1	10	(15)	759	3
21	21	1981-91	M.Marshall	3,593	247	37	3,877	971	173	8	148	.270	.324	.446	770	780	26	33	(10)	(2)	(17)	751	(14)
22	22	1962-82	M.Mota	3,779	289	28	4,096	1,149	125	52	31	.304	.358	.389	747	766	50	42	(8)	8	(20)	746	(23)
23	27	1995-	R.Cedeno	1,399	182	7	1,588	388	59	13	17	.277	.363	.375	738	686	114	32	30	10	(3)	724	(25)
24	23	1977-87	K.Landreaux	4,101	299	19	4,419	1,099	180	45	91	.268	.321	.400	721	723	145	60	6	10	4	743	(32)
25	26	1960-69	L.Johnson	2,049	110	53	2,212	529	97	14	48	.258	.313	.389	702	727	50	24	1	10	(13)	725	(34)
26	28	1906-11	A.Burch	2,185	186	1	2,372	554	48	20	4	.254	.312	.299	612	687	96	0	0	10	23	720	(45)
27	30	1995-	Hollandsworth	1,741	142	6	1,889	472	86	12	52	.271	.328	.424	752	704	55	24	3	10	(10)	707	(46)
28	25	1909-25	H.Myers	4,910	195	24	5,129	1,380	179	100	32	.281	.312	.378	690	720	107	56	(11)	10	11	731	(69)
29	31	1901-05	J.Dobbs	2,224	187	17	2,428	585	85	23	7	.263	.325	.331	656	712	78	0	0	10	(20)	702	(71)
30	24	1959-76	T.Davis	7,223	381	32	7,636	2,121	272	35	153	.294	.332	.405	736	753	136	59	2	4	(20)	739	(81)
31	33	1920-27	B.Neis	1,825	201	5	2,031	496	84	18	25	.272	.346	.379	724	696	46	39	(17)	7	(13)	673	(86)
32	34	1965-74	A.Kosko	1,963	99	6	2,068	464	75	8	73	.236	.275	.394	669	700	5	8	(5)	(4)	(21)	669	(86)
33	32	1901-08	B.Maloney	2,476	162	40	2,678	585	54	42	6	.236	.294	.299	593	654	155	0	0	10	9	673	(101)
34	35	1934-45	F.Bordagaray	2,632	173	16	2,821	745	120	28	14	.283	.331	.366	697	698	66	2	(1)	4	(37)	664	(107)
35	29	1913-25	T.Griffith	4,947	351	9	5,307	1,383	208	72	52	.280	.328	.382	711	735	70	42	(9)	(1)	(8)	716	(112)
36	36	1908-15	H.Moran	2,177	264	30	2,471	527	60	26	2	.242	.332	.296	629	664	103	10	(2)	8	(13)	657	(126)

Brooklyn/Los Angeles Dodgers
Starting Pitchers

V	R	Years	Name	G	GS	IP	W	L	SV	SO	BB	ERA	RA/9	R Wtd RA/9	V Runs /162
1	8	1966-88	D.Sutton	774	756	5,282	324	256	5	3,574	1,343	3.26	3.58	3.89	396.2
2	2	1915-35	D.Vance	442	348	2,967	197	140	11	2,045	840	3.24	3.78	3.57	341.8
3	4	1956-69	D.Drysdale	518	465	3,432	209	166	6	2,486	855	2.95	3.39	3.72	326.4
4	1	1955-66	S.Koufax	397	314	2,324	165	87	9	2,396	817	2.76	3.12	3.36	316.8
5	3	1907-16	N.Rucker	336	273	2,375	134	134	14	1,217	701	2.42	3.10	3.62	260.7
6	10	1983-	O.Hershiser	510	466	3,130	204	150	5	2,014	1,007	3.48	3.93	4.00	197.2
7	7	1911-24	J.Pfeffer	347	279	2,407	158	112	10	836	592	2.77	3.44	3.87	195.4
8	14	1978-94	B.Welch	506	462	3,092	211	146	8	1,969	1,034	3.47	3.81	4.06	176.7
9	6	1938-54	P.Roe	333	261	1,914	127	84	10	956	504	3.43	3.75	3.80	169.2
10	23	1957-75	C.Osteen	541	488	3,460	196	195	1	1,612	940	3.30	3.73	4.19	140.5
11	19	1971-85	B.Hooton	480	377	2,652	151	136	7	1,491	799	3.38	3.77	4.14	127.0
12	15	1949-60	D.Newcombe	344	294	2,155	149	90	7	1,129	490	3.56	3.99	4.07	123.5
13	18	1934-46	C.Davis	429	281	2,325	158	131	33	684	479	3.42	4.00	4.11	120.7
14	12	1924-37	W.Clark	355	206	1,747	111	97	16	643	383	3.66	4.31	4.04	106.1
15	5	1994-	I.Valdes	197	170	1,132	63	61	1	830	326	3.59	3.94	3.74	105.8
16	25	1980-97	F.Valenzuela	453	424	2,930	173	153	2	2,074	1,151	3.54	4.00	4.25	104.7
17	21	1917-27	D.Ruether	309	272	2,125	137	95	8	708	739	3.50	4.19	4.15	101.6
18	20	1931-45	V.Mungo	364	259	2,113	120	115	16	1,242	868	3.47	4.08	4.15	100.5
19	16	1896-04	N.Garvin	181	158	1,401	57	97	4	612	413	2.72	4.56	4.09	81.9
20	9	1995-	H.Nomo	183	181	1,151	69	61	0	1,212	516	3.97	3.47	4.00	72.6
21	24	1988-	R.Martinez	297	293	1,880	135	86	0	1,418	779	3.62	4.14	4.23	72.2
22	13	1972-81	D.Rau	222	187	1,261	81	60	3	697	382	3.35	3.65	4.05	72.1
23	26	1953-69	J.Podres	440	340	2,265	148	116	11	1,435	743	3.68	4.08	4.29	70.6
24	17	1915-24	L.Cadore	192	147	1,257	68	72	3	445	289	3.14	3.76	4.10	68.3
25	36	1916-34	B.Grimes	616	497	4,180	270	212	18	1,512	1,295	3.53	4.41	4.43	63.2
26	11	1994-	H.Park	185	141	950	65	43	0	880	469	3.88	4.25	4.02	57.0
27	22	1921-30	J.Petty	207	153	1,208	67	78	4	407	296	3.68	4.51	4.16	55.8
28	27	1929-45	W.Wyatt	360	210	1,761	106	95	13	872	642	3.79	4.39	4.30	53.2
29	28	1944-56	R.Branca	322	188	1,484	88	68	19	829	663	3.79	4.25	4.33	40.1
30	30	1958-72	S.Williams	482	208	1,764	109	94	43	1,305	748	3.48	4.01	4.37	36.9
31	31	1948-59	C.Erskine	335	216	1,719	122	78	13	981	646	4.00	4.35	4.39	34.1
32	33	1964-77	B.Singer	322	308	2,174	118	127	2	1,515	781	3.39	3.91	4.42	32.3
33	32	1911-27	S.Smith	373	226	2,053	114	118	21	428	440	3.32	4.23	4.42	32.2
34	29	1950-61	B.Loes	316	139	1,190	80	63	32	645	421	3.89	4.27	4.34	30.6
35	34	1937-50	K.Higbe	418	238	1,952	118	101	24	971	979	3.69	4.19	4.43	29.8
36	35	1946-52	J.Hatten	233	149	1,087	65	49	4	381	492	3.87	4.32	4.43	16.5
37	37	1994-	D.Dreifort	188	87	667	39	45	10	581	281	4.28	4.71	4.43	9.5
38	38	1912-17	F.Allen	180	127	970	50	67	3	457	373	2.93	3.81	4.48	8.9
39	39	1945-50	V.Lombardi	223	100	945	50	51	16	340	418	3.68	4.40	4.49	7.3
40	40	1987-	T.Belcher	394	373	2,443	146	140	5	1,519	860	4.16	4.62	4.54	4.7
41	41	1969-90	J.Reuss	628	547	3,670	220	191	11	1,907	1,127	3.64	4.17	4.55	3.3
42	42	1909-23	P.Ragan	283	181	1,608	77	104	6	680	470	2.99	3.88	4.55	1.4
43	43	1933-44	L.Hamlin	261	181	1,405	73	76	9	563	353	3.77	4.39	4.55	0.3
44	45	1947-56	E.Palica	246	80	839	41	55	10	423	399	4.22	4.63	4.60	(4.6)
45	44	1898-07	F.Kitson	304	250	2,223	128	118	8	731	491	3.17	4.40	4.59	(7.9)
46	46	1992-	P.Astacio	282	239	1,573	95	82	0	1,222	518	4.43	4.78	4.61	(9.3)
47	48	1903-11	D.Scanlan	181	149	1,252	65	71	5	584	608	3.00	4.01	4.66	(14.4)
48	49	1921-30	D.McWeeny	206	118	948	37	57	6	386	450	4.17	5.09	4.70	(15.9)
49	50	1907-11	G.Bell	160	124	1,086	43	79	4	376	305	2.85	3.90	4.75	(24.4)
50	47	1978-	M.Morgan	537	410	2,700	139	185	8	1,366	912	4.22	4.63	4.65	(27.2)

Brooklyn/Los Angeles Dodgers
Starting Pitchers

V	R	Years	Name	G	GS	IP	W	L	SV	SO	BB	ERA	RA/9	R Wtd RA/9	V Runs /162
51	52	1906-15	C.Barger	151	111	976	46	63	9	297	334	3.56	4.42	4.80	(27.3)
52	53	1895-04	J.Cronin	128	102	923	43	57	3	318	235	3.40	4.88	4.80	(27.6)
53	51	1955-66	R.Craig	368	186	1,536	74	98	19	803	522	3.83	4.47	4.77	(36.8)
54	54	1909-17	E.Knetzer	220	134	1,267	69	69	6	535	484	3.15	4.28	4.89	(48.9)
55	57	1903-05	O.Jones	113	97	875	44	54	1	257	225	3.20	4.84	5.06	(53.4)
56	55	1923-34	J.Elliott	252	144	1,207	63	74	12	453	414	4.24	5.13	4.98	(60.1)
57	59	1904-07	E.Stricklett	104	90	766	35	51	6	237	215	2.84	4.36	5.25	(62.5)
58	56	1981-94	T.Leary	292	224	1,491	78	105	1	888	535	4.36	4.78	5.00	(73.7)
59	60	1900-06	M.Eason	125	114	951	36	73	1	274	291	3.42	4.85	5.32	(89.6)
60	61	1943-52	H.Gregg	200	115	827	40	48	9	401	443	4.54	5.30	5.53	(93.8)
61	58	1905-13	H.McIntire	237	188	1,650	71	117	7	626	539	3.22	4.24	5.07	(98.8)
62	62	1903-21	K.Wilhelm	216	158	1,432	56	105	5	444	418	3.44	4.84	5.56	(169.1)

Brooklyn/Los Angeles Dodgers
Relief Pitchers

V	R	Years	Name	G	GS	IP	W	L	SV	SO	BB	ERA	RA/9	R Wtd RA/9	V Runs /162
1	6	1961-73	R.Perranoski	737	1	1,175	79	74	179	687	468	2.79	3.38	3.87	90.8
2	5	1960-76	J.Brewer	584	35	1,041	69	65	132	810	360	3.07	3.47	3.84	83.6
3	4	1980-94	J.Howell	568	21	845	58	53	155	666	291	3.34	3.57	3.72	81.7
4	7	1981-96	A.Pena	503	72	1,058	56	52	74	839	331	3.11	3.63	3.95	73.6
5	2	1980-96	S.Howe	497	0	606	47	41	91	328	139	3.03	3.55	3.61	69.2
6	3	1981-90	T.Niedenfuer	484	0	653	36	46	97	474	226	3.29	3.46	3.71	62.9
7	8	1935-49	H.Casey	343	56	940	75	42	55	349	321	3.45	3.96	4.13	47.2
8	9	1950-62	C.Labine	513	38	1,080	77	56	96	551	396	3.63	4.10	4.19	46.3
9	1	1995-	A.Osuna	265	0	327	24	21	10	346	141	3.27	3.61	3.47	40.3
10	12	1957-74	B.Miller	694	99	1,551	69	81	51	895	608	3.37	3.94	4.36	34.4
11	14	1977-97	R.Honeycutt	797	268	2,160	109	143	38	1,038	657	3.72	4.31	4.44	29.9
12	10	1979-86	J.Beckwith	229	5	422	18	19	7	319	150	3.54	4.03	4.28	13.2
13	11	1987-92	T.Crews	281	4	424	11	13	15	293	110	3.44	3.85	4.35	9.9
14	13	1952-57	J.Black	172	16	414	30	12	25	222	129	3.91	4.34	4.40	7.4
15	15	1955-66	E.Roebuck	460	1	791	52	31	62	477	302	3.35	4.27	4.52	3.8
16	16	1964-72	P.Mikkelsen	364	3	653	45	40	49	436	250	3.38	3.97	4.53	1.7
17	17	1958-68	L.Sherry	416	16	799	53	44	82	606	374	3.67	4.25	4.66	(9.8)
18	18	1944-53	C.King	200	21	496	32	25	11	150	189	4.14	4.77	4.81	(14.7)
19	19	1942-48	L.Webber	154	25	432	23	19	14	141	201	4.19	4.61	5.05	(24.7)
20	20	1946-49	H.Behrman	174	27	430	24	17	19	189	228	4.40	5.23	5.39	(41.7)
21	21	1957-62	D.McDevitt	155	60	456	21	27	7	303	264	4.40	5.25	5.42	(45.6)

Chicago Cubs (1900–2000)

The Cubs managed only 45 winning seasons in the past 101 years, yet 31 of these seasons occurred before 1940. The early Cubs teams dominated in every aspect of the game. The long list of early stars include Joe Tinker, Johnny Evers, Frank Chance, Three Finger Brown, Ed Reulbach, Johnny Kling, Jimmy Sheckard, Hippo Vaughn, Pete Alexander, Gabby Hartnett, Hack Wilson, Kiki Cuyler, Billy Herman, Stan Hack, Charlie Root, and Lon Warneke. Phil Cavaretta led the Cubs to their last pennant in 1945.

Cubs fans have not seen a championship game at Wrigley Field since World War II, but they still cheered on stars Ernie Banks, Ron Santo, Billy Williams, Ferguson Jenkins, Rick Reuschel, Bruce Sutter, Ryne Sandberg, Lee Smith, Mark Grace, and Sammy Sosa.

Profiled Cubs Players

Frank Chance

Chance's name anchors the famous jingle, but few people today realize just how much he contributed to the success of the great early Cubs teams. Chance's actual batting averages for the years 1903–1908 were .327, .310, .316, .319, .293, and .272. Adjusted for hitter's deflation, his batting averages were .339, .349, .345, .363, .336, and .318. Over his career, Chance hit .296 with 20 home runs and 401 stolen bases in just 4,988 total at bats. Adjusted for 9 percent career deflation, Chance hit .324 with 23 home runs, finishing sixth in league rate of success among first basemen with an 887 Total Factor, but only 11th in volume of success with 330 Hits Contribution due to his limited plate appearances.

Chance also took over as Cubs manager from an ailing Frank Selee in the middle of the 1905 campaign. Chance managed the team for the next seven and a half years to a 768–389 record, for an off-the-charts .664 winning percentage. No manager in recent memory can hope to match that win rate, as to do so would require a 108–54 record, year after year.

Ernie Banks

Banks produced two distinctly different careers, rolled up into one. In the shortstop portion through 1961, Banks hit .290 and accumulated 298 home runs in 5,151 total at bats. Adjusted for 4 percent inflation, he hit .281 with 305 home runs, for an 891 Total Factor and 593 Hits Contribution in the first half of his career. These are fantastic numbers for a shortstop.

Banks was merely ordinary at first base after 1961, hitting .258 with 214 home runs in 5,103 total at bats. Adjusted for a 2 percent deflation, he hit .266 with 220 home runs, for a 780 Total Factor, and a mere 24 Hits Contribution at this power position over the second half of his career. None of Banks' seasons at first even rate in the Cubs' own top 25 player seasons at that position.

For his career, Banks hit .274 with 512 home runs in a noninflationary period, good for an 830 Wtd. Production, a league fourth best rate of success at short with an 837 Total Factor, and league fifth best volume of success with 617 Hits Contribution.

Ron Santo

In becoming the fifth highest ranked third baseman in major league history, Ron Santo demonstrated he could do it all — except run fast. Yet underrated superstar Ron Santo remains outside of the Hall of Fame, by far the greatest omission made by today's Hall of Fame voters. This is only partially explained by Santo's playing in the semi–dead ball era of the sixties and early seventies, which lowered his statistics, especially when compared to other players who played during better hitter years.

Santo hit .277 with 342 home runs in 9,289 total at bats. Adjusted for 2 percent deflation, he hit .283 with 350 home runs, for an 847 Wtd. Production. Santo has the league's fifth best rate of success at third with an 872 Total Factor, and third best volume of success with 708 Hits Contribution. With these statistics, it is inexcusable that Santo is not in the Hall of Fame, when far more ordinary third basemen like Fred Lindstrom and George Kell found a way in.

Gabby Hartnett

Hartnett was the National League's premier all-around catcher during the first half of the twentieth century. Hartnett hit .297 over his career, with 236 home runs, and he sported a rifle arm behind the plate. Adjusted for 3 percent career inflation, he hit .288 with 240 home runs, for an 830 Wtd. Production — impressive numbers for a catcher. Hartnett's 632 Hits Contribution places him second in the league behind Johnny Bench at catcher in volume of success, while his 853 Total Factor puts him fourth among league catchers in rate of success.

Ryne Sandberg

Sandberg rose to stardom and earned the league's MVP in his third full season in 1984, leading the Cubs to their first postseason appearance in 39 years. Sandberg then put together a decade of seasons filled with power, speed, and defense. For his career, he hit .285 with 282 home runs in 9,180 total at bats, in a period with no hitter's inflation. He also stole 344 bases in 451 attempts, and earned 41 Fielding Factor points in his career. Sandberg finished third in league volume of success at second base with 775 Hits Contribution, and fourth in league rate of success with an 862 Total Factor.

Billy Williams

Williams just missed joining the upper echelon of major league stars, as his fielding was not of Gold Glove caliber, and his on-base percentage suffered from never drawing more than 77 walks in a season. Still, Williams was easily the best Cubs outfielder of all time, and his .290 average and 426 home runs ranks him as one of the better outfielders in National League history. Adjusted for a career 2 percent hitter's deflation, Williams batted .297 with 437 home runs in 18 seasons. His 891 Total Factor ranks 17th in league rate of success for outfielders, while his 661 Hits Contribution ranks eighth in league volume of success.

Three Finger Brown

Chicago's historic strength lies with its starting pitchers, as Cubs pitchers own 17 of the top 100 National League rate of success seasons since 1900, the most of any team. (The Giants are a close second with 16.) This is especially true for the years 1902–1920, when 13 of these superb Cubs seasons occurred. The best of these early pitchers—and the ace of the staff—was Three Finger Brown, with four of the top 100 seasons.

Three Finger Brown has a slight edge over the Giants' Christy Mathewson in rate of success among early National League pitchers, with a 3.40 Wtd. RA/9 to Mathewson's 3.42. Mathewson easily wins in volume of success rankings, as he worked 51 percent more innings, and it shows in his wins total and greater reputation. The point to remember is that Brown pitched just as well as Mathewson when he went to the mound. Brown went 239–130 in 3,172 innings, for a .648 winning percentage, and he achieved a 2.06 ERA and a 3.40 Wtd. RA/9 (fifth best in the league), while saving 432 runs from scoring (seventh best in the league).

Ed Reulbach

Reulbach pitched in the shadows of Three Finger Brown in his best years, and he remains a relative unknown to this day. Yet, in his first five seasons, Reulbach was one of the most unhittable pitchers in history, including a 2–0 record in World Series appearances in 1906, 1907, and 1908. Reulbach was 18–14 with a 1.42 ERA in his rookie year. He then went 60–15 in his next three seasons, before "slipping" to a 19–10 record in 1909.

Years	IP	W–L	ERA	Wtd. RA/9	Runs/162
1905–09	1,262	97–39	1.72	2.86	250
1910–17	1,370	85–67	2.80	4.20	56

In his career, Reulbach was 182–106 with a 2.28 ERA. His 3.56 Wtd. RA/9 ranks 12th in league rate of success, while his 306 Runs/162 ranks 18th in league volume of success.

Chicago Cubs   **Hitters Volume of Success**

Pos	Years	Name	AB	BB	HBP	TAB	H	2B	3B	HR	BA	OB	SA	PRO	Wtd PRO	SB	CS	SBF	SPF	FF	R TF	V HC
C	1922-41	G.Hartnett	6,432	703	35	7,170	1,912	396	64	236	.297	.370	.489	858	830	28	7	0	(10)	33	853	632
1B	1898-13	F.Chance	4,297	554	137	4,988	1,273	200	79	20	.296	.394	.394	787	862	401	0	0	10	15	887	330
2B	1981-97	R.Sandberg	8,385	761	34	9,180	2,386	403	76	282	.285	.347	.452	798	799	344	107	13	8	41	862	775
SS	1953-71	E.Banks	9,421	763	70	10,254	2,583	407	90	512	.274	.333	.500	833	830	50	53	(5)	4	8	837	617
3B	1960-74	R.Santo	8,143	1,108	38	9,289	2,254	365	67	342	.277	.366	.464	830	847	35	41	(5)	(8)	38	872	708
OF	1959-76	B.Williams	9,350	1,045	43	10,438	2,711	434	88	426	.290	.364	.492	856	875	90	49	(1)	7	9	891	661
OF	1897-13	J.Sheckard	7,605	1,135	90	8,830	2,084	354	136	56	.274	.375	.378	753	808	465	0	0	10	28	846	396
OF	1921-38	K.Cuyler	7,161	676	85	7,922	2,299	394	157	128	.321	.386	.474	860	822	328	27	3	10	18	853	377
Starters	Averages		7,599	843	67	8,509	2,188	369	95	250	.288	.364	.460	824	834	218	36	1	4	24	862	562
C	1900-13	J.Kling	4,241	281	12	4,534	1,151	181	61	20	.271	.318	.357	675	735	123	0	0	(3)	15	747	163
1B	1988-	M.Grace	7,156	946	29	8,131	2,201	456	43	148	.308	.391	.445	836	813	67	48	(3)	0	33	843	292
2B	1931-47	B.Herman	7,707	737	26	8,470	2,345	486	82	47	.304	.367	.407	774	777	67	0	0	(4)	27	801	490
SS	1902-16	J.Tinker	6,434	416	10	6,860	1,687	263	114	31	.262	.308	.353	661	716	336	0	0	0	40	755	324
3B	1932-47	S.Hack	7,278	1,092	21	8,391	2,193	363	81	57	.301	.394	.397	791	797	165	0	0	8	8	813	409
OF	1923-34	H.Wilson	4,760	674	20	5,454	1,461	266	67	244	.307	.395	.545	940	892	52	5	(0)	0	(13)	879	331
OF	1966-84	R.Monday	6,136	924	24	7,084	1,619	248	64	241	.264	.362	.443	805	828	98	91	(11)	6	6	829	246
OF	1934-49	A.Galan	5,937	979	25	6,941	1,706	336	74	100	.287	.390	.419	810	811	123	0	0	5	2	818	218
Reserves	Averages		6,206	756	21	6,983	1,795	325	73	111	.289	.368	.419	787	796	129	18	(2)	2	15	811	309
Totals	Weighted Ave.		7,135	814	51	8,000	2,057	354	88	204	.288	.365	.448	813	821	188	30	(0)	3	21	845	478

Pitchers Volume of Success

Pos	Years	Name	G	GS	IP	W	L	SV	SO	BB	ERA	RA/9	V Wtd RA/9	R Runs /162
SP	1903-16	T.Brown	481	332	3,172	239	130	49	1,375	673	2.06	2.96	3.40	432
SP	1905-17	E.Reulbach	399	300	2,632	182	106	13	1,137	892	2.28	3.03	3.56	306
SP	1965-83	F.Jenkins	664	594	4,501	284	226	7	3,192	997	3.34	3.71	4.10	233
SP	1930-45	L.Warneke	445	343	2,782	192	121	13	1,140	739	3.18	3.77	3.86	226
SP	1923-41	C.Root	632	341	3,197	201	160	40	1,459	889	3.59	4.13	4.01	203
Starters	Averages		524	382	3,257	220	149	24	1,661	838	2.94	3.55	3.82	280
RP	1980-97	L.Smith	1,022	6	1,289	71	92	478	1,251	486	3.03	3.32	3.57	148
RP	1976-88	B.Sutter	661	0	1,042	68	71	300	861	309	2.83	3.19	3.56	120
RP	1986-99	P.Assenmacher	884	1	856	61	44	56	807	315	3.53	3.90	4.00	54
RP	1989-	C.McElroy	605	2	664	36	27	17	557	316	3.74	4.24	4.13	33
Relievers	Averages		793	2	963	59	59	213	869	357	3.21	3.57	3.76	89
Totals	Averages		1,317	384	4,220	279	207	237	2,530	1,195	3.00	3.55	3.81	369

Chicago Cubs   **Hitters Rate of Success**

Pos	Years	Name	AB	BB	HBP	TAB	H	2B	3B	HR	BA	OB	SA	PRO	Wtd PRO	SB	CS	SBF	SPF	FF	R TF	V HC
C	1922-41	G.Hartnett	6,432	703	35	7,170	1,912	396	64	236	.297	.370	.489	858	830	28	7	0	(10)	33	853	632
1B	1898-13	F.Chance	4,297	554	137	4,988	1,273	200	79	20	.296	.394	.394	787	862	401	0	0	10	15	887	330
2B	1981-97	R.Sandberg	8,385	761	34	9,180	2,386	403	76	282	.285	.347	.452	798	799	344	107	13	8	41	862	775
SS	1953-71	E.Banks	9,421	763	70	10,254	2,583	407	90	512	.274	.333	.500	833	830	50	53	(5)	4	8	837	617
3B	1960-74	R.Santo	8,143	1,108	38	9,289	2,254	365	67	342	.277	.366	.464	830	847	35	41	(5)	(8)	38	872	708
OF	1959-76	B.Williams	9,350	1,045	43	10,438	2,711	434	88	426	.290	.364	.492	856	875	90	49	(1)	7	9	891	661
OF	1923-34	H.Wilson	4,760	674	20	5,454	1,461	266	67	244	.307	.395	.545	940	892	52	5	(0)	0	(13)	879	331
OF	1921-38	K.Cuyler	7,161	676	85	7,922	2,299	394	157	128	.321	.386	.474	860	822	328	27	3	10	18	853	377
Starters	Averages		7,244	786	58	8,087	2,110	358	86	274	.291	.365	.478	843	842	166	36	1	3	19	864	554
C	1900-13	J.Kling	4,241	281	12	4,534	1,151	181	61	20	.271	.318	.357	675	735	123	0	0	(3)	15	747	163
1B	1988-	M.Grace	7,156	946	29	8,131	2,201	456	43	148	.308	.391	.445	836	813	67	48	(3)	0	33	843	292
2B	1931-47	B.Herman	7,707	737	26	8,470	2,345	486	82	47	.304	.367	.407	774	777	67	0	0	(4)	27	801	490
SS	1918-24	C.Hollocher	2,936	277	26	3,239	894	145	35	14	.304	.370	.392	762	769	99	80	(29)	10	6	756	149
3B	1932-47	S.Hack	7,278	1,092	21	8,391	2,193	363	81	57	.301	.394	.397	791	797	165	0	0	8	8	813	409
OF	1897-13	J.Sheckard	7,605	1,135	90	8,830	2,084	354	136	56	.274	.375	.378	753	808	465	0	0	10	28	846	396
OF	1966-84	R.Monday	6,136	924	24	7,084	1,619	248	64	241	.264	.362	.443	805	828	98	91	(11)	6	6	829	246
OF	1936-53	B.Nicholson	5,546	800	52	6,398	1,484	272	60	235	.268	.365	.465	830	843	27	1	(0)	(10)	(13)	819	198
Reserves	Averages		6,076	774	35	6,885	1,746	313	70	102	.287	.371	.413	784	801	139	28	(6)	2	14	811	293
Totals	Weighted Ave.		6,854	782	50	7,686	1,989	343	81	217	.290	.367	.459	826	828	157	33	(1)	3	17	847	467

Pitchers Rate of Success

Pos	Years	Name	G	GS	IP	W	L	SV	SO	BB	ERA	RA/9	V Wtd RA/9	R Runs /162
SP	1903-16	T.Brown	481	332	3,172	239	130	49	1,375	673	2.06	2.96	3.40	432
SP	1905-17	E.Reulbach	399	300	2,632	182	106	13	1,137	892	2.28	3.03	3.56	306
SP	1903-09	J.Weimer	191	180	1,473	97	69	2	657	493	2.23	3.12	3.58	171
SP	1905-13	O.Overall	218	182	1,535	108	71	12	935	551	2.23	3.05	3.69	156
SP	1903-11	J.Pfiester	149	128	1,067	71	44	0	503	293	2.02	3.06	3.79	96
Starters	Averages		288	224	1,976	139	84	15	921	580	2.17	3.03	3.56	232
RP	1976-88	B.Sutter	661	0	1,042	68	71	300	861	309	2.83	3.19	3.56	120
RP	1980-97	L.Smith	1,022	6	1,289	71	92	478	1,251	486	3.03	3.32	3.57	148
RP	1986-99	P.Assenmacher	884	1	856	61	44	56	807	315	3.53	3.90	4.00	54
RP	1989-	C.McElroy	605	2	664	36	27	17	557	316	3.74	4.24	4.13	33
Relievers	Averages		793	2	963	59	59	213	869	357	3.21	3.57	3.76	89
Totals	Averages		1,081	227	2,939	198	143	228	1,790	937	2.51	3.21	3.62	321

Chicago Cubs
Catchers

V	R	Years	Name	AB	BB	HBP	TAB	H	2B	3B	HR	BA	OB	SA	PRO	Wtd PRO	SB	CS	SBF	SPF	FF	R TF	V HC
1	1	1922-41	G.Hartnett	6,432	703	35	7,170	1,912	396	64	236	.297	.370	.489	858	830	28	7	0	(10)	33	853	632
2	2	1900-13	J.Kling	4,241	281	12	4,534	1,151	181	61	20	.271	.318	.357	675	735	123	0	0	(3)	15	747	163
3	3	1915-35	B.O'Farrell	4,101	547	11	4,659	1,120	201	58	51	.273	.360	.388	748	721	35	7	1	(6)	2	719	96
4	4	1981-90	J.Davis	3,585	333	9	3,927	877	164	11	127	.245	.310	.403	713	721	7	16	(6)	(10)	12	717	73
5	5	1991-	R.Wilkins	2,092	276	13	2,381	511	94	7	80	.244	.336	.411	747	716	9	12	(6)	(4)	0	706	34
6	6	1964-77	R.Hundley	3,442	271	13	3,726	813	118	13	82	.236	.294	.350	644	664	12	17	(6)	0	23	682	9
7	7	1904-18	J.Archer	2,646	124	19	2,789	660	106	34	16	.249	.288	.333	621	658	36	6	(2)	0	11	667	(15)
8	8	1940-56	C.McCullough	3,121	265	20	3,406	785	121	28	52	.252	.314	.358	672	673	27	1	0	(7)	(7)	660	(31)
9	9	1987-97	D.Berryhill	2,030	139	6	2,175	488	106	6	47	.240	.291	.368	659	658	3	6	(4)	(7)	(9)	638	(43)
10	10	1991-	S.Servais	2,477	181	46	2,704	605	130	2	63	.244	.308	.375	682	650	3	6	(3)	(10)	(1)	636	(55)

Chicago Cubs
First basemen

V	R	Years	Name	AB	BB	HBP	TAB	H	2B	3B	HR	BA	OB	SA	PRO	Wtd PRO	SB	CS	SBF	SPF	FF	R TF	V HC
1	1	1898-13	F.Chance	4,297	554	137	4,988	1,273	200	79	20	.296	.394	.394	787	862	401	0	0	10	15	887	330
2	2	1988-	M.Grace	7,156	946	29	8,131	2,201	456	43	148	.308	.391	.445	836	813	67	48	(3)	0	33	843	292
3	3	1980-89	L.Durham	3,587	444	9	4,040	992	192	40	147	.277	.358	.475	833	840	106	61	(3)	10	(6)	841	154
4	5	1934-55	P.Cavarretta	6,754	820	37	7,611	1,977	347	99	95	.293	.372	.416	788	793	65	0	0	6	(2)	797	125
5	4	1911-19	V.Saier	2,948	378	22	3,348	775	143	61	55	.263	.351	.409	760	809	121	26	(1)	9	(11)	806	62
6	6	1951-63	D.Long	3,020	353	7	3,380	805	135	33	132	.267	.345	.464	809	785	10	3	1	(10)	(13)	763	(11)
7	7	1969-90	B.Buckner	9,397	450	42	9,889	2,715	498	49	174	.289	.324	.408	732	740	183	73	4	(0)	8	751	(72)
8	9	1951-58	D.Fondy	3,502	203	7	3,712	1,000	144	47	69	.286	.326	.413	739	715	84	53	(6)	10	(1)	718	(96)
9	8	1916-36	C.Grimm	7,917	578	31	8,526	2,299	394	108	79	.290	.341	.397	738	710	57	44	(6)	0	17	722	(207)

Chicago Cubs
Second basemen

V	R	Years	Name	AB	BB	HBP	TAB	H	2B	3B	HR	BA	OB	SA	PRO	Wtd PRO	SB	CS	SBF	SPF	FF	R TF	V HC
1	1	1981-97	R.Sandberg	8,385	761	34	9,180	2,386	403	76	282	.285	.347	.452	798	799	344	107	13	8	41	862	775
2	2	1931-47	B.Herman	7,707	737	26	8,470	2,345	486	82	47	.304	.367	.407	774	777	67	0	0	(4)	27	801	490
3	3	1902-29	J.Evers	6,137	778	39	6,954	1,659	216	70	12	.270	.356	.334	690	752	324	8	(1)	5	21	778	324
4	4	1973-89	M.Trillo	5,950	452	34	6,436	1,562	239	33	61	.263	.318	.345	663	671	56	57	(8)	1	36	699	25
5	5	1965-75	G.Beckert	5,208	260	19	5,487	1,473	196	31	22	.283	.319	.345	664	684	49	25	(0)	(2)	6	688	6
6	6	1953-61	G.Baker	2,230	184	9	2,423	590	109	21	39	.265	.323	.385	708	681	21	17	(5)	8	(13)	671	(18)
7	8	1943-48	D.Johnson	1,935	112	8	2,055	528	89	6	8	.273	.315	.337	653	660	26	0	0	0	(11)	650	(37)
8	7	1922-34	S.Adams	5,557	453	28	6,038	1,588	249	48	9	.286	.343	.353	695	666	154	50	(6)	7	3	670	(71)
9	9	1944-58	E.Miksis	3,053	215	6	3,274	722	95	17	44	.236	.288	.322	610	593	52	22	(2)	10	0	601	(171)

Chicago Cubs
Shortstops

V	R	Years	Name	AB	BB	HBP	TAB	H	2B	3B	HR	BA	OB	SA	PRO	Wtd PRO	SB	CS	SBF	SPF	FF	R TF	V HC
1	1	1953-71	E.Banks	9,421	763	70	10,254	2,583	407	90	512	.274	.333	.500	833	830	50	53	(5)	4	8	837	617
2	3	1902-16	J.Tinker	6,434	416	10	6,860	1,687	263	114	31	.262	.308	.353	661	716	336	0	0	0	40	755	324
3	4	1985-	S.Dunston	5,594	198	38	5,830	1,511	277	59	140	.270	.300	.416	715	704	208	81	6	8	6	725	158
4	2	1918-24	C.Hollocher	2,936	277	26	3,239	894	145	35	14	.304	.370	.392	762	769	99	80	(29)	10	6	756	149
5	6	1931-47	B.Jurges	6,253	568	51	6,872	1,613	245	55	43	.258	.325	.335	660	664	36	0	0	1	32	697	97
6	5	1927-38	W.English	4,746	571	29	5,346	1,356	236	52	32	.286	.366	.378	743	709	57	0	0	6	(5)	709	72
7	10	1974-88	I.DeJesus	4,602	466	16	5,084	1,167	175	48	21	.254	.324	.326	651	649	194	88	3	10	14	676	34
8	8	1991-	R.Sanchez	3,277	167	30	3,474	894	140	18	12	.273	.314	.338	652	619	40	26	(4)	1	67	683	25
9	11	1964-79	D.Kessinger	7,651	684	22	8,357	1,931	254	80	14	.252	.316	.312	628	642	100	85	(8)	8	24	666	18
10	7	1957-67	A.Rodgers	2,521	290	18	2,829	628	112	23	45	.249	.331	.365	696	700	22	20	(6)	2	(9)	687	18
11	9	1991-	J.Hernandez	2,435	195	14	2,644	608	102	24	84	.250	.309	.415	724	677	27	24	(8)	0	10	679	(14)
12	12	1948-58	R.Smalley	2,644	257	18	2,919	601	103	33	61	.227	.300	.360	661	642	4	0	0	(2)	(2)	638	(35)
13	14	1941-47	L.Merullo	2,071	136	12	2,219	497	92	8	6	.240	.291	.301	591	610	38	0	0	3	(18)	595	(75)
14	13	1916-22	Z.Terry	2,327	179	19	2,525	605	90	24	2	.260	.318	.322	640	651	32	40	(24)	0	(15)	612	(78)

Chicago Cubs
Third basemen

V	R	Years	Name	AB	BB	HBP	TAB	H	2B	3B	HR	BA	OB	SA	PRO	Wtd PRO	SB	CS	SBF	SPF	FF	R TF	V HC
1	1	1960-74	R.Santo	8,143	1,108	38	9,289	2,254	365	67	342	.277	.366	.464	830	847	35	41	(5)	(8)	38	872	708
2	2	1932-47	S.Hack	7,278	1,092	21	8,391	2,193	363	81	57	.301	.394	.397	791	797	165	0	0	8	8	813	409
3	3	1907-19	H.Zimmerman	5,304	242	38	5,584	1,566	275	105	58	.295	.331	.419	750	802	175	33	(4)	(10)	(18)	770	184
4	4	1950-59	R.Jackson	3,203	281	7	3,491	835	115	44	103	.261	.322	.421	742	718	36	16	0	5	3	726	18
5	5	1973-80	S.Ontiveros	2,193	309	16	2,518	600	111	10	24	.274	.367	.366	734	732	5	6	(3)	(6)	(4)	719	3
6	8	1922-28	H.Freigau	1,974	138	6	2,118	537	99	25	15	.272	.322	.370	692	661	32	13	(0)	0	(10)	651	(55)
7	6	1912-21	C.Deal	2,930	135	16	3,081	752	104	34	11	.257	.293	.327	620	658	65	13	(5)	0	23	676	(66)
8	7	1898-07	D.Casey	4,341	270	55	4,666	1,122	137	52	9	.258	.310	.320	630	672	191	0	0	10	(16)	666	(122)
9	9	1895-04	B.McCormick	3,645	280	25	3,950	867	110	42	15	.238	.297	.303	600	536	130	0	0	4	(7)	533	(171)

Chicago Cubs
Outfielders

V	R	Years	Name	AB	BB	HBP	TAB	H	2B	3B	HR	BA	OB	SA	PRO	Wtd PRO	SB	CS	SBF	SPF	FF	R TF	V HC
1	1	1959-76	B.Williams	9,350	1,045	43	10,438	2,711	434	88	426	.290	.364	.492	856	875	90	49	(1)	7	9	891	661
2	4	1897-13	J.Sheckard	7,605	1,135	90	8,830	2,084	354	136	56	.274	.375	.378	753	808	465	0	0	10	28	846	396
3	3	1921-38	K.Cuyler	7,161	676	85	7,922	2,299	394	157	128	.321	.386	.474	860	822	328	27	3	10	18	853	377
4	2	1923-34	H.Wilson	4,760	674	20	5,454	1,461	266	67	244	.307	.395	.545	940	892	52	5	(0)	0	(13)	879	331
5	5	1966-84	R.Monday	6,136	924	24	7,084	1,619	248	64	241	.264	.362	.443	805	828	98	91	(11)	6	6	829	246
6	7	1934-49	A.Galan	5,937	979	25	6,941	1,706	336	74	100	.287	.390	.419	810	811	123	0	0	5	2	818	218
7	6	1936-53	B.Nicholson	5,546	800	52	6,398	1,484	272	60	235	.268	.365	.465	830	843	27	1	(0)	(10)	(13)	819	198
8	8	1989-	S.Sosa	5,893	519	38	6,450	1,606	244	36	386	.273	.335	.523	858	819	231	103	4	10	(16)	817	195
9	9	1921-34	R.Stephenson	4,508	494	41	5,043	1,515	321	54	63	.336	.407	.473	880	837	53	9	(1)	(7)	(15)	815	180
10	10	1904-18	W.Schulte	6,533	545	56	7,134	1,766	288	124	92	.270	.332	.395	726	788	233	17	(2)	8	11	805	172
11	13	1943-59	A.Pafko	6,292	561	76	6,929	1,796	264	62	213	.285	.351	.449	800	785	38	13	(2)	0	10	793	140
12	12	1941-59	H.Sauer	4,796	561	34	5,391	1,278	200	19	288	.266	.347	.496	844	822	11	4	(0)	(10)	(17)	794	99
13	14	1963-80	J.Cardenal	6,964	608	26	7,598	1,913	333	46	138	.275	.335	.395	730	750	329	139	6	9	13	779	77
14	16	1903-16	S.Hofman	4,072	421	15	4,508	1,095	162	60	19	.269	.340	.352	692	749	208	0	0	9	11	769	59
15	15	1932-44	F.Demaree	4,144	359	14	4,517	1,241	190	36	72	.299	.357	.415	772	771	33	0	0	9	(2)	778	47
16	11	1964-72	A.Phillips	1,875	251	27	2,153	463	86	21	59	.247	.344	.410	754	782	82	44	(3)	10	11	800	44
17	17	1959-67	G.Altman	3,091	268	20	3,379	832	132	34	101	.269	.331	.432	763	761	52	22	2	3	(1)	765	14
18	22	1914-25	M.Flack	5,252	474	32	5,758	1,461	212	72	35	.278	.342	.366	708	733	200	71	(11)	10	6	738	5
19	18	1899-08	J.Slagle	4,996	619	23	5,638	1,340	124	56	2	.268	.352	.317	668	722	273	0	0	9	28	759	5
20	19	1962-74	J.Hickman	3,974	491	16	4,481	1,002	163	25	159	.252	.337	.426	763	777	17	19	(4)	(2)	(15)	756	(6)
21	20	1937-47	D.Dallessandro	1,945	310	3	2,258	520	110	23	22	.267	.369	.381	750	765	16	1	0	0	(18)	747	(12)
22	21	1954-61	W.Moryn	2,506	251	19	2,776	667	116	16	101	.266	.338	.446	784	762	7	7	(2)	0	(16)	743	(20)
23	28	1989-96	D.Smith	1,807	150	13	1,970	497	88	20	46	.275	.335	.422	757	751	42	37	(16)	7	(31)	711	(46)
24	23	1992-	H.Rodriguez	3,003	272	11	3,286	783	176	9	160	.261	.324	.485	810	759	10	14	(5)	(8)	(21)	725	(53)
25	26	1905-18	W.Good	2,364	190	34	2,588	609	84	44	9	.258	.322	.342	664	726	104	17	(5)	7	(14)	713	(59)
26	27	1974-84	J.Martin	2,652	207	16	2,875	666	130	17	85	.251	.309	.409	718	718	38	23	(2)	6	(11)	711	(66)
27	24	1978-89	K.Moreland	4,581	405	13	4,999	1,279	214	14	121	.279	.339	.411	751	758	28	33	(7)	(10)	(22)	719	(66)
28	32	1980-89	B.Dernier	2,483	222	8	2,713	634	92	16	23	.255	.318	.333	652	660	218	63	32	6	4	702	(71)
29	31	1919-28	J.Statz	2,585	194	9	2,788	737	114	31	17	.285	.337	.373	710	682	77	46	(10)	10	21	703	(76)
30	37	1990-	D.May	2,200	156	8	2,364	596	103	10	52	.271	.321	.398	719	697	30	12	2	0	(13)	686	(87)
31	33	1952-64	L.Walls	2,558	245	16	2,819	670	88	31	66	.262	.330	.398	728	710	21	18	(5)	0	(9)	696	(89)
32	25	1893-07	J.McCarthy	4,195	268	24	4,487	1,203	171	66	7	.287	.333	.364	697	721	145	0	0	2	(4)	719	(92)
33	38	1948-59	H.Jeffcoat	1,963	114	5	2,082	487	95	18	26	.248	.291	.355	646	632	49	7	4	9	(7)	638	(93)
34	34	1947-57	F.Baumholtz	3,477	258	17	3,752	1,010	165	51	25	.290	.342	.389	731	711	30	20	(7)	0	(9)	695	(117)
35	30	1942-55	P.Lowrey	4,317	403	11	4,731	1,177	186	45	37	.273	.336	.362	699	697	48	3	0	7	(1)	704	(117)
36	36	1970-83	L.Biittner	3,151	236	11	3,398	861	144	20	29	.273	.326	.359	685	694	10	12	(4)	(2)	0	689	(125)
37	29	1918-32	C.Heathcote	4,443	367	22	4,832	1,222	206	55	42	.275	.333	.375	708	696	191	75	(8)	9	10	707	(125)
38	35	1969-83	J.Morales	4,528	366	14	4,908	1,173	199	36	95	.259	.316	.382	698	705	37	57	(15)	5	(5)	691	(160)
39	39	1934-46	T.Stainback	2,261	64	15	2,340	585	90	14	17	.259	.284	.333	617	620	27	12	(4)	0	(16)	600	(185)

Chicago Cubs
Starting Pitchers

V	R	Years	Name	G	GS	IP	W	L	SV	SO	BB	ERA	RA/9	R Wtd RA/9	V Runs /162
1	1	1903-16	T.Brown	481	332	3,172	239	130	49	1,375	673	2.06	2.96	3.40	432.3
2	2	1905-17	E.Reulbach	399	300	2,632	182	106	13	1,137	892	2.28	3.03	3.56	306.0
3	12	1965-83	F.Jenkins	664	594	4,501	284	226	7	3,192	997	3.34	3.71	4.10	232.8
4	6	1930-45	L.Warneke	445	343	2,782	192	121	13	1,140	739	3.18	3.77	3.86	226.3
5	9	1923-41	C.Root	632	341	3,197	201	160	40	1,459	889	3.59	4.13	4.01	202.8
6	8	1908-21	H.Vaughn	390	332	2,730	178	137	5	1,416	817	2.49	3.42	4.00	184.9
7	3	1903-09	J.Weimer	191	180	1,473	97	69	2	657	493	2.23	3.12	3.58	170.7
8	4	1905-13	O.Overall	218	182	1,535	108	71	12	935	551	2.23	3.05	3.69	156.4
9	16	1972-91	R.Reuschel	557	529	3,548	214	191	5	2,015	935	3.37	3.79	4.21	141.6
10	11	1911-20	C.Hendrix	360	257	2,371	144	116	17	1,092	697	2.65	3.45	4.06	140.9
11	14	1898-07	J.Taylor	310	286	2,617	152	139	5	657	582	2.66	4.11	4.14	131.6
12	15	1935-47	C.Passeau	444	331	2,720	162	150	21	1,104	728	3.32	3.99	4.18	119.6
13	10	1928-37	P.Malone	357	220	1,915	134	92	26	1,024	705	3.74	4.40	4.06	110.6
14	7	1902-09	C.Lundgren	179	149	1,322	91	55	6	535	476	2.42	3.37	3.89	106.3
15	18	1934-47	B.Lee	462	379	2,864	169	157	13	998	893	3.54	4.10	4.25	102.9
16	5	1903-11	J.Pfiester	149	128	1,067	71	44	0	503	293	2.02	3.06	3.79	95.6
17	21	1923-45	G.Bush	542	308	2,722	176	136	34	850	859	3.86	4.52	4.28	89.4
18	20	1948-60	B.Rush	417	321	2,411	127	152	8	1,244	789	3.65	4.21	4.27	80.4
19	13	1906-13	L.Richie	241	137	1,359	74	65	9	438	495	2.54	3.60	4.14	66.8
20	22	1941-56	J.Schmitz	366	235	1,813	93	114	21	746	757	3.55	4.18	4.29	57.2
21	23	1917-28	V.Aldridge	248	204	1,601	97	80	6	526	512	3.76	4.42	4.31	46.9
22	24	1965-75	B.Hands	374	260	1,951	111	110	14	1,128	492	3.35	3.85	4.34	46.4
23	19	1942-51	H.Wyse	251	159	1,258	79	70	8	362	373	3.52	4.16	4.26	43.2
24	17	1901-06	B.Wicker	138	117	1,037	64	52	1	472	293	2.73	3.82	4.22	42.5
25	25	1932-40	T.Carleton	293	202	1,607	100	76	9	808	561	3.91	4.31	4.36	36.7
26	28	1965-79	K.Holtzman	451	410	2,867	174	150	3	1,601	910	3.49	4.00	4.49	23.0
27	27	1911-19	L.Cheney	313	225	1,881	116	100	19	926	733	2.70	3.75	4.47	18.6
28	26	1896-05	B.Briggs	106	97	856	44	47	4	338	332	3.41	5.00	4.41	16.1
29	29	1920-37	S.Blake	304	196	1,620	87	102	8	621	740	4.13	4.87	4.50	9.9
30	30	1946-56	P.Minner	253	169	1,310	69	84	10	481	393	3.94	4.50	4.51	7.2
31	31	1993-	S.Trachsel	221	220	1,347	68	84	0	939	486	4.42	4.80	4.51	6.9
32	32	1892-03	J.Menefee	139	125	1,111	58	70	0	293	273	3.81	5.73	4.54	2.3
33	33	1910-15	B.Humphries	153	91	798	50	43	9	258	151	2.79	4.10	4.55	0.8
34	34	1941-52	B.Chipman	293	87	881	51	46	14	322	386	3.72	4.48	4.59	(3.0)
35	35	1921-35	T.Kaufmann	202	123	1,086	64	62	12	345	368	4.18	4.86	4.61	(6.4)
36	36	1941-48	P.Erickson	207	86	814	37	48	6	432	425	3.86	4.35	4.63	(7.0)
37	40	1920-30	P.Jones	251	113	1,026	53	57	6	381	494	4.34	5.15	4.76	(24.5)
38	38	1912-17	J.Lavender	224	142	1,207	63	76	12	547	447	3.09	4.08	4.74	(26.1)
39	37	1977-92	D.Lamp	639	163	1,831	96	96	35	857	549	3.93	4.50	4.69	(28.5)
40	41	1948-61	W.Hacker	306	157	1,283	62	89	17	557	320	4.21	4.77	4.81	(38.4)
41	47	1957-63	B.Anderson	246	93	841	36	46	13	502	319	4.26	4.82	4.98	(41.0)
42	44	1991-	F.Castillo	232	218	1,290	66	79	1	896	407	4.52	4.88	4.84	(42.3)
43	45	1984-97	M.Bielecki	347	178	1,231	70	73	5	783	496	4.18	4.63	4.93	(51.2)
44	39	1976-94	R.Sutcliffe	457	392	2,698	171	139	6	1,679	1,081	4.08	4.42	4.75	(59.6)
45	42	1958-71	D.Ellsworth	407	310	2,156	115	137	5	1,140	595	3.72	4.31	4.81	(62.2)
46	43	1957-70	D.Cardwell	410	301	2,123	102	138	7	1,211	671	3.92	4.43	4.83	(65.5)
47	46	1971-80	B.Bonham	300	214	1,487	75	83	11	985	636	4.01	4.50	4.95	(65.6)
48	48	1978-89	S.Trout	301	236	1,501	88	92	4	656	578	4.18	4.74	4.98	(73.7)
49	50	1957-64	G.Hobbie	284	170	1,263	62	81	6	682	495	4.20	4.83	5.08	(75.8)
50	52	1979-90	D.Noles	277	96	860	36	53	11	455	338	4.56	5.13	5.48	(91.1)

**Chicago Cubs
Starting Pitchers**

V	R	Years	Name	G	GS	IP	W	L	SV	SO	BB	ERA	RA/9	R Wtd RA/9	V Runs /162
51	51	1990-98	S.Boskie	217	132	870	49	63	1	494	292	5.14	5.58	5.45	(91.8)
52	49	1973-87	R.Burris	480	302	2,188	108	134	4	1,065	764	4.17	4.66	5.03	(118.0)

**Chicago Cubs
Relief Pitchers**

V	R	Years	Name	G	GS	IP	W	L	SV	SO	BB	ERA	RA/9	R Wtd RA/9	V Runs /162
1	2	1980-97	L.Smith	1,022	6	1,289	71	92	478	1,251	486	3.03	3.32	3.57	148.0
2	1	1976-88	B.Sutter	661	0	1,042	68	71	300	861	309	2.83	3.19	3.56	120.1
3	3	1986-99	P.Assenmacher	884	1	856	61	44	56	807	315	3.53	3.90	4.00	53.8
4	4	1989-	C.McElroy	605	2	664	36	27	17	557	316	3.74	4.24	4.13	32.7
5	5	1995-	T.Adams	342	0	415	25	35	39	343	207	3.92	4.51	4.31	11.6
6	6	1979-87	B.Caudill	445	24	667	35	52	106	620	288	3.68	4.01	4.41	11.3
7	7	1953-64	D.Elston	450	15	756	49	54	63	519	327	3.69	4.22	4.44	10.3
8	9	1956-72	M.Drabowsky	589	154	1,641	88	105	55	1,162	702	3.71	4.16	4.53	5.8
9	8	1955-72	T.Abernathy	681	34	1,148	63	69	148	765	592	3.46	4.03	4.52	4.2
10	10	1955-65	B.Schultz	227	0	347	20	20	35	264	116	3.63	4.39	4.67	(4.2)
11	13	1954-57	J.Davis	154	39	406	24	26	10	197	179	4.01	4.63	4.75	(9.2)
12	17	1996-	F.Heredia	291	2	243	19	11	5	220	136	4.71	5.30	5.01	(12.3)
13	12	1987-93	L.Lancaster	323	39	704	41	28	22	408	261	4.05	4.41	4.73	(13.4)
14	11	1951-62	T.Lown	504	49	1,032	55	61	73	574	590	4.12	4.58	4.69	(16.1)
15	15	1991-98	B.Scanlan	272	39	510	20	34	17	240	195	4.46	5.10	4.94	(24.1)
16	14	1962-71	C.Koonce	334	90	971	47	49	24	504	368	3.78	4.29	4.82	(28.6)
17	19	1996-	A.Telemaco	138	42	361	17	23	0	236	128	5.03	5.58	5.35	(31.8)
18	18	1984-91	C.Schiraldi	235	47	553	32	39	21	471	267	4.28	4.64	5.08	(32.3)
19	20	1956-63	T.Phillips	147	45	439	16	22	6	233	211	4.82	5.15	5.36	(41.2)
20	16	1950-67	J.Klippstein	711	161	1,968	101	118	66	1,158	978	4.24	4.84	4.98	(95.7)

CHICAGO WHITE SOX
(1901–2000)

For most of their existence, the White Sox played Dead Ball baseball—long after every other team added power hitters to their lineup. Examples of Chicago-style Dead Ball include the Go-Go Sox of the 1950s, and the hitless wonders that challenged for the pennant in 1967. Successful Sox teams in the actual Dead Ball Era of 1901–1919 featured Fielder Jones, Big Ed Walsh, Doc White, Eddie Cicotte, Shoeless Joe Jackson, Happy Felsch, and Eddie Collins. Luke Appling, Red Faber, and Ted Lyons played for the struggling organization in the years following the Black Sox scandal. Luis Aparicio, Nellie Fox, Minnie Minoso, Billy Pierce, and Hoyt Wilhelm led the Go-Go Sox to 17 consecutive winning seasons. In the past three decades, Dick Allen, Frank Thomas, Carlton Fisk, Harold Baines, and Robin Ventura gave the Sox their first consistent power hitters, while Jack McDowell and Roberto Hernandez provided quality pitching.

Profiled White Sox Players

Carlton Fisk

Fisk split his career between two Sox teams. His very best seasons were with the Red Sox in hitter friendly Fenway Park, before coming to the White Sox in 1981 at the age of 33. Fisk's durability kept him in the game as a starting catcher until he was 44 years old, and he ended up playing the greatest portion of his career with Chicago. In 24 seasons, Fisk hit .269 with 376 home runs and 128 stolen bases in 9,748 total at bats, while catching more games than anyone else in major league history. After ad-

justing for a 1 percent career hitter's deflation, Fisk hit .273 with 384 home runs for an 811 Wtd. Production. He finished third in the American League in volume of success with 680 Hits Contribution, thanks to his endurance. Fisk is sixth in league rate of success with an 820 Total Factor. His performance by team is as follows:

Team	TAB	HR	BA	Adj. BA	Wtd. PRO	TF	HC
Boston	4,308	162	.284	.292	862	887	434
Chicago	5,440	214	.257	.259	771	768	246

While Fisk's 1983 season is tops among White Sox catchers in a single season rate of success with an 879 Total Factor, it fails to rank in the top 25 for the league. Fisk's best season, his rookie season for the Red Sox in 1972, is perhaps the best season ever among league catchers. Carlton won his only Gold Glove that year, while hitting .293 with 22 home runs. Adjusted for an 8.5 percent hitter's deflation and lost time from the player's strike, Fisk hit .318 with 25 home runs, for the league's second best 1,027 Total Factor among catchers, and the league's second best volume of success with a 89.9 Hits Contribution.

Fisk finished with the top four, and six of the top ten, Red Sox seasons for catchers. He also generated the greatest moment in Red Sox history when he won game six of the 1975 World Series with his home run off the Fenway foul pole. Given these greater Red Sox experiences and the friction with White Sox ownership at the end of his career, it is no wonder Fisk chose to wear a Red Sox hat for his induction into the Hall of Fame in 2000.

Frank Thomas

Thomas is the only player in major league history to start his career with seven consecutive .300 average, 20 homer, 100 walk, 100 RBI, and 100 runs seasons. Thomas is a powerful offensive force, hitting .321 with 344 home runs in 6,708 total at bats to date. What makes Thomas an exceptionally dangerous hitter is his career .446 on base percentage which, combined with his .579 slugging average, gives him a 1,024 career Production. Adjusted for a career 4 percent hitter's inflation, Thomas has hit .307 with 352 home runs, for a 983 Wtd. Production, while his poor fielding yields a negative 31 Fielding Factor. Thomas is currently ranked fifth in league history in both rate and volume of success at first.

Eddie Collins

Collins played only 12 of his 25 seasons with the Sox, but he starred in every one of them. In his 25-year career with the Sox and the Athletics, Collins hit .333 with 47 home runs and 744 stolen bases in 11,525 total at bats. Adjusted for a 3 percent hitter's deflation, he hit .342 with 3,600 hits, an 877 Wtd. Production and 48 Fielding Factor points. Collins ranks second to Nap Lajoie among American League second basemen in both rate and volume of success. And his 1,455 Hits Contribution ranks him sixth in volume of success among all American Leaguers at any position. Collins' lifetime results for his two teams are as follows:

Team	TAB	HR	BA	Adj. BA	Wtd. PRO	TF	HC
Philadelphia	4,461	16	.337	.365	930	997	701
Chicago	7,064	31	.331	.328	845	895	753

Collins excelled in the Dead Ball Era, primarily with the Philadelphia Athletics. Six of his seven best seasons were with the Athletics. The best of these was in 1909, when Collins hit .347 with 198 hits and 67 stolen bases in his first full season in the majors. Adjusted for 15 percent deflation that year, he hit .401 with 233 hits, a 1,001 Wtd. Production, 1,081 Total Factor, and 126.7 Hits Contribution. Collins' adjusted batting averages during his six full years with the Athletics were .401, .368, .370, .361, .368, and .378. Despite this consistent level of excellence by Collins— and despite Collins being voted the winner of the Chalmers (MVP) Award in 1914, Connie Mack's financial difficulties caused him to trade Collins to the White Sox after the 1914 season.

Much like Ty Cobb, Collins' actual results were much better than they appear early in his career during the Dead Ball Era. Again like Cobb, a fall-off in performance later in Collins' career was covered up by the hitter's inflation of the 1920s. Even the best of these later years, when Collins hit a career high .372 in 1920, does not come close to the level of performance he maintained every year from 1909 to 1915.

Collins captured the top four, and 12 of the top 25 Sox seasons at second — in just 12 seasons with the Sox. He also captured six of the top seven, and seven of the top 25 seasons at second for the Athletics. In total, 19 of Eddie's seasons ranked in the top 25 for these two teams— out of 19 seasons that he qualified for consideration.

Robin Ventura

Ventura was one of the best hitters in college baseball. He disappointed fans in his rookie season in 1990 by hitting only .249 with 5 home runs. He went on to surprise nearly everyone by becoming one of the finest fielding third basemen of all time. Over time, Ventura improved his power; he frequently drew walks; and he finally cracked the .300 mark in 1999, while seriously contesting for the league's MVP Award. In his career-to-date, 33-year-old Ventura is hitting .273 with 227 home runs, and earned 50 Fielding Factor points. Adjusted for a 4 percent career hitter's inflation, Ventura has batted .262 with 227 home runs. His 824 Total Factor ranks eighth in league rate of success at third, while his 343 Hits Contribution ranks tenth in league volume of success.

Minnie Minoso

Minoso was one of the most popular players ever in a career that spanned 17 seasons, from 1949 to pinch-hitting appearances in 1976 and in 1980. Minoso hit well, led the league in both triples and steals three times, and won three Gold Glove Awards after the award was created in 1957.

Minoso played most of his career with Chicago. Unfortunately for him, he was with Cleveland when Chicago broke through the Yankees' blockade and won the 1959 pennant. In his career, Minoso batted .298 with 186 home runs and 205 steals. Adjusted for a 1 percent career hitter's inflation, Minoso batted .295 with 193 home runs. His 870 Total Factor ranks 26th among league outfielders in rate of success, while his 426 Hits Contribution ranks 24th in volume of success. This is not a very high ranking, but it is considerably higher than any other outfielder who spent most of his career with the White Sox.

Ed Walsh

Walsh has the lowest career earned run average (1.82) in major league history, while more than earning a 195–126 record for some of the worst hitting teams ever. Although he pitched in the Dead Ball period when few earned runs were scored by anyone, after removing these favorable biases, Walsh still ranks second in league career rate of success with a 3.13 Wtd. RA/9. He gave up 1.4 runs per 9 innings less than the historic average, and only Walter Johnson can boast better results for American League pitchers. Walsh saved 494 runs from scoring, giving him the fifth best league volume of success despite his only working 2,964 innings.

Walsh and Jack Chesbro are the only two pitchers to win 40 games in the twentieth century. Walsh went 40–15 in 464 innings in 1908 for a third place team, with a 1.42 ERA, 2.85 Wtd. RA/9, and 92.6 Runs saved from scoring.

Billy Pierce and Bert Blyleven

Pierce and Blyleven are the two highest ranked, eligible starting pitchers of the twentieth century not elected to the Hall of Fame. Blyleven has just become eligible, leaving Pierce as the more glaring exclusion from the Hall. Pierce was 211–169 in 3,307 innings, with a 3.27 ERA, a 3.68 Wtd. RA/9, and he saved 338 runs from scoring. Pierce ranks 13th in league volume of success and 25th in league rate of success.

Hoyt Wilhelm

Wilhelm, a knuckleball pitcher who retired at the age of 49, produced a 143–122 record and 227 saves over 1,070 games, all but 52 in relief. In his career, Wilhelm had a 2.52 ERA and a 3.30 Wtd. RA/9 (tenth in the league), and he twice led his league in ERA — once as a reliever and once in a rare starting role. As Wilhelm gave up 1.3 runs per 9 innings less than the historic average, and as this reliever worked an incredible 2,254 innings, he actually managed to save 324 runs from scoring compared to the historic average. The next closest relief pitchers in major league history were Goose Gossage and Rollie Fingers, each with 199 runs saved. The remarkable Wilhelm saved as many runs from scoring as Sox starting pitchers Pierce, Cicotte, or Faber. In fact, only 16 American League starters in history rank ahead of Wilhelm in this volume metric.

Chicago White Sox   **Hitters Volume of Success**

Pos	Years	Name	AB	BB	HBP	TAB	H	2B	3B	HR	BA	OB	SA	PRO	Wtd PRO	SB	CS	SBF	SPF	FF	R TF	V HC
C	1969-93	C.Fisk	8,756	849	143	9,748	2,356	421	47	376	.269	.343	.457	800	811	128	58	1	(4)	12	820	680
1B	1990-	F.Thomas	5,474	1,188	46	6,708	1,755	361	10	344	.321	.446	.579	1,024	983	29	21	(2)	(0)	(31)	949	601
2B	1906-30	E.Collins	9,949	1,499	77	11,525	3,315	438	187	47	.333	.424	.429	853	877	744	173	(2)	10	48	934	1,455
SS	1930-50	L.Appling	8,856	1,302	10	10,168	2,749	440	102	45	.310	.399	.398	798	769	179	108	(3)	(0)	6	771	542
3B	1989-	R.Ventura	5,599	817	20	6,436	1,530	280	13	227	.273	.368	.450	817	783	19	32	(6)	(3)	50	824	343
OF	1949-80	M.Minoso	6,579	814	192	7,585	1,963	336	83	186	.298	.391	.459	851	841	205	130	(7)	10	26	870	426
OF	1915-20	H.Felsch	2,812	207	24	3,043	825	135	64	38	.293	.347	.427	774	812	88	31	(11)	10	49	859	159
OF	1980-	H.Baines	9,824	1,054	14	10,892	2,855	487	49	384	.291	.360	.467	828	812	34	34	(3)	(4)	(21)	785	147
Starters	Averages		7,231	966	66	8,263	2,169	362	69	206	.300	.387	.455	842	834	178	73	(4)	2	17	850	544
C	1946-63	S.Lollar	5,351	671	115	6,137	1,415	244	14	155	.264	.359	.402	761	747	20	10	(0)	(10)	40	776	304
1B	1934-40	Z.Bonura	3,582	404	17	4,003	1,099	232	29	119	.307	.380	.487	867	807	19	7	0	(10)	(21)	776	13
2B	1947-65	N.Fox	9,232	719	142	10,093	2,663	355	112	35	.288	.349	.363	712	703	76	80	(8)	3	37	735	251
SS	1956-73	L.Aparicio	10,230	736	27	10,993	2,677	394	92	83	.262	.313	.343	655	666	506	136	20	10	50	747	451
3B	1923-35	W.Kamm	5,851	824	22	6,697	1,643	348	85	29	.281	.372	.384	756	712	126	84	(6)	10	32	748	107
OF	1896-15	F.Jones	6,747	817	76	7,640	1,920	206	75	21	.285	.368	.347	715	758	359	0	0	8	26	793	140
OF	1898-05	D.Green	3,484	315	46	3,845	1,021	124	65	29	.293	.359	.391	750	797	192	0	0	10	(3)	804	94
OF	1918-29	J.Mostil	3,507	415	70	3,992	1,054	209	82	23	.301	.386	.427	812	765	176	105	(8)	10	36	803	92
Reserves	Averages		5,998	613	64	6,675	1,687	264	69	62	.281	.354	.379	733	729	184	53	(0)	4	25	757	181
Totals	Weighted Ave.		6,820	848	65	7,734	2,008	330	69	158	.294	.378	.432	810	799	180	67	(3)	3	20	819	423

Pitchers Volume of Success

Pos	Years	Name	G	GS	IP	W	L	SV	SO	BB	ERA	RA/9	R Wtd RA/9	V Runs /162
SP	1904-17	E.Walsh	430	315	2,964	195	126	35	1,736	617	1.82	2.66	3.13	494
SP	1945-64	B.Pierce	585	432	3,307	211	169	32	1,999	1,178	3.27	3.61	3.68	338
SP	1905-20	E.Cicotte	502	361	3,223	208	149	25	1,374	827	2.38	3.21	3.69	336
SP	1914-33	R.Faber	669	483	4,087	254	213	28	1,471	1,213	3.15	3.99	3.93	302
SP	1923-46	T.Lyons	594	484	4,161	260	230	23	1,073	1,121	3.67	4.45	3.97	287
Starters	Averages		556	415	3,548	226	177	29	1,531	991	2.93	3.66	3.71	351
RP	1952-72	H.Wilhelm	1,070	52	2,254	143	122	227	1,610	778	2.52	3.09	3.30	324
RP	1972-94	R.Gossage	1,002	37	1,809	124	107	310	1,502	732	3.01	3.33	3.59	199
RP	1991-	R.Hernandez	580	3	655	42	42	266	631	267	3.03	3.41	3.13	108
RP	1965-75	B.Locker	576	0	879	57	39	95	577	257	2.75	3.37	3.94	61
Relievers	Averages		807	23	1,399	92	78	225	1,080	509	2.78	3.25	3.47	173
Totals	Averages		1,363	438	4,948	317	255	253	2,611	1,500	2.89	3.55	3.65	524

Chicago White Sox   **Hitters Rate of Success**

Pos	Years	Name	AB	BB	HBP	TAB	H	2B	3B	HR	BA	OB	SA	PRO	Wtd PRO	SB	CS	SBF	SPF	FF	R TF	V HC
C	1969-93	C.Fisk	8756	849	143	9,748	2,356	421	47	376	.269	.343	.457	800	811	128	58	1	(4)	12	820	680
1B	1990-	F.Thomas	5474	1,188	46	6,708	1,755	361	10	344	.321	.446	.579	1,024	983	29	21	(2)	(0)	(31)	949	601
2B	1906-30	E.Collins	9949	1,499	77	11,525	3,315	438	187	47	.333	.424	.429	853	877	744	173	(2)	10	48	934	1,455
SS	1930-50	L.Appling	8856	1,302	10	10,168	2,749	440	102	45	.310	.399	.398	798	769	179	108	(3)	(0)	6	771	542
3B	1989-	R.Ventura	5599	817	20	6,436	1,530	280	13	227	.273	.368	.450	817	783	19	32	(6)	(3)	50	824	343
OF	1949-80	M.Minoso	6579	814	192	7,585	1,963	336	83	186	.298	.391	.459	851	841	205	130	(7)	10	26	870	426
OF	1915-20	H.Felsch	2812	207	24	3,043	825	135	64	38	.293	.347	.427	774	812	88	31	(11)	10	49	859	159
OF	1997-	M.Ordonez	1816	137	12	1,965	546	99	8	80	.301	.354	.496	850	786	41	19	1	10	21	819	58
Starters	Averages		6,230	852	66	7,147	1,880	314	64	168	.302	.391	.454	845	837	179	72	(4)	4	23	860	533
C	1946-63	S.Lollar	5351	671	115	6,137	1,415	244	14	155	.264	.359	.402	761	747	20	10	(0)	(10)	40	776	304
1B	1934-40	Z.Bonura	3582	404	17	4,003	1,099	232	29	119	.307	.380	.487	867	807	19	7	0	(10)	(21)	776	13
2B	1947-65	N.Fox	9232	719	142	10,093	2,663	355	112	35	.288	.349	.363	712	703	76	80	(8)	3	37	735	251
SS	1956-73	L.Aparicio	10230	736	27	10,993	2,677	394	92	83	.262	.313	.343	655	666	506	136	20	10	50	747	451
3B	1968-77	B.Melton	3971	479	44	4,494	1,004	162	9	160	.253	.340	.419	759	783	23	24	(5)	(6)	(6)	765	79
OF	1898-05	D.Green	3484	315	46	3,845	1,021	124	65	29	.293	.359	.391	750	797	192	0	0	10	(3)	804	94
OF	1918-29	J.Mostil	3507	415	70	3,992	1,054	209	82	23	.301	.386	.427	812	765	176	105	(8)	10	36	803	92
OF	1896-15	F.Jones	6747	817	76	7,640	1,920	206	75	21	.285	.368	.347	715	758	359	0	0	8	26	793	140
Reserves	Averages		5,763	570	67	6,400	1,607	241	60	78	.279	.351	.382	732	736	171	45	(0)	2	20	757	178
Totals	Weighted Ave.		6,074	758	66	6,898	1,789	289	63	138	.294	.379	.431	810	803	177	63	(2)	3	22	826	415

Pitchers Rate of Success

Pos	Year	Name	G	GS	IP	W	L	SV	SO	BB	ERA	RA/9	R Wtd RA/9	V Runs /162
SP	1904-17	E.Walsh	430	315	2,964	195	126	35	1,736	617	1.82	2.66	3.13	494
SP	1945-64	B.Pierce	585	432	3,307	211	169	32	1,999	1,178	3.27	3.61	3.68	338
SP	1905-20	E.Cicotte	502	361	3,223	208	149	25	1,374	827	2.38	3.21	3.69	336
SP	1901-13	D.White	427	363	3,041	189	156	5	1,384	670	2.39	3.30	3.80	276
SP	1913-19	R.Russell	242	148	1,292	80	59	13	495	267	2.33	3.15	3.81	115
Starters	Averages		437	324	2,765	177	132	22	1,398	712	2.47	3.20	3.60	312
RP	1991-	R.Hernandez	580	3	655	42	42	266	631	267	3.03	3.41	3.13	108
RP	1998-	B.Howry	178	0	193	7	10	44	191	86	3.31	3.73	3.25	28
RP	1952-72	H.Wilhelm	1,070	52	2,254	143	122	227	1,610	778	2.52	3.09	3.30	324
RP	1997-	K.Foulke	220	8	332	13	11	47	325	86	3.71	3.85	3.52	38
Relievers	Averages		512	16	859	51	46	146	689	304	2.78	3.26	3.29	125
Totals	Averages		949	340	3,624	228	178	168	2,087	1,016	2.54	3.21	3.53	436

Chicago White Sox
Catchers

V	R	Years	Name	AB	BB	HBP	TAB	H	2B	3B	HR	BA	OB	SA	PRO	Wtd PRO	SB	CS	SBF	SPF	FF	R TF	V HC
1	1	1969-93	C.Fisk	8,756	849	143	9,748	2,356	421	47	376	.269	.343	.457	800	811	128	58	1	(4)	12	820	680
2	2	1946-63	S.Lollar	5,351	671	115	6,137	1,415	244	14	155	.264	.359	.402	761	747	20	10	(0)	(10)	40	776	304
3	4	1912-29	R.Schalk	5,306	638	59	6,003	1,345	199	49	11	.253	.340	.316	656	664	177	69	(3)	0	53	714	112
4	3	1893-08	E.McFarland	3,007	254	18	3,279	826	146	49	13	.275	.335	.369	704	726	65	0	0	(3)	15	738	105
5	5	1986-97	R.Karkovice	2,597	233	26	2,856	574	120	6	96	.221	.292	.383	674	659	24	14	(2)	(4)	48	701	33
6	6	1967-78	E.Herrmann	2,729	260	29	3,018	654	92	4	80	.240	.312	.364	677	698	6	8	(3)	(10)	2	687	15
7	7	1931-47	B.Sullivan	2,840	240	11	3,091	820	152	32	29	.289	.346	.395	742	698	30	24	(7)	(1)	(11)	678	(54)
8	8	1959-72	J.Martin	2,189	201	17	2,407	487	82	12	32	.222	.293	.315	608	626	9	8	(3)	(10)	19	632	(65)
9	9	1938-49	M.Tresh	3,169	402	11	3,582	788	75	14	2	.249	.335	.283	618	616	19	21	(6)	(4)	12	618	(108)
10	10	1899-16	B.Sullivan	3,647	170	32	3,849	777	119	33	21	.213	.254	.281	535	586	98	0	0	(1)	14	599	(158)

Chicago White Sox
First basemen

V	R	Years	Name	AB	BB	HBP	TAB	H	2B	3B	HR	BA	OB	SA	PRO	Wtd PRO	SB	CS	SBF	SPF	FF	R TF	V HC
1	1	1990-	F.Thomas	5,474	1,188	46	6,708	1,755	361	10	344	.321	.446	.579	1,024	983	29	21	(2)	(0)	(31)	949	601
2	2	1934-40	Z.Bonura	3,582	404	17	4,003	1,099	232	29	119	.307	.380	.487	867	807	19	7	0	(10)	(21)	776	13
3	3	1982-90	G.Walker	2,864	268	20	3,152	746	164	19	113	.260	.328	.449	777	772	19	12	(1)	(9)	(5)	756	(21)
4	5	1900-09	J.Donahue	2,862	215	17	3,094	731	90	31	4	.255	.311	.313	624	715	143	0	0	10	16	741	(34)
5	4	1942-57	E.Robinson	4,282	521	50	4,853	1,146	172	24	172	.268	.354	.440	793	775	10	12	(3)	(10)	(14)	748	(52)
6	7	1974-82	L.Johnson	2,631	211	7	2,849	755	122	12	64	.287	.342	.415	757	759	22	19	(6)	(10)	(17)	726	(61)
7	6	1921-31	E.Sheely	4,471	563	40	5,074	1,340	244	27	48	.300	.383	.399	782	733	33	31	(7)	(1)	10	735	(89)
8	8	1963-75	T.McCraw	3,956	332	40	4,328	972	150	42	75	.246	.311	.362	672	704	143	68	1	10	(2)	714	(111)
9	10	1924-34	B.Clancy	1,796	111	8	1,915	504	69	26	12	.281	.325	.368	693	655	19	16	(6)	0	0	648	(117)
10	9	1898-09	F.Isbell	4,219	190	41	4,450	1,056	158	62	13	.250	.289	.326	616	677	253	0	0	9	(1)	685	(133)

Chicago White Sox
Second basemen

V	R	Years	Name	AB	BB	HBP	TAB	H	2B	3B	HR	BA	OB	SA	PRO	Wtd PRO	SB	CS	SBF	SPF	FF	R TF	V HC
1	1	1906-30	E.Collins	9,949	1,499	77	11,525	3,315	438	187	47	.333	.424	.429	853	877	744	173	(2)	10	48	934	1,455
2	2	1947-65	N.Fox	9,232	719	142	10,093	2,663	355	112	35	.288	.349	.363	712	703	76	80	(8)	3	37	735	251
3	4	1995-	R.Durham	3,523	371	39	3,933	980	187	41	77	.278	.353	.420	774	718	176	58	14	10	(36)	706	40
4	5	1990-	C.Grebeck	1,947	226	19	2,192	516	115	8	19	.265	.347	.362	709	683	4	11	(8)	0	22	697	16
5	6	1943-54	C.Michaels	4,367	566	24	4,957	1,142	147	46	53	.262	.349	.353	702	692	64	32	0	2	(8)	686	12
6	3	1972-87	J.Orta	5,829	500	29	6,358	1,619	267	63	130	.278	.338	.412	750	762	79	60	(6)	6	(41)	722	2
7	9	1928-38	B.Cissell	3,707	212	10	3,929	990	173	43	29	.267	.308	.360	669	630	113	63	(3)	9	(10)	627	(98)
8	7	1910-18	R.Zeider	3,210	334	22	3,566	769	89	22	5	.240	.315	.286	601	647	223	0	0	7	(14)	640	(120)
9	8	1940-53	D.Kolloway	3,993	189	10	4,192	1,081	180	30	29	.271	.305	.353	658	653	76	54	(7)	9	(15)	639	(135)
10	10	1927-40	J.Hayes	4,040	309	9	4,358	1,069	196	33	20	.265	.318	.344	663	617	34	31	(6)	0	13	625	(139)

Chicago White Sox
Shortstops

V	R	Years	Name	AB	BB	HBP	TAB	H	2B	3B	HR	BA	OB	SA	PRO	Wtd PRO	SB	CS	SBF	SPF	FF	R TF	V HC
1	1	1930-50	L.Appling	8,856	1,302	10	10,168	2,749	440	102	45	.310	.399	.398	798	769	179	108	(3)	(0)	6	771	542
2	2	1956-73	L.Aparicio	10,230	736	27	10,993	2,677	394	92	83	.262	.313	.343	655	666	506	136	20	10	50	747	451
3	4	1958-72	R.Hansen	4,311	551	19	4,881	1,007	156	17	106	.234	.323	.351	675	689	9	14	(4)	(7)	23	700	84
4	3	1912-20	B.Weaver	4,809	183	58	5,050	1,308	198	69	21	.272	.307	.355	662	700	172	70	(11)	10	10	709	58
5	5	1981-95	S.Fletcher	5,258	514	57	5,829	1,376	243	38	34	.262	.334	.342	676	670	99	58	(2)	5	7	680	15
6	6	1912-25	E.Johnson	2,619	181	15	2,815	697	91	36	19	.266	.317	.350	667	659	114	41	(10)	10	7	666	2
7	7	1950-59	C.Carrasquel	4,644	491	38	5,173	1,199	172	25	55	.258	.334	.342	676	662	31	28	(5)	7	(3)	661	(2)
8	9	1910-27	L.Blackburne	1,807	162	14	1,983	387	39	23	4	.214	.284	.268	552	608	54	26	(6)	5	17	624	(68)
9	8	1985-	O.Guillen	6,686	239	7	6,932	1,764	275	69	28	.264	.290	.338	628	612	169	108	(7)	6	16	628	(117)
10	10	1932-48	S.Webb	2,274	132	3	2,409	498	73	15	3	.219	.263	.268	531	532	33	26	(7)	10	4	538	(162)

Chicago White Sox
Third basemen

V	R	Years	Name	AB	BB	HBP	TAB	H	2B	3B	HR	BA	OB	SA	PRO	Wtd PRO	SB	CS	SBF	SPF	FF	R TF	V HC
1	1	1989-	R.Ventura	5,599	817	20	6,436	1,530	280	13	227	.273	.368	.450	817	783	19	32	(6)	(3)	50	824	343
2	4	1923-35	W.Kamm	5,851	824	22	6,697	1,643	348	85	29	.281	.372	.384	756	712	126	84	(6)	10	32	748	107
3	2	1968-77	B.Melton	3,971	479	44	4,494	1,004	162	9	160	.253	.340	.419	759	783	23	24	(5)	(6)	(6)	765	79
4	3	1962-70	P.Ward	3,060	371	40	3,471	776	136	17	98	.254	.342	.405	747	777	20	17	(4)	(2)	(9)	762	50
5	5	1907-15	H.Lord	3,691	226	38	3,955	1,024	107	70	14	.277	.326	.356	681	743	206	2	(0)	10	(41)	711	(10)
6	6	1976-86	G.Pryor	1,883	104	10	1,997	471	85	9	14	.250	.293	.327	620	617	11	12	(6)	5	45	661	(27)
7	8	1943-55	F.Baker	2,280	382	6	2,668	573	76	13	1	.251	.360	.297	658	650	23	25	(10)	0	12	652	(78)
8	7	1903-12	L.Tannehill	3,778	229	23	4,030	833	135	27	3	.220	.269	.273	542	609	63	0	0	(1)	50	657	(84)

Chicago White Sox
Outfielders

V	R	Years	Name	AB	BB	HBP	TAB	H	2B	3B	HR	BA	OB	SA	PRO	Wtd PRO	SB	CS	SBF	SPF	FF	R TF	V HC
1	1	1949-80	M.Minoso	6,579	814	192	7,585	1,963	336	83	186	.298	.391	.459	851	841	205	130	(7)	10	26	870	426
2	2	1915-20	H.Felsch	2,812	207	24	3,043	825	135	64	38	.293	.347	.427	774	812	88	31	(11)	10	49	859	159
3	8	1980-	H.Baines	9,824	1,054	14	10,892	2,855	487	49	384	.291	.360	.467	828	812	34	34	(3)	(4)	(21)	785	147
4	6	1896-15	F.Jones	6,747	817	76	7,640	1,920	206	75	21	.285	.368	.347	715	758	359	0	0	8	26	793	140
5	4	1898-05	D.Green	3,484	315	46	3,845	1,021	124	65	29	.293	.359	.391	750	797	192	0	0	10	(3)	804	94
6	5	1918-29	J.Mostil	3,507	415	70	3,992	1,054	209	82	23	.301	.386	.427	812	765	176	105	(8)	10	36	803	92
7	12	1953-64	A.Smith	5,357	674	63	6,094	1,458	258	46	164	.272	.360	.429	790	779	67	43	(3)	8	(10)	774	85
8	28	1894-13	N.Callahan	3,295	159	20	3,474	901	135	46	11	.273	.311	.352	663	718	186	0	0	10	(6)	721	83
9	7	1902-11	P.Dougherty	4,558	378	54	4,990	1,294	138	78	17	.284	.346	.360	705	792	261	0	0	10	(14)	787	76
10	3	1997-	M.Ordonez	1,816	137	12	1,965	546	99	8	80	.301	.354	.496	850	786	41	19	1	10	21	819	58
11	10	1957-67	J.Landis	4,288	588	59	4,935	1,061	169	50	93	.247	.346	.375	721	721	139	51	7	9	42	779	50
12	9	1984-93	I.Calderon	3,312	306	13	3,631	901	200	25	104	.272	.336	.442	778	780	97	49	(0)	0	2	782	43
13	11	1960-68	F.Robinson	3,284	408	27	3,719	929	140	36	67	.283	.367	.409	775	783	42	21	(0)	3	(11)	775	30
14	15	1927-39	C.Reynolds	4,495	260	40	4,795	1,357	247	107	80	.302	.346	.458	803	760	112	40	4	10	(9)	765	16
15	14	1938-49	T.Wright	3,583	346	26	3,955	1,115	175	55	38	.311	.376	.423	799	774	32	33	(8)	6	(7)	765	15
16	16	1968-77	C.May	4,120	512	45	4,677	1,127	172	23	90	.274	.360	.392	752	780	85	53	(4)	3	(15)	763	9
17	17	1987-	L.Johnson	5,379	352	7	5,738	1,565	175	117	34	.291	.335	.386	721	700	327	105	20	10	31	761	9
18	13	1995-	M.Cameron	1,909	254	26	2,189	473	98	21	63	.248	.344	.420	764	707	112	33	20	10	28	765	9
19	18	1920-31	B.Falk	4,652	412	12	5,076	1,463	300	59	69	.314	.372	.449	821	769	47	49	(9)	4	(3)	760	8
20	19	1911-21	P.Bodie	3,670	312	18	4,000	1,011	169	72	43	.275	.335	.396	731	762	83	26	(8)	10	(4)	760	6
21	20	1967-81	P.Kelly	4,338	588	29	4,955	1,147	189	35	76	.264	.356	.377	733	753	250	118	2	10	(13)	751	(15)
22	21	1985-94	D.Pasqua	2,620	335	15	2,970	638	129	15	117	.244	.333	.438	771	771	7	10	(4)	(6)	(17)	745	(20)
23	23	1982-91	R.Kittle	2,708	236	38	2,982	648	100	3	176	.239	.309	.473	783	783	16	16	(5)	(5)	(31)	742	(25)
24	27	1973-89	J.Hairston	1,699	282	8	1,989	438	91	6	30	.258	.366	.371	737	744	4	5	(3)	0	(17)	724	(34)
25	25	1978-86	R.Law	2,421	184	13	2,618	656	101	37	18	.271	.326	.366	691	691	228	65	35	10	(8)	728	(37)
26	22	1931-45	M.Kreevich	4,676	446	7	5,129	1,321	221	75	45	.283	.346	.391	737	707	115	53	2	10	25	743	(37)
27	24	1952-61	J.Rivera	3,552	365	23	3,940	911	155	56	83	.256	.330	.402	731	723	160	70	5	10	(0)	737	(39)
28	29	1929-34	E.Swanson	1,892	212	11	2,115	573	87	28	7	.303	.376	.390	766	709	69	15	1	10	(6)	714	(46)
29	39	1921-30	B.Barrett	2,395	209	8	2,612	690	151	30	23	.288	.347	.405	752	706	80	50	(7)	10	(14)	696	(49)
30	30	1905-10	E.Hahn	2,045	258	44	2,347	484	42	20	1	.237	.335	.278	613	708	59	0	0	10	(7)	711	(54)
31	33	1925-30	A.Metzler	1,968	260	18	2,246	561	85	41	9	.285	.374	.384	757	711	46	27	(3)	6	(4)	709	(54)
32	32	1964-75	W.Williams	2,373	126	18	2,517	640	106	11	33	.270	.311	.365	677	702	34	19	(1)	10	(1)	709	(58)
33	34	1942-51	T.Tucker	2,231	291	4	2,526	570	79	24	9	.255	.342	.325	667	680	77	47	(6)	10	23	707	(63)
34	26	1895-05	D.Holmes	3,601	236	64	3,901	1,014	142	58	17	.282	.337	.367	704	722	236	0	0	10	(6)	726	(66)
35	35	1984-94	D.Boston	2,629	237	8	2,874	655	131	22	83	.249	.313	.410	724	719	98	50	(1)	8	(21)	706	(70)
36	41	1987-95	D.Gallagher	2,081	187	7	2,275	564	100	10	17	.271	.333	.353	686	685	20	24	(12)	2	(3)	671	(97)
37	31	1962-75	K.Berry	4,136	298	30	4,464	1,053	150	23	58	.255	.309	.344	653	686	45	46	(10)	5	30	711	(100)
38	42	1974-85	A.Bannister	3,007	292	13	3,312	811	143	28	19	.270	.337	.355	692	691	108	37	11	10	(49)	664	(101)
39	43	1985-93	S.Lyons	2,162	156	5	2,323	545	100	17	19	.252	.304	.340	644	647	42	32	(9)	10	(11)	637	(103)
40	37	1934-43	R.Radcliff	4,074	310	14	4,398	1,267	205	50	42	.311	.362	.417	779	727	40	30	(4)	0	(21)	701	(123)
41	38	1913-25	N.Leibold	4,167	571	16	4,754	1,109	145	49	3	.266	.357	.327	683	696	134	60	(15)	6	9	696	(145)
42	36	1941-62	D.Philley	6,296	594	17	6,907	1,700	276	72	84	.270	.335	.377	711	696	101	63	(3)	7	5	705	(182)
43	40	1910-25	S.Collins	6,390	331	57	6,778	1,687	310	133	22	.264	.306	.364	671	692	225	83	(7)	5	(4)	686	(252)
44	44	1939-57	B.Kennedy	4,624	364	6	4,994	1,176	196	41	63	.254	.310	.355	665	649	45	50	(10)	7	(14)	632	(268)

Chicago White Sox
Starting Pitchers

V	R	Years	Name	G	GS	IP	W	L	SV	SO	BB	ERA	RA/9	R Wtd RA/9	V Runs /162
1	1	1904-17	E.Walsh	430	315	2,964	195	126	35	1,736	617	1.82	2.66	3.13	493.5
2	2	1945-64	B.Pierce	585	432	3,307	211	169	32	1,999	1,178	3.27	3.61	3.68	338.4
3	3	1905-20	E.Cicotte	502	361	3,223	208	149	25	1,374	827	2.38	3.21	3.69	336.0
4	12	1914-33	R.Faber	669	483	4,087	254	213	28	1,471	1,213	3.15	3.99	3.93	301.9
5	14	1923-46	T.Lyons	594	484	4,161	260	230	23	1,073	1,121	3.67	4.45	3.97	287.3
6	4	1901-13	D.White	427	363	3,041	189	156	5	1,384	670	2.39	3.30	3.80	275.6
7	20	1963-89	T.John	760	700	4,710	288	231	4	2,245	1,259	3.34	3.85	4.14	220.0
8	15	1933-48	T.Lee	374	272	2,331	117	124	10	937	838	3.56	4.27	4.03	143.8
9	11	1909-17	J.Scott	317	226	1,892	107	114	9	945	609	2.30	3.30	3.91	142.2
10	9	1990-	A.Fernandez	263	261	1,760	107	87	0	1,252	552	3.74	4.11	3.88	139.6
11	13	1987-99	J.McDowell	277	275	1,889	127	87	0	1,311	606	3.86	4.16	3.95	134.7
12	8	1901-07	R.Patterson	184	152	1,365	81	72	2	442	273	2.75	3.74	3.83	123.0
13	5	1913-19	R.Russell	242	148	1,292	80	59	13	495	267	2.33	3.15	3.81	115.4
14	17	1961-72	J.Horlen	361	290	2,002	116	117	4	1,065	554	3.11	3.52	4.07	109.6
15	10	1911-19	J.Benz	251	163	1,360	76	75	3	539	334	2.43	3.37	3.90	106.4
16	6	1937-47	J.Rigney	197	132	1,186	63	64	1	605	450	3.59	4.17	3.81	103.5
17	24	1961-78	W.Wood	651	297	2,684	164	156	57	1,411	724	3.24	3.79	4.25	91.5
18	16	1989-	W.Alvarez	250	224	1,433	86	77	1	1,074	708	3.96	4.47	4.04	88.3
19	25	1904-15	F.Smith	354	255	2,273	139	111	6	1,051	676	2.59	3.54	4.27	76.2
20	23	1950-65	D.Donovan	345	273	2,017	122	99	5	880	495	3.67	4.05	4.25	72.1
21	7	1950-57	S.Consuegra	248	71	809	51	32	26	193	246	3.37	3.84	3.83	69.0
22	18	1952-60	J.Harshman	217	155	1,169	69	65	7	741	539	3.50	3.91	4.09	64.2
23	27	1959-72	G.Peters	359	286	2,081	124	103	5	1,420	706	3.25	3.66	4.28	63.1
24	30	1926-37	T.Thomas	398	267	2,176	117	128	12	736	712	4.11	4.90	4.33	56.5
25	19	1978-85	B.Burns	193	161	1,094	70	60	3	734	362	3.66	4.10	4.13	56.2
26	26	1898-24	N.Altrock	218	161	1,514	83	75	7	425	272	2.67	3.59	4.27	50.5
27	22	1913-20	L.Williams	189	152	1,186	82	48	5	515	347	3.13	3.77	4.22	48.8
28	31	1957-74	J.Pizarro	488	245	2,034	131	105	28	1,522	888	3.43	3.93	4.35	48.2
29	29	1957-67	B.Shaw	430	223	1,778	108	98	32	880	511	3.52	4.00	4.32	48.2
30	21	1919-25	D.Kerr	140	83	811	53	34	6	235	250	3.84	4.42	4.18	37.2
31	32	1901-09	F.Owen	194	155	1,368	82	67	2	443	298	2.55	3.66	4.37	29.9
32	34	1894-03	N.Callahan	195	177	1,603	99	73	2	445	437	3.39	5.15	4.41	29.2
33	28	1935-42	J.Whitehead	172	119	944	49	54	4	254	372	4.60	5.12	4.31	27.0
34	35	1936-47	E.Smith	282	197	1,596	73	113	12	694	739	3.82	4.60	4.46	18.7
35	33	1995-	M.Sirotka	125	111	710	45	42	0	435	207	4.31	5.04	4.41	11.8
36	37	1945-58	J.Wilson	257	217	1,539	86	89	2	692	608	4.01	4.34	4.50	10.6
37	36	1958-68	J.Buzhardt	326	200	1,491	71	96	7	678	457	3.66	4.08	4.50	10.1
38	38	1946-58	B.Wight	347	198	1,563	77	99	8	574	714	3.95	4.56	4.51	8.3
39	39	1922-30	T.Blankenship	241	156	1,331	77	79	4	378	489	4.29	4.90	4.51	6.7
40	41	1936-52	R.Gumpert	261	113	1,053	51	59	7	352	346	4.17	4.69	4.53	3.2
41	40	1949-57	S.Rogovin	150	121	884	48	48	2	388	308	4.06	4.42	4.53	2.9
42	42	1977-92	F.Bannister	431	363	2,388	134	143	0	1,723	846	4.06	4.48	4.56	(0.6)
43	43	1979-86	L.Hoyt	244	172	1,311	98	68	10	681	279	3.99	4.37	4.57	(2.4)
44	44	1987-95	M.Perez	243	201	1,355	78	85	1	1,092	551	4.17	4.65	4.62	(9.2)
45	45	1923-33	S.Thurston	288	178	1,543	89	86	13	306	369	4.24	4.92	4.63	(12.8)
46	47	1955-65	F.Baumann	244	78	797	45	38	13	384	300	4.11	4.58	4.71	(14.3)
47	46	1938-46	J.Humphries	211	111	1,002	52	63	12	317	373	3.78	4.48	4.71	(17.4)
48	50	1921-34	S.Connally	303	67	994	49	60	31	345	449	4.30	5.24	4.74	(20.7)
49	52	1989-94	G.Hibbard	165	158	990	57	50	1	408	288	4.05	4.65	4.76	(23.5)
50	53	1995-	J.Baldwin	167	149	920	62	48	0	624	349	5.09	5.44	4.79	(24.1)

Chicago White Sox
Starting Pitchers

V	R	Years	Name	G	GS	IP	W	L	SV	SO	BB	ERA	RA/9	R Wtd RA/9	V Runs /162
51	54	1919-28	C.Robertson	166	141	1,005	49	80	1	310	377	4.44	5.11	4.80	(29.0)
52	48	1939-52	J.Haynes	379	147	1,581	76	82	21	475	620	4.01	4.69	4.72	(29.3)
53	56	1969-77	B.Johnson	185	97	809	43	51	17	520	348	3.94	4.39	4.92	(32.6)
54	49	1979-90	R.Dotson	305	295	1,857	111	113	0	973	740	4.23	4.67	4.72	(35.8)
55	51	1971-81	S.Stone	320	269	1,788	107	93	1	1,065	716	3.97	4.43	4.74	(37.9)
56	58	1969-75	T.Bradley	183	151	1,018	55	61	2	691	311	3.72	4.28	4.94	(43.6)
57	60	1993-	J.Bere	161	153	831	59	44	0	679	519	5.28	5.73	5.09	(53.2)
58	59	1940-49	O.Grove	207	152	1,177	63	73	4	374	444	3.78	4.55	5.02	(63.7)
59	61	1975-82	K.Kravec	160	128	859	43	56	1	557	404	4.47	4.99	5.24	(68.7)
60	55	1934-45	V.Kennedy	344	263	2,026	104	132	5	691	1,049	4.67	5.34	4.86	(72.0)
61	62	1946-56	L.Kretlow	199	104	785	27	47	1	450	522	4.87	5.50	5.51	(87.6)
62	57	1933-48	B.Dietrich	366	253	2,004	108	128	11	660	890	4.48	5.15	4.93	(88.1)

Chicago White Sox
Relief Pitchers

V	R	Years	Name	G	GS	IP	W	L	SV	SO	BB	ERA	RA/9	R Wtd RA/9	V Runs /162
1	3	1952-72	H.Wilhelm	1,070	52	2,254	143	122	227	1,610	778	2.52	3.09	3.30	323.8
2	5	1972-94	R.Gossage	1,002	37	1,809	124	107	310	1,502	732	3.01	3.33	3.59	198.8
3	1	1991-	R.Hernandez	580	3	655	42	42	266	631	267	3.03	3.41	3.13	108.1
4	9	1965-75	B.Locker	576	0	879	57	39	95	577	257	2.75	3.37	3.94	60.8
5	12	1971-86	T.Forster	614	39	1,106	54	65	127	791	457	3.23	3.70	4.12	54.8
6	8	1986-94	B.Thigpen	448	0	569	31	36	201	376	238	3.43	3.75	3.79	48.7
7	7	1990-	S.Radinsky	555	0	480	42	25	52	355	206	3.34	3.79	3.73	44.7
8	4	1997-	K.Foulke	220	8	332	13	11	47	325	86	3.71	3.85	3.52	38.3
9	14	1959-73	E.Fisher	690	63	1,539	85	70	81	812	438	3.41	3.85	4.36	33.1
10	6	1995-	B.Simas	308	0	338	18	19	23	265	149	3.83	4.23	3.68	33.0
11	11	1976-83	M.Proly	267	18	546	22	29	22	185	195	3.23	3.78	4.04	32.9
12	2	1998-	B.Howry	178	0	193	7	10	44	191	86	3.31	3.73	3.25	28.1
13	13	1988-98	D.Pall	328	0	505	24	23	10	278	139	3.63	4.11	4.13	24.5
14	15	1947-56	H.Dorish	323	40	834	45	43	44	332	301	3.83	4.38	4.39	15.9
15	10	1995-	M.Karchner	223	0	241	21	13	27	166	132	4.21	4.59	4.01	14.9
16	16	1978-87	B.James	279	2	407	24	26	73	340	157	3.80	4.29	4.41	6.7
17	17	1988-94	K.Patterson	224	4	318	14	8	5	183	166	3.88	4.31	4.50	2.0
18	18	1986-93	B.Jones	348	0	433	33	33	23	250	194	3.66	4.14	4.54	0.8
19	19	1981-91	K.Hickey	231	0	233	9	14	17	118	101	3.91	4.41	4.63	(2.1)
20	20	1948-54	H.Judson	207	48	615	17	37	14	204	319	4.29	4.93	4.74	(12.9)
21	21	1928-48	E.Caldwell	200	49	588	33	43	25	202	259	4.69	5.31	4.93	(25.4)
22	23	1945-53	E.Harrist	132	24	383	12	28	10	162	193	4.34	5.09	5.27	(32.1)
23	22	1987-93	S.Hillegas	181	62	515	24	38	10	332	238	4.61	4.96	5.18	(35.6)
24	24	1971-83	E.Farmer	370	21	624	30	43	75	395	345	4.30	4.95	5.44	(64.5)

CINCINNATI REDS (1900–2000)

The Big Red Machine survived only one decade, finishing first six times in the 1970s, yet this team goes down in history as perhaps the most famous and respected National League dynasty. The starting lineup included Hall of Famers Johnny Bench, Tony Perez, and Joe Morgan, as well as all-time hits leader Pete Rose, Dave Concepcion, George Foster, and Ken Griffey, Sr. Pitchers Gary Nolan, Don Gullett, Clay Carroll, and even Tom Seaver made this a complete team.

Reds players also starred in the other nine decades. Cy Seymour, Heinie Groh, Edd Roush, Dolf Luque, and Eppa Rixey were early stars. Ernie Lombardi, Bucky Walters, and Frank McCormick sparked the championship teams of 1939–1940. Ted Kluszewski, Frank Robinson, and Vada Pinson powered the team in the 1950s and early 1960s. Finally, Barry Larkin, Eric Davis, and John Franco led the post–Big Red Machine teams.

Profiled Reds Players

Johnny Bench

Bench won ten straight Gold Glove Awards from 1968 to 1977 with his rocket arm and on-field leadership. Bench was also one of the best hitting catchers ever, blasting 389 home runs in his 17-year career, while hitting .267. Adjusted for a 2 percent career hitter's deflation, Bench hit .273 with 399 home runs. His 896 Total Factor ranks first in league rate of success among catchers, while his 878 Hits Contribution is the best volume of success ever for a major league catcher.

After his knees gave out, Bench switched positions and covered third and first base, while often playing brutal defense. This three year extension of his career padded Bench's total numbers, but actually hurt his rate and volume of success:

Years	TAB	HR	BA	Adj. BA	Wtd. PRO	TF	HC
1967–80 (C)	7,603	356	.267	.272	844	921	886
1981–83 (1B/3B)	965	33	.267	.276	777	715	(8)

Bench should have forgone the embarrassment of playing out of position, as he could have retired in 1980 with both the best rate and volume of success ever for a catcher.

Joe Morgan

Morgan appeared in parts of nine seasons for the Astros before being traded to Cincinnati. Morgan was not a superstar during those seasons in Houston, as his fielding was erratic at best, and he failed to hit for power or a high average. All that changed once he arrived in Cincinnati in 1972. Morgan improved his fielding, and ended up winning five straight Gold Gloves for the Reds. He became a deadly hitter, and a very dangerous person on the basepaths, where he spent much of his time due to a very high on-base percentage. After his success in Cincinnati, Morgan reverted back to being inconsistent, and he spent his last five seasons playing for four different teams.

Years/Team	TAB	HR	BA	Adj. BA	Wtd. PRO	SB	TF	HC
1963–71/Hou	3,864	61	.263	.268	788	195	816	240
1972–79/Cin	4,911	152	.288	.291	899	406	978	693
1980–84	2,407	55	.251	.254	778	88	799	141

In his career, Morgan hit .271 with 268 home runs, and he drew 1,865 walks for a .395 on-base percentage, while stealing 689 bases in 851 attempts. Adjusted for a 1 percent career hitter's deflation, Morgan hit .275 with 276 home runs, for an 833 Wtd. Production. His 882 Total Factor ranks third in league rate of success for second basemen, trailing only Rogers Hornsby and Jackie Robinson. Morgan's 1,074 Hits Contribution ranks second to Hornsby in league volume of success.

Barry Larkin

When Larkin joined the Reds as a 22-year-old rookie in 1986, two of his teammates were Pete Rose and Tony Perez, both in their mid–40s. The last players of the Big Red Machine era were turning the game over to a new generation of Reds stars. The best of these new players was Larkin, who evolved into the second best shortstop of all-time, trailing only Honus Wagner. Larkin brought the same tools to the position that Wagner used so successfully — speed, hitting, power, and defense. Larkin also hit .338 in postseason play, including a .353 average in the 1990 World Series sweep of Oakland.

In his career-to-date, the 36-year-old Larkin has hit .300 with 179 home runs, while stealing 359 bases in 430 attempts, for an 83 percent success rate. Adjusted for a 3 percent career hitter's inflation, Larkin has hit .292 with 180 home runs. His 879 Total Factor ranks second in league rate of success for shortstops, while his 810 Hits Contribution has him currently ranked third in league volume of success.

Heinie Groh

Groh and Frank Baker were the best third basemen of their generation. Groh broke in with the Giants in 1912, and was traded to the Reds the next season. He led the Reds to their first pennant near the end of the Dead Ball Era with his glove and steady hitting, and he later played third for three Giants pennant-winning teams. Groh's best years clearly ended when he left the Reds, and he was a less than average player in his last six seasons with the Giants, as his batting average nose-dived even as hitter's inflation picked up steam.

Years	TAB	HR	BA	Adj. BA	Wtd. PRO	TF	HC
1912–21	5,071	17	.298	.321	833	866	408
1922–27	1,782	9	.276	.264	684	688	(25)

In his career, Groh batted .292 with 26 home runs, while stealing 180 bases. Adjusted for a 5 percent hitter's deflation, he hit .306 with 29 home runs. His 820 Total Factor ranks ninth in league rate of success for third basemen, while his 384 Hits Contribution ranks ninth in league volume of success.

Frank Robinson

Rarely has a player of Robinson's stature been traded in his prime. The Reds immediately regretted this move, as Robinson won the Triple Crown and helped the Orioles win the World Series in his first season with Baltimore. Robinson was the first player to win the MVP in each league, and he was also the first black manager in baseball. Robinson played 21 seasons for five ball clubs, and he accumulated 586 home runs, the fourth highest total in history. Robinson generated 2,943 hits in 10,006 at bats for a .294 average; he drew 1,420 walks; and he stole 204 bases in 281 attempts. Adjusted for a 1 percent career hitter's deflation, Frank hit .298 with 3,022 hits and 602 home runs, for a 941 Wtd. Production. His 963 Total Factor ranks fifth in National League rate of success for outfielders, while his 1,144 Hits Contribution ranks fifth in National League volume of success.

Pete Rose

Rose was extremely good at what he did best — hustle and hit singles over a very long period of time. Rose was able to break one of the greatest records in all of baseball, when he collected 4,256 career hits to best Ty Cobb's 4,189 hits mark. Rose was the leadoff hitter for one of the greatest dynasties in baseball history, while starting at first, second, third, and in the outfield during his career. Rose was blacklisted from baseball for betting on games while managing the Reds. For all this, he became an American icon.

Rose was a very good player, and he deserves Hall of Fame recognition for his playing credentials. But he does not deserve the same level of regard that players like Ruth, Williams, Cobb, Mantle, Mays, and Aaron earned. Rose never hit for the kind of Production these men generated. And he played years beyond being effective in his single-minded pursuit of the hits record. In the last five years of his career he couldn't run, he couldn't hit for a high average, he had no power at all, and he was a subpar fielder. In other words, he was a weak-hitting singles hitter, who hit just .261 to get those last 559 hits.

Years	TAB	HR	BA	Adj. BA	Wtd. PRO	TF	HC
1963–81	13,289	155	.310	.317	825	832	620
1982–87	2,437	5	.261	.264	674	663	(124)

Rose had a record 15,726 total at bats in his 24-year career, collecting 4,256 hits, 1,566 walks, 746 doubles, 135 triples and 160 home runs. He hit .303, and he stole 198 bases — while being caught stealing 149 times. Adjusted for a 2 percent career hitter's deflation, Rose hit .309 with

163 home runs. His 806 Total Factor ranks only 93rd among league outfielders in rate of success, while his 495 Hits Contribution ranks a much higher 19th in league volume of success.

Noodles Hahn

Unlike Pete Rose, Hahn is hardly a household name. Hahn pitched in eight seasons from 1899 to 1906, and he pitched significant innings in just the first six. But Hahn was very effective in the innings he threw, while winning 20 games four times. Hahn was 130–94 with a 2.55 ERA in his career. His 3.54 Wtd. RA/9 ranks tenth among all National League starting pitchers in rate of success, while his 256 Runs/162 ranks a respectable 26th in league volume of success, and a close second to Dolf Luque among Reds starters.

Eric Davis

Davis came within a fragile body of being one of the greatest players ever. When he first broke in with the Reds, Davis was frighteningly good on the basepaths, stealing 80 bases in 91 attempts in 1986 — despite only 484 total at bats that year. Davis peaked at age 25 in his second full season in 1987, hitting .293 with 37 home runs and 50 steals in just 56 attempts, for a 1,090 Total Factor, while winning a Gold Glove Award. Injuries and illness held Davis back through the years, but he has managed to produce a career to be proud of.

In his career, Davis is batting .271 with 278 home runs in 5,924 total at bats, while stealing 348 bases in 413 attempts. Adjusted for 2 percent hitter's inflation, Davis is batting .265 with 280 home runs, for an 890 Total Factor, the league's 18th best rate of success, and 382 Hits Contribution, currently ranked 30th in volume of success.

Cincinnati Reds   **Hitters Volume of Success**

Pos	Years	Name	AB	BB	HBP	TAB	H	2B	3B	HR	BA	OB	SA	PRO	Wtd PRO	SB	CS	SBF	SPF	FF	R TF	V HC
C	1967-83	J.Bench	7,658	891	19	8,568	2,048	381	24	389	.267	.345	.476	821	835	68	43	(2)	(3)	65	896	878
1B	1964-86	T.Perez	9,778	925	43	10,746	2,732	505	79	379	.279	.344	.463	808	821	49	33	(1)	(10)	(12)	797	230
2B	1963-84	J.Morgan	9,277	1,865	40	11,182	2,517	449	96	268	.271	.395	.427	823	833	689	162	31	10	9	882	1,074
SS	1986-	B.Larkin	6,687	812	48	7,547	2,008	361	70	179	.300	.380	.456	836	813	359	71	28	9	29	879	810
3B	1912-27	H.Groh	6,074	696	83	6,853	1,774	308	87	26	.292	.373	.384	757	794	180	66	(9)	7	27	820	384
OF	1956-76	F.Robinson	10,006	1,420	198	11,624	2,943	528	72	586	.294	.392	.537	929	941	204	77	4	7	10	963	1,144
OF	1963-86	P.Rose	14,053	1,566	107	15,726	4,256	746	135	160	.303	.377	.409	786	802	198	149	(6)	7	3	806	495
OF	1984-	E.Davis	5,165	727	32	5,924	1,398	232	23	278	.271	.364	.486	850	835	348	65	35	8	13	890	382
Starters	Averages		8,587	1,113	71	9,771	2,460	439	73	283	.286	.373	.453	826	836	262	83	10	5	18	869	675
C	1931-47	E.Lombardi	5,855	430	44	6,329	1,792	277	27	190	.306	.358	.460	818	821	8	0	0	(10)	(10)	801	394
1B	1934-48	F.McCormick	5,723	399	27	6,149	1,711	334	26	128	.299	.348	.434	781	793	27	0	0	0	24	817	146
2B	1933-48	L.Frey	5,517	752	28	6,297	1,482	263	69	61	.269	.359	.374	734	739	105	0	0	10	(4)	745	212
SS	1970-88	D.Concepcion	8,723	736	21	9,480	2,326	389	48	101	.267	.325	.357	682	691	321	109	10	9	23	733	325
3B	1898-11	H.Steinfeldt	5,896	471	79	6,446	1,576	284	90	27	.267	.330	.360	690	750	194	0	0	0	20	771	188
OF	1958-75	V.Pinson	9,645	574	54	10,273	2,757	485	127	256	.286	.330	.442	772	787	305	122	6	10	26	828	351
OF	1913-31	E.Roush	7,363	484	53	7,900	2,376	339	182	68	.323	.369	.446	815	821	268	92	(9)	10	16	838	326
OF	1969-86	G.Foster	7,023	666	52	7,741	1,925	307	47	348	.274	.341	.480	821	833	51	31	(1)	2	(2)	831	286
Reserves	Averages		6,968	564	45	7,577	1,993	335	77	147	.286	.343	.420	763	778	160	44	1	4	12	794	279
Totals	Weighted Ave.		8,048	930	62	9,040	2,304	404	75	238	.286	.365	.444	808	817	228	70	7	4	16	844	543

Pitchers Volume of Success

Pos	Years	Name	G	GS	IP	W	L	SV	SO	BB	ERA	RA/9	Wtd RA/9	V Runs /162
SP	1914-35	D.Luque	550	366	3,220	194	179	28	1,130	918	3.24	3.95	3.84	272
SP	1899-06	N.Hahn	243	231	2,029	130	94	0	917	381	2.55	3.65	3.54	256
SP	1912-33	E.Rixey	692	554	4,495	266	251	14	1,350	1,082	3.15	3.98	4.11	233
SP	1934-50	B.Walters	428	398	3,105	198	160	4	1,107	1,121	3.30	3.89	4.05	186
SP	1984-95	J.Rijo	332	260	1,786	111	87	3	1,556	634	3.16	3.62	3.77	163
Starters	Averages		449	362	2,927	180	154	10	1,212	827	3.12	3.86	3.92	222
RP	1964-78	C.Carroll	731	28	1,353	96	73	143	681	442	2.94	3.37	3.83	110
RP	1990-	J.Shaw	556	19	773	31	49	160	487	216	3.54	3.91	3.87	62
RP	1988-95	R.Dibble	385	0	477	27	25	89	645	238	2.98	3.19	3.46	58
RP	1938-48	J.Beggs	238	41	694	48	35	29	178	189	2.96	3.69	3.87	56
Relievers	Averages		478	22	824	51	46	105	498	271	3.09	3.54	3.79	72
Totals	Averages		927	384	3,751	230	200	115	1,710	1,098	3.11	3.79	3.89	294

Cincinnati Reds   **Hitters Rate of Success**

Pos	Years	Name	AB	BB	HBP	TAB	H	2B	3B	HR	BA	OB	SA	PRO	Wtd PRO	SB	CS	SBF	SPF	FF	R TF	V HC
C	1967-83	J.Bench	7,658	891	19	8,568	2,048	381	24	389	.267	.345	.476	821	835	68	43	(2)	(3)	65	896	878
1B	1934-48	F.McCormick	5,723	399	27	6,149	1,711	334	26	128	.299	.348	.434	781	793	27	0	0	0	24	817	146
2B	1963-84	J.Morgan	9,277	1,865	40	11,182	2,517	449	96	268	.271	.395	.427	823	833	689	162	31	10	9	882	1,074
SS	1986-	B.Larkin	6,687	812	48	7,547	2,008	361	70	179	.300	.380	.456	836	813	359	71	28	9	29	879	810
3B	1912-27	H.Groh	6,074	696	83	6,853	1,774	308	87	26	.292	.373	.384	757	794	180	66	(9)	7	27	820	384
OF	1956-76	F.Robinson	10,006	1,420	198	11,624	2,943	528	72	586	.294	.392	.537	929	941	204	77	4	7	10	963	1,144
OF	1984-	E.Davis	5,165	727	32	5,924	1,398	232	23	278	.271	.364	.486	850	835	348	65	35	8	13	890	382
OF	1986-92	K.Daniels	2,338	365	14	2,717	666	125	8	104	.285	.385	.479	863	873	87	26	12	2	(9)	878	155
Starters	Averages		6,616	897	58	7,571	1,883	340	51	245	.285	.375	.462	837	845	245	64	12	5	21	884	622
C	1931-47	E.Lombardi	5,855	430	44	6,329	1,792	277	27	190	.306	.358	.460	818	821	8	0	0	(10)	(10)	801	394
1B	1947-61	T.Kluszewski	5,929	492	23	6,444	1,766	290	29	279	.298	.354	.498	852	825	20	10	(1)	(9)	(12)	804	114
2B	1933-48	L.Frey	5,517	752	28	6,297	1,482	263	69	61	.269	.359	.374	734	739	105	0	0	10	(4)	745	212
SS	1970-88	D.Concepcion	8,723	736	21	9,480	2,326	389	48	101	.267	.325	.357	682	691	321	109	10	9	23	733	325
3B	1988-96	C.Sabo	3,354	274	32	3,660	898	214	17	116	.268	.329	.445	774	775	120	49	5	8	4	792	135
OF	1913-31	E.Roush	7,363	484	53	7,900	2,376	339	182	68	.323	.369	.446	815	821	268	92	(9)	10	16	838	326
OF	1969-86	G.Foster	7,023	666	52	7,741	1,925	307	47	348	.274	.341	.480	821	833	51	31	(1)	2	(2)	831	286
OF	1958-75	V.Pinson	9,645	574	54	10,273	2,757	485	127	256	.286	.330	.442	772	787	305	122	6	10	26	828	351
Reserves	Averages		6,676	551	38	7,266	1,915	321	68	177	.287	.345	.435	780	784	150	52	1	4	5	794	268
Totals	Weighted Ave.		6,636	782	51	7,469	1,894	333	57	222	.285	.365	.453	818	825	213	60	9	5	16	854	504

Pitchers Rate of Success

Pos	Years	Name	G	GS	IP	W	L	SV	SO	BB	ERA	RA/9	Wtd RA/9	R V Runs /162
SP	1899-06	N.Hahn	243	231	2,029	130	94	0	917	381	2.55	3.65	3.54	256
SP	1984-95	J.Rijo	332	260	1,786	111	87	3	1,556	634	3.16	3.62	3.77	163
SP	1970-78	D.Gullett	266	186	1,390	109	50	11	921	501	3.11	3.42	3.77	122
SP	1967-77	G.Nolan	250	247	1,675	110	70	0	1,039	413	3.08	3.35	3.78	145
SP	1914-35	D.Luque	550	366	3,220	194	179	28	1,130	918	3.24	3.95	3.84	272
Starters	Averages		328	258	2,020	131	96	8	1,113	569	3.04	3.66	3.75	192
RP	1988-95	R.Dibble	385	0	477	27	25	89	645	238	2.98	3.19	3.46	58
RP	1996-	D.Graves	233	0	339	22	13	65	199	149	3.31	3.82	3.53	39
RP	1995-	S.Sullivan	294	0	431	18	18	8	361	158	3.70	3.90	3.70	41
RP	1964-78	C.Carroll	731	28	1,353	96	73	143	681	442	2.94	3.37	3.83	110
Relievers	Averages		411	7	650	41	32	76	472	247	3.12	3.48	3.70	62
Totals	Averages		739	265	2,670	172	128	85	1,584	816	3.06	3.61	3.74	254

Cincinnati Reds
Catchers

V	R	Years	Name	AB	BB	HBP	TAB	H	2B	3B	HR	BA	OB	SA	PRO	Wtd PRO	SB	CS	SBF	SPF	FF	R TF	V HC
1	1	1967-83	J.Bench	7,658	891	19	8,568	2,048	381	24	389	.267	.345	.476	821	835	68	43	(2)	(3)	65	896	878
2	2	1931-47	E.Lombardi	5,855	430	44	6,329	1,792	277	27	190	.306	.358	.460	818	821	8	0	0	(10)	(10)	801	394
3	5	1953-66	E.Bailey	3,581	545	25	4,151	915	128	15	155	.256	.358	.429	787	776	17	18	(4)	(10)	(10)	751	152
4	3	1913-30	B.Hargrave	2,533	217	32	2,782	786	155	58	29	.310	.372	.452	824	789	29	16	(3)	(10)	(17)	758	113
5	4	1909-18	T.Clarke	1,708	216	11	1,935	453	66	37	6	.265	.351	.358	709	757	42	3	0	5	(5)	757	77
6	7	1961-74	J.Edwards	4,577	465	16	5,058	1,106	202	32	81	.242	.314	.353	667	680	15	23	(6)	(6)	31	699	54
7	6	1991-	E.Taubensee	2,758	245	8	3,011	755	149	8	91	.274	.335	.433	767	731	11	10	(3)	(7)	(22)	700	33
8	8	1904-11	A.Schlei	1,918	172	22	2,112	455	52	21	6	.237	.307	.296	603	681	38	0	0	(10)	22	693	16
9	9	1935-51	R.Mueller	2,911	250	13	3,174	733	123	23	56	.252	.314	.368	681	686	14	0	0	(10)	10	686	15
10	10	1977-89	B.Diaz	3,274	198	13	3,485	834	162	5	87	.255	.300	.387	687	700	9	17	(7)	(10)	1	683	11
11	11	1911-29	I.Wingo	4,003	264	10	4,277	1,039	147	81	25	.260	.307	.355	662	691	87	25	(6)	2	(6)	681	8
12	12	1989-	J.Oliver	3,319	246	15	3,580	819	172	3	101	.247	.302	.392	693	676	13	13	(4)	(10)	2	664	(22)
13	13	1984-	J.Reed	3,101	391	14	3,506	774	144	10	61	.250	.336	.361	698	674	7	9	(3)	(10)	(1)	661	(27)
14	14	1901-15	L.McLean	2,647	136	9	2,792	694	90	26	6	.262	.301	.323	623	674	20	0	0	(10)	(17)	647	(44)

Cincinnati Reds
First basemen

V	R	Years	Name	AB	BB	HBP	TAB	H	2B	3B	HR	BA	OB	SA	PRO	Wtd PRO	SB	CS	SBF	SPF	FF	R TF	V HC
1	3	1964-86	T.Perez	9,778	925	43	10,746	2,732	505	79	379	.279	.344	.463	808	821	49	33	(1)	(10)	(12)	797	230
2	1	1934-48	F.McCormick	5,723	399	27	6,149	1,711	334	26	128	.299	.348	.434	781	793	27	0	0	0	24	817	146
3	2	1947-61	T.Kluszewski	5,929	492	23	6,444	1,766	290	29	279	.298	.354	.498	852	825	20	10	(1)	(9)	(12)	804	114
4	5	1973-87	D.Driessen	5,479	761	28	6,268	1,464	282	23	153	.267	.359	.411	770	776	154	63	4	8	3	791	89
5	7	1983-90	N.Esasky	2,703	314	15	3,032	677	120	21	122	.250	.332	.446	778	788	18	14	(3)	(4)	(12)	769	26
6	4	1997-	S.Casey	1,386	157	20	1,563	432	96	6	52	.312	.390	.502	892	822	2	3	(2)	(10)	(12)	797	20
7	6	1988-	H.Morris	3,998	356	22	4,376	1,216	246	21	76	.304	.364	.433	797	774	45	24	(0)	(2)	1	773	8
8	9	1959-67	G.Coleman	2,384	177	11	2,572	650	102	11	98	.273	.326	.448	774	774	9	8	(3)	(5)	(12)	754	(19)
9	8	1908-18	D.Hoblitzel	4,706	407	38	5,151	1,310	194	88	27	.278	.341	.374	715	762	173	26	(3)	0	(2)	756	(38)
10	10	1937-51	B.Haas	2,440	204	7	2,651	644	93	32	22	.264	.323	.355	678	691	51	0	0	0	(10)	681	(88)
11	12	1913-19	F.Mollwitz	1,740	83	5	1,828	420	50	19	1	.241	.278	.294	572	633	70	11	(1)	10	3	645	(123)
12	11	1987-95	T.Benzinger	2,856	181	14	3,051	733	135	18	66	.257	.304	.386	690	689	21	29	(11)	(2)	(4)	673	(145)

Cincinnati Reds
Second basemen

V	R	Years	Name	AB	BB	HBP	TAB	H	2B	3B	HR	BA	OB	SA	PRO	Wtd PRO	SB	CS	SBF	SPF	FF	R TF	V HC
1	1	1963-84	J.Morgan	9,277	1,865	40	11,182	2,517	449	96	268	.271	.395	.427	823	833	689	162	31	10	9	882	1,074
2	2	1933-48	L.Frey	5,517	752	28	6,297	1,482	263	69	61	.269	.359	.374	734	739	105	0	0	10	(4)	745	212
3	3	1992-	B.Boone	3,911	307	40	4,258	996	215	14	125	.255	.315	.413	728	692	47	33	(4)	10	10	708	49
4	5	1978-90	R.Oester	4,214	369	4	4,587	1,118	190	33	42	.265	.325	.356	681	694	40	26	(3)	3	2	696	25
5	4	1997-	P.Reese	1,633	125	17	1,775	420	74	13	27	.257	.317	.368	685	633	95	19	30	10	32	704	14
6	6	1909-20	M.Rath	2,048	258	14	2,320	521	36	7	4	.254	.342	.285	626	665	82	11	(5)	10	17	687	0
7	7	1934-43	A.Kampouris	2,182	244	20	2,446	531	94	20	45	.243	.325	.367	692	688	22	1	0	0	(2)	686	(2)
8	9	1952-64	J.Temple	5,218	648	13	5,879	1,484	208	36	22	.284	.365	.351	716	696	140	48	7	9	(39)	673	(36)
9	8	1964-77	T.Helms	4,997	231	15	5,243	1,342	223	21	34	.269	.303	.342	645	662	33	40	(8)	1	19	674	(38)
10	12	1916-26	S.Bohne	2,315	193	9	2,517	605	87	45	16	.261	.321	.359	679	650	75	59	(17)	8	1	642	(53)
11	11	1908-16	D.Egan	3,080	291	6	3,377	767	87	29	4	.249	.315	.300	615	654	167	4	(1)	7	(10)	649	(66)
12	10	1924-35	H.Critz	5,930	289	9	6,228	1,591	195	95	38	.268	.303	.352	656	627	97	24	(2)	9	27	660	(77)

Cincinnati Reds
Shortstops

V	R	Years	Name	AB	BB	HBP	TAB	H	2B	3B	HR	BA	OB	SA	PRO	Wtd PRO	SB	CS	SBF	SPF	FF	R TF	V HC
1	1	1986-	B.Larkin	6,687	812	48	7,547	2,008	361	70	179	.300	.380	.456	836	813	359	71	28	9	29	879	810
2	2	1970-88	D.Concepcion	8,723	736	21	9,480	2,326	389	48	101	.267	.325	.357	682	691	321	109	10	9	23	733	325
3	3	1960-75	L.Cardenas	6,707	522	28	7,257	1,725	285	49	118	.257	.313	.367	681	698	39	48	(7)	4	14	709	163
4	5	1936-50	E.Miller	5,337	351	44	5,732	1,270	263	28	97	.238	.290	.352	643	650	64	0	0	1	39	689	74
5	4	1935-41	B.Myers	2,399	250	6	2,655	616	88	33	45	.257	.328	.377	706	697	23	0	0	0	(6)	691	38
6	7	1898-03	G.Magoon	1,834	194	28	2,056	439	62	16	2	.239	.321	.294	615	649	47	0	0	0	(2)	648	(25)
7	6	1951-66	R.McMillan	6,752	665	57	7,474	1,639	253	35	68	.243	.316	.321	637	625	41	36	(4)	0	31	653	(33)
8	9	1909-15	T.Downey	2,170	198	8	2,376	520	69	25	7	.240	.306	.304	610	642	87	0	0	2	(9)	635	(48)
9	8	1957-66	E.Kasko	3,546	265	20	3,831	935	146	13	22	.264	.318	.331	649	649	31	31	(8)	7	2	645	(80)
10	12	1947-53	V.Stallcup	2,059	51	2	2,112	497	99	13	22	.241	.260	.334	595	580	9	4	(3)	0	(5)	572	(95)
11	10	1919-33	H.Ford	4,833	351	24	5,208	1,269	200	55	16	.263	.316	.337	652	620	21	28	(9)	0	14	625	(127)
12	11	1913-23	L.Kopf	3,010	242	33	3,285	750	84	30	5	.249	.312	.302	614	640	72	48	(19)	8	(50)	580	(145)

Cincinnati Reds
Third basemen

V	R	Years	Name	AB	BB	HBP	TAB	H	2B	3B	HR	BA	OB	SA	PRO	Wtd PRO	SB	CS	SBF	SPF	FF	R TF	V HC
1	1	1912-27	H.Groh	6,074	696	83	6,853	1,774	308	87	26	.292	.373	.384	757	794	180	66	(9)	7	27	820	384
2	3	1898-11	H.Steinfeldt	5,896	471	79	6,446	1,576	284	90	27	.267	.330	.360	690	750	194	0	0	0	20	771	188
3	2	1988-96	C.Sabo	3,354	274	32	3,660	898	214	17	116	.268	.329	.445	774	775	120	49	5	8	4	792	135
4	4	1903-17	H.Lobert	4,563	395	38	4,996	1,252	159	82	32	.274	.337	.366	703	766	316	15	(3)	10	(30)	743	66
5	5	1946-60	G.Hatton	4,206	646	13	4,865	1,068	166	33	91	.254	.355	.374	729	718	42	9	(1)	0	(11)	706	(11)
6	6	1992-	W.Greene	1,902	260	6	2,168	446	76	12	86	.234	.328	.423	751	709	17	6	2	0	(8)	704	(11)
7	11	1992-	J.Branson	1,534	122	4	1,660	377	72	11	34	.246	.303	.374	677	655	9	5	(1)	3	18	676	(17)
8	7	1925-33	C.Dressen	2,215	219	18	2,452	603	123	29	11	.272	.343	.369	711	678	30	3	(0)	10	7	694	(26)
9	8	1934-46	L.Riggs	2,477	181	17	2,675	650	110	43	28	.262	.317	.375	692	690	22	0	0	(0)	4	694	(30)
10	9	1946-59	B.Adams	4,019	414	17	4,450	1,082	188	49	37	.269	.340	.368	708	690	67	30	(7)	9	(1)	691	(36)
11	12	1918-27	B.Pinelli	2,617	182	20	2,819	723	101	33	5	.276	.328	.346	674	637	71	80	(32)	10	37	652	(91)
12	10	1974-88	R.Knight	4,829	343	36	5,208	1,311	266	27	84	.271	.325	.390	714	717	14	25	(7)	(7)	(15)	688	(112)

Cincinnati Reds
Outfielders

V	R	Years	Name	AB	BB	HBP	TAB	H	2B	3B	HR	BA	OB	SA	PRO	Wtd PRO	SB	CS	SBF	SPF	FF	R TF	V HC
1	1	1956-76	F.Robinson	10,006	1,420	198	11,624	2,943	528	72	586	.294	.392	.537	929	941	204	77	4	7	10	963	1,144
2	9	1963-86	P.Rose	14,053	1,566	107	15,726	4,256	746	135	160	.303	.377	.409	786	802	198	149	(6)	7	3	806	495
3	2	1984-	E.Davis	5,165	727	32	5,924	1,398	232	23	278	.271	.364	.486	850	835	348	65	35	8	13	890	382
4	6	1958-75	V.Pinson	9,645	574	54	10,273	2,757	485	127	256	.286	.330	.442	772	787	305	122	6	10	26	828	351
5	4	1913-31	E.Roush	7,363	484	53	7,900	2,376	339	182	68	.323	.369	.446	815	821	268	92	(9)	10	16	838	326
6	5	1969-86	G.Foster	7,023	666	52	7,741	1,925	307	47	348	.274	.341	.480	821	833	51	31	(1)	2	(2)	831	286
7	10	1973-91	K.Griffey	7,229	719	14	7,962	2,143	364	77	152	.296	.361	.431	792	797	200	83	4	6	(4)	803	178
8	3	1986-92	K.Daniels	2,338	365	14	2,717	666	125	8	104	.285	.385	.479	863	873	87	26	12	2	(9)	878	155
9	7	1991-	R.Sanders	3,703	443	39	4,185	996	199	41	162	.269	.353	.476	829	791	215	80	12	10	(1)	813	119
10	8	1935-44	I.Goodman	3,928	382	49	4,359	1,104	188	85	95	.281	.352	.445	797	796	49	0	0	8	4	808	110
11	11	1907-14	M.Mitchell	4,095	368	15	4,478	1,138	130	104	27	.278	.340	.380	720	775	202	7	0	10	14	799	93
12	12	1982-94	G.Redus	3,513	481	17	4,011	886	183	51	90	.252	.345	.410	755	759	322	83	37	10	(7)	798	72
13	13	1949-64	W.Post	4,007	331	20	4,358	1,064	194	28	210	.266	.325	.485	810	784	19	13	(2)	(2)	0	781	52
14	15	1962-76	T.Harper	6,269	753	35	7,057	1,609	256	36	146	.257	.340	.379	719	744	408	116	24	10	(17)	760	43
15	14	1919-30	C.Walker	4,858	535	9	5,402	1,475	235	117	64	.304	.374	.440	813	765	96	38	(5)	10	(0)	770	35
16	17	1914-32	R.Bressler	3,881	449	28	4,358	1,170	164	87	32	.301	.378	.413	791	755	47	21	(3)	9	(6)	755	27
17	16	1908-18	B.Bescher	4,536	619	48	5,203	1,171	190	74	28	.258	.353	.351	704	753	428	31	1	10	(7)	757	(3)
18	20	1896-01	A.McBride	1,589	132	26	1,747	464	60	26	12	.292	.356	.385	741	754	36	0	0	0	(7)	747	(9)
19	18	1969-83	C.Geronimo	3,780	354	31	4,165	977	161	50	51	.258	.327	.368	695	702	82	40	1	10	40	752	(10)
20	22	1952-56	J.Greengrass	1,793	165	4	1,962	482	82	16	69	.269	.332	.448	780	744	6	9	(6)	0	2	740	(17)
21	21	1954-66	J.Lynch	2,879	224	9	3,112	798	123	34	115	.277	.331	.463	795	781	12	17	(7)	(8)	(25)	742	(23)
22	19	1950-64	G.Bell	6,478	470	27	6,975	1,823	311	66	206	.281	.333	.445	778	754	30	31	(5)	(1)	1	750	(26)
23	23	1980-88	E.Milner	2,395	286	6	2,687	607	111	28	42	.253	.335	.376	710	716	145	72	0	10	6	733	(32)
24	28	1996-	D.Young	1,819	155	10	1,984	537	129	12	51	.295	.354	.463	817	761	11	14	(8)	(10)	(24)	719	(39)
25	27	1915-24	P.Duncan	2,695	184	15	2,894	827	137	50	23	.307	.355	.420	775	756	55	84	(37)	0	3	721	(53)
26	31	1937-42	H.Craft	2,104	110	10	2,224	533	85	25	44	.253	.294	.380	674	676	14	0	0	5	25	707	(56)
27	24	1926-38	E.Allen	4,418	223	14	4,655	1,325	255	45	47	.300	.336	.410	745	712	84	4	(1)	9	9	729	(66)
28	30	1916-24	G.Neale	2,661	201	35	2,897	688	71	50	8	.259	.319	.332	651	701	139	24	(1)	10	2	712	(69)
29	25	1942-54	J.Wyrostek	4,240	482	25	4,747	1,149	209	45	58	.271	.349	.383	731	719	33	13	(4)	7	3	724	(79)
30	29	1965-79	B.Tolan	4,238	258	65	4,561	1,121	173	34	86	.265	.317	.382	699	712	193	100	(1)	10	(2)	718	(86)
31	35	1927-34	W.Roettger	1,949	99	12	2,060	556	96	23	19	.285	.324	.387	711	673	4	0	0	0	0	673	(87)
32	36	1956-66	M.Keough	1,796	164	17	1,977	434	71	23	43	.242	.311	.379	690	688	26	19	(6)	6	(21)	667	(88)
33	32	1911-18	A.Marsans	2,273	173	16	2,462	612	67	19	2	.269	.325	.318	643	680	171	26	(2)	10	(5)	682	(95)
34	26	1975-90	D.Collins	4,907	467	38	5,412	1,335	187	52	32	.272	.340	.351	691	699	395	139	20	10	(8)	722	(97)
35	33	1940-51	M.McCormick	2,325	188	3	2,516	640	100	29	14	.275	.330	.361	692	690	16	3	(2)	0	(8)	680	(98)
36	34	1990-	T.Howard	2,483	165	11	2,659	655	123	22	44	.264	.313	.384	697	674	66	41	(5)	6	(1)	673	(111)

Cincinnati Reds
Starting Pitchers

V	R	Years	Name	G	GS	IP	W	L	SV	SO	BB	ERA	RA/9	R Wtd RA/9	V Runs /162
1	5	1914-35	D.Luque	550	366	3,220	194	179	28	1,130	918	3.24	3.95	3.84	272.0
2	1	1899-06	N.Hahn	243	231	2,029	130	94	0	917	381	2.55	3.65	3.54	256.1
3	12	1912-33	E.Rixey	692	554	4,495	266	251	14	1,350	1,082	3.15	3.98	4.11	233.2
4	8	1934-50	B.Walters	428	398	3,105	198	160	4	1,107	1,121	3.30	3.89	4.05	185.5
5	2	1984-95	J.Rijo	332	260	1,786	111	87	3	1,556	634	3.16	3.62	3.77	163.1
6	15	1931-45	P.Derringer	579	445	3,645	223	212	29	1,507	761	3.46	4.08	4.20	152.6
7	4	1967-77	G.Nolan	250	247	1,675	110	70	0	1,039	413	3.08	3.35	3.78	144.6
8	11	1923-38	R.Lucas	396	301	2,542	157	135	7	602	455	3.72	4.24	4.08	143.1
9	3	1970-78	D.Gullett	266	186	1,390	109	50	11	921	501	3.11	3.42	3.77	121.7
10	13	1937-51	J.Vander Meer	346	286	2,105	119	121	2	1,294	1,132	3.44	3.91	4.12	108.2
11	10	1960-71	J.Maloney	302	262	1,849	134	84	4	1,605	810	3.19	3.55	4.06	102.0
12	6	1942-55	E.Blackwell	236	169	1,321	82	78	10	839	562	3.30	3.83	3.91	99.4
13	16	1939-54	K.Raffensberger	396	282	2,152	119	154	16	806	449	3.60	4.15	4.24	79.4
14	19	1902-12	B.Ewing	291	264	2,301	124	118	4	998	614	2.49	3.68	4.29	72.8
15	18	1921-32	P.Donohue	344	269	2,112	134	118	12	571	422	3.87	4.61	4.27	70.5
16	7	1917-21	H.Eller	160	89	863	60	40	5	381	213	2.62	3.27	3.96	64.9
17	17	1977-88	M.Soto	297	224	1,730	100	92	4	1,449	657	3.47	3.81	4.25	63.1
18	14	1939-49	E.Riddle	190	124	1,023	65	52	8	342	458	3.40	3.85	4.14	49.5
19	9	1909-12	H.Gaspar	143	98	825	46	48	13	228	217	2.69	3.63	4.05	49.0
20	20	1908-15	G.Suggs	245	185	1,652	99	91	17	588	355	3.11	3.92	4.32	45.9
21	23	1910-25	R.Benton	437	308	2,517	150	144	21	950	712	3.09	3.99	4.42	39.8
22	22	1958-67	J.O'Toole	270	238	1,615	98	84	4	1,039	546	3.57	4.07	4.40	28.6
23	21	1990-	D.Burba	376	184	1,361	95	70	1	1,100	606	4.26	4.62	4.38	27.9
24	24	1962-80	F.Norman	403	268	1,940	104	103	8	1,303	815	3.64	4.01	4.44	26.4
25	28	1954-66	B.Purkey	386	276	2,115	129	115	9	793	510	3.79	4.25	4.47	21.4
26	29	1944-66	J.Nuxhall	526	287	2,303	135	117	19	1,372	776	3.90	4.27	4.48	19.8
27	27	1953-66	J.Jay	310	203	1,546	99	91	7	999	607	3.77	4.16	4.45	18.6
28	26	1935-48	E.Heusser	266	104	1,087	56	67	18	299	300	3.69	4.37	4.45	14.0
29	30	1921-34	R.Kolp	383	174	1,688	79	95	18	439	424	4.08	4.78	4.50	10.8
30	25	1997-	B.Tomko	121	87	601	36	31	1	448	211	4.40	4.75	4.44	7.5
31	31	1906-15	A.Fromme	252	167	1,438	80	90	4	638	530	2.90	3.99	4.55	0.6
32	32	1913-16	E.Moseley	136	100	856	49	48	3	469	340	3.01	3.86	4.58	(2.7)
33	33	1984-92	R.Robinson	232	102	800	48	39	19	473	253	3.63	4.23	4.59	(2.8)
34	35	1917-32	J.May	410	160	1,562	72	95	19	765	617	3.88	4.65	4.69	(25.1)
35	34	1984-95	T.Browning	302	300	1,921	123	90	0	1,000	511	3.94	4.28	4.69	(28.8)
36	37	1954-60	B.Lawrence	275	127	1,041	69	62	22	481	385	4.25	4.66	4.80	(30.0)
37	36	1968-80	J.Billingham	476	305	2,231	145	113	15	1,141	750	3.83	4.31	4.70	(35.2)
38	38	1914-19	P.Schneider	207	157	1,274	59	86	4	487	498	2.66	3.80	4.84	(43.0)
39	44	1980-86	B.Berenyi	142	131	782	44	55	0	607	425	4.03	4.51	5.02	(43.9)
40	46	1984-90	J.Tibbs	158	133	863	39	54	0	448	319	4.20	4.72	5.05	(47.7)
41	41	1991-	P.Schourek	255	176	1,119	65	72	2	793	405	4.59	5.01	4.93	(48.8)
42	40	1929-36	B.Frey	256	127	1,160	57	82	8	179	263	4.50	5.21	4.93	(50.2)
43	39	1935-46	A.Hollingsworth	315	185	1,520	70	104	15	608	587	3.99	4.67	4.87	(55.1)
44	43	1899-06	J.Harper	158	148	1,217	80	64	1	466	438	3.55	4.94	4.96	(60.6)
45	45	1944-54	H.Fox	248	132	1,108	43	72	6	342	435	4.33	4.96	5.03	(61.4)
46	47	1979-86	F.Pastore	220	139	986	48	58	6	541	301	4.29	4.63	5.20	(74.8)
47	48	1962-69	S.Ellis	229	140	1,004	63	58	18	677	378	4.15	4.51	5.23	(75.5)
48	42	1928-47	S.Johnson	492	272	2,281	101	165	15	840	687	4.09	4.84	4.95	(104.8)
49	49	1890-03	B.Phillips	176	152	1,296	70	76	3	374	363	4.09	5.83	5.25	(115.0)
50	50	1945-58	H.Wehmeier	361	240	1,803	92	108	9	794	852	4.80	5.21	5.27	(150.9)

**Cincinnati Reds
Relief Pitchers**

V	R	Years	Name	G	GS	IP	W	L	SV	SO	BB	ERA	RA/9	R Wtd RA/9	V Runs /162
1	4	1964-78	C.Carroll	731	28	1,353	96	73	143	681	442	2.94	3.37	3.83	110.5
2	5	1990-	J.Shaw	556	19	773	31	49	160	487	216	3.54	3.91	3.87	61.8
3	1	1988-95	R.Dibble	385	0	477	27	25	89	645	238	2.98	3.19	3.46	58.5
4	6	1938-48	J.Beggs	238	41	694	48	35	29	178	189	2.96	3.69	3.87	55.6
5	7	1954-63	J.Brosnan	385	47	831	55	47	67	507	312	3.54	3.85	4.00	53.6
6	3	1995-	S.Sullivan	294	0	431	18	18	8	361	158	3.70	3.90	3.70	41.2
7	2	1996-	D.Graves	233	0	339	22	13	65	199	149	3.31	3.82	3.53	38.7
8	11	1969-80	P.Borbon	593	4	1,027	69	39	80	409	251	3.52	3.82	4.22	38.3
9	8	1974-81	R.Eastwick	326	1	525	28	27	68	295	156	3.31	3.68	4.01	33.1
10	14	1976-90	D.Bair	584	5	909	55	43	81	689	405	3.63	3.94	4.28	29.3
11	13	1988-	N.Charlton	561	37	852	47	52	96	760	398	3.75	4.23	4.25	29.1
12	12	1985-95	R.Murphy	597	0	623	32	38	30	520	247	3.64	4.00	4.24	22.5
13	10	1994-	H.Carrasco	402	1	493	24	33	14	385	249	4.11	4.56	4.19	21.5
14	9	1994-	G.White	225	15	334	21	14	16	295	84	4.10	4.23	4.12	16.8
15	15	1991-	M.Remlinger	292	59	568	34	35	15	520	298	4.15	4.43	4.35	13.9
16	16	1976-83	M.Sarmiento	228	22	514	26	22	12	283	172	3.49	3.92	4.36	11.5
17	18	1980-90	J.Price	372	84	906	45	49	13	657	337	3.65	4.05	4.47	9.0
18	17	1956-59	T.Acker	153	23	380	19	13	8	256	150	4.12	4.28	4.44	5.0
19	19	1950-56	F.Smith	271	7	496	35	33	44	277	181	3.81	4.48	4.48	4.6
20	20	1952-58	H.Freeman	204	3	359	30	16	37	158	109	3.74	4.39	4.56	0.0
21	21	1954-64	A.Fowler	362	90	1,024	54	51	32	539	308	4.03	4.43	4.56	(0.2)
22	22	1995-	R.Villone	221	45	451	23	21	5	330	268	4.67	5.03	4.58	(1.4)
23	26	1982-88	B.Scherrer	228	2	311	8	10	11	207	140	4.08	4.45	4.72	(5.7)
24	23	1968-76	W.Granger	451	0	639	35	35	108	303	201	3.14	4.08	4.68	(8.5)
25	24	1964-70	B.McCool	292	20	528	32	42	58	471	272	3.59	4.07	4.71	(9.2)
26	28	1951-62	J.Collum	171	37	464	32	28	12	171	173	4.15	4.79	4.76	(11.1)
27	29	1966-74	G.Culver	335	57	789	48	49	23	451	352	3.62	4.04	4.76	(18.3)
28	25	1981-93	T.Power	564	85	1,160	68	69	70	701	452	4.00	4.41	4.72	(20.8)
29	32	1933-37	D.Brennan	141	26	397	21	12	19	172	180	4.19	5.27	5.01	(21.1)
30	27	1977-87	T.Hume	543	55	1,086	57	71	92	536	384	3.85	4.32	4.73	(21.9)
31	33	1984-95	D.Henry	256	1	335	14	15	14	275	216	4.65	4.95	5.16	(22.4)
32	31	1945-54	J.Hetki	214	23	525	18	26	13	175	185	4.39	4.95	4.96	(25.0)
33	30	1954-59	H.Jeffcoat	245	51	697	39	37	25	239	257	4.22	4.71	4.86	(25.1)
34	34	1931-43	A.Stout	180	29	458	20	20	11	185	177	4.54	5.33	5.35	(42.3)
35	35	1944-53	K.Peterson	147	43	420	13	38	5	208	215	4.95	5.53	5.48	(45.1)

CLEVELAND INDIANS (1901–2000)

The Indians are cursed with tracking the same periods of up and down performance as the Yankees. In the 1950s, Cleveland assembled a deep pitching staff of Bob Lemon, Early Wynn, Mike Garcia, and Bob Feller. Hitters Al Rosen, Larry Doby, and Bobby Avila gave the pitchers plenty of support. Yet Cleveland finished in second place six times in the 1950s, as only the 1954 team, with 111 victories, won a pennant in a decade dominated by the Yankees.

The other Indians dynasty resided in the 1990s, as hitters Albert Belle, Kenny Lofton, Manny Ramirez, Jim Thome, Carlos Baerga and Omar Vizquel led the Tribe to five consecutive division titles and two pennants. The Yankees won the other three pennants in this five-year period.

The remaining decades of Indians history include just two pennants, along with great play from Nap Lajoie, Joe Jackson, Tris Speaker, Addie Joss, Elmer Flick, Ray Chapman, Earl Averill, Lou Boudreau, Ken Keltner, and Buddy Bell.

Profiled Indians Players

Nap Lajoie

Lajoie edges Rogers Hornsby and Eddie Collins for the honor of ranking as the best second baseman of all time. At his peak, from 1901 through 1910, Lajoie produced the best hitting results in the American League. His adjusted batting averages during that ten-year period were .428, .381, .375, .431, .379, .404, .345, .341, .374, and .437. Lajoie was so popular that Cleveland named their team after him soon after he joined their ball club.

Lajoie hit .338 with 82 home runs and 380 stolen bases in his career. Adjusted for a 7.5 percent career hitter's deflation, he hit an impressive .363 with 95 home runs, for a 910 Wtd. Production. Add 63 Fielding Factor points, and Lajoie's 978 Total Factor ranks first in league rate of success at second base, while his 1,495 Hits Contribution ranks first in major league history at his position.

Lajoie produced eight years with over 1,000 Total Factor, and five years with over 100 Hits Contribution. In his best season for Cleveland in 1910, the 35-year-old hit an adjusted .437, with an adjusted 264 hits, a 1,171 Total Factor and 159.6 Hits Contribution. As impressive as that season was—the best volume of success season by any other American Leaguer not named Ruth—Lajoie surpassed these results with his 164.7 Hits Contribution in his 1901 season with Philadelphia.

Lou Boudreau

Boudreau made up for his lack of speed with sure hands and a great understanding of the game, correctly positioning himself to compensate for his limited range. Boudreau ended up one of the best fielding shortstops of all time. He was a steady, patient hitter, batting .295 while drawing 796 walks in 6,859 career total at bats, for a .380 on-base percentage. Boudreau also became Cleveland's player-manager in 1942 at the tender age of 24. His sparkling leadership, fielding, and a career year at the plate (.355, 18 home runs) led the Indians to a World Series title in 1948.

In his career, Boudreau hit .295 with 68 home runs. Adjusted for minuscule hitter's inflation, he hit .294 with 71 home runs. Fifty Fielding Factor points helped Boudreau earn an 830 Total Factor, the league's fifth best rate of success, while his 580 Hits Contribution is the league's fifth best volume of success. Not bad for a person whose 15-year career included just 10 seasons with over 309 total at bats.

Ray Chapman

Chapman's career ended tragically at the age of 29, after less than nine full major league seasons, when a Carl Mays pitch took his life. Chapman was not the greatest shortstop ever, but he and Dave Bancroft were the best all-around shortstops of their time.

Chapman hit .278 with 17 home runs and 233 stolen bases in 4,256 career total at bats. Adjusted for a career 7 percent hitter's deflation, he hit .296 with 19 home runs. His 800 Total Factor ranks eighth in league rate of success among shortstops, while his short career ensured that his 304 Hits Contribution ranks only 16th in league volume of success. If we doubled Chapman's career span and his Hits Contribution to 608, he would rank fourth in league volume of success— ahead of fellow Tribe shortstop Lou Boudreau.

Tris Speaker

Underrated Speaker put on quite a show for 22 brilliant seasons. Acknowledged as the best fielding outfielder of his time, Speaker was also a great hitter who could run the bases. It is fitting that Speaker, the more graceful fielder and much nicer person, edges infamous peer Ty Cobb by a fraction of a point in career rate of success.

In his career, Speaker hit .345 with a record 792 doubles, 222 triples, and 117 home runs, for a 928 Production. He stole 432 bases, and earned 58 Fielding Factor points. Adjusted for a career 2 percent hitter's deflation, Speaker hit .352 with 123 home runs, for a 947 Wtd. Production. His 1,008 Total Factor ranks fourth in league rate of success among outfielders, while his 1,494 Hits Contribution ranks fourth in league volume of success.

Speaker's four best seasons were Dead Ball years playing for the Red Sox and Indians. Speaker took advantage of hitter's inflation in the 1920s to hit for more power and a high average, but he was no longer quite as good as he demonstrated in those earlier years, when he, Cobb, and Joe Jackson dominated major league offensive statistics. For example, Speaker's best raw batting averages were .389 in 1925, .388 in 1920, .386 in 1916, and .383 in 1912. But after adjusting for hitter's inflation/deflation,

he hit only .358 in 1925 and .373 in 1920, compared to .397 in 1912 and .423 in 1916.

Shoeless Joe Jackson

Jackson had earned a place in the Hall of Fame— until he was thrown out of baseball for being implicated in the Black Sox scandal. Jackson remains a sympathetic figure today as a result of his excellent on-field performance, and due to questions about his role in throwing the 1919 series, as he had team highs with a .375 average and one home run in that series.

Regardless of Jackson's Hall status, he was one of the three great offensive players in the game in his prime— along with Ty Cobb and Tris Speaker. Jackson hit .356 over his career, the third highest average in history behind Cobb and Hornsby. Jackson added 54 home runs and 202 stolen bases in 5,559 total at bats. Adjusted for a 5 percent career hitter's deflation, he hit for a sparkling .374 average and 60 home runs, for a 988 Wtd. Production. Jackson's 996 Total Factor ranks sixth in league rate of success among outfielders, while his 674 Hits Contribution ranks only 12th in league volume of success, as the 31-year-old was involuntarily retired from the game in 1920.

Elmer Flick

Flick began his career with four strong seasons with the Philadelphia National League ball club from 1898 to 1901, hitting .302, .342, .367, and .333. Flick's performance dropped off sharply when he moved to Cleveland, but this dropoff was partly due to the arrival of the Dead Ball Era:

Team	TAB	HR	BA	Adj. BA	Wtd. PRO	TF	HC
Phi NL	2,308	29	.338	.345	929	963	251
Cle AL	3,985	19	.299	.335	887	900	293

While Flick's highest batting average for Cleveland was .311, he did lead the league with a .308 average in 1905. If we adjust for hitter's deflation, he hit .349 or higher four consecutive years from 1904 to 1907.

Flick hit .313 with 48 home runs in his career, and stole 330 bases. He also had 164 triples in just 6,293 total at bats. Adjusted for a challenging career 8 percent hitter's deflation, he hit .339 with 56 home runs, for a 902 Wtd. Production. His 924 Total Factor ranks tenth in league rate of success among outfielders, while his 544 Hits Contribution ranks 17th in league volume of success. Flick would have achieved a greater historic stature if injuries hadn't all but ended his career after his 1907 season, when he was only 31.

Albert Belle

Belle is a weak fielding left fielder, and he has been a surly teammate for three ball clubs in his career-to-date. But Belle has also been capable of sustained power hitting. He had outstanding offensive numbers for Cleveland in 1994, 1995, and 1996. After a miserable first half start in 1998 that cost the White Sox any chance of the division title, Belle went on a tear after the All-Star break to bat .328 and set the Sox all-time single season home run record with 49 long balls. Belle drove in over 100 runs for his ninth straight year in 2000, despite an off year reflected in a negative Hits Contribution.

In his career-to-date, Belle is hitting .295 with 381 home runs. Adjusted for a 4 percent career hitter's inflation, he hit .282 with 386 home runs, for an 899 Wtd. Production. His 886 Total Factor ranks 19th in league rate of success among outfielders, while his 424 Hits Contribution currently ranks him 25th in league volume of success.

Bob Feller

Feller was a 17-year-old rookie in 1936, when he won 5 games in 14 appearances for the Indians. Feller was 9–7 at age 18; 17–11 at age 19; 24–9 at age 20; 27–11 at age 21 (with a league leading 2.61 ERA); and 25–13 at age 22. His cumulative record at age 22 was already 107–54, and he had struck out 1,233 batters in 1,449 innings. Feller appeared capable of challenging Cy Young's 511 career wins record, and certain to break Walter Johnson's 3,509 career strikeouts record.

Unfortunately for Feller, war service cost him the next four seasons, and probably around 100 wins and 1,000 strikeouts. Feller returned to have big seasons in 1946 and 1947, but he lost some of his high octane edge thereafter, finishing his career from age 29 onward with only one other 20 win season, and with annual ERAs always above 3.00. By the time Feller participated in his only two pennant winning seasons in 1948 and 1954, he was no longer the top, or even second best, winner on his team.

Years	IP	W–L	SO	ERA	Wtd. RA/9	Runs/162
1936–47	2,191	158–83	1,836	2.92	3.04	388
1948–56	1,636	108–79	745	3.70	4.19	71

In his career, Feller was 266–162 with a 3.25 ERA and a 3.53 Wtd. RA/9, the league's 14th best rate of success. He would have ranked number 1 if he had retired after the 1947 season. His 459 Runs/162 ranks him seventh in volume of success.

Addie Joss

Joss is the best pitcher ever whose career ended with less than ten seasons in the big leagues. Joss died from an illness two days after his 31st birthday, just before the 1912 season. Before his death, Joss was one of the great Dead Ball pitchers, along with the likes of Christy Mathewson, Three Finger Brown, Ed Walsh and Cy Young. Joss was 160–97 in his short career, with a 1.89 ERA, and a 3.32 Wtd. RA/9, the league's seventh best rate of success. His 344 Runs/162 ranks 12th in league volume of success.

Cleveland Indians   **Hitters Volume of Success**

Pos	Years	Name	AB	BB	HBP	TAB	H	2B	3B	HR	BA	OB	SA	PRO	Wtd PRO	SB	CS	SBF	SPF	FF	R TF	V HC
C	1958-67	J.Romano	2,767	414	29	3,210	706	112	10	129	.255	.358	.443	801	802	7	9	(3)	(7)	(12)	781	158
1B	1933-46	H.Trosky	5,161	545	16	5,722	1,561	331	58	228	.302	.371	.522	892	840	28	23	(3)	0	(0)	837	189
2B	1896-16	N.Lajoie	9,589	516	134	10,239	3,242	657	163	82	.338	.380	.466	846	910	380	21	(2)	6	63	978	1,495
SS	1938-52	L.Boudreau	6,029	796	34	6,859	1,779	385	66	68	.295	.380	.415	795	792	51	50	(7)	(5)	50	830	580
3B	1972-89	B.Bell	8,995	836	38	9,869	2,514	425	56	201	.279	.343	.406	750	761	55	79	(10)	(1)	38	788	336
OF	1907-28	T.Speaker	10,195	1,381	103	11,679	3,514	792	222	117	.345	.428	.500	928	947	432	129	(7)	10	58	1,008	1,494
OF	1908-20	J.Jackson	4,981	519	59	5,559	1,772	307	168	54	.356	.423	.517	940	988	202	61	(9)	10	7	996	674
OF	1898-10	E.Flick	5,597	597	99	6,293	1,752	268	164	48	.313	.389	.445	834	902	330	0	0	9	12	924	544
Starters	Averages		6,664	701	64	7,429	2,105	410	113	116	.316	.386	.464	850	873	186	47	(5)	3	27	898	684
C	1964-74	D.Sims	2,422	338	35	2,795	580	80	6	100	.239	.341	.401	742	773	6	16	(9)	(10)	(7)	747	94
1B	1897-08	C.Hickman	3,982	153	58	4,193	1,176	217	91	59	.295	.331	.440	771	838	72	0	0	(1)	(29)	807	138
2B	1990-99	C.Baerga	4,807	253	58	5,118	1,400	246	17	124	.291	.334	.427	761	740	52	23	1	(1)	1	741	127
SS	1920-33	J.Sewell	7,132	842	79	8,053	2,226	436	68	49	.312	.391	.413	804	756	74	72	(8)	0	18	766	345
3B	1991-	J.Thome	3,634	764	33	4,431	1,033	214	17	233	.284	.413	.545	958	894	17	11	(1)	(3)	(15)	874	290
OF	1989-	A.Belle	5,853	683	55	6,591	1,726	389	25	381	.295	.374	.564	938	899	88	41	1	0	(13)	886	424
OF	1947-59	L.Doby	5,348	871	38	6,257	1,515	243	52	253	.283	.387	.490	877	858	47	36	(4)	8	16	877	379
OF	1955-68	R.Colavito	6,503	951	29	7,483	1,730	283	21	374	.266	.362	.489	851	856	19	27	(5)	(9)	12	853	350
Reserves	Averages		4,960	607	48	5,615	1,423	264	37	197	.287	.370	.474	844	828	47	28	(3)	(2)	(2)	821	268
Totals	Weighted Ave.		6,096	669	59	6,824	1,878	361	88	143	.308	.382	.466	848	858	139	40	(4)	1	17	872	545

Pitchers Volume of Success

Pos	Years	Name	G	GS	IP	W	L	SV	SO	BB	ERA	RA/9	Wtd RA/9	R V Runs /162
SP	1936-56	B.Feller	570	484	3,827	266	162	21	2,581	1,764	3.25	3.66	3.53	459
SP	1912-28	S.Coveleski	450	385	3,082	215	142	21	981	802	2.89	3.60	3.63	345
SP	1902-10	A.Joss	286	260	2,327	160	97	5	920	364	1.89	2.82	3.32	344
SP	1946-58	B.Lemon	460	350	2,850	207	128	22	1,277	1,251	3.23	3.74	3.77	263
SP	1948-61	M.Garcia	428	281	2,175	142	97	23	1,117	719	3.27	3.67	3.72	212
Starters	Averages		439	352	2,852	198	125	18	1,375	980	2.95	3.53	3.59	325
RP	1982-	D.Jones	846	4	1,128	69	79	303	909	247	3.30	3.71	3.56	128
RP	1986-99	E.Plunk	714	41	1,151	72	58	35	1,081	647	3.82	4.20	4.00	73
RP	1974-86	J.Kern	416	14	793	53	57	88	651	444	3.32	3.77	3.95	55
RP	1994-	P.Shuey	275	0	313	26	18	19	341	166	3.88	4.20	3.74	29
Relievers	Averages		563	15	846	55	53	111	746	376	3.54	3.93	3.82	71
Totals	Averages		1,002	367	3,699	253	178	130	2,121	1,356	3.08	3.62	3.65	396

Cleveland Indians   **Hitters Rate of Success**

Pos	Years	Name	AB	BB	HBP	TAB	H	2B	3B	HR	BA	OB	SA	PRO	Wtd PRO	SB	CS	SBF	SPF	FF	R TF	V HC
C	1958-67	J.Romano	2,767	414	29	3,210	706	112	10	129	.255	.358	.443	801	802	7	9	(3)	(7)	(12)	781	158
1B	1933-46	H.Trosky	5,161	545	16	5,722	1,561	331	58	228	.302	.371	.522	892	840	28	23	(3)	0	(0)	837	189
2B	1896-16	N.Lajoie	9,589	516	134	10,239	3,242	657	163	82	.338	.380	.466	846	910	380	21	(2)	6	63	978	1,495
SS	1938-52	L.Boudreau	6,029	796	34	6,859	1,779	385	66	68	.295	.380	.415	795	792	51	50	(7)	(5)	50	830	580
3B	1991-	J.Thome	3,634	764	33	4,431	1,033	214	17	233	.284	.413	.545	958	894	17	11	(1)	(3)	(15)	874	290
OF	1907-28	T.Speaker	10,195	1,381	103	11,679	3,514	792	222	117	.345	.428	.500	928	947	432	129	(7)	10	58	1,008	1,494
OF	1908-20	J.Jackson	4,981	519	59	5,559	1,772	307	168	54	.356	.423	.517	940	988	202	61	(9)	10	7	996	674
OF	1898-10	E.Flick	5,597	597	99	6,293	1,752	268	164	48	.313	.389	.445	834	902	330	0	0	9	12	924	544
Starters		Averages	5,994	692	63	6,749	1,920	383	109	120	.320	.396	.480	877	895	181	38	(4)	3	20	914	678
C	1909-15	T.Easterly	2020	107	8	2,135	607	88	38	8	.300	.338	.394	732	784	42	0	0	0	(21)	763	80
1B	1897-08	C.Hickman	3982	153	58	4,193	1,176	217	91	59	.295	.331	.440	771	838	72	0	0	(1)	(29)	807	138
2B	1931-41	O.Hale	3701	353	3	4,057	1,071	240	51	73	.289	.352	.441	793	737	57	45	(8)	4	10	744	86
SS	1912-20	R.Chapman	3785	452	19	4,256	1,053	162	81	17	.278	.358	.377	735	784	233	47	0	9	7	800	304
3B	1947-56	A.Rosen	3725	587	27	4,339	1,063	165	20	192	.285	.386	.495	882	861	39	33	(6)	(1)	(18)	837	262
OF	1993-	M.Ramirez	3470	541	37	4,048	1,086	237	11	236	.313	.411	.592	1,003	929	28	24	(5)	0	(2)	922	337
OF	1989-	A.Belle	5853	683	55	6,591	1,726	389	21	381	.295	.374	.564	938	899	88	41	1	0	(13)	886	424
OF	1947-59	L.Doby	5348	871	38	6,257	1,515	243	52	253	.283	.387	.490	877	858	47	36	(4)	8	16	877	379
Reserves		Averages	3,986	468	31	4,485	1,162	218	46	152	.292	.370	.484	854	845	76	28	(3)	2	(6)	838	251
Totals		Weighted Ave.	5,325	617	52	5,994	1,667	328	88	131	.313	.390	.481	871	878	146	35	(4)	3	11	889	536

Pitchers Rate of Success

Pos	Years	Name	G	GS	IP	W	L	SV	SO	BB	ERA	RA/9	V Wtd RA/9	R Runs /162
SP	1902-10	A.Joss	286	260	2,327	160	97	5	920	364	1.89	2.82	3.32	344
SP	1936-56	B.Feller	570	484	3,827	266	162	21	2,581	1,764	3.25	3.66	3.53	459
SP	1912-28	S.Coveleski	450	385	3,082	215	142	21	981	802	2.89	3.60	3.63	345
SP	1948-61	M.Garcia	428	281	2,175	142	97	23	1,117	719	3.27	3.67	3.72	212
SP	1946-58	B.Lemon	460	350	2,850	207	128	22	1,277	1,251	3.23	3.74	3.77	263
Starters		Averages	439	352	2,852	198	125	18	1,375	980	2.95	3.53	3.59	325
RP	1982-	D.Jones	846	4	1,128	69	79	303	909	247	3.30	3.71	3.56	128
RP	1994-	P.Shuey	275	0	313	26	18	19	341	166	3.88	4.20	3.74	29
RP	1974-86	J.Kern	416	14	793	53	57	88	651	444	3.32	3.77	3.95	55
RP	1986-99	E.Plunk	714	41	1,151	72	58	35	1,081	647	3.82	4.20	4.00	73
Relievers		Averages	563	15	846	55	53	111	746	376	3.54	3.93	3.82	71
Totals		Averages	1,002	367	3,699	253	178	130	2,121	1,356	3.08	3.62	3.65	396

Cleveland Indians
Catchers

V	R	Years	Name	AB	BB	HBP	TAB	H	2B	3B	HR	BA	OB	SA	PRO	Wtd PRO	SB	CS	SBF	SPF	FF	R TF	V HC
1	1	1958-67	J.Romano	2,767	414	29	3,210	706	112	10	129	.255	.358	.443	801	802	7	9	(3)	(7)	(12)	781	158
2	3	1964-74	D.Sims	2,422	338	35	2,795	580	80	6	100	.239	.341	.401	742	773	6	16	(9)	(10)	(7)	747	94
3	2	1909-15	T.Easterly	2,020	107	8	2,135	607	88	38	8	.300	.338	.394	732	784	42	0	0	0	(21)	763	80
4	4	1978-91	R.Hassey	3,440	385	21	3,846	914	172	7	71	.266	.343	.382	725	722	14	10	(2)	(10)	8	718	78
5	5	1988-	S.Alomar Jr.	3,429	168	35	3,632	948	195	8	93	.276	.317	.419	736	706	24	22	(5)	(2)	19	718	73
6	6	1967-79	R.Fosse	2,957	203	18	3,178	758	117	13	61	.256	.308	.367	675	697	15	19	(7)	(1)	19	708	48
7	8	1911-28	S.O'Neill	4,795	592	43	5,430	1,259	248	34	13	.263	.349	.337	685	692	30	23	(6)	(10)	14	690	35
8	7	1932-46	F.Pytlak	2,399	247	24	2,670	677	100	36	7	.282	.355	.363	718	670	56	29	(1)	10	19	698	27
9	9	1960-72	J.Azcue	2,828	207	17	3,052	712	94	9	50	.252	.307	.344	651	674	5	12	(6)	(10)	24	682	6
10	11	1902-10	H.Bemis	2,229	79	36	2,344	569	92	29	5	.255	.292	.329	621	695	49	0	0	3	(27)	671	(7)
11	10	1941-60	J.Hegan	4,772	456	4	5,232	1,087	187	46	92	.228	.296	.344	640	628	15	24	(6)	(6)	58	673	(10)
12	12	1920-36	G.Myatt	2,678	248	11	2,937	722	137	37	38	.270	.334	.391	725	680	20	18	(5)	(1)	(24)	649	(50)
13	13	1921-42	L.Sewell	5,383	486	27	5,896	1,393	272	56	20	.259	.323	.341	665	622	65	44	(4)	(4)	17	631	(137)

Cleveland Indians
First basemen

V	R	Years	Name	AB	BB	HBP	TAB	H	2B	3B	HR	BA	OB	SA	PRO	Wtd PRO	SB	CS	SBF	SPF	FF	R TF	V HC
1	1	1933-46	H.Trosky	5,161	545	16	5,722	1,561	331	58	228	.302	.371	.522	892	840	28	23	(3)	0	(0)	837	189
2	2	1897-08	C.Hickman	3,982	153	58	4,193	1,176	217	91	59	.295	.331	.440	771	838	72	0	0	(1)	(29)	807	138
3	4	1973-87	A.Thornton	5,291	876	41	6,208	1,342	244	22	253	.254	.364	.452	815	815	48	37	(4)	(4)	(8)	800	94
4	5	1914-29	G.Burns	6,573	363	110	7,046	2,018	444	72	72	.307	.354	.429	783	797	154	63	(1)	0	1	796	94
5	6	1974-85	M.Hargrove	5,564	965	53	6,582	1,614	266	28	80	.290	.400	.391	791	804	24	37	(7)	(7)	1	791	77
6	3	1928-34	E.Morgan	2,810	385	10	3,205	879	186	45	52	.313	.398	.467	864	811	36	25	(4)	10	(14)	802	53
7	10	1921-33	L.Fonseca	3,404	186	22	3,612	1,075	203	50	31	.316	.355	.432	787	742	64	36	(2)	10	(1)	749	46
8	7	1949-54	L.Easter	1,725	174	28	1,927	472	54	12	93	.274	.350	.481	830	807	1	8	(7)	(10)	(10)	779	9
9	9	1964-70	T.Horton	2,228	140	13	2,381	597	102	15	76	.268	.315	.430	745	778	12	8	(2)	(7)	(16)	754	(17)
10	8	1989-	P.Sorrento	3,412	426	21	3,859	876	176	5	166	.257	.343	.457	800	763	8	15	(5)	(5)	2	755	(27)
11	11	1962-70	F.Whitfield	2,284	139	16	2,439	578	93	8	108	.253	.301	.443	743	769	7	16	(10)	(10)	(12)	737	(40)
12	14	1969-81	J.Ellis	2,672	190	19	2,881	699	116	13	69	.262	.315	.392	707	722	6	10	(5)	(10)	(25)	681	(68)
13	13	1981-92	P.Tabler	3,911	375	24	4,310	1,101	190	25	47	.282	.348	.379	727	724	16	20	(5)	(4)	(22)	693	(142)
14	12	1904-15	G.Stovall	5,222	172	33	5,427	1,382	231	56	15	.265	.292	.339	631	699	142	0	0	0	14	713	(155)
15	15	1909-22	D.Johnston	3,774	264	48	4,086	992	154	68	14	.263	.319	.351	670	693	139	48	(8)	0	(4)	681	(187)

Cleveland Indians
Second basemen

V	R	Years	Name	AB	BB	HBP	TAB	H	2B	3B	HR	BA	OB	SA	PRO	Wtd PRO	SB	CS	SBF	SPF	FF	R TF	V HC
1	1	1896-16	N.Lajoie	9,589	516	134	10,239	3,242	657	163	82	.338	.380	.466	846	910	380	21	(2)	6	63	978	1,495
2	3	1990-99	C.Baerga	4,807	253	58	5,118	1,400	246	17	124	.291	.334	.427	761	740	52	23	1	(1)	1	741	127
3	5	1949-59	B.Avila	4,620	561	14	5,195	1,296	185	35	80	.281	.360	.388	748	736	78	52	(5)	6	(7)	731	118
4	2	1931-41	O.Hale	3,701	353	3	4,057	1,071	240	51	73	.289	.352	.441	793	737	57	45	(8)	4	10	744	86
5	6	1979-91	T.Bernazard	3,700	428	17	4,145	970	177	30	75	.262	.341	.387	728	729	113	55	0	9	(12)	726	85
6	4	1925-33	J.Hodapp	2,826	163	5	2,994	880	169	34	28	.311	.350	.425	775	728	18	20	(7)	0	10	731	48
7	7	1972-80	J.Brohamer	2,500	222	8	2,730	613	91	12	30	.245	.309	.327	636	659	9	17	(9)	0	14	665	(33)
8	9	1938-47	R.Mack	2,707	261	6	2,974	629	113	24	34	.232	.301	.330	631	630	35	17	0	10	14	655	(46)
9	10	1935-46	R.Hughes	2,582	222	7	2,811	705	105	27	5	.273	.332	.340	673	644	80	18	4	10	(8)	650	(57)
10	12	1991-	M.Lewis	2,782	196	16	2,994	735	155	13	48	.264	.316	.381	697	665	29	18	(2)	0	(16)	647	(63)
11	14	1956-65	J.Kindall	2,057	145	8	2,210	439	83	9	44	.213	.268	.327	595	590	17	11	(2)	10	22	619	(68)
12	8	1986-95	J.Browne	3,190	393	13	3,596	866	135	25	23	.271	.354	.351	705	702	73	45	(4)	5	(46)	658	(80)
13	13	1974-85	D.Kuiper	3,379	248	28	3,655	917	91	29	1	.271	.326	.316	643	652	52	71	(23)	7	1	637	(87)
14	11	1914-26	Wambsganss	5,237	490	47	5,774	1,359	215	59	7	.259	.328	.327	655	656	140	74	(11)	0	3	648	(104)

Cleveland Indians
Shortstops

V	R	Years	Name	AB	BB	HBP	TAB	H	2B	3B	HR	BA	OB	SA	PRO	Wtd PRO	SB	CS	SBF	SPF	FF	R TF	V HC
1	1	1938-52	L.Boudreau	6,029	796	34	6,859	1,779	385	66	68	.295	.380	.415	795	792	51	50	(7)	(5)	50	830	580
2	4	1920-33	J.Sewell	7,132	842	79	8,053	2,226	436	68	49	.312	.391	.413	804	756	74	72	(8)	0	18	766	345
3	3	1982-	J.Franco	7,244	753	33	8,030	2,177	335	47	141	.301	.369	.418	787	778	260	101	7	7	(25)	767	309
4	2	1912-20	R.Chapman	3,785	452	19	4,256	1,053	162	81	17	.278	.358	.377	735	784	233	47	0	9	7	800	304
5	6	1989-	O.Vizquel	5,809	582	24	6,415	1,605	250	36	41	.276	.345	.353	698	664	260	101	9	10	45	727	206
6	5	1954-69	W.Held	4,019	508	56	4,583	963	150	22	179	.240	.333	.421	755	756	14	11	(2)	0	(14)	740	95
7	7	1901-19	T.Turner	5,921	435	34	6,390	1,499	207	77	8	.253	.308	.318	626	693	256	24	(3)	10	11	711	67
8	8	1961-68	D.Howser	2,483	367	13	2,863	617	90	17	16	.248	.348	.318	666	673	105	34	12	10	(21)	675	10
9	9	1970-79	F.Duffy	2,665	171	8	2,844	619	104	14	26	.232	.281	.311	592	616	49	30	(4)	10	17	639	(34)
10	13	1968-75	E.Leon	1,862	156	9	2,027	440	51	10	24	.236	.298	.313	612	627	7	16	(12)	0	14	629	(46)
11	14	1927-35	J.Burnett	1,835	163	9	2,007	521	94	15	9	.284	.345	.366	712	672	15	12	(4)	0	(40)	627	(52)
12	11	1963-74	L.Brown	3,449	317	22	3,788	803	108	13	47	.233	.301	.313	614	642	22	23	(6)	5	(9)	632	(63)
13	10	1950-60	G.Strickland	2,824	361	11	3,196	633	84	27	36	.224	.314	.311	626	618	12	10	(2)	0	18	634	(67)
14	12	1933-42	Knickerbocker	3,418	244	9	3,671	943	198	27	28	.276	.326	.374	700	657	25	46	(17)	10	(21)	630	(70)
15	15	1987-96	F.Fermin	2,767	166	24	2,957	718	86	11	4	.259	.307	.303	610	607	27	21	(5)	9	(14)	597	(97)
16	16	1973-84	T.Veryzer	2,848	143	33	3,024	687	84	12	14	.241	.285	.294	579	589	9	23	(11)	0	(4)	573	(133)

Cleveland Indians
Third basemen

V	R	Years	Name	AB	BB	HBP	TAB	H	2B	3B	HR	BA	OB	SA	PRO	Wtd PRO	SB	CS	SBF	SPF	FF	R TF	V HC
1	4	1972-89	B.Bell	8,995	836	38	9,869	2,514	425	56	201	.279	.343	.406	750	761	55	79	(10)	(1)	38	788	336
2	1	1991-	J.Thome	3,634	764	33	4,431	1,033	214	17	233	.284	.413	.545	958	894	17	11	(1)	(3)	(15)	874	290
3	2	1947-56	A.Rosen	3,725	587	27	4,339	1,063	165	20	192	.285	.386	.495	882	861	39	33	(6)	(1)	(18)	837	262
4	3	1937-50	K.Keltner	5,683	514	13	6,210	1,570	308	69	163	.276	.338	.441	778	764	39	33	(4)	0	33	793	240
5	5	1899-15	B.Bradley	5,430	290	73	5,793	1,471	275	84	34	.271	.317	.371	688	754	181	0	0	9	17	780	190
6	6	1908-15	G.Perring	1,764	154	6	1,924	438	75	34	9	.248	.311	.345	655	714	34	0	0	0	18	732	24
7	7	1962-70	M.Alvis	3,629	262	35	3,926	895	142	22	111	.247	.304	.390	693	724	43	46	(12)	9	2	723	13
8	8	1981-92	B.Jacoby	4,520	439	16	4,975	1,220	204	24	120	.270	.337	.405	742	742	16	25	(6)	(5)	(11)	719	9
9	10	1923-27	R.Lutzke	1,876	179	14	2,069	468	87	18	4	.249	.319	.321	641	605	23	14	(2)	0	10	613	(107)
10	9	1955-64	B.Phillips	3,278	182	31	3,491	835	135	8	62	.255	.300	.358	658	650	25	11	1	10	(8)	653	(113)

Cleveland Indians
Outfielders

V	R	Years	Name	AB	BB	HBP	TAB	H	2B	3B	HR	BA	OB	SA	PRO	Wtd PRO	SB	CS	SBF	SPF	FF	R TF	V HC
1	1	1907-28	T.Speaker	10,195	1,381	103	11,679	3,514	792	222	117	.345	.428	.500	928	947	432	129	(7)	10	58	1,008	1,494
2	2	1908-20	J.Jackson	4,981	519	59	5,559	1,772	307	168	54	.356	.423	.517	940	988	202	61	(9)	10	7	996	674
3	3	1898-10	E.Flick	5,597	597	99	6,293	1,752	268	164	48	.313	.389	.445	834	902	330	0	0	9	12	924	544
4	5	1989-	A.Belle	5,853	683	55	6,591	1,726	389	21	381	.295	.374	.564	938	899	88	41	1	0	(13)	886	424
5	6	1947-59	L.Doby	5,348	871	38	6,257	1,515	243	52	253	.283	.387	.490	877	858	47	36	(4)	8	16	877	379
6	10	1955-68	R.Colavito	6,503	951	29	7,483	1,730	283	21	374	.266	.362	.489	851	856	19	27	(5)	(9)	12	853	350
7	9	1929-41	E.Averill	6,353	774	33	7,160	2,019	401	128	238	.318	.395	.534	928	865	70	57	(6)	(0)	(5)	854	346
8	4	1993-	M.Ramirez	3,470	541	37	4,048	1,086	237	11	236	.313	.411	.592	1,003	929	28	24	(5)	0	(2)	922	337
9	7	1936-49	J.Heath	4,937	593	10	5,540	1,447	279	102	194	.293	.370	.509	879	870	56	47	(7)	9	(7)	866	301
10	8	1991-	K.Lofton	4,922	616	20	5,558	1,507	235	65	78	.306	.386	.428	813	774	463	114	41	10	33	858	280
11	13	1908-22	J.Wood	1,952	208	16	2,176	553	118	31	23	.283	.357	.411	768	777	23	3	1	0	(1)	776	107
12	11	1914-21	B.Roth	2,831	335	35	3,201	804	138	73	30	.284	.367	.416	783	824	189	41	0	10	(19)	815	96
13	12	1958-69	L.Wagner	4,426	435	43	4,904	1,202	150	15	211	.272	.343	.455	798	810	54	24	1	(1)	(20)	790	76
14	14	1914-25	E.Smith	3,195	319	16	3,530	881	181	62	70	.276	.344	.437	781	782	54	27	(8)	0	(10)	764	13
15	15	1961-71	C.Hinton	3,968	416	7	4,391	1,048	152	47	113	.264	.335	.412	747	763	130	50	6	10	(19)	761	3
16	16	1930-44	J.Vosmik	5,472	514	21	6,007	1,682	335	92	65	.307	.369	.438	807	757	23	24	(4)	0	5	758	1
17	18	1941-53	H.Edwards	2,191	208	2	2,401	613	116	41	51	.280	.343	.440	783	786	9	22	(14)	(10)	(9)	753	(5)
18	17	1946-56	D.Mitchell	3,984	346	5	4,335	1,244	169	61	41	.312	.368	.416	784	766	45	47	(11)	6	(6)	755	(7)
19	21	1895-04	B.Lush	1,722	291	8	2,021	429	49	35	8	.249	.360	.332	692	745	84	0	0	7	(6)	746	(13)
20	19	1930-42	B.Campbell	4,762	548	27	5,337	1,382	295	87	106	.290	.367	.455	822	776	53	50	(8)	0	(16)	752	(15)
21	22	1901-07	H.Bay	2,640	195	18	2,853	722	65	42	5	.273	.328	.336	663	731	169	0	0	10	5	746	(18)
22	20	1981-96	M.Hall	4,237	267	16	4,520	1,171	229	25	134	.276	.322	.437	759	761	31	22	(3)	2	(14)	747	(23)
23	24	1990-	M.Whiten	3,104	378	17	3,499	804	129	20	105	.259	.343	.415	758	737	78	40	(0)	0	1	738	(34)
24	26	1970-85	J.Lowenstein	3,476	446	9	3,931	881	137	18	116	.253	.340	.403	743	757	128	78	(7)	7	(25)	732	(37)
25	23	1963-80	V.Davalillo	4,017	212	10	4,239	1,122	160	37	36	.279	.317	.364	682	707	125	58	2	9	20	738	(39)
26	27	1929-34	D.Porter	2,515	268	7	2,790	774	159	37	11	.308	.376	.414	790	743	23	27	(11)	0	(10)	722	(49)
27	31	1943-49	P.Seerey	1,815	259	2	2,076	406	73	5	86	.224	.321	.412	733	747	3	8	(6)	(10)	(23)	709	(51)
28	33	1974-85	M.Dilone	2,000	142	6	2,148	530	67	25	6	.265	.316	.333	648	658	267	78	48	10	(12)	704	(59)
29	37	1972-80	C.Spikes	2,039	154	22	2,215	502	72	12	65	.246	.306	.389	695	719	27	25	(10)	(1)	(17)	692	(69)
30	25	1956-70	T.Francona	5,121	544	32	5,697	1,395	224	34	125	.272	.346	.403	749	750	46	21	1	0	(16)	735	(71)
31	36	1938-45	O.Hockett	2,165	159	10	2,334	598	112	21	13	.276	.329	.365	694	725	43	48	(21)	0	(10)	693	(75)
32	29	1986-94	C.Snyder	3,656	226	13	3,895	902	178	13	149	.247	.293	.425	718	713	28	19	(2)	0	4	715	(80)
33	35	1906-14	J.Birmingham	2,633	129	24	2,786	667	89	27	7	.253	.294	.316	610	674	108	1	(1)	10	16	699	(81)
34	34	1936-50	R.Weatherly	2,781	180	7	2,968	794	152	44	43	.286	.331	.418	749	719	42	49	(18)	6	(5)	702	(83)
35	39	1915-25	J.Evans	2,043	212	3	2,258	529	71	31	3	.259	.329	.328	658	659	67	16	4	3	(8)	658	(94)
36	28	1908-22	J.Graney	4,705	712	40	5,457	1,178	219	79	18	.250	.354	.342	696	741	148	36	(6)	0	(13)	721	(100)
37	38	1920-30	H.Summa	3,001	166	36	3,203	905	166	34	18	.302	.346	.398	743	702	44	35	(8)	0	(21)	674	(134)
38	32	1975-87	R.Manning	5,248	471	9	5,728	1,349	189	43	56	.257	.319	.341	661	669	168	78	3	10	26	709	(138)
39	30	1915-32	C.Jamieson	6,560	748	34	7,342	1,990	322	80	18	.303	.378	.385	763	730	131	110	(15)	2	(3)	714	(149)

Cleveland Indians
Starting Pitchers

V	R	Years	Name	G	GS	IP	W	L	SV	SO	BB	ERA	RA/9	R Wtd RA/9	V Runs /162
1	2	1936-56	B.Feller	570	484	3,827	266	162	21	2,581	1,764	3.25	3.66	3.53	459.3
2	3	1912-28	S.Coveleski	450	385	3,082	215	142	21	981	802	2.89	3.60	3.63	345.0
3	1	1902-10	A.Joss	286	260	2,327	160	97	5	920	364	1.89	2.82	3.32	343.9
4	5	1946-58	B.Lemon	460	350	2,850	207	128	22	1,277	1,251	3.23	3.74	3.77	263.5
5	4	1948-61	M.Garcia	428	281	2,175	142	97	23	1,117	719	3.27	3.67	3.72	211.7
6	15	1939-63	E.Wynn	691	612	4,564	300	244	15	2,334	1,775	3.54	4.02	4.17	207.0
7	13	1928-47	M.Harder	582	433	3,426	223	186	23	1,161	1,118	3.80	4.50	4.12	173.2
8	6	1932-44	J.Allen	352	241	1,950	142	75	18	1,070	738	3.75	4.26	3.86	158.4
9	12	1927-41	W.Ferrell	374	323	2,623	193	128	13	985	1,040	4.04	4.74	4.08	146.7
10	11	1941-57	S.Gromek	447	225	2,065	123	108	23	904	630	3.41	3.89	4.06	119.7
11	10	1912-23	J.Bagby	316	208	1,822	127	88	29	450	458	3.11	3.80	4.04	115.2
12	14	1961-75	S.McDowell	425	346	2,492	141	134	14	2,453	1,312	3.17	3.61	4.15	112.4
13	19	1901-14	E.Moore	388	326	2,776	162	154	7	1,403	1,108	2.78	3.99	4.27	96.6
14	18	1983-99	T.Candiotti	451	410	2,725	151	164	0	1,735	883	3.73	4.29	4.25	95.4
15	9	1911-25	V.Gregg	239	161	1,393	92	63	12	720	552	2.70	3.56	4.00	93.7
16	21	1919-36	G.Uhle	513	368	3,120	200	166	25	1,135	966	3.99	4.72	4.31	89.7
17	17	1986-	G.Swindell	566	269	2,147	121	114	5	1,477	488	3.80	4.21	4.22	83.4
18	7	1955-62	H.Score	150	127	858	55	46	3	837	573	3.36	3.82	3.88	67.6
19	20	1990-	C.Nagy	279	277	1,823	123	93	0	1,184	550	4.32	4.69	4.28	58.3
20	16	1931-40	O.Hildebrand	258	182	1,431	83	78	13	527	623	4.35	4.91	4.22	56.9
21	8	1997-	B.Colon	112	110	691	51	29	3	597	298	4.09	4.43	3.90	50.1
22	22	1899-07	B.Bernhard	231	200	1,792	116	82	3	545	365	3.04	4.31	4.37	41.7
23	23	1928-42	C.Brown	434	130	1,486	89	93	64	410	368	4.26	5.03	4.37	32.1
24	26	1964-75	S.Siebert	399	307	2,152	140	114	16	1,512	692	3.21	3.79	4.43	30.8
25	27	1902-09	B.Rhoads	218	185	1,692	97	82	2	522	494	2.61	3.73	4.45	21.2
26	24	1924-33	J.Miller	200	139	1,070	60	58	3	305	340	4.09	4.90	4.40	20.0
27	29	1958-71	M.Grant	571	293	2,442	145	119	53	1,267	849	3.63	4.07	4.50	16.0
28	31	1893-06	R.Donahue	367	340	2,966	164	175	3	787	689	3.61	4.96	4.51	15.8
29	30	1926-44	W.Hudlin	491	328	2,613	158	156	31	677	846	4.41	5.13	4.51	15.2
30	25	1911-15	G.Krapp	118	92	764	40	47	1	353	418	3.23	4.03	4.42	11.9
31	33	1903-17	C.Falkenberg	330	266	2,275	130	123	8	1,164	690	2.68	3.80	4.52	9.0
32	28	1947-53	G.Bearden	193	84	788	45	38	1	259	435	3.96	4.54	4.46	8.7
33	32	1914-24	G.Morton	317	185	1,630	98	88	6	830	583	3.13	4.13	4.52	8.2
34	34	1934-45	A.Smith	356	201	1,662	99	101	17	587	587	3.72	4.48	4.60	(7.8)
35	35	1938-47	J.Bagby	303	198	1,666	97	96	9	431	608	3.96	4.58	4.61	(9.9)
36	36	1909-19	W.Mitchell	276	190	1,632	84	92	4	921	605	2.88	4.00	4.62	(11.9)
37	41	1914-21	F.Coumbe	193	70	761	38	38	13	212	217	2.80	4.00	4.74	(17.3)
38	37	1958-69	G.Bell	519	233	2,015	121	117	51	1,378	842	3.68	4.16	4.63	(17.7)
39	42	1910-14	F.Blanding	144	86	814	45	46	4	278	277	3.13	4.36	4.75	(18.2)
40	39	1936-46	A.Milnar	188	127	996	57	58	7	350	495	4.22	4.98	4.71	(18.2)
41	40	1973-81	W.Garland	190	121	1,040	55	66	6	450	328	3.89	4.46	4.72	(19.6)
42	38	1991-	M.Clark	219	197	1,246	74	71	0	728	367	4.61	4.96	4.71	(21.7)
43	44	1957-67	B.Latman	344	134	1,219	59	68	16	829	489	3.91	4.47	4.78	(30.3)
44	43	1902-15	O.Hess	198	165	1,418	70	90	5	580	448	2.98	4.20	4.76	(33.6)
45	47	1976-87	L.Barker	248	194	1,324	74	76	5	975	513	4.34	4.73	4.87	(48.8)
46	46	1973-85	R.Waits	317	190	1,427	79	92	8	659	568	4.25	4.67	4.87	(51.9)
47	45	1944-64	C.McLish	352	209	1,609	92	92	6	713	552	4.01	4.61	4.85	(54.2)
48	48	1922-34	J.Shaute	360	208	1,818	99	109	18	512	534	4.15	5.16	4.88	(67.8)
49	49	1982-93	N.Heaton	382	202	1,507	80	96	10	699	524	4.37	4.80	4.97	(69.6)
50	50	1965-77	S.Hargan	354	215	1,632	87	107	4	891	614	3.92	4.47	5.14	(105.8)

**Cleveland Indians
Relief Pitchers**

V	R	Years	Name	G	GS	IP	W	L	SV	SO	BB	ERA	RA/9	R Wtd RA/9	V Runs /162
1	1	1982-	D.Jones	846	4	1,128	69	79	303	909	247	3.30	3.71	3.56	127.8
2	4	1986-99	E.Plunk	714	41	1,151	72	58	35	1,081	647	3.82	4.20	4.00	73.5
3	3	1974-86	J.Kern	416	14	793	53	57	88	651	444	3.32	3.77	3.95	54.5
4	2	1994-	P.Shuey	275	0	313	26	18	19	341	166	3.88	4.20	3.74	29.0
5	5	1935-42	H.Eisenstat	165	33	479	25	27	14	157	114	3.84	4.54	4.10	25.6
6	10	1988-	D.Cook	566	71	942	62	44	9	688	366	3.90	4.33	4.33	23.8
7	6	1943-50	E.Klieman	222	32	542	26	28	33	130	239	3.49	3.85	4.18	23.7
8	9	1975-84	S.Monge	435	17	764	49	40	56	471	356	3.53	4.03	4.32	20.7
9	7	1954-59	R.Narleski	266	52	702	43	33	58	454	335	3.60	4.08	4.32	19.8
10	11	1930-45	J.Heving	430	40	1,039	76	48	63	429	380	3.90	4.84	4.43	15.4
11	12	1987-	J.Mesa	556	95	1,097	58	75	138	728	454	4.42	4.75	4.45	13.6
12	8	1973-80	T.Buskey	258	0	479	21	27	34	212	167	3.66	4.09	4.32	12.6
13	13	1969-73	R.Lamb	154	31	424	20	23	4	258	174	3.54	3.88	4.47	4.0
14	14	1955-62	D.Ferrarese	183	50	507	19	36	5	350	295	4.00	4.42	4.50	3.6
15	16	1993-	A.Lopez	219	55	557	33	33	4	368	233	4.73	5.28	4.65	(5.8)
16	15	1973-83	D.Hood	297	72	848	34	35	6	374	364	3.79	4.37	4.64	(7.4)
17	17	1959-68	B.Locke	165	23	417	16	15	10	194	165	4.02	4.53	4.89	(16.0)
18	20	1961-67	B.Allen	204	0	274	7	12	19	199	132	4.11	4.99	5.46	(27.6)
19	19	1968-74	M.Paul	228	77	628	27	48	8	452	246	3.91	4.29	5.02	(32.9)
20	21	1974-87	J.Easterly	321	36	611	23	33	14	350	319	4.62	5.30	5.47	(65.1)
21	18	1974-85	D.Spillner	556	123	1,493	75	89	50	878	605	4.21	4.74	4.94	(65.6)
22	22	1986-98	S.Bailes	343	59	680	39	44	13	351	256	4.95	5.60	5.57	(76.8)

DETROIT TIGERS (1901–2000)

Four stars define Detroit's four successful periods. The first star, Ty Cobb, was 20 in 1907 when he sprinted the Tigers to the first of three consecutive pennants. Sam Crawford, Harry Heilmann, and Donie Bush helped the Tigers earn 15 winning seasons in Cobb's final 20 years with Detroit.

Hank Greenberg was 23 in 1934 when he powered the Tigers to the first of 11 winning seasons and four pennants over 13 years. His talented teammates included Charlie Gehringer, Hal Newhouser, Rudy York, and Mickey Cochrane.

Al Kaline was a 20-year-old batting champ in 1955 when he led his team to the first of 14 winning seasons in a 19-year period. Bill Freehan, Norm Cash, Denny McLain and John Hiller helped Kaline's 1968 Tigers win the pennant.

Alan Trammell was 20 in 1978 when he and 21-year-old Lou Whitaker formed a long-lasting double play tandem, beginning a streak of 11 consecutive winning seasons in which Trammell produced 471 Hits Contribution, while Whitaker added 346 Hits Contribution. The performances of Lance Parrish, Kirk Gibson, Willie Hernandez, and Jack Morris were also critical to the team's 1984 pennant.

Profiled Tigers Players

Ty Cobb

Cobb's strength was his ability to get on base, and then use his speed and aggression to intimidate opponents. Cobb hit a major league record .366 over 24 seasons, while drawing 1,249 walks, for a .433 on-base percentage. He also stole 892 bases, while scoring 2,246 runs.

Cobb's 4,189 hits and 295 triples rank second in history, while his 724 doubles rank fourth. He hit 117 home runs, and he could have hit many more, but he refused to emulate rival Babe Ruth's weapon of choice. Adjusted for a career 4 percent hitter's deflation, Cobb batted .382 with a .450 on-base percentage, and with 127 home runs, for a 983 Wtd. Production. His 1,008 Total Factor ranks fifth in league rate of success, while his 1,623 Hits Contribution ranks second among league outfielders and third among all major leaguers, behind only Babe Ruth and Honus Wagner.

Cobb's superhuman offensive statistics in his earlier years were hidden by the hitter's deflation of the Dead Ball Era, while his offensive decline after 1919 was hidden by the hitter's inflation of the 1920s:

Years	TAB	HR	BA	Adj. BA	Wtd. PRO	TF	HC
1905–19	8,104	67	.372	.408	1,041	1,068	1,314
1920–28	4,673	50	.357	.336	880	902	309

Cobb's adjusted .408 batting average, adjusted 815 stolen bases, 1,068 Total Factor and 1,314 Hits Contribution over his first 15 seasons were one of the most dominating performances in history. This period included 11 seasons with an adjusted batting average of over .400. Cobb's adjusted .336 batting average, adjusted 134 stolen bases, 902 Total Factor and 309 Hits Contribution over his last nine years were far more subdued.

Sam Crawford

Crawford owns the career record for most triples with 309. He hit 302 of those three baggers over a 17-year period from 1900 to 1916, averaging 18 triples per year.

Since the triple has become a much more infrequent event in modern baseball, Crawford's record is likely to stand for a long time.

In his career, Crawford hit .309 with those 309 triples and 97 home runs, for an 814 Production, while stealing 366 bases. Adjusted for a career 10 percent hitter's deflation — one of the worst deflation-challenged career results in history — he hit .341 with 360 triples and 113 home runs, for an 896 Wtd. Production. His 911 Total Factor ranks Crawford 13th in league rate of success among outfielders, while his 812 Hits Contribution ranks him 11th in league volume of success.

Bill Freehan

Freehan was the premier defensive catcher of the 1960s, earning 36 Fielding Factor points over his 15-year career. Freehan could also hit, drilling 200 home runs while batting .262 in his career. Adjusted for a 4 percent career hitter's deflation, Freehan batted .273 with 208 home runs, for a 787 Wtd. Production. His 823 Total Factor ranks fifth among league catchers in rate of success, while his 455 Hits Contribution ranks sixth in volume of success.

Hank Greenberg

Greenberg was a big man, at 6'4" and 210 pounds, who hit for tremendous power while playing a capable first base. Although he hit 331 home runs in a 13-year career interrupted by World War II, his best power numbers are measured in terms of extra-base hits. Greenberg slammed 781 extra-base hits in just 6,061 total at bats, or one every 7.8 times up — putting him at the same level as Babe Ruth. Greenberg produced four seasons with 96 or more extra base hits, making him an extremely dangerous hitter at his peak. He once hit 58 home runs in a season, but he "only" had 85 extra base hits that year.

Greenberg's career can be summed up in terms of what could have been. What if his career got started before 1933, when he was already 22? What if he didn't lose the 1936 season to a broken wrist, and nearly 4½ years to World War II? What if he hadn't retired in 1947 at the age of 36, with just nine full seasons in the majors? The probable answer is that Greenberg would be competing with Lou Gehrig for the honor of being called the best first baseman of all time.

In just 6,061 total at bats, Greenberg hit .313 with 331 home runs, for a 1,017 Production. Adjusted for a 5 percent career hitter's inflation, he hit .298 with 335 home runs, for a 966 Wtd. Production. His 971 Total Factor ranks third in league rate of success for first basemen, while his 616 Hits Contribution ranks fourth in league volume of success.

Charlie Gehringer

Gehringer was only a fair home run hitter; he wasn't the best fielder at his position; and, although he won the 1937 MVP, he didn't have any really spectacular seasons. What Gehringer accomplished were 14 seasons in which he assumed key supporting roles for a team that won three pennants. He hit .320 with 184 home runs and 181 stolen bases in his career. Adjusted for a 7 percent hitter's inflation, Gehringer hit .300 with 183 home runs, for an 827 Wtd. Production. His 862 Total Factor ranks fourth in league rate of success for second basemen, while his impressive 894 Hits Contribution ranks third in league volume of success — behind Lajoie and Collins.

Alan Trammell

Trammell played all-out baseball with the Tigers for 20 seasons, while teaming with talented Lou Whitaker to form the major leagues' longest lasting double play tandem. Trammell hit .285 with 185 home runs, while stealing 236 bases. Adjusted for a 1 percent career hitter's inflation, he hit .283 with 188 home runs, for a 762 Wtd. Production. His 790 Total Factor ranks tenth in league rate of success for shortstops, while his 582 Hits Contribution ranks fourth in league volume of success, thanks to 9,175 career total at bats.

Al Kaline

Kaline was the Tigers' best player from 1955 to 1967. He hit for average and power, and he won ten Gold Gloves in 11 years from the inception of the award in 1957 to 1967. After 1967, Kaline continued to hit well, but he had to fight for playing time in an outfield that included Willie Horton, Jim Northrup, and Mickey Stanley. This problem was not resolved until Kaline's final season in 1974, when he moved to DH.

Over his 22-year career, Kaline hit .297 with 399 home runs, while stealing 137 bases. Adjusted for a 1 percent career hitter's deflation, he hit .301, and he topped 400 home runs with a 410 total. His 912 Total Factor ranks 12th in league rate of success for outfielders, while his 868 Hits Contribution ranks ninth in league volume of success.

Hal Newhouser

Newhouser was only 19 when he earned a spot in Detroit's starting rotation with the 1940 pennant-winning

Tigers. Newhouser then posted three losing seasons, before suddenly blossoming in 1944 with a 29–9 record and a 2.22 ERA. He was the league's best pitcher in both wins and ERA for the 1945 pennant-winning Tigers, and he again topped the league in both wins and ERA in 1946. Newhouser's performance slipped a notch for a few years, and then he faded badly beginning in 1951, at the age of 30.

In his six peak seasons from 1944 to 1949, Newhouser was untouchable. In the other 11 years, Hal was a below average pitcher:

Years	IP	W–L	SO	ERA	Wtd. RA/9	Runs/162
1944–49	1,768	136–67	1,137	2.52	3.09	303
All others	1,225	71–83	659	3.84	4.57	(2)

In his career, Newhouser was 207–150 with a 3.06 ERA, a 3.70 Wtd. RA/9, and he saved 301 runs from scoring. Although his limited period of success prevented him from being considered one of the very best pitchers ever, at least Newhouser proved that his pitching success was not due to his facing weak-hitting wartime opponents. And few pitchers can lay claim to winning two MVP awards.

John Hiller

Hiller was one of the best relief pitchers of the 1970s. He broke in with the Tigers in 1965, but played his first significant role for the 1968 World Series champions, going 9–6 with a 2.39 ERA in 39 games, including 12 starts. Hiller was a fairly average pitcher in 1969 and 1970, and he then lost 1½ years of playing time due to an illness. By the time he was able to pitch full time again, it was 1973, and he was 30 years old. Hiller made the most of his remaining time, with a standout season in 1973, and four strong seasons in the next five years. Over his career, Hiller was 87–76 with 125 saves and a 2.83 ERA. His 3.49 Wtd. RA/9 ranks 16th among league relievers in rate of success, while his 147 Runs/162 ranks sixth in league volume of success.

Detroit Tigers

Hitters Volume of Success

Pos	Years	Name	AB	BB	HBP	TAB	H	2B	3B	HR	BA	OB	SA	PRO	Wtd PRO	SB	CS	SBF	SPF	FF	R TF	V HC
C	1961-76	B.Freehan	6,073	626	114	6,813	1,591	241	35	200	.262	.342	.412	754	787	24	21	(3)	2	36	823	455
1B	1930-47	H.Greenberg	5,193	852	16	6,061	1,628	379	71	331	.313	.412	.605	1,017	966	58	26	1	0	4	971	616
2B	1924-42	C.Gehringer	8,860	1,186	51	10,097	2,839	574	146	184	.320	.404	.480	884	827	181	89	0	5	30	862	894
SS	1977-96	A.Trammell	8,288	850	37	9,175	2,365	412	55	185	.285	.354	.415	770	762	236	109	2	8	17	790	582
3B	1943-57	G.Kell	6,702	621	36	7,359	2,054	385	50	78	.306	.368	.414	782	774	51	36	(3)	0	15	786	261
OF	1905-28	T.Cobb	11,434	1,249	94	12,777	4,189	724	295	117	.366	.433	.512	945	983	892	178	(2)	10	17	1,008	1,623
OF	1953-74	A.Kaline	10,116	1,277	55	11,448	3,007	498	75	399	.297	.379	.480	859	868	137	65	1	6	37	912	868
OF	1899-17	S.Crawford	9,570	760	23	10,353	2,961	458	309	97	.309	.362	.452	814	896	366	30	(1)	5	11	911	812
Starters		Averages	8,280	928	53	9,260	2,579	459	130	199	.312	.384	.470	855	864	243	69	(1)	5	21	889	764
C	1977-95	L.Parrish	7,067	612	37	7,716	1,782	305	27	324	.252	.315	.440	756	755	28	37	(6)	(10)	17	757	300
1B	1958-74	N.Cash	6,705	1,043	90	7,838	1,820	241	41	377	.271	.377	.488	865	886	43	30	(2)	(5)	15	893	465
2B	1977-95	L.Whitaker	8,570	1,197	20	9,787	2,369	420	65	244	.276	.366	.426	792	789	143	75	(1)	6	20	815	628
SS	1908-23	D.Bush	7,210	1,158	29	8,397	1,804	186	74	9	.250	.356	.300	656	696	404	75	(6)	9	11	710	203
3B	1990-	T.Fryman	5,750	532	36	6,318	1,602	316	37	209	.279	.343	.455	799	762	71	36	(0)	0	14	776	225
OF	1914-32	H.Heilmann	7,787	856	40	8,683	2,660	542	151	183	.342	.410	.520	930	897	113	64	(6)	(10)	(18)	863	459
OF	1975-90	C.Lemon	6,868	749	151	7,768	1,875	396	61	215	.273	.357	.442	800	805	58	76	(12)	6	31	831	279
OF	1912-25	B.Veach	6,656	571	59	7,286	2,063	393	147	64	.310	.370	.442	812	827	195	84	(7)	8	2	829	269
Reserves		Averages	7,077	840	58	7,974	1,997	350	75	203	.282	.363	.439	802	803	132	60	(5)	0	11	810	353
Totals		Weighted Ave.	7,879	898	55	8,832	2,385	423	111	200	.303	.378	.461	839	844	206	66	(2)	3	18	863	627

Pitchers Volume of Success

Pos	Years	Name	G	GS	IP	W	L	SV	SO	BB	ERA	RA/9	Wtd RA/9	R V Runs /162
SP	1939-55	H.Newhouser	488	374	2,993	207	150	26	1,796	1,249	3.06	3.60	3.70	301
SP	1930-46	T.Bridges	424	362	2,826	194	138	10	1,674	1,192	3.57	4.21	3.77	261
SP	1955-71	J.Bunning	591	519	3,760	224	184	16	2,855	1,000	3.27	3.66	3.99	240
SP	1941-58	V.Trucks	517	328	2,682	177	135	30	1,534	1,088	3.39	3.77	3.93	197
SP	1939-57	D.Trout	521	322	2,726	170	161	35	1,256	1,046	3.23	3.85	3.97	186
Starters		Averages	508	381	2,998	194	154	23	1,823	1,115	3.30	3.80	3.88	237
RP	1965-80	J.Hiller	545	43	1,242	87	76	125	1,036	535	2.83	3.17	3.49	147
RP	1987-96	M.Henneman	561	0	733	57	42	193	533	271	3.21	3.70	3.65	76
RP	1977-89	W.Hernandez	744	11	1,045	70	63	147	788	349	3.38	3.71	3.94	72
RP	1974-87	A.Lopez	459	9	910	62	36	93	635	367	3.56	3.88	4.02	57
Relievers		Averages	577	16	982	69	54	140	748	381	3.22	3.58	3.76	88
Totals		Averages	1,085	397	3,980	263	208	163	2,571	1,496	3.28	3.75	3.85	325

Detroit Tigers   **Hitters Rate of Success**

Pos	Years	Name	AB	BB	HBP	TAB	H	2B	3B	HR	BA	OB	SA	PRO	Wtd PRO	SB	CS	SBF	SPF	FF	R TF	V HC
C	1961-76	B.Freehan	6,073	626	114	6,813	1,591	241	35	200	.262	.342	.412	754	787	24	21	(3)	2	36	823	455
1B	1930-47	H.Greenberg	5,193	852	16	6,061	1,628	379	71	331	.313	.412	.605	1,017	966	58	26	1	0	4	971	616
2B	1924-42	C.Gehringer	8,860	1,186	51	10,097	2,839	574	146	184	.320	.404	.480	884	827	181	89	0	5	30	862	894
SS	1977-96	A.Trammell	8,288	850	37	9,175	2,365	412	55	185	.285	.354	.415	770	762	236	109	2	8	17	790	582
3B	1943-57	G.Kell	6,702	621	36	7,359	2,054	385	50	78	.306	.368	.414	782	774	51	36	(3)	0	15	786	261
OF	1905-28	T.Cobb	11,434	1,249	94	12,777	4,189	724	295	117	.366	.433	.512	945	983	892	178	(2)	10	17	1,008	1,623
OF	1953-74	A.Kaline	10,116	1,277	55	11,448	3,007	498	75	399	.297	.379	.480	859	868	137	65	1	6	37	912	868
OF	1899-17	S.Crawford	9,570	760	23	10,353	2,961	458	309	97	.309	.362	.452	814	896	366	30	(1)	5	11	911	812
Starters		Averages	8,280	928	53	9,260	2,579	459	130	199	.312	.384	.470	855	864	243	69	(1)	5	21	889	764
C	1984-97	M.Tettleton	4,698	949	30	5,677	1,132	210	16	245	.241	.372	.449	821	807	23	29	(6)	(6)	(28)	767	176
1B	1958-74	N.Cash	6,705	1,043	90	7,838	1,820	241	41	377	.271	.377	.488	865	886	43	30	(2)	(5)	15	893	465
2B	1977-95	L.Whitaker	8,570	1,197	20	9,787	2,369	420	65	244	.276	.366	.426	792	789	143	75	(1)	6	20	815	628
SS	1922-27	T.Rigney	2,326	377	5	2,708	669	113	39	13	.288	.388	.387	775	732	44	36	(10)	10	(10)	722	81
3B	1990-	T.Fryman	5,750	532	36	6,318	1,602	316	37	209	.279	.343	.455	799	762	71	36	(0)	0	14	776	225
OF	1914-32	H.Heilmann	7,787	856	40	8,683	2,660	542	151	183	.342	.410	.520	930	897	113	64	(6)	(10)	(18)	863	459
OF	1938-47	R.Cullenbine	3,879	853	11	4,743	1,072	209	32	110	.276	.408	.432	840	852	26	20	(3)	0	4	853	225
OF	1979-95	K.Gibson	5798	718	61	6,577	1,553	260	54	255	.268	.355	.463	818	816	284	78	18	8	(11)	831	244
Reserves		Averages	5,689	816	37	6,541	1,610	289	54	205	.283	.376	.461	837	826	93	46	(1)	0	(2)	824	313
Totals		Weighted Ave.	7,416	890	48	8,354	2,256	402	104	201	.304	.382	.468	850	852	193	62	(1)	3	13	867	613

Pitchers Rate of Success

Pos	Years	Name	G	GS	IP	W	L	SV	SO	BB	ERA	RA/9	R Wtd RA/9	V Runs /162
SP	1939-55	H.Newhouser	488	374	2,993	207	150	26	1,796	1,249	3.06	3.60	3.70	301
SP	1930-46	T.Bridges	424	362	2,826	194	138	10	1,674	1,192	3.57	4.21	3.77	261
SP	1996-	J.Thompson	101	101	647	36	43	0	427	235	3.98	4.39	3.90	47
SP	1941-58	V.Trucks	517	328	2,682	177	135	30	1,534	1,088	3.39	3.77	3.93	197
SP	1939-57	D.Trout	521	322	2,726	170	161	35	1,256	1,046	3.23	3.85	3.97	186
Starters		Averages	410	297	2,375	157	125	20	1,337	962	3.34	3.88	3.84	199
RP	1965-80	J.Hiller	545	43	1,242	87	76	125	1,036	535	2.83	3.17	3.49	147
RP	1987-96	M.Henneman	561	0	733	57	42	193	533	271	3.21	3.70	3.65	76
RP	1960-66	T.Fox	248	0	397	29	19	59	185	124	2.99	3.39	3.74	36
RP	1977-89	W.Hernandez	744	11	1,045	70	63	147	788	349	3.38	3.71	3.94	72
Relievers		Averages	525	14	854	61	50	131	636	320	3.10	3.48	3.69	83
Totals		Averages	935	311	3,229	218	175	151	1,973	1,282	3.28	3.78	3.80	281

Detroit Tigers
Catchers

V	R	Years	Name	AB	BB	HBP	TAB	H	2B	3B	HR	BA	OB	SA	PRO	Wtd PRO	SB	CS	SBF	SPF	FF	R TF	V HC
1	1	1961-76	B.Freehan	6,073	626	114	6,813	1,591	241	35	200	.262	.342	.412	754	787	24	21	(3)	2	36	823	455
2	3	1977-95	L.Parrish	7,067	612	37	7,716	1,782	305	27	324	.252	.315	.440	756	755	28	37	(6)	(10)	17	757	300
3	2	1984-97	M.Tettleton	4,698	949	30	5,677	1,132	210	16	245	.241	.372	.449	821	807	23	29	(6)	(6)	(28)	767	176
4	6	1913-27	J.Bassler	2,319	437	10	2,766	704	99	16	1	.304	.416	.361	777	732	13	8	(1)	(10)	15	736	81
5	5	1943-51	A.Robinson	1,839	337	3	2,179	478	74	11	61	.260	.375	.412	787	775	0	6	(5)	(10)	(12)	748	76
6	8	1993-	B.Ausmus	3,008	317	34	3,359	791	137	20	48	.263	.340	.370	710	664	74	37	1	7	26	697	33
7	7	1951-60	R.Wilson	1,765	215	8	1,988	455	84	8	24	.258	.341	.355	696	686	25	12	0	0	22	709	31
8	4	1974-85	J.Wockenfuss	2,072	277	7	2,356	543	73	11	86	.262	.351	.432	783	789	5	11	(7)	(10)	(24)	748	19
9	9	1936-52	B.Tebbetts	3,704	389	12	4,105	1,000	169	22	38	.270	.341	.358	700	676	29	23	(4)	(1)	9	680	5
10	10	1957-65	D.Brown	1,866	119	11	1,996	455	62	3	62	.244	.293	.380	673	670	7	6	(2)	(10)	21	679	2
11	11	1988-	C.Kreuter	2,201	307	18	2,526	525	106	7	46	.239	.337	.356	692	658	4	7	(4)	(7)	7	655	(29)
12	12	1950-61	F.House	1,994	151	11	2,156	494	64	11	47	.248	.304	.362	666	657	6	7	(4)	(10)	1	644	(36)
13	13	1926-45	R.Hayworth	2,062	198	6	2,266	546	92	16	5	.265	.331	.332	663	622	2	6	(4)	(4)	14	628	(57)
14	15	1940-53	B.Swift	2,750	324	3	3,077	635	86	3	14	.231	.313	.280	592	590	10	6	(1)	(2)	0	588	(137)
15	14	1906-25	O.Stanage	3,503	219	25	3,747	819	123	34	8	.234	.284	.295	579	619	30	2	1	(10)	(19)	591	(164)

Detroit Tigers
First basemen

V	R	Years	Name	AB	BB	HBP	TAB	H	2B	3B	HR	BA	OB	SA	PRO	Wtd PRO	SB	CS	SBF	SPF	FF	R TF	V HC
1	1	1930-47	H.Greenberg	5,193	852	16	6,061	1,628	379	71	331	.313	.412	.605	1,017	966	58	26	1	0	4	971	616
2	2	1958-74	N.Cash	6,705	1,043	90	7,838	1,820	241	41	377	.271	.377	.488	865	886	43	30	(2)	(5)	15	893	465
3	3	1934-48	R.York	5,891	792	12	6,695	1,621	291	52	277	.275	.362	.483	845	838	38	26	(2)	(3)	(21)	812	205
4	4	1929-33	D.Alexander	2,450	248	6	2,704	811	164	30	61	.331	.394	.497	891	836	20	28	(13)	(10)	(17)	796	35
5	6	1985-98	C.Fielder	5,157	693	43	5,893	1,313	200	7	319	.255	.348	.482	829	805	2	6	(2)	(10)	(17)	777	22
6	5	1904-09	C.Rossman	1,848	90	4	1,942	523	80	26	3	.283	.318	.359	677	784	49	0	0	0	(3)	781	12
7	7	1995-	T.Clark	2,403	281	12	2,696	660	127	4	140	.275	.353	.506	859	799	6	8	(3)	(10)	(20)	766	(5)
8	8	1921-33	L.Blue	5,904	1,092	43	7,039	1,696	319	109	44	.287	.402	.401	803	754	151	85	(3)	10	0	761	(30)
9	9	1975-92	D.Bergman	2,679	380	7	3,066	690	100	16	54	.258	.351	.367	719	726	19	14	(2)	(5)	9	728	(63)
10	11	1898-14	C.Carr	1,950	71	5	2,026	492	68	32	6	.252	.280	.329	610	670	49	0	0	0	2	672	(103)
11	10	1949-61	W.Dropo	4,124	328	24	4,476	1,113	168	22	152	.270	.327	.432	759	741	5	6	(1)	(10)	(14)	716	(121)

Detroit Tigers
Second basemen

V	R	Years	Name	AB	BB	HBP	TAB	H	2B	3B	HR	BA	OB	SA	PRO	Wtd PRO	SB	CS	SBF	SPF	FF	R TF	V HC
1	1	1924-42	C.Gehringer	8,860	1,186	51	10,097	2,839	574	146	184	.320	.404	.480	884	827	181	89	0	5	30	862	894
2	2	1977-95	L.Whitaker	8,570	1,197	20	9,787	2,369	420	65	244	.276	.366	.426	792	789	143	75	(1)	6	20	815	628
3	4	1960-75	D.McAuliffe	6,185	882	33	7,100	1,530	231	71	197	.247	.344	.403	748	773	63	59	(7)	8	(20)	754	261
4	6	1941-53	J.Priddy	4,720	624	13	5,357	1,252	232	46	61	.265	.353	.373	725	718	44	44	(8)	(1)	25	734	128
5	3	1901-15	J.Delahanty	4,091	378	92	4,561	1,159	191	59	19	.283	.357	.373	730	806	151	0	0	0	(40)	766	114
6	5	1907-16	B.Louden	1,942	254	30	2,226	507	61	22	12	.261	.355	.334	689	732	112	0	0	0	11	744	70
7	7	1901-18	G.Schaefer	3,784	333	13	4,130	972	117	48	9	.257	.319	.320	639	714	201	1	0	10	2	727	55
8	8	1992-	D.Easley	3,300	320	79	3,699	852	182	13	100	.258	.338	.412	750	698	94	44	1	8	10	716	49
9	9	1954-66	F.Bolling	5,562	462	30	6,054	1,415	221	40	106	.254	.315	.366	681	679	40	38	(6)	1	(3)	672	(39)
10	11	1961-67	J.Wood	1,877	159	14	2,050	469	53	26	35	.250	.313	.362	675	674	79	23	15	10	(53)	646	(43)
11	10	1936-48	E.Mayo	3,013	257	13	3,283	759	119	16	26	.252	.313	.328	641	657	29	38	(14)	0	8	652	(69)
12	12	1913-22	R.Young	3,643	495	15	4,153	898	108	30	4	.247	.339	.296	635	647	92	59	(13)	10	(11)	633	(113)
13	13	1966-78	G.Sutherland	3,104	207	10	3,321	754	109	10	24	.243	.292	.308	600	619	11	24	(11)	0	(16)	592	(145)

Detroit Tigers
Shortstops

V	R	Years	Name	AB	BB	HBP	TAB	H	2B	3B	HR	BA	OB	SA	PRO	Wtd PRO	SB	CS	SBF	SPF	FF	R TF	V HC
1	1	1977-96	A.Trammell	8,288	850	37	9,175	2,365	412	55	185	.285	.354	.415	770	762	236	109	2	8	17	790	582
2	3	1908-23	D.Bush	7,210	1,158	29	8,397	1,804	186	74	9	.250	.356	.300	656	696	404	75	(6)	9	11	710	203
3	4	1925-40	B.Rogell	5,149	649	20	5,818	1,375	256	75	42	.267	.351	.370	722	674	82	62	(7)	5	23	695	88
4	2	1922-27	T.Rigney	2,326	377	5	2,708	669	113	39	13	.288	.388	.387	775	732	44	36	(10)	10	(10)	722	81
5	5	1997-	D.Cruz	1,991	82	11	2,084	546	129	8	30	.274	.307	.392	699	648	8	18	(13)	0	35	670	9
6	6	1939-50	E.Lake	2,595	546	8	3,149	599	105	9	39	.231	.366	.323	689	703	52	45	(13)	8	(32)	666	3
7	7	1921-29	J.Tavener	2,131	186	9	2,326	543	88	53	13	.255	.317	.364	681	641	46	31	(7)	10	14	658	(4)
8	8	1942-54	J.Lipon	2,661	347	7	3,015	690	95	24	10	.259	.346	.324	671	649	28	25	(7)	10	(1)	650	(16)
9	9	1956-63	C.Fernandez	2,778	213	4	2,995	666	91	19	40	.240	.295	.329	624	610	68	28	4	10	(30)	594	(100)
10	10	1904-34	C.O'Leary	3,232	164	32	3,428	731	104	18	3	.226	.270	.272	543	609	74	0	0	(1)	(16)	592	(132)

Detroit Tigers
Third basemen

V	R	Years	Name	AB	BB	HBP	TAB	H	2B	3B	HR	BA	OB	SA	PRO	Wtd PRO	SB	CS	SBF	SPF	FF	R TF	V HC
1	1	1943-57	G.Kell	6,702	621	36	7,359	2,054	385	50	78	.306	.368	.414	782	774	51	36	(3)	0	15	786	261
2	2	1990-	T.Fryman	5,750	532	36	6,318	1,602	316	37	209	.279	.343	.455	799	762	71	36	(0)	0	14	776	225
3	3	1948-60	R.Boone	4,589	608	27	5,224	1,260	162	46	151	.275	.363	.429	791	776	21	19	(3)	(3)	(6)	763	137
4	5	1898-08	J.Yeager	1,853	110	51	2,014	467	77	29	4	.252	.312	.331	643	709	37	0	0	0	3	712	62
5	4	1930-46	P.Higgins	6,636	800	22	7,458	1,941	374	51	140	.292	.370	.428	798	768	61	59	(7)	(2)	(26)	733	61
6	9	1922-29	F.Haney	1,977	282	10	2,269	544	66	21	8	.275	.368	.342	710	669	51	25	0	10	1	680	(32)
7	6	1963-71	D.Wert	3,840	389	31	4,260	929	129	15	77	.242	.317	.343	660	687	22	24	(6)	0	16	697	(37)
8	13	1950-58	F.Hatfield	2,039	248	33	2,320	493	67	10	25	.242	.334	.321	655	646	15	14	(5)	8	20	668	(44)
9	7	1903-16	G.Moriarty	3,671	234	44	3,949	920	147	32	5	.251	.303	.312	616	682	248	16	1	10	(1)	691	(70)
10	10	1912-21	O.Vitt	3,760	455	12	4,227	894	106	48	4	.238	.322	.295	617	652	114	32	(5)	10	21	678	(79)
11	8	1967-83	A.Rodriguez	6,611	324	27	6,962	1,570	287	46	124	.237	.276	.351	627	648	35	31	(4)	6	41	691	(84)
12	11	1899-08	B.Coughlin	3,854	203	52	4,109	972	133	39	15	.252	.299	.319	617	680	159	0	0	5	(9)	676	(86)
13	12	1979-90	T.Brookens	3,865	281	14	4,160	950	175	40	71	.246	.299	.367	666	665	86	60	(8)	8	8	673	(88)
14	15	1917-25	B.Jones	2,990	208	8	3,206	791	120	38	7	.265	.314	.337	651	633	49	30	(9)	8	(0)	633	(138)
15	14	1931-40	M.Owen	3,782	338	26	4,146	1,040	167	44	31	.275	.339	.367	706	657	30	30	(7)	0	(10)	640	(146)

Detroit Tigers
Outfielders

V	R	Years	Name	AB	BB	HBP	TAB	H	2B	3B	HR	BA	OB	SA	PRO	Wtd PRO	SB	CS	SBF	SPF	FF	R TF	V HC
1	1	1905-28	T.Cobb	11,434	1,249	94	12,777	4,189	724	295	117	.366	.433	.512	945	983	892	178	(2)	10	17	1,008	1,623
2	2	1953-74	A.Kaline	10,116	1,277	55	11,448	3,007	498	75	399	.297	.379	.480	859	868	137	65	1	6	37	912	868
3	3	1899-17	S.Crawford	9,570	760	23	10,353	2,961	458	309	97	.309	.362	.452	814	896	366	30	(1)	5	11	911	812
4	4	1914-32	H.Heilmann	7,787	856	40	8,683	2,660	542	151	183	.342	.410	.520	930	897	113	64	(6)	(10)	(18)	863	459
5	7	1975-90	C.Lemon	6,868	749	151	7,768	1,875	396	61	215	.273	.357	.442	800	805	58	76	(12)	6	31	831	279
6	8	1912-25	B.Veach	6,656	571	59	7,286	2,063	393	147	64	.310	.370	.442	812	827	195	84	(7)	8	2	829	269
7	6	1979-95	K.Gibson	5,798	718	61	6,577	1,553	260	54	255	.268	.355	.463	818	816	284	78	18	8	(11)	831	244
8	5	1938-47	R.Cullenbine	3,879	853	11	4,743	1,072	209	32	110	.276	.408	.432	840	852	26	20	(3)	0	4	853	225
9	13	1947-63	V.Wertz	6,099	828	27	6,954	1,692	289	42	266	.277	.366	.469	836	817	9	19	(4)	(8)	(8)	797	120
10	11	1899-08	J.Barrett	3,306	440	29	3,775	962	83	47	16	.291	.379	.359	738	783	143	0	0	9	15	807	101
11	10	1950-64	C.Maxwell	3,245	484	22	3,751	856	110	26	148	.264	.363	.451	814	802	18	7	1	0	7	810	98
12	14	1964-75	J.Northrup	4,692	449	30	5,171	1,254	218	42	153	.267	.335	.429	765	800	39	38	(7)	9	(8)	794	91
13	9	1941-52	D.Wakefield	2,132	360	3	2,495	625	102	29	56	.293	.396	.447	843	862	10	17	(9)	(10)	(17)	826	86
14	15	1901-12	M.McIntyre	3,958	439	28	4,425	1,066	140	69	4	.269	.346	.343	689	769	120	0	0	1	24	794	82
15	16	1977-88	S.Kemp	4,058	576	19	4,653	1,128	179	25	130	.278	.370	.431	801	806	39	24	(1)	(1)	(12)	792	81
16	17	1939-53	B.McCosky	4,172	497	10	4,679	1,301	214	71	24	.312	.386	.414	801	782	58	31	(1)	5	(1)	785	66
17	18	1928-38	J.Stone	4,494	463	12	4,969	1,391	268	105	77	.310	.376	.467	843	787	45	40	(7)	10	(7)	784	65
18	12	1995-	B.Higginson	2,982	398	19	3,399	839	181	18	134	.281	.370	.489	858	796	46	26	(2)	0	3	797	65
19	19	1974-82	R.LeFlore	4,458	363	17	4,838	1,283	172	57	59	.288	.344	.392	735	744	455	142	34	10	(5)	782	59
20	22	1963-80	W.Horton	7,298	620	58	7,976	1,993	284	40	325	.273	.335	.457	791	817	20	38	(7)	(10)	(29)	772	54
21	30	1952-66	H.Kuenn	6,913	594	15	7,522	2,092	356	56	87	.303	.359	.408	767	761	68	56	(6)	(3)	(27)	725	46
22	20	1940-53	P.Mullin	2,493	330	6	2,829	676	106	43	87	.271	.358	.453	811	797	20	27	(11)	4	(7)	782	35
23	21	1963-75	G.Brown	2,262	242	15	2,519	582	78	19	84	.257	.333	.420	753	781	30	8	5	1	(7)	780	27
24	23	1901-15	D.Jones	3,772	478	22	4,272	1,020	98	40	9	.270	.356	.325	681	744	207	0	0	10	7	761	8
25	24	1941-56	H.Evers	3,801	415	27	4,243	1,055	187	41	98	.278	.353	.426	778	761	45	36	(6)	0	3	758	1
26	25	1964-78	M.Stanley	5,022	371	8	5,401	1,243	201	48	117	.248	.300	.377	677	706	44	23	(0)	9	36	751	(17)
27	26	1933-45	P.Fox	5,636	392	33	6,061	1,678	314	75	65	.298	.347	.415	762	732	158	81	(1)	10	1	742	(47)
28	29	1922-33	B.Fothergill	3,269	202	20	3,491	1,064	225	52	36	.325	.368	.459	828	779	42	52	(17)	(8)	(25)	730	(48)
29	28	1974-88	L.Herndon	4,877	353	16	5,246	1,334	186	76	107	.274	.325	.409	733	736	92	57	(4)	9	(8)	733	(64)
30	27	1931-45	G.Walker	6,771	330	44	7,145	1,991	399	76	124	.294	.331	.430	761	727	223	70	7	10	(6)	738	(70)
31	36	1937-49	J.Outlaw	1,974	188	5	2,167	529	79	17	6	.268	.333	.334	668	683	24	21	(9)	1	(8)	667	(90)
32	31	1946-60	J.Groth	3,808	419	11	4,238	1,064	197	31	60	.279	.353	.395	747	729	19	42	(14)	0	(6)	709	(102)
33	33	1948-60	J.Delsing	2,461	299	18	2,778	627	112	21	40	.255	.340	.366	706	694	15	23	(11)	0	0	684	(102)
34	34	1994-	B.Hunter	2,903	205	10	3,118	765	118	24	20	.264	.314	.341	656	617	241	58	38	10	15	679	(118)
35	35	1932-44	J.White	2,652	386	13	3,051	678	83	42	8	.256	.353	.328	681	661	92	48	(1)	10	(1)	668	(136)
36	32	1952-63	B.Tuttle	4,268	480	13	4,761	1,105	149	47	67	.259	.336	.363	699	688	38	44	(10)	6	12	696	(144)

Detroit Tigers
Starting Pitchers

V	R	Years	Name	G	GS	IP	W	L	SV	SO	BB	ERA	RA/9	R Wtd RA/9	V Runs /162
1	1	1939-55	H.Newhouser	488	374	2,993	207	150	26	1,796	1,249	3.06	3.60	3.70	300.5
2	2	1930-46	T.Bridges	424	362	2,826	194	138	10	1,674	1,192	3.57	4.21	3.77	261.4
3	6	1955-71	J.Bunning	591	519	3,760	224	184	16	2,855	1,000	3.27	3.66	3.99	240.1
4	4	1941-58	V.Trucks	517	328	2,682	177	135	30	1,534	1,088	3.39	3.77	3.93	197.3
5	5	1939-57	D.Trout	521	322	2,726	170	161	35	1,256	1,046	3.23	3.85	3.97	186.4
6	13	1898-18	B.Donovan	378	327	2,965	186	139	8	1,552	1,059	2.69	3.68	4.16	143.4
7	8	1933-49	S.Rowe	382	278	2,219	158	101	12	913	558	3.87	4.36	4.06	128.1
8	16	1977-94	J.Morris	549	527	3,824	254	186	0	2,478	1,390	3.90	4.27	4.29	119.0
9	14	1954-65	F.Lary	350	292	2,162	128	116	11	1,099	616	3.49	4.00	4.16	98.8
10	21	1963-79	M.Lolich	586	496	3,638	217	191	11	2,832	1,099	3.44	3.80	4.35	84.9
11	12	1903-10	E.Killian	214	180	1,598	102	78	6	516	482	2.38	3.29	4.11	84.1
12	9	1939-53	F.Hutchinson	242	169	1,464	95	71	7	591	388	3.73	4.18	4.07	83.6
13	11	1954-65	D.Mossi	460	165	1,548	101	80	50	932	385	3.43	3.91	4.09	82.7
14	7	1955-70	H.Aguirre	447	149	1,376	75	72	33	856	479	3.24	3.68	4.04	80.1
15	10	1977-86	D.Rozema	248	132	1,106	60	53	17	448	258	3.47	3.99	4.07	62.1
16	18	1934-52	A.Benton	455	167	1,688	98	88	66	697	733	3.66	4.43	4.30	49.8
17	3	1996-	J.Thompson	101	101	647	36	43	0	427	235	3.98	4.39	3.90	47.0
18	25	1915-30	H.Ehmke	427	338	2,821	166	166	14	1,030	1,042	3.75	4.55	4.42	46.2
19	15	1907-18	H.Coveleski	198	151	1,248	81	55	9	511	376	2.39	3.50	4.24	45.9
20	20	1901-08	E.Siever	203	174	1,507	83	82	2	470	311	2.60	4.02	4.34	40.0
21	24	1963-72	D.McLain	280	264	1,886	131	91	2	1,282	548	3.39	3.71	4.39	35.9
22	27	1979-91	D.Petry	370	300	2,080	125	104	1	1,063	852	3.95	4.43	4.45	26.4
23	30	1912-26	H.Dauss	538	388	3,391	222	182	40	1,201	1,067	3.30	4.24	4.49	25.9
24	17	1986-92	E.King	203	113	863	52	45	16	459	333	3.97	4.24	4.29	25.6
25	26	1920-31	R.Collins	311	219	1,712	108	82	5	569	674	3.99	4.88	4.43	24.8
26	22	1908-12	E.Summers	138	112	999	68	45	3	362	221	2.42	3.64	4.37	21.6
27	19	1996-	B.Moehler	127	127	781	47	51	0	431	224	4.50	4.90	4.32	20.5
28	32	1923-39	E.Whitehill	541	473	3,565	218	185	11	1,350	1,431	4.36	5.10	4.51	18.4
29	23	1901-04	R.Miller	102	88	773	39	45	5	198	229	3.45	4.81	4.38	17.0
30	29	1928-37	V.Sorrell	280	216	1,672	92	101	10	619	706	4.43	5.11	4.48	15.1
31	28	1915-21	B.Boland	209	119	1,062	68	53	12	364	432	3.25	3.89	4.48	10.7
32	31	1952-66	B.Hoeft	505	200	1,847	97	101	33	1,140	685	3.94	4.30	4.51	10.5
33	33	1933-42	E.Auker	333	261	1,963	130	101	2	594	706	4.42	5.07	4.53	5.9
34	35	1960-69	D.Wickersham	283	124	1,123	68	57	18	638	384	3.66	4.12	4.65	(11.7)
35	37	1953-64	P.Foytack	312	193	1,498	86	87	7	827	662	4.14	4.55	4.71	(26.5)
36	38	1945-57	A.Houtteman	325	181	1,555	87	91	20	639	516	4.14	4.69	4.73	(30.6)
37	39	1943-52	S.Overmire	266	137	1,131	58	67	10	301	325	3.96	4.53	4.79	(31.4)
38	36	1970-86	M.Wilcox	394	283	2,017	119	113	6	1,137	770	4.07	4.52	4.71	(35.7)
39	34	1902-15	G.Mullin	487	428	3,687	228	196	8	1,482	1,238	2.82	3.99	4.64	(36.4)
40	45	1914-26	R.Oldham	176	93	854	39	48	12	267	292	4.15	5.15	4.93	(37.1)
41	41	1922-30	K.Holloway	285	110	1,160	64	52	18	293	397	4.40	5.31	4.85	(39.9)
42	48	1930-40	R.Lawson	208	83	852	47	39	11	258	512	5.37	5.94	5.04	(47.7)
43	46	1990-99	M.Leiter	315	146	1,148	63	72	26	866	416	4.60	5.08	4.94	(51.4)
44	47	1946-55	T.Gray	222	162	1,134	59	74	4	687	595	4.37	4.96	4.96	(53.7)
45	44	1908-19	J.Dubuc	256	150	1,444	85	76	13	438	577	3.04	4.17	4.91	(61.1)
46	42	1982-92	W.Terrell	321	294	1,987	111	124	0	929	748	4.22	4.67	4.86	(66.2)
47	53	1964-70	J.Sparma	183	142	865	52	52	0	586	436	3.94	4.40	5.25	(66.7)
48	43	1906-15	E.Willett	274	203	1,773	102	100	5	600	565	3.08	4.27	4.88	(67.7)
49	50	1922-31	L.Stoner	229	111	1,004	50	58	14	299	374	4.76	5.58	5.14	(68.4)
50	40	1965-79	J.Coleman	484	340	2,569	142	135	7	1,728	1,003	3.70	4.21	4.80	(69.8)

**Detroit Tigers
Starting Pitchers**

V	R	Years	Name	G	GS	IP	W	L	SV	SO	BB	ERA	RA/9	R Wtd RA/9	V Runs /162
51	49	1911-19	B.James	203	147	1,180	65	71	4	408	578	3.20	4.27	5.09	(75.9)
52	51	1929-44	C.Hogsett	330	114	1,222	63	87	33	441	501	5.02	6.11	5.20	(91.8)
53	52	1990-	W.Blair	409	135	1,250	59	82	4	744	404	4.93	5.39	5.20	(92.9)
54	54	1925-34	O.Carroll	248	153	1,331	64	90	5	311	486	4.43	5.47	5.27	(111.3)

**Detroit Tigers
Relief Pitchers**

V	R	Years	Name	G	GS	IP	W	L	SV	SO	BB	ERA	RA/9	R Wtd RA/9	V Runs /162
1	1	1965-80	J.Hiller	545	43	1,242	87	76	125	1,036	535	2.83	3.17	3.49	146.9
2	2	1987-96	M.Henneman	561	0	733	57	42	193	533	271	3.21	3.70	3.65	75.8
3	4	1977-89	W.Hernandez	744	11	1,045	70	63	147	788	349	3.38	3.71	3.94	72.2
4	6	1974-87	A.Lopez	459	9	910	62	36	93	635	367	3.56	3.88	4.02	57.2
5	7	1961-73	F.Gladding	450	1	601	48	34	109	394	223	3.13	3.56	4.02	36.2
6	3	1960-66	T.Fox	248	0	397	29	19	59	185	124	2.99	3.39	3.74	36.1
7	5	1978-85	D.Tobik	196	2	396	14	23	28	256	153	3.70	4.00	3.99	26.7
8	8	1992-	D.Brocail	338	42	563	28	36	5	403	190	3.87	4.33	4.19	23.7
9	10	1985-96	J.Boever	516	0	754	34	45	49	541	343	3.93	4.32	4.39	13.7
10	9	1995-	M.Myers	403	0	263	6	13	10	239	125	4.31	4.69	4.22	10.0
11	11	1941-54	H.White	336	67	920	46	54	25	349	450	3.78	4.33	4.50	6.0
12	12	1988-96	P.Gibson	319	15	557	22	24	11	345	236	4.07	4.35	4.51	2.8
13	13	1978-92	J.Berenguer	490	95	1,205	67	62	32	975	604	3.90	4.30	4.55	1.3
14	14	1994-	B.Florie	254	29	485	20	23	2	388	236	4.34	5.08	4.58	(1.5)
15	16	1969-76	F.Scherman	346	11	536	33	26	39	297	245	3.66	4.16	4.77	(13.1)
16	17	1969-74	T.Timmerman	228	44	548	35	35	35	315	208	3.78	4.19	4.78	(13.8)
17	18	1950-57	A.Aber	168	30	389	24	25	14	169	160	4.18	4.73	4.92	(16.8)
18	19	1979-92	J.Gleaton	307	16	447	15	23	26	265	199	4.25	4.67	4.94	(21.1)
19	15	1960-72	P.Regan	551	105	1,373	96	81	92	743	447	3.84	4.26	4.69	(21.1)
20	21	1995-	C.Nitkowski	209	44	368	15	27	3	258	190	5.42	6.13	5.39	(35.1)
21	22	1969-73	M.Kilkenny	139	54	410	23	18	4	301	224	4.43	4.74	5.42	(39.6)
22	24	1973-78	J.Crawford	181	14	431	15	28	13	276	182	4.40	5.26	5.67	(53.1)
23	20	1970-80	L.LaGrow	309	67	779	34	55	54	375	312	4.11	4.85	5.24	(58.8)
24	23	1949-54	M.Stuart	196	31	486	23	17	15	185	256	4.65	5.56	5.64	(61.7)

NEW YORK/SAN FRANCISCO GIANTS (1900–2000)

The Giants proved to be the most successful National League team from 1900 forward, with 71 winning seasons, 17 pennants, and four additional division titles. Christy Mathewson (646 Runs/162), Mel Ott (1,075 Hits Contribution), Carl Hubbell (484 Runs/162), and Willie Mays (1,579 Hits Contribution) stand tall among the Giants stars achieving this success, due to their sustained, superior performance. Barry Bonds has joined that upper tier of Giants talent, even though he produced 489 of his career-to-date 1,290 Hits Contribution with Pittsburgh.

Mathewson starred on five pennant-winning teams in the first two decades of the century, with support from Joe McGinnity, Roger Bresnahan, Larry Doyle, and Mike Donlin. Ott and Hubbell generated their best years in the 1920s and 1930s, as did Frank Frisch, Bill Terry, Dave Bancroft, and Dick Bartell. Mays led the team in the 1950s and 1960s; he received help from Willie McCovey, Orlando Cepeda, and Juan Marichal. Barry Bonds joined Will Clark and Matt Williams on the 1993 Giants; these three stars led the Giants to its last 100-win season.

Profiled Giants Players

Willie Mays

Mays, baseball's most complete player, excelled at running, fielding, and hitting. Mays was the National League's best base stealer in the 1950s, he stole 338 bases, and he achieved a 77 percent theft success rate in his career. Mays won 12 consecutive Gold Glove awards, and he would have won more if the award had existed before 1957. Mays hit .302 with 660 home runs in his career, while racking up 3,283 hits and 1,464 walks in 12,389 total at bats. Adjusted for a 0.5 percent career hitter's inflation, Mays hit .301 with 674 home runs, for a 942 Wtd. Production. Add 20 speed-related points and 58 Fielding Factor points, and Mays earned a 1,019 Total Factor, ranking him second behind Barry Bonds in league rate of success for outfielders, and for players of any position. His 1,579 Hits Contribution ranks first in league volume of success for outfielders, and second to Honus Wagner among all National League players.

Barry Bonds

If anyone could approximate Willie Mays' excellence in all phases of the game, it would be Bonds. Bonds played his first seven seasons in Pittsburgh, and he demonstrated a superb glove and incredible speed, once stealing 52 bases in 65 attempts. In his last three seasons in Pittsburgh, he also began to unleash his home run swing. He hit even more home runs playing for the Giants, while continuing to steal bases.

Team	TAB	HR	BA	Adj. BA	Wtd. PRO	TF	HC
Pirates	4,215	176	.275	.278	899	998	488
Giants	4,844	318	.303	.286	1,009	1,087	803

And Bonds he does one thing very well that Mays was only average at — drawing an ever increasing number of walks to give himself a high on-base percentage, and a higher Production than Mays could achieve. Bonds has drawn 1,547 walks in 9,059 career total at bats, giving him a .415 on-base percentage. It is this on-base advantage that gives Bonds the edge over all National League outfielders— even Willie Mays— in rate of success.

Apparently, Bonds is baseball's most disliked player, at least according to some player polls. He is also on track to become baseball's first 500 home run/500 steals man, and he has a few years left to prove conclusively that he is the best National League outfielder of all time. At this point in his career, Bonds has a .289 average, 494 home runs, and 471 steals, and he earned 56 Fielding Factor points. Adjusting for a 2 percent hitter's inflation, Bonds hit .283 with 502 home runs, for a 959 Wtd. Production. His 1,046 Total Factor is the National League's highest rate of success, and the third highest in history behind Babe Ruth and Ted Williams. His 1,290 Hits Contribution is currently third among league outfielders in volume of success.

Bobby Bonds

Tracing the source of Bonds' talent is quite easy. His father, Bobby, was a multi-dimensional star for the Giants in his own right. Bobby Bonds hit for power, he stole bases at a higher rate than his son, and he won three Gold Gloves. Bobby was baseball's first consistent 30–30 player, hitting 30 home runs and stealing 30 bases five times in his career. The one rap against Bobby was that he struck out far too often, setting the strikeout record for a single season with 189 in 1970.

Bobby Bonds spent his first seven years with the Giants, before finishing his career with seven teams in his last seven years. Over his career, he hit .268 with 332 home runs, while stealing 461 bases at a 73 percent success rate. Adjusted for a 1 percent career hitter's deflation, Bonds hit .272 with 341 home runs, for an 839 Wtd. Production. Add 44 points for speed and fielding, and he earned an 883 Total Factor, which ranks him 22nd in league rate of success for outfielders. His 485 Hits Contribution ranks 20th in league volume of success.

Roger Bresnahan

Bresnahan was not your typical catcher. He was fast; he could play multiple positions well; and he had a higher on-base percentage than slugging average. Bresnahan also played at the peak of the Dead Ball Era, which seriously reduced his career hitting results.

In his career, Bresnahan hit .279 with 26 home runs, while stealing 212 bases. He drew 714 walks in just 5,261 total at bats, earning him a .386 on-base percentage. Adjusted for an 8 percent career hitter's deflation, he hit .302 with 30 home runs, with a .419 on-base percentage and

an 827 Wtd. Production. His 848 Total Factor ranks fifth in league rate of success for catchers, while his 404 Hits Contribution ranks seventh in league volume of success.

Willie McCovey

At 6'4", McCovey was an imposing figure at the plate for 22 seasons. McCovey broke in with a bang in 1959, hitting .354 with 13 home runs in just 192 at bats. His burst of success created a problem for the Giants, as they already had a slugging first baseman in Orlando Cepeda. The team's solution was to put one of them in the outfield, where the out-of-position star played erratic defense. McCovey outlasted Cepeda in San Francisco, and first base was finally his beginning in 1965, just as he became a consistently deadly hitter.

McCovey was the best hitter in baseball at the apex of his career in the late 1960s. McCovey teamed with Mays, Jim Ray Hart and other Giants sluggers to form a formidable lineup. The Giants finished in second place five straight years in the late 1960s, although McCovey did make it to the World Series back in 1962. Knee injuries caused McCovey's career to begin to deteriorate in 1971. He produced solid seasons in 1973, 1974, and 1978, but he proved to be ineffective otherwise:

Years	TAB	HR	BA	Adj. BA	Wtd. PRO	TF	HC
1959–70	5,808	352	.283	.289	965	940	483
1971–80	3,803	169	.249	.251	816	781	26

McCovey hit .270 with 521 home runs over his career. Adjusted for a 1.5 percent career hitter's deflation, he hit .274 with 531 home runs, for a 906 Wtd. Production. His 877 Total Factor ranks seventh in league rate of success for first basemen. His 509 Hits Contribution ranks fourth in league volume of success.

Matt Williams

Williams was hailed early in his career as the next Mike Schmidt. Williams has Schmidt's power and is an excellent fielder, but he never mastered the art of getting on base for a high percentage. In fact, Williams' career .319 on-base percentage is remarkably low for a power hitter. While Williams will not achieve the levels of success achieved by Schmidt, he has a shot at over 500 career home runs, and he is already highly ranked compared to other third basemen.

In his career to date, Williams has hit .269 with 346 home runs, and added 50 Fielding Factor points. Adjusted for a 3 percent career hitter's inflation, he hit .260 with 356 home runs. His 836 Total Factor ranks eighth in league rate of success for third basemen, while his 403 Hits Contribution ranks seventh in league volume of success.

Mel Ott

Ott's career speaks of consistency. Ott was consistently one of his league's top three outfielders from 1928 until 1945. His home runs were generally in the 30 to 35 range, which was sufficient to win six home run crowns in this period. Ott led the league in walks six times for a career 1,708 walks, and a career .414 on-base percentage. And he played long enough to hit 511 career home runs, while batting .304.

Adjusted for a 1 percent career hitter's inflation, Ott hit .300 with 532 home runs, for a 934 Wtd. Production. His 943 Total Factor ranks seventh in league rate of success for outfielders, while his 1,075 Hits Contribution ranks sixth in league volume of success. Only 21 players in major league history generated over 1,000 Hits Contribution, and Ott was one of them.

Christy Mathewson

Mathewson was the National League's premier pitcher during the Dead Ball Era. He won 20 or more games 13 times in a 14-year span, and he reached the 30-win mark four times in this period. Mathewson teamed with Joe McGinnity to pitch the Giants to two pennants early in his career. He later teamed with Rube Marquard for three more pennants in the early 1910s. Pitching was the key to the Giants' strength in this period, and Mathewson was the key to the Giants pitching. In his career, Matty was 373–188 with a 2.13 ERA. His 3.42 Wtd. RA/9 ranks eighth in league rate of success, while his 646 Runs/162 ranks second to Pete Alexander in league volume of success.

Carl Hubbell

Hubbell was the first great pitcher to come into the National League after Christy Mathewson, Pete Alexander, and Three Finger Brown retired. Hubbell was overpowering in his two best seasons, winning the league's MVP Award while pitching his team to a pennant each year. Hubbell started his career on a strong note, with a Wtd. RA/9 of 3.70 or better in each of his first 12 seasons, before becoming merely ordinary in his last four seasons. In his career, Hubbell was 253–154, with a 2.98 ERA. His 3.40 Wtd. RA/9 ranks sixth in league rate of success, while his 484 Runs/162 ranks fifth in league volume of success.

Gaylord Perry

Perry did not join the Giants starting rotation until 1964, when he was 25 years old. Perry managed to win 314 games in his career, but he only did so by pitching well past his prime, surviving in the big leagues by using experience, slow junk pitches and gimmicks. Gaylord's last four years gave him 35 wins, but they cost him both rate and volume of success, as he was a sub-par pitcher by then, with "no stuff."

Perry finished second in the 1970 Cy Young voting for the Giants, while winning the Cy Young in 1972 for the Indians. His most remarkable year was with San Diego in 1978, when he won his first National League Cy Young Award at the age of 39, with a 21–6 record and a 2.73 ERA. In his 22-year career, Perry was 314–265 with a 3.11 ERA. His 3.96 Wtd. RA/9 ranks 60th in league rate of success, while his 360 Runs/162 ranks tenth in league volume of success.

New York/San Francisco Giants   **Hitters Volume of Success**

Pos	Years	Name	AB	BB	HBP	TAB	H	2B	3B	HR	BA	OB	SA	PRO	Wtd PRO	SB	CS	SBF	SPF	FF	R TF	V HC
C	1897-15	R.Bresnahan	4,481	714	66	5,261	1,252	218	71	26	.279	.386	.377	763	827	212	3	2	9	10	848	404
1B	1959-80	W.McCovey	8,197	1,345	69	9,611	2,211	353	46	521	.270	.377	.515	892	906	26	22	(2)	(9)	(18)	877	509
2B	1907-20	L.Doyle	6,509	625	53	7,187	1,887	299	123	74	.290	.357	.408	765	824	298	27	(3)	10	(35)	796	405
SS	1927-46	D.Bartell	7,629	748	97	8,474	2,165	442	71	79	.284	.355	.391	747	729	109	3	1	10	34	774	439
3B	1987-	M.Williams	6,243	410	50	6,703	1,677	292	33	346	.269	.319	.492	811	789	49	34	(2)	0	50	836	403
OF	1951-73	W.Mays	10,881	1,464	44	12,389	3,283	523	140	660	.302	.387	.557	944	942	338	103	10	10	58	1,019	1,579
OF	1986-	B.Bonds	7,456	1,547	56	9,059	2,157	451	69	494	.289	.415	.567	982	959	471	135	21	10	56	1,046	1,290
OF	1926-47	M.Ott	9,456	1,708	64	11,228	2,876	488	72	511	.304	.414	.533	947	934	89	0	0	(1)	10	943	1,075
Starters	Averages		7,607	1,070	62	8,739	2,189	383	78	339	.288	.380	.492	872	877	199	41	3	5	20	905	763
C	1961-72	T.Haller	3,935	477	35	4,447	1,011	153	31	134	.257	.342	.414	756	778	14	30	(10)	(7)	9	769	196
1B	1958-74	O.Cepeda	7,927	588	102	8,617	2,351	417	27	379	.297	.353	.499	852	860	142	80	(2)	2	(0)	859	377
2B	1992-	J.Kent	4,329	387	71	4,787	1,228	274	25	194	.284	.352	.493	845	798	61	40	(4)	10	(2)	801	272
SS	1909-22	A.Fletcher	5,541	203	141	5,885	1,534	238	77	32	.277	.319	.365	684	726	159	28	(5)	9	33	762	305
3B	1969-89	D.Evans	8,973	1,605	35	10,613	2,223	329	36	414	.248	.364	.431	795	800	98	68	(3)	(3)	2	796	293
OF	1968-81	B.Bonds	7,043	914	53	8,010	1,886	302	66	332	.268	.356	.471	827	839	461	169	14	10	20	883	485
OF	1896-13	C.Seymour	5,682	354	30	6,066	1,723	229	96	52	.303	.347	.405	752	822	222	0	0	10	24	856	425
OF	1975-92	J.Clark	6,847	1,262	24	8,133	1,826	332	39	340	.267	.383	.476	858	864	77	61	(5)	2	(6)	855	371
Reserves	Averages		6,285	724	61	7,070	1,723	284	50	235	.274	.355	.447	802	817	154	60	(2)	4	10	828	341
Totals	Weighted Ave.		7,166	955	62	8,183	2,033	350	69	304	.284	.373	.479	852	857	184	47	2	5	17	880	622

Pitchers Volume of Success

Pos	Years	Name	G	GS	IP	W	L	SV	SO	BB	ERA	RA/9	R Wtd RA/9	V Runs /162
SP	1900-16	C.Mathewson	635	551	4,781	373	188	29	2,502	844	2.13	3.04	3.42	646
SP	1928-43	C.Hubbell	535	431	3,590	253	154	33	1,677	725	2.98	3.46	3.40	484
SP	1962-83	G.Perry	777	690	5,350	314	265	11	3,534	1,379	3.11	3.58	3.96	360
SP	1899-08	J.McGinnity	465	381	3,441	246	142	24	1,068	812	2.66	3.76	3.77	330
SP	1960-75	J.Marichal	471	457	3,507	243	142	2	2,303	709	2.89	3.41	3.83	284
Starters	Averages		577	502	4,134	286	178	20	2,217	894	2.75	3.44	3.69	421
RP	1952-68	S.Miller	704	93	1,694	105	103	154	1,164	600	3.24	3.70	3.91	126
RP	1974-87	G.Lavelle	745	3	1,085	80	77	136	769	440	2.93	3.43	3.80	95
RP	1975-90	G.Minton	710	7	1,131	59	65	150	479	483	3.10	3.60	3.90	85
RP	1991-	R.Beck	574	0	628	29	37	260	534	143	3.20	3.46	3.43	82
Relievers	Averages		683	26	1,134	68	71	175	737	417	3.12	3.58	3.81	97
Totals	Averages		1,260	528	5,268	354	249	195	2,953	1,310	2.83	3.47	3.71	518

New York/San Francisco Giants　　　**Hitters Rate of Success**

Pos	Years	Name	AB	BB	HBP	TAB	H	2B	3B	HR	BA	OB	SA	PRO	Wtd PRO	SB	CS	SBF	SPF	FF	R TF	V HC
C	1897-15	R.Bresnahan	4,481	714	66	5,261	1,252	218	71	26	.279	.386	.377	763	827	212	3	2	9	10	848	404
1B	1959-80	W.McCovey	8,197	1,345	69	9,611	2,211	353	46	521	.270	.377	.515	892	906	26	22	(2)	(9)	(18)	877	509
2B	1992-	J.Kent	4,329	387	71	4,787	1,228	274	25	194	.284	.352	.493	845	798	61	40	(4)	10	(2)	801	272
SS	1927-46	D.Bartell	7,629	748	97	8,474	2,165	442	71	79	.284	.355	.391	747	729	109	3	1	10	34	774	439
3B	1987-	M.Williams	6,243	410	50	6,703	1,677	292	33	346	.269	.319	.492	811	789	49	34	(2)	0	50	836	403
OF	1986-	B.Bonds	7,456	1,547	56	9,059	2,157	451	69	494	.289	.415	.567	982	959	471	135	21	10	56	1,046	1,290
OF	1951-73	W.Mays	10,881	1,464	44	12,389	3,283	523	140	660	.302	.387	.557	944	942	338	103	10	10	58	1,019	1,579
OF	1926-47	M.Ott	9,456	1,708	64	11,228	2,876	488	72	511	.304	.414	.533	947	934	89	0	0	(1)	10	943	1,075
Starters	Averages		7,334	1,040	65	8,439	2,106	380	66	354	.287	.381	.502	882	876	169	43	3	5	25	909	746
C	1966-73	D.Dietz	1,829	381	13	2,223	478	89	6	66	.261	.392	.425	817	834	4	6	(3)	(10)	(14)	807	130
1B	1923-36	B.Terry	6,428	537	9	6,974	2,193	373	112	154	.341	.393	.506	899	858	56	6	(1)	(2)	16	871	351
2B	1907-20	L.Doyle	6,509	625	53	7,187	1,887	299	123	74	.290	.357	.408	765	824	298	27	(3)	10	(35)	796	405
SS	1909-22	A.Fletcher	5,541	203	141	5,885	1,534	238	77	32	.277	.319	.365	684	726	159	28	(5)	9	33	762	305
3B	1904-13	A.Devlin	4,412	576	84	5,072	1,185	164	57	10	.269	.364	.338	702	772	285	0	0	9	28	809	223
OF	1912-20	B.Kauff	3,094	367	28	3,489	961	169	57	49	.311	.389	.450	838	904	234	33	(6)	10	17	925	304
OF	1899-14	M.Donlin	3,854	312	20	4,186	1,282	176	97	51	.333	.386	.468	854	916	213	0	0	10	(9)	917	347
OF	1968-81	B.Bonds	7,043	914	53	8,010	1,886	302	66	332	.268	.356	.471	827	839	461	169	14	10	20	883	485
Reserves	Averages		4,839	489	50	5,378	1,426	226	74	96	.295	.365	.432	797	829	214	34	(1)	6	7	841	319
Totals	Weighted Ave.		6,502	857	60	7,419	1,879	329	69	268	.289	.377	.484	861	861	184	40	2	5	19	886	604

Pitchers Rate of Success

Pos	Years	Name	G	GS	IP	W	L	SV	SO	BB	ERA	RA/9	R Wtd RA/9	V Runs /162
SP	1928-43	C.Hubbell	535	431	3,590	253	154	33	1,677	725	2.98	3.46	3.40	484
SP	1900-16	C.Mathewson	635	551	4,781	373	188	29	2,502	844	2.13	3.04	3.42	646
SP	1945-58	S.Maglie	303	232	1,723	119	62	14	862	562	3.15	3.57	3.62	189
SP	1912-18	J.Tesreau	247	207	1,679	115	72	9	880	572	2.43	3.17	3.77	156
SP	1899-08	J.McGinnity	465	381	3,441	246	142	24	1,068	812	2.66	3.76	3.77	330
Starters	Averages		437	360	3,043	221	124	22	1,398	703	2.60	3.38	3.56	361
RP	1991-	R.Beck	574	0	628	29	37	260	534	143	3.20	3.46	3.43	82
RP	1977-87	A.Holland	384	11	646	34	30	78	513	232	2.98	3.36	3.66	70
RP	1988-	J.Brantley	597	18	838	43	45	172	717	357	3.35	3.61	3.72	82
RP	1974-87	G.Lavelle	745	3	1,085	80	77	136	769	440	2.93	3.43	3.80	95
Relievers	Averages		575	8	799	47	47	162	633	293	3.10	3.47	3.68	82
Totals	Averages		1,012	368	3,842	268	171	183	2,031	996	2.70	3.40	3.58	443

New York/San Francisco Giants
Catchers

V	R	Years	Name	AB	BB	HBP	TAB	H	2B	3B	HR	BA	OB	SA	PRO	Wtd PRO	SB	CS	SBF	SPF	FF	R TF	V HC
1	1	1897-15	R.Bresnahan	4,481	714	66	5,261	1,252	218	71	26	.279	.386	.377	763	827	212	3	2	9	10	848	404
2	4	1961-72	T.Haller	3,935	477	35	4,447	1,011	153	31	134	.257	.342	.414	756	778	14	30	(10)	(7)	9	769	196
3	3	1909-17	C.Meyers	2,834	274	63	3,171	826	120	41	14	.291	.367	.378	744	789	44	4	(1)	(10)	13	791	181
4	2	1966-73	D.Dietz	1,829	381	13	2,223	478	89	6	66	.261	.392	.425	817	834	4	6	(3)	(10)	(14)	807	130
5	5	1933-42	H.Danning	2,971	187	14	3,172	847	162	26	57	.285	.330	.415	745	750	13	0	0	(10)	13	753	120
6	6	1947-57	W.Westrum	2,322	489	19	2,830	503	59	8	96	.217	.357	.373	730	709	10	5	(2)	(10)	39	736	85
7	7	1981-89	B.Brenly	2,615	318	17	2,950	647	119	7	91	.247	.333	.403	736	743	45	38	(10)	(1)	(13)	719	58
8	8	1925-37	S.Hogan	3,180	220	38	3,438	939	146	12	61	.295	.348	.406	754	719	6	2	(1)	(10)	3	710	56
9	9	1912-27	F.Snyder	4,229	281	11	4,521	1,122	170	44	47	.265	.313	.360	672	685	37	20	(5)	(2)	11	690	29
10	10	1970-84	M.May	3,693	305	9	4,007	971	147	11	77	.263	.321	.371	692	704	4	13	(6)	(10)	0	688	22
11	11	1928-45	G.Mancuso	4,505	418	5	4,928	1,194	197	16	53	.265	.328	.351	679	673	8	0	0	(10)	16	679	1
12	12	1971-80	D.Rader	2,405	245	11	2,661	619	107	12	30	.257	.329	.349	678	688	8	4	(0)	0	(28)	660	(23)
13	13	1895-09	F.Bowerman	3,401	129	47	3,577	852	102	38	13	.251	.287	.314	602	647	81	0	0	(1)	12	658	(36)
14	14	1895-08	J.Warner	3,494	181	91	3,766	870	81	35	6	.249	.303	.297	601	627	83	0	0	(10)	37	653	(48)
15	15	1950-63	H.Landrith	1,929	253	3	2,185	450	69	5	34	.233	.323	.327	650	633	5	12	(8)	(10)	4	619	(64)
16	17	1973-86	M.Hill	1,809	185	6	2,000	404	62	3	34	.223	.298	.317	615	614	1	7	(6)	(10)	11	609	(66)
17	16	1987-	K.Manwaring	2,982	243	50	3,275	733	111	20	21	.246	.313	.318	631	613	10	19	(8)	(6)	18	617	(99)

New York/San Francisco Giants
First basemen

V	R	Years	Name	AB	BB	HBP	TAB	H	2B	3B	HR	BA	OB	SA	PRO	Wtd PRO	SB	CS	SBF	SPF	FF	R TF	V HC
1	1	1959-80	W.McCovey	8,197	1,345	69	9,611	2,211	353	46	521	.270	.377	.515	892	906	26	22	(2)	(9)	(18)	877	509
2	4	1958-74	O.Cepeda	7,927	588	102	8,617	2,351	417	27	379	.297	.353	.499	852	860	142	80	(2)	2	(0)	859	377
3	3	1986-	W.Clark	7,173	937	59	8,169	2,176	440	47	284	.303	.388	.497	885	865	67	48	(3)	(2)	4	863	375
4	2	1923-36	B.Terry	6,428	537	9	6,974	2,193	373	112	154	.341	.393	.506	899	858	56	6	(1)	(2)	16	871	351
5	5	1896-08	D.McGann	5,222	429	230	5,881	1,482	181	100	42	.284	.364	.381	745	790	282	0	0	3	13	807	122
6	6	1907-26	F.Merkle	5,782	454	44	6,280	1,580	290	82	60	.273	.331	.383	714	765	272	20	(2)	10	10	783	41
7	8	1915-32	G.Kelly	5,993	386	28	6,407	1,778	337	76	148	.297	.342	.452	794	761	65	43	(6)	0	10	765	11
8	7	1936-48	B.Young	2,403	274	17	2,694	656	121	17	79	.273	.352	.436	788	798	9	0	0	0	(27)	770	3
9	9	1945-60	W.Lockman	5,940	552	19	6,511	1,658	222	49	114	.279	.342	.391	733	713	43	27	(5)	8	2	718	(147)

New York/San Francisco Giants
Second basemen

V	R	Years	Name	AB	BB	HBP	TAB	H	2B	3B	HR	BA	OB	SA	PRO	Wtd PRO	SB	CS	SBF	SPF	FF	R TF	V HC
1	2	1907-20	L.Doyle	6,509	625	53	7,187	1,887	299	123	74	.290	.357	.408	765	824	298	27	(3)	10	(35)	796	405
2	1	1992-	J.Kent	4,329	387	71	4,787	1,228	274	25	194	.284	.352	.493	845	798	61	40	(4)	10	(2)	801	272
3	3	1986-96	R.Thompson	4,612	439	66	5,117	1,187	238	39	119	.257	.331	.403	734	731	103	62	(4)	9	24	761	188
4	4	1908-20	B.Herzog	5,284	427	120	5,831	1,370	191	75	20	.259	.329	.335	664	712	312	53	(5)	10	4	722	115
5	5	1940-49	M.Witek	2,147	148	0	2,295	595	65	9	22	.277	.324	.347	670	695	7	0	0	0	13	708	32
6	6	1946-53	B.Rigney	1,966	208	12	2,186	510	78	14	41	.259	.334	.376	710	700	25	4	(3)	2	(5)	694	6
7	7	1901-09	B.Gilbert	2,816	270	72	3,158	695	72	17	5	.247	.328	.290	618	662	167	0	0	9	1	672	(16)
8	10	1949-55	D.Williams	1,785	164	18	1,967	450	61	10	32	.252	.321	.351	673	653	6	12	(9)	0	(13)	632	(52)
9	8	1965-78	T.Fuentes	5,566	298	33	5,897	1,491	211	46	45	.268	.309	.347	656	665	80	47	(2)	6	(5)	664	(56)
10	9	1933-46	B.Whitehead	3,316	150	29	3,495	883	100	31	17	.266	.304	.331	634	629	51	0	0	0	12	641	(87)
11	11	1961-68	C.Hiller	2,121	157	18	2,296	516	76	9	20	.243	.301	.316	617	621	14	14	(6)	0	(32)	584	(112)

New York/San Francisco Giants
Shortstops

V	R	Years	Name	AB	BB	HBP	TAB	H	2B	3B	HR	BA	OB	SA	PRO	Wtd PRO	SB	CS	SBF	SPF	FF	R TF	V HC
1	1	1927-46	D.Bartell	7,629	748	97	8,474	2,165	442	71	79	.284	.355	.391	747	729	109	3	1	10	34	774	439
2	2	1909-22	A.Fletcher	5,541	203	141	5,885	1,534	238	77	32	.277	.319	.365	684	726	159	28	(5)	9	33	762	305
3	3	1922-36	T.Jackson	6,086	412	10	6,508	1,768	291	86	135	.291	.337	.433	770	734	71	13	(1)	5	21	759	290
4	4	1946-60	A.Dark	7,219	430	54	7,703	2,089	358	72	126	.289	.334	.411	745	724	59	27	(2)	5	(3)	724	201
5	5	1905-15	A.Bridwell	4,169	557	32	4,758	1,064	95	32	2	.255	.347	.295	642	700	136	0	0	6	5	711	107
6	9	1971-89	C.Speier	7,156	847	35	8,038	1,759	302	50	112	.246	.329	.349	678	685	42	54	(8)	4	(7)	674	37
7	6	1995-	R.Aurilia	1,919	162	8	2,089	518	92	6	61	.270	.329	.419	749	697	12	10	(4)	0	(5)	688	26
8	10	1943-51	B.Kerr	3,631	324	12	3,967	903	145	25	31	.249	.312	.328	640	639	38	0	0	0	28	667	9
9	11	1991-	R.Clayton	4,376	333	25	4,734	1,128	204	39	70	.258	.314	.370	684	647	172	75	6	10	1	664	4
10	8	1952-63	D.Spencer	3,689	449	20	4,158	901	145	20	105	.244	.329	.380	709	691	13	7	(0)	(3)	(11)	676	(4)
11	7	1989-	M.Benjamin	1,806	99	24	1,929	424	107	14	24	.235	.284	.349	633	598	44	10	13	4	62	677	(7)
12	12	1984-93	J.Uribe	3,064	256	4	3,324	738	99	34	19	.241	.300	.314	614	622	74	46	(5)	10	16	643	(31)
13	13	1959-73	J.Pagan	3,689	244	22	3,955	922	138	26	52	.250	.300	.344	644	651	46	35	(6)	5	(25)	626	(115)
14	14	1975-87	J.LeMaster	3,191	241	7	3,439	709	109	19	22	.222	.278	.289	567	576	94	51	(4)	10	7	589	(126)
15	15	1964-73	H.Lanier	3,703	136	4	3,843	843	111	20	8	.228	.256	.275	531	547	11	11	(3)	0	28	572	(189)

New York/San Francisco Giants
Third basemen

V	R	Years	Name	AB	BB	HBP	TAB	H	2B	3B	HR	BA	OB	SA	PRO	Wtd PRO	SB	CS	SBF	SPF	FF	R TF	V HC
1	1	1987-	M.Williams	6,243	410	50	6,703	1,677	292	33	346	.269	.319	.492	811	789	49	34	(2)	0	50	836	403
2	4	1969-89	D.Evans	8,973	1,605	35	10,613	2,223	329	36	414	.248	.364	.431	795	800	98	68	(3)	(3)	2	796	293
3	2	1904-13	A.Devlin	4,412	576	84	5,072	1,185	164	57	10	.269	.364	.338	702	772	285	0	0	9	28	809	223
4	5	1924-36	F.Lindstrom	5,611	334	13	5,958	1,747	301	81	103	.311	.351	.449	800	764	84	10	(2)	8	26	795	187
5	3	1963-74	J.Hart	3,783	380	28	4,191	1,052	148	29	170	.278	.348	.467	816	842	17	17	(4)	5	(39)	804	169
6	6	1947-56	H.Thompson	3,003	493	22	3,518	801	104	34	129	.267	.374	.453	827	800	33	15	(3)	0	(7)	790	127
7	7	1896-08	S.Strang	2,933	464	43	3,440	790	112	28	16	.269	.377	.343	720	769	216	0	0	10	(33)	746	66
8	8	1996-	B.Mueller	2,098	268	14	2,380	607	121	8	28	.289	.374	.395	768	718	15	10	(2)	0	13	728	14
9	9	1931-36	J.Vergez	2,323	171	17	2,511	593	114	16	52	.255	.311	.385	696	690	22	0	0	0	(1)	689	(34)
10	10	1958-70	J.Davenport	4,427	382	23	4,832	1,142	177	37	77	.258	.320	.367	687	689	16	25	(7)	(3)	6	686	(54)

New York/San Francisco Giants
Outfielders

V	R	Years	Name	AB	BB	HBP	TAB	H	2B	3B	HR	BA	OB	SA	PRO	Wtd PRO	SB	CS	SBF	SPF	FF	R TF	V HC
1	2	1951-73	W.Mays	10,881	1,464	44	12,389	3,283	523	140	660	.302	.387	.557	944	942	338	103	10	10	58	1,019	1,579
2	1	1986-	B.Bonds	7,456	1,547	56	9,059	2,157	451	69	494	.289	.415	.567	982	959	471	135	21	10	56	1,046	1,290
3	3	1926-47	M.Ott	9,456	1,708	64	11,228	2,876	488	72	511	.304	.414	.533	947	934	89	0	0	(1)	10	943	1,075
4	6	1968-81	B.Bonds	7,043	914	53	8,010	1,886	302	66	332	.268	.356	.471	827	839	461	169	14	10	20	883	485
5	9	1896-13	C.Seymour	5,682	354	30	6,066	1,723	229	96	52	.303	.347	.405	752	822	222	0	0	10	24	856	425
6	10	1975-92	J.Clark	6,847	1,262	24	8,133	1,826	332	39	340	.267	.383	.476	858	864	77	61	(5)	2	(6)	855	371
7	5	1899-14	M.Donlin	3,854	312	20	4,186	1,282	176	97	51	.333	.386	.468	854	916	213	0	0	10	(9)	917	347
8	4	1912-20	B.Kauff	3,094	367	28	3,489	961	169	57	49	.311	.389	.450	838	904	234	33	(6)	10	17	925	304
9	11	1917-26	R.Youngs	4,627	550	37	5,214	1,491	236	93	42	.322	.399	.441	839	834	153	83	(12)	10	12	844	262
10	7	1984-98	K.Mitchell	4,134	491	27	4,652	1,173	224	25	234	.284	.363	.520	883	886	30	31	(6)	(1)	(18)	860	262
11	14	1941-55	S.Gordon	4,992	731	22	5,745	1,415	220	43	202	.283	.377	.466	844	830	19	5	(1)	(10)	(22)	797	157
12	8	1949-56	M.Irvin	2,499	351	23	2,873	731	97	31	99	.293	.385	.475	860	828	28	7	4	6	18	856	140
13	16	1911-25	G.Burns	7,241	872	26	8,139	2,077	362	108	41	.287	.366	.384	749	779	383	139	(14)	10	14	788	132
14	15	1946-60	B.Thomson	6,305	559	34	6,898	1,705	267	74	264	.270	.333	.462	795	773	38	20	(2)	5	15	791	132
15	12	1914-27	I.Meusel	4,900	269	17	5,186	1,521	250	93	106	.310	.348	.464	813	803	113	53	(7)	6	3	805	126
16	17	1896-06	S.Mertes	4,405	422	33	4,860	1,227	188	108	40	.279	.346	.398	744	776	396	0	0	10	(0)	785	97
17	13	1933-42	H.Leiber	2,805	274	21	3,100	808	137	24	101	.288	.356	.462	818	811	5	0	0	0	(13)	798	66
18	18	1908-16	F.Snodgrass	3,101	386	65	3,552	852	143	42	11	.275	.367	.359	725	764	215	16	(6)	10	4	772	27
19	20	1906-17	R.Murray	4,334	299	40	4,673	1,170	168	96	37	.270	.323	.379	702	760	321	8	(2)	10	(1)	768	24
20	19	1989-	G.Hill	3,649	270	20	3,939	996	187	21	185	.273	.326	.488	814	780	96	38	6	9	(27)	768	21
21	21	1965-80	K.Henderson	4,553	589	30	5,172	1,168	216	26	122	.257	.346	.396	741	757	86	42	0	8	(1)	765	18
22	22	1930-41	J.Moore	5,427	348	37	5,812	1,615	258	53	79	.298	.344	.408	752	746	46	0	0	10	2	758	2
23	23	1912-22	D.Robertson	2,830	113	15	2,958	812	117	44	47	.287	.318	.409	727	781	94	57	(16)	0	(17)	748	(14)
24	26	1908-14	J.Devore	1,874	222	23	2,119	520	58	31	11	.277	.361	.359	720	746	160	0	0	10	(26)	730	(30)
25	24	1942-55	W.Marshall	4,233	458	13	4,704	1,160	163	39	130	.274	.347	.423	770	763	14	4	(2)	(10)	(6)	745	(31)
26	30	1936-43	J.Ripple	1,809	156	13	1,978	510	92	14	28	.282	.343	.395	738	735	7	0	0	0	(10)	725	(32)
27	31	1995-	M.Benard	2,044	225	20	2,289	562	107	16	38	.275	.353	.399	751	699	89	37	6	10	9	725	(36)
28	27	1972-80	G.Thomasson	2,373	291	5	2,669	591	103	25	61	.249	.332	.391	723	726	50	16	6	10	(14)	729	(38)
29	29	1987-96	M.Carreon	2,012	140	19	2,171	557	108	5	69	.277	.330	.438	768	754	12	11	(4)	(2)	(22)	725	(39)
30	25	1977-90	J.Leonard	5,045	342	23	5,410	1,342	223	37	144	.266	.316	.411	726	734	163	61	7	7	(7)	741	(42)
31	34	1974-86	T.Whitfield	1,913	138	10	2,061	537	93	12	33	.281	.332	.394	726	728	18	24	(14)	5	(6)	713	(44)
32	35	1928-36	C.Fullis	1,855	132	14	2,001	548	92	14	12	.295	.347	.380	726	716	46	0	0	10	(28)	698	(60)
33	28	1901-12	G.Browne	4,300	259	20	4,579	1,176	119	55	18	.273	.318	.339	657	734	190	0	0	9	(15)	728	(71)
34	32	1981-95	C.Maldonado	4,106	391	41	4,538	1,042	227	17	146	.254	.325	.424	749	752	34	33	(7)	0	(21)	724	(74)
35	33	1958-66	W.Kirkland	3,494	323	15	3,832	837	134	29	148	.240	.307	.422	728	722	52	19	3	0	(10)	715	(79)
36	36	1940-46	J.Rucker	2,617	109	4	2,730	711	105	39	21	.272	.302	.366	668	685	35	0	0	10	(5)	690	(92)
37	37	1986-96	M.Aldrete	2,147	314	5	2,466	565	104	9	41	.263	.358	.377	736	722	19	18	(6)	(10)	(21)	685	(95)
38	41	1930-40	B.Seeds	1,937	160	9	2,106	537	77	21	28	.277	.335	.382	717	677	14	15	(8)	0	(20)	650	(114)
39	39	1990-	D.Lewis	3,838	388	42	4,268	956	125	35	26	.249	.325	.320	645	615	241	99	9	10	29	663	(203)
40	40	1963-79	J.Alou	4,345	138	30	4,513	1,216	170	26	32	.280	.307	.353	660	678	31	46	(13)	7	(10)	663	(204)
41	38	1948-59	D.Mueller	4,364	167	13	4,544	1,292	139	37	65	.296	.324	.390	713	691	11	8	(1)	(10)	(16)	663	(214)

New York/San Francisco Giants
Starting Pitchers

V	R	Years	Name	G	GS	IP	W	L	SV	SO	BB	ERA	RA/9	R Wtd RA/9	V Runs /162
1	2	1900-16	C.Mathewson	635	551	4,781	373	188	29	2,502	844	2.13	3.04	3.42	646.3
2	1	1928-43	C.Hubbell	535	431	3,590	253	154	33	1,677	725	2.98	3.46	3.40	483.9
3	10	1962-83	G.Perry	777	690	5,350	314	265	11	3,534	1,379	3.11	3.58	3.96	360.0
4	5	1899-08	J.McGinnity	465	381	3,441	246	142	24	1,068	812	2.66	3.76	3.77	330.0
5	6	1960-75	J.Marichal	471	457	3,507	243	142	2	2,303	709	2.89	3.41	3.83	283.8
6	3	1945-58	S.Maglie	303	232	1,723	119	62	14	862	562	3.15	3.57	3.62	188.8
7	7	1911-23	F.Toney	336	271	2,206	139	102	12	718	583	2.69	3.41	3.88	178.7
8	16	1925-43	F.Fitzsimmons	513	426	3,224	217	146	13	870	846	3.51	4.20	4.09	174.1
9	4	1912-18	J.Tesreau	247	207	1,679	115	72	9	880	572	2.43	3.17	3.77	155.7
10	11	1931-46	H.Schumacher	391	329	2,482	158	121	7	906	902	3.36	3.91	4.02	155.6
11	14	1915-29	A.Nehf	451	321	2,708	184	120	13	844	640	3.20	3.87	4.08	154.5
12	9	1904-15	H.Wiltse	357	226	2,112	139	90	33	965	498	2.47	3.35	3.95	151.0
13	8	1948-61	J.Antonelli	377	268	1,992	126	110	21	1,162	687	3.34	3.88	3.93	145.9
14	13	1954-67	B.O'Dell	479	199	1,817	105	100	48	1,133	556	3.29	3.76	4.07	101.0
15	20	1908-25	R.Marquard	536	405	3,307	201	177	19	1,593	858	3.08	3.93	4.30	99.8
16	15	1947-56	L.Jansen	291	237	1,766	122	89	10	842	410	3.58	4.10	4.09	95.7
17	12	1927-36	B.Walker	272	192	1,490	97	77	8	626	538	3.59	4.30	4.05	88.0
18	19	1971-83	J.Barr	454	252	2,065	101	112	12	741	469	3.56	3.96	4.30	59.7
19	26	1903-19	R.Ames	533	369	3,198	183	167	36	1,702	1,034	2.63	3.69	4.40	59.1
20	18	1951-64	S.Jones	322	222	1,643	102	101	9	1,376	822	3.59	4.12	4.27	54.5
21	17	1919-28	V.Barnes	205	134	1,094	61	59	11	275	293	3.66	4.32	4.16	51.2
22	21	1941-55	D.Koslo	348	189	1,591	92	107	22	606	538	3.68	4.19	4.31	45.9
23	25	1935-50	H.Gumbert	508	235	2,156	143	113	48	709	721	3.68	4.22	4.39	42.9
24	24	1974-86	J.Monetfusco	298	244	1,652	90	83	5	1,081	513	3.54	3.97	4.39	32.2
25	22	1912-19	A.Demaree	232	173	1,424	80	72	9	514	337	2.77	3.51	4.37	31.9
26	23	1937-44	C.Melton	272	179	1,454	86	80	16	660	431	3.42	4.14	4.38	29.6
27	30	1912-22	P.Douglas	299	200	1,708	94	93	8	683	411	2.80	3.84	4.46	20.6
28	32	1900-08	D.Taylor	274	237	1,916	116	106	3	767	551	2.75	4.09	4.47	20.0
29	28	1912-21	P.Perritt	256	177	1,470	92	78	8	543	390	2.89	3.70	4.45	19.7
30	31	1961-73	B.Bolin	495	164	1,576	88	75	50	1,175	597	3.40	3.92	4.47	15.7
31	29	1993-	K.Rueter	193	191	1,074	81	48	0	537	302	4.16	4.63	4.45	13.1
32	33	1908-18	D.Crandall	302	135	1,547	102	62	25	606	379	2.92	3.89	4.49	13.0
33	27	1995-	S.Estes	133	133	831	55	42	0	686	444	4.30	4.69	4.42	12.9
34	34	1956-67	J.Sanford	388	293	2,049	137	101	11	1,182	737	3.69	4.18	4.51	10.1
35	35	1916-29	J.Scott	356	195	1,815	103	109	19	657	493	3.85	4.48	4.52	8.4
36	36	1947-59	J.Hearn	396	229	1,704	109	89	8	669	655	3.81	4.47	4.52	7.0
37	37	1918-27	H.McQuillan	279	203	1,562	88	94	16	446	489	3.83	4.52	4.52	5.9
38	38	1986-93	K.Downs	237	135	964	57	53	1	598	373	3.86	4.24	4.53	3.3
39	39	1956-71	M.McCormick	484	333	2,380	134	128	12	1,321	795	3.73	4.16	4.56	(0.7)
40	40	1981-95	A.Hammaker	249	152	1,079	59	67	5	615	287	3.66	4.11	4.57	(1.2)
41	41	1942-50	B.Voiselle	245	190	1,373	74	84	3	645	588	3.83	4.43	4.59	(4.7)
42	42	1909-18	F.Anderson	178	114	986	53	57	8	514	247	2.86	3.79	4.61	(5.9)
43	43	1946-53	M.Kennedy	249	127	961	42	55	4	411	495	3.84	4.54	4.63	(8.4)
44	44	1934-44	B.Lohrman	198	121	991	60	59	8	330	240	3.69	4.35	4.63	(8.9)
45	45	1953-67	R.Gomez	289	205	1,454	76	86	5	677	574	4.09	4.55	4.64	(14.4)
46	47	1974-80	E.Halicki	192	157	1,063	55	66	1	707	334	3.62	4.31	4.69	(15.9)
47	48	1946-53	S.Jones	260	101	920	54	57	12	413	413	3.96	4.69	4.71	(16.1)
48	49	1904-11	B.Raymond	136	95	855	45	57	2	401	282	2.49	3.79	4.72	(16.8)
49	46	1987-	J.Burkett	350	330	2,074	129	107	1	1,348	533	4.35	4.73	4.65	(21.2)
50	50	1913-22	F.Schupp	216	121	1,054	61	39	6	553	464	3.32	4.01	4.73	(21.7)

New York/San Francisco Giants
Starting Pitchers

V	R	Years	Name	G	GS	IP	W	L	SV	SO	BB	ERA	RA/9	R Wtd RA/9	V Runs /162
51	52	1919-33	R.Ryan	248	75	881	52	47	19	315	278	4.14	4.96	4.78	(22.7)
52	51	1929-39	R.Parmelee	206	145	1,120	59	55	3	514	531	4.27	4.86	4.76	(26.1)
53	56	1924-29	K.Greenfield	152	101	775	41	48	1	242	297	4.54	5.20	4.97	(37.9)
54	58	1967-75	R.Bryant	205	132	917	57	56	1	509	379	4.02	4.64	5.14	(59.6)
55	55	1989-	M.Gardner	322	260	1,673	94	88	1	1,203	594	4.51	4.86	4.88	(62.1)
56	53	1976-89	M.Krukow	369	355	2,190	124	117	1	1,478	767	3.90	4.39	4.85	(73.4)
57	54	1960-77	R.Sadecki	563	328	2,501	135	131	7	1,614	922	3.78	4.34	4.87	(86.5)
58	57	1978-91	M.LaCoss	415	243	1,740	98	103	12	783	725	4.02	4.58	5.12	(111.0)

New York/San Francisco Giants
Relief Pitchers

V	R	Years	Name	G	GS	IP	W	L	SV	SO	BB	ERA	RA/9	R Wtd RA/9	V Runs /162
1	7	1952-68	S.Miller	704	93	1,694	105	103	154	1,164	600	3.24	3.70	3.91	126.5
2	4	1974-87	G.Lavelle	745	3	1,085	80	77	136	769	440	2.93	3.43	3.80	94.7
3	6	1975-90	G.Minton	710	7	1,131	59	65	150	479	483	3.10	3.60	3.90	85.4
4	1	1991-	R.Beck	574	0	628	29	37	260	534	143	3.20	3.46	3.43	81.8
5	3	1988-	J.Brantley	597	18	838	43	45	172	717	357	3.35	3.61	3.72	81.6
6	2	1977-87	A.Holland	384	11	646	34	30	78	513	232	2.98	3.36	3.66	69.7
7	8	1963-74	F.Linzy	516	2	817	62	57	111	358	282	2.85	3.47	3.97	53.6
8	12	1982-91	S.Garrelts	352	89	959	69	53	48	703	413	3.29	3.71	4.09	49.6
9	11	1946-59	M.Grissom	356	52	810	47	45	58	459	343	3.41	3.98	4.05	47.6
10	14	1953-69	A.Worthington	602	69	1,247	75	82	110	834	527	3.39	3.95	4.30	37.0
11	10	1984-89	F.Williams	333	1	472	24	14	8	314	227	3.00	3.70	4.04	27.3
12	13	1975-81	D.Heaverlo	356	0	538	26	26	26	288	188	3.41	3.93	4.13	25.5
13	5	1990-96	M.Dewey	205	0	249	12	7	8	168	102	3.65	3.80	3.84	22.0
14	9	1995-	F.Rodriguez	203	1	249	7	8	8	225	133	3.87	4.27	4.02	15.0
15	15	1941-46	A.Adams	302	7	553	41	33	49	171	224	3.47	4.01	4.35	13.3
16	16	1993-	J.Johnstone	234	0	278	15	19	3	234	115	4.01	4.46	4.35	6.5
17	17	1992-	A.Embree	303	4	292	17	15	4	258	139	4.41	4.84	4.49	2.0
18	18	1972-83	R.Moffitt	534	1	781	43	52	96	455	286	3.65	4.09	4.54	1.6
19	19	1943-49	K.Trinkle	216	19	435	21	29	21	130	208	3.74	4.38	4.66	(5.4)
20	20	1993-	J.Tavarez	364	24	553	40	24	2	318	205	4.42	5.08	4.67	(7.4)
21	21	1971-78	J.Willoughby	238	28	551	26	36	34	250	145	3.79	4.34	4.73	(10.8)
22	23	1944-53	A.Hansen	270	39	619	23	30	16	188	246	4.22	4.78	4.82	(18.8)
23	22	1984-92	J.Robinson	454	62	901	46	57	39	629	349	3.79	4.32	4.79	(23.6)
24	27	1991-95	B.Hickerson	209	36	404	21	21	2	279	143	4.72	4.92	5.14	(29.0)
25	25	1971-78	C.Williams	268	33	573	23	22	4	257	275	3.97	4.52	5.02	(29.6)
26	24	1963-71	R.Herbel	331	79	894	42	37	16	447	285	3.83	4.44	5.01	(45.1)
27	26	1980-97	M.Davis	624	85	1,145	51	84	96	1,007	534	4.17	4.58	5.04	(63.1)
28	28	1968-77	J.Johnson	365	39	771	48	51	41	489	389	4.31	4.93	5.48	(79.2)
29	29	1973-82	J.D'Acquisto	266	92	780	34	51	15	600	544	4.56	5.10	5.69	(99.6)

New York Yankees (1901–2000)

The Yankees produced 77 winning seasons, appeared in the postseason 39 times, and won 26 World Series crowns in the team's first 100 years. Not bad for a franchise that produced just eight winning seasons and no pennants in its first 20 years. Yankee stadium was home to some of the greatest legends of the game: Babe Ruth, Lou Gehrig, Mickey Mantle, Joe DiMaggio, Yogi Berra, and Whitey Ford.

So many other players also starred in Yankees pinstripes that only the best are mentioned here. The honor role: Bill Dickey, Thurman Munson, Don Mattingly, Joe Gordon, Tony Lazzeri, Willie Randolph, Derek Jeter, Graig Nettles, Dave Winfield, Willie Keeler, Charlie Keller, Bobby Murcer, Roger Maris, Bernie Williams, Reggie Jackson, Lefty Gomez, Red Ruffing, Bob Shawkey, Ron Guidry, Waite Hoyt, Spud Chandler, Sparky Lyle, Goose Gossage, and Mariano Rivera.

Profiled Yankees Players

Babe Ruth

Nowhere else in baseball is there such a combination of talent and performance as we find in the Yankees outfield. Ruth, Mantle, and DiMaggio make up a "dream team" outfield. Led by these three all-time superstars, 10 of the top 51 American League outfielders are Yankees. And the superstar of Yankees superstars, the best baseball player in major league history, is Babe Ruth.

In his career, Ruth hit .342 with 714 home runs, a .474 on base percentage, and a .690 slugging average, which equals a 1,163 Production. Adjusted for a 4.5 percent career inflation and a 162-game schedule, Ruth hit

.327 with 733 home runs, a .453 on base percentage, and a .659 slugging average, which equals a 1,112 Wtd. Production. Few sluggers ever reach these Production levels in a single season, let alone over an entire career.

Babe Ruth's career statistics are untouchable. His 1,962 Hits Contribution gives him a career volume of success that is 21 percent higher than the next best American Leaguer, Ty Cobb, and Ruth accomplished this metric in over two thousand less total at bats. His career 1,112 Total Factor is 3 percent better than that of Ted Williams, yet another all-time great with the second best rate of success in major league history.

And to think Babe was initially a pitcher, whose career 2.28 ERA and 3.50 Wtd. RA/9 places him 13th among all American League pitchers in career rate of success. Or that he was able to work enough innings before switching to the outfield to rank ninth among Red Sox pitchers in the career volume of success.

Ruth owns baseball's three greatest seasons since 1900. Normally, Babe's 1921 season would be considered his best, as he hit .378 with 59 home runs and a record 119 extra base hits, good for a 1,358 Production. But observe the results when comparing Babe's four best years, including his famous 1927 season:

	Unadjusted						Adjusted					
Year	BA	HR	OB	SA	PRO	Inflation	BA	HR	OB	SA	PRO	HC
1920	.376	54	.530	.847	1,378	4%	.361	56	.510	.815	1,325	172.7
1921	.378	59	.512	.846	1,358	8%	.349	59	.472	.781	1,253	177.0
1923	.393	41	.545	.764	1,309	5%	.375	42	.520	.730	1,250	177.5
1927	.356	60	.487	.772	1,259	6%	.334	61	.457	.726	1,183	149.2

Ruth's 1921 performance finishes a close second to his 1923 season in a three way dead heat for best volume of success, and finishes a distant second to his remarkable 1920 season in rate of success. Babe's 1920 season is the greatest performance in the history of modern baseball, and it would be clearly the greatest if Ruth had only stepped up to the plate a few more times.

Lou Gehrig

The Yankees also boast the best first baseman in major league history. Iron Man Lou Gehrig, despite his career shortening illness and untimely death, edges another legend, Jimmie Foxx of the Athletics, for top league honors in both rate and volume of success. Both hitters benefited from a 6 percent to 7 percent hitter's inflation. Adjusted for inflation, Gehrig hit 493 home runs, a .318 batting average (versus .340 unadjusted), a 996 Total Factor, and 1,083 Hits Contribution. Foxx's adjusted numbers are 536 homers, .306 batting average (versus .325 unadjusted), a 989 Total Factor, and 1,072 Hits Contribution.

Yogi Berra

The Yankees are deep with talent in many areas, including the catcher position, which resulted in decades of team success. Yogi Berra, Bill Dickey, Thurman Munson, and Wally Schang are all top 10 American League catchers for both rate and volume of success, while Elston Howard ranks in the top 20. And the very best of these talented Yankees catchers? The answer is Yogi Berra, a three-time league MVP. Berra was a stellar defensive catcher with 44 Fielding Factor points, who played on seemingly endless pennant winners, and he had an impressive World Series record. Yogi also hit .285 with 358 home runs in 8,308 total at bats over his career. Adjusted for 2 percent hitter's inflation, he hit .279 with 368 home runs, for an 816 Wtd. Production.

Berra had 37 percent more career total at bats than the Athletics' Mickey Cochrane, his rival for the league's best catcher honors. Yogi's durability gives him top volume of success league honors, with 727 Hits Contribution to Cochrane's 687. While Cochrane had a 5 percent greater rate of success, with a 904 Total Factor to Yogi's 857, Berra's success was spread out over two decades of World Series champion Yankees teams. Pick Cochrane for a game or a short series, but pick Berra to get your team into the most World Series.

Snuffy Stirnweiss

During World War II, the Yankees lost most of their star players to the war effort. They continued to challenge for the league's top honors in 1944 and 1945, as a young second baseman came out of nowhere to have two stellar seasons. In 1943, Snuffy Stirnweiss hit only .219 in his rookie season. In 1944, he hit exactly 100 points higher at

.319 despite a wartime 4 percent hitter's deflation, while stealing 55 bases in 66 attempts. His 105.1 Hits Contribution that season ranks Stirnweiss 11th in the all-time season list for league volume of success at second, with only Nap Lajoie and Eddie Collins ahead of him on that list. Stirnweiss followed his outstanding 1944 season with a 1945 campaign that, except for a lower rate of success in stealing bases, was just as impressive. Although his career tailed off quickly after 1945, Stirnweiss' career still ranks in the league's top 25 for second basemen, with 763 Total Factor and 166 Hits Contribution.

Mickey Mantle

Mantle is constantly compared to Willie Mays, as they both began long careers in the same year. Mays is usually given the nod as the better all-around player. When looking at volume-based Hits Contribution, Mays does outperform Mantle, 1,579 to 1,305. But it took Mays 2,541 more total at bats to achieve this outcome. When we look at the Total Factor rate of success metric, Mantle edges Mays 1,026 to 1,019. If Mantle had not been plagued by injuries that lowered his rate of success and eventually shortened his career, his volume of success metric would have exceeded Mays'. As it is, Mantle finished with the third best rate of success and fifth best volume of success among American League outfielders.

Mantle hit .298 with 536 home runs in his career, while winning three MVP awards and playing on numerous championship teams. Adjusted, he hit .299 with 552 home runs, for a 981 Wtd. Production. Mantle also stole 153 bases in 191 attempts, for an outstanding 80 percent success rate.

Joe DiMaggio

DiMaggio is best remembered for his remarkable 56 game hitting streak in his MVP 1941 season, and for his graceful play in center field. But what really defines DiMaggio's career is the overwhelming success of the teams the three-time MVP led into the playoffs. Nine World Series titles in 13 years is an incredible rate of success that Ruth, Mantle, and Gehrig failed to achieve.

DiMaggio lost three years in his prime to the war effort. And he chose to walk away from the game at the age of 36, limiting his career to just those special 13 seasons. In 7,657 career total at bats, DiMaggio hit .325 with 361 home runs, for a 977 Production. He also demonstrated he was fast on the basepaths by stealing 30 bases in just 39 career attempts, for a 77 percent success rate. Adjusted for a 4.5 percent career hitter's inflation, DiMaggio batted .310 with 364 home runs, for a 934 Wtd. Production. Adding 51 Fielding Factor points and 7 speed related points yields a 992 Total Factor, the league's seventh best rate of success among outfielders. DiMaggio's 900 Hits Contribution ranks sixth in volume of success in league history, despite his short career. His 69 Hits Contribution per year is about the same rate as achieved by Mantle, Mays and Cobb in longer careers.

Charlie Keller

In 1943, at the age of 26, Keller completed the best of five impressive seasons in a row to start his career. Keller appeared poised for greatness. Then a war-related two-year break interrupted his career, followed by another impressive season in 1946. Unfortunately, injuries repeatedly shelved Keller the following two years, and his career was effectively over.

Keller ended up hitting .286 with 189 home runs, 427 extra-base hits, and 784 walks in just 4,584 total at bats, in a period with a 1 percent hitter's inflation. What he accomplished in six plus seasons was a 28th place league volume of success ranking. A sense of Keller's lost potential was his 929 Total Factor, good for the ninth best league rate of success—and better numbers than those generated by Al Kaline, Sam Crawford, Carl Yastrzemski, and Al Simmons.

Whitey Ford

Historically, the Yankees hit well, but they also pitched well. This combination of hitting and pitching certainly made for some very impressive winning percentages for the better pitchers on the Yankees staff. Pitchers who won over 60 percent of their games in a Yankees uniform include Spud Chandler, Lefty Gomez, Ron Guidry, Tiny Bonham, Red Ruffing, and the best Yankees starting pitcher ever, Whitey Ford.

Ford was a model of consistency and the ace of a staff that saw nearly annual World Series duty during his career. Ford went 236–106 for a remarkable .690 winning percentage, with a 2.75 ERA and a 3.31 Wtd. RA/9, giving up 1.25 runs per 9 innings less than the historic average, the league's sixth best rate of success. As a result, Ford ranks eighth in league volume of success by saving 452 runs from scoring in his 3,170 innings pitched.

Mariano Rivera

Rivera's career-to-date results are most impressive. Rivera, in just six seasons, worked 452 innings in 332 games, for a 2.63 ERA and 2.47 Wtd. RA/9, ranking Rivera first in major league history in rate of success for his career. Subtract Rivera's first season, when he started more games than he relieved with a worse than average 5.14 Wtd. RA/9 result, and his career Wtd. RA/9 drops to an off-the-charts 1.95.

Rivera was consistently untouchable from 1996 to 1999, as his Wtd. RA/9 results were 1.76, 1.95, 1.72, and 1.70. His 2.64 Wtd. RA/9 in 2000 was sharply worse than these earlier results yet, when compared to his peers in 2000, Rivera remains one of the very best relievers around.

Rivera has already saved 107 runs from scoring, and is moving up quickly in volume of success rankings, where he currently ranks 16th in the American League. If Rivera continues to perform at his current level for another decade, he will own both the greatest rate of success and the greatest volume of success relief pitcher ratings ever.

Johnny Murphy

Murphy is the only reliever among the top 50 in American League history to throw a major league pitch before 1948, and his career spanned the period 1932–1947. Murphy worked 415 games, 375 of them in relief. He toiled 1,045 innings, going 93–53 with 107 saves, a 3.50 ERA, and 3.65 Wtd. RA/9, the league's 26th best rate of success. He saved 111 runs from scoring to rank 12th in league volume of success, surpassing the totals of most of the modern day relief specialists. The Yankees teams of the 1930s and 1940s had everything going for them, including the game's first star reliever.

New York Yankees · **Hitters Volume of Success**

Pos	Years	Name	AB	BB	HBP	TAB	H	2B	3B	HR	BA	OB	SA	PRO	Wtd PRO	SB	CS	SBF	SPF	FF	R TF	V HC
C	1946-65	Y.Berra	7,555	704	49	8,308	2,150	321	49	358	.285	.349	.482	832	816	30	26	(3)	(0)	44	857	727
1B	1923-39	L.Gehrig	8,001	1,508	45	9,554	2,721	534	163	493	.340	.447	.632	1,080	1,009	102	101	(10)	0	(3)	996	1,083
2B	1938-50	J.Gordon	5,707	759	29	6,495	1,530	264	52	253	.268	.357	.466	822	803	89	60	(5)	0	27	825	454
SS	1995-	D.Jeter	3,130	341	48	3,519	1,008	153	35	78	.322	.397	.468	865	802	108	37	9	10	13	834	291
3B	1967-88	G.Nettles	8,986	1,088	50	10,124	2,225	328	28	390	.248	.332	.421	753	769	32	36	(4)	(5)	34	794	376
OF	1914-35	B.Ruth	8,399	2,056	42	10,497	2,873	506	136	714	.342	.474	.690	1,163	1,112	123	117	(11)	3	9	1,112	1,962
OF	1951-68	M.Mantle	8,102	1,733	13	9,848	2,415	344	72	536	.298	.423	.557	979	981	153	38	7	9	28	1,026	1,305
OF	1936-51	J.DiMaggio	6,821	790	46	7,657	2,214	389	131	361	.325	.398	.579	977	934	30	9	1	6	51	992	900
Starters	Averages		7,088	1,122	40	8,250	2,142	355	83	398	.302	.401	.544	945	920	83	53	(2)	3	25	946	887
C	1928-46	B.Dickey	6,300	678	31	7,009	1,969	343	72	202	.313	.382	.486	868	820	36	29	(3)	(9)	43	850	609
1B	1982-95	D.Mattingly	7,003	588	21	7,612	2,153	442	20	222	.307	.363	.471	834	825	14	9	(1)	(4)	31	851	303
2B	1926-39	T.Lazzeri	6,297	869	21	7,187	1,840	334	115	178	.292	.380	.467	846	794	148	79	(1)	7	(3)	798	404
SS	1898-14	K.Elberfeld	4,561	427	165	5,153	1,235	169	56	10	.271	.355	.339	694	757	213	0	0	10	8	774	277
3B	1955-71	C.Boyer	5,780	470	25	6,275	1,396	200	33	162	.242	.301	.372	673	680	41	28	(2)	0	61	739	76
OF	1973-95	D.Winfield	11,003	1,216	25	12,244	3,110	540	88	465	.283	.355	.475	830	829	223	96	3	6	20	857	599
OF	1892-10	W.Keeler	8,591	524	129	9,244	2,932	241	145	33	.341	.388	.415	802	833	495	0	0	10	4	847	448
OF	1939-52	C.Keller	3,790	784	10	4,584	1,085	166	72	189	.286	.410	.518	928	922	45	23	(0)	6	0	929	395
Reserves	Averages		6,666	695	53	7,414	1,965	304	75	183	.295	.366	.445	811	809	152	33	(1)	3	20	832	389
Totals	Weighted Ave.		6,947	980	45	7,971	2,083	338	81	326	.300	.390	.513	902	883	106	46	(1)	3	24	908	721

Pitchers Volume of Success

Pos	Years	Name	G	GS	IP	W	L	SV	SO	BB	ERA	RA/9	Wtd RA/9	R V Runs /162
SP	1950-67	W.Ford	498	438	3,170	236	106	10	1,956	1,086	2.75	3.14	3.31	452
SP	1930-43	L.Gomez	368	320	2,503	189	102	9	1,468	1,095	3.34	3.92	3.43	329
SP	1924-47	R.Ruffing	624	536	4,344	273	225	16	1,987	1,541	3.80	4.39	3.95	310
SP	1913-27	B.Shawkey	488	333	2,937	195	150	28	1,360	1,018	3.09	3.68	3.77	272
SP	1975-88	R.Guidry	368	323	2,392	170	91	4	1,778	633	3.29	3.59	3.61	260
Starters	Averages		469	390	3,069	213	135	13	1,710	1,075	3.29	3.79	3.64	325
RP	1967-82	S.Lyle	899	0	1,390	99	76	238	873	481	2.88	3.36	3.75	128
RP	1932-47	J.Murphy	415	40	1,045	93	53	107	378	444	3.50	4.00	3.65	111
RP	1979-95	D.Righetti	718	89	1,404	82	79	252	1,112	591	3.46	3.86	3.90	108
RP	1995-	M.Rivera	332	10	452	33	17	165	395	144	2.63	2.77	2.47	107
Relievers	Averages		591	35	1,073	77	56	191	690	415	3.19	3.62	3.64	114
Totals	Averages		1,060	425	4,142	289	191	204	2,399	1,490	3.27	3.75	3.64	438

New York Yankees　　　　　**Hitters Rate of Success**

Pos	Years	Name	AB	BB	HBP	TAB	H	2B	3B	HR	BA	OB	SA	PRO	Wtd PRO	SB	CS	SBF	SPF	FF	R TF	V HC
C	1946-65	Y.Berra	7555	704	49	8,308	2,150	321	49	358	.285	.349	.482	832	816	30	26	(3)	(0)	44	857	727
1B	1923-39	L.Gehrig	8001	1,508	45	9,554	2,721	534	163	493	.340	.447	.632	1,080	1,009	102	101	(10)	0	(3)	996	1,083
2B	1938-50	J.Gordon	5707	759	29	6,495	1,530	264	52	253	.268	.357	.466	822	803	89	60	(5)	0	27	825	454
SS	1995-	D.Jeter	3130	341	48	3,519	1,008	153	35	78	.322	.397	.468	865	802	108	37	9	10	13	834	291
3B	1967-88	G.Nettles	8986	1,088	50	10,124	2,225	328	28	390	.248	.332	.421	753	769	32	36	(4)	(5)	34	794	376
OF	1914-35	B.Ruth	8399	2,056	42	10,497	2,873	506	136	714	.342	.474	.690	1,163	1,112	123	117	(11)	3	9	1,112	1,962
OF	1951-68	M.Mantle	8102	1,733	13	9,848	2,415	344	72	536	.298	.423	.557	979	981	153	38	7	9	28	1,026	1,305
OF	1936-51	J.DiMaggio	6821	790	46	7,657	2,214	389	131	361	.325	.398	.579	977	934	30	9	1	6	51	992	900
Starters	Averages		7,088	1,122	40	8,250	2,142	355	83	398	.302	.401	.544	945	920	83	53	(2)	3	25	946	887
C	1928-46	B.Dickey	6300	678	31	7,009	1,969	343	72	202	.313	.382	.486	868	820	36	29	(3)	(9)	43	850	609
1B	1982-95	D.Mattingly	7003	588	21	7,612	2,153	442	20	222	.307	.363	.471	834	825	14	9	(1)	(4)	31	851	303
2B	1899-09	J.Williams	5481	474	36	5,991	1,507	242	138	49	.275	.337	.396	733	794	151	0	0	0	15	809	366
SS	1898-14	K.Elberfeld	4561	427	165	5,153	1,235	169	56	10	.271	.355	.339	694	757	213	0	0	10	8	774	277
3B	1943-53	B.Johnson	3253	347	28	3,628	882	141	33	61	.271	.346	.391	737	735	13	11	(2)	0	10	742	47
OF	1939-52	C.Keller	3790	784	10	4,584	1,085	166	72	189	.286	.410	.518	928	922	45	23	(0)	6	0	929	395
OF	1991-	B.Williams	4806	666	22	5,494	1,463	278	50	181	.304	.392	.496	888	835	119	71	(4)	10	32	873	317
OF	1973-95	D.Winfield	11003	1,216	25	12,244	3,110	540	88	465	.283	.355	.475	830	829	223	96	3	6	20	857	599
Reserves	Averages		5,775	648	42	6,464	1,676	290	66	172	.290	.366	.453	819	818	102	30	(1)	2	20	839	364
Totals	Weighted Ave.		6,650	964	41	7,655	1,987	333	78	323	.299	.391	.518	909	886	90	45	(1)	3	23	911	713

Pitchers Rate of Success

Pos	Years	Name	G	GS	IP	W	L	SV	SO	BB	ERA	RA/9	R Wtd RA/9	V Runs /162
SP	1937-47	S.Chandler	211	184	1,485	109	43	6	614	463	2.84	3.33	3.31	217
SP	1950-67	W.Ford	498	438	3,170	236	106	10	1,956	1,086	2.75	3.14	3.31	452
SP	1930-43	L.Gomez	368	320	2,503	189	102	9	1,468	1,095	3.34	3.92	3.43	329
SP	1940-49	T.Bonham	231	193	1,551	103	72	9	478	287	3.06	3.36	3.58	178
SP	1975-88	R.Guidry	368	323	2,392	170	91	4	1,778	633	3.29	3.59	3.61	260
Starters	Averages		335	292	2,220	161	83	8	1,259	713	3.06	3.47	3.44	287
RP	1995-	M.Rivera	332	10	452	33	17	165	395	144	2.63	2.77	2.47	107
RP	1992-	J.Nelson	534	0	555	35	32	17	560	287	3.29	3.71	3.36	77
RP	1932-47	J.Murphy	415	40	1,045	93	53	107	378	444	3.50	4.00	3.65	111
RP	1967-82	S.Lyle	899	0	1,390	99	76	238	873	481	2.88	3.36	3.75	128
Relievers	Averages		545	13	861	65	45	132	552	339	3.10	3.53	3.49	106
Totals	Averages		880	304	3,081	226	127	139	1,810	1,052	3.07	3.49	3.45	393

**New York Yankees
Catchers**

V	R	Years	Name	AB	BB	HBP	TAB	H	2B	3B	HR	BA	OB	SA	PRO	Wtd PRO	SB	CS	SBF	SPF	FF	R TF	V HC
1	1	1946-65	Y.Berra	7,555	704	49	8,308	2,150	321	49	358	.285	.349	.482	832	816	30	26	(3)	(0)	44	857	727
2	2	1928-46	B.Dickey	6,300	678	31	7,009	1,969	343	72	202	.313	.382	.486	868	820	36	29	(3)	(9)	43	850	609
3	3	1969-79	T.Munson	5,344	438	42	5,824	1,558	229	32	113	.292	.350	.410	760	781	48	50	(8)	5	17	795	327
4	4	1913-31	W.Schang	5,307	849	107	6,263	1,506	264	90	59	.284	.393	.401	794	789	121	49	(3)	0	(5)	780	323
5	6	1955-68	E.Howard	5,363	373	26	5,762	1,471	218	50	167	.274	.325	.427	752	755	9	14	(3)	(10)	14	756	158
6	5	1995-	J.Posada	1,444	238	14	1,696	382	89	3	63	.265	.374	.461	835	774	4	5	(3)	(10)	1	762	69
7	8	1911-22	L.Nunamaker	1,990	176	14	2,180	533	75	30	2	.268	.332	.339	670	711	36	12	(3)	(7)	(2)	699	25
8	7	1990-	J.Leyritz	2,527	337	65	2,929	667	107	2	90	.264	.365	.415	780	747	7	7	(2)	(6)	(33)	707	6
9	9	1985-95	M.Nokes	2,735	200	26	2,961	695	96	4	136	.254	.311	.441	752	751	8	7	(2)	(8)	(61)	680	3
10	10	1989-	J.Girardi	3,641	239	25	3,905	986	166	24	32	.271	.320	.356	676	646	43	30	(4)	0	27	669	(17)
11	12	1908-19	E.Sweeney	1,841	181	28	2,050	427	48	13	3	.232	.310	.277	587	633	63	9	2	0	3	638	(41)
12	11	1975-92	R.Cerone	4,069	320	24	4,413	998	190	15	59	.245	.304	.343	647	649	6	22	(8)	(4)	7	643	(74)

**New York Yankees
First basemen**

V	R	Years	Name	AB	BB	HBP	TAB	H	2B	3B	HR	BA	OB	SA	PRO	Wtd PRO	SB	CS	SBF	SPF	FF	R TF	V HC
1	1	1923-39	L.Gehrig	8,001	1,508	45	9,554	2,721	534	163	493	.340	.447	.632	1,080	1,009	102	101	(10)	0	(3)	996	1,083
2	2	1982-95	D.Mattingly	7,003	588	21	7,612	2,153	442	20	222	.307	.363	.471	834	825	14	9	(1)	(4)	31	851	303
3	3	1905-19	H.Chase	7,417	276	30	7,723	2,158	322	124	57	.291	.319	.391	710	782	363	15	0	10	28	820	195
4	4	1938-47	N.Etten	3,320	480	12	3,812	921	167	25	89	.277	.371	.423	794	812	22	13	(4)	7	(21)	794	47
5	5	1954-67	B.Skowron	5,547	383	54	5,984	1,566	243	53	211	.282	.335	.459	794	793	16	18	(3)	(6)	0	784	41
6	6	1990-	T.Martinez	4,774	523	34	5,331	1,303	262	15	229	.273	.349	.478	827	782	17	14	(2)	(10)	3	772	7
7	7	1962-73	J.Pepitone	5,097	302	28	5,427	1,315	158	35	219	.258	.303	.432	735	757	41	32	(4)	0	16	768	5
8	9	1948-57	J.Collins	2,329	338	4	2,671	596	79	24	86	.256	.351	.421	772	760	27	21	(5)	2	4	760	(12)
9	8	1971-88	C.Chambliss	7,571	632	27	8,230	2,109	392	42	185	.279	.336	.415	751	769	40	35	(3)	(8)	7	765	(19)
10	10	1913-28	W.Pipp	6,914	596	38	7,548	1,941	311	148	90	.281	.341	.408	749	746	125	60	(7)	9	9	758	(46)
11	11	1898-08	J.Ganzel	2,715	136	42	2,893	682	104	50	18	.251	.297	.346	643	710	48	0	0	0	0	710	(91)
12	12	1935-46	B.Dahlgren	4,045	390	22	4,457	1,056	174	37	82	.261	.329	.383	713	705	18	11	(2)	3	(12)	693	(170)

**New York Yankees
Second basemen**

V	R	Years	Name	AB	BB	HBP	TAB	H	2B	3B	HR	BA	OB	SA	PRO	Wtd PRO	SB	CS	SBF	SPF	FF	R TF	V HC
1	1	1938-50	J.Gordon	5,707	759	29	6,495	1,530	264	52	253	.268	.357	.466	822	803	89	60	(5)	0	27	825	454
2	3	1926-39	T.Lazzeri	6,297	869	21	7,187	1,840	334	115	178	.292	.380	.467	846	794	148	79	(1)	7	(3)	798	404
3	2	1899-09	J.Williams	5,481	474	36	5,991	1,507	242	138	49	.275	.337	.396	733	794	151	0	0	0	15	809	366
4	7	1975-92	W.Randolph	8,018	1,243	38	9,299	2,210	316	65	54	.276	.375	.351	727	730	271	94	8	8	9	754	314
5	4	1951-60	G.McDougald	4,676	559	36	5,271	1,291	187	51	112	.276	.358	.410	768	758	45	44	(8)	0	13	764	189
6	5	1943-52	S.Stirnweiss	3,695	541	6	4,242	989	157	68	29	.268	.362	.371	733	743	134	55	5	10	4	763	166
7	6	1905-15	F.LaPorte	4,212	288	27	4,527	1,185	198	79	15	.281	.331	.377	708	772	101	0	0	1	(13)	760	149
8	8	1987-	R.Velarde	3,769	414	36	4,219	1,046	187	21	89	.278	.355	.409	764	726	69	35	(0)	3	(6)	723	73
9	9	1949-57	J.Coleman	2,119	235	13	2,367	558	77	18	16	.263	.341	.339	680	656	22	15	(3)	8	25	685	2
10	11	1965-74	H.Clarke	4,813	365	11	5,189	1,230	150	23	27	.256	.310	.313	623	650	151	58	6	10	12	678	(14)
11	12	1991-	P.Kelly	1,988	145	33	2,166	495	109	11	36	.249	.311	.369	680	659	61	29	1	5	12	676	(15)
12	10	1917-28	A.Ward	3,611	339	25	3,975	966	158	54	50	.268	.335	.383	717	675	36	38	(10)	0	14	679	(21)
13	13	1955-66	B.Richardson	5,386	262	7	5,655	1,432	196	37	34	.266	.301	.335	636	638	73	48	(4)	10	30	673	(33)
14	14	1950-61	B.Martin	3,419	188	32	3,639	877	137	28	64	.257	.301	.369	671	661	34	29	(6)	0	(12)	644	(69)
15	15	1917-27	C.Fewster	1,963	240	25	2,228	506	91	12	6	.258	.346	.326	672	644	57	47	(23)	7	(19)	609	(114)

New York Yankees
Shortstops

V	R	Years	Name	AB	BB	HBP	TAB	H	2B	3B	HR	BA	OB	SA	PRO	Wtd PRO	SB	CS	SBF	SPF	FF	R TF	V HC
1	1	1995-	D.Jeter	3,130	341	48	3,519	1,008	153	35	78	.322	.397	.468	865	802	108	37	9	10	13	834	291
2	2	1898-14	K.Elberfeld	4,561	427	165	5,153	1,235	169	56	10	.271	.355	.339	694	757	213	0	0	10	8	774	277
3	3	1941-56	P.Rizzuto	5,816	651	49	6,516	1,588	239	62	38	.273	.351	.355	706	695	149	58	5	10	33	742	262
4	5	1910-27	R.Peckinpaugh	7,233	814	22	8,069	1,876	256	75	48	.259	.336	.335	672	677	205	70	(3)	6	22	702	167
5	4	1929-40	L.Lary	4,603	705	24	5,332	1,239	247	56	38	.269	.369	.372	741	688	162	49	11	10	(3)	706	104
6	6	1957-65	T.Kubek	4,167	217	13	4,397	1,109	178	30	57	.266	.305	.364	669	667	29	23	(4)	7	10	680	16
7	8	1932-48	F.Crosetti	6,277	792	114	7,183	1,541	260	65	98	.245	.341	.354	695	662	113	62	(1)	0	1	662	(2)
8	9	1973-84	B.Dent	4,512	328	15	4,855	1,114	169	23	40	.247	.300	.321	621	635	17	29	(8)	0	32	659	(6)
9	7	1905-13	J.Knight	2,664	211	24	2,899	636	96	24	14	.239	.300	.309	609	676	86	0	0	7	(11)	671	(24)
10	12	1966-75	G.Michael	2,806	234	8	3,048	642	86	12	15	.229	.290	.284	574	595	22	18	(4)	3	29	622	(60)
11	11	1984-97	A.Espinoza	2,478	76	16	2,570	630	105	9	22	.254	.281	.331	611	602	13	19	(10)	0	41	634	(60)
12	10	1925-36	M.Koenig	4,271	222	11	4,504	1,190	195	49	28	.279	.316	.367	683	653	31	14	(1)	0	(11)	640	(83)

New York Yankees
Third basemen

V	R	Years	Name	AB	BB	HBP	TAB	H	2B	3B	HR	BA	OB	SA	PRO	Wtd PRO	SB	CS	SBF	SPF	FF	R TF	V HC
1	1	1967-88	G.Nettles	8,986	1,088	50	10,124	2,225	328	28	390	.248	.332	.421	753	769	32	36	(4)	(5)	34	794	376
2	3	1955-71	C.Boyer	5,780	470	25	6,275	1,396	200	33	162	.242	.301	.372	673	680	41	28	(2)	0	61	739	76
3	4	1931-42	R.Rolfe	4,827	526	10	5,363	1,394	257	67	69	.289	.360	.413	773	721	44	20	1	4	10	736	61
4	2	1943-53	B.Johnson	3,253	347	28	3,628	882	141	33	61	.271	.346	.391	737	735	13	11	(2)	0	10	742	47
5	6	1901-11	W.Conroy	5,061	345	36	5,442	1,257	176	82	22	.248	.301	.329	630	704	262	0	0	8	10	722	20
6	5	1952-62	A.Carey	2,850	268	27	3,145	741	119	38	64	.260	.329	.396	725	714	23	21	(6)	0	20	728	19
7	8	1938-46	O.Grimes	1,832	297	11	2,140	469	73	24	18	.256	.363	.352	715	720	30	12	3	4	(27)	699	(12)
8	7	1984-95	M.Pagliarulo	3,901	343	29	4,273	942	206	18	134	.241	.308	.407	714	706	18	16	(3)	0	6	710	(12)
9	9	1913-18	F.Maisel	2,111	260	7	2,378	510	56	24	6	.242	.327	.299	626	683	194	29	26	10	(25)	694	(24)
10	10	1917-31	J.Dugan	5,410	250	39	5,699	1,516	277	46	42	.280	.317	.372	688	657	37	28	(5)	0	(15)	637	(202)

New York Yankees
Outfielders

V	R	Years	Name	AB	BB	HBP	TAB	H	2B	3B	HR	BA	OB	SA	PRO	Wtd PRO	SB	CS	SBF	SPF	FF	R TF	V HC
1	1	1914-35	B.Ruth	8,399	2,056	42	10,497	2,873	506	136	714	.342	.474	.690	1,163	1,112	123	117	(11)	3	9	1,112	1,962
2	2	1951-68	M.Mantle	8,102	1,733	13	9,848	2,415	344	72	536	.298	.423	.557	979	981	153	38	7	9	28	1,026	1,305
3	3	1936-51	J.DiMaggio	6,821	790	46	7,657	2,214	389	131	361	.325	.398	.579	977	934	30	9	1	6	51	992	900
4	6	1973-95	D.Winfield	11,003	1,216	25	12,244	3,110	540	88	465	.283	.355	.475	830	829	223	96	3	6	20	857	599
5	8	1892-10	W.Keeler	8,591	524	129	9,244	2,932	241	145	33	.341	.388	.415	802	833	495	0	0	10	4	847	448
6	4	1939-52	C.Keller	3,790	784	10	4,584	1,085	166	72	189	.286	.410	.518	928	922	45	23	(0)	6	0	929	395
7	5	1991-	B.Williams	4,806	666	22	5,494	1,463	278	50	181	.304	.392	.496	888	835	119	71	(4)	10	32	873	317
8	10	1965-83	B.Murcer	6,730	862	27	7,619	1,862	285	45	252	.277	.361	.445	806	823	127	75	(3)	8	6	835	291
9	7	1957-68	R.Maris	5,101	652	38	5,791	1,325	195	42	275	.260	.348	.476	824	828	21	9	0	9	19	856	280
10	12	1965-79	R.White	6,650	934	29	7,613	1,803	300	51	160	.271	.363	.404	767	797	233	117	(0)	9	19	825	247
11	14	1985-	P.O'Neill	6,808	844	20	7,672	1,969	418	20	260	.289	.369	.471	840	816	119	70	(3)	2	6	821	240
12	9	1937-50	T.Henrich	4,603	712	34	5,349	1,297	269	73	183	.282	.382	.491	873	847	37	19	(0)	0	(5)	842	224
13	15	1924-35	E.Combs	5,746	670	17	6,433	1,866	309	154	58	.325	.397	.462	859	808	96	71	(7)	9	4	814	184
14	20	1961-69	T.Tresh	4,251	550	40	4,841	1,041	179	34	153	.245	.337	.411	748	771	45	25	(1)	5	9	785	145
15	19	1930-46	B.Chapman	6,478	824	25	7,327	1,958	407	107	90	.302	.383	.440	823	769	287	135	2	9	4	785	131
16	18	1943-62	G.Woodling	5,587	921	28	6,536	1,585	257	63	147	.284	.388	.431	819	804	29	45	(9)	(3)	(1)	791	110
17	17	1920-30	B.Meusel	5,475	375	21	5,871	1,693	368	95	156	.309	.356	.497	852	797	142	102	(10)	10	(2)	796	109
18	13	1934-42	G.Selkirk	2,790	486	23	3,299	810	131	41	108	.290	.400	.483	883	819	49	32	(4)	8	0	823	108
19	16	1969-85	O.Gamble	4,502	610	43	5,155	1,195	188	31	200	.265	.358	.454	813	825	47	37	(5)	6	(28)	798	103
20	11	1908-15	B.Cree	2,603	269	43	2,915	761	117	62	11	.292	.368	.398	766	829	132	17	(8)	8	(4)	825	97
21	22	1987-	R.Kelly	4,797	317	49	5,163	1,390	241	30	124	.290	.340	.430	770	749	235	84	11	10	13	783	66
22	21	1941-54	J.Lindell	2,795	289	16	3,100	762	124	48	72	.273	.344	.429	773	784	17	13	(3)	0	3	784	66
23	24	1970-84	M.Rivers	5,629	266	22	5,917	1,660	247	71	61	.295	.329	.397	726	740	267	90	13	10	3	766	25
24	23	1907-17	H.Wolter	1,907	268	17	2,192	514	69	42	12	.270	.365	.369	733	796	95	0	0	0	(16)	780	24
25	25	1948-61	H.Bauer	5,145	521	34	5,700	1,424	229	57	164	.277	.347	.439	786	772	50	33	(3)	0	(7)	762	12
26	26	1950-60	I.Noren	3,119	335	23	3,477	857	157	35	65	.275	.349	.410	760	741	34	24	(4)	8	9	754	(8)
27	29	1955-66	H.Lopez	4,644	418	23	5,085	1,251	193	37	136	.269	.333	.415	747	742	16	23	(6)	0	(10)	727	(9)
28	27	1910-14	B.Daniels	1,903	203	72	2,178	486	76	40	5	.255	.349	.345	695	736	159	0	0	10	0	746	(12)
29	28	1964-84	L.Piniella	5,867	368	31	6,266	1,705	305	41	102	.291	.336	.409	745	763	32	41	(8)	(6)	(9)	741	(49)
30	30	1929-36	S.Byrd	1,700	198	3	1,901	465	101	10	38	.274	.350	.412	762	725	17	10	(3)	6	(32)	696	(58)
31	31	1906-16	R.Hartzell	4,548	455	49	5,052	1,146	112	55	12	.252	.327	.309	635	698	182	44	(11)	9	(12)	685	(116)
32	32	1931-45	M.Hoag	3,147	252	12	3,411	854	141	33	28	.271	.328	.364	692	663	59	49	(11)	4	(19)	637	(206)

New York Yankees
Starting Pitchers

V	R	Years	Name	G	GS	IP	W	L	SV	SO	BB	ERA	RA/9	R Wtd RA/9	V Runs /162
1	2	1950-67	W.Ford	498	438	3,170	236	106	10	1,956	1,086	2.75	3.14	3.31	452.4
2	3	1930-43	L.Gomez	368	320	2,503	189	102	9	1,468	1,095	3.34	3.92	3.43	329.4
3	11	1924-47	R.Ruffing	624	536	4,344	273	225	16	1,987	1,541	3.80	4.39	3.95	309.7
4	6	1913-27	B.Shawkey	488	333	2,937	195	150	28	1,360	1,018	3.09	3.68	3.77	271.7
5	5	1975-88	R.Guidry	368	323	2,392	170	91	4	1,778	633	3.29	3.59	3.61	259.7
6	13	1918-38	W.Hoyt	674	423	3,762	237	182	52	1,206	1,003	3.59	4.26	3.97	258.2
7	1	1937-47	S.Chandler	211	184	1,485	109	43	6	614	463	2.84	3.33	3.31	217.2
8	16	1912-34	H.Pennock	617	419	3,572	241	162	33	1,227	916	3.60	4.28	4.06	208.4
9	8	1944-55	E.Lopat	340	318	2,439	166	112	3	859	650	3.21	3.72	3.84	203.5
10	9	1942-54	A.Reynolds	434	309	2,492	182	107	49	1,423	1,261	3.30	3.71	3.87	200.3
11	4	1940-49	T.Bonham	231	193	1,551	103	72	9	478	287	3.06	3.36	3.58	177.7
12	12	1964-74	M.Stottlemyre	360	356	2,661	164	139	1	1,257	809	2.97	3.39	3.97	174.2
13	20	1909-33	J.Quinn	756	444	3,920	247	218	57	1,329	860	3.29	4.20	4.23	153.4
14	19	1899-09	J.Chesbro	392	332	2,897	198	132	5	1,265	690	2.68	3.76	4.21	120.8
15	15	1946-55	V.Raschi	269	255	1,819	132	66	3	944	727	3.72	4.09	4.04	110.4
16	10	1932-41	M.Pearson	224	191	1,430	100	61	4	703	740	4.00	4.54	3.92	107.1
17	7	1995-	A.Pettitte	197	190	1,249	100	55	0	834	456	3.99	4.35	3.81	105.6
18	14	1909-15	R.Ford	199	170	1,487	99	71	9	710	376	2.59	3.64	3.99	98.0
19	17	1951-63	B.Turley	310	237	1,713	101	85	12	1,265	1,068	3.64	3.96	4.13	84.8
20	28	1914-35	S.Jones	647	487	3,883	229	217	31	1,223	1,396	3.84	4.65	4.38	80.2
21	21	1961-77	A.Downing	405	317	2,268	123	107	3	1,639	933	3.22	3.72	4.25	78.1
22	18	1974-81	E.Figueroa	200	179	1,310	80	67	1	571	443	3.51	3.92	4.15	60.1
23	27	1910-21	R.Caldwell	343	259	2,242	133	120	9	1,006	738	3.22	3.98	4.34	58.3
24	24	1910-20	R.Fisher	278	207	1,756	100	94	7	680	481	2.82	3.73	4.30	53.8
25	25	1942-51	H.Borowy	314	214	1,717	108	82	7	690	623	3.50	4.04	4.30	51.2
26	26	1923-35	G.Pipgras	276	189	1,488	102	73	12	714	598	4.09	4.85	4.33	39.6
27	23	1955-64	T.Sturdivant	335	101	1,137	59	51	17	704	449	3.74	4.12	4.28	36.2
28	22	1938-45	A.Donald	153	115	932	65	33	1	369	369	3.52	4.18	4.28	30.4
29	32	1956-67	R.Terry	338	257	1,849	107	99	11	1,000	446	3.62	4.11	4.41	30.1
30	35	1966-76	F.Peterson	355	330	2,218	133	131	1	1,015	426	3.30	3.85	4.47	21.6
31	38	1895-09	A.Orth	440	394	3,355	204	189	6	948	661	3.37	4.57	4.51	21.4
32	34	1953-67	D.Larsen	412	171	1,548	81	91	26	849	725	3.78	4.23	4.44	20.5
33	31	1913-21	N.Cullop	174	121	1,024	57	55	5	400	259	2.73	3.73	4.41	17.7
34	37	1967-77	P.Dobson	414	279	2,120	122	129	19	1,301	665	3.54	3.99	4.48	17.1
35	30	1991-	S.Kamieniecki	250	138	976	53	59	5	542	446	4.52	4.79	4.41	17.0
36	29	1946-57	B.Kuzava	213	99	862	49	44	13	446	415	4.05	4.47	4.40	15.4
37	33	1947-55	S.Shea	195	118	944	56	46	5	361	497	3.80	4.32	4.43	13.9
38	36	1909-16	G.McConnell	133	98	842	41	51	4	403	242	2.60	3.81	4.47	8.1
39	39	1943-57	T.Byrne	281	170	1,362	85	69	12	766	1,037	4.11	4.54	4.55	1.5
40	40	1966-82	S.Bahnsen	574	327	2,529	146	149	20	1,359	924	3.60	4.01	4.57	(2.4)
41	41	1962-78	J.Bouton	304	144	1,239	62	63	6	720	435	3.57	4.12	4.62	(8.6)
42	44	1944-52	M.Dubiel	187	97	879	45	53	11	289	349	3.87	4.46	4.70	(15.2)
43	42	1915-25	A.Russell	345	112	1,394	70	76	42	603	610	3.52	4.47	4.65	(15.7)
44	43	1908-15	J.Warhop	221	150	1,413	69	92	7	463	400	3.12	4.09	4.68	(19.9)
45	45	1954-62	A.Ditmar	287	156	1,268	72	77	14	552	461	3.98	4.61	4.72	(24.2)
46	48	1955-60	J.Kucks	207	123	938	54	56	7	338	308	4.10	4.73	4.89	(36.0)
47	46	1923-34	E.Wells	291	140	1,232	68	69	13	403	468	4.65	5.40	4.82	(37.2)
48	50	1936-47	B.Zuber	224	65	786	43	42	6	383	468	4.28	4.77	5.01	(41.9)
49	47	1900-09	D.Newton	177	139	1,201	54	72	3	502	416	3.22	4.58	4.85	(44.1)
50	49	1925-39	H.Johnson	249	116	1,066	63	56	11	568	567	4.75	5.62	4.97	(52.0)

**New York Yankees
Starting Pitchers**

V	R	Years	Name	G	GS	IP	W	L	SV	SO	BB	ERA	RA/9	R Wtd RA/9	V Runs /162
51	51	1912-16	A.Schulz	160	110	933	47	63	4	445	409	3.32	4.20	5.05	(54.0)
52	52	1912-19	R.Keating	130	92	752	30	51	1	349	293	3.29	4.42	5.29	(66.9)
53	53	1963-70	F.Talbot	195	126	854	38	56	1	449	334	4.12	4.54	5.36	(76.0)
54	54	1965-77	M.Kekich	235	112	861	39	51	6	497	442	4.59	5.08	5.86	(125.8)

**New York Yankees
Relief Pitchers**

V	R	Years	Name	G	GS	IP	W	L	SV	SO	BB	ERA	RA/9	R Wtd RA/9	V Runs /162
1	4	1967-82	S.Lyle	899	0	1,390	99	76	238	873	481	2.88	3.36	3.75	128.4
2	3	1932-47	J.Murphy	415	40	1,045	93	53	107	378	444	3.50	4.00	3.65	111.1
3	7	1979-95	D.Righetti	718	89	1,404	82	79	252	1,112	591	3.46	3.86	3.90	107.8
4	1	1995-	M.Rivera	332	10	452	33	17	165	395	144	2.63	2.77	2.47	106.7
5	2	1992-	J.Nelson	534	0	555	35	32	17	560	287	3.29	3.71	3.36	77.5
6	6	1992-	B.Wickman	521	28	761	53	42	104	537	343	3.76	4.16	3.81	66.7
7	5	1961-72	S.Hamilton	421	17	663	40	31	42	531	214	3.05	3.32	3.75	59.2
8	12	1951-63	T.Morgan	443	61	1,023	67	47	64	364	300	3.61	4.10	4.25	36.6
9	9	1927-33	W.Moore	261	32	691	51	44	49	204	232	3.70	4.64	4.17	31.5
10	8	1985-96	J.Habyan	348	18	532	26	24	12	372	186	3.85	4.29	4.15	25.1
11	13	1954-62	B.Grim	268	60	760	61	41	37	443	330	3.61	4.10	4.32	21.2
12	10	1961-67	H.Reniff	276	0	471	21	23	45	314	242	3.27	3.70	4.21	18.4
13	14	1944-54	J.Page	285	45	790	57	49	76	519	421	3.53	4.20	4.39	15.3
14	11	1987-96	R.Monteleone	210	0	353	24	17	0	212	119	3.87	4.33	4.24	13.2
15	15	1987-98	G.Cadaret	451	35	724	38	32	14	539	403	3.99	4.36	4.41	12.4
16	16	1925-41	J.Brown	249	23	597	33	31	29	301	300	4.07	4.76	4.43	9.1
17	17	1955-63	L.Arroyo	244	36	531	40	32	44	336	208	3.93	4.41	4.53	1.8
18	18	1954-65	R.Duren	311	32	589	27	44	57	630	392	3.83	4.33	4.60	(3.1)
19	20	1956-67	J.Coates	247	46	683	43	22	15	396	286	4.00	4.43	4.70	(11.3)
20	19	1972-84	D.Tidrow	620	138	1,747	100	94	55	975	579	3.68	4.16	4.63	(14.8)
21	22	1984-96	L.Guetterman	425	23	658	38	36	25	287	222	4.33	4.80	4.87	(23.1)
22	21	1978-87	G.Frazier	415	0	676	35	43	29	449	313	4.20	4.65	4.86	(23.3)
23	23	1989-	J.Grimsley	219	72	597	28	29	3	385	345	5.11	5.61	5.06	(35.7)

PHILADELPHIA/KANSAS CITY/ OAKLAND ATHLETICS (1901–2000)

The Athletics possess a Dr. Jekyll and Mr. Hyde personality. In four periods where ownership allowed the team to realize its potential, the Athletics were .500 or better in 39 of 43 seasons, or over 90 percent of the time, with 19 first place finishes — second only to the Yankees in league history. In four periods where financial considerations were more important than team success, the Athletics produced winners in only 6 of 57 seasons, or about 10 percent of the time.

From 1901 to 1914, the team's leaders were Eddie Collins, Frank Baker, Danny Murphy, Rube Waddell, Eddie Plank, and Chief Bender. From 1925 to 1933, the team's stars were Mickey Cochrane, Jimmie Foxx, Al Simmons, and Lefty Grove. From 1968 to 1981, the team featured Reggie Jackson, Rollie Fingers, Bert Campaneris, Sal Bando, Vida Blue, Catfish Hunter, Gene Tenace, and a young Rickey Henderson. From 1987 to 1992, the A's relied on Jose Canseco, Mark McGwire, Rickey Henderson, and relief ace Dennis Eckersley.

Profiled Athletics Players

Mickey Cochrane

Two-time MVP Cochrane hit .320 in his career, and added 857 walks in just 6,055 total at bats, for a .419 on-base percentage. Cochrane also hit 119 home runs and had 516 extra base hits, earning him a .478 slugging average and an 897 Production. Given his speed, and his ability to get on and drive in runs, Cochrane would have made an excellent number 1, 2, 3, or 4 hitter. The re-

markable Cochrane did all this while proving to be one of the best defensive catchers and on-field generals in history, helping his team win five pennants in a seven-year period from 1929 to 1935.

Cochrane also proved to be an excellent manager, at least as long as he was also the starting catcher. Connie Mack sold Cochrane to Detroit for $100,000 in 1934, and Cochrane became the team's player-manager. His Tigers won pennants in his first two seasons there, and he starred behind the plate. Cochrane became ill and missed most of the 1936 season, and his playing career ended in 1937 when a Bump Hadley pitch fractured his skull. Both seasons resulted in second place finishes for Detroit.

After adjusting for a 6.5 percent career hitter's inflation, Cochrane's raw statistics become an adjusted .300 average and 120 home runs, for an 842 Wtd. Production. His 904 Total Factor is the best rate of success for a catcher in major league history. And his 687 Hits Contribution ranks third in major league history in volume of success for catchers. If Cochrane's career had not unraveled at age 33, after 11 great seasons, he would probably have been the greatest catcher of all time.

Jimmie Foxx

Three-time MVP Foxx hit 379 home runs before his 30th birthday, and he hit 500 home runs before his 33rd birthday, to date the youngest player ever to hit 500 home runs. Aaron hit 342 by his 30th birthday, and 442 by his 33rd. Ruth's numbers were 284 and 416. Mantle's were 374 and 454. Eddie Mathews had 370 and 445 totals. In 1999, 29-year-old Ken Griffey, Jr., reached 398 career home runs to finally break Foxx's pre–age 30 home run record.

Foxx hit at least 30 home runs every year from 1929 to 1940 but, then, saw his career unravel in a hurry. Foxx was still going strong when he had two impressive seasons for Boston in 1938 and 1939, averaging 43 home runs with a .354 batting average. He hit 36 home runs in 1940 to reach exactly 500 home runs, but his average slid to .297. The next year, the 33-year-old hit .300 with just 19 home runs. In 1942, at the age of 34, Jimmie Foxx was washed up, with subpar statistics.

Age	TAB	HR	BA	*Adj.* *BA*	*Wtd.* *PRO*	TF	HC
17–32	8,403	500	.334	.312	1,001	1,016	1,053
33–37	1,196	34	.266	.267	798	800	19

Foxx hit .325 with 534 home runs in his career, for a 1,038 Production. Adjusted for 6 percent hitter's inflation, he hit .306 with 536 home runs, for a 976 Wtd. Production. Foxx's 989 Total Factor and his 1,072 Hits Contribution rate just behind Lou Gehrig's numbers for the league's best results for first basemen.

Mark McGwire

In 1987, McGwire displayed his enormous power and potential in his rookie season, hitting .289 with 49 home runs. McGwire's career slowed dramatically after that, and almost ended due to a spat of midcareer injuries. He hit just 18 home runs in 278 total at bats over two seasons in 1993 and 1994. At age 30, McGwire's career appeared to be finished.

McGwire started healthy in 1995, but another injury held him to just 416 total at bats—and 39 home runs. Finally free of major injuries from 1996 to 1999, Big Mac put on a home run show, hitting 52, 58, 70, and 65 home runs. In 2000, knee problems held McGwire to 32 home runs in just 319 total at bats. The only question remaining for this 37-year-old home run hitter is whether he stays healthy long enough to pass Aaron in the all-time rankings. McGwire's career tracks as follows:

Years	TAB	HR	BA	*Adj.* *BA*	*Wtd.* *PRO*	TF	HC
1986–94	3,956	238	.250	.247	865	864	183
1995–00	3,265	316	.289	.269	1,073	1,065	467

McGwire hit .267 with 554 home runs in his first 15 seasons, for a 995 Production. Adjusted for 4 percent hitter's inflation, he hit .256 with 546 home runs, for a 957 Wtd. Production. McGwire's 953 Total Factor ranks fourth in league rate of success, while his 650 Hits Contribution ranks third in league volume of success.

Frank Baker

Baker peaked at the same time as the Philadelphia Athletics, with his best years coming in 1911–1914. Baker led the league in home runs each of these years, earning him the nickname "Home Run" Baker, even though he averaged only 10.5 home runs a season over that period. In his career, he hit .307 with 96 home runs in 13 seasons. Adjusted for a 6.5 percent career hitter's deflation, Baker hit .327 with 107 home runs. His 877 Total Factor ranks second in league rate of success at third, while his 538 Hits Contribution ranks third in league volume of success.

Rickey Henderson

Henderson is the best leadoff hitter of all time. No one else comes close. If his attitude matched his results, Henderson would have been a priceless asset that any team would desperately hang onto. Instead, he found himself shuttling back and forth between teams the second half of his career.

Henderson has 1,370 career steals, or 432 (46 percent) more steals than his closest competitor, the Cardinals' Lou Brock. Better still, he has been caught only 326 times, and his career 81 percent success rate is one of the best ever. As if this isn't enough, Henderson has drawn 2,060 career walks, passing Ted Williams during the 2000 season in that category. Add a .282 batting average, and Henderson sports a .406 career on-base percentage, a deadly high percentage for a leadoff hitter with the speed he generates. Finally, Henderson has far more leadoff home runs than any player in history.

Henderson has hit .282 with 282 home runs in his career. Adjusted for a career 2 percent hitter's inflation, he has hit .278 with 286 home runs, for an 815 Wtd. Production. Add 53 Stolen Base points, 23 Fielding Factor points, and 10 Speed Factor points, and Henderson earns a 902 Total Factor, the league's 15th best rate of success. His 892 Hits Contribution is the league's seventh best volume of success.

Reggie Jackson

Jackson displayed the greatest swagger of all time. Although he was an erratic fielder, and he struck out a record 2,597 times, Jackson generated power numbers to support his ego. Jackson hit .262 with 563 home runs in his career, for an 848 Production, and he stole 228 bases to boot. Adjusted for a 2 percent career hitter's deflation, Jackson hit .267 with 582 home runs. His 847 Total Factor ranks only 47th in league rate of success, but his 494

Hits Contribution ranks 20th in league volume of success.

Jackson used the DH to hang around too long. Sadly, the enticement to hit 500 home runs overshadows all other considerations for a player like Jackson late in his career. Compare Jackson's first 16 seasons, and those last five years as a poor-hitting DH and part-time outfielder:

Years	TAB	HR	BA	Adj. BA	Wtd. PRO	TF	HC
1967–82	8,873	464	.272	.279	900	891	580
1983–87	2,462	99	.227	.225	733	683	(86)

If Jackson had retired after the 1982 season, his rate of success would be the league's 17th best, instead of his actual 47th best finish.

Lefty Grove

A contract locked Grove into a five-year, 108-win stint with Baltimore of the International (minor) League. Grove finally broke into the big leagues with Philadelphia at age 25. Grove managed a 300–141 major league record, for a .680 winning percentage, despite arm injuries that hampered the number of innings he pitched after being traded to Boston in 1934. Grove's career 3.06 ERA is not an accurate measure of his performance, as he pitched his entire career during a period of high hitter's inflation. His 3.22 Wtd. RA/9 adjusts for this inflation, and ranks Lefty third in league history in rate of success. Grove saved 616 runs from scoring over 3,941 innings, ranking him second to Walter Johnson in league volume of success.

Eddie Plank

Plank, although a Hall of Famer, is one of the most underrated pitchers of all time. Plank was a 20-game win-ner on the first Athletics pennant winner in 1902, and he won 24 for the 1905 pennant winning team. He was still going strong a decade later, winning 98 games from 1910 to 1914 to edge out Chief Bender (91) and Jack Coombs (80) for the most wins on those five successful Athletics teams. Plank was 326–194 in his career, with a 2.35 ERA, and a 3.58 Wtd. RA/9, which ranks 18th in league rate of success. He saved 524 runs from scoring, which ranks an impressive fourth in league volume of success.

Rollie Fingers

Fingers was already the team's ace relief pitcher when he helped the A's win the first of three straight World Series in 1972. As it turns out, he was just getting started. Even though his ERA through the 1972 season exactly matches his ERA for the remainder of his career, Fingers' improvement in effectiveness can be clearly seen in the dramatic drop in his Wtd. RA/9:

Years	IP	W–L	SV	ERA	Wtd. RA/9	Runs/162
1968–72	509	28–31	52	2.90	4.29	16
1973–85	1,192	86–87	289	2.90	3.22	183

Fingers is one of the best closers of all time. He was 114–118 in his career, with a 2.90 ERA over 944 games and 1,701 innings. His 3.53 Wtd. RA/9 is the 20th best rate of success among league relief pitchers, while his 199 Runs/162 ranks him in a virtual tie with Goose Gossage for the second best volume of success in history.

Philadelphia/Kansas City/Oakland Athletics   Hitters Volume of Success

Pos	Years	Name	AB	BB	HBP	TAB	H	2B	3B	HR	BA	OB	SA	PRO	Wtd PRO	SB	CS	SBF	SPF	FF	R TF	V HC
C	1925-37	M.Cochrane	5,169	857	29	6,055	1,652	333	64	119	.320	.419	.478	897	842	64	46	(4)	8	58	904	687
1B	1925-45	J.Foxx	8,134	1,452	13	9,599	2,646	458	125	534	.325	.428	.609	1,038	976	87	72	(6)	2	17	989	1,072
2B	1900-15	D.Murphy	5,399	335	47	5,781	1,563	289	102	44	.289	.336	.405	742	824	193	0	0	5	3	831	333
SS	1964-83	B.Campaneris	8,684	618	64	9,366	2,249	313	86	79	.259	.313	.342	655	680	649	199	25	10	2	717	240
3B	1908-22	F.Baker	5,984	473	50	6,507	1,838	315	103	96	.307	.363	.442	805	857	235	28	(4)	6	18	877	538
OF	1979-	R.Henderson	10,331	2,060	90	12,481	2,914	486	62	282	.282	.406	.423	829	815	1,370	326	53	10	23	902	892
OF	1924-44	A.Simmons	8,759	615	30	9,404	2,927	539	149	307	.334	.380	.535	915	857	88	64	(4)	(0)	32	886	605
OF	1933-45	B.Johnson	6,920	1,075	24	8,019	2,051	396	95	288	.296	.393	.506	899	867	96	64	(4)	8	10	882	501
Starters	Averages		7,423	936	43	8,402	2,230	391	98	219	.300	.382	.468	850	839	348	100	7	6	21	872	608
C	1969-83	G.Tenace	4,390	984	91	5,465	1,060	179	20	201	.241	.391	.429	819	838	36	42	(8)	(9)	(23)	797	215
1B	1986-	M.McGwire	5,888	1,261	72	7,221	1,570	248	6	554	.267	.402	.593	995	957	12	8	(1)	(9)	6	953	650
2B	1924-35	M.Bishop	4,494	1,153	31	5,678	1,216	236	35	41	.271	.423	.366	789	742	43	50	(9)	(0)	1	734	136
SS	1936-55	E.Joost	5,606	1,043	33	6,682	1,339	238	35	134	.239	.361	.366	727	724	61	31	(4)	1	4	725	199
3B	1966-81	S.Bando	7,060	1,031	75	8,166	1,790	289	38	242	.254	.355	.408	763	787	75	46	(2)	(7)	(15)	764	189
OF	1967-87	R.Jackson	9,864	1,375	96	11,335	2,584	463	49	563	.262	.358	.490	848	864	228	115	(0)	5	(23)	847	494
OF	1985-	J.Canseco	6,801	861	83	7,745	1,811	332	14	446	.266	.356	.516	872	846	198	87	3	1	(19)	831	284
OF	1898-11	T.Hartsel	4,848	837	12	5,697	1,336	182	92	31	.276	.384	.370	754	838	247	0	0	7	(14)	832	215
Reserves	Averages		6,119	1,068	62	7,249	1,588	271	36	277	.260	.375	.451	826	829	113	47	(3)	(1)	(10)	815	298
Totals	Weighted Ave.		6,988	980	49	8,017	2,016	351	78	238	.289	.380	.463	843	836	269	82	4	4	10	853	505

Pitchers Volume of Success

Pos	Years	Name	G	GS	IP	W	L	SV	SO	BB	ERA	RA/9	R Wtd RA/9	V Runs /162
SP	1925-41	L.Grove	616	457	3,941	300	141	55	2,266	1,187	3.06	3.64	3.22	616
SP	1901-17	E.Plank	623	529	4,496	326	194	23	2,246	1,072	2.35	3.14	3.58	524
SP	1897-10	R.Waddell	407	340	2,961	193	143	5	2,316	803	2.16	3.23	3.61	338
SP	1969-86	V.Blue	502	473	3,343	209	161	2	2,175	1,185	3.27	3.65	3.99	216
SP	1903-25	C.Bender	459	334	3,017	212	127	34	1,711	712	2.46	3.31	3.98	204
Starters	Averages		521	427	3,551	248	153	24	2,143	992	2.67	3.39	3.65	380
RP	1968-85	R.Fingers	944	37	1,701	114	118	341	1,299	492	2.90	3.25	3.53	199
RP	1988-99	J.Corsi	368	1	481	22	24	7	290	191	3.25	3.68	3.51	56
RP	1988-93	T.Burns	203	33	490	21	23	13	252	175	3.47	3.84	3.92	35
RP	1965-78	P.Lindblad	655	32	1,214	68	63	64	671	384	3.29	3.78	4.30	34
Relievers	Averages		543	26	972	56	57	106	628	311	3.14	3.55	3.82	81
Totals	Averages		1,064	452	4,523	304	210	130	2,771	1,302	2.77	3.43	3.69	461

Philadelphia/Kansas City/Oakland Athletics   Hitters Rate of Success

Pos	Years	Name	AB	BB	HBP	TAB	H	2B	3B	HR	BA	OB	SA	PRO	Wtd PRO	SB	CS	SBF	SPF	FF	R TF	V HC
C	1925-37	M.Cochrane	5,169	857	29	6,055	1,652	333	64	119	.320	.419	.478	897	842	64	46	(4)	8	58	904	687
1B	1925-45	J.Foxx	8,134	1,452	13	9,599	2,646	458	125	534	.325	.428	.609	1,038	976	87	72	(6)	2	17	989	1,072
2B	1900-15	D.Murphy	5,399	335	47	5,781	1,563	289	102	44	.289	.336	.405	742	824	193	0	0	5	3	831	333
SS	1997-	M.Tejada	1664	153	24	1,841	421	88	8	64	.253	.325	.431	756	698	21	13	(3)	10	29	734	64
3B	1908-22	F.Baker	5,984	473	50	6,507	1,838	315	103	96	.307	.363	.442	805	857	235	28	(4)	6	18	877	538
OF	1979-	R.Henderson	10,331	2,060	90	12,481	2,914	486	62	282	.282	.406	.423	829	815	1,370	326	53	10	23	902	892
OF	1924-44	A.Simmons	8,759	615	30	9,404	2,927	539	149	307	.334	.380	.535	915	857	88	64	(4)	(0)	32	886	605
OF	1933-45	B.Johnson	6,920	1,075	24	8,019	2,051	396	95	288	.296	.393	.506	899	867	96	64	(4)	8	10	882	501
Starters	Averages		6,545	878	38	7,461	2,002	363	89	217	.306	.391	.488	879	859	269	77	4	6	24	893	586
C	1969-83	G.Tenace	4,390	984	91	5,465	1,060	179	20	201	.241	.391	.429	819	838	36	42	(8)	(9)	(23)	797	215
1B	1986-	M.McGwire	5,888	1,261	72	7,221	1,570	248	6	554	.267	.402	.593	995	957	12	8	(1)	(9)	6	953	650
2B	1924-35	M.Bishop	4,494	1,153	31	5,678	1,216	236	35	41	.271	.423	.366	789	742	43	50	(9)	(0)	1	734	136
SS	1936-55	E.Joost	5606	1,043	33	6,682	1,339	238	35	134	.239	.361	.366	727	724	61	31	(4)	1	4	725	199
3B	1966-81	S.Bando	7,060	1,031	75	8,166	1,790	289	38	242	.254	.355	.408	763	787	75	46	(2)	(7)	(15)	764	189
OF	1899-08	S.Seybold	3,685	293	40	4,018	1,085	218	54	51	.294	.353	.424	777	852	66	0	0	0	2	855	204
OF	1967-87	R.Jackson	9,864	1,375	96	11,335	2,584	463	49	563	.262	.358	.490	848	864	228	115	(0)	5	(23)	847	494
OF	1898-11	T.Hartsel	4848	837	12	5,697	1,336	182	92	31	.276	.384	.370	754	838	247	0	0	7	(14)	832	215
Reserves	Averages		5,729	997	56	6,783	1,498	257	41	227	.261	.376	.439	816	829	96	37	(3)	(2)	(8)	816	288
Totals	Weighted Ave.		6,273	917	44	7,235	1,834	328	73	220	.292	.386	.473	859	849	212	63	1	3	13	867	487

Pitchers Rate of Success

Pos	Years	Name	G	GS	IP	W	L	SV	SO	BB	ERA	RA/9	R Wtd RA/9	V Runs /162
SP	1925-41	L.Grove	616	457	3,941	300	141	55	2,266	1,187	3.06	3.64	3.22	616
SP	1901-17	E.Plank	623	529	4,496	326	194	23	2,246	1,072	2.35	3.14	3.58	524
SP	1897-10	R.Waddell	407	340	2,961	193	143	5	2,316	803	2.16	3.23	3.61	338
SP	1949-64	B.Shantz	537	171	1,936	119	99	48	1,072	643	3.38	3.80	3.85	159
SP	1920-32	E.Rommel	500	249	2,556	171	119	29	599	724	3.54	4.27	3.89	198
Starters	Averages		537	349	3,178	222	139	32	1,700	886	2.81	3.54	3.58	367
RP	1988-99	J.Corsi	368	1	481	22	24	7	290	191	3.25	3.68	3.51	56
RP	1968-85	R.Fingers	944	37	1,701	114	118	341	1,299	492	2.90	3.25	3.53	199
RP	1988-93	T.Burns	203	33	490	21	23	13	252	175	3.47	3.84	3.92	35
RP	1995-	T.Mathews	320	0	379	31	25	15	315	147	3.79	4.34	3.95	26
Relievers	Averages		459	18	763	47	48	94	539	251	3.16	3.55	3.64	79
Totals	Averages		995	367	3,941	269	187	126	2,239	1,137	2.88	3.54	3.59	446

Philadelphia/Kansas City/Oakland Athletics
Catchers

V	R	Years	Name	AB	BB	HBP	TAB	H	2B	3B	HR	BA	OB	SA	PRO	Wtd PRO	SB	CS	SBF	SPF	FF	R TF	V HC
1	1	1925-37	M.Cochrane	5,169	857	29	6,055	1,652	333	64	119	.320	.419	.478	897	842	64	46	(4)	8	58	904	687
2	2	1969-83	G.Tenace	4,390	984	91	5,465	1,060	179	20	201	.241	.391	.429	819	838	36	42	(8)	(9)	(23)	797	215
3	4	1986-	T.Steinbach	5,369	418	48	5,835	1,453	273	21	162	.271	.329	.420	749	725	23	22	(3)	(9)	(2)	711	96
4	3	1897-08	Schreckengost	3,057	102	12	3,171	829	136	31	9	.271	.297	.345	642	697	52	0	0	(8)	42	731	88
5	5	1933-47	F.Hayes	4,493	564	13	5,070	1,164	213	32	119	.259	.343	.400	744	724	30	20	(2)	(2)	(13)	706	73
6	7	1973-84	J.Essian	1,855	231	6	2,092	453	85	3	33	.244	.330	.347	676	681	9	13	(8)	(2)	19	691	13
7	8	1939-51	B.Rosar	3,198	315	10	3,523	836	147	15	18	.261	.330	.334	663	666	17	18	(5)	(5)	26	682	8
8	6	1955-64	H.Smith	2,682	196	14	2,892	715	148	10	58	.267	.320	.394	714	704	7	10	(4)	(5)	(4)	691	6
9	9	1937-49	H.Wagner	1,849	253	15	2,117	458	90	12	15	.248	.343	.334	677	687	10	6	(1)	(2)	(3)	681	4
10	11	1964-76	D.Duncan	2,885	252	14	3,151	617	79	4	109	.214	.280	.357	638	668	5	13	(6)	(10)	3	655	(34)
11	12	1961-77	P.Roof	2,151	184	23	2,358	463	69	13	43	.215	.284	.319	604	628	11	10	(4)	(10)	32	646	(35)
12	10	1978-91	M.Heath	4,212	278	22	4,512	1,061	173	27	86	.252	.302	.367	669	670	54	40	(6)	(2)	(5)	657	(55)
13	13	1915-34	C.Perkins	3,604	301	15	3,920	933	175	35	30	.259	.319	.352	670	640	18	34	(12)	(10)	20	638	(78)
14	14	1976-84	J.Newman	2,123	116	6	2,245	475	85	4	63	.224	.266	.357	622	624	7	12	(8)	(10)	(2)	603	(104)
15	15	1898-09	D.Powers	2,088	72	18	2,178	450	72	13	4	.216	.248	.268	516	552	27	0	0	(6)	12	558	(136)

Philadelphia/Kansas City/Oakland Athletics
First basemen

V	R	Years	Name	AB	BB	HBP	TAB	H	2B	3B	HR	BA	OB	SA	PRO	Wtd PRO	SB	CS	SBF	SPF	FF	R TF	V HC
1	1	1925-45	J.Foxx	8,134	1,452	13	9,599	2,646	458	125	534	.325	.428	.609	1,038	976	87	72	(6)	2	17	989	1,072
2	2	1986-	M.McGwire	5,888	1,261	72	7,221	1,570	248	6	554	.267	.402	.593	995	957	12	8	(1)	(9)	6	953	650
3	5	1895-17	H.Davis	6,653	525	59	7,237	1,841	361	145	75	.277	.335	.408	743	806	285	2	(1)	(0)	(1)	804	125
4	4	1947-55	F.Fain	3,930	904	18	4,852	1,139	213	30	48	.290	.425	.396	821	803	46	28	(2)	5	15	821	121
5	3	1995-	J.Giambi	2,878	457	35	3,370	870	181	5	149	.302	.404	.524	928	860	7	6	(1)	(9)	(22)	828	106
6	6	1956-68	N.Siebern	4,481	708	10	5,199	1,217	206	38	132	.272	.372	.423	795	794	18	25	(6)	0	3	791	64
7	8	1963-71	K.Harrelson	2,941	382	6	3,329	703	94	14	131	.239	.328	.414	742	778	53	30	(2)	0	(3)	774	15
8	7	1922-29	J.Hauser	2,044	250	20	2,314	580	103	28	80	.284	.367	.479	846	801	19	19	(8)	(8)	(9)	776	7
9	9	1909-27	S.McInnis	7,822	380	38	8,240	2,405	312	101	20	.307	.343	.381	723	739	172	59	(7)	5	28	765	(9)
10	10	1954-65	V.Power	6,046	279	15	6,340	1,716	290	49	126	.284	.317	.411	728	721	45	35	(4)	10	35	762	(21)
11	11	1978-82	D.Revering	1,832	148	2	1,982	486	83	16	62	.265	.321	.430	750	749	2	10	(9)	(10)	(18)	712	(59)
12	12	1932-45	D.Siebert	3,917	276	14	4,207	1,104	204	40	32	.282	.331	.379	710	710	30	32	(8)	0	8	710	(125)
13	13	1964-75	D.Cater	4,451	254	22	4,727	1,229	191	29	66	.276	.318	.377	695	726	26	30	(7)	(10)	(11)	698	(157)

Philadelphia/Kansas City/Oakland Athletics
Second basemen

V	R	Years	Name	AB	BB	HBP	TAB	H	2B	3B	HR	BA	OB	SA	PRO	Wtd PRO	SB	CS	SBF	SPF	FF	R TF	V HC
1	1	1900-15	D.Murphy	5,399	335	47	5,781	1,563	289	102	44	.289	.336	.405	742	824	193	0	0	5	3	831	333
2	2	1924-35	M.Bishop	4,494	1,153	31	5,678	1,216	236	35	41	.271	.423	.366	789	742	43	50	(9)	(0)	1	734	136
3	5	1985-97	M.Gallego	2,931	326	32	3,289	700	111	12	42	.239	.322	.328	650	643	24	31	(11)	0	45	677	3
4	3	1963-74	D.Green	4,007	345	32	4,384	960	145	23	80	.240	.305	.347	652	675	26	20	(3)	(2)	9	679	(12)
5	4	1956-67	J.Lumpe	4,912	428	8	5,348	1,314	190	52	47	.268	.327	.356	683	685	20	15	(2)	(1)	(3)	679	(22)
6	6	1996-	S.Spiezio	1,517	161	8	1,686	377	87	6	39	.249	.324	.391	715	667	11	9	(4)	0	(7)	656	(38)
7	8	1943-46	I.Hall	1,904	97	15	2,016	496	58	19	0	.261	.302	.311	613	643	16	23	(14)	10	(1)	637	(42)
8	7	1993-	B.Gates	2,329	225	10	2,564	616	119	11	25	.264	.332	.357	689	650	18	13	(2)	0	(3)	645	(66)
9	11	1983-92	D.Hill	2,307	175	3	2,485	594	91	14	26	.257	.311	.343	654	650	22	11	0	0	(57)	593	(106)
10	10	1967-76	T.Kubiak	2,447	271	4	2,722	565	61	21	13	.231	.309	.289	598	616	13	22	(11)	0	(9)	597	(117)
11	9	1941-55	P.Suder	5,085	288	7	5,380	1,268	210	44	49	.249	.291	.337	627	623	19	28	(6)	0	6	623	(174)

Philadelphia/Kansas City/Oakland Athletics
Shortstops

V	R	Years	Name	AB	BB	HBP	TAB	H	2B	3B	HR	BA	OB	SA	PRO	Wtd PRO	SB	CS	SBF	SPF	FF	R TF	V HC
1	3	1964-83	B.Campaneris	8,684	618	64	9,366	2,249	313	86	79	.259	.313	.342	655	680	649	199	25	10	2	717	240
2	2	1936-55	E.Joost	5,606	1,043	33	6,682	1,339	238	35	134	.239	.361	.366	727	724	61	31	(4)	1	4	725	199
3	1	1997-	M.Tejada	1,664	153	24	1,841	421	88	8	64	.253	.325	.431	756	698	21	13	(3)	10	29	734	64
4	5	1990-	M.Bordick	4,831	415	52	5,298	1,264	207	25	71	.262	.327	.359	686	648	77	50	(4)	3	22	669	11
5	4	1955-68	W.Causey	3,244	390	15	3,649	819	130	26	35	.252	.335	.341	676	687	12	12	(3)	0	(8)	675	(2)
6	6	1908-19	J.Barry	4,146	396	76	4,618	1,009	142	38	10	.243	.321	.303	624	678	153	18	(2)	4	(12)	667	(6)
7	7	1892-07	M.Cross	5,821	616	82	6,519	1,364	232	68	31	.234	.316	.314	630	650	328	0	0	6	2	659	(11)
8	10	1927-32	J.Boley	1,780	130	13	1,923	478	88	22	7	.269	.323	.354	677	635	15	8	(0)	(8)	(26)	601	(59)
9	8	1929-42	E.McNair	4,519	261	24	4,804	1,240	229	29	82	.274	.317	.392	710	664	59	54	(10)	1	(24)	631	(106)
10	9	1919-28	C.Galloway	3,583	274	5	3,862	946	136	46	17	.264	.317	.342	659	620	79	71	(15)	10	(9)	606	(109)
11	12	1973-80	M.Guerrero	2,251	84	16	2,351	578	79	12	7	.257	.288	.312	600	612	8	12	(6)	6	(47)	565	(112)
12	11	1951-61	J.DeMaestri	3,441	168	17	3,626	813	114	23	49	.236	.275	.325	601	594	15	19	(6)	0	2	590	(131)

Philadelphia/Kansas City/Oakland Athletics
Third basemen

V	R	Years	Name	AB	BB	HBP	TAB	H	2B	3B	HR	BA	OB	SA	PRO	Wtd PRO	SB	CS	SBF	SPF	FF	R TF	V HC
1	1	1908-22	F.Baker	5,984	473	50	6,507	1,838	315	103	96	.307	.363	.442	805	857	235	28	(4)	6	18	877	538
2	2	1966-81	S.Bando	7,060	1,031	75	8,166	1,790	289	38	242	.254	.355	.408	763	787	75	46	(2)	(7)	(15)	764	189
3	6	1918-39	J.Dykes	8,046	958	109	9,113	2,256	453	90	108	.280	.365	.399	764	718	70	55	(4)	(2)	26	737	139
4	4	1978-92	C.Lansford	7,158	553	64	7,775	2,074	332	40	151	.290	.346	.411	757	762	224	104	2	6	(22)	747	119
5	3	1962-69	E.Charles	3,482	332	28	3,842	917	147	30	86	.263	.332	.397	729	749	86	35	4	8	(2)	760	78
6	5	1991-	S.Brosius	3,461	314	42	3,817	946	175	6	128	.273	.341	.438	779	727	54	29	(2)	0	21	746	53
7	7	1939-55	H.Majeski	3,421	299	27	3,747	956	181	27	57	.279	.342	.398	740	724	10	11	(4)	0	15	736	40
8	8	1920-30	S.Hale	2,915	130	22	3,067	880	157	54	30	.302	.336	.424	760	714	41	20	0	0	(16)	698	(28)
9	9	1976-86	W.Gross	3,125	482	20	3,627	727	126	9	121	.233	.339	.395	734	732	24	22	(5)	(8)	(35)	684	(69)
10	11	1942-53	B.Hitchcock	2,249	206	10	2,465	547	67	22	5	.243	.310	.299	609	601	15	11	(3)	0	(6)	593	(124)
11	10	1993-	C.Paquette	1,966	92	7	2,065	470	97	9	80	.239	.276	.420	695	625	23	12	(0)	0	(25)	600	(129)

Philadelphia/Kansas City/Oakland Athletics
Outfielders

V	R	Years	Name	AB	BB	HBP	TAB	H	2B	3B	HR	BA	OB	SA	PRO	Wtd PRO	SB	CS	SBF	SPF	FF	R TF	V HC
1	1	1979-	R.Henderson	10,331	2,060	90	12,481	2,914	486	62	282	.282	.406	.423	829	815	1,370	326	53	10	23	902	892
2	2	1924-44	A.Simmons	8,759	615	30	9,404	2,927	539	149	307	.334	.380	.535	915	857	88	64	(4)	(0)	32	886	605
3	3	1933-45	B.Johnson	6,920	1,075	24	8,019	2,051	396	95	288	.296	.393	.506	899	867	96	64	(4)	8	10	882	501
4	5	1967-87	R.Jackson	9,864	1,375	96	11,335	2,584	463	49	563	.262	.358	.490	848	864	228	115	(0)	5	(23)	847	494
5	7	1985-	J.Canseco	6,801	861	83	7,745	1,811	332	14	446	.266	.356	.516	872	846	198	87	3	1	(19)	831	284
6	6	1898-11	T.Hartsel	4,848	837	12	5,697	1,336	182	92	31	.276	.384	.370	754	838	247	0	0	7	(14)	832	215
7	4	1899-08	S.Seybold	3,685	293	40	4,018	1,085	218	54	51	.294	.353	.424	777	852	66	0	0	0	2	855	204
8	8	1978-89	D.Murphy	4,347	747	19	5,113	1,069	139	20	166	.246	.359	.402	761	763	100	61	(4)	9	48	816	149
9	11	1940-61	E.Valo	5,029	942	38	6,009	1,420	228	73	58	.282	.399	.391	791	780	110	79	(8)	9	7	789	95
10	12	1967-82	J.Rudi	5,556	369	35	5,960	1,468	287	39	179	.264	.314	.427	741	764	25	15	(1)	0	24	788	81
11	15	1935-51	W.Moses	7,356	821	21	8,198	2,138	435	110	89	.291	.364	.416	779	757	174	81	1	9	10	777	78
12	13	1908-24	A.Strunk	4,999	573	12	5,584	1,418	213	96	15	.284	.359	.374	732	763	185	86	(15)	7	25	779	64
13	10	1935-49	B.Estalella	2,196	350	8	2,554	620	106	33	44	.282	.383	.421	804	822	13	17	(8)	0	(21)	793	58
14	16	1911-23	T.Walker	5,067	416	27	5,510	1,423	244	71	118	.281	.339	.427	766	784	129	47	(5)	0	(2)	777	57
15	9	1951-62	B.Cerv	2,261	212	17	2,490	624	96	26	105	.276	.343	.481	823	816	12	10	(3)	(10)	(7)	796	49
16	14	1949-59	G.Zernial	4,131	383	24	4,538	1,093	159	22	237	.265	.331	.486	816	800	15	7	0	(10)	(11)	779	48
17	27	1982-99	T.Phillips	7,617	1,319	42	8,978	2,023	360	50	160	.266	.377	.389	766	749	177	114	(5)	5	(13)	736	41
18	20	1921-36	B.Miller	6,212	383	80	6,675	1,934	389	96	116	.311	.359	.461	820	770	127	82	(5)	0	0	765	24
19	19	1938-51	S.Chapman	4,988	562	15	5,565	1,329	210	52	180	.266	.342	.438	780	751	41	38	(6)	6	15	766	23
20	21	1981-94	D.Henderson	5,130	465	22	5,617	1,324	286	17	197	.258	.322	.436	758	755	50	38	(4)	4	9	764	19
21	17	1997-	B.Grieve	1,756	234	21	2,011	492	108	3	76	.280	.371	.475	846	785	9	2	2	0	(14)	773	15
22	18	1992-	M.Stairs	2,145	306	14	2,465	573	119	6	123	.267	.362	.500	863	802	19	16	(5)	(10)	(18)	769	13
23	22	1971-81	B.North	3,900	627	25	4,552	1,016	120	31	20	.261	.366	.323	689	707	395	162	16	10	30	762	9
24	24	1976-89	T.Armas	5,164	260	15	5,439	1,302	204	39	251	.252	.290	.453	742	747	18	20	(3)	(2)	16	758	2
25	25	1977-84	M.Page	2,104	245	18	2,367	560	84	21	72	.266	.348	.429	776	770	104	55	(2)	10	(23)	755	(2)
26	23	1912-26	E.Murphy	2,373	294	36	2,703	680	66	32	4	.287	.374	.346	720	774	111	50	(10)	9	(15)	758	(4)
27	26	1905-18	R.Oldring	4,690	206	45	4,941	1,268	205	76	27	.270	.307	.364	671	738	197	22	(4)	10	8	752	(8)
28	28	1980-89	M.Davis	2,999	236	10	3,245	778	161	16	91	.259	.316	.415	730	725	134	56	6	9	(8)	732	(39)
29	29	1989-	G.Berroa	2,506	276	17	2,799	692	113	9	101	.276	.352	.449	801	755	19	16	(4)	0	(23)	729	(41)
30	37	1912-17	J.Walsh	1,771	249	11	2,031	410	71	31	6	.232	.330	.317	647	702	92	49	(16)	10	(2)	694	(64)
31	35	1916-26	W.Witt	4,171	489	7	4,667	1,195	144	62	18	.287	.362	.364	726	714	78	41	(9)	10	(8)	707	(65)
32	33	1905-13	B.Lord	2,767	175	18	2,960	707	119	49	13	.256	.304	.348	652	710	74	0	0	0	2	712	(68)
33	39	1917-27	B.Lamar	2,040	86	2	2,128	633	114	23	19	.310	.339	.417	755	715	25	27	(16)	0	(14)	685	(78)
34	32	1896-08	O.Pickering	3,349	286	25	3,660	910	96	39	9	.272	.334	.332	665	710	194	0	0	10	(4)	716	(80)
35	34	1951-59	H.Simpson	2,829	271	10	3,110	752	101	41	73	.266	.332	.408	740	730	17	18	(6)	0	(16)	708	(80)
36	36	1898-05	D.Fultz	2,393	201	20	2,614	648	84	26	3	.271	.332	.331	664	702	189	0	0	10	(15)	697	(84)
37	30	1925-38	M.Haas	4,303	433	13	4,749	1,257	254	45	43	.292	.359	.402	761	713	12	16	(4)	0	14	723	(85)
38	43	1963-74	J.Gosger	1,815	217	6	2,038	411	67	16	30	.226	.311	.331	642	666	25	18	(5)	9	(1)	669	(86)
39	45	1962-70	J.Tartabull	1,857	115	1	1,973	484	56	24	2	.261	.304	.320	624	643	81	28	12	10	(2)	664	(88)
40	42	1952-65	B.Del Greco	1,982	271	32	2,285	454	95	11	42	.229	.331	.352	683	676	16	15	(6)	10	(10)	670	(97)
41	41	1919-27	F.Welch	2,310	250	18	2,578	634	100	31	41	.274	.350	.398	748	705	18	28	(14)	0	(10)	682	(98)
42	31	1984-	S.Javier	4,766	542	23	5,331	1,276	211	39	53	.268	.345	.362	707	683	235	50	24	10	0	717	(107)
43	38	1956-65	G.Cimoli	3,054	221	14	3,289	808	133	48	44	.265	.317	.383	700	687	21	6	3	10	(13)	686	(115)
44	40	1961-71	M.Hershberger	3,572	319	31	3,922	900	150	22	26	.252	.319	.328	647	668	74	36	0	10	5	684	(138)
45	44	1931-47	L.Finney	4,631	329	9	4,969	1,329	203	85	31	.287	.335	.388	723	688	39	45	(10)	0	(12)	667	(239)

Philadelphia/Kansas City/Oakland Athletics
Starting Pitchers

V	R	Years	Name	G	GS	IP	W	L	SV	SO	BB	ERA	RA/9	R Wtd RA/9	V Runs /162
1	1	1925-41	L.Grove	616	457	3,941	300	141	55	2,266	1,187	3.06	3.64	3.22	616.1
2	2	1901-17	E.Plank	623	529	4,496	326	194	23	2,246	1,072	2.35	3.14	3.58	524.0
3	3	1897-10	R.Waddell	407	340	2,961	193	143	5	2,316	803	2.16	3.23	3.61	338.0
4	7	1969-86	V.Blue	502	473	3,343	209	161	2	2,175	1,185	3.27	3.65	3.99	216.4
5	6	1903-25	C.Bender	459	334	3,017	212	127	34	1,711	712	2.46	3.31	3.98	204.5
6	5	1920-32	E.Rommel	500	249	2,556	171	119	29	599	724	3.54	4.27	3.89	198.2
7	8	1965-79	C.Hunter	500	476	3,449	224	166	1	2,012	954	3.26	3.60	4.08	184.8
8	4	1949-64	B.Shantz	537	171	1,936	119	99	48	1,072	643	3.38	3.80	3.85	158.8
9	10	1906-20	J.Coombs	354	269	2,320	158	110	8	1,052	841	2.78	3.59	4.27	80.0
10	12	1923-37	R.Walberg	544	306	2,644	155	141	32	1,085	1,031	4.16	4.84	4.30	78.3
11	17	1912-28	J.Bush	489	368	3,087	195	183	20	1,319	1,263	3.51	4.20	4.36	71.0
12	16	1978-95	D.Stewart	523	348	2,630	168	129	19	1,741	1,034	3.95	4.31	4.34	66.4
13	9	1942-50	J.Flores	176	113	973	44	59	6	352	306	3.18	3.65	4.09	52.7
14	14	1903-13	C.Morgan	210	172	1,445	78	78	3	667	578	2.51	3.65	4.32	39.5
15	15	1977-85	S.McCatty	221	161	1,188	63	63	5	541	520	3.99	4.40	4.32	33.2
16	11	1915-21	S.Perry	132	104	893	40	68	5	231	284	3.07	4.06	4.29	30.2
17	13	1947-53	L.Brissie	234	93	898	44	48	29	436	451	4.07	4.53	4.32	24.7
18	21	1928-36	G.Earnshaw	319	249	1,915	127	93	12	1,002	809	4.38	4.99	4.47	19.6
19	19	1933-39	J.Marcum	195	132	1,099	65	63	7	392	344	4.66	5.15	4.41	19.4
20	18	1991-	G.Heredia	243	110	844	50	43	4	499	192	4.32	4.78	4.37	18.6
21	20	1942-48	R.Christopher	241	97	1,000	54	64	35	424	399	3.37	3.97	4.43	15.0
22	22	1975-90	M.Norris	201	157	1,124	58	59	0	636	499	3.89	4.34	4.49	9.3
23	23	1976-86	R.Langford	260	196	1,491	73	106	0	671	416	4.01	4.50	4.56	(0.4)
24	24	1902-11	A.Coakley	150	124	1,072	58	59	3	428	314	2.35	3.66	4.57	(1.2)
25	25	1905-10	J.Dygert	175	105	986	57	49	2	583	383	2.65	3.64	4.59	(4.0)
26	26	1940-50	P.Marchildon	185	162	1,214	68	75	2	481	684	3.93	4.48	4.61	(7.6)
27	27	1966-72	J.Nash	201	167	1,107	68	64	4	771	401	3.58	3.99	4.65	(11.3)
28	29	1983-93	C.Young	251	162	1,107	69	53	0	536	366	4.31	4.72	4.74	(22.5)
29	28	1950-66	R.Herbert	407	236	1,881	104	107	15	864	571	4.01	4.43	4.67	(24.6)
30	31	1932-38	S.Cain	178	137	987	53	60	1	279	569	4.83	5.57	4.81	(29.3)
31	34	1955-64	B.Daley	248	116	967	60	64	10	549	351	4.03	4.68	4.84	(31.7)
32	33	1977-86	M.Keough	215	175	1,190	58	84	0	590	510	4.17	4.77	4.84	(39.5)
33	32	1941-52	D.Fowler	221	170	1,303	66	79	4	382	578	4.11	4.73	4.83	(41.3)
34	40	1950-57	H.Byrd	187	108	828	46	54	9	381	355	4.35	4.81	4.99	(42.2)
35	35	1966-75	C.Dobson	202	190	1,258	74	69	0	758	476	3.78	4.16	4.86	(42.8)
36	42	1954-60	A.Portocarrero	166	117	817	38	57	2	338	320	4.32	4.74	5.02	(44.5)
37	36	1942-55	J.Coleman	223	140	1,134	52	76	6	444	566	4.38	4.89	4.90	(45.1)
38	30	1920-28	S.Harriss	349	228	1,750	95	135	16	644	630	4.25	5.17	4.78	(46.3)
39	39	1926-36	R.Mahaffey	224	128	1,056	67	49	5	365	452	5.01	5.74	4.98	(51.9)
40	45	1941-47	L.Harris	151	91	820	35	63	3	232	265	4.16	4.71	5.16	(58.1)
41	37	1964-76	B.Odom	295	229	1,509	84	85	1	857	788	3.70	4.23	4.91	(60.3)
42	44	1917-24	R.Naylor	181	136	1,011	42	83	0	282	346	3.93	5.20	5.06	(60.8)
43	51	1995-	J.Haynes	139	118	722	38	47	1	467	378	5.63	6.13	5.40	(68.0)
44	43	1920-33	F.Heimach	296	127	1,289	62	69	7	334	360	4.46	5.28	5.04	(72.1)
45	41	1934-46	G.Caster	376	127	1,378	76	100	39	595	597	4.54	5.45	5.01	(72.8)
46	50	1943-48	D.Black	154	113	797	34	55	1	293	400	4.35	4.80	5.39	(77.1)
47	38	1948-59	A.Kellner	321	250	1,849	101	112	5	816	747	4.41	4.94	4.94	(83.4)
48	46	1961-74	L.Krausse	321	167	1,284	68	91	21	721	493	4.00	4.45	5.21	(93.3)
49	48	1943-54	C.Scheib	267	107	1,071	45	65	17	290	493	4.88	5.32	5.30	(93.3)
50	47	1983-95	B.Krueger	301	164	1,194	68	66	4	639	493	4.35	5.16	5.26	(95.2)

Philadelphia/Kansas City/Oakland Athletics
Starting Pitchers

V	R	Years	Name	G	GS	IP	W	L	SV	SO	BB	ERA	RA/9	R Wtd RA/9	V Runs /162
51	49	1936-45	B.Ross	237	182	1,365	56	95	2	360	573	4.94	5.82	5.33	(124.0)
52	52	1915-22	E.Myers	185	127	1,102	55	72	7	428	440	4.06	5.11	5.79	(163.1)

Philadelphia/Kansas City/Oakland Athletics
Relief Pitchers

V	R	Years	Name	G	GS	IP	W	L	SV	SO	BB	ERA	RA/9	R Wtd RA/9	V Runs /162
1	2	1968-85	R.Fingers	944	37	1,701	114	118	341	1,299	492	2.90	3.25	3.53	198.7
2	1	1988-99	J.Corsi	368	1	481	22	24	7	290	191	3.25	3.68	3.51	56.4
3	3	1988-93	T.Burns	203	33	490	21	23	13	252	175	3.47	3.84	3.92	34.5
4	8	1965-78	P.Lindblad	655	32	1,214	68	63	64	671	384	3.29	3.78	4.30	34.2
5	4	1995-	T.Mathews	320	0	379	31	25	15	315	147	3.79	4.34	3.95	25.8
6	7	1983-89	K.Atherton	342	0	566	33	41	26	349	215	3.99	4.26	4.24	20.2
7	5	1993-	S.Karsay	169	40	389	22	29	21	287	132	4.37	4.65	4.12	19.3
8	9	1961-69	J.Wyatt	435	9	687	42	44	103	540	346	3.47	3.80	4.31	19.1
9	10	1994-	C.Reyes	273	26	508	20	31	4	343	210	4.61	4.96	4.35	12.7
10	6	1994-	B.Taylor	316	0	323	16	28	100	304	133	4.21	4.77	4.23	12.6
11	12	1964-74	J.Aker	495	0	746	47	45	123	404	274	3.28	3.76	4.41	12.4
12	11	1978-87	J.Johnson	214	61	603	26	33	9	407	250	3.90	4.39	4.39	11.5
13	14	1952-59	T.Gorman	289	33	689	36	36	42	321	239	3.77	4.33	4.49	5.5
14	13	1984-96	D.Leiper	264	0	278	12	8	7	150	114	3.98	4.56	4.47	2.9
15	15	1981-93	G.Nelson	493	68	1,080	53	64	28	655	418	4.13	4.47	4.53	2.7
16	16	1977-84	B.Lacey	284	2	451	20	29	22	251	139	3.67	4.25	4.55	0.6
17	17	1958-75	O.Pena	427	93	1,202	56	77	40	818	352	3.71	4.11	4.56	(0.2)
18	18	1972-80	D.Hamilton	301	57	704	39	41	31	434	317	3.85	4.33	4.69	(10.3)
19	21	1993-	M.Mohler	332	20	402	14	26	10	272	223	4.90	5.39	4.88	(14.6)
20	22	1992-	B.Groom	479	15	468	21	21	12	306	197	5.10	5.49	4.93	(20.2)
21	20	1949-59	M.Martin	250	42	605	38	34	15	245	249	4.29	4.76	4.87	(22.1)
22	23	1974-79	J.Todd	270	8	511	25	23	24	194	239	4.23	4.97	5.24	(39.0)
23	25	1995-	D.Wengert	156	44	423	14	30	3	222	151	5.60	5.88	5.40	(39.8)
24	19	1962-77	D.Segui	639	171	1,808	92	111	71	1,298	786	3.81	4.32	4.82	(53.7)
25	24	1963-71	J.O'Donoghue	257	96	751	39	55	10	377	260	4.07	4.58	5.29	(61.5)

PHILADELPHIA PHILLIES
(1900–2000)

The Philadelphia Phillies struggled throughout the twentieth century, with just 33 winning seasons, while finishing in last place an incredible 30 times. Philadelphia did feature several star players, interspersed through time. Pete Alexander, Gavvy Cravath, and Dave Bancroft played in the 1915 World Series. Richie Ashburn, Stan Lopata, and Robin Roberts starred for the pennant-winning Whiz Kids in 1950. Mike Schmidt, Steve Carlton, and Garry Maddox played for five division winners in the 1970s and 1980s; Greg Luzinski played for four of these teams; and Dick Allen played for the 1976 team near the end of his career. Darren Daulton, John Kruk, Len Dykstra, and Curt Schilling played in the 1993 World Series. Sadly, Phillies stars Sherry Magee, Roy Thomas, Cy Williams, Chuck Klein, Dolph Camilli, Johnny Callison, Jim Bunning, Bobby Abreu and Scott Rolen have never had a chance to appear in a Phillies postseason.

Profiled Phillies Players

Mike Schmidt

Schmidt simply dominated his position, while excelling in every phase of the game. Schmidt's 548 home runs ranks eighth all-time; he drew 1,507 walks, which gave him a career .384 on-base percentage; he stole 174 bases—high for a third baseman; and he was probably the greatest fielding third baseman of all time. Adjusting for a career 1 percent hitter's deflation, he hit .271 with 568 home runs over his career, for a 924 Wtd. Production. Fifty-six career Fielding Factor points helped Schmidt

achieve a career 984 Total Factor, which is nearly 100 points higher than the next highest third baseman of all time. Schmidt's 1,283 Hits Contribution is nearly 50 percent higher than the second best third baseman, and sixth best in league history for any position behind Wagner, Mays, Aaron, Barry Bonds, and Hornsby.

Dick Allen

Allen was one of the most feared hitters of his time. His fielding and his unruly disposition were his only real weaknesses. Allen's fielding caused him to be moved from third base to the outfield, and finally to first base, where he appeared in over half his career games. His disposition caused him to be traded from team to team, and to even retire briefly during the 1974 season, when he was still near his peak level of performance.

Allen hit .292 with 351 home runs over his 15-year career. Adjusted for a career 3.5 percent hitter's deflation, Allen hit .302 with 362 home runs, for a 946 Wtd. Production, a 930 Total Factor, and the National League's third best volume of success for a first baseman with 641 Hits Contribution. Allen, as one of the best first basemen ever, deserves the Hall of Fame recognition that his attitude may have cost him.

Sherry Magee

Magee was one of the original stars of the National League. If he had played for winning teams in Pittsburgh, Chicago, or New York, Magee would probably be in the Hall of Fame, as his career statistics rank him as one of the top 15 or 20 National League outfielders of all time. Magee even missed his chance for glory with the Phillies, as he was traded to the 1914 National League pennant winner Boston just before the 1915 season, only to have the Phillies edge Boston for the pennant in 1915. He hit .291 with 83 home runs and 441 stolen bases over his career. Adjusting for a career 9 percent hitter's deflation, Magee hit .319 with 93 home runs, for an 884 Total Factor and 528 Hits Contribution.

Chuck Klein

Klein earned his Hall of Fame recognition in his first five full seasons with the Phillies. Klein's numbers in those five years are nearly unbelievable, as he averaged 224 hits, 46 doubles, 9 triples, 36 home runs, and 92 extra-base hits, while hitting .359. While the tiny Baker Bowl and the hitter's inflation over his career padded his statistics, Klein deserves respect for achieving what almost no other hitter accomplished over a similar five year period.

Of course, if his first five years were so impressive, what does that say about the rest of his career? Excluding those five years, Klein's performance was only slightly better than average, much like Ernie Banks' statistics for the Cubs after he was moved to first base:

Years	TAB	HR	BA	Adj. BA	Wtd. PRO	TF	HC
1929–33	3,404	180	.359	.342	998	1,002	418
All other	3,695	120	.284	.279	789	772	27

In his career, Klein hit .320 with 300 home runs. Adjusted for a career 3.5 percent hitter's inflation, he hit .309 with 304 home runs. His 883 Total Factor ranks Klein 21st in league rate of success among outfielders, while his 444 hits Contribution ranks 22nd in league volume of success.

Cy Williams

Williams was born ten years too soon. He arrived in the big leagues in 1912 as a 24-year-old rookie with the Cubs, but didn't get a chance to start every day until he was 27. Williams then hit with tremendous power, hitting 13 home runs in 1915 and leading the National League with 12 home runs in 1916. But these low home run totals just weren't a significant factor during the last days of the Dead Ball Era.

Williams' career took off in the 1920s, when he was arguably past his prime. Williams led the league in home runs with 15 in 1920, with 41 in 1923, and with 30 in 1927 at age 39, while hitting over .300 six times. In all, he hit 202 home runs in 1920s, trailing Hornsby's 250 total for the league's best power numbers that decade.

Years	TAB	HR	BA	Adj. BA	Wtd. PRO	TF	HC
1912–19	2,728	49	.260	.286	777	777	42
1920–30	4,828	202	.311	.301	878	871	260

In his career, Williams hit .292 with 251 home runs. Adjusted for a career 1 percent hitter's deflation, he hit .295 with 265 home runs. His 836 Total Factor ranks 61st in league rate of success for outfielders, while his 302 Hits Contribution ranks 44th in league volume of success.

Pete Alexander

Grover Cleveland (Old Pete) Alexander had such a spectacular career due to his fast start that few people realize how much his career suffered after 1917 from war duty, a war injury, epilepsy, and the ensuing alcoholism that plagued him the rest of his life. Pete broke in with the Phillies in 1911, and he proceeded to win 28, 19, 22, 27, 31, 33, and 30 games in his first seven seasons while pitching half his games in tiny Baker Bowl.

Alexander lost almost the entire 1918 season to the war effort. He returned to baseball in a Cubs uniform, and proceeded to have two stellar seasons while toiling in Wrigley Field. In 1919, he boasted his career best 2.44 Wtd. RA/9, the league's 23rd best ever rate of success season, while going 16–11 for the Cubs. In 1920, he won 27 games in his last great season. Alexander continued to pitch until 1930, and he even won 22 in 1923 and 21 in 1927, but he never again came close to the 363 innings he worked in 1920, or the 384 innings he averaged from 1915 to 1917. Alexander prewar statistics in seven seasons with the Phillies versus his post war statistics over 13 seasons appears as follows:

Years	IP	W–L	ERA	Wtd. RA/9	Runs/162
1911–17	2,492	190–88	2.12	3.27	376
1918–30	2,698	183–120	2.96	3.46	350

For his career, Alexander amassed a 373–208 record, which tied him with Christy Mathewson for the league's most wins. Alexander also had 2,198 strikeouts in 5,190 innings, a 2.56 ERA, and a 3.37 Wtd. RA/9, for the league's fourth best rate of success. He saved 726 runs from scoring — the league's best volume of success performance, and 80 runs better than runner-up Mathewson.

Robin Roberts

The Phillies rose from the National League's basement back into the competitive ranks in 1949. Leading the way from the pitcher's rubber was Roberts. Roberts made it to the majors in 1948, and he was 15–15 in his sophomore season in 1949. In 1950, his improvement to 20–11 with a 3.02 ERA and a 3.21 Wtd. RA/9 was a deciding factor in the Phillies winning their first pennant in 35 years. Roberts went on to win 21, 28, 23, 23, and 23 games the next five years. He struggled after 1955 to be better than an average pitcher, and the team struggled with him, falling below .500. The Phillies finally shipped Roberts off to Baltimore in 1962, and he finished his career with Houston in 1966. The two halves of Robin's career:

Years	IP	W–L	ERA	Wtd. RA/9	Runs/162
1948–55	2,311	160–102	3.02	3.37	320
1956–66	2,378	126–143	3.78	4.42	37

In his career, Roberts was 286–245, with a 3.41 ERA, and a 3.90 Wtd. RA/9, the league's 52nd best rate of success. He saved 357 runs from scoring, which is the league's 11th best volume of success.

Steve Carlton

Carlton put up Hall of Fame numbers in his 24 big league seasons. He won over 300 games and struck out the second most batters in history, with 4,136 Ks in 5,217 innings. Carlton won 20 or more games six times, and he was the staff ace for the Phillies during their most successful period ever in the late 1970s and early 1980s. But his career suffered by his hanging on once he turned 40, as every aspect of his performance was a miserable failure in 1985–1988:

Years	IP	W–L	SO's	ERA	Wtd. RA/9	Runs/162
1965–84	4,787	313–207	3,872	3.04	3.86	382
1985–88	430	16–37	264	5.21	6.30	(84)

In his career, Carlton was 329–244, with a 3.22 ERA. His 4.05 Wtd. RA/9 ranks 85th in league rate of success, while his 298 Runs/162 ranks 21st in league volume of success. If he had retired in 1984, when his ERA was beginning to climb, he would have finished with a much higher rate of success over his career, and with a league volume of success that ranks him tenth instead of his actual 21st place.

Philadelphia Phillies   **Hitters Volume of Success**

Pos	Years	Name	AB	BB	HBP	TAB	H	2B	3B	HR	BA	OB	SA	PRO	Wtd PRO	SB	CS	SBF	SPF	FF	R TF	V HC
C	1983-97	D.Daulton	3,630	629	24	4,283	891	197	25	137	.245	.360	.427	787	781	50	10	7	0	(6)	782	204
1B	1963-77	D.Allen	6,332	894	16	7,242	1,848	320	79	351	.292	.381	.534	914	946	133	52	4	10	(30)	930	641
2B	1983-98	J.Samuel	6,081	440	74	6,595	1,578	287	102	161	.259	.317	.420	737	739	396	143	16	10	(23)	742	127
SS	1915-30	D.Bancroft	7,182	827	23	8,032	2,004	320	77	32	.279	.355	.358	714	717	145	75	(9)	8	43	759	396
3B	1972-89	M.Schmidt	8,352	1,507	79	9,938	2,234	408	59	548	.267	.384	.527	912	924	174	92	(1)	5	56	984	1,283
OF	1904-19	S.Magee	7,441	736	109	8,286	2,169	425	166	83	.291	.364	.427	790	864	441	12	(1)	10	10	884	528
OF	1928-44	C.Klein	6,486	601	12	7,099	2,076	398	74	300	.320	.379	.543	922	890	79	0	0	(1)	(6)	883	444
OF	1908-20	G.Cravath	3,951	561	28	4,540	1,134	232	83	119	.287	.380	.478	858	930	89	9	(1)	(1)	(19)	908	352
Starters	Averages		6,182	774	46	7,002	1,742	323	83	216	.282	.366	.466	832	852	188	49	2	5	3	862	497
C	1928-45	S.Davis	4,255	386	22	4,663	1,312	244	22	77	.308	.369	.430	799	780	6	0	0	(10)	(10)	760	193
1B	1986-95	J.Kruk	3,897	649	2	4,548	1,170	199	34	100	.300	.400	.446	846	843	58	31	(1)	(2)	(7)	834	152
2B	1969-80	D.Cash	5,554	424	18	5,996	1,571	243	56	21	.283	.336	.358	694	702	120	74	(4)	10	14	721	102
SS	1970-85	L.Bowa	8,418	474	17	8,909	2,191	262	99	15	.260	.301	.320	621	630	318	105	11	10	23	673	49
3B	1996-	S.Rolen	2,196	300	33	2,529	623	147	14	108	.284	.378	.511	889	831	50	18	5	10	44	890	210
OF	1948-62	R.Ashburn	8,365	1,198	43	9,606	2,574	317	109	29	.308	.397	.382	779	757	234	92	(0)	10	62	828	339
OF	1912-30	C.Williams	6,780	690	86	7,556	1,981	306	74	251	.292	.365	.470	835	840	115	82	(11)	6	0	836	302
OF	1899-11	R.Thomas	5,296	1,042	71	6,409	1,537	100	53	7	.290	.413	.333	747	808	244	0	0	9	21	838	268
Reserves	Averages		5,595	645	37	6,277	1,620	227	58	76	.290	.367	.391	758	761	143	50	(0)	5	18	784	202
Totals	Weighted Ave.		5,986	731	43	6,760	1,701	291	75	170	.284	.366	.443	809	821	173	50	1	5	8	836	399

Pitchers Volume of Success

Pos	Years	Name	G	GS	IP	W	L	SV	SO	BB	ERA	RA/9	R Wtd RA/9	V Runs /162
SP	1911-30	P.Alexander	696	600	5,190	373	208	32	2,198	951	2.56	3.21	3.37	726
SP	1948-66	R.Roberts	676	609	4,689	286	245	25	2,357	902	3.41	3.77	3.90	357
SP	1965-88	S.Carlton	741	709	5,217	329	244	2	4,136	1,833	3.22	3.67	4.05	298
SP	1988-	C.Schilling	355	244	1,902	110	95	13	1,739	499	3.43	3.68	3.67	192
SP	1907-18	G.McQuillan	273	173	1,576	85	89	14	590	401	2.38	3.29	3.99	105
Starters	Averages		548	467	3,715	237	176	17	2,204	917	3.03	3.54	3.78	336
RP	1944-56	J.Konstanty	433	36	946	66	48	74	268	269	3.46	4.00	4.03	58
RP	1965-82	G.Jackson	692	83	1,359	86	75	79	889	511	3.46	3.90	4.33	35
RP	1994-	R.Bottalico	364	0	422	24	31	111	402	223	4.01	4.18	3.87	33
RP	1977-85	W.Brusstar	340	0	485	28	16	14	273	183	3.51	3.77	4.19	20
Relievers	Averages		457	30	803	51	43	70	458	297	3.54	3.95	4.16	36
Totals	Averages		1,005	497	4,518	288	219	87	2,662	1,214	3.12	3.61	3.85	372

Philadelphia Phillies — **Hitters Rate of Success**

Pos	Years	Name	AB	BB	HBP	TAB	H	2B	3B	HR	BA	OB	SA	PRO	Wtd PRO	SB	CS	SBF	SPF	FF	R TF	V HC
C	1983-97	D.Daulton	3,630	629	24	4,283	891	197	25	137	.245	.360	.427	787	781	50	10	7	0	(6)	782	204
1B	1963-77	D.Allen	6,332	894	16	7,242	1,848	320	79	351	.292	.381	.534	914	946	133	52	4	10	(30)	930	641
2B	1983-98	J.Samuel	6,081	440	74	6,595	1,578	287	102	161	.259	.317	.420	737	739	396	143	16	10	(23)	742	127
SS	1915-30	D.Bancroft	7,182	827	23	8,032	2,004	320	77	32	.279	.355	.358	714	717	145	75	(9)	8	43	759	396
3B	1972-89	M.Schmidt	8,352	1,507	79	9,938	2,234	408	59	548	.267	.384	.527	912	924	174	92	(1)	5	56	984	1,283
OF	1908-20	G.Cravath	3,951	561	28	4,540	1,134	232	83	119	.287	.380	.478	858	930	89	9	(1)	(1)	(19)	908	352
OF	1996-	B.Abreu	1,829	316	5	2,150	572	117	29	65	.313	.415	.515	930	862	81	29	10	10	15	898	144
OF	1904-19	S.Magee	7,441	736	109	8,286	2,169	425	166	83	.291	.364	.427	790	864	441	12	(1)	10	10	884	528
Starters	Averages		5,600	739	45	6,383	1,554	288	78	187	.277	.366	.457	823	847	189	53	3	6	6	862	459
C	1948-60	S.Lopata	2,601	393	7	3,001	661	116	25	116	.254	.354	.452	805	779	18	11	(2)	(10)	1	768	137
1B	1986-95	J.Kruk	3,897	649	2	4,548	1,170	199	34	100	.300	.400	.446	846	843	58	31	(1)	(2)	(7)	834	152
2B	1969-80	D.Cash	5,554	424	18	5,996	1,571	243	56	21	.283	.336	.358	694	702	120	74	(4)	10	14	721	102
SS	1970-85	L.Bowa	8,418	474	17	8,909	2,191	262	99	15	.260	.301	.320	621	630	318	105	11	10	23	673	49
3B	1996-	S.Rolen	2,196	300	33	2,529	623	147	14	108	.284	.378	.511	889	831	50	18	5	10	44	890	210
OF	1928-44	C.Klein	6,486	601	12	7,099	2,076	398	74	300	.320	.379	.543	922	890	79	0	0	(1)	(6)	883	444
OF	1985-96	L.Dykstra	4,559	640	31	5,230	1,298	281	43	81	.285	.376	.419	795	790	285	72	25	10	30	855	252
OF	1899-11	R.Thomas	5,296	1,042	71	6,409	1,537	100	53	7	.290	.413	.333	747	808	244	0	0	9	21	838	268
Reserves	Averages		4,876	565	24	5,465	1,391	218	50	94	.285	.362	.408	770	771	147	39	4	5	15	795	202
Totals	Weighted Ave.		5,358	681	38	6,077	1,499	265	68	156	.280	.365	.442	807	822	175	48	3	6	9	840	374

Pitchers Rate of Success

Pos	Years	Name	G	GS	IP	W	L	SV	SO	BB	ERA	RA/9	R Wtd RA/9	V Runs /162
SP	1911-30	P.Alexander	696	600	5,190	373	208	32	2,198	951	2.56	3.21	3.37	726
SP	1988-	C.Schilling	355	244	1,902	110	95	13	1,739	499	3.43	3.68	3.67	192
SP	1948-66	R.Roberts	676	609	4,689	286	245	25	2,357	902	3.41	3.77	3.90	357
SP	1907-18	G.McQuillan	273	173	1,576	85	89	14	590	401	2.38	3.29	3.99	105
SP	1965-88	S.Carlton	741	709	5,217	329	244	2	4,136	1,833	3.22	3.67	4.05	298
Starters	Averages		548	467	3,715	237	176	17	2,204	917	3.03	3.54	3.78	336
RP	1994-	R.Bottalico	364	0	422	24	31	111	402	223	4.01	4.18	3.87	33
RP	1944-56	J.Konstanty	433	36	946	66	48	74	268	269	3.46	4.00	4.03	58
RP	1977-85	W.Brusstar	340	0	485	28	16	14	273	183	3.51	3.77	4.19	20
RP	1965-82	G.Jackson	692	83	1,359	86	75	79	889	511	3.46	3.90	4.33	35
Relievers	Averages		457	30	803	51	43	70	458	297	3.54	3.95	4.16	36
Totals	Averages		1,005	497	4,518	288	219	87	2,662	1,214	3.12	3.61	3.85	372

Philadelphia Phillies
Catchers

V	R	Years	Name	AB	BB	HBP	TAB	H	2B	3B	HR	BA	OB	SA	PRO	Wtd PRO	SB	CS	SBF	SPF	FF	R TF	V HC
1	1	1983-97	D.Daulton	3,630	629	24	4,283	891	197	25	137	.245	.360	.427	787	781	50	10	7	0	(6)	782	204
2	3	1928-45	S.Davis	4,255	386	22	4,663	1,312	244	22	77	.308	.369	.430	799	780	6	0	0	(10)	(10)	760	193
3	2	1948-60	S.Lopata	2,601	393	7	3,001	661	116	25	116	.254	.354	.452	805	779	18	11	(2)	(10)	1	768	137
4	5	1943-57	A.Seminick	3,921	582	40	4,543	953	139	26	164	.243	.347	.417	764	749	23	7	(1)	(10)	(2)	735	132
5	4	1994-	M.Lieberthal	1,959	163	31	2,153	528	118	6	82	.270	.335	.461	797	740	7	5	(1)	(10)	23	752	79
6	7	1980-90	O.Virgil	2,258	248	29	2,535	549	84	6	98	.243	.326	.416	742	746	4	5	(2)	(10)	(15)	719	50
7	6	1921-31	B.Henline	2,101	192	38	2,331	611	96	21	40	.291	.361	.414	774	737	18	10	(2)	(3)	(13)	719	49
8	8	1972-90	B.Boone	7,245	663	20	7,928	1,838	303	26	105	.254	.318	.346	664	665	38	50	(7)	(8)	37	687	39
9	9	1923-40	J.Wilson	4,778	356	18	5,152	1,358	252	32	32	.284	.336	.370	707	676	86	9	(1)	(0)	5	680	7
10	10	1960-71	C.Dalrymple	3,042	387	22	3,451	710	98	23	55	.233	.324	.335	659	671	3	13	(6)	(10)	16	670	(11)
11	11	1909-21	B.Killefer	3,150	113	35	3,298	751	86	21	4	.238	.273	.283	555	600	39	8	(2)	(3)	49	644	(57)
12	12	1902-16	R.Dooin	4,004	155	20	4,179	961	139	31	10	.240	.272	.298	570	626	133	2	0	(1)	5	630	(100)
13	13	1964-74	M.Ryan	1,920	152	4	2,076	370	60	12	28	.193	.253	.280	534	555	4	4	(2)	(10)	23	567	(110)

Philadelphia Phillies
First basemen

V	R	Years	Name	AB	BB	HBP	TAB	H	2B	3B	HR	BA	OB	SA	PRO	Wtd PRO	SB	CS	SBF	SPF	FF	R TF	V HC
1	1	1963-77	D.Allen	6,332	894	16	7,242	1,848	320	79	351	.292	.381	.534	914	946	133	52	4	10	(30)	930	641
2	2	1986-95	J.Kruk	3,897	649	2	4,548	1,170	199	34	100	.300	.400	.446	846	843	58	31	(1)	(2)	(7)	834	152
3	3	1928-34	D.Hurst	3,275	391	15	3,681	976	190	28	115	.298	.375	.478	854	815	41	0	0	0	0	815	84
4	4	1909-20	F.Luderus	4,851	414	45	5,310	1,344	251	54	84	.277	.340	.403	743	797	55	8	(1)	0	3	799	78
5	5	1987-	G.Jefferies	5,520	472	24	6,016	1,593	300	27	126	.289	.347	.421	768	754	196	63	11	10	(22)	753	46
6	6	1992-	R.Brogna	2,752	213	6	2,971	744	167	13	103	.270	.324	.453	777	736	29	15	(0)	0	16	752	(27)
7	8	1956-62	E.Bouchee	2,199	340	27	2,566	583	114	21	61	.265	.370	.419	790	768	5	8	(4)	(10)	(10)	744	(34)
8	10	1988-96	R.Jordan	2,104	77	15	2,196	592	116	10	55	.281	.311	.424	736	745	10	6	(1)	0	(10)	734	(40)
9	7	1898-11	K.Bransfield	4,999	221	24	5,244	1,351	225	75	13	.270	.304	.353	657	727	175	0	0	10	8	745	(68)
10	13	1946-53	D.Sisler	2,606	226	9	2,841	720	118	28	55	.276	.336	.406	743	731	6	3	(1)	(10)	(18)	702	(90)
11	11	1941-55	E.Waitkus	4,254	372	11	4,637	1,214	215	44	24	.285	.344	.374	718	707	28	8	(2)	0	25	729	(94)
12	9	1966-82	W.Montanez	5,843	465	24	6,332	1,604	279	25	139	.275	.331	.402	733	741	32	42	(8)	(0)	3	736	(95)
13	12	1960-76	D.Johnson	5,941	585	20	6,546	1,447	247	33	245	.244	.313	.420	733	751	11	18	(4)	(10)	(18)	719	(134)

Philadelphia Phillies
Second basemen

V	R	Years	Name	AB	BB	HBP	TAB	H	2B	3B	HR	BA	OB	SA	PRO	Wtd PRO	SB	CS	SBF	SPF	FF	R TF	V HC
1	1	1983-98	J.Samuel	6,081	440	74	6,595	1,578	287	102	161	.259	.317	.420	737	739	396	143	16	10	(23)	742	127
2	2	1969-80	D.Cash	5,554	424	18	5,996	1,571	243	56	21	.283	.336	.358	694	702	120	74	(4)	10	14	721	102
3	4	1905-16	O.Knabe	4,469	485	36	4,990	1,103	178	48	8	.247	.325	.313	639	686	143	0	0	8	15	709	58
4	3	1925-34	F.Thompson	2,560	215	5	2,780	762	149	34	13	.298	.353	.398	751	699	69	1	0	10	5	714	40
5	6	1990-	M.Morandini	4,558	437	56	5,051	1,222	209	54	32	.268	.340	.359	698	671	123	45	6	10	3	690	11
6	5	1958-76	T.Taylor	7,680	613	78	8,371	2,007	298	86	75	.261	.322	.352	674	683	234	111	1	10	(1)	693	(12)
7	7	1950-58	B.Morgan	2,088	327	8	2,423	487	96	11	53	.233	.339	.366	705	680	18	11	(2)	3	(15)	666	(29)
8	10	1941-51	D.Murtaugh	2,599	287	9	2,895	661	97	21	8	.254	.331	.317	648	655	49	0	0	10	(5)	660	(30)
9	9	1913-18	B.Niehoff	2,037	131	5	2,173	489	104	19	12	.240	.288	.327	615	677	71	25	(4)	2	(14)	662	(34)
10	12	1944-50	E.Verban	2,911	108	10	3,029	793	99	26	1	.272	.301	.325	626	627	21	0	0	10	13	650	(54)
11	8	1985-97	M.Duncan	4,677	201	37	4,915	1,247	233	37	87	.267	.302	.388	690	679	174	57	11	10	(36)	665	(54)
12	11	1934-39	L.Chiozza	2,288	145	14	2,447	633	107	22	14	.277	.324	.361	685	671	45	0	0	5	(22)	654	(70)
13	13	1970-77	D.Doyle	3,290	205	11	3,506	823	113	28	16	.250	.296	.316	612	627	38	40	(11)	6	(18)	604	(138)

Philadelphia Phillies
Shortstops

V	R	Years	Name	AB	BB	HBP	TAB	H	2B	3B	HR	BA	OB	SA	PRO	Wtd PRO	SB	CS	SBF	SPF	FF	R TF	V HC
1	1	1915-30	D.Bancroft	7,182	827	23	8,032	2,004	320	77	32	.279	.355	.358	714	717	145	75	(9)	8	43	759	396
2	2	1970-85	L.Bowa	8,418	474	17	8,909	2,191	262	99	15	.260	.301	.320	621	630	318	105	11	10	23	673	49
3	3	1905-18	M.Doolan	5,977	370	32	6,379	1,376	244	81	15	.230	.279	.306	584	634	173	0	0	0	38	672	29
4	5	1899-10	R.Hulswitt	2,230	136	10	2,376	564	64	32	3	.253	.299	.314	613	679	49	0	0	0	(22)	656	(7)
5	4	1923-28	H.Sand	3,033	382	15	3,430	781	145	32	18	.258	.343	.344	688	660	21	8	(1)	10	(12)	657	(9)
6	6	1993-	K.Stocker	2,773	313	50	3,136	703	124	28	23	.254	.340	.343	683	645	45	28	(3)	0	(1)	641	(33)
7	10	1940-48	B.Bragan	1,900	110	2	2,012	456	62	12	15	.240	.282	.309	591	609	12	0	0	7	(11)	605	(60)
8	11	1983-90	S.Jeltz	1,749	248	3	2,000	367	46	20	5	.210	.309	.268	577	584	18	10	(1)	0	14	597	(63)
9	8	1958-69	R.Amaro	2,155	227	10	2,392	505	75	13	8	.234	.310	.292	603	602	11	14	(7)	0	15	610	(73)
10	9	1960-72	B.Wine	3,172	214	3	3,389	682	104	16	30	.215	.265	.286	552	562	7	7	(2)	0	48	608	(88)
11	12	1965-71	R.Pena	1,907	114	10	2,031	467	65	10	13	.245	.291	.310	601	625	10	17	(11)	0	(39)	575	(100)
12	7	1944-59	G.Hamner	5,839	351	6	6,196	1,529	272	62	104	.262	.304	.383	688	667	35	14	(0)	0	(33)	634	(122)

Philadelphia Phillies
Third basemen

V	R	Years	Name	AB	BB	HBP	TAB	H	2B	3B	HR	BA	OB	SA	PRO	Wtd PRO	SB	CS	SBF	SPF	FF	R TF	V HC
1	1	1972-89	M.Schmidt	8,352	1,507	79	9,938	2,234	408	59	548	.267	.384	.527	912	924	174	92	(1)	5	56	984	1,283
2	2	1996-	S.Rolen	2,196	300	33	2,529	623	147	14	108	.284	.378	.511	889	831	50	18	5	10	44	890	210
3	3	1928-39	P.Whitney	5,765	400	17	6,182	1,701	303	56	93	.295	.343	.415	758	728	45	0	0	0	24	752	109
4	6	1947-61	W.Jones	5,826	755	22	6,603	1,502	252	33	190	.258	.345	.410	755	732	40	17	(1)	(6)	15	741	81
5	5	1939-43	P.May	2,215	261	9	2,485	610	102	11	4	.275	.354	.337	691	706	13	0	0		42	748	40
6	4	1920-28	R.Wrightstone	2,992	215	22	3,229	889	152	34	60	.297	.349	.431	780	750	35	20	(6)	10	(6)	749	16
7	7	1898-12	H.Wolverton	3,001	166	48	3,215	833	95	53	7	.278	.326	.352	677	707	83	0	0	1	12	721	7
8	8	1990-	D.Hollins	3,324	463	65	3,852	867	166	17	112	.261	.362	.422	784	754	47	26	(1)	0	(38)	714	(11)
9	9	1988-	C.Hayes	5,212	413	21	5,646	1,369	249	16	144	.263	.319	.399	719	698	47	31	(3)	(3)	11	704	(36)
10	10	1919-33	B.Friberg	4,169	471	16	4,656	1,170	181	44	38	.281	.356	.373	728	689	51	60	(16)	0	1	675	(55)
11	11	1902-08	E.Courtney	1,921	188	25	2,134	471	52	17	5	.245	.321	.298	618	692	35	0	0	0	(30)	662	(58)
12	12	1905-15	E.Grant	3,385	233	11	3,629	844	79	30	5	.249	.300	.295	595	649	153	6	(2)	6	(8)	645	(122)

Philadelphia Phillies
Outfielders

V	R	Years	Name	AB	BB	HBP	TAB	H	2B	3B	HR	BA	OB	SA	PRO	Wtd PRO	SB	CS	SBF	SPF	FF	R TF	V HC
1	3	1904-19	S.Magee	7,441	736	109	8,286	2,169	425	166	83	.291	.364	.427	790	864	441	12	(1)	10	10	884	528
2	4	1928-44	C.Klein	6,486	601	12	7,099	2,076	398	74	300	.320	.379	.543	922	890	79	0	0	(1)	(6)	883	444
3	1	1908-20	G.Cravath	3,951	561	28	4,540	1,134	232	83	119	.287	.380	.478	858	930	89	9	(1)	(1)	(19)	908	352
4	9	1948-62	R.Ashburn	8,365	1,198	43	9,606	2,574	317	109	29	.308	.397	.382	779	757	234	92	(0)	10	62	828	339
5	7	1912-30	C.Williams	6,780	690	86	7,556	1,981	306	74	251	.292	.365	.470	835	840	115	82	(11)	6	0	836	302
6	6	1899-11	R.Thomas	5,296	1,042	71	6,409	1,537	100	53	7	.290	.413	.333	747	808	244	0	0	9	21	838	268
7	5	1985-96	L.Dykstra	4,559	640	31	5,230	1,298	281	43	81	.285	.376	.419	795	790	285	72	25	10	30	855	252
8	10	1958-73	J.Callison	6,652	650	41	7,343	1,757	321	89	226	.264	.333	.441	774	789	74	51	(4)	6	31	823	230
9	8	1903-13	J.Titus	4,960	620	94	5,674	1,401	253	72	38	.282	.373	.385	758	828	140	0	0	8	(1)	835	220
10	11	1970-84	G.Luzinski	6,505	845	84	7,434	1,795	344	24	307	.276	.366	.478	844	853	37	31	(3)	(9)	(27)	814	203
11	2	1996-	B.Abreu	1,829	316	5	2,150	572	117	29	65	.313	.415	.515	930	862	81	29	10	10	15	898	144
12	14	1972-86	G.Maddox	6,331	323	36	6,690	1,802	337	62	117	.285	.323	.413	736	742	248	92	9	8	42	801	144
13	15	1981-92	V.Hayes	5,249	712	22	5,983	1,402	282	36	143	.267	.357	.416	773	781	253	97	10	10	(2)	798	109
14	12	1973-83	B.McBride	3,853	248	40	4,141	1,153	167	55	63	.299	.348	.420	768	771	183	63	13	10	15	810	107
15	13	1940-51	D.Litwhiler	3,494	299	27	3,820	982	162	32	107	.281	.342	.438	780	795	11	0	0	6	4	804	90
16	22	1907-21	D.Paskert	6,017	715	41	6,773	1,613	279	77	42	.268	.350	.361	711	763	293	43	(5)	9	15	782	85
17	20	1960-71	T.Gonzalez	5,195	467	71	5,733	1,485	238	57	103	.286	.353	.413	766	780	79	61	(7)	10	5	787	82
18	18	1964-75	J.Briggs	4,117	663	5	4,785	1,041	170	43	139	.253	.357	.416	773	803	64	49	(7)	7	(11)	792	80
19	16	1916-29	G.Harper	3,398	389	35	3,822	1,030	158	43	91	.303	.380	.455	836	798	58	34	(9)	8	(3)	794	71
20	24	1946-59	D.Ennis	7,254	597	31	7,882	2,063	358	69	288	.284	.341	.472	813	793	45	19	(2)	(8)	(12)	772	60
21	17	1928-45	J.Moore	3,013	195	14	3,222	926	155	26	73	.307	.352	.449	801	788	23	0	0	10	(5)	793	57
22	21	1942-57	R.Northey	3,172	361	15	3,548	874	172	28	108	.276	.352	.450	802	813	7	0	0	(10)	(17)	786	52
23	19	1937-45	H.Martin	2,257	253	7	2,517	643	135	29	28	.285	.359	.408	766	774	33	3	1	6	8	789	40
24	23	1908-15	B.Becker	2,764	241	5	3,010	763	114	43	45	.276	.335	.397	732	786	129	15	(6)	10	(10)	781	34
25	25	1939-47	B.Adams	2,003	234	13	2,250	532	96	12	50	.266	.346	.400	747	763	12	0	0	10	(9)	764	7
26	26	1956-67	D.Demeter	3,443	180	42	3,665	912	147	17	163	.265	.309	.459	769	773	22	25	(7)	0	(17)	750	(13)
27	27	1923-32	F.Leach	3,733	163	27	3,923	1,147	196	53	72	.307	.341	.446	787	743	32	4	(1)	7	(1)	747	(21)
28	29	1996-	D.Glanville	2,500	148	15	2,663	730	120	25	32	.292	.335	.398	734	683	109	27	20	10	26	739	(23)
29	31	1926-38	K.Davis	1,824	142	4	1,970	515	112	16	19	.282	.338	.393	728	721	32	0	0	8	(1)	728	(29)
30	33	1936-46	M.Arnovich	2,013	185	10	2,208	577	104	12	22	.287	.350	.383	733	729	17	0	0	0	(2)	727	(33)
31	36	1937-41	J.Marty	1,832	142	10	1,984	478	78	22	44	.261	.318	.400	717	719	14	0	0	10	(8)	721	(37)
32	30	1984-96	M.Thompson	3,761	336	22	4,119	1,029	156	37	47	.274	.337	.372	709	708	214	66	19	10	1	738	(40)
33	38	1921-27	J.Mokan	1,936	206	18	2,160	563	98	17	32	.291	.364	.409	773	741	26	22	(12)	0	(16)	713	(47)
34	34	1986-95	C.James	3,040	193	21	3,254	794	145	24	90	.261	.310	.413	723	730	27	17	(2)	3	(9)	722	(54)
35	35	1912-22	P.Whitted	3,630	215	16	3,861	978	145	60	23	.269	.313	.361	675	723	116	53	(9)	9	(1)	721	(60)
36	28	1893-05	D.Cooley	5,364	365	20	5,749	1,576	180	102	26	.294	.341	.380	721	733	224	0	0	10	(4)	739	(61)
37	32	1966-85	J.Johnstone	4,703	429	22	5,154	1,254	215	38	102	.267	.331	.394	724	738	50	54	(11)	4	(4)	728	(71)
38	40	1937-47	J.Wasdell	2,866	243	13	3,122	782	109	34	29	.273	.332	.365	697	711	29	4	0	5	(9)	707	(86)
39	37	1973-89	G.Gross	3,745	523	8	4,276	1,073	130	46	7	.287	.375	.351	727	733	39	44	(11)	2	(9)	716	(87)
40	39	1982-93	G.Wilson	4,151	253	12	4,416	1,098	209	26	98	.265	.309	.398	707	710	27	25	(5)	(2)	8	711	(98)
41	41	1899-08	S.Barry	4,014	279	37	4,330	1,073	128	47	10	.267	.321	.330	651	710	140	0	0	8	(24)	695	(132)

Philadelphia Phillies
Starting Pitchers

V	R	Years	Name	G	GS	IP	W	L	SV	SO	BB	ERA	RA/9	R Wtd RA/9	V Runs /162
1	1	1911-30	P.Alexander	696	600	5,190	373	208	32	2,198	951	2.56	3.21	3.37	726.1
2	3	1948-66	R.Roberts	676	609	4,689	286	245	25	2,357	902	3.41	3.77	3.90	357.0
3	5	1965-88	S.Carlton	741	709	5,217	329	244	2	4,136	1,833	3.22	3.67	4.05	298.3
4	2	1988-	C.Schilling	355	244	1,902	110	95	13	1,739	499	3.43	3.68	3.67	192.0
5	4	1907-18	G.McQuillan	273	173	1,576	85	89	14	590	401	2.38	3.29	3.99	105.0
6	8	1947-67	C.Simmons	569	461	3,348	193	183	5	1,697	1,063	3.54	4.17	4.37	72.8
7	7	1897-10	T.Sparks	313	269	2,336	121	137	8	778	629	2.79	4.08	4.30	71.0
8	6	1959-73	C.Short	501	308	2,325	135	132	18	1,629	806	3.43	3.84	4.30	65.7
9	10	1914-19	M.Prendergast	180	98	908	41	53	4	311	207	2.74	3.55	4.44	13.0
10	11	1946-59	R.Meyer	319	219	1,531	94	73	5	672	541	3.99	4.47	4.49	11.7
11	9	1949-58	B.Miller	261	69	822	42	42	15	263	247	3.96	4.45	4.44	11.2
12	12	1904-10	F.Corridon	180	140	1,216	70	67	7	458	375	2.80	3.76	4.53	3.2
13	13	1973-83	L.Christenson	243	220	1,403	83	71	4	781	395	3.79	4.16	4.61	(7.9)
14	16	1962-68	D.Bennett	182	127	863	43	47	6	572	281	3.69	4.06	4.64	(7.9)
15	14	1898-03	W.Piatt	182	170	1,390	86	79	1	517	455	3.61	5.31	4.63	(11.9)
16	15	1912-19	E.Mayer	245	164	1,427	91	70	6	482	345	2.96	3.78	4.64	(13.6)
17	19	1912-17	T.Seaton	231	155	1,340	92	65	11	644	530	3.12	4.09	4.67	(17.1)
18	18	1937-52	K.Heintzelman	319	183	1,502	77	98	10	564	630	3.93	4.47	4.66	(18.3)
19	20	1978-89	S.Rawley	469	230	1,871	111	118	40	991	734	4.02	4.41	4.69	(28.8)
20	17	1964-82	R.Wise	506	455	3,127	188	181	0	1,647	804	3.69	4.19	4.65	(32.3)
21	22	1898-07	B.Duggleby	241	191	1,741	93	102	6	453	424	3.18	4.40	4.72	(35.7)
22	25	1960-66	A.Mahaffey	185	148	999	59	64	1	639	368	4.17	4.57	4.90	(38.4)
23	30	1941-48	O.Judd	161	99	771	40	51	7	304	397	3.90	4.66	4.99	(38.8)
24	27	1972-79	R.Schueler	291	86	912	40	48	11	563	393	4.08	4.56	4.96	(41.0)
25	28	1983-89	C.Hudson	208	140	1,008	50	60	2	580	361	4.14	4.63	4.97	(45.8)
26	32	1903-10	L.Moren	141	105	882	48	57	3	356	331	2.95	4.02	5.00	(45.9)
27	21	1983-97	K.Gross	474	368	2,488	142	158	5	1,727	986	4.11	4.50	4.72	(47.2)
28	35	1970-79	W.Twitchell	282	133	1,063	48	65	2	789	537	3.98	4.58	5.05	(58.1)
29	23	1966-83	W.Fryman	625	322	2,411	141	155	58	1,587	890	3.77	4.24	4.78	(60.9)
30	39	1955-67	J.Owens	286	103	885	42	68	21	516	340	4.31	4.91	5.21	(66.4)
31	33	1923-35	P.Collins	292	141	1,324	80	85	24	423	497	4.66	5.33	5.01	(69.9)
32	24	1986-	T.Mulholland	469	307	2,147	112	124	5	1,124	555	4.28	4.76	4.86	(73.9)
33	38	1924-45	B.Beck	265	100	1,034	38	69	6	352	342	4.30	4.88	5.17	(73.9)
34	40	1946-54	K.Drews	218	107	827	44	53	7	322	332	4.76	5.37	5.34	(75.8)
35	31	1925-38	R.Benge	346	249	1,875	101	130	19	655	598	4.52	5.31	5.00	(96.6)
36	26	1965-79	J.Lonborg	425	368	2,464	157	137	4	1,475	823	3.86	4.27	4.92	(101.2)
37	29	1911-32	C.Mitchell	390	278	2,217	125	139	9	543	624	4.12	4.93	4.98	(109.9)
38	42	1975-86	R.Lerch	253	164	1,099	60	64	3	507	432	4.53	5.01	5.46	(115.6)
39	41	1916-23	G.Smith	229	115	1,143	41	81	4	263	255	3.89	5.06	5.45	(124.4)
40	45	1901-05	F.Mitchell	97	86	718	31	49	1	216	303	4.10	5.88	5.96	(124.9)
41	43	1935-47	H.Mulcahy	220	145	1,162	45	89	9	314	487	4.49	5.38	5.49	(126.2)
42	44	1919-25	B.Hubbell	204	108	931	40	63	10	167	225	4.68	5.90	5.79	(134.1)
43	36	1917-28	J.Ring	389	294	2,357	118	149	11	833	953	4.13	5.05	5.08	(147.9)
44	37	1973-86	D.Ruthven	355	332	2,109	123	127	1	1,145	767	4.14	4.59	5.17	(148.2)
45	46	1925-31	C.Willoughby	219	101	841	38	58	9	175	406	5.84	6.74	6.08	(149.6)
46	34	1896-09	C.Fraser	433	388	3,356	175	212	6	1,098	1,332	3.68	5.35	5.01	(189.0)

**Philadelphia Phillies
Relief Pitchers**

V	R	Years	Name	G	GS	IP	W	L	SV	SO	BB	ERA	RA/9	R Wtd RA/9	V Runs /162
1	2	1944-56	J.Konstanty	433	36	946	66	48	74	268	269	3.46	4.00	4.03	58.0
2	4	1965-82	G.Jackson	692	83	1,359	86	75	79	889	511	3.46	3.90	4.33	34.7
3	1	1994-	R.Bottalico	364	0	422	24	31	111	402	223	4.01	4.18	3.87	33.1
4	3	1977-85	W.Brusstar	340	0	485	28	16	14	273	183	3.51	3.77	4.19	20.0
5	5	1991-	H.Slocumb	548	0	631	28	37	98	513	358	4.08	4.56	4.35	15.7
6	6	1986-96	J.Parrett	491	11	725	56	43	22	616	345	3.80	4.17	4.42	11.5
7	7	1943-47	A.Karl	191	4	423	18	23	26	107	130	3.51	4.26	4.54	0.7
8	8	1986-	M.Maddux	472	48	862	39	37	20	564	284	4.05	4.47	4.56	(0.2)
9	9	1997-	W.Gomes	246	0	284	23	18	27	217	150	4.44	4.86	4.57	(0.5)
10	10	1955-61	J.Meyer	202	24	455	24	34	21	375	244	3.92	4.45	4.60	(2.1)
11	11	1961-70	J.Baldschun	457	0	704	48	41	60	555	298	3.69	4.29	4.68	(10.1)
12	15	1993-	J.Spradlin	310	1	372	17	19	11	292	122	4.75	5.11	4.83	(11.4)
13	13	1984-90	K.Howell	245	54	613	38	48	31	549	275	3.95	4.34	4.81	(17.0)
14	14	1992-	M.Williams	276	55	580	23	37	48	443	246	4.50	4.97	4.83	(18.3)
15	12	1950-66	S.Ridzik	314	48	783	39	38	11	406	351	3.79	4.50	4.77	(18.8)
16	16	1983-92	D.Carman	342	102	922	53	54	11	598	378	4.11	4.51	4.98	(43.6)
17	17	1986-97	B.Ruffin	469	152	1,268	60	82	63	843	565	4.19	4.81	5.10	(78.7)
18	18	1962-69	J.Hamilton	218	65	612	32	40	20	357	348	4.53	5.26	5.87	(89.2)

PITTSBURGH PIRATES (1900–2000)

The Pirates began the twentieth century with great promise, winning pennants in 1901–1903, while featuring one of the best players of all time in Honus Wagner. The Pirates continued to win, accumulating 59 winning seasons through the 1980s. Led by superstar Barry Bonds, the Pirates opened the 1990s with division titles in 1990–1992, and the team was poised to end the century the way they began it. Unfortunately, Pittsburgh's ownership broke up the team after 1992 for financial reasons, and the Pirates slumped through eight straight losing seasons, while Bonds went on to star for the Giants.

A partial list of Pirates stars includes Fred Clarke, Sam Leever, Claude Ritchey, Tommy Leach, Babe Adams, Max Carey, Wilbur Cooper, Arky Vaughan, Pie Traynor, Bob Elliott, Ralph Kiner, Smoky Burgess, Roy Face, Bill Mazeroski, Roberto Clemente, Willie Stargell, Dave Parker, John Candelaria, Kent Tekulve, Andy Van Slyke, Jay Bell, Jason Kendall, and Brian Giles.

Profiled Pirates Players

Honus Wagner

Who is the greatest player of all time? Arguments will be heard for Babe Ruth, Ted Williams, Willie Mays, Ty Cobb, Hank Aaron, Ken Griffey, Jr., Cy Young, and Walter Johnson. The name Honus Wagner will probably not come up. Yet Wagner, with more Hits Contribution than any other hitter except for Ruth, deserves serious consideration. The Flying Dutchman made his case by leading the league in batting average eight times, in slugging six times, in stolen bases five times, and in fielding four times, while guiding his team to four pennants. And he did this while playing the critical position of shortstop, a position he owns, with nearly twice the volume of success as the next best shortstop in history.

Why doesn't Wagner receive the recognition he deserves? Perhaps the biggest reason is that Wagner played Dead Ball baseball longer than any other big name in history. Wagner hit .327 with 101 home runs over his career, with an 857 Production, and 722 stolen bases. Adjusted for a career 7.5 percent hitter's deflation, he hit an impressive .352, with 732 doubles, 289 triples, 114 home runs, and a 921 Wtd. Production. Add 40 Fielding Factor points, and Wagner attains a career 970 Total Factor, the best ever rate of success for a shortstop. His 1,685 Hits Contribution is the National League's best volume of success for any position, and ranks second to Ruth's 1,962 amount in major league history.

Wagner's 1900 season is often considered his best offensive season, as he hit .381 with 71 extra base hits. However, not only did he play in the outfield, but he also benefited from a lack of hitter's deflation that season. Actually, his 1901 season was better, and every year from 1903 to 1909 was far better than his 1900 performance. Adjusting for hitter's deflation, Wagner hit .382, .373, .369, .370, .392, .396, .386, .401, .413, and .384 over the ten years from 1900 to 1909.

Arky Vaughan

On any other team, Vaughan would receive serious consideration as that team's best shortstop of all time, despite his erratic fielding. But, on the Pirates, Vaughan has to settle for the best backup shortstop of all time. Despite voluntarily retiring for three years late in his career, he still posted impressive career numbers. In 14 seasons, Vaughan hit .318 with 96 home runs, for an 859 Production. Vaughan played in a period with a slight hitter's deflation, thus, giving him an 861 Wtd. Production. His 863 Total Factor is the National League's third best rate of success for shortstops (fifth in major league history), while his 740 Hits Contribution is the league's fourth best volume of success (sixth in major league history).

Jay Bell

With Wagner and Vaughan ahead of him at shortstop, Bell misses the Pirates all-star team altogether, even though he is arguably the third best infielder they ever had, behind these other two gentlemen. Bell was an integral part of the division-winning Pirates teams of 1990–1992, and he continued to play for the Pirates until 1996 as its sole remaining star from these winning teams. Bell moved on to Kansas City in 1997 and Arizona in 1998. In 1999, the 33-year-old Bell switched to second base, and had his best offensive season with a .289 average and 38 home runs for the division-winning Diamondbacks.

Bell is hitting .269 with 180 home runs in his career. Adjusted for a career 3.5 percent hitter's inflation, he has hit .260 with 178 home runs. His 749 Total Factor ranks 16th in league rate of success at shortstop, while his 315 Hits Contribution currently ranks him 12th in league volume of success.

Roberto Clemente

Clemente is best known for two things. First, his rifle arm in right field that gunned down many runners with deadly accuracy. Second, his untimely death at the age of 38 in a plane crash while on a mercy mission to Central America, soon after he finished a stellar 1972 season with exactly 3,000 career hits.

Clemente's career took some time to get started. In his first five seasons from 1955 to 1959, Clemente was a defensive standout, but a weak hitter, despite being aided by hitter's inflation. But, beginning with the Pirates championship season in 1960, Clemente was a critical contributor to the offense:

Years	TAB	HR	BA	Adj. BA	Wtd. PRO	TF	HC
1955–59	2,528	26	.282	.273	685	737	(26)
1960–72	7,582	214	.329	.336	897	961	745

Usually, a star player will either hit well his entire career, or, like Ernie Banks, may be slowed by injuries and suffer

a major drop-off in production. Rarely does a big star start as slowly as Clemente did. Imagine what Clemente would have accomplished if he hit at that high level his entire career, plus he lived to play two or three more seasons in the mid–1970s. Three hundred home runs, a career .333 average, and over 1,000 career Hits Contribution could have been his, ranking Clemente as a top ten outfielder of all time, rather than the top 25 status he actually achieved.

For his career, Clemente hit .317 with 240 home runs. Adjusted for 1 percent career hitter's deflation, Clemente hit .319 with 247 home runs, for an 842 Wtd. Production, and he earned 52 Fielding Factor points. His 902 Total Factor ranks Clemente 13th in league rate of success, while his 719 Hits Contribution ranks him seventh in league volume of success.

Jason Kendall

26-year-old Kendall has appeared in just five seasons, yet he is giving indications of becoming one of the greatest catchers of all time. Kendall has a career .314 average and a .406 on-base percentage, and has stolen 93 bases in 121 attempts, making him a unique catcher who can be used as a leadoff hitter. Adjusted for a 7 percent hitter's inflation, Kendall hit .294 with 43 home runs, for an 807 Wtd. Production over his brief career-to-date. Kendall's 845 Total Factor ranks him sixth in National League rate of success for catchers, while his 211 Hits Contribution to date already ranks him 13th in league volume of success.

Willie Stargell

Stargell was a key contributor to the six division winning teams of the 1970s. In 21 seasons, Stargell hit .282 with 475 home runs, despite hitting in expansive Forbes Field half his career. Stargell's most impressive statistic is his 953 extra-base hits in 8,942 career total at bats, for a rate of one extra-base hit every nine times up. Adjusted for a career 2 percent hitter's deflation, Stargell hit .288 with 485 home runs, for a 910 Wtd. Production. His 879 Total Factor is the league's 24th best rate of success for outfielders, while his 505 Hits Contribution ranks him 17th in volume of success.

Sam Leever

Pittsburgh did not have a Christy Mathewson or a Three Finger Brown to anchor its pitching staff in the first decade of the twentieth century. Instead, they used a deep rotation to stay competitive with the other two great teams of that period. The most reliable of these Pirates pitchers was Sam Leever, who worked 13 seasons with Pittsburgh from 1898 to 1910. Leever just missed 200 wins in his career, and he never led the league in wins, but he was a great pitcher for most of the years he did pitch. In his career, Leever was 194–100 for a .660 winning percentage, and he boasted an impressive 2.47 ERA. His 3.62 Wtd. RA/9 ranks him 18th in league rate of success, while his 301 Runs/162 ranks 20th in league volume of success.

Kent Tekulve

Tekulve (RP) is a great unknown to today's baseball fans. Tekulve quietly amassed 1,050 relief appearances from 1974 to 1989, with a 94–90 record and 184 saves in 1,436 innings. His career ERA was 2.85, with a 3.64 Wtd. RA/9, for the league's 23rd best rate of success. But Tekulve also saved 150 runs from scoring, the league's second best volume of success for a relief pitcher, and trailing league leader John Franco by just one run saved.

Pittsburgh Pirates

Hitters Volume of Success

Pos	Years	Name	AB	BB	HBP	TAB	H	2B	3B	HR	BA	OB	SA	PRO	Wtd PRO	SB	CS	SBF	SPF	FF	R TF	V HC
C	1949-67	S.Burgess	4,471	477	13	4,961	1,318	230	33	126	.295	.364	.446	810	794	13	14	(3)	(8)	(11)	772	232
1B	1976-86	J.Thompson	4,802	816	9	5,627	1,253	204	12	208	.261	.369	.438	808	820	8	7	(1)	(5)	(5)	809	108
2B	1956-72	B.Mazeroski	7,755	447	20	8,222	2,016	294	62	138	.260	.302	.367	669	673	27	23	(2)	4	74	748	249
SS	1897-17	H.Wagner	10,430	963	124	11,517	3,415	640	252	101	.327	.391	.466	857	921	722	15	(1)	9	40	970	1,685
3B	1920-37	P.Traynor	7,559	472	31	8,062	2,416	371	164	58	.320	.362	.435	797	762	158	46	(1)	10	41	812	390
OF	1955-72	R.Clemente	9,454	621	35	10,110	3,000	440	166	240	.317	.362	.475	837	842	83	46	(1)	10	52	902	719
OF	1926-45	P.Waner	9,459	1,091	38	10,588	3,152	605	191	113	.333	.404	.473	878	856	104	0	0	4	11	871	597
OF	1894-15	F.Clarke	8,568	874	153	9,595	2,672	361	220	67	.312	.386	.429	814	850	506	0	0	8	13	871	578
Starters		Averages	7,812	720	53	8,585	2,405	393	138	131	.308	.370	.444	814	824	203	19	(1)	4	27	853	570
C	1996-	J.Kendall	2,294	252	104	2,650	720	148	21	45	.314	.406	.456	862	807	93	28	13	10	15	845	211
1B	1934-49	E.Fletcher	4,879	851	42	5,772	1,323	228	58	79	.271	.384	.390	774	785	32	0	0	7	9	800	93
2B	1897-09	C.Ritchey	5,919	607	71	6,597	1,618	215	68	18	.273	.348	.342	690	740	155	0	0	0	3	743	211
SS	1932-48	A.Vaughan	6,622	937	46	7,605	2,103	356	128	96	.318	.406	.453	859	861	118	0	0	10	(8)	863	740
3B	1939-53	B.Elliott	7,141	967	16	8,124	2,061	382	94	170	.289	.375	.440	815	818	60	2	0	(1)	(13)	803	308
OF	1962-82	W.Stargell	7,927	937	78	8,942	2,232	423	55	475	.282	.363	.529	892	910	17	16	(2)	(7)	(23)	879	505
OF	1946-55	R.Kiner	5,205	1,011	24	6,240	1,451	216	39	369	.279	.398	.548	946	924	22	2	1	(4)	(24)	898	442
OF	1910-29	M.Carey	9,363	1,040	77	10,480	2,665	419	159	70	.285	.361	.386	747	758	738	92	18	10	38	824	356
Reserves		Averages	6,169	825	57	7,051	1,772	298	78	165	.287	.376	.441	818	826	154	18	4	3	(0)	832	358
Totals		Weighted Ave.	7,264	755	54	8,074	2,194	362	118	143	.302	.372	.443	815	824	187	18	1	4	18	846	499

Pitchers Volume of Success

Pos	Years	Name	G	GS	IP	W	L	SV	SO	BB	ERA	RA/9	R Wtd RA/9	V Runs /162
SP	1906-25	B.Adams	482	354	2,995	194	140	15	1,036	430	2.76	3.39	3.69	306
SP	1898-10	S.Leever	388	299	2,661	194	100	13	847	587	2.47	3.46	3.62	301
SP	1912-26	W.Cooper	517	407	3,480	216	178	14	1,252	853	2.89	3.63	3.95	253
SP	1899-11	D.Phillippe	372	289	2,607	189	109	12	929	363	2.59	3.72	3.84	230
SP	1929-42	L.French	570	384	3,152	197	171	17	1,187	819	3.44	4.11	4.03	193
Starters		Averages	466	347	2,979	198	140	14	1,050	610	2.85	3.67	3.84	256
RP	1974-89	K.Tekulve	1,050	0	1,436	94	90	184	779	491	2.85	3.30	3.64	150
RP	1953-69	R.Face	848	27	1,375	104	95	193	877	362	3.48	3.87	4.09	74
RP	1961-70	A.McBean	409	76	1,072	67	50	63	575	365	3.13	3.61	4.12	52
RP	1967-77	R.Hernandez	337	0	430	23	15	46	255	135	3.03	3.29	3.70	41
Relievers		Averages	661	26	1,078	72	63	122	622	338	3.14	3.56	3.91	79
Totals		Averages	1,127	372	4,057	270	202	136	1,672	949	2.93	3.64	3.86	336

Pittsburgh Pirates   **Hitters Rate of Success**

Pos	Years	Name	AB	BB	HBP	TAB	H	2B	3B	HR	BA	OB	SA	PRO	Wtd PRO	SB	CS	SBF	SPF	FF	R TF	V HC
C	1996-	J.Kendall	2,294	252	104	2,650	720	148	21	45	.314	.406	.456	862	807	93	28	13	10	15	845	211
1B	1976-86	J.Thompson	4,802	816	9	5,627	1,253	204	12	208	.261	.369	.438	808	820	8	7	(1)	(5)	(5)	809	108
2B	1922-34	G.Grantham	4,989	717	23	5,729	1,508	292	93	105	.302	.392	.461	854	812	132	53	(4)	1	(35)	773	168
SS	1897-17	H.Wagner	10,430	963	124	11,517	3,415	640	252	101	.327	.391	.466	857	921	722	15	(1)	9	40	970	1,685
3B	1920-37	P.Traynor	7,559	472	31	8,062	2,416	371	164	58	.320	.362	.435	797	762	158	46	(1)	10	41	812	390
OF	1995-	B.Giles	1,937	364	14	2,315	583	118	14	113	.301	.415	.551	966	893	38	10	7	10	5	915	173
OF	1955-72	R.Clemente	9,454	621	35	10,110	3,000	440	166	240	.317	.362	.475	837	842	83	46	(1)	10	52	902	719
OF	1946-55	R.Kiner	5,205	1,011	24	6,240	1,451	216	39	369	.279	.398	.548	946	924	22	2	1	(4)	(24)	898	442
Starters	Averages		5,834	652	46	6,531	1,793	304	95	155	.307	.381	.472	853	852	157	26	2	5	11	870	487
C	1949-67	S.Burgess	4,471	477	13	4,961	1,318	230	33	126	.295	.364	.446	810	794	13	14	(3)	(8)	(11)	772	232
1B	1934-49	E.Fletcher	4,879	851	42	5,772	1,323	228	58	79	.271	.384	.390	774	785	32	0	0	7	9	800	93
2B	1956-72	B.Mazeroski	7,755	447	20	8,222	2,016	294	62	138	.260	.302	.367	669	673	27	23	(2)	4	74	748	249
SS	1932-48	A.Vaughan	6,622	937	46	7,605	2,103	356	128	96	.318	.406	.453	859	861	118	0	0	10	(8)	863	740
3B	1939-53	B.Elliott	7,141	967	16	8,124	2,061	382	94	170	.289	.375	.440	815	818	60	2	0	(1)	(13)	803	308
OF	1962-82	W.Stargell	7,927	937	78	8,942	2,232	423	55	475	.282	.363	.529	892	910	17	16	(2)	(7)	(23)	879	505
OF	1894-15	F.Clarke	8,568	874	153	9,595	2,672	361	220	67	.312	.386	.429	814	850	506	0	0	8	13	871	578
OF	1926-45	P.Waner	9,459	1,091	38	10,588	3,152	605	191	113	.333	.404	.473	878	856	104	0	0	4	11	871	597
Reserves	Averages		7,103	823	51	7,976	2,110	360	105	158	.297	.374	.444	818	824	110	7	(1)	2	6	831	413
Totals	Weighted Ave.		6,257	709	47	7,013	1,899	322	98	156	.303	.379	.461	840	842	141	20	1	4	10	857	462

Pitchers Rate of Success

Pos	Years	Name	G	GS	IP	W	L	SV	SO	BB	ERA	RA/9	Wtd RA/9	R V Runs /162
SP	1898-10	S.Leever	388	299	2,661	194	100	13	847	587	2.47	3.46	3.62	301
SP	1906-25	B.Adams	482	354	2,995	194	140	15	1,036	430	2.76	3.39	3.69	306
SP	1899-11	D.Phillippe	372	289	2,607	189	109	12	929	363	2.59	3.72	3.84	230
SP	1912-26	W.Cooper	517	407	3,480	216	178	14	1,252	853	2.89	3.63	3.95	253
SP	1975-93	J.Candelaria	600	356	2,526	177	122	29	1,673	592	3.33	3.70	3.98	162
Starters	Averages		472	341	2,854	194	130	17	1,147	565	2.81	3.58	3.82	250
RP	1974-89	K.Tekulve	1,050	0	1,436	94	90	184	779	491	2.85	3.30	3.64	150
RP	1967-77	R.Hernandez	337	0	430	23	15	46	255	135	3.03	3.29	3.70	41
RP	1997-	R.Rincon	216	0	190	8	13	18	185	90	3.42	4.08	3.85	15
RP	1953-69	R.Face	848	27	1,375	104	95	193	877	362	3.48	3.87	4.09	74
Relievers	Averages		613	7	858	57	53	110	524	270	3.16	3.57	3.84	70
Totals	Averages		1,085	348	3,712	251	183	127	1,671	835	2.89	3.58	3.82	320

Pittsburgh Pirates
Catchers

V	R	Years	Name	AB	BB	HBP	TAB	H	2B	3B	HR	BA	OB	SA	PRO	Wtd PRO	SB	CS	SBF	SPF	FF	R TF	V HC
1	2	1949-67	S.Burgess	4,471	477	13	4,961	1,318	230	33	126	.295	.364	.446	810	794	13	14	(3)	(8)	(11)	772	232
2	1	1996-	J.Kendall	2,294	252	104	2,650	720	148	21	45	.314	.406	.456	862	807	93	28	13	10	15	845	211
3	6	1980-97	T.Pena	6,489	455	23	6,967	1,687	298	27	107	.260	.311	.364	674	680	80	63	(6)	(2)	51	722	150
4	5	1967-80	M.Sanguillen	5,062	223	23	5,308	1,500	205	57	65	.296	.329	.398	727	736	35	38	(7)	7	2	738	143
5	3	1919-30	E.Smith	2,264	247	11	2,522	686	115	19	46	.303	.374	.432	806	774	18	9	(1)	(7)	(14)	753	96
6	4	1955-69	J.Pagliaroni	2,465	330	25	2,820	622	98	7	90	.252	.346	.407	754	767	4	7	(3)	(10)	(9)	745	91
7	7	1982-97	D.Slaught	4,063	311	42	4,416	1,151	235	28	77	.283	.341	.412	752	743	18	15	(2)	(10)	(22)	708	65
8	8	1984-95	M.LaValliere	2,473	321	10	2,804	663	109	5	18	.268	.354	.338	693	694	5	15	(9)	(10)	16	691	19
9	9	1905-18	G.Gibson	3,776	286	26	4,088	893	142	49	15	.236	.295	.312	607	665	40	0	0	(4)	16	677	(0)
10	10	1929-37	E.Grace	1,877	185	6	2,068	493	83	10	31	.263	.331	.367	698	687	1	0	0	(10)	(5)	672	(6)
11	11	1932-43	A.Todd	2,785	104	21	2,910	768	119	29	35	.276	.307	.377	684	677	18	0	0	(10)	5	672	(8)
12	13	1974-81	E.Ott	1,792	138	3	1,933	465	76	10	33	.259	.314	.368	682	678	14	16	(8)	(2)	(13)	655	(22)
13	14	1902-13	E.Phelps	1,832	163	37	2,032	460	45	20	3	.251	.325	.302	627	685	31	0	0	(10)	(27)	648	(31)
14	15	1921-33	J.Gooch	2,363	206	15	2,584	662	98	29	7	.280	.342	.355	697	654	11	5	(1)	(10)	(1)	642	(46)
15	16	1916-25	W.Schmidt	2,411	137	15	2,563	619	63	20	3	.257	.301	.303	604	618	57	16	2	0	8	628	(66)
16	17	1982-94	J.Ortiz	1,894	121	18	2,033	484	71	4	5	.256	.306	.305	612	614	8	18	(13)	(10)	5	596	(80)
17	12	1884-96	D.Miller	5,167	467	45	5,679	1,380	192	57	33	.267	.333	.345	679	694	260	0	0	(0)	(37)	656	(155)

Pittsburgh Pirates
First basemen

V	R	Years	Name	AB	BB	HBP	TAB	H	2B	3B	HR	BA	OB	SA	PRO	Wtd PRO	SB	CS	SBF	SPF	FF	R TF	V HC
1	1	1976-86	J.Thompson	4,802	816	9	5,627	1,253	204	12	208	.261	.369	.438	808	820	8	7	(1)	(5)	(5)	809	108
2	2	1934-49	E.Fletcher	4,879	851	42	5,772	1,323	228	58	79	.271	.384	.390	774	785	32	0	0	7	9	800	93
3	3	1961-72	D.Clendenon	4,648	379	21	5,048	1,273	192	57	159	.274	.331	.442	774	796	90	57	(5)	8	(7)	793	55
4	4	1930-40	G.Suhr	5,176	718	10	5,904	1,446	288	114	84	.279	.368	.428	796	776	53	0	0	5	(0)	781	33
5	5	1958-69	D.Stuart	3,997	301	22	4,320	1,055	157	30	228	.264	.319	.489	808	804	2	7	(3)	(8)	(20)	773	7
6	6	1983-94	S.Bream	3,108	353	5	3,466	819	191	12	90	.264	.340	.420	759	762	50	40	(8)	(3)	23	773	5
7	7	1967-79	B.Robertson	2,385	317	13	2,715	578	93	10	115	.242	.334	.434	769	778	7	9	(4)	(8)	7	773	5
8	8	1992-	K.Young	2,896	232	47	3,175	771	172	16	112	.266	.331	.453	783	730	63	32	(1)	4	(5)	728	(59)
9	9	1909-21	D.Miller	5,805	391	45	6,241	1,526	232	108	32	.263	.314	.357	671	714	177	30	(3)	1	(5)	708	(77)
10	10	1948-59	P.Ward	2,067	231	2	2,300	522	83	15	50	.253	.328	.380	708	684	7	6	(3)	(2)	(1)	678	(107)

Pittsburgh Pirates
Second basemen

V	R	Years	Name	AB	BB	HBP	TAB	H	2B	3B	HR	BA	OB	SA	PRO	Wtd PRO	SB	CS	SBF	SPF	FF	R TF	V HC
1	2	1956-72	B.Mazeroski	7,755	447	20	8,222	2,016	294	62	138	.260	.302	.367	669	673	27	23	(2)	4	74	748	249
2	3	1897-09	C.Ritchey	5,919	607	71	6,597	1,618	215	68	18	.273	.348	.342	690	740	155	0	0	0	3	743	211
3	1	1922-34	G.Grantham	4,989	717	23	5,729	1,508	292	93	105	.302	.392	.461	854	812	132	53	(4)	1	(35)	773	168
4	4	1981-90	J.Ray	5,188	353	12	5,553	1,502	294	36	53	.290	.336	.391	727	733	80	49	(3)	0	6	736	136
5	6	1920-25	C.Tierney	2,299	109	13	2,421	681	119	30	31	.296	.332	.415	746	712	28	31	(13)	9	(7)	700	13
6	8	1912-16	J.Viox	1,703	222	12	1,937	465	76	24	7	.273	.361	.358	719	773	39	8	(2)	0	(76)	695	8
7	9	1933-45	P.Young	2,466	152	12	2,630	645	128	34	32	.262	.308	.380	688	679	18	0	0	8	(0)	687	8
8	7	1931-38	T.Piet	2,585	247	40	2,872	717	132	30	23	.277	.350	.378	728	698	80	16	0	10	(11)	698	3
9	5	1993-	T.Womack	2,593	174	11	2,778	716	111	41	20	.276	.324	.370	694	648	239	39	55	8	(6)	704	(0)
10	10	1939-50	F.Gustine	4,582	369	15	4,966	1,214	222	47	38	.265	.322	.359	681	689	60	1	(0)	10	(14)	684	(10)
11	11	1971-81	R.Stennett	4,521	207	16	4,744	1,239	177	41	41	.274	.308	.359	667	673	75	54	(7)	6	5	677	(19)
12	13	1990-	C.Garcia	2,178	115	22	2,315	580	102	17	33	.266	.310	.374	684	653	73	33	3	10	(3)	663	(27)
13	12	1923-34	E.Moore	2,474	272	11	2,757	706	108	26	13	.285	.359	.366	725	681	52	14	(1)	3	(12)	671	(41)
14	15	1938-46	P.Coscarart	2,992	295	15	3,302	728	129	22	28	.243	.314	.329	644	658	34	0	0	0	(10)	648	(55)
15	14	1987-95	J.Lind	3,677	215	8	3,900	935	145	27	9	.254	.297	.316	613	617	62	19	5	5	28	655	(59)

Pittsburgh Pirates
Shortstops

V	R	Years	Name	AB	BB	HBP	TAB	H	2B	3B	HR	BA	OB	SA	PRO	Wtd PRO	SB	CS	SBF	SPF	FF	R TF	V HC
1	1	1897-17	H.Wagner	10,430	963	124	11,517	3,415	640	252	101	.327	.391	.466	857	921	722	15	(1)	9	40	970	1,685
2	2	1932-48	A.Vaughan	6,622	937	46	7,605	2,103	356	128	96	.318	.406	.453	859	861	118	0	0	10	(8)	863	740
3	3	1986-	J.Bell	6,805	761	50	7,616	1,828	368	66	180	.269	.347	.421	768	741	91	59	(3)	1	10	749	315
4	5	1924-35	G.Wright	4,153	209	5	4,367	1,219	203	76	94	.294	.328	.447	775	737	38	13	(2)	10	(12)	733	155
5	4	1963-73	G.Alley	3,927	300	27	4,254	999	140	44	55	.254	.312	.354	666	686	63	30	1	10	43	740	152
6	6	1952-67	D.Groat	7,484	490	31	8,005	2,138	352	67	39	.286	.332	.366	698	694	14	27	(5)	(10)	2	681	75
7	9	1942-52	S.Rojek	1,764	152	8	1,924	470	67	13	4	.266	.327	.326	653	640	32	3	(3)	4	(7)	635	(26)
8	7	1977-87	D.Berra	2,553	210	12	2,775	603	109	9	49	.236	.297	.344	641	649	32	17	1	5	3	658	(30)
9	8	1953-71	D.Schofield	3,083	390	26	3,499	699	113	20	21	.227	.319	.297	615	628	12	29	(13)	2	22	640	(48)
10	10	1971-82	F.Taveras	4,043	249	24	4,316	1,029	144	44	2	.255	.302	.313	615	618	300	106	19	10	(44)	603	(126)
11	11	1924-38	T.Thevenow	4,164	210	11	4,385	1,030	124	32	2	.247	.285	.294	579	554	23	3	(0)	1	5	559	(249)

Pittsburgh Pirates
Third basemen

V	R	Years	Name	AB	BB	HBP	TAB	H	2B	3B	HR	BA	OB	SA	PRO	Wtd PRO	SB	CS	SBF	SPF	FF	R TF	V HC
1	1	1920-37	P.Traynor	7,559	472	31	8,062	2,416	371	164	58	.320	.362	.435	797	762	158	46	(1)	10	41	812	390
2	2	1939-53	B.Elliott	7,141	967	16	8,124	2,061	382	94	170	.289	.375	.440	815	818	60	2	0	(1)	(13)	803	308
3	3	1973-87	B.Madlock	6,594	605	68	7,267	2,008	348	34	163	.305	.369	.442	811	820	174	90	(0)	3	(28)	794	266
4	4	1986-	B.Bonilla	7,039	889	26	7,954	1,973	401	61	282	.280	.363	.475	838	822	44	56	(8)	0	(28)	786	192
5	5	1968-85	R.Hebner	6,144	687	74	6,905	1,694	273	57	203	.276	.356	.438	793	800	38	40	(6)	(5)	(19)	770	126
6	7	1954-64	D.Hoak	4,322	523	22	4,867	1,144	214	44	89	.265	.347	.396	743	727	64	47	(6)	10	8	739	57
7	8	1977-88	J.Morrison	3,375	213	25	3,613	876	170	16	112	.260	.308	.419	727	726	50	37	(6)	5	(4)	721	26
8	6	1989-	J.King	4,262	442	20	4,724	1,091	222	18	154	.256	.329	.425	754	727	75	32	2	0	20	749	22
9	10	1915-20	D.Baird	2,106	157	12	2,275	492	86	45	6	.234	.291	.326	616	683	118	28	(3)	10	8	698	(22)
10	9	1907-17	B.Byrne	4,831	456	49	5,336	1,225	186	60	10	.254	.324	.323	647	696	176	12	(4)	8	5	705	(28)
11	11	1936-47	L.Handley	3,356	267	3	3,626	902	122	45	15	.269	.323	.345	669	670	68	0	0	10	1	681	(53)
12	12	1955-66	G.Freese	3,446	243	20	3,709	877	161	28	115	.254	.307	.418	725	712	51	26	(0)	8	(41)	679	(63)
13	13	1907-20	B.McKechnie	2,843	190	15	3,048	713	86	33	8	.251	.301	.313	614	656	127	4	(0)	0	11	666	(80)

Pittsburgh Pirates
Outfielders

V	R	Years	Name	AB	BB	HBP	TAB	H	2B	3B	HR	BA	OB	SA	PRO	Wtd PRO	SB	CS	SBF	SPF	FF	R TF	V HC
1	2	1955-72	R.Clemente	9,454	621	35	10,110	3,000	440	166	240	.317	.362	.475	837	842	83	46	(1)	10	52	902	719
2	6	1926-45	P.Waner	9,459	1,091	38	10,588	3,152	605	191	113	.333	.404	.473	878	856	104	0	0	4	11	871	597
3	5	1894-15	F.Clarke	8,568	874	153	9,595	2,672	361	220	67	.312	.386	.429	814	850	506	0	0	8	13	871	578
4	4	1962-82	W.Stargell	7,927	937	78	8,942	2,232	423	55	475	.282	.363	.529	892	910	17	16	(2)	(7)	(23)	879	505
5	3	1946-55	R.Kiner	5,205	1,011	24	6,240	1,451	216	39	369	.279	.398	.548	946	924	22	2	1	(4)	(24)	898	442
6	9	1910-29	M.Carey	9,363	1,040	77	10,480	2,665	419	159	70	.285	.361	.386	747	758	738	92	18	10	38	824	356
7	7	1983-95	A.Van Slyke	5,711	667	27	6,405	1,562	293	91	164	.274	.352	.443	795	794	245	59	19	9	34	855	305
8	10	1973-91	D.Parker	9,358	683	56	10,097	2,712	526	75	339	.290	.342	.471	813	818	154	113	(7)	2	3	816	282
9	8	1899-10	G.Beaumont	5,660	425	30	6,115	1,759	182	82	39	.311	.362	.393	755	820	254	0	0	10	15	844	276
10	13	1898-18	T.Leach	7,959	820	32	8,811	2,143	266	172	63	.269	.340	.370	710	771	361	14	(1)	6	19	794	248
11	1	1995-	B.Giles	1,937	364	14	2,315	583	118	14	113	.301	.415	.551	966	893	38	10	7	10	5	915	173
12	11	1968-85	A.Oliver	9,049	535	82	9,666	2,743	529	77	219	.303	.348	.451	799	807	84	64	(4)	6	(12)	797	170
13	14	1971-83	R.Zisk	5,144	533	12	5,689	1,477	245	26	207	.287	.355	.466	821	830	8	15	(4)	(10)	(23)	793	100
14	12	1937-46	V.DiMaggio	3,849	412	12	4,273	959	209	24	125	.249	.324	.413	737	754	79	0	0	10	31	795	81
15	16	1942-51	J.Russell	3,595	503	22	4,120	959	175	51	67	.267	.360	.400	760	766	59	0	0	10	6	782	50
16	15	1905-20	B.Hinchman	3,043	298	48	3,389	793	128	69	20	.261	.336	.368	704	797	85	17	(5)	(1)	(7)	785	46
17	21	1927-45	L.Waner	7,772	420	26	8,218	2,459	281	118	27	.316	.353	.393	747	727	67	0	0	10	30	768	43
18	22	1972-87	L.Lacy	4,549	372	9	4,930	1,303	207	42	91	.286	.342	.410	752	756	185	86	4	10	(13)	757	40
19	19	1908-16	O.Wilson	4,624	241	37	4,902	1,246	157	114	59	.269	.311	.391	702	751	98	15	(4)	10	16	773	38
20	18	1947-56	W.Westlake	3,117	317	33	3,467	848	107	33	127	.272	.346	.450	795	779	19	7	(2)	4	(4)	777	33
21	20	1973-87	M.Easler	3,677	321	17	4,015	1,078	189	25	118	.293	.353	.454	807	808	20	26	(8)	(3)	(24)	773	27
22	17	1938-42	J.Rizzo	1,842	200	12	2,054	497	90	16	61	.270	.345	.435	781	787	7	0	0	10	(17)	780	23
23	23	1990-	O.Merced	3,398	432	10	3,840	951	193	22	88	.280	.363	.427	790	762	45	26	(1)	0	(4)	757	(7)
24	24	1954-66	B.Skinner	4,318	485	17	4,820	1,198	197	58	103	.277	.353	.421	774	759	67	36	(1)	8	(12)	753	(12)
25	25	1992-	A.Martin	3,721	336	20	4,077	1,044	193	44	122	.281	.343	.454	798	753	162	60	10	10	(27)	746	(24)
26	29	1942-46	J.Barrett	1,811	265	8	2,084	454	82	32	23	.251	.349	.369	718	742	69	0	0	10	(23)	729	(30)
27	26	1960-74	M.Alou	5,789	311	36	6,136	1,777	236	50	31	.307	.346	.381	727	745	156	80	(1)	8	(8)	744	(38)
28	27	1966-83	B.Robinson	4,364	263	16	4,643	1,127	229	29	166	.258	.303	.438	741	753	71	49	(5)	9	(13)	743	(40)
29	33	1939-46	M.Van Robays	1,844	139	8	1,991	493	94	27	20	.267	.321	.380	702	721	2	0	0	0	(7)	713	(44)
30	31	1983-90	R.Reynolds	2,270	190	5	2,465	605	121	17	35	.267	.325	.381	706	714	109	29	20	10	(24)	720	(44)
31	28	1916-26	C.Bigbee	4,192	344	21	4,557	1,205	139	75	17	.287	.345	.369	713	720	182	68	(6)	10	12	735	(47)
32	35	1986-98	D.Clark	1,964	222	5	2,191	518	81	8	62	.264	.340	.408	748	731	19	12	(3)	0	(18)	710	(52)
33	36	1920-28	C.Barnhart	2,673	265	7	2,945	788	121	61	27	.295	.360	.416	776	741	35	21	(4)	(10)	(18)	709	(56)
34	37	1926-35	A.Comorosky	2,787	214	14	3,015	795	134	51	28	.285	.339	.400	739	692	57	0	0	10	2	704	(81)
35	30	1951-66	F.Thomas	6,285	484	51	6,820	1,671	262	31	286	.266	.323	.454	777	759	15	22	(4)	(8)	(21)	725	(84)
36	42	1997-	J.Guillen	1,675	76	34	1,785	439	90	12	41	.262	.308	.404	711	668	8	8	(4)	0	(13)	651	(91)
37	39	1985-	J.Cangelosi	2,004	358	31	2,393	501	73	15	12	.250	.372	.319	691	674	154	61	13	10	(19)	679	(92)
38	38	1970-79	G.Clines	2,328	169	19	2,516	645	85	24	5	.277	.331	.341	672	688	71	40	(3)	9	(15)	679	(95)
39	32	1975-86	O.Moreno	4,992	387	17	5,396	1,257	171	87	37	.252	.308	.343	651	657	487	182	22	10	30	719	(104)
40	40	1931-39	W.Jensen	2,720	69	18	2,807	774	114	37	26	.285	.307	.382	689	678	20	0	0	10	(13)	675	(116)
41	34	1955-68	B.Virdon	5,980	442	8	6,430	1,596	237	81	91	.267	.318	.379	697	688	47	54	(9)	10	23	712	(144)
42	41	1983-90	M.Wynne	2,693	191	8	2,892	664	107	28	40	.247	.298	.352	650	661	80	58	(12)	10	(8)	651	(146)

Pittsburgh Pirates
Starting Pitchers

V	R	Years	Name	G	GS	IP	W	L	SV	SO	BB	ERA	RA/9	R Wtd RA/9	V Runs /162
1	2	1906-25	B.Adams	482	354	2,995	194	140	15	1,036	430	2.76	3.39	3.69	305.7
2	1	1898-10	S.Leever	388	299	2,661	194	100	13	847	587	2.47	3.46	3.62	300.9
3	4	1912-26	W.Cooper	517	407	3,480	216	178	14	1,252	853	2.89	3.63	3.95	252.7
4	3	1899-11	D.Phillippe	372	289	2,607	189	109	12	929	363	2.59	3.72	3.84	229.6
5	9	1929-42	L.French	570	384	3,152	197	171	17	1,187	819	3.44	4.11	4.03	193.2
6	5	1975-93	J.Candelaria	600	356	2,526	177	122	29	1,673	592	3.33	3.70	3.98	162.3
7	7	1962-74	B.Veale	397	255	1,926	120	95	21	1,703	858	3.07	3.53	3.99	120.8
8	8	1905-20	L.Leifield	296	216	1,838	124	97	7	616	554	2.47	3.39	4.01	120.0
9	14	1986-98	D.Drabek	398	387	2,535	155	134	0	1,594	704	3.73	4.05	4.15	119.0
10	10	1924-33	R.Kremer	308	247	1,955	143	85	10	516	483	3.76	4.37	4.05	116.7
11	6	1920-30	J.Morrison	297	164	1,535	103	80	23	546	506	3.65	4.32	3.99	102.0
12	17	1951-66	B.Friend	602	497	3,611	197	230	11	1,734	894	3.58	4.12	4.32	98.2
13	15	1904-15	H.Camnitz	326	236	2,085	133	106	15	915	656	2.75	3.69	4.18	92.0
14	18	1939-59	M.Dickson	625	338	3,052	172	181	23	1,281	1,058	3.66	4.22	4.34	79.1
15	12	1991-	D.Neagle	320	221	1,520	105	69	3	1,144	459	3.92	4.20	4.13	75.8
16	16	1932-43	B.Swift	336	163	1,638	95	82	20	636	351	3.58	4.14	4.18	72.2
17	19	1974-89	R.Rhoden	413	380	2,594	151	125	1	1,419	801	3.59	3.97	4.36	59.6
18	11	1915-30	C.Hill	147	85	787	49	33	8	264	267	3.44	4.21	4.11	41.7
19	20	1986-97	J.Smiley	361	280	1,908	126	103	4	1,284	496	3.80	4.19	4.37	41.6
20	13	1996-	F.Cordova	166	112	754	42	47	12	537	235	3.96	4.37	4.15	34.2
21	25	1932-49	R.Sewell	390	243	2,119	143	97	15	636	748	3.48	4.18	4.44	28.1
22	21	1934-42	C.Blanton	202	168	1,218	68	71	4	611	337	3.55	4.34	4.37	26.0
23	26	1968-79	D.Ellis	345	317	2,128	138	119	1	1,136	674	3.46	4.05	4.46	22.5
24	22	1913-23	F.Miller	163	127	1,010	52	66	4	359	254	3.01	3.77	4.39	20.3
25	23	1967-76	B.Moose	289	160	1,304	76	71	19	827	387	3.50	3.90	4.43	19.0
26	27	1971-85	B.Kison	380	246	1,810	115	88	12	1,073	662	3.66	4.17	4.49	13.6
27	24	1928-39	J.Weaver	189	108	893	57	36	3	449	336	3.88	4.58	4.43	13.3
28	30	1950-67	V.Law	483	364	2,672	162	147	13	1,092	597	3.77	4.29	4.52	10.4
29	29	1968-80	J.Rooker	319	255	1,810	103	109	7	976	703	3.46	4.05	4.51	9.7
30	28	1913-24	A.Mamaux	254	138	1,293	76	67	10	625	511	2.90	3.76	4.51	7.5
31	31	1972-84	J.Bibby	340	239	1,723	111	101	8	1,079	723	3.76	4.18	4.53	5.6
32	32	1917-30	H.Carlson	377	237	2,002	114	120	19	590	498	3.97	4.55	4.54	4.2
33	34	1965-74	L.Walker	243	100	825	45	47	9	558	408	3.65	4.09	4.58	(2.0)
34	33	1922-34	H.Meine	165	132	999	66	50	3	199	287	3.95	4.74	4.58	(2.2)
35	36	1938-47	B.Klinger	265	130	1,090	66	61	23	357	358	3.68	4.33	4.65	(12.0)
36	39	1994-	J.Lieber	217	170	1,137	60	69	2	886	258	4.32	4.91	4.69	(17.7)
37	37	1936-45	M.Butcher	334	229	1,786	95	106	9	485	583	3.73	4.46	4.65	(20.4)
38	41	1920-24	W.Glazner	142	102	784	41	48	4	266	249	4.21	5.04	4.81	(22.9)
39	35	1915-29	L.Meadows	490	406	3,161	188	180	7	1,063	956	3.37	4.26	4.62	(23.6)
40	44	1995-	J.Schmidt	137	128	799	43	47	0	586	344	4.58	5.06	4.83	(24.0)
41	43	1948-53	C.Chambers	189	113	897	48	53	1	374	361	4.29	4.84	4.82	(28.0)
42	38	1978-92	D.Robinson	524	229	1,958	109	106	57	1,251	643	3.79	4.17	4.69	(28.4)
43	40	1964-74	S.Blass	282	231	1,597	103	76	2	896	597	3.63	4.16	4.72	(28.6)
44	45	1940-48	N.Strincevich	203	103	890	46	49	6	274	270	4.05	4.68	4.91	(36.9)
45	48	1928-32	E.Brame	142	92	792	52	37	1	188	232	4.76	5.58	4.96	(37.7)
46	46	1995-	E.Loaiza	174	147	912	49	52	1	561	279	4.72	5.23	4.94	(39.5)
47	42	1967-81	K.Brett	349	184	1,526	83	85	11	807	562	3.93	4.33	4.82	(44.9)
48	51	1962-70	T.Sisk	316	99	928	40	49	10	441	358	3.92	4.43	5.12	(57.9)
49	47	1978-90	L.McWilliams	370	224	1,558	78	90	3	940	542	3.99	4.44	4.95	(69.7)
50	49	1980-93	B.Walk	350	259	1,666	105	81	5	848	606	4.03	4.48	4.97	(76.9)

Pittsburgh Pirates
Starting Pitchers

V	R	Years	Name	G	GS	IP	W	L	SV	SO	BB	ERA	RA/9	R Wtd RA/9	V Runs /162
51	50	1914-27	E.Jacobs	250	133	1,189	50	81	7	336	423	3.55	4.39	5.11	(80.8)
52	53	1950-58	D.Littlefield	243	83	762	33	54	9	495	413	4.71	5.45	5.54	(87.6)
53	52	1932-45	J.Bowman	298	184	1,466	77	96	11	502	484	4.40	5.14	5.19	(108.1)

Pittsburgh Pirates
Relief Pitchers

V	R	Years	Name	G	GS	IP	W	L	SV	SO	BB	ERA	RA/9	R Wtd RA/9	V Runs /162
1	1	1974-89	K.Tekulve	1,050	0	1,436	94	90	184	779	491	2.85	3.30	3.64	149.8
2	4	1953-69	R.Face	848	27	1,375	104	95	193	877	362	3.48	3.87	4.09	73.9
3	7	1961-70	A.McBean	409	76	1,072	67	50	63	575	365	3.13	3.61	4.12	52.5
4	2	1967-77	R.Hernandez	337	0	430	23	15	46	255	135	3.03	3.29	3.70	41.4
5	13	1935-46	M.Brown	387	55	1,075	76	57	48	435	388	3.46	4.20	4.28	35.4
6	8	1982-90	C.Guante	363	1	595	29	34	35	503	236	3.48	3.87	4.12	28.6
7	9	1980-88	R.Scurry	332	7	461	19	32	39	431	274	3.24	3.71	4.15	22.6
8	5	1986-93	B.Landrum	268	2	361	18	15	58	218	124	3.39	3.76	4.09	18.6
9	15	1989-	S.Belinda	585	0	685	41	37	79	622	285	4.15	4.41	4.33	18.4
10	14	1977-82	E.Romo	350	3	603	44	33	52	436	203	3.45	3.87	4.31	16.9
11	10	1985-92	P.Clements	288	2	360	17	11	12	158	160	3.77	4.07	4.16	16.1
12	3	1997-	R.Rincon	216	0	190	8	13	18	185	90	3.42	4.08	3.85	14.9
13	16	1985-98	B.Patterson	559	21	617	39	40	28	483	180	4.08	4.29	4.37	13.3
14	11	1996-	M.Wilkins	231	2	277	19	13	3	207	147	4.12	4.45	4.19	11.3
15	6	1996-	R.Loiselle	184	3	206	9	17	48	169	107	3.76	4.32	4.12	10.1
16	12	1995-	J.Christiansen	299	0	285	15	20	10	287	146	4.17	4.46	4.25	10.1
17	17	1960-72	J.Gibbon	419	127	1,120	61	65	32	743	414	3.52	4.06	4.49	8.7
18	19	1987-95	V.Palacios	127	44	361	17	19	7	262	153	4.36	4.48	4.71	(7.3)
19	20	1984-94	R.Mason	232	23	416	22	35	13	286	161	4.02	4.45	4.72	(8.0)
20	18	1952-70	R.Kline	736	203	2,078	114	144	108	989	731	3.75	4.29	4.59	(8.5)
21	22	1996-	C.Peters	123	43	349	17	21	2	210	142	4.57	5.09	4.84	(11.1)
22	21	1929-35	L.Chagnon	135	22	393	19	16	3	153	104	4.51	4.99	4.81	(11.6)
23	23	1993-	D.Miceli	388	9	449	31	31	31	401	206	4.71	5.13	4.88	(16.9)
24	24	1975-88	O.Jones	201	45	549	24	35	13	338	213	4.42	4.98	4.96	(25.8)
25	25	1985-92	B.Fisher	222	65	640	36	34	23	370	252	4.39	4.80	5.05	(35.3)
26	26	1951-57	P.LaPalme	253	51	616	24	45	14	277	272	4.42	5.15	5.10	(39.4)
27	27	1985-92	B.Kipper	271	45	562	27	37	11	369	217	4.34	4.82	5.23	(42.2)

St. Louis Browns/ Baltimore Orioles (1901–2000)

As the St. Louis Browns, this franchise produced just 12 winning seasons in 53 years. Several of the biggest Browns names— George Sisler, Ken Williams, Marty Mc-Manus and Urban Shocker — played for the best Browns teams in the 1920s, but they failed to win a pennant. Neither did Browns stars Bobby Wallace, George Stone, Del Pratt, or Harlond Clift. Only Vern Stephens, of the best Browns stars through the years, managed in 1944 to play for a Browns pennant winner.

The franchise prospered in Baltimore, with 30 winning seasons in 47 years. The golden era was from 1960 to 1985, when the Orioles produced 24 winning seasons and eight postseason appearances in 26 years. Pitchers Jim Palmer, Milt Pappas, Dave McNally, Mike Cuellar, and Dennis Martinez formed the team's core strength, while Brooks and Frank Robinson, Boog Powell, Davey Johnson, Bobby Grich, Ken Singleton, Doug DeCinces, Eddie Murray, and Cal Ripken produced lively lineups. Iron man Ripken became a legend in the 1990s, while playing with Brady Anderson, Rafael Palmeiro, Mike Mussina, and Gregg Olson.

Profiled Browns/Orioles Players

George Sisler

Sisler was one of the best players ever, a non–power hitter dominating a power hitter's position, until a sinus infection that created double vision caused him to sit out the entire 1923 season. He came back in 1924, but played at a below average level. This disparity in performance is even more obvious when his career is adjusted for hitter's inflation and deflation:

Years	TAB	HR	BA	Infla-tion	Adj. BA	Wtd. PRO	TF	HC
1915–22	4,458	60	.361	(1%)	.366	926	961	507
1924–30	4,329	42	.320	8%	.296	722	743	(55)

In his first eight seasons, Sisler had adjusted batting averages of .309, .334, .390, .372, .359, .392, .342, and .397. After 1924, he had only three adjusted batting averages over .300.

The best fielding first baseman of the 1920s, Sisler hit .340 with 102 home runs, and he stole 375 bases in his career. Adjusted for a career 2.5 percent hitter's inflation, he hit .332 with 105 home runs. His 855 Total Factor ranks ninth in league history for rate of success at first base, while his 452 Hits Contribution ranks tenth in league volume of success.

Eddie Murray

Murray shows what a player can do when he gets a chance to play at his full potential for a full career. In fact, Murray overstayed his time, generating a net negative contribution over his last seven seasons in order to amass over 500 home runs and over 3,000 hits in nearly 13,000 total at bats. If a player wasn't judged on gross numbers but, instead, on real contribution, Murray would have been better off retiring after the 1990 season:

Years	TAB	HR	BA	Adj. BA	Wtd. PRO	TF	HC
1977–90	9,041	379	.294	.295	871	893	545
1991–97	3,646	125	.270	.261	740	721	(90)

For his career, Murray hit .287 with 3,255 hits and 504 home runs. Adjusted for a 1 percent career hitter's inflation, he hit .284 with 521 home runs. His 842 Total Factor ranks Murray 14th in league rate of success, while his 454 Hits Contribution ranks him ninth in league volume of success. (If Murray had retired after the 1990 season, he would have ranked seventh in rate of success and sixth in volume of success.)

Cal Ripken

40-year-old Ripken is the Iron Man of baseball. He accomplished this feat while playing shortstop, which makes his endurance record even more remarkable. Ripken is no longer adding to the streak, and he has no range at third base. However, he can still hit, as he proved in 1999 by batting .340 with 18 home runs, while being limited to half a season of playing time in both 1999 and 2000 due to the first real injuries of his career.

Ripken hit .277 with 3,070 hits and 417 home runs to date. Adjusted for a career 2 percent hitter's inflation and a 162-game schedule, he has hit .271 with 3,084 hits and 416 home runs. His 788 Total Factor ranks 11th in league rate of success, while his 701 Hits Contribution ranks second behind Joe Cronin.

Vern Stephens

In his career, Stephens hit .286 with 247 home runs in a noninflationary period. Stephens' 815 Total Factor is the league's sixth best rate of success among shortstops, while his 521 Hits Contribution is the league's seventh best volume of success. What is remarkable about Stephens' career are the ten years from 1942 to 1951, when he was a consistently valuable contributor to his team's success. During that period, he generated all of his Hits Contribution, which means he averaged a 52 Hits Contribution every year for ten years.

Brooks Robinson

Robinson played so well and so long at third base that he owns most of the volume-related fielding records at that position. As a hitter, he produced nearly 3,000 hits despite a career .267 batting average. Robinson's reputation places him in the elite class of the top two or three third basemen of all time. But his low batting average, his infrequent rate of drawing walks that leads to an even lower on-base percentage, his career slugging average that barely tops .400, and his lack of speed all point to an average offensive player.

Robinson hit .267 with 268 home runs in 11,567 total at bats. Adjusting for a career 2.5 percent hitter's deflation, he hit .274 with 276 home runs, for a 744 Wtd. Production. Add in 56 career Fielding Factor points, and his 793 Total Factor ranks Robinson 15th in league rate of success, while his 429 Hits Contribution ranks him seventh in league volume of success.

Jim Palmer

Palmer issued a lot of walks with his high fastball. But the longtime ace of the Orioles staff also overpowered hitters. In his career, Palmer was 268–152, and he won 20 or more games in eight different seasons in the 1970s. Palmer achieved a 2.86 ERA and a 3.49 Wtd. RA/9, saving more than a run a game from scoring, which ranks him 11th in league rate of success. He saved 479 runs from scoring over his career, which ranks him sixth in league volume of success.

Mike Mussina

Mussina is the new Jim Palmer of the Orioles staff. The 32-year-old righty boasts a 147–81 record in his first ten seasons, with a 3.53 ERA. Mussina's ERA is high relative to history, as he is pitching in the greatest hitter's era in many decades. His 3.35 Wtd. RA/9 is the league's eighth best rate of success, showing how tough he is when compared to the league average pitcher. Mussina saves 1.2 runs from scoring every 9 innings, which over 2,010 innings gives him 282 Runs/162, currently the league's 26th best volume of success.

Ken Williams

Williams was baseball's first 30-30 man, and was nearly baseball's first 40-40 man in 1922, when he hit a league-leading 39 home runs and stole 37 bases, while batting .332. What made Williams' performance even more remarkable is that Babe Ruth was the only player to hit more than 30 home runs in a season prior to the 1922 season. And only three other players achieved the 30-30 mark in the next 37 years. Williams was an erratic outfielder, but he more than made up for his fielding problems with his speed, hitting, and power.

Williams didn't get a chance to start full-time until

he was 30. In 14 seasons, he hit .319 with 196 home runs and 154 steals in 5,456 total at bats. Adjusted for a career 5 percent hitter's inflation, Williams batted .304 with 197 home runs, for an 878 Wtd. Production. His 863 Total Factor ranks 31st in league rate of success for outfielders, while his 292 Hits Contribution ranks 40th in league volume of success.

St. Louis Browns/Baltimore Orioles   **Hitters Volume of Success**

Pos	Years	Name	AB	BB	HBP	TAB	H	2B	3B	HR	BA	OB	SA	PRO	Wtd PRO	SB	CS	SBF	SPF	FF	R TF	V HC
C	1989-98	C.Hoiles	2,820	435	44	3,299	739	122	2	151	.262	.369	.467	837	801	5	7	(2)	0	(10)	789	189
1B	1977-97	E.Murray	11,336	1,333	18	12,687	3,255	560	35	504	.287	.363	.476	839	832	110	43	2	(4)	13	842	454
2B	1912-24	D.Pratt	6,826	513	37	7,376	1,996	392	117	43	.292	.345	.403	748	766	247	108	(10)	9	19	784	373
SS	1981-	C.Ripken	11,074	1,103	64	12,241	3,070	587	44	417	.277	.346	.451	797	779	36	37	(3)	(1)	13	788	701
3B	1955-77	B.Robinson	10,654	860	53	11,567	2,848	482	68	268	.267	.325	.401	726	744	28	22	(1)	(6)	56	793	429
OF	1915-29	K.Williams	4,862	566	28	5,456	1,552	285	77	196	.319	.393	.530	924	878	154	106	(11)	10	(14)	863	292
OF	1903-10	G.Stone	3,271	282	22	3,575	984	106	68	23	.301	.360	.396	756	871	132	0	0	10	(14)	867	196
OF	1970-84	K.Singleton	7,189	1,263	17	8,469	2,029	317	25	246	.282	.391	.436	827	837	21	36	(6)	(7)	(23)	801	186
Starters		Averages	7,254	794	35	8,084	2,059	356	55	231	.284	.357	.444	801	804	92	45	(4)	1	5	806	353
C	1929-47	R.Ferrell	6,028	931	10	6,969	1,692	324	45	28	.281	.378	.363	741	708	29	35	(6)	(6)	14	710	114
1B	1915-30	G.Sisler	8,267	472	48	8,787	2,812	425	164	102	.340	.379	.468	847	826	375	127	(1)	10	20	855	452
2B	1965-78	D.Johnson	4,797	559	40	5,396	1,252	242	18	136	.261	.343	.404	747	773	33	25	(3)	0	12	783	221
SS	1941-55	V.Stephens	6,497	692	6	7,195	1,859	307	42	247	.286	.355	.460	816	817	25	22	(2)	0	0	815	521
3B	1934-45	H.Clift	5,730	1,070	41	6,841	1,558	309	62	178	.272	.390	.441	831	792	69	43	(2)	0	28	817	347
OF	1988-	B.Anderson	5,989	882	144	7,015	1,561	322	64	201	.261	.369	.436	805	768	299	96	16	10	15	809	180
OF	1915-27	B.Jacobson	5,507	355	39	5,901	1,714	328	94	83	.311	.357	.450	807	779	86	54	(7)	9	13	794	110
OF	1951-62	B.Nieman	3,452	435	9	3,896	1,018	180	32	125	.295	.375	.474	849	840	10	30	(12)	(10)	(15)	802	88
Reserves		Averages	5,783	675	42	6,500	1,683	305	65	138	.291	.369	.438	807	787	116	54	(2)	2	11	797	254
Totals		Weighted Ave.	6,764	754	38	7,556	1,934	339	58	200	.286	.361	.442	803	798	100	48	(3)	1	7	803	320

Pitchers Volume of Success

Pos	Years	Name	G	GS	IP	W	L	SV	SO	BB	ERA	RA/9	R Wtd RA/9	V Runs /162
SP	1965-84	J.Palmer	558	521	3,948	268	152	4	2,212	1,311	2.86	3.18	3.49	479
SP	1916-28	U.Shocker	412	317	2,682	187	117	25	983	657	3.17	3.78	3.65	288
SP	1991-	M.Mussina	288	288	2,010	147	81	0	1,535	467	3.53	3.75	3.35	282
SP	1897-12	J.Powell	578	516	4,389	245	254	15	1,621	1,021	2.97	4.08	4.18	199
SP	1976-98	D.Martinez	692	562	4,000	245	193	8	2,149	1,165	3.70	4.13	4.23	153
Starters		Averages	506	441	3,406	218	159	10	1,700	924	3.21	3.80	3.85	280
RP	1988-	G.Olson	594	0	647	40	38	217	564	310	3.28	3.49	3.39	85
RP	1955-71	D.Hall	495	74	1,260	93	75	68	741	236	3.32	3.66	4.01	78
RP	1978-87	S.Stewart	359	25	957	59	48	45	586	502	3.59	3.96	3.92	72
RP	1994-	A.Benitez	360	0	368	19	23	100	517	208	3.04	3.23	2.92	69
Relievers		Averages	452	25	808	53	46	108	602	314	3.36	3.67	3.73	76
Totals		Averages	958	466	4,213	271	205	118	2,302	1,238	3.24	3.77	3.83	356

St. Louis Browns/Baltimore Orioles   **Hitters Rate of Success**

Pos	Years	Name	AB	BB	HBP	TAB	H	2B	3B	HR	BA	OB	SA	PRO	Wtd PRO	SB	CS	SBF	SPF	FF	R TF	V HC
C	1989-98	C.Hoiles	2,820	435	44	3,299	739	122	2	151	.262	.369	.467	837	801	5	7	(2)	0	(10)	789	189
1B	1915-30	G.Sisler	8,267	472	48	8,787	2,812	425	164	102	.340	.379	.468	847	826	375	127	(1)	10	20	855	452
2B	1912-24	D.Pratt	6,826	513	37	7,376	1,996	392	117	43	.292	.345	.403	748	766	247	108	(10)	9	19	784	373
SS	1941-55	V.Stephens	6,497	692	6	7,195	1,859	307	42	247	.286	.355	.460	816	817	25	22	(2)	0	0	815	521
3B	1934-45	H.Clift	5,730	1,070	41	6,841	1,558	309	62	178	.272	.390	.441	831	792	69	43	(2)	0	28	817	347
OF	1903-10	G.Stone	3,271	282	22	3,575	984	106	68	23	.301	.360	.396	756	871	132	0	0	10	(14)	867	196
OF	1915-29	K.Williams	4,862	566	28	5,456	1,552	285	77	196	.319	.393	.530	924	878	154	106	(11)	10	(14)	863	292
OF	1940-49	W.Judnich	2,786	385	7	3,178	782	150	29	90	.281	.369	.452	822	813	20	24	(8)	0	9	814	86
Starters	Averages		5,132	552	29	5,713	1,535	262	70	129	.299	.370	.453	823	817	128	55	(5)	5	5	822	307
C	1953-65	G.Triandos	3,907	440	21	4,368	954	147	6	167	.244	.324	.413	737	730	1	0	0	(10)	4	724	75
1B	1977-97	E.Murray	11,336	1,333	18	12,687	3,255	560	35	504	.287	.363	.476	839	832	110	43	2	(4)	13	842	454
2B	1965-78	D.Johnson	4,797	559	40	5,396	1,252	242	18	136	.261	.343	.404	747	773	33	25	(3)	0	12	783	221
SS	1981-	C.Ripken	11,074	1,103	64	12,241	3,070	587	44	417	.277	.346	.451	797	779	36	37	(3)	(1)	13	788	701
3B	1955-77	B.Robinson	10,654	860	53	11,567	2,848	482	68	268	.267	.325	.401	726	744	28	22	(1)	(6)	56	793	429
OF	1968-80	M.Rettenmund	2,555	445	18	3,018	693	114	16	66	.271	.383	.406	789	808	68	28	4	9	(11)	810	75
OF	1988-	B.Anderson	5,989	882	144	7,015	1,561	322	64	201	.261	.369	.436	805	768	299	96	16	10	15	809	180
OF	1951-62	B.Nieman	3,452	435	9	3,896	1,018	180	32	125	.295	.375	.474	849	840	10	30	(12)	(10)	(15)	802	88
Reserves	Averages		6,721	757	46	7,524	1,831	329	35	236	.273	.350	.437	787	783	73	35	0	(2)	11	793	278
Totals	Weighted Ave.		5,662	620	35	6,317	1,634	284	59	164	.289	.362	.447	809	806	110	48	(3)	3	7	812	297

Pitchers Rate of Success

Pos	Years	Name	G	GS	IP	W	L	SV	SO	BB	ERA	RA/9	R Wtd RA/9	V Runs /162
SP	1991-	M.Mussina	288	288	2,010	147	81	0	1,535	467	3.53	3.75	3.35	282
SP	1965-84	J.Palmer	558	521	3,948	268	152	4	2,212	1,311	2.86	3.18	3.49	479
SP	1916-28	U.Shocker	412	317	2,682	187	117	25	983	657	3.17	3.78	3.65	288
SP	1989-97	B.McDonald	211	198	1,291	78	70	0	894	437	3.91	4.22	3.99	86
SP	1912-20	C.Weilman	239	179	1,521	84	93	10	536	418	2.67	3.55	4.02	96
Starters	Averages		342	301	2,290	153	103	8	1,232	658	3.14	3.59	3.63	246
RP	1994-	A.Benitez	360	0	368	19	23	100	517	208	3.04	3.23	2.92	69
RP	1988-	G.Olson	594	0	647	40	38	217	564	310	3.28	3.49	3.39	85
RP	1948-65	S.Paige	179	26	476	28	31	32	288	180	3.29	3.61	3.66	50
RP	1966-75	E.Watt	411	13	660	38	36	80	462	254	2.91	3.33	3.90	48
Relievers	Averages		386	10	538	31	32	107	458	238	3.13	3.42	3.53	63
Totals	Averages		728	310	2,828	184	135	115	1,690	896	3.14	3.56	3.61	309

St. Louis Browns/Baltimore Orioles
Catchers

V	R	Years	Name	AB	BB	HBP	TAB	H	2B	3B	HR	BA	OB	SA	PRO	Wtd PRO	SB	CS	SBF	SPF	FF	R TF	V HC
1	1	1989-98	C.Hoiles	2,820	435	44	3,299	739	122	2	151	.262	.369	.467	837	801	5	7	(2)	0	(10)	789	189
2	3	1929-47	R.Ferrell	6,028	931	10	6,969	1,692	324	45	28	.281	.378	.363	741	708	29	35	(6)	(6)	14	710	114
3	2	1953-65	G.Triandos	3,907	440	21	4,368	954	147	6	167	.244	.324	.413	737	730	1	0	0	(10)	4	724	75
4	4	1969-92	R.Dempsey	4,692	592	18	5,302	1,093	223	12	96	.233	.321	.347	668	673	20	19	(3)	(2)	24	692	39
5	5	1962-78	A.Etchebarren	2,618	246	31	2,895	615	101	17	49	.235	.308	.343	651	680	13	14	(5)	(2)	16	689	16
6	8	1911-26	H.Severeid	4,312	331	19	4,662	1,245	204	42	17	.289	.342	.367	709	699	35	19	(4)	(10)	(2)	683	11
7	7	1968-79	E.Hendricks	1,888	229	12	2,129	415	66	7	62	.220	.308	.361	669	693	1	5	(4)	(10)	8	687	9
8	6	1989-	L.Webster	1,450	140	12	1,602	368	73	2	33	.254	.325	.375	700	673	1	3	(3)	(10)	28	687	7
9	10	1946-58	L.Moss	2,234	282	6	2,522	552	75	4	63	.247	.333	.369	702	685	1	5	(3)	(10)	(22)	649	(36)
10	9	1928-47	R.Helmsley	5,047	357	4	5,408	1,321	257	72	31	.262	.311	.360	671	638	29	18	(3)	4	22	661	(44)
11	11	1948-62	J.Ginsberg	1,716	226	14	1,956	414	59	8	20	.241	.334	.320	654	644	7	5	(1)	(10)	(9)	623	(52)
12	12	1985-94	B.Melvin	1,955	98	1	2,054	456	85	6	35	.233	.270	.337	607	615	4	13	(10)	(10)	13	607	(69)

St. Louis Browns/Baltimore Orioles
First basemen

V	R	Years	Name	AB	BB	HBP	TAB	H	2B	3B	HR	BA	OB	SA	PRO	Wtd PRO	SB	CS	SBF	SPF	FF	R TF	V HC
1	2	1977-97	E.Murray	11,336	1,333	18	12,687	3,255	560	35	504	.287	.363	.476	839	832	110	43	2	(4)	13	842	454
2	1	1915-30	G.Sisler	8,267	472	48	8,787	2,812	425	164	102	.340	.379	.468	847	826	375	127	(1)	10	20	855	452
3	3	1961-77	B.Powell	6,681	1,001	29	7,711	1,776	270	11	339	.266	.364	.462	826	856	20	21	(3)	(10)	(12)	831	236
4	4	1957-66	J.Gentile	2,922	475	45	3,442	759	113	6	179	.260	.372	.486	858	854	3	1	0	(10)	(16)	829	98
5	6	1936-48	G.McQuinn	5,747	712	8	6,467	1,588	315	64	135	.276	.357	.424	781	771	32	31	(4)	0	29	796	82
6	5	1987-94	R.Milligan	2,118	447	13	2,578	553	106	10	70	.261	.393	.420	813	816	16	18	(7)	(4)	(2)	803	41
7	7	1965-82	L.May	7,609	487	49	8,145	2,031	340	31	354	.267	.315	.459	774	793	39	35	(4)	(7)	(13)	769	(3)
8	8	1951-61	B.Boyd	1,936	167	7	2,110	567	81	23	19	.293	.351	.388	739	731	9	17	(11)	5	(3)	722	(50)
9	9	1949-55	D.Kryhoski	1,794	119	12	1,925	475	85	14	45	.265	.315	.403	718	705	5	13	(10)	8	(3)	700	(67)
10	10	1930-36	J.Burns	3,506	376	8	3,890	980	199	31	44	.280	.351	.392	742	697	63	47	(8)	0	5	694	(148)
11	11	1902-10	T.Jones	3,847	193	44	4,084	964	122	34	4	.251	.294	.303	597	684	135	0	0	0	7	691	(163)

St. Louis Browns/Baltimore Orioles
Second basemen

V	R	Years	Name	AB	BB	HBP	TAB	H	2B	3B	HR	BA	OB	SA	PRO	Wtd PRO	SB	CS	SBF	SPF	FF	R TF	V HC
1	1	1912-24	D.Pratt	6,826	513	37	7,376	1,996	392	117	43	.292	.345	.403	748	766	247	108	(10)	9	19	784	373
2	2	1965-78	D.Johnson	4,797	559	40	5,396	1,252	242	18	136	.261	.343	.404	747	773	33	25	(3)	0	12	783	221
3	3	1920-34	M.McManus	6,660	675	30	7,365	1,926	401	88	120	.289	.357	.430	787	741	126	91	(8)	9	11	753	204
4	4	1958-70	J.Adair	4,019	208	17	4,244	1,022	163	19	57	.254	.294	.347	641	654	29	29	(6)	6	2	655	(47)
5	8	1939-52	J.Berardino	3,030	284	13	3,327	755	167	23	36	.249	.316	.355	671	654	27	29	(8)	0	(1)	645	(61)
6	4	1936-48	D.Gutteridge	4,202	309	5	4,516	1,075	200	64	39	.256	.308	.362	669	683	95	37	(3)	10	(20)	670	(64)
7	9	1913-20	J.Gedeon	2,109	180	25	2,314	515	82	20	1	.244	.311	.303	615	633	33	3	(2)	0	2	634	(67)
8	10	1987-98	B.Ripken	2,729	174	18	2,921	674	121	6	20	.247	.296	.318	614	611	25	16	(2)	3	22	634	(72)
9	7	1976-85	R.Dauer	3,829	297	14	4,140	984	193	3	43	.257	.313	.343	655	660	6	13	(4)	(1)	(7)	648	(77)
10	6	1926-37	O.Melillo	5,063	327	12	5,402	1,316	210	64	22	.260	.306	.340	646	607	69	65	(11)	8	44	648	(101)
11	12	1948-58	B.Young	2,447	208	2	2,657	609	68	28	15	.249	.308	.318	626	620	18	19	(7)	0	(16)	598	(116)
12	11	1954-63	B.Gardner	3,544	246	33	3,823	841	159	18	41	.237	.293	.327	620	609	19	22	(6)	1	12	616	(131)
13	13	1934-44	D.Heffner	2,526	270	9	2,805	610	99	19	6	.241	.317	.303	620	585	18	26	(11)	0	(10)	564	(166)

St. Louis Browns/Baltimore Orioles
Shortstops

V	R	Years	Name	AB	BB	HBP	TAB	H	2B	3B	HR	BA	OB	SA	PRO	Wtd PRO	SB	CS	SBF	SPF	FF	R TF	V HC
1	2	1981-	C.Ripken	11,074	1,103	64	12,241	3,070	587	44	417	.277	.346	.451	797	779	36	37	(3)	(1)	13	788	701
2	1	1941-55	V.Stephens	6,497	692	6	7,195	1,859	307	42	247	.286	.355	.460	816	817	25	22	(2)	0	0	815	521
3	3	1894-18	B.Wallace	8,618	774	47	9,439	2,309	391	143	34	.268	.332	.358	690	738	201	2	(0)	(1)	39	776	520
4	6	1965-82	M.Belanger	5,784	576	42	6,402	1,316	175	33	20	.228	.302	.280	582	600	167	75	2	10	54	667	17
5	5	1927-46	R.Kress	5,087	474	6	5,567	1,454	298	58	89	.286	.347	.420	767	717	47	56	(11)	(0)	(10)	696	4
6	4	1960-70	B.Johnson	2,307	156	10	2,473	628	88	11	44	.272	.321	.377	698	708	24	12	0	5	(12)	701	(2)
7	8	1951-59	W.Miranda	1,914	165	2	2,081	423	50	14	6	.221	.284	.271	555	546	13	16	(9)	0	35	572	(91)
8	9	1953-58	B.Hunter	1,875	111	8	1,994	410	58	18	16	.219	.265	.294	560	553	23	12	(0)	0	12	564	(102)
9	7	1914-29	W.Gerber	5,099	465	33	5,597	1,309	172	46	7	.257	.323	.313	635	611	43	47	(9)	0	4	606	(163)

St. Louis Browns/Baltimore Orioles
Third basemen

V	R	Years	Name	AB	BB	HBP	TAB	H	2B	3B	HR	BA	OB	SA	PRO	Wtd PRO	SB	CS	SBF	SPF	FF	R TF	V HC
1	2	1955-77	B.Robinson	10,654	860	53	11,567	2,848	482	68	268	.267	.325	.401	726	744	28	22	(1)	(6)	56	793	429
2	1	1934-45	H.Clift	5,730	1,070	41	6,841	1,558	309	62	178	.272	.390	.441	831	792	69	43	(2)	0	28	817	347
3	3	1973-87	D.DeCinces	5,809	618	21	6,448	1,505	312	29	237	.259	.333	.445	778	781	58	48	(6)	(4)	13	784	216
4	4	1946-51	B.Dillinger	2,904	251	12	3,167	888	123	47	10	.306	.363	.391	754	733	106	47	3	10	(18)	728	19
5	5	1990-96	L.Gomez	1,916	255	25	2,196	466	92	2	79	.243	.340	.417	757	745	4	10	(7)	(6)	(13)	720	4
6	7	1983-95	T.Hulett	2,128	145	10	2,283	529	90	13	48	.249	.300	.371	670	662	14	11	(3)	0	15	674	(43)
7	6	1909-29	J.Austin	5,388	592	44	6,024	1,328	174	76	13	.246	.326	.314	640	685	244	43	(7)	8	2	689	(82)
8	8	1919-30	G.Robertson	2,200	205	10	2,415	615	100	23	20	.280	.344	.373	717	670	29	22	(5)	10	(30)	645	(86)
9	9	1938-49	M.Christman	3,081	219	15	3,315	781	113	23	19	.253	.306	.324	630	633	17	17	(5)	5	1	634	(106)
10	10	1912-31	F.O'Rourke	4,069	314	53	4,436	1,032	196	42	15	.254	.315	.333	649	612	100	59	(6)	10	(0)	615	(186)

St. Louis Browns/Baltimore Orioles
Outfielders

V	R	Years	Name	AB	BB	HBP	TAB	H	2B	3B	HR	BA	OB	SA	PRO	Wtd PRO	SB	CS	SBF	SPF	FF	R TF	V HC
1	2	1915-29	K.Williams	4,862	566	28	5,456	1,552	285	77	196	.319	.393	.530	924	878	154	106	(11)	10	(14)	863	292
2	1	1903-10	G.Stone	3,271	282	22	3,575	984	106	68	23	.301	.360	.396	756	871	132	0	0	10	(14)	867	196
3	7	1970-84	K.Singleton	7,189	1,263	17	8,469	2,029	317	25	246	.282	.391	.436	827	837	21	36	(6)	(7)	(23)	801	186
4	5	1988-	B.Anderson	5,989	882	144	7,015	1,561	322	64	201	.261	.369	.436	805	768	299	96	16	10	15	809	180
5	8	1915-27	B.Jacobson	5,507	355	39	5,901	1,714	328	94	83	.311	.357	.450	807	779	86	54	(7)	9	13	794	110
6	6	1951-62	B.Nieman	3,452	435	9	3,896	1,018	180	32	125	.295	.375	.474	849	840	10	30	(12)	(10)	(15)	802	88
7	3	1940-49	W.Judnich	2,786	385	7	3,178	782	150	29	90	.281	.369	.452	822	813	20	24	(8)	0	9	814	86
8	14	1963-72	D.Buford	4,553	672	41	5,266	1,203	157	44	93	.264	.364	.379	743	774	200	105	(2)	10	(19)	763	83
9	4	1968-80	M.Rettenmund	2,555	445	18	3,018	693	114	16	66	.271	.383	.406	789	808	68	28	4	9	(11)	810	75
10	9	1937-47	C.Laabs	3,102	389	10	3,501	813	151	44	117	.262	.346	.452	798	794	32	22	(3)	6	(3)	794	65
11	11	1894-08	J.Anderson	6,341	310	53	6,704	1,841	328	124	49	.290	.329	.404	733	768	338	0	0	10	(4)	774	46
12	10	1898-08	E.Heidrick	3,047	146	6	3,199	914	108	73	16	.300	.333	.399	732	770	186	0	0	5	(0)	775	29
13	13	1909-17	W.Miller	2,244	318	30	2,592	623	79	35	8	.278	.375	.355	729	774	128	21	(6)	10	(7)	770	17
14	12	1993-	J.Hammonds	2,151	193	19	2,363	607	117	11	88	.282	.347	.470	816	758	56	22	5	10	(2)	771	17
15	15	1964-80	P.Blair	6,042	449	23	6,514	1,513	282	55	134	.250	.305	.382	687	715	171	93	(2)	10	40	762	16
16	16	1973-90	J.Dwyer	2,761	402	12	3,175	719	115	17	77	.260	.357	.398	755	754	26	15	(2)	4	(0)	755	(4)
17	18	1976-88	G.Roenicke	2,708	406	41	3,155	670	135	4	121	.247	.354	.434	788	786	16	20	(7)	(1)	(28)	750	(11)
18	17	1914-27	J.Tobin	6,174	508	29	6,711	1,906	294	99	64	.309	.364	.420	784	769	147	62	(8)	6	(14)	753	(15)
19	19	1903-11	D.Hoffman	2,981	226	39	3,246	762	71	52	14	.256	.316	.328	645	737	185	0	0	10	(1)	746	(19)
20	23	1965-72	C.Blefary	2,947	456	29	3,432	699	104	20	112	.237	.345	.400	745	781	24	24	(7)	(10)	(21)	743	(20)
21	28	1949-56	C.Abrams	1,611	304	7	1,922	433	64	19	32	.269	.387	.392	779	762	12	18	(12)	10	(25)	735	(23)
22	29	1982-89	M.Young	1,840	237	20	2,097	454	80	6	72	.247	.339	.414	753	748	22	17	(5)	5	(15)	733	(25)
23	20	1943-53	A.Zarilla	3,535	415	30	3,980	975	186	43	61	.276	.357	.405	761	750	33	33	(8)	8	(6)	744	(27)
24	24	1956-67	J.Brandt	3,895	351	12	4,258	1,020	175	37	112	.262	.325	.412	737	730	45	30	(3)	9	7	743	(30)
25	22	1927-37	F.Schulte	4,259	462	9	4,730	1,241	249	54	47	.291	.362	.408	770	728	56	58	(12)	9	18	744	(33)
26	26	1923-33	H.Rice	3,740	376	32	4,148	1,118	186	63	48	.299	.368	.421	789	748	59	55	(12)	0	4	740	(35)
27	21	1899-11	C.Hemphill	4,541	435	17	4,993	1,230	117	68	22	.271	.337	.341	678	742	207	0	0	10	(8)	744	(35)
28	25	1972-85	A.Bumbry	5,053	471	21	5,545	1,422	220	52	54	.281	.345	.378	723	732	254	92	11	10	(10)	743	(39)
29	35	1906-10	H.Niles	2,270	163	30	2,463	561	58	24	12	.247	.306	.310	616	710	107	0	0	10	(24)	697	(41)
30	32	1984-93	L.Sheets	2,284	175	19	2,478	607	98	5	94	.266	.323	.437	760	756	6	12	(7)	(10)	(26)	714	(53)
31	27	1909-23	B.Shotton	4,945	713	22	5,680	1,338	154	65	9	.271	.365	.333	698	749	293	93	(9)	10	(12)	738	(56)
32	30	1935-41	B.Bell	2,718	272	7	2,997	806	165	32	46	.297	.362	.432	794	729	11	12	(4)	0	(6)	719	(58)
33	31	1934-43	M.Solters	3,421	221	9	3,651	990	213	42	83	.289	.334	.449	783	728	42	23	(1)	1	(10)	718	(72)
34	37	1951-64	D.Williams	2,959	227	12	3,198	768	157	12	70	.260	.315	.392	707	698	12	21	(9)	0	(8)	681	(99)
35	33	1987-98	M.Devereaux	3,740	296	12	4,048	949	170	33	105	.254	.311	.401	712	698	85	56	(6)	10	6	707	(101)
36	34	1959-70	R.Snyder	3,631	294	9	3,934	984	150	29	42	.271	.327	.363	690	703	58	32	(1)	7	(5)	703	(102)
37	39	1958-63	W.Tasby	1,868	201	16	2,085	467	61	10	46	.250	.328	.367	695	685	12	20	(12)	6	(22)	657	(103)
38	38	1981-91	J.Shelby	3,090	182	4	3,276	739	128	24	70	.239	.282	.364	646	648	98	40	5	10	5	669	(138)
39	36	1983-97	J.Orsulak	4,293	318	23	4,634	1,173	186	37	57	.273	.327	.374	700	700	93	60	(5)	6	(4)	696	(141)

St. Louis Browns/Baltimore Orioles
Starting Pitchers

V	R	Years	Name	G	GS	IP	W	L	SV	SO	BB	ERA	RA/9	R Wtd RA/9	V Runs /162
1	2	1965-84	J.Palmer	558	521	3,948	268	152	4	2,212	1,311	2.86	3.18	3.49	479.4
2	3	1916-28	U.Shocker	412	317	2,682	187	117	25	983	657	3.17	3.78	3.65	287.9
3	1	1991-	M.Mussina	288	288	2,010	147	81	0	1,535	467	3.53	3.75	3.35	282.4
4	10	1897-12	J.Powell	578	516	4,389	245	254	15	1,621	1,021	2.97	4.08	4.18	198.9
5	12	1976-98	D.Martinez	692	562	4,000	245	193	8	2,149	1,165	3.70	4.13	4.23	153.4
6	6	1962-75	D.McNally	424	396	2,730	184	119	2	1,512	826	3.24	3.53	4.07	148.3
7	9	1957-73	M.Pappas	520	465	3,186	209	164	4	1,728	858	3.40	3.76	4.17	138.4
8	8	1959-77	M.Cuellar	453	379	2,808	185	130	11	1,632	822	3.14	3.62	4.12	136.2
9	5	1912-20	C.Weilman	239	179	1,521	84	93	10	536	418	2.67	3.55	4.02	95.6
10	4	1989-97	B.McDonald	211	198	1,291	78	70	0	894	437	3.91	4.22	3.99	86.4
11	14	1980-93	M.Boddicker	342	309	2,124	134	116	3	1,330	721	3.80	4.20	4.23	76.5
12	19	1975-92	M.Flanagan	526	404	2,770	167	143	4	1,491	890	3.90	4.23	4.32	74.6
13	18	1898-10	H.Howell	340	282	2,568	131	146	6	986	677	2.74	4.06	4.32	74.2
14	13	1903-12	B.Pelty	266	217	1,908	92	117	4	693	532	2.63	3.52	4.23	73.3
15	7	1938-46	J.Niggeling	184	161	1,251	64	69	0	620	516	3.22	3.84	4.07	70.5
16	20	1948-61	N.Garver	402	330	2,477	129	157	12	881	881	3.73	4.30	4.34	62.8
17	17	1921-35	L.Stewart	279	216	1,722	101	98	8	503	498	4.19	4.87	4.31	49.4
18	21	1934-49	D.Galehouse	375	258	2,004	109	118	13	851	735	3.97	4.49	4.35	49.3
19	22	1976-88	S.McGregor	356	309	2,141	138	108	5	904	518	3.99	4.33	4.36	47.7
20	11	1931-38	I.Andrews	249	108	1,041	50	59	8	257	342	4.14	4.86	4.18	45.4
21	16	1902-08	F.Glade	132	126	1,073	52	68	2	464	237	2.62	3.45	4.27	35.8
22	23	1960-74	S.Barber	466	272	1,999	121	106	13	1,309	950	3.36	3.92	4.40	34.8
23	15	1944-52	S.Zoldak	250	93	929	43	53	8	207	301	3.54	4.09	4.26	32.6
24	26	1990-	S.Erickson	326	322	2,106	135	116	0	1,152	745	4.43	4.81	4.43	31.0
25	24	1951-64	H.Brown	358	211	1,680	85	92	11	710	389	3.81	4.18	4.41	28.7
26	25	1982-94	S.Davis	442	239	1,781	113	96	11	1,048	687	4.02	4.38	4.42	28.1
27	28	1936-49	N.Potter	349	177	1,686	92	97	22	747	582	3.99	4.50	4.47	18.1
28	27	1966-72	T.Phoebus	201	149	1,030	56	52	6	725	489	3.33	3.73	4.44	12.9
29	30	1911-24	E.Hamilton	410	261	2,343	116	147	13	790	773	3.16	4.13	4.52	11.2
30	29	1963-71	W.Bunker	206	152	1,085	60	52	5	569	334	3.51	3.92	4.52	5.0
31	31	1971-82	R.Grimsley	345	295	2,039	124	99	3	750	559	3.81	4.18	4.54	3.5
32	32	1914-19	D.Davenport	259	186	1,537	73	83	12	719	521	2.93	3.75	4.56	0.0
33	34	1937-51	B.Muncrief	288	165	1,401	80	82	9	525	392	3.80	4.30	4.58	(4.4)
34	33	1924-33	S.Gray	379	231	1,951	111	115	22	730	639	4.18	5.14	4.58	(5.8)
35	35	1912-26	D.Davis	239	164	1,319	75	71	2	460	688	3.97	4.94	4.60	(7.0)
36	36	1914-26	A.Sothoron	264	193	1,582	91	99	9	576	596	3.31	4.47	4.62	(12.5)
37	37	1925-36	G.Blaeholder	338	251	1,914	104	125	12	572	535	4.54	5.26	4.63	(16.3)
38	40	1988-96	B.Milacki	143	125	796	39	47	1	387	301	4.38	4.69	4.78	(20.5)
39	38	1936-46	S.Sundra	168	99	859	56	41	2	214	321	4.17	4.82	4.77	(20.9)
40	41	1911-25	D.Danforth	286	112	1,186	71	66	23	484	455	3.89	4.69	4.85	(42.1)
41	46	1949-56	D.Pillette	188	119	904	38	66	2	305	391	4.40	4.96	5.03	(50.2)
42	39	1897-06	W.Sudhoff	278	239	2,075	102	135	3	516	603	3.60	4.93	4.78	(56.9)
43	43	1919-29	E.Vangilder	367	187	1,716	99	102	19	474	699	4.28	5.31	4.91	(70.8)
44	45	1927-45	D.Coffman	472	132	1,460	72	95	38	372	463	4.65	5.51	5.01	(77.1)
45	44	1939-51	J.Kramer	322	215	1,637	95	103	7	613	682	4.24	4.91	4.96	(77.2)
46	42	1924-34	M.Gaston	355	270	2,105	97	164	8	615	836	4.55	5.46	4.88	(78.4)
47	47	1933-46	J.Knott	325	192	1,557	82	103	19	484	642	4.97	5.73	5.06	(91.3)
48	48	1908-13	J.Lake	199	139	1,318	62	90	5	594	332	2.85	4.57	5.33	(118.8)
49	49	1907-22	B.Bailey	203	117	1,084	38	76	0	570	527	3.57	4.92	5.93	(175.4)

**St. Louis Browns/Baltimore Orioles
Relief Pitchers**

V	R	Years	Name	G	GS	IP	W	L	SV	SO	BB	ERA	RA/9	R Wtd RA/9	V Runs /162
1	2	1988-	G.Olson	594	0	647	40	38	217	564	310	3.28	3.49	3.39	85.4
2	8	1955-71	D.Hall	495	74	1,260	93	75	68	741	236	3.32	3.66	4.01	78.1
3	5	1978-87	S.Stewart	359	25	957	59	48	45	586	502	3.59	3.96	3.92	71.7
4	1	1994-	A.Benitez	360	0	368	19	23	100	517	208	3.04	3.23	2.92	68.8
5	6	1974-88	T.Martinez	546	2	834	55	42	115	632	425	3.45	3.85	3.95	58.3
6	3	1948-65	S.Paige	179	26	476	28	31	32	288	180	3.29	3.61	3.66	49.9
7	4	1966-75	E.Watt	411	13	660	38	36	80	462	254	2.91	3.33	3.90	48.2
8	7	1990-	A.Mills	459	5	622	38	31	15	447	384	3.99	4.21	3.95	43.3
9	9	1987-94	M.Williamson	365	15	690	46	35	21	397	226	3.86	4.19	4.11	35.7
10	14	1981-92	D.Schmidt	376	63	902	54	55	50	479	237	3.88	4.33	4.39	17.4
11	12	1951-59	G.Zuverink	265	31	642	32	36	40	223	203	3.54	4.15	4.33	17.3
12	13	1975-89	T.Stoddard	485	0	730	41	35	76	582	356	3.95	4.23	4.36	16.4
13	11	1959-67	W.Stock	321	3	517	27	13	22	365	215	3.60	3.91	4.29	15.3
14	10	1987-96	T.Frohwirth	284	0	418	20	19	11	259	172	3.60	4.09	4.25	14.6
15	15	1952-63	R.Moore	365	105	1,073	63	59	46	612	560	4.06	4.38	4.54	1.6
16	16	1991-	A.Rhodes	310	61	692	48	44	9	656	345	4.80	5.00	4.62	(5.4)
17	17	1990-	J.Poole	431	0	363	22	12	4	256	156	4.31	5.03	4.71	(6.4)
18	18	1988-97	J.Bautista	312	49	686	32	42	3	328	171	4.62	4.93	4.92	(29.2)
19	19	1929-36	C.Kimsey	198	10	509	24	29	17	121	194	5.07	6.04	5.22	(39.4)
20	20	1948-57	B.Kennedy	172	45	465	15	28	11	256	289	4.73	5.50	5.38	(44.6)
21	21	1937-44	B.Trotter	163	31	483	22	34	3	158	174	5.40	6.58	5.99	(81.1)

ST. LOUIS CARDINALS (1900–2000)

The Cardinals began the twentieth century with only four winning seasons in 21 years. Despite this slow start, the Cardinals proved to be baseball's most successful small-city franchise, with 58 winning seasons and 17 postseason appearances in the past 80 years.

St. Louis' first star was Rogers Hornsby, who teamed with Jim Bottomley, Jesse Haines, and Chick Hafey to win the first Cardinals pennant in 1926. Dizzy Dean, Joe Medwick, Ripper Collins, and Frank Frisch led the 1934 "Gashouse Gang" to a World Series crown. Wartime Cardinals teams won repeatedly with talented players Stan Musial, Walker Cooper, Red Shoendienst, Marty Marion, Whitey Kurowski, Enos Slaughter, Mort Cooper, Harry Brecheen and Max Lanier. The 1960s Cardinals featured Ken Boyer, Lou Brock, Bob Gibson and Tim McCarver. Ted Simmons, Keith Hernandez, Ozzie Smith, John Tudor, Ray Lankford, and Mark McGwire starred on more recent Cardinals teams.

Profiled Cardinals Players

Rogers Hornsby

Hornsby was a 19-year-old shortstop when he arrived in the majors in 1915. Hornsby hit for respectable Dead Ball numbers the next few years, but he was hardly the league's most dangerous slugger. He failed to hit 10 home runs in any of his first six seasons, and he waited five years to hit better than .327. Just as Hornsby started to mature into a great hitter, the hitter's inflation of the 1920s arrived, and his batting statistics exploded.

From 1915–1919, Hornsby hit an overall .310 with 27 home runs. He then hit .382 with 250 home runs in the 1920s, culminating in his MVP season for Chicago in 1929. At that point, the 33-year-old Hornsby was on the verge of establishing himself as perhaps the second greatest player ever. Unfortunately, a foot injury cost Hornsby the 1930 season, and he missed out on sharing in the 15 percent hitter's inflation that year. Hornsby came back for 357 at bats in 1931, but he never topped 100 at bats after that.

Years	TAB	HR	BA	Adj. BA	Wtd. PRO	TF	HC
1915–19	2,196	27	.310	.341	895	895	244
1920–29	6,228	250	.382	.367	1,049	1,042	1,104
1930–37	835	24	.313	.302	878	828	59

Ruth hit 244 home runs after he turned 34, while Hornsby hit just 24. Cobb churned out 1,333 hits after he turned 34, while Hornsby had just 225. As a result of Hornsby's limited performance in the 1930s, he finished his career on par with Nap Lajoie and Tris Speaker in historic rankings, while missing the top rankings earned by Ruth, Wagner, Cobb, and Williams.

In his career, Hornsby hit .358 with 301 home runs. Adjusted for a 2 percent career hitter's inflation, he hit .355 with 310 home runs, for a 995 Wtd. Production. His 986 Total Factor ranks first in major league rate of success among second basemen. His 1,407 Hits Contribution ranks first in the league in volume of success at second base.

Johnny Mize

Mize was a dangerous hitter in each of his first ten seasons for the Cardinals and Giants. During this peak period, Mize's rate of success is comparable to that of Lou Gehrig and Jimmie Foxx. Mize hit for a high average in several years, the highest being a .364 average with 25 home runs in 1937. He also hit 40 or more home runs three times, the highest being 51 home runs and a .302 average in 1947. But Mize never put together a season where he hit for both a high average and 30 or more home runs.

Mize lost three years to military service during his productive period. Worse yet, he lost his batting eye at the age of 36, and suffered through five very ordinary seasons at the end of his career.

Years	TAB	HR	BA	Adj. BA	Wtd. PRO	TF	HC
1936–48	5,937	297	.324	.324	999	992	662
1949–53	1,414	62	.264	.256	777	757	(10)

It was probably very difficult for Mize to go from being another Lou Gehrig to being Mr. Average, a part-time player for the Yankees in his last four seasons.

In his career, Mize hit .312 with 359 home runs in 7,351 total at bats. Adjusted for a 0.5 percent career hitter's inflation, he hit .311 with 375 home runs, for a 955 Wtd. Production. His 946 Total Factor ranks third in league rate of success for first basemen. Although Mize ranks far behind American League stars Gehrig and Foxx in volume of success with 652 Hits Contribution, he does rank second among National League first basemen, trailing only Jeff Bagwell.

Ozzie Smith

One of the best trades the Cardinals ever made was acquiring Smith in exchange for Garry Templeton. Smith's average improved after the trade, while Templeton's average and stolen bases dropped off sharply. And there never was any comparison when it came to playing defense. Ozzie Smith played shortstop like a circus acrobat, making unbelievable stops on balls headed through the infield while doing spins and cartwheels. Smith was the heart and soul of the successful Cardinals teams of the 1980s that relied on defense and speed to overcome a lack of power.

In his career, Smith hit .262 with 1,072 walks and 28 home runs in a noninflationary environment, and he stole 580 bases in 728 attempts, for an 80 percent success ratio. Smith's 668 Wtd. Production was average for a shortstop, but adding 65 Fielding Factor points, 24 Stolen Base Factor points, and 9 Speed Factor points made him anything

but average. His 766 Total Factor ranks seventh in league rate of success for shortstops, while his 545 Hits Contribution ranks sixth in league volume of success.

Jim Bottomley

The Cardinals employed many talented first basemen over the years. Ed Konetchy hit well in the Dead Ball Era. Bottomley had impressive statistics in the 1920s. Johnny Mize and Ripper Collins terrorized hitters in the 1930s. Stan Musial covered first for over 1,000 games in the 1940s and 1950s. Bill White and Orlando Cepeda hit and fielded well in the 1960s. Keith Hernandez was a great defensive first baseman and even won a MVP award in 1979. Jack Clark hit home runs and drew walks in the 1980s, and Mark McGwire hit even more home runs and drew even more walks in the 1990s. Of all these players, Musial, Mize, Bottomley and Cepeda are in the Hall of Fame, and McGwire will make it there soon. Who really deserves Hall of Fame recognition?

Based on their raw statistics, a case can be made that the right players are in the Hall. But if we adjust for the biases found between seasons, we find that Jim Bottomley's statistics are no better than Konetchy's, and far worse than those of Keith Hernandez, especially when we take into account their fielding abilities. Simply put, if Bottomley hit in the Dead Ball Era, there is no way he would be in the Hall of Fame today.

In his career, Jim Bottomley hit .310 with 219 home runs, while hitting one extra-base hit about every 10 times up. Adjusted for a career 5 percent hitter's inflation, he hit .295 with 220 home runs, for an 827 Wtd. Production. His 815 Total Factor ranks 22nd in league rate of success for first basemen, while his 187 Hits Contribution is 18th in volume of success, and just 10 better than Todd Helton of the Rockies—who has only three full seasons in the majors.

Ken Boyer

In the 1960s, Boyer and Ron Santo were the two best third basemen in the National League. Neither player has been elected to the Hall of Fame, even though they have sufficient credentials. Boyer won five Gold Gloves before Santo pushed him aside in 1964. However, Boyer won MVP honors in that season while leading his team to a World Series victory over the Yankees. In his career, Boyer hit .287 with 282 home runs, and he added 29 Fielding Factor points. Adjusted for 0.5 percent career hitter's inflation, Boyer hit .286 with 289 home runs, for an 810 Wtd. Production. His 843 Total Factor ranks sixth in league rate of success at third, while his 495 Hits Contribution ranks fourth in league volume of success.

Stan Musial

Musial was "The Man" to Cardinals fans for two decades. Musial displayed three distinct periods of evolving hitting in his long career. Over his first six seasons, he hit .342 with 77 triples and 71 home runs in 3,305 total at bats, while drawing 379 walks. In the prime seven years of his career, Musial hit .346 with 74 triples and 221 home runs in 4,808 total at bats, while drawing 675 walks. Over the last nine years of his career, Musial hit .307 with 26 triples and 183 home runs in 4,511 total at bats, while drawing 545 walks.

Years	TAB	HR	BA	Adj. BA	Wtd. PRO	TF	HC
1941–47	3,305	71	.342	.351	989	997	392
1948–54	4,808	221	.346	.336	1,024	1,019	620
1955–63	4,511	183	.307	.300	887	873	245

In his career, Musial hit .331 with 3,630 hits and 475 home runs. Adjusted for a 1 percent career hitter's inflation, he hit .327 with 491 home runs, for a 966 Wtd. Production. His 961 Total Factor ranks sixth in league rate of success for outfielders, while his 1,257 Hits Contribution ranks fourth in league volume of success.

Joe Medwick

In his career, Medwick teamed with three first basemen to provide his team's 1-2 offensive punch. Medwick and Ripper Collins hit over half the Cardinals' home runs while pacing the "Gashouse Gang" to a pennant in 1934 and a second place finish in 1935. Next, Medwick teamed with Johnny Mize to give the Cardinals the best 1-2 punch in the league from 1936 to 1939. In 1937, these two sluggers combined to hit .370 with 56 home runs. Unfortunately for them, the rest of the team hit .257 with 38 home runs, and the Cardinals settled for fourth place that year. After Medwick was traded to Brooklyn, he joined up with ex–Phillie Dolph Camilli to power the Dodgers to a second-place finish in 1940 and a pennant in 1941. Medwick lost his power swing in 1942, and he became a singles hitter the remainder of his career.

Years	TAB	HR	BA	Adj. BA	Wtd. PRO	TF	HC
1932–41	5,872	180	.332	.330	906	935	523
1942–48	2,226	25	.302	.313	776	789	36

Over his career, Medwick hit .324 with 205 home runs in a noninflationary period. Although Medwick never hit more than 31 home runs in a season, he hit 64 doubles one year, and 18 triples in another. Medwick ended up hitting for extra bases once every nine times up over his career. His 895 Total Factor ranks 16th in league rate of success for outfielders, while his 559 Hits Contribution ranks 15th in league volume of success.

Bob Gibson

Gibson was an imposing figure on the mound for nearly two decades, with a blazing fastball that carved out 3,117 strikeouts in 3,884 innings, a 251–174 record and a 2.91 ERA. Gibson's 3.66 Wtd. RA/9 ranks 20th in league rate of success, while his 391 Runs/162 ranks ninth in league volume of success. At his peak, Gibson won 20 or more games five times in a six-year period. As it turns out, Gibson won only 13 games in that sixth season in 1967 and, although no other Cardinals pitcher won more than 16 games, the team still managed to win 101 games, the pennant, and the World Series.

Dizzy Dean

Dean was elected to the Hall of Fame for his brilliant, albeit short, career. He was also elected for his colorful character and backwoods language, for his 30 win MVP season with the 1934 world champions, and for his teaming with brother Paul to win four World Series games that year. Perhaps the best way to measure Dizzy is to project what his career results would have been if a toe injury at age 27 hadn't led to a career-ending sore arm. Dizzy was on track to win over 300 games if he had stayed healthy.

Dean was 150–83 in his career, with a 3.02 ERA. His 3.55 Wtd. RA/9 ranks 11th in league rate of success, higher than pitchers Warren Spahn, Bob Gibson, Dazzy Vance, and Juan Marichal. Dizzy's 232 Runs/162 ranks 31st in league volume of success.

St. Louis Cardinals · **Hitters Volume of Success**

Pos	Years	Name	AB	BB	HBP	TAB	H	2B	3B	HR	BA	OB	SA	PRO	Wtd PRO	SB	CS	SBF	SPF	FF	R TF	V HC
C	1968-88	T.Simmons	8,680	855	39	9,574	2,472	483	47	248	.285	.352	.437	789	793	21	33	(4)	(8)	(7)	773	380
1B	1936-53	J.Mize	6,443	856	52	7,351	2,011	367	83	359	.312	.397	.562	959	955	28	1	(0)	(4)	(4)	946	652
2B	1915-37	R.Hornsby	8,173	1,038	48	9,259	2,930	541	169	301	.358	.434	.577	1,010	995	135	64	(7)	(0)	(2)	986	1,407
SS	1978-96	O.Smith	9,396	1,072	33	10,501	2,460	402	69	28	.262	.339	.328	668	668	580	148	24	9	65	766	545
3B	1955-69	K.Boyer	7,455	713	20	8,188	2,143	318	68	282	.287	.351	.462	813	810	105	77	(6)	9	29	843	495
OF	1941-63	S.Musial	10,972	1,599	53	12,624	3,630	725	177	475	.331	.418	.559	977	966	78	31	(2)	(1)	(1)	961	1,257
OF	1932-48	J.Medwick	7,635	437	26	8,098	2,471	540	113	205	.324	.362	.505	867	870	42	0	0	10	15	895	559
OF	1938-59	E.Slaughter	7,946	1,018	37	9,001	2,383	413	148	169	.300	.382	.453	835	830	71	15	(1)	8	8	846	397
Starters		Averages	8,338	949	39	9,325	2,563	474	109	258	.307	.381	.483	864	860	133	46	0	3	13	876	711
C	1940-57	W.Cooper	4,702	309	22	5,033	1,341	240	40	173	.285	.332	.464	796	795	18	1	0	(10)	(10)	775	246
1B	1974-90	K.Hernandez	7,370	1,070	32	8,472	2,182	426	60	162	.296	.388	.436	824	832	98	63	(3)	(1)	40	868	406
2B	1919-37	F.Frisch	9,112	728	31	9,871	2,880	466	138	105	.316	.369	.432	801	770	419	74	4	9	25	808	581
SS	1940-53	M.Marion	5,506	470	14	5,990	1,448	272	37	36	.263	.323	.345	668	675	35	2	(1)	0	32	706	133
3B	1941-49	W.Kurowski	3,229	369	36	3,634	925	162	32	106	.286	.366	.455	821	837	19	0	0	(4)	5	838	221
OF	1990-	R.Lankford	4,953	707	28	5,688	1,366	307	48	207	.276	.369	.483	852	819	244	111	3	10	26	859	288
OF	1924-37	C.Hafey	4,625	372	33	5,030	1,466	341	67	164	.317	.372	.526	898	858	70	7	(2)	9	4	870	286
OF	1961-79	L.Brock	10,332	761	49	11,142	3,023	486	141	149	.293	.344	.410	754	770	938	307	28	10	(3)	804	251
Reserves		Averages	6,229	598	31	6,858	1,829	338	70	138	.294	.358	.437	795	789	230	71	4	3	15	811	301
Totals		Weighted Ave.	7,635	832	36	8,502	2,318	428	96	218	.304	.375	.471	845	837	165	54	2	3	14	855	575

Pitchers Volume of Success

Pos	Years	Name	G	GS	IP	W	L	SV	SO	BB	ERA	RA/9	R Wtd RA/9	V Runs /162
SP	1959-75	B.Gibson	528	482	3,884	251	174	6	3,117	1,336	2.91	3.29	3.66	391
SP	1940-53	H.Brecheen	318	240	1,908	133	92	18	901	536	2.92	3.31	3.42	254
SP	1930-47	D.Dean	317	230	1,967	150	83	30	1,163	453	3.02	3.54	3.55	232
SP	1938-49	M.Cooper	295	239	1,841	128	75	14	913	571	2.97	3.44	3.69	191
SP	1908-21	S.Sallee	476	305	2,822	174	143	36	836	573	2.56	3.48	4.06	166
Starters		Averages	387	299	2,484	167	113	21	1,386	694	2.86	3.40	3.70	247
RP	1944-53	T.Wilks	385	44	913	59	30	46	403	283	3.26	3.59	3.72	89
RP	1985-97	T.Worrell	617	0	694	50	52	256	628	247	3.09	3.43	3.60	76
RP	1955-75	L.McDaniel	987	74	2,139	141	119	172	1,361	623	3.45	3.93	4.28	66
RP	1970-82	A.Hrabosky	545	1	722	64	35	97	548	315	3.10	3.54	3.78	64
Relievers		Averages	634	30	1,117	79	59	143	735	367	3.30	3.72	3.98	74
Totals		Averages	1,020	329	3,601	246	172	164	2,121	1,061	3.00	3.50	3.79	321

St. Louis Cardinals   **Hitters Rate of Success**

Pos	Years	Name	AB	BB	HBP	TAB	H	2B	3B	HR	BA	OB	SA	PRO	Wtd PRO	SB	CS	SBF	SPF	FF	R TF	V HC
C	1894-06	M.Grady	3,000	311	73	3,384	881	155	67	35	.294	.374	.425	799	809	114	0	0	8	(41)	776	138
1B	1936-53	J.Mize	6,443	856	52	7,351	2,011	367	83	359	.312	.397	.562	959	955	28	1	(0)	(4)	(4)	946	652
2B	1915-37	R.Hornsby	8,173	1,038	48	9,259	2,930	541	169	301	.358	.434	.577	1,010	995	135	64	(7)	(0)	(2)	986	1,407
SS	1978-96	O.Smith	9,396	1,072	33	10,501	2,460	402	69	28	.262	.339	.328	668	668	580	148	24	9	65	766	545
3B	1955-69	K.Boyer	7,455	713	20	8,188	2,143	318	68	282	.287	.351	.462	813	810	105	77	(6)	9	29	843	495
OF	1941-63	S.Musial	10,972	1,599	53	12,624	3,630	725	177	475	.331	.418	.559	977	966	78	31	(2)	(1)	(1)	961	1,257
OF	1932-48	J.Medwick	7,635	437	26	8,098	2,471	540	113	205	.324	.362	.505	867	870	42	0	0	10	15	895	559
OF	1924-37	C.Hafey	4,625	372	33	5,030	1,466	341	67	164	.317	.372	.526	898	858	70	7	(2)	9	4	870	286
Starters	Averages		7,212	800	42	8,054	2,249	424	102	231	.312	.384	.495	879	872	144	41	1	5	8	886	667
C	1940-57	W.Cooper	4,702	309	22	5,033	1,341	240	40	173	.285	.332	.464	796	795	18	1	0	(10)	(10)	775	246
1B	1974-90	K.Hernandez	7,370	1,070	32	8,472	2,182	426	60	162	.296	.388	.436	824	832	98	63	(3)	(1)	40	868	406
2B	1919-37	F.Frisch	9,112	728	31	9,871	2,880	466	138	105	.316	.369	.432	801	770	419	74	4	9	25	808	581
SS	1896-03	B.Keister	2,433	90	50	2,573	758	133	63	18	.312	.349	.440	789	794	131	0	0	10	(50)	755	72
3B	1941-49	W.Kurowski	3,229	369	36	3,634	925	162	32	106	.286	.366	.455	821	837	19	0	0	(4)	5	838	221
OF	1990-	R.Lankford	4,953	707	28	5,688	1,366	307	48	207	.276	.369	.483	852	819	244	111	3	10	26	859	288
OF	1938-59	E.Slaughter	7,946	1,018	37	9,001	2,383	413	148	169	.300	.382	.453	835	830	71	15	(1)	8	8	846	397
OF	1908-15	S.Evans	3,359	359	111	3,829	963	175	67	32	.287	.374	.407	782	820	86	0	0	0	(9)	811	100
Reserves	Averages		5,388	581	43	6,013	1,600	290	75	122	.297	.370	.446	816	811	136	33	0	3	4	818	289
Totals	Weighted Ave.		6,604	727	43	7,374	2,033	379	93	195	.308	.380	.482	862	852	141	38	1	4	7	863	541

Pitchers Rate of Success

Pos	Years	Name	G	GS	IP	W	L	SV	SO	BB	ERA	RA/9	Wtd RA/9	R V Runs /162
SP	1940-53	H.Brecheen	318	240	1,908	133	92	18	901	536	2.92	3.31	3.42	254
SP	1930-47	D.Dean	317	230	1,967	150	83	30	1,163	453	3.02	3.54	3.55	232
SP	1959-75	B.Gibson	528	482	3,884	251	174	6	3,117	1,336	2.91	3.29	3.66	391
SP	1938-49	M.Cooper	295	239	1,841	128	75	14	913	571	2.97	3.44	3.69	191
SP	1938-53	M.Lanier	327	204	1,619	108	82	17	821	611	3.01	3.50	3.71	160
Starters	Averages		357	279	2,244	154	101	17	1,383	701	2.95	3.39	3.61	246
RP	1985-97	T.Worrell	617	0	694	50	52	256	628	247	3.09	3.43	3.60	76
RP	1969-76	C.Taylor	305	21	607	28	20	31	282	162	3.07	3.29	3.64	62
RP	1944-53	T.Wilks	385	44	913	59	30	46	403	283	3.26	3.59	3.72	89
RP	1970-82	A.Hrabosky	545	1	722	64	35	97	548	315	3.10	3.54	3.78	64
Relievers	Averages		463	17	734	50	34	108	465	252	3.14	3.48	3.69	73
Totals	Averages		820	296	2,978	204	135	125	1,848	953	3.00	3.41	3.63	319

St. Louis Cardinals
Catchers

V	R	Years	Name	AB	BB	HBP	TAB	H	2B	3B	HR	BA	OB	SA	PRO	Wtd PRO	SB	CS	SBF	SPF	FF	R TF	V HC
1	3	1968-88	T.Simmons	8,680	855	39	9,574	2,472	483	47	248	.285	.352	.437	789	793	21	33	(4)	(8)	(7)	773	380
2	2	1940-57	W.Cooper	4,702	309	22	5,033	1,341	240	40	173	.285	.332	.464	796	795	18	1	0	(10)	(10)	775	246
3	4	1959-80	T.McCarver	5,529	548	30	6,107	1,501	242	57	97	.271	.340	.388	729	748	61	49	(6)	5	12	760	225
4	1	1894-06	M.Grady	3,000	311	73	3,384	881	155	67	35	.294	.374	.425	799	809	114	0	0	8	(41)	776	138
5	5	1935-46	K.O'Dea	2,195	273	3	2,471	560	101	20	40	.255	.338	.374	712	720	3	0	0	(10)	10	721	53
6	7	1946-54	J.Garagiola	1,872	267	16	2,155	481	82	16	42	.257	.355	.385	740	725	5	2	0	(10)	(9)	706	31
7	6	1937-48	D.Padgett	1,991	141	4	2,136	573	111	16	37	.288	.336	.415	752	750	6	0	0	(6)	(24)	720	(4)
8	8	1912-32	M.Gonzalez	2,829	231	20	3,080	717	123	19	13	.253	.314	.324	638	657	52	10	(3)	(2)	24	674	(6)
9	9	1987-98	T.Pagnozzi	2,896	189	11	3,096	733	153	11	44	.253	.301	.359	660	653	18	21	(7)	(4)	21	663	(22)
10	10	1945-61	D.Rice	3,826	382	34	4,242	908	177	20	79	.237	.312	.356	668	653	2	3	(1)	(10)	13	655	(48)

St. Louis Cardinals
First basemen

V	R	Years	Name	AB	BB	HBP	TAB	H	2B	3B	HR	BA	OB	SA	PRO	Wtd PRO	SB	CS	SBF	SPF	FF	R TF	V HC
1	1	1936-53	J.Mize	6,443	856	52	7,351	2,011	367	83	359	.312	.397	.562	959	955	28	1	(0)	(4)	(4)	946	652
2	2	1974-90	K.Hernandez	7,370	1,070	32	8,472	2,182	426	60	162	.296	.388	.436	824	832	98	63	(3)	(1)	40	868	406
3	4	1956-69	B.White	5,972	596	28	6,596	1,706	278	65	202	.286	.353	.455	809	815	103	68	(5)	9	24	843	234
4	5	1922-37	J.Bottomley	7,471	664	43	8,178	2,313	465	151	219	.310	.369	.500	869	827	58	15	(2)	0	(10)	815	187
5	6	1907-21	E.Konetchy	7,649	689	73	8,411	2,150	344	182	74	.281	.346	.403	749	800	255	5	(0)	(1)	11	810	173
6	3	1931-41	R.Collins	3,784	356	23	4,163	1,121	205	65	135	.296	.360	.492	852	842	18	0	0	0	9	851	170
7	7	1954-66	J.Cunningham	3,362	599	49	4,010	980	177	26	64	.291	.406	.417	823	807	16	27	(9)	(2)	(18)	778	27
8	8	1942-49	R.Sanders	2,182	328	7	2,517	597	114	19	42	.274	.370	.401	771	797	8	0	0	0	(20)	777	9
9	9	1949-62	S.Bilko	1,738	234	3	1,975	432	85	13	76	.249	.339	.444	782	756	2	4	(3)	(10)	4	747	(22)
10	10	1911-20	G.Paulette	1,780	108	9	1,897	478	66	19	2	.269	.314	.330	644	696	43	8	(3)	0	(5)	688	(65)

St. Louis Cardinals
Second basemen

V	R	Years	Name	AB	BB	HBP	TAB	H	2B	3B	HR	BA	OB	SA	PRO	Wtd PRO	SB	CS	SBF	SPF	FF	R TF	V HC
1	1	1915-37	R.Hornsby	8,173	1,038	48	9,259	2,930	541	169	301	.358	.434	.577	1,010	995	135	64	(7)	(0)	(2)	986	1,407
2	2	1919-37	F.Frisch	9,112	728	31	9,871	2,880	466	138	105	.316	.369	.432	801	770	419	74	4	9	25	808	581
3	3	1904-16	M.Huggins	5,558	1,003	47	6,608	1,474	146	50	9	.265	.382	.314	696	758	324	12	(2)	10	17	784	325
4	5	1945-63	Schoendienst	8,479	606	21	9,106	2,449	427	78	84	.289	.338	.387	725	708	89	27	(2)	8	31	745	250
5	6	1979-91	T.Herr	5,349	627	22	5,998	1,450	254	41	28	.271	.350	.350	700	707	188	64	10	9	9	734	145
6	4	1901-05	J.Farrell	2,172	193	10	2,375	567	93	28	4	.261	.324	.335	659	704	68	0	0	3	46	753	86
7	7	1983-95	J.Oquendo	3,202	448	5	3,655	821	104	24	14	.256	.349	.317	666	670	35	33	(8)	7	39	708	42
8	8	1988-	L.Alicea	3,347	445	43	3,835	871	165	47	42	.260	.354	.375	730	700	71	41	(3)	0	(4)	692	14
9	9	1937-46	J.Brown	3,512	231	12	3,755	980	146	42	9	.279	.326	.352	678	687	39	0	0	4	(14)	678	(12)
10	11	1936-43	S.Martin	2,237	190	8	2,435	599	112	24	16	.268	.327	.361	688	688	36	0	0	8	(23)	673	(22)
11	10	1960-72	J.Javier	5,722	314	21	6,057	1,469	216	55	78	.257	.298	.355	652	665	135	63	2	10	1	677	(24)
12	14	1972-81	M.Tyson	2,959	175	14	3,148	714	118	28	27	.241	.287	.327	614	618	23	18	(4)	5	16	635	(61)
13	13	1969-80	T.Sizemore	5,011	469	20	5,500	1,311	188	21	23	.262	.327	.321	649	655	59	46	(6)	2	3	654	(82)
14	12	1955-66	D.Blasingame	5,296	552	15	5,863	1,366	178	62	21	.258	.330	.327	657	647	105	60	(2)	10	1	655	(88)

St. Louis Cardinals
Shortstops

V	R	Years	Name	AB	BB	HBP	TAB	H	2B	3B	HR	BA	OB	SA	PRO	Wtd PRO	SB	CS	SBF	SPF	FF	R TF	V HC
1	1	1978-96	O.Smith	9,396	1,072	33	10,501	2,460	402	69	28	.262	.339	.328	668	668	580	148	24	9	65	766	545
2	4	1940-53	M.Marion	5,506	470	14	5,990	1,448	272	37	36	.263	.323	.345	668	675	35	2	(1)	0	32	706	133
3	3	1949-59	S.Hemus	2,694	456	62	3,212	736	137	41	51	.273	.390	.411	802	779	21	18	(4)	0	(22)	752	129
4	2	1896-03	B.Keister	2,433	90	50	2,573	758	133	63	18	.312	.349	.440	789	794	131	0	0	10	(50)	755	72
5	5	1929-40	C.Gelbert	2,869	290	7	3,166	766	169	43	17	.267	.336	.374	709	671	34	0	1	0	10	682	13
6	7	1954-63	A.Grammas	2,073	206	15	2,294	512	90	10	12	.247	.320	.317	637	615	17	14	(5)	0	33	644	(25)
7	6	1899-05	O.Krueger	1,704	160	31	1,895	427	40	33	5	.251	.326	.322	648	700	48	0	0	0	(42)	659	(37)
8	8	1913-24	D.Lavan	3,891	209	24	4,124	954	134	45	7	.245	.288	.308	596	627	71	56	(16)	9	19	640	(48)
9	9	1962-75	D.Maxvill	3,443	370	8	3,821	748	79	24	6	.217	.295	.259	554	571	7	11	(4)	10	58	635	(51)
10	10	1925-45	L.Durocher	5,350	377	18	5,745	1,320	210	56	24	.247	.299	.320	619	604	31	5	(1)	0	29	632	(91)

St. Louis Cardinals
Third basemen

V	R	Years	Name	AB	BB	HBP	TAB	H	2B	3B	HR	BA	OB	SA	PRO	Wtd PRO	SB	CS	SBF	SPF	FF	R TF	V HC
1	1	1955-69	K.Boyer	7,455	713	20	8,188	2,143	318	68	282	.287	.351	.462	813	810	105	77	(6)	9	29	843	495
2	2	1941-49	W.Kurowski	3,229	369	36	3,634	925	162	32	106	.286	.366	.455	821	837	19	0	0	(4)	5	838	221
3	4	1984-98	T.Pendleton	7,032	486	15	7,533	1,897	356	39	140	.270	.318	.391	710	704	127	59	1	4	43	752	133
4	3	1997-	F.Tatis	1,616	189	32	1,837	446	94	7	71	.276	.363	.475	838	775	39	17	3	10	(4)	784	61
5	5	1901-08	D.Brain	2,543	134	11	2,688	641	97	52	27	.252	.292	.363	655	726	73	0	0	0	15	741	60
6	6	1977-92	K.Oberkfell	4,874	546	23	5,443	1,354	237	44	29	.278	.353	.362	716	724	62	47	(5)	3	7	728	46
7	7	1905-17	M.Mowrey	4,291	469	35	4,795	1,099	183	54	7	.256	.334	.329	663	714	167	0	0	0	11	725	22
8	8	1923-31	L.Bell	3,239	276	2	3,517	938	184	49	66	.290	.346	.438	784	739	25	5	(1)	8	(23)	724	17
9	9	1989-	T.Zeile	5,889	728	31	6,648	1,576	323	20	205	.268	.351	.434	785	755	50	50	(7)	(4)	(24)	720	9
10	11	1913-26	M.Stock	6,249	455	13	6,717	1,806	270	58	22	.289	.339	.361	700	716	155	75	(10)	9	(11)	704	(30)
11	10	1962-70	M.Shannon	2,780	224	10	3,014	710	116	23	68	.255	.313	.387	700	727	19	17	(5)	10	(22)	710	(31)
12	12	1953-60	R.Jablonski	2,562	196	15	2,773	687	126	11	83	.268	.324	.423	747	716	16	13	(3)	(10)	(29)	673	(60)
13	14	1898-05	J.Burke	1,947	112	30	2,089	475	58	13	1	.244	.295	.289	584	626	87	0	0	10	(17)	619	(103)
14	13	1972-82	K.Reitz	4,777	184	35	4,996	1,243	243	12	68	.260	.293	.359	651	654	10	14	(3)	(10)	20	661	(135)

St. Louis Cardinals
Outfielders

V	R	Years	Name	AB	BB	HBP	TAB	H	2B	3B	HR	BA	OB	SA	PRO	Wtd PRO	SB	CS	SBF	SPF	FF	R TF	V HC
1	1	1941-63	S.Musial	10,972	1,599	53	12,624	3,630	725	177	475	.331	.418	.559	977	966	78	31	(2)	(1)	(1)	961	1,257
2	2	1932-48	J.Medwick	7,635	437	26	8,098	2,471	540	113	205	.324	.362	.505	867	870	42	0	0	10	15	895	559
3	5	1938-59	E.Slaughter	7,946	1,018	37	9,001	2,383	413	148	169	.300	.382	.453	835	830	71	15	(1)	8	8	846	397
4	4	1990-	R.Lankford	4,953	707	28	5,688	1,366	307	48	207	.276	.369	.483	852	819	244	111	3	10	26	859	288
5	3	1924-37	C.Hafey	4,625	372	33	5,030	1,466	341	67	164	.317	.372	.526	898	858	70	7	(2)	9	4	870	286
6	10	1961-79	L.Brock	10,332	761	49	11,142	3,023	486	141	149	.293	.344	.410	754	770	938	307	28	10	(3)	804	251
7	7	1954-65	W.Moon	4,843	644	13	5,500	1,399	212	60	142	.289	.374	.445	819	800	89	68	(8)	9	10	811	146
8	9	1978-94	L.Smith	5,170	623	92	5,885	1,488	273	58	98	.288	.374	.420	794	801	370	140	14	10	(18)	808	145
9	11	1956-71	C.Flood	6,357	444	52	6,853	1,861	271	44	85	.293	.344	.389	733	747	88	73	(8)	10	50	798	135
10	15	1928-44	P.Martin	4,117	369	13	4,499	1,227	270	75	59	.298	.358	.443	801	794	146	0	0	10	(14)	790	110
11	17	1971-88	G.Hendrick	7,129	567	22	7,718	1,980	343	27	267	.278	.333	.446	779	794	59	47	(4)	3	(8)	785	101
12	6	1908-15	S.Evans	3,359	359	111	3,829	963	175	67	32	.287	.374	.407	782	820	86	0	0	0	(9)	811	100
13	14	1935-48	T.Moore	4,700	406	16	5,122	1,318	263	28	80	.280	.340	.399	739	740	82	0	0	10	41	791	86
14	12	1939-52	J.Hopp	4,260	464	19	4,743	1,262	216	74	46	.296	.368	.414	782	788	128	1	1	10	(3)	796	81
15	8	1922-32	R.Blades	2,415	331	47	2,793	726	133	51	50	.301	.395	.460	855	815	33	22	(8)	8	(7)	808	70
16	16	1992-	B.Jordan	3,371	228	53	3,652	963	176	28	124	.286	.341	.465	805	760	109	41	7	10	14	790	58
17	13	1902-06	H.Smoot	2,635	149	34	2,818	763	102	45	15	.290	.336	.380	715	788	84	0	0	8	(4)	792	51
18	19	1990-	B.Gilkey	3,955	455	41	4,451	1,086	238	24	116	.275	.355	.435	790	757	115	70	(5)	10	8	771	29
19	20	1974-88	J.Mumphrey	4,993	478	4	5,475	1,442	217	55	70	.289	.351	.396	748	754	174	80	2	9	2	768	28
20	18	1918-22	A.McHenry	1,959	117	6	2,082	592	105	39	34	.302	.343	.448	791	802	35	33	(20)	(6)	0	776	20
21	21	1982-	W.McGee	7,649	448	15	8,112	2,254	350	94	79	.295	.335	.396	731	728	352	121	13	10	12	762	19
22	23	1940-55	H.Walker	2,651	245	7	2,903	786	126	37	10	.296	.358	.383	741	743	42	0	0	7	3	754	(4)
23	22	1930-36	G.Watkins	3,207	246	44	3,497	925	192	42	73	.288	.347	.443	790	766	61	0	0	6	(17)	755	(5)
24	27	1911-19	L.Magee	3,741	265	9	4,015	1,031	133	54	12	.276	.325	.350	675	723	186	25	(5)	10	6	735	(7)
25	24	1927-35	E.Orsati	2,165	176	6	2,347	663	129	39	10	.306	.360	.416	776	750	46	0	0	10	(9)	751	(8)
26	26	1988-95	F.Jose	2,490	193	9	2,692	697	134	14	51	.280	.334	.406	740	740	102	57	(6)	10	(9)	735	(30)
27	25	1923-33	T.Douthit	4,127	443	33	4,603	1,201	220	38	29	.291	.364	.384	748	704	67	3	(0)	6	33	743	(33)
28	28	1904-08	S.Shannon	2,613	286	22	2,921	677	49	15	3	.259	.337	.293	630	713	145	0	0	10	12	735	(33)
29	32	1909-12	R.Ellis	1,985	216	10	2,211	517	66	30	13	.260	.336	.344	680	719	56	0	0	3	1	724	(37)
30	31	1909-15	R.Oakes	3,619	265	32	3,916	1,011	112	42	15	.279	.334	.346	680	712	163	0	0	10	2	724	(65)
31	30	1915-29	J.Smith	4,532	334	22	4,888	1,301	182	71	40	.287	.339	.385	724	724	228	67	2	10	(8)	727	(74)
32	29	1985-97	V.Coleman	5,406	477	15	5,898	1,425	176	89	28	.264	.325	.345	670	664	752	177	63	10	(6)	732	(75)
33	33	1953-61	R.Repulski	3,088	207	33	3,328	830	153	23	106	.269	.322	.436	758	727	25	29	(9)	0	(9)	709	(81)
34	36	1912-25	J.Schultz	1,959	116	6	2,081	558	83	19	15	.285	.327	.370	696	699	35	16	(3)	(4)	(24)	668	(84)
35	35	1920-35	H.Mueller	2,118	168	26	2,312	597	87	37	22	.282	.342	.389	731	700	37	18	(8)	0	(17)	675	(96)
36	34	1994-	J.Mabry	2,207	167	11	2,385	608	122	3	49	.275	.330	.400	730	690	5	10	(6)	(6)	1	679	(98)
37	37	1973-84	T.Scott	2,803	186	16	3,005	699	111	28	17	.249	.300	.327	627	634	125	69	(4)	9	10	649	(167)

St. Louis Cardinals
Starting Pitchers

V	R	Years	Name	G	GS	IP	W	L	SV	SO	BB	ERA	RA/9	R Wtd RA/9	V Runs /162
1	3	1959-75	B.Gibson	528	482	3,884	251	174	6	3,117	1,336	2.91	3.29	3.66	391.3
2	1	1940-53	H.Brecheen	318	240	1,908	133	92	18	901	536	2.92	3.31	3.42	253.9
3	2	1930-47	D.Dean	317	230	1,967	150	83	30	1,163	453	3.02	3.54	3.55	231.6
4	4	1938-49	M.Cooper	295	239	1,841	128	75	14	913	571	2.97	3.44	3.69	191.2
5	9	1908-21	S.Sallee	476	305	2,822	174	143	36	836	573	2.56	3.48	4.06	165.7
6	5	1938-53	M.Lanier	327	204	1,619	108	82	17	821	611	3.01	3.50	3.71	159.7
7	6	1979-90	J.Tudor	281	263	1,797	117	72	1	988	475	3.12	3.51	3.78	157.9
8	12	1918-37	J.Haines	555	388	3,209	210	158	10	981	871	3.64	4.37	4.20	133.1
9	13	1955-68	L.Jackson	558	429	3,263	194	183	20	1,709	824	3.40	3.88	4.24	116.6
10	7	1943-54	A.Brazle	441	117	1,377	97	64	60	554	492	3.31	3.86	3.92	102.2
11	10	1952-65	H.Haddix	453	285	2,235	136	113	21	1,575	601	3.63	4.07	4.19	95.8
12	14	1912-29	B.Doak	453	369	2,783	169	157	16	1,014	851	2.98	3.83	4.28	93.4
13	11	1941-56	H.Pollet	403	278	2,107	131	116	20	934	745	3.51	4.09	4.20	88.1
14	15	1918-32	B.Sherdel	514	273	2,709	165	146	26	839	661	3.72	4.40	4.31	80.6
15	17	1947-61	G.Staley	640	186	1,982	134	111	61	727	529	3.70	4.30	4.32	54.7
16	19	1922-40	S.Johnson	542	209	2,166	112	117	43	920	488	4.06	4.56	4.35	53.4
17	18	1988-	K.Hill	327	315	1,966	117	108	0	1,179	847	4.03	4.42	4.34	48.6
18	8	1934-43	P.Dean	159	87	787	50	34	8	387	179	3.75	4.16	4.05	46.9
19	21	1976-88	J.Andujar	405	305	2,153	127	118	9	1,032	731	3.58	3.99	4.39	40.0
20	23	1974-86	J.Denny	325	322	2,149	123	108	0	1,146	778	3.59	4.05	4.40	37.6
21	16	1943-56	R.Munger	273	161	1,229	77	56	12	564	500	3.83	4.21	4.32	34.1
22	20	1975-86	P.Vukovich	286	186	1,455	93	69	10	882	545	3.66	4.11	4.38	30.0
23	24	1986-98	B.Tewksbury	302	277	1,807	110	102	1	812	292	3.92	4.40	4.42	28.7
24	22	1952-62	V.Mizell	268	230	1,529	90	88	0	918	680	3.85	4.27	4.40	28.4
25	25	1983-95	J.DeLeon	415	264	1,897	86	119	6	1,594	841	3.76	4.16	4.44	24.4
26	27	1965-78	N.Briles	452	279	2,112	129	112	22	1,163	547	3.44	3.96	4.46	23.5
27	26	1987-96	J.Magrane	190	166	1,097	57	67	0	564	391	3.81	4.24	4.45	13.8
28	28	1983-95	D.Cox	278	174	1,298	74	75	8	723	432	3.64	4.17	4.49	10.3
29	29	1992-99	D.Osborne	143	138	840	47	45	0	535	231	3.92	4.45	4.55	0.9
30	30	1959-66	E.Broglio	259	184	1,337	77	74	2	849	587	3.74	4.23	4.55	0.7
31	31	1925-38	B.Hallahan	324	224	1,740	102	94	8	856	779	4.03	4.73	4.56	(0.9)
32	32	1961-70	R.Washburn	239	166	1,210	72	64	5	700	354	3.53	4.06	4.57	(1.9)
33	33	1992-	K.Bottenfield	279	107	860	44	44	9	527	369	4.43	4.84	4.60	(3.8)
34	34	1967-76	A.Foster	217	148	1,025	48	63	0	501	383	3.74	4.21	4.65	(10.9)
35	36	1935-42	B.McGee	197	102	853	46	41	6	340	355	3.74	4.45	4.67	(11.2)
36	35	1912-19	G.Packard	248	153	1,410	85	69	17	488	356	3.01	3.84	4.65	(16.4)
37	39	1975-83	E.Rasmussen	238	144	1,018	50	77	5	489	309	3.85	4.32	4.73	(19.7)
38	37	1990-	O.Olivares	304	217	1,482	71	77	3	784	643	4.53	4.87	4.69	(22.2)
39	43	1906-11	E.Karger	165	123	1,092	48	67	3	415	314	2.79	3.88	4.84	(36.0)
40	42	1928-40	B.Weiland	277	179	1,388	62	94	7	614	611	4.24	5.15	4.82	(42.2)
41	40	1909-18	B.Harmon	321	240	2,054	107	133	12	634	762	3.33	4.19	4.73	(42.6)
42	41	1980-91	D.LaPoint	294	227	1,487	80	86	1	802	559	4.02	4.53	4.82	(43.0)
43	38	1974-89	B.Forsch	498	422	2,795	168	136	3	1,133	832	3.76	4.25	4.69	(43.3)
44	49	1993-	A.Watson	206	137	892	51	55	1	589	351	5.03	5.52	5.24	(72.0)
45	45	1972-82	L.McGlothen	318	201	1,498	86	93	2	939	572	3.98	4.42	4.99	(73.8)
46	47	1906-16	F.Beebe	202	153	1,294	62	83	4	634	534	2.86	4.08	5.08	(78.7)
47	44	1970-84	J.Curtis	438	199	1,641	89	97	11	825	669	3.96	4.44	4.98	(80.0)
48	48	1904-10	J.Lush	182	155	1,239	66	85	2	490	413	2.68	4.14	5.15	(86.6)
49	46	1924-36	F.Rhem	294	230	1,725	105	97	10	534	529	4.20	5.15	5.00	(90.0)

St. Louis Cardinals
Relief Pitchers

V	R	Years	Name	G	GS	IP	W	L	SV	SO	BB	ERA	RA/9	R Wtd RA/9	V Runs /162
1	3	1944-53	T.Wilks	385	44	913	59	30	46	403	283	3.26	3.59	3.72	89.4
2	1	1985-97	T.Worrell	617	0	694	50	52	256	628	247	3.09	3.43	3.60	76.3
3	9	1955-75	L.McDaniel	987	74	2,139	141	119	172	1,361	623	3.45	3.93	4.28	66.0
4	4	1970-82	A.Hrabosky	545	1	722	64	35	97	548	315	3.10	3.54	3.78	64.2
5	2	1969-76	C.Taylor	305	21	607	28	20	31	282	162	3.07	3.29	3.64	62.3
6	6	1963-77	J.Hoerner	493	0	563	39	34	99	412	181	2.99	3.40	3.84	44.8
7	7	1973-82	M.Littell	316	19	532	32	31	56	466	304	3.32	3.67	4.05	31.2
8	5	1982-86	J.Lahti	205	1	286	17	11	20	137	111	3.12	3.43	3.82	23.3
9	8	1990-97	M.Perez	313	0	346	24	16	22	224	120	3.56	3.85	4.12	18.0
10	11	1984-90	R.Horton	325	53	673	32	27	15	319	222	3.76	4.02	4.33	17.0
11	10	1994-	J.Frascatore	262	5	355	19	17	1	197	141	4.08	4.59	4.31	10.0
12	12	1924-34	H.Bell	221	46	663	32	34	24	191	143	3.69	4.62	4.43	9.8
13	13	1988-96	C.Carpenter	291	13	414	27	22	7	252	131	3.91	4.21	4.49	3.2
14	14	1969-78	M.Garman	303	8	434	22	27	42	213	202	3.63	4.12	4.60	(2.1)
15	16	1995-	J.Acevedo	204	34	397	24	25	19	232	150	4.45	4.90	4.67	(4.9)
16	20	1959-65	M.Bridges	206	5	345	23	15	25	302	191	3.75	4.45	4.75	(7.4)
17	19	1986-91	S.Terry	236	40	499	24	28	8	262	176	3.73	4.22	4.74	(10.3)
18	18	1982-93	K.Dayley	385	33	574	33	45	39	406	225	3.64	4.28	4.74	(11.4)
19	15	1935-49	C.Shoun	454	85	1,287	73	59	29	483	404	3.91	4.42	4.63	(11.6)
20	17	1991-	R.Cormier	293	108	846	43	42	1	507	183	4.18	4.69	4.68	(12.1)
21	22	1970-77	R.Folkers	195	28	423	19	23	7	242	170	4.11	4.41	4.85	(13.6)
22	21	1991-	M.Petkovsek	335	41	633	45	26	5	316	194	4.49	4.96	4.76	(14.9)
23	23	1997-	M.Aybar	151	27	326	14	17	5	217	142	5.06	5.61	5.27	(25.8)
24	24	1913-24	L.North	172	25	463	21	16	13	199	200	4.43	5.32	5.27	(38.6)

WASHINGTON SENATORS/ MINNESOTA TWINS (1901–2000)

Pitching legend Walter Johnson (1,021 Runs/162 over 21 years) salvaged an otherwise dismal 60-year performance by the Washington Senators, as Johnson pitched on over half of the 18 Senators teams with winning records, including two pennant winners. The 1933 team won the other Senators pennant behind General Crowder, Joe Cronin, Goose Goslin, Hennie Manush, Buddy Myer, veteran Sam Rice, and rookie Cecil Travis. Roy Sievers, Mickey Vernon, and Dutch Leonard starred on weak Senators teams in the 1940s and 1950s.

The Senators moved to Minnesota in 1961, and became a hitting juggernaut. Harmon Killebrew, Tony Oliva, Bob Allison, and Earl Battey powered the 1960s teams, while Rod Carew, Roy Smalley, and pitcher Bert Blyleven continued the Twins' winning ways in the 1970s. The Twins struggled in the 1980s and 1990s, but did win two World Series crowns behind Kirby Puckett, Kent Hrbek, Gary Gaetti, Frank Viola, Chuck Knoblauch, and Rick Aguilera.

Profiled Senators/Twins Players

Walter Johnson

Johnson is the best pitcher in major league history. He was practically the only reason why the Senators became a competitive team after 1911, and he was still the team's best pitcher for their 1924 and 1925 pennant winning teams. The "Big Train" won 417 games in his career, second only to Cy Young, and he would have won over 500 games if he played for Detroit or another team that

could hit. Johnson struck out 3,509 batters, a record that stood for many decades, and he had a career 2.17 ERA. Johnson boasts the second best rate of success for starting pitchers in major league history behind Pedro Martinez with a 3.10 Wtd. RA/9, giving up 1.5 runs per 9 innings less than the historic average pitcher. Johnson finished just behind Cy Young in volume of success, with 1,021 Runs saved from scoring compared to Young's 1,027. But Young had the advantage of more frequent starts in the 1890s to offset his 11 percent worse rate of success.

Johnson produced many excellent seasons. One season stands out as the best performance for a starting pitcher in the twentieth century. In 1913, Johnson went 36–7 in 346 innings, with 243 strikeouts, only 38 walks and a 1.14 ERA. His 1.68 Wtd. RA/9 that year is the third best rate of success in major league history, behind Pedro Martinez (1.55 in 2000) and Greg Maddux (1.64 in 1995). Johnson saved 117 runs from scoring compared to the league average performance, which gives him the highest volume of success for any twentieth century season. He also hit .261 that year for a 726 Production, versus his team's .252 average and 643 Production.

Bert Blyleven

The Dutchman won 20 games just once, and he had a career-long struggle to win more games than he lost. But, in the final analysis, Blyleven deserves Hall of Fame recognition as one of the best pitchers of all time, and he would already have that honor if he had won 13 more games in his career. The second best pitcher in franchise history, Blyleven went 287–250 with 3,701 strikeouts in

4,970 innings. He achieved a career 3.31 ERA and a 3.91 Wtd. RA/9, for the league's 56th best rate of success. Blyleven saved 367 runs from scoring, for the league's tenth best volume of success.

Harmon Killebrew

Killebrew was one of the most prolific home run hitters in history, as he hit a home run every 14 times up to bat to rank fifth lifetime with 573 home runs. As one of the most feared hitters in his day, Killebrew drew 1,559 walks, and had a .379 on-base percentage despite his career .256 batting average. Adjusted for a career 2 percent hitter's deflation, he hit .261 with 586 home runs, for a 906 Wtd. Production. He ranks eighth in rate of success for league first basemen with an 860 Total Factor. He ranks sixth in volume of success with 517 Hits Contribution.

Killebrew hit for so much power that he made up for his lack of speed and bad fielding. The Twins tried him at first, third, and in the outfield, before letting him finish his career as the team's DH. Killebrew played nearly as many games at third as he did at first, and was a poor fielding third baseman when he was the league's MVP in 1969, while setting the major league record for home runs by a third baseman with 49. The two years at DH extended Killebrew's career and gave him a chance to hit another 27 home runs, but they also hurt his overall performance, as he suffered through a negative 42 Hits Contribution.

Rod Carew

Carew also split his time between two positions. He was a below average fielding second baseman the first half of his career with the Twins, and a below average fielding first baseman the second half of his career with the Twins and Angels. Although he played 5 percent more games at first, most of his Hits Contribution came from his seasons at second, and Carew is considered a second baseman for the career rankings in this book:

Years	TAB	HR	BA	Adj. BA	Wtd. PRO	TF	HC
1967–75 (2B)	4,864	46	.328	.343	852	849	382
1976–85 (1B)	5,494	46	.328	.331	840	838	183

Carew did have three solid seasons his first three years as a first baseman. They were also his last three years with the Twins. After starring with the Twins, he was an average player with the Angels:

Years	TAB	HR	BA	Adj. BA	Wtd. PRO	TF	HC
1967–78 (Twins)	6,868	74	.334	.348	877	878	555
1979–85 (Angels)	3,490	18	.314	.315	787	776	11

Over his career, Carew hit .328 with 92 home runs, while stealing 353 bases. Adjusted for a career 2.5 percent hitter's deflation, he hit .336 with 95 home runs. In his peak years of 1972–1978, Carew produced adjusted batting averages of .345, .359, .381, .370, .353, .384, and .341. His 843 Total Factor ranks sixth in league rate of success for second basemen, while his 566 Hits Contribution ranks eighth in league volume of success.

Kirby Puckett

Puckett was a gifted sparkplug of a player. Standing 5'8" and weighing 210 pounds, Puckett was fast and a fine fielding outfielder who could hit for average and for power. The only real weakness in his game was an unwillingness to draw walks, keeping his career on-base percentage at a rather anemic .363.

Puckett hit .318 with 207 home runs and 134 stolen bases in his 12-year career. Adjusted for 1 percent career hitter's inflation, he hit .315 with 214 home runs. His 888 Total Factor ranks 17th in league rate of success for outfielders, while his 500 Hits Contribution ranks 19th in league volume of success. Puckett would have ranked higher in volume of success if he wasn't forced to retire with eye problems at age 34.

Goose Goslin

Goslin was one of baseball's first power hitters, hitting .316 with 248 home runs and 921 extra base hits in 9,661 total at bats, while stealing 175 bases. He even hit 37 home runs in 1930, after a sore arm caused Washington to trade him to St. Louis early in the season. Goslin played for pennant winners in Washington in 1924, 1925, and 1933, and in Detroit in 1934 and 1935.

Goslin benefited from hitter's inflation during his entire career. Adjusted for a 7 percent career inflation, he hit .296 with 246 home runs. His 847 Total Factor places him only 46th in league rate of success, but his 435 Hits Contribution ranks 23rd in league volume of success.

Chuck Knoblauch

Knoblauch was rookie of the year with a .281 average and 25 steals for the surprising 1991 Twins, who went from last the previous year to win the 1991 World Series. Knoblauch had productive seasons for a financially weak

Twins organization from 1992 to 1997, but the team's lack of talent kept him out of the playoffs. He joined the Yankees in 1998, and played on three world champion teams in 1998–2000.

The 32-year-old Knoblauch is hitting .297 with 83 home runs and 350 steals in a career that includes a Gold Glove Award in 1997, and an extremely wild throwing arm in both 1999 and 2000. Adjusted for a career 5 percent hitter's inflation, he is batting .283 with 82 home runs. His 796 Total Factor ranks 13th in league rate of success at second, while his 352 Hits Contribution also ranks him 13th in league volume of success.

Tony Oliva

In his rookie season of 1964, 23-year-old outfielder Oliva hit .323 with 217 hits, 32 home runs and 84 extra base hits. The next season, Oliva hit .321 with 40 doubles, 16 home runs and 19 steals, and the Twins organization made its first World Series appearance since 1933. Oliva followed with a .307 average, 25 home runs and a Gold Glove Award in 1966. He continued to play at a high level until bad knees forced him to miss most of the 1972 season, and he then become a DH in his last four years. Oliva's four years at DH dropped both his rate and volume of success.

In his career, Oliva hit .304 with 220 home runs. Adjusted for a career 4 percent hitter's deflation, he batted .315 with 227 home runs. His 874 Total Factor ranks 24th in league rate of success for outfielders, while his 376 Hits Contribution ranks 31st in league volume of success.

Washington Senators/Minnesota Twins   **Hitters Volume of Success**

Pos	Years	Name	AB	BB	HBP	TAB	H	2B	3B	HR	BA	OB	SA	PRO	Wtd PRO	SB	CS	SBF	SPF	FF	R TF	V HC
C	1955-67	E.Battey	3,586	421	28	4,035	969	150	17	104	.270	.351	.409	760	762	13	12	(3)	(10)	28	778	196
1B	1954-75	H.Killebrew	8,147	1,559	48	9,754	2,086	290	24	573	.256	.379	.509	887	906	19	18	(2)	(10)	(34)	860	517
2B	1967-85	R.Carew	9,315	1,018	25	10,358	3,053	445	112	92	.328	.395	.429	825	846	353	187	(2)	9	(10)	843	566
SS	1975-87	R.Smalley	5,657	771	14	6,442	1,454	244	25	163	.257	.348	.395	743	747	27	34	(6)	(3)	(8)	729	185
3B	1981-	G.Gaetti	8,951	634	96	9,681	2,280	443	39	360	.255	.311	.434	745	732	96	65	(3)	(4)	147	871	200
OF	1984-95	K.Puckett	7,244	450	56	7,750	2,304	414	57	207	.318	.363	.477	839	832	134	76	(2)	8	50	888	500
OF	1921-38	G.Goslin	8,656	949	56	9,661	2,735	500	173	248	.316	.387	.500	887	831	175	89	(0)	8	8	847	435
OF	1962-76	T.Oliva	6,301	448	59	6,808	1,917	329	48	220	.304	.356	.476	832	863	86	55	(3)	5	9	874	376
Starters		Averages	7,232	781	48	8,061	2,100	352	62	246	.290	.363	.458	821	821	113	67	(3)	0	24	842	372
C	1976-88	B.Wynegar	4,330	626	17	4,973	1,102	176	15	65	.255	.351	.347	698	701	10	13	(3)	(7)	5	696	46
1B	1981-94	K.Hrbek	6,192	838	26	7,056	1,749	312	18	293	.282	.370	.481	851	845	37	26	(2)	(5)	13	851	279
2B	1991-	C.Knoblauch	5,545	718	121	6,384	1,646	293	61	83	.297	.389	.417	806	768	350	105	21	10	(4)	796	352
SS	1933-47	C.Travis	4,914	402	31	5,347	1,544	265	78	27	.314	.370	.416	786	741	23	32	(7)	0	1	735	143
3B	1944-62	E.Yost	7,346	1,614	99	9,059	1,863	337	56	139	.254	.395	.371	766	752	72	66	(6)	6	(13)	739	105
OF	1915-34	S.Rice	9,269	708	54	10,031	2,987	498	184	34	.322	.374	.427	800	767	351	143	(0)	10	28	805	244
OF	1958-70	B.Allison	5,032	795	34	5,861	1,281	216	53	256	.255	.360	.471	831	845	84	50	(3)	6	(8)	840	231
OF	1923-39	H.Manush	7,654	506	70	8,230	2,524	491	160	110	.330	.377	.479	856	808	114	58	(1)	6	(6)	807	203
Reserves		Averages	6,285	776	57	7,118	1,837	324	78	126	.292	.375	.429	804	780	130	62	(0)	3	2	785	200
Totals		Weighted Ave.	6,917	779	51	7,747	2,012	342	67	206	.291	.367	.449	816	807	119	65	(2)	1	17	823	315

Pitchers Volume of Success

Pos	Years	Name	G	GS	IP	W	L	SV	SO	BB	ERA	RA/9	R Wtd RA/9	V Runs /162
SP	1907-27	W.Johnson	802	666	5,914	417	279	34	3,509	1,363	2.17	2.89	3.10	1021
SP	1970-92	B.Blyleven	692	685	4,970	287	250	0	3,701	1,322	3.31	3.67	3.91	367
SP	1933-53	D.Leonard	640	375	3,218	191	181	44	1,170	737	3.25	4.00	3.97	221
SP	1923-36	F.Marberry	551	186	2,067	148	88	101	822	686	3.63	4.23	3.78	188
SP	1918-36	T.Zachary	533	408	3,126	186	191	22	720	914	3.73	4.47	4.20	131
Starters		Averages	644	464	3,859	246	198	40	1,984	1,004	3.05	3.68	3.70	385
RP	1985-	R.Aguilera	732	89	1,291	86	81	318	1,030	351	3.57	3.96	3.91	96
RP	1941-52	T.Ferrick	323	7	674	40	40	56	245	227	3.47	4.09	4.03	42
RP	1973-87	B.Campbell	700	9	1,229	83	68	126	864	495	3.54	4.03	4.34	30
RP	1968-77	T.Hall	358	63	853	52	33	32	797	382	3.27	3.80	4.29	26
Relievers		Averages	528	42	1,012	65	56	133	734	364	3.48	3.97	4.14	48
Totals		Averages	1,172	506	4,871	311	253	173	2,718	1,368	3.14	3.74	3.80	434

Washington Senators/Minnesota Twins   **Hitters Rate of Success**

Pos	Years	Name	AB	BB	HBP	TAB	H	2B	3B	HR	BA	OB	SA	PRO	Wtd PRO	SB	CS	SBF	SPF	FF	R TF	V HC
C	1955-67	E.Battey	3,586	421	28	4,035	969	150	17	104	.270	.351	.409	760	762	13	12	(3)	(10)	28	778	196
1B	1954-75	H.Killebrew	8,147	1,559	48	9,754	2,086	290	24	573	.256	.379	.509	887	906	19	18	(2)	(10)	(34)	860	517
2B	1967-85	R.Carew	9,315	1,018	25	10,358	3,053	445	112	92	.328	.395	.429	825	846	353	187	(2)	9	(10)	843	566
SS	1933-47	C.Travis	4,914	402	31	5,347	1,544	265	78	27	.314	.370	.416	786	741	23	32	(7)	0	1	735	143
3B	1981-	G.Gaetti	8,951	634	96	9,681	2,280	443	39	360	.255	.311	.434	745	732	96	65	(3)	(4)	147	871	200
OF	1984-95	K.Puckett	7,244	450	56	7,750	2,304	414	57	207	.318	.363	.477	839	832	134	76	(2)	8	50	888	500
OF	1962-76	T.Oliva	6,301	448	59	6,808	1,917	329	48	220	.304	.356	.476	832	863	86	55	(3)	5	9	874	376
OF	1921-38	G.Goslin	8,656	949	56	9,661	2,735	500	173	248	.316	.387	.500	887	831	175	89	(0)	8	8	847	435
Starters	Averages		7,139	735	50	7,924	2,111	355	69	229	.296	.365	.461	826	821	112	67	(3)	1	25	844	367
C	1979-95	B.Harper	3,151	133	44	3,328	931	186	7	63	.295	.333	.419	752	751	8	17	(7)	(9)	(20)	715	45
1B	1981-94	K.Hrbek	6,192	838	26	7,056	1,749	312	18	293	.282	.370	.481	851	845	37	26	(2)	(5)	13	851	279
2B	1991-	C.Knoblauch	5,545	718	121	6,384	1,646	293	61	83	.297	.389	.417	806	768	350	105	21	10	(4)	796	352
SS	1975-87	R.Smalley	5,657	771	14	6,442	1,454	244	25	163	.257	.348	.395	743	747	27	34	(6)	(3)	(8)	729	185
3B	1971-80	E.Soderholm	2,894	295	22	3,211	764	120	14	102	.264	.337	.421	758	771	18	21	(7)	1	12	778	94
OF	1987-98	S.Mack	2,857	256	51	3,164	853	155	28	80	.299	.367	.456	823	817	90	43	1	10	14	842	133
OF	1958-70	B.Allison	5,032	795	34	5,861	1,281	216	53	256	.255	.360	.471	831	845	84	50	(3)	6	(8)	840	231
OF	1940-49	S.Spence	3,871	520	19	4,410	1,090	196	60	95	.282	.369	.437	806	820	21	23	(5)	1	20	835	170
Reserves	Averages		4,400	541	41	4,982	1,221	215	33	142	.278	.362	.438	800	798	79	40	(1)	1	2	801	186
Totals	Weighted Ave.		6,226	670	47	6,944	1,814	308	57	200	.291	.365	.455	820	814	101	58	(2)	1	17	830	307

Pitchers Rate of Success

Pos	Years	Name	G	GS	IP	W	L	SV	SO	BB	ERA	RA/9	V Wtd RA/9	R Runs /162
SP	1907-27	W.Johnson	802	666	5,914	417	279	34	3,509	1,363	2.17	2.89	3.10	1,021
SP	1923-36	F.Marberry	551	186	2,067	148	88	101	822	686	3.63	4.23	3.78	188
SP	1970-92	B.Blyleven	692	685	4,970	287	250	0	3,701	1,322	3.31	3.67	3.91	367
SP	1933-53	D.Leonard	640	375	3,218	191	181	44	1,170	737	3.25	4.00	3.97	221
SP	1995-	B.Radke	198	197	1,312	78	84	0	805	290	4.32	4.64	4.08	70
Starters	Averages		577	422	3,496	224	176	36	2,001	880	3.03	3.61	3.64	373
RP	1985-	R.Aguilera	732	89	1,291	86	81	318	1,030	351	3.57	3.96	3.91	96
RP	1941-52	T.Ferrick	323	7	674	40	40	56	245	227	3.47	4.09	4.03	42
RP	1968-77	T.Hall	358	63	853	52	33	32	797	382	3.27	3.80	4.29	26
RP	1973-87	B.Campbell	700	9	1,229	83	68	126	864	495	3.54	4.03	4.34	30
Relievers	Averages		528	42	1,012	65	56	133	734	364	3.48	3.97	4.14	48
Totals	Averages		1,105	464	4,508	289	232	169	2,735	1,243	3.13	3.69	3.76	422

Washington Senators/Minnesota Twins
Catchers

V	R	Years	Name	AB	BB	HBP	TAB	H	2B	3B	HR	BA	OB	SA	PRO	Wtd PRO	SB	CS	SBF	SPF	FF	R TF	V HC
1	1	1955-67	E.Battey	3,586	421	28	4,035	969	150	17	104	.270	.351	.409	760	762	13	12	(3)	(10)	28	778	196
2	3	1976-88	B.Wynegar	4,330	626	17	4,973	1,102	176	15	65	.255	.351	.347	698	701	10	13	(3)	(7)	5	696	46
3	2	1979-95	B.Harper	3,151	133	44	3,328	931	186	7	63	.295	.333	.419	752	751	8	17	(7)	(9)	(20)	715	45
4	4	1916-33	V.Picinich	2,877	314	11	3,202	743	166	26	26	.258	.334	.361	695	678	31	9	(2)	(0)	7	683	9
5	5	1916-30	P.Gharrity	1,961	188	14	2,163	513	92	26	20	.262	.331	.366	696	681	32	13	(3)	1	(5)	674	(13)
6	8	1939-49	J.Early	2,208	281	11	2,500	532	98	23	32	.241	.330	.350	679	679	7	8	(3)	(1)	(9)	665	(17)
7	9	1981-89	T.Laudner	2,038	190	8	2,236	458	97	5	77	.225	.293	.391	684	683	3	3	(1)	(10)	(10)	661	(17)
8	7	1951-61	C.Courtney	2,796	264	45	3,105	750	126	17	38	.268	.341	.366	707	701	3	16	(9)	(10)	(17)	665	(20)
9	6	1915-34	M.Ruel	4,514	606	29	5,149	1,242	187	29	4	.275	.365	.332	697	658	61	59	(11)	(4)	27	669	(22)
10	10	1966-77	G.Mitterwald	2,645	222	13	2,880	623	93	7	76	.236	.298	.362	660	671	14	17	(7)	(10)	1	655	(29)
11	12	1910-18	J.Henry	1,920	244	21	2,185	397	54	15	2	.207	.303	.254	557	599	55	5	3	6	25	632	(49)
12	11	1910-24	E.Ainsmith	3,048	263	12	3,323	707	108	54	22	.232	.296	.324	620	637	86	16	(2)	(1)	8	641	(60)
13	13	1939-51	A.Evans	2,053	243	7	2,303	514	70	23	13	.250	.332	.326	658	649	14	9	(2)	0	(28)	619	(67)
14	14	1948-59	E.Fitz Gerald	2,086	185	12	2,283	542	82	10	19	.260	.324	.336	660	651	9	6	(3)	(1)	(34)	613	(74)
15	15	1925-38	R.Spencer	1,814	128	11	1,953	448	57	13	3	.247	.301	.298	598	568	4	1	1	(1)	9	577	(98)
16	16	1993-	M.Walbeck	1,885	127	9	2,021	447	73	4	27	.237	.288	.323	612	566	13	11	(4)	(10)	17	569	(115)

Washington Senators/Minnesota Twins
First basemen

V	R	Years	Name	AB	BB	HBP	TAB	H	2B	3B	HR	BA	OB	SA	PRO	Wtd PRO	SB	CS	SBF	SPF	FF	R TF	V HC
1	1	1954-75	H.Killebrew	8,147	1,559	48	9,754	2,086	290	24	573	.256	.379	.509	887	906	19	18	(2)	(10)	(34)	860	517
2	2	1981-94	K.Hrbek	6,192	838	26	7,056	1,749	312	18	293	.282	.370	.481	851	845	37	26	(2)	(5)	13	851	279
3	4	1949-65	R.Sievers	6,387	841	51	7,279	1,703	292	42	318	.267	.357	.475	831	819	14	19	(3)	(6)	(10)	799	135
4	5	1915-34	J.Judge	7,898	965	50	8,913	2,352	433	159	71	.298	.378	.420	798	772	213	92	(5)	4	22	792	103
5	6	1939-60	M.Vernon	8,731	955	49	9,735	2,495	490	120	172	.286	.359	.428	788	780	137	90	(4)	6	6	788	90
6	3	1960-72	D.Mincher	4,026	606	27	4,659	1,003	176	16	200	.249	.351	.450	801	830	24	32	(8)	(10)	(4)	809	84
7	9	1951-64	P.Runnels	6,373	844	28	7,245	1,854	282	64	49	.291	.376	.378	755	747	37	51	(9)	0	(10)	728	66
8	7	1910-19	C.Gandil	4,245	273	42	4,560	1,176	173	78	11	.277	.327	.362	689	743	153	32	(3)	0	27	767	(7)
9	10	1964-73	R.Reese	2,020	158	20	2,198	512	73	17	52	.253	.314	.384	698	725	16	15	(6)	0	6	725	(49)
10	11	1904-10	B.Unglaub	2,150	88	5	2,243	554	67	35	5	.258	.288	.328	617	715	66	0	0	0	5	720	(52)
11	8	1930-47	J.Kuhel	7,984	980	39	9,003	2,212	412	111	131	.277	.359	.406	765	738	178	90	(0)	8	10	756	(67)
12	12	1987-93	G.Larkin	2,321	268	38	2,627	618	131	12	32	.266	.352	.374	726	733	23	17	(4)	0	(21)	707	(73)
13	13	1995-	R.Coomer	2,397	132	6	2,535	667	121	7	77	.278	.318	.431	749	696	13	7	(0)	(10)	(4)	681	(80)

Washington Senators/Minnesota Twins
Second basemen

V	R	Years	Name	AB	BB	HBP	TAB	H	2B	3B	HR	BA	OB	SA	PRO	Wtd PRO	SB	CS	SBF	SPF	FF	R TF	V HC
1	1	1967-85	R.Carew	9,315	1,018	25	10,358	3,053	445	112	92	.328	.395	.429	825	846	353	187	(2)	9	(10)	843	566
2	2	1991-	C.Knoblauch	5,545	718	121	6,384	1,646	293	61	83	.297	.389	.417	806	768	350	105	21	10	(4)	796	352
3	3	1925-41	B.Myer	7,038	965	32	8,035	2,131	353	130	38	.303	.389	.406	795	746	156	109	(7)	8	(6)	741	236
4	5	1911-18	R.Morgan	2,480	320	38	2,838	630	90	33	4	.254	.348	.322	670	723	87	22	(5)	10	(33)	696	15
5	4	1996-	T.Walker	1,545	141	5	1,691	445	102	12	30	.288	.349	.428	777	722	53	18	10	10	(38)	704	11
6	7	1919-31	B.Harris	4,736	472	99	5,307	1,297	224	64	9	.274	.352	.354	706	665	167	91	(3)	5	22	689	11
7	6	1977-87	R.Wilfong	2,690	205	14	2,909	668	97	23	39	.248	.305	.345	650	651	54	33	(5)	10	35	692	9
8	9	1949-60	W.Terwilliger	2,091	247	11	2,349	501	93	10	22	.240	.323	.325	648	632	31	14	(4)	9	30	668	(21)
9	8	1962-73	B.Allen	3,404	370	8	3,782	815	140	21	73	.239	.315	.357	673	693	13	16	(5)	0	(14)	674	(24)
10	10	1937-51	J.Bloodworth	3,519	202	16	3,737	874	160	20	62	.248	.292	.358	650	641	19	22	(7)	0	18	652	(62)
11	11	1985-92	A.Newman	2,107	236	6	2,349	476	68	7	1	.226	.306	.266	572	577	91	55	(8)	10	(10)	569	(127)

Washington Senators/Minnesota Twins
Shortstops

V	R	Years	Name	AB	BB	HBP	TAB	H	2B	3B	HR	BA	OB	SA	PRO	Wtd PRO	SB	CS	SBF	SPF	FF	R TF	V HC
1	2	1975-87	R.Smalley	5,657	771	14	6,442	1,454	244	25	163	.257	.348	.395	743	747	27	34	(6)	(3)	(8)	729	185
2	1	1933-47	C.Travis	4,914	402	31	5,347	1,544	265	78	27	.314	.370	.416	786	741	23	32	(7)	0	1	735	143
3	3	1959-71	Z.Versalles	5,141	318	40	5,499	1,246	230	63	95	.242	.292	.367	659	674	97	48	0	10	15	699	88
4	5	1983-97	G.Gagne	5,673	367	40	6,080	1,440	296	50	111	.254	.304	.382	686	673	108	96	(14)	7	12	678	47
5	4	1906-11	D.Altizer	1,734	140	33	1,907	433	36	21	4	.250	.318	.302	619	710	119	0	0	9	(26)	694	6
6	8	1993-	D.Hocking	1,429	120	4	1,553	364	70	13	17	.255	.314	.358	672	623	30	21	(7)	10	10	637	(32)
7	6	1901-20	G.McBride	5,526	419	64	6,009	1,203	140	47	7	.218	.281	.264	544	596	133	19	(3)	0	57	650	(34)
8	7	1992-	J.Reboulet	1,706	226	11	1,943	406	72	2	14	.238	.331	.307	638	607	20	13	(3)	2	32	638	(36)
9	10	1993-	P.Meares	3,017	140	55	3,212	792	146	23	54	.263	.307	.380	687	643	43	25	(2)	2	(11)	632	(48)
10	9	1951-61	R.Bridges	2,272	205	7	2,484	562	80	11	16	.247	.312	.313	625	612	10	15	(8)	0	30	635	(53)
11	11	1942-49	J.Sullivan	1,833	216	1	2,050	422	52	9	1	.230	.312	.270	582	596	18	11	(2)	10	(9)	595	(69)
12	12	1970-76	D.Thompson	2,218	120	8	2,346	550	70	11	15	.248	.289	.310	599	629	8	11	(6)	0	(30)	594	(81)
13	13	1947-55	S.Dente	2,320	167	4	2,491	585	78	16	4	.252	.303	.305	608	588	9	9	(3)	0	(12)	572	(117)

Washington Senators/Minnesota Twins
Third basemen

V	R	Years	Name	AB	BB	HBP	TAB	H	2B	3B	HR	BA	OB	SA	PRO	Wtd PRO	SB	CS	SBF	SPF	FF	R TF	V HC
1	1	1981-	G.Gaetti	8,951	634	96	9,681	2,280	443	39	360	.255	.311	.434	745	732	96	65	(3)	(4)	147	871	200
2	5	1944-62	E.Yost	7,346	1,614	99	9,059	1,863	337	56	139	.254	.395	.371	766	752	72	66	(6)	6	(13)	739	105
3	2	1971-80	E.Soderholm	2,894	295	22	3,211	764	120	14	102	.264	.337	.421	758	771	18	21	(7)	1	12	778	94
4	3	1979-84	J.Castino	2,320	177	5	2,502	646	86	34	41	.278	.331	.398	729	730	22	19	(7)	4	39	767	81
5	4	1935-49	B.Lewis	5,261	573	20	5,854	1,563	249	93	71	.297	.368	.420	789	752	83	59	(6)	10	(5)	751	39
6	6	1961-70	R.Rollins	3,303	266	39	3,608	887	125	20	77	.269	.330	.388	719	734	17	10	(1)	0	(16)	717	3
7	7	1974-81	M.Cubbage	1,951	215	5	2,171	503	74	20	34	.258	.333	.369	702	711	6	15	(10)	0	1	702	(21)
8	8	1910-23	E.Foster	5,652	528	25	6,205	1,490	191	71	6	.264	.329	.326	655	687	195	53	(1)	8	(15)	680	(113)
9	9	1922-39	O.Bluege	6,440	723	70	7,233	1,751	276	67	43	.272	.352	.356	707	664	140	87	(4)	5	15	679	(115)

Washington Senators/Minnesota Twins
Outfielders

V	R	Years	Name	AB	BB	HBP	TAB	H	2B	3B	HR	BA	OB	SA	PRO	Wtd PRO	SB	CS	SBF	SPF	FF	R TF	V HC
1	1	1984-95	K.Puckett	7,244	450	56	7,750	2,304	414	57	207	.318	.363	.477	839	832	134	76	(2)	8	50	888	500
2	3	1921-38	G.Goslin	8,656	949	56	9,661	2,735	500	173	248	.316	.387	.500	887	831	175	89	(0)	8	8	847	435
3	2	1962-76	T.Oliva	6,301	448	59	6,808	1,917	329	48	220	.304	.356	.476	832	863	86	55	(3)	5	9	874	376
4	10	1915-34	S.Rice	9,269	708	54	10,031	2,987	498	184	34	.322	.374	.427	800	767	351	143	(0)	10	28	805	244
5	5	1958-70	B.Allison	5,032	795	34	5,861	1,281	216	53	256	.255	.360	.471	831	845	84	50	(3)	6	(8)	840	231
6	9	1923-39	H.Manush	7,654	506	70	8,230	2,524	491	160	110	.330	.377	.479	856	808	114	58	(1)	6	(6)	807	203
7	6	1940-49	S.Spence	3,871	520	19	4,410	1,090	196	60	95	.282	.369	.437	806	820	21	23	(5)	1	20	835	170
8	8	1968-82	L.Hisle	4,205	462	39	4,706	1,146	193	32	166	.273	.350	.452	802	819	128	61	1	8	1	829	163
9	4	1987-98	S.Mack	2,857	256	51	3,164	853	155	28	80	.299	.367	.456	823	817	90	43	1	10	14	842	133
10	14	1907-22	C.Milan	7,359	685	80	8,124	2,100	240	105	17	.285	.353	.353	706	754	495	78	(3)	10	21	781	99
11	11	1903-11	D.Gessler	2,969	333	92	3,394	831	127	50	14	.280	.370	.370	741	821	142	0	0	4	(21)	804	77
12	7	1975-78	L.Bostock	2,004	171	9	2,184	624	102	30	23	.311	.368	.427	795	813	45	28	(5)	10	11	829	75
13	15	1981-94	T.Brunansky	6,289	770	30	7,089	1,543	306	33	271	.245	.331	.434	764	765	69	70	(9)	(2)	19	773	55
14	12	1995-	M.Lawton	2,296	345	45	2,686	629	138	13	62	.274	.379	.426	806	749	77	28	7	10	30	796	51
15	13	1963-70	J.Hall	2,848	287	2	3,137	724	100	24	121	.254	.323	.434	757	784	38	18	1	10	(5)	790	48
16	16	1927-42	S.West	6,148	696	5	6,849	1,838	347	101	75	.299	.371	.425	796	744	53	56	(8)	10	23	769	37
17	17	1950-63	J.Lemon	3,445	363	18	3,826	901	121	35	164	.262	.335	.460	795	783	13	18	(6)	2	(19)	760	5
18	20	1971-85	S.Braun	3,650	579	17	4,246	989	155	19	52	.271	.373	.367	740	764	45	27	(2)	2	(19)	746	1
19	18	1995-	M.Cordova	2,522	251	38	2,811	692	146	14	83	.274	.349	.442	791	737	55	27	1	2	14	755	(4)
20	19	1975-85	D.Ford	4,163	303	47	4,513	1,123	214	38	121	.270	.326	.427	753	766	61	37	(3)	6	(16)	753	(10)
21	21	1962-77	B.Darwin	2,224	160	37	2,421	559	76	16	83	.251	.312	.412	724	760	15	9	(1)	0	(15)	744	(15)
22	23	1965-76	C.Tovar	5,569	413	88	6,070	1,546	253	55	46	.278	.337	.368	705	737	226	108	2	10	(11)	737	(33)
23	22	1983-93	D.Gladden	4,501	337	42	4,880	1,215	203	40	74	.270	.327	.382	709	714	222	93	7	10	9	740	(42)
24	25	1905-09	B.Ganley	2,129	177	6	2,312	540	44	24	2	.254	.313	.300	612	706	112	0	0	10	4	720	(43)
25	29	1941-54	B.Stewart	2,041	252	9	2,302	547	96	32	32	.268	.351	.393	744	728	29	23	(9)	10	(15)	714	(50)
26	28	1993-	R.Becker	2,227	350	12	2,589	570	100	12	45	.256	.360	.372	732	677	66	26	5	9	24	714	(54)
27	24	1937-47	G.Case	5,016	426	21	5,463	1,415	233	43	21	.282	.341	.358	699	694	349	109	23	10	10	737	(57)
28	26	1965-72	T.Uhlaender	2,932	202	12	3,146	772	114	21	36	.263	.313	.353	667	696	52	35	(5)	10	19	720	(57)
29	33	1942-54	C.Vollmer	2,021	243	11	2,275	508	77	10	69	.251	.335	.402	737	720	7	6	(3)	0	(13)	704	(59)
30	35	1901-08	C.Jones	1,799	93	13	1,905	420	56	28	5	.233	.276	.304	580	667	100	0	0	10	17	693	(61)
31	34	1970-78	S.Brye	1,997	144	10	2,151	515	97	13	30	.258	.311	.365	676	701	16	14	(5)	7	(8)	695	(64)
32	32	1907-16	D.Moeller	2,538	302	17	2,857	618	83	43	15	.243	.328	.328	656	707	171	35	(4)	5	2	709	(69)
33	27	1947-56	S.Mele	3,437	311	10	3,758	916	168	39	80	.267	.329	.408	737	723	15	14	(3)	8	(9)	719	(71)
34	31	1957-68	L.Green	2,956	368	29	3,353	788	138	27	47	.267	.353	.379	733	731	78	41	(1)	8	(28)	710	(76)
35	30	1982-93	R.Bush	3,045	348	49	3,442	763	154	26	96	.251	.337	.413	750	751	33	29	(7)	(4)	(27)	713	(77)
36	39	1978-83	H.Powell	1,816	144	7	1,967	470	78	17	17	.259	.316	.349	664	666	43	17	4	10	(15)	665	(93)
37	37	1979-90	M.Hatcher	3,377	164	13	3,554	946	172	20	38	.280	.316	.377	693	694	11	15	(5)	2	(3)	689	(117)
38	38	1946-56	G.Coan	2,877	232	28	3,137	731	98	44	39	.254	.316	.359	675	659	83	38	2	10	(1)	670	(138)
39	42	1924-31	E.McNeely	2,254	183	29	2,466	614	107	33	4	.272	.335	.354	689	646	69	41	(5)	10	(10)	641	(143)
40	41	1930-45	J.Powell	2,540	173	9	2,722	689	116	26	22	.271	.320	.363	683	648	65	35	(2)	4	(5)	646	(152)
41	36	1950-62	J.Busby	4,250	310	23	4,583	1,113	162	35	48	.262	.316	.350	666	657	97	48	0	9	25	691	(153)
42	40	1912-25	H.Shanks	5,699	415	37	6,151	1,440	211	96	25	.253	.308	.337	644	658	185	64	(6)	9	(2)	659	(208)

Washington Senators/Minnesota Twins
Starting Pitchers

V	R	Years	Name	G	GS	IP	W	L	SV	SO	BB	ERA	RA/9	R Wtd RA/9	V Runs /162
1	1	1907-27	W.Johnson	802	666	5,914	417	279	34	3,509	1,363	2.17	2.89	3.10	1,021.3
2	3	1970-92	B.Blyleven	692	685	4,970	287	250	0	3,701	1,322	3.31	3.67	3.91	366.6
3	4	1933-53	D.Leonard	640	375	3,218	191	181	44	1,170	737	3.25	4.00	3.97	220.9
4	2	1923-36	F.Marberry	551	186	2,067	148	88	101	822	686	3.63	4.23	3.78	187.9
5	9	1918-36	T.Zachary	533	408	3,126	186	191	22	720	914	3.73	4.47	4.20	130.6
6	6	1911-27	G.Mogridge	398	261	2,266	132	131	20	678	565	3.23	3.99	4.09	127.4
7	7	1926-36	G.Crowder	402	292	2,344	167	115	22	799	800	4.12	4.62	4.10	124.7
8	8	1982-96	F.Viola	421	420	2,836	176	150	0	1,844	864	3.73	4.13	4.18	118.2
9	11	1959-75	J.Perry	630	447	3,286	215	174	10	1,576	998	3.45	3.85	4.28	101.9
10	19	1929-53	B.Newsom	600	483	3,759	211	222	21	2,082	1,732	3.98	4.57	4.36	84.9
11	15	1926-41	B.Hadley	528	355	2,946	161	165	25	1,318	1,442	4.24	4.92	4.33	77.8
12	5	1995-	B.Radke	198	197	1,312	78	84	0	805	290	4.32	4.64	4.08	70.2
13	13	1913-21	J.Shaw	287	194	1,600	84	98	17	767	688	3.07	3.79	4.31	49.4
14	12	1948-59	B.Porterfield	318	193	1,568	87	97	8	572	552	3.79	4.20	4.30	47.7
15	18	1989-	K.Tapani	332	325	2,097	134	111	0	1,333	514	4.34	4.61	4.36	47.3
16	14	1943-50	M.Haefner	261	179	1,467	78	91	13	508	577	3.50	4.09	4.33	39.2
17	10	1959-67	J.Kralick	235	169	1,218	67	65	1	668	318	3.56	4.00	4.28	37.8
18	20	1925-40	L.Brown	404	181	1,693	91	105	21	510	590	4.20	4.99	4.38	34.8
19	22	1954-71	C.Pascual	529	404	2,931	174	170	10	2,167	1,069	3.63	4.10	4.45	34.2
20	25	1959-83	J.Kaat	898	625	4,530	283	237	18	2,461	1,083	3.45	4.05	4.49	31.6
21	17	1913-23	H.Harper	219	171	1,256	57	76	5	623	582	2.87	3.80	4.36	30.6
22	16	1931-39	M.Weaver	201	135	1,052	71	50	4	297	435	4.36	5.06	4.33	27.4
23	24	1972-83	D.Goltz	353	264	2,040	113	109	8	1,105	646	3.69	4.19	4.48	17.8
24	21	1927-37	B.Burke	254	88	919	38	46	5	299	360	4.29	4.97	4.41	15.8
25	23	1913-21	D.Ayers	299	140	1,429	65	79	15	622	382	2.84	3.85	4.48	13.7
26	27	1973-85	G.Zahn	304	270	1,849	111	109	1	705	526	3.74	4.33	4.52	7.3
27	26	1912-20	J.Boehling	162	118	925	55	50	5	396	386	2.97	3.80	4.50	6.0
28	28	1930-37	C.Fischer	191	105	823	46	50	11	376	372	4.63	5.16	4.54	1.9
29	29	1927-45	P.Appleton	341	71	1,141	57	66	26	420	486	4.30	5.25	4.55	0.3
30	30	1941-47	R.Wolff	182	128	1,025	52	69	13	430	316	3.41	4.11	4.57	(1.2)
31	31	1965-75	J.Merritt	297	192	1,483	81	86	7	932	322	3.65	3.98	4.57	(2.3)
32	32	1921-33	G.Braxton	282	71	938	50	53	32	412	276	4.13	5.08	4.58	(2.7)
33	34	1939-49	A.Carrasquel	258	64	861	50	39	16	252	347	3.73	4.45	4.62	(6.4)
34	33	1964-71	D.Boswell	205	151	1,065	68	56	0	882	481	3.52	3.90	4.62	(7.5)
35	36	1960-66	D.Stigman	235	119	923	46	54	16	755	406	4.03	4.31	4.70	(14.9)
36	35	1936-43	K.Chase	188	160	1,165	53	84	1	582	694	4.27	5.00	4.69	(18.0)
37	38	1980-86	J.Butcher	164	113	834	36	49	6	363	229	4.42	4.79	4.76	(19.5)
38	40	1986-91	A.Anderson	148	128	819	49	54	0	339	211	4.11	4.66	4.79	(20.8)
39	37	1902-14	C.Smith	212	148	1,349	66	87	3	570	353	2.81	3.91	4.71	(23.6)
40	43	1932-39	J.DeShong	175	100	873	47	44	9	273	432	5.08	5.77	4.84	(28.9)
41	46	1978-83	R.Erickson	135	117	799	35	53	1	365	251	4.13	4.72	4.89	(31.5)
42	41	1942-53	R.Scarborough	318	168	1,429	80	85	12	564	611	4.13	4.75	4.80	(40.7)
43	51	1914-22	E.Erickson	145	93	822	34	57	4	367	379	3.85	5.01	4.99	(43.4)
44	42	1939-56	W.Masterson	399	184	1,650	78	100	20	815	886	4.15	4.85	4.82	(51.6)
45	56	1995-	F.Rodriguez	177	82	645	29	39	5	362	277	5.45	6.03	5.30	(54.4)
46	47	1912-20	B.Gallia	242	135	1,277	66	68	10	550	494	3.14	4.13	4.91	(55.3)
47	50	1982-89	M.Smithson	240	204	1,356	76	86	2	731	383	4.58	4.94	4.95	(59.7)
48	39	1909-18	B.Groom	367	288	2,336	119	150	13	1,159	783	3.10	4.11	4.79	(62.5)
49	57	1995-	L.Hawkins	165	98	609	28	49	14	358	221	5.77	6.21	5.50	(64.4)
50	54	1980-87	K.Schrom	176	137	900	51	51	1	372	320	4.81	5.35	5.25	(69.1)

Washington Senators/Minnesota Twins
Starting Pitchers

V	R	Years	Name	G	GS	IP	W	L	SV	SO	BB	ERA	RA/9	R Wtd RA/9	V Runs /162
51	44	1947-61	C.Stobbs	459	238	1,920	107	130	19	897	735	4.29	4.83	4.89	(73.9)
52	55	1954-63	R.Kemmerer	302	109	1,067	43	59	8	505	389	4.46	4.96	5.25	(85.6)
53	45	1955-70	P.Ramos	582	268	2,356	117	160	55	1,305	724	4.08	4.62	4.89	(89.9)
54	52	1898-02	B.Carrick	167	155	1,325	63	89	0	239	400	4.14	6.04	5.15	(98.0)
55	49	1940-54	S.Hudson	380	279	2,181	104	152	13	734	835	4.28	5.00	4.95	(100.2)
56	48	1900-13	T.Hughes	399	313	2,644	131	175	16	1,368	853	3.09	4.40	4.94	(120.2)
57	58	1901-06	H.Townsend	153	125	1,138	34	82	0	473	416	3.59	5.06	5.62	(147.9)
58	53	1901-08	C.Patten	270	238	2,062	106	128	5	757	557	3.36	4.71	5.17	(152.7)

Washington Senators/Minnesota Twins
Relief Pitchers

V	R	Years	Name	G	GS	IP	W	L	SV	SO	BB	ERA	RA/9	R Wtd RA/9	V Runs /162
1	1	1985-	R.Aguilera	732	89	1,291	86	81	318	1,030	351	3.57	3.96	3.91	96.0
2	2	1941-52	T.Ferrick	323	7	674	40	40	56	245	227	3.47	4.09	4.03	41.5
3	4	1973-87	B.Campbell	700	9	1,229	83	68	126	864	495	3.54	4.03	4.34	30.4
4	3	1968-77	T.Hall	358	63	853	52	33	32	797	382	3.27	3.80	4.29	25.5
5	5	1978-88	R.Davis	481	0	747	47	53	130	597	300	4.05	4.35	4.34	18.8
6	6	1992-	M.Trombley	435	36	714	34	38	38	597	281	4.43	4.79	4.39	13.5
7	7	1962-72	J.Roland	216	29	450	19	17	9	272	229	3.22	3.70	4.40	7.8
8	8	1989-	M.Guthrie	578	43	836	38	46	12	658	320	4.18	4.66	4.54	1.8
9	10	1989-94	G.Wayne	231	0	250	14	14	4	164	104	3.93	4.51	4.69	(3.7)
10	9	1943-60	B.Byerly	237	17	492	22	22	14	209	167	3.70	4.42	4.62	(3.9)
11	12	1990-98	L.Casian	245	3	241	11	13	2	125	77	4.56	4.97	4.79	(6.7)
12	11	1993-	E.Guardado	438	25	498	25	38	18	408	213	5.08	5.26	4.74	(10.7)
13	14	1984-95	C.Willis	267	2	390	22	16	13	222	115	4.25	4.85	4.93	(17.2)
14	13	1977-85	B.Castillo	250	59	689	38	40	18	434	327	3.94	4.27	4.84	(22.8)
15	21	1994-	D.Stevens	183	6	251	15	16	21	170	132	6.03	6.27	5.60	(32.2)
16	17	1988-98	D.West	204	78	569	31	38	3	437	311	4.66	5.07	5.09	(36.2)
17	16	1954-62	T.Clevenger	307	40	695	36	37	30	361	298	4.18	4.79	5.03	(38.5)
18	20	1951-57	B.Chakales	171	23	420	15	25	10	187	225	4.54	5.27	5.41	(42.0)
19	18	1981-89	B.Havens	205	61	591	24	37	3	370	246	4.81	5.12	5.16	(42.5)
20	15	1956-64	B.Fischer	281	78	831	45	58	13	313	210	4.34	4.75	5.01	(43.4)
21	19	1992-	P.Mahomes	227	56	547	34	31	5	355	308	5.55	5.96	5.34	(53.0)
22	22	1990-	S.Aldred	229	67	500	20	39	1	312	230	6.02	6.41	5.91	(75.3)

AMERICAN LEAGUE
EXPANSION TEAMS (1961–2000)

The American League added six expansion teams since 1961. These teams often struggled with losing records in their first decade of existence. They did manage to win a collective 22 division crowns in the past 25 years, as well as five pennants and three World Series championships— by the Royals in 1985, and the Blue Jays in 1992–1993.

The Angels are historically deep in starting pitchers, including Nolan Ryan, Frank Tanana, Andy Messersmith, Dean Chance, and Chuck Finley. Star hitters in club history include Jim Fregosi, Tim Salmon, Bobby Grich, and Wally Joyner.

The Senators/Rangers featured slugger Frank Howard in the 1960s and infielder Toby Harrah in the 1970s. In the 1990s, a trio of stars— Juan Gonzalez, Ivan Rodriguez, and Rafael Palmeiro— led the team to three playoff appearances.

The Brewers peaked in the early 1980s, led by Robin Yount, Paul Molitor, Cecil Cooper, and Sixto Lezcano. The Brewers struggled in the 1990s, and switched leagues in 1998.

The Royals own an expansion-team-record six division titles, with superstar George Brett playing for all six teams. Other talented Royals include Darrell Porter, John Mayberry, Frank White, Amos Otis, Bret Saberhagen, Kevin Appier, Dan Quisenberry, and Jeff Montgomery.

The Blue Jays produced 11 consecutive winning seasons from 1983 to 1993, earning five division titles and two world championships. Toronto stars include Carlos Delgado, John Olerud, Roberto Alomar, Tony Fernandez, Kelly Gruber, Jesse Barfield, Jimmy Key, Dave Stieb, David Wells, Tom Henke, and Mark Eichhorn.

The Mariners failed to produce a winning season until 1991. In the 1990s, talented sluggers Ken Griffey, Jr., Alex Rodriguez, Edgar Martinez, and Jay Buhner terrorized opposing pitchers in the hitter-friendly Kingdome, while starting pitcher Randy Johnson posted stellar results.

Profiled American League Expansion Players

Ivan Rodriguez

Twenty-eight-year-old Rodriguez (Texas Rangers) is making a run at being recognized as the best catcher of all time. He has all the ingredients: rock-solid defense, a gun for an arm, power, a high batting average, and speed, plus the advantages of having all his statistics overstated by the raging hitter's inflation of the 1990s, and playing for a winning team. Pudge broke in with Texas in 1991 at age 19, and immediately made a positive contribution. Rodriguez continues to improve, with 1999 and 2000 being outstanding seasons. With perhaps a dozen years ahead of him, he could become the first catcher to generate 1,000 Hits Contribution.

Rodriguez is hitting .304 in his first ten seasons, with 171 home runs, 65 steals, and 87 Fielding Factor points. Adjusted for a 6 percent career hitter's inflation, Pudge is hitting .287 with 169 home runs. His 868 Total Factor ranks second in league rate of success behind Cochrane, while his 483 Hits Contribution currently ranks him fifth in league volume of success.

Rafael Palmeiro

Thirty-six-year-old Palmeiro (Texas Rangers) came up with the Chicago Cubs. When Mark Grace emerged as a potential star in 1988, Palmeiro became expendable, and was traded to the Rangers after the season, where he was switched from the outfield to first base. Although Grace has played solid offense and great defense in his career, Palmeiro has been more spectacular with solid defense and great offense.

In his career to date, Palmeiro has hit .296 with 400 home runs, for an 891 Production. Adjusted for a 3 percent career hitter's inflation, he has hit .287 with 399 home runs, for an 862 Wtd. Production. His 877 Total Factor ranks seventh in league rate of success for first basemen, while his 470 Hits Contribution currently ranks seventh in league volume of success.

Roberto Alomar

Thirty-three-year-old Alomar (Toronto Blue Jays) is the best American League second baseman since Lajoie and Collins. Alomar can hit, field, run and, on occasion, even hits for power. Alomar broke in with the Padres; he made a name for himself on two world champion Blue Jays teams; he survived a spitting incident involving an umpire while with the Orioles; and he is now a key part of a powerful Indians lineup.

In his career, Alomar has hit .304 with 170 home runs, has 416 steals in 516 attempts, and has earned 42 Fielding Factor points. Adjusting for a 3.5 percent career hitter's inflation, he has hit .294 with 168 home runs. His 876 Total Factor ranks third in league rate of success for second basemen, while his 759 Hits Contribution already ranks him fourth in career volume of success.

Bobby Grich

Grich (California Angels) quietly did what it takes to win for 17 seasons with the Angels and Orioles. A four-time Gold Glove winner, Grich showed rare power for a second baseman, even tieing for the league lead in home runs in the strike-shortened 1981 season. In his career, he hit .266 with 224 home runs, and stole 104 bases. Adjusted for a 2.5 percent career hitter's deflation, Grich hit .273 with 239 home runs, for an 816 Wtd. Production. His 832 Total Factor ranks seventh in league rate of success at second, while his 586 Hits Contribution ranks seventh in league volume of success.

Robin Yount

Yount (Milwaukee Brewers) broke in as an 18-year-old shortstop in 1974, and he retired as a 38-year-old outfielder in 1993. When he first came in the league in the 1970s, Yount was a decent shortstop who had no power. In his last four seasons in the 1990s, he again lost his edge as a hitter. If we remove these years, we find Yount was one of the great players of the 1980s, with ten superlative seasons that include an MVP Award as a shortstop for the 1982 pennant winners, and an MVP Award as an outfielder in 1989.

Years	TAB	HR	BA	Adj. BA	Wtd. PRO	TF	HC
1980–89	6,261	174	.305	.304	851	898	583
All others	5,761	77	.265	.269	701	715	38

In his career, Yount hit .285 with 251 home runs and 271 steals in a noninflationary period. His 811 Total Factor ranks seventh in league rate of success for shortstops, while his 621 Hits Contribution ranks third in league volume of success.

Alex Rodriguez

The three best shortstops in American League history may be the three young stars who made headlines in 2000 — 27-year-old Derek Jeter of the Yankees, 27-year-old Nomar Garciaparra of the Red Sox, and 25-year-old Rodriguez of the Seattle Mariners. The best of these shortstops to date is the youngest player, Rodriguez. Rodriguez is a 40-40 player, hitting 40 home runs and stealing 40 bases in one year, an incredible feat for a shortstop. He won the batting title in his first full season at age 20, hitting .358. His fielding has improved steadily. And with potentially two more decades of playing time, A-Rod could end up as one of the greatest players of all time — for any position.

In his first seven seasons, Rodriguez hit .309 with 189 home runs and 133 steals in 3,467 total at bats. Adjusted for an 8 percent career hitter's inflation, he hit .286 with 178 home runs, for an 866 Wtd. Production. Rodriguez's 913 Total Factor ranks second in league rate of success — to Garciaparra — while his 422 Hits Contribution currently ranks tenth in league volume of success. Rodriguez should pass Joe Cronin's league-leading 737 Hits Contribution mark in a few years.

George Brett

Brett (Kansas City Royals) sits at the top of the list of American League third basemen in both single season and career success. Brett was a terrific player, leading the Royals to all six of their division titles in his 21-year career. He hit .305 with 317 home runs and 201 steals in his career during a noninflationary period, for an 868 Wtd. Production. His 870 Total Factor ranks fourth in league rate of success for third basemen, while his 756 Hits Contribution ranks first in league volume of success.

In 1980, Brett missed part of the season due to injury. He came back to hit .390, the highest batting mark between 1941 and 1994, and he had just enough at bats to qualify for the batting crown. He added 24 home runs and 15 steals that year, leading the Royals into the World Series. Adjusted for a 0.5 percent hitter's inflation, Brett hit .388 with 24 home runs, for a 1,120 Wtd. Production. His 1,155 Total Factor ranks first in league rate of success for a season at third base, while his 106.3 Hits Contribution ranks second in league volume of success—while playing only 117 games. Despite the lost playing time, Brett's 1980 season deserves recognition as his best season and as the best season ever for an American League third baseman.

Paul Molitor

Molitor (Milwaukee Brewers) showed flashes of a great player from 1978 to 1986. He hit over .300 with over 30 steals in 1979, 1980, and 1982. But he also lost most of two seasons to injuries, and he was just a slightly above average hitter in the other four seasons. And Molitor was never a great fielder, moving around from second to outfield to third, and doing time at DH. Then came 1987, Molitor's breakout season and career year, when he hit .353. From 1987 to 1994, he was one of the best all-around players in baseball, while helping the Blue Jays win two World Series titles.

When he finally retired in 1998, Molitor amassed 3,319 hits, 234 home runs, and 504 steals to go with a .306 batting average. Adjusted for a 1.5 percent career hitter's inflation, he hit .301 with 239 home runs. His 822 Total Factor ranks ninth in league rate of success at third, while his 515 Hits Contribution ranks fourth in league volume of success.

Ken Griffey, Jr.

Griffey (Seattle Mariners) broke into the majors as a 19-year-old in 1989, and wasted no time becoming a star. By his 30th birthday, Junior had earned 10 consecutive Gold Gloves and hit 398 home runs, the all-time record for his age. Griffey accelerated his pace over the past five years, averaging 50 home runs per season, and is considered the player most likely to break Hank Aaron's

career home run mark. Griffey was traded to the Reds in 2000, where he "struggled" to hit .271 with 40 home runs.

In his career-to-date, Griffey has hit .296 with 438 home runs and 173 steals, while earning 57 Fielding Factor points. Adjusted for 4 percent career hitter's inflation, he has hit .286 with 439 home runs. His 989 Total Factor ranks eighth in league rate of success for outfielders, while his 825 Hits Contribution currently ranks tenth in league volume of success.

Amos Otis

Otis (Kansas City Royals) was a star in his first full season in 1970, and proved to be Kansas City's most consistent player in the 1970s, when the Royals prospered. Otis was an all-around solid player, who hit .277 with 193 home runs, 341 steals, and two Gold Glove awards in 17 seasons. Adjusted for a 2 percent career hitter's deflation, he hit .284 with 202 home runs. His 857 Total Factor ranks 38th in league rate of success for outfielders, while his 395 Hits Contribution ranks 27th in league volume of success.

Juan Gonzalez

Gonzalez (Texas Rangers) hit 340 home runs before he turned 30 at the end of 1999. Gonzalez is the same age as Ken Griffey, Jr., and he has a shot at overtaking both Junior and Hank Aaron for the most home runs ever. Gonzalez has hit over 40 home runs five times, and he just missed in 1999 with 39 home runs, before sliding to 22 home runs with Detroit in 2000. Despite his power, Gonzalez's historic success ranking is hurt by his poor fielding, his average speed, his unwillingness to draw a walk, and the fact that his numbers have been overstated by the hitter's inflation of the 1990s.

In his career, Gonzalez has hit .294 with 362 home runs. Adjusted for a 5.5 percent career hitter's inflation, he has hit .279 with 358 home runs, for an 865 Wtd. Production. His 848 Total Factor ranks 44th in league rate of success for outfielders, while his 256 Hits Contribution currently ranks 50th in league volume of success.

Nolan Ryan

Ryan (California Angels) created such remarkable records that he deserves attention. Ryan played a record 27 years, threw a record seven no-hitters, and is far and away the all-time strikeout king with 5,714 strikeouts in just 5,386 innings. Ryan's winning percentage is not much higher than .500, and he did issue an awful lot of walks, especially early in his career. But he played long enough to go 324–292 with a 3.19 ERA. His 3.95 Wtd. RA/9 ranks 66th in league rate of success, while his 367 Runs/162 ranks ninth in league volume of success.

Bret Saberhagen

Saberhagen (Kansas City Royals) is one of the most inconsistent stars of all time. He was one of the league's best pitchers in 1985, 1987, 1989, 1991, 1994, 1998 and 1999. On the other hand, Saberhagen was a fairly average pitcher who often missed a lot of games in 1984, 1986, 1988, 1990, 1992, 1993, 1995, and 1997. He also missed the entire 1996 and 2000 seasons due to injuries. Sum up his seven superb seasons, and we have the makings of a Hall of Fame pitcher. Throw in the other seasons, and it's not clear if he will make the Hall.

Years	IP	W–L	SO	BB	ERA	Wtd. RA/9	Runs/162
7 best	1,422	113–48	974	232	2.98	3.10	242
Others	1,125	53–67	731	239	3.77	4.20	45

In his career, the 37-year-old Saberhagen is 166–115 with a 3.33 ERA. His Wtd. RA/9 of 3.58 ranks 17th in league rate of success, while his 287 Runs/162 currently ranks him 25th in league volume of success.

Randy Johnson

Thirty-seven-year-old Johnson (Seattle Mariners) is an imposing figure on the mound, standing 6'10" and firing a fastball that approaches 100 miles an hour. Once he mastered his control, the Big Unit became nearly unbeatable. In one three-year stretch with the Mariners, he went 43–6. The only problem Johnson had winning games the past eight seasons was his poor 9–10 showing in the first half of 1998, which was his way of forcing Seattle to trade him — he proved to be unhittable with Houston the second half of that season, going 10–1 with a 1.28 ERA.

In his career-to-date, Johnson is 179–95, with a 3.20 ERA, and 3,040 strikeouts in 2,499 innings. His 3.44 Wtd. RA/9 ranks 10th in league rate of success, while his 321 Runs/162 ranks 17th in league volume of success.

Dan Quisenberry

Quisenberry (Kansas City Royals) achieved more concentrated success than any other relief pitcher ever during a six year stretch from 1980 to 1985, which included two World Series appearances for the Royals:

Years	IP	W–L	SVS	ERA	Wtd. RA/9	Runs/162
1980–1985	725	41–33	212	2.98	2.78	149
All others	319	15–13	32	3.48	4.07	17

Gossage comes close with 145 Runs/162 from 1977 to 1982. Quisenberry topped Goose, not because of a better rate of success, but because he consistently worked around 130 innings in all years except the strike season of 1981. In his career, Quiz produced a 56–46 record with 244 saves and a 2.76 ERA. His 3.16 Wtd. RA/9 ranks seventh in league rate of success for relievers, while his 167 Runs/162 ranks fourth in league volume of success.

AL Expansion Teams　　　　　　**Hitters Volume of Success**

Pos	Years	Name	AB	BB	HBP	TAB	H	2B	3B	HR	BA	OB	SA	PRO	Wtd PRO	SB	CS	SBF	SPF	FF	R TF	V HC
C	1991-	I.Rodriguez	4,806	256	33	5,095	1,459	288	24	171	.304	.343	.480	823	777	65	33	(0)	3	87	868	483
1B	1986-	R.Palmeiro	7,846	935	61	8,842	2,321	455	36	400	.296	.375	.516	891	862	88	38	1	(1)	14	877	470
2B	1988-	R.Alomar	7,221	822	41	8,084	2,196	412	60	170	.304	.378	.448	827	799	416	100	25	9	42	876	759
SS	1974-93	R.Yount	11,008	966	48	12,022	3,142	583	126	251	.285	.346	.430	775	780	271	105	5	9	18	811	621
3B	1973-93	G.Brett	10,349	1,096	33	11,478	3,154	665	137	317	.305	.373	.487	861	868	201	97	1	2	(0)	870	756
OF	1989-	K.Griffey Jr.	6,352	841	56	7,249	1,883	342	33	438	.296	.384	.568	951	916	173	64	6	10	57	989	825
OF	1967-84	A.Otis	7,299	757	33	8,089	2,020	374	66	193	.277	.347	.425	773	791	341	93	18	10	38	857	395
OF	1992-	T.Salmon	4,051	683	37	4,771	1,180	231	16	230	.291	.398	.527	925	868	29	33	(7)	(1)	25	884	304
Starters		Averages	7,367	795	43	8,204	2,169	419	62	271	.294	.366	.479	845	831	198	70	6	5	35	878	577
C	1971-87	D.Porter	5,539	905	45	6,489	1,369	237	48	188	.247	.357	.409	766	777	39	37	(5)	(4)	(8)	760	261
1B	1989-	J.Olerud	5,330	922	64	6,316	1,595	367	11	186	.299	.409	.477	886	844	8	12	(2)	(9)	10	842	228
2B	1970-86	B.Grich	6,890	1,087	86	8,063	1,833	320	47	224	.266	.373	.424	796	816	104	83	(7)	3	20	832	586
SS	1994-	A.Rodriguez	3,126	310	31	3,467	966	194	13	189	.309	.377	.561	938	866	133	36	17	10	21	913	422
3B	1978-98	P.Molitor	10,835	1,094	47	11,976	3,319	605	114	234	.306	.372	.448	820	807	504	131	19	10	(13)	822	515
OF	1958-73	F.Howard	6,488	782	33	7,303	1,774	245	35	382	.273	.355	.499	853	880	8	9	(1)	(10)	(29)	840	287
OF	1989-	J.Gonzalez	5,292	376	50	5,718	1,554	312	21	362	.294	.346	.566	912	865	22	17	(2)	0	(15)	848	256
OF	1987-	J.Buhner	4,968	784	56	5,808	1,263	231	19	308	.254	.362	.494	856	825	6	24	(7)	(2)	24	840	237
Reserves		Averages	6,059	783	52	6,893	1,709	314	39	259	.282	.369	.475	844	830	103	44	1	(0)	1	832	349
Totals		Weighted Ave.	6,931	791	46	7,767	2,016	384	54	267	.291	.367	.478	845	831	166	61	4	3	24	862	501

Pitchers Volume of Success

Pos	Years	Name	G	GS	IP	W	L	SV	SO	BB	ERA	RA/9	Wtd RA/9	R V Runs /162
SP	1966-93	N.Ryan	807	773	5,386	324	292	3	5,714	2,795	3.19	3.64	3.95	367
SP	1988-	R.Johnson	366	357	2,499	179	95	2	3,040	1,089	3.20	3.61	3.44	321
SP	1986-	K.Brown	382	380	2,661	170	114	0	1,917	730	3.21	3.69	3.62	288
SP	1984-	B.Saberhagen	396	368	2,548	166	115	1	1,705	471	3.33	3.62	3.58	287
SP	1984-98	J.Key	470	389	2,592	186	117	10	1,538	668	3.51	3.83	3.70	253
Starters		Averages	484	453	3,137	205	147	3	2,783	1,151	3.27	3.67	3.71	303
RP	1979-90	D.Quisenberry	674	0	1,043	56	46	244	379	162	2.76	3.07	3.16	167
RP	1982-95	T.Henke	642	0	790	41	42	311	861	255	2.67	2.87	2.85	154
RP	1982-96	M.Eichhorn	563	7	886	48	43	32	640	270	3.00	3.33	3.29	129
RP	1986-	M.Jackson	835	7	1,018	53	61	138	905	414	3.26	3.62	3.57	114
Relievers		Averages	679	4	934	50	48	181	696	275	2.93	3.24	3.24	141
Totals		Averages	1,163	457	4,071	255	195	184	3,479	1,426	3.19	3.57	3.60	444

AL Expansion Teams   **Hitters Rate of Success**

Pos	Years	Name	AB	BB	HBP	TAB	H	2B	3B	HR	BA	OB	SA	PRO	Wtd PRO	SB	CS	SBF	SPF	FF	R TF	V HC
C	1991-	I.Rodriguez	4,806	256	33	5,095	1,459	288	24	171	.304	.343	.480	823	777	65	33	(0)	3	87	868	483
1B	1986-	R.Palmeiro	7,846	935	61	8,842	2,321	455	36	400	.296	.375	.516	891	862	88	38	1	(1)	14	877	470
2B	1988-	R.Alomar	7,221	822	41	8,084	2,196	412	60	170	.304	.378	.448	827	799	416	100	25	9	42	876	759
SS	1994-	A.Rodriguez	3,126	310	31	3,467	966	194	13	189	.309	.377	.561	938	866	133	36	17	10	21	913	422
3B	1987-	E.Martinez	5,432	973	65	6,470	1,738	403	14	235	.320	.429	.529	958	915	43	27	(1)	(3)	(22)	888	470
OF	1989-	K.Griffey Jr.	6,352	841	56	7,249	1,883	342	33	438	.296	.384	.568	951	916	173	64	6	10	57	989	825
OF	1992-	T.Salmon	4,051	683	37	4,771	1,180	231	16	230	.291	.398	.527	925	868	29	33	(7)	(1)	25	884	304
OF	1993-	J.Edmonds	3,169	377	21	3,567	923	186	12	163	.291	.370	.512	882	817	36	27	(5)	10	42	864	194
Starters	Averages		5,250	650	43	5,943	1,583	314	26	250	.302	.383	.514	897	855	123	45	4	5	33	897	490
C	1971-87	D.Porter	5,539	905	45	6,489	1,369	237	48	188	.247	.357	.409	766	777	39	37	(5)	(4)	(8)	760	261
1B	1993-	C.Delgado	2,901	436	61	3,398	818	214	7	190	.282	.387	.557	944	872	5	6	(2)	0	(18)	852	140
2B	1970-86	B.Grich	6,890	1,087	86	8,063	1,833	320	47	224	.266	.373	.424	796	816	104	83	(7)	3	20	832	586
SS	1974-93	R.Yount	11,008	966	48	12,022	3,142	583	126	251	.285	.346	.430	775	780	271	105	5	9	18	811	621
3B	1973-93	G.Brett	10,349	1,096	33	11,478	3,154	665	137	317	.305	.373	.487	861	868	201	97	1	2	(0)	870	756
OF	1967-84	A.Otis	7,299	757	33	8,089	2,020	374	66	193	.277	.347	.425	773	791	341	93	18	10	38	857	395
OF	1989-	J.Gonzalez	5,292	376	50	5,718	1,554	312	21	362	.294	.346	.566	912	865	22	17	(2)	0	(15)	848	256
OF	1981-92	J.Barfield	4,759	551	34	5,344	1,219	216	30	241	.256	.338	.466	804	802	66	47	(5)	6	40	843	220
Reserves	Averages		6,755	772	49	7,575	1,889	365	60	246	.280	.358	.461	818	818	131	61	0	3	9	830	404
Totals	Weighted Ave.		5,752	690	45	6,487	1,685	331	37	248	.293	.373	.493	866	843	126	50	3	4	25	875	461

Pitchers Rate of Success

Pos	Years	Name	G	GS	IP	W	L	SV	SO	BB	ERA	RA/9	R Wtd RA/9	V Runs /162
SP	1988-	R.Johnson	366	357	2,499	179	95	2	3,040	1,089	3.20	3.61	3.44	321
SP	1984-	B.Saberhagen	396	368	2,548	166	115	1	1,705	471	3.33	3.62	3.58	287
SP	1986-	K.Brown	382	380	2,661	170	114	0	1,917	730	3.21	3.69	3.62	288
SP	1989-	K.Appier	324	312	2,085	136	105	0	1,633	759	3.63	3.94	3.63	224
SP	1984-98	J.Key	470	389	2,592	186	117	10	1,538	668	3.51	3.83	3.70	253
Starters	Averages		388	361	2,477	167	109	3	1,967	743	3.36	3.73	3.59	274
RP	1982-95	T.Henke	642	0	790	41	42	311	861	255	2.67	2.87	2.85	154
RP	1987-95	B.Harvey	322	0	387	17	25	177	448	144	2.49	2.84	2.89	73
RP	1995-	T.Percival	360	0	374	19	27	171	460	168	3.16	3.40	2.96	68
RP	1979-90	D.Quisenberry	674	0	1,043	56	46	244	379	162	2.76	3.07	3.16	167
Relievers	Averages		500	0	648	33	35	226	537	182	2.75	3.02	3.00	115
Totals	Averages		887	361	3,125	201	144	228	2,504	926	3.24	3.58	3.47	390

AL Expansion Teams
Catchers

V	R	Years	Name	AB	BB	HBP	TAB	H	2B	3B	HR	BA	OB	SA	PRO	Wtd PRO	SB	CS	SBF	SPF	FF	R TF	V HC
1	1	1991-	I.Rodriguez	4,806	256	33	5,095	1,459	288	24	171	.304	.343	.480	823	777	65	33	(0)	3	87	868	483
2	2	1971-87	D.Porter	5,539	905	45	6,489	1,369	237	48	188	.247	.357	.409	766	777	39	37	(5)	(4)	(8)	760	261
3	4	1976-91	E.Whitt	3,774	436	4	4,214	938	176	15	134	.249	.327	.410	737	733	22	26	(6)	(8)	22	741	132
4	8	1974-89	J.Sundberg	6,021	699	22	6,742	1,493	243	36	95	.248	.328	.348	676	685	20	37	(8)	(9)	47	715	125
5	7	1987-	M.MacFarlane	3,602	295	97	3,994	906	221	17	129	.252	.325	.430	755	733	12	16	(4)	(10)	(2)	716	79
6	5	1987-	B.Surhoff	6,734	523	29	7,286	1,895	359	38	160	.281	.336	.417	753	726	127	76	(3)	4	2	729	41
7	3	1995-	M.Sweeney	1,884	184	37	2,105	569	110	2	70	.302	.375	.474	849	785	20	11	(1)	(6)	(20)	757	21
8	9	1984-96	D.Valle	2,775	258	63	3,096	658	121	12	77	.237	.316	.373	689	683	5	7	(3)	(10)	19	689	18
9	6	1992-	D.Nilsson	2,779	320	10	3,109	789	157	10	105	.284	.360	.461	821	770	15	18	(6)	(10)	(25)	728	7
10	10	1968-76	E.Rodriguez	2,173	332	55	2,560	533	76	6	16	.245	.359	.308	667	694	17	18	(7)	(8)	(6)	674	(4)
11	11	1982-93	G.Petralli	1,874	216	10	2,100	501	83	9	24	.267	.346	.360	706	708	8	6	(2)	(10)	(27)	669	(9)
12	13	1992-	D.Wilson	2,788	201	18	3,007	730	147	9	66	.262	.316	.392	708	656	19	10	(1)	(10)	17	662	(23)
13	14	1988-	P.Borders	3,046	149	10	3,205	779	155	12	67	.256	.293	.380	673	657	6	13	(6)	(4)	12	660	(28)
14	16	1990-	B.Mayne	2,400	251	15	2,666	648	136	3	26	.270	.343	.362	705	666	12	19	(9)	(10)	5	653	(32)
15	12	1976-85	J.Wathan	2,505	199	14	2,718	656	90	25	21	.262	.320	.343	663	664	105	36	11	9	(21)	663	(38)
16	17	1969-86	B.Martinez	2,743	230	8	2,981	618	128	10	58	.225	.287	.343	630	640	5	10	(4)	(10)	13	639	(55)
17	18	1975-92	J.Quirk	2,266	177	18	2,461	544	100	7	43	.240	.300	.347	648	649	5	16	(11)	(7)	7	638	(60)
18	19	1987-	G.Myers	2,378	181	3	2,562	602	121	7	55	.253	.307	.379	686	656	3	9	(6)	(10)	(16)	624	(67)
19	21	1994-	M.Matheny	1,752	101	26	1,879	415	84	5	28	.237	.288	.338	627	583	6	5	(2)	(10)	24	594	(76)
20	15	1973-87	C.Moore	4,033	346	11	4,390	1,052	187	43	36	.261	.321	.355	676	682	51	57	(14)	0	(10)	659	(89)
21	24	1994-	J.Fabregas	1,524	103	4	1,631	380	48	3	18	.249	.299	.320	619	576	4	5	(4)	(10)	5	568	(90)
22	20	1961-69	B.Rodgers	3,033	234	17	3,284	704	114	18	31	.232	.291	.312	603	619	17	27	(11)	6	4	619	(92)
23	22	1992-	J.Flaherty	2,484	135	14	2,633	636	117	2	60	.256	.298	.377	675	632	7	15	(8)	(10)	(22)	592	(109)
24	23	1965-74	P.Casanova	2,786	101	9	2,896	627	87	12	50	.225	.254	.319	573	597	2	10	(6)	6	(9)	588	(124)

AL Expansion Teams
First basemen

V	R	Years	Name	AB	BB	HBP	TAB	H	2B	3B	HR	BA	OB	SA	PRO	Wtd PRO	SB	CS	SBF	SPF	FF	R TF	V HC
1	1	1986-	R.Palmeiro	7,846	935	61	8,842	2,321	455	36	400	.296	.375	.516	891	862	88	38	1	(1)	14	877	470
2	3	1989-	J.Olerud	5,330	922	64	6,316	1,595	367	11	186	.299	.409	.477	886	844	8	12	(2)	(9)	10	842	228
3	4	1971-87	C.Cooper	7,349	448	17	7,814	2,192	415	47	241	.298	.340	.466	806	814	89	49	(1)	1	11	824	208
4	6	1986-	W.Joyner	6,979	820	38	7,837	2,024	404	25	201	.290	.368	.441	809	789	59	38	(2)	(3)	27	811	158
5	5	1968-82	J.Mayberry	5,447	881	55	6,383	1,379	211	19	255	.253	.363	.439	802	824	20	17	(2)	(9)	(0)	813	141
6	2	1993-	C.Delgado	2,901	436	61	3,398	818	214	7	190	.282	.387	.557	944	872	5	6	(2)	0	(18)	852	140
7	8	1984-92	A.Davis	4,240	685	28	4,953	1,189	220	10	160	.280	.384	.450	834	835	7	16	(5)	(7)	(15)	808	91
8	12	1972-86	C.Johnson	3,945	568	50	4,563	1,016	188	10	196	.258	.358	.459	817	821	9	12	(3)	(10)	(40)	768	48
9	7	1980-90	K.Phelps	1,854	390	21	2,265	443	64	7	123	.239	.377	.480	857	851	10	7	(2)	(10)	(30)	809	45
10	10	1966-74	M.Epstein	2,854	448	70	3,372	695	93	16	130	.244	.360	.424	784	821	7	17	(8)	(10)	(10)	793	40
11	9	1977-85	W.Aikens	2,492	319	18	2,829	675	125	2	110	.271	.358	.455	813	819	3	6	(3)	(10)	(10)	796	38
12	11	1992-	J.Jaha	2,730	424	50	3,204	726	123	5	141	.266	.375	.470	844	791	36	17	0	(1)	(2)	788	28
13	13	1992-	J.Snow	3,847	493	30	4,370	1,022	188	10	151	.266	.354	.437	791	737	14	21	(6)	(4)	31	758	(25)
14	17	1964-77	M.Hegan	2,080	311	7	2,398	504	73	18	53	.242	.343	.371	714	737	28	21	(5)	4	7	742	(27)
15	14	1978-88	W.Upshaw	4,203	452	23	4,678	1,103	199	45	123	.262	.337	.419	756	751	88	59	(6)	9	1	755	(33)
16	18	1982-91	G.Brock	3,202	434	15	3,651	794	141	6	110	.248	.340	.399	739	743	41	18	1	(1)	(2)	741	(51)
17	16	1974-86	B.Bochte	5,233	653	13	5,899	1,478	250	21	100	.282	.363	.396	759	765	43	41	(6)	(6)	(7)	745	(58)
18	15	1982-93	P.O'Brien	5,437	641	7	6,085	1,421	254	21	169	.261	.340	.409	749	749	24	34	(7)	(3)	10	749	(61)
19	24	1977-84	P.Putnam	1,989	144	10	2,143	508	95	8	63	.255	.309	.406	715	719	10	14	(7)	(10)	6	708	(67)
20	22	1965-75	B.Oliver	2,914	156	19	3,089	745	102	19	94	.256	.298	.400	698	724	17	14	(3)	7	(15)	712	(69)
21	21	1990-	L.Stevens	2,432	217	5	2,654	641	137	12	104	.264	.325	.458	783	742	6	15	(9)	(5)	(14)	714	(72)
22	23	1975-84	R.Jackson	2,986	213	35	3,234	774	165	22	56	.259	.316	.385	701	710	23	27	(9)	4	4	709	(77)
23	20	1981-93	S.Balboni	3,120	273	19	3,412	714	127	11	181	.229	.295	.451	745	745	1	2	(1)	(10)	(19)	714	(90)
24	19	1968-82	J.Spencer	4,908	407	17	5,332	1,227	179	27	146	.250	.310	.387	696	709	11	19	(5)	(9)	25	720	(128)
25	25	1974-85	D.Meyer	3,734	219	10	3,963	944	153	31	86	.253	.296	.379	675	680	61	29	0	5	(14)	672	(159)

AL Expansion Teams
Second basemen

V	R	Years	Name	AB	BB	HBP	TAB	H	2B	3B	HR	BA	OB	SA	PRO	Wtd PRO	SB	CS	SBF	SPF	FF	R TF	V HC
1	1	1988-	R.Alomar	7,221	822	41	8,084	2,196	412	60	170	.304	.378	.448	827	799	416	100	25	9	42	876	759
2	2	1970-86	B.Grich	6,890	1,087	86	8,063	1,833	320	47	224	.266	.373	.424	796	816	104	83	(7)	3	20	832	586
3	3	1973-90	F.White	7,859	412	30	8,301	2,006	407	58	160	.255	.295	.383	678	681	178	83	1	7	51	741	226
4	5	1977-82	B.Wills	3,030	310	17	3,357	807	128	24	36	.266	.338	.360	698	698	196	65	17	10	10	734	84
5	4	1993-	F.Vina	2,613	192	101	2,906	746	116	32	26	.285	.358	.384	742	690	76	44	(4)	10	43	739	77
6	6	1964-72	B.Knoop	3,622	305	14	3,941	856	129	29	56	.236	.298	.334	632	661	16	17	(4)	(3)	67	720	65
7	8	1977-86	J.Cruz	3,859	478	14	4,351	916	113	27	23	.237	.324	.299	622	627	343	78	42	10	36	714	61
8	9	1983-94	H.Reynolds	4,782	480	27	5,289	1,233	230	53	21	.258	.329	.341	670	668	250	138	(5)	10	33	706	53
9	7	1990-	T.Shumpert	1,409	120	15	1,544	356	78	18	37	.253	.318	.412	730	692	66	25	12	10	1	715	13
10	11	1978-89	D.Garcia	3,914	130	27	4,071	1,108	183	27	36	.283	.311	.371	682	681	203	90	6	10	(7)	690	10
11	10	1976-92	J.Gantner	6,189	383	52	6,624	1,696	262	38	47	.274	.322	.351	673	676	137	78	(3)	2	16	692	0
12	14	1996-	M.Cairo	1,411	81	17	1,509	386	62	12	9	.274	.321	.354	674	614	69	22	16	10	26	666	(14)
13	12	1958-65	B.Moran	2,076	133	11	2,220	545	88	10	28	.263	.310	.355	665	662	10	8	(3)	0	16	676	(16)
14	17	1995-	D.Bell	1,913	151	13	2,077	486	105	10	46	.254	.313	.392	704	655	12	14	(7)	0	2	649	(48)
15	19	1987-98	N.Liriano	2,216	212	7	2,435	576	105	27	25	.260	.326	.366	692	683	59	30	(1)	6	(44)	644	(49)
16	18	1990-	L.Sojo	2,488	120	12	2,620	658	101	12	36	.264	.302	.358	660	634	27	20	(4)	0	17	647	(51)
17	16	1968-77	D.Nelson	2,578	220	13	2,811	630	77	19	20	.244	.307	.312	619	649	187	73	14	10	(21)	653	(59)
18	21	1974-84	L.Milbourne	2,448	133	9	2,590	623	71	24	11	.254	.295	.317	612	620	41	33	(8)	10	12	633	(66)
19	13	1986-	M.McLemore	4,887	666	11	5,564	1,260	193	34	37	.258	.348	.334	682	646	210	95	4	10	13	673	(76)
20	20	1987-98	J.Cora	3,734	380	44	4,158	1,035	171	41	30	.277	.351	.369	720	685	117	60	(1)	6	(48)	642	(90)
21	15	1962-77	C.Rojas	6,309	396	20	6,725	1,660	254	25	54	.263	.309	.337	646	670	74	68	(9)	(2)	0	660	(96)
22	23	1975-82	D.McKay	1,928	86	17	2,031	441	70	15	21	.229	.268	.313	581	598	20	12	(1)	0	(6)	591	(107)
23	22	1964-78	S.Alomar Sr.	4,760	302	3	5,065	1,168	126	19	13	.245	.291	.288	579	601	227	80	12	10	5	629	(135)

AL Expansion Teams
Shortstops

V	R	Years	Name	AB	BB	HBP	TAB	H	2B	3B	HR	BA	OB	SA	PRO	Wtd PRO	SB	CS	SBF	SPF	FF	R TF	V HC
1	2	1974-93	R.Yount	11,008	966	48	12,022	3,142	583	126	251	.285	.346	.430	775	780	271	105	5	9	18	811	621
2	1	1994-	A.Rodriguez	3,126	310	31	3,467	966	194	13	189	.309	.377	.561	938	866	133	36	17	10	21	913	422
3	5	1983-	T.Fernandez	7,788	682	63	8,533	2,240	410	92	92	.288	.350	.399	749	736	245	135	(3)	10	13	756	351
4	4	1961-78	J.Fregosi	6,523	715	32	7,270	1,726	264	78	151	.265	.340	.398	739	764	76	40	(1)	5	1	770	318
5	6	1992-	J.Valentin	2,977	357	14	3,348	732	169	24	115	.246	.329	.435	764	710	97	34	8	10	9	737	126
6	3	1996-	T.Batista	1,858	124	18	2,000	496	98	7	100	.267	.319	.489	808	747	19	10	(0)	10	25	782	91
7	7	1968-81	F.Patek	5,530	523	31	6,084	1,340	216	55	41	.242	.311	.324	635	653	385	131	19	10	0	682	57
8	8	1994-	A.Gonzalez	2,622	214	25	2,861	637	147	15	66	.243	.306	.386	692	642	67	28	4	10	4	661	(2)
9	9	1983-96	D.Schofield	4,299	446	48	4,793	989	137	32	56	.230	.309	.316	625	622	120	41	7	6	17	651	(26)
10	11	1977-87	U.Washington	2,797	261	1	3,059	703	103	36	27	.251	.315	.343	658	660	132	53	6	10	(36)	640	(37)
11	10	1985-93	E.Riles	2,504	244	9	2,757	637	92	20	48	.254	.323	.365	687	689	20	28	(12)	0	(29)	647	(55)
12	14	1992-97	P.Listach	1,772	167	8	1,947	444	63	13	5	.251	.318	.309	627	608	116	38	19	10	(16)	621	(60)
13	13	1985-95	M.Lee	2,693	201	4	2,898	686	88	20	19	.255	.307	.323	631	631	31	20	(3)	0	0	628	(65)
14	18	1977-90	E.Romero	1,912	140	5	2,057	473	79	1	8	.247	.300	.302	603	599	9	10	(6)	7	13	613	(68)
15	12	1986-99	D.Sveum	2,526	227	6	2,759	597	125	13	69	.236	.301	.378	679	666	10	18	(9)	0	(27)	630	(75)
16	19	1981-90	W.Tolleson	2,322	219	8	2,549	559	60	17	9	.241	.308	.293	601	596	108	41	10	10	(5)	611	(78)
17	22	1988-	J.Huson	1,879	191	6	2,076	439	65	13	8	.234	.306	.295	601	592	64	21	10	7	(16)	593	(82)
18	17	1986-96	K.Stillwell	3,125	274	18	3,417	779	151	30	34	.249	.313	.349	663	666	38	29	(6)	5	(52)	614	(84)
19	21	1983-93	C.Wilkerson	2,452	138	12	2,602	600	78	23	8	.245	.288	.305	593	596	81	43	(2)	10	(1)	603	(92)
20	20	1989-	G.DiSarcina	3,744	154	36	3,934	966	186	20	28	.258	.294	.341	635	604	47	44	(10)	10	2	605	(112)
21	15	1961-75	E.Brinkman	6,045	444	40	6,529	1,355	201	38	60	.224	.282	.300	581	601	30	35	(6)	0	26	621	(130)
22	16	1976-93	A.Griffin	6,780	338	25	7,143	1,688	245	78	24	.249	.287	.319	606	605	192	134	(11)	9	15	618	(153)

AL Expansion Teams
Third basemen

V	R	Years	Name	AB	BB	HBP	TAB	H	2B	3B	HR	BA	OB	SA	PRO	Wtd PRO	SB	CS	SBF	SPF	FF	R TF	V HC
1	2	1973-93	G.Brett	10,349	1,096	33	11,478	3,154	665	137	317	.305	.373	.487	861	868	201	97	1	2	(0)	870	756
2	3	1978-98	P.Molitor	10,835	1,094	47	11,976	3,319	605	114	234	.306	.372	.448	820	807	504	131	19	10	(13)	822	515
3	1	1987-	E.Martinez	5,432	973	65	6,470	1,738	403	14	235	.320	.429	.529	958	915	43	27	(1)	(3)	(22)	888	470
4	6	1969-86	T.Harrah	7,402	1,153	63	8,618	1,954	307	40	195	.264	.368	.395	763	777	238	94	6	3	(28)	758	274
5	4	1994-	J.Cirillo	3,409	397	42	3,848	1,059	239	15	77	.311	.389	.457	847	784	35	27	(5)	2	25	806	168
6	5	1984-93	K.Gruber	3,159	197	36	3,392	818	148	24	117	.259	.310	.432	742	749	80	33	4	10	32	795	129
7	8	1968-83	D.Money	6,215	600	40	6,855	1,623	302	36	176	.261	.330	.406	736	747	80	51	(3)	2	1	747	112
8	7	1986-97	K.Seitzer	5,278	669	35	5,982	1,557	285	35	74	.295	.378	.404	782	766	80	49	(3)	(5)	(9)	749	71
9	10	1962-77	K.McMullen	5,131	510	17	5,658	1,273	172	26	156	.248	.318	.383	701	734	20	19	(3)	(10)	18	739	55
10	12	1977-92	R.Mulliniks	3,569	460	7	4,036	972	226	17	73	.272	.357	.407	763	760	15	12	(5)	(3)	(24)	731	45
11	9	1995-	J.Randa	2,550	200	23	2,773	748	139	24	54	.293	.350	.430	780	723	36	21	(2)	0	21	742	34
12	13	1985-95	S.Buechele	4,266	408	43	4,717	1,046	183	21	137	.245	.317	.394	712	707	17	28	(7)	(1)	29	727	24
13	14	1989-	D.Palmer	4,588	465	49	5,102	1,169	218	15	264	.255	.330	.481	811	768	44	30	(3)	(4)	(36)	725	24
14	11	1985-	J.Howell	2,639	300	12	2,951	632	129	16	108	.239	.320	.423	743	737	14	15	(5)	(1)	1	731	8
15	19	1972-85	B.Stein	2,811	186	14	3,011	751	122	18	44	.267	.316	.370	686	699	16	16	(5)	(1)	(4)	688	(31)
16	15	1984-91	J.Presley	3,546	210	19	3,775	875	181	14	135	.247	.292	.420	712	708	9	14	(5)	(3)	(3)	698	(32)
17	17	1989-	M.Blowers	2,300	248	6	2,554	591	116	8	78	.257	.331	.416	747	716	7	8	(3)	1	(23)	690	(39)
18	18	1964-74	P.Schaal	3,555	516	22	4,093	869	132	26	57	.244	.344	.344	688	717	43	38	(8)	0	(20)	690	(50)
19	22	1994-	R.Davis	1,813	129	15	1,957	465	95	5	77	.256	.311	.442	753	701	15	11	(3)	0	(37)	661	(52)
20	16	1974-84	R.Howell	3,791	318	23	4,132	991	183	31	80	.261	.322	.389	712	721	9	14	(4)	(10)	(10)	696	(54)
21	20	1971-82	L.Randle	3,950	372	15	4,337	1,016	145	40	27	.257	.323	.335	658	674	156	112	(14)	10	(1)	669	(76)
22	24	1973-81	D.Chalk	2,910	295	35	3,240	733	107	9	15	.252	.328	.310	638	653	36	38	(12)	8	(14)	636	(81)
23	25	1978-87	G.Iorg	2,450	114	11	2,575	633	125	16	20	.258	.294	.347	641	636	23	17	(5)	0	(4)	628	(98)
24	26	1989-98	D.Strange	1,859	155	14	2,028	434	87	7	31	.233	.297	.338	635	609	14	15	(8)	0	(7)	594	(112)
25	21	1983-97	D.Coles	2,891	237	35	3,163	709	142	14	75	.245	.310	.382	692	690	20	23	(8)	3	(23)	662	(116)
26	23	1991-	E.Sprague	4,001	347	90	4,438	982	218	12	150	.245	.320	.418	738	691	6	12	(4)	(8)	(22)	657	(132)

AL Expansion Teams
Outfielders

V	R	Years	Name	AB	BB	HBP	TAB	H	2B	3B	HR	BA	OB	SA	PRO	Wtd PRO	SB	CS	SBF	SPF	FF	R TF	V HC
1	1	1989-	K.Griffey Jr.	6,352	841	56	7,249	1,883	342	33	438	.296	.384	.568	951	916	173	64	6	10	57	989	825
2	4	1967-84	A.Otis	7,299	757	33	8,089	2,020	374	66	193	.277	.347	.425	773	791	341	93	18	10	38	857	395
3	2	1992-	T.Salmon	4,051	683	37	4,771	1,180	231	16	230	.291	.398	.527	925	868	29	33	(7)	(1)	25	884	304
4	8	1958-73	F.Howard	6,488	782	33	7,303	1,774	245	35	382	.273	.355	.499	853	880	8	9	(1)	(10)	(29)	840	287
5	5	1989-	J.Gonzalez	5,292	376	50	5,718	1,554	312	21	362	.294	.346	.566	912	865	22	17	(2)	0	(15)	848	256
6	7	1987-	J.Buhner	4,968	784	56	5,808	1,263	231	19	308	.254	.362	.494	856	825	6	24	(7)	(2)	24	840	237
7	6	1981-92	J.Barfield	4,759	551	34	5,344	1,219	216	30	241	.256	.338	.466	804	802	66	47	(5)	6	40	843	220
8	10	1984-97	D.Tartabull	5,011	768	17	5,796	1,366	289	22	262	.273	.371	.496	867	856	37	30	(4)	(5)	(20)	827	203
9	3	1993-	J.Edmonds	3,169	377	21	3,567	923	186	12	163	.291	.370	.512	882	817	36	27	(5)	10	42	864	194
10	9	1974-85	S.Lezcano	4,134	576	19	4,729	1,122	184	34	148	.271	.363	.440	803	814	37	31	(5)	6	18	833	175
11	32	1973-92	B.Downing	7,853	1,197	129	9,179	2,099	360	28	275	.267	.373	.425	798	803	50	44	(4)	(7)	(24)	768	144
12	15	1971-86	B.Oglivie	5,913	560	35	6,508	1,615	277	33	235	.273	.340	.450	790	797	87	70	(8)	5	2	796	124
13	12	1983-90	P.Bradley	3,695	432	65	4,192	1,058	179	43	78	.286	.371	.421	792	794	155	62	7	10	5	815	115
14	17	1976-94	W.Wilson	7,731	425	62	8,218	2,207	281	147	41	.285	.328	.376	704	704	668	134	46	10	26	786	113
15	13	1994-	R.Greer	3,385	473	21	3,879	1,040	226	23	111	.307	.395	.486	881	820	29	13	1	0	(6)	814	110
16	11	1993-	S.Green	3,123	296	36	3,455	882	208	19	143	.282	.351	.499	850	787	100	30	11	10	12	819	104
17	25	1981-	C.Davis	8,673	1,194	15	9,882	2,380	424	30	350	.274	.363	.451	814	803	142	98	(5)	2	(24)	777	96
18	22	1985-	D.White	6,954	513	75	7,542	1,826	353	69	194	.263	.320	.417	737	718	328	95	17	10	33	779	78
19	19	1989-	G.Vaughn	5,330	745	31	6,106	1,314	246	21	320	.247	.342	.481	823	786	107	52	0	2	(6)	782	75
20	27	1968-87	H.McRae	7,218	648	79	7,945	2,091	484	66	191	.290	.355	.454	809	819	109	78	(6)	(2)	(37)	775	71
21	23	1970-85	J.Burroughs	5,536	831	15	6,382	1,443	230	20	240	.261	.359	.439	798	812	16	22	(4)	(6)	(24)	778	67
22	24	1980-91	L.Moseby	5,815	616	58	6,489	1,494	273	66	169	.257	.334	.414	748	746	280	92	13	10	8	777	64
23	21	1973-86	G.Thomas	4,677	697	18	5,392	1,051	212	13	268	.225	.328	.448	775	784	50	49	(9)	0	4	779	53
24	16	1986-94	B.Jackson	2,393	200	14	2,607	598	86	14	141	.250	.311	.474	786	783	82	32	6	5	2	796	50
25	30	1970-88	D.Baylor	8,198	805	267	9,270	2,135	366	28	338	.260	.346	.436	782	791	285	120	4	7	(31)	771	49

AL Expansion Teams
Outfielders

V	R	Years	Name	AB	BB	HBP	TAB	H	2B	3B	HR	BA	OB	SA	PRO	Wtd PRO	SB	CS	SBF	SPF	FF	R TF	V HC
26	29	1981-93	G.Bell	6,123	331	49	6,503	1,702	308	34	265	.278	.320	.469	789	789	67	36	(1)	3	(19)	773	49
27	14	1996-	D.Erstad	2,545	222	12	2,779	767	139	19	77	.301	.360	.462	822	763	87	32	8	10	18	799	48
28	20	1995-	J.Damon	3,057	275	15	3,347	894	156	47	65	.292	.354	.438	792	734	156	42	20	10	16	781	38
29	33	1983-98	J.Carter	8,422	527	90	9,039	2,184	432	53	396	.259	.310	.464	774	758	231	66	11	6	(8)	767	37
30	28	1979-90	G.Ward	4,479	351	13	4,843	1,236	196	41	130	.276	.330	.425	755	754	83	30	4	8	6	773	36
31	36	1995-	S.Stewart	1,930	188	34	2,152	574	114	17	44	.297	.370	.442	812	752	121	40	(9)	10	9	763	32
32	18	1996-	J.Dye	1,978	163	9	2,150	566	120	11	84	.286	.343	.485	829	769	7	11	(7)	0	23	785	29
33	31	1964-74	R.Reichardt	3,307	263	66	3,636	864	109	24	116	.261	.328	.414	742	780	40	41	(11)	10	(11)	768	20
34	34	1984-96	R.Deer	3,881	575	32	4,488	853	148	13	230	.220	.325	.442	768	768	43	31	(4)	0	(0)	764	13
35	26	1973-83	O.Velez	1,802	336	11	2,149	452	87	11	78	.251	.372	.441	813	819	6	10	(7)	(10)	(27)	775	12
36	35	1962-69	D.Lock	2,695	373	15	3,083	642	92	12	122	.238	.334	.417	751	773	30	29	(9)	0	(1)	763	8
37	37	1976-87	R.Jones	4,415	534	12	4,961	1,103	215	38	147	.250	.332	.416	748	746	143	84	(6)	7	13	760	6
38	38	1997-	J.Cruz	1,699	233	2	1,934	417	84	12	82	.245	.337	.454	791	734	47	15	8	10	7	759	1
39	40	1994-	G.Anderson	3,507	163	4	3,674	1,043	205	18	107	.297	.329	.458	787	732	41	28	(4)	0	25	753	(7)
40	39	1986-	R.Sierra	6,469	495	7	6,971	1,737	341	56	240	.269	.321	.450	771	758	133	51	4	7	(14)	755	(9)
41	42	1985-94	O.McDowell	2,829	294	9	3,132	715	125	28	74	.253	.325	.395	720	714	169	53	20	10	0	744	(20)
42	45	1974-84	L.Roberts	2,737	256	22	3,015	731	126	28	78	.267	.335	.419	754	765	26	25	(8)	(5)	(13)	739	(26)
43	44	1955-67	J.King	2,918	363	23	3,304	699	112	19	117	.240	.328	.411	740	741	23	8	2	(4)	2	741	(27)
44	41	1974-86	A.Cowens	5,534	389	34	5,957	1,494	276	68	108	.270	.322	.403	725	731	120	74	(5)	9	11	747	(32)
45	52	1986-92	G.Braggs	2,336	211	24	2,571	601	102	16	70	.257	.325	.405	730	731	58	26	2	10	(14)	730	(33)
46	43	1988-	D.Hamilton	4,451	474	15	4,940	1,306	197	36	50	.293	.363	.388	751	718	160	72	3	10	10	741	(39)
47	56	1989-94	J.Felix	2,132	158	19	2,309	562	105	24	55	.264	.320	.413	733	738	49	40	(14)	7	(10)	722	(41)
48	53	1978-86	B.Sample	2,516	195	28	2,739	684	127	9	46	.272	.331	.384	715	719	98	31	12	10	(14)	727	(41)
49	54	1964-72	R.Repoz	2,145	280	10	2,435	480	73	19	82	.224	.316	.390	706	739	26	25	(9)	9	(15)	722	(41)
50	67	1995-	Q.McCracken	1,402	135	6	1,543	397	68	15	14	.283	.349	.383	732	690	70	33	2	10	(3)	699	(43)
51	50	1958-66	A.Pearson	3,077	477	12	3,566	831	130	24	28	.270	.370	.355	725	724	77	33	3	10	(5)	731	(44)
52	60	1968-78	J.LaHoud	1,925	309	16	2,250	429	68	12	65	.223	.335	.372	707	739	20	20	(8)	0	(18)	712	(49)
53	47	1964-76	A.Johnson	4,623	244	36	4,903	1,331	180	33	78	.288	.329	.392	720	750	113	63	(3)	10	(22)	736	(50)
54	48	1982-98	J.Eisenreich	3,995	324	8	4,327	1,160	221	39	52	.290	.345	.404	749	740	105	38	7	3	(17)	733	(53)
55	46	1970-87	T.Paciorek	4,121	245	38	4,404	1,162	232	30	86	.282	.328	.415	744	757	55	38	(5)	(0)	(15)	737	(54)
56	65	1970-79	T.Grieve	1,907	135	13	2,055	474	76	10	65	.249	.303	.401	704	731	7	7	(3)	0	(26)	701	(56)
57	76	1991-	R.Amaral	1,788	176	16	1,980	493	82	10	11	.276	.346	.351	697	659	112	39	17	10	(16)	670	(60)
58	66	1984-93	H.Cotto	2,178	107	16	2,301	569	87	9	44	.261	.301	.370	671	676	130	26	32	10	(16)	701	(61)
59	51	1992-	C.Curtis	3,902	496	39	4,437	1,032	192	16	98	.264	.353	.397	750	710	205	97	2	9	9	730	(62)
60	61	1970-78	L.Stanton	2,575	236	24	2,835	628	114	13	77	.244	.313	.388	701	725	36	27	(6)	6	(14)	711	(64)
61	74	1993-	M.Mieske	1,547	124	11	1,682	406	78	10	56	.262	.322	.434	756	705	7	16	(15)	3	(15)	678	(70)
62	70	1977-86	A.Woods	1,986	167	3	2,156	538	98	14	35	.271	.328	.387	716	709	23	24	(11)	10	(15)	693	(70)
63	57	1982-92	G.Pettis	3,629	521	9	4,159	855	109	49	21	.236	.333	.310	643	644	354	104	33	10	34	721	(73)
64	55	1961-68	L.Thomas	3,324	332	32	3,688	847	111	22	106	.255	.328	.397	725	732	25	11	1	0	(10)	722	(74)
65	49	1990-	B.McRae	5,114	488	57	5,659	1,336	264	58	103	.261	.332	.396	728	702	196	86	5	8	16	731	(75)
66	75	1993-	D.Buford	1,768	169	20	1,957	433	84	9	51	.245	.318	.389	707	657	56	35	(7)	10	17	677	(76)
67	63	1977-86	B.Bonnell	3,068	229	13	3,310	833	143	24	56	.272	.325	.389	713	709	64	39	(4)	3	(2)	707	(83)
68	73	1969-80	V.Joshua	2,234	108	3	2,345	610	87	31	30	.273	.307	.380	687	699	55	40	(10)	9	(18)	680	(86)
69	72	1981-91	P.Sheridan	2,419	236	6	2,661	611	91	21	51	.253	.321	.371	691	690	86	35	6	10	(20)	686	(91)
70	62	1967-78	D.May	3,670	344	28	4,042	920	130	20	96	.251	.320	.375	695	719	60	47	(8)	8	(9)	710	(92)
71	58	1987-	L.Polonia	4,840	369	15	5,224	1,417	189	70	36	.293	.345	.383	728	712	321	145	5	10	(6)	720	(96)
72	71	1962-77	E.Kirkpatrick	3,467	456	22	3,945	824	143	18	85	.238	.330	.363	693	715	34	39	(11)	0	(17)	687	(98)
73	77	1975-85	B.Bailor	2,937	187	20	3,144	775	107	23	9	.264	.312	.325	638	642	90	36	6	10	3	660	(100)
74	59	1986-98	P.Incaviglia	4,233	360	45	4,638	1,043	194	21	206	.246	.312	.448	760	751	33	26	(4)	(10)	(25)	713	(101)
75	69	1991-	T.Goodwin	3,130	309	13	3,452	853	94	32	18	.273	.340	.340	681	635	307	103	28	10	24	696	(102)
76	80	1982-86	G.Wright	2,160	126	9	2,295	529	88	18	42	.245	.289	.361	650	649	19	29	(16)	6	8	646	(122)
77	78	1985-94	M.Felder	2,262	168	6	2,436	564	59	32	14	.249	.303	.322	625	621	161	46	27	10	(7)	651	(126)
78	68	1971-88	J.Beniquez	4,651	349	31	5,031	1,274	190	30	79	.274	.329	.379	707	712	104	76	(9)	4	(10)	697	(140)
79	64	1968-82	D.Unser	5,215	481	9	5,705	1,344	179	42	87	.258	.321	.358	680	697	64	60	(9)	10	8	705	(147)
80	79	1972-86	J.Wohlford	3,049	241	8	3,298	793	125	33	21	.260	.316	.343	659	672	89	68	(13)	9	(18)	651	(169)

AL Expansion Teams
Starting Pitchers

V	R	Years	Name	G	GS	IP	W	L	SV	SO	BB	ERA	RA/9	R Wtd RA/9	V Runs /162
1	10	1966-93	N.Ryan	807	773	5,386	324	292	3	5,714	2,795	3.19	3.64	3.95	366.8
2	1	1988-	R.Johnson	366	357	2,499	179	95	2	3,040	1,089	3.20	3.61	3.44	320.9
3	3	1986-	K.Brown	382	380	2,661	170	114	0	1,917	730	3.21	3.69	3.62	287.9
4	2	1984-	B.Saberhagen	396	368	2,548	166	115	1	1,705	471	3.33	3.62	3.58	286.8
5	5	1984-98	J.Key	470	389	2,592	186	117	10	1,538	668	3.51	3.83	3.70	252.9
6	7	1979-98	D.Stieb	443	412	2,895	176	137	3	1,669	1,034	3.44	3.81	3.84	238.7
7	4	1989-	K.Appier	324	312	2,085	136	105	0	1,633	759	3.63	3.94	3.63	223.6
8	8	1986-	C.Finley	470	413	2,893	181	151	0	2,340	1,219	3.76	4.18	3.92	212.4
9	6	1968-79	A.Messersmith	344	295	2,230	130	99	15	1,625	831	2.86	3.28	3.70	212.3
10	18	1973-93	F.Tanana	638	616	4,188	240	236	1	2,773	1,255	3.66	4.10	4.24	148.2
11	13	1987-	D.Wells	479	309	2,307	161	107	13	1,576	538	4.06	4.40	4.06	130.4
12	12	1961-71	D.Chance	406	294	2,147	128	115	23	1,534	739	2.92	3.49	4.03	125.5
13	15	1984-97	M.Gubicza	384	329	2,223	132	136	2	1,371	786	3.96	4.30	4.18	97.5
14	14	1991-	P.Hentgen	285	255	1,750	120	88	0	1,113	646	4.21	4.58	4.09	94.9
15	9	1985-94	T.Higuera	213	205	1,380	94	64	0	1,081	443	3.61	3.97	3.95	94.8
16	22	1984-99	M.Langston	457	428	2,963	179	158	0	2,464	1,289	3.97	4.37	4.29	90.8
17	25	1978-98	D.Darwin	716	371	3,017	171	182	32	1,942	874	3.84	4.27	4.31	84.5
18	16	1989-	K.Rogers	536	251	1,929	127	91	28	1,241	729	4.11	4.61	4.20	79.6
19	29	1971-89	D.Alexander	561	464	3,368	194	174	3	1,528	978	3.76	4.12	4.36	76.3
20	33	1970-94	C.Hough	858	440	3,801	216	216	61	2,362	1,665	3.75	4.28	4.39	73.3
21	20	1974-86	D.Leonard	312	302	2,187	144	106	1	1,323	622	3.70	4.15	4.29	68.7
22	11	1993-	W.Williams	222	132	990	50	54	0	687	378	4.23	4.44	3.97	66.7
23	17	1991-	J.Guzman	240	240	1,483	91	79	0	1,243	667	4.08	4.55	4.22	58.4
24	24	1970-85	L.Gura	403	261	2,047	126	97	14	801	600	3.76	4.21	4.31	58.1
25	30	1965-83	R.May	535	360	2,622	152	156	12	1,760	958	3.46	3.95	4.37	57.7
26	27	1979-93	C.Leibrandt	394	346	2,308	140	119	2	1,121	656	3.71	4.16	4.35	54.6
27	21	1986-96	C.Bosio	309	246	1,710	94	93	9	1,059	481	3.96	4.39	4.29	53.4
28	28	1972-82	D.Medich	312	287	1,996	124	105	2	955	624	3.78	4.17	4.35	48.6
29	23	1988-	T.Gordon	444	203	1,645	104	96	71	1,431	807	4.15	4.57	4.31	48.2
30	31	1981-93	M.Witt	341	299	2,108	117	116	6	1,373	713	3.83	4.32	4.38	43.9
31	26	1988-98	E.Hanson	245	238	1,555	89	84	0	1,175	504	4.15	4.49	4.32	43.0
32	35	1969-81	D.Drago	519	189	1,875	108	117	58	987	558	3.62	3.97	4.43	26.9
33	36	1981-95	B.Black	398	296	2,053	121	116	11	1,039	623	3.84	4.30	4.44	26.3
34	19	1996-	J.Rosado	125	112	720	37	45	1	484	237	4.27	4.79	4.25	24.8
35	39	1986-	J.Moyer	372	320	2,082	131	111	0	1,262	620	4.30	4.69	4.46	23.7
36	34	1991-	C.Eldred	194	189	1,191	74	67	0	783	507	4.52	4.80	4.39	23.3
37	38	1968-80	M.Pattin	475	224	2,039	114	109	25	1,179	603	3.62	4.00	4.46	23.1
38	32	1972-80	S.Busby	167	150	1,061	70	54	0	659	433	3.72	4.10	4.39	20.2
39	37	1976-87	M.Haas	266	252	1,655	100	83	2	853	436	4.01	4.38	4.45	20.2
40	43	1988-	T.Stottlemyre	367	335	2,171	138	119	1	1,575	809	4.25	4.61	4.48	18.6
41	40	1969-78	A.Fitzmorris	288	159	1,277	77	59	7	458	433	3.65	4.04	4.47	12.9
42	44	1989-99	J.Abbott	263	254	1,674	87	108	0	888	620	4.25	4.73	4.50	12.2
43	46	1985-98	B.Swift	403	220	1,600	94	78	27	767	507	3.95	4.51	4.50	10.0
44	47	1985-96	K.McCaskill	380	242	1,729	106	108	7	1,003	665	4.12	4.56	4.51	9.6
45	41	1986-95	S.Bankhead	267	110	901	57	48	1	614	289	4.18	4.50	4.47	9.1
46	42	1957-66	D.Lee	244	97	828	40	44	11	467	281	3.61	4.20	4.47	8.2
47	45	1985-91	J.Cerutti	229	116	861	49	43	4	398	291	3.94	4.46	4.50	5.6
48	48	1985-94	J.Guzman	193	186	1,224	80	74	0	889	482	4.05	4.53	4.55	1.2
49	49	1985-95	B.Wegman	262	216	1,483	81	90	2	696	352	4.16	4.67	4.57	(2.9)
50	50	1974-84	T.Underwood	379	203	1,586	86	87	18	948	662	3.89	4.38	4.58	(4.0)

AL Expansion Teams
Starting Pitchers

V	R	Years	Name	G	GS	IP	W	L	SV	SO	BB	ERA	RA/9	R Wtd RA/9	V Runs /162
51	54	1959-65	K.McBride	151	122	808	40	50	3	503	363	3.79	4.32	4.60	(4.0)
52	52	1978-86	J.Beattie	203	182	1,149	52	87	1	660	461	4.17	4.55	4.59	(4.9)
53	51	1969-78	J.Colborn	301	204	1,597	83	88	7	688	475	3.80	4.22	4.59	(5.5)
54	53	1966-75	C.Wright	329	235	1,729	100	111	3	667	550	3.50	3.98	4.60	(8.0)
55	58	1995-	S.Sparks	123	101	671	34	38	1	333	307	4.92	5.35	4.66	(8.2)
56	56	1980-85	L.Leal	165	151	946	51	58	1	491	320	4.14	4.53	4.66	(11.1)
57	55	1968-79	T.Murphy	439	147	1,444	68	101	59	621	493	3.78	4.14	4.65	(15.2)
58	59	1965-73	J.McGlothlin	256	201	1,300	67	77	3	709	418	3.61	4.02	4.66	(15.4)
59	57	1956-71	G.Brunet	324	213	1,432	69	93	4	921	581	3.62	4.02	4.66	(16.5)
60	69	1995-	J.Suppan	123	108	662	30	34	0	381	222	5.15	5.42	4.82	(19.3)
61	62	1993-	D.Oliver	204	149	942	56	49	2	564	408	4.88	5.39	4.74	(19.4)
62	68	1995-	S.Karl	178	161	1,002	54	56	0	513	369	4.81	5.34	4.82	(29.4)
63	60	1970-84	P.Splittorff	429	392	2,555	166	143	1	1,057	780	3.81	4.38	4.68	(34.8)
64	61	1971-84	M.Caldwell	475	307	2,409	137	130	18	939	597	3.81	4.42	4.68	(35.1)
65	73	1975-84	J.Augustine	279	104	944	55	59	11	348	340	4.23	4.68	4.88	(35.3)
66	67	1991-	R.Bones	314	164	1,214	59	78	1	523	431	4.84	5.30	4.81	(36.5)
67	72	1974-83	B.Travers	205	168	1,121	65	71	1	488	415	4.10	4.62	4.86	(37.8)
68	66	1977-88	L.Sorensen	346	235	1,736	93	103	6	569	402	4.15	4.63	4.77	(42.0)
69	79	1995-	D.Springer	125	95	635	23	46	1	288	254	5.23	5.77	5.19	(45.0)
70	70	1966-76	D.Bosman	306	229	1,591	82	85	2	757	412	3.67	4.16	4.82	(46.6)
71	63	1983-97	D.Jackson	353	324	2,073	112	131	1	1,225	816	4.01	4.61	4.75	(47.1)
72	76	1970-77	J.Brown	214	105	893	47	53	3	516	353	4.18	4.63	5.05	(49.2)
73	80	1991-	C.Haney	172	125	795	38	52	0	427	276	5.11	5.62	5.19	(57.7)
74	64	1971-86	J.Slaton	496	360	2,684	151	158	14	1,191	1,004	4.03	4.48	4.76	(60.9)
75	77	1983-93	M.Young	333	163	1,190	55	95	25	857	565	4.40	5.00	5.06	(66.5)
76	65	1982-95	M.Moore	450	440	2,832	161	176	2	1,667	1,156	4.39	4.82	4.76	(66.9)
77	71	1977-91	J.Clancy	472	381	2,517	140	167	10	1,422	947	4.23	4.66	4.83	(79.6)
78	78	1973-84	G.Abbott	248	206	1,286	62	83	0	484	352	4.39	4.95	5.13	(86.7)
79	83	1973-80	D.Lemanczyk	185	103	913	37	63	0	429	363	4.62	5.21	5.42	(87.3)
80	81	1957-65	B.Daniels	230	139	997	45	76	5	471	383	4.44	4.99	5.34	(88.0)
81	82	1978-84	R.Gale	195	144	970	55	56	2	518	457	4.54	5.05	5.35	(89.9)
82	87	1969-76	B.Champion	202	102	804	34	50	2	360	354	4.69	5.03	5.60	(93.8)
83	85	1994-	R.Helling	167	137	896	60	47	0	612	373	4.65	4.95	5.55	(101.0)
84	84	1960-69	P.Ortega	204	141	952	46	62	2	549	378	4.43	4.71	5.52	(102.4)
85	74	1989-	J.Navarro	361	309	2,055	116	126	2	1,113	690	4.72	5.28	5.04	(113.7)
86	86	1973-81	J.Jefferson	237	144	1,086	39	81	1	522	520	4.81	5.32	5.55	(124.3)
87	88	1971-78	P.Broberg	206	134	963	41	71	1	536	478	4.56	5.16	5.81	(135.4)
88	75	1986-	B.Witt	416	390	2,422	138	156	0	1,924	1,350	4.83	5.30	5.05	(136.3)

AL Expansion Teams
Relief Pitchers

V	R	Years	Name	G	GS	IP	W	L	SV	SO	BB	ERA	RA/9	R Wtd RA/9	V Runs /162
1	4	1979-90	D.Quisenberry	674	0	1,043	56	46	244	379	162	2.76	3.07	3.16	166.6
2	1	1982-95	T.Henke	642	0	790	41	42	311	861	255	2.67	2.87	2.85	154.3
3	5	1982-96	M.Eichhorn	563	7	886	48	43	32	640	270	3.00	3.33	3.29	128.5
4	10	1986-	M.Jackson	835	7	1,018	53	61	138	905	414	3.26	3.62	3.57	114.1
5	8	1987-99	J.Montgomery	700	1	869	46	52	304	733	296	3.27	3.60	3.42	113.2
6	6	1989-	J.Wetteland	618	17	765	48	45	330	804	252	2.93	3.38	3.31	110.7
7	9	1984-94	S.Farr	509	28	824	48	45	132	668	334	3.25	3.56	3.57	91.9
8	2	1987-95	B.Harvey	322	0	387	17	25	177	448	144	2.49	2.84	2.89	72.7
9	3	1995-	T.Percival	360	0	374	19	27	171	460	168	3.16	3.40	2.96	68.0
10	23	1986-	D.Plesac	884	14	957	56	62	154	895	323	3.65	4.05	3.99	62.5
11	27	1965-80	D.Knowles	765	8	1,092	66	74	143	681	480	3.12	3.60	4.05	61.8
12	13	1986-95	D.Ward	462	2	667	32	37	121	679	286	3.28	3.62	3.74	60.7
13	12	1991-	M.Timlin	525	3	626	37	40	111	502	246	3.59	4.03	3.73	59.9
14	11	1980-87	D.Corbett	313	1	553	24	30	66	343	200	3.32	3.68	3.69	57.9
15	30	1970-83	D.LaRoche	647	15	1,049	65	58	126	819	459	3.53	3.84	4.10	54.6
16	31	1977-90	D.Aase	448	91	1,109	66	60	82	641	457	3.80	4.08	4.13	54.2
17	16	1964-76	K.Sanders	408	1	657	29	45	86	360	258	2.97	3.29	3.83	53.6
18	34	1962-74	P.Richert	429	122	1,166	80	73	51	925	424	3.19	3.58	4.17	50.3
19	19	1989-	M.Fetters	473	6	590	25	35	90	413	273	3.59	4.20	3.89	45.3
20	17	1975-81	D.Miller	251	1	465	23	17	22	235	177	3.23	3.56	3.84	38.7
21	18	1964-68	B.Lee	269	7	493	25	23	63	315	196	2.70	3.24	3.87	37.7
22	24	1970-79	S.Mingori	385	2	585	18	33	42	329	225	3.03	3.65	3.99	37.1
23	7	1995-	J.Mecir	201	0	268	18	11	5	228	118	3.62	3.89	3.40	34.4
24	37	1992-	P.Quantrill	450	64	854	41	62	16	497	250	3.97	4.52	4.22	33.9
25	14	1993-	G.Lloyd	366	0	358	16	22	11	198	107	3.62	4.22	3.79	32.5
26	15	1997-	S.Hasegawa	241	8	387	25	22	16	259	150	3.84	4.31	3.82	31.8
27	44	1983-96	J.Russell	589	79	1,100	56	73	186	693	415	3.75	4.30	4.35	26.1
28	26	1994-	R.White	225	18	407	18	26	9	254	134	3.94	4.43	4.04	25.5
29	32	1973-78	S.Foucault	277	0	497	35	36	52	307	190	3.21	3.86	4.15	22.5
30	20	1981-90	R.Searage	254	0	288	11	13	11	193	137	3.50	3.75	3.90	22.4
31	35	1988-98	T.Castillo	403	6	527	28	23	22	333	179	3.93	4.56	4.20	22.2
32	29	1995-	T.Crabtree	321	0	371	21	17	5	272	136	4.05	4.66	4.09	19.6
33	39	1974-83	B.Castro	303	9	546	31	26	45	203	145	3.33	4.04	4.24	19.4
34	28	1986-90	D.Mohorcic	254	0	364	16	21	33	174	99	3.49	4.03	4.08	19.1
35	41	1991-	D.Henry	529	0	590	32	40	82	484	296	3.95	4.47	4.28	18.7
36	43	1986-97	M.Williams	619	3	691	45	58	192	660	544	3.63	4.13	4.32	18.4
37	25	1988-93	M.Schooler	260	0	292	15	29	98	248	103	3.49	3.89	4.01	17.7
38	50	1975-93	B.McClure	698	73	1,159	68	57	52	701	497	3.81	4.28	4.42	17.7
39	21	1996-	D.Patterson	228	0	257	19	12	3	179	78	4.20	4.48	3.95	17.3
40	42	1991-	M.Magnante	387	19	534	23	29	3	313	210	4.12	4.59	4.29	16.6
41	51	1969-80	S.Lockwood	420	106	1,236	57	97	68	829	490	3.55	3.92	4.44	16.5
42	22	1996-	J.Paniagua	168	14	249	14	17	9	196	134	4.16	4.37	3.97	16.2
43	38	1968-78	H.Pina	314	7	432	23	23	38	278	216	3.25	3.67	4.23	16.0
44	36	1981-85	L.Sanchez	194	1	370	28	21	27	216	145	3.75	4.11	4.22	14.7
45	47	1987-94	C.Crim	449	6	696	47	43	45	334	209	3.83	4.32	4.38	14.6
46	46	1977-86	R.Jackson	280	18	559	28	34	34	351	203	3.77	4.19	4.36	13.1
47	33	1996-	A.Levine	172	6	284	6	9	2	132	117	4.25	4.75	4.16	12.7
48	48	1962-70	D.Osinski	324	21	590	29	28	18	400	264	3.34	3.91	4.38	11.8
49	49	1982-88	E.Vande Berg	413	17	519	25	28	22	314	200	3.92	4.37	4.41	8.3
50	45	1991-96	R.Meacham	189	9	303	22	14	9	182	81	4.16	4.69	4.35	7.5

AL Expansion Teams
Relief Pitchers

V	R	Years	Name	G	GS	IP	W	L	SV	SO	BB	ERA	RA/9	R Wtd RA/9	V Runs /162
51	40	1993-99	B.Brewer	203	0	179	11	11	5	137	93	4.79	4.84	4.26	6.7
52	54	1977-84	J.McLaughlin	250	12	449	29	28	36	268	198	3.85	4.39	4.49	3.4
53	55	1962-70	B.Humphreys	319	4	566	27	21	20	364	219	3.36	3.80	4.51	2.9
54	57	1973-79	E.Rodriguez	264	39	734	42	36	32	430	323	3.89	4.27	4.53	2.4
55	53	1990-96	R.MacDonald	197	0	234	8	9	3	142	107	4.34	4.61	4.48	2.0
56	52	1996-	M.Holtz	238	0	166	13	15	3	157	82	4.49	5.09	4.46	1.8
57	60	1992-98	H.Pichardo	319	68	735	48	42	20	377	275	4.39	4.89	4.54	1.6
58	58	1975-88	D.Moore	416	4	655	43	40	89	416	186	3.67	4.23	4.54	1.5
59	56	1986-	E.Vosberg	244	3	220	10	15	13	168	105	4.34	4.88	4.52	1.0
60	59	1977-87	R.Thomas	182	13	419	20	11	7	289	196	3.82	4.36	4.54	1.0
61	61	1981-90	J.Reed	238	12	479	20	19	18	248	172	3.94	4.47	4.55	0.4
62	62	1966-72	D.Higgins	241	2	410	22	23	46	339	223	3.42	3.91	4.61	(2.3)
63	65	1979-86	P.Ladd	205	1	287	17	23	39	209	96	4.14	4.61	4.64	(2.8)
64	63	1994-	B.Wells	301	21	509	30	22	13	338	166	4.91	5.27	4.61	(2.9)
65	66	1980-87	M.Armstrong	197	1	338	19	17	11	221	155	4.10	4.53	4.66	(3.9)
66	82	1997-	M.Whisenant	189	0	158	9	8	3	114	104	5.13	5.70	5.07	(9.0)
67	64	1982-95	J.Gott	554	96	1,120	56	74	91	837	466	3.87	4.39	4.63	(9.7)
68	67	1983-92	J.Acker	467	32	904	33	49	30	482	329	3.97	4.45	4.68	(12.1)
69	73	1961-72	J.Grzenda	219	3	308	14	13	14	173	120	4.00	4.37	4.92	(12.5)
70	81	1990-	E.Gunderson	254	5	229	8	11	2	137	84	4.95	5.50	5.06	(13.1)
71	72	1988-	S.Service	284	1	362	19	19	15	361	164	4.90	5.23	4.88	(13.4)
72	76	1992-	M.Whiteside	271	1	386	18	14	9	244	145	5.02	5.46	4.96	(18.5)
73	71	1982-94	E.Nunez	427	14	652	28	36	54	508	280	4.19	4.76	4.83	(19.7)
74	77	1990-99	J.Grahe	187	39	400	22	30	45	204	182	4.41	5.01	5.00	(20.7)
75	88	1996-	E.Yan	164	23	306	15	17	1	245	125	5.76	6.02	5.24	(23.4)
76	68	1973-83	D.Bird	432	100	1,214	73	60	60	680	296	3.99	4.38	4.74	(25.6)
77	74	1990-99	R.DeLucia	320	49	624	38	51	7	502	299	4.62	5.00	4.92	(25.8)
78	78	1992-	R.Springer	333	27	514	19	32	7	473	242	5.01	5.35	5.01	(27.1)
79	70	1967-77	B.DalCanton	316	83	931	51	49	19	485	391	3.67	4.28	4.82	(27.7)
80	80	1983-94	M.Jeffcoat	255	45	500	25	26	7	242	149	4.37	4.86	5.05	(27.7)
81	69	1971-85	A.Hassler	387	112	1,123	44	71	29	630	520	3.83	4.50	4.77	(27.8)
82	75	1986-95	W.Fraser	239	57	657	38	40	7	328	238	4.47	4.85	4.94	(28.1)
83	86	1975-85	M.Stanton	277	3	384	13	22	31	304	182	4.61	5.10	5.21	(29.4)
84	84	1966-77	J.Shellenback	165	48	454	16	30	2	222	200	3.81	4.51	5.15	(30.1)
85	87	1968-76	E.Sprague	198	23	408	17	23	9	188	206	3.84	4.58	5.22	(30.2)
86	79	1992-99	B.Ayala	406	14	576	37	44	59	541	245	4.78	5.51	5.03	(32.0)
87	93	1994-	P.Spoljaric	195	12	277	8	17	4	278	163	5.52	6.36	5.71	(35.8)
88	91	1983-91	F.Wills	154	35	436	22	26	6	281	198	5.06	5.25	5.33	(37.2)
89	90	1978-90	P.Mirabella	298	33	500	19	29	13	258	239	4.45	5.12	5.30	(41.8)
90	89	1973-80	J.Montague	223	17	547	24	26	21	260	226	4.76	5.17	5.26	(42.5)
91	83	1962-71	J.Hannan	276	101	822	41	48	7	438	406	3.88	4.41	5.07	(47.1)
92	85	1966-73	C.Cox	308	59	762	39	42	20	297	234	3.70	4.45	5.18	(53.1)
93	92	1955-63	P.Burnside	196	64	567	19	36	7	303	230	4.81	5.34	5.54	(63.2)

NATIONAL LEAGUE
EXPANSION TEAMS (1962–2000)

NL expansion teams have produced 15 division titles, compared to 22 division titles by AL expansion teams. NL expansion teams have won seven pennants versus the AL expansion teams' five pennants, while tieing with three World Series champions. The 1969 Mets were the first expansion team ever to win its division, a pennant, and a World Series crown. The 1973 Mets also appeared in the World Series. It took another seven years before another National League expansion team, the Astros, won a division title. The Mets won the World Series in 1986, and the wild-card winner Marlins surprised everyone by winning a world championship in 1997 — in just their fifth season.

Tom Seaver heads up the historically strong Mets pitching, which includes Jerry Koosman, Dwight Gooden, David Cone, Jon Matlack, Sid Fernandez, Jesse Orosco, and Tug McGraw. Mets hitters include Darryl Strawberry, Howard Johnson, Gary Carter, Keith Hernandez, Kevin McReynolds, and Mike Piazza.

Early Astros teams centered around the pitching of Larry Dierker, J.R. Richard, and Don Wilson, and hitters Jimmy Wynn, Bob Watson, Doug Rader and Cesar Cedeno. Cedeno, Jose Cruz, Ken Forsch, Dave Smith, and Joe Sambito led the Astros to a division title in 1980. Jeff Bagwell and Craig Biggio paced the Astros during their most successful period in the 1990s.

Rusty Staub, Mike Marshall and Steve Rogers played for weak Expos teams in the 1970s. Rogers, Andre Dawson, Tim Raines, and Gary Carter led the Expos to a division title in 1981. Larry Walker, Moises Alou, John Wetteland, and Pedro Martinez contributed heavily to Montreal's 74–40 record in 1994.

The Padres have produced three division titles, two pennants, and one superstar in Tony Gwynn. Dave Winfield, Trevor Hoffman, and Ken Caminiti are the best of their other players.

The Rockies and their hitter-friendly park have been home to sluggers Larry Walker, Andres Galarraga, Vinnie Castilla, Todd Helton, Ellis Burks, and Dante Bichette. The Rockies and their hitters won the 1995 wild card berth.

In 1997, the Marlins featured stars Gary Sheffield, Kevin Brown, Al Leiter, Robb Nen and Moises Alou, and won the World Series. The team's owner then chopped the payroll in 1998, and the team fell into last place.

Profiled National League Expansion Players

Gary Carter

At age 32 in 1986, Carter (Montreal Expos) completed ten outstanding seasons as a catcher for the Expos and Mets. If he had continued to play at this high level for another half dozen seasons, he would have ranked with Johnny Bench as the top volume of success catchers in history. Instead, Carter's career tailed off sharply, and he spent his last six seasons as an average catcher, whose playing time dwindled after 1988.

Years	TAB	HR	BA	Adj. BA	Wtd. PRO	TF	HC
1977–86	5,847	247	.274	.276	831	865	541
All others	3,040	77	.240	.243	692	678	(21)

In his career, Carter hit .262 with 324 home runs. Adjusted for a 1 percent career hitter's deflation, he hit .265 with 334 home runs. His 802 Total Factor ranks ninth in league rate of success for catchers, while his 520 Hits Contribution ranks third in volume of success, behind Bench and Gabby Hartnett.

Jeff Bagwell

Bagwell (Houston Astros) is the best kept secret in today's game. Even though he won an MVP Award for his outstanding 1994 season, that season was tainted when cut short by the player's strike. In the past five years, Bagwell has drawn over 100 walks a year, with this number climbing to 149 in 1999. Combine this with his .305 career batting average and his 310 home runs in 6,438 total at bats, and we have a person who excels at getting on base and in driving in runs. Bagwell's .422 on-base percentage and .552 slugging average yields a 975 Production. Add speed (30 steals in 1999) and fielding (a Gold Glove in 1994), and we have the most well rounded first baseman of all time.

Bagwell is only 33 years old in 2001 and, yet, he already ranks high in historic standings for a first baseman after just 11 seasons. After adjusting for a career 4 percent hitter's inflation, Bagwell has hit .294 with 317 home runs in his career. His 976 Total Factor ranks first in league rate of success at first, while his 657 Hits Contribution also ranks first in league volume of success.

Craig Biggio

Biggio (Houston Astros) started his career as an average fielding catcher who could steal bases. Biggio switched to second base in his fifth season, and he never looked back, improving his hitting and winning four Gold Gloves.

Years	TAB	HR	BA	Adj. BA	Wtd. PRO	TF	HC
1988–91 (C)	1,840	24	.272	.277	725	740	55
1992–00 (2B)	5,942	136	.297	.284	814	865	532

The 35-year-old Biggio is hitting .291 with 160 home runs and 358 steals in his career. Adjusted for a 3 percent hitter's inflation, he hit .282 with 160 home runs. His 836 Total Factor ranks fifth in league rate of success, while his 586 Hits Contribution currently ranks fourth in league volume of success.

Tim Raines

Raines (Montreal Expos) stole 70 or more bases for six straight seasons. Even though his theft rate dropped dramatically after 1992, his 807 career steals ranks fifth all-time, and he has a career 85 percent success rate in stealing bases. Raines could also get on base, hitting .295 with 1,290 walks for a career .388 on-base percentage, and he hit 168 home runs. Adjusted for a 1 percent career hitter's inflation, he batted .292 with 174 home runs, for an 809 Wtd. Production. Adding 58 points for steals and speed, and 18 points for fielding, and Raines earned a career 886 Total Factor, the National League's 19th best rate of success. His 642 Hits Contribution ranks ninth in league volume of success.

Tony Gwynn

Forty-one-year-old Gwynn (San Diego Padres) has the best career batting average (.338) since Ted Williams retired in 1960, and the second highest career batting average since Lou Gehrig was forced to retire back in 1939. Gwynn isn't just a one-dimensional singles hitter, even though singles make up most of his 3,108 career hits. He has won five Gold Gloves, stole 318 bases, and demonstrated enough power to hit 134 home runs. Adjusted for a 1 percent hitter's inflation, Gwynn has hit .335 with 137 home runs, for an 841 Wtd. Production. His 878 Total Factor ranks 25th in league rate of success, while his 592 Hits Contribution ranks 12th in league volume of success.

Larry Walker

Thirty-four-year-old Walker (Colorado Rockies) was a promising young outfielder in his days in Montreal. Walker more than fulfilled on this promise in Colorado and, in the process, generated three of the finest hitting seasons by a National League outfielder in 1997–1999, while winning Gold Gloves each year.

Team	TAB	HR	BA	Adj. BA	Wtd. PRO	TF	HC
Expos	2,657	99	.281	.281	843	890	179
Rockies	2,916	172	.339	.318	997	1,047	412

Walker is hitting .311 with 271 home runs in his career-to-date, with 195 steals in 256 attempts. Adjusted for a 4 percent career hitter's inflation, he is hitting .300 with 274 home runs, for a 922 Wtd. Production. His 970 Total Factor ranks fourth in league rate of success for outfielders—behind Barry Bonds, Mays and Aaron. And his 591 Hits Contribution currently ranks 13th in league volume of success.

Andre Dawson

Dawson (Montreal Expos) looked the part of a Greek god while playing outfield for the Expos. Years of playing on artificial turf took their toll on Dawson's knees, and he finally begged the Cubs to sign him in 1987 for whatever price they chose. He went on to win the 1987 MVP Award for his best power season, hitting 49 home runs for the Cubs that year. As the years progressed, his aching knees limited him more and more, until Dawson was reduced to the role of DH for Boston, and part-time outfielder for Florida. Like so many other players of his generation, Hawk would have been better off on a success basis retiring years before he finally did, as the last five years shaved 10 percent off his volume of success totals.

In his career, Dawson hit .279 with 438 home runs, he stole 314 bases in 423 attempts, and he won eight Gold Glove awards. Adjusted for a 0.5 percent career hitter's deflation, he hit .281 with 459 home runs, for an 814 Wtd. Production. Add 38 speed and fielding points, and his 852 Total Factor ranks 50th in league rate of success for outfielders, while his 499 Hits Contribution ranks 18th in league volume of success.

Tom Seaver

Seaver (New York Mets) produced such wonderful statistics for the New York Mets that few people realize that he should have done much better in the win-loss columns. Seaver pitched for weak hitting Mets teams in the 1970s. If he had pitched for the Reds or Red Sox his entire career, his typical actual records of 18–12, 21–12, and 19–10 might have looked like 23–7, 26–7, and 23–6. Seaver also lost out big in the 1981 players' strike. Seaver was 14–2 at the time of the strike. He could easily have earned a 21–3 record for the Reds that year.

The key to understanding how good Seaver was is by looking at his success factors. He was 311–205 with a 2.86 ERA in his career. His 3.47 Wtd. RA/9 ranks ninth in league rate of success, while his 589 Runs/162 ranks fourth in league volume of success. Only three phenomenal pitchers — Pete Alexander, Christy Mathewson, and Warren Spahn — rank ahead of Tom Terrific in volume of success. Seaver would have rated higher in rate of success also, but he had an overall average performance in his last five seasons for the Reds, Mets, White Sox, and Red Sox, diluting his career rate of success.

David Cone

Cone (New York Mets) started out with a bang, going 20–3 with a 2.22 ERA for the Mets in 1988, leading the team to a division title. He then struggled a bit, and the Mets teams he pitched for struggled even more, resulting in a big drop in his winning percentage. Cone picked the wrong two years to make a comeback, as he was denied 20-win seasons in 1994 and 1995 due to the players' strike. It wasn't until he had a chance to pitch for four world championship Yankees teams that Cone was given the exposure he deserved. In 1998, Cone earned his second 20-win season for a Yankees team that won 114 games.

In his career-to-date, the 38-year-old Cone is 184–116 with a 3.40 ERA, and he has 2,540 strikeouts in 2,745 innings. His 3.65 Wtd. RA/9 ranks 19th in league rate of success, while his 285 Runs/162 ranks 22nd in league volume of success.

Pedro Martinez

Twenty-nine-year-old Martinez (Montreal Expos) has been so dominant that he threatens to rewrite the record books. Pitching for Montreal in 1997, he blazed to a 17–8 record and 1.90 ERA in a year with 5.5 percent hitter's inflation. In 1999, Pedro was untouchable with the Red Sox with a 23–4 record, 313 strikeouts in 213 innings, and a 2.07 ERA, despite pitching in Fenway Park in a year with a 8.5 percent hitter's inflation. In 2000, Martinez achieved the highest rate of success season in major league history with a 1.55 Wtd. RA/9, while going 18–6 with a 1.74 ERA, along with 284 strikeouts and only 32 walks in 217 innings.

In his nine-year career to date, Pedro is 125–56 with a 2.68 ERA, and with 1,818 strikeouts in 1,576 innings. His 2.84 Wtd. RA/9 is the best rate of success in major league history, surpassing even Walter Johnson and his 3.10 performance by a wide 9 percent margin. Martinez's 317 Runs/162 has him currently ranked 15th in National League rate of success.

Trevor Hoffman

Thirty-three-year-old Hoffman (San Diego Padres) is rapidly moving up the ranks of relievers. He averaged 43 saves in his past five seasons, while boasting ERAs of 2.25, 2.66, 1.48, 2.14, and 2.99. At this current pace, he will reach 500 saves in the next six seasons, which would rate him as one of the very best relievers ever. In his first eight seasons, Hoffman accumulated 271 saves, while going 40–35 with a 2.73 ERA. His Wtd. RA/9 is 2.92, which ranks him second to Houston's Billy Wagner in league rate of success. Hoffman's 111 Runs/162 currently ranks him ninth in league volume of success.

John Franco

Franco (New York Mets) has proven to be a durable pitcher, working 940 games in relief in his first 17 seasons for New York and Cincinnati, while ranking second to Lee Smith all-time in saves with 420. Although he turned 40 in 2000, Franco had enough left in his arm to climb into first place in league volume of success for relievers with 151 Runs/162. He has a 82–74 lifetime record, and a 2.68 ERA. His 3.35 Wtd. RA/9 ranks fourth in league rate of success.

NL Expansion Teams

Hitters Volume of Success

Pos	Years	Name	AB	BB	HBP	TAB	H	2B	3B	HR	BA	OB	SA	PRO	Wtd PRO	SB	CS	SBF	SPF	FF	R TF	V HC
C	1974-92	G.Carter	7,971	848	68	8,887	2,092	371	31	324	.262	.338	.439	777	784	39	42	(5)	(6)	29	802	520
1B	1991-	J.Bagwell	5,349	992	97	6,438	1,630	351	22	310	.305	.422	.552	975	938	167	64	6	10	22	976	657
2B	1988-	C.Biggio	6,766	847	169	7,782	1,969	402	43	160	.291	.384	.434	818	793	358	106	19	10	14	836	586
SS	1979-93	D.Thon	4,449	348	9	4,806	1,176	193	42	71	.264	.319	.374	693	702	167	63	8	10	0	721	133
3B	1987-	K.Caminiti	5,932	684	27	6,643	1,629	331	16	224	.275	.352	.449	801	781	88	38	2	0	17	800	280
OF	1979-99	T.Raines	8,694	1,290	41	10,025	2,561	419	112	168	.295	.388	.427	815	809	807	146	49	9	18	886	642
OF	1982-	T.Gwynn	9,186	780	24	9,990	3,108	534	84	134	.338	.392	.459	850	841	318	125	7	8	23	878	592
OF	1989-	L.Walker	4,906	578	89	5,573	1,528	335	43	271	.311	.394	.563	957	922	195	61	12	10	26	970	591
Starters		Averages	6,657	796	66	7,518	1,962	367	49	208	.295	.375	.458	834	821	267	81	12	6	19	859	500
C	1986-	B.Santiago	5,397	343	30	5,770	1,406	242	29	178	.261	.308	.415	723	709	81	60	(6)	5	20	728	142
1B	1985-	A.Galarraga	7,123	503	154	7,780	2,070	389	31	360	.291	.351	.506	856	836	124	73	(2)	2	15	851	310
2B	1992-	E.Young	3,921	447	59	4,427	1,139	195	35	49	.290	.372	.396	767	727	346	114	25	10	2	763	158
SS	1976-91	G.Templeton	7,721	375	9	8,105	2,096	329	106	70	.271	.306	.369	675	681	242	129	(3)	5	5	689	103
3B	1991-	V.Castilla	3,847	237	30	4,114	1,122	175	18	209	.292	.338	.509	847	802	23	34	(10)	0	25	817	218
OF	1976-96	A.Dawson	9,927	589	111	10,627	2,774	503	98	438	.279	.327	.482	809	814	314	109	9	3	26	852	499
OF	1988-	G.Sheffield	5,146	858	76	6,080	1,508	265	19	279	.293	.402	.515	916	884	160	77	1	10	(21)	874	411
OF	1963-77	J.Wynn	6,653	1,224	27	7,904	1,665	285	39	291	.250	.369	.436	805	827	225	101	3	10	20	859	387
Reserves		Averages	6,217	572	62	6,851	1,723	298	47	234	.277	.344	.453	797	788	189	87	2	6	11	807	279
Totals		Weighted Ave.	6,510	721	64	7,296	1,882	344	48	217	.289	.366	.457	822	810	241	83	9	6	16	841	426

Pitchers Volume of Success

Pos	Years	Name	G	GS	IP	W	L	SV	SO	BB	ERA	RA/9	Wtd RA/9	R Runs/162
SP	1967-86	T.Seaver	656	647	4,783	311	205	1	3,640	1,390	2.86	3.15	3.47	589
SP	1992-	P.Martinez	278	211	1,576	125	56	3	1,818	442	2.68	2.96	2.84	317
SP	1986-	D.Cone	420	390	2,745	184	116	1	2,540	1,067	3.40	3.72	3.65	285
SP	1973-85	S.Rogers	399	393	2,838	158	152	2	1,621	876	3.17	3.56	3.95	198
SP	1967-85	J.Koosman	612	527	3,839	222	209	17	2,556	1,198	3.36	3.77	4.12	188
Starters		Averages	473	434	3,156	200	148	5	2,435	995	3.11	3.46	3.68	316
RP	1984-	J.Franco	940	0	1,097	82	74	420	857	430	2.68	3.19	3.35	151
RP	1979-	J.Orosco	1,096	4	1,218	84	75	141	1,107	541	3.03	3.43	3.51	146
RP	1979-94	J.Reardon	880	0	1,132	73	77	367	877	358	3.16	3.39	3.58	127
RP	1993-	T.Hoffman	509	0	581	40	35	271	665	175	2.73	3.03	2.92	111
Relievers		Averages	856	1	1,007	70	65	300	877	376	2.93	3.29	3.40	134
Totals		Averages	1,329	435	4,163	270	213	305	3,312	1,371	3.07	3.42	3.62	449

NL Expansion Teams   **Hitters Rate of Success**

Pos	Years	Name	AB	BB	HBP	TAB	H	2B	3B	HR	BA	OB	SA	PRO	Wtd PRO	SB	CS	SBF	SPF	FF	R TF	V HC
C	1974-92	G.Carter	7,971	848	68	8,887	2,092	371	31	324	.262	.338	.439	777	784	39	42	(5)	(6)	29	802	520
1B	1991-	J.Bagwell	5,349	992	97	6,438	1,630	351	22	310	.305	.422	.552	975	938	167	64	6	10	22	976	657
2B	1988-	C.Biggio	6,766	847	169	7,782	1,969	402	43	160	.291	.384	.434	818	793	358	106	19	10	14	836	586
SS	1996-	N.Perez	2,346	117	3	2,466	655	106	41	36	.279	.314	.405	720	669	27	22	(7)	10	55	727	77
3B	1991-	V.Castilla	3,847	237	30	4,114	1,122	175	18	209	.292	.338	.509	847	802	23	34	(10)	0	25	817	218
OF	1989-	L.Walker	4,906	578	89	5,573	1,528	335	43	271	.311	.394	.563	957	922	195	61	12	10	26	970	591
OF	1979-99	T.Raines	8,694	1,290	41	10,025	2,561	419	112	168	.295	.388	.427	815	809	807	146	49	9	18	886	642
OF	1982-	T.Gwynn	9,186	780	24	9,990	3,108	534	84	134	.338	.392	.459	850	841	318	125	7	8	23	878	592
Starters		Averages	6,133	711	65	6,909	1,833	337	49	202	.299	.378	.468	846	828	242	75	9	6	27	870	485
C	1994-	C.Johnson	2,434	299	15	2,748	607	116	4	110	.249	.335	.436	771	725	3	6	(3)	(8)	45	758	108
1B	1997-	T.Helton	1,781	232	16	2,029	594	137	9	107	.334	.415	.601	1,016	940	15	13	(5)	0	16	951	177
2B	1995-	E.Alfonzo	2,950	345	17	3,312	874	164	14	87	.296	.373	.450	823	768	34	14	2	0	26	795	155
SS	1979-93	D.Thon	4,449	348	9	4,806	1,176	193	42	71	.264	.319	.374	693	702	167	63	8	10	0	721	133
3B	1987-	K.Caminiti	5,932	684	27	6,643	1,629	331	16	224	.275	.352	.449	801	781	88	38	2	0	17	800	280
OF	1996-	V.Guerrero	2,156	174	29	2,359	695	124	25	136	.322	.381	.592	973	904	37	30	(9)	10	(30)	875	133
OF	1988-	G.Sheffield	5,146	858	76	6,080	1,508	265	19	279	.293	.402	.515	916	884	160	77	1	10	(21)	874	411
OF	1983-	D.Strawberry	5,418	816	38	6,272	1,401	256	38	335	.259	.360	.505	865	864	221	99	3	8	(15)	860	312
Reserves		Averages	3,783	470	28	4,281	1,061	198	21	169	.280	.364	.477	841	815	91	43	(0)	4	5	824	214
Totals		Weighted Ave.	5,350	631	53	6,033	1,576	291	40	191	.295	.374	.471	845	824	191	64	6	6	19	855	395

Pitchers Rate of Success

Pos	Years	Name	G	GS	IP	W	L	SV	SO	BB	ERA	RA/9	R Wtd RA/9	V Runs /162
SP	1992-	P.Martinez	278	211	1,576	125	56	3	1,818	442	2.68	2.96	2.84	317
SP	1967-86	T.Seaver	656	647	4,783	311	205	1	3,640	1,390	2.86	3.15	3.47	589
SP	1986-	D.Cone	420	390	2,745	184	116	1	2,540	1,067	3.40	3.72	3.65	285
SP	1987-	A.Leiter	264	234	1,503	106	79	2	1,307	759	3.73	4.01	3.78	135
SP	1993-	M.Hampton	241	187	1,261	85	53	1	852	489	3.44	4.02	3.85	102
Starters		Averages	372	334	2,373	162	102	2	2,031	829	3.13	3.46	3.51	286
RP	1995-	B.Wagner	252	0	281	19	18	107	422	126	2.73	2.92	2.78	56
RP	1993-	T.Hoffman	509	0	581	40	35	271	665	175	2.73	3.03	2.92	111
RP	1984-	J.Franco	940	0	1,097	82	74	420	857	430	2.68	3.19	3.35	151
RP	1993-	R.Nen	496	4	564	35	35	226	619	218	3.08	3.50	3.37	79
Relievers		Averages	549	1	631	44	41	256	641	237	2.79	3.19	3.19	99
Totals		Averages	921	335	3,004	206	142	258	2,672	1,067	3.06	3.40	3.44	385

NL Expansion Teams
Catchers

V	R	Years	Name	AB	BB	HBP	TAB	H	2B	3B	HR	BA	OB	SA	PRO	Wtd PRO	SB	CS	SBF	SPF	FF	R TF	V HC
1	1	1974-92	G.Carter	7,971	848	68	8,887	2,092	371	31	324	.262	.338	.439	777	784	39	42	(5)	(6)	29	802	520
2	3	1986-	B.Santiago	5,397	343	30	5,770	1,406	242	29	178	.261	.308	.415	723	709	81	60	(6)	5	20	728	142
3	2	1994-	C.Johnson	2,434	299	15	2,748	607	116	4	110	.249	.335	.436	771	725	3	6	(3)	(8)	45	758	108
4	4	1990-	T.Hundley	3,224	388	28	3,640	775	148	7	172	.240	.327	.451	778	740	14	10	(1)	(2)	(18)	719	75
5	6	1989-	D.Fletcher	3,359	227	43	3,629	926	188	8	110	.276	.330	.435	764	725	2	5	(2)	(10)	5	718	74
6	5	1974-84	J.Stearns	2,681	323	25	3,029	696	152	10	46	.260	.345	.375	720	721	91	51	(2)	4	(6)	718	62
7	7	1963-81	J.Grote	4,339	399	26	4,764	1,092	160	22	39	.252	.318	.326	644	661	15	23	(6)	(5)	37	687	24
8	8	1978-91	T.Kennedy	4,979	365	16	5,360	1,313	244	12	113	.264	.316	.386	702	710	6	15	(4)	(10)	(12)	684	16
9	9	1985-	C.O'Brien	2,213	207	60	2,480	489	118	4	55	.221	.305	.352	657	641	1	10	(7)	(10)	52	676	(1)
10	10	1973-89	A.Ashby	4,123	461	11	4,595	1,010	183	13	90	.245	.323	.361	684	693	7	10	(3)	(8)	(9)	674	(8)
11	13	1991-	T.Eusebio	1,585	165	12	1,762	440	79	5	25	.278	.350	.381	731	689	1	5	(5)	(10)	(17)	657	(19)
12	11	1983-92	M.Fitzgerald	2,316	292	9	2,617	545	95	9	48	.235	.323	.346	670	677	31	20	(3)	0	(13)	661	(19)
13	12	1973-82	B.Foote	2,127	136	10	2,273	489	103	10	57	.230	.279	.368	647	653	10	6	(1)	(10)	17	658	(20)
14	14	1968-81	D.Dyer	1,993	228	19	2,240	441	74	11	30	.221	.307	.315	622	628	10	4	1	(10)	34	653	(26)
15	16	1995-	C.Widger	1,426	112	10	1,548	342	79	7	50	.240	.300	.410	710	661	10	7	(2)	(5)	(29)	625	(39)
16	15	1978-90	A.Trevino	2,430	205	19	2,654	604	117	10	23	.249	.312	.333	645	653	19	11	(1)	0	(6)	647	(39)
17	18	1960-74	C.Cannizzaro	1,950	241	7	2,198	458	66	12	18	.235	.321	.309	630	640	3	17	(13)	(10)	(13)	603	(78)
18	17	1963-72	J.Bateman	3,330	172	27	3,529	765	123	18	81	.230	.273	.350	624	641	10	10	(3)	(10)	(7)	621	(95)
19	19	1969-80	F.Kendall	2,576	189	6	2,771	603	86	11	31	.234	.288	.312	600	609	5	5	(2)	(10)	(27)	570	(145)

NL Expansion Teams
First basemen

V	R	Years	Name	AB	BB	HBP	TAB	H	2B	3B	HR	BA	OB	SA	PRO	Wtd PRO	SB	CS	SBF	SPF	FF	R TF	V HC
1	1	1991-	J.Bagwell	5,349	992	97	6,438	1,630	351	22	310	.305	.422	.552	975	938	167	64	6	10	22	976	657
2	3	1985-	A.Galarraga	7,123	503	154	7,780	2,070	389	31	360	.291	.351	.506	856	836	124	73	(2)	2	15	851	310
3	2	1997-	T.Helton	1,781	232	16	2,029	594	137	9	107	.334	.415	.601	1,016	940	15	13	(5)	0	16	951	177
4	5	1966-84	B.Watson	6,185	653	48	6,886	1,826	307	41	184	.295	.367	.447	814	823	27	28	(4)	(10)	(13)	796	101
5	4	1984-93	G.Davis	3,719	370	55	4,144	965	177	13	190	.259	.335	.467	803	812	28	11	1	(10)	(5)	799	58
6	6	1966-76	N.Colbert	3,422	383	23	3,828	833	141	25	173	.243	.324	.451	775	787	52	31	(2)	9	(9)	786	29
7	7	1990-	D.Segui	4,177	433	8	4,618	1,220	249	14	121	.292	.360	.445	805	761	15	17	(4)	(7)	18	769	(3)
8	8	1971-82	J.Milner	3,436	504	10	3,950	855	140	16	131	.249	.347	.413	760	768	31	22	(3)	4	(12)	757	(14)
9	9	1968-85	M.Jorgensen	3,421	532	25	3,978	833	132	13	95	.243	.349	.373	722	732	58	44	(7)	7	23	755	(28)
10	10	1992-	G.Colbrunn	2,416	143	45	2,604	697	130	9	81	.288	.340	.450	790	749	29	20	(4)	2	(2)	745	(32)
11	12	1998-	T.Lee	1,341	190	2	1,533	335	60	5	40	.250	.344	.391	735	684	33	5	14	10	14	722	(35)
12	11	1971-83	M.Ivie	2,694	214	17	2,925	724	133	17	81	.269	.326	.421	747	749	22	16	(4)	(4)	(11)	730	(54)
13	13	1962-79	E.Kranepool	5,436	454	14	5,904	1,418	225	25	118	.261	.319	.377	696	714	15	27	(6)	(6)	5	707	(172)

NL Expansion Teams
Second basemen

V	R	Years	Name	AB	BB	HBP	TAB	H	2B	3B	HR	BA	OB	SA	PRO	Wtd PRO	SB	CS	SBF	SPF	FF	R TF	V HC
1	1	1988-	C.Biggio	6,766	847	169	7,782	1,969	402	43	160	.291	.384	.434	818	793	358	106	19	10	14	836	586
2	3	1992-	E.Young	3,921	447	59	4,427	1,139	195	35	49	.290	.372	.396	767	727	346	114	25	10	2	763	158
3	4	1982-93	B.Doran	5,131	709	10	5,850	1,366	220	39	84	.266	.356	.373	730	738	209	93	4	8	(8)	741	157
4	2	1995-	E.Alfonzo	2,950	345	17	3,312	874	164	14	87	.296	.373	.450	823	768	34	14	2	0	26	795	155
5	9	1990-	D.DeShields	5,282	674	19	5,975	1,438	221	68	72	.272	.357	.381	737	710	430	144	23	10	(18)	725	116
6	7	1973-88	P.Garner	6,136	564	34	6,734	1,594	299	82	109	.260	.326	.389	714	721	225	105	2	6	1	730	105
7	10	1993-	M.Lansing	3,798	277	36	4,111	1,036	231	17	76	.273	.328	.403	731	690	116	35	10	9	14	723	70
8	8	1995-	Q.Veras	2,522	403	31	2,956	685	115	13	29	.272	.379	.362	741	696	176	79	6	10	12	725	57
9	13	1963-74	R.Hunt	5,235	555	243	6,033	1,429	223	23	39	.273	.369	.347	716	737	65	55	(7)	(1)	(30)	700	32
10	12	1983-93	T.Teufel	3,112	387	12	3,511	789	185	12	86	.254	.338	.404	742	745	23	19	(4)	(4)	(30)	707	28
11	6	1986-98	B.Roberts	4,147	396	30	4,573	1,220	203	31	30	.294	.360	.380	740	726	264	95	16	10	(20)	732	26
12	11	1997-	J.Vidro	1,474	116	12	1,602	437	120	5	38	.296	.353	.462	815	750	8	10	(7)	0	(25)	718	21
13	5	1983-95	R.Ready	2,110	326	12	2,448	547	107	21	40	.259	.362	.387	748	750	27	15	(2)	(0)	(16)	733	7
14	14	1996-	L.Castillo	1,606	208	1	1,815	464	53	10	4	.289	.371	.342	713	649	148	53	22	10	(6)	675	(8)
15	15	1980-93	W.Backman	3,245	371	5	3,621	893	138	19	10	.275	.350	.339	689	698	117	52	4	9	(42)	668	(35)
16	19	1986-97	C.Candaele	1,934	161	6	2,101	483	86	20	11	.250	.309	.332	641	640	37	28	(9)	3	(2)	632	(60)
17	20	1967-77	K.Boswell	2,517	240	9	2,766	625	91	19	31	.248	.316	.337	652	668	27	17	(2)	6	(40)	631	(76)
18	18	1979-89	T.Flannery	2,473	277	32	2,782	631	77	25	9	.255	.338	.317	655	662	22	22	(7)	0	(22)	632	(81)
19	17	1981-87	A.Wiggins	2,247	235	8	2,490	581	61	19	5	.259	.331	.309	640	642	242	68	40	10	(52)	640	(82)
20	21	1975-82	R.Scott	2,132	281	10	2,423	504	43	26	3	.236	.328	.285	613	612	205	62	32	10	(46)	608	(100)
21	16	1971-85	D.Thomas	4,677	456	25	5,158	1,163	154	54	43	.249	.319	.332	651	658	140	92	(8)	10	(18)	643	(169)
22	22	1975-85	D.Flynn	3,853	151	1	4,005	918	115	39	7	.238	.267	.294	561	565	20	20	(5)	0	28	588	(191)

NL Expansion Teams
Shortstops

V	R	Years	Name	AB	BB	HBP	TAB	H	2B	3B	HR	BA	OB	SA	PRO	Wtd PRO	SB	CS	SBF	SPF	FF	R TF	V HC
1	2	1979-93	D.Thon	4,449	348	9	4,806	1,176	193	42	71	.264	.319	.374	693	702	167	63	8	10	0	721	133
2	7	1976-91	G.Templeton	7,721	375	9	8,105	2,096	329	106	70	.271	.306	.369	675	681	242	129	(3)	5	5	689	103
3	1	1996-	N.Perez	2,346	117	3	2,466	655	106	41	36	.279	.314	.405	720	669	27	22	(7)	10	55	727	77
4	6	1996-	E.Renteria	2,712	242	13	2,967	767	125	11	39	.283	.344	.380	725	677	147	60	9	10	(2)	694	46
5	3	1995-	M.Loretta	1,995	196	21	2,212	582	107	11	25	.292	.361	.394	755	702	21	17	(6)	0	18	714	23
6	5	1989-	B.Spiers	3,405	354	18	3,777	921	158	35	37	.270	.342	.370	712	683	97	43	3	10	7	703	15
7	9	1983-95	S.Owen	4,930	569	15	5,514	1,211	215	59	46	.246	.326	.341	667	666	82	62	(8)	4	11	673	12
8	11	1986-	K.Elster	2,844	295	13	3,152	648	136	12	88	.228	.303	.377	680	663	14	11	(2)	3	3	667	9
9	8	1993-	K.Abbott	2,035	133	17	2,185	521	109	23	62	.256	.307	.424	731	686	21	11	(0)	7	(18)	676	7
10	10	1995-	Grudzielanek	3,269	165	56	3,490	935	179	21	35	.286	.331	.386	717	671	102	33	10	10	(22)	669	4
11	4	1992-	W.Cordero	3,329	231	45	3,605	928	209	18	95	.279	.334	.438	772	732	45	18	3	4	(31)	708	2
12	14	1987-	W.Weiss	4,686	658	40	5,384	1,207	182	31	25	.258	.354	.326	679	657	96	35	4	4	(4)	661	(3)
13	13	1965-80	B.Harrelson	4,744	633	22	5,399	1,120	136	45	7	.236	.329	.288	617	630	127	60	1	10	21	662	(3)
14	15	1983-95	T.Foley	2,708	232	7	2,947	661	134	20	32	.244	.305	.344	649	654	32	29	(8)	0	15	661	(18)
15	12	1974-88	B.Almon	3,330	250	6	3,586	846	138	25	36	.254	.307	.343	650	658	128	60	3	10	(7)	663	(22)
16	16	1975-89	C.Reynolds	4,466	227	9	4,702	1,142	143	65	42	.256	.293	.345	638	646	58	32	(1)	3	5	653	(25)
17	17	1992-	A.Arias	1,629	163	22	1,814	439	75	6	16	.269	.344	.352	696	657	9	5	(2)	0	(17)	637	(30)
18	22	1993-	T.Bogar	1,501	141	17	1,659	340	67	9	22	.227	.300	.327	627	587	13	12	(6)	10	27	618	(43)
19	19	1993-	C.Gomez	2,570	278	25	2,873	644	126	10	33	.251	.330	.346	676	640	21	22	(7)	0	(7)	626	(53)
20	21	1993-	R.Gutierrez	2,598	293	29	2,920	682	99	22	24	.263	.344	.345	689	646	45	26	(3)	6	(26)	623	(57)
21	25	1983-90	R.Santana	2,021	138	5	2,164	497	74	5	13	.246	.296	.307	603	603	3	7	(5)	0	5	603	(61)
22	24	1990-96	A.Cedeno	2,051	143	21	2,215	485	98	13	47	.236	.293	.366	659	638	26	17	(3)	4	(32)	607	(63)
23	18	1989-	J.Vizcaino	3,748	269	11	4,028	1,016	131	33	21	.271	.322	.340	662	633	64	51	(10)	3	10	635	(67)
24	26	1971-78	E.Hernandez	2,327	189	5	2,521	522	66	13	2	.224	.284	.266	550	563	129	33	24	10	3	599	(76)
25	27	1996-	R.Ordonez	2,016	129	4	2,149	489	66	11	4	.243	.289	.292	582	546	23	18	(6)	0	45	585	(79)
26	20	1970-80	R.Metzger	4,201	355	8	4,564	972	101	71	5	.231	.293	.293	585	595	83	36	2	9	18	624	(84)
27	28	1958-67	B.Lillis	2,328	99	13	2,440	549	68	9	3	.236	.271	.277	548	553	23	25	(10)	10	2	554	(132)
28	23	1970-85	T.Foli	6,047	265	35	6,347	1,515	241	20	25	.251	.286	.309	595	602	81	55	(5)	2	14	614	(155)

NL Expansion Teams
Third basemen

V	R	Years	Name	AB	BB	HBP	TAB	H	2B	3B	HR	BA	OB	SA	PRO	Wtd PRO	SB	CS	SBF	SPF	FF	R TF	V HC
1	2	1987-	K.Caminiti	5,932	684	27	6,643	1,629	331	16	224	.275	.352	.449	801	781	88	38	2	0	17	800	280
2	1	1991-	V.Castilla	3,847	237	30	4,114	1,122	175	18	209	.292	.338	.509	847	802	23	34	(10)	0	25	817	218
3	4	1967-77	D.Rader	5,186	528	40	5,754	1,302	245	39	155	.251	.325	.403	728	742	37	33	(5)	6	30	773	152
4	3	1982-95	H.Johnson	4,940	692	17	5,649	1,229	247	22	228	.249	.343	.446	789	790	231	77	13	6	(34)	775	147
5	7	1980-96	T.Wallach	8,099	649	77	8,825	2,085	432	36	260	.257	.319	.416	735	735	51	66	(9)	(9)	22	740	95
6	9	1962-78	B.Bailey	6,082	852	17	6,951	1,564	234	43	189	.257	.350	.403	753	771	85	83	(11)	(2)	(19)	740	48
7	6	1990-	S.Berry	2,413	206	32	2,651	657	153	10	81	.272	.338	.445	782	739	47	24	1	2	(2)	740	24
8	11	1974-85	A.Howe	2,626	275	9	2,910	682	139	23	43	.260	.332	.379	711	722	10	10	(4)	(6)	14	726	24
9	5	1975-92	D.Walling	2,945	308	4	3,257	799	142	30	49	.271	.341	.390	731	737	44	18	2	6	1	747	11
10	8	1986-	D.Magadan	4,031	706	11	4,748	1,165	211	13	41	.289	.396	.378	775	760	11	11	(2)	(9)	(9)	740	7
11	12	1995-	P.Nevin	1,685	178	16	1,879	442	94	4	82	.262	.338	.469	807	724	5	1	2	0	(3)	723	4
12	14	1980-91	V.Law	3,802	408	9	4,219	972	193	26	71	.256	.329	.376	705	709	34	26	(4)	0	(7)	697	(2)
13	10	1974-88	L.Parrish	6,792	529	42	7,363	1,789	360	33	256	.263	.321	.439	760	758	30	36	(5)	(5)	(21)	727	(13)
14	15	1995-	S.Andrews	1,691	190	6	1,887	374	75	4	86	.221	.302	.423	725	680	7	10	(6)	0	17	690	(24)
15	13	1969-78	W.Garrett	3,285	561	12	3,858	786	107	22	61	.239	.352	.341	693	701	38	30	(5)	7	(1)	703	(24)
16	16	1980-92	L.Salazar	4,101	179	15	4,295	1,070	144	33	94	.261	.294	.381	675	688	117	51	3	7	(7)	690	(72)
17	18	1960-69	C.Smith	2,484	130	14	2,628	594	83	18	69	.239	.281	.370	651	663	7	12	(6)	0	(8)	649	(85)
18	20	1972-82	D.Roberts	2,017	128	8	2,153	483	77	7	49	.239	.288	.357	645	651	27	8	5	7	(32)	632	(85)
19	21	1971-85	K.Bevacqua	2,117	221	5	2,343	499	90	11	27	.236	.309	.327	636	648	12	20	(11)	(6)	(31)	599	(142)
20	19	1956-71	B.Aspromonte	4,369	333	29	4,731	1,103	135	26	60	.252	.310	.336	646	663	19	24	(6)	(10)	(7)	640	(174)
21	17	1972-86	E.Cabell	5,952	259	23	6,234	1,647	263	56	60	.277	.309	.370	679	683	238	124	(2)	10	(18)	673	(197)

NL Expansion Teams
Outfielders

V	R	Years	Name	AB	BB	HBP	TAB	H	2B	3B	HR	BA	OB	SA	PRO	Wtd PRO	SB	CS	SBF	SPF	FF	R TF	V HC
1	2	1979-99	T.Raines	8,694	1,290	41	10,025	2,561	419	112	168	.295	.388	.427	815	809	807	146	49	9	18	886	642
2	3	1982-	T.Gwynn	9,186	780	24	9,990	3,108	534	84	134	.338	.392	.459	850	841	318	125	7	8	23	878	592
3	1	1989-	L.Walker	4,906	578	89	5,573	1,528	335	43	271	.311	.394	.563	957	922	195	61	12	10	26	970	591
4	10	1976-96	A.Dawson	9,927	589	111	10,627	2,774	503	98	438	.279	.327	.482	809	814	314	109	9	3	26	852	499
5	5	1988-	G.Sheffield	5,146	858	76	6,080	1,508	265	19	279	.293	.402	.515	916	884	160	77	1	10	(21)	874	411
6	8	1963-77	J.Wynn	6,653	1,224	27	7,904	1,665	285	39	291	.250	.369	.436	805	827	225	101	3	10	20	859	387
7	9	1970-86	C.Cedeno	7,310	664	56	8,030	2,087	436	60	199	.285	.350	.443	793	802	550	179	22	10	22	855	376
8	6	1983-	D.Strawberry	5,418	816	38	6,272	1,401	256	38	335	.259	.360	.505	865	864	221	99	3	8	(15)	860	312
9	13	1970-88	J.Cruz	7,917	898	7	8,822	2,251	391	94	165	.284	.358	.420	778	784	317	136	4	8	11	808	229
10	7	1990-	M.Alou	3,725	389	30	4,144	1,127	229	28	175	.303	.373	.520	893	854	76	32	2	9	(6)	859	214
11	18	1963-85	R.Staub	9,720	1,255	79	11,054	2,716	499	47	292	.279	.366	.431	797	816	47	33	(2)	(6)	(19)	790	162
12	11	1983-94	K.McReynolds	5,423	522	14	5,959	1,439	284	35	211	.265	.331	.447	779	784	93	32	5	7	17	813	159
13	14	1988-	D.Bichette	5,990	335	38	6,363	1,794	371	26	262	.299	.341	.501	842	808	150	71	1	5	(11)	803	145
14	4	1996-	V.Guerrero	2,156	174	29	2,359	695	124	25	136	.322	.381	.592	973	904	37	30	(9)	10	(30)	875	133
15	16	1989-	S.Finley	6,327	534	37	6,898	1,737	302	90	188	.275	.335	.440	774	746	254	88	10	10	26	793	121
16	12	1993-	R.White	2,823	205	43	3,071	830	167	23	103	.294	.351	.479	830	779	88	38	4	6	20	809	79
17	20	1990-	L.Gonzalez	5,096	552	65	5,713	1,434	329	44	164	.281	.359	.460	819	778	100	73	(8)	5	8	783	73
18	19	1962-73	T.Agee	3,912	342	34	4,288	999	170	27	130	.255	.321	.412	733	756	167	81	1	10	22	789	66
19	17	1993-	J.Burnitz	2,747	429	45	3,221	711	156	19	154	.259	.368	.498	866	805	48	32	(5)	0	(10)	790	51
20	15	1993-	C.Everett	2,421	242	35	2,698	682	149	16	103	.282	.355	.484	840	783	82	37	3	10	(1)	795	49
21	24	1989-	M.Grissom	6,198	451	24	6,673	1,695	285	46	145	.273	.325	.404	730	702	402	105	28	10	31	771	45
22	22	1977-91	T.Puhl	4,855	505	26	5,386	1,361	226	56	62	.280	.351	.388	740	747	217	99	4	10	13	774	44
23	21	1975-85	E.Valentine	3,166	180	7	3,353	881	169	15	123	.278	.319	.458	776	774	59	37	(5)	0	10	778	35
24	23	1972-87	J.Grubb	4,154	566	36	4,756	1,153	207	29	99	.278	.369	.413	782	785	27	33	(8)	3	(9)	771	33
25	25	1963-76	C.Jones	4,263	360	40	4,663	1,196	183	33	93	.281	.342	.404	747	766	91	48	(1)	8	(8)	765	20

NL Expansion Teams
Outfielders

V	R	Years	Name	AB	BB	HBP	TAB	H	2B	3B	HR	BA	OB	SA	PRO	Wtd PRO	SB	CS	SBF	SPF	FF	R TF	V HC
26	26	1990-	J.Conine	3,804	379	20	4,203	1,089	206	19	132	.286	.354	.455	809	771	15	14	(3)	0	(6)	761	12
27	28	1977-88	S.Henderson	3,484	386	13	3,883	976	162	49	68	.280	.354	.413	767	772	79	58	(10)	8	(11)	759	4
28	29	1971-86	D.Kingman	6,677	608	53	7,338	1,575	240	25	442	.236	.305	.478	783	790	85	49	(1)	1	(30)	759	1
29	30	1977-84	G.Richards	3,549	356	20	3,925	1,028	127	63	26	.290	.358	.383	741	748	247	89	16	10	(17)	757	1
30	27	1974-91	W.Cromartie	3,927	325	18	4,270	1,104	229	32	61	.281	.339	.402	741	748	50	37	(6)	4	12	760	(3)
31	31	1976-89	L.Mazzilli	4,124	642	20	4,786	1,068	191	24	93	.259	.361	.385	746	748	197	90	4	9	(3)	757	(8)
32	34	1991-	J.Vander Wal	1,702	244	6	1,952	448	98	12	61	.263	.358	.442	800	758	28	11	3	(1)	(9)	750	(9)
33	32	1980-91	M.Wilson	5,094	282	23	5,399	1,397	227	71	67	.274	.315	.386	701	711	327	98	22	10	10	753	(9)
34	33	1993-	C.Floyd	2,057	212	24	2,293	565	138	13	73	.275	.349	.461	810	753	82	29	10	10	(21)	752	(10)
35	35	1983-91	C.Martinez	2,906	404	11	3,321	713	134	7	108	.245	.340	.408	747	756	10	16	(6)	(5)	1	745	(24)
36	39	1990-97	P.Plantier	1,883	237	23	2,143	457	90	3	91	.243	.335	.439	773	745	13	15	(7)	(3)	(2)	733	(27)
37	41	1997-	M.Kotsay	1,655	109	1	1,765	463	80	22	31	.280	.325	.411	736	682	39	20	(1)	10	33	725	(27)
38	37	1983-95	M.Webster	3,419	325	28	3,772	900	150	55	70	.263	.332	.401	733	737	160	73	3	9	(9)	740	(31)
39	36	1982-95	K.Bass	4,839	357	37	5,233	1,308	248	40	118	.270	.325	.411	736	739	151	73	0	7	(3)	743	(37)
40	42	1970-80	E.Maddox	2,843	409	34	3,286	742	121	16	18	.261	.361	.334	694	714	60	54	(14)	8	10	718	(47)
41	38	1991-	D.Bell	4,422	352	61	4,835	1,235	229	15	129	.279	.341	.425	766	727	170	49	14	10	(16)	735	(55)
42	40	1965-77	O.Brown	3,642	314	17	3,973	964	144	11	102	.265	.326	.394	720	736	30	27	(6)	5	(8)	727	(59)
43	53	1995-	F.Santangelo	1,620	229	78	1,927	401	83	14	21	.248	.367	.355	722	681	36	17	1	7	1	691	(62)
44	47	1986-96	M.Kingery	2,034	191	7	2,232	546	108	26	30	.268	.333	.391	725	713	45	28	(6)	10	(16)	701	(65)
45	44	1985-	D.Jackson	2,629	131	11	2,771	676	114	15	80	.257	.295	.403	698	695	43	17	4	9	2	710	(66)
46	50	1993-	B.Huskey	2,078	164	4	2,246	555	98	4	86	.267	.322	.442	764	717	21	17	(5)	0	(16)	696	(66)
47	45	1965-73	R.Swoboda	2,581	299	21	2,901	624	87	24	73	.242	.325	.379	704	731	20	14	(3)	(4)	(15)	709	(67)
48	54	1987-94	G.Young	1,815	227	6	2,048	446	58	19	3	.246	.332	.304	635	649	155	73	4	10	26	689	(68)
49	48	1959-71	A.Spangler	2,267	295	11	2,573	594	87	26	21	.262	.350	.351	701	717	37	32	(10)	7	(14)	699	(71)
50	46	1967-78	C.Gaston	3,120	185	9	3,314	799	106	30	91	.256	.300	.397	696	703	13	7	(0)	5	(6)	702	(88)
51	55	1979-91	D.Heep	1,961	220	9	2,190	503	96	6	30	.257	.334	.357	692	701	12	14	(7)	(0)	(17)	677	(88)
52	52	1980-94	H.Brooks	5,974	387	38	6,399	1,608	290	31	149	.269	.318	.403	721	732	64	56	(7)	(0)	(31)	693	(89)
53	56	1989-97	E.Anthony	1,999	217	5	2,221	462	81	8	78	.231	.308	.397	705	690	24	14	(1)	0	(12)	676	(91)
54	57	1990-97	C.Carr	1,713	149	12	1,874	435	81	7	13	.254	.318	.332	650	619	144	52	21	10	17	667	(91)
55	49	1976-89	J.Youngblood	3,659	332	36	4,027	969	180	23	80	.265	.332	.392	724	736	60	55	(12)	3	(29)	697	(93)
56	58	1994-	J.Mouton	1,432	163	16	1,611	352	67	7	16	.246	.330	.336	666	624	102	38	17	10	(12)	639	(101)
57	43	1986-	D.Martinez	5,558	546	27	6,131	1,531	227	69	89	.275	.343	.389	732	708	180	91	(1)	6	1	715	(129)
58	59	1984-92	H.Winningham	1,888	157	0	2,045	452	69	26	19	.239	.298	.334	631	637	105	53	(0)	10	(23)	624	(130)
59	51	1984-95	B.Hatcher	4,339	267	55	4,661	1,146	210	30	54	.264	.315	.364	679	676	218	87	8	10	(0)	695	(143)

NL Expansion Teams
Starting Pitchers

V	R	Years	Name	G	GS	IP	W	L	SV	SO	BB	ERA	RA/9	R Wtd RA/9	V Runs /162
1	2	1967-86	T.Seaver	656	647	4,783	311	205	1	3,640	1,390	2.86	3.15	3.47	589.0
2	1	1992-	P.Martinez	278	211	1,576	125	56	3	1,818	442	2.68	2.96	2.84	317.4
3	3	1986-	D.Cone	420	390	2,745	184	116	1	2,540	1,067	3.40	3.72	3.65	285.3
4	9	1973-85	S.Rogers	399	393	2,838	158	152	2	1,621	876	3.17	3.56	3.95	198.1
5	15	1967-85	J.Koosman	612	527	3,839	222	209	17	2,556	1,198	3.36	3.77	4.12	188.1
6	10	1984-	D.Gooden	430	410	2,801	194	112	3	2,293	954	3.51	3.85	3.97	184.2
7	11	1971-83	J.Matlack	361	318	2,363	125	126	3	1,516	638	3.18	3.69	4.02	146.3
8	7	1983-97	S.Fernandez	307	300	1,867	114	96	1	1,743	715	3.36	3.61	3.89	143.7
9	4	1987-	A.Leiter	264	234	1,503	106	79	2	1,307	759	3.73	4.01	3.78	135.3
10	12	1970-86	K.Forsch	521	241	2,127	114	113	51	1,047	586	3.37	3.73	4.03	128.5
11	6	1971-80	J.Richard	238	221	1,606	107	71	0	1,493	770	3.15	3.50	3.87	123.1
12	17	1964-77	L.Dierker	356	329	2,334	139	123	1	1,493	711	3.31	3.65	4.14	109.5
13	5	1993-	M.Hampton	241	187	1,261	85	53	1	852	489	3.44	4.02	3.85	102.5
14	14	1966-74	D.Wilson	266	245	1,748	104	92	2	1,283	640	3.15	3.59	4.10	88.8
15	20	1989-	A.Benes	358	351	2,301	143	128	1	1,858	797	3.86	4.20	4.23	86.5
16	16	1991-	J.Fassero	404	217	1,595	100	91	10	1,326	557	3.89	4.41	4.13	79.3
17	8	1982-89	D.Dravecky	226	146	1,063	64	57	10	558	315	3.13	3.57	3.89	78.3
18	13	1992-	S.Reynolds	233	207	1,366	86	69	0	1,160	296	3.85	4.27	4.08	77.1
19	21	1988-	P.Harnisch	314	311	1,924	110	100	0	1,351	699	3.84	4.20	4.26	64.7
20	18	1988-	R.Reed	181	160	1,020	60	45	1	636	199	3.93	4.24	4.17	43.7
21	19	1994-	J.Hamilton	174	166	1,066	64	53	0	710	394	4.07	4.46	4.23	41.2
22	27	1979-94	B.Gullickson	398	390	2,560	162	136	0	1,279	622	3.93	4.32	4.43	37.5
23	24	1979-91	M.Scott	347	319	2,069	124	108	3	1,469	627	3.54	3.95	4.40	36.1
24	23	1980-94	B.Ojeda	351	291	1,884	115	98	1	1,128	676	3.65	4.09	4.39	35.6
25	28	1985-99	M.Portugal	346	283	1,826	109	95	5	1,134	607	4.03	4.42	4.43	25.9
26	25	1981-91	E.Show	332	235	1,655	101	89	7	971	610	3.66	4.02	4.42	25.0
27	33	1978-96	S.Sanderson	472	407	2,562	163	143	5	1,611	625	3.84	4.25	4.48	22.0
28	22	1996-	L.Hernandez	114	113	773	44	38	0	545	293	4.19	4.61	4.32	20.2
29	36	1967-88	J.Niekro	702	500	3,584	221	204	16	1,747	1,262	3.59	4.07	4.51	18.8
30	30	1991-	A.Ashby	254	241	1,542	84	87	1	1,016	457	4.10	4.61	4.46	18.2
31	32	1981-93	B.Smith	365	255	1,791	108	94	6	1,028	432	3.53	4.06	4.47	16.4
32	26	1980-88	C.Lea	152	144	923	62	48	0	535	341	3.54	3.97	4.42	14.3
33	31	1993-	B.Jones	193	190	1,216	74	56	0	714	353	4.13	4.65	4.47	12.1
34	29	1969-75	G.Gentry	157	138	903	46	49	2	615	369	3.56	3.99	4.44	11.8
35	35	1993-	B.Anderson	154	136	863	51	38	1	413	175	4.63	4.90	4.50	6.3
36	34	1995-	D.Hermanson	170	122	805	47	48	4	559	292	4.17	4.78	4.49	6.1
37	37	1974-86	V.Ruhle	327	188	1,411	67	88	11	582	348	3.73	4.30	4.56	0.2
38	39	1992-	D.Mlicki	206	148	979	51	59	1	680	364	4.41	4.87	4.58	(2.0)
39	38	1976-90	B.Knepper	445	413	2,708	146	155	1	1,473	857	3.68	4.18	4.57	(3.2)
40	40	1973-82	R.Jones	305	285	1,933	100	123	2	735	503	3.42	4.07	4.58	(4.0)
41	42	1976-85	P.Zachry	293	154	1,177	69	67	3	669	495	3.52	4.04	4.59	(4.1)
42	43	1992-	S.Hitchcock	209	175	1,067	61	62	3	841	395	4.69	5.04	4.60	(5.0)
43	41	1983-95	R.Darling	382	364	2,360	136	116	0	1,590	906	3.87	4.34	4.58	(5.2)
44	45	1973-84	C.Swan	231	185	1,236	59	72	2	673	368	3.74	4.19	4.62	(8.7)
45	46	1977-87	B.Shirley	434	162	1,432	67	94	18	790	543	3.82	4.33	4.62	(10.5)
46	44	1977-91	E.Whitson	452	333	2,240	126	123	8	1,266	698	3.79	4.20	4.60	(11.0)
47	49	1995-	C.Perez	142	127	823	40	53	0	448	211	4.44	4.93	4.68	(11.4)
48	50	1978-89	D.Palmer	212	176	1,085	64	59	2	748	434	3.78	4.27	4.68	(14.9)
49	52	1994-	J.Lima	210	122	904	53	56	5	646	203	4.87	5.13	4.73	(18.0)
50	53	1988-95	G.Harris	243	109	909	45	64	16	605	303	3.98	4.41	4.75	(20.6)

NL Expansion Teams
Starting Pitchers

V	R	Years	Name	G	GS	IP	W	L	SV	SO	BB	ERA	RA/9	R Wtd RA/9	V Runs /162
51	47	1969-81	D.Roberts	445	277	2,099	103	125	15	957	615	3.78	4.20	4.65	(20.7)
52	48	1984-95	J.Deshaies	257	253	1,525	84	95	0	951	575	4.14	4.38	4.68	(21.0)
53	56	1960-69	D.Nottebart	296	89	928	36	51	21	525	283	3.65	4.30	4.79	(24.4)
54	54	1992-	P.Rapp	228	211	1,217	65	79	0	743	612	4.66	5.13	4.76	(29.3)
55	51	1991-	D.Kile	311	283	1,853	112	104	0	1,439	825	4.27	4.76	4.70	(30.2)
56	59	1959-67	B.Bruce	219	167	1,122	49	71	1	733	340	3.85	4.42	4.85	(36.9)
57	62	1976-86	B.Owchinko	275	104	891	37	60	7	490	363	4.28	4.66	4.93	(38.1)
58	61	1980-87	E.Lynch	248	119	940	47	54	8	396	229	4.00	4.50	4.91	(38.7)
59	60	1991-	A.Reynoso	187	177	1,031	67	56	1	537	362	4.68	5.07	4.89	(39.9)
60	65	1990-98	C.Hammond	191	136	844	46	55	1	513	313	4.54	4.96	5.01	(45.1)
61	57	1983-95	D.Rasmussen	256	235	1,461	91	77	0	835	522	4.15	4.60	4.84	(45.2)
62	58	1969-76	C.Kirby	261	239	1,548	75	104	0	1,061	713	3.84	4.38	4.85	(50.6)
63	68	1974-81	N.Espinosa	140	126	820	44	55	0	338	252	4.17	4.54	5.13	(54.8)
64	55	1969-83	S.Renko	451	365	2,494	134	146	6	1,455	1,010	3.99	4.45	4.76	(57.9)
65	63	1975-84	P.Falcone	325	217	1,435	70	90	7	865	671	4.07	4.50	4.94	(62.5)
66	64	1967-74	B.Stoneman	245	170	1,236	54	85	5	934	602	4.08	4.49	5.01	(62.6)
67	69	1980-86	T.Lollar	199	131	906	47	52	4	600	480	4.27	4.56	5.16	(63.4)
68	75	1996-	J.Wright	118	116	706	32	42	0	335	349	5.22	5.72	5.48	(72.3)
69	73	1974-79	D.Freisleben	202	121	865	34	60	4	430	430	4.30	4.96	5.34	(74.9)
70	71	1990-	B.Bohanon	284	138	1,019	49	52	2	624	442	5.00	5.54	5.21	(76.2)
71	74	1993-	S.Bergman	196	117	750	39	47	0	455	272	5.28	5.87	5.45	(76.8)
72	66	1969-82	T.Griffin	401	191	1,495	77	94	5	1,054	769	4.07	4.59	5.04	(84.2)
73	76	1969-74	S.Arlin	141	123	789	34	67	1	463	373	4.33	4.91	5.56	(89.4)
74	67	1982-91	A.Hawkins	280	249	1,558	84	91	0	706	612	4.22	4.71	5.10	(94.4)
75	77	1989-98	K.Ritz	151	130	753	45	56	2	462	377	5.35	5.79	5.73	(105.2)
76	72	1959-69	A.Jackson	302	184	1,389	67	99	10	738	407	3.98	4.70	5.30	(114.8)
77	70	1959-69	J.Fisher	400	265	1,976	86	139	9	1,017	605	4.06	4.66	5.20	(141.2)

NL Expansion Teams
Relief Pitchers

V	R	Years	Name	G	GS	IP	W	L	SV	SO	BB	ERA	RA/9	R Wtd RA/9	V Runs /162
1	3	1984-	J.Franco	940	0	1,097	82	74	420	857	430	2.68	3.19	3.35	151.1
2	7	1979-	J.Orosco	1,096	4	1,218	84	75	141	1,107	541	3.03	3.43	3.51	146.0
3	10	1979-94	J.Reardon	880	0	1,132	73	77	367	877	358	3.16	3.39	3.58	127.3
4	2	1993-	T.Hoffman	509	0	581	40	35	271	665	175	2.73	3.03	2.92	110.9
5	20	1965-84	T.McGraw	824	39	1,515	96	92	180	1,109	582	3.14	3.55	3.92	109.9
6	18	1967-81	M.Marshall	723	24	1,387	97	112	188	880	514	3.14	3.56	3.87	107.2
7	6	1980-92	D.Smith	609	1	809	53	53	216	548	283	2.67	3.11	3.50	99.8
8	11	1985-	R.Myers	728	12	885	44	63	347	884	396	3.19	3.44	3.58	98.3
9	4	1993-	R.Nen	496	4	564	35	35	226	619	218	3.08	3.50	3.37	78.5
10	8	1985-92	T.Burke	498	2	699	49	33	102	444	219	2.72	3.23	3.56	77.1
11	21	1975-94	L.Andersen	699	1	995	40	39	49	758	311	3.15	3.63	3.92	73.6
12	5	1994-	D.Veres	432	0	513	26	24	75	462	185	3.32	3.63	3.41	69.0
13	14	1976-87	J.Sambito	461	5	629	37	38	84	489	195	3.03	3.45	3.66	66.1
14	9	1993-	T.Jones	459	0	531	30	28	170	486	256	3.54	3.90	3.57	62.6
15	15	1981-93	T.Leach	376	21	700	38	27	10	331	197	3.15	3.59	3.81	59.7
16	1	1995-	B.Wagner	252	0	281	19	18	107	422	126	2.73	2.92	2.78	55.5
17	30	1985-96	R.McDowell	723	2	1,050	70	70	159	524	410	3.30	3.89	4.13	50.6
18	22	1980-87	G.Lucas	409	18	669	29	44	63	410	227	3.01	3.69	3.94	49.2
19	38	1956-69	T.Farrell	590	134	1,705	106	111	83	1,177	468	3.45	3.89	4.30	48.8
20	35	1983-94	C.Lefferts	696	45	1,146	58	72	101	719	322	3.43	3.85	4.20	45.9
21	23	1992-	S.Reed	537	0	583	35	23	16	442	194	3.69	4.12	3.95	41.6
22	33	1972-83	E.Sosa	601	3	918	59	51	83	538	334	3.32	3.80	4.18	39.6
23	29	1990-99	M.Rojas	525	0	667	34	31	126	562	254	3.82	4.12	4.09	37.1
24	31	1981-91	A.McGaffigan	363	62	833	38	33	24	610	294	3.38	3.79	4.16	36.6
25	13	1995-	U.Urbina	251	21	360	29	25	110	423	161	3.43	3.80	3.65	36.4
26	19	1983-89	B.Dawley	275	0	471	27	30	25	292	166	3.42	3.67	3.90	34.6
27	27	1985-92	L.McCullers	306	9	526	28	31	39	442	252	3.25	3.74	4.00	32.7
28	28	1993-	T.Wendell	414	6	498	29	25	31	421	250	3.83	4.12	4.06	28.1
29	17	1987-93	J.Innis	288	1	360	10	20	5	192	121	3.05	3.53	3.86	27.9
30	16	1981-89	L.DeLeon	207	1	334	17	19	32	248	77	3.12	3.53	3.83	27.6
31	34	1990-	R.Rodriguez	517	2	581	26	18	7	350	232	3.75	4.17	4.19	24.6
32	12	1995-	M.Mantei	180	0	197	6	9	58	255	136	3.70	3.88	3.65	20.0
33	26	1997-	S.Kline	289	1	276	15	19	15	246	124	3.84	4.23	3.98	17.6
34	39	1967-76	D.Frisella	351	17	609	34	40	57	471	286	3.32	3.77	4.31	16.5
35	25	1997-	A.Alfonseca	216	0	244	14	20	74	158	96	3.95	4.24	3.98	15.7
36	24	1995-	A.Reyes	173	0	211	13	7	2	202	113	4.27	4.35	3.96	14.4
37	32	1995-	J.Powell	308	0	332	24	17	15	276	168	3.94	4.39	4.17	14.1
38	36	1990-	A.Telford	305	9	425	20	23	7	307	156	3.94	4.47	4.28	13.1
39	37	1991-99	T.Mathews	324	5	422	22	21	10	300	180	4.25	4.53	4.30	13.0
40	42	1989-98	X.Hernandez	463	7	671	40	35	35	562	266	3.90	4.34	4.39	12.8
41	40	1995-	D.Wall	185	37	410	31	24	2	278	131	4.01	4.50	4.32	10.9
42	47	1979-89	N.Allen	434	59	988	58	70	75	611	417	3.88	4.23	4.47	10.2
43	43	1982-91	D.Sisk	332	0	523	22	20	33	195	267	3.27	4.09	4.42	8.2
44	44	1958-71	H.Reed	229	35	515	26	29	9	268	208	3.72	3.99	4.43	7.4
45	46	1965-74	J.Ray	308	20	618	43	30	25	407	271	3.61	3.95	4.47	6.3
46	41	1991-	J.Manzanillo	148	1	206	7	8	3	177	103	4.41	4.84	4.35	5.4
47	45	1991-97	T.Scott	276	0	314	24	13	5	253	133	4.13	4.50	4.44	4.4
48	50	1993-	T.Worrell	298	49	598	25	38	7	460	235	4.29	4.74	4.50	4.0
49	48	1995-	J.Isringhausen	146	52	428	24	26	42	302	192	4.37	4.79	4.48	3.7
50	49	1993-	J.Dipoto	390	0	496	27	24	49	352	221	4.05	4.67	4.50	3.4

NL Expansion Teams
Relief Pitchers

V	R	Years	Name	G	GS	IP	W	L	SV	SO	BB	ERA	RA/9	R Wtd RA/9	V Runs /162
51	51	1995-	B.Boehringer	152	21	298	16	19	0	240	165	4.52	4.89	4.51	1.7
52	55	1962-77	D.Giusti	668	133	1,717	100	93	145	1,103	570	3.60	4.00	4.55	1.4
53	52	1994-99	J.Hudek	194	0	201	10	15	29	206	123	4.43	4.78	4.52	0.9
54	53	1995-	D.Bochtler	220	0	260	9	18	6	215	166	4.57	4.85	4.54	0.4
55	54	1989-96	S.Frey	314	0	304	18	15	28	157	154	3.76	4.41	4.55	0.4
56	56	1956-67	H.Woodeshick	427	62	847	44	62	61	484	389	3.56	4.25	4.56	0.0
57	57	1993-	O.Daal	302	92	758	40	51	1	541	301	4.49	4.86	4.56	(0.1)
58	58	1983-90	M.Thurmond	314	97	838	40	46	21	320	262	3.69	4.24	4.57	(1.3)
59	67	1990-96	A.Osuna	218	0	193	18	10	14	143	109	3.83	4.25	4.72	(3.6)
60	59	1993-	C.Leskanic	429	11	547	40	23	32	490	272	4.59	4.82	4.63	(4.3)
61	66	1991-	Y.Perez	314	0	255	14	15	1	234	133	4.56	4.95	4.72	(4.9)
62	72	1998-	V.Darensbourg	171	0	168	5	11	1	149	79	4.89	5.21	4.83	(5.0)
63	61	1975-82	T.Hausman	160	33	441	15	23	3	180	121	3.80	4.31	4.67	(6.0)
64	64	1989-96	W.Whitehurst	163	66	488	20	37	3	313	130	4.02	4.36	4.70	(8.2)
65	60	1965-74	D.Selma	307	76	840	42	54	31	681	381	3.62	4.01	4.65	(9.2)
66	62	1972-82	D.Stanhouse	294	66	760	38	54	64	408	455	3.84	4.25	4.69	(11.4)
67	65	1981-93	F.DiPino	514	6	700	35	38	56	515	269	3.83	4.27	4.71	(11.8)
68	70	1990-	D.Holmes	454	6	583	32	29	58	488	233	4.47	4.85	4.77	(14.2)
69	69	1959-71	C.Raymond	449	7	721	46	53	83	497	225	3.66	4.22	4.75	(15.1)
70	80	1997-	M.DeJean	224	1	256	14	9	4	130	110	4.95	5.44	5.09	(15.2)
71	68	1962-72	R.Taylor	491	17	800	45	43	72	464	209	3.93	4.16	4.74	(15.8)
72	63	1977-91	D.Schatzeder	504	121	1,317	69	68	10	748	475	3.74	4.22	4.69	(20.4)
73	74	1991-96	A.Young	181	51	460	15	48	20	245	167	3.89	4.75	4.92	(20.9)
74	73	1981-93	J.Agosto	543	2	626	40	33	29	307	248	4.01	4.50	4.86	(21.4)
75	71	1974-85	D.Murray	518	1	902	53	50	60	400	329	3.85	4.47	4.77	(21.5)
76	79	1972-77	T.Walker	191	17	414	18	23	11	262	142	3.87	4.66	5.08	(24.3)
77	78	1972-86	D.Tomlin	409	1	511	25	12	12	278	198	3.82	4.59	5.06	(28.8)
78	83	1992-98	R.Lewis	217	4	293	14	15	2	244	191	4.88	5.62	5.40	(29.9)
79	82	1993-	L.Painter	269	28	403	24	16	3	300	153	5.14	5.45	5.24	(33.2)
80	75	1968-77	G.Ross	283	59	714	25	47	7	378	288	3.92	4.53	4.99	(34.3)
81	77	1986-96	M.Freeman	221	78	594	35	28	5	383	249	4.64	5.05	5.06	(36.7)
82	76	1993-99	S.Sanders	235	88	682	34	45	5	632	276	4.86	5.27	5.01	(37.3)
83	85	1989-	M.Munoz	453	0	364	18	20	11	240	174	5.19	5.61	5.45	(38.6)
84	81	1984-93	M.Grant	233	58	639	22	32	8	382	235	4.31	4.71	5.11	(39.2)
85	86	1969-74	M.Corkins	157	44	459	19	28	9	335	248	4.39	5.04	5.51	(49.4)
86	84	1991-	D.Weathers	320	67	683	34	41	3	471	311	5.12	5.59	5.43	(72.6)
87	88	1975-84	F.LaCorte	253	32	490	23	44	26	372	258	5.01	5.46	5.94	(78.6)
88	89	1968-72	D.McGinn	210	28	409	15	30	10	293	225	5.11	5.70	6.30	(79.9)
89	87	1991-	B.Williams	256	59	595	26	38	6	397	332	5.37	6.06	5.83	(89.7)

NINETEENTH CENTURY PLAYERS

The final 24 years of the nineteenth century served as an incubator for major league baseball. Leagues, teams, players, and rules came and went in a whirlwind of activity. By 1900, major league baseball settled down into the game we would recognize, albeit with primitive equipment and a level of violent play that we rarely see today.

The early days of baseball were a fun time historically due to their differences from the modern game. In the beginning, there were few power hitters. The large number of errors showed what the lack of equipment will do. Starting pitchers started nearly every game, giving nineteenth century pitchers historically high volume of success rankings. At the same time, relief pitchers did not exist. Despite the differences, the early days produced many stars deserving recognition for being so much better than the average player of their day.

Profiled 1800s Players

Buck Ewing

Ewing (C) was far and away the best catcher of the 1800s. He was a superb defensive player and intelligent on-field leader, an adequate runner who mastered the art of stealing, and a solid hitter. Ewing also played significant games at first, third, and in the outfield in his 18-year career, while hitting .303 with 71 home runs in 5,764 total at bats. Adjusted for a 4 percent career hitter's deflation and a 162-game schedule, Ewing batted .316 with 98 home runs, for an 838 Wtd. Production. Ewing's 881 Total Factor ranks fourth in history in rate of success for catchers, while his 640 Hits Contribution ranks fifth in history in volume of success.

Cap Anson

The player with by far the most adjusted hits of all time was a teenage rookie at the dawn of professional baseball. Anson (1B) was a 19-year-old when he broke in with a Rockford, Illinois National Association team in the league's founding season of 1871. Anson played 27 years of professional baseball from 1871 to 1897, tieing Nolan Ryan for the most seasons played. In those 27 years, he produced 3,418 hits in 10,278 at bats, for a .333 average. Adjusted for a career 8 percent hitter's deflation and a 162 game schedule, Anson had a staggering 6,314 hits in 17,110 at bats, for a .369 average. He also hit an adjusted 1,064 doubles, 264 triples, 138 home runs, and drew 1,493 walks, for a 907 Wtd. Production, 916 Total Factor, and 1,371 Hits Contribution. These numbers would give Anson the highest volume of success for a first baseman in major league history.

This book ignores National Association results, as teams were so unstable and schedules so short that player statistics are unreliable. More than any other player, Anson's results suffer as a result of this ruling, as he loses five seasons from his spectacular career. He now becomes a 24-year-old rookie in 1876, and he plays "only" 22 years for Chicago of the National League. His statistics from 1876 to 1897 are still impressive. Anson generated 2,995 hits in 9,101 at bats, for a .329 average, and he hit 97 home runs. Adjusted for an 8 percent career hitter's deflation and a 162-game schedule, Anson had a major league record 4,818 hits in 13,362 at bats, with a .361 average and 138 home runs, for a 907 Wtd. Production. His 918 Total Factor ranks 13th in history in rate of success at first, while his 1,079 Hits Contribution is just short of Lou Gehrig's all-time 1,083 mark for the best volume of success.

Dan Brouthers

Brouthers (1B) was Cap Anson's only rival for the title of best hitter in the nineteenth century, while playing for 11 teams in 19 years. Brouthers was a big man for his day, at 6'2" and 207 pounds, and he used his strength to hit for tremendous power in his era. He had an extra-base hit every ten times at bat, and hit over 10 home runs three times in his career. In all, Brouthers hit .342 with 106 home runs in 7,656 total at bats. Adjusted for a 5.5 percent career hitter's deflation and a 162-game schedule, he batted .363 with 3,258 hits, 660 doubles, 288 triples, and 158 home runs, for a 994 Wtd. Production. His 993 Total Factor and his 1,082 Hits Contribution ranks second all time at first base, trailing only Lou Gehrig.

Roger Connor

Connor (1B) was not only the third best first baseman of the nineteenth century, but he was also the third best overall hitter of the nineteenth century behind Brouthers and Anson. Playing 18 years for New York (NL) and other teams, Connor hit .317 with 233 triples and 138 home runs, making him the home runs leader among all nineteenth century players. Adjusted for a 5 percent career hitter's deflation and a 162-game schedule, he hit .337 with 3,541 hits, 625 doubles, 332 triples, and 180 home runs, for a 926 Wtd. Production. His 933 Total Factor ranks tenth in history in rate of success at first, while his 971 Hits Contribution ranks fifth all time in volume of success at first.

Fred Dunlap

Dunlap (2B) played just 12 seasons from 1880 to 1891, yet he played at a high rate of success. Although Dunlap produced several fine seasons, it was his huge 1884 season for St. Louis of the Union Association that draws the most attention, and that season certainly helped his overall rate of success. Not as obvious is how his last four seasons substantially lowered his career rate of success:

Years	TAB	HR	BA	Adj. BA	Wtd. PRO	TF	HC
1880–87	3,318	38	.306	.349	889	947	662
1888–91	946	3	.240	.259	653	662	(13)

In his career, Dunlap hit .292 with 41 home runs. Adjusted for a brisk 14 percent career hitter's deflation and a 162-game schedule, he batted .333 with 69 home runs, for an 848 Wtd. Production. His 897 Total Factor ranks sixth in history in rate of success among second basemen, while his 649 Hits Contribution ranks tenth in

history in volume of success. If Dunlap had retired after his first eight seasons, his 947 Total Factor would have ranked third all time in rate of success at second base.

Dunlap's best season was with St. Louis (U) in 1884, a team that used his hitting and great pitching from several players to post an incredible 94–19 record. Dunlap led the league in just about every hitting statistic that year, batting .412 with 13 home runs, for a 1,069 Production. Adjusted for a steep 20 percent hitter's deflation and a 162-game schedule, Dunlap's numbers are staggering. He hit .495 with 328 hits in 662 at bats, with 69 doubles, 14 triples, and 23 home runs, for a 1,283 Wtd. Production — the second highest Wtd. Production of all time, behind Babe Ruth's 1,325 number in 1920. Add 100 Fielding Factor points, and Dunlap's 1,383 Total Factor ranks first in history in rate of success at any position, while his 241 Hits Contribution ranks second in history in volume of success at any position behind Ross Barnes' 250 Hits Contribution in 1876.

George Davis

Davis (SS/3B) began his career as an outfielder with Cleveland (NL) in 1890. He moved to third base in 1892, and was both an offensive and defensive stalwart at third with New York (NL) from 1893 to 1896. Davis then moved over to shortstop in 1897, and proved to be one of the finest shortstops ever over the remainder of his career with New York and the Chicago White Sox, even though the hitter's deflation of the Dead Ball Era impacted his raw hitting statistics. In his 20-year career, Davis hit .295 with 72 home runs and 616 stolen bases. Adjusted for a 3.5 percent career hitter's deflation and a 162-game schedule, Davis hit .305 with 3,100 hits, 526 doubles, 190 triples, and 84 home runs. His 840 Total Factor ranks seventh all-time in rate of success at short, while his 793 Hits Contribution ranks fourth all-time in volume of success.

Jack Glasscock

Glasscock (SS) was the finest shortstop to play his entire career in the 1800s, excelling at hitting, running, and defense. He broke in with Cleveland (NL) in 1879, and played 17 seasons, but never for a first place team. In his career, Glasscock hit .290 with 27 home runs in 7,531 total at bats. Adjusted for a 6 percent hitter's deflation and a 162-game schedule, Glasscock hit .309 with 3,025 hits and 39 home runs in 10,482 total at bats. His 816 Total Factor ranks 13th in history in rate of success for shortstops, while his 760 Hits Contribution ranks fifth all-time in volume of success.

Hughie Jennings

Jennings (SS) played 12 seasons from 1891 to 1902, before effectively retiring at age 33. He then made token appearances in five seasons in the 1900s, including a brief appearance at first base at age 49 while managing the 1918 Tigers. Jennings was the captain of the three title-winning Baltimore teams in 1894–1896, while hitting .335, .386, and .401. In his career, he hit .311 with 18 home runs, while stealing 359 bases in 5,538 total at bats. Adjusted for a 1 percent career hitter's inflation and a 162-game schedule, Jennings hit .309 with 21 home runs. His 846 Total Factor ranks sixth all-time in rate of success at short, while his 482 Hits Contribution ranks 17th in volume of success.

Bill Joyce

Joyce (3B) played his entire eight-year career during the 1890s. Joyce was extremely good at drawing walks, with 718 free passes in just 4,130 career total at bats. He also hit for power, with four seasons of 10 or more home runs, and seven straight seasons with more than 10 triples. Joyce hit .294 with 70 home runs and 264 steals in his career. The combination of power and ability to get on base gave him a high 902 Production number in his career. Adjusted for a 3 percent career hitter's inflation and a 162-game schedule, Joyce hit .286 with 80 home runs, for an 878 Wtd. Production. His 875 Total Factor ranks seventh all-time in rate of success at third, while his 350 Hits Contribution ranks 22nd in volume of success.

Ed Delahanty

Delahanty (OF) was the premier outfielder of the nineteenth century, and he was still going strong at the beginning of the twentieth century. In 1902, Delahanty hit .376 to win the batting title for Washington. Then, sadly, he fell off a bridge and drowned in 1903 after being kicked off a train for being a rowdy drunk, ending a 16-year career at age 35.

During his career, Delahanty hit over .400 three times, and finished with the fourth highest lifetime batting average at .346. Delahanty also hit for power, with 19 home runs in 1893, while reaching 70 extra-base hits in a season four times. In his career, he hit .346 with 2,596 hits and 101 home runs, while stealing 455 bases. Adjusted for a 1 percent career hitter's inflation and a 162-game schedule, Delahanty hit .343 with 3,013 hits, 604 doubles, 215 triples, and 118 home runs. Imagine how many adjusted hits he would have accumulated if he had played a full career! Delahanty earned a 928 Total Factor, which ranks 19th in history in rate of success for outfielders, while his 840 Hits Contribution ranks 16th in volume of success.

King Kelly

Kelly (OF/C) was one of the early stars of the game, with great speed and a batting title to his credit. The flamboyant Kelly played every position in his career from 1878 to 1893, including over a third of his games as a catcher. He also played for more winners than anyone else in his day, participating on eight championship teams with Chicago (NL), Boston (P), and Boston (NL).

In his career, Kelly hit .308 with 1,813 hits and 69 home runs. Adjusted for a 9.5 percent career hitter's deflation and a 162-game schedule, Kelly hit .342 with 3,015 hits and 103 home runs, for an 883 Wtd. Production. His 901 Total Factor ranks 34th all-time in rate of success for outfielders, while his 785 Hits Contribution ranks 19th in volume of success.

Pete Browning

Browning (OF) was a 20-year-old rookie in 1882 when he joined Louisville of the new American Association. Browning was the league's first star, leading the league in batting, on-base percentage, and slugging average, while playing second base. He spent the next two seasons playing third, short, and the outfield, before settling in the outfield for the last ten seasons of his career, and winning two more batting titles.

Browning hit .341 with 46 home runs in his career, ranking him 11th in career average. Adjusted for a 10 percent career hitter's deflation and a 162-game schedule, he hit an even more impressive .376 with 70 home runs, for a 954 Wtd. Production. His 963 Total Factor ranks 13th all-time in rate of success for outfielders, while his 717 Hits Contribution ranks 21st in volume of success.

Harry Stovey

Stovey (OF/1B) played 14 seasons for Philadelphia (AA) and other teams. Stovey played most of his games in the outfield, but he was a first baseman in three of his four best seasons in 1883–1885. A very fast player, Stovey was credited with a league-leading 97 steals in 1890. He also hit 174 triples in his career, including three seasons of 20 or more triples. And his 122 home runs represent the third best total in the 1800s, trailing only Roger Connor and Sam Thompson.

In his career, Stovey hit .289 in 6,832 total at bats. Adjusted for a 9 percent hitter's deflation and a 162 game schedule, he hit .318 with 262 triples and 181 home runs,

202   Baseball's Best Careers

for an 899 Wtd. Production. His 918 Total Factor ranks 24th in all-time rate of success in the outfield, while his 686 Hits Contribution ranks 22nd in volume of success.

Jesse Burkett

Burkett (OF) played for Cleveland (NL) and several other teams from 1890 to 1905. He won two batting titles for Cleveland with .409 and .410 averages in 1895–1896, and he also led the National League in 1901 with a .376 average for the Cardinals. Burkett had less power than many of the other star outfielders of his day, but he used his career .415 on-base percentage to score 1,720 runs in his career, compared to only 1,029 RBI.

Burkett hit .338 with 2,850 hits and 75 home runs in 9,525 total at bats. Adjusted for a 1 percent career hitter's deflation and a 162-game schedule, he hit .343 with 3,302 hits and 87 home runs. His 882 Total Factor ranks 53rd in history in rate of success for outfielders, while his 646 Hits Contribution ranks 26th in volume of success.

Sam Thompson

Thompson (OF) was at his peak production in 1894 and 1895, with a .407 average, 27 triples and 13 home runs in 1894, and a .392 average, 21 triples and 18 home runs in 1895. Back troubles took their toll the next season, and Thompson's career was effectively over in 1896 at age 36. Thompson amassed impressive statistics in 12 full seasons, hitting .331 with 160 triples and 126 home runs in 6,497 total at bats. Adjusted for a 1 percent career hitter's deflation and a 162-game schedule, he hit .335 with 197 triples and 155 home runs, for a 900 Wtd. Production. His 928 Total Factor ranks 20th all-time in rate of success for outfielders, while his 640 Hits Contribution ranks 28th in volume of success.

Billy Hamilton

Hamilton (OF) had blazing speed, leading the league with three years of more than 100 steals in 1889–1891. Hamilton also led the league with 98 steals in 1894 and 97 steals in 1895. He stole 912 bases just 14 seasons in his career, ranking him third all-time, although some of these "steals" were just his taking an extra base on a hit. Hamilton combined his speed with an amazing ability to get on base. He hit .344 in his career, ranking him seventh all-time, and he drew 1,187 walks in just 7,545 total at bats, to give him the fourth best on-base percentage in history at .455 behind Williams, Ruth, and John McGraw.

Adjusted for a 0.5 percent hitter's inflation and a 162-game schedule, Hamilton hit .343 with 47 home runs,

while stealing 1,074 bases. His 896 Total Factor ranks 38th in history in rate of success for outfielders, while his 582 Hits Contribution ranks 36th in volume of success. Note that these success factors received no benefit from any of his steals, as caught stealing data was not kept in Hamilton's day.

Cy Young

Babe Ruth may have been the best hitter, and Walter Johnson the best pitcher, but Young (SP) is the player with a major award named after him. Playing from 1890 to 1911, Young pitched successfully in both the hitter's inflation of the mid–1890s and in the depths of the Dead Ball Era of the 1900s. His ERA fluctuated with the times, with a high of 3.94 in the 15 percent hitter's inflation of 1894, and a low of 1.26 in the 18 percent hitter's deflation year of 1908, while averaging 2.63. Young holds the volume-based career records for games started (815), innings (7,356), wins (511), and losses (316). His Wtd. RA/9 of 3.44 ranks just 19th all-time in rate of success, but Young's 1,027 Runs/162 edges Walter Johnson's 1,021 number for the best all time volume of success. Of course, Young needed 24.4 percent more innings to edge Johnson by 0.6 percent in Runs/162.

Tim Keefe

Keefe (SP) was baseball's best pitcher before Cy Young. Keefe was 342–225 lifetime, with a 2.62 ERA. His 3.60 Wtd. RA/9 ranks 40th all-time in rate of success, while his 777 Runs/162 ranks third all-time behind Young and Johnson in volume of success.

Keefe holds the tainted honor of having the best single season ERA of all time at 0.86, as he only worked 105 innings in his rookie season, with a 6–6 record, and he gave up nearly twice as many unearned runs as earned runs. The problem with the Earned Run Average for these early years is that there is no way to tell how good a pitcher is, when so many of the runs scored are impacted by errors.

Old Hoss Radbourn

Radbourn (SP) is the other great pitcher before Cy Young. He didn't have quite as many wins or as much volume of success over his career as Keefe, but he made himself famous for what he accomplished in one season. Old Hoss was considered to have won 60 games for Providence (NL) in 1884, until a recent adjustment dropped the number to 59. Regardless, no one won more games in one season than Radbourn, and he was solely responsible for winning the title that year for an 84–28 Providence team. Old Hoss went 59–12, with a 1.38 ERA. His Wtd. RA/9 of 2.32 ranks 26th all-time in rate of success over a single season, while his 239.9 Runs/162 ranks second all time in volume of success behind a season by George Bradley in 1876 — and Bradley pitched every single game in the National League's initial season.

In his career, Old Hoss was 309–195 with a 2.67 ERA, 3.59 Wtd. RA/9 (39th all time), and 717 Runs/162 (fifth all time). Take away the 1884 season, and Radbourn still managed to win 250 games.

Kid Nichols

Who was the best pitcher of the 1890s? Was it Cy Young, or Nichols? Both pitchers began their careers in 1890, but it was Nichols (SP) who won more games (297 to 267), won 30 or more games more times (7 to 3), pitched for more first place clubs (5 to 0), had a better ERA (2.97 to 3.05), had a better Wtd. RA/9 (3.38 to 3.45), and saved more runs from scoring (607 to 532). Nichols entered 1900 ahead of Young in every important category, and he was only 30 years old, while Young turned 33 before the 1900 season started. But Nichols stumbled in the 1900s, and after missing two seasons in 1902 and 1903, he had his only good season in that decade in 1904, when he went 21–13 for the Cardinals. When he was done in 1906, Nichols was 361–208 in his career, with a 2.95 ERA, for a 3.50 Wtd. RA/9 that ranks 26th all time in rate of success, while his 685 Runs/162 ranks sixth in volume of success.

1876-1887　　　　　　　　　　**Hitters Volume of Success**

Pos	Years	Name	AB	BB	HBP	TAB	H	2B	3B	HR	BA	OB	SA	PRO	Wtd PRO	SB	CS	SBF	SPF	FF	R TF	V HC
C	1878-93	C.Bennett	3,821	478	11	4,310	978	203	67	55	.256	.340	.387	728	808	42	0	0	(4)	29	833	474
1B	1876-97	C.Anson	9,101	952	32	10,085	2,995	528	124	97	.329	.395	.446	841	907	247	0	(0)	(3)	15	918	1,079
2B	1879-92	H.Richardson	5,642	377	10	6,029	1,688	303	126	70	.299	.344	.435	779	844	205	0	0	5	25	875	682
SS	1879-95	J.Glasscock	7,030	439	62	7,531	2,040	313	98	27	.290	.337	.374	712	756	372	0	0	9	51	816	760
3B	1878-90	N.Williamson	4,553	506	23	5,082	1,159	228	85	64	.255	.332	.384	716	795	88	0	0	9	21	825	470
OF	1878-93	K.Kelly	5,894	549	12	6,455	1,813	359	102	69	.308	.368	.438	806	883	368	0	0	9	9	901	785
OF	1882-94	P.Browning	4,820	466	29	5,315	1,646	295	85	46	.341	.403	.467	869	954	258	0	0	8	1	963	717
OF	1880-93	H.Stovey	6,138	663	31	6,832	1,771	347	174	122	.289	.361	.461	822	899	509	0	0	10	9	918	686
Starters		Averages	5,875	554	26	6,455	1,761	322	108	69	.300	.363	.426	789	859	261	0	(0)	6	20	884	707
C	1876-83	J.Clapp	1,765	101	0	1,866	499	60	21	2	.283	.322	.344	665	781	0	0	0	(2)	1	781	204
1B	1883-90	D.Orr	3,289	98	24	3,411	1,125	198	108	37	.342	.366	.502	867	946	66	0	0	(10)	(13)	923	314
2B	1880-91	F.Dunlap	3,974	283	7	4,264	1,159	224	53	41	.292	.340	.406	745	848	85	0	0	0	49	897	649
SS	1878-94	M.Ward	7,647	420	17	8,084	2,104	231	96	26	.275	.314	.341	655	695	540	0	0	10	25	730	328
3B	1876-90	D.White	5,335	292	41	5,668	1,619	217	73	18	.303	.344	.382	726	823	46	0	(1)	(7)	(5)	810	417
OF	1876-04	J.O'Rourke	7,435	481	36	7,952	2,304	414	132	50	.310	.355	.421	776	858	191	0	2	2	(10)	853	583
OF	1876-88	C.Jones	3,687	237	34	3,958	1,101	170	98	56	.299	.347	.443	790	910	19	0	(2)	0	21	930	567
OF	1876-91	P.Hines	6,253	366	36	6,655	1,881	368	84	56	.301	.343	.413	756	853	153	0	(2)	1	4	855	505
Reserves		Averages	4,923	285	24	5,232	1,474	235	83	36	.299	.341	.403	744	829	138	0	(0)	(1)	9	837	446
Totals		Weighted Ave.	5,558	464	26	6,047	1,666	293	99	58	.300	.356	.419	776	849	220	0	(0)	3	16	869	620

Pitchers Volume of Success

Pos	Years	Name	G	GS	IP	W	L	SV	SO	BB	ERA	RA/9	R Wtd RA/9	V Runs /162
SP	1880-93	T.Keefe	600	594	5,048	342	225	2	2,560	1,236	2.62	4.40	3.60	777
SP	1881-91	O.Radbourn	528	503	4,535	309	195	2	1,830	875	2.67	4.51	3.59	717
SP	1878-87	J.McCormick	492	485	4,276	265	214	1	1,704	749	2.43	4.41	3.74	676
SP	1876-84	T.Bond	322	314	2,780	193	115	0	860	178	2.25	4.33	3.60	669
SP	1881-94	T.Mullane	555	504	4,531	284	220	15	1,803	1,408	3.05	5.01	3.86	475
SP	1878-84	M.Ward	292	261	2,462	164	102	3	920	253	2.10	4.33	3.73	450
SP	1884-90	E.Morris	311	307	2,678	171	122	1	1,217	498	2.82	4.41	3.52	401
SP	1879-92	P.Galvin	697	681	5,941	360	308	1	1,799	744	2.87	5.03	4.18	380
SP	1877-86	W.White	403	401	3,543	229	166	0	1,041	496	2.28	4.68	4.06	374
Totals		Averages (9 Starters)	467	450	3,977	257	185	3	1,526	715	2.62	4.61	3.79	547

1876-1887 **Hitters Rate of Success**

Pos	Years	Name	AB	BB	HBP	TAB	H	2B	3B	HR	BA	OB	SA	PRO	Wtd PRO	SB	CS	SBF	SPF	FF	R TF	V HC
C	1878-93	C.Bennett	3,821	478	11	4,310	978	203	67	55	.256	.340	.387	728	808	42	0	0	(4)	29	833	474
1B	1883-90	D.Orr	3,289	98	24	3,411	1,125	198	108	37	.342	.366	.502	867	946	66	0	0	(10)	(13)	923	314
2B	1876-81	R.Barnes	1,032	59	0	1,091	329	45	17	2	.319	.356	.401	757	909	0	0	0	8	8	924	289
SS	1879-95	J.Glasscock	7,030	439	62	7,531	2,040	313	98	27	.290	.337	.374	712	756	372	0	0	9	51	816	760
3B	1878-90	N.Williamson	4,553	506	23	5,082	1,159	228	85	64	.255	.332	.384	716	795	88	0	0	9	21	825	470
OF	1882-94	P.Browning	4,820	466	29	5,315	1,646	295	85	46	.341	.403	.467	869	954	258	0	0	8	1	963	717
OF	1876-88	C.Jones	3,687	237	34	3,958	1,101	170	98	56	.299	.347	.443	790	910	19	0	(2)	0	21	930	567
OF	1880-93	H.Stovey	6,138	663	31	6,832	1,771	347	174	122	.289	.361	.461	822	899	509	0	0	10	9	918	686
Starters	Averages		4,296	368	27	4,691	1,269	225	92	51	.295	.355	.426	781	859	169	0	(0)	4	16	879	535
C	1882-90	J.O'Brien	2,169	180	31	2,380	577	106	42	11	.266	.331	.369	700	800	76	0	0	0	(6)	794	160
1B	1876-97	C.Anson	9,101	952	32	10,085	2,995	528	124	97	.329	.395	.446	841	907	247	0	(0)	(3)	15	918	1,079
2B	1880-91	F.Dunlap	3,974	283	7	4,264	1,159	224	53	41	.292	.340	.406	745	848	85	0	0	0	49	897	649
SS	1884-90	F.Fennelly	3,042	378	31	3,451	781	102	82	34	.257	.345	.378	723	800	175	0	0	10	(1)	810	300
3B	1876-90	D.White	5,335	292	41	5,668	1,619	217	73	18	.303	.344	.382	726	823	46	0	(1)	(7)	(5)	810	417
OF	1878-93	K.Kelly	5,894	549	12	6,455	1,813	359	102	69	.308	.368	.438	806	883	368	0	0	9	9	901	785
OF	1881-92	E.Swartwood	2,876	325	43	3,244	861	120	63	14	.299	.379	.400	778	888	120	0	0	6	(5)	889	280
OF	1879-92	G.Gore	5,357	717	30	6,104	1,612	262	94	46	.301	.386	.411	797	877	170	0	0	0	(3)	874	487
Reserves	Averages		4,719	460	28	5,206	1,427	240	79	41	.302	.368	.413	781	865	161	0	(0)	2	7	873	520
Totals	Weighted Ave.		4,437	399	27	4,863	1,321	230	87	48	.298	.359	.421	781	861	166	0	(0)	3	13	877	530

Pitchers Rate of Success

Pos	Years	Name	G	GS	IP	W	L	SV	SO	BB	ERA	RA/9	R Wtd RA/9	V Runs /162
SP	1876-77	A.Spalding	65	61	540	48	12	1	41	26	1.78	3.97	3.13	214
SP	1884-90	E.Morris	311	307	2,678	171	122	1	1,217	498	2.82	4.41	3.52	401
SP	1881-91	O.Radbourn	528	503	4,535	309	195	2	1,830	875	2.67	4.51	3.59	717
SP	1880-93	T.Keefe	600	594	5,048	342	225	2	2,560	1,236	2.62	4.40	3.60	777
SP	1876-84	T.Bond	322	314	2,780	193	115	0	860	178	2.25	4.33	3.60	669
SP	1876-77	J.Devlin	129	129	1,181	65	60	0	263	78	1.89	4.55	3.62	319
SP	1878-84	M.Ward	292	261	2,462	164	102	3	920	253	2.10	4.33	3.73	450
SP	1878-87	J.McCormick	492	485	4,276	265	214	1	1,704	749	2.43	4.41	3.74	676
SP	1884-94	D.Foutz	251	216	1,997	147	66	4	790	510	2.84	4.81	3.74	226
Totals	Averages (9 Starters)		332	319	2,833	189	123	2	1,132	489	2.49	4.44	3.63	494

1876-1887
Catchers

V	R	Years	Name	AB	BB	HBP	TAB	H	2B	3B	HR	BA	OB	SA	PRO	Wtd PRO	SB	CS	SBF	SPF	FF	R TF	V HC
1	1	1878-93	C.Bennett	3,821	478	11	4,310	978	203	67	55	.256	.340	.387	728	808	42	0	0	(4)	29	833	474
2	3	1876-83	J.Clapp	1,765	101	0	1,866	499	60	21	2	.283	.322	.344	665	781	0	0	0	(2)	1	781	204
3	2	1882-90	J.O'Brien	2,169	180	31	2,380	577	106	42	11	.266	.331	.369	700	800	76	0	0	0	(6)	794	160
4	4	1876-84	L.Brown	1,531	45	0	1,576	379	83	31	10	.248	.269	.362	631	748	0	0	0	(10)	17	754	98
5	5	1876-91	P.Snyder	3,122	75	10	3,207	737	110	39	7	.236	.256	.303	559	639	30	0	(5)	(2)	63	695	60
6	7	1880-88	S.Trott	1,354	54	4	1,412	338	73	22	3	.250	.280	.343	623	683	9	0	0	(10)	1	674	(6)
7	6	1878-89	S.Flint	2,852	53	1	2,906	682	129	34	21	.239	.253	.330	584	662	10	0	3	(2)	13	676	(12)
8	8	1881-88	P.Deasley	1,466	49	4	1,519	358	37	9	0	.244	.271	.282	552	628	7	0	0	(10)	31	648	(33)
9	9	1879-88	B.Gilligan	1,865	147	0	2,012	386	68	23	3	.207	.265	.273	538	601	8	0	0	(0)	16	617	(94)
10	12	1884-90	K.Baldwin	1,677	36	13	1,726	371	56	27	7	.221	.243	.299	543	584	40	0	0	0	(7)	577	(102)
11	11	1876-90	D.Bushong	2,392	124	6	2,522	511	58	12	2	.214	.254	.250	505	554	39	0	0	(10)	35	580	(174)
12	13	1884-89	G.Myers	1,578	109	12	1,699	321	43	8	5	.203	.260	.250	510	561	72	0	0	(10)	(32)	520	(178)
13	10	1876-88	B.Holbert	2,335	58	3	2,396	486	41	7	0	.208	.228	.232	460	523	16	0	0	(10)	68	581	(207)

1876-1887
First basemen

V	R	Years	Name	AB	BB	HBP	TAB	H	2B	3B	HR	BA	OB	SA	PRO	Wtd PRO	SB	CS	SBF	SPF	FF	R TF	V HC
1	2	1876-97	C.Anson	9,101	952	32	10,085	2,995	528	124	97	.329	.395	.446	841	907	247	0	(0)	(3)	15	918	1,079
2	1	1883-90	D.Orr	3,289	98	24	3,411	1,125	198	108	37	.342	.366	.502	867	946	66	0	0	(10)	(13)	923	314
3	4	1880-91	L.Reilly	4,684	157	94	4,935	1,352	215	139	69	.289	.325	.438	763	839	245	0	0	10	(2)	847	240
4	3	1876-79	C.McVey	1,199	23	0	1,222	393	52	17	3	.328	.340	.407	747	876	0	0	0	8	(27)	856	174
5	5	1876-86	J.Start	3,433	150	0	3,583	1,031	107	55	7	.300	.330	.370	699	810	4	0	(1)	(9)	8	808	126
6	9	1876-90	J.Morrill	4,912	358	4	5,274	1,275	239	80	43	.260	.310	.367	677	757	61	0	0	0	4	760	54
7	6	1884-87	A.McKinnon	1,572	45	0	1,617	465	82	30	13	.296	.315	.411	726	804	16	0	0	0	2	806	39
8	8	1884-90	J.Kerins	2,227	165	14	2,406	561	72	51	20	.252	.308	.357	665	728	95	0	0	0	38	766	26
9	7	1884-91	M.McQuery	1,581	123	9	1,713	429	73	18	13	.271	.327	.365	692	763	33	0	0	3	5	770	(0)
10	11	1881-85	M.Powell	1,238	76	2	1,316	341	43	14	3	.275	.318	.340	658	742	0	0	0	0	(11)	732	(41)
11	10	1879-88	B.Phillips	4,255	178	25	4,458	1,130	214	98	17	.266	.299	.374	673	754	39	0	0	0	3	757	(42)
12	12	1876-84	T.Murnane	947	44	0	991	244	22	7	3	.258	.291	.305	596	708	0	0	0	5	(5)	708	(64)
13	17	1883-98	J.Field	1,274	77	28	1,379	292	38	21	10	.229	.288	.316	603	689	9	0	0	(0)	(13)	676	(90)
14	15	1877-84	J.Latham	1,277	35	3	1,315	317	30	17	0	.248	.270	.298	568	684	0	0	0	3	3	689	(99)
15	13	1880-89	D.Stearns	2,025	173	12	2,210	491	72	36	8	.242	.306	.325	631	703	67	0	0	10	(7)	706	(100)
16	14	1883-90	S.Farrar	3,573	233	34	3,840	905	157	53	18	.253	.305	.342	647	691	92	0	0	(1)	5	695	(183)
17	16	1882-94	C.Comiskey	5,796	197	42	6,035	1,530	206	68	29	.264	.293	.338	631	683	419	0	0	7	(2)	689	(300)

1876-1887
Second basemen

V	R	Years	Name	AB	BB	HBP	TAB	H	2B	3B	HR	BA	OB	SA	PRO	Wtd PRO	SB	CS	SBF	SPF	FF	R TF	V HC
1	3	1879-92	H.Richardson	5,642	377	10	6,029	1,688	303	126	70	.299	.344	.435	779	844	205	0	0	5	25	875	682
2	2	1880-91	F.Dunlap	3,974	283	7	4,264	1,159	224	53	41	.292	.340	.406	745	848	85	0	0	0	49	897	649
3	1	1876-81	R.Barnes	1,032	59	0	1,091	329	45	17	2	.319	.356	.401	757	909	0	0	0	8	8	924	289
4	4	1884-89	S.Barkley	2,329	176	12	2,517	602	125	39	10	.258	.314	.359	672	758	51	0	0	0	13	771	113
5	5	1876-84	B.Ferguson	2,306	113	0	2,419	625	76	20	1	.271	.305	.323	628	728	0	0	0	0	9	737	108
6	8	1880-91	P.Smith	4,238	325	60	4,623	941	141	87	24	.222	.287	.313	600	662	169	0	0	6	21	690	32
7	7	1879-89	J.Farrell	3,613	197	5	3,815	877	148	55	23	.243	.283	.333	616	703	87	0	0	0	(12)	692	29
8	6	1876-91	J.Gerhardt	3,770	162	13	3,945	854	112	51	7	.227	.261	.289	550	642	37	0	(3)	0	58	697	14
9	9	1876-91	J.Burdock	3,873	128	10	4,011	944	131	40	15	.244	.270	.310	580	667	32	0	(0)	(0)	16	682	(11)
10	10	1876-82	M.McGeary	1,252	15	0	1,267	304	19	6	0	.243	.252	.268	519	609	0	0	0	10	20	639	(66)
11	11	1878-88	B.McClellan	3,197	274	15	3,486	773	129	33	6	.242	.305	.308	613	659	132	0	0	1	(33)	627	(129)
12	13	1878-84	G.Creamer	1,862	71	2	1,935	400	55	28	1	.215	.244	.276	520	603	0	0	0	0	2	605	(137)
13	15	1880-90	S.Crane	1,359	60	1	1,420	276	30	18	3	.203	.237	.258	496	574	25	0	0	0	(37)	537	(148)
14	14	1879-85	G.Strief	1,360	64	0	1,424	281	50	14	5	.207	.242	.275	517	599	0	0	0	0	(6)	593	(149)
15	12	1878-86	J.Quest	2,282	103	3	2,388	496	77	17	1	.217	.252	.267	519	596	5	0	0	0	9	605	(165)

1876-1887
Shortstops

V	R	Years	Name	AB	BB	HBP	TAB	H	2B	3B	HR	BA	OB	SA	PRO	Wtd PRO	SB	CS	SBF	SPF	FF	R TF	V HC
1	1	1879-95	J.Glasscock	7,030	439	62	7,531	2,040	313	98	27	.290	.337	.374	712	756	372	0	0	9	51	816	760
2	8	1878-94	M.Ward	7,647	420	17	8,084	2,104	231	96	26	.275	.314	.341	655	695	540	0	0	10	25	730	328
3	2	1884-90	F.Fennelly	3,042	378	31	3,451	781	102	82	34	.257	.345	.378	723	800	175	0	0	10	(1)	810	300
4	5	1881-93	S.Wise	4,715	389	36	5,140	1,281	221	112	48	.272	.332	.397	729	765	203	0	0	(1)	(9)	755	247
5	6	1879-90	J.Rowe	4,386	224	16	4,626	1,256	202	88	28	.286	.323	.392	715	782	59	0	0	(2)	(38)	742	230
6	4	1876-84	J.Peters	2,159	22	0	2,181	594	66	10	2	.275	.282	.318	600	721	0	0	0	6	28	755	208
7	3	1876-82	G.Wright	1,494	43	0	1,537	383	54	20	2	.256	.277	.323	600	702	0	0	0	10	54	766	171
8	9	1878-90	C.Nelson	2,457	331	27	2,815	624	70	19	3	.254	.349	.302	650	730	55	0	4	0	(8)	726	99
9	7	1879-87	S.Houck	2,659	48	20	2,727	666	106	58	4	.250	.269	.338	608	705	31	0	0	10	15	730	88
10	11	1882-89	B.Gleason	3,395	177	52	3,624	907	111	35	7	.267	.313	.327	640	731	70	0	0	1	(34)	698	87
11	10	1876-84	C.Fulmer	1,422	31	0	1,453	365	48	20	6	.257	.273	.331	604	720	0	0	0	0	(1)	719	71
12	13	1884-88	B.White	1,833	125	7	1,965	441	39	37	6	.241	.292	.312	604	666	76	0	0	0	15	681	21
13	14	1880-94	A.Irwin	3,871	309	10	4,190	934	141	45	5	.241	.299	.305	604	662	93	0	0	0	14	676	19
14	12	1879-85	J.Richmond	1,600	102	5	1,707	385	43	28	5	.241	.288	.312	600	689	0	0	0	0	(4)	686	(19)
15	17	1876-79	T.Carey	1,151	8	0	1,159	288	34	6	1	.250	.255	.293	548	640	0	0	0	0	(13)	627	(48)
16	15	1879-86	J.Macullar	1,541	155	14	1,710	319	47	19	7	.207	.285	.276	561	649	23	0	0	0	(8)	642	(61)
17	18	1879-86	E.Caskin	1,871	82	0	1,953	427	50	10	2	.228	.261	.269	529	609	0	0	0	0	7	616	(85)
18	19	1884-91	C.Bastian	1,806	179	15	2,000	342	49	26	11	.189	.268	.264	532	581	57	0	0	(2)	5	584	(114)
19	16	1876-86	D.Force	2,950	131	0	3,081	623	80	15	1	.211	.245	.249	494	569	9	0	6	0	53	628	(124)

1876-1887
Third basemen

V	R	Years	Name	AB	BB	HBP	TAB	H	2B	3B	HR	BA	OB	SA	PRO	Wtd PRO	SB	CS	SBF	SPF	FF	R TF	V HC
1	1	1878-90	N.Williamson	4,553	506	23	5,082	1,159	228	85	64	.255	.332	.384	716	795	88	0	0	9	21	825	470
2	2	1876-90	D.White	5,335	292	41	5,668	1,619	217	73	18	.303	.344	.382	726	823	46	0	(1)	(7)	(5)	810	417
3	5	1880-92	T.Burns	4,920	270	8	5,198	1,299	236	69	39	.264	.303	.364	667	741	162	0	0	10	1	752	219
4	3	1876-88	E.Sutton	4,281	164	8	4,453	1,231	190	73	21	.288	.315	.381	696	774	45	0	(2)	0	(9)	763	216
5	6	1881-94	J.Denny	4,946	173	15	5,134	1,286	238	76	74	.260	.287	.384	671	716	130	0	0	0	31	747	109
6	4	1877-86	J.Gleason	1,425	95	11	1,531	384	59	14	9	.269	.320	.349	670	794	8	0	0	0	(38)	756	46
7	8	1878-85	F.Corey	1,738	60	5	1,803	427	70	43	7	.246	.273	.348	620	704	0	0	0	0	(4)	700	(18)
8	9	1876-90	J.Battin	1,435	37	1	1,473	313	34	21	3	.218	.238	.277	516	616	8	0	3	(1)	68	687	(44)
9	7	1880-91	D.Esterbrook	2,837	70	20	2,927	741	120	34	6	.261	.284	.334	618	704	55	0	0	0	5	708	(57)
10	11	1882-86	M.Muldoon	1,932	92	6	2,030	450	88	28	10	.233	.270	.323	593	670	12	0	0	0	(10)	660	(75)
11	10	1879-92	H.Carpenter	4,637	112	28	4,777	1,202	142	47	18	.259	.281	.322	603	687	158	0	0	10	(14)	683	(125)
12	15	1876-84	W.Foley	970	20	0	990	221	22	10	0	.228	.243	.271	515	600	0	0	0	0	(3)	597	(134)
13	17	1882-86	J.Farrell	1,489	35	0	1,524	345	43	15	5	.232	.249	.291	540	606	5	0	0	0	(16)	590	(134)
14	13	1878-88	F.Hankinson	3,272	170	1	3,443	747	122	39	13	.228	.267	.301	568	627	31	0	0	0	19	647	(145)
15	18	1876-79	B.Hague	1,016	17	0	1,033	246	21	2	2	.242	.255	.273	527	615	0	0	0	0	(25)	590	(155)
16	12	1883-92	W.Kuehne	4,284	137	10	4,431	996	145	115	25	.232	.258	.338	595	649	151	0	0	8	(5)	653	(170)
17	14	1884-98	J.Donnelly	2,411	170	16	2,597	552	57	28	2	.229	.284	.278	562	593	173	0	0	10	(4)	599	(184)
18	16	1880-91	A.Whitney	3,681	302	18	4,001	820	89	32	6	.223	.285	.269	554	594	67	0	0	(10)	9	593	(313)

1876-1887
Outfielders

V	R	Years	Name	AB	BB	HBP	TAB	H	2B	3B	HR	BA	OB	SA	PRO	Wtd PRO	SB	CS	SBF	SPF	FF	R TF	V HC
1	4	1878-93	K.Kelly	5,894	549	12	6,455	1,813	359	102	69	.308	.368	.438	806	883	368	0	0	9	9	901	785
2	1	1882-94	P.Browning	4,820	466	29	5,315	1,646	295	85	46	.341	.403	.467	869	954	258	0	0	8	1	963	717
3	3	1880-93	H.Stovey	6,138	663	31	6,832	1,771	347	174	122	.289	.361	.461	822	899	509	0	0	10	9	918	686
4	8	1876-04	J.O'Rourke	7,435	481	36	7,952	2,304	414	132	50	.310	.355	.421	776	858	191	0	2	2	(10)	853	583
5	2	1876-88	C.Jones	3,687	237	34	3,958	1,101	170	98	56	.299	.347	.443	790	910	19	0	(2)	0	21	930	567
6	7	1876-91	P.Hines	6,253	366	36	6,655	1,881	368	84	56	.301	.343	.413	756	853	153	0	(2)	1	4	855	505
7	6	1879-92	G.Gore	5,357	717	30	6,104	1,612	262	94	46	.301	.386	.411	797	877	170	0	0	0	(3)	874	487
8	9	1878-91	A.Dalrymple	4,172	204	8	4,384	1,202	217	81	43	.288	.323	.410	732	840	58	0	0	2	6	847	307
9	5	1881-92	E.Swartwood	2,876	325	43	3,244	861	120	63	14	.299	.379	.400	778	888	120	0	0	6	(5)	889	280
10	10	1877-90	O.Shaffer	3,442	227	5	3,674	974	162	52	10	.283	.328	.369	697	802	32	0	1	3	36	842	266
11	13	1880-92	G.Wood	5,371	418	32	5,821	1,467	228	132	68	.273	.329	.403	732	794	113	0	0	9	3	806	185
12	11	1876-85	T.York	2,733	175	10	2,918	741	174	57	10	.271	.317	.387	705	816	0	0	0	0	(1)	815	159
13	15	1882-92	C.Wolf	4,968	229	42	5,239	1,440	213	109	18	.290	.327	.387	714	789	186	0	0	0	13	801	144
14	20	1879-83	C.Foley	1,305	34	0	1,339	373	57	12	6	.286	.304	.362	666	766	0	0	0	0	(13)	754	95
15	14	1878-85	B.Dickerson	1,762	48	2	1,812	500	84	34	4	.284	.304	.377	680	797	0	0	0	0	8	805	76
16	12	1881-86	F.Lewis	1,318	60	8	1,386	390	70	13	4	.296	.330	.378	708	802	8	0	0	0	6	807	50
17	16	1884-90	J.Fogarty	2,880	351	33	3,264	709	110	55	20	.246	.335	.343	678	720	325	0	0	10	48	778	43
18	17	1882-87	F.Mann	2,277	163	43	2,483	597	104	68	12	.262	.323	.383	707	786	67	0	0	10	(23)	773	35
19	18	1879-84	M.Mansell	1,471	61	4	1,536	352	43	42	9	.239	.271	.344	615	729	0	0	0	10	22	761	4
20	30	1883-90	J.Coleman	2,508	152	10	2,670	645	88	56	7	.257	.302	.345	648	713	71	0	0	0	5	718	(1)
21	21	1877-88	D.Rowe	1,458	42	1	1,501	383	77	32	8	.263	.284	.376	660	771	4	0	0	0	(17)	753	(5)
22	19	1879-88	P.Hotaling	3,492	224	18	3,734	931	148	63	9	.267	.314	.353	667	747	78	0	0	10	(3)	754	(10)
23	22	1880-87	P.Gillespie	2,927	106	5	3,038	809	108	45	10	.276	.303	.354	657	737	54	0	0	10	3	751	(16)
24	26	1876-86	J.Clinton	1,490	82	21	1,593	393	38	19	4	.264	.311	.323	634	736	3	0	(3)	0	(0)	733	(25)
25	23	1877-85	B.Crowley	2,020	101	0	2,121	537	83	22	8	.266	.301	.341	641	740	0	0	0	0	1	741	(31)

1876-1887
Outfielders

V	R	Years	Name	AB	BB	HBP	TAB	H	2B	3B	HR	BA	OB	SA	PRO	Wtd PRO	SB	CS	SBF	SPF	FF	R TF	V HC
26	27	1882-90	C.Roseman	2,761	133	62	2,956	726	120	49	17	.263	.312	.360	672	749	19	0	0	(1)	(18)	730	(51)
27	29	1876-86	J.Manning	2,824	176	3	3,003	725	147	31	13	.257	.301	.345	646	742	24	0	(1)	3	(22)	721	(59)
28	37	1876-85	L.Knight	2,241	97	2	2,340	549	91	37	3	.245	.277	.323	600	691	0	0	0	0	4	695	(64)
29	24	1880-92	N.Hanlon	5,074	471	18	5,563	1,317	159	79	30	.260	.325	.340	664	725	329	0	0	10	5	740	(67)
30	33	1883-86	S.Brady	1,817	92	9	1,918	479	45	19	4	.264	.302	.316	618	711	16	0	1	0	(5)	707	(71)
31	25	1879-90	J.Hornung	4,784	120	14	4,918	1,230	172	90	31	.257	.277	.350	627	705	159	0	0	10	21	736	(75)
32	43	1876-84	B.Harbidge	1,302	71	0	1,373	323	44	13	2	.248	.287	.306	593	680	0	0	0	0	(25)	655	(83)
33	28	1877-90	M.Dorgan	2,924	118	4	3,046	802	112	34	4	.274	.303	.340	643	726	39	0	0	10	(12)	724	(84)
34	36	1876-84	J.Remsen	1,339	62	0	1,401	312	42	21	5	.233	.267	.307	574	676	0	0	0	0	22	697	(87)
35	35	1879-85	J.Evans	1,831	63	4	1,898	435	70	21	1	.238	.264	.300	565	640	0	0	0	10	51	701	(91)
36	41	1876-80	A.Leonard	970	20	0	990	259	26	7	1	.267	.282	.311	593	695	0	0	0	0	(27)	668	(94)
37	39	1880-88	T.Poorman	2,043	102	16	2,161	498	65	43	12	.244	.285	.335	620	676	165	0	0	8	(1)	683	(100)
38	45	1878-84	H.Wheeler	1,122	23	0	1,145	256	29	21	2	.228	.244	.297	540	643	0	0	0	0	(17)	626	(120)
39	32	1883-92	P.Corkhill	4,404	174	36	4,614	1,120	110	80	31	.254	.288	.337	625	684	137	0	0	0	31	714	(121)
40	34	1880-90	J.Sommer	3,675	238	20	3,933	911	109	42	11	.248	.297	.309	607	692	101	0	0	0	11	703	(130)
41	31	1879-90	B.Purcell	4,563	284	28	4,875	1,217	177	60	13	.267	.314	.340	654	721	197	0	0	10	(16)	715	(133)
42	44	1882-86	L.Maskrey	1,601	61	6	1,668	360	52	26	2	.225	.256	.294	550	640	4	0	0	0	7	647	(141)
43	38	1876-85	J.Cassidy	2,454	84	5	2,543	618	83	31	4	.252	.278	.316	594	696	0	0	0	2	(12)	685	(170)
44	46	1876-85	D.Eggler	1,247	25	0	1,272	279	19	9	0	.224	.239	.253	492	587	0	0	0	10	12	609	(174)
45	42	1884-91	E.Andrews	3,233	194	9	3,436	830	117	26	12	.257	.301	.320	621	668	205	0	0	0	(4)	664	(177)
46	47	1883-86	J.Lillie	1,518	23	0	1,541	332	41	11	6	.219	.230	.272	502	571	13	0	0	0	15	586	(180)
47	40	1881-90	H.Nicol	3,465	337	23	3,825	813	91	29	5	.235	.307	.282	589	649	383	0	0	10	23	682	(188)

1876-1887
Starting Pitchers

V	R	Years	Name	G	GS	IP	W	L	SV	SO	BB	ERA	RA/9	R Wtd RA/9	V Runs /162
1	4	1880-93	T.Keefe	600	594	5,048	342	225	2	2,560	1,236	2.62	4.40	3.60	777.4
2	3	1881-91	O.Radbourn	528	503	4,535	309	195	2	1,830	875	2.67	4.51	3.59	716.6
3	8	1878-87	J.McCormick	492	485	4,276	265	214	1	1,704	749	2.43	4.41	3.74	676.1
4	5	1876-84	T.Bond	322	314	2,780	193	115	0	860	178	2.25	4.33	3.60	669.2
5	12	1881-94	T.Mullane	555	504	4,531	284	220	15	1,803	1,408	3.05	5.01	3.86	475.1
6	7	1878-84	M.Ward	292	261	2,462	164	102	3	920	253	2.10	4.33	3.73	449.7
7	2	1884-90	E.Morris	311	307	2,678	171	122	1	1,217	498	2.82	4.41	3.52	401.0
8	23	1879-92	P.Galvin	697	681	5,941	360	308	1	1,799	744	2.87	5.03	4.18	380.1
9	16	1877-86	W.White	403	401	3,543	229	166	0	1,041	496	2.28	4.68	4.06	374.4
10	19	1880-92	M.Welch	564	549	4,802	307	210	4	1,850	1,297	2.71	4.79	4.10	362.3
11	10	1882-92	C.Buffinton	414	396	3,404	233	152	3	1,700	856	2.96	4.82	3.84	358.0
12	6	1876-77	J.Devlin	129	129	1,181	65	60	0	263	78	1.89	4.55	3.62	318.8
13	13	1880-87	L.Corcoran	277	268	2,392	177	89	2	1,103	496	2.36	4.64	3.87	314.1
14	9	1884-94	D.Foutz	251	216	1,997	147	66	4	790	510	2.84	4.81	3.74	226.2
15	1	1876-77	A.Spalding	65	61	540	48	12	1	41	26	1.78	3.97	3.13	214.0
16	20	1882-90	G.Hecker	336	322	2,924	175	146	1	1,110	492	2.93	5.31	4.10	206.3
17	18	1879-84	F.Goldsmith	189	185	1,610	112	68	1	433	171	2.73	4.95	4.07	154.4
18	26	1881-90	J.Whitney	413	396	3,496	191	204	2	1,571	411	2.97	5.22	4.30	151.7
19	14	1884-87	C.Ferguson	183	170	1,515	99	64	4	728	290	2.67	4.71	3.91	150.4
20	30	1876-84	G.Bradley	287	265	2,404	138	125	1	611	179	2.50	5.21	4.33	136.5
21	15	1883-87	C.Sweeney	129	123	1,031	64	52	1	505	172	2.87	4.91	3.93	106.2
22	11	1884-90	L.Baldwin	118	116	1,017	73	41	1	582	233	2.85	4.84	3.85	106.0
23	21	1884-90	D.Casey	201	198	1,680	96	90	0	743	543	3.18	5.05	4.12	102.9
24	22	1884-89	H.Boyle	207	199	1,756	89	111	1	602	378	3.06	5.04	4.17	99.2
25	24	1883-88	D.Shaw	211	207	1,762	83	121	0	950	396	3.10	5.36	4.28	77.7
26	28	1882-87	J.McGinnis	187	186	1,604	102	79	0	562	294	2.95	5.38	4.31	69.3
27	17	1881-87	B.Taylor	100	84	800	50	36	4	376	165	3.17	5.13	4.07	64.7
28	27	1882-87	H.Daily	165	163	1,415	73	87	1	846	369	2.92	5.51	4.31	61.6
29	29	1879-83	H.McCormick	103	103	884	41	58	0	157	115	2.66	5.07	4.32	46.2
30	25	1882-84	B.Sweeney	82	80	708	49	31	0	422	116	2.67	5.25	4.29	34.6
31	33	1876-80	T.Larkin	176	176	1,567	89	80	0	406	124	2.43	5.29	4.49	29.2
32	32	1885-90	T.Ramsey	248	241	2,101	114	124	0	1,515	671	3.29	5.88	4.47	23.6
33	31	1880-84	D.Driscoll	83	80	681	38	39	0	171	67	3.08	5.47	4.38	23.3
34	34	1881-90	J.Lynch	221	216	1,924	110	105	0	859	295	3.69	5.73	4.54	5.0
35	35	1884-92	C.Getzien	296	292	2,540	145	139	1	1,070	602	3.46	5.51	4.57	(6.0)
36	36	1878-86	S.Weaver	152	149	1,302	67	80	0	346	104	3.22	5.75	4.59	(9.4)
37	40	1879-82	H.Salisbury	48	48	424	24	24	0	166	48	2.55	5.52	4.71	(15.2)
38	37	1885-91	E.Daily	151	139	1,238	66	70	1	407	380	3.39	5.67	4.65	(16.0)
39	41	1876-77	C.Cummings	43	43	372	21	22	0	37	27	2.78	5.84	4.72	(17.3)
40	42	1883-85	B.Emslie	91	90	792	44	44	0	362	165	3.19	5.76	4.74	(25.0)
41	38	1883-90	E.Cushman	147	145	1,226	62	81	1	607	359	3.86	6.22	4.70	(25.6)
42	39	1884-89	H.Porter	207	206	1,793	96	107	0	659	466	3.70	6.07	4.71	(37.9)
43	45	1884-91	P.Smith	149	137	1,231	57	78	0	532	496	3.87	6.32	4.81	(42.4)
44	47	1884-86	L.McKeon	116	115	979	46	64	0	474	206	3.71	5.91	4.84	(43.2)
45	46	1885-90	A.Mays	150	147	1,251	53	89	0	469	415	3.91	6.51	4.82	(44.1)
46	50	1884-87	A.Atkinson	106	106	915	51	51	0	435	209	3.96	6.45	5.03	(62.6)
47	53	1877-82	B.Mitchell	45	44	382	20	23	0	184	73	3.18	6.30	5.20	(63.6)
48	48	1878-85	T.Nolan	79	78	676	23	52	0	274	135	2.98	5.78	4.94	(64.2)
49	59	1884-88	J.Kirby	75	75	611	18	50	0	200	258	4.09	6.64	5.37	(73.3)
50	49	1881-83	G.Derby	110	107	964	48	56	1	428	182	3.01	5.96	4.98	(85.5)

1876-1887
Starting Pitchers

V	R	Years	Name	G	GS	IP	W	L	SV	SO	BB	ERA	RA/9	R Wtd RA/9	V Runs /162
51	44	1880-88	S.Wiedman	279	269	2,318	101	156	2	910	459	3.60	5.96	4.80	(99.2)
52	51	1880-86	F.Mountain	143	142	1,216	58	83	1	383	309	3.47	6.01	5.03	(106.4)
53	58	1878-85	F.Corey	93	74	656	27	46	2	168	98	3.32	6.25	5.34	(107.5)
54	56	1885-89	P.Conway	126	123	1,040	61	61	0	428	250	3.59	6.01	5.30	(110.6)
55	61	1879-83	C.Foley	69	50	443	27	27	0	127	64	3.54	6.32	5.76	(115.1)
56	43	1876-87	B.Mathews	323	315	2,734	166	136	3	1,199	336	3.00	5.79	4.79	(128.4)
57	57	1876-82	T.Nichols	72	65	593	24	44	0	126	82	3.37	6.48	5.33	(129.4)
58	54	1883-91	B.Barr	159	152	1,328	49	98	1	588	363	3.85	6.34	5.24	(136.9)
59	55	1883-88	H.Henderson	210	206	1,788	81	121	0	930	522	3.50	6.19	5.25	(152.8)
60	60	1884-88	J.Harkins	139	137	1,183	51	83	0	489	358	4.09	7.02	5.48	(161.6)
61	52	1879-86	L.Richmond	191	179	1,583	75	100	3	552	269	3.06	5.79	5.07	(171.4)
62	63	1879-84	J.Neagle	70	68	560	16	50	0	152	141	4.59	7.69	6.35	(174.2)
63	62	1884-88	B.Serad	95	92	787	35	55	1	278	290	4.13	7.56	6.18	(193.0)
64	65	1879-87	B.Purcell	79	57	581	15	43	0	138	84	3.73	7.52	6.57	(247.2)
65	64	1883-90	J.Coleman	107	93	843	23	72	0	224	102	4.68	8.25	6.47	(276.5)

1888-1899   **Hitters Volume of Success**

Pos	Years	Name	AB	BB	HBP	TAB	H	2B	3B	HR	BA	OB	SA	PRO	Wtd PRO	SB	CS	SBF	SPF	FF	R TF	V HC
C	1880-97	B.Ewing	5,363	392	9	5,764	1,625	250	178	71	.303	.351	.456	807	838	354	0	0	(2)	45	881	640
1B	1879-04	D.Brouthers	6,711	840	105	7,656	2,296	460	205	106	.342	.423	.519	942	994	256	0	0	(0)	(1)	993	1,082
2B	1882-99	B.McPhee	8,291	981	87	9,359	2,250	303	188	53	.271	.355	.372	727	753	568	0	0	9	64	826	784
SS	1890-09	G.Davis	9,031	870	74	9,975	2,660	451	163	72	.295	.361	.404	766	793	616	0	0	10	38	840	793
3B	1885-97	D.Lyons	4,294	621	82	4,997	1,333	244	69	62	.310	.407	.443	850	864	224	0	0	1	(8)	857	391
OF	1888-03	E.Delahanty	7,505	741	94	8,340	2,596	522	185	101	.346	.411	.505	917	909	455	0	0	10	10	928	840
OF	1890-05	J.Burkett	8,421	1,029	75	9,525	2,850	320	182	75	.338	.415	.446	862	874	389	0	0	9	(1)	882	646
OF	1885-06	S.Thompson	5,984	450	63	6,497	1,979	340	160	126	.331	.384	.504	888	900	229	0	0	9	19	928	640
Starters	Averages		6,950	741	74	7,764	2,199	361	166	83	.316	.388	.452	840	861	386	0	0	6	21	887	727
C	1884-93	J.Milligan	2,964	210	36	3,210	848	189	50	49	.286	.341	.433	774	818	41	0	0	(10)	37	845	292
1B	1880-97	R.Connor	7,794	1,002	38	8,834	2,467	441	233	138	.317	.397	.486	883	926	244	0	0	0	7	933	971
2B	1888-01	C.Childs	5,618	991	63	6,672	1,720	205	100	20	.306	.416	.389	805	801	269	0	0	9	20	830	539
SS	1891-18	H.Jennings	4,904	347	287	5,538	1,527	232	88	18	.311	.390	.406	796	788	359	0	0	9	50	846	482
3B	1891-06	J.McGraw	3,924	836	132	4,892	1,309	121	70	13	.334	.465	.410	875	856	436	0	0	10	(26)	840	358
OF	1888-01	B.Hamilton	6,269	1,187	89	7,545	2,159	242	95	40	.344	.455	.432	888	883	912	0	0	10	3	896	582
OF	1891-08	J.Kelley	7,006	911	82	7,999	2,220	358	194	65	.317	.402	.451	853	858	443	0	0	9	3	870	485
OF	1885-03	J.Ryan	8,164	803	83	9,050	2,502	451	157	118	.306	.374	.444	818	826	418	0	0	4	20	851	478
Reserves	Averages		5,830	786	101	6,718	1,844	280	123	58	.316	.407	.436	843	851	390	0	0	5	14	870	523
Totals	Weighted Ave.		6,577	756	83	7,415	2,080	334	152	75	.316	.394	.447	841	857	388	0	0	5	19	881	659

Pitchers Volume of Success

Pos	Years	Name	G	GS	IP	W	L	SV	SO	BB	ERA	RA/9	R Wtd RA/9	V Runs /162
SP	1890-11	C.Young	906	815	7,356	511	316	17	2,803	1,217	2.63	3.87	3.44	1,027
SP	1890-06	K.Nichols	620	561	5,056	361	208	17	1,873	1,268	2.95	4.41	3.50	685
SP	1882-94	J.Clarkson	531	518	4,536	328	178	5	1,978	1,191	2.81	4.71	3.79	483
SP	1884-92	B.Caruthers	340	310	2,829	218	99	3	900	597	2.83	4.43	3.45	426
SP	1889-01	A.Rusie	463	427	3,779	246	174	5	1,950	1,707	3.07	4.93	3.72	413
SP	1886-97	S.King	397	371	3,182	203	153	6	1,222	967	3.18	5.10	3.83	300
SP	1891-14	C.Griffith	453	372	3,386	237	146	6	955	774	3.31	4.92	3.97	255
SP	1892-01	N.Cuppy	302	262	2,283	162	98	5	504	609	3.48	5.30	3.87	202
SP	1889-97	S.McMahon	321	305	2,634	173	127	4	967	945	3.51	5.44	4.01	187
Totals	Averages (9 Starters)		481	438	3,893	271	167	8	1,461	1,031	3.00	4.64	3.68	442

1888-1899   **Hitters Rate of Success**

Pos	Years	Name	AB	BB	HBP	TAB	H	2B	3B	HR	BA	OB	SA	PRO	Wtd PRO	SB	CS	SBF	SPF	FF	R TF	V HC
C	1880-97	B.Ewing	5,363	392	9	5,764	1,625	250	178	71	.303	.351	.456	807	838	354	0	0	(2)	45	881	640
1B	1879-04	D.Brouthers	6,711	840	105	7,656	2,296	460	205	106	.342	.423	.519	942	994	256	0	0	(0)	(1)	993	1,082
2B	1888-01	C.Childs	5,618	991	63	6,672	1,720	205	100	20	.306	.416	.389	805	801	269	0	0	9	20	830	539
SS	1891-18	H.Jennings	4,904	347	287	5,538	1,527	232	88	18	.311	.390	.406	796	788	359	0	0	9	50	846	482
3B	1890-98	B.Joyce	3,304	718	108	4,130	970	152	106	70	.294	.435	.467	902	878	264	0	0	10	(12)	875	350
OF	1888-03	E.Delahanty	7,505	741	94	8,340	2,596	522	185	101	.346	.411	.505	917	909	455	0	0	10	10	928	840
OF	1885-06	S.Thompson	5,984	450	63	6,497	1,979	340	160	126	.331	.384	.504	888	900	229	0	0	9	19	928	640
OF	1883-92	T.O'Neill	4,255	421	44	4,720	1,386	222	92	52	.326	.392	.458	850	903	161	0	0	7	(11)	899	397
Starters	Averages		5,456	613	97	6,165	1,762	298	139	71	.323	.401	.467	868	881	293	0	0	6	15	903	621
C	1884-93	J.Milligan	2,964	210	36	3,210	848	189	50	49	.286	.341	.433	774	818	41	0	0	(10)	37	845	292
1B	1880-97	R.Connor	7,794	1,002	38	8,834	2,467	441	233	138	.317	.397	.486	883	926	244	0	0	0	7	933	971
2B	1882-99	B.McPhee	8,291	981	87	9,359	2,250	303	188	53	.271	.355	.372	727	753	568	0	0	9	64	826	784
SS	1890-09	G.Davis	9,031	870	74	9,975	2,660	451	163	72	.295	.361	.404	766	793	616	0	0	10	38	840	793
3B	1885-97	D.Lyons	4,294	621	82	4,997	1,333	244	69	62	.310	.407	.443	850	864	224	0	0	1	(8)	857	391
OF	1888-01	B.Hamilton	6,269	1,187	89	7,545	2,159	242	95	40	.344	.455	.432	888	883	912	0	0	10	3	896	582
OF	1890-05	J.Burkett	8,421	1,029	75	9,525	2,850	320	182	75	.338	.415	.446	862	874	389	0	0	9	(1)	882	646
OF	1891-08	J.Kelley	7,006	911	82	7,999	2,220	358	194	65	.317	.402	.451	853	858	443	0	0	9	3	870	485
Reserves	Averages		6,759	851	70	7,681	2,098	319	147	69	.310	.393	.432	825	845	430	0	0	5	18	868	618
Totals	Weighted Ave.		5,890	692	88	6,670	1,874	305	142	70	.318	.398	.454	852	869	339	0	0	6	16	891	620

Pitchers Rate of Success

Pos	Years	Name	G	GS	IP	W	L	SV	SO	BB	ERA	RA/9	R Wtd RA/9	V Runs /162
SP	1890-11	C.Young	906	815	7,356	511	316	17	2,803	1,217	2.63	3.87	3.44	1,027
SP	1884-92	B.Caruthers	340	310	2,829	218	99	3	900	597	2.83	4.43	3.45	426
SP	1890-06	K.Nichols	620	561	5,056	361	208	17	1,873	1,268	2.95	4.41	3.50	685
SP	1885-91	E.Seward	176	169	1,486	89	72	0	589	451	3.40	4.99	3.71	164
SP	1889-01	A.Rusie	463	427	3,779	246	174	5	1,950	1,707	3.07	4.93	3.72	413
SP	1882-94	J.Clarkson	531	518	4,536	328	178	5	1,978	1,191	2.81	4.71	3.79	483
SP	1895-01	B.Hoffer	161	142	1,254	92	46	3	314	453	3.75	5.11	3.82	121
SP	1886-97	S.King	397	371	3,182	203	153	6	1,222	967	3.18	5.10	3.83	300
SP	1892-01	N.Cuppy	302	262	2,283	162	98	5	504	609	3.48	5.30	3.87	202
Totals	Averages (9 Starters)		433	397	3,529	246	149	7	1,348	940	2.97	4.58	3.63	425

1888-1899
Catchers

V	R	Years	Name	AB	BB	HBP	TAB	H	2B	3B	HR	BA	OB	SA	PRO	Wtd PRO	SB	CS	SBF	SPF	FF	R TF	V HC
1	1	1880-97	B.Ewing	5,363	392	9	5,764	1,625	250	178	71	.303	.351	.456	807	838	354	0	0	(2)		45	881	640
2	2	1884-93	J.Milligan	2,964	210	36	3,210	848	189	50	49	.286	.341	.433	774	818	41	0	0	(10)		37	845	292
3	4	1884-00	J.Clements	4,283	339	61	4,683	1,226	226	60	77	.286	.347	.421	768	787	55	0	0	(8)	(4)		775	255
4	3	1884-91	F.Carroll	2,892	348	50	3,290	820	146	66	27	.284	.370	.408	778	830	137	0	0	0	(3)		827	252
5	5	1888-05	D.Farrell	5,679	477	58	6,214	1,564	211	123	51	.275	.338	.383	721	725	150	0	0	(3)		27	749	226
6	6	1884-03	C.Zimmer	4,546	390	91	5,027	1,224	222	76	26	.269	.339	.369	708	712	151	0	0	(2)		35	745	189
7	8	1884-12	D.McGuire	6,290	515	84	6,889	1,748	300	79	45	.278	.341	.372	713	726	117	0	0	(10)		3	719	158
8	7	1880-91	J.Keenan	1,873	177	21	2,071	452	61	36	22	.241	.314	.348	661	726	41	0	0	(8)		4	723	58
9	9	1892-13	H.Peitz	4,121	409	34	4,564	1,117	191	66	16	.271	.342	.361	703	710	91	0	0	(9)		1	702	49
10	10	1886-01	P.Schriver	2,727	223	41	2,991	720	117	40	16	.264	.329	.354	683	686	46	0	0	(10)	(6)		670	(12)
11	14	1888-95	D.Buckley	1,833	98	21	1,952	449	72	14	26	.245	.291	.342	633	657	25	0	0	(10)	(2)		645	(36)
12	12	1886-02	W.Robinson	5,075	286	27	5,388	1,388	212	51	18	.273	.316	.346	662	664	196	0	0	(4)	(2)		658	(57)
13	15	1888-99	J.Grim	2,638	85	48	2,771	705	119	37	16	.267	.302	.359	661	642	82	0	0	(3)	(1)		638	(59)
14	16	1886-96	C.Mack	2,695	169	64	2,928	659	79	28	5	.245	.305	.300	605	612	127	0	0	(2)		26	636	(76)
15	18	1893-12	J.Sugden	2,726	220	33	2,979	696	72	25	3	.255	.319	.303	622	631	48	0	0	(10)		6	627	(81)
16	13	1886-99	F.Vaughn	3,454	151	14	3,619	946	147	53	21	.274	.307	.365	672	663	92	0	0	(10)		2	655	(107)
17	20	1884-96	C.Daily	2,222	208	21	2,451	541	74	22	2	.243	.314	.299	613	630	94	0	0	(10)	(21)		599	(113)
18	11	1887-10	J.O'Connor	5,380	301	35	5,716	1,417	201	66	19	.263	.307	.336	643	658	219	0	0	(3)		6	661	(136)
19	19	1893-05	B.Clarke	3,346	176	85	3,607	858	110	32	20	.256	.310	.326	637	641	54	0	0	(10)	(8)		623	(136)
20	22	1890-01	M.Murphy	1,967	157	14	2,138	443	56	12	10	.225	.287	.281	568	557	53	0	0	(7)		4	554	(147)
21	23	1889-13	J.Ryan	2,192	85	7	2,284	476	69	29	4	.217	.249	.281	529	540	32	0	0	(6)		1	534	(181)
22	17	1886-98	J.Boyle	4,222	328	59	4,609	1,067	137	54	23	.253	.315	.327	643	632	125	0	0	(2)		1	631	(213)
23	21	1890-06	M.Kittridge	4,027	314	8	4,349	882	108	31	17	.219	.277	.274	551	570	64	0	0	(10)		20	579	(233)

1888-1899
First basemen

V	R	Years	Name	AB	BB	HBP	TAB	H	2B	3B	HR	BA	OB	SA	PRO	Wtd PRO	SB	CS	SBF	SPF	FF	R TF	V HC
1	1	1879-04	D.Brouthers	6,711	840	105	7,656	2,296	460	205	106	.342	.423	.519	942	994	256	0	0	(0)		(1)	993	1,082
2	2	1880-97	R.Connor	7,794	1,002	38	8,834	2,467	441	233	138	.317	.397	.486	883	926	244	0	0	0		7	933	971
3	3	1884-93	H.Larkin	4,718	484	100	5,302	1,429	259	114	53	.303	.380	.440	819	876	129	0	0	(6)	(6)		864	302
4	4	1888-07	J.Beckley	9,526	616	183	10,325	2,930	473	243	87	.308	.361	.436	797	819	315	0	0	1	(6)		814	253
5	6	1882-90	G.Hecker	2,876	143	33	3,052	812	117	47	19	.282	.324	.376	699	775	123	0	0	(1)		6	779	234
6	5	1884-97	P.Werden	2,740	281	46	3,067	773	109	87	26	.282	.359	.414	773	793	150	0	0	2		14	810	83
7	13	1884-96	D.Foutz	4,533	300	12	4,845	1,253	186	91	31	.276	.323	.378	701	730	280	0	0	4	(4)		730	20
8	7	1890-97	E.Cartwright	1,902	202	15	2,119	562	100	44	24	.295	.368	.432	800	751	144	0	0	10		7	768	(1)
9	8	1890-94	J.Virtue	1,764	275	15	2,054	483	60	50	7	.274	.376	.376	753	780	50	0	0	(10)	(10)		759	(10)
10	10	1889-05	J.Doyle	6,039	437	49	6,525	1,806	315	64	25	.299	.351	.385	736	736	516	0	0	10		(7)	739	(13)
11	12	1895-01	B.Everett	2,842	212	15	3,069	902	85	43	11	.317	.368	.389	757	738	186	0	0	9	(16)		731	(15)
12	11	1890-93	H.Taylor	1,762	213	13	1,988	504	30	13	3	.286	.367	.323	690	722	108	0	0	7		2	732	(38)
13	17	1887-94	W.Brown	1,589	123	12	1,724	415	70	17	6	.261	.319	.338	657	656	39	0	0	(4)		7	658	(77)
14	9	1887-99	T.Tucker	6,479	479	272	7,230	1,882	240	85	42	.290	.364	.373	737	744	352	0	0	(2)		2	744	(103)
15	16	1896-04	K.Douglas	2,797	227	40	3,064	766	85	29	10	.274	.337	.336	673	683	84	0	0	(7)	(10)		667	(106)
16	15	1887-00	P.Tebeau	4,618	319	42	4,979	1,290	196	57	27	.279	.332	.364	696	680	164	0	0	(2)		12	689	(173)
17	14	1893-05	C.LaChance	4,919	219	55	5,193	1,377	197	86	39	.280	.318	.379	697	698	192	0	0	3	(5)		697	(206)

1888-1899
Second basemen

V	R	Years	Name	AB	BB	HBP	TAB	H	2B	3B	HR	BA	OB	SA	PRO	Wtd PRO	SB	CS	SBF	SPF	FF	R TF	V HC
1	2	1882-99	B.McPhee	8,291	981	87	9,359	2,250	303	188	53	.271	.355	.372	727	753	568	0	0	9	64	826	784
2	1	1888-01	C.Childs	5,618	991	63	6,672	1,720	205	100	20	.306	.416	.389	805	801	269	0	0	9	20	830	539
3	4	1882-97	F.Pfeffer	6,555	527	21	7,103	1,671	231	119	94	.255	.312	.369	682	709	382	0	0	10	52	771	384
4	5	1887-03	T.Daly	5,684	687	52	6,423	1,582	262	103	49	.278	.361	.387	748	746	385	0	0	9	(5)	750	232
5	6	1894-04	DeMontreville	3,615	174	26	3,815	1,096	130	35	17	.303	.340	.373	712	720	228	0	0	10	14	745	146
6	3	1886-92	H.Collins	2,779	332	19	3,130	790	127	38	11	.284	.365	.369	734	780	335	0	0	10	(10)	781	111
7	9	1889-98	J.Crooks	2,780	610	44	3,434	668	74	44	21	.240	.385	.321	706	715	220	0	0	9	13	736	96
8	8	1893-99	H.Reitz	2,741	266	39	3,046	800	108	65	11	.292	.363	.391	754	717	122	0	0	0	21	738	90
9	11	1890-07	B.Lowe	7,065	473	71	7,609	1,929	230	85	71	.273	.325	.360	685	693	302	0	0	9	16	718	85
10	7	1885-90	R.Mack	2,062	275	36	2,373	524	87	36	6	.254	.352	.340	692	741	83	0	0	0	3	744	78
11	10	1882-92	Y.Robinson	3,428	664	75	4,167	825	148	44	16	.241	.375	.324	699	759	272	0	0	8	(42)	724	77
12	12	1884-94	D.Richardson	4,451	283	17	4,751	1,129	149	52	32	.254	.301	.332	633	659	225	0	0	7	42	708	48
13	13	1886-98	L.Bierbauer	5,706	268	15	5,989	1,521	208	95	33	.267	.301	.354	655	662	206	0	0	0	34	696	38
14	14	1896-05	D.Padden	3,157	224	97	3,478	814	113	46	11	.258	.326	.333	660	676	132	0	0	10	5	691	16
15	15	1884-91	A.Myers	3,222	294	32	3,548	788	135	34	13	.245	.314	.320	634	681	111	0	0	2	(18)	664	(46)
16	19	1888-12	K.Gleason	7,452	500	38	7,990	1,944	216	80	15	.261	.311	.317	628	643	328	0	0	7	(0)	650	(46)
17	16	1882-93	C.Stricker	4,635	414	34	5,083	1,106	128	47	12	.239	.306	.294	600	644	278	0	0	9	9	662	(74)
18	17	1884-92	C.Bassett	3,493	239	27	3,759	806	114	49	15	.231	.285	.304	590	631	116	0	0	0	25	656	(77)
19	22	1891-99	J.O'Brien	1,910	154	35	2,099	486	47	17	12	.254	.322	.316	637	615	45	0	0	(7)	(5)	604	(96)
20	21	1882-90	B.Greenwood	2,170	201	21	2,392	490	56	26	8	.226	.298	.287	584	627	194	0	0	6	(14)	619	(96)
21	18	1888-03	B.Hallman	6,012	425	52	6,489	1,634	234	81	21	.272	.325	.348	673	669	200	0	0	0	(17)	653	(132)
22	20	1884-01	J.Quinn	6,879	364	39	7,282	1,797	228	70	29	.261	.302	.327	629	640	268	0	0	0	(13)	626	(303)

1888-1899
Shortstops

V	R	Years	Name	AB	BB	HBP	TAB	H	2B	3B	HR	BA	OB	SA	PRO	Wtd PRO	SB	CS	SBF	SPF	FF	R TF	V HC
1	2	1890-09	G.Davis	9,031	870	74	9,975	2,660	451	163	72	.295	.361	.404	766	793	616	0	0	10	38	840	793
2	1	1891-18	H.Jennings	4,904	347	287	5,538	1,527	232	88	18	.311	.390	.406	796	788	359	0	0	9	50	846	482
3	3	1889-04	H.Long	7,675	612	56	8,343	2,128	342	97	91	.277	.335	.383	718	722	536	0	0	10	23	755	429
4	4	1887-99	E.McKean	6,890	635	39	7,564	2,083	272	158	67	.302	.364	.417	781	784	323	0	0	6	(43)	747	361
5	5	1890-00	B.Allen	2,211	297	13	2,521	532	77	44	14	.241	.334	.334	668	683	53	0	0	0	56	739	108
6	7	1884-98	G.Smith	6,552	408	16	6,976	1,592	251	94	47	.243	.289	.332	620	638	235	0	0	(1)	33	670	26
7	8	1890-07	T.Corcoran	8,804	382	35	9,221	2,252	289	155	34	.256	.289	.335	625	636	387	0	0	10	18	664	5
8	6	1890-01	F.Shugart	3,014	218	31	3,263	804	110	79	22	.267	.323	.378	700	682	131	0	0	0	(10)	673	(13)
9	10	1893-96	J.Sullivan	1,648	116	48	1,812	492	45	29	11	.299	.362	.381	743	689	49	0	0	(3)	(53)	632	(57)
10	9	1888-96	S.Fuller	3,679	444	28	4,151	867	97	43	6	.236	.323	.290	613	617	260	0	0	10	9	636	(60)
11	11	1884-02	B.Ely	5,159	257	11	5,427	1,331	149	68	24	.258	.295	.327	622	610	164	0	0	1	13	624	(143)

1888-1899
Third basemen

V	R	Years	Name	AB	BB	HBP	TAB	H	2B	3B	HR	BA	OB	SA	PRO	Wtd PRO	SB	CS	SBF	SPF	FF	R TF	V HC
1	2	1885-97	D.Lyons	4,294	621	82	4,997	1,333	244	69	62	.310	.407	.443	850	864	224	0	0	1	(8)	857	391
2	3	1891-06	J.McGraw	3,924	836	132	4,892	1,309	121	70	13	.334	.465	.410	875	856	436	0	0	10	(26)	840	358
3	1	1890-98	B.Joyce	3,304	718	108	4,130	970	152	106	70	.294	.435	.467	902	878	264	0	0	10	(12)	875	350
4	6	1887-07	L.Cross	9,072	464	31	9,567	2,645	411	135	47	.292	.328	.382	710	726	301	0	0	8	24	758	237
5	5	1884-98	B.Nash	5,849	803	41	6,693	1,606	266	87	60	.275	.366	.381	747	760	265	0	0	(1)	19	777	235
6	4	1884-91	J.Davis	1,723	108	19	1,850	468	69	37	14	.272	.322	.379	701	748	151	0	0	10	20	779	66
7	7	1880-09	A.Latham	6,822	588	85	7,495	1,833	245	85	27	.269	.334	.341	676	701	739	0	0	10	17	728	58
8	8	1884-93	G.Pinkney	4,610	526	53	5,189	1,212	170	56	21	.263	.345	.338	683	731	296	0	0	8	(24)	715	12
9	10	1890-94	T.O'Rourke	1,510	197	18	1,725	440	43	23	1	.291	.380	.352	732	724	81	0	0	10	(41)	693	(8)
10	11	1894-02	F.Hartman	2,236	118	41	2,395	622	77	47	10	.278	.326	.368	694	694	88	0	0	3	(6)	691	(32)
11	12	1889-97	C.Reilly	2,380	180	41	2,601	595	80	24	17	.250	.314	.325	639	644	132	0	0	7	32	683	(42)
12	9	1886-98	B.Shindle	5,807	388	74	6,269	1,561	226	97	31	.269	.323	.357	680	677	318	0	0	2	21	700	(57)
13	14	1890-03	B.Clingman	2,839	303	24	3,166	697	86	31	8	.246	.323	.306	630	619	98	0	0	0	40	658	(66)
14	17	1898-03	B.Lauder	1,829	77	3	1,909	476	64	14	5	.260	.291	.319	610	634	59	0	0	0	(21)	614	(103)
15	13	1893-02	C.Irwin	3,679	286	60	4,025	981	144	46	16	.267	.330	.344	674	667	180	0	0	6	(10)	663	(115)
16	16	1884-96	C.McGarr	3,253	183	14	3,450	872	116	28	9	.268	.310	.329	639	627	267	0	0	10	(8)	629	(145)
17	15	1883-95	J.Mulvey	4,063	134	15	4,212	1,059	157	71	28	.261	.287	.355	642	677	147	0	0	(2)	(17)	658	(147)

1888-1899
Outfielders

V	R	Years	Name	AB	BB	HBP	TAB	H	2B	3B	HR	BA	OB	SA	PRO	Wtd PRO	SB	CS	SBF	SPF	FF	R TF	V HC
1	1	1888-03	E.Delahanty	7,505	741	94	8,340	2,596	522	185	101	.346	.411	.505	917	909	455	0	0	10	10	928	840
2	5	1890-05	J.Burkett	8,421	1,029	75	9,525	2,850	320	182	75	.338	.415	.446	862	874	389	0	0	9	(1)	882	646
3	2	1885-06	S.Thompson	5,984	450	63	6,497	1,979	340	160	126	.331	.384	.504	888	900	229	0	0	9	19	928	640
4	4	1888-01	B.Hamilton	6,269	1,187	89	7,545	2,159	242	95	40	.344	.455	.432	888	883	912	0	0	10	3	896	582
5	6	1891-08	J.Kelley	7,006	911	82	7,999	2,220	358	194	65	.317	.402	.451	853	858	443	0	0	9	3	870	485
6	8	1885-03	J.Ryan	8,164	803	83	9,050	2,502	451	157	118	.306	.374	.444	818	826	418	0	0	4	20	851	478
7	3	1883-92	T.O'Neill	4,255	421	44	4,720	1,386	222	92	52	.326	.392	.458	850	903	161	0	0	7	(11)	899	397
8	7	1887-99	M.Tiernan	5,906	747	41	6,694	1,834	256	162	106	.311	.392	.463	854	858	428	0	0	10	(12)	856	376
9	12	1888-06	H.Duffy	7,042	662	29	7,733	2,282	325	119	106	.324	.384	.449	834	825	574	0	0	10	2	837	341
10	16	1887-03	G.Van Haltren	8,021	868	38	8,927	2,532	285	161	69	.316	.385	.417	802	802	583	0	0	10	3	814	284
11	11	1884-93	B.Caruthers	2,465	417	24	2,906	695	104	50	29	.282	.391	.400	791	850	152	0	0	0	(12)	838	268
12	14	1887-98	M.Griffin	5,914	809	77	6,800	1,753	313	108	42	.296	.388	.407	795	793	473	0	0	7	27	827	265
13	13	1884-95	O.Burns	4,637	464	41	5,142	1,389	224	129	65	.300	.368	.446	814	838	263	0	0	8	(18)	828	242
14	17	1886-01	E.Smith	4,684	636	42	5,362	1,454	196	136	37	.310	.398	.434	832	815	232	0	0	0	(2)	813	225
15	9	1893-99	B.Lange	3,195	350	25	3,570	1,055	133	80	39	.330	.401	.459	859	818	399	0	0	10	21	849	206
16	10	1890-99	J.Stenzel	3,024	299	57	3,380	1,024	190	71	32	.339	.408	.480	888	845	292	0	0	10	(14)	841	157
17	15	1889-98	B.Holliday	3,648	359	20	4,027	1,134	162	71	65	.311	.394	.448	823	823	248	0	0	9	(15)	817	132
18	18	1884-93	C.Welch	4,385	381	173	4,939	1,152	215	66	16	.263	.345	.353	698	755	453	0	0	10	36	801	120
19	19	1885-91	J.McTamany	3,102	535	45	3,682	794	135	58	19	.256	.373	.355	728	778	255	0	0	10	9	796	80
20	24	1888-02	D.Hoy	7,112	1,004	133	8,249	2,044	248	121	40	.287	.386	.373	759	759	594	0	0	10	2	771	64
21	21	1887-92	D.O'Brien	2,856	231	41	3,128	805	147	47	20	.282	.344	.387	732	779	321	0	0	10	3	792	59
22	25	1884-96	T.McCarthy	5,128	537	50	5,715	1,496	192	53	44	.292	.364	.376	740	749	468	0	0	9	13	771	47
23	22	1884-92	E.Seery	3,547	471	33	4,051	893	152	68	27	.252	.345	.356	701	753	240	0	0	10	14	777	45
24	20	1889-93	C.Duffee	1,943	180	11	2,134	518	67	33	35	.267	.332	.389	721	760	110	0	0	0	35	795	44
25	23	1889-99	D.Miller	2,557	174	30	2,761	769	139	50	22	.301	.352	.420	772	755	206	0	0	10	10	775	29

1888-1899
Outfielders

V	R	Years	Name	AB	BB	HBP	TAB	H	2B	3B	HR	BA	OB	SA	PRO	Wtd PRO	SB	CS	SBF	SPF	FF	R TF	V HC
26	27	1888-98	W.Wilmot	3,981	349	17	4,347	1,098	152	92	58	.276	.337	.404	741	747	381	0	0	10	11	767	25
27	26	1887-91	M.Sullivan	1,618	162	7	1,787	441	56	32	26	.273	.341	.395	736	772	99	0	0	3	(6)	769	11
28	28	1890-02	S.Brodie	5,699	420	132	6,251	1,726	191	89	25	.303	.364	.381	745	741	289	0	0	6	11	758	(0)
29	29	1895-03	T.McCreery	2,951	308	10	3,269	855	99	76	26	.290	.359	.401	760	765	116	0	0	1	(12)	755	(9)
30	31	1887-95	G.Tebeau	2,315	324	22	2,661	622	96	54	15	.269	.364	.376	740	746	228	0	0	7	(9)	743	(21)
31	35	1893-97	C.Abbey	1,751	167	23	1,941	492	67	46	19	.281	.351	.404	756	693	93	0	0	0	15	708	(56)
32	39	1886-97	G.Shoch	2,536	298	57	2,891	671	89	28	10	.265	.355	.334	688	683	138	0	0	(3)	(2)	679	(61)
33	30	1882-98	T.Brown	7,363	748	46	8,157	1,951	239	138	64	.265	.337	.361	698	727	657	0	0	10	7	744	(66)
34	34	1884-91	D.Johnston	2,992	133	10	3,135	751	109	68	33	.251	.285	.366	651	695	151	0	0	0	22	718	(77)
35	32	1890-97	E.Burke	3,508	317	76	3,901	979	142	57	30	.279	.352	.378	729	708	291	0	0	10	2	720	(83)
36	37	1883-94	P.Radford	4,979	790	47	5,816	1,206	176	57	13	.242	.351	.308	660	679	346	0	0	10	13	702	(108)
37	40	1883-90	B.Sunday	2,007	134	14	2,155	498	55	24	12	.248	.300	.317	617	669	246	0	0	10	(8)	671	(112)
38	38	1888-94	F.Weaver	3,082	185	54	3,321	856	114	38	9	.278	.330	.348	678	693	162	0	0	1	(1)	693	(119)
39	51	1891-97	J.Canavan	2,064	230	9	2,303	461	63	48	30	.223	.304	.344	648	638	114	0	0	3	(24)	617	(120)
40	50	1890-99	G.Stafford	2,128	164	17	2,309	583	60	19	21	.274	.331	.350	681	655	117	0	0	3	(41)	617	(125)
41	48	1887-93	H.Lyons	1,713	97	5	1,815	401	31	21	7	.234	.277	.289	566	612	120	0	0	3	14	630	(128)
42	43	1896-03	C.Dexter	2,866	198	42	3,106	749	94	24	16	.261	.318	.328	646	662	183	0	0	10	(12)	659	(134)
43	36	1882-93	C.Carroll	3,972	361	47	4,380	995	125	47	31	.251	.320	.329	649	688	197	0	0	10	7	705	(140)
44	46	1885-91	E.Daily	2,573	125	5	2,703	616	92	35	19	.239	.276	.325	601	640	235	0	0	10	(1)	649	(144)
45	49	1894-99	H.Blake	1,877	230	7	2,114	473	67	22	8	.252	.336	.324	660	633	55	0	0	(10)	7	629	(149)
46	41	1892-99	G.Decker	2,727	173	21	2,921	753	98	49	25	.276	.324	.376	700	675	112	0	0	8	(16)	667	(154)
47	42	1897-03	D.Harley	2,879	223	78	3,180	755	59	27	10	.262	.332	.312	644	656	139	0	0	10	(2)	664	(160)
48	44	1886-94	L.Twitchell	2,571	168	19	2,758	676	103	40	19	.263	.313	.356	669	685	84	0	0	(10)	(21)	654	(161)
49	33	1890-07	P.Donovan	7,496	453	83	8,032	2,253	207	75	16	.301	.347	.355	702	707	518	0	0	10	2	719	(167)
50	52	1886-91	J.McGeachy	2,464	57	9	2,530	604	106	18	9	.245	.265	.314	579	601	164	0	0	5	8	613	(213)
51	45	1889-07	J.McAleer	3,977	365	38	4,380	1,007	114	39	11	.253	.322	.310	632	627	262	0	0	6	17	650	(264)
52	47	1891-01	T.Dowd	5,511	369	22	5,902	1,492	163	88	24	.271	.319	.345	664	651	366	0	0	10	(23)	639	(321)

1888-1899
Starting Pitchers

V	R	Years	Name	G	GS	IP	W	L	SV	SO	BB	ERA	RA/9	R Wtd RA/9	V Runs /162
1	1	1890-11	C.Young	906	815	7,356	511	316	17	2,803	1,217	2.63	3.87	3.44	1,027.4
2	3	1890-06	K.Nichols	620	561	5,056	361	208	17	1,873	1,268	2.95	4.41	3.50	684.5
3	6	1882-94	J.Clarkson	531	518	4,536	328	178	5	1,978	1,191	2.81	4.71	3.79	482.9
4	2	1884-92	B.Caruthers	340	310	2,829	218	99	3	900	597	2.83	4.43	3.45	426.3
5	5	1889-01	A.Rusie	463	427	3,779	246	174	5	1,950	1,707	3.07	4.93	3.72	412.9
6	8	1886-97	S.King	397	371	3,182	203	153	6	1,222	967	3.18	5.10	3.83	300.5
7	13	1891-14	C.Griffith	453	372	3,386	237	146	6	955	774	3.31	4.92	3.97	254.7
8	9	1892-01	N.Cuppy	302	262	2,283	162	98	5	504	609	3.48	5.30	3.87	202.2
9	14	1889-97	S.McMahon	321	305	2,634	173	127	4	967	945	3.51	5.44	4.01	186.7
10	19	1891-01	T.Breitenstein	379	341	2,964	160	170	3	889	1,203	4.04	5.60	4.11	173.4
11	4	1885-91	E.Seward	176	169	1,486	89	72	0	589	451	3.40	4.99	3.71	164.0
12	20	1888-99	F.Dwyer	366	318	2,819	177	151	6	565	764	3.84	5.69	4.14	154.6
13	22	1889-99	J.Stivetts	388	333	2,888	203	132	5	1,223	1,155	3.74	5.72	4.16	150.3
14	24	1884-97	B.Hutchison	375	346	3,078	183	163	4	1,232	1,132	3.59	5.59	4.19	149.5
15	23	1892-03	B.Kennedy	405	353	3,021	187	159	9	797	1,201	3.96	5.54	4.18	146.9
16	29	1887-01	G.Weyhing	538	503	4,324	264	232	4	1,665	1,566	3.89	5.80	4.29	146.1
17	21	1886-96	E.Chamberlain	321	301	2,522	157	120	1	1,133	1,065	3.57	5.57	4.14	136.1
18	17	1890-99	B.Rhines	248	222	1,891	113	103	1	553	576	3.48	5.24	4.05	124.5
19	7	1895-01	B.Hoffer	161	142	1,254	92	46	3	314	453	3.75	5.11	3.82	121.4
20	28	1892-01	P.Hawley	393	344	3,013	167	179	3	868	974	3.96	5.76	4.28	110.3
21	12	1888-92	B.Sanders	168	157	1,385	80	70	2	468	297	3.24	5.13	3.96	108.7
22	18	1890-98	E.Stein	215	183	1,656	109	78	3	535	732	3.97	5.68	4.06	107.0
23	11	1896-01	T.Lewis	183	153	1,405	94	64	4	378	511	3.53	4.82	3.95	106.5
24	25	1891-00	F.Killen	321	300	2,511	164	131	0	725	822	3.78	5.63	4.25	100.7
25	27	1888-95	H.Staley	283	257	2,269	136	119	2	746	601	3.80	5.84	4.26	88.1
26	15	1886-98	E.Smith	149	136	1,210	75	57	0	525	422	3.35	5.33	4.03	83.0
27	30	1886-98	M.Kilroy	303	292	2,436	141	133	1	1,170	754	3.47	5.69	4.30	80.6
28	16	1898-02	J.Hughes	134	128	1,088	83	40	0	368	372	3.00	4.24	4.04	69.1
29	33	1891-00	J.Meekin	324	308	2,603	153	133	2	900	1,058	4.07	5.89	4.36	64.6
30	10	1886-89	N.Hudson	86	78	694	48	26	1	258	156	3.08	4.94	3.91	62.2
31	43	1884-97	A.Terry	440	406	3,514	197	196	6	1,553	1,298	3.74	5.87	4.44	58.8
32	38	1887-93	M.Baldwin	346	328	2,802	155	165	4	1,349	1,307	3.37	5.82	4.40	57.4
33	36	1888-95	K.Gleason	299	266	2,389	138	131	6	744	906	3.79	5.69	4.39	52.0
34	35	1888-96	A.Gumbert	262	234	1,985	123	102	1	546	634	4.27	6.10	4.39	44.7
35	26	1889-93	J.Duryea	143	130	1,088	59	67	3	416	349	3.45	5.53	4.25	43.2
36	45	1888-98	R.Ehret	362	309	2,754	139	167	4	848	841	4.02	6.15	4.45	39.8
37	34	1890-97	G.Hemming	204	168	1,588	91	82	6	362	691	4.53	6.37	4.37	39.0
38	32	1895-01	D.McJames	178	162	1,361	79	80	4	593	563	3.43	5.39	4.36	33.6
39	39	1885-94	T.Lovett	162	149	1,305	88	59	1	439	444	3.94	5.79	4.41	26.8
40	31	1896-01	J.Nops	136	122	988	72	41	1	294	281	3.70	5.29	4.34	26.4
41	40	1888-92	L.Viau	178	162	1,442	83	77	1	554	526	3.33	5.50	4.42	26.2
42	42	1888-95	P.Knell	192	163	1,452	79	90	0	575	705	4.05	6.31	4.43	23.4
43	47	1891-99	J.Taylor	270	234	2,079	120	117	9	528	581	4.23	6.13	4.49	18.5
44	41	1895-99	Z.Wilson	119	105	874	52	44	1	194	266	4.03	5.78	4.43	14.7
45	44	1892-97	D.Daub	126	103	899	45	52	0	185	327	4.75	6.58	4.44	14.6
46	37	1896-02	F.Klobedanz	89	85	702	53	25	0	181	266	4.12	5.51	4.40	14.3
47	46	1888-91	J.Ewing	129	121	1,059	53	63	2	525	390	3.68	6.08	4.47	11.8
48	48	1889-96	H.Gastright	171	143	1,301	72	63	2	514	584	4.20	6.16	4.50	9.2
49	49	1890-98	D.Esper	236	198	1,728	101	100	5	453	667	4.39	6.24	4.52	7.5
50	50	1896-02	C.Seymour	140	123	1,029	61	56	1	584	655	3.76	5.52	4.53	4.0

1888-1899
Starting Pitchers

V	R	Years	Name	G	GS	IP	W	L	SV	SO	BB	ERA	RA/9	R Wtd RA/9	V Runs /162
51	52	1887-91	E.Beatin	109	108	946	48	56	0	335	372	3.68	5.65	4.54	2.1
52	51	1888-98	D.Clarke	120	92	848	44	51	3	174	191	4.17	6.45	4.54	1.9
53	53	1887-91	K.Madden	122	109	958	54	50	3	284	336	3.92	6.06	4.61	(7.3)
54	56	1896-99	B.Hill	124	115	925	36	69	3	280	406	4.16	5.91	4.64	(10.2)
55	58	1897-04	J.Dunn	142	118	1,077	64	59	3	171	334	4.11	5.55	4.66	(13.2)
56	61	1891-96	D.Clarkson	96	81	705	39	39	0	133	325	4.90	7.23	4.69	(13.2)
57	55	1888-94	G.Haddock	204	189	1,580	95	87	2	599	714	4.07	6.33	4.63	(14.2)
58	54	1888-95	S.Stratton	230	213	1,883	97	114	1	569	432	3.87	6.16	4.62	(15.5)
59	57	1890-96	W.McGill	168	150	1,251	72	74	1	510	701	4.59	6.88	4.65	(16.4)
60	62	1890-95	P.Luby	106	88	797	40	41	2	217	311	3.88	5.91	4.72	(17.1)
61	59	1888-91	D.O'Brien	136	126	1,081	59	65	2	398	486	3.68	6.21	4.68	(17.5)
62	65	1893-96	T.Parrott	115	89	795	39	48	4	166	307	5.33	7.47	4.80	(26.5)
63	66	1897-01	P.Dowling	117	102	907	39	65	1	299	339	3.87	5.69	4.81	(27.4)
64	60	1884-02	F.Foreman	229	205	1,722	96	93	4	586	659	3.97	6.16	4.69	(29.1)
65	64	1884-01	A.Maul	187	167	1,432	84	80	1	346	518	4.43	6.75	4.80	(45.7)
66	71	1890-93	T.Vickery	97	90	718	42	42	0	265	352	3.75	6.32	5.05	(45.7)
67	67	1887-91	H.Gruber	151	139	1,239	61	78	1	346	479	3.67	6.43	4.86	(50.4)
68	63	1894-02	W.Mercer	334	300	2,482	132	164	10	531	755	3.98	6.36	4.77	(69.3)
69	78	1887-01	G.Van Haltren	93	68	689	40	31	4	281	244	4.05	6.88	5.33	(72.0)
70	80	1897-02	B.Magee	106	89	743	29	51	0	161	350	4.93	6.33	5.42	(78.2)
71	69	1884-90	H.O'Day	201	192	1,651	73	110	4	663	578	3.74	6.15	4.91	(83.8)
72	74	1889-99	M.Sullivan	163	121	1,123	54	66	4	286	577	5.11	7.27	5.22	(98.5)
73	70	1885-92	E.Healy	227	222	1,875	78	136	0	822	599	3.84	6.10	4.94	(98.7)
74	79	1891-00	J.Hughey	145	113	1,008	29	80	1	250	317	4.87	6.68	5.42	(107.5)
75	81	1890-97	L.German	129	92	850	34	63	2	147	376	5.49	7.94	5.50	(108.9)
76	68	1887-01	B.Cunningham	341	310	2,727	142	167	2	718	1,064	4.22	6.40	4.88	(112.7)
77	75	1895-03	E.Doheny	183	168	1,393	75	83	2	567	665	3.75	6.01	5.23	(117.1)
78	76	1886-01	B.Hart	206	190	1,582	66	120	3	431	704	4.65	6.91	5.25	(143.6)
79	73	1883-91	J.Bakely	215	204	1,783	76	125	0	669	564	3.66	6.67	5.14	(147.1)
80	77	1884-93	E.Crane	204	176	1,550	72	96	2	719	885	3.99	6.91	5.29	(148.9)
81	72	1891-01	K.Carsey	294	256	2,222	116	138	3	484	796	4.95	6.97	5.08	(150.2)

ALL TIME GREAT PLAYERS

The Hall of Fame has inducted over 180 major league players, as well as managers, umpires, executives, and players from the Negro Leagues. These 180 players are supposed to represent the best of the best. In many cases, this is true. But there are also many players in this elite group who do not deserve Hall of Fame recognition. They made it because they hit in hitter's eras, pitched in pitcher's eras, piled up large statistical numbers by playing a long time, or benefited from the media attention while playing in large metropolitan areas. One player, Rabbit Maranville, was a great fielder and a dreadful hitter who owes his Hall selection almost entirely to heavy campaigning by Ralph Kiner after Maranville's untimely death.

Another problem with the Hall selection process is the bias towards outfielders, and the dearth of third basemen. There are just nine third basemen in the Hall. And two of these — George Kell and Fred Lindstrom — don't belong in the Hall, based on the statistical evidence. Lindstrom benefited from hitting in a hitter's era for a New York team; his 13-year career was certainly unspectacular after we remove the benefit of hitter's inflation. The fact that Fred Lindstrom is in the Hall, while Ron Santo and Ken Boyer are not, is proof positive that Hall selections are not based on the true contributions of a player to his team.

This chapter summarizes the best players by position for American League and National League teams. Finally, an all-time ranking is presented, which provides support for which players deserve to be in the Hall of Fame. We would have a much stronger Hall of Fame if we chose the top 15 eligible players for each infield position, the top 45 or 50 eligible outfielders, and the top 60 eligible pitchers (based primarily on rate of success for pitchers).

AL All Time Greats

Hitters Volume of Success

Pos	Years	Name	AB	BB	HBP	TAB	H	2B	3B	HR	BA	OB	SA	PRO	Wtd PRO	SB	CS	SBF	SPF	FF	R TF	V HC
C	1946-65	Y.Berra	7,555	704	49	8,308	2,150	321	49	358	.285	.349	.482	832	816	30	26	(3)	(0)	44	857	727
1B	1923-39	L.Gehrig	8,001	1,508	45	9,554	2,721	534	163	493	.340	.447	.632	1,080	1,009	102	101	(10)	0	(3)	996	1,083
2B	1896-16	N.Lajoie	9,589	516	134	10,239	3,242	657	163	82	.338	.380	.466	846	910	380	21	(2)	6	63	978	1,495
SS	1926-45	J.Cronin	7,579	1,059	34	8,672	2,285	515	118	170	.301	.390	.468	857	808	87	71	(6)	7	26	835	737
3B	1973-93	G.Brett	10,349	1,096	33	11,478	3,154	665	137	317	.305	.373	.487	861	868	201	97	1	2	(0)	870	756
OF	1914-35	B.Ruth	8,399	2,056	42	10,497	2,873	506	136	714	.342	.474	.690	1,163	1,112	123	117	(11)	3	9	1,112	1,962
OF	1905-28	T.Cobb	11,434	1,249	94	12,777	4,189	724	295	117	.366	.433	.512	945	983	892	178	(2)	10	17	1,008	1,623
OF	1939-60	T.Williams	7,706	2,019	39	9,764	2,654	525	71	521	.344	.483	.634	1,116	1,093	24	17	(1)	(2)	(8)	1,082	1,599
Starters	Averages		8,827	1,276	59	10,161	2,909	556	142	347	.330	.418	.542	960	955	230	79	(4)	3	18	972	1,248
C	1925-37	M.Cochrane	5,169	857	29	6,055	1,652	333	64	119	.320	.419	.478	897	842	64	46	(4)	8	58	904	687
1B	1925-45	J.Foxx	8,134	1,452	13	9,599	2,646	458	125	534	.325	.428	.609	1,038	976	87	72	(6)	2	17	989	1,072
2B	1906-30	E.Collins	9,949	1,499	77	11,525	3,315	438	187	47	.333	.424	.429	853	877	744	173	(2)	10	48	934	1,455
SS	1981-	C.Ripken	11,074	1,103	64	12,241	3,070	587	44	417	.277	.346	.451	797	779	36	37	(3)	(1)	13	788	701
3B	1982-99	W.Boggs	9,180	1,412	23	10,615	3,010	578	61	118	.328	.419	.443	861	847	24	35	(4)	(4)	19	858	729
OF	1907-28	T.Speaker	10,195	1,381	103	11,679	3,514	792	222	117	.345	.428	.500	928	947	432	129	(7)	10	58	1,008	1,494
OF	1951-68	M.Mantle	8,102	1,733	13	9,848	2,415	344	72	536	.298	.423	.557	979	981	153	38	7	9	28	1,026	1,305
OF	1936-51	J.DiMaggio	6,821	790	46	7,657	2,214	389	131	361	.325	.398	.579	977	934	30	9	1	6	51	992	900
Reserves	Averages		8,578	1,278	46	9,902	2,730	490	113	281	.318	.409	.500	909	896	196	67	(2)	5	37	935	1,043
Totals	Weighted Ave.		8,744	1,277	55	10,075	2,849	534	132	325	.326	.415	.528	943	935	219	75	(4)	4	25	960	1,179

Pitchers Volume of Success

Pos	Years	Name	G	GS	IP	W	L	SV	SO	BB	ERA	RA/9	R Wtd RA/9	V Runs /162
SP	1907-27	W.Johnson	802	666	5,914	417	279	34	3,509	1,363	2.17	2.89	3.10	1,021
SP	1925-41	L.Grove	616	457	3,941	300	141	55	2,266	1,187	3.06	3.64	3.22	616
SP	1984-	R.Clemens	512	511	3,667	260	142	0	3,504	1,186	3.07	3.40	3.23	555
SP	1901-17	E.Plank	623	529	4,496	326	194	23	2,246	1,072	2.35	3.14	3.58	524
SP	1904-17	E.Walsh	430	315	2,964	195	126	35	1,736	617	1.82	2.66	3.13	494
Starters	Averages		597	496	4,196	300	176	29	2,652	1,085	2.48	3.14	3.25	642
RP	1952-72	H.Wilhelm	1,070	52	2,254	143	122	227	1,610	778	2.52	3.09	3.30	324
RP	1972-94	R.Gossage	1,002	37	1,809	124	107	310	1,502	732	3.01	3.33	3.59	199
RP	1968-85	R.Fingers	944	37	1,701	114	118	341	1,299	492	2.90	3.25	3.53	199
RP	1979-90	D.Quisenberry	674	0	1,043	56	46	244	379	162	2.76	3.07	3.16	167
Relievers	Averages		923	32	1,702	109	98	281	1,198	541	2.78	3.19	3.41	222
Totals	Averages		1,519	527	5,898	409	275	310	3,850	1,626	2.57	3.16	3.30	864

AL All Time Greats   **Hitters Rate of Success**

Pos	Years	Name	AB	BB	HBP	TAB	H	2B	3B	HR	BA	OB	SA	PRO	Wtd PRO	SB	CS	SBF	SPF	FF	R TF	V HC
C	1925-37	M.Cochrane	5,169	857	29	6,055	1,652	333	64	119	.320	.419	.478	897	842	64	46	(4)	8	58	904	687
1B	1923-39	L.Gehrig	8,001	1,508	45	9,554	2,721	534	163	493	.340	.447	.632	1,080	1,009	102	101	(10)	0	(3)	996	1,083
2B	1896-16	N.Lajoie	9,589	516	134	10,239	3,242	657	163	82	.338	.380	.466	846	910	380	21	(2)	6	63	978	1,495
SS	1996-	N.Garciaparra	2,436	184	24	2,644	812	176	29	117	.333	.386	.573	959	893	58	20	6	10	6	915	319
3B	1987-	E.Martinez	5,432	973	65	6,470	1,738	403	14	235	.320	.429	.529	958	915	43	27	(1)	(3)	(22)	888	470
OF	1914-35	B.Ruth	8,399	2,056	42	10,497	2,873	506	136	714	.342	.474	.690	1,163	1,112	123	117	(11)	3	9	1,112	1,962
OF	1939-60	T.Williams	7,706	2,019	39	9,764	2,654	525	71	521	.344	.483	.634	1,116	1,093	24	17	(1)	(2)	(8)	1,082	1,599
OF	1951-68	M.Mantle	8,102	1,733	13	9,848	2,415	344	72	536	.298	.423	.557	979	981	153	38	7	9	28	1,026	1,305
Starters	Averages		6,854	1,231	49	8,134	2,263	435	89	352	.330	.436	.574	1,009	989	118	48	(2)	4	16	1,007	1,115
C	1991-	I.Rodriguez	4,806	256	33	5,095	1,459	288	24	171	.304	.343	.480	823	777	65	33	(0)	3	87	868	483
1B	1925-45	J.Foxx	8,134	1,452	13	9,599	2,646	458	125	534	.325	.428	.609	1,038	976	87	72	(6)	2	17	989	1,072
2B	1906-30	E.Collins	9,949	1,499	77	11,525	3,315	438	187	47	.333	.424	.429	853	877	744	173	(2)	10	48	934	1,455
SS	1994-	A.Rodriguez	3,126	310	31	3,467	966	194	13	189	.309	.377	.561	938	866	133	36	17	10	21	913	422
3B	1908-22	F.Baker	5,984	473	50	6,507	1,838	315	103	96	.307	.363	.442	805	857	235	28	(4)	6	18	877	538
OF	1907-28	T.Speaker	10,195	1,381	103	11,679	3,514	792	222	117	.345	.428	.500	928	947	432	129	(7)	10	58	1,008	1,494
OF	1905-28	T.Cobb	11,434	1,249	94	12,777	4,189	724	295	117	.366	.433	.512	945	983	892	178	(2)	10	17	1,008	1,623
OF	1908-20	J.Jackson	4,981	519	59	5,559	1,772	307	168	54	.356	.423	.517	940	988	202	61	(9)	10	7	996	674
Reserves	Averages		7,326	892	58	8,276	2,462	440	142	166	.336	.412	.503	915	923	349	89	(2)	8	34	963	970
Totals	Weighted Ave.		7,012	1,118	52	8,181	2,330	436	107	290	.332	.428	.549	977	967	195	62	(2)	5	22	993	1,067

Pitchers Rate of Success

Pos	Years	Name	G	GS	IP	W	L	SV	SO	BB	ERA	RA/9	R Wtd RA/9	V Runs /162
SP	1907-27	W.Johnson	802	666	5,914	417	279	34	3,509	1,363	2.17	2.89	3.10	1,021
SP	1904-17	E.Walsh	430	315	2,964	195	126	35	1,736	617	1.82	2.66	3.13	494
SP	1925-41	L.Grove	616	457	3,941	300	141	55	2,266	1,187	3.06	3.64	3.22	616
SP	1984-	R.Clemens	512	511	3,667	260	142	0	3,504	1,186	3.07	3.40	3.23	555
SP	1937-47	S.Chandler	211	184	1,485	109	43	6	614	463	2.84	3.33	3.31	217
Starters	Averages		514	427	3,594	256	146	26	2,326	963	2.54	3.16	3.18	581
RP	1995-	M.Rivera	332	10	452	33	17	165	395	144	2.63	2.77	2.47	107
RP	1982-95	T.Henke	642	0	790	41	42	311	861	255	2.67	2.87	2.85	154
RP	1987-95	B.Harvey	322	0	387	17	25	177	448	144	2.49	2.84	2.89	73
RP	1994-	A.Benitez	360	0	368	19	23	100	517	208	3.04	3.23	2.92	69
Relievers	Averages		414	3	499	28	27	188	555	188	2.69	2.91	2.78	101
Totals	Averages		928	429	4,093	284	173	214	2,881	1,151	2.56	3.13	3.13	681

AL All Time Greats
Catchers

V	R	Years	Name	AB	BB	HBP	TAB	H	2B	3B	HR	BA	OB	SA	PRO	Wtd PRO	SB	CS	SBF	SPF	FF	R TF	V HC
1	3	1946-65	Y.Berra	7,555	704	49	8,308	2,150	321	49	358	.285	.349	.482	832	816	30	26	(3)	(0)	44	857	727
2	1	1925-37	M.Cochrane	5,169	857	29	6,055	1,652	333	64	119	.320	.419	.478	897	842	64	46	(4)	8	58	904	687
3	6	1969-93	C.Fisk	8,756	849	143	9,748	2,356	421	47	376	.269	.343	.457	800	811	128	58	1	(4)	12	820	680
4	4	1928-46	B.Dickey	6,300	678	31	7,009	1,969	343	72	202	.313	.382	.486	868	820	36	29	(3)	(9)	43	850	609
5	2	1991-	I.Rodriguez	4,806	256	33	5,095	1,459	288	24	171	.304	.343	.480	823	777	65	33	(0)	3	87	868	483
6	5	1961-76	B.Freehan	6,073	626	114	6,813	1,591	241	35	200	.262	.342	.412	754	787	24	21	(3)	2	36	823	455
7	8	1969-79	T.Munson	5,344	438	42	5,824	1,558	229	32	113	.292	.350	.410	760	781	48	50	(8)	5	17	795	327
8	11	1913-31	W.Schang	5,307	849	107	6,263	1,506	264	90	59	.284	.393	.401	794	789	121	49	(3)	0	(5)	780	323
9	13	1946-63	S.Lollar	5,351	671	115	6,137	1,415	244	14	155	.264	.359	.402	761	747	20	10	(0)	(10)	40	776	304
10	20	1977-95	L.Parrish	7,067	612	37	7,716	1,782	305	27	324	.252	.315	.440	756	755	28	37	(6)	(10)	17	757	300
11	18	1971-87	D.Porter	5,539	905	45	6,489	1,369	237	48	188	.247	.357	.409	766	777	39	37	(5)	(4)	(8)	760	261
12	7	1969-83	G.Tenace	4,390	984	91	5,465	1,060	179	20	201	.241	.391	.429	819	838	36	42	(8)	(9)	(23)	797	215
13	12	1955-67	E.Battey	3,586	421	28	4,035	969	150	17	104	.270	.351	.409	760	762	13	12	(3)	(10)	28	778	196
14	9	1989-98	C.Hoiles	2,820	435	44	3,299	739	122	2	151	.262	.369	.467	837	801	5	7	(2)	0	(10)	789	189
15	14	1984-97	M.Tettleton	4,698	949	30	5,677	1,132	210	16	245	.241	.372	.449	821	807	23	29	(6)	(6)	(28)	767	176
16	21	1955-68	E.Howard	5,363	373	26	5,762	1,471	218	50	167	.274	.325	.427	752	755	9	14	(3)	(10)	14	756	158
17	10	1958-67	J.Romano	2,767	414	29	3,210	706	112	10	129	.255	.358	.443	801	802	7	9	(3)	(7)	(12)	781	158
18	15	1986-	M.Stanley	4,222	652	48	4,922	1,138	220	7	187	.270	.373	.458	831	795	13	4	1	(8)	(22)	766	134
19	25	1976-91	E.Whitt	3,774	436	4	4,214	938	176	15	134	.249	.327	.410	737	733	22	26	(6)	(8)	22	741	132
20	35	1974-89	J.Sundberg	6,021	699	22	6,742	1,493	243	36	95	.248	.328	.348	676	685	20	37	(8)	(9)	47	715	125
21	39	1929-47	R.Ferrell	6,028	931	10	6,969	1,692	324	45	28	.281	.378	.363	741	708	29	35	(6)	(6)	14	710	114
22	37	1912-29	R.Schalk	5,306	638	59	6,003	1,345	199	49	11	.253	.340	.316	656	664	177	69	(3)	0	53	714	112
23	26	1893-08	E.McFarland	3,007	254	18	3,279	826	146	49	13	.275	.335	.369	704	726	65	0	0	(3)	15	738	105
24	38	1986-	T.Steinbach	5,369	418	48	5,835	1,453	273	21	162	.271	.329	.420	749	725	23	22	(3)	(9)	(2)	711	96
25	24	1964-74	D.Sims	2,422	338	35	2,795	580	80	6	100	.239	.341	.401	742	773	6	16	(9)	(10)	(7)	747	94

AL All Time Greats
First Basemen

V	R	Years	Name	AB	BB	HBP	TAB	H	2B	3B	HR	BA	OB	SA	PRO	Wtd PRO	SB	CS	SBF	SPF	FF	R TF	V HC
1	1	1923-39	L.Gehrig	8,001	1,508	45	9,554	2,721	534	163	493	.340	.447	.632	1,080	1,009	102	101	(10)	0	(3)	996	1,083
2	2	1925-45	J.Foxx	8,134	1,452	13	9,599	2,646	458	125	534	.325	.428	.609	1,038	976	87	72	(6)	2	17	989	1,072
3	4	1986-	M.McGwire	5,888	1,261	72	7,221	1,570	248	6	554	.267	.402	.593	995	957	12	8	(1)	(9)	6	953	650
4	3	1930-47	H.Greenberg	5,193	852	16	6,061	1,628	379	71	331	.313	.412	.605	1,017	966	58	26	1	0	4	971	616
5	5	1990-	F.Thomas	5,474	1,188	46	6,708	1,755	361	10	344	.321	.446	.579	1,024	983	29	21	(2)	(0)	(31)	949	601
6	8	1954-75	H.Killebrew	8,147	1,559	48	9,754	2,086	290	24	573	.256	.379	.509	887	906	19	18	(2)	(10)	(34)	860	517
7	7	1986-	R.Palmeiro	7,846	935	61	8,842	2,321	455	36	400	.296	.375	.516	891	862	88	38	1	(1)	14	877	470
8	6	1958-74	N.Cash	6,705	1,043	90	7,838	1,820	241	41	377	.271	.377	.488	865	886	43	30	(2)	(5)	15	893	465
9	14	1977-97	E.Murray	11,336	1,333	18	12,687	3,255	560	35	504	.287	.363	.476	839	832	110	43	2	(4)	13	842	454
10	9	1915-30	G.Sisler	8,267	472	48	8,787	2,812	425	164	102	.340	.379	.468	847	826	375	127	(1)	10	20	855	452
11	12	1982-95	D.Mattingly	7,003	588	21	7,612	2,153	442	20	222	.307	.363	.471	834	825	14	9	(1)	(4)	31	851	303
12	11	1981-94	K.Hrbek	6,192	838	26	7,056	1,749	312	18	293	.282	.370	.481	851	845	37	26	(2)	(5)	13	851	279
13	18	1961-77	B.Powell	6,681	1,001	29	7,711	1,776	270	11	339	.266	.364	.462	826	856	20	21	(3)	(10)	(12)	831	236
14	15	1989-	J.Olerud	5,330	922	64	6,316	1,595	367	11	186	.299	.409	.477	886	844	8	12	(2)	(9)	9	841	225
15	13	1991-	M.Vaughn	4,966	652	96	5,714	1,479	250	10	299	.298	.390	.533	923	872	30	17	(1)	(6)	(19)	846	218
16	21	1971-87	C.Cooper	7,349	448	17	7,814	2,192	415	47	241	.298	.340	.466	806	814	89	49	(1)	1	11	824	208
17	24	1966-79	G.Scott	7,433	699	53	8,185	1,992	306	60	271	.268	.335	.435	770	798	69	57	(5)	5	17	815	207
18	27	1934-48	R.York	5,891	792	12	6,695	1,621	291	52	277	.275	.362	.483	845	838	38	26	(2)	(3)	(21)	812	205
19	23	1905-19	H.Chase	7,417	276	30	7,723	2,158	322	124	57	.291	.319	.391	710	782	363	15	0	10	28	820	195
20	16	1933-46	H.Trosky	5,161	545	16	5,722	1,561	331	58	228	.302	.371	.522	892	840	28	23	(3)	0	(0)	837	189
21	28	1986-	W.Joyner	6,979	820	38	7,837	2,024	404	25	201	.290	.368	.441	809	789	59	38	(2)	(3)	27	811	158
22	26	1968-82	J.Mayberry	5,447	881	55	6,383	1,379	211	19	255	.253	.363	.439	802	824	20	17	(2)	(9)	(0)	813	141
23	10	1993-	C.Delgado	2,901	436	61	3,398	818	214	7	190	.282	.387	.557	944	872	5	6	(2)	0	(18)	852	140
24	32	1897-08	C.Hickman	3,982	153	58	4,193	1,176	217	91	59	.295	.331	.440	771	838	72	0	0	(1)	(29)	807	138
25	37	1949-65	R.Sievers	6,387	841	51	7,279	1,703	292	42	318	.267	.357	.475	831	819	14	19	(3)	(6)	(10)	799	135

AL All Time Greats
Second basemen

V	R	Years	Name	AB	BB	HBP	TAB	H	2B	3B	HR	BA	OB	SA	PRO	Wtd PRO	SB	CS	SBF	SPF	FF	R TF	V HC
1	1	1896-16	N.Lajoie	9,589	516	134	10,239	3,242	657	163	82	.338	.380	.466	846	910	380	21	(2)	6	63	978	1,495
2	2	1906-30	E.Collins	9,949	1,499	77	11,525	3,315	438	187	47	.333	.424	.429	853	877	744	173	(2)	10	48	934	1,455
3	4	1924-42	C.Gehringer	8,860	1,186	51	10,097	2,839	574	146	184	.320	.404	.480	884	884	827	181	89	0	5	30	862	894
4	3	1988-	R.Alomar	7,221	822	41	8,084	2,196	412	60	170	.304	.378	.448	827	799	416	100	25	9	42	876	759
5	5	1937-51	B.Doerr	7,093	809	11	7,913	2,042	381	89	223	.288	.362	.461	823	806	54	64	(9)	0	48	845	637
6	10	1977-95	L.Whitaker	8,570	1,197	20	9,787	2,369	420	65	244	.276	.366	.426	792	789	143	75	(1)	6	20	815	628
7	7	1970-86	B.Grich	6,890	1,087	86	8,063	1,833	320	47	224	.266	.373	.424	796	816	104	83	(7)	3	20	832	586
8	6	1967-85	R.Carew	9,315	1,018	25	10,358	3,053	445	112	92	.328	.395	.429	825	846	353	187	(2)	9	(10)	843	566
9	9	1938-50	J.Gordon	5,707	759	29	6,495	1,530	264	52	253	.268	.357	.466	822	803	89	60	(5)	0	27	825	454
10	12	1926-39	T.Lazzeri	6,297	869	21	7,187	1,840	334	115	178	.292	.380	.467	846	794	148	79	(1)	7	(3)	798	404
11	14	1912-24	D.Pratt	6,826	513	37	7,376	1,996	392	117	43	.292	.345	.403	748	766	247	108	(10)	9	19	784	373
12	11	1899-09	J.Williams	5,481	474	36	5,991	1,507	242	138	49	.275	.337	.396	733	794	151	0	0	0	15	809	366
13	13	1991-	C.Knoblauch	5,545	718	121	6,384	1,646	293	61	83	.297	.389	.417	806	768	350	105	21	10	(4)	796	352
14	8	1900-15	D.Murphy	5,399	335	47	5,781	1,563	289	102	44	.289	.336	.405	742	824	193	0	0	5	3	831	333
15	20	1975-92	W.Randolph	8,018	1,243	38	9,299	2,210	316	65	54	.276	.375	.351	727	730	271	94	8	8	9	754	314
16	21	1960-75	D.McAuliffe	6,185	882	33	7,100	1,530	231	71	197	.247	.344	.403	748	773	63	59	(7)	8	(20)	754	261
17	29	1947-65	N.Fox	9,232	719	142	10,093	2,663	355	112	35	.288	.349	.363	712	703	76	80	(8)	3	37	735	251
18	26	1925-41	B.Myer	7,038	965	32	8,035	2,131	353	130	38	.303	.389	.406	795	746	156	109	(7)	8	(6)	741	236
19	27	1973-90	F.White	7,859	412	30	8,301	2,006	407	58	160	.255	.295	.383	678	681	178	83	1	7	51	741	226
20	15	1965-78	D.Johnson	4,797	559	40	5,396	1,252	242	18	136	.261	.343	.404	747	773	33	25	(3)	0	12	783	221
21	22	1920-34	M.McManus	6,660	675	30	7,365	1,926	401	88	120	.289	.357	.430	787	741	126	91	(8)	9	11	753	204
22	17	1951-60	G.McDougald	4,676	559	36	5,271	1,291	187	51	112	.276	.358	.410	768	758	45	44	(8)	0	13	764	189
23	18	1943-52	S.Stirnweiss	3,695	541	6	4,242	989	157	68	29	.268	.362	.371	733	743	134	55	5	10	4	763	166
24	19	1905-15	F.LaPorte	4,212	288	27	4,527	1,185	198	79	15	.281	.331	.377	708	772	101	0	0	1	(13)	760	149
25	32	1924-35	M.Bishop	4,494	1,153	31	5,678	1,216	236	35	41	.271	.423	.366	789	742	43	50	(9)	(0)	1	734	136

AL All Time Greats
Shortstops

V	R	Years	Name	AB	BB	HBP	TAB	H	2B	3B	HR	BA	OB	SA	PRO	Wtd PRO	SB	CS	SBF	SPF	FF	R TF	V HC
1	3	1926-45	J.Cronin	7,579	1,059	34	8,672	2,285	515	118	170	.301	.390	.468	857	808	87	71	(6)	7	26	835	737
2	11	1981-	C.Ripken	11,074	1,103	64	12,241	3,070	587	44	417	.277	.346	.451	797	779	36	37	(3)	(1)	13	788	701
3	7	1974-93	R.Yount	11,008	966	48	12,022	3,142	583	126	251	.285	.346	.430	775	780	271	105	5	9	18	811	621
4	10	1977-96	A.Trammell	8,288	850	37	9,175	2,365	412	55	185	.285	.354	.415	770	762	236	109	2	8	17	790	582
5	5	1938-52	L.Boudreau	6,029	796	34	6,859	1,779	385	66	68	.295	.380	.415	795	792	51	50	(7)	(5)	50	830	580
6	16	1930-50	L.Appling	8,856	1,302	10	10,168	2,749	440	102	45	.310	.399	.398	798	769	179	108	(3)	(0)	6	771	542
7	6	1941-55	V.Stephens	6,497	692	6	7,195	1,859	307	42	247	.286	.355	.460	816	817	25	22	(2)	0	0	815	521
8	14	1894-18	B.Wallace	8,618	774	47	9,439	2,309	391	143	34	.268	.332	.358	690	738	201	2	(0)	(1)	39	776	520
9	22	1956-73	L.Aparicio	10,230	736	27	10,993	2,677	394	92	83	.262	.313	.343	655	666	506	136	20	10	50	747	451
10	2	1994-	A.Rodriguez	3,126	310	31	3,467	966	194	13	189	.309	.377	.561	938	866	133	36	17	10	21	913	422
11	21	1983-	T.Fernandez	7,788	682	63	8,533	2,240	410	92	92	.288	.350	.399	749	736	245	135	(3)	10	13	756	351
12	20	1920-33	J.Sewell	7,132	842	79	8,053	2,226	436	68	49	.312	.391	.413	804	756	74	72	(8)	0	18	766	345
13	1	1996-	N.Garciaparra	2,436	184	24	2,644	812	176	29	117	.333	.386	.573	959	893	58	20	6	10	6	915	319
14	18	1961-78	J.Fregosi	6,523	715	32	7,270	1,726	264	78	151	.265	.340	.398	739	764	76	40	(1)	5	1	770	318
15	19	1982-	J.Franco	7,244	753	33	8,030	2,177	335	47	141	.301	.369	.418	787	778	260	101	7	7	(25)	767	309
16	8	1912-20	R.Chapman	3,785	452	19	4,256	1,053	162	81	17	.278	.358	.377	735	784	233	47	0	9	7	800	304
17	4	1995-	D.Jeter	3,130	341	48	3,519	1,008	153	35	78	.322	.397	.468	865	802	108	37	9	10	13	834	291
18	15	1898-14	K.Elberfeld	4,561	427	165	5,153	1,235	169	56	10	.271	.355	.339	694	757	213	0	0	10	8	774	277
19	12	1942-54	J.Pesky	4,745	662	25	5,432	1,455	226	50	17	.307	.394	.386	780	771	53	49	(8)	8	14	786	275
20	23	1941-56	P.Rizzuto	5,816	651	49	6,516	1,588	239	62	38	.273	.351	.355	706	695	149	58	5	10	33	742	262
21	17	1963-76	R.Petrocelli	5,390	661	26	6,077	1,352	237	22	210	.251	.336	.420	755	788	10	22	(5)	(10)	(3)	770	243
22	34	1964-83	B.Campaneris	8,684	618	64	9,366	2,249	313	86	79	.259	.313	.342	655	680	649	199	25	10	2	717	240
23	9	1992-	J.Valentin	3,649	432	42	4,123	1,031	264	17	120	.283	.365	.463	828	785	47	31	(3)	(1)	12	792	232
24	30	1989-	O.Vizquel	5,809	582	24	6,415	1,605	250	36	41	.276	.345	.353	698	664	260	101	9	10	45	727	206
25	37	1908-23	D.Bush	7,210	1,158	29	8,397	1,804	186	74	9	.250	.356	.300	656	696	404	75	(6)	9	11	710	203

AL All Time Greats
Third basemen

V	R	Years	Name	AB	BB	HBP	TAB	H	2B	3B	HR	BA	OB	SA	PRO	Wtd PRO	SB	CS	SBF	SPF	FF	R TF	V HC
1	4	1973-93	G.Brett	10,349	1,096	33	11,478	3,154	665	137	317	.305	.373	.487	861	868	201	97	1	2	(0)	870	756
2	5	1982-99	W.Boggs	9,180	1,412	23	10,615	3,010	578	61	118	.328	.419	.443	861	847	24	35	(4)	(4)	19	858	729
3	2	1908-22	F.Baker	5,984	473	50	6,507	1,838	315	103	96	.307	.363	.442	805	857	235	28	(4)	6	18	877	538
4	9	1978-98	P.Molitor	10,835	1,094	47	11,976	3,319	605	114	234	.306	.372	.448	820	807	504	131	19	10	(13)	822	515
5	1	1987-	E.Martinez	5,432	973	65	6,470	1,738	403	14	235	.320	.429	.529	958	915	43	27	(1)	(3)	(22)	888	470
6	6	1895-08	J.Collins	6,795	426	84	7,305	1,999	352	116	65	.294	.343	.409	752	786	194	0	0	8	43	837	457
7	15	1955-77	B.Robinson	10,654	860	53	11,567	2,848	482	68	268	.267	.325	.401	726	744	28	22	(1)	(6)	56	793	429
8	13	1967-88	G.Nettles	8,986	1,088	50	10,124	2,225	328	28	390	.248	.332	.421	753	769	32	36	(4)	(5)	34	794	376
9	10	1934-45	H.Clift	5,730	1,070	41	6,841	1,558	309	62	178	.272	.390	.441	831	792	69	43	(2)	0	28	817	347
10	8	1989-	R.Ventura	5,599	817	20	6,436	1,530	280	13	227	.273	.368	.450	817	783	19	32	(6)	(3)	50	824	343
11	16	1972-89	B.Bell	8,995	836	38	9,869	2,514	425	56	201	.279	.343	.406	750	761	55	79	(10)	(1)	38	788	336
12	3	1991-	J.Thome	3,634	764	33	4,431	1,033	214	17	233	.284	.413	.545	958	894	17	11	(1)	(3)	(15)	874	290
13	30	1969-86	T.Harrah	7,402	1,153	63	8,618	1,954	307	40	195	.264	.368	.395	763	777	238	94	6	3	(28)	758	274
14	7	1947-56	A.Rosen	3,725	587	27	4,339	1,063	165	20	192	.285	.386	.495	882	861	39	33	(6)	(1)	(18)	837	262
15	17	1943-57	G.Kell	6,702	621	36	7,359	2,054	385	50	78	.306	.368	.414	782	774	51	36	(3)	0	15	786	261
16	14	1937-50	K.Keltner	5,683	514	13	6,210	1,570	308	69	163	.276	.338	.441	778	764	39	33	(4)	0	33	793	240
17	21	1990-	T.Fryman	5,750	532	36	6,318	1,602	316	37	209	.279	.343	.455	799	762	71	36	(0)	0	14	776	225
18	18	1973-87	D.DeCinces	5,809	618	21	6,448	1,505	312	29	237	.259	.333	.445	778	781	58	48	(6)	(4)	13	784	216
19	29	1981-	G.Gaetti	8,951	634	96	9,681	2,280	443	39	360	.255	.311	.434	745	732	96	65	(3)	(4)	34	758	200
20	23	1908-24	L.Gardner	6,688	654	32	7,374	1,931	301	129	27	.289	.355	.384	739	767	165	68	(12)	7	5	766	196
21	19	1899-15	B.Bradley	5,430	290	73	5,793	1,471	275	84	34	.271	.317	.371	688	754	181	0	0	9	17	780	190
22	25	1966-81	S.Bando	7,060	1,031	75	8,166	1,790	289	38	242	.254	.355	.408	763	787	75	46	(2)	(7)	(15)	764	189
23	11	1994-	J.Cirillo	3,409	397	42	3,848	1,059	239	15	77	.311	.389	.457	847	784	35	27	(5)	2	25	806	168
24	45	1918-39	J.Dykes	8,046	958	109	9,113	2,256	453	90	108	.280	.365	.399	764	718	70	55	(4)	(2)	26	737	139
25	26	1948-60	R.Boone	4,589	608	27	5,224	1,260	162	46	151	.275	.363	.429	791	776	21	19	(3)	(3)	(6)	763	137

AL All Time Greats
Outfielders

V	R	Years	Name	AB	BB	HBP	TAB	H	2B	3B	HR	BA	OB	SA	PRO	Wtd PRO	SB	CS	SBF	SPF	FF	R TF	V HC
1	1	1914-35	B.Ruth	8,399	2,056	42	10,497	2,873	506	136	714	.342	.474	.690	1,163	1,112	123	117	(11)	3	9	1,112	1,962
2	5	1905-28	T.Cobb	11,434	1,249	94	12,777	4,189	724	295	117	.366	.433	.512	945	983	892	178	(2)	10	17	1,008	1,623
3	2	1939-60	T.Williams	7,706	2,019	39	9,764	2,654	525	71	521	.344	.483	.634	1,116	1,093	24	17	(1)	(2)	(8)	1,082	1,599
4	4	1907-28	T.Speaker	10,195	1,381	103	11,679	3,514	792	222	117	.345	.428	.500	928	947	432	129	(7)	10	58	1,008	1,494
5	3	1951-68	M.Mantle	8,102	1,733	13	9,848	2,415	344	72	536	.298	.423	.557	979	981	153	38	7	9	28	1,026	1,305
6	7	1936-51	J.DiMaggio	6,821	790	46	7,657	2,214	389	131	361	.325	.398	.579	977	934	30	9	1	6	51	992	900
7	15	1979-	R.Henderson	10,331	2,060	90	12,481	2,914	486	62	282	.282	.406	.423	829	815	1,370	326	53	10	23	902	892
8	16	1961-83	C.Yastrzemski	11,988	1,845	40	13,873	3,419	646	59	452	.285	.382	.462	844	864	168	116	(4)	3	30	892	881
9	12	1953-74	A.Kaline	10,116	1,277	55	11,448	3,007	498	75	399	.297	.379	.480	859	868	137	65	1	6	37	912	868
10	8	1989-	K.Griffey Jr.	6,352	841	56	7,249	1,883	342	33	438	.296	.384	.568	951	916	173	64	6	10	57	989	825
11	13	1899-17	S.Crawford	9,570	760	23	10,353	2,961	458	309	97	.309	.362	.452	814	896	366	30	(1)	5	11	911	812
12	6	1908-20	J.Jackson	4,981	519	59	5,559	1,772	307	168	54	.356	.423	.517	940	988	202	61	(9)	10	7	996	674
13	18	1972-91	D.Evans	8,996	1,391	53	10,440	2,446	483	73	385	.272	.373	.470	843	854	78	59	(4)	4	33	887	657
14	20	1924-44	A.Simmons	8,759	615	30	9,404	2,927	539	149	307	.334	.380	.535	915	857	88	64	(4)	(0)	32	886	605
15	37	1973-95	D.Winfield	11,003	1,216	25	12,244	3,110	540	88	465	.283	.355	.475	830	829	223	96	3	6	20	857	599
16	14	1966-82	R.Smith	7,033	890	33	7,956	2,020	363	57	314	.287	.370	.489	859	882	137	86	(4)	4	21	903	556
17	10	1898-10	E.Flick	5,597	597	99	6,293	1,752	268	164	48	.313	.389	.445	834	902	330	0	0	9	12	924	544
18	22	1933-45	B.Johnson	6,920	1,075	24	8,019	2,051	396	95	288	.296	.393	.506	899	867	96	64	(4)	8	10	882	501
19	17	1984-95	K.Puckett	7,244	450	56	7,750	2,304	414	57	207	.318	.363	.477	839	832	134	76	(2)	8	50	888	500
20	47	1967-87	R.Jackson	9,864	1,375	96	11,335	2,584	463	49	563	.262	.358	.490	848	864	228	115	(0)	5	(23)	847	494
21	32	1914-32	H.Heilmann	7,787	856	40	8,683	2,660	542	151	183	.342	.410	.520	930	897	113	64	(6)	(10)	(18)	863	459
22	45	1892-10	W.Keeler	8,591	524	129	9,244	2,932	241	145	33	.341	.388	.415	802	833	495	0	0	10	4	847	448
23	46	1921-38	G.Goslin	8,656	949	56	9,661	2,735	500	173	248	.316	.387	.500	887	831	175	89	(0)	8	8	847	435
24	26	1949-80	M.Minoso	6,579	814	192	7,585	1,963	336	83	186	.298	.391	.459	851	841	205	130	(7)	10	26	870	426
25	19	1989-	A.Belle	5,853	683	55	6,591	1,726	389	21	381	.295	.374	.564	938	899	88	41	1	0	(13)	886	424

AL All Time Greats
Outfielders

V	R	Years	Name	AB	BB	HBP	TAB	H	2B	3B	HR	BA	OB	SA	PRO	Wtd PRO	SB	CS	SBF	SPF	FF	R TF	V HC
26	27	1974-90	F.Lynn	6,925	857	30	7,812	1,960	388	43	306	.283	.364	.484	848	851	72	54	(4)	(2)	25	869	423
27	38	1967-84	A.Otis	7,299	757	33	8,089	2,020	374	66	193	.277	.347	.425	773	791	341	93	18	10	38	857	395
28	9	1939-52	C.Keller	3,790	784	10	4,584	1,085	166	72	189	.286	.410	.518	928	922	45	23	(0)	6	0	929	395
29	48	1974-89	J.Rice	8,225	670	64	8,959	2,452	373	79	382	.298	.356	.502	858	862	58	34	(1)	(2)	(12)	846	389
30	23	1947-59	L.Doby	5,348	871	38	6,257	1,515	243	52	253	.283	.387	.490	877	858	47	36	(4)	8	16	877	379
31	24	1962-76	T.Oliva	6,301	448	59	6,808	1,917	329	48	220	.304	.356	.476	832	863	86	55	(3)	5	9	874	376
32	30	1987-	E.Burks	6,044	657	45	6,746	1,770	334	61	285	.293	.366	.510	876	851	171	79	2	5	7	866	354
33	42	1955-68	R.Colavito	6,503	951	29	7,483	1,730	283	21	374	.266	.362	.489	851	856	19	27	(5)	(9)	12	853	350
34	41	1929-41	E.Averill	6,353	774	33	7,160	2,019	401	128	238	.318	.395	.534	928	865	70	57	(6)	(0)	(5)	854	346
35	11	1993-	M.Ramirez	3,470	541	37	4,048	1,086	237	11	236	.313	.411	.592	1,003	929	28	24	(5)	0	(2)	922	337
36	25	1991-	B.Williams	4,806	666	22	5,494	1,463	278	50	181	.304	.392	.496	888	835	119	71	(4)	10	32	873	317
37	35	1950-61	J.Jensen	5,236	750	23	6,009	1,463	259	45	199	.279	.372	.460	832	822	143	55	5	10	22	859	306
38	21	1992-	T.Salmon	4,051	683	37	4,771	1,180	231	16	230	.291	.398	.527	925	868	29	33	(7)	(1)	25	884	304
39	29	1936-49	J.Heath	4,937	593	10	5,540	1,447	279	102	194	.293	.370	.509	879	870	56	47	(7)	9	(7)	866	301
40	31	1915-29	K.Williams	4,862	566	28	5,456	1,552	285	77	196	.319	.393	.530	924	878	154	106	(11)	10	(14)	863	292
41	58	1965-83	B.Murcer	6,730	862	27	7,619	1,862	285	45	252	.277	.361	.445	806	823	127	75	(3)	8	6	835	291
42	54	1958-73	F.Howard	6,488	782	33	7,303	1,774	245	35	382	.273	.355	.499	853	880	8	9	(1)	(10)	(29)	840	287
43	63	1985-	J.Canseco	6,801	861	83	7,745	1,811	332	14	446	.266	.356	.516	872	846	198	87	3	1	(19)	831	284
44	36	1991-	K.Lofton	4,922	616	20	5,558	1,507	235	65	78	.306	.386	.428	813	774	463	114	41	10	33	858	280
45	39	1957-68	R.Maris	5,101	652	38	5,791	1,325	195	42	275	.260	.348	.476	824	828	21	9	0	9	19	856	280
46	65	1975-90	C.Lemon	6,868	749	151	7,768	1,875	396	61	215	.273	.357	.442	800	805	58	76	(12)	6	31	831	279
47	84	1909-25	H.Hooper	8,785	1,136	76	9,997	2,466	389	160	75	.281	.368	.387	755	776	375	121	(8)	8	36	812	278
48	66	1912-25	B.Veach	6,656	571	59	7,286	2,063	393	147	64	.310	.370	.442	812	827	195	84	(7)	8	2	829	269
49	55	1940-53	D.DiMaggio	5,640	750	31	6,421	1,680	308	57	87	.298	.383	.419	802	787	100	62	(4)	10	44	838	258
50	44	1989-	J.Gonzalez	5,292	376	50	5,718	1,554	312	21	362	.294	.346	.566	912	865	22	17	(2)	0	(15)	848	256
51	72	1965-79	R.White	6,650	934	29	7,613	1,803	300	51	160	.271	.363	.404	767	797	233	117	(0)	9	19	825	247
52	64	1979-95	K.Gibson	5,798	718	61	6,577	1,553	260	54	255	.268	.355	.463	818	816	284	78	18	8	(11)	831	244
53	93	1915-34	S.Rice	9,269	708	54	10,031	2,987	498	184	34	.322	.374	.427	800	767	351	143	(0)	10	28	805	244
54	74	1985-	P.O'Neill	6,808	844	20	7,672	1,969	418	20	260	.289	.369	.471	840	816	119	70	(3)	2	6	821	240
55	75	1894-06	K.Selbach	6,158	783	41	6,982	1,803	299	149	44	.293	.376	.411	787	799	334	0	0	7	14	820	238
56	53	1987-	J.Buhner	4,968	784	56	5,808	1,263	231	19	308	.254	.362	.494	856	825	6	24	(7)	(2)	24	840	237
57	52	1958-70	B.Allison	5,032	795	34	5,861	1,281	216	53	256	.255	.360	.471	831	845	84	50	(3)	6	(8)	840	231
58	60	1897-06	C.Stahl	5,069	470	44	5,583	1,546	219	118	36	.305	.369	.416	785	822	189	0	0	10	2	834	226
59	43	1938-47	R.Cullenbine	3,879	853	11	4,743	1,072	209	32	110	.276	.408	.432	840	852	26	20	(3)	0	4	853	225
60	51	1937-50	T.Henrich	4,603	712	34	5,349	1,297	269	73	183	.282	.382	.491	873	847	37	19	(0)	0	(5)	842	224
61	49	1981-92	J.Barfield	4,759	551	34	5,344	1,219	216	30	241	.256	.338	.466	804	802	66	47	(5)	6	40	843	220
62	62	1898-11	T.Hartsel	4,848	837	12	5,697	1,336	182	92	31	.276	.384	.370	754	838	247	0	0	7	(14)	832	215
63	40	1899-08	S.Seybold	3,685	293	40	4,018	1,085	218	54	51	.294	.353	.424	777	852	66	0	0	0	2	855	204
64	69	1984-97	D.Tartabull	5,011	768	17	5,796	1,366	289	22	262	.273	.371	.496	867	856	37	30	(4)	(5)	(20)	827	203
65	91	1923-39	H.Manush	7,654	506	70	8,230	2,524	491	160	110	.330	.377	.479	856	808	114	58	(1)	6	(6)	807	203
66	28	1903-10	G.Stone	3,271	282	22	3,575	984	106	68	23	.301	.360	.396	756	871	132	0	0	10	(14)	867	196
67	33	1993-	J.Edmonds	3,169	377	21	3,567	923	186	12	163	.291	.370	.512	882	817	36	27	(5)	10	39	861	188
68	98	1970-84	K.Singleton	7,189	1,263	17	8,469	2,029	317	25	246	.282	.391	.436	827	837	21	36	(6)	(7)	(23)	801	186
69	81	1924-35	E.Combs	5,746	670	17	6,433	1,866	309	154	58	.325	.397	.462	859	808	96	71	(7)	9	4	814	184
70	87	1988-	B.Anderson	5,989	882	144	7,015	1,561	322	64	201	.261	.369	.436	805	768	299	96	16	10	15	809	180
71	57	1891-07	B.Freeman	4,208	272	66	4,546	1,235	199	131	82	.293	.346	.462	808	855	92	0	0	0	(20)	835	179
72	61	1974-85	S.Lezcano	4,134	576	19	4,729	1,122	184	34	148	.271	.363	.440	803	814	37	31	(5)	6	18	833	175
73	59	1940-49	S.Spence	3,871	520	19	4,410	1,090	196	60	95	.282	.369	.437	806	820	21	23	(5)	1	20	835	170
74	68	1968-82	L.Hisle	4,205	462	39	4,706	1,146	193	32	166	.273	.350	.452	802	819	128	61	1	8	1	829	163
75	34	1915-20	H.Felsch	2,812	207	24	3,043	825	135	64	38	.293	.347	.427	774	812	88	31	(11)	10	49	859	159

AL All Time Greats
Starting Pitchers

V	R	Years	Name	G	GS	IP	W	L	SV	SO	BB	ERA	RA/9	R Wtd RA/9	V Runs /162
1	1	1907-27	W.Johnson	802	666	5,914	417	279	34	3,509	1,363	2.17	2.89	3.10	1,021.3
2	3	1925-41	L.Grove	616	457	3,941	300	141	55	2,266	1,187	3.06	3.64	3.22	616.1
3	4	1984-	R.Clemens	512	511	3,667	260	142	0	3,504	1,186	3.07	3.40	3.23	555.2
4	18	1901-17	E.Plank	623	529	4,496	326	194	23	2,246	1,072	2.35	3.14	3.58	524.0
5	2	1904-17	E.Walsh	430	315	2,964	195	126	35	1,736	617	1.82	2.66	3.13	493.5
6	11	1965-84	J.Palmer	558	521	3,948	268	152	4	2,212	1,311	2.86	3.18	3.49	479.4
7	14	1936-56	B.Feller	570	484	3,827	266	162	21	2,581	1,764	3.25	3.66	3.53	459.3
8	6	1950-67	W.Ford	498	438	3,170	236	106	10	1,956	1,086	2.75	3.14	3.31	452.4
9	66	1966-93	N.Ryan	807	773	5,386	324	292	3	5,714	2,795	3.19	3.64	3.95	366.8
10	56	1970-92	B.Blyleven	692	685	4,970	287	250	0	3,701	1,322	3.31	3.67	3.91	366.6
11	22	1912-28	S.Coveleski	450	385	3,082	215	142	21	981	802	2.89	3.60	3.63	345.0
12	7	1902-10	A.Joss	286	260	2,327	160	97	5	920	364	1.89	2.82	3.32	343.9
13	25	1945-64	B.Pierce	585	432	3,307	211	169	32	1,999	1,178	3.27	3.61	3.68	338.4
14	20	1897-10	R.Waddell	407	340	2,961	193	143	5	2,316	803	2.16	3.23	3.61	338.0
15	26	1905-20	E.Cicotte	502	361	3,223	208	149	25	1,374	827	2.38	3.21	3.69	336.0
16	9	1930-43	L.Gomez	368	320	2,503	189	102	9	1,468	1,095	3.34	3.92	3.43	329.4
17	10	1988-	R.Johnson	366	357	2,499	179	95	2	3,040	1,089	3.20	3.61	3.44	320.9
18	63	1924-47	R.Ruffing	624	536	4,344	273	225	16	1,987	1,541	3.80	4.39	3.95	309.7
19	30	1915-29	C.Mays	490	324	3,021	208	126	31	862	734	2.92	3.61	3.71	308.9
20	62	1914-33	R.Faber	669	483	4,087	254	213	28	1,471	1,213	3.15	3.99	3.93	301.9
21	27	1939-55	H.Newhouser	488	374	2,993	207	150	26	1,796	1,249	3.06	3.60	3.70	300.5
22	24	1916-28	U.Shocker	412	317	2,682	187	117	25	983	657	3.17	3.78	3.65	287.9
23	21	1986-	K.Brown	382	380	2,661	170	114	0	1,917	730	3.21	3.69	3.62	287.9
24	68	1923-46	T.Lyons	594	484	4,161	260	230	23	1,073	1,121	3.67	4.45	3.97	287.3
25	17	1984-	B.Saberhagen	396	368	2,548	166	115	1	1,705	471	3.33	3.62	3.58	286.8
26	8	1991-	M.Mussina	288	288	2,010	147	81	0	1,535	467	3.53	3.75	3.35	282.4
27	38	1901-13	D.White	427	363	3,041	189	156	5	1,384	670	2.39	3.30	3.80	275.6
28	34	1913-27	B.Shawkey	488	333	2,937	195	150	28	1,360	1,018	3.09	3.68	3.77	271.7
29	33	1946-58	B.Lemon	460	350	2,850	207	128	22	1,277	1,251	3.23	3.74	3.77	263.5
30	32	1930-46	T.Bridges	424	362	2,826	194	138	10	1,674	1,192	3.57	4.21	3.77	261.4
31	19	1975-88	R.Guidry	368	323	2,392	170	91	4	1,778	633	3.29	3.59	3.61	259.7
32	73	1918-38	W.Hoyt	674	423	3,762	237	182	52	1,206	1,003	3.59	4.26	3.97	258.2
33	28	1984-98	J.Key	470	389	2,592	186	117	10	1,538	668	3.51	3.83	3.70	252.9
34	78	1955-71	J.Bunning	591	519	3,760	224	184	16	2,855	1,000	3.27	3.66	3.99	240.1
35	45	1979-98	D.Stieb	443	412	2,895	176	137	3	1,669	1,034	3.44	3.81	3.84	238.7
36	67	1975-98	D.Eckersley	1,071	361	3,286	197	171	390	2,401	738	3.50	3.79	3.96	226.1
37	23	1989-	K.Appier	324	312	2,085	136	105	0	1,633	759	3.63	3.94	3.63	223.6
38	70	1933-53	D.Leonard	640	375	3,218	191	181	44	1,170	737	3.25	4.00	3.97	220.9
39	115	1963-89	T.John	760	700	4,710	288	231	4	2,245	1,259	3.34	3.85	4.14	220.0
40	5	1937-47	S.Chandler	211	184	1,485	109	43	6	614	463	2.84	3.33	3.31	217.2
41	76	1969-86	V.Blue	502	473	3,343	209	161	2	2,175	1,185	3.27	3.65	3.99	216.4
42	81	1964-82	L.Tiant	573	484	3,486	229	172	15	2,416	1,104	3.30	3.61	4.01	214.4
43	60	1986-	C.Finley	470	413	2,893	181	151	0	2,340	1,219	3.76	4.18	3.92	212.4
44	29	1968-79	A.Messersmith	344	295	2,230	130	99	15	1,625	831	2.86	3.28	3.70	212.3
45	31	1948-61	M.Garcia	428	281	2,175	142	97	23	1,117	719	3.27	3.67	3.72	211.7
46	92	1912-34	H.Pennock	617	419	3,572	241	162	33	1,227	916	3.60	4.28	4.06	208.4
47	120	1939-63	E.Wynn	691	612	4,564	300	244	15	2,334	1,775	3.54	4.02	4.17	207.0
48	75	1903-25	C.Bender	459	334	3,017	212	127	34	1,711	712	2.46	3.31	3.98	204.5
49	46	1944-55	E.Lopat	340	318	2,439	166	112	3	859	650	3.21	3.72	3.84	203.5
50	36	1913-25	D.Leonard	331	272	2,192	139	112	13	1,160	664	2.76	3.50	3.79	201.0

AL All Time Greats
Starting Pitchers

V	R	Years	Name	G	GS	IP	W	L	SV	SO	BB	ERA	RA/9	R Wtd RA/9	V Runs /162
51	49	1942-54	A.Reynolds	434	309	2,492	182	107	49	1,423	1,261	3.30	3.71	3.87	200.3
52	124	1897-12	J.Powell	578	516	4,389	245	254	15	1,621	1,021	2.97	4.08	4.18	198.9
53	52	1920-32	E.Rommel	500	249	2,556	171	119	29	599	724	3.54	4.27	3.89	198.2
54	61	1941-58	V.Trucks	517	328	2,682	177	135	30	1,534	1,088	3.39	3.77	3.93	197.3
55	71	1894-11	J.Tannehill	358	320	2,750	197	117	7	940	477	2.79	3.91	3.97	197.2
56	35	1923-36	F.Marberry	551	186	2,067	148	88	101	822	686	3.63	4.23	3.78	187.9
57	74	1939-57	D.Trout	521	322	2,726	170	161	35	1,256	1,046	3.23	3.85	3.97	186.4
58	101	1965-79	C.Hunter	500	476	3,449	224	166	1	2,012	954	3.26	3.60	4.08	184.8
59	12	1908-20	J.Wood	225	158	1,434	117	57	10	989	421	2.03	3.11	3.50	178.0
60	16	1940-49	T.Bonham	231	193	1,551	103	72	9	478	287	3.06	3.36	3.58	177.7
61	72	1964-74	M.Stottlemyre	360	356	2,661	164	139	1	1,257	809	2.97	3.39	3.97	174.2
62	112	1928-47	M.Harder	582	433	3,426	223	186	23	1,161	1,118	3.80	4.50	4.12	173.2
63	47	1949-64	B.Shantz	537	171	1,936	119	99	48	1,072	643	3.38	3.80	3.85	158.8
64	48	1932-44	J.Allen	352	241	1,950	142	75	18	1,070	738	3.75	4.26	3.86	158.4
65	15	1941-49	T.Hughson	225	156	1,376	96	54	17	693	372	2.94	3.30	3.57	158.1
66	13	1914-33	B.Ruth	163	148	1,221	94	46	4	488	441	2.28	2.94	3.50	157.6
67	135	1976-98	D.Martinez	692	562	4,000	245	193	8	2,149	1,165	3.70	4.13	4.23	153.4
68	134	1909-33	J.Quinn	756	444	3,920	247	218	57	1,329	860	3.29	4.20	4.23	153.4
69	98	1962-75	D.McNally	424	396	2,730	184	119	2	1,512	826	3.24	3.53	4.07	148.3
70	139	1973-93	F.Tanana	638	616	4,188	240	236	1	2,773	1,255	3.66	4.10	4.24	148.2
71	102	1927-41	W.Ferrell	374	323	2,623	193	128	13	985	1,040	4.04	4.74	4.08	146.7
72	84	1933-48	T.Lee	374	272	2,331	117	124	10	937	838	3.56	4.27	4.03	143.8
73	118	1898-18	B.Donovan	378	327	2,965	186	139	8	1,552	1,059	2.69	3.68	4.16	143.4
74	57	1909-17	J.Scott	317	226	1,892	107	114	9	945	609	2.30	3.30	3.91	142.2
75	50	1990-	A.Fernandez	263	261	1,760	107	87	0	1,252	552	3.74	4.11	3.88	139.6
76	121	1957-73	M.Pappas	520	465	3,186	209	164	4	1,728	858	3.40	3.76	4.17	138.4
77	111	1959-77	M.Cuellar	453	379	2,808	185	130	11	1,632	822	3.14	3.62	4.12	136.2
78	64	1987-99	J.McDowell	277	275	1,889	127	87	0	1,311	606	3.86	4.16	3.95	134.7
79	127	1918-36	T.Zachary	533	408	3,126	186	191	22	720	914	3.73	4.47	4.20	130.6
80	95	1987-	D.Wells	479	309	2,307	161	107	13	1,576	538	4.06	4.40	4.06	130.4
81	39	1946-57	E.Kinder	484	122	1,480	102	71	102	749	539	3.43	3.81	3.81	129.6
82	94	1933-49	S.Rowe	382	278	2,219	158	101	12	913	558	3.87	4.36	4.06	128.1
83	105	1911-27	G.Mogridge	398	261	2,266	132	131	20	678	565	3.23	3.99	4.09	127.4
84	91	1939-54	J.Dobson	414	273	2,170	137	103	18	992	851	3.62	4.06	4.06	126.3
85	85	1961-71	D.Chance	406	294	2,147	128	115	23	1,534	739	2.92	3.49	4.03	125.5
86	109	1926-36	G.Crowder	402	292	2,344	167	115	22	799	800	4.12	4.62	4.10	124.7
87	44	1901-07	R.Patterson	184	152	1,365	81	72	2	442	273	2.75	3.74	3.83	123.0
88	129	1899-09	J.Chesbro	392	332	2,897	198	132	5	1,265	690	2.68	3.76	4.21	120.8
89	93	1941-57	S.Gromek	447	225	2,065	123	108	23	904	630	3.41	3.89	4.06	119.7
90	162	1977-94	J.Morris	549	527	3,824	254	186	0	2,478	1,390	3.90	4.27	4.29	119.0
91	37	1909-15	R.Collins	199	151	1,336	84	62	4	511	269	2.51	3.33	3.80	118.3
92	125	1982-96	F.Viola	421	420	2,836	176	150	0	1,844	864	3.73	4.13	4.18	118.2
93	40	1913-19	R.Russell	242	148	1,292	80	59	13	495	267	2.33	3.15	3.81	115.4
94	88	1912-23	J.Bagby	316	208	1,822	127	88	29	450	458	3.11	3.80	4.04	115.2
95	143	1898-09	B.Dinneen	391	352	3,075	170	177	7	1,127	829	3.01	4.13	4.25	114.5
96	117	1961-75	S.McDowell	425	346	2,492	141	134	14	2,453	1,312	3.17	3.61	4.15	112.4
97	86	1946-55	V.Raschi	269	255	1,819	132	66	3	944	727	3.72	4.09	4.04	110.4
98	96	1961-72	J.Horlen	361	290	2,002	116	117	4	1,065	554	3.11	3.52	4.07	109.6
99	58	1932-41	M.Pearson	224	191	1,430	100	61	4	703	740	4.00	4.54	3.92	107.1
100	53	1911-19	J.Benz	251	163	1,360	76	75	3	539	334	2.43	3.37	3.90	106.4

AL All Time Greats
Relief Pitchers

V	R	Years	Name	G	GS	IP	W	L	SV	SO	BB	ERA	RA/9	R Wtd RA/9	V Runs /162
1	10	1952-72	H.Wilhelm	1,070	52	2,254	143	122	227	1,610	778	2.52	3.09	3.30	323.8
2	25	1972-94	R.Gossage	1,002	37	1,809	124	107	310	1,502	732	3.01	3.33	3.59	198.8
3	20	1968-85	R.Fingers	944	37	1,701	114	118	341	1,299	492	2.90	3.25	3.53	198.7
4	7	1979-90	D.Quisenberry	674	0	1,043	56	46	244	379	162	2.76	3.07	3.16	166.6
5	2	1982-95	T.Henke	642	0	790	41	42	311	861	255	2.67	2.87	2.85	154.3
6	16	1965-80	J.Hiller	545	43	1,242	87	76	125	1,036	535	2.83	3.17	3.49	146.9
7	9	1982-96	M.Eichhorn	563	7	886	48	43	32	640	270	3.00	3.33	3.29	128.5
8	36	1967-82	S.Lyle	899	0	1,390	99	76	238	873	481	2.88	3.36	3.75	128.4
9	21	1982-	D.Jones	846	4	1,128	69	79	303	909	247	3.30	3.71	3.56	127.8
10	23	1986-	M.Jackson	835	7	1,018	53	61	138	905	414	3.26	3.62	3.57	114.1
11	15	1987-99	J.Montgomery	700	1	869	46	52	304	733	296	3.27	3.60	3.42	113.2
12	26	1932-47	J.Murphy	415	40	1,045	93	53	107	378	444	3.50	4.00	3.65	111.1
13	11	1989-	J.Wetteland	618	17	765	48	45	330	804	252	2.93	3.38	3.31	110.7
14	6	1991-	R.Hernandez	580	3	655	42	42	266	631	267	3.03	3.41	3.13	108.1
15	47	1979-95	D.Righetti	718	89	1,404	82	79	252	1,112	591	3.46	3.86	3.90	107.8
16	1	1995-	M.Rivera	332	10	452	33	17	165	395	144	2.63	2.77	2.47	106.7
17	50	1985-	R.Aguilera	732	89	1,291	86	81	318	1,030	351	3.57	3.96	3.91	96.0
18	22	1984-94	S.Farr	509	28	824	48	45	132	668	334	3.25	3.56	3.57	91.9
19	13	1988-	G.Olson	594	0	647	40	38	217	564	310	3.28	3.49	3.39	85.4
20	65	1955-71	D.Hall	495	74	1,260	93	75	68	741	236	3.32	3.66	4.01	78.1
21	12	1992-	J.Nelson	534	0	555	35	32	17	560	287	3.29	3.71	3.36	77.5
22	27	1987-96	M.Henneman	561	0	733	57	42	193	533	271	3.21	3.70	3.65	75.8
23	64	1986-99	E.Plunk	714	41	1,151	72	58	35	1,081	647	3.82	4.20	4.00	73.5
24	3	1987-95	B.Harvey	322	0	387	17	25	177	448	144	2.49	2.84	2.89	72.7
25	54	1977-89	W.Hernandez	744	11	1,045	70	63	147	788	349	3.38	3.71	3.94	72.2
26	51	1978-87	S.Stewart	359	25	957	59	48	45	586	502	3.59	3.96	3.92	71.7
27	4	1994-	A.Benitez	360	0	368	19	23	100	517	208	3.04	3.23	2.92	68.8
28	5	1995-	T.Percival	360	0	374	19	27	171	460	168	3.16	3.40	2.96	68.0
29	77	1968-84	T.Burgmeier	745	3	1,259	79	55	102	584	384	3.23	3.74	4.09	66.8
30	41	1992-	B.Wickman	521	28	761	53	42	104	537	343	3.76	4.16	3.81	66.7
31	101	1977-89	B.Stanley	637	85	1,707	115	97	132	693	471	3.64	4.20	4.24	62.6
32	61	1986-	D.Plesac	884	14	957	56	62	154	895	323	3.65	4.05	3.99	62.5
33	73	1965-80	D.Knowles	765	8	1,092	66	74	143	681	480	3.12	3.60	4.05	61.8
34	53	1965-75	B.Locker	576	0	879	57	39	95	577	257	2.75	3.37	3.94	60.8
35	34	1986-95	D.Ward	462	2	667	32	37	121	679	286	3.28	3.62	3.74	60.7
36	31	1991-	M.Timlin	525	3	626	37	40	111	502	246	3.59	4.03	3.73	59.9
37	37	1961-72	S.Hamilton	421	17	663	40	31	42	531	214	3.05	3.32	3.75	59.2
38	56	1974-88	T.Martinez	546	2	834	55	42	115	632	425	3.45	3.85	3.95	58.3
39	40	1962-69	D.Radatz	381	0	694	52	43	122	745	296	3.13	3.37	3.80	58.0
40	30	1980-87	D.Corbett	313	1	553	24	30	66	343	200	3.32	3.68	3.69	57.9
41	68	1974-87	A.Lopez	459	9	910	62	36	93	635	367	3.56	3.88	4.02	57.2
42	18	1988-99	J.Corsi	368	1	481	22	24	7	290	191	3.25	3.68	3.51	56.4
43	82	1971-86	T.Forster	614	39	1,106	54	65	127	791	457	3.23	3.70	4.12	54.8
44	79	1970-83	D.LaRoche	647	15	1,049	65	58	126	819	459	3.53	3.84	4.10	54.6
45	55	1974-86	J.Kern	416	14	793	53	57	88	651	444	3.32	3.77	3.95	54.5
46	84	1977-90	D.Aase	448	91	1,109	66	60	82	641	457	3.80	4.08	4.13	54.2
47	43	1964-76	K.Sanders	408	1	657	29	45	86	360	258	2.97	3.29	3.83	53.6
48	90	1962-74	P.Richert	429	122	1,166	80	73	51	925	424	3.19	3.58	4.17	50.3
49	28	1948-65	S.Paige	179	26	476	28	31	32	288	180	3.29	3.61	3.66	49.9
50	39	1986-94	B.Thigpen	448	0	569	31	36	201	376	238	3.43	3.75	3.79	48.7

NL All Time Greats　　　　　　**Hitters Volume of Success**

Pos	Years	Name	AB	BB	HBP	TAB	H	2B	3B	HR	BA	OB	SA	PRO	Wtd PRO	SB	CS	SBF	SPF	FF	R TF	V HC
C	1967-83	J.Bench	7,658	891	19	8,568	2,048	381	24	389	.267	.345	.476	821	835	68	43	(2)	(3)	65	896	878
1B	1991-	J.Bagwell	5,349	992	97	6,438	1,630	351	22	310	.305	.422	.552	975	938	167	64	6	10	22	976	657
2B	1915-37	R.Hornsby	8,173	1,038	48	9,259	2,930	541	169	301	.358	.434	.577	1,010	995	135	64	(7)	(0)	(2)	986	1,407
SS	1897-17	H.Wagner	10,430	963	124	11,517	3,415	640	252	101	.327	.391	.466	857	921	722	15	(1)	9	40	970	1,685
3B	1972-89	M.Schmidt	8,352	1,507	79	9,938	2,234	408	59	548	.267	.384	.527	912	924	174	92	(1)	5	56	984	1,283
OF	1951-73	W.Mays	10,881	1,464	44	12,389	3,283	523	140	660	.302	.387	.557	944	942	338	103	10	10	58	1,019	1,579
OF	1954-76	H.Aaron	12,364	1,402	32	13,798	3,771	624	98	755	.305	.377	.555	932	935	240	73	6	8	22	971	1,429
OF	1986-	B.Bonds	7,456	1,547	56	9,059	2,157	451	69	494	.289	.415	.567	982	959	471	135	21	10	56	1,046	1,290
Starters		Averages	8,833	1,226	62	10,121	2,684	490	104	445	.304	.392	.534	926	932	289	74	4	6	40	982	1,276
C	1922-41	G.Hartnett	6,432	703	35	7,170	1,912	396	64	236	.297	.370	.489	858	830	28	7	0	(10)	33	853	632
1B	1936-53	J.Mize	6,443	856	52	7,351	2,011	367	83	359	.312	.397	.562	959	955	28	1	(0)	(4)	(4)	946	652
2B	1963-84	J.Morgan	9,277	1,865	40	11,182	2,517	449	96	268	.271	.395	.427	823	833	689	162	31	10	9	882	1,074
SS	1891-11	B.Dahlen	9,031	1,064	140	10,235	2,457	413	163	84	.272	.358	.382	739	767	547	0	0	9	50	826	880
3B	1952-68	E.Mathews	8,537	1,444	26	10,007	2,315	354	72	512	.271	.378	.509	888	877	68	39	(1)	7	4	887	829
OF	1941-63	S.Musial	10,972	1,599	53	12,624	3,630	725	177	475	.331	.418	.559	977	966	78	31	(2)	(1)	(1)	961	1,257
OF	1956-76	F.Robinson	10,006	1,420	198	11,624	2,943	528	72	586	.294	.392	.537	929	941	204	77	4	7	10	963	1,144
OF	1926-47	M.Ott	9,456	1,708	64	11,228	2,876	488	72	511	.304	.414	.533	947	934	89	0	0	(1)	10	943	1,075
Reserves		Averages	8,769	1,332	76	10,178	2,583	465	100	379	.295	.392	.500	892	891	216	40	4	2	14	911	943
Totals		Weighted Ave.	8,812	1,261	67	10,140	2,650	482	103	423	.301	.392	.523	915	918	265	62	4	5	31	958	1,165

Pitchers Volume of Success

Pos	Years	Name	G	GS	IP	W	L	SV	SO	BB	ERA	RA/9	R Wtd RA/9	V Runs /162
SP	1911-30	P.Alexander	696	600	5,190	373	208	32	2,198	951	2.56	3.21	3.37	726
SP	1900-16	C.Mathewson	635	551	4,781	373	188	29	2,502	844	2.13	3.04	3.42	646
SP	1942-65	W.Spahn	750	665	5,244	363	245	29	2,583	1,434	3.09	3.46	3.59	590
SP	1967-86	T.Seaver	656	647	4,783	311	205	1	3,640	1,390	2.86	3.15	3.47	589
SP	1928-43	C.Hubbell	535	431	3,590	253	154	33	1,677	725	2.98	3.46	3.40	484
Starters		Averages	654	579	4,717	335	200	25	2,520	1,069	2.71	3.26	3.45	607
RP	1984-	J.Franco	940	0	1,097	82	74	420	857	430	2.68	3.19	3.35	151
RP	1974-89	K.Tekulve	1,050	0	1,436	94	90	184	779	491	2.85	3.30	3.64	150
RP	1980-97	L.Smith	1,022	6	1,289	71	92	478	1,251	486	3.03	3.32	3.57	148
RP	1979-	J.Orosco	1,096	4	1,218	84	75	141	1,107	541	3.03	3.43	3.51	146
Relievers		Averages	1,027	3	1,260	83	83	306	999	487	2.90	3.31	3.53	149
Totals		Averages	1,681	581	5,978	417	283	331	3,519	1,556	2.75	3.27	3.47	756

NL All Time Greats — **Hitters Rate of Success**

Pos	Years	Name	AB	BB	HBP	TAB	H	2B	3B	HR	BA	OB	SA	PRO	Wtd PRO	SB	CS	SBF	SPF	FF	R TF	V HC
C	1967-83	J.Bench	7,658	891	19	8,568	2,048	381	24	389	.267	.345	.476	821	835	68	43	(2)	(3)	65	896	878
1B	1991-	J.Bagwell	5,349	992	97	6,438	1,630	351	22	310	.305	.422	.552	975	938	167	64	6	10	22	976	657
2B	1915-37	R.Hornsby	8,173	1,038	48	9,259	2,930	541	169	301	.358	.434	.577	1,010	995	135	64	(7)	(0)	(2)	986	1,407
SS	1897-17	H.Wagner	10,430	963	124	11,517	3,415	640	252	101	.327	.391	.466	857	921	722	15	(1)	9	40	970	1,685
3B	1972-89	M.Schmidt	8,352	1,507	79	9,938	2,234	408	59	548	.267	.384	.527	912	924	174	92	(1)	5	56	984	1,283
OF	1986-	B.Bonds	7,456	1,547	56	9,059	2,157	451	69	494	.289	.415	.567	982	959	471	135	21	10	56	1,046	1,290
OF	1951-73	W.Mays	10,881	1,464	44	12,389	3,283	523	140	660	.302	.387	.557	944	942	338	103	10	10	58	1,019	1,579
OF	1954-76	H.Aaron	12,364	1,402	32	13,798	3,771	624	98	755	.305	.377	.555	932	935	240	73	6	8	22	971	1,429
Starters		Averages	8,833	1,226	62	10,121	2,684	490	104	445	.304	.392	.534	926	932	289	74	4	6	40	982	1,276
C	1992-	M.Piazza	4,135	439	16	4,590	1,356	199	4	278	.328	.395	.580	974	918	17	15	(3)	(10)	(18)	887	483
1B	1997-	T.Helton	1,781	232	16	2,029	594	137	9	107	.334	.415	.601	1,016	940	15	13	(5)	0	16	951	177
2B	1947-56	J.Robinson	4,877	740	72	5,689	1,518	273	54	137	.311	.410	.474	883	858	197	30	6	10	24	899	531
SS	1986-	B.Larkin	6,687	812	48	7,547	2,008	361	70	179	.300	.380	.456	836	813	359	71	28	9	29	879	810
3B	1993-	C.Jones	3,469	554	5	4,028	1,051	204	18	189	.303	.400	.536	935	875	97	26	10	10	(5)	891	343
OF	1989-	L.Walker	4,906	578	89	5,573	1,528	335	43	271	.311	.394	.563	957	922	195	61	12	10	26	970	591
OF	1956-76	F.Robinson	10,006	1,420	198	11,624	2,943	528	72	586	.294	.392	.537	929	941	204	77	4	7	10	963	1,144
OF	1941-63	S.Musial	10,972	1,599	53	12,624	3,630	725	177	475	.331	.418	.559	977	966	78	31	(2)	(1)	(1)	961	1,257
Reserves		Averages	5,854	797	62	6,713	1,829	345	56	278	.312	.400	.533	933	911	145	41	6	4	10	932	667
Totals		Weighted Ave.	7,840	1,083	62	8,985	2,399	442	88	389	.306	.394	.534	928	925	241	63	5	5	30	965	1,073

Pitchers Rate of Success

Pos	Years	Name	G	GS	IP	W	L	SV	SO	BB	ERA	RA/9	R Wtd RA/9	V Runs /162
SP	1992-	P.Martinez	278	211	1,576	125	56	3	1,818	442	2.68	2.96	2.84	317
SP	1986-	G.Maddux	471	467	3,318	240	135	0	2,350	733	2.83	3.24	3.31	476
SP	1955-66	S.Koufax	397	314	2,324	165	87	9	2,396	817	2.76	3.12	3.36	317
SP	1911-30	P.Alexander	696	600	5,190	373	208	32	2,198	951	2.56	3.21	3.37	726
SP	1903-16	T.Brown	481	332	3,172	239	130	49	1,375	673	2.06	2.96	3.40	432
Starters		Averages	465	385	3,116	228	123	19	2,027	723	2.56	3.13	3.31	454
RP	1995-	B.Wagner	252	0	281	19	18	107	422	126	2.73	2.92	2.78	56
RP	1993-	T.Hoffman	509	0	581	40	35	271	665	175	2.73	3.03	2.92	111
RP	1998-	J.Rocker	180	0	163	6	10	64	223	107	2.54	3.25	2.98	29
RP	1984-	J.Franco	940	0	1,097	82	74	420	857	430	2.68	3.19	3.35	151
Relievers		Averages	470	0	531	37	34	216	542	210	2.69	3.12	3.13	87
Totals		Averages	935	385	3,647	265	157	234	2,569	933	2.58	3.13	3.28	540

NL All Time Greats
Catchers

V	R	Years	Name	AB	BB	HBP	TAB	H	2B	3B	HR	BA	OB	SA	PRO	Wtd PRO	SB	CS	SBF	SPF	FF	R TF	V HC
1	1	1967-83	J.Bench	7,658	891	19	8,568	2,048	381	24	389	.267	.345	.476	821	835	68	43	(2)	(3)	65	896	878
2	4	1922-41	G.Hartnett	6,432	703	35	7,170	1,912	396	64	236	.297	.370	.489	858	830	28	7	0	(10)	33	853	632
3	9	1974-92	G.Carter	7,971	848	68	8,887	2,092	371	31	324	.262	.338	.439	777	784	39	42	(5)	(6)	29	802	520
4	2	1992-	M.Piazza	4,135	439	16	4,590	1,356	199	4	278	.328	.395	.580	974	918	17	15	(3)	(10)	(18)	887	483
5	3	1948-57	R.Campanella	4,205	533	30	4,768	1,161	178	18	242	.276	.362	.500	861	835	25	15	(2)	(4)	48	877	476
6	7	1960-77	J.Torre	7,874	779	85	8,738	2,342	344	59	252	.297	.367	.452	819	836	23	29	(4)	(9)	(0)	822	475
7	5	1897-15	R.Bresnahan	4,481	714	66	5,261	1,252	218	71	26	.279	.386	.377	763	827	212	3	2	9	10	848	404
8	10	1931-47	E.Lombardi	5,855	430	44	6,329	1,792	277	27	190	.306	.358	.460	818	821	8	0	0	(10)	(10)	801	394
9	18	1968-88	T.Simmons	8,680	855	39	9,574	2,472	483	47	248	.285	.352	.437	789	793	21	33	(4)	(8)	(7)	773	380
10	15	1940-57	W.Cooper	4,702	309	22	5,033	1,341	240	40	173	.285	.332	.464	796	795	18	1	0	(10)	(10)	775	246
11	19	1949-67	S.Burgess	4,471	477	13	4,961	1,318	230	33	126	.295	.364	.446	810	794	13	14	(3)	(8)	(11)	772	232
12	23	1959-80	T.McCarver	5,529	548	30	6,107	1,501	242	57	97	.271	.340	.388	729	748	61	49	(6)	5	12	760	225
13	6	1996-	J.Kendall	2,294	252	104	2,650	720	148	21	45	.314	.406	.456	862	807	93	28	13	10	15	845	211
14	13	1983-97	D.Daulton	3,630	629	24	4,283	891	197	25	137	.245	.360	.427	787	781	50	10	7	0	(6)	782	204
15	20	1961-72	T.Haller	3,935	477	35	4,447	1,011	153	31	134	.257	.342	.414	756	778	14	30	(10)	(7)	9	769	196
16	24	1928-45	S.Davis	4,255	386	22	4,663	1,312	244	22	77	.308	.369	.430	799	780	6	0	0	(10)	(10)	760	193
17	12	1909-17	C.Meyers	2,834	274	63	3,171	826	120	41	14	.291	.367	.378	744	789	44	4	(1)	(10)	13	791	181
18	32	1900-13	J.Kling	4,241	281	12	4,534	1,151	181	61	20	.271	.318	.357	675	735	123	0	0	(3)	15	747	163
19	31	1953-66	E.Bailey	3,581	545	25	4,151	915	128	15	155	.256	.358	.429	787	776	17	18	(4)	(10)	(10)	751	152
20	22	1970-83	J.Ferguson	3,001	562	9	3,572	719	121	11	122	.240	.361	.409	770	775	22	12	(1)	(8)	(1)	765	151
21	40	1980-97	T.Pena	6,489	455	23	6,967	1,687	298	27	107	.260	.311	.364	674	680	80	63	(6)	(2)	51	722	150
22	16	1992-	J.Lopez	2,761	184	29	2,974	800	130	10	143	.290	.341	.499	840	786	7	16	(8)	(7)	4	775	146
23	38	1949-66	D.Crandall	5,026	424	21	5,471	1,276	179	18	179	.254	.315	.404	718	701	26	28	(5)	(3)	38	731	146
24	34	1967-80	M.Sanguillen	5,062	223	23	5,308	1,500	205	57	65	.296	.329	.398	727	736	35	38	(7)	7	2	738	143
25	39	1986-	B.Santiago	5,397	343	30	5,770	1,406	242	29	178	.261	.308	.415	723	709	81	60	(6)	5	20	728	142

NL All Time Greats
First basemen

V	R	Years	Name	AB	BB	HBP	TAB	H	2B	3B	HR	BA	OB	SA	PRO	Wtd PRO	SB	CS	SBF	SPF	FF	R TF	V HC
1	1	1991-	J.Bagwell	5,349	992	97	6,438	1,630	351	22	310	.305	.422	.552	975	938	167	64	6	10	22	976	657
2	3	1936-53	J.Mize	6,443	856	52	7,351	2,011	367	83	359	.312	.397	.562	959	955	28	1	(0)	(4)	(4)	946	652
3	4	1963-77	D.Allen	6,332	894	16	7,242	1,848	320	79	351	.292	.381	.534	914	946	133	52	4	10	(30)	930	641
4	7	1959-80	W.McCovey	8,197	1,345	69	9,611	2,211	353	46	521	.270	.377	.515	892	906	26	22	(2)	(9)	(18)	877	509
5	9	1974-90	K.Hernandez	7,370	1,070	32	8,472	2,182	426	60	162	.296	.388	.436	824	832	98	63	(3)	(1)	40	868	406
6	11	1986-	F.McGriff	7,352	1,136	31	8,519	2,103	372	20	417	.286	.384	.512	896	874	70	34	0	(3)	(9)	862	387
7	5	1933-45	D.Camilli	5,353	947	28	6,328	1,482	261	86	239	.277	.388	.492	880	883	60	0	0	0	5	888	379
8	13	1958-74	O.Cepeda	7,927	588	102	8,617	2,351	417	27	379	.297	.353	.499	852	860	142	80	(2)	2	(0)	859	377
9	10	1986-	W.Clark	7,173	937	59	8,169	2,176	440	47	284	.303	.388	.497	885	865	67	48	(3)	(2)	4	863	375
10	8	1923-36	B.Terry	6,428	537	9	6,974	2,193	373	112	154	.341	.393	.506	899	858	56	6	(1)	(2)	16	871	351
11	6	1898-13	F.Chance	4,297	554	137	4,988	1,273	200	79	20	.296	.394	.394	787	862	401	0	0	10	15	887	330
12	16	1943-63	G.Hodges	7,030	943	25	7,998	1,921	295	48	370	.273	.361	.487	848	823	63	31	(3)	0	27	847	314
13	15	1985-	A.Galarraga	7,123	503	154	7,780	2,070	389	31	360	.291	.351	.506	856	836	124	73	(2)	2	15	851	310
14	17	1988-	M.Grace	7,156	946	29	8,131	2,201	456	43	148	.308	.391	.445	836	813	67	48	(3)	0	33	843	292
15	12	1912-27	J.Fournier	5,208	587	89	5,884	1,631	252	113	136	.313	.392	.483	875	872	145	94	(13)	5	(4)	860	268
16	18	1956-69	B.White	5,972	596	28	6,596	1,706	278	65	202	.286	.353	.455	809	815	103	68	(5)	9	24	843	234
17	35	1964-86	T.Perez	9,778	925	43	10,746	2,732	505	79	379	.279	.344	.463	808	821	49	33	(1)	(10)	(12)	797	230
18	22	1922-37	J.Bottomley	7,471	664	43	8,178	2,313	465	151	219	.310	.369	.500	869	827	58	15	(2)	0	(10)	815	187
19	2	1997-	T.Helton	1,781	232	16	2,029	594	137	9	107	.334	.415	.601	1,016	940	15	13	(5)	0	16	951	177
20	25	1907-21	E.Konetchy	7,649	689	73	8,411	2,150	344	182	74	.281	.346	.403	749	800	255	5	(0)	(1)	11	810	173
21	14	1931-41	R.Collins	3,784	356	23	4,163	1,121	205	65	135	.296	.360	.492	852	842	18	0	0	0	9	851	170
22	31	1969-87	S.Garvey	8,835	479	29	9,343	2,599	440	43	272	.294	.333	.446	779	786	83	62	(4)	(0)	19	801	158
23	27	1910-24	J.Daubert	7,673	623	53	8,349	2,326	250	165	56	.303	.360	.401	760	788	251	78	(8)	9	18	807	156
24	19	1980-89	L.Durham	3,587	444	9	4,040	992	192	40	147	.277	.358	.475	833	840	106	61	(3)	10	(6)	841	154
25	20	1986-95	J.Kruk	3,897	649	2	4,548	1,170	199	34	100	.300	.400	.446	846	843	58	31	(1)	(2)	(7)	834	152

NL All Time Greats
Second basemen

V	R	Years	Name	AB	BB	HBP	TAB	H	2B	3B	HR	BA	OB	SA	PRO	Wtd PRO	SB	CS	SBF	SPF	FF	R TF	V HC
1	1	1915-37	R.Hornsby	8,173	1,038	48	9,259	2,930	541	169	301	.358	.434	.577	1,010	995	135	64	(7)	(0)	(2)	986	1,407
2	3	1963-84	J.Morgan	9,277	1,865	40	11,182	2,517	449	96	268	.271	.395	.427	823	833	689	162	31	10	9	882	1,074
3	4	1981-97	R.Sandberg	8,385	761	34	9,180	2,386	403	76	282	.285	.347	.452	798	799	344	107	13	8	41	862	775
4	5	1988-	C.Biggio	6,766	847	169	7,782	1,969	402	43	160	.291	.384	.434	818	793	358	106	19	10	14	836	586
5	6	1919-37	F.Frisch	9,112	728	31	9,871	2,880	466	138	105	.316	.369	.432	801	770	419	74	4	9	25	808	581
6	2	1947-56	J.Robinson	4,877	740	72	5,689	1,518	273	54	137	.311	.410	.474	883	858	197	30	6	10	24	899	531
7	7	1931-47	B.Herman	7,707	737	26	8,470	2,345	486	82	47	.304	.367	.407	774	777	67	0	0	(4)	27	801	490
8	9	1907-20	L.Doyle	6,509	625	53	7,187	1,887	299	123	74	.290	.357	.408	765	824	298	27	(3)	10	(35)	796	405
9	11	1904-16	M.Huggins	5,558	1,003	47	6,608	1,474	146	50	9	.265	.382	.314	696	758	324	12	(2)	10	17	784	325
10	12	1902-29	J.Evers	6,137	778	39	6,954	1,659	216	70	12	.270	.356	.334	690	752	324	8	(1)	5	21	778	324
11	8	1992-	J.Kent	4,329	387	71	4,787	1,228	274	25	194	.284	.352	.493	845	798	61	40	(4)	10	(2)	801	272
12	22	1945-63	Schoendienst	8,479	606	21	9,106	2,449	427	78	84	.289	.338	.387	725	708	89	27	(2)	8	31	745	250
13	20	1956-72	B.Mazeroski	7,755	447	20	8,222	2,016	294	62	138	.260	.302	.367	669	673	27	23	(2)	4	74	748	249
14	14	1972-87	D.Lopes	6,354	833	31	7,218	1,671	232	50	155	.263	.351	.388	740	741	557	114	43	10	(29)	765	248
15	21	1933-48	L.Frey	5,517	752	28	6,297	1,482	263	69	61	.269	.359	.374	734	739	105	0	0	10	(4)	745	212
16	23	1897-09	C.Ritchey	5,919	607	71	6,597	1,618	215	68	18	.273	.348	.342	690	740	155	0	0	0	3	743	211
17	16	1943-53	E.Stanky	4,301	996	35	5,332	1,154	185	35	29	.268	.410	.348	758	755	48	5	(0)	0	7	761	205
18	17	1986-96	R.Thompson	4,612	439	66	5,117	1,187	238	39	119	.257	.331	.403	734	731	103	62	(4)	9	24	761	188
19	13	1922-34	G.Grantham	4,989	717	23	5,729	1,508	292	93	105	.302	.392	.461	854	812	132	53	(4)	1	(35)	773	168
20	15	1992-	E.Young	3,921	447	59	4,427	1,139	195	35	49	.290	.372	.396	767	727	346	114	25	10	2	763	158
21	25	1982-93	B.Doran	5,131	709	10	5,850	1,366	220	39	84	.266	.356	.373	730	738	209	93	4	8	(8)	741	157
22	10	1995-	E.Alfonzo	2,950	345	17	3,312	874	164	14	87	.296	.373	.450	823	768	34	14	2	0	26	795	155
23	27	1979-91	T.Herr	5,349	627	22	5,998	1,450	254	41	28	.271	.350	.350	700	707	188	64	10	9	9	734	145
24	18	1907-14	B.Sweeney	3,692	423	12	4,127	1,004	153	40	11	.272	.349	.344	693	736	172	0	0	9	13	758	139
25	26	1981-90	J.Ray	5,188	353	12	5,553	1,502	294	36	53	.290	.336	.391	727	733	80	49	(3)	0	6	736	136

NL All Time Greats
Shortstops

V	R	Years	Name	AB	BB	HBP	TAB	H	2B	3B	HR	BA	OB	SA	PRO	Wtd PRO	SB	CS	SBF	SPF	FF	R TF	V HC
1	1	1897-17	H.Wagner	10,430	963	124	11,517	3,415	640	252	101	.327	.391	.466	857	921	722	15	(1)	9	40	970	1,685
2	5	1891-11	B.Dahlen	9,031	1,064	140	10,235	2,457	413	163	84	.272	.358	.382	739	767	547	0	0	9	50	826	880
3	2	1986-	B.Larkin	6,687	812	48	7,547	2,008	361	70	179	.300	.380	.456	836	813	359	71	28	9	29	879	810
4	3	1932-48	A.Vaughan	6,622	937	46	7,605	2,103	356	128	96	.318	.406	.453	859	861	118	0	0	10	(8)	863	740
5	4	1953-71	E.Banks	9,421	763	70	10,254	2,583	407	90	512	.274	.333	.500	833	830	50	53	(5)	4	8	837	617
6	7	1978-96	O.Smith	9,396	1,072	33	10,501	2,460	402	69	28	.262	.339	.328	668	668	580	148	24	9	65	766	545
7	9	1940-58	P.Reese	8,058	1,210	26	9,294	2,170	330	80	126	.269	.366	.377	743	733	232	45	2	9	19	762	458
8	6	1927-46	D.Bartell	7,629	748	97	8,474	2,165	442	71	79	.284	.355	.391	747	729	109	3	1	10	34	774	439
9	11	1915-30	D.Bancroft	7,182	827	23	8,032	2,004	320	77	32	.279	.355	.358	714	717	145	75	(9)	8	43	759	396
10	18	1970-88	D.Concepcion	8,723	736	21	9,480	2,326	389	48	101	.267	.325	.357	682	691	321	109	10	9	23	733	325
11	13	1902-16	J.Tinker	6,434	416	10	6,860	1,687	263	114	31	.262	.308	.353	661	716	336	0	0	0	40	755	324
12	16	1986-	J.Bell	6,805	761	50	7,616	1,828	368	66	180	.269	.347	.421	768	741	91	59	(3)	1	10	749	315
13	8	1909-22	A.Fletcher	5,541	203	141	5,885	1,534	238	77	32	.277	.319	.365	684	726	159	28	(5)	9	33	762	305
14	10	1922-36	T.Jackson	6,086	412	10	6,508	1,768	291	86	135	.291	.337	.433	770	734	71	13	(1)	5	21	759	290
15	34	1912-35	R.Maranville	10,078	839	39	10,956	2,605	380	177	28	.258	.318	.340	658	659	291	93	(3)	8	42	706	220
16	22	1946-60	A.Dark	7,219	430	54	7,703	2,089	358	72	126	.289	.334	.411	745	724	59	27	(2)	5	(3)	724	201
17	23	1959-72	M.Wills	7,588	552	16	8,156	2,134	177	71	20	.281	.331	.331	662	673	586	208	20	10	18	721	198
18	31	1960-75	L.Cardenas	6,707	522	28	7,257	1,725	285	49	118	.257	.313	.367	681	698	39	48	(7)	4	14	709	163
19	21	1985-	S.Dunston	5,594	198	38	5,830	1,511	277	59	140	.270	.300	.416	715	704	208	81	6	8	6	725	158
20	19	1924-35	G.Wright	4,153	209	5	4,367	1,219	203	76	94	.294	.328	.447	775	737	38	13	(2)	10	(12)	733	155
21	17	1963-73	G.Alley	3,927	300	27	4,254	999	140	44	55	.254	.312	.354	666	686	63	30	1	10	43	740	152
22	26	1951-63	J.Logan	5,244	451	43	5,738	1,407	216	41	93	.268	.331	.378	710	690	19	13	(1)	0	27	715	150
23	12	1918-24	C.Hollocher	2,936	277	26	3,239	894	145	35	14	.304	.370	.392	762	769	99	80	(29)	10	6	756	149
24	24	1979-93	D.Thon	4,449	348	9	4,806	1,176	193	42	71	.264	.319	.374	693	702	167	63	8	10	0	721	133
25	33	1940-53	M.Marion	5,506	470	14	5,990	1,448	272	37	36	.263	.323	.345	668	675	35	2	(1)	0	32	706	133

NL All Time Greats
Third basemen

V	R	Years	Name	AB	BB	HBP	TAB	H	2B	3B	HR	BA	OB	SA	PRO	Wtd PRO	SB	CS	SBF	SPF	FF	R TF	V HC
1	1	1972-89	M.Schmidt	8,352	1,507	79	9,938	2,234	408	59	548	.267	.384	.527	912	924	174	92	(1)	5	56	984	1,283
2	4	1952-68	E.Mathews	8,537	1,444	26	10,007	2,315	354	72	512	.271	.378	.509	888	877	68	39	(1)	7	4	887	829
3	5	1960-74	R.Santo	8,143	1,108	38	9,289	2,254	365	67	342	.277	.366	.464	830	847	35	41	(5)	(8)	38	872	708
4	6	1955-69	K.Boyer	7,455	713	20	8,188	2,143	318	68	282	.287	.351	.462	813	810	105	77	(6)	9	29	843	495
5	13	1932-47	S.Hack	7,278	1,092	21	8,391	2,193	363	81	57	.301	.394	.397	791	797	165	0	0	8	8	813	409
6	10	1971-87	R.Cey	7,162	1,012	62	8,236	1,868	328	21	316	.261	.357	.445	802	811	24	29	(4)	(6)	18	819	408
7	8	1987-	M.Williams	6,243	410	50	6,703	1,677	292	33	346	.269	.319	.492	811	789	49	34	(2)	0	50	836	403
8	14	1920-37	P.Traynor	7,559	472	31	8,062	2,416	371	164	58	.320	.362	.435	797	762	158	46	(1)	10	41	812	390
9	9	1912-27	H.Groh	6,074	696	83	6,853	1,774	308	87	26	.292	.373	.384	757	794	180	66	(9)	7	27	820	384
10	2	1993-	C.Jones	3,469	554	5	4,028	1,051	204	18	189	.303	.400	.536	935	875	97	26	10	10	(5)	891	343
11	17	1939-53	B.Elliott	7,141	967	16	8,124	2,061	382	94	170	.289	.375	.440	815	818	60	2	0	(1)	(13)	803	308
12	19	1969-89	D.Evans	8,973	1,605	35	10,613	2,223	329	36	414	.248	.364	.431	795	800	98	68	(3)	(3)	2	796	293
13	18	1987-	K.Caminiti	5,932	684	27	6,643	1,629	331	16	224	.275	.352	.449	801	781	88	38	2	0	17	800	280
14	21	1973-87	B.Madlock	6,594	605	68	7,267	2,008	348	34	163	.305	.369	.442	811	820	174	90	(0)	3	(28)	794	266
15	15	1904-13	A.Devlin	4,412	576	84	5,072	1,185	164	57	10	.269	.364	.338	702	772	285	0	0	9	28	809	223
16	7	1941-49	W.Kurowski	3,229	369	36	3,634	925	162	32	106	.286	.366	.455	821	837	19	0	0	(4)	5	838	221
17	11	1991-	V.Castilla	3,847	237	30	4,114	1,122	175	18	209	.292	.338	.509	847	802	23	34	(10)	0	25	817	218
18	3	1996-	S.Rolen	2,196	300	33	2,529	623	147	14	108	.284	.378	.511	889	831	50	18	5	10	44	890	210
19	25	1986-	B.Bonilla	7,039	889	26	7,954	1,973	401	61	282	.280	.363	.475	838	822	44	56	(8)	0	(28)	786	192
20	29	1898-11	H.Steinfeldt	5,896	471	79	6,446	1,576	284	90	27	.267	.330	.360	690	750	194	0	0	0	20	771	188
21	20	1924-36	F.Lindstrom	5,611	334	13	5,958	1,747	301	81	103	.311	.351	.449	800	764	84	10	(2)	8	26	795	187
22	30	1907-19	H.Zimmerman	5,304	242	38	5,584	1,566	275	105	58	.295	.331	.419	750	802	175	33	(4)	(10)	(18)	770	184
23	16	1963-74	J.Hart	3,783	380	28	4,191	1,052	148	29	170	.278	.348	.467	816	842	17	17	(4)	5	(39)	804	169
24	12	1978-88	B.Horner	3,777	369	16	4,162	1,047	169	8	218	.277	.344	.499	843	853	14	18	(5)	(8)	(25)	814	166
25	24	1911-19	R.Smith	3,907	420	34	4,361	1,087	208	49	27	.278	.353	.377	731	788	117	5	0	0	2	790	159

NL All Time Greats
Outfielders

V	R	Years	Name	AB	BB	HBP	TAB	H	2B	3B	HR	BA	OB	SA	PRO	Wtd PRO	SB	CS	SBF	SPF	FF	R TF	V HC
1	2	1951-73	W.Mays	10,881	1,464	44	12,389	3,283	523	140	660	.302	.387	.557	944	942	338	103	10	10	58	1,019	1,579
2	3	1954-76	H.Aaron	12,364	1,402	32	13,798	3,771	624	98	755	.305	.377	.555	932	935	240	73	6	8	22	971	1,429
3	1	1986-	B.Bonds	7,456	1,547	56	9,059	2,157	451	69	494	.289	.415	.567	982	959	471	135	21	10	56	1,046	1,290
4	6	1941-63	S.Musial	10,972	1,599	53	12,624	3,630	725	177	475	.331	.418	.559	977	966	78	31	(2)	(1)	(1)	961	1,257
5	5	1956-76	F.Robinson	10,006	1,420	198	11,624	2,943	528	72	586	.294	.392	.537	929	941	204	77	4	7	10	963	1,144
6	7	1926-47	M.Ott	9,456	1,708	64	11,228	2,876	488	72	511	.304	.414	.533	947	934	89	0	0	(1)	10	943	1,075
7	13	1955-72	R.Clemente	9,454	621	35	10,110	3,000	440	166	240	.317	.362	.475	837	842	83	46	(1)	10	52	902	719
8	17	1959-76	B.Williams	9,350	1,045	43	10,438	2,711	434	88	426	.290	.364	.492	856	875	90	49	(1)	7	9	891	661
9	19	1979-99	T.Raines	8,694	1,290	41	10,025	2,561	419	112	168	.295	.388	.427	815	809	807	146	49	9	18	886	642
10	31	1926-45	P.Waner	9,459	1,091	38	10,588	3,152	605	191	113	.333	.404	.473	878	856	104	0	0	4	11	871	597
11	12	1947-64	D.Snider	7,161	971	21	8,153	2,116	358	85	407	.295	.381	.540	921	897	99	50	(4)	1	10	903	596
12	25	1982-	T.Gwynn	9,186	780	24	9,990	3,108	534	84	134	.338	.392	.459	850	841	318	125	7	8	23	878	592
13	4	1989-	L.Walker	4,906	578	89	5,573	1,528	335	43	271	.311	.394	.563	957	922	195	61	12	10	26	970	591
14	30	1894-15	F.Clarke	8,568	874	153	9,595	2,672	361	220	67	.312	.386	.429	814	850	506	0	0	8	13	871	578
15	16	1932-48	J.Medwick	7,635	437	26	8,098	2,471	540	113	205	.324	.362	.505	867	870	42	0	0	10	15	895	559
16	20	1904-19	S.Magee	7,441	736	109	8,286	2,169	425	166	83	.291	.364	.427	790	864	441	12	(1)	10	10	884	528
17	24	1962-82	W.Stargell	7,927	937	78	8,942	2,232	423	55	475	.282	.363	.529	892	910	17	16	(2)	(7)	(23)	879	505
18	50	1976-96	A.Dawson	9,927	589	111	10,627	2,774	503	98	438	.279	.327	.482	809	814	314	109	9	3	26	852	499
19	93	1963-86	P.Rose	14,053	1,566	107	15,726	4,256	746	135	160	.303	.377	.409	786	802	198	149	(6)	7	3	806	495
20	22	1968-81	B.Bonds	7,043	914	53	8,010	1,886	302	66	332	.268	.356	.471	827	839	461	169	14	10	20	883	485
21	51	1909-27	Z.Wheat	9,106	650	72	9,828	2,884	476	172	132	.317	.367	.450	817	835	205	49	(4)	5	14	850	464
22	21	1928-44	C.Klein	6,486	601	12	7,099	2,076	398	74	300	.320	.379	.543	922	890	79	0	0	(1)	(6)	883	444
23	14	1946-55	R.Kiner	5,205	1,011	24	6,240	1,451	216	39	369	.279	.398	.548	946	924	22	2	1	(4)	(24)	898	442
24	47	1976-93	D.Murphy	7,960	986	28	8,974	2,111	350	39	398	.265	.348	.469	817	824	161	68	3	6	21	854	430
25	42	1896-13	C.Seymour	5,682	354	30	6,066	1,723	229	96	52	.303	.347	.405	752	822	222	0	0	10	24	856	425

NL All Time Greats
Outfielders

V	R	Years	Name	AB	BB	HBP	TAB	H	2B	3B	HR	BA	OB	SA	PRO	Wtd PRO	SB	CS	SBF	SPF	FF	R TF	V HC
26	28	1988-	G.Sheffield	5,146	858	76	6,080	1,508	265	19	279	.293	.402	.515	916	884	160	77	1	10	(21)	874	411
27	55	1938-59	E.Slaughter	7,946	1,018	37	9,001	2,383	413	148	169	.300	.382	.453	835	830	71	15	(1)	8	8	846	397
28	54	1897-13	J.Sheckard	7,605	1,135	90	8,830	2,084	354	136	56	.274	.375	.378	753	808	465	0	0	10	28	846	396
29	38	1963-77	J.Wynn	6,653	1,224	27	7,904	1,665	285	39	291	.250	.369	.436	805	827	225	101	3	10	20	859	387
30	18	1984-	E.Davis	5,165	727	32	5,924	1,398	232	23	278	.271	.364	.486	850	835	348	65	35	8	13	890	382
31	49	1921-38	K.Cuyler	7,161	676	85	7,922	2,299	394	157	128	.321	.386	.474	860	822	328	27	3	10	18	853	377
32	43	1970-86	C.Cedeno	7,310	664	56	8,030	2,087	436	60	199	.285	.350	.443	793	802	550	179	22	10	22	855	376
33	44	1975-92	J.Clark	6,847	1,262	24	8,133	1,826	332	39	340	.267	.383	.476	858	864	77	61	(5)	2	(6)	855	371
34	69	1910-29	M.Carey	9,363	1,040	77	10,480	2,665	419	159	70	.285	.361	.386	747	758	738	92	18	10	38	824	356
35	11	1908-20	G.Cravath	3,951	561	28	4,540	1,134	232	83	119	.287	.380	.478	858	930	89	9	(1)	(1)	(19)	908	352
36	67	1958-75	V.Pinson	9,645	574	54	10,273	2,757	485	127	256	.286	.330	.442	772	787	305	122	6	10	26	828	351
37	9	1899-14	M.Donlin	3,854	312	20	4,186	1,282	176	97	51	.333	.386	.468	854	916	213	0	0	10	(9)	917	347
38	66	1948-62	R.Ashburn	8,365	1,198	43	9,606	2,574	317	109	29	.308	.397	.382	779	757	234	92	(0)	10	62	828	339
39	23	1923-34	H.Wilson	4,760	674	20	5,454	1,461	266	67	244	.307	.395	.545	940	892	52	5	(0)	0	(13)	879	331
40	58	1913-31	E.Roush	7,363	484	53	7,900	2,376	339	182	68	.323	.369	.446	815	821	268	92	(9)	10	16	838	326
41	36	1983-	D.Strawberry	5,418	816	38	6,272	1,401	256	38	335	.259	.360	.505	865	864	221	99	3	8	(15)	860	312
42	45	1983-95	A.Van Slyke	5,711	667	27	6,405	1,562	293	91	164	.274	.352	.443	795	794	245	59	19	9	34	855	305
43	8	1912-20	B.Kauff	3,094	367	28	3,489	961	169	57	49	.311	.389	.450	838	904	234	33	(6)	10	17	925	304
44	61	1912-30	C.Williams	6,780	690	86	7,556	1,981	306	74	251	.292	.365	.470	835	840	115	82	(11)	6	0	836	302
45	40	1926-45	B.Herman	5,603	520	11	6,134	1,818	399	110	181	.324	.383	.532	915	875	94	0	0	8	(26)	857	299
46	39	1990-	R.Lankford	4,953	707	28	5,688	1,366	307	48	207	.276	.369	.483	852	819	244	111	3	10	26	859	288
47	33	1924-37	C.Hafey	4,625	372	33	5,030	1,466	341	67	164	.317	.372	.526	898	858	70	7	(2)	9	4	870	286
48	64	1969-86	G.Foster	7,023	666	52	7,741	1,925	307	47	348	.274	.341	.480	821	833	51	31	(1)	2	(2)	831	286
49	76	1973-91	D.Parker	9,358	683	56	10,097	2,712	526	75	339	.290	.342	.471	813	818	154	113	(7)	2	3	816	282
50	53	1978-92	P.Guerrero	5,392	609	32	6,033	1,618	267	29	215	.300	.374	.480	854	865	97	47	(1)	(0)	(18)	847	279
51	56	1899-10	G.Beaumont	5,660	425	30	6,115	1,759	182	82	39	.311	.362	.393	755	820	254	0	0	10	15	844	276
52	48	1930-40	W.Berger	5,163	435	38	5,636	1,550	299	59	242	.300	.359	.522	881	857	36	0	0	4	(8)	854	272
53	60	1899-11	R.Thomas	5,296	1,042	71	6,409	1,537	100	53	7	.290	.413	.333	747	808	244	0	0	9	21	838	268
54	57	1917-26	R.Youngs	4,627	550	37	5,214	1,491	236	93	42	.322	.399	.441	839	834	153	83	(12)	10	12	844	262
55	35	1984-98	K.Mitchell	4,134	491	27	4,652	1,173	224	25	234	.284	.363	.520	883	886	30	31	(6)	(1)	(18)	860	262
56	46	1985-96	L.Dykstra	4,559	640	31	5,230	1,298	281	43	81	.285	.376	.419	795	790	285	72	25	10	30	855	252
57	97	1961-79	L.Brock	10,332	761	49	11,142	3,023	486	141	149	.293	.344	.410	754	770	938	307	28	10	(3)	804	251
58	72	1972-87	G.Matthews	7,147	940	21	8,108	2,011	319	51	234	.281	.367	.439	805	815	183	74	5	9	(8)	820	249
59	118	1898-18	T.Leach	7,959	820	32	8,811	2,143	266	172	63	.269	.340	.370	710	771	361	14	(1)	6	19	794	248
60	52	1989-	D.Justice	4,846	779	17	5,642	1,373	246	20	276	.283	.384	.513	898	864	48	43	(7)	1	(11)	847	247
61	65	1966-84	R.Monday	6,136	924	24	7,084	1,619	248	64	241	.264	.362	.443	805	828	98	91	(11)	6	6	829	246
62	71	1931-49	D.Walker	6,740	817	16	7,573	2,064	376	96	105	.306	.383	.437	820	815	59	10	(1)	(0)	7	821	241
63	70	1958-73	J.Callison	6,652	650	41	7,343	1,757	321	89	226	.264	.333	.441	774	789	74	51	(4)	6	31	823	230
64	89	1970-88	J.Cruz	7,917	898	7	8,822	2,251	391	94	165	.284	.342	.420	778	784	317	136	4	8	11	808	229
65	29	1919-34	L.O'Doul	3,264	333	23	3,620	1,140	175	41	113	.349	.413	.532	945	893	36	0	0	0	(20)	872	222
66	62	1903-13	J.Titus	4,960	620	94	5,674	1,401	253	72	38	.282	.373	.385	758	828	140	0	0	8	(1)	835	220
67	74	1934-49	A.Galan	5,937	979	25	6,941	1,706	336	74	100	.287	.390	.419	810	811	123	0	0	5	2	818	218
68	37	1990-	M.Alou	3,725	389	30	4,144	1,127	229	28	175	.303	.373	.520	893	854	76	32	2	9	(6)	859	214
69	63	1942-52	T.Holmes	4,992	480	24	5,496	1,507	292	47	88	.302	.366	.432	798	807	40	0	0	(3)	27	832	207
70	78	1970-84	G.Luzinski	6,505	845	84	7,434	1,795	344	24	307	.276	.366	.478	844	853	37	31	(3)	(9)	(27)	814	203
71	73	1936-53	B.Nicholson	5,546	800	52	6,398	1,484	272	60	235	.268	.365	.465	830	843	27	1	(0)	(10)	(13)	819	198
72	75	1989-	S.Sosa	5,893	519	38	6,450	1,606	244	36	386	.273	.335	.523	858	819	231	103	4	10	(16)	817	195
73	105	1981-97	B.Butler	8,180	1,129	38	9,347	2,375	277	131	54	.290	.379	.376	755	752	558	257	5	10	31	799	192
74	77	1921-34	R.Stephenson	4,508	494	41	5,043	1,515	321	54	63	.336	.407	.473	880	837	53	9	(1)	(7)	(15)	815	180
75	100	1973-91	K.Griffey	7,229	719	14	7,962	2,143	364	77	152	.296	.361	.431	792	797	200	83	4	6	(4)	803	178

NL All Time Greats
Starting Pitchers

V	R	Years	Name	G	GS	IP	W	L	SV	SO	BB	ERA	RA/9	R Wtd RA/9	V Runs /162
1	4	1911-30	P.Alexander	696	600	5,190	373	208	32	2,198	951	2.56	3.21	3.37	726.1
2	8	1900-16	C.Mathewson	635	551	4,781	373	188	29	2,502	844	2.13	3.04	3.42	646.3
3	15	1942-65	W.Spahn	750	665	5,244	363	245	29	2,583	1,434	3.09	3.46	3.59	589.5
4	9	1967-86	T.Seaver	656	647	4,783	311	205	1	3,640	1,390	2.86	3.15	3.47	589.0
5	6	1928-43	C.Hubbell	535	431	3,590	253	154	33	1,677	725	2.98	3.46	3.40	483.9
6	2	1986-	G.Maddux	471	467	3,318	240	135	0	2,350	733	2.83	3.24	3.31	476.4
7	5	1903-16	T.Brown	481	332	3,172	239	130	49	1,375	673	2.06	2.96	3.40	432.3
8	50	1966-88	D.Sutton	774	756	5,282	324	256	5	3,574	1,343	3.26	3.58	3.89	396.2
9	20	1959-75	B.Gibson	528	482	3,884	251	174	6	3,117	1,336	2.91	3.29	3.66	391.3
10	60	1962-83	G.Perry	777	690	5,350	314	265	11	3,534	1,379	3.11	3.58	3.96	360.0
11	52	1948-66	R.Roberts	676	609	4,689	286	245	25	2,357	902	3.41	3.77	3.90	357.0
12	13	1915-35	D.Vance	442	348	2,967	197	140	11	2,045	840	3.24	3.78	3.57	341.8
13	30	1899-08	J.McGinnity	465	381	3,441	246	142	24	1,068	812	2.66	3.76	3.77	330.0
14	26	1956-69	D.Drysdale	518	465	3,432	209	166	6	2,486	855	2.95	3.39	3.72	326.4
15	1	1992-	P.Martinez	278	211	1,576	125	56	3	1,818	442	2.68	2.96	2.84	317.4
16	3	1955-66	S.Koufax	397	314	2,324	165	87	9	2,396	817	2.76	3.12	3.36	316.8
17	53	1898-10	V.Willis	513	471	3,996	249	205	11	1,651	1,212	2.63	3.67	3.90	315.9
18	12	1905-17	E.Reulbach	399	300	2,632	182	106	13	1,137	892	2.28	3.03	3.56	306.0
19	24	1906-25	B.Adams	482	354	2,995	194	140	15	1,036	430	2.76	3.39	3.69	305.7
20	18	1898-10	S.Leever	388	299	2,661	194	100	13	847	587	2.47	3.46	3.62	300.9
21	85	1965-88	S.Carlton	741	709	5,217	329	244	2	4,136	1,833	3.22	3.67	4.05	298.3
22	19	1986-	D.Cone	420	390	2,745	184	116	1	2,540	1,067	3.40	3.72	3.65	285.3
23	37	1960-75	J.Marichal	471	457	3,507	243	142	2	2,303	709	2.89	3.41	3.83	283.8
24	40	1914-35	D.Luque	550	366	3,220	194	179	28	1,130	918	3.24	3.95	3.84	272.0
25	16	1907-16	N.Rucker	336	273	2,375	134	134	14	1,217	701	2.42	3.10	3.62	260.7
26	10	1899-06	N.Hahn	243	231	2,029	130	94	0	917	381	2.55	3.65	3.54	256.1
27	7	1940-53	H.Brecheen	318	240	1,908	133	92	18	901	536	2.92	3.31	3.42	253.9
28	59	1912-26	W.Cooper	517	407	3,480	216	178	14	1,252	853	2.89	3.63	3.95	252.7
29	105	1912-33	E.Rixey	692	554	4,495	266	251	14	1,350	1,082	3.15	3.98	4.11	233.2
30	100	1965-83	F.Jenkins	664	594	4,501	284	226	7	3,192	997	3.34	3.71	4.10	232.8
31	11	1930-47	D.Dean	317	230	1,967	150	83	30	1,163	453	3.02	3.54	3.55	231.6
32	38	1899-11	D.Phillippe	372	289	2,607	189	109	12	929	363	2.59	3.72	3.84	229.6
33	45	1987-	T.Glavine	434	434	2,901	208	125	0	1,811	965	3.38	3.76	3.87	228.9
34	42	1930-45	L.Warneke	445	343	2,782	192	121	13	1,140	739	3.18	3.77	3.86	226.3
35	72	1923-41	C.Root	632	341	3,197	201	160	40	1,459	889	3.59	4.13	4.01	202.8
36	39	1988-	J.Smoltz	356	356	2,414	157	113	0	2,098	774	3.35	3.68	3.84	199.6
37	58	1973-85	S.Rogers	399	393	2,838	158	152	2	1,621	876	3.17	3.56	3.95	198.1
38	70	1983-	O.Hershiser	510	466	3,130	204	150	5	2,014	1,007	3.48	3.93	4.00	197.2
39	46	1911-24	J.Pfeffer	347	279	2,407	158	112	10	836	592	2.77	3.44	3.87	195.4
40	76	1929-42	L.French	570	384	3,152	197	171	17	1,187	819	3.44	4.11	4.03	193.2
41	21	1988-	C.Schilling	355	244	1,902	110	95	13	1,739	499	3.43	3.68	3.67	192.0
42	23	1938-49	M.Cooper	295	239	1,841	128	75	14	913	571	2.97	3.44	3.69	191.2
43	17	1945-58	S.Maglie	303	232	1,723	119	62	14	862	562	3.15	3.57	3.62	188.8
44	108	1967-85	J.Koosman	612	527	3,839	222	209	17	2,556	1,198	3.36	3.77	4.12	188.1
45	80	1934-50	B.Walters	428	398	3,105	198	160	4	1,107	1,121	3.30	3.89	4.05	185.5
46	67	1908-21	H.Vaughn	390	332	2,730	178	137	5	1,416	817	2.49	3.42	4.00	184.9
47	62	1984-	D.Gooden	430	410	2,801	194	112	3	2,293	954	3.51	3.85	3.97	184.2
48	145	1964-87	P.Niekro	864	716	5,404	318	274	29	3,342	1,809	3.35	3.89	4.26	183.9
49	47	1911-23	F.Toney	336	271	2,206	139	102	12	718	583	2.69	3.41	3.88	178.7
50	86	1978-94	B.Welch	506	462	3,092	211	146	8	1,969	1,034	3.47	3.81	4.06	176.7

NL All Time Greats
Starting Pitchers

V	R	Years	Name	G	GS	IP	W	L	SV	SO	BB	ERA	RA/9	R Wtd RA/9	V Runs /162
51	98	1925-43	F.Fitzsimmons	513	426	3,224	217	146	13	870	846	3.51	4.20	4.09	174.1
52	14	1903-09	J.Weimer	191	180	1,473	97	69	2	657	493	2.23	3.12	3.58	170.7
53	36	1938-54	P.Roe	333	261	1,914	127	84	10	956	504	3.43	3.75	3.80	169.2
54	90	1908-21	S.Sallee	476	305	2,822	174	143	36	836	573	2.56	3.48	4.06	165.7
55	28	1984-95	J.Rijo	332	260	1,786	111	87	3	1,556	634	3.16	3.62	3.77	163.1
56	63	1975-93	J.Candelaria	600	356	2,526	177	122	29	1,673	592	3.33	3.70	3.98	162.3
57	25	1938-53	M.Lanier	327	204	1,619	108	82	17	821	611	3.01	3.50	3.71	159.7
58	33	1979-90	J.Tudor	281	263	1,797	117	72	1	988	475	3.12	3.51	3.78	157.9
59	22	1905-13	O.Overall	218	182	1,535	108	71	12	935	551	2.23	3.05	3.69	156.4
60	29	1912-18	J.Tesreau	247	207	1,679	115	72	9	880	572	2.43	3.17	3.77	155.7
61	75	1931-46	H.Schumacher	391	329	2,482	158	121	7	906	902	3.36	3.91	4.02	155.6
62	95	1915-29	A.Nehf	451	321	2,708	184	120	13	844	640	3.20	3.87	4.08	154.5
63	131	1931-45	P.Derringer	579	445	3,645	223	212	29	1,507	761	3.46	4.08	4.20	152.6
64	57	1904-15	H.Wiltse	357	226	2,112	139	90	33	965	498	2.47	3.35	3.95	151.0
65	73	1971-83	J.Matlack	361	318	2,363	125	126	3	1,516	638	3.18	3.69	4.02	146.3
66	56	1948-61	J.Antonelli	377	268	1,992	126	110	21	1,162	687	3.34	3.88	3.93	145.9
67	34	1967-77	G.Nolan	250	247	1,675	110	70	0	1,039	413	3.08	3.35	3.78	144.6
68	48	1983-97	S.Fernandez	307	300	1,867	114	96	1	1,743	715	3.36	3.61	3.89	143.7
69	94	1923-38	R.Lucas	396	301	2,542	157	135	7	602	455	3.72	4.24	4.08	143.1
70	134	1972-91	R.Reuschel	557	529	3,548	214	191	5	2,015	935	3.37	3.79	4.21	141.6
71	89	1911-20	C.Hendrix	360	257	2,371	144	116	17	1,092	697	2.65	3.45	4.06	140.9
72	130	1957-75	C.Osteen	541	488	3,460	196	195	1	1,612	940	3.30	3.73	4.19	140.5
73	32	1987-	A.Leiter	264	234	1,503	106	79	2	1,307	759	3.73	4.01	3.78	135.3
74	133	1918-37	J.Haines	555	388	3,209	210	158	10	981	871	3.64	4.37	4.20	133.1
75	116	1898-07	J.Taylor	310	286	2,617	152	139	5	657	582	2.66	4.11	4.14	131.6
76	77	1970-86	K.Forsch	521	241	2,127	114	113	51	1,047	586	3.37	3.73	4.03	128.5
77	113	1971-85	B.Hooton	480	377	2,652	151	136	7	1,491	799	3.38	3.77	4.14	127.0
78	91	1949-60	D.Newcombe	344	294	2,155	149	90	7	1,129	490	3.56	3.99	4.07	123.5
79	44	1971-80	J.Richard	238	221	1,606	107	71	0	1,493	770	3.15	3.50	3.87	123.1
80	31	1970-78	D.Gullett	266	186	1,390	109	50	11	921	501	3.11	3.42	3.77	121.7
81	66	1962-74	B.Veale	397	255	1,926	120	95	21	1,703	858	3.07	3.53	3.99	120.8
82	104	1934-46	C.Davis	429	281	2,325	158	131	33	684	479	3.42	4.00	4.11	120.7
83	71	1905-20	L.Leifield	296	216	1,838	124	97	7	616	554	2.47	3.39	4.01	120.0
84	127	1935-47	C.Passeau	444	331	2,720	162	150	21	1,104	728	3.32	3.99	4.18	119.6
85	118	1986-98	D.Drabek	398	387	2,535	155	134	0	1,594	704	3.73	4.05	4.15	119.0
86	81	1924-33	R.Kremer	308	247	1,955	143	85	10	516	483	3.76	4.37	4.05	116.7
87	140	1955-68	L.Jackson	558	429	3,263	194	183	20	1,709	824	3.40	3.88	4.24	116.6
88	88	1928-37	P.Malone	357	220	1,915	134	92	26	1,024	705	3.74	4.40	4.06	110.6
89	114	1928-38	E.Brandt	378	277	2,268	121	146	17	877	778	3.86	4.31	4.14	110.6
90	112	1964-77	L.Dierker	356	329	2,334	139	123	1	1,493	711	3.31	3.65	4.14	109.5
91	106	1937-51	J.Vander Meer	346	286	2,105	119	121	2	1,294	1,132	3.44	3.91	4.12	108.2
92	107	1942-55	J.Sain	412	245	2,126	139	116	51	910	619	3.49	4.01	4.12	107.7
93	49	1902-09	C.Lundgren	179	149	1,322	91	55	6	535	476	2.42	3.37	3.89	106.3
94	78	1924-37	W.Clark	355	206	1,747	111	97	16	643	383	3.66	4.31	4.04	106.1
95	27	1994-	I.Valdes	197	170	1,132	63	61	1	830	326	3.59	3.94	3.74	105.8
96	65	1907-18	G.McQuillan	273	173	1,576	85	89	14	590	401	2.38	3.29	3.99	105.0
97	142	1980-97	F.Valenzuela	453	424	2,930	173	153	2	2,074	1,151	3.54	4.00	4.25	104.7
98	143	1934-47	B.Lee	462	379	2,864	169	157	13	998	893	3.54	4.10	4.25	102.9
99	41	1993-	M.Hampton	241	187	1,261	85	53	1	852	489	3.44	4.02	3.85	102.5
100	55	1943-54	A.Brazle	441	117	1,377	97	64	60	554	492	3.31	3.86	3.92	102.2

NL All Time Greats
Relief Pitchers

V	R	Years	Name	G	GS	IP	W	L	SV	SO	BB	ERA	RA/9	R Wtd RA/9	V Runs /162
1	4	1984-	J.Franco	940	0	1,097	82	74	420	857	430	2.68	3.19	3.35	151.1
2	23	1974-89	K.Tekulve	1,050	0	1,436	94	90	184	779	491	2.85	3.30	3.64	149.8
3	15	1980-97	L.Smith	1,022	6	1,289	71	92	478	1,251	486	3.03	3.32	3.57	148.0
4	11	1979-	J.Orosco	1,096	4	1,218	84	75	141	1,107	541	3.03	3.43	3.51	146.0
5	17	1979-94	J.Reardon	880	0	1,132	73	77	367	877	358	3.16	3.39	3.58	127.3
6	29	1957-74	D.McMahon	874	2	1,311	90	68	153	1,003	579	2.96	3.31	3.70	127.2
7	53	1952-68	S.Miller	704	93	1,694	105	103	154	1,164	600	3.24	3.70	3.91	126.5
8	13	1976-88	B.Sutter	661	0	1,042	68	71	300	861	309	2.83	3.19	3.56	120.1
9	2	1993-	T.Hoffman	509	0	581	40	35	271	665	175	2.73	3.03	2.92	110.9
10	39	1964-78	C.Carroll	731	28	1,353	96	73	143	681	442	2.94	3.37	3.83	110.5
11	54	1965-84	T.McGraw	824	39	1,515	96	92	180	1,109	582	3.14	3.55	3.92	109.9
12	50	1967-81	M.Marshall	723	24	1,387	97	112	188	880	514	3.14	3.56	3.87	107.2
13	10	1980-92	D.Smith	609	1	809	53	53	216	548	283	2.67	3.11	3.50	99.8
14	18	1985-	R.Myers	728	12	885	44	63	347	884	396	3.19	3.44	3.58	98.3
15	36	1974-87	G.Lavelle	745	3	1,085	80	77	136	769	440	2.93	3.43	3.80	94.7
16	46	1961-73	R.Perranoski	737	1	1,175	79	74	179	687	468	2.79	3.38	3.87	90.8
17	34	1944-53	T.Wilks	385	44	913	59	30	46	403	283	3.26	3.59	3.72	89.4
18	52	1975-90	G.Minton	710	7	1,131	59	65	150	479	483	3.10	3.60	3.90	85.4
19	42	1960-76	J.Brewer	584	35	1,041	69	65	132	810	360	3.07	3.47	3.84	83.6
20	7	1991-	R.Beck	574	0	628	29	37	260	534	143	3.20	3.46	3.43	81.8
21	32	1980-94	J.Howell	568	21	845	58	53	155	666	291	3.34	3.57	3.72	81.7
22	33	1988-	J.Brantley	597	18	838	43	45	172	717	357	3.35	3.61	3.72	81.6
23	5	1993-	R.Nen	496	4	564	35	35	226	619	218	3.08	3.50	3.37	78.5
24	14	1985-92	T.Burke	498	2	699	49	33	102	444	219	2.72	3.23	3.56	77.1
25	19	1985-97	T.Worrell	617	0	694	50	52	256	628	247	3.09	3.43	3.60	76.3
26	74	1953-69	R.Face	848	27	1,375	104	95	193	877	362	3.48	3.87	4.09	73.9
27	55	1975-94	L.Andersen	699	1	995	40	39	49	758	311	3.15	3.63	3.92	73.6
28	57	1981-96	A.Pena	503	72	1,058	56	52	74	839	331	3.11	3.63	3.95	73.6
29	27	1977-87	A.Holland	384	11	646	34	30	78	513	232	2.98	3.36	3.66	69.7
30	20	1980-96	S.Howe	497	0	606	47	41	91	328	139	3.03	3.55	3.61	69.2
31	6	1994-	D.Veres	432	0	513	26	24	75	462	185	3.32	3.63	3.41	69.0
32	26	1976-87	J.Sambito	461	5	629	37	38	84	489	195	3.03	3.45	3.66	66.1
33	110	1955-75	L.McDaniel	987	74	2,139	141	119	172	1,361	623	3.45	3.93	4.28	66.0
34	35	1970-82	A.Hrabosky	545	1	722	64	35	97	548	315	3.10	3.54	3.78	64.2
35	31	1981-90	T.Niedenfuer	484	0	653	36	46	97	474	226	3.29	3.46	3.71	62.9
36	16	1993-	T.Jones	459	0	531	30	28	170	486	256	3.54	3.90	3.57	62.6
37	22	1969-76	C.Taylor	305	21	607	28	20	31	282	162	3.07	3.29	3.64	62.3
38	48	1990-	J.Shaw	556	19	773	31	49	160	487	216	3.54	3.91	3.87	61.8
39	77	1981-95	S.Bedrosian	732	46	1,191	76	79	184	921	518	3.38	3.75	4.11	60.9
40	37	1981-93	T.Leach	376	21	700	38	27	10	331	197	3.15	3.59	3.81	59.7
41	8	1988-95	R.Dibble	385	0	477	27	25	89	645	238	2.98	3.19	3.46	58.5
42	21	1993-	G.McMichael	453	0	523	31	29	53	459	193	3.25	3.70	3.62	58.3
43	68	1944-56	J.Konstanty	433	36	946	66	48	74	268	269	3.46	4.00	4.03	58.0
44	49	1938-48	J.Beggs	238	41	694	48	35	29	178	189	2.96	3.69	3.87	55.6
45	1	1995-	B.Wagner	252	0	281	19	18	107	422	126	2.73	2.92	2.78	55.5
46	65	1986-99	P.Assenmacher	884	1	856	61	44	56	807	315	3.53	3.90	4.00	53.8
47	64	1954-63	J.Brosnan	385	47	831	55	47	67	507	312	3.54	3.85	4.00	53.6
48	60	1963-74	F.Linzy	516	2	817	62	57	111	358	282	2.85	3.47	3.97	53.6
49	81	1961-70	A.McBean	409	76	1,072	67	50	63	575	365	3.13	3.61	4.12	52.5
50	105	1969-88	G.Garber	931	9	1,510	96	113	218	940	445	3.34	3.90	4.26	51.3

All Time Greats   **Hitters Volume of Success**

Pos	Years	Name	AB	BB	HBP	TAB	H	2B	3B	HR	BA	OB	SA	PRO	Wtd PRO	SB	CS	SBF	SPF	FF	R TF	V HC
C	1967-83	J.Bench	7,658	891	19	8,568	2,048	381	24	389	.267	.345	.476	821	835	68	43	(2)	(3)	65	896	878
1B	1923-39	L.Gehrig	8,001	1,508	45	9,554	2,721	534	163	493	.340	.447	.632	1,080	1,009	102	101	(10)	0	(3)	996	1,083
2B	1896-16	N.Lajoie	9,589	516	134	10,239	3,242	657	163	82	.338	.380	.466	846	910	380	21	(2)	6	63	978	1,495
SS	1897-17	H.Wagner	10,430	963	124	11,517	3,415	640	252	101	.327	.391	.466	857	921	722	15	(1)	9	40	970	1,685
3B	1972-89	M.Schmidt	8,352	1,507	79	9,938	2,234	408	59	548	.267	.384	.527	912	924	174	92	(1)	5	56	984	1,283
OF	1914-35	B.Ruth	8,399	2,056	42	10,497	2,873	506	136	714	.342	.474	.690	1,163	1,112	123	117	(11)	3	9	1,112	1,962
OF	1905-28	T.Cobb	11,434	1,249	94	12,777	4,189	724	295	117	.366	.433	.512	945	983	892	178	(2)	10	17	1,008	1,623
OF	1939-60	T.Williams	7,706	2,019	39	9,764	2,654	525	71	521	.344	.483	.634	1,116	1,093	24	17	(1)	(2)	(8)	1,082	1,599
Starters	Averages		8,946	1,339	72	10,357	2,922	547	145	371	.327	.418	.545	963	975	311	73	(4)	4	30	1,005	1,251
C	1946-65	Y.Berra	7,555	704	49	8,308	2,150	321	49	358	.285	.349	.482	832	816	30	26	(3)	(0)	44	857	727
1B	1879-04	D.Brouthers	6,711	840	105	7,656	2,296	460	205	106	.342	.423	.519	942	994	256	0	0	(0)	(1)	993	1,082
2B	1906-30	E.Collins	9,949	1,499	77	11,525	3,315	438	187	47	.333	.424	.429	853	877	744	173	(2)	10	48	934	1,455
SS	1891-11	B.Dahlen	9,031	1,064	140	10,235	2,457	413	163	84	.272	.358	.382	739	767	547	0	0	9	50	826	880
3B	1952-68	E.Mathews	8,537	1,444	26	10,007	2,315	354	72	512	.271	.378	.509	888	877	68	39	(1)	7	4	887	829
OF	1951-73	W.Mays	10,881	1,464	44	12,389	3,283	523	140	660	.302	.387	.557	944	942	338	103	10	10	58	1,019	1,579
OF	1907-28	T.Speaker	10,195	1,381	103	11,679	3,514	792	222	117	.345	.428	.500	928	947	432	129	(7)	10	58	1,008	1,494
OF	1954-76	H.Aaron	12,364	1,402	32	13,798	3,771	624	98	755	.305	.377	.555	932	935	240	73	6	8	22	971	1,429
Reserves	Averages		9,403	1,225	72	10,700	2,888	491	142	330	.307	.391	.495	886	897	332	68	0	7	35	939	1,184
Totals	Weighted Ave.		9,098	1,301	72	10,471	2,911	528	144	357	.320	.409	.527	936	949	318	71	(2)	5	32	983	1,229

Pitchers Volume of Success

Pos	Years	Name	G	GS	IP	W	L	SV	SO	BB	ERA	RA/9	R Wtd RA/9	V Runs /162
SP	1890-11	C.Young	906	815	7,356	511	316	17	2,803	1,217	2.63	3.87	3.44	1,027
SP	1907-27	W.Johnson	802	666	5,914	417	279	34	3,509	1,363	2.17	2.89	3.10	1,021
SP	1880-93	T.Keefe	600	594	5,048	342	225	2	2,560	1,236	2.62	4.40	3.60	777
SP	1911-30	P.Alexander	696	600	5,190	373	208	32	2,198	951	2.56	3.21	3.37	726
SP	1881-91	O.Radbourn	528	503	4,535	309	195	2	1,830	875	2.67	4.51	3.59	717
Starters	Averages		706	636	5,609	390	245	17	2,580	1,128	2.52	3.74	3.41	854
RP	1952-72	H.Wilhelm	1,070	52	2,254	143	122	227	1,610	778	2.52	3.09	3.30	324
RP	1972-94	R.Gossage	1,002	37	1,809	124	107	310	1,502	732	3.01	3.33	3.59	199
RP	1968-85	R.Fingers	944	37	1,701	114	118	341	1,299	492	2.90	3.25	3.53	199
RP	1979-90	D.Quisenberry	674	0	1,043	56	46	244	379	162	2.76	3.07	3.16	167
Relievers	Averages		923	32	1,702	109	98	281	1,198	541	2.78	3.19	3.41	222
Totals	Averages		1,629	667	7,311	500	343	298	3,778	1,669	2.58	3.61	3.41	1,076

All Time Greats

Hitters Rate of Success

Pos	Years	Name	AB	BB	HBP	TAB	H	2B	3B	HR	BA	OB	SA	PRO	Wtd PRO	SB	CS	SBF	SPF	FF	R TF	V HC
C	1925-37	M.Cochrane	5,169	857	29	6,055	1,652	333	64	119	.320	.419	.478	897	842	64	46	(4)	8	58	904	687
1B	1923-39	L.Gehrig	8,001	1,508	45	9,554	2,721	534	163	493	.340	.447	.632	1,080	1,009	102	101	(10)	0	(3)	996	1,083
2B	1915-37	R.Hornsby	8,173	1,038	48	9,259	2,930	541	169	301	.358	.434	.577	1,010	995	135	64	(7)	(0)	(2)	986	1,407
SS	1897-17	H.Wagner	10,430	963	124	11,517	3,415	640	252	101	.327	.391	.466	857	921	722	15	(1)	9	40	970	1,685
3B	1972-89	M.Schmidt	8,352	1,507	79	9,938	2,234	408	59	548	.267	.384	.527	912	924	174	92	(1)	5	56	984	1,283
OF	1914-35	B.Ruth	8,399	2,056	42	10,497	2,873	506	136	714	.342	.474	.690	1,163	1,112	123	117	(11)	3	9	1,112	1,962
OF	1939-60	T.Williams	7,706	2,019	39	9,764	2,654	525	71	521	.344	.483	.634	1,116	1,093	24	17	(1)	(2)	(8)	1,082	1,599
OF	1986-	B.Bonds	7,456	1,547	56	9,059	2,157	451	69	494	.289	.415	.567	982	959	471	135	21	10	56	1,046	1,290
Starters	Averages		7,961	1,437	58	9,455	2,580	492	123	411	.324	.431	.572	1,003	989	227	73	(2)	4	26	1,017	1,375
C	1967-83	J.Bench	7,658	891	19	8,568	2,048	381	24	389	.267	.345	.476	821	835	68	43	(2)	(3)	65	896	878
1B	1879-04	D.Brouthers	6,711	840	105	7,656	2,296	460	205	106	.342	.423	.519	942	994	256	0	0	(0)	(1)	993	1,082
2B	1896-16	N.Lajoie	9,589	516	134	10,239	3,242	657	163	82	.338	.380	.466	846	910	380	21	(2)	6	63	978	1,495
SS	1996-	N.Garciaparra	2,436	184	24	2,644	812	176	29	117	.333	.386	.573	959	893	58	20	6	10	6	915	319
3B	1993-	C.Jones	3,469	554	5	4,028	1,051	204	18	189	.303	.400	.536	935	875	97	26	10	10	(5)	891	343
OF	1951-68	M.Mantle	8,102	1,733	13	9,848	2,415	344	72	536	.298	.423	.557	979	981	153	38	7	9	28	1,026	1,305
OF	1951-73	W.Mays	10,881	1,464	44	12,389	3,283	523	140	660	.302	.387	.557	944	942	338	103	10	10	58	1,019	1,579
OF	1907-28	T.Speaker	10,195	1,381	103	11,679	3,514	792	222	117	.345	.428	.500	928	947	432	129	(7)	10	58	1,008	1,494
Reserves	Averages		7,380	945	56	8,381	2,333	442	109	275	.316	.398	.517	915	930	223	48	3	7	34	974	1,062
Totals	Weighted Ave.		7,767	1,273	57	9,097	2,497	476	118	366	.322	.421	.554	975	969	226	65	(0)	5	29	1,002	1,270

Pitchers Rate of Success

Pos	Years	Name	G	GS	IP	W	L	SV	SO	BB	ERA	RA/9	R Wtd RA/9	V Runs /162
SP	1992-	P.Martinez	278	211	1,576	125	56	3	1,818	442	2.68	2.96	2.84	317
SP	1907-27	W.Johnson	802	666	5,914	417	279	34	3,509	1,363	2.17	2.89	3.10	1,021
SP	1876-77	A.Spalding	65	61	540	48	12	1	41	26	1.78	3.97	3.13	214
SP	1904-17	E.Walsh	430	315	2,964	195	126	35	1,736	617	1.82	2.66	3.13	494
SP	1925-41	L.Grove	616	457	3,941	300	141	55	2,266	1,187	3.06	3.64	3.22	616
Starters	Averages		438	342	2,987	217	123	26	1,874	727	2.37	3.09	3.11	532
RP	1995-	M.Rivera	332	10	452	33	17	165	395	144	2.63	2.77	2.47	107
RP	1995-	B.Wagner	252	0	281	19	18	107	422	126	2.73	2.92	2.78	56
RP	1982-95	T.Henke	642	0	790	41	42	311	861	255	2.67	2.87	2.85	154
RP	1987-95	B.Harvey	322	0	387	17	25	177	448	144	2.49	2.84	2.89	73
Relievers	Averages		387	3	477	28	26	190	532	167	2.63	2.85	2.76	97
Totals	Averages		825	345	3,464	245	148	216	2,406	894	2.41	3.06	3.06	630

All Time Greats
Catchers

V	R	Years	Name	AB	BB	HBP	TAB	H	2B	3B	HR	BA	OB	SA	PRO	Wtd PRO	SB	CS	SBF	SPF	FF	R TF	V HC
1	2	1967-83	J.Bench	7,658	891	19	8,568	2,048	381	24	389	.267	.345	.476	821	835	68	43	(2)	(3)	65	896	878
2	7	1946-65	Y.Berra	7,555	704	49	8,308	2,150	321	49	358	.285	.349	.482	832	816	30	26	(3)	(0)	44	857	727
3	1	1925-37	M.Cochrane	5,169	857	29	6,055	1,652	333	64	119	.320	.419	.478	897	842	64	46	(4)	8	58	904	687
4	17	1969-93	C.Fisk	8,756	849	143	9,748	2,356	421	47	376	.269	.343	.457	800	811	128	58	1	(4)	12	820	680
5	4	1880-97	B.Ewing	5,363	392	9	5,764	1,625	250	178	71	.303	.351	.456	807	838	354	0	0	(2)	45	881	640
6	8	1922-41	G.Hartnett	6,432	703	35	7,170	1,912	396	64	236	.297	.370	.489	858	830	28	7	0	(10)	33	853	632
7	9	1928-46	B.Dickey	6,300	678	31	7,009	1,969	343	72	202	.313	.382	.486	868	820	36	29	(3)	(9)	43	850	609
8	19	1974-92	G.Carter	7,971	848	68	8,887	2,092	371	31	324	.262	.338	.439	777	784	39	42	(5)	(6)	29	802	520
9	3	1992-	M.Piazza	4,135	439	16	4,590	1,356	199	4	278	.328	.395	.580	974	918	17	15	(3)	(10)	(18)	887	483
10	6	1991-	I.Rodriguez	4,806	256	33	5,095	1,459	288	24	171	.304	.343	.480	823	777	65	33	(0)	3	87	868	483
11	5	1948-57	R.Campanella	4,205	533	30	4,768	1,161	178	18	242	.276	.362	.500	861	835	25	15	(2)	(4)	48	877	476
12	16	1960-77	J.Torre	7,874	779	85	8,738	2,342	344	59	252	.297	.367	.452	819	836	23	29	(4)	(9)	(0)	822	475
13	13	1878-93	C.Bennett	3,821	478	11	4,310	978	203	67	55	.256	.340	.387	728	808	42	0	0	(4)	29	833	474
14	15	1961-76	B.Freehan	6,073	626	114	6,813	1,591	241	35	200	.262	.342	.412	754	787	24	21	(3)	2	36	823	455
15	10	1897-15	R.Bresnahan	4,481	714	66	5,261	1,252	218	71	26	.279	.386	.377	763	827	212	3	2	9	10	848	404
16	20	1931-47	E.Lombardi	5,855	430	44	6,329	1,792	277	27	190	.306	.358	.460	818	821	8	0	0	(10)	(10)	801	394
17	38	1968-88	T.Simmons	8,680	855	39	9,574	2,472	483	47	248	.285	.352	.437	789	793	21	33	(4)	(8)	(7)	773	380
18	23	1969-79	T.Munson	5,344	438	42	5,824	1,558	229	32	113	.292	.350	.410	760	781	48	50	(8)	5	17	795	327
19	30	1913-31	W.Schang	5,307	849	107	6,263	1,506	264	90	59	.284	.393	.401	794	789	121	49	(3)	0	(5)	780	323
20	32	1946-63	S.Lollar	5,351	671	115	6,137	1,415	244	14	155	.264	.359	.402	761	747	20	10	(0)	(10)	40	776	304
21	54	1977-95	L.Parrish	7,067	612	37	7,716	1,782	305	27	324	.252	.315	.440	756	755	28	37	(6)	(10)	17	757	300
22	11	1884-93	J.Milligan	2,964	210	36	3,210	848	189	50	49	.286	.341	.433	774	818	41	0	0	(10)	37	845	292
23	48	1971-87	D.Porter	5,539	905	45	6,489	1,369	237	48	188	.247	.357	.409	766	777	39	37	(5)	(4)	(8)	760	261
24	35	1884-00	J.Clements	4,283	339	61	4,683	1,226	226	60	77	.286	.347	.421	768	787	55	0	0	(8)	(4)	775	255
25	14	1884-91	F.Carroll	2,892	348	50	3,290	820	146	66	27	.284	.370	.408	778	830	137	0	0	0	(3)	827	252

All Time Greats
First Basemen

V	R	Years	Name	AB	BB	HBP	TAB	H	2B	3B	HR	BA	OB	SA	PRO	Wtd PRO	SB	CS	SBF	SPF	FF	R TF	V HC
1	1	1923-39	L.Gehrig	8,001	1,508	45	9,554	2,721	534	163	493	.340	.447	.632	1,080	1,009	102	101	(10)	0	(3)	996	1,083
2	2	1879-04	D.Brouthers	6,711	840	105	7,656	2,296	460	205	106	.342	.423	.519	942	994	256	0	0	(0)	(1)	993	1,082
3	13	1876-97	C.Anson	9,101	952	32	10,085	2,995	528	124	97	.329	.395	.446	841	907	247	0	(0)	(3)	15	918	1,079
4	3	1925-45	J.Foxx	8,134	1,452	13	9,599	2,646	458	125	534	.325	.428	.609	1,038	976	87	72	(6)	2	17	989	1,072
5	10	1880-97	R.Connor	7,794	1,002	38	8,834	2,467	441	233	138	.317	.397	.486	883	926	244	0	0	0	7	933	971
6	6	1991-	J.Bagwell	5,349	992	97	6,438	1,630	351	22	310	.305	.422	.552	975	938	167	64	6	10	22	976	657
7	9	1936-53	J.Mize	6,443	856	52	7,351	2,011	367	83	359	.312	.397	.562	959	955	28	1	(0)	(4)	(4)	946	652
8	6	1986-	M.McGwire	5,888	1,261	72	7,221	1,570	248	6	554	.267	.402	.593	995	957	12	8	(1)	(9)	6	953	650
9	11	1963-77	D.Allen	6,332	894	16	7,242	1,848	320	79	351	.292	.381	.534	914	946	133	52	4	10	(30)	930	641
10	5	1930-47	H.Greenberg	5,193	852	16	6,061	1,628	379	71	331	.313	.412	.605	1,017	966	58	26	1	0	4	971	616
11	8	1990-	F.Thomas	5,474	1,188	46	6,708	1,755	361	10	344	.321	.446	.579	1,024	983	29	21	(2)	(0)	(31)	949	601
12	25	1954-75	H.Killebrew	8,147	1,559	48	9,754	2,086	290	24	573	.256	.379	.509	887	906	19	18	(2)	(10)	(34)	860	517
13	17	1959-80	W.McCovey	8,197	1,345	69	9,611	2,211	353	46	521	.270	.377	.515	892	906	26	22	(2)	(9)	(18)	877	509
14	18	1986-	R.Palmeiro	7,846	935	61	8,842	2,321	455	36	400	.296	.375	.516	891	862	88	38	1	(1)	14	877	470
15	14	1958-74	N.Cash	6,705	1,043	90	7,838	1,820	241	41	377	.271	.377	.488	865	886	43	30	(2)	(5)	15	893	465
16	39	1977-97	E.Murray	11,336	1,333	18	12,687	3,255	560	35	504	.287	.363	.476	839	832	110	43	2	(4)	13	842	454
17	28	1915-30	G.Sisler	8,267	472	48	8,787	2,812	425	164	102	.340	.379	.468	847	826	375	127	(1)	10	20	855	452
18	20	1974-90	K.Hernandez	7,370	1,070	32	8,472	2,182	426	60	162	.296	.388	.436	824	832	98	63	(3)	(1)	40	868	406
19	23	1986-	F.McGriff	7,352	1,136	31	8,519	2,103	372	20	417	.286	.384	.512	896	874	70	34	0	(3)	(9)	862	387
20	15	1933-45	D.Camilli	5,353	947	28	6,328	1,482	261	86	239	.277	.388	.492	880	883	60	0	0	0	5	888	379
21	26	1958-74	O.Cepeda	7,927	588	102	8,617	2,351	417	27	379	.297	.353	.499	852	860	142	80	(2)	2	(0)	859	377
22	22	1986-	W.Clark	7,173	937	59	8,169	2,176	440	47	284	.303	.388	.497	885	865	67	48	(3)	(2)	4	863	375
23	19	1923-36	B.Terry	6,428	537	9	6,974	2,193	373	112	154	.341	.393	.506	899	858	56	6	(1)	(2)	16	871	351
24	16	1898-13	F.Chance	4,297	554	137	4,988	1,273	200	79	20	.296	.394	.394	787	862	401	0	0	10	15	887	330
25	35	1943-63	G.Hodges	7,030	943	25	7,998	1,921	295	48	370	.273	.361	.487	848	823	63	31	(3)	0	27	847	314

All Time Greats
Second basemen

V	R	Years	Name	AB	BB	HBP	TAB	H	2B	3B	HR	BA	OB	SA	PRO	Wtd PRO	SB	CS	SBF	SPF	FF	R TF	V HC
1	2	1896-16	N.Lajoie	9,589	516	134	10,239	3,242	657	163	82	.338	.380	.466	846	910	380	21	(2)	6	63	978	1,495
2	3	1906-30	E.Collins	9,949	1,499	77	11,525	3,315	438	187	47	.333	.424	.429	853	877	744	173	(2)	10	48	934	1,455
3	1	1915-37	R.Hornsby	8,173	1,038	48	9,259	2,930	541	169	301	.358	.434	.577	1,010	995	135	64	(7)	(0)	(2)	986	1,407
4	7	1963-84	J.Morgan	9,277	1,865	40	11,182	2,517	449	96	268	.271	.395	.427	823	833	689	162	31	10	9	882	1,074
5	10	1924-42	C.Gehringer	8,860	1,186	51	10,097	2,839	574	146	184	.320	.404	.480	884	827	181	89	0	5	30	862	894
6	18	1882-99	B.McPhee	8,291	981	87	9,359	2,250	303	188	53	.271	.355	.372	727	753	568	0	0	9	64	826	784
7	11	1981-97	R.Sandberg	8,385	761	34	9,180	2,386	403	76	282	.285	.347	.452	798	799	344	107	13	8	41	862	775
8	8	1988-	R.Alomar	7,221	822	41	8,084	2,196	412	60	170	.304	.378	.448	827	799	416	100	25	9	42	876	759
9	9	1879-92	H.Richardson	5,642	377	10	6,029	1,688	303	126	70	.299	.344	.435	779	844	205	0	0	5	25	875	682
10	6	1880-91	F.Dunlap	3,974	283	7	4,264	1,159	224	53	41	.292	.340	.406	745	848	85	0	0	0	49	897	649
11	12	1937-51	B.Doerr	7,093	809	11	7,913	2,042	381	89	223	.288	.362	.461	823	806	54	64	(9)	0	48	845	637
12	20	1977-95	L.Whitaker	8,570	1,197	20	9,787	2,369	420	65	244	.276	.366	.426	792	789	143	75	(1)	6	20	815	628
13	14	1988-	C.Biggio	6,766	847	169	7,782	1,969	402	43	160	.291	.384	.434	818	793	358	106	19	10	14	836	586
14	15	1970-86	B.Grich	6,890	1,087	86	8,063	1,833	320	47	224	.266	.373	.424	796	816	104	83	(7)	3	20	832	586
15	22	1919-37	F.Frisch	9,112	728	31	9,871	2,880	466	138	105	.316	.369	.432	801	770	419	74	4	9	25	808	581
16	13	1967-85	R.Carew	9,315	1,018	25	10,358	3,053	445	112	92	.328	.395	.429	825	846	353	187	(2)	9	(10)	843	566
17	17	1888-01	C.Childs	5,618	991	63	6,672	1,720	205	100	20	.306	.416	.389	805	801	269	0	0	9	20	830	539
18	5	1947-56	J.Robinson	4,877	740	72	5,689	1,518	273	54	137	.311	.410	.474	883	858	197	30	6	10	24	899	531
19	23	1931-47	B.Herman	7,707	737	26	8,470	2,345	486	82	47	.304	.367	.407	774	777	67	0	0	(4)	27	801	490
20	19	1938-50	J.Gordon	5,707	759	29	6,495	1,530	264	52	253	.268	.357	.466	822	803	89	60	(5)	0	27	825	454
21	26	1907-20	L.Doyle	6,509	625	53	7,187	1,887	299	123	74	.290	.357	.408	765	824	298	27	(3)	10	(35)	796	405
22	25	1926-39	T.Lazzeri	6,297	869	21	7,187	1,840	334	115	178	.292	.380	.467	846	794	148	79	(1)	7	(3)	798	404
23	36	1882-97	F.Pfeffer	6,555	527	21	7,103	1,671	231	119	94	.255	.312	.369	682	709	382	0	0	10	52	771	384
24	29	1912-24	D.Pratt	6,826	513	37	7,376	1,996	392	117	43	.292	.345	.403	748	766	247	108	(10)	9	19	784	373
25	21	1899-09	J.Williams	5,481	474	36	5,991	1,507	242	138	49	.275	.337	.396	733	794	151	0	0	0	15	809	366

All Time Greats
Shortstops

V	R	Years	Name	AB	BB	HBP	TAB	H	2B	3B	HR	BA	OB	SA	PRO	Wtd PRO	SB	CS	SBF	SPF	FF	R TF	V HC
1	1	1897-17	H.Wagner	10,430	963	124	11,517	3,415	640	252	101	.327	.391	.466	857	921	722	15	(1)	9	40	970	1,685
2	12	1891-11	B.Dahlen	9,031	1,064	140	10,235	2,457	413	163	84	.272	.358	.382	739	767	547	0	0	9	50	826	880
3	4	1986-	B.Larkin	6,687	812	48	7,547	2,008	361	70	179	.300	.380	.456	836	813	359	71	28	9	29	879	810
4	7	1890-09	G.Davis	9,031	870	74	9,975	2,660	451	163	72	.295	.361	.404	766	793	616	0	0	10	38	840	793
5	13	1879-95	J.Glasscock	7,030	439	62	7,531	2,040	313	98	27	.290	.337	.374	712	756	372	0	0	9	51	816	760
6	5	1932-48	A.Vaughan	6,622	937	46	7,605	2,103	356	128	96	.318	.406	.453	859	861	118	0	0	10	(8)	863	740
7	9	1926-45	J.Cronin	7,579	1,059	34	8,672	2,285	515	118	170	.301	.390	.468	857	808	87	71	(6)	7	26	835	737
8	20	1981-	C.Ripken	11,074	1,103	64	12,241	3,070	587	44	417	.277	.346	.451	797	779	36	37	(3)	(1)	13	788	701
9	15	1974-93	R.Yount	11,008	966	48	12,022	3,142	583	126	251	.285	.346	.430	775	780	271	105	5	9	18	811	621
10	8	1953-71	E.Banks	9,421	763	70	10,254	2,583	407	90	512	.274	.333	.500	833	830	50	53	(5)	4	8	837	617
11	19	1977-96	A.Trammell	8,288	850	37	9,175	2,365	412	55	185	.285	.354	.415	770	762	236	109	2	8	17	790	582
12	11	1938-52	L.Boudreau	6,029	796	34	6,859	1,779	385	66	68	.295	.380	.415	795	792	51	50	(7)	(5)	50	830	580
13	30	1978-96	O.Smith	9,396	1,072	33	10,501	2,460	402	69	28	.262	.339	.328	668	668	580	148	24	9	65	766	545
14	26	1930-50	L.Appling	8,856	1,302	10	10,168	2,749	440	102	45	.310	.399	.398	798	769	179	108	(3)	(0)	6	771	542
15	14	1941-55	V.Stephens	6,497	692	6	7,195	1,859	307	42	247	.286	.355	.460	816	817	25	22	(2)	0	0	815	521
16	23	1894-18	B.Wallace	8,618	774	47	9,439	2,309	391	143	34	.268	.332	.358	690	738	201	2	(0)	(1)	39	776	520
17	6	1891-18	H.Jennings	4,904	347	287	5,538	1,527	232	88	18	.311	.390	.406	796	788	359	0	0	9	50	846	482
18	34	1940-58	P.Reese	8,058	1,210	26	9,294	2,170	330	80	126	.269	.366	.377	743	733	232	45	2	9	19	762	458
19	47	1956-73	L.Aparicio	10,230	736	27	10,993	2,677	394	92	83	.262	.313	.343	655	666	506	136	20	10	50	747	451
20	25	1927-46	D.Bartell	7,629	748	97	8,474	2,165	442	71	79	.284	.355	.391	747	729	109	3	1	10	34	774	439
21	42	1889-04	H.Long	7,675	612	56	8,343	2,128	342	97	91	.277	.335	.383	718	722	536	0	0	10	23	755	429
22	3	1994-	A.Rodriguez	3,126	310	31	3,467	966	194	13	189	.309	.377	.561	938	866	133	36	17	10	21	913	422
23	36	1915-30	D.Bancroft	7,182	827	23	8,032	2,004	320	77	32	.279	.355	.358	714	717	145	75	(9)	8	43	759	396
24	46	1887-99	E.McKean	6,890	635	39	7,564	2,083	272	158	67	.302	.364	.417	781	784	323	0	0	6	(43)	747	361
25	37	1983-	T.Fernandez	7,788	682	63	8,533	2,240	410	92	92	.288	.350	.399	749	736	245	135	(3)	10	13	756	351

All Time Greats
Third basemen

V	R	Years	Name	AB	BB	HBP	TAB	H	2B	3B	HR	BA	OB	SA	PRO	Wtd PRO	SB	CS	SBF	SPF	FF	R TF	V HC
1	1	1972-89	M.Schmidt	8,352	1,507	79	9,938	2,234	408	59	548	.267	.384	.527	912	924	174	92	(1)	5	56	984	1,283
2	5	1952-68	E.Mathews	8,537	1,444	26	10,007	2,315	354	72	512	.271	.378	.509	888	877	68	39	(1)	7	4	887	829
3	11	1973-93	G.Brett	10,349	1,096	33	11,478	3,154	665	137	317	.305	.373	.487	861	868	201	97	1	2	(0)	870	756
4	12	1982-99	W.Boggs	9,180	1,412	23	10,615	3,010	578	61	118	.328	.419	.443	861	847	24	35	(4)	(4)	19	858	729
5	9	1960-74	R.Santo	8,143	1,108	38	9,289	2,254	365	67	342	.277	.366	.464	830	847	35	41	(5)	(8)	38	872	708
6	6	1908-22	F.Baker	5,984	473	50	6,507	1,838	315	103	96	.307	.363	.442	805	857	235	28	(4)	6	18	877	538
7	22	1978-98	P.Molitor	10,835	1,094	47	11,976	3,319	605	114	234	.306	.372	.448	820	807	504	131	19	10	(13)	822	515
8	14	1955-69	K.Boyer	7,455	713	20	8,188	2,143	318	68	282	.287	.351	.462	813	810	105	77	(6)	9	29	843	495
9	4	1987-	E.Martinez	5,432	973	65	6,470	1,738	403	14	235	.320	.429	.529	958	915	43	27	(1)	(3)	(22)	888	470
10	20	1878-90	N.Williamson	4,553	506	23	5,082	1,159	228	85	64	.255	.332	.384	716	795	88	0	0	9	21	825	470
11	17	1895-08	J.Collins	6,795	426	84	7,305	1,999	352	116	65	.294	.343	.409	752	786	194	0	0	8	43	837	457
12	42	1955-77	B.Robinson	10,654	860	53	11,567	2,848	482	68	268	.267	.325	.401	726	744	28	22	(1)	(6)	56	793	429
13	30	1876-90	D.White	5,335	292	41	5,668	1,619	217	73	18	.303	.344	.382	726	823	46	0	(1)	(7)	(5)	810	417
14	28	1932-47	S.Hack	7,278	1,092	21	8,391	2,193	363	81	57	.301	.394	.397	791	797	165	0	0	8	8	813	409
15	24	1971-87	R.Cey	7,162	1,012	62	8,236	1,868	328	21	316	.261	.357	.445	802	811	24	29	(4)	(6)	18	819	408
16	19	1987-	M.Williams	6,243	410	50	6,703	1,677	292	33	346	.269	.319	.492	811	789	49	34	(2)	0	50	836	403
17	13	1885-97	D.Lyons	4,294	621	82	4,997	1,333	244	69	62	.310	.407	.443	850	864	224	0	0	1	(8)	857	391
18	29	1920-37	P.Traynor	7,559	472	31	8,062	2,416	371	164	58	.320	.362	.435	797	762	158	46	(1)	10	41	812	390
19	23	1912-27	H.Groh	6,074	696	83	6,853	1,774	308	87	26	.292	.373	.384	757	794	180	66	(9)	7	27	820	384
20	40	1967-88	G.Nettles	8,986	1,088	50	10,124	2,225	328	28	390	.248	.332	.421	753	769	32	36	(4)	(5)	34	794	376
21	15	1891-06	J.McGraw	3,924	836	132	4,892	1,309	121	70	13	.334	.465	.410	875	856	436	0	0	10	(26)	840	358
22	7	1890-98	B.Joyce	3,304	718	108	4,130	970	152	106	70	.294	.435	.467	902	878	264	0	0	10	(12)	875	350
23	25	1934-45	H.Clift	5,730	1,070	41	6,841	1,558	309	62	178	.272	.390	.441	831	792	69	43	(2)	0	28	817	347
24	21	1989-	R.Ventura	5,599	817	20	6,436	1,530	280	13	227	.273	.368	.450	817	783	19	32	(6)	(3)	50	824	343
25	2	1993-	C.Jones	3,469	554	5	4,028	1,051	204	18	189	.303	.400	.536	935	875	97	26	10	10	(5)	891	343

All Time Greats
Outfielders

V	R	Years	Name	AB	BB	HBP	TAB	H	2B	3B	HR	BA	OB	SA	PRO	Wtd PRO	SB	CS	SBF	SPF	FF	R TF	V HC
1	1	1914-35	B.Ruth	8,399	2,056	42	10,497	2,873	506	136	714	.342	.474	.690	1,163	1,112	123	117	(11)	3	9	1,112	1,962
2	7	1905-28	T.Cobb	11,434	1,249	94	12,777	4,189	724	295	117	.366	.433	.512	945	983	892	178	(2)	10	17	1,008	1,623
3	2	1939-60	T.Williams	7,706	2,019	39	9,764	2,654	525	71	521	.344	.483	.634	1,116	1,093	24	17	(1)	(2)	(8)	1,082	1,599
4	5	1951-73	W.Mays	10,881	1,464	44	12,389	3,283	523	140	660	.302	.387	.557	944	942	338	103	10	10	58	1,019	1,579
5	6	1907-28	T.Speaker	10,195	1,381	103	11,679	3,514	792	222	117	.345	.428	.500	928	947	432	129	(7)	10	58	1,008	1,494
6	11	1954-76	H.Aaron	12,364	1,402	32	13,798	3,771	624	98	755	.305	.377	.555	932	935	240	73	6	8	22	971	1,429
7	4	1951-68	M.Mantle	8,102	1,733	13	9,848	2,415	344	72	536	.298	.423	.557	979	981	153	38	7	9	28	1,026	1,305
8	3	1986-	B.Bonds	7,456	1,547	56	9,059	2,157	451	69	494	.289	.415	.567	982	959	471	135	21	10	56	1,046	1,290
9	15	1941-63	S.Musial	10,972	1,599	53	12,624	3,630	725	177	475	.331	.418	.559	977	966	78	31	(2)	(1)	(1)	961	1,257
10	14	1956-76	F.Robinson	10,006	1,420	198	11,624	2,943	528	72	586	.294	.392	.537	929	941	204	77	4	7	10	963	1,144
11	16	1926-47	M.Ott	9,456	1,708	64	11,228	2,876	488	72	511	.304	.414	.533	947	934	89	0	0	(1)	10	943	1,075
12	9	1936-51	J.DiMaggio	6,821	790	46	7,657	2,214	389	131	361	.325	.398	.579	977	934	30	9	1	6	51	992	900
13	33	1979-	R.Henderson	10,331	2,060	90	12,481	2,914	486	62	282	.282	.406	.423	829	815	1,370	326	53	10	23	902	892
14	40	1961-83	C.Yastrzemski	11,988	1,845	40	13,873	3,419	646	59	452	.285	.382	.462	844	864	168	116	(4)	3	30	892	881
15	27	1953-74	A.Kaline	10,116	1,277	55	11,448	3,007	498	75	399	.297	.379	.480	859	868	137	65	1	6	37	912	868
16	19	1888-03	E.Delahanty	7,505	741	94	8,340	2,596	522	185	101	.346	.411	.505	917	909	455	0	0	10	10	928	840
17	10	1989-	K.Griffey Jr.	6,352	841	56	7,249	1,883	342	33	438	.296	.384	.568	951	916	173	64	6	10	57	989	825
18	28	1899-17	S.Crawford	9,570	760	23	10,353	2,961	458	309	97	.309	.362	.452	814	896	366	30	(1)	5	11	911	812
19	34	1878-93	K.Kelly	5,894	549	12	6,455	1,813	359	102	69	.308	.368	.438	806	883	368	0	0	9	9	901	785
20	32	1955-72	R.Clemente	9,454	621	35	10,110	3,000	440	166	240	.317	.362	.475	837	842	83	46	(1)	10	52	902	719
21	13	1882-94	P.Browning	4,820	466	29	5,315	1,646	295	85	46	.341	.403	.467	869	954	258	0	0	8	1	963	717
22	24	1880-93	H.Stovey	6,138	663	31	6,832	1,771	347	174	122	.289	.361	.461	822	899	509	0	0	10	9	918	686
23	8	1908-20	J.Jackson	4,981	519	59	5,559	1,772	307	168	54	.356	.423	.517	940	988	202	61	(9)	10	7	996	674
24	41	1959-76	B.Williams	9,350	1,045	43	10,438	2,711	434	88	426	.290	.364	.492	856	875	90	49	(1)	7	9	891	661
25	45	1972-91	D.Evans	8,996	1,391	53	10,440	2,446	483	73	385	.272	.373	.470	843	854	78	59	(4)	4	33	887	657

All Time Greats
Outfielders

V	R	Years	Name	AB	BB	HBP	TAB	H	2B	3B	HR	BA	OB	SA	PRO	Wtd PRO	SB	CS	SBF	SPF	FF	R TF	V HC
26	53	1890-05	J.Burkett	8,421	1,029	75	9,525	2,850	320	182	75	.338	.415	.446	862	874	389	0	0	9	(1)	882	646
27	46	1979-99	T.Raines	8,694	1,290	41	10,025	2,561	419	112	168	.295	.388	.427	815	809	807	146	49	9	18	886	642
28	20	1885-06	S.Thompson	5,984	450	63	6,497	1,979	340	160	126	.331	.384	.504	888	900	229	0	0	9	19	928	640
29	48	1924-44	A.Simmons	8,759	615	30	9,404	2,927	539	149	307	.334	.380	.535	915	857	88	64	(4)	(0)	32	886	605
30	88	1973-95	D.Winfield	11,003	1,216	25	12,244	3,110	540	88	465	.283	.355	.475	830	829	223	96	3	6	20	857	599
31	67	1926-45	P.Waner	9,459	1,091	38	10,588	3,152	605	191	113	.333	.404	.473	878	856	104	0	0	4	11	871	597
32	31	1947-64	D.Snider	7,161	971	21	8,153	2,116	358	85	407	.295	.381	.540	921	897	99	50	(4)	1	10	903	596
33	57	1982-	T.Gwynn	9,186	780	24	9,990	3,108	534	84	134	.338	.392	.459	850	841	318	125	7	8	23	878	592
34	12	1989-	L.Walker	4,906	578	89	5,573	1,528	335	43	271	.311	.394	.563	957	922	195	61	12	10	26	970	591
35	106	1876-04	J.O'Rourke	7,435	481	36	7,952	2,304	414	132	50	.310	.355	.421	776	858	191	0	2	5	(10)	853	583
36	38	1888-01	B.Hamilton	6,269	1,187	89	7,545	2,159	242	95	40	.344	.455	.432	888	883	912	0	0	10	3	896	582
37	66	1894-15	F.Clarke	8,568	874	153	9,595	2,672	361	220	67	.312	.386	.429	814	850	506	0	0	8	13	871	578
38	17	1876-88	C.Jones	3,687	237	34	3,958	1,101	170	98	56	.299	.347	.443	790	910	19	0	(2)	0	21	930	567
39	39	1932-48	J.Medwick	7,635	437	26	8,098	2,471	540	113	205	.324	.362	.505	867	870	42	0	0	10	15	895	559
40	30	1966-82	R.Smith	7,033	890	33	7,956	2,020	363	57	314	.287	.370	.489	859	882	137	86	(4)	4	21	903	556
41	22	1898-10	E.Flick	5,597	597	99	6,293	1,752	268	164	48	.313	.389	.445	834	902	330	0	0	9	12	924	544
42	50	1904-19	S.Magee	7,441	736	109	8,286	2,169	425	166	83	.291	.364	.427	790	864	441	12	(1)	10	10	884	528
43	95	1876-91	P.Hines	6,253	366	36	6,655	1,881	368	84	56	.301	.343	.413	756	853	153	0	(2)	1	4	855	505
44	56	1962-82	W.Stargell	7,927	937	78	8,942	2,232	423	55	475	.282	.363	.529	892	910	17	16	(2)	(7)	(23)	879	505
45	54	1933-45	B.Johnson	6,920	1,075	24	8,019	2,051	396	95	288	.296	.393	.506	899	867	96	64	(4)	8	10	882	501
46	44	1984-95	K.Puckett	7,244	450	56	7,750	2,304	414	57	207	.318	.363	.477	839	832	134	76	(2)	8	50	888	500
47	108	1976-96	A.Dawson	9,927	589	111	10,627	2,774	503	98	438	.279	.327	.482	809	814	314	109	9	3	26	852	499
48	214	1963-86	P.Rose	14,053	1,566	107	15,726	4,256	746	135	160	.303	.377	.409	786	802	198	149	(6)	7	3	806	495
49	117	1967-87	R.Jackson	9,864	1,375	96	11,335	2,584	463	49	563	.262	.358	.490	848	864	228	115	(0)	5	(23)	847	494
50	61	1879-92	G.Gore	5,357	717	30	6,104	1,612	262	94	46	.301	.386	.411	797	877	170	0	0	0	(3)	874	487
51	52	1968-81	B.Bonds	7,043	914	53	8,010	1,886	302	66	332	.268	.356	.471	827	839	461	169	14	10	20	883	485
52	71	1891-08	J.Kelley	7,006	911	82	7,999	2,220	358	194	65	.317	.402	.451	853	858	443	0	0	9	3	870	485
53	109	1885-03	J.Ryan	8,164	803	83	9,050	2,502	451	157	118	.306	.374	.444	818	826	418	0	0	4	20	851	478
54	110	1909-27	Z.Wheat	9,106	650	72	9,828	2,884	476	172	132	.317	.367	.450	817	835	205	49	(4)	5	14	850	464
55	77	1914-32	H.Heilmann	7,787	856	40	8,683	2,660	542	151	183	.342	.410	.520	930	897	113	64	(6)	(10)	(18)	863	459
56	113	1892-10	W.Keeler	8,591	524	129	9,244	2,932	241	145	33	.341	.388	.415	802	833	495	0	0	10	4	847	448
57	51	1928-44	C.Klein	6,486	601	12	7,099	2,076	398	74	300	.320	.379	.543	922	890	79	0	(1)	(6)	(6)	883	444
58	36	1946-55	R.Kiner	5,205	1,011	24	6,240	1,451	216	39	369	.279	.398	.548	946	924	22	2	1	(4)	(24)	898	442
59	115	1921-38	G.Goslin	8,656	949	56	9,661	2,735	500	173	248	.316	.387	.500	887	831	175	89	(0)	8	8	847	435
60	101	1976-93	D.Murphy	7,960	986	28	8,974	2,111	350	39	398	.265	.348	.469	817	824	161	68	3	6	21	854	430
61	70	1949-80	M.Minoso	6,579	814	192	7,585	1,963	336	83	186	.298	.391	.459	851	841	205	130	(7)	10	26	870	426
62	94	1896-13	C.Seymour	5,682	354	30	6,066	1,723	229	96	52	.303	.347	.405	752	822	222	0	0	10	24	856	425
63	47	1989-	A.Belle	5,853	683	55	6,591	1,726	389	21	381	.295	.374	.564	938	899	88	41	1	0	(13)	886	424
64	72	1974-90	F.Lynn	6,925	857	30	7,812	1,960	388	43	306	.283	.364	.484	848	851	72	54	(4)	(2)	25	869	423
65	62	1988-	G.Sheffield	5,146	858	76	6,080	1,508	265	19	279	.293	.402	.515	916	884	160	77	1	10	(21)	874	411
66	121	1938-59	E.Slaughter	7,946	1,018	37	9,001	2,383	413	148	169	.300	.382	.453	835	830	71	15	(1)	8	8	846	397
67	35	1883-92	T.O'Neill	4,255	421	44	4,720	1,386	222	92	52	.326	.392	.458	850	903	161	0	0	7	(11)	899	397
68	120	1897-13	J.Sheckard	7,605	1,135	90	8,830	2,084	354	136	56	.274	.375	.378	753	808	465	0	0	10	28	846	396
69	90	1967-84	A.Otis	7,299	757	33	8,089	2,020	374	66	193	.277	.347	.425	773	791	341	93	18	10	38	857	395
70	18	1939-52	C.Keller	3,790	784	10	4,584	1,085	166	72	189	.286	.410	.518	928	922	45	23	(0)	6	0	929	395
71	119	1974-89	J.Rice	8,225	670	64	8,959	2,452	373	79	382	.298	.356	.502	858	862	58	34	(1)	(2)	(12)	846	389
72	84	1963-77	J.Wynn	6,653	1,224	27	7,904	1,665	285	39	291	.250	.369	.436	805	827	225	101	3	10	20	859	387
73	42	1984-	E.Davis	5,165	727	32	5,924	1,398	232	23	278	.271	.364	.486	850	835	348	65	35	8	13	890	382
74	59	1947-59	L.Doby	5,348	871	38	6,257	1,515	243	52	253	.283	.387	.490	877	858	47	36	(4)	8	16	877	379
75	107	1921-38	K.Cuyler	7,161	676	85	7,922	2,299	394	157	128	.321	.386	.474	860	822	328	27	3	10	18	853	377

All Time Greats
Starting Pitchers

V	R	Years	Name	G	GS	IP	W	L	SV	SO	BB	ERA	RA/9	R Wtd RA/9	V Runs /162
1	19	1890-11	C.Young	906	815	7,356	511	316	17	2,803	1,217	2.63	3.87	3.44	1,027.4
2	2	1907-27	W.Johnson	802	666	5,914	417	279	34	3,509	1,363	2.17	2.89	3.10	1,021.3
3	40	1880-93	T.Keefe	600	594	5,048	342	225	2	2,560	1,236	2.62	4.40	3.60	777.4
4	13	1911-30	P.Alexander	696	600	5,190	373	208	32	2,198	951	2.56	3.21	3.37	726.1
5	39	1881-91	O.Radbourn	528	503	4,535	309	195	2	1,830	875	2.67	4.51	3.59	716.6
6	26	1890-06	K.Nichols	620	561	5,056	361	208	17	1,873	1,268	2.95	4.41	3.50	684.5
7	70	1878-87	J.McCormick	492	485	4,276	265	214	1	1,704	749	2.43	4.41	3.74	676.1
8	41	1876-84	T.Bond	322	314	2,780	193	115	0	860	178	2.25	4.33	3.60	669.2
9	17	1900-16	C.Mathewson	635	551	4,781	373	188	29	2,502	844	2.13	3.04	3.42	646.3
10	5	1925-41	L.Grove	616	457	3,941	300	141	55	2,266	1,187	3.06	3.64	3.22	616.1
11	38	1942-65	W.Spahn	750	665	5,244	363	245	29	2,583	1,434	3.09	3.46	3.59	589.5
12	22	1967-86	T.Seaver	656	647	4,783	311	205	1	3,640	1,390	2.86	3.15	3.47	589.0
13	6	1984-	R.Clemens	512	511	3,667	260	142	0	3,504	1,186	3.07	3.40	3.23	555.2
14	36	1901-17	E.Plank	623	529	4,496	326	194	23	2,246	1,072	2.35	3.14	3.58	524.0
15	4	1904-17	E.Walsh	430	315	2,964	195	126	35	1,736	617	1.82	2.66	3.13	493.5
16	15	1928-43	C.Hubbell	535	431	3,590	253	154	33	1,677	725	2.98	3.46	3.40	483.9
17	86	1882-94	J.Clarkson	531	518	4,536	328	178	5	1,978	1,191	2.81	4.71	3.79	482.9
18	23	1965-84	J.Palmer	558	521	3,948	268	152	4	2,212	1,311	2.86	3.18	3.49	479.4
19	8	1986-	G.Maddux	471	467	3,318	240	135	0	2,350	733	2.83	3.24	3.31	476.4
20	110	1881-94	T.Mullane	555	504	4,531	284	220	15	1,803	1,408	3.05	5.01	3.86	475.1
21	28	1936-56	B.Feller	570	484	3,827	266	162	21	2,581	1,764	3.25	3.66	3.53	459.3
22	9	1950-67	W.Ford	498	438	3,170	236	106	10	1,956	1,086	2.75	3.14	3.31	452.4
23	69	1878-84	M.Ward	292	261	2,462	164	102	3	920	253	2.10	4.33	3.73	449.7
24	14	1903-16	T.Brown	481	332	3,172	239	130	49	1,375	673	2.06	2.96	3.40	432.3
25	21	1884-92	B.Caruthers	340	310	2,829	218	99	3	900	597	2.83	4.43	3.45	426.3
26	67	1889-01	A.Rusie	463	427	3,779	246	174	5	1,950	1,707	3.07	4.93	3.72	412.9
27	27	1884-90	E.Morris	311	307	2,678	171	122	1	1,217	498	2.82	4.41	3.52	401.0
28	124	1966-88	D.Sutton	774	756	5,282	324	256	5	3,574	1,343	3.26	3.58	3.89	396.2
29	53	1959-75	B.Gibson	528	482	3,884	251	174	6	3,117	1,336	2.91	3.29	3.66	391.3
30	296	1879-92	P.Galvin	697	681	5,941	360	308	1	1,799	744	2.87	5.03	4.18	380.1
31	212	1877-86	W.White	403	401	3,543	229	166	0	1,041	496	2.28	4.68	4.06	374.4
32	151	1966-93	N.Ryan	807	773	5,386	324	292	3	5,714	2,795	3.19	3.64	3.95	366.8
33	131	1970-92	B.Blyleven	692	685	4,970	287	250	0	3,701	1,322	3.31	3.67	3.91	366.6
34	245	1880-92	M.Welch	564	549	4,802	307	210	4	1,850	1,297	2.71	4.79	4.10	362.3
35	154	1962-83	G.Perry	777	690	5,350	314	265	11	3,534	1,379	3.11	3.58	3.96	360.0
36	104	1882-92	C.Buffinton	414	396	3,404	233	152	3	1,700	856	2.96	4.82	3.84	358.0
37	126	1948-66	R.Roberts	676	609	4,689	286	245	25	2,357	902	3.41	3.77	3.90	357.0
38	49	1912-28	S.Coveleski	450	385	3,082	215	142	21	981	802	2.89	3.60	3.63	345.0
39	10	1902-10	A.Joss	286	260	2,327	160	97	5	920	364	1.89	2.82	3.32	343.9
40	32	1915-35	D.Vance	442	348	2,967	197	140	11	2,045	840	3.24	3.78	3.57	341.8
41	55	1945-64	B.Pierce	585	432	3,307	211	169	32	1,999	1,178	3.27	3.61	3.68	338.4
42	43	1897-10	R.Waddell	407	340	2,961	193	143	5	2,316	803	2.16	3.23	3.61	338.0
43	57	1905-20	E.Cicotte	502	361	3,223	208	149	25	1,374	827	2.38	3.21	3.69	336.0
44	77	1899-08	J.McGinnity	465	381	3,441	246	142	24	1,068	812	2.66	3.76	3.77	330.0
45	18	1930-43	L.Gomez	368	320	2,503	189	102	9	1,468	1,095	3.34	3.92	3.43	329.4
46	66	1956-69	D.Drysdale	518	465	3,432	209	166	6	2,486	855	2.95	3.39	3.72	326.4
47	20	1988-	R.Johnson	366	357	2,499	179	95	2	3,040	1,089	3.20	3.61	3.44	320.9
48	47	1876-77	J.Devlin	129	129	1,181	65	60	0	263	78	1.89	4.55	3.62	318.8
49	1	1992-	P.Martinez	278	211	1,576	125	56	3	1,818	442	2.68	2.96	2.84	317.4
50	12	1955-66	S.Koufax	397	314	2,324	165	87	9	2,396	817	2.76	3.12	3.36	316.8

All Time Greats
Starting Pitchers

V	R	Years	Name	G	GS	IP	W	L	SV	SO	BB	ERA	RA/9	R Wtd RA/9	V Runs /162
51	127	1898-10	V.Willis	513	471	3,996	249	205	11	1,651	1,212	2.63	3.67	3.90	315.9
52	116	1880-87	L.Corcoran	277	268	2,392	177	89	2	1,103	496	2.36	4.64	3.87	314.1
53	146	1924-47	R.Ruffing	624	536	4,344	273	225	16	1,987	1,541	3.80	4.39	3.95	309.7
54	63	1915-29	C.Mays	490	324	3,021	208	126	31	862	734	2.92	3.61	3.71	308.9
55	31	1905-17	E.Reulbach	399	300	2,632	182	106	13	1,137	892	2.28	3.03	3.56	306.0
56	59	1906-25	B.Adams	482	354	2,995	194	140	15	1,036	430	2.76	3.39	3.69	305.7
57	142	1914-33	R.Faber	669	483	4,087	254	213	28	1,471	1,213	3.15	3.99	3.93	301.9
58	48	1898-10	S.Leever	388	299	2,661	194	100	13	847	587	2.47	3.46	3.62	300.9
59	60	1939-55	H.Newhouser	488	374	2,993	207	150	26	1,796	1,249	3.06	3.60	3.70	300.5
60	97	1886-97	S.King	397	371	3,182	203	153	6	1,222	967	3.18	5.10	3.83	300.5
61	206	1965-88	S.Carlton	741	709	5,217	329	244	2	4,136	1,833	3.22	3.67	4.05	298.3
62	51	1916-28	U.Shocker	412	317	2,682	187	117	25	983	657	3.17	3.78	3.65	287.9
63	44	1986-	K.Brown	382	380	2,661	170	114	0	1,917	730	3.21	3.69	3.62	287.9
64	156	1923-46	T.Lyons	594	484	4,161	260	230	23	1,073	1,121	3.67	4.45	3.97	287.3
65	35	1984-	B.Saberhagen	396	368	2,548	166	115	1	1,705	471	3.33	3.62	3.58	286.8
66	52	1986-	D.Cone	420	390	2,745	184	116	1	2,540	1,067	3.40	3.72	3.65	285.3
67	98	1960-75	J.Marichal	471	457	3,507	243	142	2	2,303	709	2.89	3.41	3.83	283.8
68	11	1991-	M.Mussina	288	288	2,010	147	81	0	1,535	467	3.53	3.75	3.35	282.4
69	89	1901-13	D.White	427	363	3,041	189	156	5	1,384	670	2.39	3.30	3.80	275.6
70	102	1914-35	D.Luque	550	366	3,220	194	179	28	1,130	918	3.24	3.95	3.84	272.0
71	79	1913-27	B.Shawkey	488	333	2,937	195	150	28	1,360	1,018	3.09	3.68	3.77	271.7
72	74	1946-58	B.Lemon	460	350	2,850	207	128	22	1,277	1,251	3.23	3.74	3.77	263.5
73	73	1930-46	T.Bridges	424	362	2,826	194	138	10	1,674	1,192	3.57	4.21	3.77	261.4
74	45	1907-16	N.Rucker	336	273	2,375	134	134	14	1,217	701	2.42	3.10	3.62	260.7
75	42	1975-88	R.Guidry	368	323	2,392	170	91	4	1,778	633	3.29	3.59	3.61	259.7
76	163	1918-38	W.Hoyt	674	423	3,762	237	182	52	1,206	1,003	3.59	4.26	3.97	258.2
77	29	1899-06	N.Hahn	243	231	2,029	130	94	0	917	381	2.55	3.65	3.54	256.1
78	159	1891-14	C.Griffith	453	372	3,386	237	146	6	955	774	3.31	4.92	3.97	254.7
79	16	1940-53	H.Brecheen	318	240	1,908	133	92	18	901	536	2.92	3.31	3.42	253.9
80	61	1984-98	J.Key	470	389	2,592	186	117	10	1,538	668	3.51	3.83	3.70	252.9
81	149	1912-26	W.Cooper	517	407	3,480	216	178	14	1,252	853	2.89	3.63	3.95	252.7
82	171	1955-71	J.Bunning	591	519	3,760	224	184	16	2,855	1,000	3.27	3.66	3.99	240.1
83	101	1979-98	D.Stieb	443	412	2,895	176	137	3	1,669	1,034	3.44	3.81	3.84	238.7
84	254	1912-33	E.Rixey	692	554	4,495	266	251	14	1,350	1,082	3.15	3.98	4.11	233.2
85	244	1965-83	F.Jenkins	664	594	4,501	284	226	7	3,192	997	3.34	3.71	4.10	232.8
86	30	1930-47	D.Dean	317	230	1,967	150	83	30	1,163	453	3.02	3.54	3.55	231.6
87	99	1899-11	D.Phillippe	372	289	2,607	189	109	12	929	363	2.59	3.72	3.84	229.6
88	113	1987-	T.Glavine	434	434	2,901	208	125	0	1,811	965	3.38	3.76	3.87	228.9
89	108	1930-45	L.Warneke	445	343	2,782	192	121	13	1,140	739	3.18	3.77	3.86	226.3
90	72	1884-94	D.Foutz	251	216	1,997	147	66	4	790	510	2.84	4.81	3.74	226.2
91	152	1975-98	D.Eckersley	1,071	361	3,286	197	171	390	2,401	738	3.50	3.79	3.96	226.1
92	50	1989-	K.Appier	324	312	2,085	136	105	0	1,633	759	3.63	3.94	3.63	223.6
93	160	1933-53	D.Leonard	640	375	3,218	191	181	44	1,170	737	3.25	4.00	3.97	220.9
94	272	1963-89	T.John	760	700	4,710	288	231	4	2,245	1,259	3.34	3.85	4.14	220.0
95	7	1937-47	S.Chandler	211	184	1,485	109	43	6	614	463	2.84	3.33	3.31	217.2
96	167	1969-86	V.Blue	502	473	3,343	209	161	2	2,175	1,185	3.27	3.65	3.99	216.4
97	180	1964-82	L.Tiant	573	484	3,486	229	172	15	2,416	1,104	3.30	3.61	4.01	214.4
98	3	1876-77	A.Spalding	65	61	540	48	12	1	41	26	1.78	3.97	3.13	214.0
99	138	1986-	C.Finley	470	413	2,893	181	151	0	2,340	1,219	3.76	4.18	3.92	212.4
100	62	1968-79	A.Messersmith	344	295	2,230	130	99	15	1,625	831	2.86	3.28	3.70	212.3

All Time Greats
Relief Pitchers

V	R	Years	Name	G	GS	IP	W	L	SV	SO	BB	ERA	RA/9	R Wtd RA/9	V Runs /162
1	13	1952-72	H.Wilhelm	1,070	52	2,254	143	122	227	1,610	778	2.52	3.09	3.30	323.8
2	43	1972-94	R.Gossage	1,002	37	1,809	124	107	310	1,502	732	3.01	3.33	3.59	198.8
3	32	1968-85	R.Fingers	944	37	1,701	114	118	341	1,299	492	2.90	3.25	3.53	198.7
4	10	1979-90	D.Quisenberry	674	0	1,043	56	46	244	379	162	2.76	3.07	3.16	166.6
5	3	1982-95	T.Henke	642	0	790	41	42	311	861	255	2.67	2.87	2.85	154.3
6	15	1984-	J.Franco	940	0	1,097	82	74	420	857	430	2.68	3.19	3.35	151.1
7	48	1974-89	K.Tekulve	1,050	0	1,436	94	90	184	779	491	2.85	3.30	3.64	149.8
8	36	1980-97	L.Smith	1,022	6	1,289	71	92	478	1,251	486	3.03	3.32	3.57	148.0
9	25	1965-80	J.Hiller	545	43	1,242	87	76	125	1,036	535	2.83	3.17	3.49	146.9
10	28	1979-	J.Orosco	1,096	4	1,218	84	75	141	1,107	541	3.03	3.43	3.51	146.0
11	12	1982-96	M.Eichhorn	563	7	886	48	43	32	640	270	3.00	3.33	3.29	128.5
12	70	1967-82	S.Lyle	899	0	1,390	99	76	238	873	481	2.88	3.36	3.75	128.4
13	34	1982-	D.Jones	846	4	1,128	69	79	303	909	247	3.30	3.71	3.56	127.8
14	40	1979-94	J.Reardon	880	0	1,132	73	77	367	877	358	3.16	3.39	3.58	127.3
15	59	1957-74	D.McMahon	874	2	1,311	90	68	153	1,003	579	2.96	3.31	3.70	127.2
16	102	1952-68	S.Miller	704	93	1,694	105	103	154	1,164	600	3.24	3.70	3.91	126.5
17	33	1976-88	B.Sutter	661	0	1,042	68	71	300	861	309	2.83	3.19	3.56	120.1
18	38	1986-	M.Jackson	835	7	1,018	53	61	138	905	414	3.26	3.62	3.57	114.1
19	21	1987-99	J.Montgomery	700	1	869	46	52	304	733	296	3.27	3.60	3.42	113.2
20	49	1932-47	J.Murphy	415	40	1,045	93	53	107	378	444	3.50	4.00	3.65	111.1
21	6	1993-	T.Hoffman	509	0	581	40	35	271	665	175	2.73	3.03	2.92	110.9
22	14	1989-	J.Wetteland	618	17	765	48	45	330	804	252	2.93	3.38	3.31	110.7
23	81	1964-78	C.Carroll	731	28	1,353	96	73	143	681	442	2.94	3.37	3.83	110.5
24	104	1965-84	T.McGraw	824	39	1,515	96	92	180	1,109	582	3.14	3.55	3.92	109.9
25	9	1991-	R.Hernandez	580	3	655	42	42	266	631	267	3.03	3.41	3.13	108.1
26	98	1979-95	D.Righetti	718	89	1,404	82	79	252	1,112	591	3.46	3.86	3.90	107.8
27	95	1967-81	M.Marshall	723	24	1,387	97	112	188	880	514	3.14	3.56	3.87	107.2
28	1	1995-	M.Rivera	332	10	452	33	17	165	395	144	2.63	2.77	2.47	106.7
29	27	1980-92	D.Smith	609	1	809	53	53	216	548	283	2.67	3.11	3.50	99.8
30	41	1985-	R.Myers	728	12	885	44	63	347	884	396	3.19	3.44	3.58	98.3
31	103	1985-	R.Aguilera	732	89	1,291	86	81	318	1,030	351	3.57	3.96	3.91	96.0
32	75	1974-87	G.Lavelle	745	3	1,085	80	77	136	769	440	2.93	3.43	3.80	94.7
33	37	1984-94	S.Farr	509	28	824	48	45	132	668	334	3.25	3.56	3.57	91.9
34	90	1961-73	R.Perranoski	737	1	1,175	79	74	179	687	468	2.79	3.38	3.87	90.8
35	64	1944-53	T.Wilks	385	44	913	59	30	46	403	283	3.26	3.59	3.72	89.4
36	18	1988-	G.Olson	594	0	647	40	38	217	564	310	3.28	3.49	3.39	85.4
37	101	1975-90	G.Minton	710	7	1,131	59	65	150	479	483	3.10	3.60	3.90	85.4
38	86	1960-76	J.Brewer	584	35	1,041	69	65	132	810	360	3.07	3.47	3.84	83.6
39	22	1991-	R.Beck	574	0	628	29	37	260	534	143	3.20	3.46	3.43	81.8
40	62	1980-94	J.Howell	568	21	845	58	53	155	666	291	3.34	3.57	3.72	81.7
41	63	1988-	J.Brantley	597	18	838	43	45	172	717	357	3.35	3.61	3.72	81.6
42	17	1993-	R.Nen	496	4	564	35	35	226	619	218	3.08	3.50	3.37	78.5
43	130	1955-71	D.Hall	495	74	1,260	93	75	68	741	236	3.32	3.66	4.01	78.1
44	16	1992-	J.Nelson	534	0	555	35	32	17	560	287	3.29	3.71	3.36	77.5
45	35	1985-92	T.Burke	498	2	699	49	33	102	444	219	2.72	3.23	3.56	77.1
46	44	1985-97	T.Worrell	617	0	694	50	52	256	628	247	3.09	3.43	3.60	76.3
47	50	1987-96	M.Henneman	561	0	733	57	42	193	533	271	3.21	3.70	3.65	75.8
48	150	1953-69	R.Face	848	27	1,375	104	95	193	877	362	3.48	3.87	4.09	73.9
49	106	1975-94	L.Andersen	699	1	995	40	39	49	758	311	3.15	3.63	3.92	73.6
50	111	1981-96	A.Pena	503	72	1,058	56	52	74	839	331	3.11	3.63	3.95	73.6

APPENDIX:
125 GREATEST PLAYERS
OF ALL TIME

Johnny Bench **Reds** **Catcher** **Actual**

Year	T	L	P	AB	BB	HBP	TAB	H	2B	3B	HR	BA	OB	SA	PRO	SB	CS	SBF	SPF	FF	Actual TF	Actual HC
1967	Cin	NL	C	86	5	0	91	14	3	1	1	.163	.209	.256	465	0	1	(21)	0	100	544	(5.8)
1968	Cin	NL	C	564	31	2	597	155	40	2	15	.275	.315	.433	748	1	5	(14)	0	80	813	38.6
1969	Cin	NL	C	532	49	4	585	156	23	1	26	.293	.357	.487	844	6	6	(10)	0	90	924	68.8
1970	Cin	NL	C	605	54	0	659	177	35	4	45	.293	.351	.587	937	5	2	1	0	100	1,039	113.4
1971	Cin	NL	C	562	49	0	611	134	19	2	27	.238	.300	.423	723	2	1	0	0	80	803	36.6
1972	Cin	NL	C	538	100	2	640	145	22	2	40	.270	.386	.541	927	6	6	(9)	0	90	1,008	106.0
1973	Cin	NL	C	557	83	0	640	141	17	3	25	.253	.350	.429	779	4	1	3	0	100	882	62.4
1974	Cin	NL	C	621	80	3	704	174	38	2	33	.280	.365	.507	872	5	4	(4)	0	90	958	94.2
1975	Cin	NL	C	530	65	2	597	150	39	1	28	.283	.363	.519	882	11	0	17	0	100	1,000	91.7
1976	Cin	NL	C	465	81	2	548	109	24	1	16	.234	.350	.394	744	13	2	16	0	90	849	44.9
1977	Cin	NL	C	494	58	1	553	136	34	2	31	.275	.353	.540	893	2	4	(10)	0	70	953	72.6
1978	Cin	NL	C	393	50	1	444	102	17	1	23	.260	.345	.483	828	4	2	0	(10)	50	868	40.3
1979	Cin	NL	C	464	67	0	531	128	19	0	22	.276	.367	.459	826	4	2	0	(10)	40	856	45.3
1980	Cin	NL	C	360	41	2	403	90	12	0	24	.250	.330	.483	813	4	2	0	(10)	20	823	28.0
1981	Cin	NL	1B	178	17	0	195	55	8	0	8	.309	.369	.489	858	0	2	(19)	(10)	(20)	809	5.4
1982	Cin	NL	3B	399	37	0	436	103	16	0	13	.258	.321	.396	717	1	2	(7)	(10)	(50)	651	(13.6)
1983	Cin	NL	3B	310	24	0	334	79	15	2	12	.255	.308	.432	741	0	1	(6)	(10)	(50)	675	(6.6)
12.9 Totals				7,658	891	19	8,568	2,048	381	24	389					68	43					822.4
1.0 Averages				595	69	1	666	159	30	2	30	.267	.345	.476	821	5	3	(2)	(3)	65	881	63.9

Johnny Bench **Reds** **Catcher** **Adjusted**

Year	T	L	P	AB	BB	HBP	TAB	H	2B	3B	HR	BA	OB	SA	Wtd PRO	SB	CS	SBF	SPF	FF	Wtd TF	HC
1967	Cin	NL	C	86	5	0	91	15	3	1	1	.170	.218	.268	486	0	1	(21)	0	100	565	(4.9)
1968	Cin	NL	C	559	35	2	597	169	44	2	16	.302	.346	.475	821	1	5	(14)	0	80	886	59.4
1969	Cin	NL	C	530	51	4	585	159	23	1	27	.300	.365	.498	864	6	6	(10)	0	90	944	74.3
1970	Cin	NL	C	607	52	0	659	173	34	4	44	.285	.342	.572	914	5	2	1	0	100	1,015	106.1
1971	Cin	NL	C	560	51	0	611	138	20	2	28	.246	.309	.436	745	2	1	0	0	80	825	43.0
1972	Cin	NL	C	561	110	2	673	156	24	2	43	.279	.399	.560	959	6	6	(9)	0	90	1,040	116.4
1973	Cin	NL	C	556	84	0	640	142	17	3	25	.255	.353	.433	786	4	1	3	0	100	889	64.4
1974	Cin	NL	C	619	82	3	704	176	38	2	33	.285	.371	.515	886	5	4	(4)	0	90	972	98.8
1975	Cin	NL	C	529	66	2	597	151	39	1	28	.286	.368	.525	892	11	0	17	0	100	1,010	94.5
1976	Cin	NL	C	461	84	2	548	112	25	1	16	.242	.362	.406	768	13	2	16	0	90	873	51.1
1977	Cin	NL	C	496	56	1	553	133	33	2	30	.267	.342	.525	867	2	4	(10)	0	70	927	65.7
1978	Cin	NL	C	392	51	1	444	103	17	1	23	.264	.351	.492	842	4	2	0	(10)	50	882	43.3
1979	Cin	NL	C	465	66	0	531	127	19	0	22	.273	.364	.455	819	4	2	0	(10)	40	849	43.5
1980	Cin	NL	C	359	42	2	403	91	12	0	24	.253	.334	.490	824	4	2	0	(10)	20	834	30.0
1981	Cin	NL	1B	268	27	0	295	85	12	0	12	.318	.380	.503	883	0	3	(19)	(10)	(20)	833	8.9
1982	Cin	NL	3B	398	38	0	436	104	16	0	13	.262	.326	.402	728	1	2	(7)	(10)	(50)	662	(11.3)
1983	Cin	NL	3B	310	24	0	334	80	15	2	12	.257	.311	.436	747	0	1	(6)	(10)	(50)	681	(5.6)
12.9 Totals				7,757	924	20	8,701	2,114	392	24	399					68	44					877.8
1.0 Averages				603	72	2	676	164	30	2	31	.273	.352	.484	835	5	3	(2)	(3)	65	896	68.2

Mickey Cochrane Athletics   Catcher   Actual

Year	T	L	P	AB	BB	HBP	TAB	H	2B	3B	HR	BA	OB	SA	PRO	SB	CS	SBF	SPF	FF	Actual TF	Actual HC
1925	Phi	AL	C	420	44	2	466	139	21	5	6	.331	.397	.448	845	7	4	(2)	10	30	883	47.9
1926	Phi	AL	C	370	56	0	426	101	8	9	8	.273	.369	.408	777	5	2	2	10	50	839	34.5
1927	Phi	AL	C	432	50	2	484	146	20	6	12	.338	.409	.495	904	9	6	(6)	10	60	969	70.6
1928	Phi	AL	C	468	76	3	547	137	26	12	10	.293	.395	.464	859	7	7	(12)	10	40	896	60.1
1929	Phi	AL	C	514	69	2	585	170	37	8	7	.331	.412	.475	887	7	6	(8)	10	70	959	82.4
1930	Phi	AL	C	487	55	1	543	174	42	5	10	.357	.424	.526	949	5	0	9	10	90	1,058	103.6
1931	Phi	AL	C	459	56	3	518	160	31	6	17	.349	.423	.553	976	2	3	(7)	10	80	1,059	99.0
1932	Phi	AL	C	518	100	4	622	152	35	4	23	.293	.412	.510	921	0	1	(3)	10	90	1,018	106.2
1933	Phi	AL	C	429	106	3	538	138	30	4	15	.322	.459	.515	974	8	6	(7)	10	60	1,037	97.0
1934	Det	AL	C	437	78	4	519	140	32	1	2	.320	.428	.412	840	8	4	0	0	50	890	55.2
1935	Det	AL	C	411	96	4	511	131	33	3	5	.319	.452	.450	902	5	5	(9)	0	50	943	68.0
1936	Det	AL	C	126	46	0	172	34	8	0	2	.270	.465	.381	846	1	1	(5)	0	(20)	821	12.3
1937	Det	AL	C	98	25	1	124	30	10	1	2	.306	.452	.490	941	0	1	(15)	0	0	926	15.5
9.4 Totals				5,169	857	29	6,055	1,652	333	64	119					64	46					852.4
1.0 Averages				549	91	3	643	175	35	7	13	.320	.419	.478	897	7	5	(4)	8	58	959	90.5

Mickey Cochrane Athletics   Catcher   Adjusted

Year	T	L	P	AB	BB	HBP	TAB	H	2B	3B	HR	BA	OB	SA	Wtd PRO	SB	CS	SBF	SPF	FF	Wtd TF	HC
1925	Phi	AL	C	447	41	2	490	136	21	5	6	.304	.365	.411	776	7	4	(2)	10	30	814	32.0
1926	Phi	AL	C	393	55	0	448	102	8	9	8	.259	.350	.388	738	5	2	2	10	50	800	26.2
1927	Phi	AL	C	459	48	2	509	146	20	6	12	.318	.385	.466	850	9	6	(6)	10	60	914	57.5
1928	Phi	AL	C	498	75	3	575	139	26	12	10	.279	.376	.442	818	7	7	(12)	10	40	856	48.9
1929	Phi	AL	C	548	66	2	615	169	37	8	7	.309	.385	.443	828	7	6	(8)	10	70	900	65.2
1930	Phi	AL	C	520	50	1	571	170	41	5	10	.327	.387	.481	868	5	0	9	10	90	977	81.4
1931	Phi	AL	C	487	55	3	545	162	31	6	17	.333	.403	.528	931	2	3	(7)	10	80	1,014	87.4
1932	Phi	AL	C	554	97	4	654	153	35	4	23	.276	.387	.480	867	0	1	(3)	10	90	964	89.3
1933	Phi	AL	C	457	106	3	566	142	31	4	15	.310	.443	.497	940	8	6	(7)	10	60	1,002	87.7
1934	Det	AL	C	467	75	4	546	141	32	1	2	.302	.403	.388	790	8	4	0	0	50	840	42.4
1935	Det	AL	C	442	92	4	538	132	33	3	5	.299	.424	.422	846	5	5	(9)	0	50	886	53.5
1936	Det	AL	C	139	42	0	181	34	8	0	2	.243	.419	.343	762	1	1	(5)	0	(20)	736	5.1
1937	Det	AL	C	106	23	1	130	30	10	1	2	.281	.414	.449	863	0	1	(15)	0	0	848	10.6
9.4 Totals				5,517	824	28	6,370	1,655	334	64	120					67	48					687.1
1.0 Averages				586	87	3	676	176	35	7	13	.300	.394	.449	842	7	5	(4)	8	58	904	72.9

Yogi Berra   **Yankees**   **Catcher**   **Actual**

Year	T	L	P	AB	BB	HBP	TAB	H	2B	3B	HR	BA	OB	SA	PRO	SB	CS	SBF	SPF	FF	Actual TF	Actual HC
1946	NY	AL	C	22	1	0	23	8	1	0	2	.364	.391	.682	1,073	0	0	0	0	90	1,163	5.6
1947	NY	AL	C	293	13	0	306	82	15	3	11	.280	.310	.464	775	0	1	(6)	0	(10)	758	12.4
1948	NY	AL	C	469	25	1	495	143	24	10	14	.305	.341	.488	830	3	3	(6)	0	10	834	38.8
1949	NY	AL	C	415	22	6	443	115	20	2	20	.277	.323	.480	802	2	1	0	0	70	872	43.3
1950	NY	AL	C	597	55	1	653	192	30	6	28	.322	.380	.533	912	4	2	0	0	40	952	90.0
1951	NY	AL	C	547	44	3	594	161	19	4	27	.294	.350	.492	842	5	4	(5)	0	50	887	62.4
1952	NY	AL	C	534	66	4	604	146	17	1	30	.273	.358	.478	835	2	3	(6)	0	50	879	61.0
1953	NY	AL	C	503	50	3	556	149	23	5	27	.296	.363	.523	886	0	3	(10)	0	50	926	69.3
1954	NY	AL	C	584	56	4	644	179	28	6	22	.307	.371	.488	859	0	1	(3)	0	50	906	73.8
1955	NY	AL	C	541	60	7	608	147	20	3	27	.272	.352	.470	821	1	0	2	0	40	863	56.6
1956	NY	AL	C	521	65	5	591	155	29	2	30	.298	.381	.534	914	3	2	(2)	0	50	963	84.5
1957	NY	AL	C	482	57	1	540	121	14	2	24	.251	.331	.438	769	1	2	(5)	0	90	854	47.8
1958	NY	AL	C	433	35	2	470	115	17	3	22	.266	.323	.471	795	3	0	6	0	60	861	43.1
1959	NY	AL	C	472	43	4	519	134	25	1	19	.284	.349	.462	811	1	2	(5)	0	50	855	46.2
1960	NY	AL	C	359	38	3	400	99	14	1	15	.276	.350	.446	796	2	1	0	0	10	806	25.7
1961	NY	AL	OF	395	35	2	432	107	11	0	22	.271	.333	.466	799	2	0	4	0	0	804	9.5
1962	NY	AL	C	232	24	2	258	52	8	0	10	.224	.302	.388	690	0	1	(7)	(10)	50	723	5.6
1963	NY	AL	C	147	15	1	163	43	6	0	8	.293	.362	.497	859	1	0	6	(10)	60	914	18.4
1965	NY	NL	C	9	0	0	9	2	0	0	0	.222	.222	.222	444	0	0	0	(10)	20	454	(1.0)
12.9 Totals				7,555	704	49	8,308	2,150	321	49	358					30	26					793.2
1.0 Averages				587	55	4	646	167	25	4	28	.285	.349	.482	832	2	2	(3)	(0)	44	873	61.7

Yogi Berra   **Yankees**   **Catcher**   **Adjusted**

Year	T	L	P	AB	BB	HBP	TAB	H	2B	3B	HR	BA	OB	SA	Wtd PRO	SB	CS	SBF	SPF	FF	Wtd TF	HC
1946	NY	AL	C	23	1	0	24	9	1	0	2	.371	.399	.696	1,095	0	0	0	0	90	1,185	5.8
1947	NY	AL	C	308	14	0	322	87	16	3	12	.283	.314	.469	783	0	1	(6)	0	(10)	767	13.8
1948	NY	AL	C	495	25	1	521	146	24	10	14	.294	.330	.472	801	3	3	(6)	0	10	805	31.8
1949	NY	AL	C	438	22	6	466	117	20	2	20	.267	.311	.462	774	2	1	0	0	70	844	36.9
1950	NY	AL	C	634	52	1	687	190	30	6	28	.299	.353	.495	849	4	2	0	0	40	889	69.1
1951	NY	AL	C	577	45	3	625	166	20	4	28	.287	.342	.480	822	5	4	(5)	0	50	867	56.5
1952	NY	AL	C	560	71	4	635	156	18	1	32	.278	.363	.485	848	2	3	(6)	0	50	892	65.0
1953	NY	AL	C	531	51	3	585	154	24	5	28	.290	.356	.513	869	0	3	(10)	0	50	909	64.4
1954	NY	AL	C	614	59	4	677	188	29	6	23	.306	.371	.487	858	0	1	(3)	0	50	905	73.4
1955	NY	AL	C	571	61	7	640	152	21	3	28	.266	.345	.460	805	1	0	2	0	40	847	51.7
1956	NY	AL	C	552	64	5	622	157	29	2	30	.285	.365	.511	876	3	2	(2)	0	50	924	73.1
1957	NY	AL	C	508	59	1	568	127	15	2	25	.250	.330	.435	765	1	2	(5)	0	90	850	46.6
1958	NY	AL	C	456	37	2	494	121	18	3	23	.265	.323	.470	793	3	0	6	0	60	859	42.9
1959	NY	AL	C	497	45	4	546	140	26	1	20	.283	.347	.460	807	1	2	(5)	0	50	852	45.3
1960	NY	AL	C	379	39	3	421	103	15	1	16	.271	.344	.438	782	2	1	0	0	10	792	23.0
1961	NY	AL	OF	396	34	2	432	104	11	0	21	.263	.324	.453	777	2	0	4	0	0	781	4.9
1962	NY	AL	C	233	23	2	258	51	8	0	10	.219	.296	.379	675	0	1	(7)	(10)	50	708	3.7
1963	NY	AL	C	147	15	1	163	44	6	0	8	.298	.368	.505	873	1	0	6	(10)	60	929	19.5
1965	NY	NL	C	9	0	0	9	2	0	0	0	.228	.228	.228	457	0	0	0	(10)	20	467	(0.9)
12.9 Totals				7,927	718	50	8,695	2,213	330	50	368					31	27					726.6
1.0 Averages				616	56	4	676	172	26	4	29	.279	.343	.473	816	2	2	(3)	(0)	44	857	56.5

Buck Ewing   **NY NL**   **Catcher**   **Actual**

| | | | | | | | | | | | | | | | | | | | | | Actual | Actual |
Year	T	L	P	AB	BB	HBP	TAB	H	2B	3B	HR	BA	OB	SA	PRO	SB	CS	SBF	SPF	FF	TF	HC
1880	Tro	NL	C	45	1	0	46	8	1	0	0	.178	.196	.200	396				0	(50)	346	(13.9)
1881	Tro	NL	C	272	7	0	279	68	14	7	0	.250	.269	.353	622				0	120	742	16.5
1882	Tro	NL	3B	328	10	0	338	89	16	11	2	.271	.293	.405	698				0	60	758	13.0
1883	NY	NL	C	376	20	0	396	114	11	13	10	.303	.338	.481	820				0	40	860	56.3
1884	NY	NL	C	382	28	0	410	106	15	20	3	.277	.327	.445	772				0	50	822	40.1
1885	NY	NL	C	342	13	0	355	104	15	12	6	.304	.330	.471	800				0	60	860	45.2
1886	NY	NL	C	275	16	0	291	85	11	7	4	.309	.347	.444	791	18			0	40	831	27.8
1887	NY	NL	3B	318	30	3	351	97	17	13	6	.305	.370	.497	867	26			0	0	867	32.2
1888	NY	NL	C	415	24	3	442	127	18	15	6	.306	.348	.465	813	53			0	50	863	46.7
1889	NY	NL	C	407	37	0	444	133	23	13	4	.327	.383	.477	860	34			0	90	950	70.1
1890	NY	P	C	352	39	1	392	119	19	15	8	.338	.406	.545	951	36			0	100	1,051	85.6
1891	NY	NL	2B	49	5	0	54	17	2	1	0	.347	.407	.429	836	5			0	(50)	786	3.0
1892	NY	NL	1B	393	38	0	431	122	10	15	8	.310	.371	.473	845	42			0	30	875	22.6
1893	Cle	NL	OF	500	41	0	541	172	28	15	6	.344	.394	.496	890	47			0	0	890	42.2
1894	Cle	NL	OF	211	24	0	235	53	12	4	2	.251	.328	.374	702	18			(10)	(10)	682	(10.4)
1895	Cin	NL	1B	434	30	1	465	138	24	13	5	.318	.363	.468	831	34			(10)	20	841	19.2
1896	Cin	NL	1B	263	29	0	292	73	14	4	1	.278	.349	.373	722	41			(10)	20	732	(6.5)
1897	Cin	NL	1B	1	0	1	2	0	0	0	0	.000	.500	.000	500	0			(10)	(30)	460	(0.4)
11.5 Totals				5,363	392	9	5,764	1,625	250	178	71					354	0					489.5
1.0 Averages				465	34	1	499	141	22	15	6	.303	.351	.456	807	31	0	0	(2)	45	850	42.4

Buck Ewing   **NY NL**   **Catcher**   **Adjusted**

| | | | | | | | | | | | | | | | Wtd | | | | | | Wtd | |
Year	T	L	P	AB	BB	HBP	TAB	H	2B	3B	HR	BA	OB	SA	PRO	SB	CS	SBF	SPF	FF	TF	HC
1880	Tro	NL	C	85	2	0	88	18	2	0	0	.214	.235	.241	476				0	(50)	426	(10.5)
1881	Tro	NL	C	522	16	0	538	147	30	15	0	.281	.303	.397	700				0	120	820	36.6
1882	Tro	NL	3B	625	23	0	648	192	35	24	4	.308	.332	.460	793				0	60	853	42.1
1883	NY	NL	C	611	37	0	648	201	19	23	18	.329	.367	.523	890				0	40	930	78.1
1884	NY	NL	C	535	47	0	583	168	24	32	5	.313	.369	.502	870				0	50	920	67.4
1885	NY	NL	C	494	24	0	518	175	25	20	10	.354	.384	.548	932				0	60	992	77.7
1886	NY	NL	C	356	24	0	380	121	16	10	6	.340	.382	.489	871	24			0	40	911	42.3
1887	NY	NL	3B	406	38	4	448	124	22	17	8	.305	.370	.496	866	33			0	0	866	31.9
1888	NY	NL	C	486	36	4	527	173	24	20	8	.355	.404	.539	943	63			0	50	993	79.1
1889	NY	NL	C	494	46	0	541	165	28	16	5	.333	.390	.486	876	41			0	90	966	74.2
1890	NY	P	C	434	46	1	481	142	23	18	10	.327	.393	.528	921	44			0	100	1,021	78.7
1891	NY	NL	2B	57	6	0	63	21	2	1	0	.367	.431	.454	885	6			0	(50)	835	4.5
1892	NY	NL	1B	409	46	0	455	139	11	17	9	.340	.407	.519	926	44			0	30	956	40.2
1893	Cle	NL	OF	621	48	0	669	205	33	18	7	.330	.378	.476	853	58			0	0	853	30.6
1894	Cle	NL	OF	264	24	0	288	57	13	4	2	.218	.284	.325	609	22			(10)	(10)	589	(23.2)
1895	Cin	NL	1B	533	33	1	566	157	27	15	6	.295	.337	.434	771	41			(10)	20	781	3.0
1896	Cin	NL	1B	325	33	0	358	86	16	5	1	.264	.333	.355	688	50			(10)	20	698	(12.3)
1897	Cin	NL	1B	1	0	1	2	0	0	0	0	.000	.476	.000	476	0			(10)	(30)	436	(0.4)
11.5 Totals				7,260	529	12	7,802	2,291	353	255	98					428	0					640.1
1.0 Averages				629	46	1	676	199	31	22	9	.316	.363	.475	838	37	0	0	(2)	45	881	55.5

Gabby Hartnett Cubs Catcher Actual

Year	T	L	P	AB	BB	HBP	TAB	H	2B	3B	HR	BA	OB	SA	PRO	SB	CS	SBF	SPF	FF	Actual TF	Actual HC
1922	Chi	NL	C	72	6	0	78	14	1	1	0	.194	.256	.236	493	1	0	12	(10)	70	565	(4.4)
1923	Chi	NL	C	231	25	3	259	62	12	2	8	.268	.347	.442	789	4	0	15	(10)	30	824	19.0
1924	Chi	NL	C	354	39	5	398	106	17	7	16	.299	.377	.523	899	10	2	14	(10)	0	904	45.1
1925	Chi	NL	C	398	36	2	436	115	28	3	24	.289	.351	.555	906	1	5	(20)	(10)	10	887	45.7
1926	Chi	NL	C	284	32	2	318	78	25	3	8	.275	.352	.468	821	0			(10)	30	841	26.0
1927	Chi	NL	C	449	44	3	496	132	32	5	10	.294	.361	.454	815	2			(10)	30	835	39.2
1928	Chi	NL	C	388	65	2	455	117	26	9	14	.302	.404	.523	928	3			(10)	60	978	68.5
1929	Chi	NL	C	22	5	0	27	6	2	1	1	.273	.407	.591	998	1			(10)	60	1,048	5.0
1930	Chi	NL	C	508	55	1	564	172	31	3	37	.339	.404	.630	1,034	0			(10)	40	1,064	109.3
1931	Chi	NL	C	380	52	1	433	107	32	1	8	.282	.370	.434	804	3			(10)	30	824	31.8
1932	Chi	NL	C	406	51	1	458	110	25	3	12	.271	.354	.436	790	0			(10)	30	810	30.4
1933	Chi	NL	C	490	37	0	527	135	21	4	16	.276	.326	.433	759	1			(10)	40	789	29.5
1934	Chi	NL	C	438	37	3	478	131	21	1	22	.299	.358	.502	860	0			(10)	70	920	58.1
1935	Chi	NL	C	413	41	1	455	142	32	6	13	.344	.404	.545	949	1			(10)	30	969	66.5
1936	Chi	NL	C	424	30	6	460	130	25	6	7	.307	.361	.443	804	0			(10)	50	844	38.5
1937	Chi	NL	C	356	43	0	399	126	21	6	12	.354	.424	.548	971	0			(10)	40	1,001	64.8
1938	Chi	NL	C	299	48	3	350	82	19	1	10	.274	.380	.445	825	1			(10)	30	845	29.4
1939	Chi	NL	C	306	37	1	344	85	18	2	12	.278	.358	.467	825	0			(10)	0	815	23.7
1940	Chi	NL	C	64	8	0	72	17	3	0	1	.266	.347	.359	707	0			(10)	(20)	677	(0.0)
1941	NY	NL	C	150	12	1	163	45	5	0	5	.300	.356	.433	789	0			(10)	(20)	759	6.7
11.2	Totals			6,432	703	35	7,170	1,912	396	64	236					28	7					732.7
1.0	Averages			576	63	3	643	171	35	6	21	.297	.370	.489	858	3	1	0	(10)	33	881	65.7

Gabby Hartnett Cubs Catcher Adjusted

Year	T	L	P	AB	BB	HBP	TAB	H	2B	3B	HR	BA	OB	SA	Wtd PRO	SB	CS	SBF	SPF	FF	Wtd TF	HC
1922	Chi	NL	C	76	6	0	82	14	1	1	0	.182	.240	.221	462	1	0	12	(10)	70	534	(5.6)
1923	Chi	NL	C	245	25	3	272	63	12	2	8	.257	.333	.423	756	4	0	15	(10)	30	790	14.7
1924	Chi	NL	C	374	39	5	419	109	17	7	16	.290	.365	.506	871	11	2	14	(10)	0	875	39.5
1925	Chi	NL	C	423	34	2	459	113	28	3	24	.268	.325	.514	839	1	5	(20)	(10)	10	820	31.2
1926	Chi	NL	C	300	33	2	335	80	26	3	8	.268	.343	.457	800	0			(10)	30	820	22.7
1927	Chi	NL	C	474	45	3	522	136	33	5	10	.286	.351	.442	794	2			(10)	30	814	33.9
1928	Chi	NL	C	413	64	2	479	119	26	9	14	.287	.385	.498	884	3			(10)	60	934	58.4
1929	Chi	NL	C	24	5	0	28	6	2	1	1	.246	.367	.533	900	1			(10)	60	950	3.7
1930	Chi	NL	C	545	47	1	593	161	29	3	35	.296	.353	.550	903	0			(10)	40	933	72.4
1931	Chi	NL	C	401	53	1	455	111	33	1	8	.276	.362	.425	787	3			(10)	30	807	28.1
1932	Chi	NL	C	429	52	1	482	113	26	3	12	.264	.345	.425	770	0			(10)	30	790	25.8
1933	Chi	NL	C	513	41	0	554	147	23	4	17	.286	.339	.450	789	1			(10)	40	819	37.4
1934	Chi	NL	C	462	37	3	503	134	22	1	23	.290	.347	.488	835	0			(10)	70	895	52.1
1935	Chi	NL	C	436	42	1	479	147	33	6	13	.336	.395	.533	928	1			(10)	30	948	61.7
1936	Chi	NL	C	447	31	6	484	134	26	6	7	.300	.353	.434	786	0			(10)	50	826	34.3
1937	Chi	NL	C	375	44	0	420	131	22	6	13	.350	.419	.542	960	0			(10)	40	990	62.6
1938	Chi	NL	C	314	51	3	368	86	20	1	11	.275	.380	.445	826	1			(10)	30	846	29.6
1939	Chi	NL	C	323	38	1	362	88	19	2	12	.272	.350	.458	808	0			(10)	0	798	20.7
1940	Chi	NL	C	67	8	0	76	18	3	0	1	.267	.349	.361	711	0			(10)	(20)	681	0.1
1941	NY	NL	C	157	13	1	171	48	5	0	5	.308	.365	.445	810	0			(10)	(20)	780	8.4
11.2	Totals			6,800	707	35	7,542	1,958	405	66	240					29	7					631.6
1.0	Averages			609	63	3	676	175	36	6	21	.288	.358	.472	830	3	1	0	(10)	33	853	56.6

Mike Piazza   **Dodgers**   **Catcher**   **Actual**

Year	T	L	P	AB	BB	HBP	TAB	H	2B	3B	HR	BA	OB	SA	PRO	SB	CS	SBF	SPF	FF	Actual TF	Actual HC
1992	LA	NL	C	69	4	1	74	16	3	0	1	.232	.284	.319	603	0	0	0	(10)	(40)	553	(4.4)
1993	LA	NL	C	547	46	3	596	174	24	2	35	.318	.374	.561	935	3	4	(8)	(10)	(10)	907	65.3
1994	LA	NL	C	405	33	1	439	129	18	0	24	.319	.371	.541	912	1	3	(11)	(10)	(30)	861	54.4
1995	LA	NL	C	434	39	1	474	150	17	0	32	.346	.401	.606	1,007	1	0	2	(10)	(20)	979	76.6
1996	LA	NL	C	547	81	1	629	184	16	0	36	.336	.423	.563	986	0	3	(9)	(10)	(20)	947	80.8
1997	LA	NL	C	556	69	3	628	201	32	1	40	.362	.435	.638	1,073	5	1	5	(10)	(20)	1,048	110.8
1998	NY	NL	C	561	58	2	621	184	38	1	32	.328	.393	.570	963	1	0	2	(10)	(10)	945	79.1
1999	NY	NL	C	534	51	1	586	162	25	0	40	.303	.365	.575	940	2	2	(3)	(10)	(20)	907	64.1
2000	NY	NL	C	482	58	3	543	156	26	0	38	.324	.400	.614	1,014	4	2	0	(10)	(10)	994	81.8
7.1 Totals				4,135	439	16	4,590	1,356	199	4	278					17	15					608.5
1.0 Averages				579	61	2	642	190	28	1	39	.328	.395	.580	974	2	2	(3)	(10)	(18)	944	85.1

Mike Piazza   **Dodgers**   **Catcher**   **Adjusted**

Year	T	L	P	AB	BB	HBP	TAB	H	2B	3B	HR	BA	OB	SA	Wtd PRO	SB	CS	SBF	SPF	FF	Wtd TF	HC
1992	LA	NL	C	69	4	1	74	16	3	0	1	.239	.292	.328	620	0	0	0	(10)	(40)	570	(3.8)
1993	LA	NL	C	549	44	3	596	169	23	2	34	.308	.362	.543	906	3	4	(8)	(10)	(10)	878	56.9
1994	LA	NL	C	577	43	1	621	173	24	0	32	.300	.349	.509	858	1	4	(11)	(10)	(30)	808	38.5
1995	LA	NL	C	491	41	1	533	162	18	0	35	.329	.382	.577	959	1	0	2	(10)	(20)	931	64.5
1996	LA	NL	C	553	75	1	629	177	15	0	35	.320	.403	.536	939	0	3	(9)	(10)	(20)	900	66.8
1997	LA	NL	C	562	64	3	628	193	31	1	38	.343	.413	.606	1,019	5	1	5	(10)	(20)	993	94.4
1998	NY	NL	C	565	54	2	621	176	36	1	31	.312	.374	.543	917	1	0	2	(10)	(10)	898	65.3
1999	NY	NL	C	540	45	1	586	150	23	0	37	.278	.334	.526	860	2	2	(3)	(10)	(20)	827	41.7
2000	NY	NL	C	490	51	3	543	145	24	0	35	.295	.365	.560	925	4	2	0	(10)	(10)	905	58.9
7.1 Totals				4,396	420	15	4,831	1,361	199	4	278					18	16					483.3
1.0 Averages				615	59	2	676	190	28	1	39	.310	.372	.546	918	2	2	(3)	(10)	(18)	887	67.6

Bill Dickey Yankees Catcher Actual

Year	T	L	P	AB	BB	HBP	TAB	H	2B	3B	HR	BA	OB	SA	PRO	SB	CS	SBF	SPF	FF	Actual TF	Actual HC
1928	NY	AL	C	15	0	0	15	3	1	1	0	.200	.200	.400	600	0	0	0	0	0	600	(0.6)
1929	NY	AL	C	447	14	1	462	145	30	6	10	.324	.346	.485	832	4	3	(4)	0	0	828	34.8
1930	NY	AL	C	366	21	0	387	124	25	7	5	.339	.375	.486	861	7	1	12	0	0	873	38.0
1931	NY	AL	C	477	39	0	516	156	17	10	6	.327	.378	.442	820	2	1	0	(10)	70	880	52.5
1932	NY	AL	C	423	34	0	457	131	20	4	15	.310	.361	.482	843	2	4	(12)	(10)	40	861	42.0
1933	NY	AL	C	478	47	2	527	152	24	8	14	.318	.381	.490	871	3	4	(9)	(10)	50	902	59.3
1934	NY	AL	C	395	38	2	435	127	24	4	12	.322	.384	.494	878	0	3	(13)	(10)	30	885	45.2
1935	NY	AL	C	448	35	6	489	125	26	6	14	.279	.339	.458	797	1	1	(2)	(10)	50	835	38.7
1936	NY	AL	C	423	46	3	472	153	26	8	22	.362	.428	.617	1,045	0	2	(8)	(10)	40	1,067	92.2
1937	NY	AL	C	530	73	4	607	176	35	2	29	.332	.417	.570	987	3	2	(2)	(10)	70	1,045	111.8
1938	NY	AL	C	454	75	2	531	142	27	4	27	.313	.412	.568	981	3	0	5	(10)	40	1,016	90.1
1939	NY	AL	C	480	77	4	561	145	23	3	24	.302	.403	.513	915	5	0	8	(10)	70	984	86.1
1940	NY	AL	C	372	48	2	422	92	11	1	9	.247	.336	.355	691	0	3	(13)	(10)	50	718	8.6
1941	NY	AL	C	348	45	3	396	99	15	5	7	.284	.371	.417	788	2	1	0	(10)	50	828	29.9
1942	NY	AL	C	268	26	1	295	79	13	1	2	.295	.359	.373	732	2	2	(6)	(10)	20	736	8.7
1943	NY	AL	C	242	41	0	283	85	18	2	4	.351	.445	.492	937	2	1	0	(10)	10	937	36.8
1946	NY	AL	C	134	19	1	154	35	8	0	2	.261	.357	.366	723	0	1	(12)	(10)	60	761	6.4
10.9	Totals			6,300	678	31	7,009	1,969	343	72	202					36	29					780.4
1.0	Averages			578	62	3	643	181	31	7	19	.313	.382	.486	868	3	3	(3)	(9)	43	899	71.6

Bill Dickey Yankees Catcher Adjusted

Year	T	L	P	AB	BB	HBP	TAB	H	2B	3B	HR	BA	OB	SA	Wtd PRO	SB	CS	SBF	SPF	FF	Wtd TF	HC
1928	NY	AL	C	16	0	0	16	3	1	1	0	.191	.191	.381	572	0	0	0	0	0	572	(0.8)
1929	NY	AL	C	472	13	1	486	143	30	6	10	.303	.323	.453	777	4	3	(4)	0	0	773	22.0
1930	NY	AL	C	388	19	0	407	120	24	7	5	.310	.343	.445	787	7	1	12	0	0	800	23.7
1931	NY	AL	C	505	38	0	543	157	17	10	6	.312	.360	.422	782	2	1	0	(10)	70	842	42.7
1932	NY	AL	C	448	33	0	481	131	20	4	15	.291	.340	.454	794	2	4	(12)	(10)	40	811	30.7
1933	NY	AL	C	505	47	2	554	155	24	8	14	.307	.368	.472	840	3	4	(9)	(10)	50	871	51.1
1934	NY	AL	C	419	37	2	458	127	24	4	12	.303	.361	.465	826	0	3	(13)	(10)	30	833	33.9
1935	NY	AL	C	475	34	6	514	124	26	6	14	.262	.318	.429	747	1	1	(2)	(10)	50	785	26.4
1936	NY	AL	C	453	41	3	497	147	25	8	21	.326	.385	.556	941	0	2	(8)	(10)	40	963	67.5
1937	NY	AL	C	567	68	4	639	173	34	2	28	.304	.382	.522	904	3	2	(2)	(10)	70	963	86.9
1938	NY	AL	C	487	69	2	559	139	26	4	26	.286	.377	.519	896	3	0	5	(10)	40	931	67.5
1939	NY	AL	C	513	73	4	590	144	23	3	24	.281	.375	.477	851	5	0	8	(10)	70	920	68.1
1940	NY	AL	C	395	47	2	444	92	11	1	9	.233	.317	.334	651	0	3	(13)	(10)	50	677	(0.0)
1941	NY	AL	C	368	45	3	417	101	15	5	7	.275	.359	.403	762	2	1	0	(10)	50	802	24.7
1942	NY	AL	C	281	28	1	310	85	14	1	2	.303	.370	.384	754	2	2	(6)	(10)	20	757	11.8
1943	NY	AL	C	250	48	0	298	94	20	2	4	.374	.474	.524	998	2	1	0	(10)	10	998	45.4
1946	NY	AL	C	140	21	1	162	37	9	0	2	.266	.364	.373	737	0	1	(12)	(10)	60	775	7.5
10.9	Totals			6,683	661	30	7,373	1,973	344	72	201					38	31					609.2
1.0	Averages			613	61	3	676	181	32	7	18	.295	.361	.458	820	3	3	(3)	(9)	43	850	55.9

Carlton Fisk **White Sox** **Catcher** **Actual**

Year	T	L	P	AB	BB	HBP	TAB	H	2B	3B	HR	BA	OB	SA	PRO	SB	CS	SBF	SPF	FF	Actual TF	Actual HC
1969	Bos	AL	C	5	0	0	5	0	0	0	0	.000	.000	.000	0	0	0	0	0	0	0	(1.6)
1971	Bos	AL	C	48	1	0	49	15	2	1	2	.313	.327	.521	847	0	0	0	0	(10)	837	3.7
1972	Bos	AL	C	457	52	4	513	134	28	9	22	.293	.370	.538	909	5	2	2	0	40	951	70.2
1973	Bos	AL	C	508	37	10	555	125	21	0	26	.246	.310	.441	751	7	2	5	0	30	786	28.7
1974	Bos	AL	C	187	24	2	213	56	12	1	11	.299	.385	.551	936	5	1	13	0	30	979	30.6
1975	Bos	AL	C	263	27	2	292	87	14	4	10	.331	.397	.529	926	4	3	(6)	0	0	919	33.7
1976	Bos	AL	C	487	56	6	549	124	17	5	17	.255	.339	.415	754	12	5	3	0	40	797	31.3
1977	Bos	AL	C	536	75	9	620	169	26	3	26	.315	.408	.521	929	7	6	(8)	0	30	951	80.8
1978	Bos	AL	C	571	71	7	649	162	39	5	20	.284	.370	.475	844	7	2	4	0	30	879	62.3
1979	Bos	AL	DH	320	10	6	336	87	23	2	10	.272	.307	.450	757	3	0	8	0	(30)	735	9.2
1980	Bos	AL	C	478	36	13	527	138	25	3	18	.289	.355	.467	821	11	5	2	0	10	833	39.1
1981	Chi	AL	C	338	38	12	388	89	12	0	7	.263	.358	.361	719	3	2	(2)	0	10	727	13.8
1982	Chi	AL	C	476	46	6	528	127	17	3	14	.267	.339	.403	742	17	2	23	0	10	776	24.7
1983	Chi	AL	C	488	46	6	540	141	26	4	26	.289	.357	.518	876	9	6	(5)	0	10	881	52.3
1984	Chi	AL	C	359	26	5	390	83	20	1	21	.231	.292	.468	760	6	0	15	0	(10)	765	16.2
1985	Chi	AL	C	543	52	17	612	129	23	1	37	.238	.324	.488	812	17	9	(2)	(10)	10	810	38.7
1986	Chi	AL	C	457	22	6	485	101	11	0	14	.221	.266	.337	603	2	4	(12)	(10)	10	591	(19.9)
1987	Chi	AL	C	454	39	8	501	116	22	1	23	.256	.325	.460	786	1	4	(13)	(10)	10	772	22.7
1988	Chi	AL	C	253	37	5	295	70	8	1	19	.277	.380	.542	921	0	0	0	(10)	10	921	34.3
1989	Chi	AL	C	375	36	3	414	110	25	2	13	.293	.360	.475	835	1	0	2	(10)	(10)	817	27.5
1990	Chi	AL	C	452	61	7	520	129	21	0	18	.285	.379	.451	830	7	2	5	(10)	10	836	39.2
1991	Chi	AL	C	460	32	7	499	111	25	0	18	.241	.301	.413	714	1	2	(6)	(10)	(10)	688	2.5
1992	Chi	AL	C	188	23	1	212	43	4	1	3	.229	.316	.309	625	3	0	13	(10)	(30)	598	(8.0)
1993	Chi	AL	C	53	2	1	56	10	0	0	1	.189	.232	.245	477	0	1	(34)	(10)	(60)	374	(8.1)
14.8 Totals				8,756	849	143	9,748	2,356	421	47	376					128	58					623.8
1.0 Averages				593	58	10	661	160	29	3	25	.269	.343	.457	800	9	4	1	(4)	12	809	42.3

Carlton Fisk **White Sox** **Catcher** **Adjusted**

Year	T	L	P	AB	BB	HBP	TAB	H	2B	3B	HR	BA	OB	SA	Wtd PRO	SB	CS	SBF	SPF	FF	Wtd TF	HC
1969	Bos	AL	C	5	0	0	5	0	0	0	0	.000	.000	.000	0	0	0	0	0	0	0	(1.6)
1971	Bos	AL	C	48	1	0	49	15	2	1	2	.323	.337	.538	874	0	0	0	0	(10)	864	4.4
1972	Bos	AL	C	473	61	5	540	151	31	10	25	.318	.402	.584	985	5	2	2	0	40	1,027	89.9
1973	Bos	AL	C	506	38	10	555	128	21	0	27	.252	.318	.452	770	7	2	5	0	30	805	33.7
1974	Bos	AL	C	185	26	2	213	58	12	1	11	.314	.403	.577	980	5	1	13	0	30	1,023	35.1
1975	Bos	AL	C	262	28	2	292	89	14	4	10	.341	.409	.544	953	4	3	(6)	0	0	947	37.5
1976	Bos	AL	C	481	61	7	549	131	18	5	18	.272	.362	.443	804	12	5	3	0	40	848	44.5
1977	Bos	AL	C	537	74	9	620	168	26	3	26	.312	.404	.515	919	7	6	(8)	0	30	941	77.8
1978	Bos	AL	C	569	73	7	649	165	40	5	20	.290	.378	.485	863	7	2	4	0	30	898	68.1
1979	Bos	AL	DH	320	10	6	336	85	23	2	10	.266	.300	.440	740	3	0	8	0	(30)	719	6.6
1980	Bos	AL	C	478	36	13	527	138	25	3	18	.288	.353	.465	818	11	5	2	0	10	830	38.3
1981	Chi	AL	C	507	61	19	587	140	19	0	11	.276	.376	.379	754	5	3	(2)	0	10	762	23.6
1982	Chi	AL	C	476	46	6	528	127	17	3	14	.266	.338	.402	739	17	2	23	0	10	773	23.9
1983	Chi	AL	C	488	46	6	540	141	26	4	26	.289	.357	.518	875	9	6	(5)	0	10	879	52.0
1984	Chi	AL	C	359	26	5	390	83	20	1	21	.232	.294	.470	763	6	0	15	0	(10)	768	16.8
1985	Chi	AL	C	544	52	17	612	128	23	1	37	.236	.321	.485	806	17	9	(2)	(10)	10	804	37.1
1986	Chi	AL	C	457	22	6	485	100	11	0	14	.218	.262	.332	595	2	4	(12)	(10)	10	583	(21.8)
1987	Chi	AL	C	457	37	8	501	112	21	1	22	.245	.312	.442	754	1	4	(13)	(10)	10	740	15.1
1988	Chi	AL	C	252	38	5	295	71	8	1	19	.281	.386	.551	937	0	0	0	(10)	10	937	36.4
1989	Chi	AL	C	374	37	3	414	112	26	2	13	.301	.369	.487	856	1	0	2	(10)	(10)	838	31.7
1990	Chi	AL	C	450	62	7	520	131	21	0	18	.290	.385	.459	844	7	2	5	(10)	10	849	42.6
1991	Chi	AL	C	460	32	7	499	112	25	0	18	.243	.302	.415	718	1	2	(6)	(10)	(10)	692	3.4
1992	Chi	AL	C	187	24	1	212	44	4	1	3	.233	.322	.315	637	3	0	13	(10)	(30)	610	(6.8)
1993	Chi	AL	C	53	2	1	56	10	0	0	1	.184	.227	.239	466	0	1	(34)	(10)	(60)	362	(8.4)
14.8 Totals				8,929	893	152	9,974	2,436	434	49	384					130	59					680.0
1.0 Averages				605	61	10	676	165	29	3	26	.273	.349	.461	811	9	4	1	(4)	12	820	46.1

Roy Campanella   **Dodgers**   **Catcher**   **Actual**

| | | | | | | | | | | | | | | | | | | | | | Actual | Actual |
Year	T	L	P	AB	BB	HBP	TAB	H	2B	3B	HR	BA	OB	SA	PRO	SB	CS	SBF	SPF	FF	TF	HC
1948	Bkn	NL	C	279	36	1	316	72	11	3	9	.258	.345	.416	761	3			0	50	811	21.1
1949	Bkn	NL	C	436	67	3	506	125	22	2	22	.287	.385	.498	883	3			0	30	913	59.8
1950	Bkn	NL	C	437	55	2	494	123	19	3	31	.281	.364	.551	916	1			0	40	956	68.9
1951	Bkn	NL	C	505	53	4	562	164	33	1	33	.325	.393	.590	983	1	2	(5)	0	50	1,028	98.8
1952	Bkn	NL	C	468	57	3	528	126	18	1	22	.269	.352	.453	805	8	4	0	0	60	865	49.7
1953	Bkn	NL	C	519	67	4	590	162	26	3	41	.312	.395	.611	1,006	4	2	0	0	50	1,056	111.9
1954	Bkn	NL	C	397	42	2	441	82	14	3	19	.207	.286	.401	686	1	4	(15)	(10)	40	701	5.3
1955	Bkn	NL	C	446	56	6	508	142	20	1	32	.318	.402	.583	985	2	3	(7)	(10)	50	1,017	86.5
1956	Bkn	NL	C	388	66	1	455	85	6	1	20	.219	.334	.394	728	1	0	2	(10)	40	760	18.9
1957	Bkn	NL	C	330	34	4	368	80	9	0	13	.242	.321	.388	709	1	0	3	(10)	70	771	17.3
7.4	Totals			4,205	533	30	4,768	1,161	178	18	242					25	15					538.2
1.0	Averages			567	72	4	643	156	24	2	33	.276	.362	.500	861	3	2	(2)	(4)	48	903	72.5

Roy Campanella   **Dodgers**   **Catcher**   **Adjusted**

| | | | | | | | | | | | | | | | Wtd | | | | | | Wtd | |
Year	T	L	P	AB	BB	HBP	TAB	H	2B	3B	HR	BA	OB	SA	PRO	SB	CS	SBF	SPF	FF	TF	HC
1948	Bkn	NL	C	294	37	1	332	75	11	3	9	.255	.341	.410	751	3			0	50	801	19.6
1949	Bkn	NL	C	461	68	3	532	129	23	2	23	.280	.376	.486	862	3			0	30	892	54.5
1950	Bkn	NL	C	463	55	2	520	125	19	3	31	.270	.349	.528	877	1			0	40	917	59.4
1951	Bkn	NL	C	533	54	4	591	169	34	1	34	.318	.385	.578	963	1	2	(5)	0	50	1,008	93.0
1952	Bkn	NL	C	491	61	3	555	134	19	1	23	.273	.357	.459	816	8	4	0	0	60	876	52.4
1953	Bkn	NL	C	552	65	4	621	163	26	3	41	.295	.373	.577	950	4	2	0	0	50	1,000	95.5
1954	Bkn	NL	C	421	41	2	464	82	14	3	19	.196	.271	.379	650	1	4	(15)	(10)	40	665	(2.7)
1955	Bkn	NL	C	473	55	6	534	144	20	1	33	.305	.385	.558	943	2	3	(7)	(10)	50	976	75.9
1956	Bkn	NL	C	411	67	1	479	88	6	1	21	.213	.325	.384	709	1	0	2	(10)	40	741	14.6
1957	Bkn	NL	C	348	35	4	387	82	9	0	13	.236	.313	.378	691	1	0	3	(10)	70	753	14.0
7.4	Totals			4,447	538	30	5,016	1,192	183	18	248					26	16					476.2
1.0	Averages			599	73	4	676	161	25	2	33	.268	.351	.484	835	4	2	(2)	(4)	48	877	64.2

Ivan Rodriguez · **Rangers** · **Catcher** · **Actual**

Year	T	L	P	AB	BB	HBP	TAB	H	2B	3B	HR	BA	OB	SA	PRO	SB	CS	SBF	SPF	FF	Actual TF	Actual HC
1991	Tex	AL	C	280	5	0	285	74	16	0	3	.264	.277	.354	631	0	1	(7)	10	90	724	6.3
1992	Tex	AL	C	420	24	1	445	109	16	1	8	.260	.301	.360	661	0	0	0	10	60	731	11.3
1993	Tex	AL	C	473	29	4	506	129	28	4	10	.273	.320	.412	732	8	7	(11)	10	90	821	34.7
1994	Tex	AL	C	363	31	7	401	108	19	1	16	.298	.364	.488	852	6	3	0	10	80	942	71.4
1995	Tex	AL	C	492	16	4	512	149	32	2	12	.303	.330	.449	779	0	2	(7)	0	80	852	47.9
1996	Tex	AL	C	639	38	4	681	192	47	3	19	.300	.344	.473	816	5	0	7	0	100	923	79.7
1997	Tex	AL	C	597	38	8	643	187	34	4	20	.313	.362	.484	846	7	3	1	0	90	938	79.8
1998	Tex	AL	C	579	32	3	614	186	40	4	21	.321	.360	.513	873	9	0	14	0	90	977	87.6
1999	Tex	AL	C	600	24	1	625	199	29	1	35	.332	.358	.558	917	25	12	2	0	90	1,008	98.5
2000	Tex	AL	C	363	19	1	383	126	27	4	27	.347	.381	.667	1,048	5	5	(12)	0	100	1,136	83.6
7.9 Totals				4,806	256	33	5,095	1,459	288	24	171					65	33					600.8
1.0 Averages				610	32	4	647	185	37	3	22	.304	.343	.480	823	8	4	(0)	3	87	914	76.3

Ivan Rodriguez · **Rangers** · **Catcher** · **Adjusted**

Year	T	L	P	AB	BB	HBP	TAB	H	2B	3B	HR	BA	OB	SA	Wtd PRO	SB	CS	SBF	SPF	FF	Wtd TF	HC
1991	Tex	AL	C	280	5	0	285	74	16	0	3	.266	.279	.356	634	0	1	(7)	10	90	728	6.8
1992	Tex	AL	C	419	25	1	445	111	16	1	8	.265	.307	.367	674	0	0	0	10	60	744	14.0
1993	Tex	AL	C	474	28	4	506	126	27	4	10	.266	.312	.402	715	8	7	(11)	10	90	804	30.4
1994	Tex	AL	C	519	40	9	567	144	25	1	21	.278	.340	.455	795	8	4	0	10	80	885	56.1
1995	Tex	AL	C	555	17	4	576	159	34	2	13	.286	.311	.424	735	0	2	(7)	0	80	808	35.7
1996	Tex	AL	C	644	34	4	681	177	43	3	18	.275	.314	.432	747	5	0	7	0	100	854	57.2
1997	Tex	AL	C	601	35	7	643	178	32	4	19	.296	.342	.457	799	7	3	1	0	90	890	65.3
1998	Tex	AL	C	582	29	3	614	176	38	4	20	.302	.338	.482	821	9	0	14	0	90	925	72.3
1999	Tex	AL	C	603	21	1	625	184	27	1	32	.306	.331	.515	846	25	12	2	0	90	937	77.3
2000	Tex	AL	C	365	17	1	383	116	25	4	25	.318	.349	.610	959	5	5	(12)	0	100	1,047	67.4
7.9 Totals				5,042	250	33	5,325	1,445	284	23	169					67	34					482.6
1.0 Averages				640	32	4	676	183	36	3	21	.287	.325	.453	777	9	4	(0)	3	87	868	61.3

Lou Gehrig Yankees **First Baseman** Actual

				AB	BB	HBP	TAB	H	2B	3B	HR	BA	OB	SA	PRO	SB	CS	SBF	SPF	FF	Actual TF	Actual HC
Year	T	L	P																			
1923	NY	AL	1B	26	2	0	28	11	4	1	1	.423	.464	.769	1,234	0	0	0	0	(50)	1,184	5.8
1924	NY	AL	1B	12	1	0	13	6	1	0	0	.500	.538	.583	1,122	0	0	0	0	0	1,122	2.3
1925	NY	AL	1B	437	46	2	485	129	23	10	20	.295	.365	.531	896	6	3	0	0	(10)	886	28.2
1926	NY	AL	1B	572	105	1	678	179	47	20	16	.313	.420	.549	969	6	5	(6)	0	(10)	954	62.4
1927	NY	AL	1B	584	109	3	696	218	52	18	47	.373	.474	.765	1,240	10	8	(8)	0	0	1,231	160.9
1928	NY	AL	1B	562	95	4	661	210	47	13	27	.374	.467	.648	1,115	4	11	(26)	0	0	1,089	105.8
1929	NY	AL	1B	553	122	5	680	166	32	10	35	.300	.431	.584	1,015	4	4	(6)	0	0	1,009	81.6
1930	NY	AL	1B	581	101	3	685	220	42	17	41	.379	.473	.721	1,194	12	14	(22)	0	0	1,172	138.0
1931	NY	AL	1B	619	117	0	736	211	31	15	46	.341	.446	.662	1,108	17	12	(9)	0	0	1,099	121.4
1932	NY	AL	1B	596	108	3	707	208	42	9	34	.349	.451	.621	1,072	4	11	(24)	0	(10)	1,038	94.9
1933	NY	AL	1B	593	92	1	686	198	41	12	32	.334	.424	.605	1,030	9	13	(23)	0	0	1,006	81.2
1934	NY	AL	1B	579	109	2	690	210	40	6	49	.363	.465	.706	1,172	9	5	(1)	0	0	1,170	138.4
1935	NY	AL	1B	535	132	5	672	176	26	10	30	.329	.466	.583	1,049	8	7	(8)	0	0	1,041	91.1
1936	NY	AL	1B	579	130	7	716	205	37	7	49	.354	.478	.696	1,174	3	4	(7)	0	0	1,167	142.5
1937	NY	AL	1B	569	127	4	700	200	37	9	37	.351	.473	.643	1,116	4	3	(3)	0	(10)	1,103	117.0
1938	NY	AL	1B	576	107	5	688	170	32	6	29	.295	.410	.523	932	6	1	5	0	0	938	57.9
1939	NY	AL	1B	28	5	0	33	4	0	0	0	.143	.273	.143	416	0	0	0	0	(40)	376	(6.5)
14.9 Totals				8,001	1,508	45	9,554	2,721	534	163	493					102	101					1,422.9
1.0 Averages				538	101	3	643	183	36	11	33	.340	.447	.632	1,080	7	7	(10)	0	(3)	1,067	95.7

Lou Gehrig Yankees **First Baseman** Adjusted

				AB	BB	HBP	TAB	H	2B	3B	HR	BA	OB	SA	Wtd PRO	SB	CS	SBF	SPF	FF	Wtd TF	HC
Year	T	L	P																			
1923	NY	AL	1B	28	2	0	29	11	4	1	1	.404	.443	.735	1,178	0	0	0	0	(50)	1,128	5.0
1924	NY	AL	1B	13	1	0	14	6	1	0	0	.467	.503	.545	1,049	0	0	0	0	0	1,049	1.8
1925	NY	AL	1B	465	43	2	510	126	23	10	20	.271	.335	.488	823	6	3	0	0	(10)	813	10.5
1926	NY	AL	1B	610	103	1	713	181	48	20	16	.297	.399	.522	921	6	5	(6)	0	(10)	905	46.0
1927	NY	AL	1B	625	104	3	732	219	52	18	47	.351	.446	.719	1,165	11	8	(8)	0	0	1,157	135.0
1928	NY	AL	1B	599	93	4	695	213	48	13	27	.356	.445	.617	1,062	4	12	(26)	0	0	1,037	88.3
1929	NY	AL	1B	594	117	5	715	166	32	10	35	.280	.402	.545	948	4	4	(6)	0	0	942	58.7
1930	NY	AL	1B	626	92	3	721	217	41	17	40	.346	.432	.659	1,092	13	15	(22)	0	0	1,070	102.9
1931	NY	AL	1B	660	115	0	774	214	32	15	47	.325	.425	.632	1,057	18	13	(9)	0	0	1,048	102.5
1932	NY	AL	1B	637	104	3	744	209	42	9	34	.328	.425	.584	1,009	4	12	(24)	0	(10)	975	72.6
1933	NY	AL	1B	629	92	1	722	203	42	12	33	.322	.409	.584	993	9	14	(23)	0	0	969	68.6
1934	NY	AL	1B	620	104	2	726	211	40	6	49	.341	.438	.665	1,103	9	5	(1)	0	0	1,101	114.6
1935	NY	AL	1B	576	126	5	707	178	26	10	30	.308	.437	.547	983	8	7	(8)	0	0	975	69.0
1936	NY	AL	1B	630	117	6	753	201	36	7	48	.319	.430	.627	1,057	3	4	(7)	0	0	1,050	100.5
1937	NY	AL	1B	615	117	4	736	198	37	9	37	.322	.433	.590	1,023	4	3	(3)	0	(10)	1,010	84.4
1938	NY	AL	1B	620	99	5	724	167	31	6	29	.270	.374	.477	852	6	1	5	0	0	857	30.0
1939	NY	AL	1B	30	5	0	35	4	0	0	0	.133	.254	.133	387	0	0	0	0	(40)	347	(7.0)
14.9 Totals				8,575	1,433	42	10,050	2,726	535	164	493					107	106					1,083.5
1.0 Averages				577	96	3	676	183	36	11	33	.318	.418	.591	1,009	7	7	(10)	0	(3)	996	72.9

Dan Brouthers   **Buf NL**   **First Baseman**   **Actual**

Year	T	L	P	AB	BB	HBP	TAB	H	2B	3B	HR	BA	OB	SA	PRO	SB	CS	SBF	SPF	FF	Actual TF	Actual HC
1879	Tro	NL	1B	168	1	0	169	46	12	1	4	.274	.278	.429	707				0	(30)	677	(15.2)
1880	Tro	NL	1B	12	1	0	13	2	0	0	0	.167	.231	.167	397				0	(30)	367	(4.8)
1881	Buf	NL	OF	270	18	0	288	86	18	9	8	.319	.361	.541	902				0	(20)	882	32.9
1882	Buf	NL	1B	351	21	0	372	129	23	11	6	.368	.403	.547	950				0	20	970	68.0
1883	Buf	NL	1B	425	16	0	441	159	41	17	3	.374	.397	.572	969				0	10	979	71.7
1884	Buf	NL	1B	398	33	0	431	130	22	15	14	.327	.378	.563	941				0	0	941	49.9
1885	Buf	NL	1B	407	34	0	441	146	32	11	7	.359	.408	.543	951				0	0	951	55.5
1886	Det	NL	1B	489	66	0	555	181	40	15	11	.370	.445	.581	1,026	21			0	(10)	1,016	84.9
1887	Det	NL	1B	500	71	6	577	169	36	20	12	.338	.426	.562	988	34			0	(10)	978	73.1
1888	Det	NL	1B	522	68	12	602	160	33	11	9	.307	.399	.464	862	34			0	0	862	31.5
1889	Bos	NL	1B	485	66	14	565	181	26	9	7	.373	.462	.507	969	22			0	0	969	65.3
1890	Bos	P	1B	460	99	18	577	152	36	9	1	.330	.466	.454	921	28			0	0	921	50.8
1891	Bos	AA	1B	486	87	24	597	170	26	19	5	.350	.471	.512	983	31			0	(10)	973	66.8
1892	Bkn	NL	1B	588	84	16	688	197	30	20	5	.335	.432	.480	911	31			0	20	931	55.8
1893	Bkn	NL	1B	282	52	6	340	95	21	11	2	.337	.450	.511	961	9			0	10	971	40.2
1894	Bal	NL	1B	525	67	5	597	182	39	23	9	.347	.425	.560	985	38			0	0	985	75.2
1895	Lou	NL	1B	120	12	0	132	36	12	1	2	.300	.364	.467	830	1		(10)	(20)	800	2.3
1896	Phi	NL	1B	218	44	4	266	75	13	3	1	.344	.462	.445	907	7		(10)	(10)	887	18.3
1904	NY	NL	1B	5	0	0	5	0	0	0	0	.000	.000	.000	0	0		(10)	(20)	(30)	(2.0)
15.2 Totals				6,711	840	105	7,656	2,296	460	205	106					256	0					820.3
1.0 Averages				443	55	7	505	151	30	14	7	.342	.423	.519	942	17	0	0	(0)	(1)	941	54.1

Dan Brouthers   **Buf NL**   **First Baseman**   **Adjusted**

Year	T	L	P	AB	BB	HBP	TAB	H	2B	3B	HR	BA	OB	SA	Wtd PRO	SB	CS	SBF	SPF	FF	Wtd TF	HC
1879	Tro	NL	1B	340	3	0	342	110	29	2	10	.323	.328	.505	833				0	(30)	803	5.3
1880	Tro	NL	1B	22	2	0	25	4	0	0	0	.200	.278	.200	478				0	(30)	448	(3.8)
1881	Buf	NL	OF	514	42	0	555	184	39	19	17	.359	.407	.609	1,015				0	(20)	995	63.0
1882	Buf	NL	1B	664	50	0	713	277	49	24	13	.417	.458	.621	1,078				0	20	1,098	111.6
1883	Buf	NL	1B	692	30	0	722	281	72	30	5	.406	.431	.621	1,052				0	10	1,062	100.4
1884	Buf	NL	1B	556	56	0	612	205	35	24	22	.368	.426	.635	1,061				0	0	1,061	84.9
1885	Buf	NL	1B	580	64	0	644	242	53	18	12	.418	.475	.633	1,108				0	0	1,108	103.6
1886	Det	NL	1B	624	101	0	725	254	56	21	15	.408	.490	.640	1,130	27			0	(10)	1,120	120.8
1887	Det	NL	1B	638	90	8	736	215	46	25	15	.337	.426	.561	987	43			0	(10)	977	72.5
1888	Det	NL	1B	598	101	18	717	213	44	15	12	.355	.462	.537	999	41			0	0	999	78.4
1889	Bos	NL	1B	588	83	18	688	223	32	11	9	.380	.471	.517	987	27			0	0	987	71.2
1890	Bos	P	1B	571	116	21	708	183	43	11	1	.320	.451	.440	891	34			0	0	891	41.0
1891	Bos	AA	1B	555	106	29	691	201	31	22	6	.362	.487	.530	1,017	36			0	(10)	1,007	78.2
1892	Bkn	NL	1B	605	102	19	726	222	34	23	6	.367	.473	.526	999	33			0	20	1,019	86.1
1893	Bkn	NL	1B	353	60	7	420	114	25	13	2	.323	.432	.490	921	11			0	10	931	32.3
1894	Bal	NL	1B	661	67	5	733	199	43	25	10	.301	.369	.486	855	47			0	0	855	29.5
1895	Lou	NL	1B	148	13	0	161	41	14	1	2	.278	.337	.433	770	1		(10)	(20)	740	(2.3)
1896	Phi	NL	1B	272	50	5	326	89	15	4	1	.328	.441	.424	864	9		(10)	(10)	844	11.6
1904	NY	NL	1B	5	0	0	5	0	0	0	0	.000	.000	.000	0	0		(10)	(20)	(30)	(2.0)
15.2 Totals				8,985	1,136	129	10,250	3,258	660	288	158					309	0					1,082.3
1.0 Averages				593	75	9	676	215	43	19	10	.363	.441	.553	994	20	0	0	(0)	(1)	993	71.4

Jimmie Foxx   **Athletics**   **First Baseman**   **Actual**

Year	T	L	P	AB	BB	HBP	TAB	H	2B	3B	HR	BA	OB	SA	PRO	SB	CS	SBF	SPF	FF	Actual TF	Actual HC
1925	Phi	AL	C	9	0	0	9	6	1	0	0	.667	.667	.778	1,444	0	0	0	10	0	1,454	3.5
1926	Phi	AL	C	32	1	0	33	10	2	1	0	.313	.333	.438	771	1	0	29	10	0	809	2.2
1927	Phi	AL	1B	130	14	1	145	42	6	5	3	.323	.393	.515	908	2	1	0	10	(20)	898	9.3
1928	Phi	AL	3B	400	60	1	461	131	29	10	13	.328	.416	.548	964	3	8	(27)	10	(10)	937	51.1
1929	Phi	AL	1B	517	103	2	622	183	23	9	33	.354	.463	.625	1,088	9	7	(8)	10	10	1,100	102.9
1930	Phi	AL	1B	562	93	0	655	188	33	13	37	.335	.429	.637	1,066	7	7	(10)	10	10	1,076	100.4
1931	Phi	AL	1B	515	73	1	589	150	32	10	30	.291	.380	.567	947	4	3	(3)	0	20	964	57.3
1932	Phi	AL	1B	585	116	0	701	213	33	9	58	.364	.469	.749	1,218	3	7	(15)	0	20	1,223	159.2
1933	Phi	AL	1B	573	96	1	670	204	37	9	48	.356	.449	.703	1,153	2	2	(3)	0	20	1,170	134.2
1934	Phi	AL	1B	539	111	1	651	180	28	6	44	.334	.449	.653	1,102	11	2	10	0	20	1,132	118.0
1935	Phi	AL	1B	535	114	0	649	185	33	7	36	.346	.461	.636	1,096	6	4	(3)	0	30	1,123	114.9
1936	Bos	AL	1B	585	105	1	691	198	32	8	41	.338	.440	.631	1,071	13	4	7	0	20	1,098	113.4
1937	Bos	AL	1B	569	99	1	669	162	24	6	36	.285	.392	.538	929	10	8	(8)	0	40	961	64.0
1938	Bos	AL	1B	565	119	0	684	197	33	9	50	.349	.462	.704	1,166	5	4	(4)	0	20	1,182	141.3
1939	Bos	AL	1B	467	89	2	558	168	31	10	35	.360	.464	.694	1,158	4	3	(3)	0	30	1,185	115.9
1940	Bos	AL	1B	515	101	0	616	153	30	4	36	.297	.412	.581	993	4	7	(15)	0	10	988	67.2
1941	Bos	AL	1B	487	93	0	580	146	27	8	19	.300	.412	.505	917	2	5	(13)	0	30	934	47.7
1942	Chi	NL	1B	305	40	2	347	69	12	0	8	.226	.320	.344	664	1	0		0	0	664	(18.4)
1944	Chi	NL	3B	20	2	0	22	1	1	0	0	.050	.136	.100	236	0			(10)	0	226	(5.4)
1945	Phi	NL	1B	224	23	0	247	60	11	1	7	.268	.336	.420	756	0			(10)	(20)	726	(5.5)
14.9	Totals			8,134	1,452	13	9,599	2,646	458	125	534					87	72					1,373.5
1.0	Averages			545	97	1	643	177	31	8	36	.325	.428	.609	1,038	6	5	(6)	2	17	1,051	91.9

Jimmie Foxx   **Athletics**   **First Baseman**   **Adjusted**

Year	T	L	P	AB	BB	HBP	TAB	H	2B	3B	HR	BA	OB	SA	Wtd PRO	SB	CS	SBF	SPF	FF	Wtd TF	HC
1925	Phi	AL	C	9	0	0	9	6	1	0	0	.613	.613	.715	1,328	0	0	0	10	0	1,338	3.0
1926	Phi	AL	C	34	1	0	35	10	2	1	0	.297	.317	.416	732	1	0	29	10	0	771	1.5
1927	Phi	AL	1B	138	13	1	153	42	6	5	3	.304	.369	.484	854	2	1	0	10	(20)	844	5.4
1928	Phi	AL	3B	425	59	1	485	133	29	10	13	.312	.397	.522	918	3	8	(27)	10	(10)	892	40.5
1929	Phi	AL	1B	555	98	2	654	183	23	9	33	.331	.432	.583	1,016	9	7	(8)	10	10	1,028	80.5
1930	Phi	AL	1B	603	86	0	689	185	32	13	36	.306	.392	.582	975	7	7	(10)	10	10	985	70.5
1931	Phi	AL	1B	547	72	1	620	152	32	10	30	.278	.363	.541	904	4	3	(3)	0	20	920	44.4
1932	Phi	AL	1B	626	111	0	737	215	33	9	58	.343	.442	.705	1,146	3	7	(15)	0	20	1,152	134.1
1933	Phi	AL	1B	608	96	1	705	209	38	9	49	.343	.433	.678	1,111	2	2	(3)	0	20	1,129	120.4
1934	Phi	AL	1B	577	107	1	685	181	28	6	44	.314	.422	.615	1,037	12	2	10	0	20	1,067	96.9
1935	Phi	AL	1B	574	109	0	683	186	33	7	36	.324	.432	.596	1,028	6	4	(3)	0	30	1,055	92.6
1936	Bos	AL	1B	631	95	1	727	192	31	8	40	.305	.396	.568	964	14	4	7	0	20	991	76.5
1937	Bos	AL	1B	610	92	1	704	159	24	6	35	.261	.359	.493	852	11	8	(8)	0	40	884	38.1
1938	Bos	AL	1B	610	109	0	720	194	33	9	49	.318	.422	.643	1,065	5	4	(4)	0	20	1,081	106.6
1939	Bos	AL	1B	501	84	2	587	168	31	10	35	.335	.432	.645	1,077	4	3	(3)	0	30	1,104	93.3
1940	Bos	AL	1B	550	98	0	648	154	30	4	36	.280	.388	.546	935	4	7	(15)	0	10	929	49.1
1941	Bos	AL	1B	517	93	0	610	150	28	8	19	.290	.398	.488	887	2	5	(13)	0	30	904	38.9
1942	Chi	NL	1B	317	46	2	365	77	13	0	9	.242	.342	.368	709	1	0		0	0	709	(10.6)
1944	Chi	NL	3B	21	2	0	23	1	1	0	0	.051	.140	.102	242	0			(10)	0	232	(5.3)
1945	Phi	NL	1B	235	25	0	260	64	12	1	7	.272	.341	.426	766	0			(10)	(20)	736	(4.2)
14.9	Totals			8,691	1,394	13	10,098	2,660	461	125	536					92	76					1,072.2
1.0	Averages			582	93	1	676	178	31	8	36	.306	.403	.573	976	6	5	(6)	2	17	989	71.8

Cap Anson   Chicago NL   First Baseman   Actual

Year	T	L	P	AB	BB	HBP	TAB	H	2B	3B	HR	BA	OB	SA	PRO	SB	CS	SBF	SPF	FF	Actual TF	Actual HC
1876	Chi	NL	3B	309	12		321	110	9	7	2	.356	.380	.450	830				0	50	880	62.4
1877	Chi	NL	3B	255	9		264	86	19	1	0	.337	.360	.420	779				0	50	829	38.5
1878	Chi	NL	OF	261	13		274	89	12	2	0	.341	.372	.402	775				0	(40)	735	(7.9)
1879	Chi	NL	1B	227	2		229	72	20	1	0	.317	.323	.414	737				0	10	747	(5.0)
1880	Chi	NL	1B	356	14		370	120	24	1	1	.337	.362	.419	781				0	20	801	10.3
1881	Chi	NL	1B	343	26		369	137	21	7	1	.399	.442	.510	952				0	40	992	75.2
1882	Chi	NL	1B	348	20		368	126	29	8	1	.362	.397	.500	897				0	0	897	42.6
1883	Chi	NL	1B	413	18		431	127	36	5	0	.308	.336	.419	755				0	20	775	1.8
1884	Chi	NL	1B	475	29		504	159	30	3	21	.335	.373	.543	916				0	10	926	53.3
1885	Chi	NL	1B	464	34		498	144	35	7	7	.310	.357	.461	819				0	0	819	16.8
1886	Chi	NL	1B	504	55		559	187	35	11	10	.371	.433	.544	977	29			0	20	997	78.8
1887	Chi	NL	1B	472	60	1	533	164	33	13	7	.347	.422	.517	939	27			0	30	969	64.5
1888	Chi	NL	1B	515	47	1	563	177	20	12	12	.344	.400	.499	899	28			0	40	939	53.9
1889	Chi	NL	1B	518	86	5	609	161	32	7	7	.311	.414	.440	854	27			0	40	894	43.8
1890	Chi	NL	1B	504	113	6	623	157	14	5	7	.312	.443	.401	844	29			0	10	854	29.9
1891	Chi	NL	1B	540	75	1	616	157	24	8	8	.291	.378	.409	788	17		(10)		20	798	9.5
1892	Chi	NL	1B	559	67	4	630	152	25	9	1	.272	.354	.354	708	13		(10)	(10)	688	(25.9)
1893	Chi	NL	1B	398	68	1	467	125	24	2	0	.314	.415	.384	800	13		(10)	(10)	780	2.7
1894	Chi	NL	1B	340	40	3	383	132	28	4	5	.388	.457	.538	995	17		(10)	10	995	50.4
1895	Chi	NL	1B	474	55	3	532	159	23	6	2	.335	.408	.422	830	12		(10)	0	820	15.4
1896	Chi	NL	1B	402	49	3	454	133	18	2	2	.331	.407	.400	808	24		(10)	0	798	7.4
1897	Chi	NL	1B	424	60	4	488	121	17	3	3	.285	.379	.361	740	11		(10)	0	730	(11.2)
21.9 Totals				9,101	952	32	10,085	2,995	528	124	97					247	0					607.2
1.0 Averages				416	44	1	462	137	24	6	4	.329	.395	.446	841	11	0	(0)	(3)	15	853	27.8

Cap Anson   Chicago NL   First Baseman   Adjusted

Year	T	L	P	AB	BB	HBP	TAB	H	2B	3B	HR	BA	OB	SA	Wtd PRO	SB	CS	SBF	SPF	FF	Wtd TF	HC
1876	Chi	NL	3B	761	39	0	800	320	26	20	6	.420	.449	.531	980	0			0	50	1,030	119.5
1877	Chi	NL	3B	684	29	0	713	260	57	3	0	.380	.405	.472	878	0			0	50	928	71.8
1878	Chi	NL	OF	683	45	0	728	275	37	6	0	.403	.439	.475	914	0			0	(40)	874	40.5
1879	Chi	NL	1B	459	5	0	464	171	48	2	0	.374	.381	.488	869	0			0	10	879	24.0
1880	Chi	NL	1B	669	36	0	705	271	54	2	2	.405	.436	.503	939	0			0	20	959	63.4
1881	Chi	NL	1B	650	62	0	712	292	45	15	2	.450	.497	.574	1,072	0			0	40	1,112	115.9
1882	Chi	NL	1B	658	47	0	706	271	62	17	2	.411	.450	.567	1,018	0			0	0	1,018	83.3
1883	Chi	NL	1B	672	33	0	705	224	64	9	0	.334	.365	.455	820	0			0	20	840	23.6
1884	Chi	NL	1B	667	50	0	716	252	47	5	33	.377	.421	.612	1,033	0			0	10	1,043	93.2
1885	Chi	NL	1B	664	62	0	727	240	58	12	12	.362	.416	.537	954	0			0	0	954	63.6
1886	Chi	NL	1B	646	84	0	730	264	49	16	14	.409	.477	.599	1,075	38			0	20	1,095	113.2
1887	Chi	NL	1B	602	76	1	680	209	42	17	9	.347	.421	.516	938	34			0	30	968	64.0
1888	Chi	NL	1B	598	71	2	671	238	27	16	16	.398	.463	.578	1,042	33			0	40	1,082	99.6
1889	Chi	NL	1B	628	108	6	742	199	40	9	9	.317	.421	.448	870	33			0	40	910	49.4
1890	Chi	NL	1B	594	146	8	748	195	17	6	9	.328	.466	.422	888	35			0	10	898	45.5
1891	Chi	NL	1B	626	95	1	723	193	29	10	10	.308	.400	.433	833	20		(10)		20	843	25.3
1892	Chi	NL	1B	580	80	5	665	173	28	10	1	.298	.388	.388	776	14		(10)	(10)	756	(4.4)
1893	Chi	NL	1B	497	79	1	578	150	29	2	0	.301	.398	.369	767	16		(10)	(10)	747	(6.3)
1894	Chi	NL	1B	428	39	3	470	144	31	4	5	.337	.396	.467	863	21		(10)	10	863	20.8
1895	Chi	NL	1B	585	60	3	648	182	26	7	2	.311	.378	.391	770	15		(10)	0	760	(3.2)
1896	Chi	NL	1B	498	56	3	557	157	21	2	2	.315	.388	.382	770	29		(10)	0	760	(2.7)
1897	Chi	NL	1B	514	67	4	586	140	20	3	3	.272	.361	.344	705	13		(10)	0	695	(21.0)
21.9 Totals				13,362	1,371	38	14,771	4,818	859	194	138					301	0					1,079.1
1.0 Averages				612	63	2	676	221	39	9	6	.361	.422	.485	907	14	0	(0)	(3)	15	918	49.4

Roger Connor NY NL **First Baseman** Actual

Year	T	L	P	AB	BB	HBP	TAB	H	2B	3B	HR	BA	OB	SA	PRO	SB	CS	SBF	SPF	FF	Actual TF	Actual HC
1880	Tro	NL	3B	340	13	0	353	113	18	8	3	.332	.357	.459	816				0	(30)	786	22.3
1881	Tro	NL	1B	367	15	0	382	107	17	6	2	.292	.319	.387	706				0	10	716	(18.9)
1882	Tro	NL	1B	349	13	0	362	115	22	18	4	.330	.354	.530	884				0	10	894	40.9
1883	NY	NL	1B	409	25	0	434	146	28	15	1	.357	.394	.506	900				0	10	910	47.4
1884	NY	NL	2B	477	38	0	515	151	28	4	4	.317	.367	.417	784				0	0	784	34.5
1885	NY	NL	1B	455	51	0	506	169	23	15	1	.371	.435	.495	929				0	10	939	59.6
1886	NY	NL	1B	485	41	0	526	172	29	20	7	.355	.405	.540	945	17			0	20	965	63.9
1887	NY	NL	1B	471	75	8	554	134	26	22	17	.285	.392	.541	933	43			0	20	953	61.6
1888	NY	NL	1B	481	73	4	558	140	15	17	14	.291	.389	.480	869	27			0	0	869	31.4
1889	NY	NL	1B	496	93	2	591	157	32	17	13	.317	.426	.528	955	21			0	(10)	945	59.9
1890	NY	P	1B	484	88	1	573	169	24	15	14	.349	.450	.548	998	22			0	30	1,028	86.4
1891	NY	NL	1B	479	83	4	566	139	29	13	7	.290	.399	.449	848	27			0	0	848	24.7
1892	Phi	NL	1B	564	116	6	686	166	37	11	12	.294	.420	.463	883	22			0	0	883	38.8
1893	NY	NL	1B	511	91	3	605	156	25	8	11	.305	.413	.450	863	24			0	0	863	33.3
1894	StL	NL	1B	462	59	6	527	146	35	25	8	.316	.400	.552	952	19			0	10	962	59.3
1895	StL	NL	1B	398	63	2	463	131	29	9	8	.329	.423	.508	931	9			0	10	941	45.9
1896	StL	NL	1B	483	52	2	537	137	21	9	11	.284	.356	.433	788	10			0	30	818	15.2
1897	StL	NL	1B	83	13	0	96	19	3	1	1	.229	.333	.325	659	3			0	0	659	(6.1)
17.6 Totals				7,794	1,002	38	8,834	2,467	441	233	138					244	0					700.1
1.0 Averages				443	57	2	502	140	25	13	8	.317	.397	.486	883	14	0	0	0	7	890	39.8

Roger Connor NY NL **First Baseman** Adjusted

Year	T	L	P	AB	BB	HBP	TAB	H	2B	3B	HR	BA	OB	SA	Wtd PRO	SB	CS	SBF	SPF	FF	Wtd TF	HC
1880	Tro	NL	3B	640	33	0	673	256	41	18	7	.400	.429	.552	981				0	(30)	951	75.3
1881	Tro	NL	1B	702	34	0	737	231	37	13	4	.328	.360	.436	795				0	10	805	12.3
1882	Tro	NL	1B	664	30	0	694	248	47	39	9	.374	.401	.602	1,003				0	10	1,013	80.3
1883	NY	NL	1B	664	47	0	710	257	49	26	2	.388	.428	.550	978				0	10	988	73.6
1884	NY	NL	2B	667	65	0	732	238	44	6	6	.357	.414	.470	884				0	0	884	69.4
1885	NY	NL	1B	642	96	0	738	278	38	25	2	.433	.506	.576	1,082				0	10	1,092	113.5
1886	NY	NL	1B	625	62	0	687	244	41	28	10	.391	.446	.595	1,041	22			0	20	1,061	95.2
1887	NY	NL	1B	601	95	10	707	171	33	28	22	.284	.391	.541	932	55			0	20	952	61.2
1888	NY	NL	1B	551	108	6	665	186	20	23	19	.337	.451	.557	1,007	32			0	0	1,007	75.2
1889	NY	NL	1B	601	116	3	720	194	39	21	16	.322	.434	.538	972	26			0	(10)	962	66.0
1890	NY	P	1B	599	103	1	703	203	29	18	17	.338	.436	.530	966	27			0	30	996	75.8
1891	NY	NL	1B	554	106	5	664	170	35	16	9	.307	.423	.475	898	32			0	0	898	40.4
1892	Phi	NL	1B	577	140	7	724	186	41	12	13	.323	.460	.507	967	23			0	0	967	68.1
1893	NY	NL	1B	639	106	3	748	187	30	10	13	.293	.396	.432	828	30			0	0	828	20.7
1894	StL	NL	1B	582	59	6	647	159	38	27	9	.274	.347	.479	826	23			0	10	836	20.3
1895	StL	NL	1B	493	69	2	564	151	33	10	9	.305	.393	.471	863	11			0	10	873	27.8
1896	StL	NL	1B	597	60	2	659	161	25	11	13	.270	.339	.412	751	12			0	30	781	3.5
1897	StL	NL	1B	101	15	0	115	22	3	1	1	.218	.318	.310	627	4			0	0	627	(7.8)
17.6 Totals				10,497	1,344	46	11,887	3,541	625	332	180					297	0					970.6
1.0 Averages				597	76	3	676	201	36	19	10	.337	.415	.512	926	17	0	0	0	7	933	55.2

Jeff Bagwell   **Astros**   **First Baseman**   **Actual**

Year	T	L	P	AB	BB	HBP	TAB	H	2B	3B	HR	BA	OB	SA	PRO	SB	CS	SBF	SPF	FF	Actual TF	Actual HC
1991	Hou	NL	1B	554	75	13	642	163	26	4	15	.294	.391	.437	828	7	4	(1)	10	0	836	20.3
1992	Hou	NL	1B	586	84	12	682	160	34	6	18	.273	.375	.444	819	10	6	(3)	10	10	836	21.5
1993	Hou	NL	1B	535	62	3	600	171	37	4	20	.320	.393	.516	909	13	4	8	10	10	937	47.8
1994	Hou	NL	1B	400	65	4	469	147	32	2	39	.368	.461	.750	1,211	15	4	14	10	40	1,275	159.5
1995	Hou	NL	1B	448	79	6	533	130	29	0	21	.290	.403	.496	899	12	5	4	10	40	952	52.1
1996	Hou	NL	1B	568	135	10	713	179	48	2	31	.315	.454	.570	1,025	21	7	9	10	20	1,064	99.9
1997	Hou	NL	1B	566	127	16	709	162	40	2	43	.286	.430	.592	1,022	31	10	15	10	20	1,067	100.2
1998	Hou	NL	1B	540	109	7	656	164	33	1	34	.304	.427	.557	984	19	7	7	10	30	1,031	81.7
1999	Hou	NL	1B	562	149	11	722	171	35	0	42	.304	.458	.591	1,049	30	11	10	10	30	1,100	113.4
2000	Hou	NL	1B	590	107	15	712	183	37	1	47	.310	.428	.615	1,044	9	6	(4)	10	20	1,070	101.6
9.9 Totals				5,349	992	97	6,438	1,630	351	22	310					167	64					798.1
1.0 Averages				540	100	10	650	164	35	2	31	.305	.422	.552	975	17	6	6	10	22	1,012	80.5

Jeff Bagwell   **Astros**   **First Baseman**   **Adjusted**

Year	T	L	P	AB	BB	HBP	TAB	H	2B	3B	HR	BA	OB	SA	Wtd PRO	SB	CS	SBF	SPF	FF	Wtd TF	HC
1991	Hou	NL	1B	551	77	13	642	166	26	4	15	.300	.399	.446	844	7	4	(1)	10	0	853	25.4
1992	Hou	NL	1B	582	87	12	682	164	35	6	18	.281	.386	.457	843	10	6	(3)	10	10	860	29.3
1993	Hou	NL	1B	538	59	3	600	167	36	4	19	.309	.381	.500	880	13	4	8	10	10	908	39.5
1994	Hou	NL	1B	575	84	5	664	199	43	3	53	.346	.433	.706	1,139	21	6	14	10	40	1,203	137.0
1995	Hou	NL	1B	510	83	6	600	141	31	0	23	.276	.384	.472	856	14	6	4	10	40	910	40.0
1996	Hou	NL	1B	578	126	9	713	173	47	2	30	.300	.433	.543	976	21	7	9	10	20	1,016	83.4
1997	Hou	NL	1B	576	118	15	709	156	39	2	42	.272	.408	.562	970	31	10	15	10	20	1,015	82.7
1998	Hou	NL	1B	548	102	7	656	158	32	1	33	.289	.406	.530	937	19	7	7	10	30	984	66.8
1999	Hou	NL	1B	581	131	10	722	162	33	0	40	.278	.419	.540	960	30	11	10	10	30	1,010	82.6
2000	Hou	NL	1B	605	94	13	712	171	35	1	44	.283	.391	.561	952	9	6	(4)	10	20	978	70.6
9.9 Totals				5,644	961	94	6,699	1,657	357	23	317					175	66					657.3
1.0 Averages				570	97	9	676	167	36	2	32	.294	.405	.533	938	18	7	6	10	22	976	66.3

Hank Greenberg   Tigers   First Baseman   Actual

Year	T	L	P	AB	BB	HBP	TAB	H	2B	3B	HR	BA	OB	SA	PRO	SB	CS	SBF	SPF	FF	Actual TF	Actual HC
1930	Det	AL	PH	1	0	0	1	0	0	0	0	.000	.000	.000	0	0	0	0	0	0	0	(0.4)
1933	Det	AL	1B	449	46	1	496	135	33	3	12	.301	.367	.468	835	6	2	4	0	10	848	19.5
1934	Det	AL	1B	593	63	2	658	201	63	7	26	.339	.404	.600	1,005	9	5	(1)	0	10	1,013	80.2
1935	Det	AL	1B	619	87	0	706	203	46	16	36	.328	.411	.628	1,039	4	3	(3)	0	10	1,047	97.8
1936	Det	AL	1B	46	9	0	55	16	6	2	1	.348	.455	.630	1,085	1	0	17	0	10	1,112	9.4
1937	Det	AL	1B	594	102	3	699	200	49	14	40	.337	.436	.668	1,105	8	3	3	0	10	1,117	121.7
1938	Det	AL	1B	556	119	3	678	175	23	4	58	.315	.438	.683	1,122	7	5	(4)	0	10	1,127	121.4
1939	Det	AL	1B	500	91	2	593	156	42	7	33	.312	.420	.622	1,042	8	3	3	0	10	1,055	84.7
1940	Det	AL	OF	573	93	1	667	195	50	8	41	.340	.433	.670	1,103	6	3	0	0	(10)	1,093	112.3
1941	Det	AL	OF	67	16	0	83	18	5	1	2	.269	.410	.463	872	1	0	11	0	(50)	834	3.2
1945	Det	AL	OF	270	42	0	312	84	20	2	13	.311	.404	.544	948	3	1	3	0	(10)	941	28.8
1946	Det	AL	1B	523	80	0	603	145	29	5	44	.277	.373	.604	977	5	1	5	0	0	982	64.1
1947	Pit	NL	1B	402	104	4	510	100	13	2	25	.249	.408	.478	885	0			0	0	885	29.5
9.4 Totals				5,193	852	16	6,061	1,628	379	71	331					58	26					772.3
1.0 Averages				551	90	2	643	173	40	8	35	.313	.412	.605	1,017	6	3	1	0	4	1,022	81.9

Hank Greenberg   Tigers   First Baseman   Adjusted

Year	T	L	P	AB	BB	HBP	TAB	H	2B	3B	HR	BA	OB	SA	Wtd PRO	SB	CS	SBF	SPF	FF	Wtd TF	HC
1930	Det	AL	PH	1	0	0	1	0	0	0	0	.000	.000	.000	0	0	0	0	0	0	0	(0.4)
1933	Det	AL	1B	475	46	1	522	138	34	3	12	.290	.354	.451	805	6	2	4	0	10	819	12.1
1934	Det	AL	1B	630	61	2	692	201	63	7	26	.319	.380	.565	946	9	5	(1)	0	10	954	60.7
1935	Det	AL	1B	659	83	0	743	203	46	16	36	.307	.385	.589	974	4	3	(3)	0	10	982	74.8
1936	Det	AL	1B	50	8	0	58	16	6	2	1	.313	.409	.568	977	1	0	17	0	10	1,004	6.5
1937	Det	AL	1B	638	94	3	735	197	48	14	39	.309	.400	.613	1,013	8	3	3	0	10	1,025	89.5
1938	Det	AL	1B	601	110	3	713	173	23	4	57	.287	.400	.624	1,024	7	5	(4)	0	10	1,030	88.3
1939	Det	AL	1B	536	86	2	624	155	42	7	33	.290	.391	.578	969	8	3	3	0	10	982	63.1
1940	Det	AL	OF	611	89	1	702	196	50	8	41	.320	.408	.631	1,039	6	3	0	0	(10)	1,029	90.6
1941	Det	AL	OF	71	16	0	87	19	5	1	2	.260	.396	.447	844	1	0	11	0	(50)	805	2.0
1945	Det	AL	OF	281	48	0	328	92	22	2	14	.327	.425	.573	998	3	1	3	0	(10)	991	36.5
1946	Det	AL	1B	548	87	0	634	155	31	5	47	.283	.381	.616	997	5	1	5	0	0	1,002	70.0
1947	Pit	NL	1B	428	105	4	536	103	13	2	26	.241	.395	.462	857	0			0	0	857	22.3
9.4 Totals				5,528	833	15	6,376	1,646	383	71	335					61	27					616.0
1.0 Averages				586	88	2	676	175	41	8	36	.298	.391	.575	966	6	3	1	0	4	971	65.3

Mark McGwire   **Athletics**   **First Baseman**   **Actual**

Year	T	L	P	AB	BB	HBP	TAB	H	2B	3B	HR	BA	OB	SA	PRO	SB	CS	SBF	SPF	FF	Actual TF	Actual HC
1986	Oak	AL	3B	53	4	1	58	10	1	0	3	.189	.259	.377	636	0	1	(33)	0	(120)	483	(6.4)
1987	Oak	AL	1B	557	71	5	633	161	28	4	49	.289	.374	.618	992	1	1	(1)	0	0	991	66.5
1988	Oak	AL	1B	550	76	4	630	143	22	1	32	.260	.354	.478	832	0	0	0	(10)	0	822	15.7
1989	Oak	AL	1B	490	83	3	576	113	17	0	33	.231	.345	.467	813	1	1	(2)	(10)	10	811	11.3
1990	Oak	AL	1B	523	110	7	640	123	16	0	39	.235	.375	.489	864	2	1	0	(10)	30	884	34.9
1991	Oak	AL	1B	483	93	3	579	97	22	0	22	.201	.333	.383	716	2	1	0	(10)	20	726	(12.0)
1992	Oak	AL	1B	467	90	5	562	125	22	0	42	.268	.391	.585	976	0	1	(3)	(10)	10	973	54.3
1993	Oak	AL	1B	84	21	1	106	28	6	0	9	.333	.472	.726	1,198	0	1	(18)	(10)	30	1,200	21.7
1994	Oak	AL	1B	135	37	0	172	34	3	0	9	.252	.413	.474	887	0	0	0	(10)	0	877	12.4
1995	Oak	AL	1B	317	88	11	416	87	13	0	39	.274	.447	.685	1,132	1	1	(2)	(10)	0	1,119	77.9
1996	Oak	AL	1B	423	116	8	547	132	21	0	52	.312	.468	.730	1,199	0	0	0	(10)	0	1,189	109.1
1997	Oak	AL	1B	540	101	9	650	148	27	0	58	.274	.397	.646	1,043	3	0	4	(10)	20	1,058	89.1
1998	StL	NL	1B	509	162	6	677	152	21	0	70	.299	.473	.752	1,225	1	0	1	(10)	(10)	1,207	140.8
1999	StL	NL	1B	521	133	2	656	145	21	1	65	.278	.427	.697	1,124	0	0	0	(10)	(10)	1,104	104.2
2000	StL	NL	1B	236	76	7	319	72	8	0	32	.305	.486	.746	1,232	1	0	3	(10)	10	1,235	70.6
10.9 Totals				5,888	1,261	72	7,221	1,570	248	6	554					12	8					789.9
1.0 Averages				542	116	7	665	145	23	1	51	.267	.402	.593	995	1	1	(1)	(9)	6	991	72.7

Mark McGwire   **Athletics**   **First Baseman**   **Adjusted**

Year	T	L	P	AB	BB	HBP	TAB	H	2B	3B	HR	BA	OB	SA	Wtd PRO	SB	CS	SBF	SPF	FF	Wtd TF	HC
1986	Oak	AL	3B	53	4	1	58	0	0	0	0	.000	.085	.000	85	0	1	(33)	0	(120)	-68	(21.7)
1987	Oak	AL	1B	561	67	5	633	156	27	4	47	.277	.359	.592	952	1	1	(1)	0	0	950	54.3
1988	Oak	AL	1B	548	78	4	630	145	22	1	32	.264	.360	.486	846	0	0	0	(10)	0	836	19.8
1989	Oak	AL	1B	487	86	3	576	115	17	0	34	.236	.354	.479	833	1	1	(2)	(10)	10	832	16.9
1990	Oak	AL	1B	520	112	7	640	124	16	0	39	.239	.381	.498	879	2	1	0	(10)	30	899	39.3
1991	Oak	AL	1B	482	94	3	579	97	22	0	22	.202	.335	.385	720	2	1	0	(10)	20	730	(11.0)
1992	Oak	AL	1B	464	92	5	562	127	22	0	43	.273	.399	.596	995	0	1	(3)	(10)	10	992	59.4
1993	Oak	AL	1B	85	20	1	106	28	6	0	9	.325	.460	.709	1,169	0	1	(18)	(10)	30	1,171	20.3
1994	Oak	AL	1B	196	48	0	243	46	4	0	12	.235	.385	.443	828	0	0	0	(10)	0	818	5.6
1995	Oak	AL	1B	365	91	11	468	95	14	0	42	.259	.422	.646	1,067	1	1	(2)	(10)	0	1,055	63.6
1996	Oak	AL	1B	438	102	7	547	125	20	0	49	.285	.428	.668	1,096	0	0	0	(10)	0	1,086	82.4
1997	Oak	AL	1B	548	93	8	650	142	26	0	56	.259	.375	.610	985	3	0	4	(10)	20	999	70.9
1998	StL	NL	1B	520	151	6	677	148	20	0	68	.284	.450	.716	1,166	1	0	1	(10)	(10)	1,147	121.7
1999	StL	NL	1B	536	118	2	656	137	20	1	61	.255	.390	.637	1,028	0	0	0	(10)	(10)	1,008	74.3
2000	StL	NL	1B	246	67	6	319	68	8	0	30	.278	.443	.680	1,124	1	0	3	(10)	10	1,127	54.2
10.9 Totals				6,051	1,223	69	7,344	1,552	245	6	546					12	8					650.1
1.0 Averages				557	113	6	676	143	23	1	50	.256	.387	.569	957	1	1	(1)	(9)	6	953	59.8

Johnny Mize **Cardinals** **First Baseman** **Actual**

Year	T	L	P	AB	BB	HBP	TAB	H	2B	3B	HR	BA	OB	SA	PRO	SB	CS	SBF	SPF	FF	Actual TF	Actual HC
1936	StL	NL	1B	414	50	1	465	136	30	8	19	.329	.402	.577	979	1			0	0	979	48.8
1937	StL	NL	1B	560	56	5	621	204	40	7	25	.364	.427	.595	1,021	2			0	(20)	1,001	72.0
1938	StL	NL	1B	531	74	4	609	179	34	16	27	.337	.422	.614	1,036	0			0	0	1,036	81.2
1939	StL	NL	1B	564	92	4	660	197	44	14	28	.349	.444	.626	1,070	0			0	0	1,070	99.2
1940	StL	NL	1B	579	82	5	666	182	31	13	43	.314	.404	.636	1,039	7			0	0	1,039	89.9
1941	StL	NL	1B	473	70	1	544	150	39	8	16	.317	.406	.535	941	4			0	0	941	46.7
1942	NY	NL	1B	541	60	5	606	165	25	7	26	.305	.380	.521	901	3			0	0	901	39.7
1946	NY	NL	1B	377	62	5	444	127	18	3	22	.337	.437	.576	1,013	3			(10)	0	1,003	51.7
1947	NY	NL	1B	586	74	4	664	177	26	2	51	.302	.384	.614	998	2			(10)	0	988	72.7
1948	NY	NL	1B	560	94	4	658	162	26	4	40	.289	.395	.564	959	4			(10)	(10)	939	55.9
1949	NY	NL	1B	411	54	4	469	108	16	0	19	.263	.354	.440	794	1			(10)	(10)	774	1.0
1950	NY	AL	1B	274	29	2	305	76	12	0	25	.277	.351	.595	946	0	0	0	(10)	0	936	25.3
1951	NY	AL	1B	332	36	4	372	86	14	1	10	.259	.339	.398	736	1	1	(3)	(10)	(20)	704	(12.3)
1952	NY	AL	1B	137	11	2	150	36	9	0	4	.263	.327	.416	743	0	0	0	(10)	(10)	723	(3.6)
1953	NY	AL	1B	104	12	2	118	26	3	0	4	.250	.339	.394	733	0	0	0	(10)	0	723	(2.8)
11.4 Totals				6,443	856	52	7,351	2,011	367	83	359					28	1					665.4
1.0 Averages				563	75	5	643	176	32	7	31	.312	.397	.562	959	2	0	(0)	(4)	(4)	950	58.2

Johnny Mize **Cardinals** **First Baseman** **Adjusted**

Year	T	L	P	AB	BB	HBP	TAB	H	2B	3B	HR	BA	OB	SA	Wtd PRO	SB	CS	SBF	SPF	FF	Wtd TF	HC
1936	StL	NL	1B	437	51	1	489	140	31	8	20	.321	.393	.564	958	1			0	0	958	43.7
1937	StL	NL	1B	590	58	5	653	213	42	7	26	.360	.422	.588	1,010	2			0	(20)	990	68.4
1938	StL	NL	1B	558	78	4	641	188	36	17	28	.338	.423	.615	1,037	0			0	0	1,037	81.6
1939	StL	NL	1B	597	94	4	694	204	46	14	29	.342	.435	.613	1,047	0			0	0	1,047	91.8
1940	StL	NL	1B	608	87	5	701	192	33	14	45	.316	.406	.639	1,045	7			0	0	1,045	91.9
1941	StL	NL	1B	495	76	1	572	161	42	9	17	.325	.417	.549	966	4			0	0	966	53.3
1942	NY	NL	1B	562	69	6	637	183	28	8	29	.326	.405	.557	962	3			0	0	962	58.3
1946	NY	NL	1B	393	68	6	467	137	19	3	24	.348	.451	.594	1,045	3			(10)	0	1,035	59.0
1947	NY	NL	1B	620	74	4	698	181	27	2	52	.292	.372	.595	967	2			(10)	0	957	62.1
1948	NY	NL	1B	591	97	4	692	169	27	4	42	.286	.390	.557	947	4			(10)	(10)	927	51.8
1949	NY	NL	1B	434	55	4	493	111	17	0	20	.257	.346	.430	776	1			(10)	(10)	756	(3.4)
1950	NY	AL	1B	291	28	2	321	75	12	0	25	.258	.326	.553	880	0	0	0	(10)	0	870	15.2
1951	NY	AL	1B	351	37	4	391	89	14	1	10	.253	.331	.388	719	1	1	(3)	(10)	(20)	686	(15.6)
1952	NY	AL	1B	144	12	2	158	38	10	0	4	.267	.332	.423	754	0	0	0	(10)	(10)	734	(2.7)
1953	NY	AL	1B	110	12	2	124	27	3	0	4	.245	.332	.387	719	0	0	0	(10)	0	709	(3.6)
11.4 Totals				6,782	897	55	7,733	2,109	385	87	375					29	1					651.8
1.0 Averages				593	78	5	676	184	34	8	33	.311	.396	.560	955	3	0	(0)	(4)	(4)	946	57.0

Frank Thomas   **White Sox**   **First Baseman**   **Actual**

Year	T	L	P	AB	BB	HBP	TAB	H	2B	3B	HR	BA	OB	SA	PRO	SB	CS	SBF	SPF	FF	Actual TF	Actual HC
1990	Chi	AL	1B	191	44	2	237	63	11	3	7	.330	.460	.529	989	0	1	(8)	10	(40)	951	20.4
1991	Chi	AL	DH	559	138	1	698	178	31	2	32	.318	.454	.553	1,007	1	2	(4)	10	(30)	983	70.8
1992	Chi	AL	1B	573	122	5	700	185	46	2	24	.323	.446	.536	981	6	3	0	0	(30)	951	60.5
1993	Chi	AL	1B	549	112	2	663	174	36	0	41	.317	.434	.607	1,041	4	2	0	0	(30)	1,011	76.1
1994	Chi	AL	1B	399	109	2	510	141	34	1	38	.353	.494	.729	1,223	2	3	(7)	0	(30)	1,186	143.0
1995	Chi	AL	1B	493	136	6	635	152	27	0	40	.308	.463	.606	1,069	3	2	(1)	0	(30)	1,038	91.2
1996	Chi	AL	1B	527	109	5	641	184	26	0	40	.349	.465	.626	1,091	1	1	(1)	0	(30)	1,060	88.4
1997	Chi	AL	1B	530	109	3	642	184	35	0	35	.347	.461	.611	1,072	1	1	(1)	0	(40)	1,031	79.8
1998	Chi	AL	DH	585	110	6	701	155	35	2	29	.265	.387	.480	867	7	0	9	0	(30)	846	25.5
1999	Chi	AL	DH	486	87	9	582	148	36	0	15	.305	.419	.471	890	3	3	(5)	(10)	(40)	836	18.2
2000	Chi	AL	DH	582	112	5	699	191	44	0	43	.328	.441	.625	1,066	1	3	(7)	(10)	(20)	1,029	86.4
10.4 Totals				5,474	1,188	46	6,708	1,755	361	10	344					29	21					760.3
1.0 Averages				529	115	4	648	170	35	1	33	.321	.446	.579	1,024	3	2	(2)	(0)	(31)	991	73.4

Frank Thomas   **White Sox**   **First Baseman**   **Adjusted**

Year	T	L	P	AB	BB	HBP	TAB	H	2B	3B	HR	BA	OB	SA	Wtd PRO	SB	CS	SBF	SPF	FF	Wtd TF	HC
1990	Chi	AL	1B	190	45	2	237	64	11	3	7	.335	.468	.538	1,005	0	1	(8)	10	(40)	967	22.3
1991	Chi	AL	DH	558	139	1	698	179	31	2	32	.320	.457	.556	1,012	1	2	(4)	10	(30)	988	72.6
1992	Chi	AL	1B	569	126	5	700	187	47	2	24	.329	.454	.546	1,001	6	3	0	0	(30)	971	66.9
1993	Chi	AL	1B	553	108	2	663	171	35	0	40	.309	.424	.592	1,016	4	2	0	0	(30)	986	68.2
1994	Chi	AL	1B	580	139	3	722	191	46	1	52	.330	.461	.681	1,142	3	4	(7)	0	(30)	1,105	115.0
1995	Chi	AL	1B	567	141	6	714	165	29	0	43	.291	.437	.572	1,009	3	2	(1)	0	(30)	977	70.5
1996	Chi	AL	1B	541	95	4	641	173	24	0	38	.319	.425	.573	998	1	1	(1)	0	(30)	967	60.0
1997	Chi	AL	1B	539	100	3	642	177	34	0	34	.328	.435	.577	1,012	1	1	(1)	0	(40)	971	61.4
1998	Chi	AL	DH	594	101	6	701	148	33	2	28	.249	.363	.452	815	7	0	9	0	(30)	795	8.2
1999	Chi	AL	DH	496	78	8	582	139	34	0	14	.281	.387	.435	821	3	3	(5)	(10)	(40)	766	(1.0)
2000	Chi	AL	DH	596	98	4	699	179	41	0	40	.300	.403	.573	976	1	3	(7)	(10)	(20)	939	56.3
10.4 Totals				5,785	1,170	44	6,999	1,773	366	10	352					30	22					600.5
1.0 Averages				559	113	4	676	171	35	1	34	.307	.427	.556	983	3	2	(2)	(0)	(31)	949	58.0

Nap Lajoie **Indians** **Second Baseman** **Actual**

Year	T	L	P	AB	BB	HBP	TAB	H	2B	3B	HR	BA	OB	SA	PRO	SB	CS	SBF	SPF	FF	Actual TF	Actual HC
1896	Phi	NL	1B	175	1	0	176	57	12	7	4	.326	.330	.543	872	7			10	0	882	11.6
1897	Phi	NL	1B	545	15	12	572	197	40	23	9	.361	.392	.569	960	20			10	(10)	960	62.3
1898	Phi	NL	2B	608	21	7	636	197	43	11	6	.324	.354	.461	814	25			10	10	834	47.6
1899	Phi	NL	2B	312	12	10	334	118	19	9	6	.378	.419	.554	974	13			10	100	1,084	66.9
1900	Phi	NL	2B	451	10	8	469	152	33	12	7	.337	.362	.510	872	22			10	90	972	74.2
1901	Phi	AL	2B	544	24	13	581	232	48	14	14	.426	.463	.643	1,106	27			10	80	1,196	163.7
1902	Cle	AL	2B	352	19	6	377	133	35	5	7	.378	.419	.565	984	20			10	110	1,104	87.1
1903	Cle	AL	2B	485	24	3	512	167	41	11	7	.344	.379	.518	896	21			10	100	1,006	90.6
1904	Cle	AL	2B	553	27	8	588	208	49	15	5	.376	.413	.546	959	29			10	50	1,019	98.4
1905	Cle	AL	2B	249	17	2	268	82	12	2	2	.329	.377	.418	795	11			10	70	875	25.4
1906	Cle	AL	2B	602	30	6	638	214	48	9	0	.355	.392	.465	857	20			10	90	957	86.9
1907	Cle	AL	2B	509	30	6	545	152	30	6	2	.299	.345	.393	738	24			10	120	868	49.9
1908	Cle	AL	2B	581	47	9	637	168	32	6	2	.289	.352	.375	727	15			10	120	857	54.8
1909	Cle	AL	2B	469	35	6	510	152	33	7	1	.324	.378	.431	809	13			0	80	889	52.1
1910	Cle	AL	2B	591	60	5	656	227	51	7	4	.384	.445	.514	960	26			0	80	1,040	116.5
1911	Cle	AL	1B	315	26	4	345	115	20	1	2	.365	.420	.454	874	13			0	(10)	864	16.3
1912	Cle	AL	2B	448	28	7	483	165	34	4	0	.368	.414	.462	876	18			0	30	906	53.5
1913	Cle	AL	2B	465	33	15	513	156	25	2	1	.335	.398	.404	802	17			0	50	852	42.8
1914	Cle	AL	2B	419	32	2	453	108	14	3	0	.258	.313	.305	619	14	15	(33)	0	30	616	(15.8)
1915	Phi	AL	2B	490	11	4	505	137	24	5	1	.280	.301	.355	656	10	6	(4)	0	30	682	(0.7)
1916	Phi	AL	2B	426	14	1	441	105	14	4	2	.246	.272	.312	584	15			0	50	634	(11.3)
16.4		Totals		9,589	516	134	10,239	3,242	657	163	82					380	21					1,172.7
1.0		Averages		584	31	8	624	198	40	10	5	.338	.380	.466	846	23	1	(2)	6	63	914	71.5

Nap Lajoie **Indians** **Second Baseman** **Adjusted**

Year	T	L	P	AB	BB	HBP	TAB	H	2B	3B	HR	BA	OB	SA	Wtd PRO	SB	CS	SBF	SPF	FF	Wtd TF	HC
1896	Phi	NL	1B	215	1	0	216	67	14	8	5	.310	.314	.517	831	9			10	0	841	7.3
1897	Phi	NL	1B	656	17	13	686	226	46	26	10	.344	.373	.542	915	24			10	(10)	915	47.4
1898	Phi	NL	2B	640	23	8	671	215	47	12	7	.336	.367	.477	844	26			10	10	864	57.2
1899	Phi	NL	2B	329	13	10	352	124	20	9	6	.376	.417	.551	968	14			10	100	1,078	66.0
1900	Phi	NL	2B	522	12	9	543	176	38	14	8	.337	.363	.511	874	25			10	90	974	74.5
1901	Phi	AL	2B	629	28	15	672	269	56	16	16	.428	.464	.645	1,109	31			10	80	1,199	164.7
1902	Cle	AL	2B	407	22	7	436	155	41	6	8	.381	.423	.570	993	23			10	110	1,113	88.8
1903	Cle	AL	2B	557	32	4	592	209	51	14	9	.375	.413	.564	977	24			10	100	1,087	113.2
1904	Cle	AL	2B	572	36	11	619	247	58	18	6	.431	.474	.626	1,099	31			10	50	1,159	139.7
1905	Cle	AL	2B	257	22	3	282	97	14	2	2	.379	.434	.481	915	12			10	70	995	41.6
1906	Cle	AL	2B	625	39	8	671	252	57	11	0	.404	.445	.529	974	21			10	90	1,074	124.3
1907	Cle	AL	2B	526	39	8	573	182	36	7	2	.345	.399	.454	852	25			10	120	982	81.2
1908	Cle	AL	2B	595	63	12	670	203	39	7	2	.341	.415	.443	858	16			10	120	988	96.6
1909	Cle	AL	2B	483	46	8	536	181	39	8	1	.374	.437	.498	935	14			0	80	1,015	84.2
1910	Cle	AL	2B	605	78	7	690	264	59	8	5	.437	.506	.585	1,091	27			0	80	1,171	159.6
1911	Cle	AL	1B	331	28	4	363	122	21	1	2	.370	.426	.460	887	14			0	(10)	877	18.4
1912	Cle	AL	2B	469	31	8	508	179	37	4	0	.382	.429	.479	908	19			0	30	938	61.2
1913	Cle	AL	2B	484	38	17	540	173	28	2	1	.358	.425	.432	856	18			0	50	906	56.9
1914	Cle	AL	2B	436	38	2	477	124	16	3	0	.283	.345	.336	681	15	16	(33)	0	30	677	(1.8)
1915	Phi	AL	2B	514	13	5	531	156	27	6	1	.303	.326	.385	711	11	6	(4)	0	30	738	13.3
1916	Phi	AL	2B	446	17	1	464	120	16	5	2	.270	.298	.342	639	16			0	50	689	0.9
16.4		Totals		10,298	636	160	11,094	3,741	760	189	95					414	22					1,495.2
1.0		Averages		627	39	10	676	228	46	12	6	.363	.409	.501	910	25	1	(2)	6	63	978	91.1

Rogers Hornsby   Cardinals   Second Baseman   Actual

Year	T	L	P	AB	BB	HBP	TAB	H	2B	3B	HR	BA	OB	SA	PRO	SB	CS	SBF	SPF	FF	Actual TF	Actual HC
1915	StL	NL	SS	57	2	0	59	14	2	0	0	.246	.271	.281	552	0	2	(64)	0	0	488	(5.2)
1916	StL	NL	3B	495	40	4	539	155	17	15	6	.313	.369	.444	814	17			0	0	814	26.3
1917	StL	NL	SS	523	45	4	572	171	24	17	8	.327	.385	.484	868	17			0	10	878	62.0
1918	StL	NL	3B	416	40	3	459	117	19	11	5	.281	.349	.416	764	8			0	10	774	16.2
1919	StL	NL	2B	512	48	7	567	163	15	9	8	.318	.384	.430	814	17			0	10	824	43.4
1920	StL	NL	2B	589	60	3	652	218	44	20	9	.370	.431	.559	990	12	15	(26)	0	20	983	97.4
1921	StL	NL	2B	592	60	7	659	235	44	18	21	.397	.458	.639	1,097	13	13	(19)	0	10	1,088	133.0
1922	StL	NL	2B	623	65	1	689	250	46	14	42	.401	.459	.722	1,181	17	12	(10)	0	10	1,181	171.3
1923	StL	NL	2B	424	55	3	482	163	32	10	17	.384	.459	.627	1,086	3	7	(22)	0	(10)	1,054	89.1
1924	StL	NL	2B	536	89	2	627	227	43	14	25	.424	.507	.696	1,203	5	12	(29)	0	0	1,174	153.7
1925	StL	NL	2B	504	83	2	589	203	41	10	39	.403	.489	.756	1,245	5	3	(2)	0	(10)	1,233	161.8
1926	StL	NL	2B	527	61	0	588	167	34	5	11	.317	.388	.463	851	3			0	(30)	821	39.9
1927	NY	NL	2B	568	86	4	658	205	32	9	26	.361	.448	.586	1,035	9			0	20	1,055	121.8
1928	Bos	NL	2B	486	107	1	594	188	42	7	21	.387	.498	.632	1,130	5			0	(20)	1,110	126.4
1929	Chi	NL	2B	602	87	1	690	229	47	8	39	.380	.459	.679	1,139	2			0	0	1,139	156.8
1930	Chi	NL	2B	104	12	1	117	32	5	1	2	.308	.385	.433	817	0			0	(40)	777	5.4
1931	Chi	NL	2B	357	56	0	413	118	37	1	16	.331	.421	.574	996	1			0	(30)	966	58.0
1932	Chi	NL	OF	58	10	2	70	13	2	0	1	.224	.357	.310	667	0			(10)	(30)	627	(4.6)
1933	StL	NL	2B	92	14	2	108	30	7	0	3	.326	.426	.500	926	1			(10)	(80)	836	8.2
1934	StL	AL	3B	23	7	1	31	7	2	0	1	.304	.484	.522	1,006	0	0	0	(10)	0	996	4.3
1935	StL	AL	1B	24	3	0	27	5	3	0	0	.208	.296	.333	630	0	0	0	(10)	0	620	(2.0)
1936	StL	AL	1B	5	1	0	6	2	0	0	0	.400	.500	.400	900	0	0	0	(10)	(10)	880	0.3
1937	StL	AL	2B	56	7	0	63	18	3	0	1	.321	.397	.429	825	0	0	0	(10)	(70)	745	1.9
14.6 Totals				8,173	1,038	48	9,259	2,930	541	169	301					135	64					1,465.7
1.0 Averages				558	71	3	632	200	37	12	21	.358	.434	.577	1,010	9	4	(7)	(0)	(2)	1,001	100.1

Rogers Hornsby   Cardinals   Second Baseman   Adjusted

Year	T	L	P	AB	BB	HBP	TAB	H	2B	3B	HR	BA	OB	SA	Wtd PRO	SB	CS	SBF	SPF	FF	Wtd TF	HC
1915	StL	NL	SS	60	2	0	62	16	2	0	0	.271	.299	.310	609	0	2	(64)	0	0	545	(3.5)
1916	StL	NL	3B	512	50	5	567	179	20	17	7	.350	.412	.496	909	18			0	0	909	52.0
1917	StL	NL	SS	541	56	5	602	197	28	20	9	.365	.429	.539	968	18			0	10	978	90.7
1918	StL	NL	3B	522	59	4	585	162	26	15	7	.311	.386	.460	846	10			0	10	856	38.9
1919	StL	NL	2B	584	63	9	656	202	19	11	10	.347	.419	.468	887	20			0	10	897	66.1
1920	StL	NL	2B	615	67	3	686	237	48	22	10	.385	.448	.581	1,029	13	16	(26)	0	20	1,023	110.2
1921	StL	NL	2B	627	59	7	693	239	45	18	21	.381	.440	.612	1,052	14	14	(19)	0	10	1,043	118.2
1922	StL	NL	2B	662	62	1	725	249	46	14	42	.376	.430	.677	1,107	18	13	(10)	0	10	1,107	145.8
1923	StL	NL	2B	450	54	3	507	166	33	10	17	.368	.439	.601	1,040	3	7	(22)	0	(10)	1,008	78.1
1924	StL	NL	2B	569	89	2	660	233	44	14	26	.410	.491	.674	1,165	5	13	(29)	0	0	1,136	141.7
1925	StL	NL	2B	541	77	2	620	202	41	10	39	.373	.453	.700	1,153	5	3	(2)	0	(10)	1,142	134.7
1926	StL	NL	2B	557	62	0	619	172	35	5	11	.309	.378	.451	829	3			0	(30)	799	33.6
1927	NY	NL	2B	601	87	4	692	211	33	9	27	.351	.437	.571	1,007	9			0	20	1,027	112.8
1928	Bos	NL	2B	520	104	1	625	192	43	7	21	.369	.475	.602	1,076	5			0	(20)	1,056	110.5
1929	Chi	NL	2B	647	78	1	726	222	46	8	38	.343	.414	.613	1,027	2			0	0	1,027	118.1
1930	Chi	NL	2B	112	10	1	123	30	5	1	2	.269	.336	.378	714	0			0	(40)	674	(0.7)
1931	Chi	NL	2B	377	57	0	434	122	38	1	17	.324	.412	.562	975	1			0	(30)	945	53.7
1932	Chi	NL	OF	61	10	2	74	13	2	0	1	.219	.348	.303	651	0			(10)	(30)	611	(5.1)
1933	StL	NL	2B	96	16	2	114	32	8	0	3	.339	.443	.520	963	1			(10)	(80)	873	10.1
1934	StL	AL	3B	25	7	1	33	7	2	0	1	.286	.455	.491	946	0	0	0	(10)	0	936	3.4
1935	StL	AL	1B	25	3	0	28	5	3	0	0	.195	.278	.312	590	0	0	0	(10)	0	580	(2.6)
1936	StL	AL	1B	5	1	0	6	2	0	0	0	.360	.450	.360	810	0	0	0	(10)	(10)	790	0.1
1937	StL	AL	2B	60	6	0	66	18	3	0	1	.295	.364	.393	757	0	0	0	(10)	(70)	677	(0.3)
14.6 Totals				8,771	1,078	54	9,902	3,110	567	183	310					146	67					1,406.7
1.0 Averages				599	74	4	676	212	39	13	21	.355	.428	.567	995	10	5	(7)	(0)	(2)	986	96.0

Eddie Collins　　**White Sox**　　**Second Baseman**　　**Actual**

Year	T	L	P	AB	BB	HBP	TAB	H	2B	3B	HR	BA	OB	SA	PRO	SB	CS	SBF	SPF	FF	Actual TF	Actual HC
1906	Phi	AL	SS	15	0	0	15	3	0	0	0	.200	.200	.200	400	0			10	0	410	(1.9)
1907	Phi	AL	SS	23	0	0	23	8	0	1	0	.348	.348	.435	783	0			10	(50)	743	0.9
1908	Phi	AL	2B	330	16	3	349	90	18	7	1	.273	.312	.379	691	8			10	0	701	2.8
1909	Phi	AL	2B	571	62	6	639	198	30	10	3	.347	.416	.450	866	67			10	70	946	83.6
1910	Phi	AL	2B	581	49	6	636	188	16	15	3	.324	.382	.418	800	81			10	110	920	74.9
1911	Phi	AL	2B	493	62	15	570	180	22	13	3	.365	.451	.481	932	38			10	50	992	87.5
1912	Phi	AL	2B	543	101	0	644	189	25	11	3	.348	.450	.435	885	63			10	70	965	90.3
1913	Phi	AL	2B	534	85	7	626	184	23	13	3	.345	.441	.453	894	55			10	80	984	93.7
1914	Phi	AL	2B	526	97	6	629	181	23	14	2	.344	.452	.452	904	58	30	(3)	10	50	961	86.9
1915	Chi	AL	2B	521	119	5	645	173	22	10	4	.332	.460	.436	896	46	30	(21)	10	70	956	87.4
1916	Chi	AL	2B	545	86	3	634	168	14	17	0	.308	.405	.396	802	40	21	(3)	10	40	849	51.9
1917	Chi	AL	2B	564	89	3	656	163	18	12	0	.289	.389	.363	752	53			10	10	772	28.6
1918	Chi	AL	2B	330	73	0	403	91	8	2	2	.276	.407	.330	737	22			10	30	777	22.5
1919	Chi	AL	2B	518	68	2	588	165	19	7	4	.319	.400	.405	805	33			10	40	855	55.0
1920	Chi	AL	2B	602	69	2	673	224	38	13	3	.372	.438	.493	932	20	8	6	10	60	1,007	108.6
1921	Chi	AL	2B	526	66	2	594	177	20	10	2	.337	.412	.424	836	12	10	(13)	10	80	914	68.0
1922	Chi	AL	2B	598	73	3	674	194	20	12	1	.324	.401	.403	804	20	12	(6)	10	40	848	55.0
1923	Chi	AL	2B	505	84	4	593	182	22	5	5	.360	.455	.453	909	48	29	(16)	10	40	943	76.5
1924	Chi	AL	2B	556	89	3	648	194	27	7	6	.349	.441	.455	896	42	17	12	10	40	958	88.6
1925	Chi	AL	2B	425	87	4	516	147	26	3	3	.346	.461	.442	904	19	6	13	10	20	946	67.5
1926	Chi	AL	2B	375	62	3	440	129	32	4	1	.344	.441	.459	900	13	8	(6)	10	20	923	52.4
1927	Phi	AL	2B	226	56	0	282	76	12	1	1	.336	.468	.412	880	6	2	7	10	(10)	886	28.4
1928	Phi	AL	2B	33	4	0	37	10	3	0	0	.303	.378	.394	772	0	0	0	0	(30)	742	1.1
1929	Phi	AL	PH	7	2	0	9	0	0	0	0	.000	.222	.000	222	0	0	0	0	0	222	(2.1)
1930	Phi	AL	PH	2	0	0	2	1	0	0	0	.500	.500	.500	1,000	0	0	0	0	0	1,000	0.3
18.2 Totals				9,949	1,499	77	11,525	3,315	438	187	47					744	173					1,308.5
1.0 Averages				548	83	4	635	183	24	10	3	.333	.424	.429	853	41	10	(2)	10	48	910	72.1

Eddie Collins　　**White Sox**　　**Second Baseman**　　**Adjusted**

Year	T	L	P	AB	BB	HBP	TAB	H	2B	3B	HR	BA	OB	SA	Wtd PRO	SB	CS	SBF	SPF	FF	Wtd TF	HC
1906	Phi	AL	SS	16	0	0	16	4	0	0	0	.227	.227	.227	455	0			10	0	465	(1.5)
1907	Phi	AL	SS	24	0	0	24	10	0	1	0	.402	.402	.502	904	0			10	(50)	864	2.3
1908	Phi	AL	2B	342	21	4	367	110	22	9	1	.322	.369	.447	816	8			10	0	826	24.6
1909	Phi	AL	2B	582	82	8	672	233	35	12	4	.401	.481	.520	1,001	70			10	70	1,081	126.7
1910	Phi	AL	2B	599	63	8	669	220	19	18	4	.368	.434	.475	910	85			10	110	1,030	109.8
1911	Phi	AL	2B	517	67	16	600	191	23	14	3	.370	.457	.488	945	40			10	50	1,005	91.3
1912	Phi	AL	2B	565	112	0	677	204	27	12	0	.361	.467	.451	917	66			10	70	997	100.7
1913	Phi	AL	2B	551	99	8	659	203	25	14	3	.368	.471	.484	955	58			10	80	1,045	112.8
1914	Phi	AL	2B	536	118	7	662	203	26	16	2	.378	.496	.498	994	61	32	(3)	10	50	1,051	115.3
1915	Chi	AL	2B	531	142	6	679	191	24	11	4	.360	.499	.472	972	48	32	(21)	10	70	1,031	111.8
1916	Chi	AL	2B	560	103	4	667	189	16	19	0	.337	.444	.434	877	42	22	(3)	10	40	924	76.0
1917	Chi	AL	2B	578	108	4	690	185	20	14	0	.320	.430	.402	832	56			10	10	852	54.9
1918	Chi	AL	2B	409	105	0	514	123	11	3	3	.301	.445	.361	806	28			10	30	846	39.3
1919	Chi	AL	2B	597	81	2	680	194	22	8	5	.325	.408	.414	821	38			10	40	871	60.3
1920	Chi	AL	2B	638	68	2	708	228	39	13	3	.358	.422	.474	896	21	8	6	10	60	972	96.6
1921	Chi	AL	2B	561	62	2	625	174	20	10	2	.311	.381	.391	772	13	11	(13)	10	80	849	48.8
1922	Chi	AL	2B	635	71	3	709	195	20	12	1	.307	.379	.381	760	21	13	(6)	10	40	805	40.4
1923	Chi	AL	2B	538	82	4	624	185	22	5	5	.344	.435	.433	868	50	31	(16)	10	40	902	64.4
1924	Chi	AL	2B	594	85	3	682	194	27	7	6	.326	.413	.425	838	44	18	12	10	40	900	69.6
1925	Chi	AL	2B	458	81	4	543	146	26	3	3	.318	.424	.407	831	20	6	13	10	20	873	48.6
1926	Chi	AL	2B	400	60	3	463	131	32	4	1	.327	.419	.436	855	14	8	(6)	10	20	878	42.5
1927	Phi	AL	2B	243	54	0	297	77	12	1	1	.316	.440	.387	827	6	2	7	10	(10)	833	20.9
1928	Phi	AL	2B	35	4	0	39	10	3	0	0	.289	.360	.375	736	0	0	0	0	(30)	706	0.4
1929	Phi	AL	PH	8	2	0	9	0	0	0	0	.000	.207	.000	207	0	0	0	0	0	207	(2.2)
1930	Phi	AL	PH	2	0	0	2	1	0	0	0	.457	.457	.457	914	0	0	0	0	0	914	0.2
18.2 Totals				10,518	1,671	87	12,276	3,600	472	205	51					791	182					1,454.5
1.0 Averages				579	92	5	676	198	26	11	3	.342	.436	.441	877	44	10	(2)	10	48	934	80.1

Joe Morgan   **Reds**   **Second Baseman**   **Actual**

Year	T	L	P	AB	BB	HBP	TAB	H	2B	3B	HR	BA	OB	SA	PRO	SB	CS	SBF	SPF	FF	Actual TF	Actual HC
1963	Hou	NL	2B	25	5	0	30	6	0	1	0	.240	.367	.320	687	1	0	32	10	(90)	638	(0.7)
1964	Hou	NL	2B	37	6	0	43	7	0	0	0	.189	.302	.189	492	0	1	(44)	10	(30)	428	(5.3)
1965	Hou	NL	2B	601	97	3	701	163	22	12	14	.271	.375	.418	793	20	9	3	10	(10)	796	36.8
1966	Hou	NL	2B	425	89	3	517	121	14	8	5	.285	.412	.391	803	11	8	(9)	10	(20)	783	24.2
1967	Hou	NL	2B	494	81	2	577	136	27	11	6	.275	.380	.411	790	29	5	31	10	(10)	822	37.5
1968	Hou	NL	2B	20	7	0	27	5	0	1	0	.250	.444	.350	794	3	0	105	10	(150)	759	1.0
1969	Hou	NL	2B	535	110	1	646	126	18	5	15	.236	.367	.372	739	49	14	31	10	0	780	29.0
1970	Hou	NL	2B	548	102	1	651	147	28	9	8	.268	.384	.396	780	42	13	23	10	20	833	45.9
1971	Hou	NL	2B	583	88	1	672	149	27	11	13	.256	.354	.407	761	40	8	34	10	20	824	44.5
1972	Cin	NL	2B	552	115	6	673	161	23	4	16	.292	.419	.435	854	58	17	34	10	30	928	81.7
1973	Cin	NL	2B	576	111	4	691	167	35	2	26	.290	.408	.493	901	67	15	51	10	40	1,002	104.2
1974	Cin	NL	2B	512	120	3	635	150	31	3	22	.293	.430	.494	924	58	12	51	10	20	1,005	96.6
1975	Cin	NL	2B	498	132	3	633	163	27	6	17	.327	.471	.508	979	67	10	70	10	40	1,099	124.8
1976	Cin	NL	2B	472	114	1	587	151	30	5	27	.320	.453	.576	1,029	60	9	68	10	20	1,127	123.5
1977	Cin	NL	2B	521	117	2	640	150	21	6	22	.288	.420	.478	898	49	10	43	10	30	981	90.2
1978	Cin	NL	2B	441	79	2	522	104	27	0	13	.236	.354	.385	740	19	5	16	10	(10)	756	17.6
1979	Cin	NL	2B	436	93	1	530	109	26	1	9	.250	.383	.376	759	28	6	29	10	10	808	30.9
1980	Hou	NL	2B	461	93	0	554	112	17	5	11	.243	.370	.373	743	24	6	20	10	10	784	25.9
1981	SF	NL	2B	308	66	0	374	74	16	1	8	.240	.374	.377	751	14	5	10	10	10	781	25.8
1982	SF	NL	2B	463	85	2	550	134	19	4	14	.289	.402	.438	840	24	4	27	10	10	888	53.0
1983	Phi	NL	2B	404	89	4	497	93	20	1	16	.230	.374	.403	778	18	2	27	10	0	814	30.6
1984	Oak	AL	2B	365	66	1	432	89	21	0	6	.244	.361	.351	712	8	3	4	0	(70)	646	(8.1)
16.9	Totals			9,277	1,865	40	11,182	2,517	449	96	268					689	162					1,009.7
1.0	Averages			550	111	2	663	149	27	6	16	.271	.395	.427	823	41	10	31	10	9	872	59.8

Joe Morgan   **Reds**   **Second Baseman**   **Adjusted**

Year	T	L	P	AB	BB	HBP	TAB	H	2B	3B	HR	BA	OB	SA	Wtd PRO	SB	CS	SBF	SPF	FF	Wtd TF	HC
1963	Hou	NL	2B	25	5	0	30	6	0	1	0	.252	.386	.337	722	1	0	32	10	(90)	674	(0.2)
1964	Hou	NL	2B	37	6	0	43	7	0	0	0	.194	.311	.194	505	0	1	(44)	10	(30)	441	(5.0)
1965	Hou	NL	2B	597	101	3	701	166	22	12	14	.279	.385	.429	815	20	9	3	10	(10)	817	44.1
1966	Hou	NL	2B	424	90	3	517	122	14	8	5	.288	.416	.394	811	11	8	(9)	10	(20)	791	26.1
1967	Hou	NL	2B	489	86	2	577	141	28	11	6	.288	.397	.430	827	29	5	31	10	(10)	858	47.4
1968	Hou	NL	2B	19	8	0	27	5	0	1	0	.274	.488	.384	872	3	0	105	10	(150)	837	2.0
1969	Hou	NL	2B	532	113	1	646	128	18	5	15	.241	.375	.381	756	49	14	31	10	0	797	34.2
1970	Hou	NL	2B	551	99	1	651	144	27	9	8	.262	.374	.386	761	42	13	23	10	20	814	39.8
1971	Hou	NL	2B	579	92	1	672	153	28	11	13	.263	.365	.419	784	40	8	34	10	20	848	52.0
1972	Cin	NL	2B	574	127	7	708	173	25	4	17	.302	.434	.450	884	61	18	34	10	30	957	91.8
1973	Cin	NL	2B	575	112	4	691	168	35	2	26	.292	.412	.497	909	67	15	51	10	40	1,009	106.7
1974	Cin	NL	2B	509	123	3	635	152	31	3	22	.298	.437	.502	939	58	12	51	10	20	1,019	101.0
1975	Cin	NL	2B	496	134	3	633	164	27	6	17	.331	.476	.514	990	67	10	70	10	40	1,110	128.1
1976	Cin	NL	2B	467	119	1	587	154	31	5	28	.330	.468	.595	1,062	60	9	68	10	20	1,160	132.8
1977	Cin	NL	2B	526	112	2	640	147	21	6	22	.280	.408	.464	872	49	10	43	10	30	955	82.2
1978	Cin	NL	2B	439	81	2	522	105	27	0	13	.240	.360	.392	753	19	5	16	10	(10)	769	20.8
1979	Cin	NL	2B	437	92	1	530	108	26	1	9	.248	.380	.373	753	28	6	29	10	10	801	29.3
1980	Hou	NL	2B	459	95	0	554	113	17	5	11	.246	.375	.378	753	24	6	20	10	10	793	28.5
1981	SF	NL	2B	462	104	0	566	114	25	2	12	.247	.385	.388	773	21	8	10	10	10	803	31.7
1982	SF	NL	2B	461	87	2	550	136	19	4	14	.294	.408	.445	853	24	4	27	10	10	901	56.5
1983	Phi	NL	2B	403	90	4	497	94	20	1	16	.232	.377	.407	784	18	2	27	10	0	821	32.1
1984	Oak	AL	2B	365	66	1	432	89	21	0	6	.245	.363	.352	715	8	3	4	0	(70)	649	(7.5)
16.9	Totals			9,426	1,942	41	11,409	2,590	463	98	276					699	165					1,074.4
1.0	Averages			558	115	2	676	153	27	6	16	.275	.401	.432	833	41	10	31	10	9	882	63.7

Charlie Gehringer Tigers   Second Baseman   Actual

Year	T	L	P	AB	BB	HBP	TAB	H	2B	3B	HR	BA	OB	SA	PRO	SB	CS	SBF	SPF	FF	Actual TF	Actual HC
1924	Det	AL	2B	13	0	1	14	6	0	0	0	.462	.500	.462	962	1	1	(68)	10	60	964	2.0
1925	Det	AL	2B	18	2	0	20	3	0	0	0	.167	.250	.167	417	0	1	(95)	10	90	422	(2.6)
1926	Det	AL	2B	459	30	1	490	127	19	17	1	.277	.322	.399	721	9	7	(10)	10	0	721	8.9
1927	Det	AL	2B	508	52	2	562	161	29	11	4	.317	.383	.441	824	17	8	2	10	60	895	59.1
1928	Det	AL	2B	603	69	6	678	193	29	16	6	.320	.395	.451	846	15	9	(4)	10	20	872	63.5
1929	Det	AL	2B	634	64	6	704	215	45	19	13	.339	.405	.532	936	27	9	12	10	30	988	107.0
1930	Det	AL	2B	610	69	7	686	201	47	15	16	.330	.404	.534	938	19	15	(15)	10	30	963	95.5
1931	Det	AL	2B	383	29	0	412	119	24	5	4	.311	.359	.431	790	13	4	11	10	20	832	30.2
1932	Det	AL	2B	618	68	3	689	184	44	11	19	.298	.370	.497	867	9	8	(10)	10	10	877	66.3
1933	Det	AL	2B	628	68	3	699	204	42	6	12	.325	.393	.468	862	5	4	(4)	10	40	908	77.8
1934	Det	AL	2B	601	99	3	703	214	50	7	11	.356	.450	.517	967	11	8	(7)	0	40	1,000	111.0
1935	Det	AL	2B	610	79	3	692	201	32	8	19	.330	.409	.502	911	11	4	4	0	40	955	93.4
1936	Det	AL	2B	641	83	4	728	227	60	12	15	.354	.431	.555	987	4	1	3	0	70	1,059	136.5
1937	Det	AL	2B	564	90	1	655	209	40	1	14	.371	.458	.520	978	11	4	4	0	50	1,032	113.8
1938	Det	AL	2B	568	113	4	685	174	32	5	20	.306	.425	.486	911	14	1	17	0	20	947	89.9
1939	Det	AL	2B	406	68	1	475	132	29	6	16	.325	.423	.544	967	4	3	(4)	0	30	994	73.4
1940	Det	AL	2B	515	101	3	619	161	33	3	10	.313	.428	.447	875	10	0	15	0	(10)	880	60.4
1941	Det	AL	2B	436	95	3	534	96	19	4	3	.220	.363	.303	666	1	2	(5)	0	10	671	(3.9)
1942	Det	AL	2B	45	7	0	52	12	0	0	1	.267	.365	.333	699	0	0	0	0	30	729	1.1
15.7	Totals			8,860	1,186	51	10,097	2,839	574	146	184					181	89					1,183.1
1.0	Averages			564	75	3	643	181	37	9	12	.320	.404	.480	884	12	6	0	5	30	919	75.3

Charlie Gehringer Tigers   Second Baseman   Adjusted

Year	T	L	P	AB	BB	HBP	TAB	H	2B	3B	HR	BA	OB	SA	Wtd PRO	SB	CS	SBF	SPF	FF	Wtd TF	HC
1924	Det	AL	2B	14	0	1	15	6	0	0	0	.432	.467	.432	899	1	1	(68)	10	60	902	1.5
1925	Det	AL	2B	19	2	0	21	3	0	0	0	.153	.230	.153	383	0	1	(95)	10	90	388	(3.0)
1926	Det	AL	2B	485	29	1	515	128	19	17	1	.263	.306	.379	685	9	7	(10)	10	0	685	0.0
1927	Det	AL	2B	539	50	2	591	161	29	11	4	.298	.360	.414	774	18	8	2	10	60	846	45.2
1928	Det	AL	2B	640	68	6	713	195	29	16	6	.305	.377	.430	806	16	9	(4)	10	20	832	49.9
1929	Det	AL	2B	674	61	6	741	213	45	19	13	.317	.378	.496	874	28	9	12	10	30	926	85.1
1930	Det	AL	2B	651	64	6	722	196	46	15	16	.301	.369	.489	858	20	16	(15)	10	30	883	67.9
1931	Det	AL	2B	405	29	0	433	120	24	5	4	.296	.343	.411	754	14	4	11	10	20	795	22.7
1932	Det	AL	2B	656	66	3	725	184	44	11	19	.280	.348	.468	816	9	8	(10)	10	10	826	48.7
1933	Det	AL	2B	665	68	3	735	208	43	6	12	.313	.379	.451	831	5	4	(4)	10	40	877	67.1
1934	Det	AL	2B	642	95	3	740	215	50	7	11	.335	.423	.487	910	12	8	(7)	0	40	943	90.9
1935	Det	AL	2B	649	76	3	728	201	32	8	19	.309	.383	.470	854	12	4	4	0	40	898	73.7
1936	Det	AL	2B	688	75	4	766	219	58	12	14	.319	.388	.500	888	4	1	3	0	70	961	100.6
1937	Det	AL	2B	605	83	1	689	206	39	1	14	.340	.420	.476	896	12	4	4	0	50	950	87.0
1938	Det	AL	2B	612	105	4	721	171	32	5	20	.280	.388	.444	832	15	1	17	0	20	868	62.8
1939	Det	AL	2B	434	64	1	500	131	29	6	16	.302	.394	.506	900	4	3	(4)	0	30	926	57.3
1940	Det	AL	2B	551	97	3	651	162	33	3	10	.294	.403	.420	823	11	0	15	0	(10)	829	44.4
1941	Det	AL	2B	463	96	3	562	99	20	4	3	.213	.351	.293	644	1	2	(5)	0	10	649	(9.8)
1942	Det	AL	2B	47	8	0	55	13	0	0	1	.274	.376	.343	719	0	0	0	0	30	749	1.7
15.7	Totals			9,440	1,133	49	10,622	2,831	572	145	183					190	94					893.7
1.0	Averages			601	72	3	676	180	36	9	12	.300	.378	.449	827	12	6	0	5	30	862	56.9

Roberto Alomar **Blue Jays** **Second Baseman** **Actual**

Year	T	L	P	AB	BB	HBP	TAB	H	2B	3B	HR	BA	OB	SA	PRO	SB	CS	SBF	SPF	FF	Actual TF	Actual HC
1988	SD	NL	2B	545	47	3	595	145	24	6	9	.266	.328	.382	709	24	6	19	10	50	788	29.2
1989	SD	NL	2B	623	53	1	677	184	27	1	7	.295	.352	.376	727	42	17	11	10	20	768	26.8
1990	SD	NL	2B	586	48	2	636	168	27	5	6	.287	.343	.381	723	24	7	15	10	30	778	28.1
1991	Tor	AL	2B	637	57	4	698	188	41	11	9	.295	.357	.436	793	53	11	42	10	30	875	63.1
1992	Tor	AL	2B	571	87	5	663	177	27	8	8	.310	.406	.427	833	49	9	44	10	40	927	76.4
1993	Tor	AL	2B	589	80	5	674	192	35	6	17	.326	.411	.492	903	55	15	35	10	30	978	94.1
1994	Tor	AL	2B	392	51	2	445	120	25	4	8	.306	.389	.452	840	19	8	6	0	50	897	63.4
1995	Tor	AL	2B	517	47	0	564	155	24	7	13	.300	.358	.449	807	30	3	40	10	50	907	67.1
1996	Bal	AL	2B	588	90	1	679	193	43	4	22	.328	.418	.527	945	17	6	7	10	60	1,022	109.1
1997	Bal	AL	2B	412	40	3	455	137	23	2	14	.333	.396	.500	896	9	3	6	10	40	952	57.8
1998	Bal	AL	2B	588	59	2	649	166	36	1	14	.282	.350	.418	768	18	5	12	10	50	840	47.8
1999	Cle	AL	2B	563	99	7	669	182	40	3	24	.323	.430	.533	963	37	6	35	10	60	1,069	122.2
2000	Cle	AL	2B	610	64	6	680	189	40	2	19	.310	.381	.475	856	39	4	43	10	40	949	85.6
12.3 Totals				7,221	822	41	8,084	2,196	412	60	170					416	100					870.6
1.0 Averages				585	67	3	655	178	33	5	14	.304	.378	.448	827	34	8	25	9	42	904	70.6

Roberto Alomar **Blue Jays** **Second Baseman** **Adjusted**

Year	T	L	P	AB	BB	HBP	TAB	H	2B	3B	HR	BA	OB	SA	Wtd PRO	SB	CS	SBF	SPF	FF	Wtd TF	HC
1988	SD	NL	2B	542	50	3	595	151	25	6	9	.278	.343	.399	742	24	6	19	10	50	821	38.4
1989	SD	NL	2B	620	56	1	677	190	28	1	7	.307	.365	.390	755	42	17	11	10	20	796	35.7
1990	SD	NL	2B	586	48	2	636	168	27	5	6	.286	.342	.380	722	24	7	15	10	30	777	27.8
1991	Tor	AL	2B	637	57	4	698	189	41	11	9	.297	.359	.439	798	53	11	42	10	30	879	64.6
1992	Tor	AL	2B	568	89	5	663	180	27	8	8	.316	.414	.436	849	49	9	44	10	40	944	81.6
1993	Tor	AL	2B	592	77	5	674	188	34	6	17	.318	.401	.481	882	55	15	35	10	30	957	87.1
1994	Tor	AL	2B	562	65	3	630	160	33	5	11	.286	.363	.421	784	27	11	6	0	50	841	46.6
1995	Tor	AL	2B	586	49	0	635	166	26	7	14	.283	.338	.423	761	34	3	40	10	50	861	53.2
1996	Bal	AL	2B	599	79	1	679	180	40	4	21	.300	.383	.482	865	17	6	7	10	60	942	83.0
1997	Bal	AL	2B	416	37	3	455	130	22	2	13	.314	.373	.472	845	9	3	6	10	40	902	46.9
1998	Bal	AL	2B	593	54	2	649	157	34	1	13	.265	.329	.393	722	18	5	12	10	50	794	33.6
1999	Cle	AL	2B	575	88	6	669	171	38	3	23	.298	.397	.491	889	37	6	35	10	60	994	98.3
2000	Cle	AL	2B	618	56	5	680	175	37	2	18	.284	.349	.435	784	39	4	43	10	40	877	62.1
12.3 Totals				7,493	806	40	8,339	2,206	413	61	168					428	104					758.9
1.0 Averages				607	65	3	676	179	33	5	14	.294	.366	.433	799	35	8	25	9	42	876	61.5

Ryne Sandberg   **Cubs**   **Second Baseman**   **Actual**

Year	T	L	P	AB	BB	HBP	TAB	H	2B	3B	HR	BA	OB	SA	PRO	SB	CS	SBF	SPF	FF	Actual TF	Actual HC
1981	Phil	NL	SS	6	0	0	6	1	0	0	0	.167	.167	.167	333	0	0	0	10	90	433	(1.0)
1982	Chi	NL	3B	635	36	4	675	172	33	5	7	.271	.314	.372	686	32	12	11	10	30	737	6.7
1983	Chi	NL	2B	633	51	3	687	165	25	4	8	.261	.319	.351	669	37	11	21	10	90	790	34.3
1984	Chi	NL	2B	636	52	3	691	200	36	19	19	.314	.369	.520	889	32	7	25	10	70	994	101.7
1985	Chi	NL	2B	609	57	1	667	186	31	6	26	.305	.366	.504	870	54	11	45	10	60	985	95.3
1986	Chi	NL	2B	627	46	0	673	178	28	5	14	.284	.333	.411	744	34	11	17	10	60	831	46.8
1987	Chi	NL	2B	523	59	2	584	154	25	2	16	.294	.368	.442	810	21	2	28	10	50	897	59.0
1988	Chi	NL	2B	618	54	1	673	163	23	8	19	.264	.324	.419	743	25	10	7	10	40	800	36.8
1989	Chi	NL	2B	606	59	4	669	176	25	5	30	.290	.357	.497	854	15	5	7	10	40	911	71.9
1990	Chi	NL	2B	615	50	1	666	188	30	3	40	.306	.359	.559	918	25	7	16	10	50	994	97.9
1991	Chi	NL	2B	585	87	2	674	170	32	2	26	.291	.384	.485	870	22	8	8	10	70	958	87.6
1992	Chi	NL	2B	612	68	1	681	186	32	8	26	.304	.374	.510	884	17	6	7	10	30	931	79.8
1993	Chi	NL	2B	456	37	2	495	141	20	0	9	.309	.364	.412	776	9	2	10	10	10	805	28.3
1994	Chi	NL	2B	223	23	1	247	53	9	5	5	.238	.312	.390	702	2	3	(15)	0	20	707	3.5
1996	Chi	NL	2B	554	54	7	615	135	28	4	25	.244	.319	.444	763	12	8	(6)	0	(10)	747	18.0
1997	Chi	NL	2B	447	28	2	477	118	26	0	12	.264	.310	.403	713	7	4	(2)	0	(40)	671	(3.3)
13.7	Totals			8,385	761	34	9,180	2,386	403	76	282					344	107					763.3
1.0	Averages			610	55	2	668	174	29	6	21	.285	.347	.452	798	25	8	13	8	41	861	55.6

Ryne Sandberg   **Cubs**   **Second Baseman**   **Adjusted**

Year	T	L	P	AB	BB	HBP	TAB	H	2B	3B	HR	BA	OB	SA	Wtd PRO	SB	CS	SBF	SPF	FF	Wtd TF	HC
1981	Phil	NL	SS	9	0	0	9	2	0	0	0	.172	.172	.172	343	0	0	0	10	90	443	(0.9)
1982	Chi	NL	3B	634	37	4	675	174	33	5	7	.275	.319	.377	696	32	12	11	10	30	748	10.1
1983	Chi	NL	2B	632	52	3	687	166	25	4	8	.263	.321	.354	675	37	11	21	10	90	796	36.2
1984	Chi	NL	2B	634	54	3	691	204	37	19	19	.321	.377	.532	909	32	7	25	10	70	1,013	108.0
1985	Chi	NL	2B	608	58	1	667	189	31	6	26	.310	.372	.512	884	54	11	45	10	60	999	99.7
1986	Chi	NL	2B	627	46	0	673	178	28	5	14	.285	.334	.413	746	34	11	17	10	60	833	47.4
1987	Chi	NL	2B	526	56	2	584	149	24	2	15	.283	.354	.425	779	21	2	28	10	50	866	50.4
1988	Chi	NL	2B	615	57	1	673	170	24	8	20	.276	.339	.438	777	25	10	7	10	40	834	47.7
1989	Chi	NL	2B	603	62	4	669	182	26	5	31	.301	.371	.516	886	15	5	7	10	40	944	82.3
1990	Chi	NL	2B	615	50	1	666	188	30	3	40	.305	.358	.558	917	25	7	16	10	50	992	97.4
1991	Chi	NL	2B	582	89	2	674	173	33	2	26	.296	.392	.495	887	22	8	8	10	70	976	93.2
1992	Chi	NL	2B	609	71	1	681	190	33	8	27	.313	.385	.525	910	17	6	7	10	30	957	88.1
1993	Chi	NL	2B	458	35	2	495	137	19	0	9	.299	.352	.399	751	9	2	10	10	10	781	22.5
1994	Chi	NL	2B	318	30	1	349	71	12	7	7	.224	.293	.367	661	3	4	(15)	0	20	665	(3.3)
1996	Chi	NL	2B	558	51	7	615	129	27	4	24	.232	.304	.423	727	12	8	(6)	0	(10)	710	7.4
1997	Chi	NL	2B	449	26	2	477	113	25	0	11	.251	.294	.382	677	7	4	(2)	0	(40)	635	(11.5)
13.7	Totals			8,477	774	34	9,286	2,414	407	79	285					345	108					774.6
1.0	Averages			617	56	2	676	176	30	6	21	.285	.347	.452	799	25	8	13	8	41	862	56.4

Fred Dunlap   Cle NL   Second Baseman   Actual

Year	T	L	P	AB	BB	HBP	TAB	H	2B	3B	HR	BA	OB	SA	PRO	SB	CS	SBF	SPF	Actual FF	Actual TF	Actual HC
1880	Cle	NL	2B	373	7	0	380	103	27	9	4	.276	.289	.429	718				0	30	748	21.8
1881	Cle	NL	2B	351	18	0	369	114	25	4	3	.325	.358	.444	802				0	20	822	46.4
1882	Cle	NL	2B	364	23	0	387	102	19	4	0	.280	.323	.354	677				0	60	737	18.4
1883	Cle	NL	2B	396	22	0	418	129	34	2	4	.326	.361	.452	813				0	30	843	51.5
1884	StL	U	2B	449	29	0	478	185	39	8	13	.412	.448	.621	1,069				0	100	1,169	166.8
1885	StL	NL	2B	423	41	0	464	114	11	5	2	.270	.334	.333	667				0	90	757	23.3
1886	StL	NL	2B	481	44	0	525	132	23	5	7	.274	.335	.387	722	20			0	50	772	28.3
1887	Det	NL	2B	272	25	0	297	72	13	10	5	.265	.327	.441	768	15			0	100	868	32.9
1888	Pit	NL	2B	321	16	3	340	84	12	4	1	.262	.303	.333	636	24			0	50	686	0.2
1889	Pit	NL	2B	451	46	2	499	106	19	0	2	.235	.309	.290	599	21			0	0	599	(25.0)
1890	Pit	NL	2B	68	7	1	76	13	1	1	0	.191	.276	.235	512	2			0	(70)	442	(10.6)
1891	Was	AA	2B	25	5	1	31	5	1	1	0	.200	.355	.320	675	3			0	(110)	565	(2.1)
9.6 Totals				3,974	283	7	4,264	1,159	224	53	41					85	0					351.9
1.0 Averages				415	30	1	446	121	23	6	4	.292	.340	.406	745	9	0	0	0	49	794	36.8

Fred Dunlap   Cle NL   Second Baseman   Adjusted

Year	T	L	P	AB	BB	HBP	TAB	H	2B	3B	HR	BA	OB	SA	Wtd PRO	SB	CS	SBF	SPF	FF	Wtd TF	HC
1880	Cle	NL	2B	707	17	0	724	235	62	21	9	.332	.348	.516	864				0	30	894	72.0
1881	Cle	NL	2B	670	42	0	712	245	54	9	6	.366	.403	.500	903				0	20	923	80.6
1882	Cle	NL	2B	689	53	0	742	219	41	9	0	.318	.367	.402	769				0	60	829	50.7
1883	Cle	NL	2B	643	41	0	684	228	60	4	7	.354	.392	.491	883				0	30	913	74.3
1884	StL	U	2B	662	61	0	724	328	69	14	23	.495	.537	.746	1,283				0	100	1,383	240.7
1885	StL	NL	2B	603	74	0	677	189	18	8	3	.314	.389	.388	777				0	90	867	58.8
1886	StL	NL	2B	620	66	0	686	187	33	7	10	.302	.369	.426	795	26			0	50	845	52.2
1887	Det	NL	2B	347	32	0	379	92	17	13	6	.264	.326	.440	767	19			0	100	867	32.7
1888	Pit	NL	2B	377	23	4	405	114	16	5	1	.303	.351	.386	738	29			0	50	788	19.7
1889	Pit	NL	2B	548	57	2	608	131	24	0	2	.239	.314	.296	610	26			0	0	610	(21.7)
1890	Pit	NL	2B	81	9	1	91	16	1	1	0	.201	.291	.248	538	2			0	(70)	468	(9.4)
1891	Was	AA	2B	29	6	1	36	6	1	1	0	.207	.367	.331	698	3			0	(110)	588	(1.7)
9.6 Totals				5,976	482	9	6,467	1,990	395	91	69					105	0					648.9
1.0 Averages				625	50	1	676	208	41	10	7	.333	.384	.464	848	11	0	0	0	49	897	67.8

Hardy Richardson Buf NL   Second Baseman   Actual

Year	T	L	P	AB	BB	HBP	TAB	H	2B	3B	HR	BA	OB	SA	PRO	SB	CS	SBF	SPF	FF	Actual TF	Actual HC
1879	Buf	NL	3B	336	16	0	352	95	18	10	0	.283	.315	.396	711				10	(20)	701	(5.1)
1880	Buf	NL	3B	343	14	0	357	89	18	8	0	.259	.289	.359	647				10	(20)	637	(25.6)
1881	Buf	NL	OF	344	12	0	356	100	18	9	2	.291	.315	.413	727				10	80	817	19.6
1882	Buf	NL	2B	354	11	0	365	96	20	8	2	.271	.293	.390	683				10	60	753	22.6
1883	Buf	NL	2B	399	22	0	421	124	34	7	1	.311	.347	.439	785				10	60	855	55.8
1884	Buf	NL	2B	439	22	0	461	132	27	9	6	.301	.334	.444	778				10	20	808	38.4
1885	Buf	NL	2B	426	20	0	446	136	19	11	6	.319	.350	.458	808				10	40	858	53.4
1886	Det	NL	OF	538	46	0	584	189	27	11	11	.351	.402	.504	906	42			0	20	926	61.3
1887	Det	NL	2B	543	31	2	576	178	25	18	8	.328	.366	.484	851	29			0	40	891	71.9
1888	Det	NL	2B	266	17	1	284	77	18	2	6	.289	.335	.440	774	13			0	20	794	17.6
1889	Bos	NL	2B	536	48	5	589	163	33	10	6	.304	.367	.437	803	47			0	30	833	50.6
1890	Bos	P	OF	555	52	0	607	181	26	14	13	.326	.384	.494	878	42			0	0	878	42.6
1891	Bos	AA	OF	278	40	1	319	71	9	4	7	.255	.351	.392	743	16			0	0	743	(2.5)
1892	NY	NL	2B	285	26	1	312	57	11	5	2	.200	.269	.295	564	16			0	(10)	554	(20.6)
13.0	Totals			5,642	377	10	6,029	1,688	303	126	70					205	0					380.0
1.0	Averages			435	29	1	465	130	23	10	5	.299	.344	.435	779	16	0	0	5	25	809	29.3

Hardy Richardson Buf NL   Second Baseman   Adjusted

Year	T	L	P	AB	BB	HBP	TAB	H	2B	3B	HR	BA	OB	SA	Wtd PRO	SB	CS	SBF	SPF	FF	Wtd TF	HC
1879	Buf	NL	3B	672	41	0	713	224	42	24	0	.333	.372	.466	838				10	(20)	828	38.0
1880	Buf	NL	3B	646	35	0	680	202	41	18	0	.312	.347	.431	778				10	(20)	768	16.9
1881	Buf	NL	OF	659	27	0	687	216	39	19	4	.327	.354	.465	819				10	80	909	49.6
1882	Buf	NL	2B	675	25	0	700	208	43	17	4	.308	.333	.442	775				10	60	845	53.3
1883	Buf	NL	2B	648	41	0	689	219	60	12	2	.338	.377	.476	853				10	60	923	78.0
1884	Buf	NL	2B	618	37	0	655	209	43	14	10	.339	.377	.501	878				10	20	908	69.4
1885	Buf	NL	2B	614	37	0	651	228	32	18	10	.372	.407	.533	941				10	40	991	94.7
1886	Det	NL	OF	693	70	0	763	268	38	16	16	.387	.443	.555	998	55			0	20	1,018	94.7
1887	Det	NL	2B	693	39	3	735	227	32	23	10	.327	.366	.484	849	37			0	40	889	71.4
1888	Det	NL	2B	312	25	1	338	105	24	3	8	.336	.388	.510	898	15			0	20	918	37.4
1889	Bos	NL	2B	651	60	6	717	202	41	12	7	.310	.374	.445	818	57			0	30	848	55.7
1890	Bos	P	OF	684	61	0	745	216	31	17	16	.316	.372	.478	850	52			0	0	850	32.8
1891	Bos	AA	OF	319	48	1	369	84	11	5	8	.264	.363	.406	769	19			0	0	769	2.1
1892	NY	NL	2B	297	31	1	329	65	13	6	2	.219	.295	.323	618	17			0	(10)	608	(12.1)
13.0	Totals			8,181	578	13	8,771	2,672	490	204	97					252	0					681.7
1.0	Averages			630	45	1	676	206	38	16	8	.327	.372	.472	844	19	0	0	5	25	875	52.5

Jackie Robinson   Dodgers   Second Baseman   Actual

Year	T	L	P	AB	BB	HBP	TAB	H	2B	3B	HR	BA	OB	SA	PRO	SB	CS	SBF	SPF	FF	Actual TF	Actual HC
1947	Bkn	NL	1B	590	74	9	673	175	31	5	12	.297	.383	.427	810	29			10	10	830	20.4
1948	Bkn	NL	2B	574	57	7	638	170	38	8	12	.296	.367	.453	820	22			10	30	860	55.8
1949	Bkn	NL	2B	593	86	8	687	203	38	12	16	.342	.432	.528	960	37			10	20	990	105.0
1950	Bkn	NL	2B	518	80	5	603	170	39	4	14	.328	.423	.500	923	12			10	40	973	86.9
1951	Bkn	NL	2B	548	79	9	636	185	33	7	19	.338	.429	.527	957	25	8	13	10	50	1,030	109.9
1952	Bkn	NL	2B	510	106	14	630	157	17	3	19	.308	.440	.465	904	24	7	15	10	20	949	83.4
1953	Bkn	NL	OF	484	74	7	565	159	34	7	12	.329	.425	.502	927	17	4	15	10	10	962	57.9
1954	Bkn	NL	OF	386	63	7	456	120	22	4	15	.311	.417	.505	922	7	3	2	10	0	934	40.3
1955	Bkn	NL	3B	317	61	3	381	81	6	2	8	.256	.381	.363	743	12	3	15	10	20	788	13.8
1956	Bkn	NL	3B	357	60	3	420	98	15	2	10	.275	.383	.412	795	12	5	5	10	40	850	28.1
8.9		Totals		4,877	740	72	5,689	1,518	273	54	137					197	30					601.4
1.0		Averages		551	84	8	643	171	31	6	15	.311	.410	.474	883	22	3	6	10	24	924	67.9

Jackie Robinson   Dodgers   Second Baseman   Adjusted

Year	T	L	P	AB	BB	HBP	TAB	H	2B	3B	HR	BA	OB	SA	Wtd PRO	SB	CS	SBF	SPF	FF	Wtd TF	HC
1947	Bkn	NL	1B	625	74	9	708	179	32	5	12	.287	.371	.414	785	31			10	10	805	11.7
1948	Bkn	NL	2B	605	59	7	671	177	40	8	12	.292	.362	.447	809	23			10	30	849	52.4
1949	Bkn	NL	2B	627	87	8	723	210	39	12	17	.334	.422	.515	937	39			10	20	967	97.1
1950	Bkn	NL	2B	550	79	5	634	173	40	4	14	.314	.405	.479	884	13			10	40	934	75.1
1951	Bkn	NL	2B	579	81	9	669	191	34	7	20	.331	.420	.516	937	26	8	13	10	50	1,010	103.5
1952	Bkn	NL	2B	534	114	15	663	167	18	3	20	.312	.445	.471	916	25	7	15	10	20	961	87.0
1953	Bkn	NL	OF	516	72	7	594	160	34	7	12	.310	.401	.474	876	18	4	15	10	10	911	43.5
1954	Bkn	NL	OF	412	61	7	480	121	22	4	15	.295	.395	.479	873	7	3	2	10	0	886	29.3
1955	Bkn	NL	3B	337	61	3	401	83	6	2	8	.245	.365	.347	712	13	3	15	10	20	757	7.8
1956	Bkn	NL	3B	378	61	3	442	101	15	2	10	.267	.373	.401	774	13	5	5	10	40	829	23.7
8.9		Totals		5,163	748	73	5,985	1,562	280	56	141					207	32					531.1
1.0		Averages		583	84	8	676	176	32	6	16	.302	.398	.460	858	23	4	6	10	24	899	60.0

Honus Wagner   **Pirates**   **Shortstop**   **Actual**

Year	T	L	P	AB	BB	HBP	TAB	H	2B	3B	HR	BA	OB	SA	PRO	SB	CS	SBF	SPF	FF	Actual TF	Actual HC
1897	Lou	NL	OF	237	15	1	253	80	17	4	2	.338	.379	.468	848	19			10	20	878	17.4
1898	Lou	NL	1B	588	31	6	625	176	29	3	10	.299	.341	.410	751	27			10	0	761	(2.9)
1899	Lou	NL	3B	571	40	11	622	192	43	13	7	.336	.391	.494	885	37			10	20	915	62.0
1900	Pit	NL	OF	527	41	8	576	201	45	22	4	.381	.434	.573	1,007	38			10	20	1,037	88.8
1901	Pit	NL	SS	549	53	6	608	194	37	11	6	.353	.416	.494	910	49			10	50	970	103.1
1902	Pit	NL	OF	534	43	14	591	176	30	16	3	.330	.394	.463	857	42			10	40	907	48.7
1903	Pit	NL	SS	512	44	7	563	182	30	19	5	.355	.414	.518	931	46			10	80	1,021	111.6
1904	Pit	NL	SS	490	59	4	553	171	44	14	4	.349	.423	.520	944	53			10	30	984	89.1
1905	Pit	NL	SS	548	54	7	609	199	32	14	6	.363	.427	.505	932	57			10	70	1,012	106.9
1906	Pit	NL	SS	516	58	10	584	175	38	9	2	.339	.416	.459	875	53			10	80	965	88.8
1907	Pit	NL	SS	515	46	5	566	180	38	14	6	.350	.408	.513	921	61			10	40	971	87.6
1908	Pit	NL	SS	568	54	5	627	201	39	19	10	.354	.415	.542	957	53			10	40	1,007	108.4
1909	Pit	NL	SS	495	66	3	564	168	39	10	5	.339	.420	.489	909	35			10	50	969	86.8
1910	Pit	NL	SS	556	59	5	620	178	34	8	4	.320	.390	.432	822	24			10	30	862	62.1
1911	Pit	NL	SS	473	67	6	546	158	23	16	9	.334	.423	.507	930	20			10	30	970	84.4
1912	Pit	NL	SS	558	59	6	623	181	35	20	7	.324	.395	.496	891	26			10	80	981	99.7
1913	Pit	NL	SS	413	26	5	444	124	18	4	3	.300	.349	.385	734	21			10	60	804	31.6
1914	Pit	NL	SS	552	51	2	605	139	15	9	1	.252	.317	.317	634	23			10	40	684	6.8
1915	Pit	NL	SS	566	39	4	609	155	32	17	6	.274	.325	.422	747	22	15	(12)	10	30	775	34.5
1916	Pit	NL	SS	432	34	8	474	124	15	9	1	.287	.350	.370	721	11			0	0	721	13.9
1917	Pit	NL	1B	230	24	1	255	61	7	1	0	.265	.337	.304	642	5			0	(10)	632	(17.7)
18.3 Totals				10,430	963	124	11,517	3,415	640	252	101					722	15					1,311.7
1.0 Averages				568	52	7	628	186	35	14	6	.327	.391	.466	857	39	1	(1)	9	40	906	71.5

Honus Wagner   **Pirates**   **Shortstop**   **Adjusted**

Year	T	L	P	AB	BB	HBP	TAB	H	2B	3B	HR	BA	OB	SA	Wtd PRO	SB	CS	SBF	SPF	FF	Wtd TF	HC
1897	Lou	NL	OF	286	17	1	304	92	20	5	2	.322	.361	.446	808	23			10	20	838	11.6
1898	Lou	NL	1B	618	34	7	660	192	32	3	11	.310	.353	.425	778	28			10	0	788	5.7
1899	Lou	NL	3B	603	42	12	656	202	45	14	7	.334	.388	.491	879	39			10	20	909	60.4
1900	Pit	NL	OF	610	48	9	667	233	52	25	5	.382	.435	.574	1,008	44			10	20	1,038	89.2
1901	Pit	NL	SS	629	67	8	704	235	45	13	7	.373	.439	.521	960	57			10	50	1,020	120.0
1902	Pit	NL	OF	606	59	19	684	223	38	20	4	.369	.441	.517	958	49			10	40	1,008	81.8
1903	Pit	NL	SS	589	54	9	651	218	36	23	6	.370	.430	.538	968	53			10	80	1,058	123.0
1904	Pit	NL	SS	502	75	5	582	197	51	16	5	.392	.476	.585	1,061	56			10	30	1,101	121.6
1905	Pit	NL	SS	567	65	8	641	225	36	16	7	.396	.466	.551	1,017	60			10	70	1,097	132.9
1906	Pit	NL	SS	527	75	13	614	203	44	10	2	.386	.474	.523	997	56			10	80	1,087	124.3
1907	Pit	NL	SS	529	60	7	595	212	45	16	7	.401	.468	.587	1,055	64			10	40	1,105	125.7
1908	Pit	NL	SS	580	73	7	660	239	46	23	12	.413	.484	.633	1,117	56			10	40	1,167	158.5
1909	Pit	NL	SS	505	84	4	593	194	45	12	6	.384	.475	.553	1,028	37			10	50	1,088	120.5
1910	Pit	NL	SS	579	68	6	652	196	38	9	4	.339	.414	.458	871	25			10	30	911	77.4
1911	Pit	NL	SS	495	73	7	574	169	25	17	10	.341	.432	.518	951	21			10	30	991	89.9
1912	Pit	NL	SS	588	62	6	655	189	37	21	7	.322	.393	.494	886	27			10	80	976	98.1
1913	Pit	NL	SS	433	29	6	467	135	20	4	3	.312	.363	.400	763	22			10	60	833	38.1
1914	Pit	NL	SS	574	60	2	636	157	17	10	1	.273	.344	.344	688	24			10	40	738	23.0
1915	Pit	NL	SS	589	47	5	641	178	37	20	7	.302	.359	.466	824	23	16	(12)	10	30	852	58.0
1916	Pit	NL	SS	447	42	10	499	143	17	10	1	.321	.391	.414	805	12			0	0	805	33.9
1917	Pit	NL	1B	238	29	1	268	70	8	1	0	.296	.376	.339	715	5			0	(10)	705	(8.2)
18.3 Totals				11,091	1,162	150	12,403	3,902	732	289	114					781	16					1,685.4
1.0 Averages				605	63	8	676	213	40	16	6	.352	.420	.501	921	43	1	(1)	9	40	970	91.9

Barry Larkin   **Reds**   **Shortstop**   **Actual**

Year	T	L	P	AB	BB	HBP	TAB	H	2B	3B	HR	BA	OB	SA	PRO	SB	CS	SBF	SPF	FF	Actual TF	Actual HC
1986	Cin	NL	SS	159	9	0	168	45	4	3	3	.283	.321	.403	724	8	0	45	10	0	779	9.4
1987	Cin	NL	SS	439	36	5	480	107	16	2	12	.244	.308	.371	680	21	6	18	10	0	707	10.4
1988	Cin	NL	SS	588	41	8	637	174	32	5	12	.296	.350	.429	779	40	7	39	10	30	857	59.2
1989	Cin	NL	SS	325	20	2	347	111	14	4	4	.342	.383	.446	829	10	5	0	10	90	929	44.2
1990	Cin	NL	SS	614	49	7	670	185	25	6	7	.301	.360	.396	755	30	5	28	10	60	854	61.2
1991	Cin	NL	SS	464	55	3	522	140	27	4	20	.302	.379	.506	886	24	6	22	10	70	988	80.9
1992	Cin	NL	SS	533	63	4	600	162	32	6	12	.304	.382	.454	836	15	4	11	10	40	897	67.1
1993	Cin	NL	SS	384	51	1	436	121	20	3	8	.315	.397	.445	842	14	1	26	10	20	898	49.0
1994	Cin	NL	SS	427	64	0	491	119	23	5	9	.279	.373	.419	792	26	2	42	10	40	884	73.6
1995	Cin	NL	SS	496	61	3	560	158	29	6	15	.319	.396	.492	888	51	5	69	10	30	998	100.7
1996	Cin	NL	SS	517	96	7	620	154	32	4	33	.298	.415	.567	981	36	10	24	10	40	1,056	116.3
1997	Cin	NL	SS	224	47	3	274	71	17	3	4	.317	.442	.473	915	14	3	28	10	20	972	40.5
1998	Cin	NL	SS	538	79	2	619	166	34	10	17	.309	.399	.504	903	26	3	31	10	(10)	933	80.0
1999	Cin	NL	SS	583	93	2	678	171	30	4	12	.293	.392	.420	813	30	8	20	10	(10)	832	54.9
2000	Cin	NL	SS	396	48	1	445	124	26	5	11	.313	.389	.487	876	14	6	4	10	(10)	880	46.3
11.6	Totals			6,687	812	48	7,547	2,008	361	70	179					359	71					893.8
1.0	Averages			578	70	4	652	174	31	6	15	.300	.380	.456	836	31	6	27	9	29	901	77.3

Barry Larkin   **Reds**   **Shortstop**   **Adjusted**

Year	T	L	P	AB	BB	HBP	TAB	H	2B	3B	HR	BA	OB	SA	Wtd PRO	SB	CS	SBF	SPF	FF	Wtd TF	HC
1986	Cin	NL	SS	159	9	0	168	45	4	3	3	.284	.322	.404	726	8	0	45	10	0	781	9.5
1987	Cin	NL	SS	441	34	5	480	103	15	2	12	.234	.297	.357	654	21	6	18	10	0	681	4.4
1988	Cin	NL	SS	585	44	9	637	181	33	5	12	.309	.366	.448	814	40	7	39	10	30	893	70.1
1989	Cin	NL	SS	324	21	2	347	115	14	4	4	.355	.398	.463	861	10	5	0	10	90	961	49.4
1990	Cin	NL	SS	614	49	7	670	185	25	6	7	.301	.359	.395	754	30	5	28	10	60	853	60.8
1991	Cin	NL	SS	462	57	3	522	142	27	4	20	.308	.387	.517	904	24	6	22	10	70	1,005	85.4
1992	Cin	NL	SS	530	66	4	600	166	33	6	12	.313	.393	.467	860	15	4	11	10	40	921	74.0
1993	Cin	NL	SS	386	49	1	436	118	19	3	8	.305	.384	.431	815	14	1	26	10	20	871	43.5
1994	Cin	NL	SS	611	83	0	695	160	31	7	12	.262	.351	.395	745	37	3	42	10	40	838	58.1
1995	Cin	NL	SS	563	64	3	630	171	31	6	16	.303	.378	.469	846	57	6	69	10	30	955	88.1
1996	Cin	NL	SS	524	90	7	620	149	31	4	32	.284	.395	.540	935	36	10	24	10	40	1,009	102.5
1997	Cin	NL	SS	228	44	3	274	68	16	3	4	.301	.419	.449	868	14	3	28	10	20	926	34.4
1998	Cin	NL	SS	544	74	2	619	160	33	10	16	.294	.380	.479	859	26	3	31	10	(10)	890	67.1
1999	Cin	NL	SS	594	82	2	678	159	28	4	11	.268	.359	.384	743	30	8	20	10	(10)	763	32.6
2000	Cin	NL	SS	402	42	1	445	115	24	5	10	.286	.355	.445	799	14	6	4	10	(10)	804	30.0
11.6	Totals			6,967	806	48	7,821	2,037	366	71	180					376	72					810.1
1.0	Averages			602	70	4	676	176	32	6	16	.292	.370	.443	813	33	6	28	9	29	879	70.0

Bill Dahlen **Dodgers** **Shortstop** **Actual**

Year	T	L	P	AB	BB	HBP	TAB	H	2B	3B	HR	BA	OB	SA	PRO	SB	CS	SBF	SPF	FF	Actual TF	Actual HC
1891	Chi	NL	3B	549	67	7	623	143	18	13	9	.260	.348	.390	738	21			10	20	768	18.1
1892	Chi	NL	SS	581	45	5	631	169	23	19	5	.291	.347	.422	769	60			10	60	839	56.1
1893	Chi	NL	SS	485	58	5	548	146	28	15	5	.301	.381	.452	833	31			10	20	863	64.9
1894	Chi	NL	SS	502	76	3	581	179	32	14	15	.357	.444	.566	1,010	42			10	80	1,100	148.7
1895	Chi	NL	SS	516	61	10	587	131	19	10	7	.254	.344	.370	714	38			10	90	814	51.9
1896	Chi	NL	SS	474	64	8	546	167	30	19	9	.352	.438	.553	990	51			10	70	1,070	130.4
1897	Chi	NL	SS	276	43	7	326	80	18	8	6	.290	.399	.478	877	15			10	120	1,007	64.3
1898	Chi	NL	SS	521	58	23	602	151	35	8	1	.290	.385	.393	779	27			10	60	849	56.6
1899	Bkn	NL	SS	428	67	15	510	121	22	7	4	.283	.398	.395	793	29			10	80	883	56.6
1900	Bkn	NL	SS	483	73	7	563	125	16	11	1	.259	.364	.344	708	31			10	50	768	32.8
1901	Bkn	NL	SS	511	30	5	546	136	17	9	4	.266	.313	.358	671	23			10	30	711	14.8
1902	Bkn	NL	SS	527	43	8	578	139	25	8	2	.264	.329	.353	682	20			10	10	702	12.6
1903	Bkn	NL	SS	474	82	2	558	124	17	9	1	.262	.373	.342	715	34			10	60	785	37.7
1904	NY	NL	SS	523	44	1	568	140	26	2	2	.268	.326	.337	662	47			10	40	712	14.3
1905	NY	NL	SS	520	62	12	594	126	20	4	7	.242	.337	.337	673	37			10	30	713	15.3
1906	NY	NL	SS	471	76	10	557	113	18	3	1	.240	.357	.297	655	16			10	10	675	3.5
1907	NY	NL	SS	464	51	4	519	96	20	1	0	.207	.291	.254	545	11			10	20	575	(22.6)
1908	Bos	NL	SS	524	35	8	567	125	23	2	3	.239	.296	.307	604	10			0	70	674	3.3
1909	Bos	NL	SS	197	29	0	226	46	6	1	2	.234	.332	.305	636	4			0	40	676	1.6
1910	Bkn	NL	PH	2	0	0	2	0	0	0	0	.000	.000	.000	0	0			0	0	0	(0.7)
1911	Bkn	NL	SS	3	0	0	3	0	0	0	0	.000	.000	.000	0	0			0	50	50	(0.9)
17.1	Totals			9,031	1,064	140	10,235	2,457	413	163	84					547	0					759.4
1.0	Averages			530	62	8	600	144	24	10	5	.272	.358	.382	739	32	0	0	9	50	798	44.5

Bill Dahlen **Dodgers** **Shortstop** **Adjusted**

Year	T	L	P	AB	BB	HBP	TAB	H	2B	3B	HR	BA	OB	SA	Wtd PRO	SB	CS	SBF	SPF	FF	Wtd TF	HC
1891	Chi	NL	3B	637	85	9	731	176	22	16	11	.276	.369	.413	781	25			10	20	811	33.1
1892	Chi	NL	SS	606	54	6	666	193	26	22	6	.319	.380	.462	843	63			10	60	913	79.5
1893	Chi	NL	SS	604	68	6	678	174	33	18	6	.289	.366	.433	799	38			10	20	829	53.9
1894	Chi	NL	SS	635	75	3	713	196	35	15	16	.309	.385	.491	876	52			10	80	966	103.2
1895	Chi	NL	SS	637	67	11	715	150	22	11	8	.235	.319	.343	663	46			10	90	763	34.3
1896	Chi	NL	SS	588	73	9	670	197	35	22	11	.336	.417	.527	944	63			10	70	1,024	115.4
1897	Chi	NL	SS	335	48	8	391	93	21	9	7	.276	.380	.456	835	18			10	120	965	56.6
1898	Chi	NL	SS	545	64	26	635	164	38	9	1	.300	.399	.408	807	28			10	60	877	65.2
1899	Bkn	NL	SS	452	70	16	538	127	23	7	4	.281	.396	.393	788	31			10	80	878	55.5
1900	Bkn	NL	SS	559	85	8	651	145	19	13	1	.259	.365	.344	709	36			10	50	769	33.1
1901	Bkn	NL	SS	588	37	6	632	165	21	11	5	.281	.330	.378	708	27			10	30	748	26.0
1902	Bkn	NL	SS	600	58	11	669	177	32	10	3	.295	.368	.395	763	23			10	10	783	38.4
1903	Bkn	NL	SS	543	100	2	646	148	20	11	1	.272	.388	.355	743	39			10	60	813	46.4
1904	NY	NL	SS	542	54	1	598	163	30	2	2	.301	.366	.378	744	49			10	40	794	37.7
1905	NY	NL	SS	537	73	14	625	142	23	5	8	.264	.367	.367	735	39			10	30	775	33.5
1906	NY	NL	SS	478	95	13	586	131	21	3	1	.273	.407	.338	745	17			10	10	765	28.8
1907	NY	NL	SS	477	64	5	546	113	24	1	0	.237	.333	.291	625	12			10	20	655	(1.9)
1908	Bos	NL	SS	541	45	10	596	151	28	2	4	.278	.346	.358	704	11			0	70	774	31.9
1909	Bos	NL	SS	202	36	0	238	53	7	1	2	.264	.375	.345	720	4			0	40	760	11.1
1910	Bkn	NL	PH	2	0	0	2	0	0	0	0	.000	.000	.000	0	0			0	0	0	(0.7)
1911	Bkn	NL	SS	3	0	0	3	0	0	0	0	.000	.000	.000	0	0			0	50	50	(0.9)
17.1	Totals			10,112	1,253	164	11,529	2,858	479	190	97					620	0					880.0
1.0	Averages			593	73	10	676	168	28	11	6	.283	.371	.396	767	36	0	0	9	50	826	51.6

Arky Vaughan   **Pirates**   **Shortstop**   **Actual**

Year	T	L	P	AB	BB	HBP	TAB	H	2B	3B	HR	BA	OB	SA	PRO	SB	CS	SBF	SPF	FF	Actual TF	Actual HC
1932	Pit	NL	SS	497	39	6	542	158	15	10	4	.318	.375	.412	787	10			10	(40)	757	25.8
1933	Pit	NL	SS	573	64	5	642	180	29	19	9	.314	.388	.478	866	3			10	(20)	856	62.4
1934	Pit	NL	SS	558	94	2	654	186	41	11	12	.333	.431	.511	942	10			10	0	952	95.0
1935	Pit	NL	SS	499	97	7	603	192	34	10	19	.385	.491	.607	1,098	4			10	(10)	1,098	131.8
1936	Pit	NL	SS	568	118	5	691	190	30	11	9	.335	.453	.474	927	6			10	(20)	917	88.2
1937	Pit	NL	SS	469	54	2	525	151	17	17	5	.322	.394	.463	857	7			10	0	867	53.9
1938	Pit	NL	SS	541	104	2	647	174	35	5	7	.322	.433	.444	876	14			10	20	906	79.2
1939	Pit	NL	SS	595	70	6	671	182	30	11	6	.306	.385	.424	808	12			10	20	838	59.2
1940	Pit	NL	SS	594	88	3	685	178	40	15	7	.300	.393	.453	846	12			10	10	866	69.9
1941	Pit	NL	SS	374	50	2	426	118	20	7	6	.316	.399	.455	854	8			10	(10)	854	40.9
1942	Bkn	NL	3B	495	51	3	549	137	18	4	2	.277	.348	.341	689	8			10	(20)	679	(10.1)
1943	Bkn	NL	SS	610	60	3	673	186	39	6	5	.305	.370	.413	783	20			10	(40)	753	30.7
1947	Bkn	NL	OF	126	27	0	153	41	5	2	2	.325	.444	.444	889	4			10	10	909	11.6
1948	Bkn	NL	OF	123	21	0	144	30	3	0	3	.244	.354	.341	696	0			10	10	716	(3.0)
11.8 Totals				6,622	937	46	7,605	2,103	356	128	96					118	0					735.6
1.0 Averages				560	79	4	643	178	30	11	8	.318	.406	.453	859	10	0	0	10	(8)	861	62.2

Arky Vaughan   **Pirates**   **Shortstop**   **Adjusted**

Year	T	L	P	AB	BB	HBP	TAB	H	2B	3B	HR	BA	OB	SA	Wtd PRO	SB	CS	SBF	SPF	FF	Wtd TF	HC
1932	Pit	NL	SS	525	40	6	570	163	15	10	4	.310	.365	.402	767	11			10	(40)	737	20.5
1933	Pit	NL	SS	598	71	6	675	195	31	21	10	.327	.403	.497	900	3			10	(20)	890	73.5
1934	Pit	NL	SS	591	95	2	688	191	42	11	12	.324	.419	.496	915	11			10	0	925	86.1
1935	Pit	NL	SS	529	98	7	634	199	35	10	20	.376	.480	.594	1,074	4			10	(10)	1,074	124.4
1936	Pit	NL	SS	602	120	5	727	197	31	11	9	.327	.443	.463	906	6			10	(20)	896	81.0
1937	Pit	NL	SS	494	56	2	552	157	18	18	5	.318	.390	.457	847	7			10	0	857	51.4
1938	Pit	NL	SS	569	110	2	681	183	37	5	7	.322	.433	.444	878	15			10	20	908	79.6
1939	Pit	NL	SS	628	71	6	706	188	31	11	6	.299	.376	.415	791	13			10	20	821	53.5
1940	Pit	NL	SS	624	93	3	721	188	42	16	7	.301	.395	.455	850	13			10	10	870	71.5
1941	Pit	NL	SS	391	55	2	448	127	21	8	6	.324	.409	.466	876	8			10	(10)	876	45.6
1942	Bkn	NL	3B	515	59	3	578	152	20	4	2	.296	.372	.365	736	8			10	(20)	726	2.7
1943	Bkn	NL	SS	637	68	3	708	204	43	7	5	.320	.389	.434	823	21			10	(40)	793	44.1
1947	Bkn	NL	OF	134	27	0	161	42	5	2	2	.315	.430	.430	861	4			10	10	881	9.5
1948	Bkn	NL	OF	130	22	0	151	31	3	0	3	.241	.350	.337	687	0			10	10	707	(3.7)
11.8 Totals				6,968	984	48	8,000	2,218	376	135	101					124	0					739.6
1.0 Averages				589	83	4	676	187	32	11	9	.318	.406	.454	861	10	0	0	10	(8)	863	62.5

George Davis NY NL Shortstop Actual

Year	T	L	P	AB	BB	HBP	TAB	H	2B	3B	HR	BA	OB	SA	PRO	SB	CS	SBF	SPF	FF	Actual TF	Actual HC
1890	Cle	NL	OF	526	53	4	583	139	22	9	6	.264	.336	.375	711	22			10	30	751	(2.2)
1891	Cle	NL	OF	570	53	4	627	165	35	12	3	.289	.354	.409	763	42			10	30	803	15.9
1892	Cle	NL	3B	597	58	3	658	144	27	12	5	.241	.312	.352	663	36			10	0	673	(14.2)
1893	NY	NL	3B	549	42	9	600	195	22	27	11	.355	.410	.554	964	37			10	10	984	94.6
1894	NY	NL	3B	477	66	4	547	168	26	19	8	.352	.435	.537	972	40			10	10	992	88.1
1895	NY	NL	3B	430	55	2	487	146	36	9	5	.340	.417	.500	917	48			10	50	977	73.7
1896	NY	NL	3B	494	50	4	548	158	25	12	5	.320	.387	.449	836	48			10	40	886	54.5
1897	NY	NL	SS	519	41	6	566	183	31	10	10	.353	.406	.509	915	65			10	60	985	104.5
1898	NY	NL	SS	486	32	1	519	149	20	5	2	.307	.351	.381	731	26			10	100	841	46.8
1899	NY	NL	SS	416	37	2	455	140	21	5	1	.337	.393	.418	812	34			10	140	962	68.6
1900	NY	NL	SS	426	35	4	465	136	20	4	3	.319	.376	.406	782	29			10	50	842	46.3
1901	NY	NL	SS	491	40	2	533	148	26	7	7	.301	.356	.426	782	27			10	40	832	50.0
1902	Chi	AL	SS	485	65	4	554	145	27	7	3	.299	.386	.402	788	31			10	20	818	47.7
1903	NY	NL	SS	15	1	0	16	4	0	0	0	.267	.313	.267	579	0			10	(90)	499	(1.4)
1904	Chi	AL	SS	563	43	5	611	142	27	15	1	.252	.311	.359	670	32			10	30	710	14.6
1905	Chi	AL	SS	550	60	4	614	153	29	1	1	.278	.353	.340	693	31			10	50	753	28.1
1906	Chi	AL	SS	484	41	4	529	134	26	6	0	.277	.338	.355	694	27			10	30	734	19.0
1907	Chi	AL	SS	466	47	4	517	111	16	2	1	.238	.313	.288	601	15			10	20	631	(8.1)
1908	Chi	AL	2B	419	41	7	467	91	14	1	0	.217	.298	.255	553	22			10	10	573	(26.3)
1909	Chi	AL	1B	68	10	1	79	9	1	0	0	.132	.253	.147	400	4			0	20	420	(13.8)
16.7	Totals			9,031	870	74	9,975	2,660	451	163	72					616	0					686.4
1.0	Averages			541	52	4	597	159	27	10	4	.295	.361	.404	766	37	0	0	10	38	813	41.1

George Davis NY NL Shortstop Adjusted

Year	T	L	P	AB	BB	HBP	TAB	H	2B	3B	HR	BA	OB	SA	Wtd PRO	SB	CS	SBF	SPF	FF	Wtd TF	HC
1890	Cle	NL	OF	626	68	5	700	174	28	11	8	.278	.354	.394	748	26			10	30	788	10.1
1891	Cle	NL	OF	664	67	5	736	203	43	15	4	.306	.375	.433	807	49			10	30	847	31.5
1892	Cle	NL	3B	622	69	4	694	164	31	14	6	.264	.341	.386	727	38			10	0	737	6.9
1893	NY	NL	3B	683	49	10	742	233	26	32	13	.341	.393	.531	924	46			10	10	944	80.6
1894	NY	NL	3B	602	66	4	671	184	28	21	9	.305	.377	.465	843	49			10	10	863	46.9
1895	NY	NL	3B	531	60	2	593	167	41	10	6	.315	.387	.464	850	58			10	50	910	54.9
1896	NY	NL	3B	611	57	5	673	186	29	14	6	.305	.369	.428	797	59			10	40	847	41.8
1897	NY	NL	SS	627	46	7	679	211	36	12	12	.336	.387	.485	872	78			10	60	942	90.5
1898	NY	NL	SS	511	36	1	548	162	22	5	2	.318	.363	.395	758	27			10	100	868	53.8
1899	NY	NL	SS	439	39	2	480	147	22	5	1	.335	.391	.416	807	36			10	140	957	67.5
1900	NY	NL	SS	493	41	5	538	158	23	5	3	.320	.377	.407	783	34			10	50	843	46.5
1901	NY	NL	SS	564	50	3	617	179	32	8	8	.318	.376	.449	825	31			10	40	875	62.7
1902	Chi	AL	SS	560	76	5	641	169	31	8	3	.301	.390	.405	795	36			10	20	825	49.8
1903	NY	NL	SS	17	1	0	19	5	0	0	0	.277	.325	.277	602	0			10	(90)	522	(1.2)
1904	Chi	AL	SS	582	55	6	643	168	32	18	1	.289	.356	.411	768	34			10	30	808	44.6
1905	Chi	AL	SS	564	77	5	646	181	34	1	1	.320	.407	.392	799	33			10	50	859	60.5
1906	Chi	AL	SS	500	52	5	556	157	31	7	0	.315	.385	.404	789	28			10	30	829	44.2
1907	Chi	AL	SS	479	60	5	544	132	19	2	1	.275	.362	.332	694	16			10	20	724	16.1
1908	Chi	AL	2B	429	54	9	491	110	17	1	0	.256	.351	.301	653	23			10	10	673	(2.9)
1909	Chi	AL	1B	69	12	1	83	11	1	0	0	.153	.292	.170	462	4			0	20	482	(11.4)
16.7	Totals			10,172	1,034	89	11,294	3,100	526	190	84					706	0					793.2
1.0	Averages			609	62	5	676	186	32	11	5	.305	.374	.419	793	42	0	0	10	38	840	47.5

Joe Cronin **Red Sox** **Shortstop** **Actual**

Year	T	L	P	AB	BB	HBP	TAB	H	2B	3B	HR	BA	OB	SA	PRO	SB	CS	SBF	SPF	FF	Actual TF	Actual HC
1926	Pit	NL	2B	83	6	0	89	22	2	2	0	.265	.315	.337	652	0			10	60	722	1.6
1927	Pit	NL	2B	22	2	0	24	5	1	0	0	.227	.292	.273	564	0			10	0	574	(1.3)
1928	Was	AL	SS	227	22	0	249	55	10	4	0	.242	.309	.322	631	4	0	15	10	50	706	5.5
1929	Was	AL	SS	494	85	1	580	139	29	8	8	.281	.388	.421	809	5	9	(21)	10	20	818	45.3
1930	Was	AL	SS	587	72	5	664	203	41	9	13	.346	.422	.513	934	17	10	(4)	10	80	1,020	119.2
1931	Was	AL	SS	611	81	4	696	187	44	13	12	.306	.391	.480	870	10	9	(11)	10	40	909	86.3
1932	Was	AL	SS	557	66	3	626	177	43	18	6	.318	.393	.492	885	7	5	(5)	10	40	930	84.2
1933	Was	AL	SS	602	87	2	691	186	45	11	5	.309	.398	.445	843	5	4	(4)	10	50	899	82.1
1934	Was	AL	SS	504	53	1	558	143	30	9	7	.284	.353	.421	774	8	0	14	10	60	857	54.6
1935	Bos	AL	SS	556	63	3	622	164	37	14	9	.295	.370	.460	830	3	3	(5)	10	0	836	54.1
1936	Bos	AL	SS	295	32	1	328	83	22	4	2	.281	.354	.403	757	1	3	(14)	10	0	753	14.9
1937	Bos	AL	SS	570	84	6	660	175	40	4	18	.307	.402	.486	887	5	3	(1)	10	0	896	77.4
1938	Bos	AL	SS	530	91	5	626	172	51	5	17	.325	.428	.536	964	7	5	(5)	10	20	989	102.7
1939	Bos	AL	SS	520	87	0	607	160	33	3	19	.308	.407	.492	899	6	6	(9)	0	20	910	75.4
1940	Bos	AL	SS	548	83	1	632	156	35	6	24	.285	.380	.502	882	7	5	(4)	0	10	887	71.3
1941	Bos	AL	SS	518	82	1	601	161	38	8	16	.311	.406	.508	914	1	4	(11)	0	0	903	72.5
1942	Bos	AL	3B	79	15	0	94	24	3	0	4	.304	.415	.494	909	0	1	(20)	0	(30)	858	6.7
1943	Bos	AL	3B	77	11	0	88	24	4	0	5	.312	.398	.558	956	0	0	0	0	0	956	10.6
1944	Bos	AL	1B	191	34	1	226	46	7	0	5	.241	.358	.356	714	1	4	(29)	0	(10)	675	(10.7)
1945	Bos	AL	3B	8	3	0	11	3	0	0	0	.375	.545	.375	920	0	0	0	0	0	920	1.1
13.5	Totals			7,579	1,059	34	8,672	2,285	515	118	170					87	71					953.5
1.0	Averages			562	78	3	643	169	38	9	13	.301	.390	.468	857	6	5	(6)	7	26	885	70.7

Joe Cronin **Red Sox** **Shortstop** **Adjusted**

Year	T	L	P	AB	BB	HBP	TAB	H	2B	3B	HR	BA	OB	SA	Wtd PRO	SB	CS	SBF	SPF	FF	Wtd TF	HC
1926	Pit	NL	2B	88	6	0	94	23	2	2	0	.258	.307	.329	636	0			10	60	706	0.9
1927	Pit	NL	2B	23	2	0	25	5	1	0	0	.221	.284	.266	550	0			10	0	560	(1.5)
1928	Was	AL	SS	240	22	0	262	55	10	4	0	.231	.295	.306	601	4	0	15	10	50	676	1.8
1929	Was	AL	SS	528	81	1	610	139	29	8	8	.263	.362	.393	755	5	9	(21)	10	20	764	29.7
1930	Was	AL	SS	628	66	5	698	198	40	9	13	.316	.386	.469	854	18	11	(4)	10	80	940	92.6
1931	Was	AL	SS	649	80	4	732	189	45	13	12	.292	.373	.457	830	11	9	(11)	10	40	869	72.3
1932	Was	AL	SS	592	64	3	659	177	43	18	6	.299	.370	.463	833	7	5	(5)	10	40	878	67.9
1933	Was	AL	SS	638	87	2	727	190	46	11	5	.298	.384	.429	813	5	4	(4)	10	50	869	71.7
1934	Was	AL	SS	535	51	1	587	143	30	9	7	.267	.332	.396	728	8	0	14	10	60	812	41.9
1935	Bos	AL	SS	591	61	3	654	163	37	14	9	.277	.347	.432	778	3	3	(5)	10	0	784	37.9
1936	Bos	AL	SS	315	29	1	345	80	21	4	2	.253	.318	.363	682	1	3	(14)	10	0	677	2.5
1937	Bos	AL	SS	611	78	6	694	172	39	4	18	.281	.368	.446	814	5	3	(1)	10	0	822	53.0
1938	Bos	AL	SS	570	84	5	659	169	50	5	17	.296	.391	.489	880	7	5	(5)	10	20	906	76.5
1939	Bos	AL	SS	556	83	0	639	159	33	3	19	.286	.378	.458	836	6	6	(9)	0	20	847	56.3
1940	Bos	AL	SS	584	80	1	665	156	35	6	24	.268	.357	.472	830	7	5	(4)	0	10	835	54.9
1941	Bos	AL	SS	549	82	1	632	165	39	8	16	.301	.393	.491	884	1	4	(11)	0	0	873	63.4
1942	Bos	AL	3B	82	16	0	99	26	3	0	4	.313	.427	.508	935	0	1	(20)	0	(30)	885	7.9
1943	Bos	AL	3B	80	13	0	93	27	4	0	6	.332	.423	.595	1,018	0	0	0	0	0	1,018	13.3
1944	Bos	AL	1B	199	38	1	238	50	8	0	5	.251	.373	.371	744	1	4	(29)	0	(10)	705	(7.4)
1945	Bos	AL	3B	8	3	0	12	3	0	0	0	.395	.574	.395	968	0	0	0	0	0	968	1.4
13.5	Totals			8,064	1,026	32	9,122	2,289	515	118	171					92	75					736.9
1.0	Averages			598	76	2	676	170	38	9	13	.284	.367	.441	808	7	6	(6)	7	26	835	54.6

Jack Glasscock **Cle NL** **Shortstop** **Actual**

Year	T	L	P	AB	BB	HBP	TAB	H	2B	3B	HR	BA	OB	SA	PRO	SB	CS	SBF	SPF	FF	Actual TF	Actual HC
1879	Cle	NL	2B	325	6	0	331	68	9	3	0	.209	.224	.255	479				10	(20)	469	(69.1)
1880	Cle	NL	SS	296	2	0	298	72	13	3	0	.243	.248	.307	556				10	30	596	(17.9)
1881	Cle	NL	SS	335	15	0	350	86	9	5	0	.257	.289	.313	602				10	40	652	(3.2)
1882	Cle	NL	SS	358	13	0	371	104	27	9	4	.291	.315	.450	765				10	100	875	72.2
1883	Cle	NL	SS	383	13	0	396	110	19	6	0	.287	.311	.368	679				10	60	749	26.8
1884	Cle	NL	SS	453	33	0	486	142	13	9	3	.313	.360	.402	762				10	80	852	62.5
1885	StL	NL	SS	446	29	0	475	125	18	3	1	.280	.324	.341	665				10	70	745	27.4
1886	StL	NL	SS	486	38	0	524	158	29	7	3	.325	.374	.432	806	38			10	50	866	66.6
1887	Ind	NL	SS	483	41	10	534	142	18	7	0	.294	.361	.360	722	62			10	100	832	55.1
1888	Ind	NL	SS	442	14	7	463	119	17	3	1	.269	.302	.328	630	48			10	40	680	4.8
1889	Ind	NL	SS	582	31	5	618	205	40	3	7	.352	.390	.467	857	57			10	90	957	105.9
1890	NY	NL	SS	512	41	9	562	172	32	9	1	.336	.395	.439	834	54			10	60	904	77.9
1891	NY	NL	SS	369	36	5	410	89	12	6	0	.241	.317	.306	623	29			10	10	643	(4.3)
1892	StL	NL	SS	566	44	7	617	151	27	5	3	.267	.327	.348	675	26			10	20	705	13.5
1893	Pit	NL	SS	488	42	9	539	156	15	12	2	.320	.384	.412	796	36			10	20	826	52.1
1894	Pit	NL	SS	332	31	4	367	93	10	7	1	.280	.349	.361	710	18			0	30	740	16.8
1895	Was	NL	SS	174	10	6	190	48	5	1	1	.276	.337	.333	670	4			0	40	710	5.3
15.5	Totals			7,030	439	62	7,531	2,040	313	98	27					372	0					492.3
1.0	Averages			453	28	4	486	132	20	6	2	.290	.337	.374	712	24	0	0	9	51	772	31.7

Jack Glasscock **Cle NL** **Shortstop** **Adjusted**

Year	T	L	P	AB	BB	HBP	TAB	H	2B	3B	HR	BA	OB	SA	Wtd PRO	SB	CS	SBF	SPF	FF	Wtd TF	HC
1879	Cle	NL	2B	655	15	0	670	162	21	7	0	.247	.263	.301	564				10	(20)	554	(41.8)
1880	Cle	NL	SS	563	5	0	568	165	30	7	0	.293	.299	.370	668				10	30	708	12.5
1881	Cle	NL	SS	641	34	0	675	185	19	11	0	.289	.325	.353	678				10	40	728	21.1
1882	Cle	NL	SS	681	30	0	711	225	58	19	9	.330	.358	.510	868				10	100	978	107.2
1883	Cle	NL	SS	624	24	0	648	195	34	11	0	.312	.337	.400	737				10	60	807	44.8
1884	Cle	NL	SS	634	56	0	691	224	21	14	5	.353	.406	.453	859				10	80	949	94.5
1885	StL	NL	SS	641	53	0	693	209	30	5	2	.326	.378	.397	775				10	70	855	63.6
1886	StL	NL	SS	627	57	0	685	225	41	10	4	.358	.412	.476	888	50			10	50	948	93.2
1887	Ind	NL	SS	616	52	13	681	181	23	9	0	.294	.361	.360	721	79			10	100	831	54.7
1888	Ind	NL	SS	521	21	10	552	162	23	4	1	.312	.350	.380	731	57			10	40	781	31.2
1889	Ind	NL	SS	708	39	6	753	254	50	4	9	.359	.397	.476	873	69			10	90	973	111.6
1890	NY	NL	SS	610	53	12	674	215	40	11	1	.353	.416	.462	878	65			10	60	948	91.8
1891	NY	NL	SS	429	46	6	481	110	15	7	0	.255	.336	.324	660	34			10	10	680	4.0
1892	StL	NL	SS	590	53	8	651	173	31	6	3	.292	.359	.382	740	27			10	20	770	33.6
1893	Pit	NL	SS	607	49	10	667	186	18	14	2	.307	.368	.395	763	45			10	20	793	41.7
1894	Pit	NL	SS	415	31	4	450	101	11	8	1	.243	.302	.313	616	22			0	30	646	(3.5)
1895	Was	NL	SS	214	11	7	231	55	6	1	1	.256	.312	.309	622	5			0	40	662	(0.0)
15.5	Totals			9,776	628	77	10,482	3,025	470	148	39					453	0					760.4
1.0	Averages			631	41	5	676	195	30	10	2	.309	.356	.400	756	29	0	0	9	51	816	49.0

Alex Rodriguez **Mariners** **Shortstop** **Actual**

Year	T	L	P	AB	BB	HBP	TAB	H	2B	3B	HR	BA	OB	SA	PRO	SB	CS	SBF	SPF	FF	Actual TF	Actual HC
1994	Sea	AL	SS	54	3	0	57	11	0	0	0	.204	.246	.204	449	3	0	50	10	0	509	(5.9)
1995	Sea	AL	SS	142	6	0	148	33	6	2	5	.232	.264	.408	672	4	2	0	10	(20)	662	(0.0)
1996	Sea	AL	SS	601	59	4	664	215	54	1	36	.358	.419	.631	1,049	15	4	10	10	0	1,069	128.8
1997	Sea	AL	SS	587	41	5	633	176	40	3	23	.300	.351	.496	846	29	6	25	10	10	892	69.3
1998	Sea	AL	SS	686	45	10	741	213	35	5	42	.310	.362	.560	921	46	13	26	10	20	977	111.2
1999	Sea	AL	SS	502	56	5	563	143	25	0	42	.285	.362	.586	948	21	7	12	10	40	1,010	93.3
2000	Sea	AL	SS	554	100	7	661	175	34	2	41	.316	.427	.606	1,033	15	4	10	10	50	1,103	138.9
5.2 Totals				3,126	310	31	3,467	966	194	13	189					133	36					535.6
1.0 Averages				602	60	6	668	186	37	3	36	.309	.377	.561	938	26	7	17	10	21	985	103.2

Alex Rodriguez **Mariners** **Shortstop** **Adjusted**

Year	T	L	P	AB	BB	HBP	TAB	H	2B	3B	HR	BA	OB	SA	Wtd PRO	SB	CS	SBF	SPF	FF	Wtd TF	HC
1994	Sea	AL	SS	77	4	0	81	15	0	0	0	.190	.229	.190	419	4	0	50	10	0	479	(7.0)
1995	Sea	AL	SS	160	6	0	167	35	6	2	5	.219	.249	.385	634	5	2	0	10	(20)	624	(3.0)
1996	Sea	AL	SS	609	52	3	664	199	50	1	33	.327	.383	.577	960	15	4	10	10	0	980	100.5
1997	Sea	AL	SS	591	38	5	633	167	38	3	22	.283	.331	.468	799	29	6	25	10	10	844	55.0
1998	Sea	AL	SS	691	41	9	741	202	33	5	40	.292	.340	.526	866	46	13	26	10	20	922	91.7
1999	Sea	AL	SS	508	50	4	563	134	23	0	39	.263	.334	.540	874	21	7	12	10	40	936	73.5
2000	Sea	AL	SS	567	88	6	661	164	32	2	38	.289	.391	.555	946	15	4	10	10	50	1,016	111.4
5.2 Totals				3,202	279	28	3,509	915	183	13	178					135	36					422.1
1.0 Averages				617	54	5	676	176	35	2	34	.286	.348	.517	866	26	7	17	10	21	913	81.3

Ernie Banks   **Cubs**   **Shortstop (First Base)**   **Actual**

Year	T	L	P	AB	BB	HBP	TAB	H	2B	3B	HR	BA	OB	SA	PRO	SB	CS	SBF	SPF	FF	Actual TF	Actual HC
1953	Chi	NL	SS	35	4	0	39	11	1	1	2	.314	.385	.571	956	0	0	0	10	80	1,046	7.5
1954	Chi	NL	SS	593	40	7	640	163	19	7	19	.275	.328	.427	755	6	10	(21)	10	(10)	734	23.1
1955	Chi	NL	SS	596	45	2	643	176	29	9	44	.295	.347	.596	942	9	3	4	10	10	967	98.2
1956	Chi	NL	SS	538	52	0	590	160	25	8	28	.297	.359	.530	889	6	9	(19)	10	0	880	64.4
1957	Chi	NL	SS	594	70	3	667	169	34	6	43	.285	.363	.579	942	8	4	0	10	0	952	96.9
1958	Chi	NL	SS	617	52	4	673	193	23	11	47	.313	.370	.614	984	4	4	(6)	10	10	999	113.5
1959	Chi	NL	SS	589	64	7	660	179	25	6	45	.304	.379	.596	975	2	4	(9)	10	30	1,006	113.8
1960	Chi	NL	SS	597	71	4	672	162	32	7	41	.271	.353	.554	907	1	3	(7)	0	40	940	93.7
1961	Chi	NL	SS	511	54	2	567	142	22	4	29	.278	.349	.507	856	1	2	(5)	0	10	861	56.6
1962	Chi	NL	1B	610	30	7	647	164	20	6	37	.269	.311	.503	814	5	1	4	0	0	818	14.9
1963	Chi	NL	1B	432	39	4	475	98	20	1	18	.227	.297	.403	700	0	3	(12)	0	10	698	(16.4)
1964	Chi	NL	1B	591	36	3	630	156	29	6	23	.264	.310	.450	760	1	2	(5)	0	10	765	(1.5)
1965	Chi	NL	1B	612	55	6	673	162	25	3	28	.265	.331	.453	784	3	5	(10)	0	10	784	4.5
1966	Chi	NL	1B	511	29	5	545	139	23	7	15	.272	.317	.432	750	0	1	(3)	0	10	756	(3.5)
1967	Chi	NL	1B	573	27	3	603	158	26	4	23	.276	.312	.455	767	2	2	(3)	0	0	764	(1.7)
1968	Chi	NL	1B	552	27	5	584	136	27	0	32	.246	.288	.469	757	2	0	3	0	0	760	(2.8)
1969	Chi	NL	1B	565	42	7	614	143	19	2	23	.253	.313	.416	729	0	0	0	0	0	729	(12.1)
1970	Chi	NL	1B	222	20	1	243	56	6	2	12	.252	.317	.459	776	0	0	0	(10)	0	766	(0.4)
1971	Chi	NL	1B	83	6	0	89	16	2	0	3	.193	.247	.325	572	0	0	0	(10)	0	562	(8.8)
15.6	Totals			9,421	763	70	10,254	2,583	407	90	512					50	53					640.1
1.0	Averages			605	49	4	659	166	26	6	33	.274	.333	.500	833	3	3	(5)	4	8	840	41.1

Ernie Banks   **Cubs**   **Shortstop (First Base)**   **Adjusted**

Year	T	L	P	AB	BB	HBP	TAB	H	2B	3B	HR	BA	OB	SA	Wtd PRO	SB	CS	SBF	SPF	FF	Wtd TF	HC
1953	Chi	NL	SS	37	4	0	41	11	1	1	2	.297	.363	.540	903	0	0	0	10	80	993	6.5
1954	Chi	NL	SS	627	39	7	673	163	19	7	19	.260	.311	.404	715	6	11	(21)	10	(10)	694	10.4
1955	Chi	NL	SS	630	45	2	676	178	29	9	45	.283	.332	.571	903	9	3	4	10	10	927	85.4
1956	Chi	NL	SS	568	53	0	621	164	26	8	29	.290	.350	.516	866	6	9	(19)	10	0	856	57.5
1957	Chi	NL	SS	628	71	3	702	174	35	6	44	.277	.354	.565	918	8	4	0	10	0	928	89.0
1958	Chi	NL	SS	652	52	4	708	196	23	11	48	.300	.355	.590	945	4	4	(6)	10	10	960	100.4
1959	Chi	NL	SS	623	65	7	694	184	26	6	46	.295	.368	.579	946	2	4	(9)	10	30	978	104.5
1960	Chi	NL	SS	629	74	4	707	170	34	7	43	.270	.351	.551	902	1	3	(7)	0	40	935	91.9
1961	Chi	NL	SS	541	54	2	596	144	22	4	29	.267	.335	.487	822	1	2	(5)	0	10	827	46.9
1962	Chi	NL	1B	611	29	7	647	161	20	6	36	.263	.304	.492	796	5	1	4	0	0	800	9.3
1963	Chi	NL	1B	429	42	4	475	102	21	1	19	.239	.312	.424	736	0	3	(12)	0	10	734	(8.1)
1964	Chi	NL	1B	590	37	3	630	160	30	6	24	.271	.318	.462	781	1	2	(5)	0	10	786	4.8
1965	Chi	NL	1B	610	57	6	673	166	26	3	29	.272	.340	.465	806	3	5	(10)	0	10	806	11.4
1966	Chi	NL	1B	511	29	5	545	140	23	7	15	.275	.321	.437	757	0	1	(3)	0	10	764	(1.6)
1967	Chi	NL	1B	571	29	3	603	165	27	4	24	.288	.326	.476	802	2	2	(3)	0	0	799	8.4
1968	Chi	NL	1B	548	31	6	584	148	29	0	35	.270	.316	.515	831	2	0	3	0	0	834	17.8
1969	Chi	NL	1B	563	43	7	614	146	19	2	23	.259	.320	.426	745	0	0	0	0	0	745	(7.2)
1970	Chi	NL	1B	223	19	1	243	55	6	2	12	.246	.309	.448	757	0	0	0	(10)	0	747	(2.7)
1971	Chi	NL	1B	83	6	0	89	16	2	0	3	.199	.255	.335	590	0	0	0	(10)	0	580	(8.1)
15.6	Totals			9,672	778	72	10,522	2,644	418	92	525					52	55					616.7
1.0	Averages			621	50	5	676	170	27	6	34	.273	.332	.498	830	3	4	(5)	4	8	837	39.6

Cal Ripken **Orioles** **Shortstop** **Actual**

Year	T	L	P	AB	BB	HBP	TAB	H	2B	3B	HR	BA	OB	SA	PRO	SB	CS	SBF	SPF	FF	Actual TF	Actual HC
1981	Bal	AL	SS	39	1	0	40	5	0	0	0	.128	.150	.128	278	0	0	0	0	(10)	268	(11.4)
1982	Bal	AL	SS	598	46	3	647	158	32	5	28	.264	.320	.475	795	3	3	(4)	0	(10)	780	36.5
1983	Bal	AL	SS	663	58	0	721	211	47	2	27	.318	.373	.517	890	0	4	(10)	0	40	920	88.6
1984	Bal	AL	SS	641	71	2	714	195	37	7	27	.304	.375	.510	885	2	1	0	0	70	955	99.8
1985	Bal	AL	SS	642	67	1	710	181	32	5	26	.282	.351	.469	820	2	3	(5)	0	10	824	54.9
1986	Bal	AL	SS	627	70	4	701	177	35	1	25	.282	.358	.461	819	4	2	0	0	30	849	62.4
1987	Bal	AL	SS	624	81	1	706	157	28	3	27	.252	.339	.436	774	3	5	(9)	0	10	775	38.0
1988	Bal	AL	SS	575	102	2	679	152	25	1	23	.264	.377	.431	808	2	2	(3)	0	10	816	49.7
1989	Bal	AL	SS	646	57	3	706	166	30	0	21	.257	.320	.401	721	3	2	(1)	0	30	750	29.5
1990	Bal	AL	SS	600	82	5	687	150	28	4	21	.250	.345	.415	760	3	1	1	0	(20)	741	26.0
1991	Bal	AL	SS	650	53	5	708	210	46	5	34	.323	.379	.566	945	6	1	5	0	60	1,010	117.4
1992	Bal	AL	SS	637	64	7	708	160	29	1	14	.251	.326	.366	692	4	3	(3)	0	30	719	19.4
1993	Bal	AL	SS	641	65	6	712	165	26	3	24	.257	.331	.420	751	1	4	(9)	0	10	752	30.5
1994	Bal	AL	SS	444	32	4	480	140	19	3	13	.315	.367	.459	826	1	0	2	0	(10)	818	50.5
1995	Bal	AL	SS	550	52	2	604	144	33	2	17	.262	.328	.422	750	0	1	(3)	0	20	767	33.8
1996	Bal	AL	SS	640	59	4	703	178	40	1	26	.278	.343	.466	808	1	2	(4)	0	0	804	47.7
1997	Bal	AL	3B	615	56	5	676	166	30	0	17	.270	.336	.402	737	1	0	1	0	(10)	729	4.1
1998	Bal	AL	3B	601	51	4	656	163	27	1	14	.271	.332	.389	722	0	2	(6)	(10)	(10)	696	(6.3)
1999	Bal	AL	3B	332	13	3	348	113	27	0	18	.340	.371	.584	955	0	1	(5)	(10)	(50)	890	28.7
2000	Bal	AL	3B	309	23	3	335	79	16	0	15	.256	.313	.453	767	0	0	0	(10)	0	757	6.4
18.5 Totals				11,074	1,103	64	12,241	3,070	587	44	417					36	37					806.2
1.0 Averages				597	59	3	660	166	32	2	22	.277	.346	.451	797	2	2	(3)	(1)	13	807	43.5

Cal Ripken **Orioles** **Shortstop** **Adjusted**

Year	T	L	P	AB	BB	HBP	TAB	H	2B	3B	HR	BA	OB	SA	Wtd PRO	SB	CS	SBF	SPF	FF	Wtd TF	HC
1981	Bal	AL	SS	59	2	0	61	8	0	0	0	.134	.157	.134	292	0	0	0	0	(10)	282	(11.0)
1982	Bal	AL	SS	598	46	3	647	157	32	5	28	.263	.319	.473	792	3	3	(4)	0	(10)	777	35.5
1983	Bal	AL	SS	663	58	0	721	211	47	2	27	.318	.373	.517	889	0	4	(10)	0	40	919	88.2
1984	Bal	AL	SS	641	71	2	714	196	37	7	27	.305	.377	.512	889	2	1	0	0	70	959	101.1
1985	Bal	AL	SS	643	66	1	710	180	32	5	26	.280	.348	.466	814	2	3	(5)	0	10	819	53.0
1986	Bal	AL	SS	628	69	4	701	175	35	1	25	.278	.353	.455	808	4	2	0	0	30	838	58.7
1987	Bal	AL	SS	628	77	1	706	152	27	3	26	.241	.325	.418	743	3	5	(9)	0	10	743	27.4
1988	Bal	AL	SS	573	104	2	679	154	25	1	23	.269	.383	.439	822	2	2	(3)	0	10	829	54.0
1989	Bal	AL	SS	644	59	3	706	170	31	0	21	.263	.328	.411	739	3	2	(1)	0	30	768	35.6
1990	Bal	AL	SS	598	84	5	687	152	28	4	21	.254	.351	.422	773	3	1	1	0	(20)	754	30.1
1991	Bal	AL	SS	650	53	5	708	211	46	5	34	.325	.381	.569	950	6	1	5	0	60	1,015	119.1
1992	Bal	AL	SS	635	66	7	708	163	29	1	14	.256	.333	.373	706	4	3	(3)	0	30	733	23.9
1993	Bal	AL	SS	643	63	6	712	162	25	3	24	.251	.323	.410	733	1	4	(9)	0	10	734	24.3
1994	Bal	AL	SS	633	41	5	679	186	25	4	17	.294	.342	.429	771	1	0	2	0	(10)	763	32.7
1995	Bal	AL	SS	623	54	2	680	154	35	2	18	.247	.309	.398	707	0	1	(3)	0	20	724	20.0
1996	Bal	AL	SS	647	52	4	703	165	37	1	24	.254	.314	.426	740	1	2	(4)	0	0	736	24.6
1997	Bal	AL	3B	620	52	5	676	158	29	0	16	.255	.317	.379	696	1	0	1	0	(10)	687	(9.3)
1998	Bal	AL	3B	605	47	4	656	154	26	1	13	.255	.312	.366	679	0	2	(6)	(10)	(10)	653	(19.8)
1999	Bal	AL	3B	334	12	3	348	105	25	0	17	.314	.342	.539	881	0	1	(5)	(10)	(50)	815	16.5
2000	Bal	AL	3B	312	20	3	335	73	15	0	14	.234	.287	.415	702	0	0	0	(10)	0	692	(3.9)
18.5 Totals				11,377	1,096	64	12,536	3,084	586	45	416					36	37					700.9
1.0 Averages				613	59	3	676	166	32	2	22	.271	.338	.440	779	2	2	(3)	(1)	13	788	37.8

Mike Schmidt **Phillies** **Third Baseman** **Actual**

Year	T	L	P	AB	BB	HBP	TAB	H	2B	3B	HR	BA	OB	SA	PRO	SB	CS	SBF	SPF	FF	Actual TF	Actual HC
1972	Phi	NL	3B	34	5	1	40	7	0	0	1	.206	.325	.294	619	0	0	0	10	40	669	(0.9)
1973	Phi	NL	3B	367	62	9	438	72	11	0	18	.196	.326	.373	700	8	2	9	10	70	788	15.1
1974	Phi	NL	3B	568	106	4	678	160	28	7	36	.282	.398	.546	944	23	12	(1)	10	70	1,023	99.0
1975	Phi	NL	3B	562	101	4	667	140	34	3	38	.249	.367	.523	890	29	12	7	10	70	978	83.0
1976	Phi	NL	3B	584	100	11	695	153	31	4	38	.262	.380	.524	904	14	9	(5)	10	80	988	90.1
1977	Phi	NL	3B	544	104	9	657	149	27	11	38	.274	.399	.574	972	15	8	(1)	10	80	1,061	107.9
1978	Phi	NL	3B	513	91	4	608	129	27	2	21	.251	.368	.435	803	19	6	11	10	60	884	48.6
1979	Phi	NL	3B	541	120	3	664	137	25	4	45	.253	.392	.564	955	9	5	(1)	10	70	1,034	100.5
1980	Phi	NL	3B	548	89	2	639	157	25	8	48	.286	.388	.624	1,012	12	5	3	10	60	1,085	112.3
1981	Phi	NL	3B	354	73	4	431	112	19	2	31	.316	.439	.644	1,083	12	4	9	10	90	1,191	147.7
1982	Phi	NL	3B	514	107	3	624	144	26	3	35	.280	.407	.547	954	14	7	0	0	70	1,024	91.4
1983	Phi	NL	3B	534	128	3	665	136	16	4	40	.255	.402	.524	926	7	8	(13)	0	70	983	84.5
1984	Phi	NL	3B	528	92	4	624	146	23	3	36	.277	.388	.536	924	5	7	(14)	(10)	40	940	66.6
1985	Phi	NL	1B	549	87	3	639	152	31	5	33	.277	.379	.532	911	1	3	(7)	0	0	903	40.5
1986	Phi	NL	3B	552	89	7	648	160	29	1	37	.290	.395	.547	942	1	2	(4)	0	40	978	80.8
1987	Phi	NL	3B	522	83	2	607	153	28	0	35	.293	.392	.548	940	2	1	0	0	30	970	73.4
1988	Phi	NL	3B	390	49	6	445	97	21	2	12	.249	.342	.405	747	3	0	6	0	0	753	7.8
1989	Phi	NL	3B	148	21	0	169	30	7	0	6	.203	.302	.372	673	0	1	(11)	(10)	(30)	622	(7.6)
15.0 Totals				8,352	1,507	79	9,938	2,234	408	59	548					174	92					1,240.8
1.0 Averages				556	100	5	661	149	27	4	36	.267	.384	.527	912	12	6	(1)	5	56	972	82.5

Mike Schmidt **Phillies** **Third Baseman** **Adjusted**

Year	T	L	P	AB	BB	HBP	TAB	H	2B	3B	HR	BA	OB	SA	Wtd PRO	SB	CS	SBF	SPF	FF	Wtd TF	HC
1972	Phi	NL	3B	35	5	1	42	8	0	0	1	.213	.336	.304	641	0	0	0	10	40	691	(0.5)
1973	Phi	NL	3B	366	63	9	438	72	11	0	18	.198	.329	.376	706	8	2	9	10	70	794	16.3
1974	Phi	NL	3B	566	108	4	678	162	28	7	36	.286	.404	.554	959	23	12	(1)	10	70	1,037	103.8
1975	Phi	NL	3B	560	103	4	667	141	34	3	38	.252	.371	.529	901	29	12	7	10	70	988	86.2
1976	Phi	NL	3B	579	104	11	695	157	32	4	39	.270	.392	.541	933	14	9	(5)	10	80	1,017	99.7
1977	Phi	NL	3B	548	100	9	657	146	26	11	37	.266	.387	.557	944	15	8	(1)	10	80	1,033	99.1
1978	Phi	NL	3B	511	93	4	608	131	27	2	21	.256	.375	.442	817	19	6	11	10	60	898	52.6
1979	Phi	NL	3B	542	119	3	664	136	25	4	45	.251	.388	.559	947	9	5	(1)	10	70	1,026	97.9
1980	Phi	NL	3B	546	91	2	639	159	25	8	48	.290	.393	.632	1,025	12	5	3	10	60	1,098	116.3
1981	Phi	NL	3B	531	115	6	653	173	29	3	48	.326	.451	.663	1,114	18	6	9	10	90	1,223	157.5
1982	Phi	NL	3B	512	109	3	624	146	26	3	35	.285	.413	.555	969	14	7	0	0	70	1,039	95.9
1983	Phi	NL	3B	533	129	3	665	137	16	4	40	.257	.405	.529	934	7	8	(13)	0	70	991	87.0
1984	Phi	NL	3B	525	95	4	624	148	23	3	37	.282	.396	.548	944	5	7	(14)	(10)	40	960	72.5
1985	Phi	NL	1B	547	89	3	639	154	31	5	33	.281	.385	.540	925	1	3	(7)	0	0	917	44.9
1986	Phi	NL	3B	552	89	7	648	160	29	1	37	.291	.396	.549	945	1	2	(4)	0	40	980	81.5
1987	Phi	NL	3B	527	79	2	607	148	27	0	34	.282	.377	.527	904	2	1	0	0	30	934	63.0
1988	Phi	NL	3B	387	52	6	445	101	22	2	12	.260	.357	.424	781	3	0	6	0	0	787	15.1
1989	Phi	NL	3B	147	22	0	169	31	7	0	6	.210	.313	.386	699	0	1	(11)	(10)	(30)	648	(5.5)
15.0 Totals				8,514	1,565	82	10,162	2,308	421	60	568					180	94					1,283.2
1.0 Averages				566	104	5	676	154	28	4	38	.271	.389	.535	924	12	6	(1)	5	56	984	85.4

Eddie Mathews **Braves** **Third Baseman** **Actual**

Year T L P	AB	BB	HBP	TAB	H	2B	3B	HR	BA	OB	SA	PRO	SB	CS	SBF	SPF	FF	Actual TF	Actual HC
1952 Bos NL 3B	528	59	1	588	128	23	5	25	.242	.320	.447	767	6	4	(3)	10	(20)	753	11.0
1953 Mil NL 3B	579	99	2	680	175	31	8	47	.302	.406	.627	1,033	1	3	(7)	10	(20)	1,016	102.1
1954 Mil NL 3B	476	113	2	591	138	21	4	40	.290	.428	.603	1,031	10	3	6	10	0	1,047	98.1
1955 Mil NL 3B	499	109	1	609	144	23	5	41	.289	.417	.601	1,018	3	4	(8)	10	0	1,021	92.9
1956 Mil NL 3B	552	91	1	644	150	21	2	37	.272	.376	.518	894	6	0	9	0	(20)	883	53.7
1957 Mil NL 3B	572	90	0	662	167	28	9	32	.292	.388	.540	928	3	1	1	0	0	930	70.9
1958 Mil NL 3B	546	85	2	633	137	18	1	31	.251	.354	.458	812	5	0	7	10	20	849	42.2
1959 Mil NL 3B	594	80	3	677	182	16	8	46	.306	.391	.593	984	2	1	0	10	20	1,014	101.0
1960 Mil NL 3B	548	111	2	661	152	19	7	39	.277	.401	.551	952	7	3	1	10	0	963	81.9
1961 Mil NL 3B	572	93	2	667	175	23	6	32	.306	.405	.535	940	12	7	(3)	10	0	947	77.1
1962 Mil NL 3B	536	101	2	639	142	25	6	29	.265	.383	.496	880	4	2	0	10	20	910	58.9
1963 Mil NL 3B	547	124	1	672	144	27	4	23	.263	.400	.453	854	3	4	(7)	10	40	897	57.8
1964 Mil NL 3B	502	85	1	588	117	19	1	23	.233	.345	.412	758	2	2	(3)	10	20	784	19.1
1965 Mil NL 3B	546	73	3	622	137	23	0	32	.251	.342	.469	811	1	0	2	0	20	833	34.6
1966 Mil NL 3B	452	63	0	515	113	21	4	16	.250	.342	.420	762	1	1	(2)	0	0	760	10.8
1967 Hou NL 1B	436	63	3	502	103	16	2	16	.236	.337	.392	729	2	4	(11)	0	(20)	698	(17.3)
1968 Det AL 1B	52	5	0	57	11	0	0	3	.212	.281	.385	665	0	0	0	0	(20)	645	(3.4)
15.3 Totals	8,537	1,444	26	10,007	2,315	354	72	512					68	39					891.4
1.0 Averages	558	94	2	654	151	23	5	33	.271	.378	.509	888	4	3	(1)	7	4	898	58.3

Eddie Mathews **Braves** **Third Baseman** **Adjusted**

Year T L P	AB	BB	HBP	TAB	H	2B	3B	HR	BA	OB	SA	Wtd PRO	SB	CS	SBF	SPF	FF	Wtd TF	HC
1952 Bos NL 3B	554	63	1	619	136	24	5	27	.246	.324	.453	776	6	4	(3)	10	(20)	763	13.9
1953 Mil NL 3B	617	96	2	715	176	31	8	47	.286	.384	.592	976	1	3	(7)	10	(20)	959	82.8
1954 Mil NL 3B	509	110	2	622	140	21	4	41	.275	.406	.571	977	11	3	6	10	0	993	82.1
1955 Mil NL 3B	532	108	1	641	147	23	5	42	.276	.399	.576	975	3	4	(8)	10	0	978	79.8
1956 Mil NL 3B	584	92	1	677	155	22	2	38	.265	.366	.504	870	6	0	9	0	(20)	859	46.1
1957 Mil NL 3B	605	91	0	696	172	29	9	33	.285	.379	.527	905	3	1	1	0	0	907	63.2
1958 Mil NL 3B	579	85	2	666	140	18	1	32	.241	.340	.440	780	5	0	7	10	20	817	32.0
1959 Mil NL 3B	628	81	3	712	187	16	8	47	.298	.380	.575	955	2	1	0	10	20	985	91.4
1960 Mil NL 3B	577	116	2	695	159	20	7	41	.276	.399	.548	947	7	3	1	10	0	958	80.1
1961 Mil NL 3B	607	92	2	702	178	23	6	33	.294	.389	.514	903	13	7	(3)	10	0	910	64.7
1962 Mil NL 3B	539	98	2	639	140	25	6	29	.259	.375	.485	860	4	2	0	10	20	890	52.9
1963 Mil NL 3B	538	133	1	672	149	28	4	24	.277	.421	.477	898	3	4	(7)	10	40	941	72.0
1964 Mil NL 3B	499	88	1	588	119	19	1	23	.239	.355	.424	778	2	2	(3)	10	20	805	24.9
1965 Mil NL 3B	543	76	3	622	140	24	0	33	.258	.352	.482	834	1	0	2	0	20	855	41.2
1966 Mil NL 3B	451	64	0	515	114	21	4	16	.252	.345	.425	770	1	1	(2)	0	0	768	12.7
1967 Hou NL 1B	432	67	3	502	107	17	2	17	.247	.352	.410	762	2	4	(11)	0	(20)	731	(9.3)
1968 Det AL 1B	51	6	0	57	12	0	0	3	.234	.310	.425	735	0	0	0	0	(20)	715	(1.5)
15.3 Totals	8,848	1,466	26	10,340	2,371	362	74	524					71	40					828.8
1.0 Averages	578	96	2	676	155	24	5	34	.268	.374	.503	877	5	3	(1)	7	4	887	54.2

George Brett **Royals** **Third Baseman** **Actual**

Year	T	L	P	AB	BB	HBP	TAB	H	2B	3B	HR	BA	OB	SA	PRO	SB	CS	SBF	SPF	FF	Actual TF	Actual HC
1973	KC	AL	3B	40	0	0	40	5	2	0	0	.125	.125	.175	300	0	0	0	10	60	370	(6.6)
1974	KC	AL	3B	457	21	0	478	129	21	5	2	.282	.314	.363	677	8	5	(4)	10	(20)	663	(12.1)
1975	KC	AL	3B	634	46	2	682	195	35	13	11	.308	.356	.456	812	13	10	(10)	10	0	812	31.3
1976	KC	AL	3B	645	49	1	695	215	34	14	7	.333	.381	.462	843	21	11	(1)	10	10	862	48.3
1977	KC	AL	3B	564	55	2	621	176	32	13	22	.312	.375	.532	907	14	12	(15)	10	30	932	63.8
1978	KC	AL	3B	510	39	1	550	150	45	8	9	.294	.345	.467	812	23	7	15	0	20	848	34.4
1979	KC	AL	3B	645	51	0	696	212	42	20	23	.329	.378	.563	941	17	10	(4)	10	20	967	83.0
1980	KC	AL	3B	449	58	1	508	175	33	9	24	.390	.461	.664	1,124	15	6	6	10	20	1,160	107.4
1981	KC	AL	3B	347	27	1	375	109	27	7	6	.314	.365	.484	849	14	6	5	10	(10)	855	37.4
1982	KC	AL	3B	552	71	1	624	166	32	9	21	.301	.381	.505	887	6	1	6	0	0	893	52.5
1983	KC	AL	3B	464	57	1	522	144	38	2	25	.310	.387	.563	949	0	1	(4)	0	(40)	906	47.2
1984	KC	AL	3B	377	38	0	415	107	21	3	13	.284	.349	.459	808	0	2	(9)	(10)	0	789	14.4
1985	KC	AL	3B	550	103	3	656	184	38	5	30	.335	.442	.585	1,028	9	1	10	0	40	1,078	113.0
1986	KC	AL	3B	441	80	4	525	128	28	4	16	.290	.404	.481	885	1	2	(5)	0	0	879	40.8
1987	KC	AL	1B	427	72	1	500	124	18	2	22	.290	.394	.496	890	6	3	0	0	(10)	880	26.3
1988	KC	AL	1B	589	82	3	674	180	42	3	24	.306	.393	.509	903	14	3	11	0	(10)	904	42.9
1989	KC	AL	1B	457	59	3	519	129	26	3	12	.282	.368	.431	799	14	4	11	0	10	820	12.4
1990	KC	AL	1B	544	56	0	600	179	45	7	14	.329	.392	.515	906	9	2	8	0	0	914	41.2
1991	KC	AL	DH	505	58	0	563	129	40	2	10	.255	.332	.402	734	2	0	3	(10)	(20)	707	(16.8)
1992	KC	AL	DH	592	35	6	633	169	35	5	7	.285	.332	.397	729	8	6	(6)	(10)	(20)	693	(23.3)
1993	KC	AL	DH	560	39	3	602	149	31	3	19	.266	.317	.434	751	7	5	(5)	(10)	(40)	696	(21.1)
17.3	Totals			10,349	1,096	33	11,478	3,154	665	137	317					201	97					716.4
1.0	Averages			599	63	2	665	183	39	8	18	.305	.373	.487	861	12	6	1	2	(0)	863	41.5

George Brett **Royals** **Third Baseman** **Adjusted**

Year	T	L	P	AB	BB	HBP	TAB	H	2B	3B	HR	BA	OB	SA	Wtd PRO	SB	CS	SBF	SPF	FF	Wtd TF	HC
1973	KC	AL	3B	40	0	0	40	5	2	0	0	.128	.128	.179	308	0	0	0	10	60	378	(6.5)
1974	KC	AL	3B	456	22	0	478	135	22	5	2	.296	.329	.380	709	8	5	(4)	10	(20)	695	(4.8)
1975	KC	AL	3B	632	48	2	682	200	36	13	11	.317	.367	.469	836	13	10	(10)	10	0	836	39.1
1976	KC	AL	3B	640	54	1	695	228	36	15	7	.356	.407	.493	900	21	11	(1)	10	10	919	67.0
1977	KC	AL	3B	565	54	2	621	174	32	13	22	.309	.371	.526	897	14	12	(15)	10	30	922	60.9
1978	KC	AL	3B	509	40	1	550	153	46	8	9	.301	.353	.477	830	23	7	15	0	20	866	39.2
1979	KC	AL	3B	647	49	0	696	208	41	20	23	.322	.370	.551	920	17	10	(4)	10	20	946	76.3
1980	KC	AL	3B	449	58	1	508	174	33	9	24	.388	.459	.661	1,120	15	6	6	10	20	1,155	106.3
1981	KC	AL	3B	522	44	2	568	172	43	11	9	.329	.383	.508	891	21	9	5	10	(10)	896	48.6
1982	KC	AL	3B	552	71	1	624	165	32	9	21	.299	.380	.503	883	6	1	6	0	0	889	51.4
1983	KC	AL	3B	464	57	1	522	144	38	2	25	.310	.386	.562	948	0	1	(4)	0	(40)	905	46.8
1984	KC	AL	3B	377	38	0	415	107	21	3	13	.285	.351	.461	812	0	2	(9)	(10)	0	792	15.1
1985	KC	AL	3B	551	102	3	656	183	38	5	30	.332	.439	.581	1,021	9	1	10	0	40	1,071	110.8
1986	KC	AL	3B	443	78	4	525	127	28	4	16	.286	.398	.474	873	1	2	(5)	0	0	867	37.8
1987	KC	AL	1B	431	68	1	500	120	17	2	21	.279	.378	.476	854	6	3	0	0	(10)	844	17.7
1988	KC	AL	1B	587	84	3	674	182	43	3	24	.311	.400	.518	918	14	3	11	0	(10)	919	47.8
1989	KC	AL	1B	455	61	3	519	132	27	3	12	.289	.377	.442	819	14	4	11	0	10	840	17.4
1990	KC	AL	1B	543	57	0	600	182	46	7	14	.335	.398	.523	922	9	2	8	0	0	929	45.6
1991	KC	AL	DH	505	58	0	563	130	40	2	10	.257	.334	.404	738	2	0	3	(10)	(20)	712	(15.7)
1992	KC	AL	DH	591	36	6	633	172	36	5	7	.291	.338	.405	743	8	6	(6)	(10)	(20)	707	(19.0)
1993	KC	AL	DH	561	38	3	602	146	30	3	19	.260	.310	.423	733	7	5	(5)	(10)	(40)	678	(26.3)
17.3	Totals			10,518	1,118	34	11,671	3,239	685	142	320					208	100					755.5
1.0	Averages			609	65	2	676	188	40	8	19	.308	.376	.491	868	12	6	1	2	(0)	870	43.8

Ron Santo **Cubs** **Third Baseman** **Actual**

Year	T	L	P	AB	BB	HBP	TAB	H	2B	3B	HR	BA	OB	SA	PRO	SB	CS	SBF	SPF	FF	Actual TF	Actual HC
1960	Chi	NL	3B	347	31	0	378	87	24	2	9	.251	.312	.409	721	0	3	(15)	0	0	706	(1.9)
1961	Chi	NL	3B	578	73	0	651	164	32	6	23	.284	.364	.479	843	2	3	(6)	0	10	847	42.8
1962	Chi	NL	3B	604	65	2	671	137	20	4	17	.227	.304	.358	662	4	1	3	0	30	694	(7.0)
1963	Chi	NL	3B	630	42	4	676	187	29	6	25	.297	.345	.481	826	6	4	(3)	(10)	40	853	44.0
1964	Chi	NL	3B	592	86	2	680	185	33	13	30	.313	.401	.564	966	3	4	(7)	(10)	60	1,009	94.8
1965	Chi	NL	3B	608	88	5	701	173	30	4	33	.285	.379	.510	889	3	1	1	(10)	60	941	75.0
1966	Chi	NL	3B	561	95	6	662	175	21	8	30	.312	.417	.538	955	4	5	(9)	(10)	70	1,007	91.6
1967	Chi	NL	3B	586	96	3	685	176	23	4	31	.300	.401	.512	913	1	5	(12)	(10)	80	971	83.1
1968	Chi	NL	3B	577	96	3	676	142	17	3	26	.246	.357	.421	778	3	4	(7)	(10)	60	821	33.6
1969	Chi	NL	3B	575	96	2	673	166	18	4	29	.289	.392	.485	877	1	3	(7)	(10)	40	900	59.1
1970	Chi	NL	3B	555	92	1	648	148	30	4	26	.267	.372	.476	848	2	0	3	(10)	30	871	47.6
1971	Chi	NL	3B	555	79	0	634	148	22	1	21	.267	.358	.423	781	4	0	6	(10)	20	797	24.5
1972	Chi	NL	3B	464	69	4	537	140	25	5	17	.302	.397	.487	884	1	4	(12)	(10)	20	881	44.5
1973	Chi	NL	3B	536	63	4	603	143	29	2	20	.267	.348	.440	789	1	2	(5)	(10)	10	784	19.4
1974	Chi	AL	DH	375	37	2	414	83	12	1	5	.221	.295	.299	593	0	2	(9)	(10)	0	574	(21.9)
13.9 Totals				8,143	1,108	38	9,289	2,254	365	67	342					35	41					629.4
1.0 Averages				587	80	3	670	163	26	5	25	.277	.366	.464	830	3	3	(5)	(8)	38	855	45.4

Ron Santo **Cubs** **Third Baseman** **Adjusted**

Year	T	L	P	AB	BB	HBP	TAB	H	2B	3B	HR	BA	OB	SA	Wtd PRO	SB	CS	SBF	SPF	FF	Wtd TF	HC
1960	Chi	NL	3B	365	32	0	398	91	25	2	9	.249	.310	.407	717	0	3	(15)	0	0	702	(2.6)
1961	Chi	NL	3B	612	73	0	685	167	33	6	23	.273	.350	.460	810	2	3	(6)	0	10	814	31.9
1962	Chi	NL	3B	606	63	2	671	134	20	4	17	.222	.297	.350	647	4	1	3	0	30	680	(11.7)
1963	Chi	NL	3B	627	45	4	676	196	30	6	26	.312	.363	.506	869	6	4	(3)	(10)	40	896	57.8
1964	Chi	NL	3B	588	89	2	680	189	34	13	31	.321	.413	.580	992	3	4	(7)	(10)	60	1,035	103.4
1965	Chi	NL	3B	604	91	5	701	177	31	4	34	.292	.390	.524	914	3	1	1	(10)	60	965	83.1
1966	Chi	NL	3B	560	96	6	662	176	21	8	30	.315	.421	.544	965	4	5	(9)	(10)	70	1,016	94.6
1967	Chi	NL	3B	579	102	3	685	182	24	4	32	.314	.420	.535	955	1	5	(12)	(10)	80	1,013	96.8
1968	Chi	NL	3B	564	109	3	676	152	18	3	28	.270	.391	.462	854	3	4	(7)	(10)	60	897	58.1
1969	Chi	NL	3B	572	99	2	673	169	18	4	30	.295	.401	.496	898	1	3	(7)	(10)	40	921	65.6
1970	Chi	NL	3B	558	89	1	648	145	29	4	25	.260	.363	.464	826	2	0	3	(10)	30	849	41.1
1971	Chi	NL	3B	552	82	0	634	152	23	1	22	.275	.369	.436	805	4	0	6	(10)	20	821	31.7
1972	Chi	NL	3B	484	76	4	565	151	27	5	18	.312	.411	.504	915	1	4	(12)	(10)	20	912	52.8
1973	Chi	NL	3B	535	64	4	603	144	29	2	20	.269	.351	.444	795	1	2	(5)	(10)	10	791	21.3
1974	Chi	AL	DH	373	39	2	414	86	12	1	5	.232	.309	.313	621	0	2	(9)	(10)	0	602	(16.4)
13.9 Totals				8,179	1,151	40	9,370	2,311	374	69	350					35	42					707.7
1.0 Averages				590	83	3	676	167	27	5	25	.283	.374	.474	847	3	3	(5)	(8)	38	872	51.1

Wade Boggs **Red Sox** **Third Baseman** **Actual**

Year	T	L	P	AB	BB	HBP	TAB	H	2B	3B	HR	BA	OB	SA	PRO	SB	CS	SBF	SPF	FF	Actual TF	Actual HC
1982	Bos	AL	1B	338	35	0	373	118	14	1	5	.349	.410	.441	851	1	0	3	0	0	854	14.8
1983	Bos	AL	3B	582	92	1	675	210	44	7	5	.361	.449	.486	935	3	3	(4)	0	20	951	75.5
1984	Bos	AL	3B	625	89	0	714	203	31	4	6	.325	.409	.416	825	3	2	(1)	0	50	874	53.6
1985	Bos	AL	3B	653	96	4	753	240	42	3	8	.368	.452	.478	929	2	1	0	0	20	949	83.6
1986	Bos	AL	3B	580	105	0	685	207	47	2	8	.357	.455	.486	942	0	4	(11)	0	10	941	73.2
1987	Bos	AL	3B	551	105	2	658	200	40	6	24	.363	.467	.588	1,055	1	3	(7)	0	20	1,067	110.1
1988	Bos	AL	3B	584	125	3	712	214	45	6	5	.366	.480	.490	970	2	3	(5)	0	10	975	87.7
1989	Bos	AL	3B	621	107	7	735	205	51	7	3	.330	.434	.449	883	2	6	(13)	0	10	880	57.5
1990	Bos	AL	3B	619	87	1	707	187	44	5	6	.302	.389	.418	807	0	0	0	0	(30)	777	20.6
1991	Bos	AL	3B	546	89	0	635	181	42	2	8	.332	.425	.460	885	1	2	(4)	0	20	900	55.7
1992	Bos	AL	3B	514	74	4	592	133	22	4	7	.259	.356	.358	714	1	3	(8)	(10)	10	706	(2.8)
1993	NY	AL	3B	560	74	0	634	169	26	1	2	.302	.383	.363	746	0	1	(3)	(10)	60	793	23.1
1994	NY	AL	3B	366	61	1	428	125	19	1	11	.342	.437	.489	926	2	1	0	(10)	50	966	72.1
1995	NY	AL	3B	460	74	0	534	149	22	4	5	.324	.418	.422	839	1	1	(2)	(10)	30	858	40.5
1996	NY	AL	3B	501	67	0	568	156	29	2	2	.311	.393	.389	782	1	2	(5)	(10)	20	787	19.1
1997	NY	AL	3B	353	48	0	401	103	23	1	4	.292	.377	.397	773	0	1	(5)	(10)	30	788	13.8
1998	TB	AL	3B	435	46	0	481	122	23	4	7	.280	.349	.400	749	3	2	(2)	(10)	10	747	7.1
1999	TB	AL	3B	292	38	0	330	88	14	1	2	.301	.382	.377	759	1	0	3	(10)	(20)	731	2.4
16.1	Totals			9,180	1,412	23	10,615	3,010	578	61	118					24	35					807.8
1.0	Averages			571	88	1	661	187	36	4	7	.328	.419	.443	861	1	2	(4)	(4)	19	872	50.3

Wade Boggs **Red Sox** **Third Baseman** **Adjusted**

Year	T	L	P	AB	BB	HBP	TAB	H	2B	3B	HR	BA	OB	SA	Wtd PRO	SB	CS	SBF	SPF	FF	Wtd TF	HC
1982	Bos	AL	1B	338	35	0	373	118	14	1	5	.348	.409	.439	848	1	0	3	0	0	850	14.2
1983	Bos	AL	3B	582	92	1	675	210	44	7	5	.360	.448	.486	934	3	3	(4)	0	20	950	75.1
1984	Bos	AL	3B	624	90	0	714	204	31	4	6	.326	.411	.418	828	3	2	(1)	0	50	877	54.7
1985	Bos	AL	3B	654	95	4	753	239	42	3	8	.365	.448	.475	923	2	1	0	0	20	943	81.4
1986	Bos	AL	3B	582	103	0	685	205	47	2	8	.352	.449	.480	929	0	4	(11)	0	10	928	69.1
1987	Bos	AL	3B	558	98	2	658	194	39	6	23	.348	.448	.564	1,012	1	3	(7)	0	20	1,024	96.6
1988	Bos	AL	3B	581	128	3	712	216	45	6	5	.373	.488	.498	986	2	3	(5)	0	10	991	93.2
1989	Bos	AL	3B	617	111	7	735	209	52	7	3	.338	.445	.461	906	2	6	(13)	0	10	903	65.3
1990	Bos	AL	3B	617	89	1	707	189	45	5	6	.307	.395	.425	821	0	0	0	0	(30)	791	25.1
1991	Bos	AL	3B	545	90	0	635	182	42	2	8	.333	.428	.462	890	1	2	(4)	0	20	905	57.2
1992	Bos	AL	3B	512	76	4	592	135	22	4	7	.264	.363	.365	728	1	3	(8)	(10)	10	720	1.2
1993	NY	AL	3B	563	71	0	634	166	25	1	2	.295	.374	.354	728	0	1	(3)	(10)	60	775	17.7
1994	NY	AL	3B	526	78	1	606	168	26	1	15	.319	.408	.457	864	3	1	0	(10)	50	904	54.3
1995	NY	AL	3B	524	76	0	601	160	24	4	5	.305	.394	.398	792	1	1	(2)	(10)	30	810	26.8
1996	NY	AL	3B	509	59	0	568	145	27	2	2	.285	.359	.356	715	1	2	(5)	(10)	20	720	1.1
1997	NY	AL	3B	357	44	0	401	98	22	1	4	.275	.355	.374	730	0	1	(5)	(10)	30	745	5.5
1998	TB	AL	3B	439	42	0	481	116	22	4	7	.264	.328	.376	704	3	2	(2)	(10)	10	703	(3.1)
1999	TB	AL	3B	296	34	0	330	82	13	1	2	.278	.352	.347	700	1	0	3	(10)	(20)	672	(6.9)
16.1	Totals			9,424	1,412	24	10,859	3,035	581	61	121					25	36					728.5
1.0	Averages			587	88	1	676	189	36	4	8	.322	.412	.435	847	2	2	(4)	(4)	19	858	45.4

Frank Baker   **Athletics**   **Third Baseman**   **Actual**

Year	T	L	P	AB	BB	HBP	TAB	H	2B	3B	HR	BA	OB	SA	PRO	SB	CS	SBF	SPF	FF	Actual TF	Actual HC
1908	Phi	AL	3B	31	0	0	31	9	3	0	0	.290	.290	.387	677	0			10	60	747	0.5
1909	Phi	AL	3B	541	26	5	572	165	27	19	4	.305	.343	.447	790	20			10	(10)	790	21.1
1910	Phi	AL	3B	561	34	4	599	159	25	15	2	.283	.329	.392	721	21			10	20	751	10.5
1911	Phi	AL	3B	592	40	2	634	198	42	14	11	.334	.379	.508	887	38			10	20	917	63.8
1912	Phi	AL	3B	577	50	6	633	200	40	21	10	.347	.404	.541	945	40			10	40	995	88.5
1913	Phi	AL	3B	564	63	10	637	190	34	9	12	.337	.413	.493	906	34			10	20	936	70.1
1914	Phi	AL	3B	570	53	3	626	182	23	10	9	.319	.380	.442	822	19	20	(32)	10	40	841	39.0
1916	NY	AL	3B	360	36	5	401	97	23	2	10	.269	.344	.428	772	15			0	10	782	13.2
1917	NY	AL	3B	553	48	5	606	156	24	2	6	.282	.345	.365	710	18			0	30	740	7.3
1918	NY	AL	3B	504	38	2	544	154	24	5	6	.306	.357	.409	765	8			0	40	805	29.5
1919	NY	AL	3B	567	44	2	613	166	22	1	10	.293	.346	.388	734	13			0	0	734	6.0
1921	NY	AL	3B	330	26	4	360	97	16	2	9	.294	.353	.436	789	8	5	(5)	0	0	784	12.2
1922	NY	AL	3B	234	15	2	251	65	12	3	7	.278	.327	.444	771	1	3	(19)	0	(40)	712	(0.5)
10.4	Totals			5,984	473	50	6,507	1,838	315	103	96					235	28					361.2
1.0	Averages			575	45	5	626	177	30	10	9	.307	.363	.442	805	23	3	(4)	6	18	825	34.7

Frank Baker   **Athletics**   **Third Baseman**   **Adjusted**

Year	T	L	P	AB	BB	HBP	TAB	H	2B	3B	HR	BA	OB	SA	Wtd PRO	SB	CS	SBF	SPF	FF	Wtd TF	HC
1908	Phi	AL	3B	33	0	0	33	11	4	0	0	.343	.343	.457	800	0			10	60	870	2.4
1909	Phi	AL	3B	561	34	7	602	198	32	23	5	.352	.396	.517	913	21			10	(10)	913	56.3
1910	Phi	AL	3B	582	43	5	630	188	29	18	2	.322	.374	.446	820	22			10	20	850	40.1
1911	Phi	AL	3B	622	43	2	667	211	45	15	12	.339	.384	.516	900	40			10	20	930	67.8
1912	Phi	AL	3B	604	56	7	666	217	43	23	11	.359	.419	.560	980	42			10	40	1,030	99.5
1913	Phi	AL	3B	585	73	12	670	211	38	10	13	.360	.441	.526	967	36			10	20	997	89.7
1914	Phi	AL	3B	591	64	4	659	207	26	11	10	.351	.418	.486	904	20	21	(32)	10	40	922	64.7
1916	NY	AL	3B	373	43	6	422	110	26	2	11	.295	.377	.468	845	16			0	10	855	27.9
1917	NY	AL	3B	573	58	6	637	179	28	2	7	.312	.382	.404	786	19			0	30	816	30.2
1918	NY	AL	3B	636	55	3	694	212	33	7	8	.334	.390	.447	836	10			0	40	876	52.9
1919	NY	AL	3B	655	52	2	709	195	26	1	12	.299	.353	.396	749	15			0	0	749	10.9
1921	NY	AL	3B	350	24	4	379	95	16	2	9	.271	.326	.403	728	8	5	(5)	0	0	723	1.2
1922	NY	AL	3B	247	15	2	264	65	12	3	7	.263	.309	.421	730	1	3	(19)	0	(40)	671	(5.7)
10.4	Totals			6,411	561	59	7,031	2,099	358	117	107					250	29					537.9
1.0	Averages			616	54	6	676	202	34	11	10	.327	.387	.470	857	24	3	(4)	6	18	877	51.7

Edgar Martinez **Mariners** **DH / Third Baseman** **Actual**

Year	T	L	P	AB	BB	HBP	TAB	H	2B	3B	HR	BA	OB	SA	PRO	SB	CS	SBF	SPF	FF	Actual TF	Actual HC
1987	Sea	AL	3B	43	2	1	46	16	5	2	0	.372	.413	.581	994	0	0	0	0	0	994	6.1
1988	Sea	AL	3B	32	4	0	36	9	4	0	0	.281	.361	.406	767	0	0	0	0	(90)	677	(0.7)
1989	Sea	AL	3B	171	17	3	191	41	5	0	2	.240	.319	.304	623	2	1	0	0	(40)	583	(12.1)
1990	Sea	AL	3B	487	74	5	566	147	27	2	11	.302	.399	.433	833	1	4	(12)	0	(20)	801	22.8
1991	Sea	AL	3B	544	84	8	636	167	35	1	14	.307	.407	.452	859	0	3	(9)	0	0	851	40.7
1992	Sea	AL	3B	528	54	4	586	181	46	3	18	.343	.408	.544	951	14	4	10	0	0	961	68.4
1993	Sea	AL	DH	135	28	0	163	32	7	0	4	.237	.368	.378	746	0	0	0	0	(50)	696	(1.6)
1994	Sea	AL	3B	326	53	3	382	93	23	1	13	.285	.390	.482	872	6	2	5	0	0	877	41.3
1995	Sea	AL	DH	511	116	8	635	182	52	0	29	.356	.482	.628	1,110	4	3	(3)	0	(30)	1,077	122.8
1996	Sea	AL	DH	499	123	8	630	163	52	2	26	.327	.467	.595	1,062	3	3	(5)	0	(30)	1,027	77.2
1997	Sea	AL	DH	542	119	11	672	179	35	1	28	.330	.460	.554	1,013	2	4	(8)	0	(30)	975	65.6
1998	Sea	AL	DH	556	106	3	665	179	46	1	29	.322	.433	.565	998	1	1	(1)	(10)	(30)	956	59.1
1999	Sea	AL	DH	502	97	6	605	169	35	1	24	.337	.450	.554	1,003	7	2	5	(10)	(30)	968	57.1
2000	Sea	AL	DH	556	96	5	657	180	31	0	37	.324	.428	.579	1,007	3	0	4	(10)	(30)	971	63.0
9.9 Totals				5,432	973	65	6,470	1,738	403	14	235					43	27					609.7
1.0 Averages				547	98	7	652	175	41	1	24	.320	.429	.529	958	4	3	(2)	(3)	(22)	932	61.4

Edgar Martinez **Mariners** **DH / Third Baseman** **Adjusted**

Year	T	L	P	AB	BB	HBP	TAB	H	2B	3B	HR	BA	OB	SA	Wtd PRO	SB	CS	SBF	SPF	FF	Wtd TF	HC
1987	Sea	AL	3B	43	2	1	46	15	5	2	0	.357	.396	.558	954	0	0	0	0	0	954	5.2
1988	Sea	AL	3B	32	4	0	36	9	4	0	0	.286	.367	.413	780	0	0	0	0	(90)	690	(0.4)
1989	Sea	AL	3B	170	18	3	191	42	5	0	2	.246	.327	.312	639	2	1	0	0	(40)	599	(10.6)
1990	Sea	AL	3B	485	76	5	566	149	27	2	11	.307	.406	.440	846	1	4	(12)	0	(20)	815	26.6
1991	Sea	AL	3B	543	85	8	636	168	35	1	14	.309	.409	.455	864	0	3	(9)	0	0	855	42.1
1992	Sea	AL	3B	526	56	4	586	184	47	3	18	.350	.416	.554	970	14	4	10	0	0	980	73.6
1993	Sea	AL	DH	136	27	0	163	31	7	0	4	.231	.359	.369	728	0	0	0	0	(50)	678	(3.0)
1994	Sea	AL	3B	468	68	4	540	125	31	1	17	.266	.364	.450	814	8	3	5	0	0	819	26.4
1995	Sea	AL	DH	587	119	8	714	197	56	0	31	.336	.454	.592	1,047	5	3	(3)	0	(30)	1,014	101.3
1996	Sea	AL	DH	515	108	7	630	154	49	2	25	.299	.427	.544	971	3	3	(5)	0	(30)	937	50.1
1997	Sea	AL	DH	553	109	10	672	172	34	1	27	.312	.434	.522	956	2	4	(8)	0	(30)	918	47.4
1998	Sea	AL	DH	565	97	3	665	171	44	1	28	.303	.407	.531	938	1	1	(1)	(10)	(30)	897	40.2
1999	Sea	AL	DH	514	86	5	605	159	33	1	23	.311	.415	.511	925	7	2	5	(10)	(30)	890	34.6
2000	Sea	AL	DH	568	84	4	657	168	29	0	35	.296	.392	.530	922	3	0	4	(10)	(30)	886	36.3
9.9 Totals				5,706	939	63	6,708	1,745	406	14	235					46	28					469.7
1.0 Averages				575	95	6	676	176	41	1	24	.306	.410	.505	915	5	3	(1)	(3)	(22)	888	47.3

Chipper Jones **Braves** **Third Baseman** **Actual**

Year	T	L	P	AB	BB	HBP	TAB	H	2B	3B	HR	BA	OB	SA	PRO	SB	CS	SBF	SPF	FF	Actual TF	Actual HC
1993	Atl	NL	SS	3	1	0	4	2	1	0	0	.667	.750	1.000	1,750	0	0	0	10	90	1,850	2.3
1995	Atl	NL	3B	524	73	0	597	139	22	3	23	.265	.355	.450	805	8	4	0	10	0	815	31.8
1996	Atl	NL	3B	598	87	0	685	185	32	5	30	.309	.397	.530	927	14	1	17	10	(20)	934	71.0
1997	Atl	NL	3B	597	76	0	673	176	41	3	21	.295	.374	.479	854	20	5	14	10	(20)	858	45.3
1998	Atl	NL	3B	601	96	1	698	188	29	5	34	.313	.408	.547	956	16	6	5	10	20	991	91.4
1999	Atl	NL	3B	567	126	2	695	181	41	1	45	.319	.445	.633	1,078	25	3	26	10	0	1,114	131.6
2000	Atl	NL	3B	579	95	2	676	180	38	1	36	.311	.410	.566	976	14	7	0	10	(10)	976	83.8
6.1 Totals				3,469	554	5	4,028	1,051	204	18	189					97	26					457.1
1.0 Averages				572	91	1	664	173	34	3	31	.303	.400	.536	935	16	4	11	10	(5)	951	75.3

Chipper Jones **Braves** **Third Baseman** **Adjusted**

Year	T	L	P	AB	BB	HBP	TAB	H	2B	3B	HR	BA	OB	SA	Wtd PRO	SB	CS	SBF	SPF	FF	Wtd TF	HC
1993	Atl	NL	SS	3	1	0	4	2	1	0	0	.646	.726	.968	1,695	0	0	0	10	90	1,795	2.2
1995	Atl	NL	3B	595	77	0	672	150	24	3	25	.253	.338	.429	767	9	5	0	10	0	777	19.6
1996	Atl	NL	3B	604	81	0	685	178	31	5	29	.295	.378	.505	883	14	1	17	10	(20)	890	56.7
1997	Atl	NL	3B	602	71	0	673	169	39	3	20	.280	.355	.455	810	20	5	14	10	(20)	814	31.4
1998	Atl	NL	3B	608	89	1	698	181	28	5	33	.298	.389	.521	910	16	6	5	10	20	945	76.1
1999	Atl	NL	3B	582	111	2	695	170	39	1	42	.292	.407	.579	986	25	3	26	10	0	1,022	101.2
2000	Atl	NL	3B	591	83	2	676	168	35	1	34	.284	.374	.517	891	14	7	0	10	(10)	891	56.2
6.1 Totals				3,585	513	4	4,103	1,017	197	18	182					98	27					343.2
1.0 Averages				591	85	1	676	168	32	3	30	.284	.374	.501	875	16	4	10	10	(5)	891	56.6

Ken Boyer **Cardinals** **Third Baseman** **Actual**

Year	T	L	P	AB	BB	HBP	TAB	H	2B	3B	HR	BA	OB	SA	PRO	SB	CS	SBF	SPF	FF	Actual TF	Actual HC
1955	StL	NL	3B	530	37	1	568	140	27	2	18	.264	.313	.425	738	22	17	(20)	10	20	748	9.0
1956	StL	NL	3B	595	38	1	634	182	30	2	26	.306	.349	.494	843	8	3	3	10	30	886	53.9
1957	StL	NL	OF	544	44	1	589	144	18	3	19	.265	.321	.414	734	12	8	(6)	10	10	748	(2.8)
1958	StL	NL	3B	570	49	3	622	175	21	9	23	.307	.365	.496	861	11	6	(2)	10	70	940	69.7
1959	StL	NL	3B	563	67	2	632	174	18	5	28	.309	.384	.508	892	12	6	0	10	50	952	74.8
1960	StL	NL	3B	552	56	4	612	168	26	10	32	.304	.373	.562	934	8	7	(9)	10	60	995	85.5
1961	StL	NL	3B	589	68	1	658	194	26	11	24	.329	.400	.533	933	6	3	0	10	40	983	87.9
1962	StL	NL	3B	611	75	1	687	178	27	5	24	.291	.370	.470	839	12	7	(3)	10	30	877	52.5
1963	StL	NL	3B	617	70	2	689	176	28	2	24	.285	.360	.454	814	1	0	1	10	30	855	45.6
1964	StL	NL	3B	628	70	2	700	185	30	10	24	.295	.367	.489	856	3	5	(9)	10	10	867	50.1
1965	StL	NL	3B	535	57	1	593	139	18	2	13	.260	.332	.374	706	2	7	(19)	10	10	707	(2.6)
1966	NY	NL	3B	496	30	0	526	132	28	2	14	.266	.308	.415	723	4	3	(4)	10	30	760	10.9
1967	NY	NL	3B	346	33	0	379	86	12	3	7	.249	.314	.361	675	2	3	(10)	0	0	665	(9.2)
1968	LA	NL	3B	245	17	1	263	63	7	2	6	.257	.308	.376	683	2	2	(7)	0	(30)	646	(8.8)
1969	LA	NL	1B	34	2	0	36	7	2	0	0	.206	.250	.265	515	0	0	0	0	0	515	(4.4)
12.4 Totals				7,455	713	20	8,188	2,143	318	68	282					105	77					512.3
1.0 Averages				599	57	2	658	172	26	5	23	.287	.351	.462	813	8	6	(6)	9	29	846	41.2

Ken Boyer **Cardinals** **Third Baseman** **Adjusted**

Year	T	L	P	AB	BB	HBP	TAB	H	2B	3B	HR	BA	OB	SA	Wtd PRO	SB	CS	SBF	SPF	FF	Wtd TF	HC
1955	StL	NL	3B	560	37	1	598	142	27	2	18	.253	.300	.407	707	23	18	(20)	10	20	717	0.2
1956	StL	NL	3B	627	38	1	667	187	31	2	27	.298	.339	.481	820	8	3	3	10	30	863	46.8
1957	StL	NL	OF	574	45	1	620	148	19	3	20	.258	.313	.403	716	13	8	(6)	10	10	730	(8.2)
1958	StL	NL	3B	603	49	3	654	178	21	9	23	.295	.351	.477	827	12	6	(2)	10	70	906	59.1
1959	StL	NL	3B	595	68	2	665	179	18	5	29	.300	.373	.493	867	13	6	0	10	50	927	66.6
1960	StL	NL	3B	581	58	4	644	176	27	10	33	.303	.370	.558	929	8	7	(9)	10	60	989	83.8
1961	StL	NL	3B	624	67	1	692	197	26	11	24	.316	.384	.512	896	6	3	0	10	40	946	75.7
1962	StL	NL	3B	613	73	1	687	175	27	5	24	.285	.361	.459	821	12	7	(3)	10	30	858	46.4
1963	StL	NL	3B	612	75	2	689	184	29	2	25	.300	.379	.477	856	1	0	1	10	30	897	59.5
1964	StL	NL	3B	625	73	2	700	189	31	10	25	.303	.377	.502	880	3	5	(9)	10	10	890	58.0
1965	StL	NL	3B	533	59	1	593	142	18	2	13	.267	.341	.384	725	2	7	(19)	10	10	726	2.9
1966	NY	NL	3B	496	30	0	526	133	28	2	14	.269	.311	.419	730	4	3	(4)	10	30	767	12.7
1967	NY	NL	3B	344	35	0	379	89	12	3	7	.260	.328	.378	706	2	3	(10)	0	0	696	(3.6)
1968	LA	NL	3B	243	19	1	263	68	8	2	7	.282	.338	.412	750	2	2	(7)	0	(30)	713	(0.4)
1969	LA	NL	1B	34	2	0	36	7	2	0	0	.211	.256	.271	527	0	0	0	0	0	527	(4.2)
12.4 Totals				7,663	729	21	8,412	2,194	325	70	289					109	80					495.4
1.0 Averages				616	59	2	676	176	26	6	23	.286	.350	.460	810	9	6	(6)	9	29	843	39.8

Paul Molitor **Brewers** **DH/Third Baseman** **Actual**

Year	T	L	P	AB	BB	HBP	TAB	H	2B	3B	HR	BA	OB	SA	PRO	SB	CS	SBF	SPF	FF	Actual TF	Actual HC
1978	Mil	AL	2B	521	19	4	544	142	26	4	6	.273	.303	.372	676	30	12	10	10	(20)	676	(2.4)
1979	Mil	AL	2B	584	48	2	634	188	27	16	9	.322	.375	.469	845	33	13	10	10	0	865	54.3
1980	Mil	AL	2B	450	48	3	501	137	29	2	9	.304	.375	.438	813	34	7	38	10	0	861	41.9
1981	Mil	AL	OF	251	25	3	279	67	11	0	2	.267	.341	.335	675	10	6	(7)	10	0	678	(15.9)
1982	Mil	AL	3B	666	69	1	736	201	26	8	19	.302	.368	.450	819	41	9	30	10	0	858	49.8
1983	Mil	AL	3B	608	59	2	669	164	28	6	15	.270	.336	.410	746	41	8	35	10	0	791	23.9
1984	Mil	AL	3B	46	2	0	48	10	1	0	0	.217	.250	.239	489	1	0	20	10	0	519	(4.5)
1985	Mil	AL	3B	576	54	1	631	171	28	3	10	.297	.358	.408	766	21	7	10	10	0	787	21.2
1986	Mil	AL	3B	437	40	0	477	123	24	6	9	.281	.342	.426	767	20	5	20	10	0	797	18.4
1987	Mil	AL	DH	465	69	2	536	164	41	5	16	.353	.438	.566	1,004	45	10	44	10	(20)	1,038	82.2
1988	Mil	AL	3B	609	71	2	682	190	34	6	13	.312	.386	.452	837	41	10	29	10	(20)	856	45.5
1989	Mil	AL	3B	615	64	4	683	194	35	4	11	.315	.384	.439	823	27	11	7	10	0	840	40.1
1990	Mil	AL	2B	418	37	1	456	119	27	6	12	.285	.344	.464	808	18	3	25	10	(10)	833	32.1
1991	Mil	AL	DH	665	77	6	748	216	32	13	17	.325	.400	.489	888	19	8	4	10	(20)	882	40.0
1992	Mil	AL	DH	609	73	3	685	195	36	7	12	.320	.396	.461	857	31	6	26	10	(20)	873	33.7
1993	Tor	AL	DH	636	77	3	716	211	37	5	22	.332	.406	.509	916	22	4	18	10	(20)	924	52.6
1994	Tor	AL	DH	454	55	1	510	155	30	4	14	.341	.414	.518	931	20	0	37	10	(20)	958	64.8
1995	Tor	AL	DH	525	61	5	591	142	31	2	15	.270	.352	.423	775	12	0	19	10	(20)	784	4.4
1996	Min	AL	DH	660	56	3	719	225	41	8	9	.341	.395	.468	863	18	6	8	10	(30)	851	27.8
1997	Min	AL	DH	538	45	0	583	164	32	4	10	.305	.358	.435	793	11	4	5	10	(30)	778	2.3
1998	Min	AL	DH	502	45	1	548	141	29	5	4	.281	.341	.382	724	9	2	9	10	(30)	712	(15.1)
18.4 Totals				10,835	1,094	47	11,976	3,319	605	114	234					504	131					597.2
1.0 Averages				590	60	3	653	181	33	6	13	.306	.372	.448	820	27	7	19	10	(13)	836	32.5

Paul Molitor **Brewers** **DH/Third Baseman** **Adjusted**

Year	T	L	P	AB	BB	HBP	TAB	H	2B	3B	HR	BA	OB	SA	Wtd PRO	SB	CS	SBF	SPF	FF	Wtd TF	HC
1978	Mil	AL	2B	520	20	4	544	145	27	4	6	.279	.310	.381	691	30	12	10	10	(20)	691	1.5
1979	Mil	AL	2B	586	46	2	634	184	26	16	9	.315	.367	.459	826	33	13	10	10	0	847	48.8
1980	Mil	AL	2B	450	48	3	501	137	29	2	9	.303	.374	.436	810	34	7	38	10	0	857	41.1
1981	Mil	AL	OF	377	40	5	422	106	17	0	3	.280	.357	.351	708	15	9	(7)	10	0	711	(9.3)
1982	Mil	AL	3B	666	69	1	736	200	26	8	19	.301	.367	.449	815	41	9	30	10	0	855	48.6
1983	Mil	AL	3B	608	59	2	669	164	28	6	15	.269	.336	.409	745	41	8	35	10	0	790	23.6
1984	Mil	AL	3B	46	2	0	48	10	1	0	0	.218	.251	.240	491	1	0	20	10	0	521	(4.5)
1985	Mil	AL	3B	577	53	1	631	170	28	3	10	.295	.356	.405	761	21	7	10	10	0	781	19.6
1986	Mil	AL	3B	438	39	0	477	122	24	6	9	.278	.337	.420	757	20	5	20	10	0	787	16.0
1987	Mil	AL	DH	469	65	2	536	159	40	5	15	.338	.421	.543	963	45	10	44	10	(20)	997	71.8
1988	Mil	AL	3B	607	73	2	682	193	34	6	13	.317	.392	.459	851	41	10	29	10	(20)	870	50.1
1989	Mil	AL	3B	612	66	4	683	198	36	4	11	.323	.393	.450	843	27	11	7	10	0	860	46.9
1990	Mil	AL	2B	417	38	1	456	121	27	6	12	.289	.350	.472	822	18	3	25	10	(10)	847	35.1
1991	Mil	AL	DH	664	78	6	748	217	32	13	17	.327	.402	.491	893	19	8	4	10	(20)	887	41.7
1992	Mil	AL	DH	607	75	3	685	198	37	7	12	.326	.403	.470	874	31	6	26	10	(20)	890	39.2
1993	Tor	AL	DH	639	74	3	716	207	36	5	22	.324	.397	.497	894	22	4	18	10	(20)	902	45.1
1994	Tor	AL	DH	650	70	1	722	207	40	5	19	.319	.386	.483	869	28	0	37	10	(20)	896	43.5
1995	Tor	AL	DH	596	63	5	665	152	33	2	16	.255	.332	.399	731	14	0	19	10	(20)	740	(9.5)
1996	Min	AL	DH	667	49	3	719	208	38	7	8	.312	.361	.428	790	18	6	8	10	(30)	777	2.6
1997	Min	AL	DH	542	41	0	583	156	30	4	10	.288	.338	.411	749	11	4	5	10	(30)	734	(10.1)
1998	Min	AL	DH	506	41	1	548	134	27	5	4	.264	.321	.360	680	9	2	9	10	(30)	669	(26.4)
18.4 Totals				11,245	1,111	49	12,405	3,386	617	114	239					519	134					515.4
1.0 Averages				613	61	3	676	185	34	6	13	.301	.366	.440	807	28	7	19	10	(13)	822	28.1

Babe Ruth   **Yankees**   **Outfielder**   **Actual**

Year	T	L	P	AB	BB	HBP	TAB	H	2B	3B	HR	BA	OB	SA	PRO	SB	CS	SBF	SPF	FF	Actual TF	Actual HC
1914	Bos	AL	P	10	0	0	10	2	1	0	0	.200	.200	.300	500	0			10	10	520	0.4
1915	Bos	AL	P	92	9	0	101	29	10	1	4	.315	.376	.576	952	0			10	20	982	27.3
1916	Bos	AL	P	136	10	0	146	37	5	3	3	.272	.322	.419	741	0			10	20	771	24.1
1917	Bos	AL	P	123	12	0	135	40	6	3	2	.325	.385	.472	857	0			10	30	897	30.8
1918	Bos	AL	OF	317	57	2	376	95	26	11	11	.300	.410	.555	965	6			10	20	995	54.2
1919	Bos	AL	OF	432	101	6	539	139	34	12	29	.322	.456	.657	1,114	7			10	50	1,174	123.7
1920	NY	AL	OF	458	148	3	609	172	36	9	54	.376	.530	.847	1,378	14	14	(22)	10	10	1,376	188.7
1921	NY	AL	OF	540	144	4	688	204	44	16	59	.378	.512	.846	1,358	17	13	(12)	10	20	1,376	213.1
1922	NY	AL	OF	406	84	1	491	128	24	8	35	.315	.434	.672	1,106	2	5	(15)	10	10	1,111	87.0
1923	NY	AL	OF	522	170	4	696	205	45	13	41	.393	.545	.764	1,309	17	21	(34)	10	40	1,325	198.0
1924	NY	AL	OF	529	142	4	675	200	39	7	46	.378	.513	.739	1,252	9	13	(24)	0	20	1,248	165.9
1925	NY	AL	OF	359	59	2	420	104	12	2	25	.290	.393	.543	936	2	4	(14)	0	30	953	41.1
1926	NY	AL	OF	495	144	3	642	184	30	5	47	.372	.516	.737	1,253	11	9	(10)	0	20	1,263	162.6
1927	NY	AL	OF	540	138	0	678	192	29	8	60	.356	.487	.772	1,259	7	6	(7)	0	20	1,272	174.8
1928	NY	AL	OF	536	135	3	674	173	29	8	54	.323	.461	.709	1,170	4	5	(8)	0	0	1,162	136.7
1929	NY	AL	OF	499	72	3	574	172	26	6	46	.345	.430	.697	1,128	5	3	(2)	0	(10)	1,116	103.2
1930	NY	AL	OF	518	136	1	655	186	28	9	49	.359	.493	.732	1,225	10	10	(14)	0	(10)	1,200	145.4
1931	NY	AL	OF	534	128	0	662	199	31	3	46	.373	.494	.700	1,194	5	4	(4)	0	(20)	1,170	136.9
1932	NY	AL	OF	457	130	2	589	156	13	5	41	.341	.489	.661	1,150	2	2	(3)	0	(20)	1,127	109.0
1933	NY	AL	OF	459	114	2	575	138	21	3	34	.301	.442	.582	1,023	4	5	(10)	0	(20)	994	68.1
1934	NY	AL	OF	365	103	2	470	105	17	4	22	.288	.447	.537	984	1	3	(10)	(10)	(20)	944	43.9
1935	Bos	NL	OF	72	20	0	92	13	0	0	6	.181	.359	.431	789	0			(10)	(40)	739	(0.8)
16.5	Totals			8,399	2,056	42	10,497	2,873	506	136	714					123	117					2,234.0
1.0	Averages			508	124	3	635	174	31	8	43	.342	.474	.690	1,163	7	7	(11)	3	9	1,164	135.0

Babe Ruth   **Yankees**   **Outfielder**   **Adjusted**

Year	T	L	P	AB	BB	HBP	TAB	H	2B	3B	HR	BA	OB	SA	Wtd PRO	SB	CS	SBF	SPF	FF	Wtd TF	HC
1914	Bos	AL	P	11	0	0	11	2	1	0	0	.220	.220	.330	550	0			10	10	570	0.6
1915	Bos	AL	P	96	11	0	106	33	11	1	5	.342	.408	.625	1,033	0			10	20	1,063	31.4
1916	Bos	AL	P	142	12	0	154	42	6	3	3	.298	.352	.459	811	0			10	20	841	29.2
1917	Bos	AL	P	127	15	0	142	46	7	3	2	.360	.426	.522	948	0			10	30	988	36.9
1918	Bos	AL	OF	394	83	3	480	129	35	15	15	.327	.448	.607	1,054	8			10	20	1,084	74.7
1919	Bos	AL	OF	496	120	7	624	163	40	14	34	.328	.466	.671	1,136	8			10	50	1,196	130.4
1920	NY	AL	OF	491	146	3	641	177	37	9	56	.361	.510	.815	1,325	15	15	(22)	10	10	1,323	172.7
1921	NY	AL	OF	587	134	4	724	204	44	16	59	.349	.472	.781	1,253	18	14	(12)	10	20	1,271	177.0
1922	NY	AL	OF	434	82	1	517	129	24	8	35	.298	.410	.636	1,047	2	5	(15)	10	10	1,051	72.3
1923	NY	AL	OF	562	166	4	732	211	46	13	42	.375	.520	.730	1,250	18	22	(34)	10	40	1,266	177.5
1924	NY	AL	OF	572	134	4	710	202	39	7	46	.353	.479	.691	1,170	9	14	(24)	0	20	1,167	138.4
1925	NY	AL	OF	385	55	2	442	102	12	2	25	.266	.361	.499	860	2	4	(14)	0	30	877	25.1
1926	NY	AL	OF	533	140	3	675	188	31	5	48	.353	.490	.701	1,190	12	9	(10)	0	20	1,200	142.4
1927	NY	AL	OF	581	132	0	713	194	29	8	61	.334	.457	.726	1,183	7	6	(7)	0	20	1,196	149.2
1928	NY	AL	OF	574	132	3	709	176	30	8	55	.307	.440	.675	1,115	4	5	(8)	0	0	1,107	117.9
1929	NY	AL	OF	533	68	3	604	171	26	6	46	.322	.402	.651	1,053	5	3	(2)	0	(10)	1,041	81.7
1930	NY	AL	OF	563	125	1	689	185	28	9	49	.328	.451	.669	1,120	11	11	(14)	0	(10)	1,095	111.0
1931	NY	AL	OF	571	125	0	696	203	32	3	47	.355	.471	.668	1,139	5	4	(4)	0	(20)	1,115	118.6
1932	NY	AL	OF	493	125	2	620	158	13	5	42	.321	.460	.622	1,082	2	2	(3)	0	(20)	1,059	89.0
1933	NY	AL	OF	489	114	2	605	142	22	3	35	.290	.426	.561	987	4	5	(10)	0	(20)	957	57.5
1934	NY	AL	OF	393	100	2	494	106	17	4	22	.271	.421	.505	926	1	3	(10)	(10)	(20)	886	30.3
1935	Bos	NL	OF	76	20	0	97	13	0	0	6	.177	.351	.421	772	0			(10)	(40)	722	(1.6)
16.5	Totals			9,102	2,039	43	11,183	2,980	530	144	733					131	123					1,962.2
1.0	Averages			550	123	3	676	180	32	9	44	.327	.453	.659	1,112	8	7	(11)	3	9	1,112	118.6

Ted Williams **Red Sox** **Outfielder** **Actual**

Year	T	L	P	AB	BB	HBP	TAB	H	2B	3B	HR	BA	OB	SA	PRO	SB	CS	SBF	SPF	FF	Actual TF	Actual HC
1939	Bos	AL	OF	565	107	2	674	185	44	11	31	.327	.436	.609	1,045	2	1	0	0	(20)	1,025	90.4
1940	Bos	AL	OF	561	96	3	660	193	43	14	23	.344	.442	.594	1,036	4	4	(6)	0	0	1,030	90.3
1941	Bos	AL	OF	456	145	3	604	185	33	3	37	.406	.551	.735	1,286	2	4	(9)	0	0	1,277	157.2
1942	Bos	AL	OF	522	145	4	671	186	34	5	36	.356	.499	.648	1,147	3	2	(1)	0	0	1,145	130.5
1946	Bos	AL	OF	514	156	2	672	176	37	8	38	.342	.497	.667	1,164	0	0	0	0	0	1,164	137.1
1947	Bos	AL	OF	528	162	2	692	181	40	9	32	.343	.499	.634	1,133	0	1	(3)	0	0	1,130	129.3
1948	Bos	AL	OF	509	126	3	638	188	44	3	25	.369	.497	.615	1,112	4	0	6	0	0	1,118	115.2
1949	Bos	AL	OF	566	162	2	730	194	39	3	43	.343	.490	.650	1,141	1	1	(1)	0	0	1,139	139.7
1950	Bos	AL	OF	334	82	0	416	106	24	1	28	.317	.452	.647	1,099	3	0	7	0	(20)	1,085	68.4
1951	Bos	AL	OF	531	144	0	675	169	28	4	30	.318	.464	.556	1,019	1	1	(1)	0	0	1,018	88.1
1952	Bos	AL	OF	10	2	0	12	4	0	1	1	.400	.500	.900	1,400	0	0	0	0	0	1,400	3.9
1953	Bos	AL	OF	91	19	0	110	37	6	0	13	.407	.509	.901	1,410	0	1	(17)	0	(30)	1,363	33.4
1954	Bos	AL	OF	386	136	1	523	133	23	1	29	.345	.516	.635	1,151	0	0	0	0	(10)	1,141	100.5
1955	Bos	AL	OF	320	91	2	413	114	21	3	28	.356	.501	.703	1,204	2	0	5	0	0	1,209	93.5
1956	Bos	AL	OF	400	102	1	503	138	28	2	24	.345	.479	.605	1,084	0	0	0	(10)	(10)	1,064	77.3
1957	Bos	AL	OF	420	119	5	544	163	28	1	38	.388	.528	.731	1,259	0	1	(3)	(10)	(10)	1,235	130.2
1958	Bos	AL	OF	411	98	4	513	135	23	2	26	.328	.462	.584	1,046	1	0	2	(10)	(30)	1,008	64.4
1959	Bos	AL	OF	272	52	2	326	69	15	0	10	.254	.377	.419	796	0	0	0	(10)	(30)	756	(0.2)
1960	Bos	AL	OF	310	75	3	388	98	15	0	29	.316	.454	.645	1,099	1	1	(2)	(10)	(20)	1,066	60.1
15.2	Totals			7,706	2,019	39	9,764	2,654	525	71	521					24	17					1,709.2
1.0	Averages			507	133	3	643	175	35	5	34	.344	.483	.634	1,116	2	1	(1)	(2)	(8)	1,106	112.5

Ted Williams **Red Sox** **Outfielder** **Adjusted**

Year	T	L	P	AB	BB	HBP	TAB	H	2B	3B	HR	BA	OB	SA	Wtd PRO	SB	CS	SBF	SPF	FF	Wtd TF	HC
1939	Bos	AL	OF	606	101	2	709	185	44	11	31	.305	.406	.566	972	2	1	0	0	(20)	952	65.7
1940	Bos	AL	OF	599	92	3	694	194	43	14	23	.324	.416	.559	975	4	4	(6)	0	0	969	70.1
1941	Bos	AL	OF	488	144	3	635	192	34	3	38	.392	.533	.710	1,244	2	4	(9)	0	0	1,234	144.3
1942	Bos	AL	OF	542	160	4	706	199	36	5	38	.367	.514	.666	1,180	3	2	(1)	0	0	1,179	141.6
1946	Bos	AL	OF	536	169	2	707	187	39	9	40	.349	.507	.681	1,188	0	0	0	0	0	1,188	144.9
1947	Bos	AL	OF	552	173	2	728	192	42	10	34	.347	.504	.642	1,146	0	1	(3)	0	0	1,143	133.8
1948	Bos	AL	OF	543	125	3	671	194	45	3	26	.357	.480	.594	1,074	4	0	6	0	0	1,080	103.0
1949	Bos	AL	OF	605	161	2	768	200	40	3	44	.331	.473	.627	1,100	1	1	(1)	0	0	1,099	124.8
1950	Bos	AL	OF	360	78	0	438	106	24	1	28	.295	.420	.601	1,022	3	0	7	0	(20)	1,009	52.4
1951	Bos	AL	OF	564	146	0	710	175	29	4	31	.311	.453	.542	995	1	1	(1)	0	0	994	80.0
1952	Bos	AL	OF	10	2	0	13	4	0	1	1	.406	.508	.914	1,422	0	0	0	0	0	1,422	4.0
1953	Bos	AL	OF	96	19	0	116	38	6	0	13	.399	.499	.883	1,383	0	1	(17)	0	(30)	1,335	31.9
1954	Bos	AL	OF	406	143	1	550	140	24	1	30	.344	.515	.634	1,149	0	0	0	0	(10)	1,139	100.1
1955	Bos	AL	OF	340	93	2	434	119	22	3	29	.349	.491	.689	1,181	2	0	5	0	0	1,185	88.6
1956	Bos	AL	OF	428	101	1	529	141	29	2	25	.330	.459	.579	1,038	0	0	0	(10)	(10)	1,018	65.8
1957	Bos	AL	OF	443	124	5	572	171	29	1	40	.386	.525	.727	1,251	0	1	(3)	(10)	(10)	1,228	128.2
1958	Bos	AL	OF	433	103	4	540	142	24	2	27	.328	.461	.583	1,044	1	0	2	(10)	(30)	1,006	64.0
1959	Bos	AL	OF	286	54	2	343	72	16	0	10	.253	.376	.417	793	0	0	0	(10)	(30)	753	(0.7)
1960	Bos	AL	OF	328	77	3	408	102	16	0	30	.311	.446	.634	1,080	1	1	(2)	(10)	(20)	1,048	56.5
15.2	Totals			8,165	2,066	40	10,271	2,752	544	73	541					25	18					1,598.9
1.0	Averages			537	136	3	676	181	36	5	36	.337	.473	.620	1,093	2	1	(1)	(2)	(8)	1,082	105.2

Ty Cobb **Tigers** **Outfielder** **Actual**

Year	T	L	P	AB	BB	HBP	TAB	H	2B	3B	HR	BA	OB	SA	PRO	SB	CS	SBF	SPF	FF	Actual TF	Actual HC
1905	Det	AL	OF	150	10	0	160	36	6	0	1	.240	.288	.300	588	2			10	30	628	(10.4)
1906	Det	AL	OF	358	19	3	380	113	15	5	1	.316	.355	.394	749	23			10	30	789	6.0
1907	Det	AL	OF	605	24	5	634	212	28	14	5	.350	.380	.468	848	49			10	30	888	41.5
1908	Det	AL	OF	581	34	6	621	188	36	20	4	.324	.367	.475	842	39			10	20	872	35.7
1909	Det	AL	OF	573	48	6	627	216	33	10	9	.377	.431	.517	947	76			10	20	977	69.1
1910	Det	AL	OF	506	64	4	574	194	35	13	8	.383	.456	.551	1,008	65			10	30	1,048	83.5
1911	Det	AL	OF	591	44	8	643	248	47	24	8	.420	.467	.621	1,088	83			10	30	1,128	119.3
1912	Det	AL	OF	553	43	5	601	226	30	23	7	.409	.456	.584	1,040	61			10	10	1,060	91.1
1913	Det	AL	OF	428	58	4	490	167	18	16	4	.390	.467	.535	1,002	51			10	10	1,022	65.1
1914	Det	AL	OF	345	57	6	408	127	22	11	2	.368	.466	.513	979	35	17	2	10	(10)	981	45.7
1915	Det	AL	OF	563	118	10	691	208	31	13	3	.369	.486	.487	973	96	38	27	10	10	1,020	91.0
1916	Det	AL	OF	542	78	2	622	201	31	10	5	.371	.452	.493	944	68	24	30	10	10	995	74.0
1917	Det	AL	OF	588	61	4	653	225	44	24	6	.383	.444	.570	1,014	55			10	40	1,064	100.3
1918	Det	AL	OF	421	41	2	464	161	19	14	3	.382	.440	.515	955	34			10	20	985	64.2
1919	Det	AL	OF	497	38	1	536	191	36	13	1	.384	.429	.515	944	28			10	10	964	61.1
1920	Det	AL	OF	428	58	2	488	143	28	8	2	.334	.416	.451	867	15	10	(10)	10	0	867	26.9
1921	Det	AL	OF	507	56	3	566	197	37	16	12	.389	.452	.596	1,048	22	15	(13)	10	40	1,085	92.8
1922	Det	AL	OF	526	55	4	585	211	42	16	4	.401	.462	.565	1,026	9	13	(27)	10	20	1,029	79.5
1923	Det	AL	OF	556	66	3	625	189	40	7	6	.340	.413	.469	882	9	10	(17)	10	10	886	40.2
1924	Det	AL	OF	625	85	1	711	211	38	10	4	.338	.418	.450	867	23	14	(7)	10	30	901	51.1
1925	Det	AL	OF	415	65	5	485	157	31	12	12	.378	.468	.598	1,066	13	9	(10)	10	0	1,066	75.0
1926	Det	AL	OF	233	26	1	260	79	18	5	4	.339	.408	.511	918	9	4	4	10	(20)	912	20.2
1927	Phi	AL	OF	490	67	5	562	175	32	7	5	.357	.440	.482	921	22	16	(17)	10	0	914	44.2
1928	Phi	AL	OF	353	34	4	391	114	27	4	1	.323	.389	.431	819	5	8	(27)	10	0	803	8.9
20.1 Totals				11,434	1,249	94	12,777	4,189	724	295	117					892	178					1,375.9
1.0 Averages				568	62	5	635	208	36	15	6	.366	.433	.512	945	44	9	(2)	10	17	969	68.4

Ty Cobb **Tigers** **Outfielder** **Adjusted**

Year	T	L	P	AB	BB	HBP	TAB	H	2B	3B	HR	BA	OB	SA	Wtd PRO	SB	CS	SBF	SPF	FF	Wtd TF	HC
1905	Det	AL	OF	156	13	0	168	43	7	0	1	.276	.331	.345	677	2			10	30	717	(3.3)
1906	Det	AL	OF	372	24	4	400	133	18	6	1	.359	.404	.448	852	24			10	30	892	25.5
1907	Det	AL	OF	628	32	7	667	254	34	17	6	.405	.439	.540	980	52			10	30	1,020	83.3
1908	Det	AL	OF	599	46	8	653	229	44	24	5	.382	.433	.561	994	41			10	20	1,024	83.0
1909	Det	AL	OF	587	64	8	660	256	39	12	11	.436	.498	.597	1,094	80			10	20	1,124	115.3
1910	Det	AL	OF	515	84	5	604	224	40	15	9	.436	.519	.627	1,146	68			10	30	1,186	123.2
1911	Det	AL	OF	620	47	9	676	264	50	26	9	.426	.473	.630	1,103	87			10	30	1,143	124.3
1912	Det	AL	OF	579	48	6	632	245	33	25	8	.424	.473	.605	1,078	64			10	10	1,098	102.6
1913	Det	AL	OF	443	68	5	515	184	20	18	4	.417	.499	.571	1,070	54			10	10	1,090	81.8
1914	Det	AL	OF	352	70	7	429	142	25	12	2	.405	.512	.564	1,076	37	18	2	10	(10)	1,078	65.6
1915	Det	AL	OF	573	142	12	727	230	34	14	3	.401	.527	.528	1,055	101	40	27	10	10	1,102	119.5
1916	Det	AL	OF	557	95	2	654	226	35	11	6	.406	.494	.539	1,034	72	25	30	10	10	1,084	101.8
1917	Det	AL	OF	606	76	5	687	257	50	27	7	.423	.491	.630	1,122	58			10	40	1,172	135.6
1918	Det	AL	OF	528	61	3	592	221	26	19	4	.418	.480	.563	1,044	43			10	20	1,074	89.2
1919	Det	AL	OF	574	45	1	620	225	42	15	1	.392	.438	.525	963	32			10	10	983	66.7
1920	Det	AL	OF	454	58	2	513	146	29	8	2	.321	.400	.434	834	16	11	(10)	10	0	834	18.7
1921	Det	AL	OF	541	52	3	595	194	36	16	12	.359	.417	.550	967	23	16	(13)	10	40	1,004	69.8
1922	Det	AL	OF	559	53	4	615	212	42	16	4	.380	.437	.534	971	9	14	(27)	10	20	974	63.4
1923	Det	AL	OF	590	65	3	657	191	41	7	6	.325	.394	.448	843	9	11	(17)	10	10	846	27.8
1924	Det	AL	OF	666	81	1	748	210	38	10	4	.316	.391	.420	811	24	15	(7)	10	30	844	31.0
1925	Det	AL	OF	446	60	5	510	155	31	12	12	.348	.430	.549	979	14	9	(10)	10	0	980	54.0
1926	Det	AL	OF	247	25	1	274	80	18	5	4	.322	.387	.485	873	9	4	4	10	(20)	866	14.2
1927	Phi	AL	OF	522	64	5	591	175	32	7	5	.336	.413	.453	866	23	17	(17)	10	0	859	28.6
1928	Phi	AL	OF	374	33	4	411	115	27	4	1	.308	.370	.410	781	5	8	(27)	10	0	764	1.3
20.1 Totals				12,086	1,406	109	13,601	4,612	790	327	127					949	187					1,622.9
1.0 Averages				601	70	5	676	229	39	16	6	.382	.450	.533	983	47	9	(2)	10	17	1,008	80.7

Willie Mays   Giants   Outfielder   Actual

Year	T	L	P	AB	BB	HBP	TAB	H	2B	3B	HR	BA	OB	SA	PRO	SB	CS	SBF	SPF	FF	Actual TF	Actual HC
1951	NY	NL	OF	464	57	2	523	127	22	5	20	.274	.356	.472	828	7	4	(2)	10	50	886	33.7
1952	NY	NL	OF	127	16	1	144	30	2	4	4	.236	.326	.409	736	4	1	13	10	0	759	0.1
1954	NY	NL	OF	565	66	2	633	195	33	13	41	.345	.415	.667	1,083	8	5	(3)	10	80	1,170	130.8
1955	NY	NL	OF	580	79	4	663	185	18	13	51	.319	.404	.659	1,063	24	4	23	10	80	1,176	139.0
1956	NY	NL	OF	578	68	1	647	171	27	8	36	.296	.371	.557	928	40	10	29	10	60	1,027	87.5
1957	NY	NL	OF	585	76	1	662	195	26	20	35	.333	.411	.626	1,037	38	19	0	10	60	1,107	115.8
1958	SF	NL	OF	600	78	1	679	208	33	11	29	.347	.423	.583	1,006	31	6	26	10	70	1,112	120.8
1959	SF	NL	OF	575	65	2	642	180	43	5	34	.313	.385	.583	967	27	4	28	10	60	1,065	99.1
1960	SF	NL	OF	595	61	4	660	190	29	12	29	.319	.386	.555	941	25	10	7	10	70	1,028	89.6
1961	SF	NL	OF	572	81	2	655	176	32	3	40	.308	.395	.584	979	18	9	0	10	60	1,049	95.8
1962	SF	NL	OF	621	78	4	703	189	36	5	49	.304	.385	.615	1,001	18	2	19	10	80	1,109	117.9
1963	SF	NL	OF	596	66	2	664	187	32	7	38	.314	.384	.582	966	8	3	3	10	70	1,049	92.3
1964	SF	NL	OF	578	82	1	661	171	21	9	47	.296	.384	.607	992	19	5	13	10	70	1,084	103.0
1965	SF	NL	OF	558	76	0	634	177	21	3	52	.317	.399	.645	1,044	9	4	1	10	80	1,136	114.3
1966	SF	NL	OF	552	70	2	624	159	29	4	37	.288	.370	.556	926	5	1	5	10	70	1,011	75.4
1967	SF	NL	OF	486	51	2	539	128	22	2	22	.263	.336	.453	788	6	0	11	10	40	849	23.5
1968	SF	NL	OF	498	67	2	567	144	20	5	23	.289	.376	.488	864	12	6	0	10	40	914	42.2
1969	SF	NL	OF	403	49	3	455	114	17	3	13	.283	.365	.437	802	6	2	4	10	30	846	19.1
1970	SF	NL	OF	478	79	3	560	139	15	2	28	.291	.395	.506	901	5	0	8	10	30	949	51.2
1971	SF	NL	OF	417	112	3	532	113	24	5	18	.271	.429	.482	911	23	3	30	10	20	971	54.1
1972	NY	NL	OF	244	60	1	305	61	11	1	8	.250	.400	.402	802	4	5	(19)	0	10	793	5.4
1973	NY	NL	OF	209	27	1	237	44	10	0	6	.211	.304	.344	648	1	0	4	0	0	652	(11.9)
18.8 Totals				10,881	1,464	44	12,389	3,283	523	140	660					338	103					1,598.7
1.0 Averages				579	78	2	659	175	28	7	35	.302	.387	.557	944	18	5	10	10	58	1,021	85.0

Willie Mays   Giants   Outfielder   Adjusted

Year	T	L	P	AB	BB	HBP	TAB	H	2B	3B	HR	BA	OB	SA	Wtd PRO	SB	CS	SBF	SPF	FF	Wtd TF	HC
1951	NY	NL	OF	490	58	2	550	131	23	5	21	.268	.348	.462	810	7	4	(2)	10	50	868	29.1
1952	NY	NL	OF	133	17	1	151	32	2	4	4	.239	.331	.415	745	4	1	13	10	0	768	0.8
1954	NY	NL	OF	600	64	2	666	196	33	13	41	.327	.394	.632	1,026	8	5	(3)	10	80	1,113	112.8
1955	NY	NL	OF	615	78	4	697	188	18	13	52	.306	.387	.631	1,018	25	4	23	10	80	1,131	124.1
1956	NY	NL	OF	611	69	1	681	176	28	8	37	.288	.361	.542	904	42	11	29	10	60	1,003	79.6
1957	NY	NL	OF	618	77	1	696	201	27	21	36	.325	.401	.610	1,011	40	20	0	10	60	1,081	107.2
1958	SF	NL	OF	636	77	1	714	212	34	11	30	.333	.406	.560	966	33	6	26	10	70	1,073	107.3
1959	SF	NL	OF	608	66	2	675	185	44	5	35	.304	.374	.566	939	28	4	28	10	60	1,037	90.0
1960	SF	NL	OF	626	64	4	694	199	30	13	30	.317	.384	.551	936	26	11	7	10	70	1,023	87.8
1961	SF	NL	OF	607	80	2	689	179	33	3	41	.296	.380	.561	941	19	9	0	10	60	1,011	83.1
1962	SF	NL	OF	624	76	4	703	186	35	5	48	.298	.377	.601	978	18	2	19	10	80	1,087	110.4
1963	SF	NL	OF	591	71	2	664	195	33	7	40	.330	.404	.612	1,017	8	3	3	10	70	1,099	108.2
1964	SF	NL	OF	575	85	1	661	175	21	9	48	.304	.395	.624	1,019	19	5	13	10	70	1,112	111.6
1965	SF	NL	OF	555	79	0	634	181	21	3	53	.326	.410	.663	1,073	9	4	1	10	80	1,164	122.9
1966	SF	NL	OF	551	71	2	624	160	29	4	37	.291	.374	.562	935	5	1	5	10	70	1,020	78.1
1967	SF	NL	OF	483	54	2	539	133	23	2	23	.275	.351	.473	825	6	0	11	10	40	885	32.8
1968	SF	NL	OF	488	77	2	567	155	22	5	25	.317	.412	.536	948	12	6	0	10	40	998	65.0
1969	SF	NL	OF	401	51	3	455	116	17	3	13	.289	.373	.447	820	6	2	4	10	30	864	23.1
1970	SF	NL	OF	481	76	3	560	136	15	2	27	.284	.385	.494	878	5	0	8	10	30	927	45.2
1971	SF	NL	OF	412	117	3	532	115	24	5	18	.279	.442	.497	938	23	3	30	10	20	999	61.1
1972	NY	NL	OF	254	66	1	321	66	12	1	9	.259	.414	.416	830	4	5	(19)	0	10	821	9.7
1973	NY	NL	OF	209	27	1	237	44	10	0	6	.212	.306	.347	654	1	0	4	0	0	658	(11.3)
18.8 Totals				11,167	1,500	45	12,712	3,361	535	144	674					350	107					1,578.7
1.0 Averages				594	80	2	676	179	28	8	36	.301	.386	.556	942	19	6	10	10	58	1,019	84.0

Tris Speaker   **Indians**   **Outfielder**   **Actual**

Year	T	L	P	AB	BB	HBP	TAB	H	2B	3B	HR	BA	OB	SA	PRO	SB	CS	SBF	SPF	FF	Actual TF	Actual HC
1907	Bos	AL	OF	19	1	0	20	3	0	0	0	.158	.200	.158	358	0			10	80	448	(3.1)
1908	Bos	AL	OF	116	4	2	122	26	2	2	0	.224	.262	.276	538	3			10	80	628	(7.9)
1909	Bos	AL	OF	544	38	7	589	168	26	13	7	.309	.362	.443	805	35			10	80	895	40.5
1910	Bos	AL	OF	538	52	6	596	183	20	14	7	.340	.404	.468	873	35			10	60	943	55.4
1911	Bos	AL	OF	500	59	13	572	167	34	13	8	.334	.418	.502	920	25			10	40	970	60.9
1912	Bos	AL	OF	580	82	6	668	222	53	12	10	.383	.464	.567	1,031	52			10	70	1,111	118.5
1913	Bos	AL	OF	520	65	7	592	189	35	22	3	.363	.441	.533	974	46			10	70	1,054	87.9
1914	Bos	AL	OF	571	77	7	655	193	46	18	4	.338	.423	.503	926	42	29	(23)	10	90	1,002	80.4
1915	Bos	AL	OF	547	81	7	635	176	25	12	0	.322	.416	.411	827	29	25	(31)	10	70	876	37.7
1916	Cle	AL	OF	546	82	4	632	211	41	8	2	.386	.470	.502	972	35	27	(28)	10	50	1,003	77.9
1917	Cle	AL	OF	523	67	7	597	184	42	11	2	.352	.432	.486	918	30			10	60	988	68.9
1918	Cle	AL	OF	471	64	3	538	150	33	11	0	.318	.403	.435	839	27			10	50	899	46.2
1919	Cle	AL	OF	494	73	8	575	146	38	12	2	.296	.395	.433	828	15			10	80	918	50.9
1920	Cle	AL	OF	552	97	5	654	214	50	11	8	.388	.483	.562	1,045	10	13	(23)	10	50	1,082	106.3
1921	Cle	AL	OF	506	68	2	576	183	52	14	3	.362	.439	.538	977	2	4	(10)	10	70	1,047	83.6
1922	Cle	AL	OF	426	77	1	504	161	48	8	11	.378	.474	.606	1,080	8	3	4	10	60	1,154	100.1
1923	Cle	AL	OF	574	93	4	671	218	59	11	17	.380	.469	.610	1,079	8	9	(14)	10	50	1,125	123.7
1924	Cle	AL	OF	486	72	4	562	167	36	9	9	.344	.432	.510	943	5	7	(15)	10	30	968	59.2
1925	Cle	AL	OF	429	70	4	503	167	35	5	12	.389	.479	.578	1,057	5	2	2	10	50	1,119	91.2
1926	Cle	AL	OF	539	94	0	633	164	52	8	7	.304	.408	.469	877	6	1	6	10	60	953	62.0
1927	Was	AL	OF	523	55	4	582	171	43	6	2	.327	.395	.444	839	9	8	(11)	10	20	857	29.2
1928	Phi	AL	OF	191	10	2	203	51	22	2	3	.267	.310	.450	761	5	1	14	10	20	805	4.8
18.4 Totals				10,195	1,381	103	11,679	3,514	792	222	117					432	129					1,374.1
1.0 Averages				553	75	6	633	191	43	12	6	.345	.428	.500	928	23	7	(8)	10	58	989	74.5

Tris Speaker   **Indians**   **Outfielder**   **Adjusted**

Year	T	L	P	AB	BB	HBP	TAB	H	2B	3B	HR	BA	OB	SA	Wtd PRO	SB	CS	SBF	SPF	FF	Wtd TF	HC
1907	Bos	AL	OF	20	1	0	21	4	0	0	0	.182	.231	.182	413	0			10	80	503	(2.5)
1908	Bos	AL	OF	120	5	3	128	32	2	2	0	.265	.310	.326	635	3			10	80	725	(2.0)
1909	Bos	AL	OF	561	50	9	620	200	31	15	8	.357	.418	.512	930	37			10	80	1,020	77.4
1910	Bos	AL	OF	552	67	8	627	214	23	16	8	.387	.460	.532	992	37			10	60	1,062	91.0
1911	Bos	AL	OF	524	63	14	602	178	36	14	9	.339	.424	.509	933	26			10	40	983	64.6
1912	Bos	AL	OF	605	91	7	703	240	57	13	11	.397	.481	.588	1,069	55			10	70	1,149	131.1
1913	Bos	AL	OF	539	76	8	623	209	39	24	3	.388	.471	.569	1,040	48			10	70	1,120	107.5
1914	Bos	AL	OF	587	94	9	689	218	52	20	5	.372	.465	.553	1,018	44	31	(23)	10	90	1,095	110.7
1915	Bos	AL	OF	563	96	8	668	197	28	13	0	.349	.451	.446	897	31	26	(31)	10	70	946	59.9
1916	Cle	AL	OF	560	100	5	665	237	46	9	2	.423	.514	.549	1,064	37	28	(28)	10	50	1,095	107.0
1917	Cle	AL	OF	537	83	9	628	209	48	12	2	.389	.478	.537	1,016	32			10	60	1,086	98.2
1918	Cle	AL	OF	589	93	4	686	205	45	15	0	.348	.441	.476	916	34			10	50	976	71.6
1919	Cle	AL	OF	569	87	10	665	172	45	14	2	.301	.403	.442	845	17			10	80	935	56.2
1920	Cle	AL	OF	587	96	5	688	219	51	11	8	.373	.465	.540	1,005	11	14	(23)	10	50	1,042	93.2
1921	Cle	AL	OF	541	63	2	606	180	51	14	3	.334	.405	.496	901	2	4	(10)	10	70	971	61.8
1922	Cle	AL	OF	455	74	1	530	163	49	8	11	.358	.449	.573	1,022	8	3	4	10	60	1,096	85.4
1923	Cle	AL	OF	611	91	4	706	222	60	11	17	.363	.448	.582	1,031	8	9	(14)	10	50	1,077	107.4
1924	Cle	AL	OF	519	68	4	591	167	36	9	9	.321	.404	.477	881	5	7	(15)	10	30	906	41.9
1925	Cle	AL	OF	461	64	4	529	165	35	5	12	.358	.440	.531	972	5	2	2	10	50	1,034	69.6
1926	Cle	AL	OF	574	92	0	666	166	53	8	7	.289	.387	.446	833	6	1	6	10	60	909	48.1
1927	Was	AL	OF	556	53	4	612	171	43	6	2	.307	.371	.417	788	9	8	(11)	10	20	807	14.5
1928	Phi	AL	OF	202	10	2	214	51	22	2	3	.254	.296	.429	725	5	1	14	10	20	769	1.1
18.4 Totals				10,830	1,519	118	12,467	3,816	851	244	123					462	136					1,493.7
1.0 Averages				587	82	6	676	207	46	13	7	.352	.437	.510	947	25	7	(7)	10	58	1,008	81.0

Barry Bonds Giants Outfielder Actual

Year	T	L	P	AB	BB	HBP	TAB	H	2B	3B	HR	BA	OB	SA	PRO	SB	CS	SBF	SPF	FF	Actual TF	Actual HC
1986	Pit	NL	OF	413	65	2	480	92	26	3	16	.223	.331	.416	748	36	7	43	10	60	861	23.7
1987	Pit	NL	OF	551	54	3	608	144	34	9	25	.261	.331	.492	822	32	10	19	10	80	931	50.3
1988	Pit	NL	OF	538	72	2	612	152	30	5	24	.283	.369	.491	860	17	11	(8)	10	40	902	42.2
1989	Pit	NL	OF	580	93	1	674	144	34	6	19	.248	.353	.426	779	32	10	17	10	80	886	41.2
1990	Pit	NL	OF	519	93	3	615	156	32	3	33	.301	.410	.565	974	52	13	40	10	60	1,084	95.8
1991	Pit	NL	OF	510	107	4	621	149	28	5	25	.292	.419	.514	932	43	13	26	10	70	1,038	83.1
1992	Pit	NL	OF	473	127	5	605	147	36	5	34	.311	.461	.624	1,085	39	8	36	10	60	1,191	124.9
1993	SF	NL	OF	539	126	2	667	181	38	4	46	.336	.463	.677	1,140	29	12	7	10	50	1,208	143.0
1994	SF	NL	OF	391	74	6	471	122	18	1	37	.312	.429	.647	1,076	29	9	22	10	50	1,158	127.2
1995	SF	NL	OF	506	120	5	631	149	30	7	33	.294	.434	.577	1,011	31	10	16	10	70	1,108	118.5
1996	SF	NL	OF	517	151	1	669	159	27	3	42	.308	.465	.615	1,080	40	7	37	10	50	1,177	133.6
1997	SF	NL	OF	532	145	8	685	155	26	5	40	.291	.450	.585	1,034	37	8	29	10	40	1,113	116.1
1998	SF	NL	OF	552	130	8	690	167	44	7	37	.303	.442	.609	1,051	28	12	5	10	40	1,106	114.7
1999	SF	NL	OF	355	73	3	431	93	20	2	34	.262	.392	.617	1,009	15	2	24	10	40	1,083	66.9
2000	SF	NL	OF	480	117	3	600	147	28	4	49	.306	.445	.688	1,133	11	3	8	10	50	1,200	126.6
13.8	Totals			7,456	1,547	56	9,059	2,157	451	69	494					471	135					1,407.9
1.0	Averages			540	112	4	656	156	33	5	36	.289	.415	.567	982	34	10	21	10	56	1,069	102.0

Barry Bonds Giants Outfielder Adjusted

Year	T	L	P	AB	BB	HBP	TAB	H	2B	3B	HR	BA	OB	SA	Wtd PRO	SB	CS	SBF	SPF	FF	Wtd TF	HC
1986	Pit	NL	OF	413	65	2	480	92	26	3	16	.223	.332	.418	750	36	7	43	10	60	863	24.2
1987	Pit	NL	OF	554	51	3	608	139	33	9	24	.251	.318	.473	791	32	10	19	10	80	900	41.2
1988	Pit	NL	OF	533	77	2	612	158	31	5	25	.295	.386	.513	899	17	11	(8)	10	40	942	53.7
1989	Pit	NL	OF	575	98	1	674	148	35	6	20	.258	.367	.442	809	32	10	17	10	80	915	50.8
1990	Pit	NL	OF	519	93	3	615	156	32	3	33	.300	.409	.564	973	52	13	40	10	60	1,083	95.3
1991	Pit	NL	OF	507	110	4	621	151	28	5	25	.298	.427	.524	951	43	13	26	10	70	1,057	88.6
1992	Pit	NL	OF	467	132	5	605	149	37	5	35	.320	.475	.642	1,116	39	8	36	10	60	1,222	134.0
1993	SF	NL	OF	545	120	2	667	177	37	4	45	.325	.449	.656	1,104	29	12	7	10	50	1,171	131.6
1994	SF	NL	OF	563	96	8	666	165	24	1	50	.294	.404	.609	1,013	41	13	22	10	50	1,095	107.1
1995	SF	NL	OF	579	126	5	710	162	33	8	36	.281	.414	.550	963	35	11	16	10	70	1,060	102.3
1996	SF	NL	OF	527	141	1	669	154	26	3	41	.293	.443	.586	1,029	40	7	37	10	50	1,126	117.3
1997	SF	NL	OF	543	135	7	685	150	25	5	39	.277	.427	.555	982	37	8	29	10	40	1,061	98.9
1998	SF	NL	OF	561	121	7	690	162	43	7	36	.288	.421	.579	1,000	28	12	5	10	40	1,055	98.0
1999	SF	NL	OF	364	65	3	431	87	19	2	32	.240	.359	.564	923	15	2	24	10	40	997	49.2
2000	SF	NL	OF	495	103	3	600	138	26	4	46	.279	.406	.627	1,033	11	3	8	10	50	1,101	98.3
13.8	Totals			7,744	1,533	56	9,333	2,190	455	69	502					487	140					1,290.4
1.0	Averages			561	111	4	676	159	33	5	36	.283	.405	.554	959	35	10	21	10	56	1,046	93.5

Mickey Mantle   **Yankees**   **Outfielder**   **Actual**

Year	T	L	P	AB	BB	HBP	TAB	H	2B	3B	HR	BA	OB	SA	PRO	SB	CS	SBF	SPF	FF	Actual TF	Actual HC
1951	NY	AL	OF	341	43	0	384	91	11	5	13	.267	.349	.443	792	8	7	(15)	10	0	787	5.7
1952	NY	AL	OF	549	75	0	624	171	37	7	23	.311	.394	.530	924	4	1	3	10	20	957	62.5
1953	NY	AL	OF	461	79	0	540	136	24	3	21	.295	.398	.497	895	8	4	0	10	40	945	50.7
1954	NY	AL	OF	543	102	0	645	163	17	12	27	.300	.411	.525	936	5	2	1	10	30	977	71.0
1955	NY	AL	OF	517	113	3	633	158	25	11	37	.306	.433	.611	1,044	8	1	9	10	70	1,133	119.2
1956	NY	AL	OF	533	112	2	647	188	22	5	52	.353	.467	.705	1,172	10	1	12	10	70	1,264	164.2
1957	NY	AL	OF	474	146	0	620	173	28	6	34	.365	.515	.665	1,179	16	3	15	10	30	1,234	148.2
1958	NY	AL	OF	519	129	2	650	158	21	1	42	.304	.445	.592	1,036	18	3	17	10	30	1,094	109.5
1959	NY	AL	OF	541	93	2	636	154	23	4	31	.285	.392	.514	905	21	3	22	10	50	988	73.4
1960	NY	AL	OF	527	111	1	639	145	17	6	40	.275	.402	.558	960	14	3	12	10	30	1,012	81.5
1961	NY	AL	OF	514	126	0	640	163	16	6	54	.317	.452	.687	1,138	12	1	15	10	30	1,193	132.8
1962	NY	AL	OF	377	122	1	500	121	15	1	30	.321	.488	.605	1,093	9	0	17	10	30	1,150	93.5
1963	NY	AL	OF	172	40	0	212	54	8	0	15	.314	.443	.622	1,065	2	1	0	10	10	1,085	33.1
1964	NY	AL	OF	465	99	0	564	141	25	2	35	.303	.426	.591	1,017	6	3	0	10	10	1,037	75.1
1965	NY	AL	OF	361	73	0	434	92	12	1	19	.255	.380	.452	832	4	1	4	10	10	856	20.4
1966	NY	AL	OF	333	57	0	390	96	12	1	23	.288	.392	.538	930	1	1	(2)	10	10	947	35.3
1967	NY	AL	1B	440	107	1	548	108	17	0	22	.245	.394	.434	828	1	1	(2)	10	(10)	827	14.8
1968	NY	AL	1B	435	106	1	542	103	14	1	18	.237	.387	.398	785	6	2	3	0	(10)	779	2.2
15.0	Totals			8,102	1,733	13	9,848	2,415	344	72	536					153	38					1,293.3
1.0	Averages			539	115	1	655	161	23	5	36	.298	.423	.557	979	10	3	7	9	28	1,024	86.0

Mickey Mantle   **Yankees**   **Outfielder**   **Adjusted**

Year	T	L	P	AB	BB	HBP	TAB	H	2B	3B	HR	BA	OB	SA	Wtd PRO	SB	CS	SBF	SPF	FF	Wtd TF	HC
1951	NY	AL	OF	360	44	0	404	94	11	5	13	.261	.341	.432	773	8	7	(15)	10	0	768	2.1
1952	NY	AL	OF	576	81	0	656	182	39	7	24	.316	.400	.538	939	4	1	3	10	20	972	67.1
1953	NY	AL	OF	487	81	0	568	141	25	3	22	.289	.390	.487	877	8	4	0	10	40	927	46.0
1954	NY	AL	OF	571	107	0	679	171	18	13	28	.300	.410	.524	934	5	2	1	10	30	976	70.6
1955	NY	AL	OF	547	116	3	666	164	26	11	38	.300	.424	.599	1,024	8	1	9	10	70	1,113	112.7
1956	NY	AL	OF	568	110	2	681	192	22	5	53	.338	.447	.676	1,123	11	1	12	10	70	1,214	148.2
1957	NY	AL	OF	500	152	0	652	181	29	6	36	.363	.512	.661	1,172	17	3	15	10	30	1,228	146.1
1958	NY	AL	OF	546	135	2	684	166	22	1	44	.304	.444	.591	1,035	19	3	17	10	30	1,092	109.0
1959	NY	AL	OF	570	97	2	669	161	24	4	33	.283	.390	.512	901	22	3	22	10	50	984	72.1
1960	NY	AL	OF	557	114	1	672	151	18	6	42	.271	.395	.548	944	15	3	12	10	30	996	76.3
1961	NY	AL	OF	519	121	0	640	160	16	6	53	.308	.439	.668	1,107	12	1	15	10	30	1,162	123.2
1962	NY	AL	OF	381	118	1	500	120	15	1	30	.314	.477	.591	1,068	9	0	17	10	30	1,125	87.7
1963	NY	AL	OF	171	41	0	212	55	8	0	15	.319	.451	.633	1,084	2	1	0	10	10	1,104	35.0
1964	NY	AL	OF	463	101	0	564	142	25	2	35	.307	.430	.598	1,028	6	3	0	10	10	1,048	78.2
1965	NY	AL	OF	358	76	0	434	94	12	1	19	.264	.394	.467	861	4	1	4	10	10	885	26.4
1966	NY	AL	OF	329	61	0	390	99	12	1	24	.301	.410	.561	971	1	1	(2)	10	10	989	42.9
1967	NY	AL	1B	429	118	1	548	113	18	0	23	.264	.424	.467	891	1	1	(2)	10	(10)	890	34.5
1968	NY	AL	1B	420	121	1	542	110	15	1	19	.262	.428	.439	867	6	2	3	0	(10)	861	26.7
15.0	Totals			8,353	1,794	13	10,161	2,497	356	75	552					159	39					1,304.8
1.0	Averages			556	119	1	676	166	24	5	37	.299	.424	.558	981	11	3	7	9	28	1,026	86.8

Hank Aaron   **Braves**   **Outfielder**   **Actual**

Year	T	L	P	AB	BB	HBP	TAB	H	2B	3B	HR	BA	OB	SA	PRO	SB	CS	SBF	SPF	FF	Actual TF	Actual HC
1954	Mil	NL	OF	468	28	3	499	131	27	6	13	.280	.325	.447	771	2	2	(4)	10	10	787	7.5
1955	Mil	NL	OF	602	49	3	654	189	37	9	27	.314	.369	.540	908	3	1	1	10	20	940	59.8
1956	Mil	NL	OF	609	37	2	648	200	34	14	26	.328	.369	.558	927	2	4	(9)	10	30	958	65.3
1957	Mil	NL	OF	615	57	0	672	198	27	6	44	.322	.379	.600	979	1	1	(1)	10	30	1,018	87.8
1958	Mil	NL	OF	601	59	1	661	196	34	4	30	.326	.387	.546	933	4	1	3	10	30	976	72.4
1959	Mil	NL	OF	629	51	4	684	223	46	7	39	.355	.406	.636	1,042	8	0	11	10	30	1,093	115.2
1960	Mil	NL	OF	590	60	2	652	172	20	11	40	.292	.359	.566	925	16	7	3	10	40	978	72.0
1961	Mil	NL	OF	603	56	2	661	197	39	10	34	.327	.386	.594	979	21	9	4	10	40	1,034	91.6
1962	Mil	NL	OF	592	66	3	661	191	28	6	45	.323	.393	.618	1,012	15	7	1	10	30	1,053	93.1
1963	Mil	NL	OF	631	78	0	709	201	29	4	44	.319	.394	.586	980	31	5	28	10	20	1,038	94.7
1964	Mil	NL	OF	570	62	0	632	187	30	2	24	.328	.394	.514	908	22	4	21	10	30	969	63.7
1965	Mil	NL	OF	570	60	1	631	181	40	1	32	.318	.384	.560	943	24	4	24	10	40	1,017	78.1
1966	Atl	NL	OF	603	76	1	680	168	23	1	44	.279	.360	.539	899	21	3	21	10	30	960	65.7
1967	Atl	NL	OF	600	63	0	663	184	37	3	39	.307	.373	.573	946	17	6	7	10	30	993	74.4
1968	Atl	NL	OF	606	64	1	671	174	33	4	29	.287	.356	.498	855	28	5	25	10	50	940	58.3
1969	Atl	NL	OF	547	87	2	636	164	30	3	44	.300	.398	.607	1,005	9	10	(16)	10	20	1,018	79.1
1970	Atl	NL	OF	516	74	2	592	154	26	1	38	.298	.389	.574	962	9	0	14	10	20	1,007	70.3
1971	Atl	NL	1B	495	71	2	568	162	22	3	47	.327	.414	.669	1,082	1	1	(2)	10	0	1,091	86.8
1972	Atl	NL	1B	449	92	1	542	119	10	0	34	.265	.391	.514	906	4	0	7	0	0	913	38.7
1973	Atl	NL	OF	392	68	1	461	118	12	1	40	.301	.406	.643	1,048	1	1	(2)	0	0	1,046	63.5
1974	Atl	NL	OF	340	39	0	379	91	16	0	20	.268	.343	.491	834	1	0	2	(10)	(10)	817	10.7
1975	Mil	AL	DH	465	70	1	536	109	16	2	12	.234	.336	.355	691	0	1	(4)	(10)	(30)	647	(28.2)
1976	Mil	AL	DH	271	35	0	306	62	8	0	10	.229	.317	.369	686	0	1	(6)	(10)	(30)	640	(17.1)
20.8 Totals				12,364	1,402	32	13,798	3,771	624	98	755					240	73					1,403.3
1.0 Averages				593	67	2	662	181	30	5	36	.305	.377	.555	932	12	4	6	8	22	967	67.3

Hank Aaron   **Braves**   **Outfielder**   **Adjusted**

Year	T	L	P	AB	BB	HBP	TAB	H	2B	3B	HR	BA	OB	SA	Wtd PRO	SB	CS	SBF	SPF	FF	Wtd TF	HC
1954	Mil	NL	OF	495	27	3	525	131	27	6	13	.265	.308	.423	731	2	2	(4)	10	10	747	(2.6)
1955	Mil	NL	OF	637	48	3	688	191	37	9	27	.301	.353	.517	870	3	1	1	10	20	901	47.2
1956	Mil	NL	OF	642	37	2	682	205	35	14	27	.320	.359	.544	903	2	4	(9)	10	30	934	57.3
1957	Mil	NL	OF	649	58	0	707	204	28	6	45	.314	.370	.585	955	1	1	(1)	10	30	994	79.5
1958	Mil	NL	OF	636	58	1	695	199	35	4	30	.313	.372	.524	896	4	1	3	10	30	939	60.1
1959	Mil	NL	OF	664	51	4	720	229	47	7	40	.344	.395	.617	1,012	8	0	11	10	30	1,063	104.8
1960	Mil	NL	OF	621	63	2	686	180	21	12	42	.290	.357	.563	920	17	7	3	10	40	973	70.3
1961	Mil	NL	OF	638	56	2	695	200	40	10	35	.314	.371	.570	941	22	9	4	10	40	995	78.7
1962	Mil	NL	OF	594	64	3	661	187	27	6	44	.315	.385	.604	989	15	7	1	10	30	1,030	86.0
1963	Mil	NL	OF	625	84	0	709	209	30	4	46	.335	.414	.617	1,031	31	5	28	10	20	1,089	112.0
1964	Mil	NL	OF	567	65	0	632	191	31	2	25	.337	.405	.528	933	22	4	21	10	30	994	71.2
1965	Mil	NL	OF	568	62	1	631	185	41	1	33	.326	.394	.575	969	24	4	24	10	40	1,043	85.9
1966	Atl	NL	OF	602	77	1	680	169	23	1	44	.281	.364	.544	908	21	3	21	10	30	969	68.5
1967	Atl	NL	OF	596	67	0	663	191	38	3	40	.321	.390	.600	989	17	6	7	10	30	1,036	88.1
1968	Atl	NL	OF	597	73	1	671	188	36	4	31	.315	.391	.547	938	28	5	25	10	50	1,023	85.1
1969	Atl	NL	OF	544	90	2	636	167	31	3	45	.307	.407	.621	1,028	9	10	(16)	10	20	1,042	86.1
1970	Atl	NL	OF	519	71	2	592	151	25	1	37	.291	.379	.559	938	9	0	14	10	20	982	63.5
1971	Atl	NL	1B	492	74	2	568	166	23	3	48	.337	.426	.689	1,115	1	1	(2)	10	0	1,124	95.7
1972	Atl	NL	1B	468	101	1	570	128	11	0	37	.274	.405	.533	937	4	0	7	0	0	944	47.4
1973	Atl	NL	OF	391	69	1	461	119	12	1	40	.304	.409	.648	1,057	1	1	(2)	0	0	1,055	65.4
1974	Atl	NL	OF	339	40	0	379	92	16	0	20	.272	.348	.499	847	1	0	2	(10)	(10)	830	13.1
1975	Mil	AL	DH	463	72	1	536	111	16	2	12	.241	.345	.364	709	0	1	(4)	(10)	(30)	665	(23.5)
1976	Mil	AL	DH	268	38	0	306	65	8	0	11	.243	.337	.393	730	0	1	(6)	(10)	(30)	684	(10.7)
20.8 Totals				12,613	1,447	32	14,093	3,861	638	100	773					243	74					1,429.1
1.0 Averages				605	69	2	676	185	31	5	37	.306	.379	.556	935	12	4	6	8	22	971	68.6

Stan Musial **Cardinals** **Outfielder** **Actual**

Year	T	L	P	AB	BB	HBP	TAB	H	2B	3B	HR	BA	OB	SA	PRO	SB	CS	SBF	SPF	FF	Actual TF	Actual HC
1941	StL	NL	OF	47	2	0	49	20	4	0	1	.426	.449	.574	1,023	1			0	0	1,023	6.5
1942	StL	NL	OF	467	62	2	531	147	32	10	10	.315	.397	.490	888	6			0	0	888	34.7
1943	StL	NL	OF	617	72	2	691	220	48	20	13	.357	.425	.562	988	9			0	20	1,008	86.7
1944	StL	NL	OF	568	90	5	663	197	51	14	12	.347	.440	.549	990	7			0	10	1,000	80.5
1946	StL	NL	1B	624	73	3	700	228	50	20	16	.365	.434	.587	1,021	7			0	10	1,031	91.5
1947	StL	NL	1B	587	80	4	671	183	30	13	19	.312	.398	.504	902	4			0	10	912	47.8
1948	StL	NL	OF	611	79	3	693	230	46	18	39	.376	.450	.702	1,152	7			0	0	1,152	137.2
1949	StL	NL	OF	612	107	2	721	207	41	13	36	.338	.438	.624	1,062	3			0	(10)	1,052	106.6
1950	StL	NL	OF	555	87	3	645	192	41	7	28	.346	.437	.596	1,034	5			0	(10)	1,024	86.1
1951	StL	NL	OF	578	98	1	677	205	30	12	32	.355	.449	.614	1,063	4	5	(8)	0	0	1,055	100.9
1952	StL	NL	OF	578	96	2	676	194	42	6	21	.336	.432	.538	970	7	7	(10)	0	0	960	68.7
1953	StL	NL	OF	593	105	0	698	200	53	9	30	.337	.437	.609	1,046	3	4	(7)	0	(10)	1,029	95.0
1954	StL	NL	OF	591	103	4	698	195	41	9	35	.330	.433	.607	1,040	1	7	(18)	0	10	1,033	96.2
1955	StL	NL	1B	562	80	8	650	179	30	5	33	.319	.411	.566	977	5	4	(4)	0	0	972	65.9
1956	StL	NL	1B	594	75	3	672	184	33	6	27	.310	.390	.522	912	2	0	3	0	0	915	48.7
1957	StL	NL	1B	502	66	2	570	176	38	3	29	.351	.428	.612	1,040	1	1	(2)	0	0	1,038	76.5
1958	StL	NL	1B	472	72	1	545	159	35	2	17	.337	.426	.528	953	0	0	0	0	0	953	50.0
1959	StL	NL	1B	341	60	0	401	87	13	2	14	.255	.367	.428	795	0	2	(9)	0	(10)	775	1.1
1960	StL	NL	OF	331	41	2	374	91	17	1	17	.275	.358	.486	845	1	1	(3)	(10)	(20)	812	10.3
1961	StL	NL	OF	372	52	1	425	107	22	4	15	.288	.376	.489	866	0	0	0	(10)	(10)	846	18.8
1962	StL	NL	OF	433	64	3	500	143	18	1	19	.330	.420	.508	928	3	0	6	(10)	(20)	904	34.9
1963	StL	NL	OF	337	35	2	374	86	10	2	12	.255	.329	.404	732	2	0	5	(10)	(30)	697	(10.7)
19.6 Totals				10,972	1,599	53	12,624	3,630	725	177	475					78	31					1,334.0
1.0 Averages				560	82	3	645	185	37	9	24	.331	.418	.559	977	4	2	(2)	(1)	(1)	972	68.1

Stan Musial **Cardinals** **Outfielder** **Adjusted**

Year	T	L	P	AB	BB	HBP	TAB	H	2B	3B	HR	BA	OB	SA	Wtd PRO	SB	CS	SBF	SPF	FF	Wtd TF	HC
1941	StL	NL	OF	49	2	0	52	22	4	0	1	.437	.461	.589	1,050	1			0	0	1,050	7.2
1942	StL	NL	OF	484	72	2	559	163	35	11	11	.336	.424	.524	948	6			0	0	948	50.7
1943	StL	NL	OF	643	82	2	727	241	53	22	14	.375	.447	.591	1,038	9			0	20	1,058	104.0
1944	StL	NL	OF	594	98	5	697	211	55	15	13	.355	.451	.563	1,014	7			0	10	1,024	88.6
1946	StL	NL	1B	652	81	3	736	246	54	22	17	.377	.448	.605	1,054	7			0	10	1,064	103.0
1947	StL	NL	1B	622	80	4	706	188	31	13	19	.302	.385	.488	874	4			0	10	884	38.2
1948	StL	NL	OF	644	81	3	729	240	48	19	41	.372	.444	.693	1,138	7			0	0	1,138	132.1
1949	StL	NL	OF	648	109	2	758	214	42	13	37	.330	.428	.609	1,037	3			0	(10)	1,027	97.5
1950	StL	NL	OF	590	86	3	679	195	42	7	29	.331	.419	.571	990	5			0	(10)	980	72.0
1951	StL	NL	OF	611	100	1	712	212	31	12	33	.347	.440	.601	1,041	4	5	(8)	0	0	1,033	93.4
1952	StL	NL	OF	606	103	2	711	206	45	6	22	.340	.437	.545	982	7	7	(10)	0	0	973	72.9
1953	StL	NL	OF	633	102	0	734	202	53	9	30	.319	.413	.575	988	3	4	(7)	0	(10)	971	74.9
1954	StL	NL	OF	630	100	4	734	197	41	9	35	.313	.410	.576	986	1	7	(18)	0	10	978	77.1
1955	StL	NL	1B	597	79	8	684	182	31	5	34	.305	.393	.542	935	5	4	(4)	0	0	931	52.5
1956	StL	NL	1B	628	76	3	707	189	34	6	28	.302	.380	.508	888	2	0	3	0	0	891	40.6
1957	StL	NL	1B	531	67	2	600	181	39	3	30	.342	.417	.596	1,014	1	1	(2)	0	0	1,012	69.1
1958	StL	NL	1B	501	71	1	573	162	36	2	17	.324	.409	.507	915	0	0	0	0	0	915	39.7
1959	StL	NL	1B	361	61	0	422	89	13	2	14	.248	.356	.416	772	0	2	(9)	0	(10)	752	(3.6)
1960	StL	NL	OF	349	43	2	393	95	18	1	18	.273	.356	.484	840	1	1	(3)	(10)	(20)	807	9.4
1961	StL	NL	OF	394	52	1	447	109	22	4	15	.276	.362	.470	831	0	0	0	(10)	(10)	811	11.5
1962	StL	NL	OF	435	62	3	500	141	18	1	19	.323	.411	.497	907	3	0	6	(10)	(20)	883	29.9
1963	StL	NL	OF	334	37	2	374	90	10	2	13	.268	.346	.425	771	2	0	5	(10)	(30)	736	(3.9)
19.6 Totals				11,537	1,643	55	13,234	3,775	755	186	491					82	33					1,256.8
1.0 Averages				589	84	3	676	193	39	9	25	.327	.413	.552	966	4	2	(2)	(1)	(1)	961	64.2

Frank Robinson   **Reds**   **Outfielder**   **Actual**

Year	T	L	P	AB	BB	HBP	TAB	H	2B	3B	HR	BA	OB	SA	PRO	SB	CS	SBF	SPF	FF	Actual TF	Actual HC
1956	Cin	NL	OF	572	64	20	656	166	27	6	38	.290	.381	.558	939	8	4	0	10	20	969	69.5
1957	Cin	NL	OF	611	44	12	667	197	29	5	29	.322	.379	.529	908	10	2	9	10	40	966	69.9
1958	Cin	NL	OF	554	62	7	623	149	25	6	31	.269	.350	.504	854	10	1	12	10	40	916	49.4
1959	Cin	NL	1B	540	69	8	617	168	31	4	36	.311	.397	.583	980	18	8	3	10	0	993	69.1
1960	Cin	NL	1B	464	82	9	555	138	33	6	31	.297	.413	.595	1,007	13	6	2	10	0	1,019	69.3
1961	Cin	NL	OF	545	71	10	626	176	32	7	37	.323	.411	.611	1,022	22	3	24	10	30	1,086	103.0
1962	Cin	NL	OF	609	76	11	696	208	51	2	39	.342	.424	.624	1,048	18	9	0	10	30	1,088	109.6
1963	Cin	NL	OF	482	81	14	577	125	19	3	21	.259	.381	.442	823	26	10	10	10	30	873	31.8
1964	Cin	NL	OF	568	79	9	656	174	38	6	29	.306	.399	.548	947	23	5	19	10	20	996	74.5
1965	Cin	NL	OF	582	70	18	670	172	33	5	33	.296	.388	.540	928	13	9	(7)	10	20	951	61.6
1966	Bal	AL	OF	576	87	10	673	182	34	2	49	.316	.415	.637	1,052	8	5	(3)	10	0	1,059	96.7
1967	Bal	AL	OF	479	71	7	557	149	23	7	30	.311	.408	.576	984	2	3	(7)	10	10	997	63.6
1968	Bal	AL	OF	421	73	12	506	113	27	1	15	.268	.391	.444	835	11	2	13	10	0	859	24.4
1969	Bal	AL	OF	539	88	13	640	166	19	5	32	.308	.417	.540	957	9	3	4	10	0	972	65.3
1970	Bal	AL	OF	471	69	7	547	144	24	1	25	.306	.402	.520	922	2	1	0	10	20	952	50.8
1971	Bal	AL	OF	455	72	9	536	128	16	2	28	.281	.390	.510	900	3	0	5	10	(10)	905	37.7
1972	LA	NL	OF	342	55	2	399	86	6	1	19	.251	.358	.442	800	2	3	(9)	0	0	790	6.6
1973	Cal	AL	DH	534	82	10	626	142	29	0	30	.266	.374	.489	863	1	1	(2)	(10)	(20)	831	22.0
1974	Cal	AL	DH	477	85	10	572	117	27	3	22	.245	.371	.453	823	5	2	2	(10)	(40)	775	1.4
1975	Cle	AL	DH	118	29	0	147	28	5	0	9	.237	.388	.508	896	0	0	0	(10)	(40)	846	5.3
1976	Cle	AL	DH	67	11	0	78	15	0	0	3	.224	.333	.358	692	0	0	0	(10)	(40)	642	(4.8)
17.5 Totals				10,006	1,420	198	11,624	2,943	528	72	586					204	77					1,076.6
1.0 Averages				571	81	11	664	168	30	4	33	.294	.392	.537	929	12	4	4	7	10	951	61.5

Frank Robinson   **Reds**   **Outfielder**   **Adjusted**

Year	T	L	P	AB	BB	HBP	TAB	H	2B	3B	HR	BA	OB	SA	Wtd PRO	SB	CS	SBF	SPF	FF	Wtd TF	HC
1956	Cin	NL	OF	605	65	20	690	171	28	6	39	.283	.371	.543	914	8	4	0	10	20	944	61.4
1957	Cin	NL	OF	645	45	12	702	203	30	5	30	.314	.370	.515	885	11	2	9	10	40	944	62.3
1958	Cin	NL	OF	587	62	7	655	152	25	6	32	.258	.336	.484	820	11	1	12	10	40	882	38.9
1959	Cin	NL	1B	571	70	8	649	173	32	4	37	.302	.386	.566	952	19	8	3	10	0	965	60.3
1960	Cin	NL	1B	489	86	9	584	145	35	6	32	.296	.410	.591	1,002	14	6	2	10	0	1,013	67.7
1961	Cin	NL	OF	578	70	10	659	179	33	7	38	.310	.394	.587	981	23	3	24	10	30	1,045	90.3
1962	Cin	NL	OF	612	73	11	696	204	50	2	38	.334	.414	.610	1,024	18	9	0	10	30	1,064	101.8
1963	Cin	NL	OF	475	87	15	577	130	20	3	22	.273	.401	.465	866	26	10	10	10	30	916	43.6
1964	Cin	NL	OF	564	82	9	656	178	39	6	30	.315	.410	.563	973	23	5	19	10	20	1,022	82.6
1965	Cin	NL	OF	579	73	19	670	176	34	5	34	.304	.399	.554	953	13	9	(7)	10	20	976	69.8
1966	Bal	AL	OF	570	93	11	673	188	35	2	51	.330	.433	.665	1,098	8	5	(3)	10	0	1,105	111.6
1967	Bal	AL	OF	470	79	8	557	157	24	7	32	.335	.439	.620	1,059	2	3	(7)	10	10	1,072	83.4
1968	Bal	AL	OF	408	84	14	506	121	29	1	16	.297	.432	.491	923	11	2	13	10	0	946	45.5
1969	Bal	AL	OF	536	90	13	640	168	19	5	32	.314	.425	.550	975	9	3	4	10	0	989	70.7
1970	Bal	AL	OF	471	69	7	547	144	24	1	25	.307	.404	.522	926	2	1	0	10	20	956	51.8
1971	Bal	AL	OF	451	75	9	536	131	16	2	29	.290	.402	.526	929	3	0	5	10	(10)	934	45.1
1972	LA	NL	OF	357	61	2	420	93	6	1	21	.260	.371	.457	828	2	3	(9)	0	0	818	12.2
1973	Cal	AL	DH	531	85	10	626	145	30	0	31	.273	.383	.501	884	1	1	(2)	(10)	(20)	853	28.5
1974	Cal	AL	DH	471	90	11	572	121	28	3	23	.257	.388	.474	862	5	2	2	(10)	(40)	814	12.0
1975	Cle	AL	DH	117	30	0	147	29	5	0	9	.244	.399	.524	923	0	0	0	(10)	(40)	873	7.2
1976	Cle	AL	DH	66	12	0	78	16	0	0	3	.239	.356	.382	738	0	0	0	(10)	(40)	688	(3.0)
17.5 Totals				10,153	1,481	206	11,839	3,022	542	74	602					208	78					1,143.5
1.0 Averages				580	85	12	676	173	31	4	34	.298	.398	.543	941	12	4	4	7	10	963	65.3

Mel Ott Giants Outfielder Actual

Year	T	L	P	AB	BB	HBP	TAB	H	2B	3B	HR	BA	OB	SA	PRO	SB	CS	SBF	SPF	FF	Actual TF	Actual HC
1926	NY	NL	OF	60	1	0	61	23	2	0	0	.383	.393	.417	810	1			0	(30)	780	0.7
1927	NY	NL	OF	163	13	0	176	46	7	3	1	.282	.335	.380	716	2			0	(30)	686	(6.3)
1928	NY	NL	OF	435	52	2	489	140	26	4	18	.322	.397	.524	921	3			0	(10)	911	37.6
1929	NY	NL	OF	545	113	6	664	179	37	2	42	.328	.449	.635	1,084	6			0	20	1,104	115.2
1930	NY	NL	OF	521	103	2	626	182	34	5	25	.349	.458	.578	1,036	9			0	20	1,056	93.7
1931	NY	NL	OF	497	80	2	579	145	23	8	29	.292	.392	.545	937	10			0	20	957	58.0
1932	NY	NL	OF	566	100	4	670	180	30	8	38	.318	.424	.601	1,025	6			0	20	1,045	96.4
1933	NY	NL	OF	580	75	2	657	164	36	1	23	.283	.367	.467	834	1			0	0	834	25.2
1934	NY	NL	OF	582	85	3	670	190	29	10	35	.326	.415	.591	1,006	0			0	0	1,006	83.5
1935	NY	NL	OF	593	82	3	678	191	33	6	31	.322	.407	.555	962	7			0	30	992	79.7
1936	NY	NL	OF	534	111	5	650	175	28	6	33	.328	.448	.588	1,036	6			0	10	1,046	93.9
1937	NY	NL	3B	545	102	3	650	160	28	2	31	.294	.408	.523	931	7			0	0	931	69.9
1938	NY	NL	3B	527	118	5	650	164	23	6	36	.311	.442	.583	1,024	2			0	0	1,024	100.3
1939	NY	NL	OF	396	100	1	497	122	23	2	27	.308	.449	.581	1,030	2			0	10	1,040	70.3
1940	NY	NL	OF	536	100	6	642	155	27	3	19	.289	.407	.457	864	6			0	20	884	40.6
1941	NY	NL	OF	525	100	3	628	150	29	0	27	.286	.403	.495	898	5			0	20	918	50.6
1942	NY	NL	OF	549	109	3	661	162	21	0	30	.295	.415	.497	912	6			0	20	932	57.8
1943	NY	NL	OF	380	95	3	478	89	12	2	18	.234	.391	.418	810	7			0	10	820	14.9
1944	NY	NL	OF	399	90	3	492	115	16	4	26	.288	.423	.544	967	2			0	0	967	51.6
1945	NY	NL	OF	451	71	8	530	139	23	0	21	.308	.411	.499	910	1			(10)	0	900	37.9
1946	NY	NL	OF	68	8	0	76	5	1	0	1	.074	.171	.132	303	0			(10)	0	293	(17.7)
1947	NY	NL	PH	4	0	0	4	0	0	0	0	.000	.000	.000	0	0			(10)	0	(10)	(1.5)
17.5 Totals				9,456	1,708	64	11,228	2,876	488	72	511					89	0					1,152.3
1.0 Averages				541	98	4	643	165	28	4	29	.304	.414	.533	947	5	0	0	(1)	10	957	65.9

Mel Ott Giants Outfielder Adjusted

Year	T	L	P	AB	BB	HBP	TAB	H	2B	3B	HR	BA	OB	SA	Wtd PRO	SB	CS	SBF	SPF	FF	Wtd TF	HC
1926	NY	NL	OF	63	1	0	64	24	2	0	0	.374	.384	.406	790	1			0	(30)	760	0.1
1927	NY	NL	OF	172	13	0	185	47	7	3	1	.275	.326	.370	697	2			0	(30)	667	(8.0)
1928	NY	NL	OF	461	51	2	514	141	26	4	18	.307	.378	.499	877	3			0	(10)	867	26.9
1929	NY	NL	OF	591	102	5	698	175	36	2	41	.296	.405	.572	977	6			0	20	997	79.7
1930	NY	NL	OF	568	89	2	659	173	32	5	24	.305	.401	.505	905	9			0	20	925	52.7
1931	NY	NL	OF	525	82	2	609	150	24	8	30	.286	.384	.534	918	11			0	20	938	52.3
1932	NY	NL	OF	599	101	4	705	186	31	8	39	.310	.413	.586	999	6			0	20	1,019	87.8
1933	NY	NL	OF	606	83	2	691	178	39	1	25	.294	.381	.486	867	1			0	0	867	36.1
1934	NY	NL	OF	616	86	3	705	195	30	10	36	.317	.403	.574	977	0			0	0	977	73.7
1935	NY	NL	OF	627	83	3	713	197	34	6	32	.315	.398	.542	940	7			0	30	970	72.4
1936	NY	NL	OF	566	113	5	684	181	29	6	34	.320	.438	.575	1,013	6			0	10	1,023	86.4
1937	NY	NL	3B	575	106	3	684	167	29	2	32	.290	.403	.517	920	7			0	0	920	66.4
1938	NY	NL	3B	554	124	5	684	173	24	6	38	.312	.442	.583	1,025	2			0	0	1,025	100.7
1939	NY	NL	OF	420	102	1	523	127	24	2	28	.302	.439	.569	1,008	2			0	10	1,018	64.9
1940	NY	NL	OF	563	106	6	675	164	29	3	20	.291	.409	.460	868	6			0	20	888	42.2
1941	NY	NL	OF	548	109	3	661	161	31	0	29	.293	.413	.508	921	5			0	20	941	57.9
1942	NY	NL	OF	566	126	3	695	178	23	0	33	.315	.443	.531	974	6			0	20	994	78.3
1943	NY	NL	OF	393	107	3	503	97	13	2	20	.246	.411	.440	850	7			0	10	860	24.7
1944	NY	NL	OF	416	98	3	518	123	17	4	28	.295	.433	.557	990	2			0	0	990	57.4
1945	NY	NL	OF	473	76	9	558	148	24	0	22	.313	.417	.506	923	1			(10)	0	913	41.4
1946	NY	NL	OF	71	9	0	80	5	1	0	1	.076	.177	.137	313	0			(10)	0	303	(17.3)
1947	NY	NL	PH	4	0	0	4	0	0	0	0	.000	.000	.000	0	0			(10)	0	(10)	(1.5)
17.5 Totals				9,978	1,767	66	11,811	2,990	507	74	532					94	0					1,075.2
1.0 Averages				571	101	4	676	171	29	4	30	.300	.408	.525	934	5	0	0	(1)	10	943	61.5

Joe DiMaggio **Yankees** **Outfielder** **Actual**

Year	T	L	P	AB	BB	HBP	TAB	H	2B	3B	HR	BA	OB	SA	PRO	SB	CS	SBF	SPF	FF	Actual TF	Actual HC
1936	NY	AL	OF	637	24	4	665	206	44	15	29	.323	.352	.576	928	4	0	6	10	80	1,024	88.8
1937	NY	AL	OF	621	64	5	690	215	35	15	46	.346	.412	.673	1,085	3	0	4	10	60	1,159	138.8
1938	NY	AL	OF	599	59	2	660	194	32	13	32	.324	.386	.581	967	6	1	6	10	40	1,023	87.9
1939	NY	AL	OF	462	52	4	518	176	32	6	30	.381	.448	.671	1,119	3	0	5	10	80	1,214	118.6
1940	NY	AL	OF	508	61	3	572	179	28	9	31	.352	.425	.626	1,051	1	2	(5)	10	40	1,096	97.0
1941	NY	AL	OF	541	76	4	621	193	43	11	30	.357	.440	.643	1,083	4	2	0	10	70	1,163	126.2
1942	NY	AL	OF	610	68	2	680	186	29	13	21	.305	.376	.498	875	4	2	0	10	50	935	60.5
1946	NY	AL	OF	503	59	2	564	146	20	8	25	.290	.367	.511	878	1	0	2	0	60	940	51.5
1947	NY	AL	OF	534	64	3	601	168	31	10	20	.315	.391	.522	913	3	0	5	0	40	958	60.5
1948	NY	AL	OF	594	67	8	669	190	26	11	39	.320	.396	.598	994	1	1	(1)	0	30	1,022	88.8
1949	NY	AL	OF	272	55	2	329	94	14	6	14	.346	.459	.596	1,055	0	1	(6)	0	30	1,079	53.0
1950	NY	AL	OF	525	80	1	606	158	33	10	32	.301	.394	.585	979	0	0	0	0	30	1,009	76.5
1951	NY	AL	OF	415	61	6	482	109	22	4	12	.263	.365	.422	787	0	0	0	0	40	827	16.8
11.9 Totals				6,821	790	46	7,657	2,214	389	131	361					30	9					1,064.8
1.0 Averages				572	66	4	643	186	33	11	30	.325	.398	.579	977	3	1	1	6	51	1,035	89.4

Joe DiMaggio **Yankees** **Outfielder ·** **Adjusted**

Year	T	L	P	AB	BB	HBP	TAB	H	2B	3B	HR	BA	OB	SA	Wtd PRO	SB	CS	SBF	SPF	FF	Wtd TF	HC
1936	NY	AL	OF	674	22	4	700	196	42	14	28	.291	.317	.519	836	4	0	6	10	80	931	57.9
1937	NY	AL	OF	662	59	5	726	210	34	15	45	.317	.377	.617	994	3	0	4	10	60	1,069	107.6
1938	NY	AL	OF	638	54	2	694	189	31	13	31	.296	.353	.531	883	6	1	6	10	40	939	60.1
1939	NY	AL	OF	492	49	4	545	174	32	6	30	.354	.417	.624	1,041	3	0	5	10	80	1,136	98.3
1940	NY	AL	OF	540	59	3	602	179	28	9	31	.332	.400	.589	989	1	2	(5)	10	40	1,034	79.3
1941	NY	AL	OF	573	76	4	653	198	44	11	31	.345	.425	.622	1,047	4	2	0	10	70	1,127	115.1
1942	NY	AL	OF	639	75	2	715	200	31	14	23	.314	.387	.513	900	4	2	0	10	50	960	69.1
1946	NY	AL	OF	527	64	2	593	156	21	9	27	.296	.374	.521	896	1	0	2	0	60	957	56.5
1947	NY	AL	OF	561	68	3	632	178	33	11	21	.318	.395	.528	924	3	0	5	0	40	969	63.6
1948	NY	AL	OF	629	67	8	704	194	27	11	40	.309	.383	.577	960	1	1	(1)	0	30	988	77.4
1949	NY	AL	OF	289	55	2	346	96	14	6	14	.333	.443	.574	1,017	0	1	(6)	0	30	1,041	46.8
1950	NY	AL	OF	561	76	1	637	157	33	10	32	.280	.367	.544	911	0	0	0	0	30	941	55.7
1951	NY	AL	OF	439	62	6	507	113	23	4	12	.256	.357	.412	768	0	0	0	0	40	808	12.3
11.9 Totals				7,224	785	45	8,055	2,242	393	132	364					32	9					899.6
1.0 Averages				606	66	4	676	188	33	11	31	.310	.381	.553	934	3	1	1	6	51	992	75.5

Ken Griffey Jr.   **Mariners**   **Outfielder**   **Actual**

Year	T	L	P	AB	BB	HBP	TAB	H	2B	3B	HR	BA	OB	SA	PRO	SB	CS	SBF	SPF	FF	Actual TF	Actual HC
1989	Sea	AL	OF	455	44	2	501	120	23	0	16	.264	.331	.420	751	16	7	4	10	20	785	6.6
1990	Sea	AL	OF	597	63	2	662	179	28	7	22	.300	.369	.481	849	16	11	(9)	10	30	881	38.9
1991	Sea	AL	OF	548	71	1	620	179	42	1	22	.327	.405	.527	932	18	6	9	10	60	1,011	75.0
1992	Sea	AL	OF	565	44	5	614	174	39	4	27	.308	.363	.535	898	10	5	0	10	60	968	61.5
1993	Sea	AL	OF	582	96	6	684	180	38	3	45	.309	.412	.617	1,029	17	9	(1)	10	40	1,078	104.4
1994	Sea	AL	OF	433	56	2	491	140	24	4	40	.323	.403	.674	1,078	11	3	10	10	40	1,137	125.7
1995	Sea	AL	OF	260	52	0	312	67	7	0	17	.258	.381	.481	862	4	2	0	10	90	962	34.2
1996	Sea	AL	OF	545	78	7	630	165	26	2	49	.303	.397	.628	1,024	16	1	21	10	90	1,145	116.4
1997	Sea	AL	OF	608	76	8	692	185	34	3	56	.304	.389	.646	1,035	15	4	10	10	60	1,115	117.8
1998	Sea	AL	OF	633	76	7	716	180	33	3	56	.284	.367	.611	979	20	5	13	10	70	1,072	107.3
1999	Sea	AL	OF	606	91	7	704	173	26	3	48	.285	.385	.576	961	24	7	13	10	60	1,044	96.2
2000	Cin	NL	OF	520	94	9	623	141	22	3	40	.271	.392	.556	947	6	4	(3)	10	70	1,024	79.2
11.1	Totals			6,352	841	56	7,249	1,883	342	33	438					173	64					963.3
1.0	Averages			573	76	5	654	170	31	3	40	.296	.384	.568	951	16	6	6	10	57	1,024	86.9

Ken Griffey Jr.   **Mariners**   **Outfielder**   **Adjusted**

Year	T	L	P	AB	BB	HBP	TAB	H	2B	3B	HR	BA	OB	SA	Wtd PRO	SB	CS	SBF	SPF	FF	Wtd TF	HC
1989	Sea	AL	OF	453	46	2	501	123	23	0	16	.270	.340	.430	770	16	7	4	10	20	804	11.1
1990	Sea	AL	OF	595	65	2	662	182	28	7	22	.305	.375	.489	863	16	11	(9)	10	30	895	43.4
1991	Sea	AL	OF	547	72	1	620	180	42	1	22	.328	.407	.530	937	18	6	9	10	60	1,016	76.5
1992	Sea	AL	OF	564	45	5	614	177	40	4	27	.314	.370	.545	915	10	5	0	10	60	985	66.6
1993	Sea	AL	OF	586	93	6	684	177	37	3	44	.302	.402	.602	1,004	17	9	(1)	10	40	1,053	96.3
1994	Sea	AL	OF	620	72	3	695	187	32	5	54	.302	.376	.630	1,006	16	4	10	10	40	1,066	102.0
1995	Sea	AL	OF	297	54	0	351	72	8	0	18	.243	.360	.453	813	5	2	0	10	90	913	26.0
1996	Sea	AL	OF	555	69	6	630	154	24	2	46	.277	.363	.574	937	16	1	21	10	90	1,058	90.2
1997	Sea	AL	OF	615	70	7	692	177	32	3	53	.287	.367	.610	977	15	4	10	10	60	1,057	98.6
1998	Sea	AL	OF	640	70	6	716	171	31	3	53	.267	.345	.575	920	20	5	13	10	70	1,013	87.3
1999	Sea	AL	OF	616	81	6	704	162	24	3	45	.263	.355	.531	886	24	7	13	10	60	970	71.2
2000	Cin	NL	OF	532	83	8	623	132	21	3	37	.248	.359	.509	867	6	4	(3)	10	70	944	55.5
11.1	Totals			6,620	819	53	7,492	1,893	344	34	439					178	65					824.8
1.0	Averages			597	74	5	676	171	31	3	40	.286	.369	.547	916	16	6	6	10	57	989	74.4

Joe Jackson **Indians** **Outfielder** **Actual**

Year	T	L	P	AB	BB	HBP	TAB	H	2B	3B	HR	BA	OB	SA	PRO	SB	CS	SBF	SPF	FF	Actual TF	Actual HC
1908	Phi	AL	OF	23	0	0	23	3	0	0	0	.130	.130	.130	261	0			10	(30)	241	(6.0)
1909	Phi	AL	OF	17	1	0	18	3	0	0	0	.176	.222	.176	399	0			10	(50)	359	(3.6)
1910	Cle	AL	OF	75	8	0	83	29	2	5	1	.387	.446	.587	1,032	4			10	10	1,052	12.3
1911	Cle	AL	OF	571	56	8	635	233	45	19	7	.408	.468	.590	1,058	41			10	20	1,088	105.2
1912	Cle	AL	OF	572	54	12	638	226	44	26	3	.395	.458	.579	1,036	35			10	20	1,066	98.8
1913	Cle	AL	OF	528	80	5	613	197	39	17	7	.373	.460	.551	1,011	26			10	0	1,021	81.0
1914	Cle	AL	OF	453	41	5	499	153	22	13	3	.338	.399	.464	862	22	15	(15)	10	10	867	27.5
1915	Cle	AL	OF	461	52	6	519	142	20	14	5	.308	.385	.445	830	16	20	(44)	10	(10)	786	7.5
1916	Chi	AL	OF	592	46	5	643	202	40	21	3	.341	.393	.495	888	24	14	(6)	10	0	893	43.5
1917	Chi	AL	OF	538	57	7	602	162	20	17	5	.301	.375	.429	805	13			10	20	835	23.3
1918	Chi	AL	OF	65	8	0	73	23	2	2	1	.354	.425	.492	917	3			10	10	937	8.0
1919	Chi	AL	OF	516	60	4	580	181	31	14	7	.351	.422	.506	928	9			10	0	938	57.8
1920	Chi	AL	OF	570	56	7	633	218	42	20	12	.382	.444	.589	1,033	9	12	(22)	10	0	1,021	83.6
8.8 Totals				4,981	519	59	5,559	1,772	307	168	54					202	61					539.0
1.0 Averages				568	59	7	634	202	35	19	6	.356	.423	.517	940	23	7	(9)	10	7	948	61.5

Joe Jackson **Indians** **Outfielder** **Adjusted**

Year	T	L	P	AB	BB	HBP	TAB	H	2B	3B	HR	BA	OB	SA	Wtd PRO	SB	CS	SBF	SPF	FF	Wtd TF	HC
1908	Phi	AL	OF	24	0	0	24	4	0	0	0	.154	.154	.154	308	0			10	(30)	288	(5.4)
1909	Phi	AL	OF	18	1	0	19	4	0	0	0	.204	.257	.204	461	0			10	(50)	421	(3.0)
1910	Cle	AL	OF	77	10	0	87	34	2	6	1	.440	.507	.667	1,174	4			10	10	1,194	18.1
1911	Cle	AL	OF	599	60	9	668	248	48	20	7	.414	.474	.599	1,073	43			10	20	1,103	110.0
1912	Cle	AL	OF	597	60	13	671	245	48	28	3	.410	.474	.600	1,074	37			10	20	1,104	110.9
1913	Cle	AL	OF	545	94	6	645	217	43	19	8	.398	.491	.589	1,080	27			10	0	1,090	102.1
1914	Cle	AL	OF	469	50	6	525	174	25	15	3	.371	.438	.510	948	23	16	(15)	10	10	953	48.9
1915	Cle	AL	OF	477	62	7	546	159	22	16	6	.334	.418	.482	900	17	21	(44)	10	(10)	856	25.7
1916	Chi	AL	OF	615	56	6	676	230	45	24	3	.373	.431	.542	972	25	15	(6)	10	0	976	70.6
1917	Chi	AL	OF	555	70	9	633	185	23	19	6	.333	.415	.475	890	14			10	20	920	49.2
1918	Chi	AL	OF	81	12	0	93	31	3	3	1	.387	.464	.538	1,002	4			10	10	1,022	11.7
1919	Chi	AL	OF	595	72	5	671	213	36	16	8	.358	.431	.516	947	10			10	0	957	63.8
1920	Chi	AL	OF	604	55	7	666	222	43	20	12	.368	.427	.567	994	9	13	(22)	10	0	981	71.1
8.8 Totals				5,256	602	67	5,925	1,965	339	186	60					214	64					673.7
1.0 Averages				600	69	8	676	224	39	21	7	.374	.445	.543	988	24	7	(9)	10	7	996	76.9

Ed Delahanty　　Phi NL　　　Outfielder　　　　Actual

| | | | | | | | | | | | | | | | | | | | | Actual | Actual |
Year	T L P	AB	BB	HBP	TAB	H	2B	3B	HR	BA	OB	SA	PRO	SB	CS	SBF	SPF	FF	TF	HC
1888	Phi NL 2B	290	12	1	303	66	12	2	1	.228	.261	.293	554	38			10	(60)	504	(31.2)
1889	Phi NL OF	246	14	1	261	72	13	3	0	.293	.333	.370	703	19			10	(50)	663	(14.3)
1890	Cle P SS	517	24	8	549	153	26	13	3	.296	.337	.414	751	25			10	(20)	741	25.3
1891	Phi NL OF	543	33	8	584	132	19	9	5	.243	.296	.339	635	25			10	0	645	(36.7)
1892	Phi NL OF	477	31	9	517	146	30	21	6	.306	.360	.495	855	29			10	30	895	35.6
1893	Phi NL OF	595	47	10	652	219	35	18	19	.368	.423	.583	1,007	37			10	60	1,077	122.6
1894	Phi NL OF	489	60	7	556	199	39	18	4	.407	.478	.585	1,063	21			10	40	1,113	115.7
1895	Phi NL OF	480	86	6	572	194	49	10	11	.404	.500	.617	1,117	46			10	0	1,127	122.6
1896	Phi NL OF	499	62	9	570	198	44	17	13	.397	.472	.631	1,103	37			10	40	1,153	131.9
1897	Phi NL OF	530	60	3	593	200	40	15	5	.377	.444	.538	981	26			10	30	1,021	89.4
1898	Phi NL OF	548	77	11	636	183	36	9	4	.334	.426	.454	880	58			10	10	900	45.8
1899	Phi NL OF	581	55	4	640	238	55	9	9	.410	.464	.582	1,046	30			10	0	1,056	96.0
1900	Phi NL 1B	539	41	7	587	174	32	10	2	.323	.378	.430	809	16			10	0	819	15.7
1901	Phi NL OF	542	65	4	611	192	38	16	8	.354	.427	.528	955	29			10	0	965	69.9
1902	Was AL OF	473	62	4	539	178	43	14	10	.376	.453	.590	1,043	16			10	0	1,053	87.7
1903	Was AL OF	156	12	2	170	52	11	1	1	.333	.388	.436	824	3			0	0	824	6.3
14.4	Totals	7,505	741	94	8,340	2,596	522	185	101					455	0					882.4
1.0	Averages	521	51	7	579	180	36	13	7	.346	.411	.505	917	32	0	0	10	10	936	61.3

Ed Delahanty　　Phi NL　　　Outfielder　　　　Adjusted

| | | | | | | | | | | | | | Wtd | | | | | | Wtd | |
Year	T L P	AB	BB	HBP	TAB	H	2B	3B	HR	BA	OB	SA	PRO	SB	CS	SBF	SPF	FF	TF	HC
1888	Phi NL 2B	342	17	1	361	90	16	3	1	.264	.302	.340	642	45			10	(60)	592	(16.1)
1889	Phi NL OF	299	18	1	318	89	16	4	0	.298	.340	.377	716	23			10	(50)	676	(12.3)
1890	Cle P SS	636	28	9	674	182	31	15	4	.287	.326	.401	727	31			10	(20)	717	17.7
1891	Phi NL OF	634	42	10	686	163	23	11	6	.257	.314	.359	672	29			10	0	682	(24.6)
1892	Phi NL OF	497	37	11	546	167	34	24	7	.335	.394	.542	937	31			10	30	977	57.0
1893	Phi NL OF	740	54	12	806	261	42	21	23	.353	.406	.559	965	46			10	60	1,035	106.8
1894	Phi NL OF	617	59	7	682	218	43	20	4	.353	.415	.507	922	26			10	40	972	69.8
1895	Phi NL OF	598	93	6	697	224	57	12	13	.375	.464	.572	1,036	56			10	0	1,046	95.7
1896	Phi NL OF	619	70	10	700	234	52	20	15	.378	.450	.601	1,051	45			10	40	1,101	114.5
1897	Phi NL OF	642	67	3	712	231	46	17	6	.359	.422	.512	935	31			10	30	975	73.7
1898	Phi NL OF	573	86	12	671	198	39	10	4	.346	.442	.471	913	61			10	10	933	56.0
1899	Phi NL OF	614	57	4	675	250	58	9	9	.407	.461	.578	1,040	32			10	0	1,050	94.1
1900	Phi NL 1B	624	48	8	679	202	37	12	2	.323	.379	.431	810	19			10	0	820	16.1
1901	Phi NL OF	620	82	5	707	232	46	19	10	.374	.451	.557	1,008	34			10	0	1,018	87.6
1902	Was AL OF	546	73	5	624	207	50	16	12	.379	.457	.595	1,051	19			10	0	1,061	90.3
1903	Was AL OF	178	16	3	197	65	14	1	1	.363	.423	.475	898	3			0	0	898	13.2
14.4	Totals	8,779	846	108	9,734	3,013	604	215	118					530	0					839.5
1.0	Averages	610	59	8	676	209	42	15	8	.343	.408	.501	909	37	0	0	10	10	928	58.3

Pete Browning Lou AA Outfielder Actual

Year T L P	AB	BB	HBP	TAB	H	2B	3B	HR	BA	OB	SA	PRO	SB	CS	SBF	SPF	FF	Actual TF	Actual HC
1882 Lou AA 2B	288	26	0	314	109	17	3	5	.378	.430	.510	940				10	50	1,000	97.9
1883 Lou AA OF	358	23	0	381	121	15	9	4	.338	.378	.464	842				10	(20)	832	22.4
1884 Lou AA 3B	447	13	2	462	150	33	8	4	.336	.357	.472	829				10	(30)	809	30.1
1885 Lou AA OF	481	25	0	506	174	34	10	9	.362	.393	.530	923				10	20	953	69.0
1886 Lou AA OF	467	30	7	504	159	29	6	2	.340	.389	.441	830	26			10	(20)	820	17.5
1887 Lou AA OF	547	55	8	610	220	35	16	4	.402	.464	.547	1,011	103			10	0	1,021	90.1
1888 Lou AA OF	383	37	4	424	120	22	8	3	.313	.380	.436	816	36			10	0	826	16.3
1889 Lou AA OF	324	34	0	358	83	19	5	2	.256	.327	.364	691	21			10	(10)	691	(13.1)
1890 Cle P OF	493	75	3	571	184	40	8	5	.373	.459	.517	976	35			10	10	996	79.7
1891 Cin NL OF	419	51	3	473	133	24	4	4	.317	.395	.422	818	16			0	20	838	21.3
1892 Cin NL OF	384	52	0	436	112	16	5	3	.292	.376	.383	759	13			0	(10)	749	(1.9)
1893 Lou NL OF	220	44	2	266	78	11	3	1	.355	.466	.445	912	8			0	(20)	892	21.0
1894 StL NL OF	9	1	0	10	3	0	0	0	.333	.400	.333	733	0			0	0	733	(0.1)
10.3 Totals	4,820	466	29	5,315	1,646	295	85	46					258	0					450.2
1.0 Averages	467	45	3	515	159	29	8	4	.341	.403	.467	869	25	0	0	8	1	878	43.6

Pete Browning Lou AA Outfielder Adjusted

Year T L P	AB	BB	HBP	TAB	H	2B	3B	HR	BA	OB	SA	Wtd PRO	SB	CS	SBF	SPF	FF	Wtd TF	HC
1882 Lou AA 2B	577	75	0	652	265	41	7	12	.459	.521	.619	1,141				10	50	1,201	160.1
1883 Lou AA OF	585	48	0	633	228	28	17	8	.389	.435	.534	969				10	(20)	959	60.9
1884 Lou AA 3B	652	24	4	680	256	56	14	7	.392	.417	.552	969				10	(30)	949	75.5
1885 Lou AA OF	693	45	0	738	286	56	16	15	.412	.448	.604	1,051				10	20	1,081	114.0
1886 Lou AA OF	536	42	10	587	205	37	8	3	.383	.437	.496	933	30			10	(20)	923	46.3
1887 Lou AA OF	644	65	9	719	260	41	19	5	.403	.465	.548	1,013	121			10	0	1,023	91.0
1888 Lou AA OF	441	54	6	501	159	29	11	4	.361	.438	.503	941	43			10	0	951	46.2
1889 Lou AA OF	373	41	0	414	98	23	6	2	.263	.336	.374	710	24			10	(10)	710	(9.4)
1890 Cle P OF	610	87	3	701	220	48	10	6	.361	.444	.501	945	43			10	10	965	69.4
1891 Cin NL OF	486	65	4	555	163	29	5	5	.336	.418	.447	865	19			0	20	885	33.9
1892 Cin NL OF	398	63	0	460	127	18	6	3	.320	.412	.420	832	14			0	(10)	822	14.1
1893 Lou NL OF	276	51	2	329	94	13	4	1	.340	.447	.427	874	10			0	(20)	854	15.2
1894 StL NL OF	11	1	0	12	3	0	0	0	.289	.347	.289	636	0			0	0	636	(0.7)
10.3 Totals	6,283	662	39	6,983	2,364	421	121	70					304	0					716.5
1.0 Averages	608	64	4	676	229	41	12	7	.376	.439	.516	954	29	0	0	8	1	963	69.4

Al Kaline **Tigers** **Outfielder** **Actual**

Year	T	L	P	AB	BB	HBP	TAB	H	2B	3B	HR	BA	OB	SA	PRO	SB	CS	SBF	SPF	FF	Actual TF	Actual HC
1953	Det	AL	OF	28	1	1	30	7	0	0	1	.250	.300	.357	657	1	0	32	10	10	709	(0.7)
1954	Det	AL	OF	504	22	0	526	139	18	3	4	.276	.306	.347	653	9	5	(2)	10	30	692	(17.4)
1955	Det	AL	OF	588	82	5	675	200	24	8	27	.340	.425	.546	971	6	8	(14)	10	30	997	81.1
1956	Det	AL	OF	617	70	1	688	194	32	10	27	.314	.385	.530	915	7	1	7	10	70	1,002	84.3
1957	Det	AL	OF	577	43	3	623	170	29	4	23	.295	.347	.478	825	11	9	(11)	10	40	864	33.4
1958	Det	AL	OF	543	54	2	599	170	34	7	16	.313	.377	.490	867	7	4	(2)	10	80	956	59.5
1959	Det	AL	OF	511	72	4	587	167	19	2	27	.327	.414	.530	944	10	4	3	10	50	1,008	73.6
1960	Det	AL	OF	551	65	3	619	153	29	4	15	.278	.357	.426	784	19	4	17	10	40	850	28.8
1961	Det	AL	OF	586	66	4	656	190	41	7	19	.324	.396	.515	912	14	1	17	10	70	1,009	78.6
1962	Det	AL	OF	398	47	1	446	121	16	6	29	.304	.379	.593	972	4	0	8	10	50	1,040	60.1
1963	Det	AL	OF	551	54	4	609	172	24	3	27	.312	.378	.514	891	6	4	(3)	10	30	928	49.5
1964	Det	AL	OF	525	75	3	603	154	31	5	17	.293	.385	.469	853	4	1	3	10	70	936	51.4
1965	Det	AL	OF	399	72	0	471	112	18	2	18	.281	.391	.471	862	6	0	12	10	30	914	35.1
1966	Det	AL	OF	479	81	5	565	138	29	1	29	.288	.396	.534	931	5	5	(8)	0	40	963	55.2
1967	Det	AL	OF	458	83	1	542	141	28	2	25	.308	.415	.541	957	8	2	7	0	40	1,004	63.6
1968	Det	AL	OF	327	55	3	385	94	14	1	10	.287	.395	.428	823	6	4	(5)	0	20	838	14.8
1969	Det	AL	OF	456	54	1	511	124	17	0	21	.272	.350	.447	798	1	2	(6)	0	20	812	13.3
1970	Det	AL	OF	467	77	1	545	130	24	4	16	.278	.382	.450	831	2	2	(3)	0	20	848	23.5
1971	Det	AL	OF	405	82	7	494	119	19	2	15	.294	.421	.462	883	4	6	(15)	0	20	887	30.6
1972	Det	AL	OF	278	28	2	308	87	11	2	10	.313	.380	.475	855	1	0	3	0	0	858	15.5
1973	Det	AL	OF	310	29	3	342	79	13	0	10	.255	.325	.394	718	4	1	6	0	0	724	(5.5)
1974	Det	AL	DH	558	65	1	624	146	28	2	13	.262	.340	.389	729	2	2	(3)	0	(20)	706	(15.4)
17.3 Totals				10,116	1,277	55	11,448	3,007	498	75	399					137	65					813.1
1.0 Averages				585	74	3	662	174	29	4	23	.297	.379	.480	859	8	4	1	6	37	903	47.0

Al Kaline **Tigers** **Outfielder** **Adjusted**

Year	T	L	P	AB	BB	HBP	TAB	H	2B	3B	HR	BA	OB	SA	Wtd PRO	SB	CS	SBF	SPF	FF	Wtd TF	HC
1953	Det	AL	OF	30	1	1	32	7	0	0	1	.245	.294	.350	644	1	0	32	10	10	696	(0.9)
1954	Det	AL	OF	530	23	0	553	146	19	3	4	.275	.306	.347	652	9	5	(2)	10	30	690	(17.6)
1955	Det	AL	OF	621	84	5	710	207	25	8	28	.333	.417	.535	952	6	8	(14)	10	30	978	74.7
1956	Det	AL	OF	654	69	1	724	197	32	10	27	.301	.369	.508	877	7	1	7	10	70	963	71.0
1957	Det	AL	OF	607	45	3	655	178	30	4	24	.293	.345	.476	820	12	9	(11)	10	40	860	31.9
1958	Det	AL	OF	571	57	2	630	179	36	7	17	.313	.377	.489	866	7	4	(2)	10	80	954	59.1
1959	Det	AL	OF	538	75	4	617	175	20	2	28	.325	.412	.528	940	11	4	3	10	50	1,003	72.4
1960	Det	AL	OF	581	67	3	651	159	30	4	16	.273	.351	.419	770	20	4	17	10	40	837	24.7
1961	Det	AL	OF	589	63	4	656	186	40	7	19	.315	.385	.501	886	14	1	17	10	70	984	70.7
1962	Det	AL	OF	400	46	1	446	119	16	6	28	.297	.370	.580	950	4	0	8	10	50	1,019	55.5
1963	Det	AL	OF	550	55	4	609	174	24	3	27	.318	.384	.522	907	6	4	(3)	10	30	943	54.0
1964	Det	AL	OF	524	76	3	603	155	31	5	17	.297	.389	.474	863	4	1	3	10	70	946	54.2
1965	Det	AL	OF	395	76	0	471	115	18	2	18	.291	.404	.488	892	6	0	12	10	30	944	41.9
1966	Det	AL	OF	474	86	5	565	142	30	1	30	.301	.414	.558	972	5	5	(8)	0	40	1,004	66.3
1967	Det	AL	OF	448	92	1	542	149	30	2	26	.331	.447	.583	1,029	8	2	7	0	40	1,076	82.4
1968	Det	AL	OF	318	63	3	385	101	15	1	11	.318	.436	.473	909	6	4	(5)	0	20	924	30.6
1969	Det	AL	OF	455	55	1	511	126	17	0	21	.277	.357	.456	813	1	2	(6)	0	20	827	16.9
1970	Det	AL	OF	467	77	1	545	130	24	4	16	.280	.383	.452	835	2	2	(3)	0	20	851	24.4
1971	Det	AL	OF	401	86	7	494	122	19	2	15	.303	.435	.477	911	4	6	(15)	0	20	916	37.3
1972	Det	AL	OF	288	33	2	324	98	12	2	11	.339	.412	.515	927	1	0	3	0	0	930	26.6
1973	Det	AL	OF	309	30	3	342	81	13	0	10	.261	.333	.403	736	4	1	6	0	0	742	(2.5)
1974	Det	AL	DH	554	69	1	624	152	29	2	14	.274	.356	.407	763	2	2	(3)	0	(20)	740	(5.1)
17.3 Totals				10,303	1,330	57	11,690	3,097	512	77	410					141	67					868.3
1.0 Averages				596	77	3	676	179	30	4	24	.301	.384	.485	868	8	4	1	6	37	912	50.2

Rickey Henderson   Athletics   Outfielder   Actual

Year	T	L	P	AB	BB	HBP	TAB	H	2B	3B	HR	BA	OB	SA	PRO	SB	CS	SBF	SPF	FF	Actual TF	Actual HC
1979	Oak	AL	OF	351	34	2	387	96	13	3	1	.274	.341	.336	677	33	11	27	10	20	734	(4.3)
1980	Oak	AL	OF	591	117	5	713	179	22	4	9	.303	.422	.399	821	100	26	64	10	50	945	63.8
1981	Oak	AL	OF	423	64	2	489	135	18	7	6	.319	.411	.437	848	56	22	23	10	60	942	65.0
1982	Oak	AL	OF	536	116	2	654	143	24	4	10	.267	.399	.382	782	130	42	66	10	30	888	40.7
1983	Oak	AL	OF	513	103	4	620	150	25	7	9	.292	.415	.421	836	108	19	107	10	40	992	69.4
1984	Oak	AL	OF	502	86	5	593	147	27	4	16	.293	.401	.458	860	66	18	48	10	10	927	48.0
1985	NY	AL	OF	547	99	3	649	172	28	5	24	.314	.422	.516	938	80	10	87	10	50	1,085	101.3
1986	NY	AL	OF	608	89	2	699	160	31	5	28	.263	.359	.469	828	87	18	69	10	40	947	63.1
1987	NY	AL	OF	358	80	2	440	104	17	3	17	.291	.423	.497	920	41	8	54	10	20	1,004	51.6
1988	NY	AL	OF	554	82	3	639	169	30	2	6	.305	.397	.399	796	93	13	99	10	20	925	51.2
1989	Oak	AL	OF	541	126	3	670	148	26	3	12	.274	.413	.399	813	77	14	69	10	30	922	52.5
1990	Oak	AL	OF	489	97	4	590	159	33	3	28	.325	.441	.577	1,017	65	10	72	10	40	1,139	107.4
1991	Oak	AL	OF	470	98	7	575	126	17	1	18	.268	.402	.423	825	58	18	36	10	20	891	36.7
1992	Oak	AL	OF	396	95	6	497	112	18	3	15	.283	.429	.457	886	48	11	49	10	20	965	49.2
1993	Oak	AL	OF	481	120	4	605	139	22	2	21	.289	.435	.474	909	53	8	58	10	10	987	66.0
1994	Oak	AL	OF	296	72	5	373	77	13	0	6	.260	.413	.365	778	22	7	20	10	30	838	20.3
1995	Oak	AL	OF	407	72	4	483	122	31	1	9	.300	.410	.447	857	32	10	23	10	0	891	34.5
1996	SD	NL	OF	465	125	10	600	112	17	2	9	.241	.412	.344	756	37	15	11	10	(10)	767	2.7
1997	SD	NL	OF	403	97	6	506	100	14	0	8	.248	.401	.342	744	45	8	54	10	(10)	798	9.7
1998	Oak	AL	OF	542	118	5	665	128	16	1	14	.236	.377	.347	724	66	13	57	10	20	811	17.0
1999	NY	NL	OF	438	82	2	522	138	30	0	12	.315	.425	.466	891	37	14	16	10	(10)	907	37.3
2000	Sea	AL	OF	420	88	4	512	98	14	2	4	.233	.371	.305	676	36	11	26	10	0	712	(11.1)
19.2 Totals				10,331	2,060	90	12,481	2,914	486	62	282					1,370	326					971.8
1.0 Averages				539	108	5	652	152	25	3	15	.282	.406	.423	829	72	17	54	10	23	917	50.7

Rickey Henderson   Athletics   Outfielder   Adjusted

Year	T	L	P	AB	BB	HBP	TAB	H	2B	3B	HR	BA	OB	SA	Wtd PRO	SB	CS	SBF	SPF	FF	Wtd TF	HC
1979	Oak	AL	OF	352	33	2	387	94	13	3	1	.268	.334	.329	663	33	11	27	10	20	720	(7.0)
1980	Oak	AL	OF	592	116	5	713	178	22	4	9	.302	.420	.398	818	100	26	64	10	50	942	62.6
1981	Oak	AL	OF	633	104	3	740	212	28	11	9	.335	.431	.459	890	85	33	23	10	60	983	79.6
1982	Oak	AL	OF	537	115	2	654	143	24	4	10	.266	.397	.381	778	130	42	66	10	30	885	39.7
1983	Oak	AL	OF	513	103	4	620	150	25	7	9	.292	.414	.420	834	108	19	107	10	40	991	69.0
1984	Oak	AL	OF	501	87	5	593	147	27	4	16	.294	.403	.460	863	66	18	48	10	10	931	49.0
1985	NY	AL	OF	548	98	3	649	171	28	5	24	.312	.419	.512	931	80	10	87	10	50	1,079	99.3
1986	NY	AL	OF	610	87	2	699	158	31	5	28	.260	.354	.462	817	87	18	69	10	40	936	59.3
1987	NY	AL	OF	363	75	2	440	101	17	3	17	.279	.406	.477	882	41	8	54	10	20	966	43.8
1988	NY	AL	OF	552	84	3	639	171	30	2	6	.310	.404	.406	810	93	13	99	10	20	939	55.2
1989	Oak	AL	OF	536	130	3	670	150	26	3	12	.280	.424	.409	833	77	14	69	10	30	942	59.0
1990	Oak	AL	OF	486	99	4	590	161	33	3	28	.331	.448	.586	1,034	65	10	72	10	40	1,156	112.2
1991	Oak	AL	OF	469	99	7	575	126	17	1	18	.270	.404	.426	830	58	18	36	10	20	896	37.9
1992	Oak	AL	OF	393	98	6	497	113	18	3	15	.288	.437	.466	903	48	11	49	10	20	982	53.3
1993	Oak	AL	OF	485	116	4	605	137	22	2	21	.282	.424	.463	887	53	8	58	10	10	965	59.7
1994	Oak	AL	OF	428	93	6	528	104	18	0	8	.243	.385	.341	726	31	10	20	10	30	786	7.3
1995	Oak	AL	OF	465	75	4	543	131	33	1	10	.283	.387	.422	808	36	11	23	10	0	842	21.9
1996	SD	NL	OF	473	117	9	600	109	16	2	9	.229	.392	.328	720	37	15	11	10	(10)	731	(7.6)
1997	SD	NL	OF	410	91	6	506	97	14	0	8	.236	.381	.325	706	45	8	54	10	(10)	760	0.6
1998	Oak	AL	OF	551	109	5	665	122	15	1	13	.222	.355	.326	681	66	13	57	10	20	768	3.3
1999	NY	NL	OF	448	72	2	522	129	28	0	11	.288	.389	.426	815	37	14	16	10	(10)	831	18.4
2000	Sea	AL	OF	430	79	4	512	92	13	2	4	.214	.340	.279	619	36	11	26	10	0	655	(25.1)
19.2 Totals				10,777	2,080	91	12,947	2,998	499	66	286					1,412	341					891.5
1.0 Averages				563	109	5	676	157	26	3	15	.278	.399	.416	815	74	18	53	10	23	902	46.5

Carl Yastrzemski Red Sox   Outfielder   Actual

Year	T	L	P	AB	BB	HBP	TAB	H	2B	3B	HR	BA	OB	SA	PRO	SB	CS	SBF	SPF	FF	Actual TF	Actual HC
1961	Bos	AL	OF	583	50	3	636	155	31	6	11	.266	.327	.396	723	6	5	(6)	10	0	727	(9.1)
1962	Bos	AL	OF	646	66	3	715	191	43	6	19	.296	.364	.469	833	7	4	(1)	10	40	881	42.2
1963	Bos	AL	OF	570	95	1	666	183	40	3	14	.321	.419	.475	894	8	5	(3)	10	60	962	64.8
1964	Bos	AL	OF	567	75	2	644	164	29	9	15	.289	.374	.451	826	6	5	(6)	10	70	900	43.7
1965	Bos	AL	OF	494	70	1	565	154	45	3	20	.312	.398	.536	935	7	6	(8)	10	40	976	58.9
1966	Bos	AL	OF	594	84	1	679	165	39	2	16	.278	.368	.431	799	8	9	(14)	0	70	855	31.7
1967	Bos	AL	OF	579	91	4	674	189	31	4	44	.326	.421	.622	1,043	10	8	(8)	0	60	1,095	108.3
1968	Bos	AL	OF	539	119	2	660	162	32	2	23	.301	.429	.495	924	13	6	1	0	80	1,006	78.0
1969	Bos	AL	OF	603	101	1	705	154	28	2	40	.255	.363	.507	871	15	7	1	0	60	932	58.6
1970	Bos	AL	1B	566	128	1	695	186	29	0	40	.329	.453	.592	1,045	23	13	(4)	10	10	1,061	96.4
1971	Bos	AL	OF	508	106	1	615	129	21	2	15	.254	.384	.392	775	8	7	(9)	10	70	846	26.0
1972	Bos	AL	OF	455	67	4	526	120	18	2	12	.264	.363	.391	754	5	4	(5)	10	20	779	5.7
1973	Bos	AL	1B	540	105	0	645	160	25	4	19	.296	.411	.463	874	9	7	(7)	10	0	876	32.7
1974	Bos	AL	1B	515	104	3	622	155	25	2	15	.301	.421	.445	866	12	7	(3)	10	0	873	30.5
1975	Bos	AL	1B	543	87	2	632	146	30	1	14	.269	.372	.405	777	8	4	0	10	0	787	5.1
1976	Bos	AL	1B	546	80	1	627	146	23	2	21	.267	.362	.432	794	5	6	(11)	0	0	784	4.1
1977	Bos	AL	OF	558	73	1	632	165	27	3	28	.296	.378	.505	884	11	1	13	0	70	967	63.1
1978	Bos	AL	OF	523	76	3	602	145	21	2	17	.277	.372	.423	795	4	5	(9)	0	30	815	16.6
1979	Bos	AL	DH	518	62	2	582	140	28	1	21	.270	.351	.450	800	3	3	(5)	(10)	0	785	4.3
1980	Bos	AL	DH	364	44	0	408	100	21	1	15	.275	.353	.462	814	0	2	(9)	(10)	0	795	7.4
1981	Bos	AL	DH	338	49	0	387	83	14	1	7	.246	.341	.355	696	0	1	(5)	(10)	(10)	671	(27.6)
1982	Bos	AL	DH	459	59	2	520	126	22	1	16	.275	.360	.431	791	0	1	(4)	(10)	(10)	767	(0.7)
1983	Bos	AL	DH	380	54	2	436	101	24	0	10	.266	.360	.408	768	0	0	0	(10)	(30)	728	(8.7)
20.9 Totals				11,988	1,845	40	13,873	3,419	646	59	452					168	116					732.0
1.0 Averages				575	88	2	665	164	31	3	22	.285	.382	.462	844	8	6	(4)	3	30	873	35.1

Carl Yastrzemski Red Sox   Outfielder   Adjusted

Year	T	L	P	AB	BB	HBP	TAB	H	2B	3B	HR	BA	OB	SA	Wtd PRO	SB	CS	SBF	SPF	FF	Wtd TF	HC
1961	Bos	AL	OF	585	48	3	636	151	30	6	11	.259	.318	.385	703	6	5	(6)	10	0	707	(15.2)
1962	Bos	AL	OF	648	64	3	715	187	42	6	19	.289	.356	.459	814	7	4	(1)	10	40	863	35.9
1963	Bos	AL	OF	568	97	1	666	185	41	3	14	.327	.426	.484	910	8	5	(3)	10	60	977	69.6
1964	Bos	AL	OF	566	76	2	644	165	29	9	15	.293	.378	.457	835	6	5	(6)	10	70	909	46.6
1965	Bos	AL	OF	490	74	1	565	158	46	3	21	.323	.412	.555	967	7	6	(8)	10	40	1,009	67.7
1966	Bos	AL	OF	589	89	1	679	171	40	2	17	.290	.384	.450	835	8	9	(14)	0	70	891	43.1
1967	Bos	AL	OF	568	102	4	674	199	33	4	46	.351	.453	.669	1,122	10	8	(8)	0	60	1,174	133.8
1968	Bos	AL	OF	520	138	2	660	173	34	2	25	.332	.474	.547	1,021	13	6	1	0	80	1,102	108.5
1969	Bos	AL	OF	600	104	1	705	156	28	2	41	.260	.370	.517	887	15	7	1	0	60	948	64.1
1970	Bos	AL	1B	565	129	1	695	187	29	0	40	.330	.455	.594	1,049	23	13	(4)	10	10	1,065	97.8
1971	Bos	AL	OF	503	111	1	615	132	21	2	15	.262	.396	.404	800	8	7	(9)	10	70	871	33.3
1972	Bos	AL	OF	470	79	5	553	134	20	2	13	.286	.394	.424	818	5	4	(5)	10	20	843	22.4
1973	Bos	AL	1B	536	109	0	645	163	25	4	19	.304	.421	.475	896	9	7	(7)	10	0	899	39.5
1974	Bos	AL	1B	508	111	3	622	160	26	2	15	.315	.441	.466	907	12	7	(3)	10	0	914	42.6
1975	Bos	AL	1B	539	91	2	632	149	31	1	14	.277	.383	.417	800	8	4	0	10	0	810	12.0
1976	Bos	AL	1B	538	88	1	627	154	24	2	22	.285	.386	.461	848	5	6	(11)	0	0	837	20.1
1977	Bos	AL	OF	559	72	1	632	164	27	3	28	.292	.374	.500	874	11	1	13	0	70	957	60.2
1978	Bos	AL	OF	521	78	3	602	148	21	2	17	.283	.380	.432	812	4	5	(9)	0	30	833	21.7
1979	Bos	AL	DH	520	60	2	582	137	27	1	21	.264	.343	.440	783	3	3	(5)	(10)	0	768	(0.5)
1980	Bos	AL	DH	364	44	0	408	100	21	1	15	.274	.351	.460	811	0	2	(9)	(10)	0	792	6.7
1981	Bos	AL	DH	507	79	0	586	131	22	2	11	.258	.358	.372	730	0	2	(5)	(10)	(10)	705	(18.1)
1982	Bos	AL	DH	459	59	2	520	126	22	1	16	.273	.358	.430	788	0	1	(4)	(10)	(10)	764	(1.5)
1983	Bos	AL	DH	380	54	2	436	101	24	0	10	.265	.360	.407	767	0	0	0	(10)	(30)	727	(8.9)
20.9 Totals				12,104	1,954	42	14,099	3,531	665	60	465					168	117					881.5
1.0 Averages				580	94	2	676	169	32	3	22	.292	.392	.472	864	8	6	(4)	3	30	892	42.3

Sam Crawford **Tigers** **Outfielder** **Actual**

Year	T	L	P	AB	BB	HBP	TAB	H	2B	3B	HR	BA	OB	SA	PRO	SB	CS	SBF	SPF	FF	Actual TF	Actual HC
1899	Cin	NL	OF	127	2	0	129	39	3	7	1	.307	.318	.465	782	6			10	40	832	4.9
1900	Cin	NL	OF	389	28	3	420	101	15	15	7	.260	.314	.429	744	14			10	40	794	8.4
1901	Cin	NL	OF	515	37	3	555	170	20	16	16	.330	.378	.524	903	13			10	20	933	53.6
1902	Cin	NL	OF	555	47	1	603	185	18	22	3	.333	.386	.461	848	16			10	20	878	40.0
1903	Det	AL	OF	550	25	2	577	184	23	25	4	.335	.366	.489	855	18			10	20	885	40.5
1904	Det	AL	OF	562	44	0	606	143	22	16	2	.254	.309	.361	670	20			10	20	700	(17.5)
1905	Det	AL	OF	575	50	3	628	171	38	10	6	.297	.357	.430	786	22			10	40	836	24.8
1906	Det	AL	OF	563	38	1	602	166	25	16	2	.295	.341	.407	747	24			10	30	787	9.0
1907	Det	AL	OF	582	37	2	621	188	34	17	4	.323	.366	.460	826	18			10	40	876	36.9
1908	Det	AL	OF	591	37	3	631	184	33	16	7	.311	.355	.457	812	15			0	10	822	20.4
1909	Det	AL	OF	589	47	1	637	185	35	14	6	.314	.366	.452	817	30			0	10	827	22.3
1910	Det	AL	OF	588	37	1	626	170	26	19	5	.289	.332	.423	756	20			0	0	756	(0.5)
1911	Det	AL	OF	574	61	0	635	217	36	14	7	.378	.438	.526	964	37			0	0	964	65.7
1912	Det	AL	OF	581	42	2	625	189	30	21	4	.325	.373	.470	843	41			0	(10)	833	23.6
1913	Det	AL	OF	609	52	0	661	193	32	23	9	.317	.371	.489	860	13			0	(10)	850	30.7
1914	Det	AL	OF	582	69	1	652	183	22	26	8	.314	.388	.483	871	25	16	(10)	0	(10)	851	30.5
1915	Det	AL	OF	612	66	0	678	183	31	19	4	.299	.367	.431	799	24	14	(6)	0	(10)	783	8.7
1916	Det	AL	OF	322	37	0	359	92	11	13	0	.286	.359	.401	760	10			0	(20)	740	(3.1)
1917	Det	AL	OF	104	4	0	108	18	4	0	2	.173	.204	.269	473	0			(10)	(20)	443	(17.0)
16.4 Totals				9,570	760	23	10,353	2,961	458	309	97					366	30					381.8
1.0 Averages				582	46	1	629	180	28	19	6	.309	.362	.452	814	22	2	(1)	5	11	829	23.2

Sam Crawford **Tigers** **Outfielder** **Adjusted**

Year	T	L	P	AB	BB	HBP	TAB	H	2B	3B	HR	BA	OB	SA	Wtd PRO	SB	CS	SBF	SPF	FF	Wtd TF	HC
1899	Cin	NL	OF	134	2	0	136	41	3	7	1	.305	.316	.462	778	6			10	40	828	4.6
1900	Cin	NL	OF	450	32	3	486	117	17	17	8	.260	.315	.430	745	16			10	40	795	8.6
1901	Cin	NL	OF	592	46	4	642	206	24	19	19	.348	.399	.553	952	15			10	20	982	68.9
1902	Cin	NL	OF	632	65	1	698	236	23	28	4	.373	.432	.516	948	19			10	20	978	73.4
1903	Det	AL	OF	632	33	3	668	230	29	31	5	.364	.398	.533	931	21			10	20	961	64.8
1904	Det	AL	OF	582	56	0	637	170	26	19	2	.292	.354	.414	768	21			10	20	798	12.2
1905	Det	AL	OF	592	65	4	661	203	45	12	7	.342	.411	.495	905	23			10	40	955	62.3
1906	Det	AL	OF	584	48	1	633	196	29	19	2	.335	.387	.462	849	25			10	30	889	39.8
1907	Det	AL	OF	602	49	3	653	225	41	20	5	.373	.422	.532	954	19			10	40	1,004	76.8
1908	Det	AL	OF	610	50	4	664	224	40	19	9	.368	.419	.539	958	16			0	10	968	66.7
1909	Det	AL	OF	607	61	1	670	220	42	17	7	.363	.423	.522	944	32			0	10	954	62.9
1910	Det	AL	OF	610	47	1	659	201	31	22	6	.329	.378	.481	859	21			0	0	859	31.9
1911	Det	AL	OF	602	66	0	668	231	38	15	7	.383	.444	.534	978	39			0	0	978	70.1
1912	Det	AL	OF	609	47	2	657	205	33	23	4	.337	.386	.487	873	43			0	(10)	863	33.2
1913	Det	AL	OF	635	60	0	695	215	36	26	10	.338	.396	.523	918	14			0	(10)	908	50.0
1914	Det	AL	OF	601	84	1	686	208	25	30	9	.346	.427	.531	958	26	17	(10)	0	(10)	937	58.8
1915	Det	AL	OF	635	78	0	713	206	35	21	5	.324	.398	.468	866	25	15	(6)	0	(10)	850	31.6
1916	Det	AL	OF	333	44	0	378	104	12	15	0	.313	.393	.438	832	11			0	(20)	812	9.8
1917	Det	AL	OF	109	5	0	114	21	5	0	2	.191	.225	.298	523	0			(10)	(20)	493	(14.3)
16.4 Totals				10,151	938	29	11,118	3,458	534	361	113					391	32					812.2
1.0 Averages				617	57	2	676	210	32	22	7	.341	.398	.498	896	24	2	(1)	5	11	911	49.4

Larry Walker **Rockies** **Outfielder** **Actual**

Year	T	L	P	AB	BB	HBP	TAB	H	2B	3B	HR	BA	OB	SA	PRO	SB	CS	SBF	SPF	FF	Actual TF	Actual HC
1989	Mon	NL	OF	47	5	1	53	8	0	0	0	.170	.264	.170	434	1	1	(18)	10	20	447	(7.8)
1990	Mon	NL	OF	419	49	5	473	101	18	3	19	.241	.328	.434	762	21	7	14	10	20	806	11.0
1991	Mon	NL	OF	487	42	5	534	141	30	2	16	.290	.352	.458	810	14	9	(7)	10	40	853	24.3
1992	Mon	NL	OF	528	41	6	575	159	31	4	23	.301	.358	.506	864	18	6	10	10	40	924	45.6
1993	Mon	NL	OF	490	80	6	576	130	24	5	22	.265	.375	.469	844	29	7	25	10	30	909	41.6
1994	Mon	NL	OF	395	47	4	446	127	44	2	19	.322	.399	.587	986	15	5	11	10	10	1,017	78.1
1995	Col	NL	OF	494	49	14	557	151	31	5	36	.306	.384	.607	991	16	3	17	10	10	1,028	80.9
1996	Col	NL	OF	272	20	9	301	75	18	4	18	.276	.346	.570	915	18	2	44	10	20	989	33.3
1997	Col	NL	OF	568	78	14	660	208	46	4	49	.366	.455	.720	1,175	33	8	24	10	30	1,239	151.4
1998	Col	NL	OF	454	64	4	522	165	46	3	23	.363	.446	.630	1,076	14	4	11	10	30	1,127	92.0
1999	Col	NL	OF	438	57	12	507	166	26	4	37	.379	.464	.710	1,174	11	4	6	10	30	1,219	111.5
2000	Col	NL	OF	314	46	9	369	97	21	7	9	.309	.412	.506	918	5	5	(13)	10	30	945	33.1
8.6 Totals				4,906	578	89	5,573	1,528	335	43	271					195	61					694.8
1.0 Averages				569	67	10	646	177	39	5	31	.311	.394	.563	957	23	7	12	10	26	1,005	80.6

Larry Walker **Rockies** **Outfielder** **Adjusted**

Year	T	L	P	AB	BB	HBP	TAB	H	2B	3B	HR	BA	OB	SA	Wtd PRO	SB	CS	SBF	SPF	FF	Wtd TF	HC
1989	Mon	NL	OF	47	5	1	53	8	0	0	0	.177	.274	.177	451	1	1	(18)	10	20	463	(7.4)
1990	Mon	NL	OF	419	49	5	473	101	18	3	19	.241	.327	.434	761	21	7	14	10	20	805	10.7
1991	Mon	NL	OF	486	43	5	534	143	31	2	16	.295	.359	.467	826	14	9	(7)	10	40	869	28.4
1992	Mon	NL	OF	526	43	6	575	163	32	4	24	.310	.369	.520	889	18	6	10	10	40	949	52.5
1993	Mon	NL	OF	494	77	6	576	127	23	5	21	.257	.363	.455	818	29	7	25	10	30	882	34.3
1994	Mon	NL	OF	565	61	5	631	171	59	3	26	.303	.376	.553	928	21	7	11	10	10	959	60.6
1995	Col	NL	OF	560	51	15	627	163	34	5	39	.291	.366	.579	945	18	3	17	10	10	981	66.9
1996	Col	NL	OF	274	19	8	301	72	17	4	17	.263	.329	.543	872	18	2	44	10	20	946	27.0
1997	Col	NL	OF	575	72	13	660	200	44	4	47	.348	.431	.683	1,115	33	8	24	10	30	1,179	132.6
1998	Col	NL	OF	459	59	4	522	159	44	3	22	.346	.425	.599	1,024	14	4	11	10	30	1,075	79.0
1999	Col	NL	OF	447	50	10	507	155	24	4	35	.347	.424	.650	1,074	11	4	6	10	30	1,119	87.4
2000	Col	NL	OF	321	40	8	369	90	20	7	8	.282	.376	.462	838	5	5	(13)	10	30	865	18.9
8.6 Totals				5,172	569	86	5,828	1,553	346	43	274					203	63					590.9
1.0 Averages				600	66	10	676	180	40	5	32	.300	.379	.543	922	24	7	12	10	26	970	68.5

King Kelly   **Chi NL**   **Outfielder**   **Actual**

Year	T	L	P	AB	BB	HBP	TAB	H	2B	3B	HR	BA	OB	SA	PRO	SB	CS	SBF	SPF	FF	Actual TF	Actual HC
1878	Cin	NL	OF	237	7	0	244	67	7	1	0	.283	.303	.321	624				10	60	694	(19.6)
1879	Cin	NL	3B	345	8	0	353	120	20	12	2	.348	.363	.493	855				10	50	915	67.8
1880	Chi	NL	OF	344	12	0	356	100	17	9	1	.291	.315	.401	716				10	0	726	(10.2)
1881	Chi	NL	OF	353	16	0	369	114	27	3	2	.323	.352	.433	786				10	0	796	13.0
1882	Chi	NL	SS	377	10	0	387	115	37	4	1	.305	.323	.432	755				10	0	765	36.5
1883	Chi	NL	OF	428	16	0	444	109	28	10	3	.255	.282	.388	669				10	10	689	(23.5)
1884	Chi	NL	OF	452	46	0	498	160	28	5	13	.354	.414	.524	938				10	(10)	938	60.9
1885	Chi	NL	OF	438	46	0	484	126	24	7	9	.288	.355	.436	791				10	10	811	18.2
1886	Chi	NL	OF	451	83	0	534	175	32	11	4	.388	.483	.534	1,018	53			10	10	1,038	93.1
1887	Bos	NL	OF	484	55	1	540	156	34	11	8	.322	.393	.488	880	84			10	(20)	870	37.0
1888	Bos	NL	C	440	31	4	475	140	22	11	9	.318	.368	.480	848	56			10	0	858	48.7
1889	Bos	NL	OF	507	65	2	574	149	41	5	9	.294	.376	.448	824	68			10	(20)	814	18.9
1890	Bos	P	C	340	52	2	394	111	18	6	4	.326	.419	.450	869	51			10	0	879	46.4
1891	Bos	AA	C	350	57	3	410	100	16	7	2	.286	.390	.389	779	29			0	60	839	36.5
1892	Bos	NL	C	281	39	0	320	53	7	0	2	.189	.288	.235	522	24			0	10	532	(23.3)
1893	NY	NL	C	67	6	0	73	18	1	0	0	.269	.329	.284	612	3			0	(50)	562	(4.9)
14.3	Totals			5,894	549	12	6,455	1,813	359	102	69					368	0					395.3
1.0	Averages			412	38	1	451	127	25	7	5	.308	.368	.438	806	26	0	0	9	9	824	27.6

King Kelly   **Chi NL**   **Outfielder**   **Adjusted**

Year	T	L	P	AB	BB	HBP	TAB	H	2B	3B	HR	BA	OB	SA	Wtd PRO	SB	CS	SBF	SPF	FF	Wtd TF	HC
1878	Cin	NL	OF	624	24	0	648	208	22	3	0	.334	.358	.379	737				10	60	807	15.2
1879	Cin	NL	3B	694	21	0	715	284	47	28	5	.410	.427	.581	1,008				10	50	1,068	119.8
1880	Chi	NL	OF	649	30	0	678	227	39	20	2	.350	.378	.482	861				10	0	871	36.6
1881	Chi	NL	OF	675	37	0	712	245	58	6	4	.364	.397	.488	885				10	0	895	46.5
1882	Chi	NL	SS	719	23	0	742	249	80	9	2	.346	.367	.491	857				10	0	867	72.5
1883	Chi	NL	OF	697	29	0	727	193	50	18	5	.277	.306	.421	727				10	10	747	(3.6)
1884	Chi	NL	OF	628	79	0	708	251	44	8	20	.399	.466	.591	1,058				10	(10)	1,058	101.3
1885	Chi	NL	OF	623	84	0	706	209	40	12	15	.335	.414	.508	922				10	10	942	62.1
1886	Chi	NL	OF	570	128	0	698	244	45	15	6	.427	.532	.588	1,121	69			10	10	1,141	127.3
1887	Bos	NL	OF	618	70	1	689	199	43	14	10	.322	.392	.487	879	107			10	(20)	869	36.6
1888	Bos	NL	C	514	46	6	566	189	30	15	12	.369	.427	.556	983	67			10	0	993	85.0
1889	Bos	NL	OF	615	81	3	699	184	51	6	11	.299	.383	.456	839	83			10	(20)	829	24.0
1890	Bos	P	C	420	61	2	484	133	22	7	5	.316	.406	.436	841	63			10	0	851	40.1
1891	Bos	AA	C	402	69	4	474	119	19	8	2	.296	.404	.402	806	34			0	60	866	42.7
1892	Bos	NL	C	292	46	0	338	60	8	0	2	.207	.315	.257	573	25			0	10	583	(15.3)
1893	NY	NL	C	83	7	0	90	21	1	0	0	.258	.315	.272	587	4			0	(50)	537	(6.0)
14.3	Totals			8,822	836	16	9,673	3,015	597	170	103					451	0					784.8
1.0	Averages			617	58	1	676	211	42	12	7	.342	.400	.483	883	32	0	0	9	9	901	54.8

Harry Stovey Phi AA Outfielder Actual

Year	T	L	P	AB	BB	HBP	TAB	H	2B	3B	HR	BA	OB	SA	PRO	SB	CS	SBF	SPF	FF	Actual TF	Actual HC
1880	Wor	NL	OF	355	12	0	367	94	21	14	6	.265	.289	.454	742				10	(20)	732	(8.3)
1881	Wor	NL	1B	341	12	0	353	92	25	7	2	.270	.295	.402	696				10	(10)	696	(23.9)
1882	Wor	NL	1B	360	22	0	382	104	13	10	5	.289	.330	.422	752				10	10	772	0.7
1883	Phi	AA	1B	421	27	0	448	128	31	6	14	.304	.346	.506	852				10	10	872	36.1
1884	Phi	AA	1B	448	26	4	478	146	22	23	10	.326	.368	.545	913				10	0	923	51.3
1885	Phi	AA	1B	486	39	4	529	153	27	9	13	.315	.371	.488	858				10	10	878	39.8
1886	Phi	AA	OF	489	64	1	554	144	28	11	7	.294	.377	.440	817	68			10	10	837	24.5
1887	Phi	AA	OF	497	56	7	560	142	31	12	4	.286	.366	.421	787	74			10	30	827	21.8
1888	Phi	AA	OF	530	62	3	595	152	25	20	9	.287	.365	.460	825	87			10	10	845	29.4
1889	Bos	AA	OF	556	77	1	634	171	38	13	19	.308	.393	.525	918	63			10	40	968	73.6
1890	Bos	P	OF	481	81	5	567	144	25	11	12	.299	.406	.472	878	97			10	10	898	46.5
1891	Bos	NL	OF	544	79	2	625	152	31	20	16	.279	.373	.498	871	57			10	20	901	50.2
1892	Bal	NL	OF	429	54	4	487	101	22	12	4	.235	.326	.371	697	40			10	0	707	(12.3)
1893	Bkn	NL	OF	201	52	0	253	48	8	6	1	.239	.395	.353	748	23			10	(10)	748	(1.3)
13.8 Totals				6,138	663	31	6,832	1,771	347	174	122					509	0					327.9
1.0 Averages				445	48	2	495	128	25	13	9	.289	.361	.461	822	37	0	0	10	9	841	23.8

Harry Stovey Phi AA Outfielder Adjusted

Year	T	L	P	AB	BB	HBP	TAB	H	2B	3B	HR	BA	OB	SA	Wtd PRO	SB	CS	SBF	SPF	FF	Wtd TF	HC
1880	Wor	NL	OF	670	30	0	699	213	48	32	14	.318	.347	.545	893				10	(20)	883	41.8
1881	Wor	NL	1B	653	27	0	681	198	54	15	4	.304	.332	.452	784				10	(10)	784	4.5
1882	Wor	NL	1B	682	51	0	732	224	28	21	11	.328	.374	.479	854				10	10	874	36.1
1883	Phi	AA	1B	689	55	0	744	241	58	11	26	.350	.398	.583	981				10	10	1,001	81.9
1884	Phi	AA	1B	648	49	7	704	247	37	39	17	.381	.430	.637	1,067				10	0	1,077	102.9
1885	Phi	AA	1B	696	69	7	772	249	44	15	21	.358	.422	.555	977				10	10	997	83.5
1886	Phi	AA	OF	556	88	1	646	184	36	14	9	.331	.424	.494	918	79			10	10	938	55.6
1887	Phi	AA	OF	585	66	8	660	168	37	14	5	.286	.367	.422	789	87			10	30	829	22.4
1888	Phi	AA	OF	609	90	4	704	201	33	27	12	.331	.421	.531	952	103			10	10	972	71.8
1889	Bos	AA	OF	640	93	1	734	202	45	15	22	.316	.404	.540	943	73			10	40	993	82.4
1890	Bos	P	OF	595	95	6	696	172	30	13	14	.290	.393	.457	850	119			10	10	870	37.3
1891	Bos	NL	OF	631	100	3	734	187	38	25	20	.296	.395	.527	922	67			10	20	952	67.9
1892	Bal	NL	OF	445	64	5	514	115	25	14	5	.258	.358	.406	764	42			10	0	774	4.1
1893	Bkn	NL	OF	252	61	0	313	58	10	7	1	.229	.379	.339	718	28			10	(10)	718	(5.9)
13.8 Totals				8,350	939	43	9,332	2,659	522	262	181					599	0					686.5
1.0 Averages				605	68	3	676	193	38	19	13	.318	.390	.509	899	43	0	0	10	9	918	49.7

Sam Thompson   **Phi NL**   **Outfielder**   **Actual**

Year	T	L	P	AB	BB	HBP	TAB	H	2B	3B	HR	BA	OB	SA	PRO	SB	CS	SBF	SPF	FF	Actual TF	Actual HC
1885	Det	NL	OF	254	16	0	270	77	11	9	7	.303	.344	.500	844				10	40	894	25.7
1886	Det	NL	OF	503	35	0	538	156	18	13	8	.310	.355	.445	800	13			10	30	840	27.8
1887	Det	NL	OF	545	32	9	586	203	29	23	10	.372	.416	.565	982	22			10	20	1,012	90.5
1888	Det	NL	OF	238	23	3	264	67	10	8	6	.282	.352	.466	819	5			10	(20)	809	7.7
1889	Phi	NL	OF	533	36	6	575	158	36	4	20	.296	.348	.492	839	24			10	(10)	839	27.4
1890	Phi	NL	OF	549	42	8	599	172	41	9	4	.313	.371	.443	813	25			10	10	833	26.0
1891	Phi	NL	OF	554	52	8	614	163	23	10	7	.294	.363	.410	773	29			10	50	833	25.9
1892	Phi	NL	OF	609	59	11	679	186	28	11	9	.305	.377	.432	809	28			10	10	829	24.4
1893	Phi	NL	OF	600	50	6	656	222	37	13	11	.370	.424	.530	954	18			10	(10)	954	75.9
1894	Phi	NL	OF	437	40	1	478	178	29	27	13	.407	.458	.686	1,145	24			10	20	1,175	116.6
1895	Phi	NL	OF	538	31	5	574	211	45	21	18	.392	.430	.654	1,085	27			10	30	1,125	122.3
1896	Phi	NL	OF	517	28	6	551	154	28	7	12	.298	.341	.449	790	12			0	50	840	26.6
1897	Phi	NL	OF	13	1	0	14	3	0	1	0	.231	.286	.385	670	0			0	(30)	640	(0.9)
1898	Phi	NL	OF	63	4	0	67	22	5	3	1	.349	.388	.571	959	2			0	40	999	8.2
1906	Det	AL	OF	31	1	0	32	7	0	1	0	.226	.250	.290	540	0			(10)	(20)	510	(4.0)
11.7	Totals			5,984	450	63	6,497	1,979	340	160	126					229	0					600.0
1.0	Averages			511	38	5	555	169	29	14	11	.331	.384	.504	888	20	0	0	9	19	916	51.3

Sam Thompson   **Phi NL**   **Outfielder**   **Adjusted**

Year	T	L	P	AB	BB	HBP	TAB	H	2B	3B	HR	BA	OB	SA	Wtd PRO	SB	CS	SBF	SPF	FF	Wtd TF	HC
1885	Det	NL	OF	365	29	0	394	129	18	15	12	.353	.401	.582	984				10	40	1,034	51.9
1886	Det	NL	OF	650	53	0	703	222	26	19	11	.342	.391	.490	881	17			10	30	921	54.9
1887	Det	NL	OF	695	41	11	747	259	37	29	13	.372	.416	.564	980	28			10	20	1,010	90.0
1888	Det	NL	OF	276	34	4	314	90	13	11	8	.326	.408	.541	949	6			10	(20)	939	27.2
1889	Phi	NL	OF	648	45	8	700	196	45	5	25	.302	.354	.501	855	29			10	(10)	855	32.6
1890	Phi	NL	OF	654	54	10	719	216	51	11	5	.330	.390	.466	856	30			10	10	876	40.5
1891	Phi	NL	OF	644	66	10	721	201	28	12	9	.311	.384	.434	818	34			10	50	878	41.4
1892	Phi	NL	OF	632	71	13	717	212	32	13	10	.335	.413	.473	887	30			10	10	907	50.9
1893	Phi	NL	OF	746	58	7	811	265	44	16	13	.355	.406	.508	915	22			10	(10)	915	60.8
1894	Phi	NL	OF	547	39	1	587	193	31	29	14	.353	.397	.595	993	29			10	20	1,023	74.1
1895	Phi	NL	OF	660	33	5	699	240	51	24	20	.364	.399	.607	1,006	33			10	30	1,046	96.1
1896	Phi	NL	OF	637	32	7	676	181	33	8	14	.284	.325	.427	753	15			0	50	803	14.5
1897	Phi	NL	OF	16	1	0	17	3	0	1	0	.220	.272	.366	639	0			0	(30)	609	(1.2)
1898	Phi	NL	OF	66	4	0	71	24	5	3	1	.362	.402	.592	995	2			0	40	1,035	9.3
1906	Det	AL	OF	32	1	0	34	8	0	1	0	.257	.284	.330	614	0			(10)	(20)	584	(2.8)
11.7	Totals			7,270	563	77	7,910	2,438	416	197	155					275	0					640.3
1.0	Averages			621	48	7	676	208	36	17	13	.335	.389	.511	900	24	0	0	9	19	928	54.7

Roberto Clemente **Pirates** **Outfielder** **Actual**

Year	T	L	P	AB	BB	HBP	TAB	H	2B	3B	HR	BA	OB	SA	PRO	SB	CS	SBF	SPF	FF	Actual TF	Actual HC
1955	Pit	NL	OF	474	18	2	494	121	23	11	5	.255	.285	.382	667	2	5	(15)	10	40	702	(13.7)
1956	Pit	NL	OF	543	13	4	560	169	30	7	7	.311	.332	.431	763	6	6	(10)	10	30	793	10.0
1957	Pit	NL	OF	451	23	0	474	114	17	7	4	.253	.289	.348	637	0	4	(16)	10	70	701	(13.4)
1958	Pit	NL	OF	519	31	0	550	150	24	10	6	.289	.329	.408	738	8	2	7	10	80	834	21.2
1959	Pit	NL	OF	432	15	3	450	128	17	7	4	.296	.324	.396	720	2	3	(8)	10	30	752	(1.2)
1960	Pit	NL	OF	570	39	2	611	179	22	6	16	.314	.360	.458	818	4	5	(9)	10	30	849	28.0
1961	Pit	NL	OF	572	35	3	610	201	30	10	23	.351	.392	.559	951	4	1	3	10	70	1,034	84.7
1962	Pit	NL	OF	538	35	1	574	168	28	9	10	.312	.355	.454	809	6	4	(3)	10	70	886	35.1
1963	Pit	NL	OF	600	31	4	635	192	23	8	17	.320	.357	.470	827	12	2	12	10	30	879	36.9
1964	Pit	NL	OF	622	51	2	675	211	40	7	12	.339	.391	.484	875	5	2	1	10	50	936	57.6
1965	Pit	NL	OF	589	43	5	637	194	21	14	10	.329	.380	.463	843	8	0	12	10	50	915	47.9
1966	Pit	NL	OF	638	46	0	684	202	31	11	29	.317	.363	.536	899	7	5	(4)	10	60	964	67.5
1967	Pit	NL	OF	585	41	3	629	209	26	10	23	.357	.402	.554	956	9	1	11	10	50	1,027	80.7
1968	Pit	NL	OF	502	51	1	554	146	18	12	18	.291	.357	.482	839	2	3	(7)	10	70	913	41.0
1969	Pit	NL	OF	507	56	3	566	175	20	12	19	.345	.413	.544	958	4	1	3	10	50	1,021	71.1
1970	Pit	NL	OF	412	38	2	452	145	22	10	14	.352	.409	.556	965	3	0	6	10	30	1,011	54.7
1971	Pit	NL	OF	522	26	0	548	178	29	8	13	.341	.372	.502	874	1	2	(5)	10	60	939	47.4
1972	Pit	NL	OF	378	29	0	407	118	19	7	10	.312	.361	.479	840	0	0	0	10	60	910	31.1
15.3	Totals			9,454	621	35	10,110	3,000	440	166	240					83	46					686.4
1.0	Averages			619	41	2	662	196	29	11	16	.317	.362	.475	837	5	3	(1)	10	52	898	44.9

Roberto Clemente **Pirates** **Outfielder** **Adjusted**

Year	T	L	P	AB	BB	HBP	TAB	H	2B	3B	HR	BA	OB	SA	Wtd PRO	SB	CS	SBF	SPF	FF	Wtd TF	HC
1955	Pit	NL	OF	500	18	2	520	122	23	11	5	.245	.273	.366	639	2	5	(15)	10	40	674	(20.7)
1956	Pit	NL	OF	572	13	4	589	173	31	7	7	.303	.323	.420	743	6	6	(10)	10	30	773	4.3
1957	Pit	NL	OF	475	23	0	499	117	17	7	4	.246	.282	.339	621	0	4	(16)	10	70	685	(17.1)
1958	Pit	NL	OF	548	31	0	579	152	24	10	6	.278	.316	.392	708	8	2	7	10	80	805	13.2
1959	Pit	NL	OF	455	15	3	473	131	17	7	4	.288	.315	.384	699	2	3	(8)	10	30	731	(6.0)
1960	Pit	NL	OF	600	41	2	643	187	23	6	17	.312	.358	.455	813	4	5	(9)	10	30	844	26.5
1961	Pit	NL	OF	604	35	3	642	204	30	10	23	.337	.376	.537	914	4	1	3	10	70	997	73.2
1962	Pit	NL	OF	539	34	1	574	165	27	9	10	.305	.347	.443	791	6	4	(3)	10	70	868	30.1
1963	Pit	NL	OF	597	33	4	635	201	24	8	18	.337	.376	.494	871	12	2	12	10	30	922	49.9
1964	Pit	NL	OF	620	53	2	675	216	41	7	12	.349	.402	.497	899	5	2	1	10	50	961	65.3
1965	Pit	NL	OF	587	45	5	637	199	22	14	10	.338	.390	.476	867	8	0	12	10	50	938	55.0
1966	Pit	NL	OF	637	47	0	684	204	31	11	29	.320	.366	.541	907	7	5	(4)	10	60	973	70.4
1967	Pit	NL	OF	582	44	3	629	217	27	10	24	.374	.421	.579	1,000	9	1	11	10	50	1,070	93.8
1968	Pit	NL	OF	495	58	1	554	158	19	13	19	.319	.392	.529	922	2	3	(7)	10	70	995	62.6
1969	Pit	NL	OF	505	58	3	566	178	20	12	19	.353	.423	.557	980	4	1	3	10	50	1,043	77.1
1970	Pit	NL	OF	414	37	2	452	142	22	10	14	.343	.399	.542	941	3	0	6	10	30	987	49.5
1971	Pit	NL	OF	521	27	0	548	183	30	8	13	.351	.384	.517	901	1	2	(5)	10	60	966	54.4
1972	Pit	NL	OF	396	32	0	428	128	21	8	11	.323	.374	.496	869	0	0	0	10	60	939	37.1
15.3	Totals			9,646	644	36	10,326	3,077	451	170	247					84	47					718.6
1.0	Averages			631	42	2	676	201	30	11	16	.319	.364	.478	842	6	3	(1)	10	52	902	47.0

Charley Jones   **Cin AA**   **Outfielder**   **Actual**

Year	T	L	P	AB	BB	HBP	TAB	H	2B	3B	HR	BA	OB	SA	PRO	SB	CS	SBF	SPF	FF	Actual TF	Actual HC
1876	Cin	NL	OF	276	7	0	283	79	17	4	4	.286	.304	.420	724				0	10	734	(7.8)
1877	Cin	NL	OF	240	15	0	255	75	12	10	2	.313	.353	.471	824				0	60	884	41.5
1878	Cin	NL	OF	261	4	0	265	81	11	7	3	.310	.321	.441	761				0	30	791	11.4
1879	Bos	NL	OF	355	29	0	384	112	22	10	9	.315	.367	.510	877				0	50	927	62.8
1880	Bos	NL	OF	280	11	0	291	84	15	3	5	.300	.326	.429	755				0	(10)	745	(3.3)
1883	Cin	AA	OF	391	20	0	411	115	15	12	10	.294	.328	.471	799				0	10	809	16.8
1884	Cin	AA	OF	472	37	10	519	148	19	17	7	.314	.376	.470	846				0	10	856	35.9
1885	Cin	AA	OF	487	21	9	517	157	19	17	5	.322	.362	.462	824				0	30	854	34.6
1886	Cin	AA	OF	500	61	6	567	135	22	10	6	.270	.356	.390	746	3			0	10	756	(0.4)
1887	NY	AA	OF	400	31	9	440	111	18	7	5	.278	.343	.395	738	15			0	10	748	(2.3)
1888	KC	AA	OF	25	1	0	26	4	0	1	0	.160	.192	.240	432	1			0	(200)	232	(7.7)
10.1 Totals				3,687	237	34	3,958	1,101	170	98	56					19	0					181.6
1.0 Averages				364	23	3	391	109	17	10	6	.299	.347	.443	790	2	0	(0)	0	21	811	17.9

Charley Jones   **Cin AA**   **Outfielder**   **Adjusted**

Year	T	L	P	AB	BB	HBP	TAB	H	2B	3B	HR	BA	OB	SA	Wtd PRO	SB	CS	SBF	SPF	FF	Wtd TF	HC
1876	Cin	NL	OF	683	22	0	705	231	50	12	12	.338	.359	.496	855				0	10	865	36.1
1877	Cin	NL	OF	640	48	0	689	225	36	30	6	.352	.397	.530	927				0	60	987	75.5
1878	Cin	NL	OF	690	14	0	704	253	34	22	9	.366	.379	.520	899				0	30	929	57.4
1879	Bos	NL	OF	702	75	0	778	261	51	23	21	.372	.433	.601	1,034				0	50	1,084	120.8
1880	Bos	NL	OF	527	28	0	555	190	34	7	11	.361	.393	.515	908				0	(10)	898	37.1
1883	Cin	AA	OF	642	41	0	683	217	28	23	19	.339	.378	.542	920				0	10	930	56.2
1884	Cin	AA	OF	677	69	19	764	248	32	28	12	.366	.439	.550	989				0	10	999	87.9
1885	Cin	AA	OF	701	37	16	755	257	31	28	8	.367	.412	.526	938				0	30	968	75.6
1886	Cin	AA	OF	569	84	8	661	173	28	13	8	.303	.400	.438	839	3			0	10	849	28.8
1887	NY	AA	OF	471	37	11	518	131	21	8	6	.278	.344	.396	740	18			0	10	750	(1.8)
1888	KC	AA	OF	29	1	0	31	5	0	1	0	.185	.222	.277	499	1			0	(200)	299	(6.7)
10.1 Totals				6,332	456	54	6,842	2,192	346	195	112					22	0					567.0
1.0 Averages				626	45	5	676	217	34	19	11	.346	.395	.515	910	2	0	(2)	0	21	930	56.0

Billy Williams Cubs Outfielder Actual

Year	T	L	P	AB	BB	HBP	TAB	H	2B	3B	HR	BA	OB	SA	PRO	SB	CS	SBF	SPF	FF	Actual TF	Actual HC
1959	Chi	NL	OF	33	1	0	34	5	0	1	0	.152	.176	.212	389	0	0	0	10	0	399	(6.1)
1960	Chi	NL	OF	47	5	0	52	13	0	2	2	.277	.346	.489	836	0	0	0	10	0	846	2.3
1961	Chi	NL	OF	529	45	5	579	147	20	7	25	.278	.340	.484	824	6	0	10	10	(10)	834	22.2
1962	Chi	NL	OF	618	70	4	692	184	22	8	22	.298	.373	.466	839	9	9	(12)	10	20	857	32.7
1963	Chi	NL	OF	612	68	2	682	175	36	9	25	.286	.359	.497	856	7	6	(7)	10	40	899	46.0
1964	Chi	NL	OF	645	59	2	706	201	39	2	33	.312	.371	.532	903	10	7	(5)	10	10	918	53.9
1965	Chi	NL	OF	645	65	3	713	203	39	6	34	.315	.380	.552	932	10	1	11	10	10	963	69.7
1966	Chi	NL	OF	648	69	4	721	179	23	5	29	.276	.350	.461	811	6	3	0	10	20	841	28.7
1967	Chi	NL	OF	634	68	2	704	176	21	12	28	.278	.349	.481	831	6	3	0	10	10	851	31.2
1968	Chi	NL	OF	642	48	2	692	185	30	8	30	.288	.340	.500	840	4	1	3	10	10	862	34.6
1969	Chi	NL	OF	642	59	4	705	188	33	10	21	.293	.356	.474	830	3	2	(1)	10	10	848	30.5
1970	Chi	NL	OF	636	72	2	710	205	34	4	42	.322	.393	.586	979	7	1	7	10	30	1,026	90.9
1971	Chi	NL	OF	594	77	3	674	179	27	5	28	.301	.384	.505	889	7	5	(4)	10	20	915	50.6
1972	Chi	NL	OF	574	62	6	642	191	34	6	37	.333	.403	.606	1,010	3	1	1	10	0	1,021	84.9
1973	Chi	NL	OF	576	76	1	653	166	22	2	20	.288	.372	.438	810	4	3	(3)	0	20	827	21.6
1974	Chi	NL	1B	404	67	1	472	113	22	0	16	.280	.383	.453	836	4	5	(12)	0	(20)	804	7.7
1975	Oak	AL	DH	520	76	2	598	127	20	1	23	.244	.343	.419	762	0	0	0	(10)	(20)	732	(10.8)
1976	Oak	AL	DH	351	58	0	409	74	12	0	11	.211	.323	.339	662	4	2	0	(10)	(30)	622	(26.4)
15.5 Totals				9,350	1,045	43	10,438	2,711	434	88	426					90	49					564.2
1.0 Averages				602	67	3	672	174	28	6	27	.290	.364	.492	856	6	3	(1)	7	9	872	36.3

Billy Williams Cubs Outfielder Adjusted

Year	T	L	P	AB	BB	HBP	TAB	H	2B	3B	HR	BA	OB	SA	Wtd PRO	SB	CS	SBF	SPF	FF	Wtd TF	HC
1959	Chi	NL	OF	35	1	0	36	5	0	1	0	.147	.171	.206	377	0	0	0	10	0	387	(6.3)
1960	Chi	NL	OF	49	5	0	55	14	0	2	2	.275	.344	.487	831	0	0	0	10	0	841	2.2
1961	Chi	NL	OF	559	45	5	609	149	20	7	25	.267	.327	.465	792	6	0	10	10	(10)	801	12.7
1962	Chi	NL	OF	620	68	4	692	181	22	8	22	.291	.365	.456	820	9	9	(12)	10	20	838	26.5
1963	Chi	NL	OF	607	73	2	682	183	38	9	26	.301	.378	.523	900	7	6	(7)	10	40	944	60.5
1964	Chi	NL	OF	643	61	2	706	206	40	2	34	.320	.381	.546	928	10	7	(5)	10	10	942	62.2
1965	Chi	NL	OF	642	68	3	713	208	40	6	35	.323	.391	.567	958	10	1	11	10	10	988	78.4
1966	Chi	NL	OF	647	70	4	721	180	23	5	29	.279	.353	.466	819	6	3	0	10	20	849	31.4
1967	Chi	NL	OF	629	72	2	704	183	22	12	29	.290	.365	.503	869	6	3	0	10	10	889	44.0
1968	Chi	NL	OF	635	55	2	692	201	33	9	33	.316	.373	.549	922	4	1	3	10	10	944	61.7
1969	Chi	NL	OF	640	61	4	705	192	34	10	21	.300	.364	.484	849	3	2	(1)	10	10	867	36.9
1970	Chi	NL	OF	639	69	2	710	201	33	4	41	.314	.383	.572	955	7	1	7	10	30	1,002	82.6
1971	Chi	NL	OF	590	80	3	674	183	28	5	29	.311	.396	.520	916	7	5	(4)	10	20	942	59.4
1972	Chi	NL	OF	600	69	7	675	207	37	6	40	.344	.418	.628	1,045	3	1	1	10	0	1,057	96.3
1973	Chi	NL	OF	575	77	1	653	167	22	2	20	.291	.375	.441	816	4	3	(3)	0	20	834	23.7
1974	Chi	NL	1B	403	68	1	472	114	22	0	16	.284	.389	.460	850	4	5	(12)	0	(20)	818	10.7
1975	Oak	AL	DH	517	79	2	598	130	20	1	24	.251	.353	.432	785	0	0	0	(10)	(20)	755	(4.4)
1976	Oak	AL	DH	346	63	0	409	78	13	0	12	.225	.344	.362	706	4	2	0	(10)	(30)	666	(17.8)
15.5 Totals				9,376	1,085	45	10,506	2,780	446	91	437					90	49					660.7
1.0 Averages				603	70	3	676	179	29	6	28	.297	.372	.503	875	6	3	(1)	7	9	891	42.5

Elmer Flick   **Indians**   **Outfielder**   **Actual**

Year	T	L	P	AB	BB	HBP	TAB	H	2B	3B	HR	BA	OB	SA	PRO	SB	CS	SBF	SPF	FF	Actual TF	Actual HC
1898	Phi	NL	OF	453	86	15	554	137	16	13	8	.302	.430	.448	878	23			10	20	908	41.9
1899	Phi	NL	OF	485	42	11	538	166	22	11	2	.342	.407	.445	852	31			10	30	892	36.5
1900	Phi	NL	OF	545	56	16	617	200	32	16	11	.367	.441	.545	986	35			10	10	1,006	84.5
1901	Phi	NL	OF	540	52	7	599	180	32	17	8	.333	.399	.500	899	30			10	40	949	63.3
1902	Cle	AL	OF	461	53	6	520	137	21	12	2	.297	.377	.408	785	24			10	0	795	10.7
1903	Cle	AL	OF	523	51	8	582	155	23	16	2	.296	.368	.413	781	24			10	10	801	13.9
1904	Cle	AL	OF	579	51	9	639	177	31	17	6	.306	.371	.449	820	38			10	30	860	32.8
1905	Cle	AL	OF	500	53	8	561	154	29	18	4	.308	.383	.462	845	35			10	10	865	30.3
1906	Cle	AL	OF	624	54	7	685	194	34	22	1	.311	.372	.441	813	39			10	(10)	813	19.1
1907	Cle	AL	OF	549	64	11	624	166	15	18	3	.302	.386	.412	798	41			10	0	808	15.8
1908	Cle	AL	OF	35	3	0	38	8	1	1	0	.229	.289	.314	604	0			0	0	604	(2.9)
1909	Cle	AL	OF	235	22	1	258	60	10	2	0	.255	.322	.315	637	9			0	(20)	617	(18.2)
1910	Cle	AL	OF	68	10	0	78	18	2	1	1	.265	.359	.368	727	1			0	(40)	687	(2.8)
10.2 Totals				5,597	597	99	6,293	1,752	268	164	48					330	0					324.9
1.0 Averages				551	59	10	619	172	26	16	5	.313	.389	.445	834	32	0	0	9	12	855	32.0

Elmer Flick   **Indians**   **Outfielder**   **Adjusted**

Year	T	L	P	AB	BB	HBP	TAB	H	2B	3B	HR	BA	OB	SA	Wtd PRO	SB	CS	SBF	SPF	FF	Wtd TF	HC
1898	Phi	NL	OF	472	96	17	585	148	17	14	9	.313	.445	.465	910	24			10	20	940	50.8
1899	Phi	NL	OF	512	44	12	568	174	23	12	2	.340	.405	.443	848	33			10	30	888	35.2
1900	Phi	NL	OF	630	65	19	714	232	37	19	13	.367	.441	.546	987	41			10	10	1,007	84.9
1901	Phi	NL	OF	619	65	9	693	218	39	21	10	.352	.421	.528	949	35			10	40	999	79.6
1902	Cle	AL	OF	533	62	7	602	160	24	14	2	.300	.380	.411	791	28			10	0	801	12.6
1903	Cle	AL	OF	596	67	10	673	192	29	20	2	.323	.401	.450	850	28			10	10	870	36.3
1904	Cle	AL	OF	595	66	12	672	208	36	20	7	.350	.425	.515	940	40			10	30	980	71.2
1905	Cle	AL	OF	511	69	10	590	181	34	21	5	.355	.441	.532	973	37			10	10	993	66.3
1906	Cle	AL	OF	643	69	9	721	227	40	26	1	.353	.423	.501	924	41			10	(10)	924	57.2
1907	Cle	AL	OF	559	83	14	656	195	18	21	4	.349	.446	.476	922	43			10	0	932	54.5
1908	Cle	AL	OF	36	4	0	40	10	1	1	0	.270	.342	.371	713	0			0	0	713	(0.9)
1909	Cle	AL	OF	242	28	1	271	71	12	2	0	.295	.372	.364	735	9			0	(20)	715	(5.4)
1910	Cle	AL	OF	69	13	0	82	21	2	1	1	.301	.408	.418	826	1			0	(40)	786	1.1
10.2 Totals				6,018	730	120	6,867	2,038	313	191	56					359	0					543.6
1.0 Averages				592	72	12	676	201	31	19	5	.339	.420	.482	902	35	0	0	9	12	924	53.5

Dwight Evans **Red Sox** **Outfielder** **Actual**

Year	T	L	P	AB	BB	HBP	TAB	H	2B	3B	HR	BA	OB	SA	PRO	SB	CS	SBF	SPF	FF	Actual TF	Actual HC
1972	Bos	AL	OF	57	7	0	64	15	3	1	1	.263	.344	.404	747	0	0	0	10	40	797	1.3
1973	Bos	AL	OF	282	40	1	323	63	13	1	10	.223	.322	.383	705	5	0	15	10	10	740	(2.7)
1974	Bos	AL	OF	463	38	2	503	130	19	8	10	.281	.338	.421	759	4	4	(8)	10	70	832	17.8
1975	Bos	AL	OF	412	47	4	463	113	24	6	13	.274	.354	.456	811	3	4	(10)	10	80	890	29.3
1976	Bos	AL	OF	501	57	6	564	121	34	5	17	.242	.326	.431	757	6	7	(13)	10	70	824	17.9
1977	Bos	AL	OF	230	28	0	258	66	9	2	14	.287	.364	.526	890	4	2	0	10	10	910	18.8
1978	Bos	AL	OF	497	65	2	564	123	24	2	24	.247	.337	.449	786	8	5	(3)	10	50	842	22.8
1979	Bos	AL	OF	489	69	1	559	134	24	1	21	.274	.365	.456	821	6	9	(20)	10	60	871	30.2
1980	Bos	AL	OF	463	64	5	532	123	37	5	18	.266	.361	.484	845	3	1	2	10	30	886	32.7
1981	Bos	AL	OF	412	85	1	498	122	19	4	22	.296	.418	.522	940	3	2	(2)	10	80	1,028	97.1
1982	Bos	AL	OF	609	112	1	722	178	37	7	32	.292	.403	.534	937	3	2	(1)	0	30	965	71.5
1983	Bos	AL	OF	470	70	2	542	112	19	4	22	.238	.339	.436	776	3	0	5	0	50	831	19.0
1984	Bos	AL	OF	630	96	4	730	186	37	8	32	.295	.392	.532	924	3	1	1	0	30	955	68.7
1985	Bos	AL	OF	617	114	5	736	162	29	1	29	.263	.382	.454	836	7	2	4	0	30	869	39.3
1986	Bos	AL	OF	529	97	6	632	137	33	2	26	.259	.380	.476	856	3	3	(4)	0	20	872	34.4
1987	Bos	AL	1B	541	106	3	650	165	37	2	34	.305	.422	.569	991	4	6	(12)	0	(10)	969	61.7
1988	Bos	AL	OF	559	76	1	636	164	31	7	21	.293	.379	.487	866	5	1	4	0	0	870	34.1
1989	Bos	AL	OF	520	99	3	622	148	27	3	20	.285	.402	.463	865	3	3	(5)	0	10	871	33.6
1990	Bos	AL	DH	445	67	4	516	111	18	3	13	.249	.353	.391	744	3	4	(9)	(10)	(20)	705	(13.0)
1991	Bal	AL	OF	270	54	2	326	73	9	1	6	.270	.396	.378	773	2	3	(12)	(10)	0	752	(0.9)
15.8 Totals				8,996	1,391	53	10,440	2,446	483	73	385					78	59					613.5
1.0 Averages				568	88	3	660	155	31	5	24	.272	.373	.470	843	5	4	(4)	4	33	876	38.8

Dwight Evans **Red Sox** **Outfielder** **Adjusted**

Year	T	L	P	AB	BB	HBP	TAB	H	2B	3B	HR	BA	OB	SA	Wtd PRO	SB	CS	SBF	SPF	FF	Wtd TF	HC
1972	Bos	AL	OF	59	8	0	67	17	3	1	1	.285	.373	.438	810	0	0	0	10	40	860	3.3
1973	Bos	AL	OF	281	41	1	323	64	13	1	10	.229	.330	.393	723	5	0	15	10	10	757	0.0
1974	Bos	AL	OF	460	41	2	503	135	20	8	10	.294	.354	.441	795	4	4	(8)	10	70	868	26.4
1975	Bos	AL	OF	410	49	4	463	116	25	6	13	.282	.365	.470	835	3	4	(10)	10	80	914	34.6
1976	Bos	AL	OF	495	62	7	564	128	36	5	18	.258	.348	.460	808	6	7	(13)	10	70	875	31.6
1977	Bos	AL	OF	230	28	0	258	65	9	2	14	.284	.360	.520	881	4	2	0	10	10	901	17.6
1978	Bos	AL	OF	495	67	2	564	125	24	2	24	.253	.344	.459	803	8	5	(3)	10	50	860	27.5
1979	Bos	AL	OF	491	67	1	559	132	24	1	21	.268	.357	.446	803	6	9	(20)	10	60	853	25.5
1980	Bos	AL	OF	463	64	5	532	123	37	5	18	.265	.359	.482	841	3	1	2	10	30	883	31.8
1981	Bos	AL	OF	615	138	2	754	191	30	6	34	.311	.438	.547	985	5	3	(2)	10	80	1,073	113.5
1982	Bos	AL	OF	610	111	1	722	177	37	7	32	.291	.401	.531	933	3	2	(1)	0	30	962	70.2
1983	Bos	AL	OF	470	70	2	542	112	19	4	22	.238	.339	.436	775	3	0	5	0	50	830	18.7
1984	Bos	AL	OF	629	97	4	730	187	37	8	32	.296	.393	.534	927	3	1	1	0	30	959	70.0
1985	Bos	AL	OF	618	113	5	736	161	29	1	29	.261	.379	.451	830	7	2	4	0	30	864	37.3
1986	Bos	AL	OF	531	95	6	632	136	33	2	26	.255	.375	.470	845	3	3	(4)	0	20	860	30.9
1987	Bos	AL	1B	547	100	3	650	160	36	2	33	.293	.404	.546	950	4	6	(12)	0	(10)	929	49.2
1988	Bos	AL	OF	557	78	1	636	166	31	7	21	.298	.385	.495	880	5	1	4	0	0	884	38.5
1989	Bos	AL	OF	516	103	3	622	151	27	3	20	.292	.412	.475	887	3	3	(5)	0	10	893	40.1
1990	Bos	AL	DH	443	68	4	516	112	18	3	13	.254	.359	.398	756	3	4	(9)	(10)	(20)	717	(9.9)
1991	Bal	AL	OF	270	54	2	326	73	9	1	6	.272	.398	.380	778	2	3	(12)	(10)	0	756	(0.2)
15.8 Totals				9,192	1,453	54	10,699	2,531	497	76	399					80	60					656.6
1.0 Averages				581	92	3	676	160	31	5	25	.275	.377	.476	854	5	4	(4)	4	33	887	41.5

Duke Snider   **Dodgers**   **Outfielder**   **Actual**

Year	T	L	P	AB	BB	HBP	TAB	H	2B	3B	HR	BA	OB	SA	PRO	SB	CS	SBF	SPF	FF	Actual TF	Actual HC
1947	Bkn	NL	OF	83	3	1	87	20	3	1	0	.241	.276	.301	577	2			10	0	587	(7.4)
1948	Bkn	NL	OF	160	12	0	172	39	6	6	5	.244	.297	.450	747	4			10	0	757	(0.1)
1949	Bkn	NL	OF	552	56	4	612	161	28	7	23	.292	.361	.493	854	12			10	20	884	38.8
1950	Bkn	NL	OF	620	58	0	678	199	31	10	31	.321	.379	.553	932	16			10	30	972	73.0
1951	Bkn	NL	OF	606	62	0	668	168	26	6	29	.277	.344	.483	828	14	10	(8)	10	30	859	34.1
1952	Bkn	NL	OF	534	55	0	589	162	25	7	21	.303	.368	.494	863	7	4	(2)	0	30	891	39.5
1953	Bkn	NL	OF	590	82	3	675	198	38	4	42	.336	.419	.627	1,046	16	7	3	0	20	1,069	105.5
1954	Bkn	NL	OF	584	84	4	672	199	39	10	40	.341	.427	.647	1,074	6	6	(8)	0	10	1,076	107.3
1955	Bkn	NL	OF	538	104	1	643	166	34	6	42	.309	.421	.628	1,050	9	7	(7)	0	30	1,072	101.5
1956	Bkn	NL	OF	542	99	1	642	158	33	2	43	.292	.402	.598	1,000	3	3	(4)	0	20	1,015	83.0
1957	Bkn	NL	OF	508	77	1	586	139	25	7	40	.274	.370	.587	957	3	4	(8)	0	10	959	59.2
1958	LA	NL	OF	327	32	1	360	102	12	3	15	.312	.375	.505	880	2	2	(5)	0	(10)	864	19.3
1959	LA	NL	OF	370	58	0	428	114	11	2	23	.308	.402	.535	937	1	5	(20)	(10)	(20)	887	27.8
1960	LA	NL	OF	235	46	1	282	57	13	5	14	.243	.369	.519	888	1	0	3	(10)	(50)	831	10.4
1961	LA	NL	OF	233	29	1	263	69	8	3	16	.296	.376	.562	939	1	1	(4)	(10)	(10)	915	20.8
1962	LA	NL	OF	158	36	2	196	44	11	3	5	.278	.418	.481	899	2	0	10	(10)	(10)	889	12.3
1963	NY	NL	OF	354	56	1	411	86	8	3	14	.243	.348	.401	749	0	1	(5)	(10)	(30)	704	(10.4)
1964	SF	NL	OF	167	22	0	189	35	7	0	4	.210	.302	.323	625	0	0	0	(10)	(40)	575	(16.4)
12.6 Totals				7,161	971	21	8,153	2,116	358	85	407					99	50					698.1
1.0 Averages				567	77	2	646	168	28	7	32	.295	.381	.540	921	8	4	(4)	1	10	927	55.3

Duke Snider   **Dodgers**   **Outfielder**   **Adjusted**

Year	T	L	P	AB	BB	HBP	TAB	H	2B	3B	HR	BA	OB	SA	Wtd PRO	SB	CS	SBF	SPF	FF	Wtd TF	HC
1947	Bkn	NL	OF	87	3	1	92	20	3	1	0	.233	.267	.292	559	2			10	0	569	(8.2)
1948	Bkn	NL	OF	169	12	0	181	41	6	6	5	.241	.293	.444	737	4			10	0	747	(0.9)
1949	Bkn	NL	OF	583	57	4	644	166	29	7	24	.285	.353	.481	834	13			10	20	864	32.6
1950	Bkn	NL	OF	656	57	0	713	202	31	10	31	.307	.363	.530	893	17			10	30	933	59.6
1951	Bkn	NL	OF	639	63	0	703	174	27	6	30	.271	.337	.473	810	15	11	(8)	10	30	842	28.3
1952	Bkn	NL	OF	561	59	0	620	172	27	7	22	.307	.373	.501	874	7	4	(2)	0	30	902	42.7
1953	Bkn	NL	OF	628	79	3	710	199	38	4	42	.317	.396	.593	989	17	7	3	0	20	1,012	86.0
1954	Bkn	NL	OF	622	82	4	707	201	39	10	40	.323	.405	.613	1,018	6	6	(8)	0	10	1,020	88.3
1955	Bkn	NL	OF	573	103	1	676	169	35	6	43	.296	.404	.602	1,005	9	7	(7)	0	30	1,028	87.2
1956	Bkn	NL	OF	574	100	1	675	163	34	2	44	.284	.391	.582	973	3	3	(4)	0	20	989	74.5
1957	Bkn	NL	OF	537	78	1	616	143	26	7	41	.267	.361	.572	933	3	4	(8)	0	10	935	52.1
1958	LA	NL	OF	346	32	1	379	104	12	3	15	.300	.360	.485	845	2	2	(5)	0	(10)	830	13.0
1959	LA	NL	OF	392	58	0	450	117	11	2	24	.299	.390	.520	910	1	5	(20)	(10)	(20)	860	22.0
1960	LA	NL	OF	248	48	1	297	60	14	5	15	.241	.367	.516	883	1	0	3	(10)	(50)	826	9.7
1961	LA	NL	OF	247	29	1	277	70	8	3	16	.284	.362	.540	901	1	1	(4)	(10)	(10)	878	15.9
1962	LA	NL	OF	159	35	2	196	43	11	3	5	.272	.409	.470	879	2	0	10	(10)	(10)	869	10.4
1963	NY	NL	OF	350	60	1	411	89	8	3	15	.256	.366	.422	788	0	1	(5)	(10)	(30)	743	(2.7)
1964	SF	NL	OF	166	23	0	189	36	7	0	4	.215	.310	.332	642	0	0	0	(10)	(40)	592	(14.9)
12.6 Totals				7,535	979	21	8,535	2,169	367	87	417					104	53					595.7
1.0 Averages				597	78	2	676	172	29	7	33	.288	.371	.526	897	8	4	(4)	1	10	903	47.2

Walter Johnson — **Senators** — **Starter** — **Actual**

Year	T	L	G	GS	IP	W	L	SV	SO	BB	ERA	Actual RA/9	Actual Runs /162
1907	Was	AL	14	12	110	5	9	0	71	20	1.88	2.85	20.9
1908	Was	AL	36	30	256	14	14	1	160	53	1.65	2.63	54.9
1909	Was	AL	40	36	296	13	25	1	164	84	2.22	3.40	38.1
1910	Was	AL	45	42	370	25	17	1	313	76	1.36	2.24	95.3
1911	Was	AL	40	37	322	25	13	1	207	70	1.90	3.32	44.3
1912	Was	AL	50	37	369	33	12	2	303	76	1.39	2.17	97.9
1913	Was	AL	48	36	346	36	7	2	243	38	1.14	1.46	119.1
1914	Was	AL	51	40	372	28	18	1	225	74	1.72	2.13	100.2
1915	Was	AL	47	39	337	27	13	4	203	56	1.55	2.22	87.4
1916	Was	AL	48	38	370	25	20	1	228	82	1.90	2.56	82.0
1917	Was	AL	47	34	326	23	16	3	188	68	2.21	2.90	60.0
1918	Was	AL	39	29	326	23	13	3	162	70	1.27	1.96	94.1
1919	Was	AL	39	29	290	20	14	2	147	51	1.49	2.26	74.1
1920	Was	AL	21	15	144	8	10	3	78	27	3.13	4.26	4.7
1921	Was	AL	35	32	264	17	14	1	143	92	3.51	4.16	11.6
1922	Was	AL	41	31	280	15	16	4	105	99	2.99	3.70	26.7
1923	Was	AL	42	34	261	17	12	4	130	73	3.48	3.86	20.2
1924	Was	AL	38	38	278	23	7	0	158	77	2.72	3.14	43.7
1925	Was	AL	30	29	229	20	7	0	108	78	3.07	3.73	21.0
1926	Was	AL	33	33	261	15	16	0	125	73	3.63	4.14	12.1
1927	Was	AL	18	15	108	5	6	0	48	26	5.10	5.85	(15.5)
Totals			802	666	5,914	417	279	34	3,509	1,363	2.17	2.89	1,092.9
Average/9			1.2	1.0	9.0	0.6	0.4	0.1	5.3	2.1	2.17	2.89	1.7

Walter Johnson — **Senators** — **Starter** — **Adjusted**

Year	T	L	G	GS	IP	W	L	SV	SO	BB	Wtd RA/9	Runs /162
1907	Was	AL	15	13	116	5	9	0	75	21	3.51	13.5
1908	Was	AL	38	32	270	15	15	1	168	56	3.45	33.1
1909	Was	AL	42	38	312	14	26	1	173	88	4.45	3.6
1910	Was	AL	47	44	389	26	18	1	329	80	2.79	76.5
1911	Was	AL	42	39	339	26	14	1	218	74	3.25	49.1
1912	Was	AL	53	39	388	35	13	2	319	80	2.19	102.0
1913	Was	AL	50	38	364	38	7	2	256	40	1.68	116.5
1914	Was	AL	54	42	391	29	19	1	237	78	2.63	83.7
1915	Was	AL	49	41	354	28	14	4	214	59	2.54	79.5
1916	Was	AL	50	40	389	26	21	1	240	86	3.18	59.6
1917	Was	AL	49	36	343	24	17	3	198	72	3.64	34.9
1918	Was	AL	50	37	416	29	17	4	207	89	2.47	96.6
1919	Was	AL	45	34	336	23	16	2	170	59	2.49	77.0
1920	Was	AL	22	16	151	8	11	3	82	28	4.05	8.5
1921	Was	AL	37	34	278	18	15	1	150	97	3.70	26.6
1922	Was	AL	43	33	295	16	17	4	110	104	3.54	33.2
1923	Was	AL	44	36	275	18	13	4	137	77	3.66	27.5
1924	Was	AL	40	40	292	24	7	0	166	81	2.84	55.6
1925	Was	AL	32	31	241	21	7	0	114	82	3.24	35.3
1926	Was	AL	35	35	274	16	17	0	131	77	3.92	19.3
1927	Was	AL	19	16	113	5	6	0	50	27	5.36	(10.2)
Totals			856	710	6,325	446	298	37	3,743	1,455	3.10	1,021.3
Average/9			1.2	1.0	9.0	0.6	0.4	0.1	5.3	2.1	3.10	1.5

Cy Young   **Cle NL**   **Starter**   **Actual**

Year	T	L	G	GS	IP	W	L	SV	SO	BB	ERA	Actual RA/9	Actual Runs /162
1890	Cle	NL	17	16	148	9	7	0	39	30	3.47	5.30	(12.2)
1891	Cle	NL	55	46	424	27	22	2	147	140	2.85	5.18	(29.3)
1892	Cle	NL	53	49	453	36	12	0	168	118	1.93	3.14	71.3
1893	Cle	NL	53	46	423	34	16	1	102	103	3.36	4.90	(16.1)
1894	Cle	NL	52	47	409	26	21	1	108	106	3.94	5.84	(58.3)
1895	Cle	NL	47	40	370	35	10	0	121	75	3.26	4.31	10.1
1896	Cle	NL	51	46	414	28	15	3	140	62	3.24	4.65	(4.3)
1897	Cle	NL	46	38	336	21	19	0	88	49	3.78	5.08	(19.5)
1898	Cle	NL	46	41	378	25	13	0	101	41	2.53	3.98	24.2
1899	StL	NL	44	42	369	26	16	1	111	44	2.58	4.22	13.8
1900	StL	NL	41	35	321	19	19	0	115	36	3.00	4.03	18.8
1901	Bos	AL	43	41	371	33	10	0	158	37	1.62	2.71	76.2
1902	Bos	AL	45	43	385	32	11	0	160	53	2.15	3.18	58.9
1903	Bos	AL	40	35	342	28	9	2	176	37	2.08	3.03	58.0
1904	Bos	AL	43	41	380	26	16	1	200	29	1.97	2.46	88.5
1905	Bos	AL	38	33	321	18	19	0	210	30	1.82	2.78	63.3
1906	Bos	AL	39	34	288	13	21	2	140	25	3.19	4.29	8.5
1907	Bos	AL	43	37	343	21	15	2	147	51	1.99	2.65	72.7
1908	Bos	AL	36	33	299	21	11	2	150	37	1.26	2.05	83.3
1909	Cle	AL	35	34	294	19	15	0	109	59	2.26	3.36	39.1
1910	Cle	AL	21	20	163	7	10	0	58	27	2.53	3.42	20.6
1911	Bos	NL	18	18	126	7	9	0	55	28	3.78	5.34	(11.0)
Totals			906	815	7,356	511	316	17	2,803	1,217	2.63	3.87	556.9
Average/9			1.1	1.0	9.0	0.6	0.4	0.0	3.4	1.5	2.63	3.87	0.7

Cy Young   **Cle NL**   **Starter**   **Adjusted**

Year	T	L	G	GS	IP	W	L	SV	SO	BB	Wtd RA/9	Runs /162
1890	Cle	NL	20	19	177	11	8	0	47	36	4.24	6.3
1891	Cle	NL	65	54	497	32	26	2	173	164	4.19	20.5
1892	Cle	NL	56	52	478	38	13	0	177	125	2.73	97.3
1893	Cle	NL	66	57	523	42	20	1	126	127	3.33	71.1
1894	Cle	NL	64	58	502	32	26	1	133	130	3.47	60.3
1895	Cle	NL	57	49	450	43	12	0	147	91	2.86	84.7
1896	Cle	NL	63	56	508	34	18	4	172	76	3.39	65.9
1897	Cle	NL	55	46	403	25	23	0	106	59	3.78	34.9
1898	Cle	NL	49	43	399	26	14	0	107	43	3.52	45.8
1899	StL	NL	46	44	390	27	17	1	117	46	3.51	45.4
1900	StL	NL	47	41	372	22	22	0	133	42	3.41	47.5
1901	Bos	AL	50	47	430	38	12	0	183	43	2.23	110.9
1902	Bos	AL	52	50	445	37	13	0	185	61	2.90	82.0
1903	Bos	AL	46	41	395	32	10	2	204	43	3.30	55.1
1904	Bos	AL	45	43	400	27	17	1	210	31	3.11	64.1
1905	Bos	AL	40	35	337	19	20	0	221	32	3.40	43.5
1906	Bos	AL	41	36	303	14	22	2	147	26	5.24	(23.0)
1907	Bos	AL	45	39	361	22	16	2	155	54	3.26	51.9
1908	Bos	AL	38	35	315	22	12	2	158	39	2.69	65.2
1909	Cle	AL	37	36	310	20	16	0	115	62	4.40	5.4
1910	Cle	AL	22	21	172	7	11	0	61	28	4.26	5.7
1911	Bos	NL	19	19	133	7	9	0	58	29	5.46	(13.3)
Totals			1,023	919	8,298	579	355	19	3,133	1,388	3.44	1,027.4
Average/9			1.1	1.0	9.0	0.6	0.4	0.0	3.4	1.5	3.44	1.1

Pete Alexander   **Phillies**   **Starter**   **Actual**

Year	T	L	G	GS	IP	W	L	SV	SO	BB	ERA	Actual RA/9	Actual Runs /162
1911	Phi	NL	48	37	367	28	13	3	227	129	2.57	3.26	52.9
1912	Phi	NL	46	34	310	19	17	3	195	105	2.81	3.86	24.0
1913	Phi	NL	47	36	306	22	8	2	159	75	2.79	3.12	48.9
1914	Phi	NL	46	39	355	27	15	1	214	76	2.38	3.37	46.8
1915	Phi	NL	49	42	376	31	10	3	241	64	1.22	2.06	104.4
1916	Phi	NL	48	45	389	33	12	3	167	50	1.55	2.08	107.1
1917	Phi	NL	45	44	388	30	13	0	200	56	1.83	2.48	89.5
1918	Chi	NL	3	3	26	2	1	0	15	3	1.73	2.42	6.2
1919	Chi	NL	30	27	235	16	11	1	121	38	1.72	1.95	68.1
1920	Chi	NL	46	40	363	27	14	5	173	69	1.91	2.38	87.9
1921	Chi	NL	31	30	252	15	13	1	77	33	3.39	3.93	17.6
1922	Chi	NL	33	31	246	16	13	1	48	34	3.63	4.06	13.6
1923	Chi	NL	39	36	305	22	12	2	72	30	3.19	3.78	26.3
1924	Chi	NL	21	20	169	12	5	0	33	25	3.03	4.37	3.5
1925	Chi	NL	32	30	236	15	11	0	63	29	3.39	4.04	13.6
1926	StL	NL	30	23	200	12	10	2	47	31	3.05	3.74	18.2
1927	StL	NL	37	30	268	21	10	3	48	38	2.52	3.16	41.6
1928	StL	NL	34	31	244	16	9	2	59	37	3.36	3.91	17.5
1929	StL	NL	22	19	132	9	8	0	33	23	3.89	4.43	1.9
1930	Phi	NL	9	3	22	0	3	0	6	6	9.14	9.82	(12.7)
Totals			696	600	5,190	373	208	32	2,198	951	2.56	3.21	776.8
Average/9			1.2	1.0	9.0	0.6	0.4	0.1	3.8	1.6	2.56	3.21	1.3

Pete Alexander   **Phillies**   **Starter**   **Adjusted**

Year	T	L	G	GS	IP	W	L	SV	SO	BB	Wtd RA/9	Runs /162
1911	Phi	NL	50	39	386	29	14	3	239	136	3.33	52.6
1912	Phi	NL	48	36	326	20	18	3	205	110	3.78	28.1
1913	Phi	NL	49	38	322	23	8	2	167	79	3.41	41.1
1914	Phi	NL	48	41	373	28	16	1	225	80	3.99	23.6
1915	Phi	NL	52	44	396	33	11	3	254	67	2.57	87.3
1916	Phi	NL	50	47	409	35	13	3	176	53	2.76	81.9
1917	Phi	NL	47	46	408	32	14	0	210	59	3.20	61.5
1918	Chi	NL	4	4	33	3	1	0	19	4	3.05	5.5
1919	Chi	NL	35	31	272	19	13	1	140	44	2.44	63.9
1920	Chi	NL	48	42	382	28	15	5	182	73	2.77	76.0
1921	Chi	NL	33	32	265	16	14	1	81	35	3.88	20.0
1922	Chi	NL	35	33	258	17	14	1	50	36	3.66	25.7
1923	Chi	NL	41	38	321	23	13	2	76	32	3.54	36.4
1924	Chi	NL	22	21	178	13	5	0	35	26	4.37	3.8
1925	Chi	NL	34	32	248	16	12	0	66	31	3.58	26.9
1926	StL	NL	32	24	211	13	11	2	49	33	3.71	19.9
1927	StL	NL	39	32	282	22	11	3	50	40	3.12	45.1
1928	StL	NL	36	33	256	17	9	2	62	39	3.79	21.8
1929	StL	NL	23	20	139	9	8	0	35	24	3.71	13.1
1930	Phi	NL	9	3	23	0	3	0	6	6	7.74	(8.1)
Totals			736	635	5,490	395	220	34	2,328	1,005	3.37	726.1
Average/9			1.2	1.0	9.0	0.6	0.4	0.1	3.8	1.6	3.37	1.2

Roger Clemens   **Red Sox**   **Starter**   **Actual**

Year	T	L	G	GS	IP	W	L	SV	SO	BB	ERA	Actual RA/9	Actual Runs /162
1984	Bos	AL	21	20	133	9	4	0	126	29	4.32	4.52	0.5
1985	Bos	AL	15	15	98	7	5	0	74	37	3.29	3.48	11.8
1986	Bos	AL	33	33	254	24	4	0	238	67	2.48	2.73	51.6
1987	Bos	AL	36	36	282	20	9	0	256	83	2.97	3.20	42.5
1988	Bos	AL	35	35	264	18	12	0	291	62	2.93	3.17	40.7
1989	Bos	AL	35	35	253	17	11	0	230	93	3.13	3.59	27.2
1990	Bos	AL	31	31	228	21	6	0	209	54	1.93	2.33	56.5
1991	Bos	AL	35	35	271	18	10	0	241	65	2.62	3.08	44.5
1992	Bos	AL	32	32	247	18	11	0	208	62	2.41	2.92	44.9
1993	Bos	AL	29	29	192	11	14	0	160	67	4.46	4.65	(2.0)
1994	Bos	AL	24	24	171	9	7	0	168	71	2.85	3.28	24.2
1995	Bos	AL	23	23	140	10	5	0	132	60	4.18	4.50	0.9
1996	Bos	AL	34	34	243	10	13	0	257	106	3.63	3.93	16.9
1997	Tor	AL	34	34	264	21	7	0	292	68	2.05	2.22	68.6
1998	Tor	AL	33	33	235	20	6	0	271	88	2.65	2.99	40.9
1999	NY	AL	30	30	188	14	10	0	163	90	4.60	4.84	(5.9)
2000	NY	AL	32	32	204	13	8	0	188	84	3.70	4.23	7.4
	Totals		512	511	3,667	260	142	0	3,504	1,186	3.07	3.40	471.1
	Average/9		1.3	1.3	9.0	0.6	0.3	0.0	8.6	2.9	3.07	3.40	1.2

Roger Clemens   **Red Sox**   **Starter**   **Adjusted**

Year	T	L	G	GS	IP	W	L	SV	SO	BB	Wtd RA/9	Runs /162
1984	Bos	AL	21	20	133	9	4	0	126	29	4.63	(1.1)
1985	Bos	AL	15	15	98	7	5	0	74	37	3.45	12.1
1986	Bos	AL	33	33	254	24	4	0	238	67	2.68	53.1
1987	Bos	AL	36	36	282	20	9	0	256	83	2.95	50.4
1988	Bos	AL	35	35	264	18	12	0	291	62	3.28	37.4
1989	Bos	AL	35	35	253	17	11	0	230	93	3.77	22.2
1990	Bos	AL	31	31	228	21	6	0	209	54	2.44	53.7
1991	Bos	AL	35	35	271	18	10	0	241	65	3.13	43.1
1992	Bos	AL	32	32	247	18	11	0	208	62	3.07	40.9
1993	Bos	AL	29	29	192	11	14	0	160	67	4.46	2.0
1994	Bos	AL	34	34	241	13	10	0	238	100	2.84	46.2
1995	Bos	AL	26	26	158	11	6	0	149	68	4.01	9.7
1996	Bos	AL	34	34	243	10	13	0	257	106	3.30	33.8
1997	Tor	AL	34	34	264	21	7	0	292	68	2.03	74.1
1998	Tor	AL	33	33	235	20	6	0	271	88	2.69	48.6
1999	NY	AL	30	30	188	14	10	0	163	90	4.19	7.6
2000	NY	AL	32	32	204	13	8	0	188	84	3.61	21.5
	Totals		525	524	3,755	265	146	0	3,590	1,223	3.23	555.2
	Average/9		1.3	1.3	9.0	0.6	0.3	0.0	8.6	2.9	3.23	1.3

Tom Seaver | **Mets** | **Starter** | **Actual**

Year	T	L	G	GS	IP	W	L	SV	SO	BB	ERA	Actual RA/9	Actual Runs /162
1967	NY	NL	35	34	251	16	13	0	170	78	2.76	3.05	42.0
1968	NY	NL	36	35	278	16	12	1	205	48	2.20	2.37	67.5
1969	NY	NL	36	35	273	25	7	0	208	82	2.21	2.47	63.4
1970	NY	NL	37	36	291	18	12	0	283	83	2.82	3.19	44.1
1971	NY	NL	36	35	286	20	10	0	289	61	1.76	1.92	83.9
1972	NY	NL	35	35	262	21	12	0	249	77	2.92	3.16	40.7
1973	NY	NL	36	36	290	19	10	0	251	64	2.08	2.30	72.7
1974	NY	NL	32	32	236	11	11	0	201	75	3.20	3.39	30.6
1975	NY	NL	36	36	280	22	9	0	243	88	2.38	2.60	61.0
1976	NY	NL	35	34	271	14	11	0	235	77	2.59	2.76	54.1
1977	Cin	NL	33	33	261	21	6	0	196	66	2.58	2.69	54.2
1978	Cin	NL	36	36	260	16	14	0	226	89	2.88	3.36	34.5
1979	Cin	NL	32	32	215	16	6	0	131	61	3.14	3.56	23.8
1980	Cin	NL	26	26	168	10	8	0	101	59	3.64	3.96	11.1
1981	Cin	NL	23	23	166	14	2	0	87	66	2.54	2.76	33.2
1982	Cin	NL	21	21	111	5	13	0	62	44	5.50	6.06	(18.6)
1983	NY	NL	34	34	231	9	14	0	135	86	3.55	4.05	13.0
1984	Chi	AL	34	33	237	15	11	0	131	61	3.95	4.11	11.8
1985	Chi	AL	35	33	239	16	11	0	134	69	3.17	3.88	18.0
1986	Bos	AL	28	28	176	7	13	0	103	56	4.03	4.24	6.2
Totals			656	647	4,783	311	205	1	3,640	1,390	2.86	3.15	747.2
Average/9			1.2	1.2	9.0	0.6	0.4	0.0	6.8	2.6	2.86	3.15	1.4

Tom Seaver | **Mets** | **Starter** | **Adjusted**

Year	T	L	G	GS	IP	W	L	SV	SO	BB	Wtd RA/9	Runs /162
1967	NY	NL	35	34	251	16	13	0	170	78	3.62	26.1
1968	NY	NL	36	35	278	16	12	1	205	48	3.16	43.2
1969	NY	NL	36	35	273	25	7	0	208	82	2.76	54.6
1970	NY	NL	37	36	291	18	12	0	283	83	3.21	43.5
1971	NY	NL	36	35	286	20	10	0	289	61	2.24	73.8
1972	NY	NL	37	37	276	22	13	0	262	81	3.70	26.2
1973	NY	NL	36	36	290	19	10	0	251	64	2.53	65.5
1974	NY	NL	32	32	236	11	11	0	201	75	3.72	21.9
1975	NY	NL	36	36	280	22	9	0	243	88	2.87	52.6
1976	NY	NL	35	34	271	14	11	0	235	77	3.15	42.3
1977	Cin	NL	33	33	261	21	6	0	196	66	2.79	51.4
1978	Cin	NL	36	36	260	16	14	0	226	89	3.81	21.6
1979	Cin	NL	32	32	215	16	6	0	131	61	3.84	17.2
1980	Cin	NL	26	26	168	10	8	0	101	59	4.48	1.5
1981	Cin	NL	35	35	252	21	3	0	132	100	3.23	37.0
1982	Cin	NL	21	21	111	5	13	0	62	44	6.77	(27.4)
1983	NY	NL	34	34	231	9	14	0	135	86	4.48	2.0
1984	Chi	AL	34	33	237	15	11	0	131	61	4.21	9.2
1985	Chi	AL	35	33	239	16	11	0	134	69	3.84	18.9
1986	Bos	AL	28	28	176	7	13	0	103	56	4.16	7.9
Totals			670	661	4,882	319	207	1	3,698	1,428	3.47	589.0
Average/9			1.2	1.2	9.0	0.6	0.4	0.0	6.8	2.6	3.47	1.1

Lefty Grove

Year	T	L	G	GS	IP	W	L	SV	SO	BB	ERA	Actual RA/9	Actual Runs /162
										Athletics		Starter	Actual
1925	Phi	AL	45	18	197	10	12	1	116	131	4.75	5.48	(20.2)
1926	Phi	AL	45	33	258	13	13	6	194	101	2.51	3.38	33.7
1927	Phi	AL	51	28	262	20	13	9	174	79	3.19	3.98	16.8
1928	Phi	AL	39	31	262	24	8	4	183	64	2.58	3.19	39.7
1929	Phi	AL	42	37	275	20	6	4	170	81	2.81	3.40	35.4
1930	Phi	AL	50	32	291	28	5	9	209	60	2.54	3.12	46.5
1931	Phi	AL	41	30	289	31	4	5	175	62	2.06	2.62	62.1
1932	Phi	AL	44	30	292	25	10	7	188	79	2.84	3.11	46.9
1933	Phi	AL	45	28	275	24	8	6	114	83	3.20	3.70	26.2
1934	Bos	AL	22	12	109	8	8	0	43	32	6.50	6.94	(28.9)
1935	Bos	AL	35	30	273	20	12	1	121	65	2.70	3.46	33.3
1936	Bos	AL	35	30	253	17	12	2	130	65	2.81	3.20	38.2
1937	Bos	AL	32	32	262	17	9	0	153	83	3.02	3.47	31.6
1938	Bos	AL	24	21	164	14	4	1	99	52	3.08	3.57	17.9
1939	Bos	AL	23	23	191	15	4	0	81	58	2.54	2.97	33.7
1940	Bos	AL	22	21	153	7	6	0	62	50	3.99	4.29	4.5
1941	Bos	AL	21	21	134	7	7	0	54	42	4.37	5.64	(16.1)
Totals			616	457	3,941	300	141	55	2,266	1,187	3.06	3.64	401.4
Average/9			1.4	1.0	9.0	0.7	0.3	0.1	5.2	2.7	3.06	3.64	0.9

Lefty Grove   Athletics   Starter   Adjusted

Year	T	L	G	GS	IP	W	L	SV	SO	BB	Wtd RA/9	Runs /162
1925	Phi	AL	47	19	207	11	13	1	122	138	4.76	(4.6)
1926	Phi	AL	47	35	271	14	14	6	204	106	3.20	40.9
1927	Phi	AL	54	29	276	21	14	9	183	83	3.65	27.8
1928	Phi	AL	41	33	275	25	8	4	193	67	3.02	46.9
1929	Phi	AL	44	39	290	21	6	4	179	85	3.06	48.1
1930	Phi	AL	53	34	306	29	5	9	220	63	2.59	66.9
1931	Phi	AL	43	32	304	33	4	5	184	65	2.30	76.0
1932	Phi	AL	46	32	307	26	11	7	198	83	2.69	63.5
1933	Phi	AL	47	29	290	25	8	6	120	87	3.36	38.6
1934	Bos	AL	23	13	115	8	8	0	45	34	6.08	(19.5)
1935	Bos	AL	37	32	287	21	13	1	127	68	3.07	47.3
1936	Bos	AL	37	32	266	18	13	2	137	68	2.53	60.1
1937	Bos	AL	34	34	276	18	9	0	161	87	2.96	48.9
1938	Bos	AL	25	22	172	15	4	1	104	55	2.95	30.8
1939	Bos	AL	24	24	201	16	4	0	85	61	2.55	44.7
1940	Bos	AL	23	22	161	7	6	0	65	53	3.87	12.3
1941	Bos	AL	22	22	141	7	7	0	57	44	5.37	(12.7)
Totals			648	481	4,145	316	148	58	2,384	1,249	3.22	616.1
Average/9			1.4	1.0	9.0	0.7	0.3	0.1	5.2	2.7	3.22	1.3

Warren Spahn — Braves — Starter — Actual

Year	T	L	G	GS	IP	W	L	SV	SO	BB	ERA	Actual RA/9	Actual Runs /162
1942	Bos	NL	4	2	16	0	0	0	7	11	5.74	8.44	(6.8)
1946	Bos	NL	24	16	126	8	5	1	67	36	2.94	3.29	17.7
1947	Bos	NL	40	35	290	21	10	3	123	84	2.33	2.70	59.8
1948	Bos	NL	36	35	257	15	12	1	114	77	3.71	4.03	15.0
1949	Bos	NL	38	38	302	21	14	0	151	86	3.07	3.73	27.8
1950	Bos	NL	41	39	293	21	17	1	191	111	3.16	3.78	25.3
1951	Bos	NL	39	36	311	22	14	0	164	109	2.98	3.21	46.5
1952	Bos	NL	40	35	290	14	19	3	183	73	2.98	3.38	37.9
1953	Mil	NL	35	32	266	23	7	3	148	70	2.10	2.54	59.5
1954	Mil	NL	39	34	283	21	12	3	136	86	3.14	3.40	36.4
1955	Mil	NL	39	32	246	17	14	1	110	65	3.26	3.62	25.6
1956	Mil	NL	39	35	281	20	11	3	128	52	2.78	2.95	50.2
1957	Mil	NL	39	35	271	21	11	3	111	78	2.69	3.12	43.3
1958	Mil	NL	38	36	290	22	11	1	150	76	3.07	3.29	40.8
1959	Mil	NL	40	36	292	21	15	0	143	70	2.96	3.27	41.8
1960	Mil	NL	40	33	268	21	10	2	154	74	3.50	3.83	21.6
1961	Mil	NL	38	34	263	21	13	0	115	64	3.02	3.29	37.0
1962	Mil	NL	34	34	269	18	14	0	118	55	3.04	3.25	39.1
1963	Mil	NL	33	33	260	23	7	0	102	49	2.60	2.94	46.7
1964	Mil	NL	38	25	174	6	13	4	78	52	5.29	5.69	(21.9)
1965	NY	NL	36	30	198	7	16	0	90	56	4.01	4.74	(4.0)
Totals			750	665	5,244	363	245	29	2,583	1,434	3.09	3.46	639.4
Average/9			1.3	1.1	9.0	0.6	0.4	0.0	4.4	2.5	3.09	3.46	1.1

Warren Spahn — Braves — Starter — Adjusted

Year	T	L	G	GS	IP	W	L	SV	SO	BB	Wtd RA/9	Runs /162
1942	Bos	NL	4	2	16	0	0	0	7	12	9.84	(9.7)
1946	Bos	NL	25	17	132	8	5	1	70	38	3.76	11.7
1947	Bos	NL	42	37	305	22	11	3	129	88	2.65	64.7
1948	Bos	NL	38	37	270	16	13	1	120	81	4.08	14.3
1949	Bos	NL	40	40	318	22	15	0	159	90	3.71	29.9
1950	Bos	NL	43	41	308	22	18	1	201	117	3.66	30.8
1951	Bos	NL	41	38	327	23	15	0	173	115	3.27	46.9
1952	Bos	NL	42	37	305	15	20	3	193	77	3.66	30.5
1953	Mil	NL	37	34	279	24	7	3	156	74	2.39	67.4
1954	Mil	NL	41	36	298	22	13	3	143	90	3.38	39.1
1955	Mil	NL	41	34	258	18	15	1	116	68	3.61	27.2
1956	Mil	NL	41	37	296	21	12	3	135	55	3.13	46.8
1957	Mil	NL	41	37	285	22	12	3	117	82	3.27	40.8
1958	Mil	NL	40	38	305	23	12	1	158	80	3.39	39.5
1959	Mil	NL	42	38	307	22	16	0	150	74	3.35	41.2
1960	Mil	NL	42	35	282	22	11	2	162	78	4.11	14.1
1961	Mil	NL	40	36	276	22	14	0	121	67	3.28	39.2
1962	Mil	NL	34	34	269	18	14	0	118	55	3.28	38.3
1963	Mil	NL	33	33	260	23	7	0	102	49	3.51	30.3
1964	Mil	NL	38	25	174	6	13	4	78	52	6.42	(35.9)
1965	NY	NL	36	30	198	7	16	0	90	56	5.36	(17.6)
Totals			782	693	5,469	379	255	30	2,697	1,497	3.59	589.5
Average/9			1.3	1.1	9.0	0.6	0.4	0.0	4.4	2.5	3.59	1.0

Christy Mathewson Giants Starter Actual Actual

Year	T	L	G	GS	IP	W	L	SV	SO	BB	ERA	Actual RA/9	Actual Runs /162
1900	NY	NL	6	1	34	0	3	0	15	20	5.08	8.55	(14.9)
1901	NY	NL	40	38	336	20	17	0	221	97	2.41	3.51	39.1
1902	NY	NL	34	32	277	14	17	0	159	73	2.11	3.71	26.0
1903	NY	NL	45	42	366	30	13	2	267	100	2.26	3.34	49.5
1904	NY	NL	48	46	368	33	12	1	212	78	2.03	2.94	66.1
1905	NY	NL	43	37	339	31	9	3	206	64	1.28	2.26	86.4
1906	NY	NL	38	35	267	22	12	1	128	77	2.97	3.38	34.9
1907	NY	NL	41	36	315	24	12	2	178	53	2.00	2.51	71.6
1908	NY	NL	56	44	391	37	11	5	259	42	1.43	1.96	112.7
1909	NY	NL	37	33	275	25	6	2	149	36	1.14	1.88	81.9
1910	NY	NL	38	35	318	27	9	0	184	60	1.89	2.83	61.1
1911	NY	NL	45	37	307	26	13	3	141	38	1.99	2.99	53.5
1912	NY	NL	43	34	310	23	12	4	134	34	2.12	3.11	49.8
1913	NY	NL	40	35	306	25	11	2	93	21	2.06	2.76	61.1
1914	NY	NL	41	35	312	24	13	2	80	23	3.00	3.84	24.9
1915	NY	NL	27	24	186	8	14	0	57	20	3.58	4.69	(2.7)
1916	NY	NL	13	7	75	4	4	2	19	8	3.01	4.22	2.8
Totals			635	551	4,781	373	188	29	2,502	844	2.13	3.04	803.7
Average/9			1.2	1.0	9.0	0.7	0.4	0.1	4.7	1.6	2.13	3.04	1.5

Christy Mathewson Giants Starter Adjusted

Year	T	L	G	GS	IP	W	L	SV	SO	BB	Wtd RA/9	Runs /162
1900	NY	NL	7	1	39	0	3	0	17	23	7.23	(11.6)
1901	NY	NL	46	44	389	23	20	0	256	112	3.42	49.2
1902	NY	NL	39	37	320	16	20	0	184	84	4.18	13.2
1903	NY	NL	52	49	424	35	15	2	309	116	3.11	68.3
1904	NY	NL	50	48	387	35	13	1	223	82	3.33	52.6
1905	NY	NL	45	39	356	33	9	3	217	67	2.48	82.4
1906	NY	NL	40	37	281	23	13	1	135	81	4.23	10.1
1907	NY	NL	43	38	331	25	13	2	187	56	3.28	47.1
1908	NY	NL	59	46	411	39	12	5	272	44	2.69	85.2
1909	NY	NL	39	35	290	26	6	2	157	38	2.34	71.3
1910	NY	NL	40	37	335	28	9	0	194	63	3.18	51.4
1911	NY	NL	47	39	323	27	14	3	148	40	3.06	53.9
1912	NY	NL	45	36	326	24	13	4	141	36	3.05	54.7
1913	NY	NL	42	37	322	26	12	2	98	22	3.02	55.1
1914	NY	NL	43	37	328	25	14	2	84	24	4.55	0.4
1915	NY	NL	28	25	196	8	15	0	60	21	5.86	(28.2)
1916	NY	NL	14	7	79	4	4	2	20	8	5.59	(9.0)
Totals			681	592	5,136	399	203	31	2,702	918	3.42	646.3
Average/9			1.2	1.0	9.0	0.7	0.4	0.1	4.7	1.6	3.42	1.1

Greg Maddux   **Braves**   **Starter**   **Actual**

Year	T	L	G	GS	IP	W	L	SV	SO	BB	ERA	Actual RA/9	Actual Runs /162
1986	Chi	NL	6	5	31	2	4	0	20	11	5.52	5.81	(4.3)
1987	Chi	NL	30	27	156	6	14	0	101	74	5.61	6.42	(32.2)
1988	Chi	NL	34	34	249	18	8	0	140	81	3.18	3.51	29.0
1989	Chi	NL	35	35	238	19	12	0	135	82	2.95	3.40	30.6
1990	Chi	NL	35	35	237	15	15	0	144	71	3.46	4.41	3.9
1991	Chi	NL	37	37	263	15	11	0	198	66	3.35	3.87	20.1
1992	Chi	NL	35	35	268	20	11	0	199	70	2.18	2.28	67.8
1993	Atl	NL	36	36	267	20	10	0	197	52	2.36	2.87	50.0
1994	Atl	NL	25	25	202	16	6	0	156	31	1.56	1.96	58.3
1995	Atl	NL	28	28	210	19	2	0	181	23	1.63	1.67	67.3
1996	Atl	NL	35	35	245	15	11	0	172	28	2.72	3.12	39.1
1997	Atl	NL	33	33	233	19	4	0	177	20	2.20	2.24	59.9
1998	Atl	NL	34	34	251	18	9	0	204	45	2.22	2.69	52.1
1999	Atl	NL	33	33	219	19	9	0	136	37	3.57	4.23	8.0
2000	Atl	NL	35	35	249	19	9	0	190	42	3.00	3.28	35.4
Totals			471	467	3,318	240	135	0	2,350	733	2.83	3.24	484.8
Average/9			1.3	1.3	9.0	0.7	0.4	0.0	6.4	2.0	2.83	3.24	1.3

Greg Maddux   **Braves**   **Starter**   **Adjusted**

Year	T	L	G	GS	IP	W	L	SV	SO	BB	Wtd RA/9	Runs /162
1986	Chi	NL	6	5	31	2	4	0	20	11	6.35	(6.2)
1987	Chi	NL	30	27	156	6	14	0	101	74	6.44	(32.6)
1988	Chi	NL	34	34	249	18	8	0	140	81	4.13	11.7
1989	Chi	NL	35	35	238	19	12	0	135	82	3.93	16.5
1990	Chi	NL	35	35	237	15	15	0	144	71	4.75	(5.1)
1991	Chi	NL	37	37	263	15	11	0	198	66	4.28	8.1
1992	Chi	NL	35	35	268	20	11	0	199	70	2.68	56.0
1993	Atl	NL	36	36	267	20	10	0	197	52	2.89	49.4
1994	Atl	NL	35	35	286	23	8	0	221	44	1.92	83.7
1995	Atl	NL	32	32	236	21	2	0	204	26	1.64	76.5
1996	Atl	NL	35	35	245	15	11	0	172	28	3.02	41.9
1997	Atl	NL	33	33	233	19	4	0	177	20	2.20	60.8
1998	Atl	NL	34	34	251	18	9	0	204	45	2.65	53.3
1999	Atl	NL	33	33	219	19	9	0	136	37	3.82	17.8
2000	Atl	NL	35	35	249	19	9	0	190	42	2.95	44.6
Totals			485	481	3,428	249	138	0	2,437	749	3.31	476.4
Average/9			1.3	1.3	9.0	0.7	0.4	0.0	6.4	2.0	3.31	1.3

Kid Nichols | | | | | | | |Bos NL| | | |Starter| |Actual| | |

Year	T	L	G	GS	IP	W	L	SV	SO	BB	ERA	Actual RA/9	Actual Runs /162
1890	Bos	NL	48	47	424	27	19	0	222	112	2.23	3.71	39.9
1891	Bos	NL	52	48	425	30	17	3	240	103	2.39	4.63	(3.4)
1892	Bos	NL	53	51	453	35	16	0	192	121	2.84	4.19	18.5
1893	Bos	NL	52	44	425	34	14	1	94	118	3.52	4.70	(6.8)
1894	Bos	NL	50	46	407	32	13	0	113	121	4.75	6.81	(101.9)
1895	Bos	NL	47	42	380	26	16	3	140	86	3.41	5.19	(26.7)
1896	Bos	NL	49	43	372	30	14	1	102	101	2.83	5.10	(22.5)
1897	Bos	NL	46	40	368	31	11	3	127	68	2.64	3.72	34.2
1898	Bos	NL	50	42	388	31	12	4	138	85	2.13	3.15	60.7
1899	Bos	NL	42	37	343	21	19	1	108	82	2.99	4.06	19.0
1900	Bos	NL	29	27	231	13	16	0	53	72	3.07	4.51	1.2
1901	Bos	NL	38	34	321	19	16	0	143	90	3.22	4.09	16.7
1904	StL	NL	36	35	317	21	13	1	134	50	2.02	2.75	63.6
1905	Phi	NL	24	23	190	11	11	0	66	46	3.12	4.43	2.7
1906	Phi	NL	4	2	11	0	1	0	1	13	9.82	13.09	(10.4)
Totals			620	561	5,056	361	208	17	1,873	1,268	2.95	4.41	84.7
Average/9			1.1	1.0	9.0	0.6	0.4	0.0	3.3	2.3	2.95	4.41	0.2

Kid Nichols | | | | | | | |Bos NL| | | |Starter| |Adjusted| |

Year	T	L	G	GS	IP	W	L	SV	SO	BB	Wtd RA/9	Runs /162
1890	Bos	NL	58	56	509	32	23	0	266	134	2.97	89.9
1891	Bos	NL	61	56	499	35	20	4	282	121	3.74	45.3
1892	Bos	NL	56	54	478	37	17	0	203	128	3.64	48.9
1893	Bos	NL	64	54	526	42	17	1	116	146	3.20	79.4
1894	Bos	NL	61	56	500	39	16	0	139	149	4.05	28.1
1895	Bos	NL	57	51	462	32	19	4	171	105	3.45	57.0
1896	Bos	NL	60	53	457	37	17	1	125	124	3.72	42.6
1897	Bos	NL	55	48	442	37	13	4	152	82	2.77	87.9
1898	Bos	NL	53	44	409	33	13	4	146	90	2.79	80.5
1899	Bos	NL	44	39	362	22	20	1	114	87	3.38	47.5
1900	Bos	NL	34	31	268	15	19	0	61	83	3.81	22.1
1901	Bos	NL	44	39	371	22	19	0	165	104	3.98	23.7
1904	StL	NL	38	37	333	22	14	1	141	53	3.12	53.3
1905	Phi	NL	25	24	200	12	12	0	69	48	4.85	(6.6)
1906	Phi	NL	4	2	12	0	1	0	1	14	16.39	(15.2)
Totals			715	646	5,828	417	239	20	2,152	1,466	3.50	684.5
Average/9			1.1	1.0	9.0	0.6	0.4	0.0	3.3	2.3	3.50	1.1

Carl Hubbell   Giants   Starter   Actual

Year	T	L	G	GS	IP	W	L	SV	SO	BB	ERA	Actual RA/9	Actual Runs /162
1928	NY	NL	20	14	124	10	6	1	37	21	2.83	3.56	13.7
1929	NY	NL	39	35	268	18	11	1	106	67	3.69	4.30	7.7
1930	NY	NL	37	32	242	17	12	2	117	58	3.87	4.46	2.6
1931	NY	NL	36	30	248	14	12	3	155	67	2.65	3.19	37.7
1932	NY	NL	40	32	284	18	11	2	137	40	2.50	3.04	47.9
1933	NY	NL	45	33	309	23	12	5	156	47	1.66	2.01	87.4
1934	NY	NL	49	34	313	21	12	8	118	37	2.30	2.88	58.3
1935	NY	NL	42	35	303	23	12	0	150	49	3.27	3.71	28.5
1936	NY	NL	42	34	304	26	6	3	123	57	2.31	2.40	72.9
1937	NY	NL	39	32	262	22	8	4	159	55	3.20	3.71	24.6
1938	NY	NL	24	22	179	13	10	1	104	33	3.07	3.52	20.6
1939	NY	NL	29	18	154	11	9	2	62	24	2.75	3.51	17.9
1940	NY	NL	31	27	214	11	12	0	86	59	3.65	4.29	6.4
1941	NY	NL	26	22	164	11	9	1	75	53	3.57	4.01	10.0
1942	NY	NL	24	20	157	11	8	0	61	34	3.95	4.30	4.5
1943	NY	NL	12	11	66	4	4	0	31	24	4.91	4.91	(2.6)
Totals			535	431	3,590	253	154	33	1,677	725	2.98	3.46	437.9
Average/9			1.3	1.1	9.0	0.6	0.4	0.1	4.2	1.8	2.98	3.46	1.1

Carl Hubbell   Giants   Starter   Adjusted

Year	T	L	G	GS	IP	W	L	SV	SO	BB	Wtd RA/9	Runs /162
1928	NY	NL	21	15	130	11	6	1	39	22	3.45	16.0
1929	NY	NL	41	37	282	19	12	1	112	70	3.60	29.9
1930	NY	NL	39	34	254	18	13	2	123	61	3.52	29.4
1931	NY	NL	38	32	261	15	13	3	163	70	3.19	39.5
1932	NY	NL	42	34	299	19	12	2	144	42	3.02	51.1
1933	NY	NL	47	35	325	24	13	5	164	49	2.28	82.0
1934	NY	NL	52	36	329	22	13	8	124	39	2.77	65.4
1935	NY	NL	44	37	318	24	13	0	158	52	3.54	35.8
1936	NY	NL	44	36	320	27	6	3	129	60	2.31	79.9
1937	NY	NL	41	34	275	23	8	4	167	58	3.70	26.2
1938	NY	NL	25	23	188	14	11	1	109	35	3.61	19.8
1939	NY	NL	31	19	162	12	9	2	65	25	3.56	17.9
1940	NY	NL	33	28	225	12	13	0	90	62	4.44	2.9
1941	NY	NL	27	23	173	12	9	1	79	56	4.28	5.3
1942	NY	NL	25	21	166	12	8	0	64	36	5.01	(8.4)
1943	NY	NL	13	12	69	4	4	0	33	25	5.71	(8.9)
Totals			563	453	3,777	266	162	35	1,764	763	3.40	483.9
Average/9			1.3	1.1	9.0	0.6	0.4	0.1	4.2	1.8	3.40	1.2

Jim Palmer   Orioles   Starter   Actual

Year	T	L	G	GS	IP	W	L	SV	SO	BB	ERA	Actual RA/9	Actual Runs /162
1965	Bal	AL	27	6	92	5	4	1	75	56	3.72	4.79	(2.4)
1966	Bal	AL	30	30	208	15	10	0	147	91	3.46	3.59	22.4
1967	Bal	AL	9	9	49	3	1	0	23	20	2.94	3.31	6.8
1969	Bal	AL	26	23	181	16	4	0	123	64	2.34	2.39	43.6
1970	Bal	AL	39	39	305	20	10	0	199	100	2.71	2.89	56.5
1971	Bal	AL	37	37	282	20	9	0	184	106	2.68	3.00	48.8
1972	Bal	AL	36	36	274	21	10	0	184	70	2.07	2.39	66.1
1973	Bal	AL	38	37	296	22	9	1	158	113	2.40	2.61	64.1
1974	Bal	AL	26	26	179	7	12	0	84	69	3.27	3.93	12.4
1975	Bal	AL	39	38	323	23	11	1	193	80	2.09	2.42	76.7
1976	Bal	AL	40	40	315	22	13	0	159	84	2.51	2.89	58.3
1977	Bal	AL	39	39	319	20	11	0	193	99	2.91	2.99	55.5
1978	Bal	AL	38	38	296	21	12	0	138	97	2.46	2.86	55.8
1979	Bal	AL	23	22	156	10	6	0	67	43	3.30	3.82	12.7
1980	Bal	AL	34	33	224	16	10	0	109	74	3.98	4.34	5.4
1981	Bal	AL	22	22	127	7	8	0	35	46	3.75	4.24	4.5
1982	Bal	AL	36	32	227	15	5	1	103	63	3.13	3.37	29.9
1983	Bal	AL	14	11	77	5	4	0	34	19	4.23	4.93	(3.2)
1984	Bal	AL	5	3	18	0	3	0	4	17	9.17	9.68	(10.1)
Totals			558	521	3,948	268	152	4	2,212	1,311	2.86	3.18	604.0
Average/9			1.3	1.2	9.0	0.6	0.3	0.0	5.0	3.0	2.86	3.18	1.4

Jim Palmer   Orioles   Starter   Adjusted

Year	T	L	G	GS	IP	W	L	SV	SO	BB	Wtd RA/9	Runs /162
1965	Bal	AL	27	6	92	5	4	1	75	56	5.51	(9.8)
1966	Bal	AL	30	30	208	15	10	0	147	91	4.19	8.4
1967	Bal	AL	9	9	49	3	1	0	23	20	4.09	2.6
1969	Bal	AL	26	23	181	16	4	0	123	64	2.66	38.1
1970	Bal	AL	39	39	305	20	10	0	199	100	3.15	47.7
1971	Bal	AL	37	37	282	20	9	0	184	106	3.51	32.7
1972	Bal	AL	38	38	289	22	11	0	194	74	3.13	45.8
1973	Bal	AL	38	37	296	22	9	1	158	113	2.77	59.0
1974	Bal	AL	26	26	179	7	12	0	84	69	4.36	4.0
1975	Bal	AL	39	38	323	23	11	1	193	80	2.55	71.9
1976	Bal	AL	40	40	315	22	13	0	159	84	3.30	44.0
1977	Bal	AL	39	39	319	20	11	0	193	99	2.99	55.6
1978	Bal	AL	38	38	296	21	12	0	138	97	3.07	48.8
1979	Bal	AL	23	22	156	10	6	0	67	43	3.69	15.0
1980	Bal	AL	34	33	224	16	10	0	109	74	4.38	4.5
1981	Bal	AL	33	33	193	11	12	0	53	70	4.72	(3.6)
1982	Bal	AL	36	32	227	15	5	1	103	63	3.41	28.9
1983	Bal	AL	14	11	77	5	4	0	34	19	4.97	(3.5)
1984	Bal	AL	5	3	18	0	3	0	4	17	9.91	(10.5)
Totals			571	534	4,028	273	157	4	2,240	1,338	3.49	479.4
Average/9			1.3	1.2	9.0	0.6	0.3	0.0	5.0	3.0	3.49	1.1

Bob Feller — Indians — Starter — Actual

Year	T	L	G	GS	IP	W	L	SV	SO	BB	ERA	Actual RA/9	Actual Runs /162
1936	Cle	AL	14	8	62	5	3	1	76	47	3.34	4.21	2.4
1937	Cle	AL	26	19	149	9	7	1	150	106	3.39	4.11	7.4
1938	Cle	AL	39	36	278	17	11	1	240	208	4.08	4.40	4.8
1939	Cle	AL	39	35	297	24	9	1	246	142	2.85	3.18	45.4
1940	Cle	AL	43	37	320	27	11	4	261	118	2.61	2.87	60.0
1941	Cle	AL	44	40	343	25	13	2	260	194	3.15	3.38	44.9
1945	Cle	AL	9	9	72	5	3	0	59	35	2.50	2.63	15.4
1946	Cle	AL	48	42	371	26	15	4	348	153	2.18	2.45	86.9
1947	Cle	AL	42	37	299	20	11	3	196	127	2.68	2.92	54.4
1948	Cle	AL	44	38	280	19	15	3	164	116	3.56	3.95	18.9
1949	Cle	AL	36	28	211	15	14	0	108	84	3.75	4.44	2.7
1950	Cle	AL	35	34	247	16	11	0	119	103	3.43	3.83	20.0
1951	Cle	AL	33	32	250	22	8	0	111	95	3.50	3.78	21.6
1952	Cle	AL	30	30	192	9	13	0	81	83	4.74	5.81	(26.7)
1953	Cle	AL	25	25	176	10	7	0	60	60	3.59	3.99	11.1
1954	Cle	AL	19	19	140	13	3	0	59	39	3.09	3.41	17.8
1955	Cle	AL	25	11	83	4	4	0	25	31	3.47	4.66	(0.9)
1956	Cle	AL	19	4	58	0	4	1	18	23	4.97	5.28	(4.7)
Totals			570	484	3,827	266	162	21	2,581	1,764	3.25	3.66	381.4
Average/9			1.3	1.1	9.0	0.6	0.4	0.0	6.1	4.1	3.25	3.66	0.9

Bob Feller — Indians — Starter — Adjusted

Year	T	L	G	GS	IP	W	L	SV	SO	BB	Wtd RA/9	Runs /162
1936	Cle	AL	15	8	65	5	3	1	80	49	3.32	8.9
1937	Cle	AL	27	20	156	9	7	1	158	112	3.51	18.2
1938	Cle	AL	41	38	292	18	12	1	252	219	3.63	30.0
1939	Cle	AL	41	37	312	25	9	1	259	149	2.73	63.2
1940	Cle	AL	45	39	337	28	12	4	275	124	2.59	73.7
1941	Cle	AL	46	42	361	26	14	2	274	204	3.22	53.8
1945	Cle	AL	9	9	76	5	3	0	62	37	3.05	12.7
1946	Cle	AL	50	44	391	27	16	4	366	161	2.72	79.6
1947	Cle	AL	44	39	315	21	12	3	206	134	3.18	48.3
1948	Cle	AL	46	40	295	20	16	3	173	122	3.76	26.2
1949	Cle	AL	38	29	222	16	15	0	114	88	4.26	7.3
1950	Cle	AL	37	36	260	17	12	0	125	108	3.40	33.3
1951	Cle	AL	35	34	263	23	8	0	117	100	3.70	24.9
1952	Cle	AL	32	32	202	9	14	0	85	87	6.33	(39.8)
1953	Cle	AL	26	26	185	11	7	0	63	63	4.06	10.2
1954	Cle	AL	20	20	147	14	3	0	62	41	3.68	14.3
1955	Cle	AL	26	12	87	4	4	0	26	33	4.74	(1.8)
1956	Cle	AL	20	4	61	0	4	1	19	24	5.12	(3.8)
Totals			600	509	4,026	280	170	22	2,715	1,856	3.53	459.3
Average/9			1.3	1.1	9.0	0.6	0.4	0.0	6.1	4.1	3.53	1.0

Appendix

Whitey Ford — Yankees — Starter — Actual

Year	T	L	G	GS	IP	W	L	SV	SO	BB	ERA	Actual RA/9	Actual Runs /162
1950	NY	AL	20	12	112	9	1	1	59	52	2.81	3.13	17.8
1953	NY	AL	32	30	207	18	6	0	110	110	3.00	3.35	27.8
1954	NY	AL	34	28	211	16	8	1	125	101	2.82	3.07	34.8
1955	NY	AL	39	33	254	18	7	2	137	113	2.63	2.94	45.6
1956	NY	AL	31	30	226	19	6	1	141	84	2.47	2.79	44.3
1957	NY	AL	24	17	129	11	5	0	84	53	2.57	3.21	19.4
1958	NY	AL	30	29	219	14	7	1	145	62	2.01	2.55	48.9
1959	NY	AL	35	29	204	16	10	1	114	89	3.04	3.62	21.2
1960	NY	AL	33	29	193	12	9	0	85	65	3.08	3.54	21.8
1961	NY	AL	39	39	283	25	4	0	209	92	3.21	3.43	35.4
1962	NY	AL	38	37	258	17	8	0	160	69	2.90	3.14	40.6
1963	NY	AL	38	37	269	24	7	1	189	56	2.74	3.14	42.4
1964	NY	AL	39	36	245	17	6	1	172	57	2.13	2.46	57.0
1965	NY	AL	37	36	244	16	13	1	162	50	3.24	3.58	26.5
1966	NY	AL	22	9	73	2	5	0	43	24	2.47	4.07	4.0
1967	NY	AL	7	7	44	2	4	0	21	9	1.64	2.25	11.3
Totals			498	438	3,170	236	106	10	1,956	1,086	2.75	3.14	498.7
Average/9			1.4	1.2	9.0	0.7	0.3	0.0	5.6	3.1	2.75	3.14	1.4

Whitey Ford — Yankees — Starter — Adjusted

Year	T	L	G	GS	IP	W	L	SV	SO	BB	Wtd RA/9	Runs /162
1950	NY	AL	21	13	118	9	1	1	62	55	2.78	23.3
1953	NY	AL	34	32	218	19	6	0	116	116	3.41	27.8
1954	NY	AL	36	29	222	17	8	1	131	106	3.32	30.6
1955	NY	AL	41	35	267	19	7	2	144	119	2.99	46.4
1956	NY	AL	33	32	237	20	6	1	148	88	2.71	48.8
1957	NY	AL	25	18	136	12	5	0	88	56	3.47	16.5
1958	NY	AL	32	31	231	15	7	1	153	65	2.76	46.1
1959	NY	AL	37	31	215	17	11	1	120	94	3.76	19.1
1960	NY	AL	35	31	203	13	9	0	89	68	3.67	20.1
1961	NY	AL	39	39	283	25	4	0	209	92	3.41	36.0
1962	NY	AL	38	37	258	17	8	0	160	69	3.22	38.4
1963	NY	AL	38	37	269	24	7	1	189	56	3.51	31.4
1964	NY	AL	39	36	245	17	6	1	172	57	2.75	49.0
1965	NY	AL	37	36	244	16	13	1	162	50	4.12	11.9
1966	NY	AL	22	9	73	2	5	0	43	24	4.76	(1.6)
1967	NY	AL	7	7	44	2	4	0	21	9	2.78	8.7
Totals			512	450	3,261	243	109	10	2,008	1,124	3.31	452.4
Average/9			1.4	1.2	9.0	0.7	0.3	0.0	5.5	3.1	3.31	1.2

Eddie Plank   Athletics   Starter   Actual

Year	T	L	G	GS	IP	W	L	SV	SO	BB	ERA	Actual RA/9	Actual Runs /162
1901	Phi	AL	33	32	261	17	13	0	90	68	3.31	4.59	(1.0)
1902	Phi	AL	36	32	300	20	15	0	107	61	3.30	4.20	11.9
1903	Phi	AL	43	40	336	23	16	0	176	65	2.38	3.43	42.1
1904	Phi	AL	44	43	357	26	17	0	201	86	2.17	2.80	69.8
1905	Phi	AL	41	41	347	24	12	0	210	75	2.26	2.93	62.7
1906	Phi	AL	26	25	212	19	6	0	108	51	2.25	2.98	37.1
1907	Phi	AL	43	40	344	24	16	0	183	85	2.20	3.01	59.1
1908	Phi	AL	34	28	245	14	16	1	135	46	2.17	2.83	46.9
1909	Phi	AL	34	33	265	19	10	0	132	62	1.76	2.51	60.3
1910	Phi	AL	38	32	250	16	10	2	123	55	2.01	3.20	37.7
1911	Phi	AL	40	30	257	23	8	4	149	77	2.10	2.98	45.0
1912	Phi	AL	37	30	260	26	6	2	110	83	2.22	3.12	41.5
1913	Phi	AL	41	30	243	18	10	4	151	57	2.60	3.12	38.7
1914	Phi	AL	34	22	185	15	7	3	110	42	2.87	3.30	25.9
1915	StL	FL	42	31	268	21	11	3	147	54	2.08	2.52	60.7
1916	StL	AL	37	26	236	16	15	3	88	67	2.33	2.98	41.3
1917	StL	AL	20	14	131	5	6	1	26	38	1.79	2.68	27.3
Totals			623	529	4,496	326	194	23	2,246	1,072	2.35	3.14	707.1
Average/9			1.2	1.1	9.0	0.7	0.4	0.0	4.5	2.1	2.35	3.14	1.4

Eddie Plank   Athletics   Starter   Adjusted

Year	T	L	G	GS	IP	W	L	SV	SO	BB	Wtd RA/9	Runs /162
1901	Phi	AL	38	37	302	20	15	0	104	79	3.78	26.0
1902	Phi	AL	42	37	347	23	17	0	124	71	3.83	28.1
1903	Phi	AL	50	46	389	27	19	0	204	75	3.74	35.3
1904	Phi	AL	46	45	376	27	18	0	211	90	3.54	42.3
1905	Phi	AL	43	43	365	25	13	0	221	79	3.58	39.6
1906	Phi	AL	27	26	223	20	6	0	114	54	3.64	22.7
1907	Phi	AL	45	42	362	25	17	0	193	89	3.71	34.1
1908	Phi	AL	36	29	257	15	17	1	142	48	3.72	24.0
1909	Phi	AL	36	35	279	20	11	0	139	65	3.29	39.4
1910	Phi	AL	40	34	263	17	11	2	129	58	3.98	16.8
1911	Phi	AL	42	32	270	24	8	4	157	81	2.92	49.1
1912	Phi	AL	39	32	273	27	6	2	116	87	3.15	42.6
1913	Phi	AL	43	32	255	19	11	4	159	60	3.58	27.7
1914	Phi	AL	36	23	195	16	7	3	116	44	4.08	10.4
1915	StL	FL	44	33	282	22	12	3	155	57	3.15	44.0
1916	StL	AL	39	27	248	17	16	3	93	70	3.70	23.6
1917	StL	AL	21	15	138	5	6	1	27	40	3.36	18.3
Totals			667	567	4,824	349	209	24	2,402	1,148	3.58	524.0
Average/9			1.2	1.1	9.0	0.7	0.4	0.0	4.5	2.1	3.58	1.0

Ed Walsh

											White Sox			**Starter**	**Actual**		Actual

Ed Walsh   **White Sox**   **Starter**   **Actual**   Actual Runs

Year	T	L	G	GS	IP	W	L	SV	SO	BB	ERA	Actual RA/9	/162
1904	Chi	AL	18	8	111	6	3	1	57	32	2.60	3.66	11.0
1905	Chi	AL	22	13	137	8	3	0	71	29	2.17	3.49	16.2
1906	Chi	AL	41	31	278	17	13	2	171	58	1.88	2.68	58.0
1907	Chi	AL	56	46	422	24	18	4	206	87	1.60	2.56	93.7
1908	Chi	AL	66	49	464	40	15	6	269	56	1.42	2.17	123.1
1909	Chi	AL	31	28	230	15	11	2	127	50	1.41	2.03	64.7
1910	Chi	AL	45	36	370	18	20	5	258	61	1.27	2.19	97.2
1911	Chi	AL	56	37	369	27	18	4	255	72	2.22	3.05	61.7
1912	Chi	AL	62	41	393	27	17	10	254	94	2.15	2.86	74.1
1913	Chi	AL	16	14	98	8	3	1	34	39	2.58	3.41	12.4
1914	Chi	AL	8	5	45	2	3	0	15	20	2.82	3.74	4.1
1915	Chi	AL	3	3	27	3	0	0	12	7	1.33	1.33	9.7
1916	Chi	AL	2	1	3	0	1	0	3	3	2.70	8.10	(1.3)
1917	Bos	NL	4	3	18	0	1	0	4	9	3.50	4.50	0.1
Totals			430	315	2,964	195	126	35	1,736	617	1.82	2.66	624.8
Average/9			1.3	1.0	9.0	0.6	0.4	0.1	5.3	1.9	1.82	2.66	1.9

Ed Walsh   **White Sox**   **Starter**   **Adjusted**

Year	T	L	G	GS	IP	W	L	SV	SO	BB	Wtd RA/9	Runs /162
1904	Chi	AL	19	8	116	6	3	1	60	34	4.63	(1.0)
1905	Chi	AL	23	14	144	8	3	0	75	31	4.26	4.7
1906	Chi	AL	43	33	293	18	14	2	180	61	3.27	41.7
1907	Chi	AL	59	48	444	25	19	4	217	92	3.15	69.3
1908	Chi	AL	69	52	488	42	16	6	283	59	2.85	92.6
1909	Chi	AL	33	29	242	16	12	2	134	53	2.66	51.1
1910	Chi	AL	47	38	389	19	21	5	271	64	2.73	79.1
1911	Chi	AL	59	39	388	28	19	4	268	76	2.99	67.6
1912	Chi	AL	65	43	413	28	18	11	267	99	2.89	76.6
1913	Chi	AL	17	15	103	8	3	1	36	41	3.91	7.3
1914	Chi	AL	8	5	47	2	3	0	16	21	4.62	(0.3)
1915	Chi	AL	3	3	28	3	0	0	13	7	1.52	9.6
1916	Chi	AL	2	1	4	0	1	0	3	3	10.06	(2.1)
1917	Bos	NL	4	3	19	0	1	0	4	9	5.81	(2.6)
Totals			452	331	3,118	205	133	37	1,826	649	3.13	493.5
Average/9			1.3	1.0	9.0	0.6	0.4	0.1	5.3	1.9	3.13	1.4

Don Sutton   **Dodgers**   **Starter**   **Actual**

Year	T	L	G	GS	IP	W	L	SV	SO	BB	ERA	Actual RA/9	Actual Runs /162
1966	LA	NL	37	35	226	12	12	0	209	52	2.99	3.27	32.3
1967	LA	NL	37	34	233	11	15	1	169	57	3.95	4.10	11.8
1968	LA	NL	35	27	208	11	15	1	162	59	2.60	2.77	41.2
1969	LA	NL	41	41	293	17	18	0	217	91	3.47	3.77	25.7
1970	LA	NL	38	38	260	15	13	0	201	78	4.08	4.39	4.8
1971	LA	NL	38	37	265	17	12	1	194	55	2.54	2.88	49.4
1972	LA	NL	33	33	273	19	9	0	207	63	2.08	2.57	60.2
1973	LA	NL	33	33	256	18	10	0	200	56	2.42	2.74	51.8
1974	LA	NL	40	40	276	19	9	0	179	80	3.23	3.62	28.7
1975	LA	NL	35	35	254	16	13	0	175	62	2.87	3.08	41.7
1976	LA	NL	35	34	268	21	10	0	161	82	3.06	3.30	37.4
1977	LA	NL	33	33	240	14	8	0	150	69	3.18	3.48	28.8
1978	LA	NL	34	34	238	15	11	0	154	54	3.55	4.12	11.6
1979	LA	NL	33	32	226	12	15	1	146	61	3.82	4.34	5.4
1980	LA	NL	32	31	212	13	5	1	128	47	2.20	2.37	51.6
1981	Hou	NL	23	23	159	11	9	0	104	29	2.61	2.89	29.4
1982	Hou	NL	34	34	250	17	9	0	175	64	3.06	3.46	30.4
1983	Mil	AL	31	31	220	8	13	0	134	54	4.08	4.45	2.6
1984	Mil	AL	33	33	213	14	12	0	143	51	3.77	4.36	4.7
1985	Oak	AL	34	34	226	15	10	0	107	59	3.86	4.02	13.5
1986	Cal	AL	34	34	207	15	11	0	116	49	3.74	4.04	11.9
1987	Cal	AL	35	34	192	11	11	0	99	41	4.70	4.74	(3.9)
1988	LA	NL	16	16	87	3	6	0	44	30	3.92	4.53	0.3
Totals			774	756	5,282	324	256	5	3,574	1,343	3.26	3.58	571.3
Average/9			1.3	1.3	9.0	0.6	0.4	0.0	6.1	2.3	3.26	3.58	1.0

Don Sutton   **Dodgers**   **Starter**   **Adjusted**

Year	T	L	G	GS	IP	W	L	SV	SO	BB	Wtd RA/9	Runs /162
1966	LA	NL	37	35	226	12	12	0	209	52	3.63	23.1
1967	LA	NL	37	34	233	11	15	1	169	57	4.87	(8.0)
1968	LA	NL	35	27	208	11	15	1	162	59	3.69	20.0
1969	LA	NL	41	41	293	17	18	0	217	91	4.21	11.3
1970	LA	NL	38	38	260	15	13	0	201	78	4.42	4.1
1971	LA	NL	38	37	265	17	12	1	194	55	3.36	35.4
1972	LA	NL	35	35	287	20	9	0	218	66	3.01	49.3
1973	LA	NL	33	33	256	18	10	0	200	56	3.01	44.1
1974	LA	NL	40	40	276	19	9	0	179	80	3.98	17.8
1975	LA	NL	35	35	254	16	13	0	175	62	3.40	32.7
1976	LA	NL	35	34	268	21	10	0	161	82	3.77	23.4
1977	LA	NL	33	33	240	14	8	0	150	69	3.60	25.4
1978	LA	NL	34	34	238	15	11	0	154	54	4.67	(3.0)
1979	LA	NL	33	32	226	12	15	1	146	61	4.68	(3.0)
1980	LA	NL	32	31	212	13	5	1	128	47	2.68	44.3
1981	Hou	NL	35	35	240	17	14	0	157	44	3.39	31.3
1982	Hou	NL	34	34	250	17	9	0	175	64	3.86	19.2
1983	Mil	AL	31	31	220	8	13	0	134	54	4.49	1.7
1984	Mil	AL	33	33	213	14	12	0	143	51	4.46	2.2
1985	Oak	AL	34	34	226	15	10	0	107	59	3.98	14.4
1986	Cal	AL	34	34	207	15	11	0	116	49	3.96	13.7
1987	Cal	AL	35	34	192	11	11	0	99	41	4.36	4.1
1988	LA	NL	16	16	87	3	6	0	44	30	5.33	(7.5)
Totals			788	770	5,378	331	261	5	3,638	1,361	3.89	396.2
Average/9			1.3	1.3	9.0	0.6	0.4	0.0	6.1	2.3	3.89	0.7

Bob Gibson

Year	T	L	G	GS	IP	W	L	SV	SO	BB	ERA	Actual RA/9	Actual Runs /162
					Cardinals				**Starter**		**Actual**		
1959	StL	NL	13	9	76	3	5	0	48	39	3.33	4.14	3.5
1960	StL	NL	27	12	87	3	6	0	69	48	5.61	6.31	(16.9)
1961	StL	NL	35	27	211	13	12	1	166	119	3.24	3.88	15.9
1962	StL	NL	32	30	234	15	13	1	208	95	2.85	3.23	34.5
1963	StL	NL	36	33	255	18	9	0	204	96	3.39	3.88	19.2
1964	StL	NL	40	36	287	19	12	1	245	86	3.01	3.32	39.5
1965	StL	NL	38	36	299	20	12	1	270	103	3.07	3.31	41.4
1966	StL	NL	35	35	280	21	12	0	225	78	2.44	2.89	51.9
1967	StL	NL	24	24	175	13	7	0	147	40	2.98	3.19	26.6
1968	StL	NL	34	34	305	22	9	0	268	62	1.12	1.45	105.2
1969	StL	NL	35	35	314	20	13	0	269	95	2.18	2.41	74.9
1970	StL	NL	34	34	294	23	7	0	274	88	3.12	3.40	37.8
1971	StL	NL	31	31	246	16	13	0	185	76	3.04	3.51	28.6
1972	StL	NL	34	34	278	19	11	0	208	88	2.46	2.69	57.7
1973	StL	NL	25	25	195	12	10	0	142	57	2.77	3.28	27.7
1974	StL	NL	33	33	240	11	13	0	129	104	3.83	4.16	10.6
1975	StL	NL	22	14	109	3	10	2	60	62	5.04	5.45	(10.8)
Totals			528	482	3,884	251	174	6	3,117	1,336	2.91	3.29	547.2
Average/9			1.2	1.1	9.0	0.6	0.4	0.0	7.2	3.1	2.91	3.29	1.3

Bob Gibson

Year	T	L	G	GS	IP	W	L	SV	SO	BB	Wtd RA/9	Runs /162
					Cardinals				**Starter**		**Adjusted**	
1959	StL	NL	14	9	80	3	5	0	50	41	4.24	2.8
1960	StL	NL	28	13	91	3	6	0	73	50	6.77	(22.4)
1961	StL	NL	37	28	222	14	13	1	175	125	3.87	17.0
1962	StL	NL	32	30	234	15	13	1	208	95	3.26	33.8
1963	StL	NL	36	33	255	18	9	0	204	96	4.63	(2.0)
1964	StL	NL	40	36	287	19	12	1	245	86	3.74	25.9
1965	StL	NL	38	36	299	20	12	1	270	103	3.74	27.0
1966	StL	NL	35	35	280	21	12	0	225	78	3.21	41.9
1967	StL	NL	24	24	175	13	7	0	147	40	3.79	15.0
1968	StL	NL	34	34	305	22	9	0	268	62	1.93	88.9
1969	StL	NL	35	35	314	20	13	0	269	95	2.69	65.1
1970	StL	NL	34	34	294	23	7	0	274	88	3.42	37.1
1971	StL	NL	31	31	246	16	13	0	185	76	4.09	12.7
1972	StL	NL	36	36	292	20	12	0	219	93	3.15	45.7
1973	StL	NL	25	25	195	12	10	0	142	57	3.60	20.7
1974	StL	NL	33	33	240	11	13	0	129	104	4.57	(0.3)
1975	StL	NL	22	14	109	3	10	2	60	62	6.01	(17.6)
Totals			534	486	3,918	253	176	6	3,143	1,351	3.66	391.3
Average/9			1.2	1.1	9.0	0.6	0.4	0.0	7.2	3.1	3.66	0.9

Tim Keefe NY NL Starter Actual

Year	T	L	G	GS	IP	W	L	SV	SO	BB	ERA	Actual RA/9	Actual Runs /162
1880	Tro	NL	12	12	105	6	6	0	39	16	0.86	2.31	26.2
1881	Tro	NL	45	45	402	18	27	0	103	81	3.25	5.44	(39.4)
1882	Tro	NL	43	42	375	17	26	0	116	81	2.50	5.30	(31.0)
1883	NY	AA	68	68	619	41	27	0	359	108	2.41	3.55	69.3
1884	NY	AA	58	58	483	37	17	0	334	71	2.25	3.64	49.2
1885	NY	NL	46	46	400	32	13	0	227	102	1.58	3.48	47.9
1886	NY	NL	64	64	535	42	20	0	297	102	2.56	4.17	23.0
1887	NY	NL	56	56	477	35	19	0	189	108	3.12	4.89	(17.6)
1888	NY	NL	51	51	434	35	12	0	335	90	1.74	2.90	80.0
1889	NY	NL	47	45	364	28	13	1	225	151	3.31	5.24	(27.6)
1890	NY	P	30	30	229	17	11	0	89	89	3.38	5.38	(20.9)
1891	Phi	NL	19	17	133	5	11	1	64	57	4.45	7.56	(44.5)
1892	Phi	NL	39	38	313	19	16	0	127	100	2.36	4.08	16.6
1893	Phi	NL	22	22	178	10	7	0	56	80	4.40	6.62	(40.8)
Totals			600	594	5,048	342	225	2	2,560	1,236	2.62	4.40	90.2
Average/9			1.1	1.1	9.0	0.6	0.4	0.0	4.6	2.2	2.62	4.40	0.2

Tim Keefe NY NL Starter Adjusted

Year	T	L	G	GS	IP	W	L	SV	SO	BB	Wtd RA/9	Runs /162
1880	Tro	NL	23	23	200	11	11	0	74	30	2.21	52.2
1881	Tro	NL	87	87	775	35	52	0	199	156	4.81	(22.1)
1882	Tro	NL	82	81	719	33	50	0	222	155	4.43	10.0
1883	NY	AA	113	113	1,028	68	45	0	596	179	2.78	202.6
1884	NY	AA	85	85	711	54	25	0	492	105	3.08	116.9
1885	NY	NL	67	67	584	47	19	0	331	149	3.12	93.1
1886	NY	NL	84	84	699	55	26	0	388	133	3.47	84.6
1887	NY	NL	71	71	608	45	24	0	241	138	3.55	67.8
1888	NY	NL	61	61	517	42	14	0	399	107	2.85	98.2
1889	NY	NL	57	55	443	34	16	1	274	184	3.98	28.4
1890	NY	P	37	37	281	21	14	0	109	109	3.47	34.0
1891	Phi	NL	22	20	157	6	13	1	75	67	6.11	(27.0)
1892	Phi	NL	41	40	331	20	17	0	134	106	3.54	37.3
1893	Phi	NL	27	27	220	12	9	0	69	99	4.50	1.3
Totals			858	850	7,274	483	335	2	3,605	1,718	3.60	777.4
Average/9			1.1	1.1	9.0	0.6	0.4	0.0	4.5	2.1	3.60	1.0

Three Finger Brown   **Cubs**   **Starter**   **Actual**

Year	T	L	G	GS	IP	W	L	SV	SO	BB	ERA	Actual RA/9	Actual Runs /162
1903	StL	NL	26	24	201	9	13	0	83	59	2.60	4.70	(3.2)
1904	Chi	NL	26	23	212	15	10	1	81	50	1.86	3.14	33.4
1905	Chi	NL	30	24	249	18	12	0	89	44	2.17	3.22	37.0
1906	Chi	NL	36	32	277	26	6	3	144	61	1.04	1.82	84.3
1907	Chi	NL	34	27	233	20	6	3	107	40	1.39	1.97	67.0
1908	Chi	NL	44	31	312	29	9	5	123	49	1.47	1.84	94.3
1909	Chi	NL	50	34	343	27	9	7	172	53	1.31	2.05	95.5
1910	Chi	NL	46	31	295	25	14	7	143	64	1.86	2.90	54.4
1911	Chi	NL	53	27	270	21	11	13	129	55	2.80	3.67	26.6
1912	Chi	NL	15	8	89	5	6	0	34	20	2.64	3.55	9.9
1913	Cin	NL	39	16	173	11	12	6	41	44	2.91	4.10	8.8
1914	StL	FL	35	26	233	14	11	0	113	61	3.52	4.10	11.8
1915	Chi	FL	35	25	236	17	8	4	95	64	2.09	2.86	44.6
1916	Chi	NL	12	4	48	2	3	0	21	9	3.91	5.03	(2.5)
Totals			481	332	3,172	239	130	49	1,375	673	2.06	2.96	561.8
Average/9			1.4	0.9	9.0	0.7	0.4	0.1	3.9	1.9	2.06	2.96	1.6

Three Finger Brown   **Cubs**   **Starter**   **Adjusted**

Year	T	L	G	GS	IP	W	L	SV	SO	BB	Wtd RA/9	Runs /162
1903	StL	NL	30	28	233	10	15	0	96	68	4.37	4.8
1904	Chi	NL	27	24	223	16	11	1	85	53	3.56	24.8
1905	Chi	NL	32	25	262	19	13	0	94	46	3.53	30.0
1906	Chi	NL	38	34	292	27	6	3	151	64	2.28	73.9
1907	Chi	NL	36	28	245	21	6	3	113	42	2.57	54.1
1908	Chi	NL	46	33	329	31	9	5	129	52	2.53	74.2
1909	Chi	NL	53	36	360	28	9	7	181	56	2.55	80.3
1910	Chi	NL	48	33	311	26	15	7	150	67	3.26	44.9
1911	Chi	NL	56	28	284	22	12	14	136	58	3.75	25.5
1912	Chi	NL	16	8	93	5	6	0	36	21	3.48	11.2
1913	Cin	NL	41	17	182	12	13	6	43	46	4.48	1.5
1914	StL	FL	37	27	245	15	12	0	119	64	4.85	(8.0)
1915	Chi	FL	37	26	249	18	8	4	100	67	3.57	27.2
1916	Chi	NL	13	4	51	2	3	0	22	9	6.66	(11.9)
Totals			509	352	3,358	252	138	52	1,455	714	3.40	432.3
Average/9			1.4	0.9	9.0	0.7	0.4	0.1	3.9	1.9	3.40	1.2

Bert Blyleven   **Twins**   **Starter**   **Actual**

Year	T	L	G	GS	IP	W	L	SV	SO	BB	ERA	Actual RA/9	Actual Runs /162
1970	Min	AL	27	25	164	10	9	0	135	47	3.18	3.62	17.1
1971	Min	AL	38	38	278	16	15	0	224	59	2.81	3.07	46.0
1972	Min	AL	39	38	287	17	17	0	228	69	2.73	2.91	52.6
1973	Min	AL	40	40	325	20	17	0	258	67	2.52	3.02	55.5
1974	Min	AL	37	37	281	17	17	0	249	77	2.66	3.17	43.3
1975	Min	AL	35	35	276	15	10	0	233	84	3.00	3.40	35.4
1976	Tex	AL	36	36	298	13	16	0	219	81	2.87	3.20	44.9
1977	Tex	AL	30	30	235	14	12	0	182	69	2.72	3.11	37.7
1978	Pit	NL	34	34	244	14	10	0	182	66	3.03	3.47	29.4
1979	Pit	NL	37	37	237	12	5	0	172	92	3.60	3.87	18.1
1980	Pit	NL	34	32	217	8	13	0	168	59	3.82	4.24	7.6
1981	Cle	AL	20	20	159	11	7	0	107	40	2.88	2.94	28.6
1982	Cle	AL	4	4	20	2	2	0	19	11	4.87	6.20	(3.7)
1983	Cle	AL	24	24	156	7	10	0	123	44	3.91	4.26	5.2
1984	Cle	AL	33	32	245	19	7	0	170	74	2.87	3.16	38.0
1985	Cle	AL	37	37	294	17	16	0	206	75	3.16	3.71	27.6
1986	Min	AL	36	36	272	17	14	0	215	58	4.01	4.44	3.5
1987	Min	AL	37	37	267	15	12	0	196	101	4.01	4.45	3.2
1988	Min	AL	33	33	207	10	17	0	145	51	5.43	5.56	(23.1)
1989	Cal	AL	33	33	241	17	5	0	131	44	2.73	2.84	46.0
1990	Cal	AL	23	23	134	8	7	0	69	25	5.24	5.71	(17.2)
1992	Cal	AL	25	24	133	8	12	0	70	29	4.74	5.14	(8.6)
Totals			692	685	4,970	287	250	0	3,701	1,322	3.31	3.67	487.2
Average/9			1.3	1.2	9.0	0.5	0.5	0.0	6.7	2.4	3.31	3.67	0.9

Bert Blyleven   **Twins**   **Starter**   **Adjusted**

Year	T	L	G	GS	IP	W	L	SV	SO	BB	Wtd RA/9	Runs /162
1970	Min	AL	27	25	164	10	9	0	135	47	3.95	11.1
1971	Min	AL	38	38	278	16	15	0	224	59	3.60	29.7
1972	Min	AL	41	40	302	18	18	0	240	73	3.81	25.1
1973	Min	AL	40	40	325	20	17	0	258	67	3.20	49.0
1974	Min	AL	37	37	281	17	17	0	249	77	3.51	32.5
1975	Min	AL	35	35	276	15	10	0	233	84	3.59	29.7
1976	Tex	AL	36	36	298	13	16	0	219	81	3.65	29.8
1977	Tex	AL	30	30	235	14	12	0	182	69	3.11	37.8
1978	Pit	NL	34	34	244	14	10	0	182	66	3.93	16.9
1979	Pit	NL	37	37	237	12	5	0	172	92	4.17	10.2
1980	Pit	NL	34	32	217	8	13	0	168	59	4.79	(5.7)
1981	Cle	AL	30	30	241	17	11	0	162	61	3.28	34.3
1982	Cle	AL	4	4	20	2	2	0	19	11	6.28	(3.9)
1983	Cle	AL	24	24	156	7	10	0	123	44	4.29	4.6
1984	Cle	AL	33	32	245	19	7	0	170	74	3.24	36.0
1985	Cle	AL	37	37	294	17	16	0	206	75	3.68	28.8
1986	Min	AL	36	36	272	17	14	0	215	58	4.35	6.2
1987	Min	AL	37	37	267	15	12	0	196	101	4.10	13.7
1988	Min	AL	33	33	207	10	17	0	145	51	5.76	(27.7)
1989	Cal	AL	33	33	241	17	5	0	131	44	2.98	42.2
1990	Cal	AL	23	23	134	8	7	0	69	25	5.98	(21.2)
1992	Cal	AL	25	24	133	8	12	0	70	29	5.40	(12.4)
Totals			704	697	5,067	294	254	0	3,768	1,346	3.91	366.6
Average/9			1.3	1.2	9.0	0.5	0.5	0.0	6.7	2.4	3.91	0.7

Nolan Ryan   Angels   Starter   Actual

Year	T	L	G	GS	IP	W	L	SV	SO	BB	ERA	Actual RA/9	Actual Runs /162
1966	NY	NL	2	1	3	0	1	0	6	3	15.00	15.00	(3.5)
1968	NY	NL	21	18	134	6	9	0	133	75	3.09	3.36	17.8
1969	NY	NL	25	10	89	6	3	1	92	53	3.53	3.83	7.2
1970	NY	NL	27	19	132	7	11	1	125	97	3.42	4.03	7.7
1971	NY	NL	30	26	152	10	14	0	137	116	3.97	4.62	(1.1)
1972	Cal	AL	39	39	284	19	16	0	329	157	2.28	2.54	63.6
1973	Cal	AL	41	39	326	21	16	1	383	162	2.87	3.12	52.1
1974	Cal	AL	42	41	333	22	16	0	367	202	2.89	3.44	41.3
1975	Cal	AL	28	28	198	14	12	0	186	132	3.45	4.09	10.3
1976	Cal	AL	39	39	284	17	18	0	327	183	3.36	3.70	27.1
1977	Cal	AL	37	37	299	19	16	0	341	204	2.77	3.31	41.4
1978	Cal	AL	31	31	235	10	13	0	260	148	3.72	4.07	12.7
1979	Cal	AL	34	34	223	16	14	0	223	114	3.60	4.20	8.8
1980	Hou	NL	35	35	234	11	10	0	200	98	3.35	3.85	18.4
1981	Hou	NL	21	21	149	11	5	0	140	68	1.69	2.05	41.5
1982	Hou	NL	35	35	250	16	12	0	245	109	3.16	3.60	26.6
1983	Hou	NL	29	29	196	14	9	0	183	101	2.98	3.39	25.5
1984	Hou	NL	30	30	184	12	11	0	197	69	3.04	3.82	15.0
1985	Hou	NL	35	35	232	10	12	0	209	95	3.80	4.19	9.5
1986	Hou	NL	30	30	178	12	8	0	194	82	3.34	3.64	18.1
1987	Hou	NL	34	34	212	8	16	0	270	87	2.76	3.19	32.1
1988	Hou	NL	33	33	220	12	11	0	228	87	3.52	4.01	13.4
1989	Tex	AL	32	32	239	16	10	0	301	98	3.20	3.61	25.2
1990	Tex	AL	30	30	204	13	9	0	232	74	3.44	3.79	17.4
1991	Tex	AL	27	27	173	12	6	0	203	72	2.91	3.02	29.5
1992	Tex	AL	27	27	157	5	9	0	157	69	3.72	4.29	4.7
1993	Tex	AL	13	13	66	5	5	0	46	40	4.88	6.38	(13.4)
Totals			807	773	5,386	324	292	3	5,714	2,795	3.19	3.64	548.9
Average/9			1.3	1.3	9.0	0.5	0.5	0.0	9.5	4.7	3.19	3.64	0.9

Nolan Ryan   Angels   Starter   Adjusted

Year	T	L	G	GS	IP	W	L	SV	SO	BB	Wtd RA/9	Runs /162
1966	NY	NL	2	1	3	0	1	0	6	3	16.67	(4.0)
1968	NY	NL	21	18	134	6	9	0	133	75	4.48	1.2
1969	NY	NL	25	10	89	6	3	1	92	53	4.28	2.8
1970	NY	NL	27	19	132	7	11	1	125	97	4.05	7.4
1971	NY	NL	30	26	152	10	14	0	137	116	5.38	(14.0)
1972	Cal	AL	41	41	299	20	17	0	346	165	3.33	40.9
1973	Cal	AL	41	39	326	21	16	1	383	162	3.31	45.3
1974	Cal	AL	42	41	333	22	16	0	367	202	3.81	27.5
1975	Cal	AL	28	28	198	14	12	0	186	132	4.31	5.3
1976	Cal	AL	39	39	284	17	18	0	327	183	4.23	10.5
1977	Cal	AL	37	37	299	19	16	0	341	204	3.31	41.5
1978	Cal	AL	31	31	235	10	13	0	260	148	4.37	4.8
1979	Cal	AL	34	34	223	16	14	0	223	114	4.05	12.4
1980	Hou	NL	35	35	234	11	10	0	200	98	4.35	5.3
1981	Hou	NL	32	32	226	17	8	0	212	103	2.40	54.0
1982	Hou	NL	35	35	250	16	12	0	245	109	4.02	14.9
1983	Hou	NL	29	29	196	14	9	0	183	101	3.75	17.6
1984	Hou	NL	30	30	184	12	11	0	197	69	4.27	5.9
1985	Hou	NL	35	35	232	10	12	0	209	95	4.69	(3.5)
1986	Hou	NL	30	30	178	12	8	0	194	82	3.98	11.5
1987	Hou	NL	34	34	212	8	16	0	270	87	3.20	31.9
1988	Hou	NL	33	33	220	12	11	0	228	87	4.72	(4.0)
1989	Tex	AL	32	32	239	16	10	0	301	98	3.79	20.4
1990	Tex	AL	30	30	204	13	9	0	232	74	3.97	13.3
1991	Tex	AL	27	27	173	12	6	0	203	72	3.07	28.7
1992	Tex	AL	27	27	157	5	9	0	157	69	4.50	0.9
1993	Tex	AL	13	13	66	5	5	0	46	40	6.12	(11.5)
Totals			820	786	5,477	331	295	3	5,803	2,838	3.95	366.8
Average/9			1.3	1.3	9.0	0.5	0.5	0.0	9.5	4.7	3.95	0.6

Pedro Martinez			Expos						Starter		Actual		Actual
												Actual	Runs
Year	T	L	G	GS	IP	W	L	SV	SO	BB	ERA	RA/9	/162
1992	LA	NL	2	1	8	0	1	0	8	1	2.25	2.25	2.1
1993	LA	NL	65	2	107	10	5	2	119	57	2.61	2.86	20.2
1994	Mon	NL	24	23	145	11	5	1	142	45	3.42	3.61	15.2
1995	Mon	NL	30	30	195	14	10	0	174	66	3.51	3.61	20.5
1996	Mon	NL	33	33	217	13	10	0	222	70	3.70	4.15	9.8
1997	Mon	NL	31	31	241	17	8	0	305	67	1.90	2.42	57.3
1998	Bos	AL	33	33	234	19	7	0	251	67	2.89	3.16	36.3
1999	Bos	AL	31	29	213	23	4	0	313	37	2.07	2.36	52.1
2000	Bos	AL	29	29	217	18	6	0	284	32	1.74	1.82	66.0
	Totals		278	211	1,576	125	56	3	1,818	442	2.68	2.96	279.4
	Average/9		1.6	1.2	9.0	0.7	0.3	0.0	10.4	2.5	2.68	2.96	1.6

Pedro Martinez			Expos						Starter		Adjusted		
												Wtd	Runs
Year	T	L	G	GS	IP	W	L	SV	SO	BB		RA/9	/162
1992	LA	NL	2	1	8	0	1	0	8	1		2.64	1.7
1993	LA	NL	65	2	107	10	5	2	119	57		2.88	19.9
1994	Mon	NL	34	33	205	16	7	1	201	64		3.54	23.2
1995	Mon	NL	34	34	219	16	11	0	196	74		3.54	24.8
1996	Mon	NL	33	33	217	13	10	0	222	70		4.02	13.0
1997	Mon	NL	31	31	241	17	8	0	305	67		2.38	58.3
1998	Bos	AL	33	33	234	19	7	0	251	67		2.85	44.4
1999	Bos	AL	31	29	213	23	4	0	313	37		2.04	59.6
2000	Bos	AL	29	29	217	18	6	0	284	32		1.55	72.4
	Totals		292	224	1,661	131	59	3	1,899	469		2.84	317.4
	Average/9		1.6	1.2	9.0	0.7	0.3	0.0	10.3	2.5		2.84	1.7

Appendix

Randy Johnson — Mariners — Starter — Actual

Year	T	L	G	GS	IP	W	L	SV	SO	BB	ERA	Actual RA/9	Actual Runs /162
1988	Mon	NL	4	4	26	3	0	0	25	7	2.42	2.77	5.2
1989	Sea	AL	29	28	161	7	13	0	130	96	4.82	5.60	(18.6)
1990	Sea	AL	33	33	220	14	11	0	194	120	3.65	4.22	8.2
1991	Sea	AL	33	33	201	13	10	0	228	152	3.98	4.29	6.0
1992	Sea	AL	31	31	210	12	14	0	241	144	3.77	4.45	2.5
1993	Sea	AL	35	34	255	19	8	1	308	99	3.24	3.42	32.3
1994	Sea	AL	23	23	172	13	6	0	204	72	3.19	3.40	22.1
1995	Sea	AL	30	30	214	18	2	0	294	65	2.48	2.73	43.5
1996	Sea	AL	14	8	61	5	0	1	85	25	3.67	3.96	4.1
1997	Sea	AL	30	29	213	20	4	0	291	77	2.28	2.54	47.7
1998	Sea	AL	34	34	244	19	11	0	329	86	3.28	3.76	21.6
1999	Ari	NL	35	35	272	17	9	0	364	70	2.48	2.85	51.5
2000	Ari	NL	35	35	249	19	7	0	347	76	2.64	3.22	36.9
Totals			366	357	2,499	179	95	2	3,040	1,089	3.20	3.61	263.0
Average/9			1.3	1.3	9.0	0.6	0.3	0.0	10.9	3.9	3.20	3.61	0.9

Randy Johnson — Mariners — Starter — Adjusted

Year	T	L	G	GS	IP	W	L	SV	SO	BB	Wtd RA/9	Runs /162
1988	Mon	NL	4	4	26	3	0	0	25	7	3.26	3.7
1989	Sea	AL	29	28	161	7	13	0	130	96	5.88	(23.6)
1990	Sea	AL	33	33	220	14	11	0	194	120	4.42	3.3
1991	Sea	AL	33	33	201	13	10	0	228	152	4.35	4.5
1992	Sea	AL	31	31	210	12	14	0	241	144	4.67	(2.7)
1993	Sea	AL	35	34	255	19	8	1	308	99	3.28	36.2
1994	Sea	AL	33	33	243	18	8	0	289	102	2.94	43.7
1995	Sea	AL	34	34	241	20	2	0	331	73	2.43	57.0
1996	Sea	AL	14	8	61	5	0	1	85	25	3.33	8.4
1997	Sea	AL	30	29	213	20	4	0	291	77	2.32	52.8
1998	Sea	AL	34	34	244	19	11	0	329	86	3.39	31.8
1999	Ari	NL	35	35	272	17	9	0	364	70	2.58	59.8
2000	Ari	NL	35	35	249	19	7	0	347	76	2.89	45.9
Totals			379	370	2,597	187	98	2	3,161	1,127	3.44	320.9
Average/9			1.3	1.3	9.0	0.6	0.3	0.0	11.0	3.9	3.44	1.1

Old Hoss Radbourn — Pro NL — Starter — Actual

Year	T	L	G	GS	IP	W	L	SV	SO	BB	ERA	Actual RA/9	Actual Runs /162
1881	Pro	NL	41	36	325	25	11	0	117	64	2.43	4.48	2.8
1882	Pro	NL	55	52	474	33	20	0	201	51	2.09	4.08	25.1
1883	Pro	NL	76	68	632	48	25	1	315	56	2.05	3.91	45.5
1884	Pro	NL	75	73	679	59	12	1	441	98	1.38	2.86	128.0
1885	Pro	NL	49	49	446	28	21	0	154	83	2.20	4.22	16.7
1886	Bos	NL	58	58	509	27	31	0	218	111	3.00	5.30	(42.0)
1887	Bos	NL	50	50	425	24	23	0	87	133	4.55	6.46	(89.9)
1888	Bos	NL	24	24	207	7	16	0	64	45	2.87	4.78	(5.1)
1889	Bos	NL	33	31	277	20	11	0	99	72	3.67	4.91	(10.9)
1890	Bos	P	41	38	343	27	12	0	80	100	3.31	4.80	(9.3)
1891	Cin	NL	26	24	218	11	13	0	54	62	4.25	6.15	(38.6)
Totals			528	503	4,535	309	195	2	1,830	875	2.67	4.51	22.3
Average/9			1.0	1.0	9.0	0.6	0.4	0.0	3.6	1.7	2.67	4.51	0.0

Old Hoss Radbourn — Pro NL — Starter — Adjusted

Year	T	L	G	GS	IP	W	L	SV	SO	BB	Wtd RA/9	Runs /162
1881	Pro	NL	79	69	627	48	21	0	226	123	3.96	41.3
1882	Pro	NL	105	100	909	63	38	0	385	98	3.41	115.7
1883	Pro	NL	124	111	1,035	79	41	2	515	92	3.01	177.3
1884	Pro	NL	107	104	964	84	17	1	627	139	2.32	239.8
1885	Pro	NL	72	72	650	41	31	0	225	121	3.79	55.8
1886	Bos	NL	76	76	665	35	41	0	285	145	4.41	11.1
1887	Bos	NL	64	64	542	31	29	0	111	170	4.70	(8.3)
1888	Bos	NL	29	29	247	8	19	0	76	54	4.69	(3.8)
1889	Bos	NL	40	38	337	24	13	0	121	88	3.73	31.0
1890	Bos	P	50	47	421	33	15	0	98	123	3.09	68.4
1891	Cin	NL	31	28	256	13	15	0	63	73	4.97	(11.7)
Totals			776	736	6,654	459	280	3	2,732	1,225	3.59	716.6
Average/9			1.0	1.0	9.0	0.6	0.4	0.0	3.7	1.7	3.59	1.0

Gaylord Perry | | | | | **Giants** | | | | | **Starter** | | **Actual** | | **Actual**

Year	T	L	G	GS	IP	W	L	SV	SO	BB	ERA	Actual RA/9	Actual Runs /162
1962	SF	NL	13	7	43	3	1	0	20	14	5.23	6.07	(7.2)
1963	SF	NL	31	4	76	1	6	2	52	29	4.03	4.86	(2.6)
1964	SF	NL	44	19	206	12	11	5	155	43	2.75	2.84	39.4
1965	SF	NL	47	26	196	8	12	1	170	70	4.19	4.83	(5.9)
1966	SF	NL	36	35	256	21	8	0	201	40	2.99	3.24	37.4
1967	SF	NL	39	37	293	15	17	1	230	84	2.61	3.01	50.4
1968	SF	NL	39	38	291	16	15	1	173	59	2.44	2.88	54.2
1969	SF	NL	40	39	325	19	14	0	233	91	2.49	3.18	49.8
1970	SF	NL	41	41	329	23	13	0	214	84	3.20	3.78	28.4
1971	SF	NL	37	37	280	16	12	0	158	67	2.76	3.73	25.7
1972	Cle	AL	41	40	343	24	16	1	234	82	1.92	2.07	94.7
1973	Cle	AL	41	41	344	19	19	0	238	115	3.38	3.74	31.2
1974	Cle	AL	37	37	322	21	13	0	216	99	2.51	2.74	65.1
1975	Tex	AL	37	37	306	18	17	0	233	70	3.24	3.74	27.7
1976	Tex	AL	32	32	250	15	14	0	143	52	3.24	3.34	33.9
1977	Tex	AL	34	34	238	15	12	0	177	56	3.37	4.08	12.6
1978	SD	NL	37	37	261	21	6	0	154	66	2.73	3.31	36.1
1979	SD	NL	32	32	233	12	11	0	140	67	3.06	3.48	27.8
1980	Tex	AL	34	32	206	10	13	0	135	64	3.68	4.68	(2.8)
1981	Atl	NL	23	23	151	8	9	0	60	24	3.94	4.18	6.3
1982	Sea	AL	32	32	217	10	12	0	116	54	4.40	4.86	(7.3)
1983	Sea	AL	30	30	186	7	14	0	82	49	4.64	5.22	(13.7)
	Totals		777	690	5,350	314	265	11	3,534	1,379	3.11	3.58	581.2
	Average/9		1.3	1.2	9.0	0.5	0.4	0.0	5.9	2.3	3.11	3.58	1.0

Gaylord Perry | | | | | **Giants** | | | | | **Starter** | | **Adjusted**

Year	T	L	G	GS	IP	W	L	SV	SO	BB	Wtd RA/9	Runs /162
1962	SF	NL	13	7	43	3	1	0	20	14	6.12	(7.5)
1963	SF	NL	31	4	76	1	6	2	52	29	5.80	(10.5)
1964	SF	NL	44	19	206	12	11	5	155	43	3.20	31.0
1965	SF	NL	47	26	196	8	12	1	170	70	5.46	(19.7)
1966	SF	NL	36	35	256	21	8	0	201	40	3.60	27.2
1967	SF	NL	39	37	293	15	17	1	230	84	3.57	32.1
1968	SF	NL	39	38	291	16	15	1	173	59	3.84	23.3
1969	SF	NL	40	39	325	19	14	0	233	91	3.55	36.3
1970	SF	NL	41	41	329	23	13	0	214	84	3.80	27.6
1971	SF	NL	37	37	280	16	12	0	158	67	4.35	6.5
1972	Cle	AL	43	42	360	25	17	1	246	86	2.71	73.9
1973	Cle	AL	41	41	344	19	19	0	238	115	3.96	22.7
1974	Cle	AL	37	37	322	21	13	0	216	99	3.04	54.4
1975	Tex	AL	37	37	306	18	17	0	233	70	3.95	20.8
1976	Tex	AL	32	32	250	15	14	0	143	52	3.81	20.6
1977	Tex	AL	34	34	238	15	12	0	177	56	4.08	12.7
1978	SD	NL	37	37	261	21	6	0	154	66	3.75	23.3
1979	SD	NL	32	32	233	12	11	0	140	67	3.75	20.9
1980	Tex	AL	34	32	206	10	13	0	135	64	4.72	(3.7)
1981	Atl	NL	35	35	228	12	14	0	91	36	4.90	(8.6)
1982	Sea	AL	32	32	217	10	12	0	116	54	4.92	(8.8)
1983	Sea	AL	30	30	186	7	14	0	82	49	5.26	(14.6)
	Totals		791	704	5,446	319	270	11	3,577	1,396	3.96	360.0
	Average/9		1.3	1.2	9.0	0.5	0.4	0.0	5.9	2.3	3.96	0.6

Robin Roberts Phillies Starter Actual

Year	T	L	G	GS	IP	W	L	SV	SO	BB	ERA	Actual RA/9	Actual Runs /162
1948	Phi	NL	20	20	147	7	9	0	84	61	3.19	3.86	11.4
1949	Phi	NL	43	31	227	15	15	4	95	75	3.69	4.00	14.0
1950	Phi	NL	40	39	304	20	11	1	146	77	3.02	3.32	41.8
1951	Phi	NL	44	39	315	21	15	2	127	64	3.03	3.29	44.3
1952	Phi	NL	39	37	330	28	7	2	148	45	2.59	2.84	63.0
1953	Phi	NL	44	41	347	23	16	2	198	61	2.75	3.09	56.5
1954	Phi	NL	45	38	337	23	15	4	185	56	2.97	3.10	54.5
1955	Phi	NL	41	38	305	23	14	3	160	53	3.28	4.04	17.5
1956	Phi	NL	43	37	297	19	18	3	157	40	4.45	4.70	(4.7)
1957	Phi	NL	39	32	250	10	22	2	128	43	4.07	4.39	4.6
1958	Phi	NL	35	34	270	17	14	0	130	51	3.24	3.73	24.8
1959	Phi	NL	35	35	257	15	17	0	137	35	4.27	4.80	(6.9)
1960	Phi	NL	35	33	237	12	16	1	122	34	4.02	4.29	7.0
1961	Phi	NL	26	18	117	1	10	0	54	23	5.85	6.54	(25.8)
1962	Bal	AL	27	25	191	10	9	0	102	41	2.78	2.97	33.7
1963	Bal	AL	35	35	251	14	13	0	124	40	3.33	3.59	27.0
1964	Bal	AL	31	31	204	13	7	0	109	52	2.91	3.04	34.4
1965	Bal	AL	30	25	191	10	9	0	97	30	2.78	3.44	23.7
1966	Hou	NL	24	21	112	5	8	1	54	21	4.82	5.30	(9.2)
Totals			676	609	4,689	286	245	25	2,357	902	3.41	3.77	411.6
Average/9			1.3	1.2	9.0	0.5	0.5	0.0	4.5	1.7	3.41	3.77	0.8

Robin Roberts Phillies Starter Adjusted

Year	T	L	G	GS	IP	W	L	SV	SO	BB	Wtd RA/9	Runs /162
1948	Phi	NL	21	21	154	7	9	0	88	64	3.91	11.1
1949	Phi	NL	45	33	238	16	16	4	100	79	3.98	15.3
1950	Phi	NL	42	41	320	21	12	1	154	81	3.21	47.8
1951	Phi	NL	46	41	331	22	16	2	134	67	3.35	44.6
1952	Phi	NL	41	39	347	29	7	2	156	47	3.07	57.2
1953	Phi	NL	46	43	365	24	17	2	208	64	2.90	67.0
1954	Phi	NL	47	40	354	24	16	4	195	59	3.08	58.2
1955	Phi	NL	43	40	321	24	15	3	168	56	4.03	18.8
1956	Phi	NL	45	39	313	20	19	3	165	42	4.99	(15.1)
1957	Phi	NL	41	34	263	11	23	2	135	45	4.60	(1.2)
1958	Phi	NL	37	36	284	18	15	0	137	54	3.85	22.4
1959	Phi	NL	37	37	271	16	18	0	144	37	4.92	(10.8)
1960	Phi	NL	37	35	250	13	17	1	128	36	4.60	(1.2)
1961	Phi	NL	27	19	123	1	11	0	57	24	6.52	(26.9)
1962	Bal	AL	27	25	191	10	9	0	102	41	3.04	32.2
1963	Bal	AL	35	35	251	14	13	0	124	40	4.01	15.3
1964	Bal	AL	31	31	204	13	7	0	109	52	3.40	26.1
1965	Bal	AL	30	25	191	10	9	0	97	30	3.96	12.7
1966	Hou	NL	24	21	112	5	8	1	54	21	5.89	(16.6)
Totals			703	634	4,883	298	255	26	2,454	939	3.90	357.0
Average/9			1.3	1.2	9.0	0.5	0.5	0.0	4.5	1.7	3.90	0.7

Dazzy Vance   **Dodgers**   **Starter**   **Actual**   **Actual Runs /162**

Year	T	L	G	GS	IP	W	L	SV	SO	BB	ERA	Actual RA/9	Actual Runs /162
1915	NY	AL	9	4	31	0	4	0	18	21	4.11	4.99	(1.5)
1918	NY	AL	2	0	2	0	0	0	0	2	15.43	19.29	(3.8)
1922	Bkn	NL	36	31	246	18	12	0	134	94	3.70	4.47	2.4
1923	Bkn	NL	37	35	280	18	15	0	197	100	3.50	4.08	14.9
1924	Bkn	NL	35	34	308	28	6	0	262	77	2.16	2.60	67.0
1925	Bkn	NL	31	31	265	22	9	0	221	66	3.53	3.90	19.4
1926	Bkn	NL	24	22	169	9	10	1	140	58	3.89	4.26	5.6
1927	Bkn	NL	34	32	273	16	15	1	184	69	2.70	3.23	40.3
1928	Bkn	NL	38	32	280	22	10	2	200	72	2.09	2.54	62.8
1929	Bkn	NL	31	26	231	14	13	0	126	47	3.89	4.28	7.1
1930	Bkn	NL	35	31	259	17	15	0	173	55	2.61	3.38	33.8
1931	Bkn	NL	30	29	219	11	13	0	150	53	3.38	4.07	11.8
1932	Bkn	NL	27	24	176	12	11	1	103	57	4.20	4.61	(1.0)
1933	StL	NL	28	11	99	6	2	3	67	28	3.55	3.82	8.1
1934	StL	NL	25	6	77	1	3	1	42	25	4.56	5.49	(8.0)
1935	Bkn	NL	20	0	51	3	2	2	28	16	4.41	5.12	(3.2)
Totals			442	348	2,967	197	140	11	2,045	840	3.24	3.78	255.7
Average/9			1.3	1.1	9.0	0.6	0.4	0.0	6.2	2.5	3.24	3.78	0.8

Dazzy Vance   **Dodgers**   **Starter**   **Adjusted**

Year	T	L	G	GS	IP	W	L	SV	SO	BB	Wtd RA/9	Runs /162
1915	NY	AL	9	4	32	0	4	0	19	22	5.70	(4.1)
1918	NY	AL	3	0	3	0	0	0	0	3	24.28	(6.5)
1922	Bkn	NL	38	33	258	19	13	0	141	99	4.03	15.0
1923	Bkn	NL	39	37	295	19	16	0	207	105	3.82	24.2
1924	Bkn	NL	37	36	324	29	6	0	276	81	2.60	70.6
1925	Bkn	NL	33	33	279	23	9	0	232	69	3.46	34.1
1926	Bkn	NL	25	23	178	9	11	1	147	61	4.22	6.7
1927	Bkn	NL	36	34	288	17	16	1	194	73	3.19	43.8
1928	Bkn	NL	40	34	295	23	11	2	210	76	2.46	68.6
1929	Bkn	NL	33	27	243	15	14	0	133	49	3.59	26.3
1930	Bkn	NL	37	33	272	18	16	0	182	58	2.66	57.2
1931	Bkn	NL	32	31	230	12	14	0	158	56	4.08	12.3
1932	Bkn	NL	28	25	185	13	12	1	108	60	4.58	(0.4)
1933	StL	NL	29	12	104	6	2	3	70	29	4.34	2.5
1934	StL	NL	26	6	81	1	3	1	44	26	5.28	(6.5)
1935	Bkn	NL	21	0	54	3	2	2	29	17	4.89	(2.0)
Totals			465	366	3,121	207	147	12	2,151	884	3.57	341.8
Average/9			1.3	1.1	9.0	0.6	0.4	0.0	6.2	2.5	3.57	1.0

Billy Pierce | White Sox | Starter | Actual | | Actual

Year	T	L	G	GS	IP	W	L	SV	SO	BB	ERA	Actual RA/9	Actual Runs /162
1945	Det	AL	5	0	10	0	0	0	10	10	1.80	1.80	3.1
1948	Det	AL	22	5	55	3	0	0	36	51	6.34	6.55	(12.3)
1949	Chi	AL	32	26	172	7	15	0	95	112	3.88	4.66	(2.0)
1950	Chi	AL	33	29	219	12	16	1	118	137	3.98	4.60	(1.0)
1951	Chi	AL	37	28	240	15	14	2	113	73	3.03	3.49	28.5
1952	Chi	AL	33	32	255	15	12	1	144	79	2.57	2.68	53.3
1953	Chi	AL	40	33	271	18	12	3	186	102	2.72	3.12	43.3
1954	Chi	AL	36	26	189	9	10	3	148	86	3.48	4.10	9.6
1955	Chi	AL	33	26	206	15	10	1	157	64	1.97	2.18	54.3
1956	Chi	AL	35	33	276	20	9	1	192	100	3.32	3.52	31.8
1957	Chi	AL	37	34	257	20	12	2	171	71	3.26	3.43	32.2
1958	Chi	AL	35	32	245	17	11	2	144	66	2.68	3.05	41.0
1959	Chi	AL	34	33	224	14	15	0	114	62	3.62	3.94	15.4
1960	Chi	AL	32	30	196	14	7	0	108	46	3.62	3.72	18.3
1961	Chi	AL	39	28	180	10	9	3	106	54	3.80	4.25	6.1
1962	SF	NL	30	23	162	16	6	1	76	35	3.49	3.72	15.1
1963	SF	NL	38	13	99	3	11	8	52	20	4.27	4.45	1.2
1964	SF	NL	34	1	49	3	4	4	29	10	2.20	2.57	10.8
	Totals		585	432	3,307	211	169	32	1,999	1,178	3.27	3.61	348.7
	Average/9		1.6	1.2	9.0	0.6	0.5	0.1	5.4	3.2	3.27	3.61	0.9

Billy Pierce | White Sox | Starter | Adjusted

Year	T	L	G	GS	IP	W	L	SV	SO	BB	Wtd RA/9	Runs /162
1945	Det	AL	5	0	11	0	0	0	11	11	2.09	2.9
1948	Det	AL	23	5	58	3	0	0	38	54	6.23	(10.8)
1949	Chi	AL	34	27	181	7	16	0	100	118	4.47	1.7
1950	Chi	AL	35	31	231	13	17	1	124	144	4.09	12.1
1951	Chi	AL	39	29	253	16	15	2	119	77	3.42	31.9
1952	Chi	AL	35	34	269	16	13	1	151	83	2.92	48.8
1953	Chi	AL	42	35	285	19	13	3	196	107	3.17	43.9
1954	Chi	AL	38	27	198	9	11	3	156	90	4.43	2.9
1955	Chi	AL	35	27	216	16	11	1	165	67	2.22	56.2
1956	Chi	AL	37	35	291	21	9	1	202	105	3.41	37.0
1957	Chi	AL	39	36	270	21	13	2	180	75	3.70	25.6
1958	Chi	AL	37	34	258	18	12	2	151	69	3.30	36.0
1959	Chi	AL	36	35	236	15	16	0	120	65	4.09	12.2
1960	Chi	AL	34	32	207	15	7	0	114	48	3.85	16.2
1961	Chi	AL	39	28	180	10	9	3	106	54	4.23	6.6
1962	SF	NL	30	23	162	16	6	1	76	35	3.75	14.5
1963	SF	NL	38	13	99	3	11	8	52	20	5.31	(8.3)
1964	SF	NL	34	1	49	3	0	4	29	10	2.90	9.0
	Totals		608	451	3,453	220	176	33	2,089	1,233	3.68	338.4
	Average/9		1.6	1.2	9.0	0.6	0.5	0.1	5.4	3.2	3.68	0.9

Lefty Gomez — Yankees — Starter — Actual

Year	T	L	G	GS	IP	W	L	SV	SO	BB	ERA	Actual RA/9	Actual Runs /162
1930	NY	AL	15	6	60	2	5	1	22	28	5.55	6.15	(10.6)
1931	NY	AL	40	26	243	21	9	3	150	85	2.67	3.26	35.0
1932	NY	AL	37	31	265	24	7	1	176	105	4.21	4.75	(5.7)
1933	NY	AL	35	30	235	16	10	2	163	106	3.18	4.14	10.9
1934	NY	AL	38	33	282	26	5	1	158	96	2.33	2.74	56.9
1935	NY	AL	34	30	246	12	15	1	138	86	3.18	3.80	20.7
1936	NY	AL	31	30	189	13	7	0	105	122	4.39	4.95	(8.2)
1937	NY	AL	34	34	278	21	11	0	194	93	2.33	2.85	52.8
1938	NY	AL	32	32	239	18	12	0	129	99	3.35	4.14	11.1
1939	NY	AL	26	26	198	12	8	0	102	84	3.41	3.64	20.2
1940	NY	AL	9	5	27	3	3	0	14	18	6.59	6.51	(5.9)
1941	NY	AL	23	23	156	15	5	0	76	103	3.74	4.38	3.1
1942	NY	AL	13	13	80	6	4	0	41	65	4.27	4.72	(1.4)
1943	Was	AL	1	1	5	0	1	0	0	5	5.79	7.20	(1.4)
Totals			368	320	2,503	189	102	9	1,468	1,095	3.34	3.92	177.3
Average/9			1.3	1.2	9.0	0.7	0.4	0.0	5.3	3.9	3.34	3.92	0.6

Lefty Gomez — Yankees — Starter — Adjusted

Year	T	L	G	GS	IP	W	L	SV	SO	BB	Wtd RA/9	Runs /162
1930	NY	AL	16	6	63	2	5	1	23	29	5.10	(3.8)
1931	NY	AL	42	27	256	22	9	3	158	89	2.87	48.0
1932	NY	AL	39	33	279	25	7	1	185	110	4.12	13.7
1933	NY	AL	37	32	247	17	11	2	171	112	3.76	21.9
1934	NY	AL	40	35	296	27	5	1	166	101	2.40	71.0
1935	NY	AL	36	32	259	13	16	1	145	90	3.38	34.0
1936	NY	AL	33	32	198	14	7	0	110	128	3.91	14.3
1937	NY	AL	36	36	293	22	12	0	204	98	2.43	69.1
1938	NY	AL	34	34	251	19	13	0	136	104	3.42	31.8
1939	NY	AL	27	27	208	13	8	0	107	88	3.13	33.0
1940	NY	AL	9	5	29	3	3	0	15	19	5.87	(4.2)
1941	NY	AL	24	24	164	16	5	0	80	108	4.17	7.1
1942	NY	AL	14	14	84	6	4	0	43	68	5.01	(4.3)
1943	Was	AL	1	1	5	0	1	0	0	5	8.52	(2.2)
Totals			387	337	2,633	199	107	9	1,544	1,152	3.43	329.4
Average/9			1.3	1.2	9.0	0.7	0.4	0.0	5.3	3.9	3.43	1.1

Mike Mussina   Orioles   Starter   Actual

Year	T	L	G	GS	IP	W	L	SV	SO	BB	ERA	Actual RA/9	Actual Runs /162
1991	Bal	AL	12	12	88	4	5	0	52	21	2.87	3.18	13.4
1992	Bal	AL	32	32	241	18	5	0	130	48	2.54	2.61	52.1
1993	Bal	AL	25	25	168	14	6	0	117	44	4.46	4.51	0.9
1994	Bal	AL	24	24	176	16	5	0	99	42	3.06	3.22	26.2
1995	Bal	AL	32	32	222	19	9	0	158	50	3.29	3.49	26.3
1996	Bal	AL	36	36	243	19	11	0	204	69	4.81	5.07	(13.9)
1997	Bal	AL	33	33	225	15	8	0	218	54	3.20	3.49	26.6
1998	Bal	AL	29	29	206	13	10	0	175	41	3.49	3.71	19.4
1999	Bal	AL	31	31	203	18	7	0	172	52	3.50	3.90	14.8
2000	Bal	AL	34	34	238	11	15	0	210	46	3.79	3.98	15.2
Totals			288	288	2,010	147	81	0	1,535	467	3.53	3.75	181.2
Average/9			1.3	1.3	9.0	0.7	0.4	0.0	6.9	2.1	3.53	3.75	0.8

Mike Mussina   Orioles   Starter   Adjusted

Year	T	L	G	GS	IP	W	L	SV	SO	BB	Wtd RA/9	Runs /162
1991	Bal	AL	12	12	88	4	5	0	52	21	3.23	13.0
1992	Bal	AL	32	32	241	18	5	0	130	48	2.74	48.6
1993	Bal	AL	25	25	168	14	6	0	117	44	4.33	4.3
1994	Bal	AL	34	34	249	23	7	0	140	59	2.78	49.1
1995	Bal	AL	36	36	249	21	10	0	178	56	3.11	40.2
1996	Bal	AL	36	36	243	19	11	0	204	69	4.26	8.0
1997	Bal	AL	33	33	225	15	8	0	218	54	3.19	34.0
1998	Bal	AL	29	29	206	13	10	0	175	41	3.34	27.9
1999	Bal	AL	31	31	203	18	7	0	172	52	3.38	26.6
2000	Bal	AL	34	34	238	11	15	0	210	46	3.40	30.6
Totals			302	302	2,111	156	84	0	1,596	491	3.35	282.4
Average/9			1.3	1.3	9.0	0.7	0.4	0.0	6.8	2.1	3.35	1.2

Kevin Brown   Rangers   Starter   Actual

Year	T	L	G	GS	IP	W	L	SV	SO	BB	ERA	Actual RA/9	Actual Runs /162
1986	Tex	AL	1	1	5	1	0	0	4	0	3.60	3.60	0.5
1988	Tex	AL	4	4	23	1	1	0	12	8	4.24	5.79	(3.2)
1989	Tex	AL	28	28	191	12	9	0	104	70	3.35	3.82	15.6
1990	Tex	AL	26	26	180	12	10	0	88	60	3.60	4.20	7.1
1991	Tex	AL	33	33	211	9	12	0	96	90	4.40	4.96	(9.4)
1992	Tex	AL	35	35	266	21	11	0	173	76	3.32	3.96	17.6
1993	Tex	AL	34	34	233	15	12	0	142	74	3.59	4.06	12.9
1994	Tex	AL	26	25	170	7	9	0	123	50	4.82	5.77	(22.9)
1995	Bal	AL	26	26	172	10	9	0	117	48	3.60	3.81	14.3
1996	Fla	NL	32	32	233	17	11	0	159	33	1.89	2.32	57.9
1997	Fla	NL	33	33	237	16	8	0	205	66	2.69	2.92	43.2
1998	SD	NL	36	35	257	18	7	0	257	49	2.38	2.70	53.0
1999	LA	NL	35	35	252	18	9	0	221	59	3.00	3.53	28.8
2000	LA	NL	33	33	230	13	6	0	216	47	2.58	2.97	40.6
Totals			382	380	2,661	170	114	0	1,917	730	3.21	3.69	256.0
Average/9			1.3	1.3	9.0	0.6	0.4	0.0	6.5	2.5	3.21	3.69	0.9

Kevin Brown   Rangers   Starter   Adjusted

Year	T	L	G	GS	IP	W	L	SV	SO	BB	Wtd RA/9	Runs /162
1986	Tex	AL	1	1	5	1	0	0	4	0	3.53	0.6
1988	Tex	AL	4	4	23	1	1	0	12	8	6.00	(3.7)
1989	Tex	AL	28	28	191	12	9	0	104	70	4.01	11.6
1990	Tex	AL	26	26	180	12	10	0	88	60	4.40	3.1
1991	Tex	AL	33	33	211	9	12	0	96	90	5.03	(11.2)
1992	Tex	AL	35	35	266	21	11	0	173	76	4.16	11.8
1993	Tex	AL	34	34	233	15	12	0	142	74	3.90	17.1
1994	Tex	AL	37	35	241	10	13	0	174	71	4.99	(11.6)
1995	Bal	AL	29	29	194	11	10	0	132	54	3.39	25.1
1996	Fla	NL	32	32	233	17	11	0	159	33	2.24	59.9
1997	Fla	NL	33	33	237	16	8	0	205	66	2.87	44.4
1998	SD	NL	36	35	257	18	7	0	257	49	2.66	54.2
1999	LA	NL	35	35	252	18	9	0	221	59	3.19	38.3
2000	LA	NL	33	33	230	13	6	0	216	47	2.67	48.2
Totals			396	394	2,753	174	119	0	1,983	757	3.62	287.9
Average/9			1.3	1.3	9.0	0.6	0.4	0.0	6.5	2.5	3.62	0.9

Don Drysdale **Dodgers** **Starter** **Actual**

Year	T	L	G	GS	IP	W	L	SV	SO	BB	ERA	Actual RA/9	Actual Runs /162
1956	Bkn	NL	25	12	99	5	5	0	55	31	2.64	3.18	15.1
1957	Bkn	NL	34	29	221	17	9	0	148	61	2.69	3.10	35.8
1958	LA	NL	44	29	212	12	13	0	131	72	4.17	4.54	0.4
1959	LA	NL	44	36	271	17	13	2	242	93	3.46	3.75	24.3
1960	LA	NL	41	36	269	15	14	2	246	72	2.84	3.11	43.2
1961	LA	NL	40	37	244	13	10	0	182	83	3.69	4.09	12.7
1962	LA	NL	43	41	314	25	9	1	232	78	2.83	3.50	36.9
1963	LA	NL	42	42	315	19	17	0	251	57	2.63	3.26	45.4
1964	LA	NL	40	40	321	18	16	0	237	68	2.18	2.55	71.7
1965	LA	NL	44	42	308	23	12	1	210	66	2.77	3.30	43.1
1966	LA	NL	40	40	274	13	16	0	177	45	3.42	3.74	24.8
1967	LA	NL	38	38	282	13	16	0	196	60	2.74	3.22	41.9
1968	LA	NL	31	31	239	14	12	0	155	56	2.15	2.56	53.0
1969	LA	NL	12	12	63	5	4	0	24	13	4.45	4.86	(2.1)
Totals			518	465	3,432	209	166	6	2,486	855	2.95	3.39	446.2
Average/9			1.4	1.2	9.0	0.5	0.4	0.0	6.5	2.2	2.95	3.39	1.2

Don Drysdale **Dodgers** **Starter** **Adjusted**

Year	T	L	G	GS	IP	W	L	SV	SO	BB	Wtd RA/9	Runs /162
1956	Bkn	NL	26	13	104	5	5	0	58	33	3.38	13.6
1957	Bkn	NL	36	31	232	18	9	0	156	64	3.25	33.8
1958	LA	NL	46	31	223	13	14	0	138	76	4.68	(3.1)
1959	LA	NL	46	38	285	18	14	2	255	98	3.84	22.7
1960	LA	NL	43	38	283	16	15	2	259	76	3.33	38.4
1961	LA	NL	42	39	257	14	11	0	191	87	4.08	13.7
1962	LA	NL	43	41	314	25	9	1	232	78	3.53	35.9
1963	LA	NL	42	42	315	19	17	0	251	57	3.89	23.4
1964	LA	NL	40	40	321	18	16	0	237	68	2.88	60.0
1965	LA	NL	44	42	308	23	12	1	210	66	3.73	28.3
1966	LA	NL	40	40	274	13	16	0	177	45	4.16	12.2
1967	LA	NL	38	38	282	13	16	0	196	60	3.82	23.1
1968	LA	NL	31	31	239	14	12	0	155	56	3.41	30.4
1969	LA	NL	12	12	63	5	4	0	24	13	5.43	(6.1)
Totals			530	474	3,500	213	169	6	2,538	876	3.72	326.4
Average/9			1.4	1.2	9.0	0.5	0.4	0.0	6.5	2.3	3.72	0.8

Bret Saberhagen   **Royals**   **Starter**   **Actual**

Year	T	L	G	GS	IP	W	L	SV	SO	BB	ERA	Actual RA/9	Actual Runs /162
1984	KC	AL	38	18	158	10	11	1	73	36	3.48	4.05	8.9
1985	KC	AL	32	32	235	20	6	0	158	38	2.87	3.02	40.2
1986	KC	AL	30	25	156	7	12	0	112	29	4.15	4.44	2.0
1987	KC	AL	33	33	257	18	10	0	163	53	3.36	3.47	31.0
1988	KC	AL	35	35	261	14	16	0	171	59	3.80	4.21	10.1
1989	KC	AL	36	35	262	23	6	0	193	43	2.16	2.54	58.8
1990	KC	AL	20	20	135	5	9	0	87	28	3.27	3.47	16.3
1991	KC	AL	28	28	196	13	8	0	136	45	3.07	3.48	23.5
1992	NY	NL	17	15	98	3	5	0	81	27	3.50	3.59	10.5
1993	NY	NL	19	19	139	7	7	0	93	17	3.29	3.55	15.6
1994	NY	NL	24	24	177	14	4	0	143	13	2.74	2.94	31.9
1995	NY	NL	25	25	153	7	6	0	100	33	4.18	4.59	(0.6)
1997	Bos	AL	6	6	26	0	1	0	14	10	6.58	6.92	(6.8)
1998	Bos	AL	31	31	175	15	8	0	100	29	3.96	4.22	6.6
1999	Bos	AL	22	22	119	10	6	0	81	11	2.95	3.25	17.3
Totals			396	368	2,548	166	115	1	1,705	471	3.33	3.62	265.2
Average/9			1.4	1.3	9.0	0.6	0.4	0.0	6.0	1.7	3.33	3.62	0.9

Bret Saberhagen   **Royals**   **Starter**   **Adjusted**

Year	T	L	G	GS	IP	W	L	SV	SO	BB	Wtd RA/9	Runs /162
1984	KC	AL	38	18	158	10	11	1	73	36	4.15	7.2
1985	KC	AL	32	32	235	20	6	0	158	38	2.99	40.9
1986	KC	AL	30	25	156	7	12	0	112	29	4.35	3.6
1987	KC	AL	33	33	257	18	10	0	163	53	3.19	38.9
1988	KC	AL	35	35	261	14	16	0	171	59	4.36	5.7
1989	KC	AL	36	35	262	23	6	0	193	43	2.67	55.1
1990	KC	AL	20	20	135	5	9	0	87	28	3.64	13.8
1991	KC	AL	28	28	196	13	8	0	136	45	3.53	22.4
1992	NY	NL	17	15	98	3	5	0	81	27	4.22	3.7
1993	NY	NL	19	19	139	7	7	0	93	17	3.58	15.1
1994	NY	NL	34	34	251	20	6	0	202	18	2.88	46.7
1995	NY	NL	28	28	172	8	7	0	113	37	4.50	1.1
1997	Bos	AL	6	6	26	0	1	0	14	10	6.33	(5.1)
1998	Bos	AL	31	31	175	15	8	0	100	29	3.80	14.7
1999	Bos	AL	22	22	119	10	6	0	81	11	2.82	23.0
Totals			409	381	2,640	173	117	1	1,777	481	3.58	286.8
Average/9			1.4	1.3	9.0	0.6	0.4	0.0	6.1	1.6	3.58	1.0

Sandy Koufax   **Dodgers**   **Starter**   **Actual**

Year	T	L	G	GS	IP	W	L	SV	SO	BB	ERA	Actual RA/9	Actual Runs /162
1955	Bkn	NL	12	5	42	2	2	0	30	28	3.02	3.21	6.2
1956	Bkn	NL	16	10	59	2	4	0	30	29	4.91	5.64	(7.1)
1957	Bkn	NL	34	13	104	5	4	0	122	51	3.88	4.24	3.7
1958	LA	NL	40	26	159	11	11	1	131	105	4.48	5.04	(8.5)
1959	LA	NL	35	23	153	8	6	2	173	92	4.05	4.35	3.5
1960	LA	NL	37	26	175	8	13	1	197	100	3.91	4.27	5.6
1961	LA	NL	42	35	256	18	13	1	269	96	3.52	4.11	12.7
1962	LA	NL	28	26	184	14	7	1	216	57	2.54	2.98	32.3
1963	LA	NL	40	40	311	25	5	0	306	58	1.88	1.97	89.4
1964	LA	NL	29	28	223	19	5	1	223	53	1.74	1.98	63.9
1965	LA	NL	43	41	336	26	8	2	382	71	2.04	2.41	80.1
1966	LA	NL	41	41	323	27	9	0	317	77	1.73	2.06	89.6
Totals			397	314	2,324	165	87	9	2,396	817	2.76	3.12	371.4
Average/9			1.5	1.2	9.0	0.6	0.3	0.0	9.3	3.2	2.76	3.12	1.4

Sandy Koufax   **Dodgers**   **Starter**   **Adjusted**

Year	T	L	G	GS	IP	W	L	SV	SO	BB	Wtd RA/9	Runs /162
1955	Bkn	NL	13	5	44	2	2	0	32	29	3.20	6.6
1956	Bkn	NL	17	11	62	2	4	0	32	31	5.99	(9.8)
1957	Bkn	NL	36	14	110	5	4	0	128	54	4.44	1.4
1958	LA	NL	42	27	167	12	12	1	138	110	5.20	(11.9)
1959	LA	NL	37	24	161	8	6	2	182	97	4.45	1.8
1960	LA	NL	39	27	184	8	14	1	207	105	4.58	(0.4)
1961	LA	NL	44	37	269	19	14	1	283	101	4.10	13.7
1962	LA	NL	28	26	184	14	7	1	216	57	3.00	31.8
1963	LA	NL	40	40	311	25	5	0	306	58	2.35	76.3
1964	LA	NL	29	28	223	19	5	1	223	53	2.23	57.6
1965	LA	NL	43	41	336	26	8	2	382	71	2.73	68.3
1966	LA	NL	41	41	323	27	9	0	317	77	2.29	81.4
Totals			408	321	2,374	168	90	9	2,445	843	3.36	316.8
Average/9			1.5	1.2	9.0	0.6	0.3	0.0	9.3	3.2	3.36	1.2

Stan Coveleski — Indians — Starter — Actual

Year	T	L	G	GS	IP	W	L	SV	SO	BB	ERA	Actual RA/9	Actual Runs /162
1912	Phi	AL	5	2	21	2	1	0	9	4	3.43	3.86	1.6
1916	Cle	AL	45	27	232	15	13	3	76	58	3.41	3.88	17.5
1917	Cle	AL	45	36	298	19	14	4	133	94	1.81	2.35	73.2
1918	Cle	AL	38	33	311	22	13	1	87	76	1.82	2.60	67.6
1919	Cle	AL	43	34	286	24	12	4	118	60	2.61	3.01	49.2
1920	Cle	AL	41	38	315	24	14	2	133	65	2.49	3.14	49.6
1921	Cle	AL	43	40	315	23	13	2	99	84	3.37	3.90	23.0
1922	Cle	AL	35	33	277	17	14	2	98	64	3.32	3.90	20.2
1923	Cle	AL	33	31	228	13	14	2	54	42	2.76	3.87	17.4
1924	Cle	AL	37	33	240	15	16	0	58	73	4.04	5.25	(18.5)
1925	Was	AL	32	32	241	20	5	0	58	73	2.84	3.21	36.1
1926	Was	AL	36	34	245	14	11	1	50	81	3.12	4.48	2.1
1927	Was	AL	5	4	14	2	1	0	3	8	3.14	4.50	0.1
1928	NY	AL	12	8	58	5	1	0	5	20	5.74	6.36	(11.6)
Totals			450	385	3,082	215	142	21	981	802	2.89	3.60	327.3
Average/9			1.3	1.1	9.0	0.6	0.4	0.1	2.9	2.3	2.89	3.60	1.0

Stan Coveleski — Indians — Starter — Adjusted

Year	T	L	G	GS	IP	W	L	SV	SO	BB	Wtd RA/9	Runs /162
1912	Phi	AL	5	2	22	2	1	0	9	4	3.90	1.6
1916	Cle	AL	47	28	244	16	14	3	80	61	4.82	(7.1)
1917	Cle	AL	47	38	314	20	15	4	140	99	2.95	56.0
1918	Cle	AL	48	42	397	28	17	1	111	97	3.27	56.6
1919	Cle	AL	50	39	331	28	14	5	137	69	3.32	45.4
1920	Cle	AL	43	40	331	25	15	2	140	68	2.99	57.8
1921	Cle	AL	45	42	331	24	14	2	104	88	3.46	40.2
1922	Cle	AL	37	35	291	18	15	2	103	67	3.73	26.6
1923	Cle	AL	35	33	240	14	15	2	57	44	3.67	23.7
1924	Cle	AL	39	35	253	16	17	0	61	77	4.76	(5.6)
1925	Was	AL	34	34	254	21	5	0	61	77	2.79	49.9
1926	Was	AL	38	36	258	15	12	1	53	85	4.24	9.0
1927	Was	AL	5	4	15	2	1	0	3	8	4.13	0.7
1928	NY	AL	13	8	61	5	1	0	5	21	6.03	(10.0)
Totals			486	416	3,342	234	154	23	1,064	867	3.63	345.0
Average/9			1.3	1.1	9.0	0.6	0.4	0.1	2.9	2.3	3.63	0.9

David Cone   **Mets**   **Starter**   **Actual**

Year	T	L	G	GS	IP	W	L	SV	SO	BB	ERA	Actual RA/9	Actual Runs /162
1986	KC	AL	11	0	23	0	0	0	21	13	5.56	5.56	(2.5)
1987	NY	NL	21	13	99	5	6	1	68	44	3.71	4.17	4.3
1988	NY	NL	35	28	231	20	3	0	213	80	2.22	2.61	50.0
1989	NY	NL	34	33	220	14	8	0	190	74	3.52	3.77	19.2
1990	NY	NL	31	30	212	14	10	0	233	65	3.23	3.57	23.2
1991	NY	NL	34	34	233	14	14	0	241	73	3.29	3.67	22.9
1992	NY	NL	35	34	250	17	10	0	261	111	2.81	3.28	35.4
1993	KC	AL	34	34	254	11	14	0	191	114	3.33	3.61	26.7
1994	KC	AL	23	23	172	16	5	0	132	54	2.94	3.15	26.8
1995	Tor	AL	30	30	229	18	8	0	191	88	3.57	3.73	21.1
1996	NY	AL	11	11	72	7	2	0	71	34	2.88	3.13	11.4
1997	NY	AL	29	29	195	12	6	0	222	86	2.82	3.09	31.8
1998	NY	AL	31	31	208	20	7	0	209	59	3.55	3.86	16.1
1999	NY	AL	31	31	193	12	9	0	177	90	3.44	3.91	13.9
2000	NY	AL	30	29	155	4	14	0	120	82	6.91	7.20	(45.5)
Totals			420	390	2,745	184	116	1	2,540	1,067	3.40	3.72	254.9
Average/9			1.4	1.3	9.0	0.6	0.4	0.0	8.3	3.5	3.40	3.72	0.8

David Cone   **Mets**   **Starter**   **Adjusted**

Year	T	L	G	GS	IP	W	L	SV	SO	BB	Wtd RA/9	Runs /162
1986	KC	AL	11	0	23	0	0	0	21	13	5.45	(2.2)
1987	NY	NL	21	13	99	5	6	1	68	44	4.19	4.1
1988	NY	NL	35	28	231	20	3	0	213	80	3.07	38.1
1989	NY	NL	34	33	220	14	8	0	190	74	4.36	4.8
1990	NY	NL	31	30	212	14	10	0	233	65	3.85	16.7
1991	NY	NL	34	34	233	14	14	0	241	73	4.06	12.9
1992	NY	NL	35	34	250	17	10	0	261	111	3.85	19.5
1993	KC	AL	34	34	254	11	14	0	191	114	3.46	30.9
1994	KC	AL	33	33	243	23	7	0	187	76	2.72	49.5
1995	Tor	AL	34	34	258	20	9	0	215	99	3.32	35.5
1996	NY	AL	11	11	72	7	2	0	71	34	2.63	15.4
1997	NY	AL	29	29	195	12	6	0	222	86	2.83	37.5
1998	NY	AL	31	31	208	20	7	0	209	59	3.48	24.9
1999	NY	AL	31	31	193	12	9	0	177	90	3.39	25.1
2000	NY	AL	30	29	155	4	14	0	120	82	6.14	(27.3)
Totals			433	403	2,845	193	119	1	2,619	1,100	3.65	285.3
Average/9			1.4	1.3	9.0	0.6	0.4	0.0	8.3	3.5	3.65	0.9

Addie Joss   **Indians**   **Starter**   **Actual**

Year	T	L	G	GS	IP	W	L	SV	SO	BB	ERA	Actual RA/9	Actual Runs /162
1902	Cle	AL	32	29	269	17	13	0	106	75	2.77	4.01	16.4
1903	Cle	AL	32	31	284	18	13	0	120	37	2.19	3.30	39.6
1904	Cle	AL	25	24	192	14	10	0	83	30	1.59	2.39	46.3
1905	Cle	AL	33	32	286	20	12	0	132	46	2.01	2.83	54.9
1906	Cle	AL	34	31	282	21	9	1	106	43	1.72	2.59	61.6
1907	Cle	AL	42	38	339	27	11	2	127	54	1.83	2.66	71.4
1908	Cle	AL	42	35	325	24	11	2	130	30	1.16	2.13	87.6
1909	Cle	AL	33	28	243	14	13	0	67	31	1.71	2.63	52.0
1910	Cle	AL	13	12	107	5	5	0	49	18	2.26	2.93	19.4
Totals			286	260	2,327	160	97	5	920	364	1.89	2.82	449.2
Average/9			1.1	1.0	9.0	0.6	0.4	0.0	3.6	1.4	1.89	2.82	1.7

Addie Joss   **Indians**   **Starter**   **Adjusted**

Year	T	L	G	GS	IP	W	L	SV	SO	BB	Wtd RA/9	Runs /162
1902	Cle	AL	37	34	312	20	15	0	123	87	3.65	31.2
1903	Cle	AL	37	36	328	21	15	0	139	43	3.60	35.0
1904	Cle	AL	26	25	202	15	11	0	87	32	3.03	34.4
1905	Cle	AL	35	34	301	21	13	0	139	48	3.46	36.8
1906	Cle	AL	36	33	297	22	9	1	112	45	3.16	45.9
1907	Cle	AL	44	40	356	28	12	2	134	57	3.28	50.7
1908	Cle	AL	44	37	342	25	12	2	137	32	2.80	66.8
1909	Cle	AL	35	29	255	15	14	0	70	33	3.44	31.6
1910	Cle	AL	14	13	113	5	5	0	52	19	3.65	11.4
Totals			308	280	2,506	172	105	5	992	395	3.32	343.9
Average/9			1.1	1.0	9.0	0.6	0.4	0.0	3.6	1.4	3.32	1.2

Carl Mays   **Red Sox**   **Starter**   **Actual**

Year	T	L	G	GS	IP	W	L	SV	SO	BB	ERA	Actual RA/9	Actual Runs /162
1915	Bos	AL	38	6	132	6	5	7	65	21	2.60	3.69	12.7
1916	Bos	AL	44	24	245	18	13	3	76	74	2.39	2.90	45.1
1917	Bos	AL	35	33	289	22	9	0	91	74	1.74	2.52	65.4
1918	Bos	AL	35	33	293	21	13	0	114	81	2.21	2.89	54.3
1919	Bos	AL	34	29	266	14	14	2	107	77	2.10	3.09	43.4
1920	NY	AL	45	37	312	26	11	2	92	84	3.06	3.66	31.1
1921	NY	AL	49	38	337	27	9	7	70	76	3.05	3.87	25.7
1922	NY	AL	34	29	240	13	14	2	41	50	3.60	4.16	10.6
1923	NY	AL	23	7	81	5	2	0	16	32	6.20	6.56	(18.1)
1924	Cin	NL	37	27	226	20	9	0	63	36	3.15	3.86	17.5
1925	Cin	NL	12	5	52	3	5	2	10	13	3.31	3.81	4.3
1926	Cin	NL	39	33	281	19	12	1	58	53	3.14	3.59	30.2
1927	Cin	NL	14	9	82	3	7	0	17	10	3.51	4.28	2.5
1928	Cin	NL	14	6	63	4	1	1	10	22	3.88	4.71	(1.1)
1929	NY	NL	37	8	123	7	2	4	32	31	4.22	4.90	(4.7)
Totals			490	324	3,021	208	126	31	862	734	2.92	3.61	318.9
Average/9			1.5	1.0	9.0	0.6	0.4	0.1	2.6	2.2	2.92	3.61	1.0

Carl Mays   **Red Sox**   **Starter**   **Adjusted**

Year	T	L	G	GS	IP	W	L	SV	SO	BB	Wtd RA/9	Runs /162
1915	Bos	AL	40	6	139	6	5	7	68	22	4.21	5.3
1916	Bos	AL	46	25	258	19	14	3	80	78	3.60	27.4
1917	Bos	AL	37	35	304	23	9	0	96	78	3.16	47.1
1918	Bos	AL	45	42	374	27	17	0	145	103	3.64	38.2
1919	Bos	AL	39	34	308	16	16	2	124	89	3.41	39.2
1920	NY	AL	47	39	328	27	12	2	97	88	3.48	39.2
1921	NY	AL	52	40	354	28	9	7	74	80	3.44	44.0
1922	NY	AL	36	31	252	14	15	2	43	53	3.98	16.1
1923	NY	AL	24	7	86	5	2	0	17	34	6.21	(15.8)
1924	Cin	NL	39	28	238	21	9	0	66	38	3.86	18.5
1925	Cin	NL	13	5	54	3	5	2	11	14	3.38	7.1
1926	Cin	NL	41	35	296	20	13	1	61	56	3.56	32.9
1927	Cin	NL	15	9	86	3	7	0	18	11	4.22	3.2
1928	Cin	NL	15	6	66	4	1	1	11	23	4.57	(0.1)
1929	NY	NL	39	8	129	7	2	4	34	33	4.10	6.5
Totals			527	351	3,272	225	137	33	944	798	3.71	308.9
Average/9			1.4	1.0	9.0	0.6	0.4	0.1	2.6	2.2	3.71	0.8

Steve Carlton — Phillies — Starter — Actual

Year	T	L	G	GS	IP	W	L	SV	SO	BB	ERA	Actual RA/9	Actual Runs /162
1965	StL	NL	15	2	25	0	0	0	21	8	2.52	2.52	5.7
1966	StL	NL	9	9	52	3	3	0	25	18	3.12	3.81	4.3
1967	StL	NL	30	28	193	14	9	1	168	62	2.98	3.31	26.7
1968	StL	NL	34	33	232	13	11	0	162	61	2.99	3.38	30.3
1969	StL	NL	31	31	236	17	11	0	210	93	2.17	2.51	53.8
1970	StL	NL	34	33	254	10	19	0	193	109	3.73	4.36	5.6
1971	StL	NL	37	36	273	20	9	0	172	98	3.56	3.95	18.4
1972	Phi	NL	41	41	346	27	10	0	310	87	1.97	2.18	91.5
1973	Phi	NL	40	40	293	13	20	0	223	113	3.90	4.48	2.5
1974	Phi	NL	39	39	291	16	13	0	240	136	3.22	3.65	29.3
1975	Phi	NL	37	37	255	15	14	0	192	104	3.56	4.09	13.2
1976	Phi	NL	35	35	253	20	7	0	195	72	3.13	3.35	33.9
1977	Phi	NL	36	36	283	23	10	0	198	89	2.64	3.15	44.2
1978	Phi	NL	34	34	247	16	13	0	161	63	2.84	3.31	34.3
1979	Phi	NL	35	35	251	18	11	0	213	89	3.62	4.02	15.0
1980	Phi	NL	38	38	304	24	9	0	286	90	2.34	2.58	66.8
1981	Phi	NL	24	24	190	13	4	0	179	62	2.42	2.79	37.3
1982	Phi	NL	38	38	296	23	11	0	286	86	3.10	3.47	35.7
1983	Phi	NL	37	37	284	15	16	0	275	84	3.11	3.71	26.7
1984	Phi	NL	33	33	229	13	7	0	163	79	3.58	4.09	11.9
1985	Phi	NL	16	16	92	1	8	0	48	53	3.33	4.21	3.5
1986	Phi	NL	32	32	176	9	14	0	120	86	5.10	6.12	(30.6)
1987	Cle	AL	32	21	152	6	14	1	91	86	5.74	6.58	(34.2)
1988	Min	AL	4	1	10	0	1	0	5	5	16.76	17.69	(14.1)
Totals			741	709	5,217	329	244	2	4,136	1,833	3.22	3.67	511.7
Average/9			1.3	1.2	9.0	0.6	0.4	0.0	7.1	3.2	3.22	3.67	0.9

Steve Carlton — Phillies — Starter — Adjusted

Year	T	L	G	GS	IP	W	L	SV	SO	BB	Wtd RA/9	Runs /162
1965	StL	NL	15	2	25	0	0	0	21	8	2.85	4.7
1966	StL	NL	9	9	52	3	3	0	25	18	4.23	1.9
1967	StL	NL	30	28	193	14	9	1	168	62	3.93	13.5
1968	StL	NL	34	33	232	13	11	0	162	61	4.50	1.4
1969	StL	NL	31	31	236	17	11	0	210	93	2.80	46.0
1970	StL	NL	34	33	254	10	19	0	193	109	4.39	4.8
1971	StL	NL	37	36	273	20	9	0	172	98	4.60	(1.4)
1972	Phi	NL	43	43	364	28	11	0	326	92	2.55	81.1
1973	Phi	NL	40	40	293	13	20	0	223	113	4.92	(11.8)
1974	Phi	NL	39	39	291	16	13	0	240	136	4.01	17.8
1975	Phi	NL	37	37	255	15	14	0	192	104	4.51	1.3
1976	Phi	NL	35	35	253	20	7	0	195	72	3.83	20.5
1977	Phi	NL	36	36	283	23	10	0	198	89	3.26	40.7
1978	Phi	NL	34	34	247	16	13	0	161	63	3.75	22.1
1979	Phi	NL	35	35	251	18	11	0	213	89	4.33	6.3
1980	Phi	NL	38	38	304	24	9	0	286	90	2.92	55.4
1981	Phi	NL	36	36	288	20	6	0	271	94	3.27	41.2
1982	Phi	NL	38	38	296	23	11	0	286	86	3.88	22.4
1983	Phi	NL	37	37	284	15	16	0	275	84	4.10	14.3
1984	Phi	NL	33	33	229	13	7	0	163	79	4.57	(0.3)
1985	Phi	NL	16	16	92	1	8	0	48	53	4.71	(1.6)
1986	Phi	NL	32	32	176	9	14	0	120	86	6.69	(41.8)
1987	Cle	AL	32	21	152	6	14	1	91	86	6.06	(25.3)
1988	Min	AL	4	1	10	0	1	0	5	5	18.32	(14.8)
Totals			755	723	5,333	337	247	2	4,244	1,869	4.05	298.3
Average/9			1.3	1.2	9.0	0.6	0.4	0.0	7.2	3.2	4.05	0.5

Hoyt Wilhelm — **White Sox** — **Reliever** — **Actual**

Year	T	L	G	GS	IP	W	L	SV	SO	BB	ERA	Actual RA/9	Actual Runs /162
1952	NY	NL	71	0	159	15	3	11	108	57	2.43	3.40	20.5
1953	NY	NL	68	0	145	7	8	15	71	77	3.04	3.79	12.4
1954	NY	NL	57	0	111	12	4	7	64	52	2.10	2.59	24.3
1955	NY	NL	59	0	103	4	1	0	71	40	3.93	4.63	(0.8)
1956	NY	NL	64	0	89	4	9	8	71	43	3.83	4.55	0.1
1957	StL	NL	42	0	59	2	4	12	29	22	4.12	4.42	0.9
1958	Cle	AL	39	10	131	3	10	5	92	45	2.34	2.82	25.3
1959	Bal	AL	32	27	226	15	11	0	139	77	2.19	2.55	50.4
1960	Bal	AL	41	11	147	11	8	7	107	39	3.31	4.22	5.5
1961	Bal	AL	51	1	110	9	7	18	87	41	2.30	2.86	20.7
1962	Bal	AL	52	0	93	7	10	15	90	34	1.94	2.71	19.1
1963	Chi	AL	55	3	136	5	8	21	111	30	2.64	3.11	21.9
1964	Chi	AL	73	0	131	12	9	27	95	30	1.99	2.40	31.5
1965	Chi	AL	66	0	144	7	7	20	106	32	1.81	2.13	38.8
1966	Chi	AL	46	0	81	5	2	6	61	17	1.66	2.33	20.1
1967	Chi	AL	49	0	89	8	3	12	76	34	1.31	2.12	24.1
1968	Chi	AL	72	0	94	4	4	12	72	24	1.73	1.91	27.5
1969	Cal	AL	52	0	78	7	7	14	67	22	2.19	2.54	17.5
1970	Atl	NL	53	0	82	6	5	13	68	42	3.40	3.62	8.5
1971	LA	NL	12	0	20	0	1	3	16	5	2.70	3.15	3.1
1972	LA	NL	16	0	25	0	1	1	9	15	4.62	5.76	(3.4)
Totals			1,070	52	2,254	143	122	227	1,610	778	2.52	3.09	368.0
Average/9			4.3	0.2	9.0	0.6	0.5	0.9	6.4	3.1	2.52	3.09	1.5

Hoyt Wilhelm — **White Sox** — **Reliever** — **Adjusted**

Year	T	L	G	GS	IP	W	L	SV	SO	BB	Wtd RA/9	Runs /162
1952	NY	NL	75	0	168	16	3	12	114	60	3.68	16.3
1953	NY	NL	72	0	153	7	8	16	75	81	3.56	16.9
1954	NY	NL	60	0	117	13	4	7	67	55	2.57	25.8
1955	NY	NL	62	0	108	4	1	0	75	42	4.62	(0.7)
1956	NY	NL	67	0	94	4	9	8	75	45	4.83	(2.9)
1957	StL	NL	44	0	62	2	4	13	31	23	4.63	(0.5)
1958	Cle	AL	41	11	138	3	11	5	97	47	3.05	23.0
1959	Bal	AL	34	28	238	16	12	0	146	81	2.65	50.5
1960	Bal	AL	43	12	155	12	8	7	113	41	4.37	3.2
1961	Bal	AL	51	1	110	9	7	18	87	41	2.85	20.9
1962	Bal	AL	52	0	93	7	10	15	90	34	2.78	18.4
1963	Chi	AL	55	3	136	5	8	21	111	30	3.47	16.4
1964	Chi	AL	73	0	131	12	9	27	95	30	2.69	27.3
1965	Chi	AL	66	0	144	7	7	20	106	32	2.45	33.7
1966	Chi	AL	46	0	81	5	2	6	61	17	2.72	16.6
1967	Chi	AL	49	0	89	8	3	12	76	34	2.62	19.2
1968	Chi	AL	72	0	94	4	4	12	72	24	2.54	20.9
1969	Cal	AL	52	0	78	7	7	14	67	22	2.83	15.0
1970	Atl	NL	53	0	82	6	5	13	68	42	3.64	8.3
1971	LA	NL	12	0	20	0	1	3	16	5	3.67	2.0
1972	LA	NL	17	0	27	0	1	1	9	16	6.75	(6.5)
Totals			1,095	54	2,316	147	125	230	1,650	802	3.30	323.8
Average/9			4.3	0.2	9.0	0.6	0.5	0.9	6.4	3.1	3.30	1.3

Tom Henke   **Blue Jays**   **Reliever**   **Actual**

Year	T	L	G	GS	IP	W	L	SV	SO	BB	ERA	Actual RA/9	Actual Runs /162
1982	Tex	AL	8	0	16	1	0	0	9	8	1.15	1.15	5.9
1983	Tex	AL	8	0	16	1	0	1	17	4	3.38	3.38	2.1
1984	Tex	AL	25	0	28	1	1	2	25	20	6.35	6.67	(6.7)
1985	Tor	AL	28	0	40	3	3	13	42	8	2.02	2.70	8.3
1986	Tor	AL	63	0	91	9	5	27	118	32	3.35	3.84	7.3
1987	Tor	AL	72	0	94	0	6	34	128	25	2.49	2.59	20.5
1988	Tor	AL	52	0	68	4	4	25	66	24	2.91	3.04	11.5
1989	Tor	AL	64	0	89	8	3	20	116	25	1.92	2.02	25.1
1990	Tor	AL	61	0	75	2	4	32	75	19	2.17	2.17	19.8
1991	Tor	AL	49	0	50	0	2	32	53	11	2.32	2.32	12.5
1992	Tor	AL	57	0	56	3	2	34	46	22	2.26	3.07	9.2
1993	Tex	AL	66	0	74	5	5	40	79	27	2.91	3.03	12.6
1994	Tex	AL	37	0	38	3	6	15	39	12	3.79	3.79	3.2
1995	StL	NL	52	0	54	1	1	36	48	18	1.82	1.82	16.5
Totals			642	0	790	41	42	311	861	255	2.67	2.87	147.9
Average/9			7.3	0.0	9.0	0.5	0.5	3.5	9.8	2.9	2.67	2.87	1.7

Tom Henke   **Blue Jays**   **Reliever**   **Adjusted**

Year	T	L	G	GS	IP	W	L	SV	SO	BB	Wtd RA/9	Runs /162
1982	Tex	AL	8	0	16	1	0	0	9	8	1.16	5.9
1983	Tex	AL	8	0	16	1	0	1	17	4	3.41	2.0
1984	Tex	AL	25	0	28	1	1	2	25	20	6.83	(7.2)
1985	Tor	AL	28	0	40	3	3	13	42	8	2.67	8.4
1986	Tor	AL	63	0	91	9	5	27	118	32	3.76	8.1
1987	Tor	AL	72	0	94	0	6	34	128	25	2.38	22.7
1988	Tor	AL	52	0	68	4	4	25	66	24	3.15	10.6
1989	Tor	AL	64	0	89	8	3	20	116	25	2.12	24.1
1990	Tor	AL	61	0	75	2	4	32	75	19	2.27	18.9
1991	Tor	AL	49	0	50	0	2	32	53	11	2.35	12.3
1992	Tor	AL	57	0	56	3	2	34	46	22	3.22	8.2
1993	Tex	AL	66	0	74	5	5	40	79	27	2.91	13.6
1994	Tex	AL	52	0	54	4	8	21	55	17	3.28	7.6
1995	StL	NL	59	0	61	1	1	41	54	20	1.78	18.8
Totals			664	0	812	42	45	322	883	262	2.85	154.3
Average/9			7.4	0.0	9.0	0.5	0.5	3.6	9.8	2.9	2.85	1.7

Mariano Rivera   **Yankees**   **Reliever**   **Actual**

Year	T	L	G	GS	IP	W	L	SV	SO	BB	ERA	Actual RA/9	Actual Runs /162
1995	NY	AL	19	10	67	5	3	0	51	30	5.51	5.78	(9.1)
1996	NY	AL	61	0	108	8	3	5	130	34	2.09	2.09	29.5
1997	NY	AL	66	0	72	6	4	43	68	20	1.88	2.13	19.3
1998	NY	AL	54	0	61	3	0	36	36	17	1.91	1.91	18.0
1999	NY	AL	66	0	69	4	3	45	52	18	1.83	1.96	19.9
2000	NY	AL	66	0	76	7	4	36	58	25	2.85	3.09	12.3
Totals			332	10	452	33	17	165	395	144	2.63	2.77	90.0
Average/9			6.6	0.2	9.0	0.7	0.3	3.3	7.9	2.9	2.63	2.77	1.8

Mariano Rivera   **Yankees**   **Reliever**   **Adjusted**

Year	T	L	G	GS	IP	W	L	SV	SO	BB	Wtd RA/9	Runs /162
1995	NY	AL	21	11	75	6	3	0	57	34	5.14	(4.9)
1996	NY	AL	61	0	108	8	3	5	130	34	1.76	33.5
1997	NY	AL	66	0	72	6	4	43	68	20	1.95	20.8
1998	NY	AL	54	0	61	3	0	36	36	17	1.72	19.3
1999	NY	AL	66	0	69	4	3	45	52	18	1.70	21.9
2000	NY	AL	66	0	76	7	4	36	58	25	2.64	16.1
Totals			334	11	461	34	17	165	401	148	2.47	106.7
Average/9			6.5	0.2	9.0	0.7	0.3	3.2	7.8	2.9	2.47	2.1

Dan Quisenberry   **Royals**   **Reliever**   **Actual**

Year	T	L	G	GS	IP	W	L	SV	SO	BB	ERA	Actual RA/9	Actual Runs /162
1979	KC	AL	32	0	40	3	2	5	13	7	3.15	3.60	4.3
1980	KC	AL	75	0	128	12	7	33	37	27	3.09	3.30	17.9
1981	KC	AL	40	0	62	1	4	18	20	15	1.73	2.31	15.6
1982	KC	AL	72	0	137	9	7	35	46	12	2.57	2.83	26.2
1983	KC	AL	69	0	139	5	3	45	48	11	1.94	2.27	35.3
1984	KC	AL	72	0	129	6	3	44	41	12	2.64	2.71	26.5
1985	KC	AL	84	0	129	8	9	37	54	16	2.37	2.86	24.3
1986	KC	AL	62	0	81	3	7	12	36	24	2.77	3.32	11.2
1987	KC	AL	47	0	49	4	1	8	17	10	2.76	2.76	9.8
1988	StL	NL	53	0	63	2	1	1	28	11	5.12	5.26	(4.9)
1989	StL	NL	63	0	78	3	1	6	37	14	2.64	2.87	14.7
1990	SF	NL	5	0	7	0	1	0	2	3	13.50	16.20	(8.6)
Totals			674	0	1,043	56	46	244	379	162	2.76	3.07	172.2
Average/9			5.8	0.0	9.0	0.5	0.4	2.1	3.3	1.4	2.76	3.07	1.5

Dan Quisenberry   **Royals**   **Reliever**   **Adjusted**

Year	T	L	G	GS	IP	W	L	SV	SO	BB	Wtd RA/9	Runs /162
1979	KC	AL	32	0	40	3	2	5	13	7	3.48	4.8
1980	KC	AL	75	0	128	12	7	33	37	27	3.33	17.5
1981	KC	AL	61	0	94	2	6	27	30	23	2.57	20.8
1982	KC	AL	72	0	137	9	7	35	46	12	2.87	25.7
1983	KC	AL	69	0	139	5	3	45	48	11	2.29	35.0
1984	KC	AL	72	0	129	6	3	44	41	12	2.78	25.6
1985	KC	AL	84	0	129	8	9	37	54	16	2.83	24.7
1986	KC	AL	62	0	81	3	7	12	36	24	3.25	11.8
1987	KC	AL	47	0	49	4	1	8	17	10	2.54	11.0
1988	StL	NL	53	0	63	2	1	1	28	11	6.19	(11.5)
1989	StL	NL	63	0	78	3	1	6	37	14	3.32	10.8
1990	SF	NL	5	0	7	0	1	0	2	3	17.45	(9.6)
Totals			695	0	1,075	57	48	253	389	170	3.16	166.6
Average/9			5.8	0.0	9.0	0.5	0.4	2.1	3.3	1.4	3.16	1.4

Rollie Fingers   Athletics   Reliever   Actual   Actual

Year	T	L	G	GS	IP	W	L	SV	SO	BB	ERA	Actual RA/9	Actual Runs /162
1968	Oak	AL	1	0	1	0	0	0	0	1	27.00	27.00	(3.3)
1969	Oak	AL	60	8	119	6	7	12	61	41	3.71	4.54	0.2
1970	Oak	AL	45	19	148	7	9	2	79	48	3.65	3.95	10.0
1971	Oak	AL	48	8	129	4	6	17	98	30	2.99	3.20	19.5
1972	Oak	AL	65	0	111	11	9	21	113	32	2.51	2.83	21.4
1973	Oak	AL	62	2	127	7	8	22	110	39	1.92	2.91	23.2
1974	Oak	AL	76	0	119	9	5	18	95	29	2.65	3.10	19.3
1975	Oak	AL	75	0	127	10	6	24	115	33	2.98	3.06	21.1
1976	Oak	AL	70	0	135	13	11	20	113	40	2.47	2.67	28.2
1977	SD	NL	78	0	132	8	9	35	113	36	2.99	3.20	20.0
1978	SD	NL	67	0	107	6	13	37	72	29	2.52	2.77	21.3
1979	SD	NL	54	0	84	9	9	13	65	37	4.52	5.06	(4.7)
1980	SD	NL	66	0	103	11	9	23	69	32	2.80	3.06	17.1
1981	Mil	AL	47	0	78	6	3	28	61	13	1.04	1.04	30.5
1982	Mil	AL	50	0	80	5	6	29	71	20	2.60	2.60	17.3
1984	Mil	AL	33	0	46	1	2	23	40	13	1.96	2.54	10.3
1985	Mil	AL	47	0	55	1	6	17	24	19	5.04	5.37	(5.0)
Totals			944	37	1,701	114	118	341	1,299	492	2.90	3.25	246.3
Average/9			5.0	0.2	9.0	0.6	0.6	1.8	6.9	2.6	2.90	3.25	1.3

Rollie Fingers   Athletics   Reliever   Adjusted

Year	T	L	G	GS	IP	W	L	SV	SO	BB	Wtd RA/9	Runs /162
1968	Oak	AL	1	0	1	0	0	0	0	1	35.98	(4.7)
1969	Oak	AL	60	8	119	6	7	12	61	41	5.06	(6.6)
1970	Oak	AL	45	19	148	7	9	2	79	48	4.31	4.1
1971	Oak	AL	48	8	129	4	6	17	98	30	3.75	11.6
1972	Oak	AL	68	0	117	12	9	22	119	34	3.71	11.1
1973	Oak	AL	62	2	127	7	8	22	110	39	3.08	20.7
1974	Oak	AL	76	0	119	9	5	18	95	29	3.44	14.8
1975	Oak	AL	75	0	127	10	6	24	115	33	3.23	18.7
1976	Oak	AL	70	0	135	13	11	20	113	40	3.05	22.6
1977	SD	NL	78	0	132	8	9	35	113	36	3.31	18.3
1978	SD	NL	67	0	107	6	13	37	72	29	3.14	16.9
1979	SD	NL	54	0	84	9	9	13	65	37	5.45	(8.3)
1980	SD	NL	66	0	103	11	9	23	69	32	3.46	12.6
1981	Mil	AL	71	0	118	9	5	42	92	20	1.16	44.6
1982	Mil	AL	50	0	80	5	6	29	71	20	2.63	17.0
1984	Mil	AL	33	0	46	1	2	23	40	13	2.60	10.0
1985	Mil	AL	47	0	55	1	6	17	24	19	5.32	(4.7)
Totals			972	37	1,747	118	120	356	1,336	500	3.53	198.7
Average/9			5.0	0.2	9.0	0.6	0.6	1.8	6.9	2.6	3.53	1.0

INDEX